Weiss Ratings' Guide to Property and Casualty Insurers

Weiss Ratings'
Guide to Property and
Casualty Insurers

A Quarterly Compilation of Insurance Company
Ratings and Analyses

Spring 2015

GREY HOUSE PUBLISHING

Weiss Ratings
4400 Northcorp Parkway
Palm Beach Gardens, FL 33410
561-627-3300

Published by Grey House Publishing, Inc., located at 4919 Route 22, Amenia, NY 12501; telephone 518-789-8700. Grey House Publishing neither guarantees the accuracy of the data contained herein nor assumes any responsibility for errors, omissions or discrepancies. Grey House Publishing accepts no payment for listing; inclusion in the publication of any organization, agency, institution, publication, service or individual does not imply endorsement of the publisher.

4919 Route 22
PO Box 56
Amenia, NY 12501-0056

Edition No. 84, Spring 2015

ISBN: 978-1-61925-601-9
ISSN: 2158-5989

Contents

Terms and Conditions

This Document is prepared strictly for the confidential use of our customer(s). It has been provided to you at your specific request. It is not directed to, or intended for distribution to or use by, any person or entity who is a citizen or resident of or located in any locality, state, country or other jurisdiction where such distribution, publication, availability or use would be contrary to law or regulation or which would subject Weiss Ratings or its affiliates to any registration or licensing requirement within such jurisdiction.

No part of the analysts' compensation was, is, or will be, directly or indirectly, related to the specific recommendations or views expressed in this research report.

This Document is not intended for the direct or indirect solicitation of business. Weiss Ratings and its affiliates disclaims any and all liability to any person or entity for any loss or damage caused, in whole or in part, by any error (negligent or otherwise) or other circumstances involved in, resulting from or relating to the procurement, compilation, analysis, interpretation, editing, transcribing, publishing and/or dissemination or transmittal of any information contained herein.

Weiss Ratings has not taken any steps to ensure that the securities or investment vehicle referred to in this report are suitable for any particular investor. The investment or services contained or referred to in this report may not be suitable for you and it is recommended that you consult an independent investment advisor if you are in doubt about such investments or investment services. Nothing in this report constitutes investment, legal, accounting or tax advice or a representation that any investment or strategy is suitable or appropriate to your individual circumstances or otherwise constitutes a personal recommendation to you.

The ratings and other opinions contained in this Document must be construed solely as statements of opinion from Weiss Ratings, and not statements of fact. Each rating or opinion must be weighed solely as a factor in your choice of an institution and should not be construed as a recommendation to buy, sell or otherwise act with respect to the particular product or company involved.

Past performance should not be taken as an indication or guarantee of future performance, and no representation or warranty, expressed or implied, is made regarding future performance. Information, opinions and estimates contained in this report reflect a judgment at its original date of publication and are subject to change without notice. Weiss Ratings offers a notification service for rating changes on companies you specify. For more information visit WeissRatings.com or call 1-877-934-7778. The price, value and income from any of the securities or financial instruments mentioned in this report can fall as well as rise.

This Document and the information contained herein is copyrighted by Weiss Ratings, LLC. Any copying, displaying, selling, distributing or otherwise reproducing or delivering this information or any part of this Document to any other person entity is prohibited without the express written consent of Weiss Ratings, LLC, with the exception of a reviewer or editor who may quote brief passages in connection with a review or a news story, is prohibited.

Message To Insurers

All survey data received on or before January 23, 2015 has been considered or incorporated into this edition of the Directory. If there are particular circumstances which you believe could affect your rating, please use the online survey (**http://weissratings.com/survey/**) or e-mail Weiss Ratings, LLC (**insurancesurvey@weissinc.com**) with documentation to support your request. If warranted, we will make every effort to incorporate the changes in our next edition.

Welcome to Weiss Ratings'

Guide to Property and Casualty Insurers

Most people automatically assume their insurance company will survive, year after year. However, prudent consumers and professionals realize that in this world of shifting risks, the solvency of insurance companies can't be taken for granted.

If you are looking for accurate, unbiased ratings and data to help you choose property and casualty insurance for yourself, your family, your company or your clients, Weiss Ratings' *Guide to Property and Casualty Insurers* gives you precisely what you need.

In fact, it's the only source that currently provides ratings and analyses on over 2,400 property and casualty insurers.

Weiss Ratings' Mission Statement

Weiss Ratings' mission is to empower consumers, professionals, and institutions with high quality advisory information for selecting or monitoring a financial services company or financial investment.

In doing so, Weiss Ratings will adhere to the highest ethical standards by maintaining our independent, unbiased outlook and approach to advising our customers.

Why rely on Weiss Ratings?

Weiss Ratings provides fair, objective ratings to help professionals and consumers alike make educated purchasing decisions.

At Weiss Ratings, integrity is number one. Weiss Ratings never takes a penny from insurance companies for issuing a rating. We publish Weiss Financial Strength Ratings without regard for insurers' preferences. However, other rating agencies like A.M. Best, Fitch, Moody's and Standard & Poor's are paid by insurance companies for their ratings and may even suppress unfavorable ratings at an insurer's request.

Our ratings are reviewed and updated more frequently than the other agencies' ratings. You can be sure that the information you receive is accurate and current, providing you with advance warning of financial vulnerability early enough to do something about it.

Other rating agencies focus primarily on a company's current claims paying ability and consider only mild economic adversity. Weiss Ratings also considers these issues, but our analysis also covers a company's ability to deal with severe economic adversity and a sharp increase in claims.

Our use of more rigorous standards stems from the viewpoint that an insurance company's obligations to its policyholders should not depend on favorable business conditions. An insurer must be able to honor its policy commitments in bad times as well as good.

Our rating scale, from A to F, is easy to understand. Only a few outstanding companies receive an A (Excellent) rating, although there are many to choose from within the B (Good) category. An even larger group falls into the broad average range which receives C (Fair) ratings. Companies that demonstrate marked vulnerabilities receive either D (Weak) or E (Very Weak) ratings.

How to Use This Guide

The purpose of the *Guide to Property and Casualty Insurers* is to provide policyholders and prospective policy purchasers with a reliable source of insurance company ratings and analyses on a timely basis. We realize that the financial strength of an insurer is an important factor to consider when making the decision to purchase a policy or change companies. The ratings and analyses in this Guide can make that evaluation easier when you are considering:

- Homeowners insurance

- Business insurance

- Auto insurance

- Workers' compensation insurance

- Product liability insurance

- Medical malpractice and other professional liability insurance

This Guide does not include companies that strictly provide life and health insurance or annuities. For information on those companies, please refer to our *Guide to Life and Annuity Insurers*. Also, only a few of the property and casualty companies in this Guide provide any form of health insurance. For a complete listing of health insurance providers, please refer to our *Guide to Health Insurers*.

The rating for a particular company indicates our opinion regarding that company's ability to meet its commitments to the policyholder – not only under current economic conditions, but also during a declining economy or in the event of a sharp increase in claims. Such an increase in claims and related expenses may be triggered by any number of occurrences including a strong earthquake or hurricane, rising medical or legal costs, or large court awards. The safest companies, however, should be prepared to deal with harsh and unforeseen circumstances.

To use this Guide most effectively, we recommend you follow the steps outlined below:

Step 1   To ensure you evaluate the correct company, verify the company's exact name and state of domicile as it was given to you or appears on your policy. Many companies have similar names but are not related to one another, so you want to make sure the company you look up is really the one you are interested in evaluating.

Step 2   Turn to Section I, the Index of Companies, and locate the company you are evaluating. This section contains all companies analyzed by Weiss Ratings including those that did not receive a Financial Strength Rating. It is sorted alphabetically by the name of the company and shows the state of domicile following the name for additional verification. Once you have located your specific company, the first column after the state of domicile shows its Weiss Financial Strength Rating. Turn to *About Weiss Financial Strength Ratings* for information about what this rating means. If the rating has changed since the last issue of this Guide, a downgrade will be indicated with a down triangle ▼ to the left of the company name; an upgrade will be indicated with an up triangle ▲.

Step 3   Following Weiss Financial Strength Rating are some of the various indexes that our analysts used in rating the company. Refer to the Critical Ranges In Our Indexes table for an interpretation of which index values are considered strong, good, fair or weak. You can also turn to the introduction of Section I to see what each of these factors measures. In most cases, lower-rated companies will have a low index value in one or more of the factors shown. Bear in mind, however, that the Financial Strength Rating is the result of a complex qualitative and quantitative analysis which cannot be reproduced using only the data provided here.

Step 4   Our analysts evaluate a great number of ratios and performance measures when assigning a rating. The right hand page of Section I shows you some of the key financial ratios we consider. Again, refer to the introduction of Section I for a description of each ratio.

Step 5   Some insurers have a bullet • preceding the company name on the right hand page of Section I. This means that more detailed information about the company is available in Section II. If the company you are evaluating is identified with a bullet, turn to Section II, the Analysis of Largest Companies, and locate it there (otherwise skip to step 8). Section II contains the largest insurers rated by Weiss Ratings, regardless of rating. It too is sorted alphabetically by the name of the company.

Step 6   Once you have identified your company in Section II, you will find its Financial Strength Rating and a description of the rating immediately to the right of the company name. Then, below the company name is a description of the various rating factors that were considered in assigning the company's rating. These factors and the information below them are designed to give you a better feel for the company and its strengths and weaknesses. See the Section II introduction to get a better understanding of what each of these factors means.

Step 7   To the right, you will find a five-year summary of the company's Financial Strength Rating, capitialization and income. Look for positive or negative trends in these data. Below the five-year summary, we have included a graphic illustration of the most critical factor or factors impacting the company's rating. Again, the Section II introduction provides an overview of the content of each graph or table.

Step 8   If the company you are evaluating is not highly rated and you want to find an insurer with a higher rating, turn to the page in Section V that has your state's name at the top. This section contains those Recommended Companies (rating of A+, A, A- or B+) that are licensed to underwrite insurance in your state, sorted by rating. Then turn to the page in Section IV that shows the type of insurance you are interested in at the top. Insurers appearing on both lists will be those Recomended Companies which are licensed to sell that particular type of insurance in your state. From here you can select a company and then refer back to Sections I and II to analyze it.

Step 9   If you decide that you would like to contact one of Weiss Recommended Companies about obtaining a policy or for additional information, refer to Section III. Following each company's name is its address and phone number to assist you in making contact.

Step 10 In order to use Weiss Financial Strength Ratings most effectively, we strongly recommend you consult the Important Warnings and Cautions listed. These are more than just "standard disclaimers"; they are very important factors you should be aware of before using this Guide. If you have any questions regarding the precise meaning of specific terms used in the Guide, refer to the Glossary.

Step 11 The Appendix contains information about State Guaranty Associations and the types of coverage they provide to policyholders when an insurance company fails. Keep in mind that while guaranty funds have now been established in all states, many do not cover all types of insurance. Furthermore, all of these funds have limits on their amount of coverage. Use the table to determine whether the level of coverage is applicable to your policy and the limits are adequate for your needs. You should pay particular attention to the notes regarding coverage limitations.

Step 12 If you want more information on your state's guaranty fund, call the State Commissioner's Office directly.

Step 13 Keep in mind that good coverage from a state guaranty association is no substitute for dealing with a financially strong company. Weiss Ratings only recommends those companies which we feel are most able to stand on their own, without regard to what might happen in case the company does fail.

Step 14 Make sure you stay up to date with the latest information available since the publication of this Guide. For information on how to set up a rating change notification service, acquire follow-up reports, or receive a more in-depth analysis of an individual company, call 1-877-934-7778 or visit www.weissratings.com.

Data Sources: Annual and quarterly statutory statements filed with state insurance commissioners and data provided by the insurance companies being rated. The National Association of Insurance Commissioners has provided some of the raw data. Any analyses or conclusions are not provided or endorsed by the NAIC.

Date of data analyzed September 30, 2014 unless otherwise noted.

About Weiss Financial Strength Ratings

Weiss Financial Strength Ratings represent a completely independent, unbiased opinion of an insurance company's financial strength. The ratings are derived, for the most part, from annual and quarterly financial statements obtained from state insurance commissioners. These data are supplemented by information that we request from the insurance companies themselves. Although we seek to maintain an open line of communication with the companies being rated, we do not grant them the right to influence the ratings or stop their publication.

Weiss Financial Strength Ratings are assigned by our analysts based on a complex analysis of hundreds of factors that are synthesized into five indexes: risk-adjusted capital, reserve adequacy, profitability, liquidity and stability. These indexes are then used to arrive at a letter grade rating. A good rating requires consistency across all indexes. A weak score on any one index can result in a low rating, as insolvency can be caused by any one of a number of factors, such as inadequate capital, unpredictable claims experience, poor liquidity, inadequate reserving, or operating losses.

The primary components of Weiss Financial Strength Rating are as follows:

- **Risk-Adjusted Capital Indexes** gauge capital adequacy in terms of each insurer's risk profile under both *moderate* and *severe* loss scenarios.

- **Reserve Adequacy Index** measures the adequacy of the company's reserves and its ability to accurately anticipate the level of claims it will receive.

- **Profitability Index** measures the soundness of the company's operations and the contribution of profits to the company's financial strength. The profitability index is a composite of five sub-factors: 1) gain or loss on underwriting; (2) gain or loss on overall operations; 3) consistency of operating results; 4) impact of operating results on surplus; and 5) expenses in relation to industry norms for the types of policies that the company offers.

- **Liquidity Index** values a company's ability to raise the cash necessary to pay claims. We model various cash flow scenarios, applying liquidity tests to determine how the company might fare in the event of an unexpected spike in claims.

- **Stability Index** integrates a number of sub-factors that affect consistency (or lack thereof) in maintaining financial strength over time. Sub-factors include 1) risk diversification in terms of company size, group size, number of policies in force, types of policies written and use of reinsurance; 2) deterioration of operations as reported in critical asset, liability, income and expense items; 3) years in operation; 4) former problem areas where, despite recent improvement, the company has yet to establish a record of stable performance over a suitable period of time; 5) a substantial shift in the company's operations; 6) potential instabilities such as reinsurance quality, asset/liability matching, and sources of capital; and 7) relationships with holding companies and affiliates.

Each of these indexes is measured according to the following range of values.

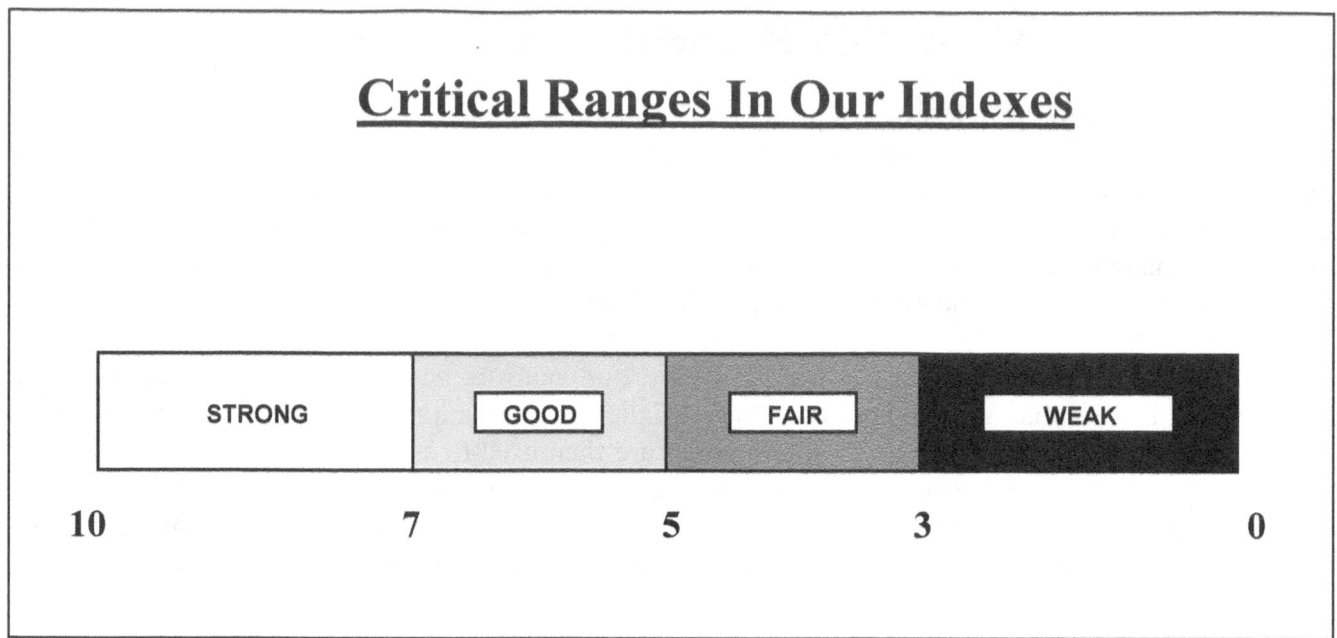

What Our Ratings Mean

A   **Excellent.** The company offers excellent financial security. It has maintained a conservative stance in its investment strategies, business operations and underwriting commitments. While the financial position of any company is subject to change, we believe that this company has the resources necessary to deal with severe economic conditions.

B   **Good.** The company offers good financial security and has the resources to deal with a variety of adverse economic conditions. It comfortably exceeds the minimum levels for all of our rating criteria, and is likely to remain healthy for the near future. However, in the event of a *severe* recession or major financial crisis, we feel that this assessment should be reviewed to make sure that the firm is still maintaining adequate financial strength.

C   **Fair.** The company offers fair financial security and is currently stable. But during an economic downturn or other financial pressures, we feel it may encounter difficulties in maintaining its financial stability.

D   **Weak.** The company currently demonstrates what we consider to be significant weaknesses which could negatively impact policyholders. In an unfavorable economic environment, these weaknesses could be magnified.

E   **Very Weak.** The company currently demonstrates what we consider to be significant weaknesses and has also failed some of the basic tests that we use to identify fiscal stability. Therefore, even in a favorable economic environment, it is our opinion that policyholders could incur significant risks.

F   **Failed.** The company is deemed failed if it is either 1) under supervision of an insurance regulatory authority; 2) in the process of rehabilitation; 3) in the process of liquidation; or 4) voluntarily dissolved after disciplinary or other regulatory action by an insurance regulatory authority.

+   **The plus sign** is an indication that the company is at the upper end of the letter grade rating.

-   **The minus sign** is an indication that the company is at the lower end of the letter grade rating.

U   **Unrated Companies.** The company is unrated for one or more of the following reasons: 1) total assets are less than $1 million; 2) premium income for the current year is less than $100,000; 3) the company functions almost exclusively as a holding company rather than as an underwriter; or 4) we do not have enough information to reliably issue a rating.

How Our Ratings Differ From Those of Other Services

Weiss Financial Strength Ratings are conservative and consumer-oriented. We use tougher standards than other rating agencies because our system is specifically designed to inform risk-averse consumers about the financial strength of property and casualty insurers.

Our rating scale (A to F) is easy to understand by the general public. Users can intuitively understand that an A+ rating is at the top of the scale rather than in the middle like some of the other rating agencies.

Other rating agencies give top ratings more generously so that most companies receive excellent ratings.

More importantly, other rating agencies focus primarily on a company's *current* claims paying ability or consider only relatively mild economic adversity. We also consider these scenarios but extend our analyses to cover a company's ability to deal with severe economic adversity and potential liquidity problems. This stems from the viewpoint that an insurance company's obligations to its policyholders should not be contingent upon a healthy economy. The company must be capable of honoring its policy commitments in bad times as well.

Looking at the insurance industry as a whole, we note that several major rating firms have poor historical track records in identifying troubled companies. The 1980s saw a persistent decline in capital ratios, increased holdings of risky investments in the life and health industry as well as recurring long-term claims liabilities in the property and casualty industry. Despite these clear signs that insolvency risk was rising, other rating firms failed to downgrade at-risk insurance companies. Instead, they often rated companies by shades of excellence, understating the gravity of potential problems.

They have not issued clear warnings that the ordinary consumer can understand. Few, if any, companies receive "weak" or "poor" ratings. Surely, weak companies do exist. However, the other rating agencies apparently do not view themselves as consumer advocates with the responsibility of warning the public about the risks involved in doing business with such companies.

Additionally, these firms will at times agree *not* to issue a rating if a company denies them permission to do so. In short, too often insurance rating agencies work hand-in-glove with the companies they rate.

At Weiss Ratings, although we seek to maintain good relationships with the firms, we owe our primary obligation to the consumer, not the industry. We reserve the right to rate companies based on publicly available data and make the necessary conservative assumptions when companies choose not to provide the additional data we request.

Comparison of Insurance Company Rating Agency Scales

Weiss Ratings [a]	Best [a,b]	S&P [c]	Moody's	Fitch [d]
A+, A, A-	A++, A+	AAA	Aaa	AAA
B+, B, B-	A, A-	AA+, AA AA-	Aa1, Aa2, Aa3	AA+, AA, AA-
C+, C, C-	B++, B+,	A+, A, A-, BBB+, BBB, BBB-	A1, A2, A3, Baa1, Baa2, Baa3	A+, A, A-, BBB+, BBB, BBB-
D+, D, D-	B, B- C++, C+, C, C-	BB+, BB, BB-, B+, B, B-	Ba1, Ba2, Ba3, B1, B2, B3	BB+, BB, BB-, B+, B, B-
E+, E, E- F	D E, F	CCC R	Caa, Ca, C	CCC+, CCC, CCC- DD

[a] Weiss Ratings and Best use additional symbols to designate that they recognize an insurer's existence but do not provide a rating. These symbols are not included in this table.

[b] Best added the A++, B++ and C++ ratings in 1992. In 1994, Best classified its ratings into "secure" and "vulnerable" categories, changed the definition of its "B" and "B-" ratings from "good" to "adequate" and assigned these ratings to the "vulnerable" category. This table contains GAO's assignment of Best's ratings to bands based on our interpretation of their rating descriptions prior to 1994.

[c] S&P discontinued CCC "+" and "-" signs, CC, C and D ratings and added the R rating in 1992.
Source: 1994 GAO *Insurance Ratings* study.

[d] Duff & Phelps Credit Rating Co. merged with Fitch IBCA in 2000, and minor changes were made to the rating scale at that time. These changes were not reflected in the GAO's 1994 study, but *are* reflected in the chart.

Rate of Insurance Company Failures

Weiss Ratings provides quarterly financial strength ratings for thousands of insurance companies each year. Weiss Ratings strives for fairness and objectivity in its ratings and analyses, ensuring that each company receives the rating that most accurately depicts its current financial status, and more importantly, its ability to deal with severe economic adversity and a sharp increase in claims. Weiss Ratings has every confidence that its financial strength ratings provide an accurate representation of a company's stability.

In order for these ratings to be of any true value, it is important that they prove accurate over time. One way to determine the accuracy of a rating is to examine those insurance companies that have failed, and their respective Weiss Financial Strength Ratings. A high percentage of failed companies with "A" ratings would indicate that Weiss Ratings is not being conservative enough with its "secure" ratings, while conversely, a low percentage of failures with "vulnerable" ratings would show that Weiss Ratings is overly conservative.

Over the past 25 years (1989–2013) Weiss Ratings has rated 563 insurance companies, for all industries, that subsequently failed. The chart below shows the number of failed companies in each rating category, the average number of companies rated in each category per year, and the percentage of annual failures for each letter grade.

	Financial Strength Rating	Number of Failed Companies	Average Number of Companies Rated per year	Percentage of Failed Companies per year (by ratings category)*
Secure	A	1	154	0.03%
	B	6	1095	0.02%
	C	71	1619	0.18%
Vulnerable	D	253	753	1.34%
	E	249	213	4.68%

A=Excellent, B=Good, C=Fair, D=Weak, E=Very Weak

On average, only 0.11% of the companies Weiss Ratings rates as "secure" fail each year. On the other hand, an average of 2.08% of the companies Weiss Ratings rates as "vulnerable" fail annually. That means that a company rated by Weiss Ratings as "Vulnerable" is 19 times more likely to fail than a company rated as "Secure".

When considering a Weiss financial strength rating, one can be sure that they are getting the most fair, objective, and accurate financial rating available anywhere.

*Percentage of Failed Companies per year = (Number of Failed Companies) / [(Average Number of Companies Rated per year) x (years in study)]

Data as of December 2013 for Life and Annuity Insurers and Property and Casualty Insurers and Health Insurers

What Does Average Mean?

At Weiss Ratings, we consider the words average and fair to mean just that – average and fair. So when we assign our ratings to insurers, the largest percentage of companies receives an average C rating. That way, you can be sure that a company receiving Weiss B or A rating is truly above average. Likewise, you can feel confident that companies with D or E ratings are truly below average.

Percentage for Property and Casualty Insurers in Each Rating Category

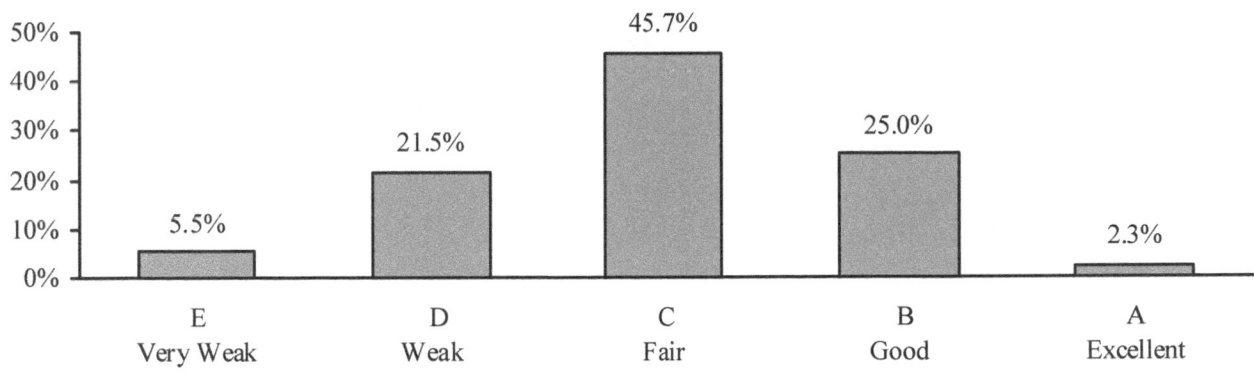

2014 Weiss Ratings Distribution

Important Warnings and Cautions

1. A rating alone cannot tell the whole story. Please read the explanatory information contained in this publication. It is provided in order to give you an understanding of our rating philosophy, as well as paint a more complete picture of how we arrive at our opinion of a company's strengths and weaknesses.

2. Weiss Financial Strength Ratings represent our opinion of a company's insolvency risk. As such, a high rating means we feel that the company has less chance of running into financial difficulties. A high rating is not a guarantee of solvency nor is a low rating a prediction of insolvency. Weiss Financial Strength Ratings are not deemed to be a recommendation concerning the purchase or sale of the securities of any insurance company that is publicly owned.

3. Company performance is only one factor in determining a rating. Conditions in the marketplace and overall economic conditions are additional factors that may affect the company's financial strength. Therefore, a rating upgrade or downgrade does not necessarily reflect changes in the company's profits, capital or other financial measures, but may be due to external factors. Likewise, changes in Weiss indexes may reflect changes in our risk assessment of business or economic conditions as well as changes in company performance.

4. All firms that have the same Financial Strength Rating should be considered to be essentially equal in strength. This is true regardless of any differences in the underlying numbers which might appear to indicate greater strengths. Weiss Financial Strength Rating already takes into account a number of lesser factors which, due to space limitations, cannot be included in this publication.

5. A good rating requires consistency. If a company is excellent on four indicators and fair on one, the company may receive a fair rating. This requirement is necessary due to the fact that fiscal problems can arise from any *one* of several causes including speculative investments, inadequate capital resources or operating losses.

6. We are an independent rating agency and do not depend on the cooperation of the companies we rate. Our data are derived, for the most part, from annual and quarterly financial statements that we obtain from federal banking regulators and state insurance commissioners. The latter may be supplemented by information insurance companies voluntarily provide upon request. Although we seek to maintain an open line of communication with the companies, we do not grant them the right to stop or influence publication of the ratings. This policy stems from the fact that this publication is designed for the protection of the consumer.

7. Affiliated companies do not automatically receive the same rating. We recognize that a troubled company may expect financial support from its parent or affiliates. Weiss Financial Strength Ratings reflect our opinion of the measure of support that may become available to a subsidiary, if the subsidiary were to experience serious financial difficulties. In the case of a strong parent and a weaker subsidiary, the affiliate relationship will generally result in a higher rating for the subsidiary than it would have on a stand-alone basis. Seldom, however, would the rating be brought up to the level of the parent. This treatment is appropriate because we do not assume the parent would have either the resources or the will to "bail out" a troubled subsidiary during a severe economic crisis. Even when there is a binding legal obligation for a parent corporation to honor the policy obligations of its subsidiaries, the possibility exists that the subsidiary could be sold and lose its parental support. Therefore, it is quite common for one affiliate to have a higher rating than another. This is another reason why it is especially important that you have the precise name of the company you are evaluating.

Section I

Index of Companies

An analysis of all rated and unrated

U.S. Property and Casualty Insurers.

Companies are listed in alphabetical order.

Section I Contents

This section contains the key rating factors and performance measures for all rated and unrated insurers analyzed by Weiss Ratings. An explanation of each of the footnotes and stability factors appears at the end of this section.

Left Pages

1. **Insurance Company Name**

The legally registered name, which can sometimes differ from the name that the company uses for advertising. If you cannot find the company you are interested in, or if you have any doubts regarding the precise name, verify the information with the company before looking the name up in this Guide. Also, determine the domicile state for confirmation. (See column 2.)

2. **Domicile State**

The state which has primary regulatory responsibility for the company. It may differ from the location of the company's corporate headquarters. You do not have to be living in the domicile state to purchase insurance from this firm, provided it is licensed to do business in your state.

Also use this column to confirm that you have located the correct company. It is possible for two unrelated companies to have the same name if they are domiciled in different states.

3. **Financial Strength Rating**

Our rating is measured on a scale from A to F and considers a wide range of factors. Please see *What Our Ratings Mean* for specific descriptions of each letter grade. Also, refer to how our ratings differ from those of other rating agencies. Most important, when using this rating, please be sure to consider the warnings regarding the ratings' limitations and the underlying assumptions. Notes in this column refer to the date of the data included in the rating evaluation and are explained.

4. **Total Assets**

All assets admitted by state insurance regulators in millions of dollars through the most recent quarter available. This includes investments and current business assets such as receivables from agents and reinsurers.

The overall size is an important factor which affects the ability of a company to manage risk. Generally speaking, risks can be more effectively diversified by large companies. Because the insurance business is based on probability, the number of policies must be large enough so that actuarial statistics are valid. The larger the number of policyholders, the more reliable the actuarial projections will be. A large company with a correspondingly large policy base can spread its risk and minimize the effects of claims experience that exceeds actuarial expectations.

5. Capital and Surplus

The company's statutory net worth in millions of dollars through the most recent quarter available. Consumers may wish to limit the size of any policy so that the policyholder's maximum potential claims do not exceed approximately 1% of the company's capital and surplus. For example, when buying a policy from a company with capital and surplus of $10,000,000, the 1% limit would be $100,000. (When performing this calculation, do not forget that figures in this column are expressed in millions of dollars.)

6. Net Premium

The amount of insurance premiums received from policyholders less any premiums that have been transferred to other companies through reinsurance agreements. This figure is updated through the most recent annual report available.

Generally speaking, companies with large net premium volume generally have more predictable claims experience.

Critical Ranges In Our Indexes and Ratios				
Indicators	*Strong*	*Good*	*Fair*	*Weak*
Risk-Adjusted Capital Ratio #1	—	1.0 or more	0.75 - 0.99	0.74 or less
Risk-Adjusted Capital Ratio #2	1.0 or more	0.75 - 0.99	0.5 - 0.74	0.49 or less
Capitalization Index	7 – 10	5 - 6.9	3 - 4.9	2.9 or less
Reserve Adequacy Index	7 – 10	5 - 6.9	3 - 4.9	2.9 or less
Profitability Index	7 – 10	5 - 6.9	3 - 4.9	2.9 or less
Liquidity Index	7 – 10	5 - 6.9	3 - 4.9	2.9 or less
Stability Index	7 – 10	5 - 6.9	3 - 4.9	2.9 or less

7. Net Income

The company's profit for the period. Profit is defined as revenues minus expenses. In the case of an insurance company, revenues include premiums and investment income, and expenses include claims payments and underwriting expenses.

8. Capitalization Index

An index that measures the adequacy of the company's capital resources to deal with a variety of business and economic scenarios. It combines Risk-Adjusted Capital Ratios #1 and #2 as well as a leverage test that examines pricing risk. (See the table above for the ranges which we believe are critical.)

9. Reserve Adequacy Index

An index that uses annual and quarterly data to measure the adequacy of the company's reserves. Reserves are funds the company sets aside to cover unsettled claims it estimates each year. Included are claims that the company has already received but have not yet been settled and claims that they expect to receive, but which have not yet been reported.

If a company consistently estimates its claims accurately, that is good. Or if it errs on the side of being conservative and overestimates its claims from time to time, that is even better. Either case will cause this index to move higher.

On the other hand, some companies may have trouble accurately predicting the claims they will have to pay. Others may intentionally underestimate their claims to inflate their profits for stockholders or to make their capital appear higher than it really is. In either case, inadequate reserve levels will result in a low Reserve Adequacy Index.

If a company has chronically deficient reserves, it calls into question the company's ability to manage its policy risk effectively.

10. Profitability Index

An index that uses annual and quarterly data to measure the soundness of the company's operations and the contribution of profits to the company's fiscal strength. The Profitability Index is a composite of five factors: (1) gain or loss on underwriting; (2) gain or loss on overall operations; (3) consistency of operating results; (4) impact of operating results on surplus; and (5) expenses in relation to industry averages for the types of policies that the company offers.

11. Liquidity Index

An index which uses annual and quarterly data to measure the company's ability to raise the necessary cash to settle claims. Sometimes a company may appear to have the necessary resources to pay claims on paper, but in reality, it may be unable to raise the necessary cash. This can occur, for example, when a company is owed a great deal of money from its agents or reinsurers, or when it cannot sell its investments at the prices at which they are valued in the company's financial statements.

We look at various cash flow scenarios. Then we apply liquidity tests which tell us how the company might fare in each of those circumstances.

12. Stability Index

An index which uses annual and quarterly data to integrate a number of factors such as: (1) risk diversification in terms of company size, number of policies in force, use of reinsurance, and single largest risk exposure; (2) deterioration of operations as reported in critical asset, liability, income, or expense items such as premium volume and/or surplus (See the table prior page for the levels which we believe are critical.)

13. Stability Factors

Indicates those specific areas that have negatively impacted the company's Stability Index.

<u>*Right Pages*</u>

1. Risk-Adjusted Capital Ratio #1

This ratio examines the adequacy of the company's capital base and whether the company has sufficient capital resources to cover potential losses which might occur in an average recession or other moderate loss scenario. Specifically, the figure, calculated from annual and quarterly data, answers the question: For every dollar of capital that we feel would be needed, how many dollars in capital resources does the company actually have?

You may find that some companies have unusually high levels of capital. This often reflects special circumstances related to the small size or unusual operations of the company.

See the table prior page for the levels which we believe are critical. See the Appendix for more details on how this ratio is calculated.

2. Risk-Adjusted Capital Ratio #2

This is similar to the Risk-Adjusted Capital Ratio #1. But in this case, the question relates to whether the company has enough capital cushion to withstand a *severe* recession or other severe loss scenario.

See the table prior page for the levels which we believe are critical. See the Appendix for more details on how this ratio is calculated.

3. Premium to Surplus

The ratio of net premiums written compared to the company's capital and surplus level. This ratio, calculated from the company's annual report, answers the question: For every dollar of capital and surplus, how many dollars of premium does the company take in? Results of over 300% are considered perilous and could indicate that the insurer does not have adequate capital to support the volume of business that it is underwriting. A large figure could also help explain why a company has poor results on its risk-adjusted capital tests.

4. Reserves to Surplus

The ratio of reserves for expected claims compared to the company's capital and surplus level. If a company does not set aside enough reserves, it may have to withdraw capital to pay claims. This ratio, calculated from the annual report, is a rough measure of how much capital cushion the company has against claims reserves. The industry average is around 180%.

High ratios signify that reserve deficiencies would have a strong impact on capital and could help explain why a company has poor risk-adjusted capital results.

5. One-Year Reserve Development

The percentage increase or decrease in the company's annual reserve estimate compared to the previous year. If last year's estimate is below that of this year, this will result in a positive ratio meaning that the company underestimated its future claims and set aside insufficient reserves. Making this error consistently is viewed negatively because it means the company is inflating its income and capital.

6.	Two-Year Reserve Development	This ratio is similar to the One-Year Reserve Development ratio. However, instead of comparing the latest estimates with those from the prior year, it compares them to the estimates from two years ago.

Again, a positive ratio means the company underestimated its reserve needs while a negative ratio indicates that reserve needs were overestimated.

7.	Loss Ratio	The ratio of claims paid to premiums collected, calculated from the annual report, measures the company's underwriting profits. Needless to say, if an insurer pays out a very high percentage of what it collects, there may not be enough left over for other expenses, let alone enough to build the company's capital and financial strength over time.

8.	Expense Ratio	The ratio of overhead expenses to premiums collected, calculated from the annual report, and answers the question: How many cents is the company paying out in executive salaries, agents' commissions, and other administrative expenses for every dollar in premiums that it collects from policyholders? A low Expense Ratio is good for both the company and its policyholders because it means that the company is efficient and can utilize more of each premium dollar to pay claims. A high Expense Ratio is a bad sign because it signals that too much of the company's premiums are being used for things which do not directly benefit its policyholders.

9.	Combined Ratio	The sum of the Loss Ratio and the Expense Ratio. The Combined Ratio shows how much the company is paying out in administrative expenses and claims for every dollar of premium collected.

Values over 100% indicate that the company is losing money on its underwriting. This is very common in the industry, but it's still a sign of possible weakness.

Underwriting losses can often be offset by income the company realizes on its investments. This is especially true for companies that issue policies on which they do not have to pay claims for several years (long-tail policies). With these policies, the premiums can be invested in order to earn income for the company until the claims are paid.

10.	Cash from Underwriting	The ratio of cash received from premiums (net of reinsurance) to cash outlays for claims and underwriting expenses, compiled from the annual report. A figure under 100% indicates that the company is paying out more in claims and expenses than it is receiving in premiums, whereas a figure over 100% indicates a positive cash flow. A negative figure generally indicates that the company has sold more business to a reinsurance company than it has taken in during the current year.

When a company has a positive net cash flow from its underwriting, it can generate additional funds for investing. On the other hand, if net cash flow is negative, the company may have to rely on its investment income to make up the shortfall. And if that isn't enough, it may even have to sell assets to meet its obligations.

11. Net Premium Growth

The annual percentage change in net premiums compared to the previous year. A company can increase its premium volume by: (1) issuing more new policies; (2) raising its rates; or (3) selling less of its insurance to other insurance companies. Slow and steady growth is healthy but rapid growth is often an indicator of trouble ahead. It may mean that the company is underpricing as a means of gaining market share. Indeed, a high percentage of insurance company failures are related to rapid growth. Regulators consider a fluctuation of more than 33% as a cautionary flag.

A rapid decline in premium volume is also a negative sign. It indicates that the company is losing its customer base. However, if the decline is the result of premium redistribution among a group of affiliates, the significance of the decline is minimal.

12. Investments In Affiliates

The percentage of the company's investment portfolio from the annual report dedicated to investments in affiliates. These investments can be bonds, preferred and common stocks, as well as other vehicles which many insurance companies use to invest in – and establish a corporate link with – affiliated companies. Large investments of this type can pose problems as these investments often produce no income and can be difficult to sell.

Footnotes:

(1)   Data items shown are from the company's 2013 annual statutory statement except for Risk-Adjusted Capital Indexes 1 and 2, Profitability Index, Investment Safety Index, Liquidity Index and Stability Index which have been updated using the company's June 2014 quarterly statutory statement. Other more recent data may have been factored into the rating when available.

(2)   Data items shown are from the company's 2013 annual statutory statement except for Risk-Adjusted Capital Indexes 1 and 2, Profitability Index, Investment Safety Index, Liquidity Index and Stability Index which have been updated using the company's March 2014 quarterly statutory statement. Other more recent data may have been factored into the rating when available.

(3)   Data items shown are from the company's 2013 annual statutory statement. Other more recent data may have been factored into the rating when available.

(4)   Data items shown are from the company's 2012 annual statutory statement except for Risk-Adjusted Capital Indexes 1 and 2, Profitability Index, Investment Safety Index, Liquidity Index and Stability Index which have been updated using the company's September 2013 quarterly statutory statement. Other more recent data may have been factored into the rating when available.

(5)   These companies have data items that are older than December 31, 2012. They will be unrated (U) if they are not failed companies (F).

Stability Factors

(A)   Stability Index was negatively impacted by the financial problems or weaknesses of a parent or **affiliate** company.

(C)   Stability Index was negatively impacted by past results on our Risk-Adjusted **Capital** tests. In general, the Stability Index of any company can be affected by past results even if current results show improvement. While such improvement is a plus, the improved results must be maintained for a period of time to assure that the improvement is not a temporary fluctuation. During a five-year period, the impact of poor past results on the Stability Index gradually diminishes.

(D)   Stability Index was negatively impacted by limited **diversification** of general business, policy, and/or investment risk. This factor especially affects smaller companies that do not issue as many policies as larger firms. It can also affect firms that specialize in only one line of business.

(E)   Stability Index was negatively impacted due to a lack of operating **experience**. The company has been in operation for less than five years. Consequently, it has not been able to establish the kind of stable track record that we believe is needed to demonstrate financial permanence and strength.

(F)   Stability Index was negatively impacted by negative cash **flow**. In other words, the company paid out more in claims and expenses than it received in premiums and investment income.

(G)   Stability Index was negatively impacted by fast asset or premium **growth**. Fast growth can pose a serious problem for insurers. It is generally achieved by offering policies with premiums that are too low, benefits that are too costly, or agents commissions that are too high. Due to the highly competitive nature of the insurance marketplace, rapid growth has been a factor in many insurance insolvencies.

(L)   Stability Index was negatively impacted by results on our **liquidity** tests. While the company may have sufficient cash flow to meet its current obligations, it could encounter difficulties under adverse scenarios, such as a dramatic increase in claims.

(O)   Stability Index was negatively impacted by significant changes in the company's business **operations**. These changes can include shifts in the kinds of insurance offered by the company, a temporary or permanent freeze on the sale of new policies, or recent release from conservatorship. In these circumstances, past performance cannot be a reliable indicator of future financial strength.

(R)   Stability Index was negatively impacted by concerns about the financial strength of its **reinsurers**.

(T)   Stability Index was negatively impacted by significant **trends** in critical asset, liability, income or expense items. Examples include fluctuations in premium volume, changes in the types of investments the company makes, and changes in the types of policies the company writes.

(Z)   This company is unrated due to data, as received by Weiss Ratings, that are either incomplete in substantial ways or contains items that, in the opinion of Weiss Ratings analysts, may not be reliable.

INSURANCE COMPANY NAME	DOM. STATE	RATING	TOTAL ASSETS ($MIL)	CAPITAL & SURPLUS ($MIL)	ANNUAL NET PREMIUM ($MIL)	NET INCOME ($MIL)	CAPITAL-IZATION INDEX (PTS)	RESERVE ADQ INDEX (PTS)	PROFIT-ABILITY INDEX (PTS)	LIQUIDITY INDEX (PTS)	STAB. INDEX (PTS)	STABILITY FACTORS
1ST ATLANTIC SURETY CO	NC	U	3.2	2.4	0.1	-0.1	N/A	N/A	3.1	10.0	3.0	FT
1ST AUTO & CASUALTY INS CO	WI	C	29.8	11.7	20.3	-1.1	7.4	5.5	2.9	5.2	3.9	DR
1ST CHOICE AUTO INS CO	PA	C	17.2	8.4	8.7	0.3	8.6	8.0	4.7	6.3	3.5	DR
2-10 HOME BUYERS WARRANTY OF VA	VA	U (5)	0.0	0.0	9.7	0.0	N/A	5.3	8.0	5.5	4.5	ADGT
21ST CENTURY ADVANTAGE INS CO	MN	B	28.5	28.2	0.0	0.5	10.0	6.0	7.8	9.1	5.6	D
21ST CENTURY ASR CO	DE	B	69.0	67.8	0.0	1.3	10.0	4.9	8.2	9.7	5.8	
21ST CENTURY AUTO INS CO OF NJ	NJ	U	25.6	24.7	0.0	0.1	N/A	5.9	6.3	10.0	7.4	FT
21ST CENTURY CASUALTY CO	CA	B	12.4	11.9	0.0	0.0	10.0	5.0	6.0	10.0	4.7	DF
21ST CENTURY CENTENNIAL INS CO	PA	B	568.4	555.8	0.0	7.6	8.2	6.0	7.9	7.0	5.8	FT
21ST CENTURY INDEMNITY INS CO	PA	B	64.9	63.7	0.0	2.9	10.0	6.0	8.4	9.0	5.4	
21ST CENTURY INS CO	CA	B	889.9	878.1	0.0	15.9	10.0	5.0	5.9	9.7	5.9	
21ST CENTURY INS CO OF THE SW	TX	U	5.4	5.4	0.0	0.0	N/A	N/A	7.3	10.0	4.6	T
21ST CENTURY NATIONAL INS CO INC	NY	B	24.2	23.6	0.0	0.2	10.0	6.0	7.8	9.3	4.1	DFT
21ST CENTURY NORTH AMERICA INS	NY	B	566.3	542.2	0.0	4.6	10.0	6.0	8.2	10.0	5.8	
21ST CENTURY PACIFIC INS	CO	B	44.3	43.1	0.0	0.4	10.0	6.0	7.0	10.0	5.6	F
21ST CENTURY PINNACLE INS CO	NJ	B	42.2	41.2	0.0	0.5	10.0	6.0	7.9	10.0	5.6	DT
21ST CENTURY PREFERRED INS CO	PA	B	41.3	40.1	0.0	0.5	10.0	6.0	8.0	9.2	5.4	DFT
21ST CENTURY PREMIER INS CO	PA	B-	271.0	267.3	0.0	6.7	10.0	6.0	8.1	10.0	5.2	T
21ST CENTURY SECURITY INS CO	PA	B	195.7	190.9	0.0	2.4	10.0	6.0	7.9	10.0	4.6	DFT
21ST CENTURY SUPERIOR INS CO	CA	U	30.4	29.8	0.0	0.6	N/A	6.0	8.3	10.0	5.7	T
360 INS CO	CO	C+	26.6	23.1	0.2	0.6	10.0	3.7	6.9	10.0	3.5	DGOT
A CENTRAL INS CO	NY	E+	98.2	35.0	46.9	-0.1	7.8	7.5	3.0	6.1	0.5	T
A-ONE COMM INS RRG GROUP INC	TN	U	3.0	3.0	0.0	0.0	N/A	0.0	4.9	0.0	0.0	LT
AAA TEXAS COUNTY MUTUAL INS CO	TX	C-	75.4	8.2	0.0	0.0	7.0	N/A	6.5	6.6	2.9	D
ACA FINANCIAL GUARANTY CORP	MD	B+	374.0	94.7	0.1	13.5	7.6	6.8	1.6	9.4	5.3	DF
ACADEMIC HLTH PROFESSIONALS INS	NY	E-	288.7	-23.4	71.7	-15.8	0.0	1.8	0.5	7.0	0.0	CDRT
ACADEMIC MEDICAL PROFESSIONALS RRG	VT	D	3.1	2.1	0.3	0.0	5.2	4.7	3.8	7.0	1.6	DFT
ACADIA INS CO	NH	C	153.8	51.2	0.0	0.6	10.0	N/A	5.0	7.0	4.1	
ACCC INS CO	TX	D	315.2	65.3	267.3	6.3	1.8	9.4	7.6	2.2	2.1	CGLT
ACCEPTANCE CASUALTY INS CO	NE	D	69.1	49.5	10.6	0.8	7.8	6.1	6.8	7.7	2.1	DGRT
ACCEPTANCE INDEMNITY INS CO	NE	C-	238.5	126.8	56.9	1.0	7.1	5.8	5.1	6.6	2.7	GRT
ACCEPTANCE INS CO	NE	F	29.1	-4.2	0.0	-1.3	0.0	0.3	0.1	10.0	0.0	CDFR
ACCESS HOME INS CO	LA	D	29.6	7.9	17.5	1.8	2.0	3.7	7.2	7.2	2.1	DGT
ACCESS INS CO	TX	C-	139.7	29.1	55.0	-0.7	4.0	2.1	2.9	7.2	2.9	CGR
ACCIDENT FUND GENERAL INS CO	MI	B-	247.0	42.8	28.6	4.9	8.0	3.7	6.8	6.8	3.9	RT
ACCIDENT FUND INS CO OF AMERICA	MI	C+	2,514.9	734.6	546.7	42.6	7.2	3.3	5.2	6.4	4.6	FR
ACCIDENT FUND NATIONAL INS CO	MI	C+	226.6	59.7	42.9	6.3	8.1	3.6	4.9	6.5	4.6	R
ACCIDENT INS CO INC	SC	E+	143.9	20.0	10.0	1.5	5.3	7.0	6.2	7.4	0.6	DGR
ACCREDITED SURETY & CAS CO INC	FL	C-	24.1	20.5	9.4	1.0	8.2	5.9	7.9	7.4	2.1	DR
ACE AMERICAN INS CO	PA	B-	12,524.0	2,988.0	1,610.8	131.4	7.0	8.2	8.2	7.1	4.9	R
ACE FIRE UNDERWRITERS INS CO	PA	C	100.8	72.5	8.7	1.2	10.0	7.3	7.2	8.9	3.9	RT
ACE INS CO	PR	B-	137.8	46.8	34.4	4.3	6.2	9.5	8.6	7.1	3.9	T
ACE INS CO OF THE MIDWEST	IN	C	74.3	62.4	2.5	1.7	10.0	5.1	7.9	9.7	3.9	T
ACE PROPERTY & CASUALTY INS CO	PA	C	7,350.7	2,042.8	1,523.8	88.8	8.2	8.4	7.6	6.8	4.2	R
ACIG INS CO	IL	D+	412.6	119.5	75.2	1.6	6.5	9.3	6.0	6.8	2.2	R
ACSTAR INS CO	IL	C	63.7	29.9	2.0	1.8	8.4	8.7	5.5	9.6	3.1	DR
ACUITY A MUTUAL INS CO	WI	B	3,017.8	1,283.5	1,074.0	71.0	9.0	9.3	8.8	6.7	5.7	T
ADDISON INS CO	IA	C+	100.8	38.1	28.9	0.9	7.7	6.8	6.7	6.7	4.7	T
ADIRONDACK INS EXCH	NY	D+	196.9	48.6	109.9	-7.5	6.9	9.3	1.8	4.9	2.5	LR
ADM INS CO	AZ	C-	438.6	21.5	0.0	-0.6	8.1	5.1	4.3	7.0	3.2	FGT
ADMIRAL INDEMNITY CO	DE	C	51.3	39.5	-6.1	0.9	10.0	4.9	7.7	7.1	4.2	FRT
ADMIRAL INS CO	DE	C-	682.0	605.3	-255.7	4.1	7.8	4.8	1.9	6.6	3.2	AFRT

See Page 27 for explanation of footnotes and
Page 28 for explanation of stability factors.
Arrows denote recent upgrades ▲ or downgrades ▼   (see Section VII for explanations)

30

www.weissratings.com

RISK ADJ. CAPITAL RATIO #1	RATIO #2	PREMIUM TO SURPLUS (%)	RESV. TO SURPLUS (%)	RESV. DEVELOP. 1 YEAR (%)	2 YEAR (%)	LOSS RATIO (%)	EXP. RATIO (%)	COMB RATIO (%)	CASH FROM UNDER-WRITING (%)	NET PREMIUM GROWTH (%)	INVEST. IN AFFIL (%)	INSURANCE COMPANY NAME
N/A	N/A	2.5	0.1	N/A	N/A	12.6	266.2	278.8	74.3	0.0	0.0	1ST ATLANTIC SURETY CO
1.5	1.2	171.2	84.0	-8.5	2.1	68.3	31.0	99.3	92.3	10.1	0.0	1ST AUTO & CASUALTY INS CO
2.8	1.9	109.2	22.7	-1.3	-2.5	74.7	26.1	100.8	110.7	30.3	0.0	1ST CHOICE AUTO INS CO
N/A	N/A	212.3	10.6	0.6	4.6	54.9	42.2	97.1	113.2	15.9	0.0	2-10 HOME BUYERS WARRANTY OF VA
109.1	57.2	N/A	2.9	0.3	1.4	N/A	N/A	N/A	-11.8	0.0	0.0	21ST CENTURY ADVANTAGE INS CO
136.0	80.8	N/A	2.4	0.3	1.2	N/A	N/A	N/A	N/A	0.0	0.0	21ST CENTURY ASR CO
N/A	N/A	N/A	4.8	0.5	2.3	N/A	N/A	N/A	N/A	0.0	0.0	21ST CENTURY AUTO INS CO OF NJ
59.7	53.7	N/A	1.7	0.2	0.8	N/A	N/A	N/A	N/A	0.0	0.0	21ST CENTURY CASUALTY CO
1.8	1.8	N/A	2.9	0.3	1.5	N/A	N/A	N/A	2.5	0.0	58.9 ●	21ST CENTURY CENTENNIAL INS CO
127.8	86.1	N/A	2.6	0.3	1.5	N/A	N/A	N/A	N/A	0.0	0.0	21ST CENTURY INDEMNITY INS CO
76.4	41.3	N/A	1.8	0.2	0.8	N/A	N/A	N/A	N/A	0.0	0.0 ●	21ST CENTURY INS CO
N/A	N/A	N/A	N/A	N/A	N/A	N/A	N/A	N/A	N/A	0.0	0.0	21ST CENTURY INS CO OF THE SW
52.4	40.3	N/A	3.4	0.4	1.6	N/A	N/A	N/A	N/A	0.0	0.0	21ST CENTURY NATIONAL INS CO INC
5.8	5.5	N/A	3.4	0.4	1.7	N/A	N/A	N/A	6.0	0.0	17.5 ●	21ST CENTURY NORTH AMERICA INS
85.3	52.1	N/A	3.7	0.4	1.8	N/A	N/A	N/A	N/A	0.0	0.0	21ST CENTURY PACIFIC INS
89.8	55.1	N/A	3.4	0.4	1.7	N/A	N/A	N/A	N/A	0.0	0.0	21ST CENTURY PINNACLE INS CO
80.4	59.0	N/A	4.0	0.4	1.9	N/A	N/A	N/A	N/A	0.0	0.0	21ST CENTURY PREFERRED INS CO
4.6	4.5	N/A	3.1	0.3	1.6	N/A	N/A	N/A	-19.2	0.0	23.4 ●	21ST CENTURY PREMIER INS CO
8.4	7.9	N/A	3.4	0.4	1.6	N/A	N/A	N/A	N/A	0.0	12.2	21ST CENTURY SECURITY INS CO
N/A	N/A	N/A	2.7	0.3	1.3	N/A	N/A	N/A	N/A	0.0	0.0	21ST CENTURY SUPERIOR INS CO
20.6	18.5	1.0	0.6	-1.7	-1.9	-100.1	-104.3	-204.4	381.3	-65.3	0.0	360 INS CO
2.6	2.0	131.8	75.2	0.2	-0.4	68.8	31.8	100.6	102.9	1.7	0.0	A CENTRAL INS CO
N/A	N/A	N/A	N/A	N/A	N/A	N/A	N/A	N/A	N/A	0.0	0.0	A-ONE COMM INS RRG GROUP INC
1.0	0.9	N/A	N/A	N/A	N/A	N/A	N/A	N/A	155.6	0.0	0.0	AAA TEXAS COUNTY MUTUAL INS CO
2.0	1.6	0.2	100.3	3.9	-8.7	141.0	999 +	999 +	0.3	136.4	0.0 ●	ACA FINANCIAL GUARANTY CORP
-0.0	-0.0	-814.1	999 +	-113.5	-155.0	107.0	2.6	109.6	182.9	15.4	-0.1	ACADEMIC HLTH PROFESSIONALS INS
1.9	1.2	18.1	21.8	-1.1	-7.6	32.8	72.0	104.8	-32.3	24.5	0.0	ACADEMIC MEDICAL PROFESSIONALS
5.6	5.1	N/A	N/A	N/A	N/A	N/A	N/A	N/A	-408.1	0.0	0.0	ACADIA INS CO
0.5	0.4	460.8	233.5	-0.5	-7.4	81.7	15.3	97.0	123.2	58.9	0.8	ACCC INS CO
2.4	1.4	21.2	14.3	-1.6	-4.0	55.4	33.3	88.7	114.2	164.2	0.0	ACCEPTANCE CASUALTY INS CO
1.3	0.9	45.8	31.2	0.2	-1.9	69.1	33.3	102.4	110.4	44.0	24.2	ACCEPTANCE INDEMNITY INS CO
-0.6	-0.2	N/A	-734.5	84.9	113.8	N/A	N/A	N/A	N/A	0.0	0.0	ACCEPTANCE INS CO
0.7	0.4	285.0	10.9	4.0	-2.0	30.8	38.6	69.4	116.9	31.9	0.0	ACCESS HOME INS CO
0.6	0.5	185.3	92.2	15.1	27.5	94.6	11.2	105.8	163.0	50.1	0.0	ACCESS INS CO
1.9	1.5	74.8	92.3	2.1	4.0	66.0	16.6	82.6	134.9	13.2	0.0	ACCIDENT FUND GENERAL INS CO
1.4	1.1	79.9	98.6	2.1	6.5	65.9	29.2	95.1	94.5	11.8	16.3 ●	ACCIDENT FUND INS CO OF AMERICA
2.1	1.7	80.2	99.0	2.5	5.2	66.0	29.9	95.9	123.8	13.2	0.0	ACCIDENT FUND NATIONAL INS CO
0.3	0.2	59.1	52.0	11.7	7.7	60.5	53.0	113.5	91.1	36.2	0.0	ACCIDENT INS CO INC
2.3	2.1	45.6	2.0	-2.6	-0.2	-4.1	88.0	83.9	122.4	-4.9	0.0	ACCREDITED SURETY & CAS CO INC
1.5	1.2	60.2	106.4	-4.4	-3.7	72.2	17.7	89.9	151.8	-2.8	21.2 ●	ACE AMERICAN INS CO
16.4	10.8	12.2	21.6	-0.8	-0.6	72.2	19.7	91.9	135.4	-2.8	0.0	ACE FIRE UNDERWRITERS INS CO
1.5	1.0	77.5	117.9	-11.2	-19.8	25.5	64.5	90.0	103.5	18.0	0.0	ACE INS CO
23.8	21.4	4.2	2.3	-0.1	-0.4	66.7	-31.0	35.7	-745.4	18.4	0.0	ACE INS CO OF THE MIDWEST
2.9	2.0	79.3	140.2	-5.6	-4.3	72.2	24.4	96.6	102.9	-2.8	3.4 ●	ACE PROPERTY & CASUALTY INS CO
1.7	1.1	65.2	191.5	-8.8	-7.2	73.9	31.5	105.4	107.6	-14.2	0.0	ACIG INS CO
3.3	2.0	7.1	46.8	-2.3	-5.1	10.0	81.4	91.4	104.1	-0.2	0.0	ACSTAR INS CO
3.8	2.3	89.3	82.8	-6.1	-11.9	62.0	28.2	90.2	120.7	14.5	0.1 ●	ACUITY A MUTUAL INS CO
2.2	1.4	78.1	94.4	-6.0	-8.4	63.3	31.6	94.9	115.9	10.3	0.0	ADDISON INS CO
1.3	0.9	184.5	97.4	-3.7	-4.9	68.1	44.0	112.1	93.1	9.9	11.1	ADIRONDACK INS EXCH
1.9	1.7	N/A	N/A	N/A	N/A	N/A	N/A	N/A	121.1	0.0	0.0	ADM INS CO
15.2	13.7	-15.8	N/A	N/A	N/A	N/A	N/A	N/A	-61.3	-154.9	0.0	ADMIRAL INDEMNITY CO
1.7	1.8	-42.8	N/A	N/A	N/A	N/A	N/A	N/A	-14.0	-149.1	51.5 ●	ADMIRAL INS CO

999 + Denotes number greater than 999.9%
999 - Denotes number less than -999.99%
● Bullets denote a more detailed analysis is available in Section II.

INSURANCE COMPANY NAME	DOM. STATE	RATING	TOTAL ASSETS ($MIL)	CAPITAL & SURPLUS ($MIL)	ANNUAL NET PREMIUM ($MIL)	NET INCOME ($MIL)	CAPITAL- IZATION INDEX (PTS)	RESERVE ADQ INDEX (PTS)	PROFIT- ABILITY INDEX (PTS)	LIQUIDITY INDEX (PTS)	STAB. INDEX (PTS)	STABILITY FACTORS
ADRIATIC INS CO	ND	C	70.8	60.1	14.5	1.2	10.0	7.8	5.9	9.2	4.0	DR
ADVANCED PHYSICIANS INS RRG INC	AZ	D	1.9	1.7	0.2	0.2	10.0	N/A	6.9	8.7	1.4	DT
ADVANTAGE WORKERS COMP INS CO	IN	C	104.1	50.6	8.9	0.3	8.6	4.8	2.0	7.5	3.8	DFT
AEGIS HEALTHCARE RRG INC	DC	E	3.3	1.4	1.0	-0.1	5.6	7.1	4.2	7.1	0.0	DFRT
AEGIS SECURITY INS CO	PA	B-	106.3	52.5	69.4	1.6	7.7	9.3	8.7	7.0	4.7	R
AETNA INS CO OF CT	CT	C	15.7	14.7	3.0	0.2	8.7	6.1	3.1	6.0	4.1	DFRT
▼AF&L INS CO	PA	E-	157.9	-0.3	25.0	-0.2	0.0	0.1	1.5	0.0	0.0	CDFL
AFFILIATED FM INS CO	RI	C	2,524.3	1,343.1	387.6	78.6	8.9	6.7	7.0	6.8	3.9	R
AFFILIATES INS CO	IN	C+	63.6	47.2	4.5	0.3	10.0	N/A	5.2	8.0	3.2	DGT
AFFILIATES INS RECIPROCAL A RRG	VT	B-	9.2	3.2	0.4	0.0	10.0	3.8	4.1	9.6	3.5	DF
AFFINITY MUTUAL INS CO	OH	C	15.4	8.7	5.4	-1.1	8.1	7.9	3.5	7.6	3.0	DR
AFFIRMATIVE INS CO	IL	D	197.5	31.8	128.6	-36.1	4.2	3.1	0.4	0.0	1.8	AFLR
AFFIRMATIVE INS CO OF MI	MI	U	9.2	9.2	0.0	0.0	N/A	N/A	5.8	10.0	4.9	FRT
AG SECURITY INS CO	OK	C+	58.0	30.1	18.6	1.0	10.0	7.0	5.4	7.0	4.6	T
AGCS MARINE INS CO	IL	D+	368.1	157.9	217.1	20.3	3.0	9.5	3.3	5.7	1.8	DR
AGENCY INS CO OF MARYLAND INC	MD	C	96.6	33.7	66.3	3.2	6.7	4.4	6.5	5.2	4.0	R
AGENT ALLIANCE INS CO	AL	C-	18.1	16.5	0.0	-0.2	10.0	3.2	3.7	7.0	3.3	DFT
AGENTS MUTUAL INS CO	AR	D	3.6	1.6	1.4	0.3	7.4	7.8	6.0	7.9	1.2	DRT
AGGREGATE SECURITY INS GROUP A RRG	NV	E-	4.0	0.7	0.5	0.1	0.0	1.9	0.5	8.3	0.0	CDGT
AGIC INC	FL	D	6.9	4.1	3.0	-1.1	4.3	2.1	1.2	5.7	2.3	DFT
AGRI GENERAL INS CO	IA	C-	254.6	253.8	-0.8	4.0	10.0	7.8	1.9	7.0	3.1	RT
AGRI INS EXCHANGE RISK RETENTION GRP	IN	C-	16.3	13.2	0.9	0.4	7.7	6.7	8.2	9.7	3.0	D
AGRICULTURAL WORKERS MUT AUTO INS	TX	B-	78.1	35.9	35.9	3.0	7.5	6.0	5.6	6.1	4.5	R
AGRINATIONAL INS CO	VT	E	1,114.9	226.4	229.9	2.4	2.2	9.4	2.9	0.6	0.3	DGLR
AIG ASR CO	PA	B	32.2	30.7	0.0	0.9	10.0	N/A	5.6	7.0	5.3	DT
AIG INS CO - PUERTO RICO	PR	B	180.4	85.6	19.1	-0.5	10.0	7.8	3.9	8.6	5.7	
AIG PROPERTY CASUALTY CO	PA	C+	4,865.6	1,454.7	713.5	156.8	7.6	3.6	3.3	6.8	4.8	A
AIG SPECIALTY INS CO	IL	C	307.1	246.3	417.3	271.7	7.5	5.9	1.9	6.9	2.8	A
AIMCO MUTUAL INS CO	NC	U	9.1	5.7	0.0	-0.3	N/A	7.0	4.3	9.6	3.5	FT
AIOI NISSAY DOWA INS CO LTD	GU	D+	24.3	10.4	9.5	2.2	5.3	4.0	0.9	8.6	1.3	DT
AIOI NISSAY DOWA INS CO OF AMERICA	NY	C+	103.7	60.1	11.6	2.8	10.0	9.3	8.0	7.5	4.5	R
AIU INS CO	NY	C	243.7	238.7	-446.8	2.9	8.6	6.7	1.9	6.8	2.8	ADRT
AIX SPECIALTY INS CO	DE	B-	52.4	50.0	0.0	1.0	10.0	3.6	6.9	9.3	5.3	
ALABAMA MUNICIPAL INS CORP	AL	C-	94.5	37.9	32.1	2.2	7.2	7.0	3.1	6.9	3.3	R
ALAMANCE FARMERS MUTUAL INS CO	NC	B-	7.7	5.3	2.0	0.2	7.5	6.0	4.9	6.9	3.5	D
ALAMANCE INS CO	IL	C-	486.7	368.4	40.7	7.0	7.6	8.0	8.3	7.8	2.6	R
ALASKA NATIONAL INS CO	AK	B	853.2	371.5	200.6	33.9	8.8	9.4	8.0	7.3	6.1	T
ALASKA TIMBER INS EXCHANGE	AK	C	19.2	8.9	4.8	-0.4	8.0	9.4	4.9	8.4	2.9	DFR
ALEA NORTH AMERICA INS CO	NY	U	146.2	95.0	0.0	13.0	N/A	5.7	2.0	10.0	4.2	FRT
ALFA ALLIANCE INS CORP	VA	C	27.6	13.4	10.9	-0.1	8.6	8.0	2.7	6.9	3.4	D
ALFA GENERAL INS CORP	AL	B-	98.0	55.1	43.6	1.2	10.0	8.1	5.1	6.9	5.0	
ALFA INS CORP	AL	B+	99.4	54.1	32.7	1.0	10.0	8.1	5.2	6.8	6.5	D
ALFA MUTUAL FIRE INS CO	AL	B	687.7	399.2	327.1	-7.7	7.4	7.7	5.2	5.1	6.3	L
ALFA MUTUAL GENERAL INS CO	AL	B+	100.9	55.9	43.6	1.4	7.5	7.5	5.0	6.4	6.4	D
ALFA MUTUAL INS CO	AL	B	1,293.2	570.5	566.7	-9.0	7.2	6.2	4.0	2.2	6.0	L
ALFA SPECIALTY INS CORP	VA	C+	53.9	26.2	21.8	0.1	5.6	6.4	4.8	5.4	4.6	D
ALFA VISION INS CORP	VA	C+	97.0	46.4	43.6	0.3	8.9	7.5	3.8	6.9	4.4	
ALICOT INS CO	TX	U (5)	0.0	0.0	0.0	0.0	N/A	N/A	6.3	7.0	4.0	T
ALINSCO INS CO	TX	U	20.2	5.4	0.0	0.2	N/A	0.0	4.9	0.0	0.0	LT
ALL AMERICA INS CO	OH	B+	256.6	127.9	76.6	3.6	10.0	7.0	6.4	6.8	6.4	
ALLEGANY CO-OP INS CO	NY	C+	47.5	31.1	13.0	1.4	10.0	6.5	8.8	7.0	4.8	DR
ALLEGHENY CASUALTY CO	PA	C	39.5	23.0	21.4	0.4	5.4	5.4	8.2	6.9	3.7	DF

See Page 27 for explanation of footnotes and
Page 28 for explanation of stability factors.
Arrows denote recent upgrades ▲ or downgrades ▼   (see Section VII for explanations)

32

www.weissratings.com

RISK ADJ. CAPITAL RATIO #1	RATIO #2	PREMIUM TO SURPLUS (%)	RESV. TO SURPLUS (%)	RESV. DEVELOP. 1 YEAR (%)	2 YEAR (%)	LOSS RATIO (%)	EXP. RATIO (%)	COMB RATIO (%)	CASH FROM UNDER- WRITING (%)	NET PREMIUM GROWTH (%)	INVEST. IN AFFIL (%)	INSURANCE COMPANY NAME
10.2	6.4	24.6	6.4	-2.2	-2.1	67.1	28.2	95.3	112.4	23.1	0.0	ADRIATIC INS CO
7.7	5.8	13.5	12.7	N/A	N/A	93.9	62.1	156.0	257.1	-43.0	0.0	ADVANCED PHYSICIANS INS RRG INC
4.1	2.6	17.7	113.0	5.0	3.4	107.7	31.3	139.0	35.3	-26.5	0.0	ADVANTAGE WORKERS COMP INS CO
1.5	1.2	65.2	97.8	-46.9	-43.3	13.1	41.3	54.4	99.4	9.8	0.0	AEGIS HEALTHCARE RRG INC
2.2	1.7	134.7	32.6	-10.3	-12.0	48.5	38.9	87.4	116.3	10.7	18.4	AEGIS SECURITY INS CO
16.8	14.3	20.2	3.9	-0.2	-0.6	77.6	70.9	148.5	82.3	-77.1	0.0	AETNA INS CO OF CT
-0.0	-0.0	999 +	999 +	999 +	999 +	145.3	14.3	159.6	56.9	-11.9	0.0	AF&L INS CO
3.8	2.4	30.7	33.1	-1.1	4.5	50.6	28.0	78.6	163.2	-12.7	0.0 ●	AFFILIATED FM INS CO
7.9	4.9	9.6	0.3	N/A	N/A	1.6	20.1	21.7	254.0	42.2	0.0	AFFILIATES INS CO
1.8	1.7	12.0	21.3	-8.4	-6.9	77.8	15.2	93.0	64.5	0.9	0.0	AFFILIATES INS RECIPROCAL A RRG
2.4	1.5	54.6	19.5	-0.4	-2.9	57.0	45.1	102.1	135.9	10.1	0.0	AFFINITY MUTUAL INS CO
0.5	0.4	277.9	131.9	22.6	15.8	89.1	31.6	120.7	89.0	-24.6	26.9	AFFIRMATIVE INS CO
N/A	N/A	N/A	N/A	N/A	N/A	N/A	N/A	N/A	-55.5	0.0	0.0	AFFIRMATIVE INS CO OF MI
5.6	3.6	64.0	30.6	-7.4	-15.3	64.6	26.6	91.2	115.0	17.4	0.0	AG SECURITY INS CO
6.3	4.5	137.2	195.2	-8.2	-15.4	78.1	27.8	105.9	131.8	-5.2	0.3	AGCS MARINE INS CO
1.2	1.1	217.0	95.4	-2.4	13.0	68.6	26.2	94.8	107.0	2.1	0.0	AGENCY INS CO OF MARYLAND INC
26.4	20.9	N/A	N/A	N/A	N/A	N/A	N/A	N/A	999 +	0.0	0.0	AGENT ALLIANCE INS CO
2.1	1.5	116.8	10.8	-9.8	-2.5	60.5	13.6	74.1	138.0	21.4	0.0	AGENTS MUTUAL INS CO
0.0	0.0	-58.7	-425.2	999 +	284.2	397.1	N/A	397.1	511.1	11.1	0.0	AGGREGATE SECURITY INS GROUP A
1.2	0.9	68.0	51.3	13.2	40.4	93.1	59.0	152.1	72.5	57.1	0.0	AGIC INC
82.9	40.7	-0.3	N/A	-0.3	-1.2	170.5	-121.6	48.9	208.1	61.7	0.0 ●	AGRI GENERAL INS CO
2.0	1.2	7.0	16.9	-1.8	-3.8	40.5	28.7	69.2	242.5	21.9	0.0	AGRI INS EXCHANGE RISK RETENTION
1.9	1.3	104.8	23.2	-0.3	1.2	72.3	15.3	87.6	120.6	6.2	12.3	AGRICULTURAL WORKERS MUT AUTO
0.7	0.6	138.7	147.3	-36.8	-28.9	90.2	10.8	101.0	106.0	19.2	54.0	AGRINATIONAL INS CO
54.5	46.4	N/A	N/A	N/A	N/A	N/A	N/A	N/A	N/A	0.0	0.0	AIG ASR CO
6.2	3.9	14.2	11.8	-1.4	-1.9	24.2	56.6	80.8	122.5	-2.8	0.1	AIG INS CO - PUERTO RICO
2.2	1.4	61.2	142.2	3.0	4.3	76.6	32.5	109.1	95.9	16.0	0.1 ●	AIG PROPERTY CASUALTY CO
3.4	2.3	56.3	166.4	-5.0	-3.5	69.4	20.8	90.2	84.6	3.7	0.0 ●	AIG SPECIALTY INS CO
N/A	N/A	0.1	57.5	-20.2	-14.6	999 +	999 +	999 +	0.3	N/A	0.0	AIMCO MUTUAL INS CO
1.5	0.9	114.5	32.9	-8.7	-20.4	36.8	36.9	73.7	144.5	24.3	0.0	AIOI NISSAY DOWA INS CO LTD
10.2	7.7	19.7	44.2	-3.9	-7.0	60.6	17.7	78.3	116.2	-58.6	0.0	AIOI NISSAY DOWA INS CO OF AMERICA
2.7	2.6	-198.6	11.3	-26.9	-12.2	438.2	7.3	445.5	108.0	-164.8	36.7 ●	AIU INS CO
57.4	25.0	N/A	N/A	N/A	N/A	N/A	N/A	N/A	N/A	0.0	0.0	AIX SPECIALTY INS CO
1.7	1.5	88.6	121.1	-16.5	-24.6	59.2	21.9	81.1	109.2	6.2	0.0	ALABAMA MUNICIPAL INS CORP
2.1	1.2	39.9	15.4	-1.7	0.6	50.3	48.4	98.7	123.1	7.3	0.0	ALAMANCE FARMERS MUTUAL INS CO
1.4	1.4	11.4	27.1	-2.3	-3.7	50.6	38.6	89.2	105.2	-5.6	57.1 ●	ALAMANCE INS CO
3.1	2.1	56.9	97.6	-15.4	-16.4	51.3	26.3	77.6	127.0	9.1	0.0 ●	ALASKA NATIONAL INS CO
2.1	1.6	52.1	96.6	-15.2	-21.1	41.2	18.4	59.6	134.1	21.9	0.0	ALASKA TIMBER INS EXCHANGE
N/A	N/A	N/A	25.6	1.1	0.7	999 +	999 +	999 +	N/A	-97.7	0.0	ALEA NORTH AMERICA INS CO
3.0	2.0	76.9	29.8	-1.8	-2.7	68.4	32.0	100.4	105.0	5.1	0.0	ALFA ALLIANCE INS CORP
3.7	2.4	73.8	26.2	-3.4	-5.1	66.4	29.1	95.5	100.5	5.1	0.0	ALFA GENERAL INS CORP
5.0	3.3	55.3	20.1	-2.9	-4.9	65.6	28.4	94.0	99.6	5.2	0.0 ●	ALFA INS CORP
1.9	1.4	81.9	26.8	-2.2	-2.4	68.6	29.6	98.2	100.4	5.1	37.6 ●	ALFA MUTUAL FIRE INS CO
2.2	1.4	80.3	26.3	-2.1	-1.9	68.8	29.4	98.2	100.6	5.1	0.7 ●	ALFA MUTUAL GENERAL INS CO
1.4	1.1	97.6	35.6	-2.6	-1.8	68.7	30.0	98.7	101.6	5.1	45.3 ●	ALFA MUTUAL INS CO
1.9	1.3	117.4	38.3	-2.8	-2.4	68.8	29.4	98.2	97.0	5.1	0.0	ALFA SPECIALTY INS CORP
3.3	2.1	95.0	31.2	-2.7	-2.4	68.4	29.3	97.7	98.1	5.1	0.0	ALFA VISION INS CORP
N/A	N/A	N/A	N/A	N/A	N/A	N/A	N/A	N/A	N/A	0.0	0.0	ALICOT INS CO
N/A	N/A	N/A	N/A	N/A	N/A	N/A	N/A	N/A	N/A	0.0	0.0	ALINSCO INS CO
5.2	3.4	61.4	56.2	-6.2	-12.5	58.4	32.9	91.3	98.1	8.8	0.1 ●	ALL AMERICA INS CO
4.4	2.9	44.4	18.5	-0.9	0.3	43.4	36.4	79.8	134.4	4.0	0.0	ALLEGANY CO-OP INS CO
0.8	0.7	104.4	0.4	-0.8	-1.5	-0.2	98.1	97.9	89.2	10.1	0.0	ALLEGHENY CASUALTY CO

999 + Denotes number greater than 999.9%
999 - Denotes number less than -999.99%
● Bullets denote a more detailed analysis is available in Section II.

INSURANCE COMPANY NAME	DOM. STATE	RATING	TOTAL ASSETS ($MIL)	CAPITAL & SURPLUS ($MIL)	ANNUAL NET PREMIUM ($MIL)	NET INCOME ($MIL)	CAPITAL-IZATION INDEX (PTS)	RESERVE ADQ INDEX (PTS)	PROFIT-ABILITY INDEX (PTS)	LIQUIDITY INDEX (PTS)	STAB. INDEX (PTS)	STABILITY FACTORS
ALLEGHENY SURETY CO	PA	D	4.6	3.0	1.6	0.0	7.9	7.8	4.9	6.6	2.1	DR
ALLEGIANT INS CO INC A RRG	HI	E	20.2	6.1	3.4	1.2	1.2	0.4	3.7	9.0	0.0	DG
ALLIANCE INDEMNITY CO	KS	C+	9.5	6.1	3.5	0.1	10.0	7.7	4.4	6.8	3.8	DR
ALLIANCE INS CO INC	KS	C	22.3	8.8	14.1	-0.1	7.8	8.4	2.7	6.0	3.7	DR
ALLIANCE MUTUAL INS CO	NC	D (1)	2.1	2.1	-0.7	-0.2	10.0	9.5	1.7	10.0	1.9	DFT
ALLIANCE NATIONAL INS CO	NY	E	47.5	8.4	10.8	2.8	0.0	3.0	2.1	2.5	0.1	CDGL
ALLIANCE OF NONPROFITS FOR INS RRG	VT	D	73.2	28.2	21.5	0.7	7.1	7.0	6.9	7.4	2.3	R
ALLIANCE UNITED INS CO	CA	D	252.4	48.4	161.9	-0.9	3.0	5.8	3.5	3.9	2.3	GLT
ALLIANZ GLOBAL RISKS US INS CO	IL	C-	3,442.4	893.7	868.2	32.9	3.2	7.9	1.9	6.2	3.1	CFR
ALLIANZ UNDERWRITERS INS CO	IL	C-	96.3	66.8	0.0	1.1	10.0	3.6	6.6	8.0	2.4	DRT
ALLIED EASTERN INDEMNITY CO	PA	C+	68.4	13.9	17.2	0.9	5.3	4.6	7.0	6.8	4.5	DGR
ALLIED INS CO OF AMERICA	OH	U	13.9	13.9	0.0	0.0	N/A	N/A	7.0	7.0	5.1	GT
ALLIED PROFESSIONALS INS CO RRG	AZ	D+	39.3	14.1	15.7	0.1	7.4	6.9	8.0	7.3	2.4	DR
ALLIED PROPERTY & CASUALTY INS CO	IA	B	362.1	58.7	0.0	0.4	10.0	N/A	4.2	7.3	5.4	
ALLIED SERVICES RRG	SC	E	7.4	4.5	1.0	0.5	2.7	4.5	4.2	7.4	0.0	D
ALLIED WORLD ASR CO (US) INC	DE	C	339.1	137.7	39.4	3.0	9.3	8.5	4.9	8.0	4.2	ART
ALLIED WORLD INS CO	NH	C	1,834.2	1,057.3	177.2	21.4	7.7	5.6	7.6	7.0	3.4	ART
ALLIED WORLD NATL ASR CO	NH	B-	300.4	127.3	39.4	1.2	10.0	8.4	5.2	7.5	4.6	ART
ALLIED WORLD SURPLUS LINES INS	AR	C	238.9	62.7	39.4	1.2	7.9	8.3	5.6	7.4	3.9	RT
ALLMERICA FINANCIAL ALLIANCE INS CO	NH	C+	19.3	19.3	0.0	0.3	10.0	N/A	7.4	7.0	4.4	DR
ALLMERICA FINANCIAL BENEFIT INS CO	MI	C+	33.0	33.0	0.0	0.5	10.0	N/A	7.5	7.0	4.5	R
ALLSTATE COUNTY MUTUAL INS CO	TX	B	14.6	14.6	0.0	0.0	10.0	N/A	6.1	7.0	4.9	DT
ALLSTATE FIRE & CASUALTY INS CO	IL	C	150.7	148.4	0.0	1.2	10.0	N/A	7.4	10.0	3.9	
ALLSTATE INDEMNITY CO	IL	B	154.3	144.0	0.0	1.2	10.0	N/A	5.2	10.0	5.4	T
ALLSTATE INS CO	IL	A-	44,425.2	16,990.1	25,108.5	1,436.0	7.9	5.6	7.9	5.9	7.2	
ALLSTATE NJ INS CO	IL	B	2,569.7	896.6	1,190.1	117.0	8.2	4.8	5.3	6.2	6.1	
ALLSTATE NJ PROPERTY & CASUALTY INS	IL	C-	49.7	48.5	0.0	0.6	10.0	N/A	7.6	10.0	3.3	T
ALLSTATE NORTH AMERICAN INS CO	IL	U	11.0	11.0	0.0	0.1	N/A	N/A	5.0	7.0	5.4	T
ALLSTATE NORTHBROOK INDEMNITY CO	IL	B-	39.5	39.3	0.0	0.5	10.0	N/A	6.5	10.0	5.0	
ALLSTATE PROPERTY & CASUALTY INS CO	IL	B	218.3	205.4	0.0	1.7	10.0	N/A	7.6	10.0	6.1	
ALLSTATE TEXAS LLOYDS	TX	B	17.1	16.9	0.0	0.1	10.0	N/A	6.3	7.0	4.9	DT
ALLSTATE VEHICLE & PROPERTY INS CO	IL	B	25.4	23.4	0.0	0.5	10.0	N/A	7.0	10.0	4.7	DT
ALPHA PROPERTY & CASUALTY INS CO	WI	B	34.3	13.0	0.0	0.3	10.0	N/A	6.8	10.0	4.9	DR
ALPS PROPERTY & CASUALTY INS CO	MT	C	98.8	36.7	28.1	1.8	7.3	9.4	6.2	6.9	3.4	R
ALTERRA AMERICA INS CO	DE	B	225.8	155.1	21.3	-1.9	7.2	5.0	3.6	6.8	4.7	FGT
ALTERRA EXCESS & SURPLUS INS CO	DE	C	381.9	149.9	52.1	4.2	5.9	4.0	3.2	7.5	3.5	GR
ALTERRA REINS USA INC	CT	B+	1,467.0	733.7	186.9	13.0	9.4	5.2	6.8	8.2	6.5	
AMALGAMATED CASUALTY INS CO	DC	C	45.8	38.5	5.0	0.5	10.0	8.3	7.8	9.0	3.5	D
AMBAC ASR CORP SEGREGATED ACCT	WI	U	13.6	441.7	0.0	0.0	N/A	N/A	0.8	7.0	0.0	CFT
AMBAC ASSURANCE CORP	WI	E	5,940.7	897.7	90.3	224.6	1.6	2.6	1.7	10.0	-0.5	CRT
AMC RE INC	AR	U (3)	0.0	0.0	0.0	0.0	N/A	4.1	4.2	7.0	1.4	FT
AMCO INS CO	IA	C+	971.4	205.0	0.0	31.5	10.0	N/A	1.9	10.0	4.5	T
AMERICA FIRST INS CO	NH	B-	13.9	13.9	0.0	0.2	10.0	N/A	7.7	6.8	4.9	DR
AMERICA FIRST LLOYD'S INS CO	TX	C-	6.9	6.3	0.0	0.0	10.0	N/A	6.3	4.8	2.9	DGLR
AMERICAN ACCESS CASUALTY CO	IL	C	228.3	53.3	175.9	5.1	4.6	5.8	5.4	1.8	3.6	CL
AMERICAN AGRI BUSINESS INS CO	TX	C+	1,387.1	29.6	0.0	2.9	8.0	4.6	8.9	7.0	4.4	R
AMERICAN AGRICULTURAL INS CO	IN	C+	1,168.6	509.6	342.2	32.8	7.5	7.0	5.0	6.8	4.5	R
AMERICAN ALLIANCE CASUALTY CO	IL	D-	12.7	3.5	7.8	0.3	0.9	3.1	3.9	7.6	1.2	CDT
AMERICAN ALTERNATIVE INS CORP	DE	C	550.0	188.0	0.0	25.8	10.0	N/A	8.0	7.0	3.6	R
AMERICAN ASSOC OF ORTHODONTIST RRG	AZ	D	41.9	12.9	7.4	0.7	5.9	10.0	8.7	9.0	1.7	DR
AMERICAN AUTOMOBILE INS CO	MO	C	181.7	162.0	0.0	2.9	10.0	4.3	5.0	7.0	4.2	RT
AMERICAN BANKERS INS CO OF FL	FL	B	2,020.9	584.1	884.0	96.4	7.7	6.6	8.2	6.4	5.5	A

See Page 27 for explanation of footnotes and
Page 28 for explanation of stability factors.
Arrows denote recent upgrades ▲ or downgrades ▼   (see Section VII for explanations)

34

www.weissratings.com

RISK ADJ. CAPITAL RATIO #1	CAPITAL RATIO #2	PREMIUM TO SURPLUS (%)	RESV. TO SURPLUS (%)	RESV. DEVELOP. 1 YEAR (%)	DEVELOP. 2 YEAR (%)	LOSS RATIO (%)	EXP. RATIO (%)	COMB RATIO (%)	CASH FROM UNDER-WRITING (%)	NET PREMIUM GROWTH (%)	INVEST. IN AFFIL (%)	INSURANCE COMPANY NAME
1.7	1.5	51.3	16.7	9.0	-0.8	20.0	85.1	105.1	97.3	2.3	0.0	ALLEGHENY SURETY CO
0.5	0.3	67.1	178.6	24.3	94.9	70.4	19.4	89.8	117.6	66.2	0.0	ALLEGIANT INS CO INC A RRG
5.0	3.7	58.7	21.8	-3.1	-2.3	69.4	30.8	100.2	97.5	2.7	0.0	ALLIANCE INDEMNITY CO
1.8	1.5	158.7	58.8	-8.3	-5.8	69.4	30.8	100.2	97.5	2.7	0.0	ALLIANCE INS CO INC
495.5	445.9	-31.5	N/A	-17.1	-24.1	13.8	2.1	15.9	-122.6	N/A	0.0	ALLIANCE MUTUAL INS CO
0.0	0.0	187.3	630.3	29.3	42.6	78.2	21.3	99.5	81.0	8.9	0.0	ALLIANCE NATIONAL INS CO
1.2	0.9	79.5	95.1	1.4	1.3	69.9	28.1	98.0	140.1	39.0	0.0	ALLIANCE OF NONPROFITS FOR INS
0.6	0.5	329.7	155.6	1.9	4.7	88.4	11.3	99.7	128.9	52.0	0.0	ALLIANCE UNITED INS CO
0.6	0.4	100.1	147.4	-6.2	-0.6	79.5	28.7	108.2	78.2	-5.2	8.8 ●	ALLIANZ GLOBAL RISKS US INS CO
14.7	13.2	N/A	N/A	N/A	N/A	N/A	N/A	N/A	167.0	0.0	0.0	ALLIANZ UNDERWRITERS INS CO
1.1	0.9	132.7	102.4	7.7	15.0	71.6	16.1	87.7	128.2	10.1	0.0	ALLIED EASTERN INDEMNITY CO
N/A	N/A	N/A	N/A	N/A	N/A	N/A	N/A	N/A	N/A	0.0	0.0	ALLIED INS CO OF AMERICA
1.4	1.1	109.9	77.2	13.7	5.0	49.9	41.6	91.5	131.1	2.2	0.0	ALLIED PROFESSIONALS INS CO RRG
5.4	4.8	N/A	N/A	N/A	N/A	N/A	N/A	N/A	374.6	0.0	6.8	ALLIED PROPERTY & CASUALTY INS CO
1.0	0.7	25.9	52.7	-50.4	-24.6	-52.3	23.7	-28.6	123.3	0.0	0.0	ALLIED SERVICES RRG
3.8	2.3	29.7	53.9	-0.4	-4.4	67.8	24.7	92.5	122.1	125.8	0.0	ALLIED WORLD ASR CO (US) INC
1.5	1.4	17.0	30.8	-0.3	-2.7	67.8	24.7	92.5	122.0	5.4	47.1 ●	ALLIED WORLD INS CO
4.5	2.9	32.2	58.4	-0.4	-4.4	67.8	24.7	92.5	111.9	69.2	0.0	ALLIED WORLD NATL ASR CO
2.2	1.4	62.2	113.0	-0.8	-8.1	67.8	24.6	92.4	121.7	58.8	0.0	ALLIED WORLD SURPLUS LINES INS
83.7	38.2	N/A	N/A	N/A	N/A	N/A	N/A	N/A	N/A	0.0	0.0	ALLMERICA FINANCIAL ALLIANCE INS CO
100.9	47.8	N/A	N/A	N/A	N/A	N/A	N/A	N/A	N/A	0.0	0.0	ALLMERICA FINANCIAL BENEFIT INS CO
255.3	127.6	N/A	N/A	N/A	N/A	N/A	N/A	N/A	190.0	0.0	0.0	ALLSTATE COUNTY MUTUAL INS CO
123.4	54.4	N/A	N/A	N/A	N/A	N/A	N/A	N/A	-188.0	0.0	0.0	ALLSTATE FIRE & CASUALTY INS CO
58.2	52.4	N/A	N/A	N/A	N/A	N/A	N/A	N/A	-222.2	0.0	0.0	ALLSTATE INDEMNITY CO
2.2	1.7	145.5	84.3	-0.2	-3.4	66.4	26.8	93.2	108.1	3.8	12.5 ●	ALLSTATE INS CO
2.5	1.9	127.8	137.7	-6.3	-4.9	62.4	24.4	86.8	101.6	-0.8	3.9 ●	ALLSTATE NJ INS CO
97.0	61.9	N/A	N/A	N/A	N/A	N/A	N/A	N/A	43.2	0.0	0.0	ALLSTATE NJ PROPERTY & CASUALTY
N/A	N/A	N/A	N/A	N/A	N/A	N/A	N/A	N/A	N/A	0.0	0.0	ALLSTATE NORTH AMERICAN INS CO
130.9	65.4	N/A	N/A	N/A	N/A	N/A	N/A	N/A	-311.0	0.0	0.0	ALLSTATE NORTHBROOK INDEMNITY CO
74.8	57.0	N/A	N/A	N/A	N/A	N/A	N/A	N/A	-14.8	0.0	0.0 ●	ALLSTATE PROPERTY & CASUALTY INS
141.6	114.5	N/A	N/A	N/A	N/A	N/A	N/A	N/A	61.4	0.0	0.0	ALLSTATE TEXAS LLOYDS
31.8	28.6	N/A	N/A	N/A	N/A	N/A	N/A	N/A	999 +	0.0	0.0	ALLSTATE VEHICLE & PROPERTY INS CO
3.5	3.1	N/A	N/A	N/A	N/A	N/A	N/A	N/A	-5.8	0.0	0.0	ALPHA PROPERTY & CASUALTY INS CO
2.1	1.5	78.8	113.3	-3.2	-17.4	63.7	34.5	98.2	99.9	0.8	0.0	ALPS PROPERTY & CASUALTY INS CO
1.1	1.0	14.2	13.6	-0.4	-0.4	76.1	44.2	120.3	63.1	38.1	91.4	ALTERRA AMERICA INS CO
1.1	0.8	36.4	62.4	19.0	18.0	96.8	10.2	107.0	419.2	19.7	0.0	ALTERRA EXCESS & SURPLUS INS CO
3.4	2.4	26.1	43.8	-1.3	-0.8	68.0	30.0	98.0	139.4	-7.3	14.3 ●	ALTERRA REINS USA INC
14.0	8.3	13.2	16.3	-1.0	-3.1	67.0	31.9	98.9	96.7	3.9	0.0	AMALGAMATED CASUALTY INS CO
N/A	N/A	N/A	N/A	N/A	N/A	N/A	N/A	N/A	N/A	0.0	0.0	AMBAC ASR CORP SEGREGATED ACCT
0.6	0.3	10.7	421.5	-200.1	-5.9	145.2	685.0	830.2	-25.2	-13.2	4.0 ●	AMBAC ASSURANCE CORP
N/A	N/A	N/A	N/A	N/A	N/A	N/A	N/A	N/A	N/A	0.0	0.0	AMC RE INC
4.6	3.9	N/A	N/A	N/A	N/A	N/A	N/A	N/A	-60.4	0.0	10.0 ●	AMCO INS CO
103.5	51.7	N/A	N/A	N/A	N/A	N/A	N/A	N/A	122.4	0.0	0.0	AMERICA FIRST INS CO
22.2	20.0	N/A	N/A	N/A	N/A	N/A	N/A	N/A	208.1	0.0	0.0	AMERICA FIRST LLOYD'S INS CO
0.7	0.6	370.7	156.5	19.2	11.3	70.2	31.0	101.2	102.8	24.6	0.0	AMERICAN ACCESS CASUALTY CO
1.4	0.8	N/A	N/A	N/A	N/A	N/A	N/A	N/A	N/A	0.0	0.0	AMERICAN AGRI BUSINESS INS CO
1.8	1.3	70.0	92.1	2.9	-7.4	73.3	17.2	90.5	147.2	20.7	0.1 ●	AMERICAN AGRICULTURAL INS CO
0.4	0.3	238.8	176.8	17.0	21.8	67.4	33.1	100.5	115.3	12.5	0.0	AMERICAN ALLIANCE CASUALTY CO
16.5	13.5	N/A	N/A	N/A	N/A	N/A	N/A	N/A	13.8	0.0	0.0	AMERICAN ALTERNATIVE INS CORP
1.2	0.9	62.2	190.0	-49.7	-85.7	57.1	25.3	82.4	183.0	9.3	0.0	AMERICAN ASSOC OF ORTHODONTIST
46.2	41.5	N/A	N/A	N/A	N/A	N/A	N/A	N/A	9.1	100.0	0.0	AMERICAN AUTOMOBILE INS CO
2.6	1.5	163.1	27.1	-3.5	-5.2	40.1	42.3	82.4	119.2	8.1	0.7 ●	AMERICAN BANKERS INS CO OF FL

999 + Denotes number greater than 999.9%
999 - Denotes number less than -999.99%
● Bullets denote a more detailed analysis is available in Section II.

INSURANCE COMPANY NAME	DOM. STATE	RATING	TOTAL ASSETS ($MIL)	CAPITAL & SURPLUS ($MIL)	ANNUAL NET PREMIUM ($MIL)	NET INCOME ($MIL)	CAPITAL- IZATION INDEX (PTS)	RESERVE ADQ INDEX (PTS)	PROFIT- ABILITY INDEX (PTS)	LIQUIDITY INDEX (PTS)	STAB. INDEX (PTS)	STABILITY FACTORS
AMERICAN BUILDERS INS CO RRG INC	MT	U	1.0	0.7	0.0	-0.1	N/A	6.4	2.8	10.0	0.0	FT
▼AMERICAN BUS & MERCANTILE INS MUT	DE	D+	58.7	28.5	2.9	-2.3	2.1	3.8	3.1	7.4	2.4	CDGR
AMERICAN CAPITAL ASR CORP	FL	B	200.2	92.8	84.0	13.3	7.9	8.7	7.6	7.1	6.1	T
AMERICAN CASUALTY CO OF READING	PA	C	145.1	145.1	0.0	2.0	8.7	N/A	7.8	8.3	3.8	AR
AMERICAN CENTENNIAL INS CO	DE	U	40.6	9.7	0.0	0.0	N/A	6.0	1.2	10.0	2.4	CT
AMERICAN COASTAL INS CO	FL	C-	357.4	215.5	176.3	27.5	8.1	8.7	9.4	7.9	3.3	T
AMERICAN COLONIAL INS CO	FL	C-	32.0	25.1	9.4	-0.9	2.8	5.9	1.5	7.6	2.7	DGT
AMERICAN COMMERCE INS CO	OH	C+	324.7	100.7	168.7	0.4	9.1	5.8	3.6	5.6	4.8	
AMERICAN COMPENSATION INS CO	MN	D	71.5	51.8	0.0	0.3	10.0	3.6	4.1	7.0	2.1	R
AMERICAN CONTRACTORS INDEMNITY CO	CA	B	322.0	98.5	69.1	8.4	7.8	6.0	7.9	7.2	5.5	
AMERICAN CONTRACTORS INS CO RISK	TX	D	21.1	8.0	0.0	0.4	10.0	N/A	8.5	10.0	1.4	DFRT
AMERICAN COUNTRY INS CO	IL	C-	75.6	18.4	27.0	1.0	2.6	3.8	3.9	7.2	3.1	DGRT
AMERICAN ECONOMY INS CO	IN	C	65.5	60.9	-292.6	-2.3	10.0	4.9	1.9	0.0	4.1	AFLR
AMERICAN EMPIRE INS CO	OH	C	41.2	21.9	8.0	0.8	8.8	7.0	3.7	8.6	3.8	DGRT
AMERICAN EMPIRE SURPLUS LINES INS CO	DE	C	299.6	115.8	71.6	6.9	7.8	7.0	4.8	7.4	4.0	GRT
AMERICAN EQUITY INS CO	AZ	U	103.8	103.6	0.0	1.5	N/A	N/A	5.3	7.0	5.4	T
AMERICAN EQUITY SPECIALTY INS CO	CT	B	79.6	31.0	20.1	2.3	8.2	8.2	5.4	6.9	5.5	D
AMERICAN EUROPEAN INS CO	NH	B-	148.5	67.1	30.6	-2.3	8.4	6.3	4.2	7.0	4.6	FR
AMERICAN EXCESS INS EXCHANGE RRG	VT	D	388.5	236.0	23.6	24.9	9.9	9.5	8.4	9.3	2.2	R
AMERICAN FAMILY HOME INS CO	FL	C+	551.7	155.8	245.4	3.9	7.9	8.1	4.5	6.3	4.7	
AMERICAN FAMILY INS CO	OH	B	27.8	17.0	0.0	0.6	10.0	N/A	8.5	6.2	5.3	D
AMERICAN FAMILY MUT INS CO	WI	B+	14,543.2	5,894.7	5,595.6	346.8	8.1	9.1	6.5	5.9	6.5	L
AMERICAN FARMERS & RANCHERS INS CO	OK	U	8.7	8.0	-0.2	-0.1	N/A	6.0	3.7	10.0	4.9	FRT
AMERICAN FARMERS & RANCHERS	OK	C	123.5	44.7	84.0	10.9	5.1	7.0	4.0	3.5	3.5	LR
AMERICAN FEDERATED INS CO	MS	C-	36.7	12.5	17.0	2.8	3.5	7.7	6.8	6.6	3.1	CD
AMERICAN FEED INDUSTRY INS CO RRG	IA	U	1.5	1.4	0.0	0.0	N/A	9.6	1.9	10.0	0.3	FRT
AMERICAN FIRE & CASUALTY CO	NH	C-	41.8	39.0	-31.3	0.5	10.0	4.9	3.6	2.2	3.1	AFLR
AMERICAN FOREST CASUALTY CO RRG	SC	D	9.8	4.7	1.4	0.2	5.3	6.1	5.9	6.9	1.7	DR
AMERICAN FREEDOM INS CO	IL	C	40.0	13.2	23.1	1.6	6.5	7.1	3.8	6.6	3.5	D
AMERICAN GUARANTEE & LIABILITY INS	NY	C	251.0	178.8	0.0	2.2	10.0	N/A	6.4	7.0	3.5	R
AMERICAN HALLMARK INS CO OF TX	TX	C	329.5	118.9	107.5	4.8	7.5	4.6	5.3	6.6	4.0	R
AMERICAN HEALTHCARE INDEMNITY CO	DE	U	105.1	71.1	-0.2	-0.7	N/A	9.7	1.9	10.0	3.1	FRT
AMERICAN HEARTLAND INS CO	IL	D-	17.3	3.0	10.7	0.3	1.9	4.9	2.9	5.9	1.3	D
AMERICAN HOME ASR CO	NY	C	26,660.0	7,054.1	5,852.4	575.6	7.3	2.5	3.3	6.5	4.2	A
AMERICAN INDEPENDENT INS CO	PA	C-	58.0	21.4	26.9	-1.8	7.7	4.6	3.2	4.8	3.0	DFL
AMERICAN INS CO	OH	C-	330.2	287.9	0.0	6.3	10.0	3.4	3.6	7.0	3.3	RT
AMERICAN INTEGRITY INS CO OF FL	FL	D	195.3	49.9	90.2	9.0	5.9	2.7	5.2	5.8	2.1	T
AMERICAN INTER FIDELITY EXCHANGE	IN	C	51.3	18.7	20.3	0.9	4.8	9.4	8.6	7.1	2.7	CDGR
AMERICAN INTERNATIONAL OVERSEAS LTD		U (5)	0.0	0.0	1,655.6	0.0	N/A	9.4	6.9	6.7	3.7	T
AMERICAN INTERSTATE INS CO	NE	B-	1,214.8	389.4	284.8	26.3	7.5	8.8	8.7	7.3	4.6	R
AMERICAN INTERSTATE INS CO OF TEXAS	TX	C	58.6	20.7	17.2	1.4	5.3	8.8	8.7	7.0	3.6	CDR
AMERICAN LIBERTY INS CO	UT	E	10.5	2.7	10.5	0.6	0.0	1.7	1.2	0.0	0.1	CDLR
AMERICAN MEDICAL ASR CO	IL	U	3.5	2.9	0.0	-0.1	N/A	7.7	2.8	10.0	3.1	FRT
AMERICAN MEDICAL INS EXCHANGE	IN	U	0.5	0.5	0.0	0.0	N/A	N/A	3.3	7.0	2.6	FT
AMERICAN MERCURY INS CO	OK	B	354.4	152.5	174.2	18.0	7.9	5.5	5.6	6.4	6.2	
AMERICAN MERCURY LLOYDS INS CO	TX	B	5.7	4.5	0.0	0.0	10.0	N/A	6.6	7.0	4.9	D
AMERICAN MILLENNIUM INS CO	NJ	D+	17.2	7.0	1.5	0.4	4.9	2.3	3.7	8.9	2.1	DGRT
AMERICAN MINING INS CO	IA	B-	33.6	24.8	0.0	0.4	10.0	N/A	4.2	7.8	4.9	D
AMERICAN MODERN HOME INS CO	OH	C+	1,235.6	383.5	431.7	9.6	8.0	7.9	6.8	6.5	4.3	R
AMERICAN MODERN INS CO OF FLORIDA	FL	C	31.0	7.8	18.2	-0.1	5.4	8.6	4.3	3.0	4.0	DL
AMERICAN MODERN LLOYDS INS CO	TX	C	7.0	3.8	0.0	0.0	10.0	N/A	3.3	7.0	3.3	DF
AMERICAN MODERN PROPERTY &	OH	B	20.8	16.3	4.5	0.1	8.9	7.6	5.6	7.0	4.0	D

See Page 27 for explanation of footnotes and Page 28 for explanation of stability factors.
Arrows denote recent upgrades ▲ or downgrades ▼ (see Section VII for explanations)

36

www.weissratings.com

RISK ADJ. RATIO #1	CAPITAL RATIO #2	PREMIUM TO SURPLUS (%)	RESV. TO SURPLUS (%)	RESV. DEVELOP. 1 YEAR (%)	RESV. DEVELOP. 2 YEAR (%)	LOSS RATIO (%)	EXP. RATIO (%)	COMB RATIO (%)	CASH FROM UNDER-WRITING (%)	NET PREMIUM GROWTH (%)	INVEST. IN AFFIL (%)	INSURANCE COMPANY NAME
N/A	N/A	N/A	12.5	0.6	0.4	N/A	N/A	N/A	-8.5	100.0	0.0	AMERICAN BUILDERS INS CO RRG INC
0.4	0.2	8.4	72.9	14.0	17.7	348.3	33.3	381.6	102.6	70.5	31.6	AMERICAN BUS & MERCANTILE INS MUT
2.6	1.7	103.1	31.9	-12.2	-14.0	19.1	47.8	66.9	149.0	48.2	9.9	AMERICAN CAPITAL ASR CORP
2.2	2.1	N/A	N/A	N/A	N/A	N/A	N/A	N/A	N/A	0.0	51.6	AMERICAN CASUALTY CO OF READING
N/A	N/A	N/A	317.1	7.3	-6.7	N/A	N/A	N/A	N/A	0.0	0.0	AMERICAN CENTENNIAL INS CO
3.3	2.3	94.5	6.9	-1.8	-2.1	11.5	44.5	56.0	156.8	26.8	0.0	AMERICAN COASTAL INS CO
2.6	1.9	146.8	79.0	2.9	-0.7	95.4	33.2	128.6	127.2	85.2	0.0	AMERICAN COLONIAL INS CO
2.6	2.0	150.7	62.0	4.6	7.4	73.5	26.7	100.2	104.7	0.3	0.0	AMERICAN COMMERCE INS CO
4.0	3.7	N/A	N/A	N/A	N/A	N/A	N/A	N/A	-10.9	0.0	37.3	AMERICAN COMPENSATION INS CO
2.5	2.0	77.1	44.6	-14.3	-36.9	12.6	62.6	75.2	123.0	-7.3	0.0	AMERICAN CONTRACTORS INDEMNITY
2.9	2.6	N/A	N/A	N/A	N/A	N/A	N/A	N/A	91.6	0.0	0.0	AMERICAN CONTRACTORS INS CO RISK
1.1	0.7	179.0	177.3	0.3	13.0	63.0	25.9	89.8	185.4	85.3	0.0	AMERICAN COUNTRY INS CO
6.5	6.2	-458.8	N/A	N/A	N/A	N/A	N/A	N/A	-14.1	-147.8	43.0	AMERICAN ECONOMY INS CO
2.2	1.8	38.0	51.6	2.7	0.1	79.7	16.0	95.7	223.6	44.3	0.0	AMERICAN EMPIRE INS CO
1.7	1.3	66.6	90.5	4.9	0.1	79.7	16.0	95.7	228.5	44.3	9.4	AMERICAN EMPIRE SURPLUS LINES INS
N/A	N/A	N/A	N/A	N/A	N/A	N/A	N/A	N/A	8.4	0.0	29.0	AMERICAN EQUITY INS CO
3.0	1.9	70.1	126.2	-1.7	-3.8	60.9	29.6	90.5	107.5	3.0	0.0	AMERICAN EQUITY SPECIALTY INS CO
2.7	2.0	43.5	87.6	-0.4	1.9	64.3	37.8	102.1	89.0	-10.8	12.5	AMERICAN EUROPEAN INS CO
4.7	3.1	9.7	61.4	-3.9	-14.5	25.0	21.1	46.1	270.8	1.1	0.0 •	AMERICAN EXCESS INS EXCHANGE RRG
2.2	1.4	163.8	27.7	-5.1	-6.3	43.8	50.1	93.9	110.3	19.4	9.0	AMERICAN FAMILY HOME INS CO
6.7	6.0	N/A	N/A	N/A	N/A	N/A	N/A	N/A	51.8	0.0	0.0	AMERICAN FAMILY INS CO
2.1	1.6	96.6	58.7	-2.2	-6.7	72.6	28.6	101.2	99.3	3.0	17.9 •	AMERICAN FAMILY MUT INS CO
N/A	N/A	-3.0	13.0	0.7	-0.3	-71.6	-48.4	-120.0	-43.4	0.0	0.0	AMERICAN FARMERS & RANCHERS INS
1.8	1.3	258.0	51.6	-17.1	-30.7	65.0	23.9	88.9	113.1	9.4	12.3	AMERICAN FARMERS & RANCHERS
0.8	0.7	183.9	5.1	-2.3	-2.7	5.7	84.4	90.1	127.8	-8.9	0.0	AMERICAN FEDERATED INS CO
N/A	N/A	N/A	9.5	-14.6	-24.5	N/A	N/A	N/A	N/A	0.0	0.0	AMERICAN FEED INDUSTRY INS CO RRG
42.1	37.9	-81.5	N/A	N/A	N/A	N/A	N/A	N/A	-10.5	-147.8	0.0	AMERICAN FIRE & CASUALTY CO
1.9	1.2	33.7	92.0	-26.2	-55.7	18.4	45.4	63.8	152.2	-14.6	0.0	AMERICAN FOREST CASUALTY CO RRG
1.2	1.0	203.9	114.3	-4.8	0.4	55.1	35.0	90.1	130.7	21.8	0.0	AMERICAN FREEDOM INS CO
23.0	20.7	N/A	N/A	N/A	N/A	N/A	N/A	N/A	-15.7	0.0	0.0	AMERICAN GUARANTEE & LIABILITY INS
1.6	1.3	93.2	79.5	1.7	N/A	72.4	32.3	104.7	110.2	12.7	29.3	AMERICAN HALLMARK INS CO OF TX
N/A	N/A	-0.5	85.0	-4.9	-0.8	-179.3	-456.4	-635.7	-750.5	-110.1	0.0	AMERICAN HEALTHCARE INDEMNITY CO
0.4	0.4	384.8	317.9	-0.6	-41.3	61.3	46.6	107.9	133.1	19.1	0.0	AMERICAN HEARTLAND INS CO
2.3	1.5	114.9	244.4	3.9	9.3	70.0	37.4	107.4	93.9	12.5	0.3 •	AMERICAN HOME ASR CO
1.6	1.5	120.2	68.5	10.7	13.4	77.5	20.1	97.6	87.0	-12.1	25.4	AMERICAN INDEPENDENT INS CO
47.8	43.0	N/A	N/A	N/A	N/A	N/A	N/A	N/A	6.6	100.0	0.0 •	AMERICAN INS CO
1.5	1.1	219.6	54.2	-3.6	25.1	44.4	29.1	73.5	145.0	18.0	0.0	AMERICAN INTEGRITY INS CO OF FL
0.9	0.5	116.6	71.3	-13.9	-21.2	65.6	27.6	93.2	134.4	173.5	0.0	AMERICAN INTER FIDELITY EXCHANGE
N/A	N/A	93.4	80.8	-7.5	-11.6	57.6	36.8	94.4	115.5	0.0	15.5	AMERICAN INTERNATIONAL OVERSEAS
1.7	1.3	80.4	128.7	-3.4	-4.5	69.4	18.0	87.4	133.6	13.4	9.9 •	AMERICAN INTERSTATE INS CO
1.1	0.5	90.1	130.3	-4.4	-5.2	69.3	18.4	87.7	143.0	12.4	0.0	AMERICAN INTERSTATE INS CO OF
0.1	0.0	503.9	241.2	152.8	85.5	64.7	32.0	96.7	109.3	25.6	0.0	AMERICAN LIBERTY INS CO
N/A	N/A	N/A	19.8	-1.8	-2.0	N/A	N/A	N/A	N/A	0.0	0.0	AMERICAN MEDICAL ASR CO
N/A	N/A	N/A	N/A	N/A	N/A	N/A	N/A	N/A	N/A	0.0	0.0	AMERICAN MEDICAL INS EXCHANGE
2.4	1.7	128.4	35.6	1.8	5.0	72.9	26.5	99.4	95.7	-4.9	9.4	AMERICAN MERCURY INS CO
9.0	8.1	N/A	N/A	N/A	N/A	N/A	N/A	N/A	43.0	0.0	0.0	AMERICAN MERCURY LLOYDS INS CO
1.6	1.2	30.8	77.8	8.3	22.7	142.2	-18.5	123.7	149.6	2.0	0.0	AMERICAN MILLENNIUM INS CO
11.1	10.0	N/A	N/A	N/A	N/A	N/A	N/A	N/A	297.4	0.0	0.0	AMERICAN MINING INS CO
2.0	1.5	115.5	19.6	-3.6	-4.9	43.8	50.2	94.0	113.9	19.4	26.7 •	AMERICAN MODERN HOME INS CO
1.1	0.7	231.6	39.2	-7.6	-9.2	43.8	50.7	94.5	109.6	19.4	0.0	AMERICAN MODERN INS CO OF FLORIDA
3.7	3.3	N/A	N/A	N/A	N/A	N/A	N/A	N/A	268.4	0.0	0.0	AMERICAN MODERN LLOYDS INS CO
8.9	5.6	79.7	13.5	-2.6	-3.3	43.8	51.1	94.9	111.1	19.4	0.0	AMERICAN MODERN PROPERTY &

999 + Denotes number greater than 999.9%
999 - Denotes number less than -999.99%
• Bullets denote a more detailed analysis is available in Section II.

INSURANCE COMPANY NAME	DOM. STATE	RATING	TOTAL ASSETS ($MIL)	CAPITAL & SURPLUS ($MIL)	ANNUAL NET PREMIUM ($MIL)	NET INCOME ($MIL)	CAPITAL-IZATION INDEX (PTS)	RESERVE ADQ INDEX (PTS)	PROFIT-ABILITY INDEX (PTS)	LIQUIDITY INDEX (PTS)	STAB. INDEX (PTS)	STABILITY FACTORS
AMERICAN MODERN SELECT INS CO	OH	C	287.7	43.9	45.4	2.9	9.1	8.1	8.4	7.2	3.9	F
AMERICAN MODERN SURPLUS LINES INS	OH	B	84.4	26.9	45.4	0.4	7.1	8.2	4.6	6.1	5.5	D
AMERICAN MUTUAL SHARE INS CORP	OH	C-	221.7	194.6	0.2	5.5	10.0	4.8	4.2	10.0	1.5	D
AMERICAN NATIONAL GENERAL INS CO	MO	B-	103.3	60.6	39.1	3.1	8.6	4.8	2.9	6.3	5.1	F
AMERICAN NATIONAL LLOYDS INS CO	TX	B	77.4	60.7	18.0	2.4	10.0	4.8	6.6	7.0	6.1	
AMERICAN NATIONAL PROPERTY & CAS CO	MO	B	1,216.0	572.7	468.0	19.3	7.7	8.3	5.5	6.4	6.3	
AMERICAN NATL COUNTY MUT INS CO	TX	B	19.9	8.9	0.0	0.0	8.4	N/A	3.9	6.9	4.7	D
AMERICAN PACIFIC INS COMPANY	HI	B	11.6	11.3	0.0	0.1	10.0	6.0	6.5	10.0	4.5	DF
AMERICAN PET INS CO INC	NY	D	37.0	22.4	69.7	1.0	1.9	4.9	6.5	0.4	2.3	DGLT
AMERICAN PHYSICIANS ASR CORP	MI	U	455.1	259.1	1.3	49.2	N/A	10.0	7.6	7.7	6.5	FT
AMERICAN PLATINUM PROP & CAS INS CO	FL	C	20.3	13.5	1.8	-0.3	8.8	N/A	3.4	6.8	3.1	DFGT
AMERICAN PROPERTY INS CO	NJ	U	28.3	6.4	0.0	-0.3	N/A	7.0	1.9	10.0	3.1	FRT
AMERICAN RELIABLE INS CO	AZ	C+	275.3	82.8	170.9	3.2	7.5	6.9	3.1	6.3	4.5	R
AMERICAN RESOURCES INS CO INC	AL	C-	21.9	7.3	4.4	-1.3	3.6	7.0	1.6	7.0	2.2	DFGR
AMERICAN RISK INS CO INC	TX	D+	21.1	8.5	8.0	0.0	3.9	4.7	4.9	2.5	2.4	DFL
AMERICAN ROAD INS CO	MI	C+	589.2	263.8	118.1	-11.4	10.0	7.5	6.1	7.2	4.4	R
AMERICAN SAFETY CASUALTY INS CO	OK	C-	180.9	131.3	11.8	-4.9	7.4	7.0	3.7	6.9	2.9	FRT
AMERICAN SAFETY INDEMNITY CO	OK	D	282.8	109.5	47.0	11.8	7.2	10.0	5.5	7.8	2.2	RT
AMERICAN SAFETY INS CO	GA	C	20.5	18.8	0.0	0.5	10.0	N/A	5.1	7.0	3.8	DR
AMERICAN SAFETY RRG INC	VT	D	11.7	6.9	-1.9	-0.3	10.0	5.1	4.2	7.0	1.9	DFRT
AMERICAN SECURITY INS CO	DE	B	2,104.9	790.8	1,601.9	208.2	8.2	8.0	8.6	6.5	5.8	A
AMERICAN SELECT INS CO	OH	C+	226.9	94.9	83.8	3.2	8.5	9.3	6.6	6.4	4.6	T
AMERICAN SENTINEL INS CO	PA	C	34.6	15.5	23.1	0.3	8.0	9.3	8.7	6.8	4.3	D
AMERICAN SERVICE INS CO INC	IL	D	118.3	31.3	40.3	1.8	4.9	4.1	1.8	6.7	1.8	RT
AMERICAN SHIELD INS CO	MO	U	5.0	5.0	0.0	0.0	N/A	0.0	3.9	0.0	0.0	LT
AMERICAN SOUTHERN HOME INS CO	FL	B	143.9	38.5	36.4	0.8	8.5	7.9	8.3	6.8	4.8	F
AMERICAN SOUTHERN INS CO	KS	C+	108.2	38.9	50.8	2.3	7.9	9.4	6.1	6.5	4.5	R
AMERICAN SPECIAL RISK INS CO	DE	U	0.9	0.8	0.0	0.0	N/A	4.2	1.9	7.0	2.6	T
AMERICAN STANDARD INS CO OF OH	OH	B	8.8	7.6	0.0	0.2	10.0	N/A	8.0	9.3	4.9	DG
AMERICAN STANDARD INS CO OF WI	WI	B+	415.8	325.5	0.0	6.8	10.0	N/A	7.9	10.0	6.4	
AMERICAN STATES INS CO	IN	C	135.0	116.0	-397.0	-3.2	10.0	4.9	1.9	0.0	4.1	AFLR
AMERICAN STATES INS CO OF TX	TX	B-	11.9	11.6	0.0	0.3	10.0	N/A	2.3	10.0	4.6	DRT
AMERICAN STATES LLOYDS INS CO	TX	B-	3.5	3.5	0.0	0.1	10.0	N/A	6.8	10.0	3.7	DR
AMERICAN STATES PREFERRED INS CO	IN	C+	23.8	20.9	-41.8	0.0	10.0	4.9	2.3	0.0	4.2	ADFL
AMERICAN STEAMSHIP O M PROT & IND AS	NY	D	313.1	61.4	86.2	-1.3	4.4	4.9	3.7	5.2	2.1	DFR
AMERICAN STRATEGIC INS CO	FL	C+	812.0	298.9	409.5	-9.4	8.3	9.2	4.7	6.8	3.9	
AMERICAN SUMMIT INS CO	TX	C+	46.0	27.6	24.5	1.0	8.5	6.5	4.8	6.9	4.7	R
AMERICAN SURETY CO	IN	C	14.4	11.3	7.9	0.7	7.4	8.3	6.9	7.0	3.2	D
AMERICAN TRADITIONS INS CO	FL	C-	45.3	18.3	24.9	2.2	4.5	3.7	5.7	6.6	3.3	CDR
AMERICAN TRANSIT INS CO	NY	E+	145.2	33.1	141.1	1.5	0.9	0.1	1.2	0.0	0.4	CFLR
AMERICAN TRUCKING & TRANSP INS RRG	MT	D-	19.8	6.4	4.6	0.4	4.9	6.0	6.3	8.9	1.2	DGR
AMERICAN UNDERWRITERS INS CO	AR	D+	7.5	5.0	0.0	0.0	10.0	3.6	3.8	10.0	2.5	DFR
AMERICAN WEST INS CO	ND	C	16.3	11.1	6.9	0.5	8.2	6.0	5.9	6.4	4.2	D
AMERICAN WESTERN HOME INS CO	OK	C	202.5	63.4	81.8	1.4	8.5	8.1	8.3	6.4	3.9	T
AMERICAN ZURICH INS CO	IL	C	236.8	155.4	0.0	1.5	10.0	N/A	6.7	8.4	3.5	R
AMERICAS INS CO	LA	D+	21.1	5.8	5.5	0.0	5.2	6.9	3.0	8.1	2.1	DFGR
AMERIGUARD RRG INC	VT	D-	11.2	7.1	2.0	0.0	7.4	7.0	5.4	9.2	0.6	DF
AMERIHEALTH CASUALTY INS CO	DE	C	268.8	49.9	99.0	4.0	3.9	2.7	4.3	5.6	3.9	CR
AMERIPRISE INS CO	WI	B	48.0	44.8	0.0	0.8	10.0	N/A	5.9	10.0	4.0	T
AMERISURE INS CO	MI	B-	745.1	217.0	199.3	2.8	8.1	8.6	6.5	7.0	4.7	R
AMERISURE MUTUAL INS CO	MI	B-	2,027.5	818.4	445.2	33.2	8.0	8.1	6.6	7.0	4.7	T
AMERISURE PARTNERS INS CO	MI	C+	73.8	22.1	19.9	0.1	6.4	9.3	3.8	6.9	4.5	DF

See Page 27 for explanation of footnotes and Page 28 for explanation of stability factors.

Arrows denote recent upgrades ▲ or downgrades ▼ (see Section VII for explanations)

38

www.weissratings.com

RISK ADJ. RATIO #1	CAPITAL RATIO #2	PREMIUM TO SURPLUS (%)	RESV. TO SURPLUS (%)	RESV. DEVELOP. 1 YEAR (%)	RESV. DEVELOP. 2 YEAR (%)	LOSS RATIO (%)	EXP. RATIO (%)	COMB RATIO (%)	CASH FROM UNDER- WRITING (%)	NET PREMIUM GROWTH (%)	INVEST. IN AFFIL (%)	INSURANCE COMPANY NAME
3.8	2.2	113.2	19.2	-4.0	-5.5	43.8	44.5	88.3	83.8	19.4	0.0	AMERICAN MODERN SELECT INS CO
1.4	0.9	172.5	29.2	-5.6	-6.9	43.8	51.0	94.8	104.9	19.4	0.0	AMERICAN MODERN SURPLUS LINES
8.8	7.6	0.1	19.8	-2.9	-2.8	999 +	999 +	93.1	2.2	-9.0	9.5	AMERICAN MUTUAL SHARE INS CORP
3.8	2.6	69.6	48.0	-2.0	-6.2	86.5	21.7	108.2	88.7	-19.1	0.0	AMERICAN NATIONAL GENERAL INS CO
7.9	6.9	31.0	4.1	1.7	-0.2	64.4	19.4	83.8	117.6	-2.6	0.0	AMERICAN NATIONAL LLOYDS INS CO
2.0	1.6	87.1	49.6	-3.2	-5.6	75.2	25.0	100.2	98.6	0.1	20.8 ●	AMERICAN NATIONAL PROPERTY & CAS
3.1	1.8	N/A	N/A	N/A	N/A	N/A	999 +	999 +	491.8	0.0	0.0	AMERICAN NATL COUNTY MUT INS CO
84.8	76.3	N/A	3.6	0.4	1.7	N/A	N/A	N/A	0.3	0.0	0.0	AMERICAN PACIFIC INS COMPANY
0.9	0.5	413.3	25.5	N/A	1.5	66.5	28.2	94.7	108.4	64.9	0.0	AMERICAN PET INS CO INC
N/A	N/A	0.6	125.2	-24.7	-61.2	999 +	722.6	999 +	7.1	-87.0	0.4	AMERICAN PHYSICIANS ASR CORP
3.4	2.3	13.2	6.5	N/A	N/A	46.4	158.8	205.2	70.0	-69.8	0.0	AMERICAN PLATINUM PROP & CAS INS
N/A	N/A	0.1	34.0	-19.5	-20.3	999 +	999 +	999 +	-3.0	N/A	0.0	AMERICAN PROPERTY INS CO
2.0	1.4	215.9	50.8	2.3	2.5	56.8	41.6	98.4	105.9	-0.6	0.7	AMERICAN RELIABLE INS CO
0.8	0.5	58.0	126.9	-6.5	-10.8	41.3	74.8	116.1	53.2	445.5	0.0	AMERICAN RESOURCES INS CO INC
1.1	0.7	95.2	31.5	21.8	16.1	57.4	37.7	95.1	80.0	-41.8	0.0	AMERICAN RISK INS CO INC
23.2	11.6	42.8	3.3	-1.0	-0.9	64.2	0.5	64.7	160.4	18.7	0.0 ●	AMERICAN ROAD INS CO
1.4	1.3	9.6	18.7	-2.3	-26.4	52.9	80.5	133.4	44.0	418.9	64.6	AMERICAN SAFETY CASUALTY INS CO
2.6	1.9	48.5	161.3	-35.6	-325.8	47.4	38.7	86.1	140.5	161.3	0.8	AMERICAN SAFETY INDEMNITY CO
28.8	12.3	N/A	N/A	N/A	N/A	N/A	N/A	N/A	N/A	0.0	0.0	AMERICAN SAFETY INS CO
4.9	3.8	-25.9	55.8	N/A	-549.4	66.7	-27.2	39.5	291.5	95.3	0.0	AMERICAN SAFETY RRG INC
2.4	1.7	216.2	27.9	-0.4	-3.2	33.6	38.1	71.7	121.5	7.1	9.5 ●	AMERICAN SECURITY INS CO
3.3	2.1	91.2	81.3	-6.4	-11.3	59.8	34.6	94.4	107.1	4.3	0.0	AMERICAN SELECT INS CO
2.5	1.7	154.9	37.6	-10.9	-12.4	48.5	39.1	87.6	112.2	10.7	0.0	AMERICAN SENTINEL INS CO
1.5	1.0	150.6	166.4	0.2	7.3	63.9	29.1	93.0	104.3	18.6	0.0	AMERICAN SERVICE INS CO INC
N/A	N/A	N/A	N/A	N/A	N/A	N/A	N/A	N/A	N/A	0.0	0.0	AMERICAN SHIELD INS CO
2.9	1.9	98.6	16.7	-3.3	-4.3	43.8	49.2	93.0	81.8	19.4	9.9	AMERICAN SOUTHERN HOME INS CO
1.9	1.4	129.9	94.6	-11.6	-13.4	65.9	31.6	97.5	112.6	40.3	18.3	AMERICAN SOUTHERN INS CO
N/A	N/A	N/A	N/A	N/A	4.2	N/A	N/A	N/A	N/A	0.0	0.0	AMERICAN SPECIAL RISK INS CO
15.0	13.5	N/A	N/A	N/A	N/A	N/A	N/A	N/A	161.6	0.0	0.0	AMERICAN STANDARD INS CO OF OH
38.0	34.2	N/A	N/A	N/A	N/A	N/A	N/A	N/A	39.3	0.0	0.0 ●	AMERICAN STANDARD INS CO OF WI
38.0	34.2	-329.2	N/A	N/A	N/A	N/A	N/A	N/A	-13.6	-147.8	0.0	AMERICAN STATES INS CO
92.7	50.5	N/A	N/A	N/A	N/A	N/A	N/A	N/A	18.0	0.0	0.0	AMERICAN STATES INS CO OF TX
149.6	74.7	N/A	N/A	N/A	N/A	N/A	N/A	N/A	163.8	0.0	0.0	AMERICAN STATES LLOYDS INS CO
23.1	20.7	-198.8	N/A	N/A	N/A	N/A	N/A	N/A	-12.9	-147.8	0.0	AMERICAN STATES PREFERRED INS CO
1.0	0.7	135.5	279.8	-20.8	2.4	78.6	33.0	111.6	90.3	0.5	0.0	AMERICAN STEAMSHIP O M PROT & IND
1.9	1.6	133.2	41.2	-8.9	-7.2	54.1	34.0	88.1	123.7	19.1	1.2 ●	AMERICAN STRATEGIC INS CO
2.4	1.9	92.6	14.7	-1.6	-3.7	69.4	29.9	99.3	103.1	5.4	0.0	AMERICAN SUMMIT INS CO
1.3	1.2	68.2	7.3	-8.9	-8.9	-0.3	89.3	89.0	101.6	7.9	0.0	AMERICAN SURETY CO
1.2	0.8	155.8	33.1	-4.5	11.0	35.9	45.0	80.9	127.1	5.1	0.0	AMERICAN TRADITIONS INS CO
0.3	0.2	459.6	153.4	118.6	167.6	77.9	33.3	111.2	77.5	3.0	0.0	AMERICAN TRANSIT INS CO
0.9	0.6	81.0	135.1	-24.1	-44.2	81.5	16.6	98.1	280.9	113.2	0.0	AMERICAN TRUCKING & TRANSP INS
5.8	5.3	N/A	N/A	N/A	N/A	N/A	N/A	N/A	-91.9	0.0	0.0	AMERICAN UNDERWRITERS INS CO
2.2	1.7	66.0	8.2	0.3	-0.7	62.4	19.4	81.8	149.5	17.1	0.0	AMERICAN WEST INS CO
2.8	1.8	133.0	22.5	-4.5	-5.9	43.8	50.8	94.6	104.4	19.4	0.0	AMERICAN WESTERN HOME INS CO
4.8	4.6	N/A	N/A	N/A	N/A	N/A	N/A	N/A	-553.3	0.0	20.8	AMERICAN ZURICH INS CO
1.7	1.2	97.9	10.5	1.9	-1.3	57.4	35.7	93.1	80.0	13.2	7.8	AMERICAS INS CO
1.0	0.8	27.6	38.3	9.2	4.8	125.5	10.9	136.4	83.9	37.7	0.0	AMERIGUARD RRG INC
0.8	0.5	205.7	287.5	-6.5	N/A	75.8	28.3	104.1	112.0	7.4	0.0	AMERIHEALTH CASUALTY INS CO
43.4	22.0	N/A	N/A	N/A	N/A	N/A	N/A	N/A	N/A	0.0	0.0	AMERIPRISE INS CO
2.4	1.6	92.4	165.7	-0.4	-6.3	73.1	30.1	103.2	105.4	15.1	0.0 ●	AMERISURE INS CO
2.1	1.6	55.4	99.3	-0.3	-4.3	73.1	29.7	102.8	110.8	15.1	14.8 ●	AMERISURE MUTUAL INS CO
1.7	1.1	90.0	161.3	-0.7	-9.5	73.1	30.1	103.2	85.3	15.1	0.0	AMERISURE PARTNERS INS CO

999 + Denotes number greater than 999.9%
999 - Denotes number less than -999.99%
● Bullets denote a more detailed analysis is available in Section II.

INSURANCE COMPANY NAME	DOM. STATE	RATING	TOTAL ASSETS ($MIL)	CAPITAL & SURPLUS ($MIL)	ANNUAL NET PREMIUM ($MIL)	NET INCOME ($MIL)	CAPITAL-IZATION INDEX (PTS)	RESERVE ADQ INDEX (PTS)	PROFIT-ABILITY INDEX (PTS)	LIQUIDITY INDEX (PTS)	STAB. INDEX (PTS)	STABILITY FACTORS
AMERITRUST INS CORP	MI	C-	136.9	30.7	40.5	1.8	7.0	3.4	6.3	6.5	3.1	R
AMEX ASSURANCE CO	IL	B	299.7	205.8	177.5	53.7	10.0	8.3	4.9	6.8	5.9	
AMFED CAS INS CO	MS	D	4.4	1.2	0.0	0.0	10.0	N/A	6.4	10.0	1.3	DRT
AMFED NATIONAL INS CO	MS	D	69.6	25.3	-0.9	0.3	10.0	9.5	8.3	10.0	1.5	D
AMGUARD INS CO	PA	C+	404.3	103.1	59.1	4.5	7.4	10.0	8.1	6.5	4.3	GRT
AMICA LLOYDS OF TEXAS	TX	A-	77.6	72.8	17.7	2.5	10.0	6.2	8.3	7.4	7.0	
AMICA MUTUAL INS CO	RI	B+	5,054.3	2,733.6	1,746.7	103.0	8.4	7.9	8.1	6.2	6.8	
AMICA PROPERTY & CASUALTY INS CO	RI	C-	30.0	26.1	-4.9	0.2	10.0	7.0	2.7	9.0	3.2	FT
AMTRUST INS CO OF KANSAS INC	KS	B-	52.9	18.5	7.0	2.9	8.8	5.0	8.3	8.7	3.9	DFGR
AMTRUST LLOYDS INS CO OF TEXAS	TX	U	2.2	2.2	0.0	0.0	N/A	N/A	5.2	10.0	3.7	RT
ANCHOR GENERAL INS CO	CA	C	93.6	20.9	40.5	0.5	7.1	8.5	3.1	2.9	3.5	DLR
ANPAC LOUISIANA INS CO	LA	B	120.4	68.4	44.7	4.6	7.4	6.6	4.7	5.8	5.7	F
ANSUR AMERICA INS CO	MI	B	100.6	34.3	42.1	0.9	8.5	9.3	5.6	6.6	4.6	
ANTHRACITE MUTUAL FIRE INS CO	PA	C-	3.7	3.7	0.3	0.1	10.0	5.0	8.5	10.0	3.2	D
ANTILLES INS CO	PR	B	108.6	69.8	39.9	3.0	5.8	8.0	8.9	6.0	5.5	C
APOLLO CASUALTY CO	IL	C	17.5	6.5	8.3	-0.7	7.2	3.0	2.9	7.1	3.5	D
APOLLO MUTUAL FIRE INS CO	PA	D+(3)	0.0	0.0	0.1	0.1	10.0	4.6	6.9	10.0	2.1	D
APPALACHIAN INS CO	RI	C	281.6	191.6	64.5	8.7	9.5	3.6	6.3	6.9	3.3	R
APPLIANCE MANUFACTURERS ASR CO RRG	IA	U (5)	0.0	0.0	0.1	0.0	N/A	3.7	1.6	10.0	1.1	CDFG
APPLIED MEDICO LEGAL SOLUTIONS RRG	AZ	D	116.1	33.2	37.7	1.2	7.0	7.1	6.9	7.3	1.8	R
APPLIED UNDERWRITERS CAPTIVE RISK	IA	E	611.7	31.6	0.0	1.9	8.4	0.5	3.8	10.0	0.3	T
AQUAGARDIAN INS CO INC	AZ	U (5)	0.0	0.0	3.2	0.0	N/A	4.0	2.8	6.8	3.3	CDFG
ARAG INS CO	IA	B-	79.6	59.5	64.7	11.6	9.0	8.5	9.6	6.5	5.1	T
ARBELLA INDEMNITY INS CO	MA	C	46.0	16.1	21.6	0.6	7.5	8.2	4.1	6.6	3.4	DR
ARBELLA MUTUAL INS CO	MA	C+	1,266.0	555.7	496.4	15.6	8.6	8.1	4.6	6.3	4.3	R
ARBELLA PROTECTION INS CO	MA	C+	315.9	94.4	143.9	8.4	8.0	8.5	4.9	5.5	4.3	R
ARCH EXCESS & SURPLUS INS CO	MO	U	61.5	60.5	0.0	-0.4	N/A	6.1	6.0	10.0	6.0	T
ARCH INDEMNITY INS CO	MO	C	41.1	24.2	0.0	5.6	10.0	N/A	2.6	7.1	4.3	DGRT
ARCH INS CO	MO	C	3,201.7	777.2	659.6	28.3	5.8	7.8	5.2	6.9	3.4	R
ARCH MORTGAGE ASR CO	WI	B	13.0	12.7	0.1	-0.1	7.9	6.4	2.0	9.6	4.4	DF
ARCH MORTGAGE GUARANTY CO	WI	B-	9.0	7.7	0.4	0.0	10.0	N/A	1.9	10.0	3.8	DFT
ARCH MORTGAGE INS CO	WI	C+	404.6	158.6	87.1	-25.7	7.1	2.9	3.3	6.9	4.8	FR
ARCH MORTGAGE REINS CO	WI	D-	26.8	12.3	11.2	-3.1	3.9	2.1	2.1	7.6	1.2	DFT
ARCH REINSURANCE CO	DE	C-	1,724.7	1,050.5	204.0	20.6	7.9	7.9	7.5	7.0	2.7	R
ARCH SPECIALTY INS CO	MO	B	577.2	293.3	0.0	9.6	10.0	5.0	3.4	7.0	5.5	FGT
ARCHITECTS & ENGINEERS INS CO RRG	DE	C-	19.2	8.3	1.2	1.0	10.0	6.6	6.5	9.4	2.9	DGR
ARCOA RRG INC	NV	E	11.4	3.7	8.8	0.9	0.0	0.2	2.9	0.0	0.0	CDFG
ARECA INS EXCHANGE	AK	C	28.9	21.4	4.7	1.8	8.5	5.6	6.8	7.4	4.3	DR
ARGONAUT GREAT CENTRAL INS CO	IL	D	52.6	24.7	0.0	0.3	10.0	N/A	3.7	10.0	2.2	DFR
ARGONAUT INS CO	IL	C	1,294.7	406.7	196.9	1.8	7.1	3.3	5.8	7.2	3.3	FR
ARGONAUT LIMITED RISK INS CO	IL	U	11.4	11.3	0.0	0.2	N/A	N/A	7.1	7.0	5.4	T
ARGONAUT-MIDWEST INS CO	IL	D	29.6	17.4	0.0	0.2	10.0	N/A	3.8	7.0	2.3	DRT
ARGONAUT-SOUTHWEST INS CO	IL	C-	17.6	17.6	0.0	0.2	10.0	N/A	7.1	7.0	2.9	DR
ARGUS FIRE & CASUALTY INS CO	FL	F	5.1	4.2	0.0	1.0	7.8	4.6	1.0	7.4	0.0	DFT
ARI CASUALTY CO	NJ	U	7.8	7.8	0.0	0.0	N/A	4.3	2.7	7.0	3.9	RT
ARI MUTUAL INS CO	PA	C	90.2	26.8	36.4	-2.1	5.1	3.7	2.3	6.7	3.1	CGRT
ARISE BOILER INSPECT & INS CO RRG	KY	B-	3.2	2.4	0.8	0.3	9.0	5.8	3.9	7.4	3.5	DT
ARIZONA AUTOMOBILE INS CO	AZ	D	20.1	8.9	6.8	0.4	8.5	9.3	8.1	6.7	2.3	DRT
ARIZONA HOME INS CO	AZ	D	23.6	15.5	7.7	0.7	6.3	8.3	8.9	6.2	1.9	DR
ARK ROYAL INS CO	FL	C-	91.4	32.1	41.3	6.5	5.0	6.3	5.6	6.7	3.1	GT
▼ARKANSAS MUTUAL INS CO	AR	D	7.2	2.1	2.7	-0.7	2.6	4.7	1.7	6.6	1.9	CDFG
ARMED FORCES INS EXCHANGE	KS	C	134.4	65.0	64.2	1.9	8.3	8.9	3.8	6.4	3.5	R

See Page 27 for explanation of footnotes and
Page 28 for explanation of stability factors.
Arrows denote recent upgrades ▲ or downgrades ▼   (see Section VII for explanations)

40

www.weissratings.com

RISK ADJ. CAPITAL RATIO #1	CAPITAL RATIO #2	PREMIUM TO SURPLUS (%)	RESV. TO SURPLUS (%)	RESV. DEVELOP. 1 YEAR (%)	DEVELOP. 2 YEAR (%)	LOSS RATIO (%)	EXP. RATIO (%)	COMB RATIO (%)	CASH FROM UNDER-WRITING (%)	NET PREMIUM GROWTH (%)	INVEST. IN AFFIL (%)	INSURANCE COMPANY NAME
2.0	1.4	137.6	221.8	13.4	36.2	79.2	33.3	112.5	100.4	-14.0	0.0	AMERITRUST INS CORP
9.8	5.7	90.2	20.1	-10.0	-4.4	49.3	-11.7	37.6	184.6	-27.4	0.0 ●	AMEX ASSURANCE CO
1.1	1.0	N/A	N/A	N/A	N/A	N/A	N/A	N/A	N/A	0.0	0.0	AMFED CAS INS CO
3.8	2.2	-7.3	28.7	2.1	-1.3	N/A	-12.1	N/A	N/A	56.2	7.7	AMFED NATIONAL INS CO
1.5	1.1	57.3	117.6	-1.6	-77.3	69.9	26.3	96.2	132.5	145.8	2.5	AMGUARD INS CO
13.1	10.7	24.6	4.1	-0.4	-1.0	49.1	11.7	60.8	163.0	18.3	0.0 ●	AMICA LLOYDS OF TEXAS
3.0	1.9	65.9	40.8	-2.2	-3.4	69.9	21.5	91.4	116.0	6.9	5.8 ●	AMICA MUTUAL INS CO
22.6	20.4	-18.0	N/A	-175.0	-74.8	N/A	-299.2	N/A	-31.7	-150.4	0.0	AMICA PROPERTY & CASUALTY INS CO
3.6	2.2	45.7	31.9	-1.3	1.4	57.2	-33.0	24.2	999 +	102.5	0.0	AMTRUST INS CO OF KANSAS INC
N/A	N/A	N/A	N/A	N/A	N/A	N/A	N/A	N/A	-0.4	0.0	0.0	AMTRUST LLOYDS INS CO OF TEXAS
1.3	1.1	198.4	84.2	-2.3	-4.8	70.1	29.5	99.6	104.1	-9.0	18.3	ANCHOR GENERAL INS CO
1.6	1.5	72.2	40.0	-1.2	-10.1	80.2	20.7	112.9	90.2	8.1	0.0	ANPAC LOUISIANA INS CO
3.3	2.4	126.3	93.8	-12.0	-15.7	63.2	29.3	92.5	124.6	3.6	0.0	ANSUR AMERICA INS CO
12.5	7.4	9.4	1.7	-0.2	-0.2	32.6	38.9	71.5	169.9	2.2	0.0	ANTHRACITE MUTUAL FIRE INS CO
0.8	0.6	56.9	8.4	-1.9	-4.3	40.4	-30.7	9.7	108.3	22.1	0.0	ANTILLES INS CO
1.7	1.5	116.0	66.1	12.1	19.1	77.5	20.9	98.4	93.6	-12.1	0.0	APOLLO CASUALTY CO
13.8	8.5	3.4	0.1	-0.1	-0.1	51.1	76.7	127.8	77.9	-2.9	0.0	APOLLO MUTUAL FIRE INS CO
4.5	2.8	35.3	33.2	18.3	20.0	50.6	28.0	78.6	127.0	-2.4	0.0	APPALACHIAN INS CO
N/A	N/A	2.3	125.1	4.2	14.3	130.2	398.1	528.3	-10.3	-81.9	0.0	APPLIANCE MANUFACTURERS ASR CO
2.0	1.4	129.0	178.6	-8.9	-31.6	68.0	27.8	95.8	122.7	14.5	0.0	APPLIED MEDICO LEGAL SOLUTIONS
2.2	2.0	N/A	24.6	0.5	-7.9	N/A	N/A	N/A	98.6	0.0	0.0	APPLIED UNDERWRITERS CAPTIVE RISK
N/A	N/A	48.4	136.6	-25.4	-113.9	65.3	64.4	129.7	77.7	-32.7	0.0	AQUAGARDIAN INS CO INC
5.3	3.4	127.8	34.7	-10.9	-12.3	40.6	31.7	72.3	133.4	3.2	0.0	ARAG INS CO
2.0	1.3	139.5	68.2	-3.0	-6.4	64.5	33.0	97.5	111.2	6.8	0.0	ARBELLA INDEMNITY INS CO
2.6	1.9	94.7	46.3	-2.2	-5.1	64.5	32.4	96.9	106.6	6.8	14.8 ●	ARBELLA MUTUAL INS CO
2.8	1.8	167.9	82.1	-3.8	-8.4	64.5	33.0	97.5	97.4	6.8	0.0	ARBELLA PROTECTION INS CO
N/A	N/A	N/A	0.7	-0.1	-0.8	529.1	999 +	999 +	2.7	0.0	34.3	ARCH EXCESS & SURPLUS INS CO
7.6	6.8	N/A	0.4	N/A	N/A	N/A	N/A	N/A	-481.2	0.0	0.0	ARCH INDEMNITY INS CO
1.3	1.0	89.5	163.0	1.1	-0.6	68.2	32.4	100.6	109.8	-12.0	18.6 ●	ARCH INS CO
1.8	1.4	2.2	3.6	-0.8	-5.5	112.9	93.5	206.4	75.1	-28.5	64.1	ARCH MORTGAGE ASR CO
6.5	6.1	1.6	0.2	N/A	N/A	8.5	248.9	257.4	37.4	-27.2	0.0	ARCH MORTGAGE GUARANTY CO
1.9	1.5	54.0	61.0	4.3	20.6	67.8	41.6	109.4	79.0	8.5	0.0	ARCH MORTGAGE INS CO
1.2	0.9	72.4	97.1	-1.0	20.3	80.2	28.7	108.9	67.1	8.9	0.0	ARCH MORTGAGE REINS CO
1.6	1.6	20.1	28.1	-3.0	-4.5	46.8	30.8	77.6	168.1	7.4	50.2 ●	ARCH REINSURANCE CO
21.7	13.8	N/A	16.1	0.1	-0.1	999 +	999 +	999 +	17.3	340.4	0.0 ●	ARCH SPECIALTY INS CO
3.4	2.6	11.4	39.0	-1.0	-3.6	65.0	30.6	95.6	161.2	76.7	0.0	ARCHITECTS & ENGINEERS INS CO RRG
0.1	0.1	328.6	277.0	1.6	120.3	46.9	45.8	92.7	80.9	71.0	0.0	ARCOA RRG INC
3.1	1.8	20.6	20.4	6.1	1.2	45.9	30.9	76.8	108.3	21.5	0.0	ARECA INS EXCHANGE
5.6	5.1	N/A	N/A	N/A	N/A	N/A	N/A	N/A	999 +	0.0	1.2	ARGONAUT GREAT CENTRAL INS CO
1.8	1.2	48.1	130.8	8.8	17.5	82.8	34.8	117.6	72.1	-9.6	8.8 ●	ARGONAUT INS CO
N/A	N/A	N/A	N/A	N/A	N/A	N/A	N/A	N/A	N/A	0.0	0.0	ARGONAUT LIMITED RISK INS CO
6.5	5.9	N/A	N/A	N/A	N/A	N/A	N/A	N/A	N/A	0.0	0.0	ARGONAUT-MIDWEST INS CO
89.7	42.9	N/A	N/A	N/A	N/A	N/A	N/A	N/A	-159.3	0.0	0.0	ARGONAUT-SOUTHWEST INS CO
11.1	10.0	-0.1	34.7	21.3	29.2	999 +	999 +	999 +	-0.5	-100.3	0.0	ARGUS FIRE & CASUALTY INS CO
N/A	N/A	N/A	N/A	N/A	N/A	N/A	N/A	N/A	N/A	0.0	0.0	ARI CASUALTY CO
0.8	0.6	127.2	115.1	10.3	9.5	80.5	27.0	107.5	121.2	57.7	11.9	ARI MUTUAL INS CO
3.5	2.9	38.4	7.0	-7.9	-7.3	N/A	62.7	62.7	242.6	23.0	0.0	ARISE BOILER INSPECT & INS CO RRG
3.0	2.2	80.3	63.4	-1.8	-3.3	68.7	28.7	97.4	102.8	9.7	0.0	ARIZONA AUTOMOBILE INS CO
1.4	0.9	52.2	16.8	-3.4	-3.7	60.2	27.4	87.6	120.8	4.3	0.0	ARIZONA HOME INS CO
1.5	1.1	164.8	40.6	3.5	-2.9	42.6	33.7	76.3	213.9	33.9	0.0	ARK ROYAL INS CO
0.3	0.3	97.7	56.3	0.6	-7.5	62.6	66.2	128.8	82.1	44.2	0.0	ARKANSAS MUTUAL INS CO
3.0	2.1	104.2	22.2	-8.8	-10.3	59.4	33.6	93.0	95.2	-1.8	3.5	ARMED FORCES INS EXCHANGE

999 + Denotes number greater than 999.9%
999 - Denotes number less than -999.99%
● Bullets denote a more detailed analysis is available in Section II.

INSURANCE COMPANY NAME	DOM. STATE	RATING	TOTAL ASSETS ($MIL)	CAPITAL & SURPLUS ($MIL)	ANNUAL NET PREMIUM ($MIL)	NET INCOME ($MIL)	CAPITAL-IZATION INDEX (PTS)	RESERVE ADQ INDEX (PTS)	PROFIT-ABILITY INDEX (PTS)	LIQUIDITY INDEX (PTS)	STAB. INDEX (PTS)	STABILITY FACTORS
ARROW MUTUAL LIABILITY INS CO	MA	B-	47.3	31.4	5.9	0.9	8.3	7.0	5.0	7.9	5.1	D
ARROWOOD INDEMNITY CO	DE	U	1,499.6	236.4	1.5	-33.3	N/A	5.7	1.7	7.0	0.9	CRT
ARROWOOD SURPLUS LINES INS CO	DE	U	174.6	157.0	0.0	3.7	N/A	5.9	3.8	10.0	6.2	FT
ARTISAN & TRUCKERS CASUALTY CO	WI	C	287.9	54.8	40.0	2.2	10.0	6.0	7.8	6.5	3.6	R
ARTISAN CONTRACTORS INS CO RRG LLC	MT	U (5)	0.0	0.0	0.2	0.0	N/A	N/A	2.9	9.2	0.0	T
ASCENDANT COMMERCIAL INS INC	FL	E+	40.0	8.7	14.4	0.3	1.6	0.4	3.9	8.1	0.5	DF
ASHLAND MUTUAL FIRE INS CO OF PA	PA	U	0.5	0.5	0.0	0.0	N/A	5.2	3.4	10.0	1.7	FT
ASHMERE INS CO	IL	U	36.5	12.2	0.0	-0.5	N/A	5.9	1.8	7.0	3.0	CRT
ASI ASR CORP	FL	C+	148.4	67.0	75.0	12.0	7.8	9.3	8.3	7.2	4.8	T
ASI HOME INS CORP	FL	B-	16.7	16.5	0.1	0.1	10.0	3.9	5.6	10.0	5.2	D
ASI LLOYDS	TX	C	197.1	77.8	86.5	3.8	8.8	9.3	6.0	7.2	3.6	R
ASI PREFERRED INS CORP	FL	C	57.9	20.9	15.3	-0.2	6.3	5.8	6.9	6.7	4.3	D
ASI SELECT INS CORP	DE	D	6.3	5.6	0.4	-0.1	10.0	3.6	0.2	9.4	1.4	DFGT
ASOC DE SUSCRIPCION CONJUNTA DEL	PR	C	256.5	119.7	157.2	18.2	10.0	6.2	2.0	6.4	3.5	T
ASPEN AMERICAN INS CO	TX	C	481.1	233.2	26.8	-22.3	10.0	9.4	2.8	7.1	4.0	FGRT
ASPEN SPECIALTY INS CO	ND	C	291.9	118.3	41.0	6.6	6.3	9.0	3.9	6.6	3.5	FGR
ASPEN SPECIALTY RRG INC	DC	U	1.0	0.9	0.0	-0.1	N/A	0.0	2.3	0.0	0.0	LT
ASSET PROTECTION PROGRAM RRG INC	SC	U	1.5	0.9	0.0	0.0	N/A	3.4	0.7	10.0	0.8	CFT
ASSN OF CERTIFIED MTG ORIG RRG	NV	U	1.2	1.0	0.0	0.0	N/A	N/A	3.2	7.0	0.0	FT
ASSOCIATED EMPLOYERS INS CO	MA	C	5.3	4.4	0.0	0.0	10.0	N/A	7.6	10.0	3.5	DR
ASSOCIATED INDEMNITY CORP	CA	C	99.6	83.6	0.0	1.5	10.0	4.4	5.6	7.6	4.2	FRT
ASSOCIATED INDUSTRIES INS CO INC	FL	D	202.8	72.5	11.6	5.8	8.3	9.5	7.8	10.0	2.0	FGRT
ASSOCIATED INDUSTRIES OF MA MUT INS	MA	C	528.3	185.9	126.1	5.7	7.7	9.4	6.8	6.8	4.0	R
ASSOCIATED INTERNATIONAL INS CO	IL	C-	274.9	102.1	35.5	3.3	4.4	3.9	3.8	7.2	3.3	CR
ASSOCIATED LOGGERS EXCHANGE	ID	C-	30.4	13.0	10.1	0.3	5.9	9.5	6.0	6.5	3.0	DR
ASSOCIATED MUTUAL INS CO	NY	D+	26.9	10.0	5.5	-0.3	7.4	5.9	3.8	7.6	2.6	DFR
ASSOCIATION CASUALTY INS CO	TX	C	46.7	18.5	20.3	0.8	7.4	5.3	3.5	6.1	3.5	D
ASSOCIATION INS CO	DE	C	112.4	32.2	20.9	0.2	7.9	9.3	8.2	6.9	3.4	RT
ASSURANCE COMPANY OF AMERICA	NY	C+	26.9	20.2	0.0	0.3	10.0	N/A	7.0	7.0	4.5	DFRT
ASSURANCEAMERICA INS CO	SC	D	51.3	12.3	23.3	0.1	5.7	3.3	3.2	6.6	1.5	DR
ASSURED GUARANTY CORP	MD	D+	2,485.9	507.9	-186.7	67.4	8.2	4.8	1.9	9.3	1.1	AFRT
ASSURED GUARANTY MUNICIPAL CORP	NY	D+	5,751.6	1,610.0	-191.3	198.0	7.3	4.4	7.9	7.0	2.4	ACR
ASURE WORLDWIDE INS CO	MI	C	37.0	13.8	15.8	0.4	8.8	6.9	5.5	6.6	4.0	D
ATAIN INS CO	TX	C-	65.4	39.8	10.9	1.7	8.2	9.3	8.9	7.5	3.2	DGR
ATAIN SPECIALTY INS CO	MI	C	292.1	148.4	61.5	8.7	7.3	9.3	8.9	7.3	3.8	GR
ATHENS FINANCIAL INS CO	OK	B-	2.1	1.8	0.3	0.1	10.0	N/A	6.9	9.7	3.5	DGT
ATLANTA INTERNATIONAL INS CO	NY	U	44.1	21.3	0.0	0.3	N/A	2.3	3.5	7.0	3.5	RT
ATLANTIC BONDING CO	MD	D	11.8	10.7	0.9	0.2	7.7	4.9	3.7	7.9	1.5	DF
ATLANTIC CASUALTY INS CO	NC	B-	236.7	83.1	66.8	1.7	7.5	9.3	6.7	7.0	4.5	R
ATLANTIC CHARTER INS CO	MA	B-	181.3	51.8	54.9	4.5	7.1	9.6	3.7	6.9	4.9	R
ATLANTIC SPECIALTY INS CO	NY	C	2,431.5	688.2	969.2	14.3	6.7	7.1	5.6	6.3	3.6	GRT
ATLANTIC STATES INS CO	PA	B-	636.4	191.4	346.9	5.2	8.5	5.1	4.7	5.8	4.7	R
ATRADIUS TRADE CREDIT INS CO	MD	C	91.4	65.8	15.6	1.0	10.0	7.0	6.9	8.4	3.7	R
ATRIUM INS CORP	NY	U	1.8	1.7	0.0	0.0	N/A	5.1	2.4	7.0	2.3	FT
ATTORNEYS INS MUTUAL OF SOUTH RRG	DC	C-	13.2	7.2	3.0	-0.5	8.6	9.6	2.7	9.3	2.7	DFGR
ATTORNEYS INS MUTUAL RRG	HI	D-	16.5	8.3	3.6	0.3	3.3	4.2	4.2	8.6	0.9	DR
ATTORNEYS LIAB ASR SOCIETY INC RRG	VT	C-	1,997.4	588.8	25.9	-46.2	9.6	4.6	4.2	9.2	2.9	GR
ATTORNEYS LIABILITY PROTECTION SOCIE (See ALPS PROPERTY & CASUALTY INS CO)												
ATTPRO RRG RECIPROCAL RRG	DC	D	1.7	1.3	0.0	0.0	10.0	N/A	2.7	10.0	1.5	DFGT
ATX PREMIER INS CO	TX	C	9.7	5.7	0.2	-0.7	10.0	4.6	3.4	9.0	3.4	DFT
AUSTIN MUTUAL INS CO	MN	E	45.3	34.6	-17.5	0.7	9.5	3.7	2.2	5.2	0.1	FRT
AUTO CLUB CASUALTY CO	TX	U	2.8	2.8	0.0	0.0	N/A	N/A	6.3	10.0	4.0	T

See Page 27 for explanation of footnotes and
Page 28 for explanation of stability factors.
Arrows denote recent upgrades ▲ or downgrades ▼ (see Section VII for explanations)

42

www.weissratings.com

RISK ADJ. RATIO #1	CAPITAL RATIO #2	PREMIUM TO SURPLUS (%)	RESV. TO SURPLUS (%)	RESV. DEVELOP. 1 YEAR (%)	RESV. DEVELOP. 2 YEAR (%)	LOSS RATIO (%)	EXP. RATIO (%)	COMB RATIO (%)	CASH FROM UNDER-WRITING (%)	NET PREMIUM GROWTH (%)	INVEST. IN AFFIL (%)	INSURANCE COMPANY NAME
2.7	1.8	19.4	39.9	-3.7	-9.8	106.1	10.6	116.7	89.9	8.9	0.0	ARROW MUTUAL LIABILITY INS CO
N/A	N/A	0.6	420.2	-12.1	-13.3	673.6	999 +	999 +	74.1	156.9	10.8	ARROWOOD INDEMNITY CO
N/A	N/A	N/A	10.9	-0.5	-0.5	N/A	N/A	N/A	N/A	0.0	0.0	ARROWOOD SURPLUS LINES INS CO
5.4	4.0	77.9	47.5	2.2	4.9	80.3	18.1	98.4	119.3	8.6	0.0	ARTISAN & TRUCKERS CASUALTY CO
N/A	N/A	42.8	8.8	N/A	N/A	41.7	46.0	87.7	156.2	0.0	0.0	ARTISAN CONTRACTORS INS CO RRG
0.6	0.4	172.4	151.8	10.3	54.6	65.9	23.8	89.7	93.8	10.1	0.0	ASCENDANT COMMERCIAL INS INC
N/A	N/A	0.4	0.5	-0.5	-0.6	N/A	999 +	999 +	5.4	-40.8	0.0	ASHLAND MUTUAL FIRE INS CO OF PA
N/A	N/A	N/A	192.8	1.4	1.0	999 +	999 +	999 +	0.1	145.1	0.0	ASHMERE INS CO
3.3	2.1	134.9	51.3	-14.1	-11.5	39.3	34.8	74.1	158.1	37.0	0.0	ASI ASR CORP
107.6	54.6	0.6	N/A	N/A	N/A	100.1	44.1	144.2	72.7	-16.7	0.0	ASI HOME INS CORP
2.4	2.1	117.5	25.1	-3.1	-10.0	47.3	34.7	82.0	158.7	54.9	0.0	ASI LLOYDS
2.1	1.3	75.7	26.0	-7.7	6.2	30.4	44.1	82.5	121.9	-24.4	0.0	ASI PREFERRED INS CORP
6.8	4.6	8.3	5.0	-0.6	N/A	62.5	147.9	210.4	34.1	50.7	0.0	ASI SELECT INS CORP
7.8	4.7	131.9	21.5	-2.5	-1.5	68.7	10.1	78.8	111.7	-7.4	0.0	ASOC DE SUSCRIPCION CONJUNTA DEL
4.3	2.9	10.4	5.8	1.4	-14.1	102.9	107.7	210.6	70.7	27.3	0.0 ●	ASPEN AMERICAN INS CO
1.2	0.8	35.2	24.1	4.0	-15.5	55.9	36.7	92.6	33.2	40.4	0.0	ASPEN SPECIALTY INS CO
N/A	N/A	N/A	N/A	N/A	N/A	N/A	N/A	N/A	N/A	0.0	0.0	ASPEN SPECIALTY RRG INC
N/A	N/A	N/A	95.4	14.2	5.2	N/A	N/A	N/A	N/A	0.0	0.0	ASSET PROTECTION PROGRAM RRG INC
N/A	N/A	N/A	N/A	N/A	N/A	N/A	N/A	N/A	N/A	0.0	0.0	ASSN OF CERTIFIED MTG ORIG RRG
11.8	10.6	N/A	N/A	N/A	N/A	N/A	N/A	N/A	-193.0	0.0	0.0	ASSOCIATED EMPLOYERS INS CO
27.0	24.3	N/A	N/A	N/A	N/A	N/A	N/A	N/A	31.9	100.0	0.0	ASSOCIATED INDEMNITY CORP
3.8	2.1	15.6	80.1	-14.4	-7.5	-43.3	31.8	-11.5	-15.1	97.1	0.0	ASSOCIATED INDUSTRIES INS CO INC
1.9	1.4	70.8	132.4	-8.2	-14.7	76.7	23.9	100.6	117.6	11.6	2.6	ASSOCIATED INDUSTRIES OF MA MUT
0.9	0.5	36.4	135.3	6.7	34.3	73.8	48.2	122.0	95.4	1.8	0.0	ASSOCIATED INTERNATIONAL INS CO
1.2	0.8	80.7	121.8	-5.2	-14.7	74.0	23.2	97.2	103.6	28.8	2.0	ASSOCIATED LOGGERS EXCHANGE
1.7	1.3	54.1	116.3	-3.6	0.2	71.6	33.7	105.3	85.4	13.3	0.0	ASSOCIATED MUTUAL INS CO
2.8	1.8	114.1	101.2	1.2	8.4	74.2	27.9	102.1	96.9	-13.4	0.0	ASSOCIATION CASUALTY INS CO
2.1	1.5	66.1	78.1	-1.9	-6.0	71.6	19.1	90.7	140.5	1.2	0.0	ASSOCIATION INS CO
10.9	9.8	N/A	N/A	N/A	N/A	N/A	N/A	N/A	178.8	0.0	0.0	ASSURANCE COMPANY OF AMERICA
1.0	0.8	192.9	89.7	-2.8	-6.4	73.7	32.1	105.8	101.0	0.5	0.0	ASSURANCEAMERICA INS CO
1.5	1.3	-27.0	22.1	-1.3	-4.6	-38.4	-32.9	-71.3	-98.4	-311.8	13.6 ●	ASSURED GUARANTY CORP
2.5	1.6	-11.0	19.6	-0.1	11.0	-19.2	-63.4	-82.6	58.8	-197.6	9.7 ●	ASSURED GUARANTY MUNICIPAL CORP
2.9	2.1	118.1	87.7	-11.3	-14.6	63.2	29.3	92.5	108.7	3.6	0.0	ASURE WORLDWIDE INS CO
2.8	2.1	28.7	38.2	-2.0	-8.2	62.1	23.1	85.2	171.5	33.8	0.0	ATAIN INS CO
1.8	1.4	45.6	60.7	-2.9	-10.5	62.4	22.0	84.4	178.7	33.8	15.0	ATAIN SPECIALTY INS CO
8.1	4.9	19.7	N/A	N/A	N/A	N/A	42.7	42.7	252.6	76.1	0.0	ATHENS FINANCIAL INS CO
N/A	N/A	N/A	96.0	6.9	15.7	999 +	357.9	999 +	N/A	0.0	0.0	ATLANTA INTERNATIONAL INS CO
2.2	1.4	9.5	2.3	-2.9	5.3	-32.4	84.8	52.4	90.5	30.5	0.0	ATLANTIC BONDING CO
1.5	1.3	80.6	124.2	-5.2	-12.7	63.1	37.0	100.1	118.0	2.9	0.0	ATLANTIC CASUALTY INS CO
1.4	1.0	117.4	208.6	-7.2	-20.4	66.6	23.6	90.2	122.5	9.3	0.0	ATLANTIC CHARTER INS CO
1.4	1.0	145.6	144.2	-0.3	0.4	54.5	37.3	91.8	105.4	14.0	9.7 ●	ATLANTIC SPECIALTY INS CO
2.8	2.0	185.9	94.5	0.8	2.2	64.7	30.9	95.6	110.3	14.4	0.0	ATLANTIC STATES INS CO
12.9	8.6	24.1	9.2	-1.5	0.4	49.1	35.6	84.7	105.7	12.9	0.0	ATRADIUS TRADE CREDIT INS CO
N/A	N/A	N/A	N/A	N/A	N/A	N/A	N/A	N/A	N/A	0.0	0.0	ATRIUM INS CORP
2.7	1.9	38.3	49.7	-7.2	-17.6	42.9	54.1	97.0	63.4	62.6	0.0	ATTORNEYS INS MUTUAL OF SOUTH
0.9	0.7	44.5	63.6	0.4	-2.0	66.1	35.0	101.1	111.7	0.5	0.0	ATTORNEYS INS MUTUAL RRG
1.8	1.2	32.3	87.8	6.3	9.8	102.4	-1.5	100.9	-338.4	11.5	0.0	ATTORNEYS LIAB ASR SOCIETY INC
7.4	6.6	1.4	1.0	N/A	N/A	159.7	340.7	500.4	34.4	136.6	0.0	ATTPRO RRG RECIPROCAL RRG
4.5	4.1	2.4	1.5	N/A	N/A	158.0	254.1	412.1	40.1	-60.7	0.0	ATX PREMIER INS CO
13.3	6.1	-51.4	N/A	N/A	7.4	N/A	N/A	N/A	-47.6	-147.3	0.0	AUSTIN MUTUAL INS CO
N/A	N/A	N/A	N/A	N/A	N/A	N/A	N/A	N/A	37.1	0.0	0.0	AUTO CLUB CASUALTY CO

999 + Denotes number greater than 999.9%
999 - Denotes number less than -999.99%
● Bullets denote a more detailed analysis is available in Section II.

INSURANCE COMPANY NAME	DOM. STATE	RATING	TOTAL ASSETS ($MIL)	CAPITAL & SURPLUS ($MIL)	ANNUAL NET PREMIUM ($MIL)	NET INCOME ($MIL)	CAPITAL-IZATION INDEX (PTS)	RESERVE ADQ INDEX (PTS)	PROFIT-ABILITY INDEX (PTS)	LIQUIDITY INDEX (PTS)	STAB. INDEX (PTS)	STABILITY FACTORS
AUTO CLUB FAMILY INS CO	MO	C	107.7	41.2	29.0	1.2	8.7	7.6	8.7	7.6	3.8	T
AUTO CLUB GROUP INS CO	MI	B-	350.7	107.5	127.8	-2.9	9.2	4.2	3.7	6.4	4.9	F
AUTO CLUB INDEMNITY CO	TX	B+	21.8	5.3	0.0	0.0	8.1	N/A	7.2	10.0	5.0	D
AUTO CLUB INS ASSN	MI	B	3,680.4	1,538.0	1,351.3	-14.7	7.8	4.4	3.7	6.1	4.9	R
AUTO CLUB INS CO OF FL	FL	C	310.0	128.5	153.1	12.7	8.5	5.0	6.8	6.6	3.4	T
AUTO CLUB PROPERTY & CASUALTY INS	MI	C	80.4	27.6	37.2	-0.7	8.1	4.1	2.6	6.3	3.7	T
AUTO CLUB SOUTH INS CO	FL	C	115.9	52.0	49.5	1.5	9.0	8.3	8.3	6.5	4.0	T
AUTO-OWNERS INS CO	MI	A	11,867.2	7,798.4	2,325.4	195.0	8.6	6.0	6.9	6.9	7.7	
AUTOMOBILE CLUB INTERINSURANCE	MO	C	400.5	202.9	115.9	9.3	8.5	7.5	5.2	6.7	4.3	T
AUTOMOBILE INS CO OF HARTFORD CT	CT	B	1,038.3	347.2	275.9	30.4	8.2	8.6	7.7	7.0	6.0	T
AUTOONE INS CO	NY	C-	47.5	13.9	15.0	-2.2	6.0	4.6	1.5	6.0	3.1	FRT
AVATAR PROPERTY & CASUALTY INS CO	FL	C	27.6	16.4	9.1	1.1	7.7	3.5	6.9	6.7	3.6	D
AVEMCO INS CO	MD	B	114.0	77.3	29.8	7.5	9.5	8.7	7.6	6.8	5.4	R
AVERA PROPERTY INS INC	SD	E+ (5)	0.0	0.0	0.6	0.0	6.3	10.0	4.7	8.6	0.0	DT
AVIATION ALLIANCE INS RRG INC	MT	D+	3.1	1.4	0.9	0.1	4.4	4.9	4.2	8.4	1.0	DGT
AVIVA INS CO OF CANADA (US BR)	NY	U	16.3	10.5	0.0	0.0	N/A	5.7	4.3	10.0	4.1	FT
AXA ART INS CORP	NY	C	42.8	31.7	14.5	14.9	9.0	6.4	5.2	7.0	3.4	R
AXA INS CO	NY	C-	224.9	127.1	27.0	13.1	10.0	5.5	6.8	9.1	3.3	R
AXIS INS CO	IL	C+	1,462.3	536.1	306.8	-21.8	7.4	6.1	3.8	7.0	4.6	AR
AXIS REINS CO	NY	C+	2,884.6	809.3	494.2	2.7	7.5	9.4	6.7	7.3	4.2	AR
AXIS SPECIALTY INS CO	CT	U	80.4	62.1	-0.1	4.6	N/A	8.8	3.2	9.0	4.9	FRT
AXIS SURPLUS INS CO	IL	C-	460.6	213.4	33.4	5.6	10.0	8.7	8.1	7.0	3.0	R
AZTEC INS CO	FL	U (5)	0.0	0.0	0.0	0.0	N/A	N/A	8.7	10.0	3.6	T
BADGER MUTUAL INS CO	WI	C	162.7	56.1	92.9	-1.2	8.1	3.8	2.7	5.8	4.3	R
BALBOA INS CO	CA	C-	242.0	197.2	-2.9	2.6	8.1	6.1	1.9	7.0	3.1	FRT
BALDWIN MUTUAL INS CO	AL	E+	11.3	7.0	5.4	0.6	8.3	6.1	1.6	9.1	0.5	DGT
BALTIMORE EQUITABLE SOCIETY	MD	U	157.6	93.6	-1.4	0.7	N/A	5.0	4.5	10.0	6.2	FT
BANKERS INDEPENDENT INS CO	PA	C	24.8	8.4	12.4	-0.8	7.5	4.5	2.7	6.5	3.7	DFR
BANKERS INS CO	FL	C	157.8	67.6	62.4	2.8	5.3	4.3	4.1	6.6	4.1	R
BANKERS SPECIALTY INS CO	LA	D+	58.2	44.8	13.3	-1.6	3.0	6.1	3.6	5.5	2.6	CDGT
BANKERS STANDARD FIRE & MARINE CO	PA	C	195.1	77.6	39.2	2.5	9.5	8.0	8.3	7.1	4.0	R
BANKERS STANDARD INS CO	PA	C	415.4	138.6	91.4	4.0	7.6	8.1	6.6	7.2	4.1	R
BAR PLAN MUTUAL INS CO	MO	C-	50.0	19.1	10.7	0.4	4.7	3.4	1.8	6.9	2.9	DFR
BAR PLAN SURETY & FIDELITY CO	MO	C	4.9	4.1	0.4	0.0	10.0	7.9	7.9	10.0	3.3	DOR
BAR VERMONT RRG INC	VT	D	25.1	16.7	2.0	0.6	8.2	9.3	7.0	9.2	1.6	DFR
BARNSTABLE COUNTY INS CO	MA	C	22.4	19.8	1.3	0.3	10.0	6.0	8.3	9.2	3.9	DR
BARNSTABLE COUNTY MUTUAL INS CO	MA	B-	102.0	79.5	15.7	2.7	8.5	7.5	8.3	7.2	5.0	F
BATTLE CREEK MUTUAL INS CO	NE	D	5.9	5.4	0.0	0.1	10.0	7.0	2.9	7.9	1.5	DGRT
BAY INS RRG INC	SC	U	0.6	0.5	0.0	0.0	N/A	0.0	4.6	0.0	0.0	LT
BAY STATE INS CO	MA	B-	429.0	273.9	73.9	11.0	8.6	6.2	6.4	7.4	4.8	T
BCS INS CO	OH	B	291.2	158.1	131.9	5.1	10.0	6.0	6.9	6.6	5.4	R
BEACON MUTUAL INS CO	RI	C (5)	387.1	153.3	81.2	0.0	2.3	6.2	3.8	7.5	2.3	CFT
BEACONHARBOR MUTUAL RRG	ME	U	1.0	1.0	0.0	0.0	N/A	0.0	4.9	0.0	0.0	LT
BEAR RIVER MUTUAL INS CO	UT	B-	233.8	125.5	99.2	7.6	9.5	8.5	8.5	6.4	5.3	T
BEARING MIDWEST CASUALTY CO	KS	D+	5.8	5.6	0.0	0.0	10.0	N/A	4.9	7.0	2.4	DT
BEAZLEY INS CO INC	CT	C+	259.1	123.9	37.5	1.2	10.0	6.7	6.2	8.7	4.5	R
BEDFORD GRANGE MUTUAL INS CO	PA	C-	7.6	3.5	3.6	0.1	7.7	5.3	5.8	7.1	2.1	D
BEDFORD PHYSICIANS RRG INC	VT	D	39.3	7.3	6.8	0.8	1.9	7.1	5.8	9.5	2.3	DR
BELL UNITED INS CO	NV	C	34.9	21.0	7.6	2.0	7.4	6.0	8.7	9.2	4.2	D
BENCHMARK INS CO	KS	B-	173.5	56.2	36.6	3.7	7.4	4.4	8.2	7.1	4.9	R
BENEFIT SECURITY INS CO	IL	B-	8.1	3.6	1.6	0.0	7.5	5.0	5.8	8.4	3.5	D
BERKLEY ASR CO	IA	C-	57.1	51.5	0.0	0.6	10.0	4.8	7.6	10.0	2.9	RT

See Page 27 for explanation of footnotes and Page 28 for explanation of stability factors.
Arrows denote recent upgrades ▲ or downgrades ▼   (see Section VII for explanations)

44

www.weissratings.com

RISK ADJ. CAPITAL RATIO #1	CAPITAL RATIO #2	PREMIUM TO SURPLUS (%)	RESV. TO SURPLUS (%)	RESV. DEVELOP. 1 YEAR (%)	2 YEAR (%)	LOSS RATIO (%)	EXP. RATIO (%)	COMB RATIO (%)	CASH FROM UNDER-WRITING (%)	NET PREMIUM GROWTH (%)	INVEST. IN AFFIL (%)	INSURANCE COMPANY NAME
3.4	2.2	71.6	25.0	-0.7	-1.4	71.1	21.9	93.0	102.2	5.3	0.0	AUTO CLUB FAMILY INS CO
3.0	2.3	115.8	95.2	2.6	12.6	73.9	30.3	104.2	74.4	-5.7	0.0	AUTO CLUB GROUP INS CO
1.6	1.5	N/A	N/A	N/A	N/A	N/A	N/A	N/A	-2.5	0.0	0.0 ●	AUTO CLUB INDEMNITY CO
1.8	1.4	85.8	71.6	2.0	9.9	74.0	30.3	104.3	111.9	9.9	20.7 ●	AUTO CLUB INS ASSN
2.8	2.1	134.0	59.3	-6.0	-2.5	61.3	23.6	84.9	146.0	17.0	0.0	AUTO CLUB INS CO OF FL
2.1	1.6	131.4	94.1	2.9	12.1	72.6	31.1	103.7	112.6	-21.4	0.0	AUTO CLUB PROPERTY & CASUALTY INS
3.0	2.6	99.3	52.7	-1.9	-3.7	75.2	22.1	97.3	115.1	1.0	0.0	AUTO CLUB SOUTH INS CO
2.4	2.1	31.0	30.2	1.1	0.6	60.9	32.0	92.9	111.1	4.3	26.1 ●	AUTO-OWNERS INS CO
2.9	2.2	58.5	20.5	-0.5	-1.1	71.1	21.9	93.0	115.9	5.3	13.4 ●	AUTOMOBILE CLUB INTERINSURANCE
3.1	2.0	87.0	156.5	-2.3	-5.3	60.9	29.8	90.7	116.8	3.0	0.0 ●	AUTOMOBILE INS CO OF HARTFORD CT
1.3	1.0	103.9	184.5	-3.7	3.0	87.4	31.3	118.7	60.8	-24.4	0.0	AUTOONE INS CO
1.9	1.4	59.6	12.0	1.1	9.3	33.7	46.2	79.9	111.8	30.0	0.0	AVATAR PROPERTY & CASUALTY INS CO
4.0	3.6	42.9	22.8	-8.4	-8.4	42.4	29.9	72.3	125.2	-5.0	17.0	AVEMCO INS CO
1.5	0.9	97.5	87.1	-89.3	-85.4	39.6	15.6	55.2	173.6	8.5	0.0	AVERA PROPERTY INS INC
0.9	0.5	73.2	32.3	-12.6	-14.0	17.0	55.0	72.0	205.0	68.3	0.0	AVIATION ALLIANCE INS RRG INC
N/A	N/A	N/A	41.1	-0.6	4.9	999 +	999 +	999 +	0.2	0.0	0.0	AVIVA INS CO OF CANADA (US BR)
3.6	2.9	48.9	15.6	-3.7	-3.4	35.9	62.9	98.8	115.9	1.4	0.0	AXA ART INS CORP
6.9	4.2	22.9	21.3	-1.5	2.8	44.7	20.9	65.6	227.9	2.1	0.0	AXA INS CO
1.7	1.1	58.3	97.6	4.2	0.3	80.0	34.3	114.3	155.1	34.9	22.4 ●	AXIS INS CO
2.4	1.5	60.1	152.3	-10.8	-17.2	57.8	35.0	92.8	85.5	21.3	0.0 ●	AXIS REINS CO
N/A	N/A	-0.2	42.5	4.1	-3.3	999 +	-411.8	999 +	-11.7	-21.2	0.0	AXIS SPECIALTY INS CO
6.9	4.5	16.2	35.9	-3.8	-7.5	31.1	33.6	64.7	162.4	13.2	0.0 ●	AXIS SURPLUS INS CO
N/A	N/A	N/A	0.6	N/A	N/A	367.0	999 +	999 +	-1.1	144.3	0.0	AZTEC INS CO
2.6	1.6	160.4	92.2	13.7	9.0	79.9	28.6	108.5	98.1	2.3	0.0	BADGER MUTUAL INS CO
1.7	1.7	-1.5	8.8	0.9	1.0	-94.5	96.0	1.5	115.7	68.6	50.4 ●	BALBOA INS CO
5.3	4.8	83.0	10.4	-40.7	-103.0	31.2	-33.7	-2.5	107.4	-13.3	4.1	BALDWIN MUTUAL INS CO
N/A	N/A	-1.6	1.1	-0.4	0.2	-139.5	-166.5	-306.0	-30.3	-14.8	0.0	BALTIMORE EQUITABLE SOCIETY
1.5	1.3	139.2	79.3	12.3	13.4	77.5	20.1	97.6	86.9	-12.1	0.0	BANKERS INDEPENDENT INS CO
1.0	0.8	105.9	81.0	-3.0	3.4	39.7	58.4	98.1	98.0	67.7	50.5	BANKERS INS CO
0.6	0.5	43.6	7.1	-2.6	-4.9	35.5	51.7	87.2	137.6	719.2	55.7	BANKERS SPECIALTY INS CO
4.4	2.9	52.2	92.2	-3.7	-2.6	72.2	19.1	91.3	100.6	-2.8	0.0	BANKERS STANDARD FIRE & MARINE CO
1.7	1.4	69.2	122.4	-5.1	-3.7	72.2	19.1	91.3	136.8	-2.8	24.2	BANKERS STANDARD INS CO
0.9	0.7	60.1	126.0	-14.2	17.7	63.4	35.5	98.9	75.2	1.1	11.6	BAR PLAN MUTUAL INS CO
10.3	8.5	10.1	9.9	-0.6	-3.5	32.9	33.9	66.8	238.5	5.9	0.0	BAR PLAN SURETY & FIDELITY CO
2.6	1.6	12.6	25.1	-7.5	-10.9	-0.9	73.8	72.9	60.4	0.7	0.0	BAR VERMONT RRG INC
6.7	4.0	6.9	0.8	-0.4	-1.2	23.1	51.2	74.3	119.5	1.0	0.0	BARNSTABLE COUNTY INS CO
2.8	2.2	20.1	5.2	-0.9	-2.3	48.7	51.9	100.6	93.5	-4.0	21.0	BARNSTABLE COUNTY MUTUAL INS CO
22.7	14.8	N/A	N/A	N/A	5.5	N/A	N/A	N/A	-890.2	100.0	0.0	BATTLE CREEK MUTUAL INS CO
N/A	N/A	N/A	N/A	N/A	N/A	N/A	N/A	N/A	N/A	0.0	0.0	BAY INS RRG INC
3.1	1.9	28.4	18.3	-1.1	-1.8	43.3	39.5	82.8	113.9	2.8	0.0 ●	BAY STATE INS CO
6.8	3.8	86.3	28.4	1.5	-2.0	70.2	26.8	97.0	104.5	18.1	1.3	BCS INS CO
2.5	1.6	51.9	127.8	-11.7	-25.2	84.2	37.9	122.1	69.8	-7.2	2.3	BEACON MUTUAL INS CO
N/A	N/A	N/A	N/A	N/A	N/A	N/A	N/A	N/A	N/A	0.0	0.0	BEACONHARBOR MUTUAL RRG
4.0	2.6	83.1	35.4	-5.3	-5.1	75.3	25.7	101.0	106.6	6.5	0.0	BEAR RIVER MUTUAL INS CO
40.3	22.3	N/A	N/A	N/A	N/A	N/A	N/A	N/A	N/A	0.0	0.0	BEARING MIDWEST CASUALTY CO
4.9	3.6	30.8	52.2	-4.5	-7.3	46.4	37.0	83.4	106.5	33.4	0.0	BEAZLEY INS CO INC
1.7	1.2	106.1	16.9	-1.5	1.1	46.8	42.5	89.3	103.5	11.9	6.7	BEDFORD GRANGE MUTUAL INS CO
0.7	0.5	104.3	325.2	-4.1	-15.9	94.4	4.0	98.4	519.5	33.0	0.0	BEDFORD PHYSICIANS RRG INC
3.7	2.5	39.7	68.6	-30.4	-40.1	23.1	11.9	35.0	155.6	0.9	0.0	BELL UNITED INS CO
2.5	1.7	70.0	79.1	3.3	6.3	59.8	34.4	94.2	132.6	6.0	0.0	BENCHMARK INS CO
1.5	1.2	44.2	53.1	N/A	0.1	36.5	69.0	105.5	116.5	3.7	0.0	BENEFIT SECURITY INS CO
32.0	21.0	N/A	N/A	N/A	N/A	N/A	N/A	N/A	-43.8	0.0	0.0	BERKLEY ASR CO

999 + Denotes number greater than 999.9%
999 - Denotes number less than -999.99%
● Bullets denote a more detailed analysis is available in Section II.

INSURANCE COMPANY NAME	DOM. STATE	RATING	TOTAL ASSETS ($MIL)	CAPITAL & SURPLUS ($MIL)	ANNUAL NET PREMIUM ($MIL)	NET INCOME ($MIL)	CAPITAL- IZATION INDEX (PTS)	RESERVE ADQ INDEX (PTS)	PROFIT- ABILITY INDEX (PTS)	LIQUIDITY INDEX (PTS)	STAB. INDEX (PTS)	STABILITY FACTORS
BERKLEY INS CO	DE	C	16,852.4	5,125.2	5,744.1	431.0	7.1	8.0	8.3	8.6	4.3	AGRT
BERKLEY NATIONAL INS CO	IA	C	84.9	49.4	-2.8	0.7	10.0	3.6	7.4	10.0	4.0	FT
BERKLEY REGIONAL INS CO	DE	C+	700.0	645.9	-547.4	-7.0	7.7	4.9	3.9	0.7	4.4	AFLR
BERKLEY REGIONAL SPECIALTY INS CO	DE	C	65.9	51.8	0.0	0.7	10.0	N/A	5.6	10.0	4.2	D
BERKSHIRE HATHAWAY ASR CORP	NY	A+	2,246.2	1,432.0	12.4	74.1	9.5	N/A	8.8	10.0	7.6	T
BERKSHIRE HATHAWAY HOMESTATE INS	NE	C+	1,860.9	1,089.3	280.1	136.3	5.4	7.6	6.8	6.4	4.4	GRT
BERKSHIRE HATHAWAY SPECIALTY INS CO	NE	C+	3,448.0	3,183.8	1.6	51.3	7.3	2.9	4.5	9.9	4.4	FGRT
BITCO GENERAL INS CORP	IL	A-	796.8	286.0	204.3	35.2	9.2	9.3	8.3	7.1	6.9	A
BITCO NATIONAL INS CO	IL	A-	468.3	151.2	128.8	20.7	8.5	9.4	8.0	6.9	7.0	A
BLACK DIAMOND INS CO	NV	B- (3)	0.0	0.0	0.0	0.0	10.0	N/A	3.9	10.0	3.5	DFT
BLOOMFIELD MUTUAL INS CO	MN	D+	9.6	7.1	3.2	0.0	10.0	7.7	8.1	6.7	2.6	D
BLOOMINGTON COMPENSATION INS CO	MN	C+	17.0	13.4	0.0	0.2	10.0	3.6	5.1	7.0	4.7	DR
BLUE CROSS BLUE SHIELD OF INDIANA (See ANTHEM INS COMPANIES INC)												
BLUE CROSS BLUE SHIELD OF OHIO (See COMMUNITY INS CO)												
BLUE RIDGE INDEMNITY CO	WI	C	27.6	5.7	4.8	-0.2	7.3	3.8	2.0	7.5	3.5	DFRT
BLUESHORE INS CO	CO	U	5.5	5.3	0.0	-0.2	N/A	4.9	2.6	7.0	3.4	FT
BOLD LEGAL DEFENSE INS INC	FL	U (5)	0.0	0.0	0.0	0.0	N/A	0.0	3.6	0.0	0.0	CLT
BOND SAFEGUARD INS CO	SD	D	70.9	29.9	30.0	4.3	4.4	0.4	3.4	6.2	2.3	FR
BONDED BUILDERS INS CO RRG	NV	D	3.5	1.5	1.3	0.2	5.3	4.7	7.3	9.2	1.2	DGT
BONDEX INS CO	NJ	B-	5.2	3.2	1.3	0.1	7.9	8.6	5.7	7.6	3.5	D
BOSTON INDEMNITY CO INC	SD	D	6.8	4.5	1.9	-0.3	7.5	3.6	3.1	6.8	2.3	DGT
BRACKEN HILL SPECIALTY INS CO INC	IL	U	45.6	45.5	0.0	0.2	N/A	N/A	6.9	7.0	5.4	GT
BREMEN FARMERS MUTUAL INS CO	KS	C	34.9	13.2	21.8	0.5	7.3	6.7	3.8	4.9	3.4	DLR
BRETHREN MUTUAL INS CO	MD	B	240.0	119.5	112.2	4.7	9.3	6.1	5.9	6.7	5.9	
BRIAR CREEK MUTUAL INS CO	PA	C-	12.3	9.6	2.2	0.0	10.0	7.5	7.7	9.0	2.9	DR
BRICKSTREET MUTUAL INS CO	WV	C-	1,873.7	634.8	301.3	31.3	6.8	9.5	6.9	7.0	2.9	R
BRIDGEFIELD CASUALTY INS CO	FL	C	82.8	72.7	0.0	0.7	10.0	N/A	6.8	10.0	4.3	FR
BRIDGEFIELD EMPLOYERS INS CO	FL	B-	156.7	156.7	0.0	1.0	9.4	N/A	7.2	9.8	4.9	R
BRIERFIELD INS CO	MS	C	12.4	8.3	0.0	0.2	10.0	3.7	6.7	9.1	3.4	DR
BRISTOL WEST CASUALTY INS CO	OH	D+	19.6	8.8	0.0	0.0	10.0	4.6	5.6	10.0	2.4	DFRT
BRISTOL WEST INS CO	OH	C-	125.7	46.2	0.0	2.4	10.0	4.4	4.3	8.9	2.9	FR
BRISTOL WEST PREFERRED INS CO	MI	D	22.0	11.3	0.0	0.0	10.0	5.6	4.5	8.0	2.3	DFRT
BRITISH AMERICAN INS CO	TX	C+	54.6	32.7	3.9	0.9	5.0	5.2	5.6	8.4	4.5	DFR
BROADLINE RRG INC	VT	C+	109.1	37.8	25.5	-1.8	7.4	5.1	7.5	5.6	4.1	T
BROADWAY INS & SURETY CO	NJ	D (3)	0.0	0.0	0.6	0.0	10.0	N/A	5.9	9.8	0.6	DT
BROOKWOOD INS CO	IA	C	8.1	7.5	0.0	0.1	10.0	N/A	3.9	7.0	4.1	DT
BROOME CO OPERATIVE INS CO	NY	C-	18.9	12.1	5.7	0.1	9.8	6.1	5.8	6.9	3.1	D
BROTHERHOOD MUTUAL INS CO	IN	A-	443.2	181.0	252.5	0.2	7.8	5.8	5.2	5.7	7.0	
BROWARD FACTORY SERVICE INC	NV	U (5)	0.0	0.0	0.7	0.0	N/A	N/A	2.9	8.5	1.2	T
BTTS INS RRG GROUP INC	SC	U	0.6	0.5	0.0	0.0	N/A	0.0	4.5	0.0	0.0	LT
BUCKEYE STATE MUTUAL INS CO	OH	C	65.5	21.5	44.4	-0.7	7.2	9.4	3.4	4.6	4.0	DGLR
BUCKS COUNTY CONTRIBUTIONSHIP	PA	U	6.5	5.7	0.0	0.0	N/A	N/A	6.7	10.0	3.4	FRT
BUILD AMERICA MUTUAL ASR CO	NY	D+	492.2	454.2	3.0	-23.7	10.0	N/A	2.7	10.0	1.1	DFT
BUILDERS INS (A MUTUAL CAPTIVE CO)	GA	C	471.9	193.4	125.9	6.7	7.5	9.4	5.9	6.7	3.5	R
BUILDERS MUTUAL INS CO	NC	B+	625.9	258.2	181.7	14.1	7.8	9.3	7.7	6.8	6.5	T
BUILDERS PREMIER INS CO	NC	C-	11.4	11.3	0.0	0.1	10.0	N/A	6.9	10.0	3.0	DT
BUILDING INDUSTRY INS ASSN INC	VA	E	20.0	5.4	9.4	0.6	0.3	1.2	0.6	0.5	0.3	CDFG
BUNKER HILL INS CASUALTY CO	MA	D+	14.0	6.5	6.2	0.6	5.0	5.9	6.2	6.4	2.0	DGT
BUNKER HILL INS CO	MA	C	52.2	29.0	19.8	1.1	6.6	8.4	3.6	6.2	4.0	R
BURLINGTON INS CO	NC	C-	388.6	181.1	57.6	6.2	9.0	9.3	8.3	8.1	2.6	R
BUSINESS ALLIANCE INS CO	CA	D	23.8	16.6	4.8	0.6	9.0	6.0	2.9	7.7	2.1	DR
BUSINESSFIRST INS CO	FL	D+	37.9	15.0	10.5	0.0	7.3	8.7	4.6	6.5	2.5	DRT

See Page 27 for explanation of footnotes and
Page 28 for explanation of stability factors.
Arrows denote recent upgrades ▲ or downgrades ▼   (see Section VII for explanations)

46   www.weissratings.com

RISK ADJ. CAPITAL RATIO #1	RATIO #2	PREMIUM TO SURPLUS (%)	RESV. TO SURPLUS (%)	RESV. DEVELOP. 1 YEAR (%)	RESV. DEVELOP. 2 YEAR (%)	LOSS RATIO (%)	EXP. RATIO (%)	COMB RATIO (%)	CASH FROM UNDER- WRITING (%)	NET PREMIUM GROWTH (%)	INVEST. IN AFFIL (%)	INSURANCE COMPANY NAME
1.3	1.0	117.1	169.5	-2.0	-4.9	61.6	26.4	88.0	999 +	234.1	17.4 ●	BERKLEY INS CO
9.5	8.5	-5.7	N/A	N/A	N/A	N/A	N/A	N/A	-96.6	-147.2	0.0	BERKLEY NATIONAL INS CO
1.6	1.7	-85.1	N/A	N/A	N/A	N/A	N/A	N/A	-19.2	-146.2	46.3 ●	BERKLEY REGIONAL INS CO
18.0	16.2	N/A	N/A	N/A	N/A	N/A	N/A	N/A	167.4	0.0	0.0	BERKLEY REGIONAL SPECIALTY INS CO
4.0	2.4	0.9	0.7	N/A	N/A	31.1	13.8	44.9	322.8	21.3	0.0 ●	BERKSHIRE HATHAWAY ASR CORP
1.1	0.7	29.1	34.0	0.1	-1.1	77.8	21.4	99.2	431.6	63.7	0.0 ●	BERKSHIRE HATHAWAY HOMESTATE
3.4	2.0	0.1	3.2	0.2	2.9	156.6	54.2	210.8	22.9	-33.0	0.0 ●	BERKSHIRE HATHAWAY SPECIALTY INS
3.4	2.2	70.4	132.1	-5.4	-11.9	67.1	25.2	92.3	143.5	14.7	0.0 ●	BITCO GENERAL INS CORP
2.8	1.8	82.0	169.8	-7.0	-20.4	64.2	33.9	98.1	107.1	13.3	0.0 ●	BITCO NATIONAL INS CO
16.8	16.3	2.3	N/A	N/A	N/A	N/A	202.9	202.9	75.3	-45.8	0.0	BLACK DIAMOND INS CO
5.5	3.6	44.3	6.0	-1.7	-1.6	52.4	30.2	82.6	129.3	5.8	0.0	BLOOMFIELD MUTUAL INS CO
11.6	10.4	N/A	N/A	N/A	N/A	N/A	N/A	N/A	113.3	0.0	0.0	BLOOMINGTON COMPENSATION INS CO
1.3	0.9	89.4	105.2	6.8	14.1	75.2	43.1	118.3	50.8	-50.7	0.0	BLUE RIDGE INDEMNITY CO
N/A	N/A	N/A	N/A	N/A	N/A	N/A	N/A	N/A	N/A	0.0	0.0	BLUESHORE INS CO
N/A	N/A	N/A	N/A	N/A	N/A	N/A	N/A	N/A	N/A	0.0	0.0	BOLD LEGAL DEFENSE INS INC
0.9	0.7	108.1	58.6	21.0	46.9	53.9	61.1	115.0	82.6	-20.1	0.0	BOND SAFEGUARD INS CO
1.1	0.7	97.0	6.8	5.9	3.7	3.9	43.9	47.8	245.7	78.4	0.0	BONDED BUILDERS INS CO RRG
2.4	1.9	46.0	11.1	-3.3	-9.4	18.5	77.9	96.4	107.2	9.7	0.0	BONDEX INS CO
1.6	1.3	39.6	13.1	-5.6	0.2	16.0	93.3	109.3	105.8	31.4	0.0	BOSTON INDEMNITY CO INC
N/A	N/A	N/A	N/A	N/A	N/A	N/A	N/A	N/A	N/A	0.0	0.0	BRACKEN HILL SPECIALTY INS CO INC
1.2	1.1	170.7	23.5	-1.1	-3.4	67.3	27.4	94.7	105.4	16.2	0.0	BREMEN FARMERS MUTUAL INS CO
4.1	2.5	94.4	36.6	1.2	3.9	62.1	33.0	95.1	106.5	7.3	0.0	BRETHREN MUTUAL INS CO
6.1	3.8	22.6	6.4	1.5	-0.1	43.6	41.9	85.5	116.4	-2.5	0.0	BRIAR CREEK MUTUAL INS CO
2.3	0.8	49.9	162.8	-9.5	-23.7	75.1	22.6	97.7	109.2	4.8	1.9 ●	BRICKSTREET MUTUAL INS CO
29.7	26.8	N/A	N/A	N/A	N/A	N/A	N/A	N/A	-73.8	0.0	0.0	BRIDGEFIELD CASUALTY INS CO
3.0	2.7	N/A	N/A	N/A	N/A	N/A	N/A	N/A	-154.5	0.0	38.7	BRIDGEFIELD EMPLOYERS INS CO
6.4	5.8	N/A	N/A	N/A	N/A	N/A	N/A	N/A	-689.5	0.0	0.0	BRIERFIELD INS CO
3.4	3.1	N/A	0.3	0.2	N/A	N/A	N/A	N/A	177.1	0.0	0.0	BRISTOL WEST CASUALTY INS CO
5.6	5.0	N/A	7.7	5.0	7.6	N/A	N/A	N/A	-131.7	0.0	0.0	BRISTOL WEST INS CO
4.4	4.0	N/A	5.3	1.2	2.9	N/A	N/A	N/A	-6.5	0.0	0.0	BRISTOL WEST PREFERRED INS CO
1.1	0.7	11.8	60.9	-0.1	0.5	53.4	22.9	76.3	71.8	0.0	0.0	BRITISH AMERICAN INS CO
2.4	1.5	68.6	141.9	-16.5	-37.7	81.1	5.7	86.8	115.1	30.5	0.0	BROADLINE RRG INC
5.5	3.7	41.3	1.4	N/A	N/A	17.0	8.9	25.9	999 +	0.0	0.0	BROADWAY INS & SURETY CO
25.2	22.7	N/A	3.0	N/A	N/A	N/A	N/A	N/A	69.5	0.0	0.0	BROOKWOOD INS CO
4.2	2.7	48.6	17.0	-5.0	-1.0	49.9	39.9	89.8	117.4	9.6	0.0	BROOME CO OPERATIVE INS CO
1.9	1.4	141.7	56.8	2.0	2.3	64.5	31.3	95.8	113.6	16.2	0.0 ●	BROTHERHOOD MUTUAL INS CO
N/A	N/A	191.3	3.2	N/A	N/A	47.9	53.9	101.8	99.9	-10.0	0.0	BROWARD FACTORY SERVICE INC
N/A	N/A	N/A	N/A	N/A	N/A	N/A	N/A	N/A	N/A	0.0	0.0	BTTS INS RRG GROUP INC
1.6	1.2	189.5	58.3	-8.0	-11.6	67.2	34.9	102.1	109.0	69.8	12.3	BUCKEYE STATE MUTUAL INS CO
N/A	N/A	N/A	N/A	N/A	N/A	N/A	999 +	999 +	0.5	-7.9	0.0	BUCKS COUNTY CONTRIBUTIONSHIP
9.1	8.9	0.6	N/A	N/A	N/A	N/A	999 +	999 +	16.8	N/A	0.0 ●	BUILD AMERICA MUTUAL ASR CO
1.7	1.3	67.7	104.9	-4.0	-10.3	69.8	32.9	102.7	114.5	18.5	13.3	BUILDERS INS (A MUTUAL CAPTIVE CO)
2.1	1.4	75.1	103.7	-3.8	-10.2	61.5	34.4	95.9	107.9	22.5	2.3 ●	BUILDERS MUTUAL INS CO
105.8	52.9	N/A	N/A	N/A	N/A	N/A	N/A	N/A	N/A	0.0	0.0	BUILDERS PREMIER INS CO
0.2	0.1	186.9	106.7	48.3	54.1	69.5	36.1	105.6	72.8	53.5	0.0	BUILDING INDUSTRY INS ASSN INC
1.0	0.7	104.7	23.5	-7.4	-10.5	43.3	41.1	84.4	151.1	25.0	0.0	BUNKER HILL INS CASUALTY CO
1.3	0.9	76.0	17.0	-5.7	-8.1	43.3	40.6	83.9	127.2	45.4	15.8	BUNKER HILL INS CO
2.9	2.5	32.4	77.8	-6.4	-10.6	50.4	40.2	90.6	103.9	-5.6	0.0	BURLINGTON INS CO
2.9	2.1	30.3	20.0	4.3	1.6	78.5	38.8	117.3	99.4	22.2	0.0	BUSINESS ALLIANCE INS CO
1.4	1.1	71.0	83.2	-0.2	-1.5	71.1	31.6	102.7	103.9	21.2	0.0	BUSINESSFIRST INS CO

999 + Denotes number greater than 999.9%
999 - Denotes number less than -999.99%
● Bullets denote a more detailed analysis is available in Section II.

INSURANCE COMPANY NAME	DOM. STATE	RATING	TOTAL ASSETS ($MIL)	CAPITAL & SURPLUS ($MIL)	ANNUAL NET PREMIUM ($MIL)	NET INCOME ($MIL)	CAPITAL- IZATION INDEX (PTS)	RESERVE ADQ INDEX (PTS)	PROFIT- ABILITY INDEX (PTS)	LIQUIDITY INDEX (PTS)	STAB. INDEX (PTS)	STABILITY FACTORS
BUTTE MUTUAL INS CO	NM	D-	1.1	1.0	0.1	0.0	10.0	N/A	4.0	10.0	1.0	DT
CAGC INS CO	NC	F (5)	0.0	0.0	5.9	0.0	0.0	2.2	0.2	7.0	0.0	CDFG
CALIFORNIA AUTOMOBILE INS CO	CA	B	420.0	124.1	410.8	3.1	7.2	6.0	2.8	2.9	4.1	GLT
CALIFORNIA CAPITAL INS CO	CA	B-	590.0	305.2	234.0	4.1	8.1	6.0	6.7	6.3	4.7	R
CALIFORNIA CAS COMPENSATION INS CO	CA	C+	72.7	68.7	0.5	0.6	7.0	4.4	5.9	10.0	4.6	DR
CALIFORNIA CAS GEN INS CO OF OREGON	OR	C+	103.8	32.0	27.2	-0.8	9.2	8.2	3.1	6.6	4.5	FR
CALIFORNIA CASUALTY & FIRE INS CO	CA	C	62.2	26.4	22.7	-0.6	9.2	8.3	3.0	6.4	4.1	R
CALIFORNIA CASUALTY INDEMNITY EXCH	CA	C+	575.1	332.5	158.7	-2.2	8.3	7.8	4.0	6.7	4.7	FR
CALIFORNIA CASUALTY INS CO	OR	C+	113.8	86.3	18.1	-0.4	7.9	7.4	3.5	6.9	4.4	FR
CALIFORNIA GENERAL UNDERWRITERS INS	CA	B	20.5	19.5	0.4	0.5	10.0	5.9	6.7	10.0	4.9	D
CALIFORNIA HEALTHCARE INS CO INC RRG	HI	C	120.8	49.0	15.8	1.2	9.9	9.7	8.8	8.9	4.1	R
CALIFORNIA INS CO	CA	B-	614.3	365.6	186.9	44.5	8.4	9.4	7.5	8.7	4.7	RT
CALIFORNIA MEDICAL GROUP INS CO RRG	AZ	E	13.4	6.2	3.9	1.6	9.4	10.0	4.9	9.2	0.0	DFR
CALIFORNIA MUTUAL INS CO	CA	D-	14.3	10.5	3.1	-0.1	9.6	8.1	5.0	7.2	1.2	DR
CALLICOON CO-OPERATIVE INS CO	NY	C	27.7	22.1	5.1	0.9	10.0	7.8	8.5	6.9	3.6	DR
CAMBRIA COUNTY MUTUAL INS CO	PA	U (3)	0.0	0.0	0.0	0.0	N/A	3.6	2.3	10.0	1.5	FT
CAMBRIDGE MUTUAL FIRE INS CO	MA	B-	794.4	467.8	172.5	17.1	8.5	6.3	6.6	7.2	4.8	T
CAMERON MUTUAL INS CO	MO	C	78.2	34.0	47.2	-1.6	7.0	8.7	3.8	5.8	4.0	R
CAMERON NATIONAL INS CO	MO	C-	11.6	9.2	0.0	0.4	10.0	N/A	6.5	9.0	3.2	DR
CAMICO MUTUAL INS CO	CA	C	90.8	38.6	32.5	0.4	7.3	5.8	4.8	7.6	3.5	FR
CAMPMED CAS & INDEM CO INC OF MD	NH	C	20.0	19.9	0.0	0.3	10.0	4.8	7.9	10.0	3.5	DR
CANAL INDEMNITY CO	SC	B	44.4	41.4	0.0	1.3	10.0	N/A	8.2	10.0	5.8	DT
CANAL INS CO	SC	B	858.0	460.8	191.9	6.4	8.2	5.0	4.0	6.8	5.6	F
CANOPIUS US INS INC	DE	B-	139.5	52.5	46.6	-5.1	7.4	5.6	2.9	6.8	5.3	
CAPACITY INS CO	FL	D	19.5	8.7	7.3	0.2	1.9	6.9	3.9	6.6	2.1	CDT
CAPITOL CASUALTY CO	NE	C	26.0	23.1	0.4	0.4	8.1	7.3	6.8	9.8	4.3	D
CAPITOL COUNTY MUTUAL FIRE INS CO	TX	C	14.2	10.3	0.0	-0.3	7.5	N/A	1.8	9.3	3.4	DFRT
CAPITOL INDEMNITY CORP	WI	C	450.7	217.0	120.0	-0.8	7.3	4.4	3.3	6.9	3.9	FR
CAPITOL INS CO	PA	D+	20.7	4.3	8.9	0.1	3.1	3.7	3.2	5.5	2.2	CDGR
CAPITOL PREFERRED INS CO	FL	D	42.5	21.8	8.8	3.4	7.9	8.4	8.9	7.1	2.3	DFR
CAPITOL SPECIALTY INS CORP	WI	C+	106.6	52.8	25.7	-0.2	8.7	4.1	4.8	6.8	4.6	FR
CAPSON PHYSICIANS INS CO	TX	D	20.1	6.3	9.3	-1.1	3.2	3.6	1.0	7.9	2.2	DGT
CARE RRG INC	DC	D	20.3	4.9	6.9	0.1	7.2	9.6	6.8	9.1	1.5	DGR
CARE WEST INS CO	CA	E+	117.7	15.2	27.9	1.2	1.0	0.4	2.1	5.9	0.4	CDFR
CARECONCEPTS INS INC A RRG	MT	D	3.0	0.9	0.8	0.0	5.2	N/A	3.7	9.0	0.6	DT
CAREGIVERS UNITED LIAB INS CO RRG	SC	D-	40.6	25.9	5.5	0.6	9.8	9.7	7.6	8.0	1.3	DR
CARIBBEAN AMERICAN PROPERTY INS CO	PR	C+	47.2	25.3	31.8	4.8	4.5	8.8	8.2	5.3	4.8	CD
CARING COMMUNITIES RECIP RRG	DC	C-	104.0	40.9	6.8	1.1	8.4	7.7	8.7	9.1	2.9	DFR
CAROLINA CASUALTY INS CO	IA	C	186.0	95.9	0.0	1.6	10.0	N/A	1.9	7.0	3.5	RT
CAROLINA FARMERS MUTUAL INS CO	NC	C-	8.8	6.3	3.4	0.3	7.7	6.2	2.8	6.7	2.4	DR
CAROLINA MUTUAL INS INC	NC	B-	78.3	32.6	24.3	1.1	7.6	9.6	8.9	7.4	3.5	T
CASCO INDEMNITY CO	ME	C-	26.7	10.9	14.6	0.7	7.4	7.0	2.9	6.5	2.9	DR
CASSATT RISK RETENTION GROUP INC	VT	D-	12.4	4.0	0.1	-0.1	8.7	6.9	5.4	9.3	1.3	DR
CASTLE HILL INS CO	RI	U (5)	0.0	0.0	0.0	0.0	N/A	N/A	1.9	7.0	3.1	T
CASTLE KEY INDEMNITY CO	IL	B	7.0	5.5	0.0	0.1	10.0	N/A	2.4	6.9	4.9	DT
CASTLE KEY INS CO	IL	B-	354.2	186.6	153.5	22.7	2.8	5.8	4.3	2.3	5.3	CL
CASTLEPOINT FLORIDA INS	FL	D+	40.2	3.3	5.1	-3.6	7.3	4.3	1.3	8.3	1.5	CDFT
▼CASTLEPOINT INS CO	NY	E-	194.0	-5.1	148.8	-4.2	7.2	4.5	0.9	5.8	0.0	CDFR
CASTLEPOINT NATIONAL INS CO	CA	C-	415.2	31.1	142.7	-2.1	7.1	4.6	3.7	6.0	2.6	CFRT
CASUALTY CORP OF AMERICA	OK	D-	7.2	1.8	7.4	0.4	2.5	0.5	2.9	0.0	0.9	DLRT
CASUALTY UNDERWRITERS INS CO	UT	D	4.4	4.3	0.0	0.0	10.0	5.9	2.5	10.0	2.1	DFRT
CATASTROPHE REINS CO	TX	D-	1,979.8	1,784.8	356.9	204.1	10.0	4.7	6.6	7.0	0.9	T

See Page 27 for explanation of footnotes and
Page 28 for explanation of stability factors.
Arrows denote recent upgrades ▲ or downgrades ▼   (see Section VII for explanations)

48

www.weissratings.com

RISK ADJ. RATIO #1	CAPITAL RATIO #2	PREMIUM TO SURPLUS (%)	RESV. TO SURPLUS (%)	RESV. DEVELOP. 1 YEAR (%)	RESV. DEVELOP. 2 YEAR (%)	LOSS RATIO (%)	EXP. RATIO (%)	COMB RATIO (%)	CASH FROM UNDER- WRITING (%)	NET PREMIUM GROWTH (%)	INVEST. IN AFFIL (%)	INSURANCE COMPANY NAME
14.5	12.8	10.4	N/A	N/A	N/A	1.0	69.8	70.8	167.4	-33.5	0.0	BUTTE MUTUAL INS CO
-0.1	-0.0	-351.0	-737.3	82.4	17.7	130.7	41.4	172.1	69.8	-39.7	0.0	CAGC INS CO
1.2	1.0	342.7	96.0	1.2	1.2	80.3	23.8	104.1	112.3	75.3	5.6	CALIFORNIA AUTOMOBILE INS CO
2.1	1.6	77.2	44.6	-2.2	0.7	65.1	32.6	97.7	108.3	11.0	24.7 ●	CALIFORNIA CAPITAL INS CO
1.7	1.0	0.7	39.1	2.5	5.4	465.1	-307.3	157.8	24.9	1.4	0.0	CALIFORNIA CAS COMPENSATION INS
3.3	2.3	83.0	37.6	-2.2	-3.0	79.4	28.9	108.3	90.9	4.0	0.0	CALIFORNIA CAS GEN INS CO OF
3.4	2.3	83.8	38.0	-2.2	-3.0	79.4	28.9	108.3	93.2	4.0	0.0	CALIFORNIA CASUALTY & FIRE INS CO
2.0	1.8	47.2	21.4	-1.3	-1.9	79.4	28.9	108.3	90.1	4.0	38.2 ●	CALIFORNIA CASUALTY INDEMNITY
1.5	1.5	20.6	9.3	-0.5	-0.8	79.4	28.9	108.3	87.4	4.0	62.7	CALIFORNIA CASUALTY INS CO
17.0	13.2	2.1	2.5	1.5	3.3	110.2	33.2	143.4	70.0	-5.1	0.0	CALIFORNIA GENERAL UNDERWRITERS
3.8	2.8	33.1	114.8	-19.8	-26.9	87.0	11.6	98.6	127.9	-8.8	0.4	CALIFORNIA HEALTHCARE INS CO INC
3.6	2.0	68.0	45.4	0.2	-9.1	32.2	28.8	61.0	381.0	37.2	0.0 ●	CALIFORNIA INS CO
4.1	2.6	67.9	79.8	-26.6	-55.4	24.9	19.3	44.2	164.5	41.6	0.0	CALIFORNIA MEDICAL GROUP INS CO
4.3	2.7	28.9	10.9	-1.6	-4.5	48.5	58.0	106.5	98.3	29.1	2.4	CALIFORNIA MUTUAL INS CO
11.6	7.8	25.0	11.3	-1.6	-3.1	49.0	37.7	86.7	106.9	7.2	0.0	CALLICOON CO-OPERATIVE INS CO
N/A	N/A	3.0	N/A	N/A	2.9	197.8	159.3	357.1	16.5	-38.3	0.0	CAMBRIA COUNTY MUTUAL INS CO
3.0	1.9	40.9	26.3	-1.5	-2.5	43.3	39.5	82.8	109.1	2.8	0.0 ●	CAMBRIDGE MUTUAL FIRE INS CO
1.7	1.1	135.5	55.9	-0.9	-11.4	61.8	35.8	97.6	102.8	10.1	13.6	CAMERON MUTUAL INS CO
10.9	9.8	N/A	N/A	N/A	N/A	N/A	N/A	N/A	276.9	0.0	0.0	CAMERON NATIONAL INS CO
1.4	1.1	84.5	87.2	2.2	-7.5	65.1	35.5	100.6	65.8	30.4	1.3	CAMICO MUTUAL INS CO
82.2	37.4	N/A	N/A	N/A	N/A	N/A	N/A	N/A	-113.4	0.0	0.0	CAMPMED CAS & INDEM CO INC OF MD
5.9	3.3	N/A	N/A	N/A	N/A	N/A	N/A	N/A	15.4	0.0	0.0	CANAL INDEMNITY CO
2.7	1.9	43.1	62.2	1.2	-4.1	86.6	32.6	119.2	78.5	-4.1	5.2 ●	CANAL INS CO
2.2	1.1	97.8	80.4	4.8	-0.2	82.1	32.2	114.3	109.4	17.2	0.0	CANOPIUS US INS INC
0.4	0.3	90.8	42.2	4.7	-1.1	52.4	38.4	90.8	148.5	32.7	0.0	CAPACITY INS CO
2.8	1.6	1.8	0.7	-1.3	-1.0	5.9	113.4	119.3	76.8	-6.1	0.0	CAPITOL CASUALTY CO
1.3	1.2	N/A	N/A	N/A	N/A	N/A	N/A	N/A	4.8	0.0	65.1	CAPITOL COUNTY MUTUAL FIRE INS CO
1.8	1.2	69.4	81.4	10.7	14.9	65.6	55.6	121.2	93.4	14.9	14.4	CAPITOL INDEMNITY CORP
0.6	0.5	216.8	77.6	19.4	15.6	78.3	11.8	90.1	94.4	54.6	0.0	CAPITOL INS CO
2.4	1.7	44.8	28.0	-1.9	-8.8	168.7	-85.1	83.6	5.9	44.5	0.0	CAPITOL PREFERRED INS CO
3.9	2.2	48.6	52.4	8.1	16.5	67.8	51.8	119.6	88.1	14.9	0.0	CAPITOL SPECIALTY INS CORP
0.6	0.4	122.9	76.7	2.6	0.8	61.5	50.9	112.4	121.7	45.7	0.0	CAPSON PHYSICIANS INS CO
1.1	0.8	145.7	178.9	-19.1	-33.9	72.2	28.5	100.7	170.2	36.6	0.0	CARE RRG INC
0.5	0.3	201.1	584.9	-14.3	103.7	78.6	24.1	102.7	94.2	12.1	0.0	CARE WEST INS CO
0.8	0.5	94.8	50.9	N/A	N/A	45.8	46.3	92.1	283.8	0.0	0.0	CARECONCEPTS INS INC A RRG
4.3	2.8	19.9	31.9	-4.1	-22.9	25.2	14.6	39.8	206.6	-7.0	0.0	CAREGIVERS UNITED LIAB INS CO RRG
1.1	0.7	147.4	28.4	-7.3	-7.4	44.1	33.3	77.4	134.8	-1.5	0.0	CARIBBEAN AMERICAN PROPERTY INS
1.9	1.7	17.5	28.5	-2.7	-3.8	48.5	9.3	57.8	237.7	4.8	40.3	CARING COMMUNITIES RECIP RRG
11.2	10.0	N/A	N/A	N/A	N/A	N/A	N/A	N/A	-10.6	0.0	0.0	CAROLINA CASUALTY INS CO
2.4	1.5	58.2	6.6	-2.2	-1.9	61.8	34.8	96.6	106.2	14.9	0.0	CAROLINA FARMERS MUTUAL INS CO
1.7	1.3	77.6	103.9	-17.5	-35.0	61.1	15.3	76.4	135.2	20.1	0.0	CAROLINA MUTUAL INS INC
2.5	1.7	139.5	67.3	-12.3	-23.6	65.8	31.5	97.3	108.6	9.1	0.0	CASCO INDEMNITY CO
1.8	1.7	2.5	2.1	-13.7	-10.8	-382.0	-20.9	-402.9	999 +	0.0	0.0	CASSATT RISK RETENTION GROUP INC
N/A	N/A	N/A	N/A	N/A	N/A	N/A	N/A	N/A	N/A	0.0	0.0	CASTLE HILL INS CO
9.3	8.4	N/A	N/A	N/A	N/A	N/A	N/A	N/A	N/A	0.0	0.0	CASTLE KEY INDEMNITY CO
0.8	0.6	92.6	33.0	-1.0	-15.1	50.6	31.4	82.0	112.6	17.5	5.1	CASTLE KEY INS CO
0.5	0.5	73.6	94.3	7.8	17.7	92.5	23.9	116.4	75.9	-1.7	0.0	CASTLEPOINT FLORIDA INS
-0.3	-0.2	999 +	999 +	62.0	59.4	105.8	56.4	162.2	53.7	-30.1	2.9	CASTLEPOINT INS CO
0.5	0.4	467.8	742.0	52.8	52.6	105.8	56.8	162.6	55.3	-23.8	11.1	CASTLEPOINT NATIONAL INS CO
0.5	0.3	475.0	42.0	15.1	54.1	82.6	20.5	103.1	92.0	3.0	0.0	CASUALTY CORP OF AMERICA
7.0	4.0	0.3	N/A	-0.1	-0.1	59.6	999 +	999 +	-2.6	-97.7	0.0	CASUALTY UNDERWRITERS INS CO
9.5	5.9	22.5	10.3	11.0	1.2	67.6	-0.3	67.3	200.7	-20.1	0.0 ●	CATASTROPHE REINS CO

999 + Denotes number greater than 999.9%
999 - Denotes number less than -999.99%
● Bullets denote a more detailed analysis is available in Section II.

INSURANCE COMPANY NAME	DOM. STATE	RATING	TOTAL ASSETS ($MIL)	CAPITAL & SURPLUS ($MIL)	ANNUAL NET PREMIUM ($MIL)	NET INCOME ($MIL)	CAPITAL-IZATION INDEX (PTS)	RESERVE ADQ INDEX (PTS)	PROFIT-ABILITY INDEX (PTS)	LIQUIDITY INDEX (PTS)	STAB. INDEX (PTS)	STABILITY FACTORS
CATAWBA INS CO	SC	U	7.1	5.7	0.0	0.0	N/A	4.7	1.8	10.0	3.0	FRT
CATERPILLAR INS CO	MO	B-	683.8	264.2	214.6	23.7	8.7	9.2	8.9	7.1	5.3	T
CATLIN INDEMNITY CO	DE	C	143.2	77.8	6.5	0.1	7.4	4.9	4.0	9.1	3.2	T
CATLIN INS CO	TX	C+	283.9	64.5	45.5	1.0	7.3	5.9	6.8	6.9	4.1	R
CATLIN SPECIALTY INS CO	DE	C+	628.7	201.2	78.0	1.9	7.6	5.9	7.7	7.6	4.3	GR
CATTLEMANS INS CO A RRG	MT	D	1.6	1.5	0.4	0.1	8.4	4.8	5.5	9.3	0.6	DT
CBIA COMP SERVICES INC	CT	D	23.5	5.9	5.1	0.1	2.1	6.0	4.5	6.5	2.3	CDR
CELINA MUTUAL INS CO	OH	C	67.0	25.8	35.6	0.7	7.5	8.6	5.9	5.9	4.1	R
CEM INS CO	IL	D-	31.5	11.5	11.3	2.0	3.8	2.8	4.4	5.6	1.3	DGRT
CENSTAT CASUALTY CO	NE	C-	18.4	16.4	0.8	0.5	10.0	8.5	8.2	10.0	3.2	DR
CENTAURI SPECIALTY INS CO	FL	D	58.7	20.8	24.0	0.3	5.3	3.6	4.9	7.0	2.3	DGOR
CENTENNIAL CASUALTY CO	AL	B	110.9	64.5	8.2	3.6	7.6	7.4	8.8	7.7	5.2	D
CENTER MUTUAL INS CO	ND	C	46.8	24.9	24.1	1.2	8.7	8.7	5.4	6.1	4.2	DR
CENTER VALLEY MUTUAL FIRE INS CO	PA	D+(3)	0.0	0.0	0.2	0.0	10.0	3.6	6.0	10.0	1.9	D
CENTRAL CO-OPERATIVE INS CO	NY	D	14.5	8.9	4.9	0.1	9.3	6.9	8.6	7.0	1.5	DR
CENTRAL MUTUAL INS CO	OH	B	1,330.2	638.5	402.3	13.8	8.4	7.0	6.0	6.7	5.9	
CENTRAL PA PHYSICIANS RRG INC	SC	D	60.0	22.1	14.2	2.0	6.3	4.4	6.5	6.9	1.9	DF
CENTRAL STATES INDEMNITY CO OF	NE	B+	427.1	358.1	43.0	4.3	9.5	7.7	8.1	9.1	5.3	T
CENTRE COUNTY MUTUAL FIRE INS CO	PA	D+	5.3	3.2	2.0	0.0	7.5	9.3	5.6	6.7	2.1	D
CENTRE INS CO	DE	U	89.8	40.7	0.0	0.9	N/A	8.9	5.5	7.0	1.2	T
CENTURION CASUALTY CO	IA	B+	140.4	139.4	15.1	8.7	10.0	6.1	3.0	9.3	6.4	DT
CENTURION MEDICAL LIAB PROTECT RRG	AZ	D-	19.6	10.1	3.1	1.7	9.7	9.9	9.0	7.6	1.0	DFR
CENTURY CASUALTY CO	GA	D+	6.5	3.1	2.2	-1.0	8.2	9.2	2.1	7.0	2.2	DR
CENTURY INDEMNITY CO	PA	U	890.2	25.0	0.0	-2.0	N/A	1.1	0.9	9.8	0.0	CFRT
CENTURY INS CO GUAM LTD	GU	B	21.0	10.7	6.8	0.2	7.5	3.3	7.2	6.2	4.0	D
CENTURY MUTUAL INS CO	NC	D+	8.5	6.9	1.8	0.2	7.3	6.0	4.7	6.7	2.2	DT
CENTURY SURETY CO	OH	C+	630.7	180.5	199.3	10.2	7.2	4.0	6.3	6.4	4.5	R
CENTURY-NATIONAL INS CO	CA	B	615.6	395.0	124.8	20.0	8.8	8.9	6.8	6.8	5.5	T
CGB INS CO	IN	U	187.2	87.6	-2.0	3.0	N/A	8.1	4.3	6.8	5.2	FT
CHARITABLE SERVICE PROVIDERS RRG	AZ	D	3.5	2.7	0.9	0.3	10.0	8.4	5.3	7.3	2.0	DR
CHARTER INDEMNITY CO	TX	B	12.5	7.6	0.0	0.3	10.0	N/A	3.2	10.0	4.1	DR
CHARTER OAK FIRE INS CO	CT	B	959.3	278.9	255.8	32.4	7.8	8.8	7.8	6.9	6.0	T
CHATTAHOCHEE RRG CAPTIVE INS CO	GA	D (5)	0.0	0.0	1.2	0.0	7.8	9.6	7.7	9.3	1.9	DGT
CHAUTAUQUA PATRONS INS CO	NY	C-	20.2	11.2	7.2	0.0	8.3	8.4	5.2	6.8	3.1	DR
CHEROKEE GUARANTEE CO INC A RRG	AZ	D	13.6	2.6	4.2	0.4	2.0	3.6	4.4	7.9	1.7	CDGT
CHEROKEE INS CO	MI	C-	430.1	163.4	154.0	10.2	7.8	3.9	6.7	5.2	3.3	R
CHERRY VALLEY COOPERATIVE INS CO	NY	D	1.7	1.4	0.3	-0.1	10.0	7.6	4.6	9.7	2.0	DRT
CHICAGO INS CO	IL	C	108.3	54.0	0.0	0.5	10.0	4.0	3.9	6.0	4.0	FGRT
CHUBB CUSTOM INS CO	NJ	B-	363.5	183.3	45.1	10.3	10.0	8.2	8.8	7.6	4.9	T
CHUBB INDEMNITY INS CO	NY	B	354.3	136.3	45.1	9.0	10.0	8.4	8.8	6.9	6.0	T
CHUBB INS CO OF NEW JERSEY	NJ	B (3)	0.0	0.0	0.0	0.8	10.0	N/A	7.8	7.0	5.4	D
CHUBB LLOYDS INS CO OF TX	TX	B	38.8	5.2	0.0	0.1	7.0	N/A	7.0	7.0	4.9	D
CHUBB NATIONAL INS CO	IN	B	304.8	136.8	45.1	9.1	10.0	8.4	8.8	7.2	6.0	T
CHUNG KUO INS CO LTD GUAM BRANCH	GU	C	35.7	18.6	15.3	2.1	7.1	4.9	8.2	9.0	3.6	D
CHURCH INS CO	NY	U	25.4	16.4	0.0	0.3	N/A	7.0	3.4	10.0	1.5	FT
CHURCH MUTUAL INS CO	WI	A	1,452.0	507.1	557.3	39.6	8.2	9.3	6.0	6.3	7.4	
CIFG ASR NORTH AMERICA INC	NY	E	785.1	611.7	19.4	43.9	10.0	4.0	2.9	8.1	0.0	DFR
CIM INS CORP	MI	C	18.6	17.2	0.0	0.2	10.0	N/A	6.5	7.0	3.3	DRT
CIMARRON INS EXCH RRG	VT	D (5)	0.0	0.0	0.8	0.0	6.2	4.3	4.3	10.0	1.4	DRT
CINCINNATI CASUALTY CO	OH	B	362.0	326.0	0.0	8.6	10.0	N/A	8.1	10.0	5.8	T
CINCINNATI EQUITABLE INS CO	OH	U	4.1	4.0	0.0	0.0	N/A	7.5	3.4	7.0	3.8	RT
CINCINNATI INDEMNITY CO	OH	A-	115.5	84.6	0.0	2.3	10.0	N/A	8.0	7.9	5.5	T

See Page 27 for explanation of footnotes and
Page 28 for explanation of stability factors.
Arrows denote recent upgrades ▲ or downgrades ▼   (see Section VII for explanations)

50

www.weissratings.com

RISK ADJ. CAPITAL RATIO #1	CAPITAL RATIO #2	PREMIUM TO SURPLUS (%)	RESV. TO SURPLUS (%)	RESV. DEVELOP. 1 YEAR (%)	RESV. DEVELOP. 2 YEAR (%)	LOSS RATIO (%)	EXP. RATIO (%)	COMB RATIO (%)	CASH FROM UNDER-WRITING (%)	NET PREMIUM GROWTH (%)	INVEST. IN AFFIL (%)	INSURANCE COMPANY NAME
N/A	N/A	N/A	28.2	12.0	14.1	N/A	N/A	N/A	N/A	100.0	0.0	CATAWBA INS CO
2.7	2.1	88.2	4.9	-3.5	-14.8	55.2	13.2	68.4	169.8	7.7	0.0 •	CATERPILLAR INS CO
1.3	1.2	8.4	10.3	-0.4	0.3	62.0	21.4	83.4	150.2	22.5	74.4	CATLIN INDEMNITY CO
1.7	1.0	70.8	86.8	-3.5	2.4	62.0	21.0	83.0	262.0	22.5	0.0	CATLIN INS CO
2.0	1.5	38.7	47.4	-3.5	2.4	62.0	20.2	82.2	164.2	22.5	22.5 •	CATLIN SPECIALTY INS CO
4.4	2.7	27.1	1.6	-2.3	-7.3	-1.2	46.7	45.5	235.4	9.9	0.0	CATTLEMANS INS CO A RRG
0.6	0.4	96.9	301.1	-2.4	-52.6	96.7	25.6	122.3	101.2	13.9	0.0	CBIA COMP SERVICES INC
2.3	1.4	142.4	52.5	-2.8	-6.2	67.1	30.8	97.9	103.3	-1.6	0.0	CELINA MUTUAL INS CO
1.3	0.9	113.3	44.4	25.9	37.2	71.1	29.3	100.4	102.0	45.5	0.0	CEM INS CO
22.6	17.6	4.8	3.2	-0.3	-2.6	54.2	29.6	83.8	133.4	-5.0	0.0	CENSTAT CASUALTY CO
1.3	0.8	130.3	7.7	-1.7	N/A	37.2	48.5	85.7	165.1	63.3	0.0	CENTAURI SPECIALTY INS CO
2.0	1.0	13.3	2.4	-0.5	-0.7	55.7	20.4	76.1	131.6	11.1	0.0	CENTENNIAL CASUALTY CO
3.1	2.1	102.4	32.9	-4.2	-6.8	72.0	27.4	99.4	103.5	8.4	0.0	CENTER MUTUAL INS CO
20.5	18.6	6.4	N/A	N/A	N/A	40.5	77.1	117.6	85.6	-3.1	0.0	CENTER VALLEY MUTUAL FIRE INS CO
3.8	2.6	56.1	19.5	-2.6	1.1	45.5	39.2	84.7	116.0	6.5	0.0	CENTRAL CO-OPERATIVE INS CO
2.8	2.0	64.9	59.4	-7.2	-15.4	58.4	32.7	91.1	98.8	8.8	11.8 •	CENTRAL MUTUAL INS CO
1.5	0.9	67.2	138.7	2.9	15.4	88.3	27.6	115.9	74.3	6.8	0.0	CENTRAL PA PHYSICIANS RRG INC
4.3	2.7	12.4	1.7	-1.1	-1.8	36.2	58.1	94.3	103.3	33.5	3.5 •	CENTRAL STATES INDEMNITY CO OF
2.0	1.2	63.0	14.3	-7.1	-15.8	28.0	38.9	66.9	142.7	26.2	0.0	CENTRE COUNTY MUTUAL FIRE INS CO
N/A	N/A	N/A	22.6	-0.8	-13.7	N/A	N/A	N/A	3.7	100.0	0.0	CENTRE INS CO
41.8	19.0	11.6	0.8	-0.2	-0.8	6.9	10.0	16.9	484.4	-14.2	0.0 •	CENTURION CASUALTY CO
4.5	2.9	37.6	55.2	-10.5	-47.0	63.4	24.0	87.4	74.4	-14.3	0.0	CENTURION MEDICAL LIAB PROTECT
1.7	1.2	52.1	52.8	-11.2	-15.5	72.5	37.9	110.4	97.1	34.6	0.0	CENTURY CASUALTY CO
N/A	N/A	N/A	999 +	999 +	773.0	N/A	N/A	N/A	N/A	0.0	10.7	CENTURY INDEMNITY CO
2.2	1.3	59.8	21.2	17.9	23.4	51.9	53.9	105.8	123.6	5.6	0.0	CENTURY INS CO GUAM LTD
1.7	1.2	27.6	2.8	-0.2	0.9	54.0	45.1	99.1	104.3	2.8	0.0	CENTURY MUTUAL INS CO
1.7	1.2	111.6	179.9	11.1	22.9	79.2	34.5	113.7	97.4	-14.0	8.6	CENTURY SURETY CO
3.5	2.2	32.3	27.5	N/A	-4.0	78.4	35.0	113.4	100.8	6.4	0.0 •	CENTURY-NATIONAL INS CO
N/A	N/A	-9.3	N/A	-0.1	-0.1	N/A	-5.3	N/A	-5.0	-146.0	0.0	CGB INS CO
5.0	3.3	30.9	13.7	1.7	-5.6	28.8	47.8	76.6	206.0	-4.1	0.0	CHARITABLE SERVICE PROVIDERS RRG
5.0	4.5	N/A	N/A	N/A	N/A	N/A	N/A	N/A	-2.2	0.0	0.0	CHARTER INDEMNITY CO
2.7	1.7	104.0	187.1	-2.7	-6.2	60.9	30.1	91.0	128.9	3.0	0.0 •	CHARTER OAK FIRE INS CO
2.8	1.9	48.8	112.9	-10.6	-27.9	56.9	31.5	88.4	545.2	-12.0	0.0	CHATTAHOCHEE RRG CAPTIVE INS CO
2.8	1.9	64.9	28.3	-0.5	-8.9	65.6	37.2	102.8	102.6	9.6	0.0	CHAUTAUQUA PATRONS INS CO
0.8	0.5	201.6	198.9	17.8	N/A	79.7	-2.5	77.2	999 +	51.1	0.0	CHEROKEE GUARANTEE CO INC A RRG
2.5	1.4	101.6	107.6	3.8	10.7	92.5	9.5	102.0	123.3	14.3	0.0	CHEROKEE INS CO
5.2	3.6	16.7	3.2	-0.5	-2.2	45.4	50.7	96.1	101.7	-12.0	0.0	CHERRY VALLEY COOPERATIVE INS CO
7.6	6.9	N/A	N/A	N/A	N/A	N/A	N/A	N/A	-2.8	100.0	0.0	CHICAGO INS CO
7.9	5.0	25.9	46.9	-2.1	-3.6	51.1	29.9	81.0	110.1	4.1	0.0	CHUBB CUSTOM INS CO
6.2	4.0	35.5	63.7	-2.4	-4.1	52.7	29.9	82.6	153.8	3.9	0.0	CHUBB INDEMNITY INS CO
8.2	7.3	N/A	N/A	N/A	N/A	N/A	N/A	N/A	N/A	0.0	0.0	CHUBB INS CO OF NEW JERSEY
1.0	0.9	N/A	N/A	N/A	N/A	N/A	N/A	N/A	N/A	0.0	0.0	CHUBB LLOYDS INS CO OF TX
6.4	4.1	35.1	62.9	-2.3	-4.1	52.7	29.9	82.6	108.5	3.9	0.0	CHUBB NATIONAL INS CO
2.1	1.3	92.3	30.3	-1.7	-4.4	35.4	45.9	81.3	103.1	0.4	0.0	CHUNG KUO INS CO LTD GUAM BRANCH
N/A	N/A	-0.2	48.4	-5.5	-25.3	999 +	999 +	-689.2	-2.4	-101.2	0.0	CHURCH INS CO
2.6	1.8	117.8	83.8	-4.0	-8.4	63.6	38.2	101.8	115.8	13.2	0.0 •	CHURCH MUTUAL INS CO
9.5	7.7	3.5	3.3	-72.6	6.8	-420.4	88.0	-332.4	17.5	-41.3	8.1 •	CIFG ASR NORTH AMERICA INC
30.6	27.5	N/A	N/A	N/A	N/A	N/A	N/A	N/A	26.3	0.0	0.0	CIM INS CORP
1.2	1.1	46.3	171.3	25.3	34.0	134.0	-36.4	97.6	43.2	-53.5	0.0	CIMARRON INS EXCH RRG
10.7	6.2	N/A	N/A	N/A	N/A	N/A	N/A	N/A	35.1	0.0	0.0 •	CINCINNATI CASUALTY CO
N/A	N/A	N/A	0.3	-0.1	-0.3	N/A	N/A	N/A	-0.3	0.0	0.0	CINCINNATI EQUITABLE INS CO
9.9	5.6	N/A	N/A	N/A	N/A	N/A	N/A	N/A	50.2	0.0	0.0 •	CINCINNATI INDEMNITY CO

999 + Denotes number greater than 999.9%
999 - Denotes number less than -999.99%
• Bullets denote a more detailed analysis is available in Section II.

INSURANCE COMPANY NAME	DOM. STATE	RATING	TOTAL ASSETS ($MIL)	CAPITAL & SURPLUS ($MIL)	ANNUAL NET PREMIUM ($MIL)	NET INCOME ($MIL)	CAPITAL-IZATION INDEX (PTS)	RESERVE ADQ INDEX (PTS)	PROFIT-ABILITY INDEX (PTS)	LIQUIDITY INDEX (PTS)	STAB. INDEX (PTS)	STABILITY FACTORS
CINCINNATI INS CO	OH	A	10,791.2	4,363.9	3,769.2	281.0	8.1	9.3	7.4	6.5	7.6	
CINCINNATI SPECIALTY UNDERWRITER	DE	B	531.6	253.2	127.7	22.7	7.8	6.5	6.3	6.8	5.5	T
CIRCLE STAR INS CO RRG	VT	D-	4.9	1.7	0.4	0.2	9.9	3.8	7.9	9.8	1.3	DT
CITATION INS CO	MA	B	250.8	82.8	137.2	1.3	9.0	5.7	3.5	5.7	4.8	
CITIES & VILLAGES MUTUAL INS CO	WI	D+	52.8	31.1	13.0	3.1	7.9	7.7	8.3	6.9	2.5	D
CITIZENS INS CO OF AMERICA	MI	B	1,480.7	677.0	679.8	11.4	10.0	8.2	4.2	6.1	5.2	
CITIZENS INS CO OF ILLINOIS	IL	C+	4.6	4.6	0.0	0.0	10.0	N/A	6.4	7.0	3.5	DR
CITIZENS INS CO OF OH	OH	C	15.0	15.0	0.0	0.3	10.0	N/A	7.5	7.0	4.1	D
CITIZENS INS CO OF THE MIDWEST	IN	C	45.3	45.2	0.0	0.7	10.0	N/A	7.6	7.0	4.2	
CITIZENS PROPERTY INS CORP	FL	A+	14,582.0	7,434.7	1,702.1	415.2	10.0	5.9	8.9	8.4	8.5	
CITIZENS UNITED RECIP EXCH	NJ	D	90.4	20.5	41.4	-6.5	3.0	1.7	2.0	5.6	2.2	CDFT
CIVIC PROPERTY & CASUALTY CO INC	CA	C+	272.2	112.9	136.4	13.8	8.7	8.2	6.3	6.4	4.5	FR
CIVIL SERVICE EMPLOYEES INS CO	CA	C	231.6	117.3	91.9	2.7	8.1	6.9	5.0	6.7	4.3	R
CLAIM PROFESSIONALS LIAB INS CO RRG	VT	E+	3.6	1.9	0.7	0.0	7.1	5.0	5.2	8.7	0.6	DRT
CLAREMONT LIABILITY INS CO	CA	U	15.0	14.8	0.0	-0.4	N/A	5.0	3.0	7.0	4.2	FRT
CLARENDON AMERICA INS CO	IL	U	250.8	137.4	-25.3	2.5	N/A	7.0	4.9	7.0	6.4	FT
CLARENDON NATIONAL INS CO	IL	C	607.4	176.0	-12.8	7.1	4.1	7.0	2.4	10.0	3.4	CFRT
CLEARFIELD CTY GRNGE MUT FIRE INS CO	PA	C-	3.8	3.0	0.6	-0.2	10.0	6.3	4.1	9.4	2.1	D
CLEARWATER INS CO	DE	D	1,197.0	410.7	0.1	9.3	4.9	1.1	3.0	7.0	1.9	FRT
CLEARWATER SELECT INS CO	CT	D	1,167.6	408.6	808.4	22.3	0.0	0.9	8.1	0.0	1.7	CGLR
CLERMONT INS CO	IA	C	23.4	21.7	0.0	0.3	10.0	N/A	6.7	9.7	4.2	DR
CLINIC MUTUAL INS CO RRG	HI	U	4.8	4.6	0.1	0.0	N/A	5.8	2.7	10.0	3.2	FRT
CLOISTER MUTUAL CASUALTY INS CO	PA	U	4.7	4.7	-0.2	0.1	N/A	7.2	3.9	10.0	4.5	FT
CLUB INS CO	OH	C	13.8	12.9	1.3	0.6	10.0	7.4	5.6	8.9	3.3	D
CMIC RRG	DC	B-	3.8	2.9	0.0	0.0	10.0	3.6	3.3	10.0	3.5	DFT
CO-OPERATIVE INS COMPANIES	VT	B-	122.2	64.7	56.8	0.2	9.5	8.2	6.8	6.6	5.0	T
COAST NATIONAL INS CO	CA	D+	613.8	410.5	0.0	4.9	10.0	6.0	6.8	10.0	2.6	R
COASTAL AMERICAN INS CO	MS	C-	7.0	3.3	2.9	0.1	5.5	3.7	2.2	6.8	2.2	DT
COASTAL INS RRG INC	AL	D-	43.4	17.7	5.2	-1.4	9.1	9.8	3.6	8.4	1.3	DFR
COASTAL SELECT INS CO	CA	D+	110.1	44.5	41.5	8.0	1.0	6.3	6.9	1.7	2.4	CGLR
COFACE NORTH AMERICA INS CO	MA	C	163.7	73.0	55.2	9.1	9.6	9.7	6.5	8.9	3.7	R
COLISEUM REINS CO	DE	C	323.3	203.5	0.1	18.6	10.0	6.2	1.9	8.8	3.2	RT
COLLEGE LIAB INS CO LTD RRG	HI	D	15.5	10.6	2.2	0.7	8.2	9.3	8.7	8.0	1.4	D
COLLEGE RRG INC	VT	D+	22.3	6.3	5.1	0.1	3.3	6.1	5.7	7.5	2.0	CD
COLONIAL AMERICAN CAS & SURETY CO	MD	C+	24.6	22.6	0.0	0.3	10.0	N/A	4.5	7.0	4.5	DFR
COLONIAL COUNTY MUTUAL INS CO	TX	B	120.6	14.1	0.0	0.0	7.7	N/A	3.9	6.0	4.9	D
COLONIAL LLOYDS	TX	D	9.1	5.8	1.4	0.0	7.2	5.5	0.8	6.5	2.1	DFT
COLONIAL MORTGAGE INS CO	TX	D+	2.9	2.0	0.6	0.1	3.7	0.2	1.6	7.7	2.4	DFT
COLONIAL SURETY CO	PA	C-	49.0	28.0	7.8	1.5	8.9	9.4	8.7	8.9	3.3	DR
COLONY INS CO	VA	C	1,367.1	369.0	199.8	38.0	7.5	9.4	4.2	7.6	3.3	R
COLONY NATIONAL INS CO	VA	U	87.6	47.5	0.0	1.6	N/A	3.9	3.7	7.0	5.7	T
COLONY SPECIALTY INS CO	OH	D+	71.0	28.0	0.0	0.5	8.5	3.9	3.4	9.7	2.5	DR
COLORADO CASUALTY INS CO	NH	C+	24.0	23.4	0.0	0.1	10.0	N/A	7.2	7.0	4.4	DRT
COLORADO FARM BUREAU MUTUAL INS CO	CO	C	79.3	30.2	24.5	-5.5	8.4	9.4	1.9	6.4	3.6	F
COLUMBIA CASUALTY CO	IL	C	240.2	239.9	0.0	5.2	10.0	N/A	5.4	9.6	3.5	AR
COLUMBIA FEDERAL INS CO	DC	D	3.5	2.1	0.9	0.0	7.4	9.4	7.5	7.5	1.6	DFT
COLUMBIA INS CO	NE	B-	19,280.1	14,397.3	546.8	534.7	7.4	7.6	8.2	8.2	4.9	R
COLUMBIA LLOYDS INS CO	TX	D	38.4	16.9	19.7	1.5	2.6	4.3	1.9	5.4	2.2	DGR
COLUMBIA MUTUAL INS CO	MO	C+	369.7	160.8	148.9	4.5	7.7	5.8	3.1	5.9	4.4	FR
COLUMBIA NATIONAL INS CO	NE	C+	90.9	36.8	38.4	1.6	8.4	5.4	4.1	6.3	4.5	
COLUMBIA NATIONAL RRG INC	VT	E	1.7	1.2	0.2	0.0	9.7	N/A	4.6	10.0	0.0	DT
COMCARE PRO INS RECIPROCAL RRG	VT	D-	5.3	3.5	1.4	0.2	4.8	4.0	7.5	6.8	0.9	D

See Page 27 for explanation of footnotes and
Page 28 for explanation of stability factors.
Arrows denote recent upgrades ▲ or downgrades ▼   (see Section VII for explanations)

52

www.weissratings.com

RISK ADJ. CAPITAL RATIO #1	RATIO #2	PREMIUM TO SURPLUS (%)	RESV. TO SURPLUS (%)	RESV. DEVELOP. 1 YEAR (%)	2 YEAR (%)	LOSS RATIO (%)	EXP. RATIO (%)	COMB RATIO (%)	CASH FROM UNDER- WRITING (%)	NET PREMIUM GROWTH (%)	INVEST. IN AFFIL (%)	INSURANCE COMPANY NAME
2.3	1.7	87.1	87.8	-4.2	-11.7	62.1	30.3	92.4	113.0	11.5	9.7 ●	CINCINNATI INS CO
2.7	1.3	55.9	65.2	-7.4	-5.9	56.6	31.2	87.8	173.6	21.6	0.0 ●	CINCINNATI SPECIALTY UNDERWRITER
1.6	1.5	27.9	36.2	-10.3	-6.5	43.0	-144.3	-101.3	-85.5	4.0	0.0	CIRCLE STAR INS CO RRG
2.6	2.0	154.3	63.5	4.3	7.6	73.5	28.0	101.5	103.0	16.0	0.0	CITATION INS CO
2.6	1.6	44.7	50.7	1.9	-2.3	67.5	25.2	92.7	130.9	18.4	0.0	CITIES & VILLAGES MUTUAL INS CO
4.5	3.0	102.7	69.6	-0.5	-0.3	67.1	28.2	95.3	104.4	-5.2	0.0 ●	CITIZENS INS CO OF AMERICA
279.2	139.6	N/A	N/A	N/A	N/A	N/A	N/A	N/A	N/A	0.0	0.0	CITIZENS INS CO OF ILLINOIS
76.0	34.6	N/A	N/A	N/A	N/A	N/A	N/A	N/A	N/A	0.0	0.0	CITIZENS INS CO OF OH
79.4	36.4	N/A	N/A	N/A	N/A	N/A	N/A	N/A	N/A	0.0	0.0	CITIZENS INS CO OF THE MIDWEST
15.8	10.0	24.3	17.9	1.2	1.6	39.9	26.2	66.1	120.9	-19.3	0.0 ●	CITIZENS PROPERTY INS CORP
0.4	0.3	189.9	142.0	12.5	43.8	92.8	21.4	114.2	75.3	-6.8	0.0	CITIZENS UNITED RECIP EXCH
4.0	2.9	125.7	73.2	0.2	0.0	67.1	34.1	101.2	97.7	-1.6	0.0	CIVIC PROPERTY & CASUALTY CO INC
2.3	1.9	81.9	46.1	N/A	0.7	67.2	35.0	102.2	97.6	5.9	20.4	CIVIL SERVICE EMPLOYEES INS CO
1.3	1.0	36.6	38.8	5.6	6.3	30.5	48.5	79.0	133.7	26.1	0.0	CLAIM PROFESSIONALS LIAB INS CO
N/A	N/A	N/A	N/A	N/A	N/A	N/A	N/A	N/A	N/A	0.0	0.0	CLAREMONT LIABILITY INS CO
N/A	N/A	-18.7	45.6	-46.6	-47.8	181.8	-8.0	173.8	-841.4	N/A	0.0	CLARENDON AMERICA INS CO
0.5	0.3	-4.4	100.7	-19.0	-25.3	195.9	-57.8	138.1	-67.0	-350.7	26.8 ●	CLARENDON NATIONAL INS CO
8.8	5.9	18.6	1.5	-2.4	-1.7	27.0	41.2	68.2	117.6	8.3	0.0	CLEARFIELD CTY GRNGE MUT FIRE INS
1.3	0.9	N/A	205.7	9.9	48.5	999 +	999 +	999 +	-2.3	-32.6	9.6 ●	CLEARWATER INS CO
0.2	0.1	217.0	173.8	478.4	400.5	93.1	5.4	98.5	999 +	N/A	1.9 ●	CLEARWATER SELECT INS CO
33.5	30.2	N/A	N/A	N/A	N/A	N/A	N/A	N/A	-132.8	0.0	0.0	CLERMONT INS CO
N/A	N/A	1.6	3.4	1.5	0.6	243.6	223.3	466.9	27.1	11.0	0.0	CLINIC MUTUAL INS CO RRG
N/A	N/A	-3.8	0.3	-0.3	-0.3	-1.5	-53.7	-55.2	-234.3	N/A	0.0	CLOISTER MUTUAL CASUALTY INS CO
8.3	4.9	10.3	0.7	-0.5	-0.9	19.8	48.8	68.6	137.0	-5.4	0.0	CLUB INS CO
7.1	6.4	1.7	2.7	-0.2	-0.2	-64.9	-143.6	-208.5	132.3	-13.5	0.0	CMIC RRG
4.2	2.9	86.6	29.0	0.3	-3.6	64.7	34.9	99.6	101.7	3.6	1.4	CO-OPERATIVE INS COMPANIES
7.8	7.2	N/A	N/A	N/A	0.1	N/A	N/A	N/A	117.4	0.0	12.3 ●	COAST NATIONAL INS CO
0.9	0.6	91.5	9.7	-2.5	-2.4	22.8	65.1	87.9	128.8	-8.3	0.0	COASTAL AMERICAN INS CO
2.6	2.1	28.0	88.4	-14.7	-32.5	49.5	58.1	107.6	109.4	-29.4	0.2	COASTAL INS RRG INC
0.3	0.2	98.2	17.4	-1.1	-2.8	27.2	18.3	45.5	272.1	95.5	0.0	COASTAL SELECT INS CO
4.9	3.3	84.9	52.6	-16.5	-57.8	41.8	27.8	69.6	232.2	30.2	0.0	COFACE NORTH AMERICA INS CO
4.7	3.3	N/A	45.3	N/A	0.1	19.5	999 +	999 +	6.6	-94.7	7.7 ●	COLISEUM REINS CO
3.3	2.0	21.6	31.4	-24.0	-14.0	58.5	24.1	82.6	129.0	-4.6	0.0	COLLEGE LIAB INS CO LTD RRG
0.9	0.4	81.0	120.2	-12.8	-52.1	50.5	28.7	79.2	162.4	4.7	0.0	COLLEGE RRG INC
31.1	28.0	N/A	N/A	N/A	N/A	N/A	N/A	N/A	4.3	0.0	0.0	COLONIAL AMERICAN CAS & SURETY CO
1.5	1.4	N/A	N/A	N/A	N/A	N/A	N/A	N/A	174.1	0.0	0.0	COLONIAL COUNTY MUTUAL INS CO
3.5	2.8	23.8	12.9	1.9	6.2	74.9	113.4	188.3	28.9	-85.0	0.0	COLONIAL LLOYDS
1.4	1.2	33.8	51.4	16.5	61.5	48.2	55.2	103.4	44.5	-21.3	0.0	COLONIAL MORTGAGE INS CO
4.0	2.7	30.2	46.0	-1.8	-8.4	27.6	30.4	58.0	200.8	0.6	0.0	COLONIAL SURETY CO
2.1	1.4	60.6	124.0	-11.9	-21.2	42.5	38.8	81.3	109.3	13.8	6.2 ●	COLONY INS CO
N/A	N/A	N/A	N/A	N/A	N/A	N/A	N/A	N/A	-0.1	0.0	0.0	COLONY NATIONAL INS CO
3.3	1.9	N/A	N/A	N/A	N/A	N/A	N/A	N/A	118.3	0.0	0.0	COLONY SPECIALTY INS CO
92.1	82.9	N/A	N/A	N/A	N/A	N/A	N/A	N/A	80.9	0.0	0.0	COLORADO CASUALTY INS CO
2.1	1.4	69.6	38.3	-10.2	-13.4	82.0	34.8	116.8	85.3	5.2	1.8	COLORADO FARM BUREAU MUTUAL INS
68.5	28.5	N/A	N/A	N/A	N/A	N/A	N/A	N/A	N/A	0.0	0.0 ●	COLUMBIA CASUALTY CO
1.9	1.1	44.7	54.6	-7.1	-17.1	76.3	21.8	98.1	105.0	-3.4	0.0	COLUMBIA FEDERAL INS CO
1.9	1.4	4.1	16.9	-1.3	-1.4	37.1	24.3	61.4	134.5	-10.5	21.6 ●	COLUMBIA INS CO
0.7	0.4	128.7	15.8	-0.6	-2.9	61.0	25.3	86.3	150.7	78.6	18.9	COLUMBIA LLOYDS INS CO
1.8	1.5	95.8	84.9	1.0	6.9	74.3	28.3	102.6	91.3	-13.4	24.7	COLUMBIA MUTUAL INS CO
3.5	2.3	107.1	95.0	1.1	8.2	74.2	27.3	101.5	94.4	-13.4	0.0	COLUMBIA NATIONAL INS CO
4.7	4.2	18.5	N/A	N/A	N/A	N/A	69.2	69.2	119.7	43.8	0.0	COLUMBIA NATIONAL RRG INC
1.3	0.9	42.2	17.7	1.4	11.7	52.7	32.9	85.6	97.8	-3.8	0.0	COMCARE PRO INS RECIPROCAL RRG

999 + Denotes number greater than 999.9%
999 - Denotes number less than -999.99%
● Bullets denote a more detailed analysis is available in Section II.

INSURANCE COMPANY NAME	DOM. STATE	RATING	TOTAL ASSETS ($MIL)	CAPITAL & SURPLUS ($MIL)	ANNUAL NET PREMIUM ($MIL)	NET INCOME ($MIL)	CAPITAL-IZATION INDEX (PTS)	RESERVE ADQ INDEX (PTS)	PROFIT-ABILITY INDEX (PTS)	LIQUIDITY INDEX (PTS)	STAB. INDEX (PTS)	STABILITY FACTORS
COMMERCE & INDUSTRY INS CO	NY	C	4,847.9	1,570.2	1,569.7	244.7	7.6	3.1	3.9	6.7	4.0	A
COMMERCE INS CO	MA	B-	2,349.1	803.8	1,320.3	35.2	9.1	5.7	3.4	5.4	4.8	
COMMERCE WEST INS CO	CA	C	162.9	60.7	85.3	1.5	9.3	5.7	3.8	5.8	4.2	
COMMERCIAL ALLIANCE INS CO	TX	C	60.2	29.1	42.1	0.1	5.1	6.3	4.4	4.9	3.6	GLR
COMMERCIAL CASUALTY INS CO	CA	U	117.6	63.1	0.0	0.3	N/A	4.9	3.4	10.0	5.3	FGT
COMMERCIAL GUARANTY INS CO	DE	U	34.8	33.9	0.0	0.7	N/A	N/A	5.7	7.0	5.4	T
COMMERCIAL MUT INS CO	GA	F (5)	0.0	0.0	7.9	0.0	0.0	2.3	0.1	0.0	0.0	CDFL
COMMONWEALTH CASUALTY CO	AZ	D-	7.2	1.7	2.1	0.3	0.5	3.6	1.3	0.4	1.1	CDFG
COMMONWEALTH INS CO	PA	F (4)	0.0	0.0	0.7	0.1	0.0	N/A	0.0	8.0	0.0	CDFG
COMMONWEALTH INS CO OF AMERICA	WA	U	22.1	19.7	-0.5	-0.1	N/A	9.3	3.7	10.0	4.9	FRT
COMMONWEALTH MUTUAL INS CO	MD	U (2)	0.5	0.2	1.0	0.0	N/A	6.5	0.5	0.0	0.6	CFLT
COMMUNITIES OF FAITH RRG INC	SC	D	13.6	12.4	1.0	0.3	10.0	8.9	7.3	9.4	1.8	DR
COMMUNITY BLOOD CENTERS EXCHANGE	IN	C-	23.7	13.8	2.9	1.9	10.0	9.7	7.8	8.5	3.3	DR
COMMUNITY HEALTH ALLIANCE RECIP RRG	VT	E	95.5	14.5	11.5	0.1	0.1	2.3	1.5	8.4	0.0	CDR
COMMUNITY HOSPITAL ALTERNATIVE RRG	VT	C-	246.8	100.3	41.7	20.3	8.3	9.5	9.3	7.6	3.0	R
COMMUNITY INS CORP	WI	C	10.5	5.8	0.0	0.1	10.0	4.7	3.5	10.0	2.6	DRT
COMMUNITY MUTUAL INS CO	NY	D-	2.6	0.9	-0.5	-0.1	7.1	7.1	1.5	9.4	1.3	DFRT
COMP OPTIONS INS CO INC	FL	D	117.0	25.5	27.9	-1.9	6.9	5.8	2.8	6.7	2.2	GT
COMPANION CAPTIVE INS CO	SC	U (5)	0.0	0.0	0.0	0.0	N/A	N/A	5.9	7.0	0.5	FT
COMPANION COMMERCIAL INS CO	SC	B	21.7	19.2	0.0	0.1	10.0	N/A	7.1	9.8	5.3	DF
COMPANION INC	VI	D (4)	0.0	0.0	0.5	-0.3	8.4	9.4	2.6	9.3	1.9	DFGR
▼COMPANION PROPERTY & CASUALTY INS	SC	C+	1,119.6	242.4	214.4	-86.5	7.1	4.9	2.7	7.1	4.5	F
COMPANION SPECIALTY INS CO	DC	B	62.2	63.5	0.0	0.6	10.0	N/A	7.4	10.0	4.3	FT
COMPASS INS CO	NY	U	11.9	10.5	0.0	0.1	N/A	4.6	4.5	10.0	4.2	FRT
COMPSOURCE OKLAHOMA	OK	U	--	--	--	--	N/A	--	--	--	--	Z
COMPTRUST AGC MUT CAPTIVE INS CO	GA	C	30.1	15.8	6.6	0.4	8.2	9.6	7.5	7.3	3.5	D
COMPUTER INS CO	RI	U	24.0	24.3	0.0	-0.1	N/A	7.2	4.1	7.0	5.1	FT
COMPWEST INS CO	CA	D+	230.8	119.5	28.6	7.1	10.0	4.1	6.8	7.0	2.5	RT
CONCORD GENERAL MUTUAL INS CO	NH	B-	439.9	216.6	164.6	1.0	8.1	9.1	5.2	6.6	4.6	
CONEMAUGH VALLEY MUTUAL INS CO	PA	D	7.5	3.7	1.6	0.0	7.8	8.2	4.2	6.9	2.3	DFR
CONIFER INS CO	MI	D	62.5	23.7	26.0	-4.3	1.6	8.9	2.7	6.4	1.9	CDGT
CONNECTICUT MEDICAL INS CO	CT	C+	476.3	271.5	35.9	4.9	7.7	9.7	8.8	8.2	4.8	R
CONSOLIDATED INS ASN	TX	D+	4.7	2.8	1.8	0.0	4.8	6.6	4.9	9.1	2.7	DFT
CONSOLIDATED INS CO	IN	C	14.3	13.0	0.0	0.1	10.0	N/A	2.4	6.5	4.1	DRT
CONSOLIDATED LLOYDS	TX	D+	1.7	1.4	0.1	0.0	9.1	7.6	2.8	9.8	1.8	DFRT
CONSTELLATION REINSURANCE CO	NY	U	15.3	4.9	0.1	-0.1	N/A	0.4	2.3	10.0	0.7	CFT
CONSTITUTION INS CO	NY	C-	18.0	14.3	4.1	1.1	10.0	N/A	7.1	10.0	2.5	DGT
CONSUMER SPECIALTIES INS CO RRG	VT	D	5.1	3.2	0.5	-0.1	8.1	9.3	2.5	9.8	2.1	DR
CONSUMERS COUNTY MUTUAL INS CO	TX	D	111.4	2.3	0.0	0.0	1.0	N/A	6.2	7.0	2.0	CDT
CONSUMERS INS USA INC	TN	C	50.5	14.4	36.3	-5.0	7.2	3.2	1.8	6.2	3.4	DFR
CONTINENTAL AMERICAN INS CO	IN	U (5)	0.0	0.0	0.0	0.0	N/A	3.3	4.9	10.0	2.6	T
CONTINENTAL CASUALTY CO	IL	C+	43,193.4	11,404.5	6,246.7	760.7	7.8	6.5	5.8	6.9	4.1	AR
CONTINENTAL DIVIDE INS CO	CO	C+	12.6	10.0	0.0	1.8	10.0	N/A	6.1	10.0	3.3	DT
CONTINENTAL HERITAGE INS CO	FL	C	7.4	7.0	1.4	0.3	10.0	7.2	7.2	9.4	2.6	DR
CONTINENTAL INDEMNITY CO	IA	C	153.7	63.6	39.1	9.1	7.3	9.4	7.1	9.1	3.8	GRT
CONTINENTAL INS CO	PA	C	2,067.4	1,430.1	0.0	45.0	9.4	3.5	3.7	10.0	4.0	AR
CONTINENTAL INS CO OF NJ	NJ	C (3)	0.0	0.0	0.0	0.4	10.0	N/A	3.7	9.0	3.8	ADR
CONTINENTAL MUTUAL INS CO	PA	D	1.4	1.0	1.5	-0.1	5.4	5.0	4.2	6.5	1.3	DRT
CONTINENTAL RISK UNDERWRITERS RRG	NV	U	0.8	0.6	0.0	-0.1	N/A	N/A	2.8	7.0	2.1	FT
CONTINENTAL WESTERN INS CO	IA	C	181.6	87.3	0.0	1.8	10.0	N/A	6.4	8.6	3.9	
CONTINUING CARE RRG INC	SC	D+	5.3	2.2	3.2	-0.8	8.0	5.9	1.6	4.4	2.0	DLR
CONTRACTORS BONDING & INS CO	WA	B-	198.5	112.9	50.0	6.0	10.0	9.3	5.0	7.0	4.9	R

See Page 27 for explanation of footnotes and
Page 28 for explanation of stability factors.
Arrows denote recent upgrades ▲ or downgrades ▼   (see Section VII for explanations)

54   www.weissratings.com

RISK ADJ. CAPITAL RATIO #1	CAPITAL RATIO #2	PREMIUM TO SURPLUS (%)	RESV. TO SURPLUS (%)	RESV. DEVELOP. 1 YEAR (%)	RESV. DEVELOP. 2 YEAR (%)	LOSS RATIO (%)	EXP. RATIO (%)	COMB RATIO (%)	CASH FROM UNDER-WRITING (%)	NET PREMIUM GROWTH (%)	INVEST. IN AFFIL (%)	INSURANCE COMPANY NAME
2.3	1.5	82.4	196.4	3.5	8.8	73.0	32.7	105.7	95.3	16.0	1.2 ●	COMMERCE & INDUSTRY INS CO
2.7	2.1	158.2	65.1	4.3	7.6	73.5	25.3	98.8	100.2	9.1	3.5 ●	COMMERCE INS CO
3.1	2.5	145.5	59.9	4.5	7.5	73.5	24.0	97.5	104.5	-4.8	0.0	COMMERCE WEST INS CO
1.1	0.7	143.3	51.6	8.6	6.8	64.2	39.6	103.8	104.6	41.5	0.0	COMMERCIAL ALLIANCE INS CO
N/A	N/A	N/A	92.2	-0.1	N/A	-361.2	999 +	999 +	0.2	N/A	0.0	COMMERCIAL CASUALTY INS CO
N/A	N/A	N/A	N/A	N/A	N/A	N/A	N/A	N/A	N/A	0.0	0.0	COMMERCIAL GUARANTY INS CO
0.0	0.0	544.6	674.2	9.5	40.7	76.4	80.1	156.5	91.3	-17.7	0.0	COMMERCIAL MUT INS CO
0.2	0.1	147.9	31.6	-0.7	N/A	73.3	41.0	114.3	75.0	187.5	0.0	COMMONWEALTH CASUALTY CO
0.0	0.0	999 +	620.0	N/A	N/A	26.3	110.3	136.6	95.5	-13.5	0.0	COMMONWEALTH INS CO
N/A	N/A	-2.5	3.5	-10.6	-10.6	999 +	-53.7	999 +	10.2	71.9	0.0	COMMONWEALTH INS CO OF AMERICA
N/A	N/A	560.5	38.2	0.4	-2.6	30.6	84.9	115.5	82.5	3.1	0.0	COMMONWEALTH MUTUAL INS CO
5.3	3.2	7.6	7.7	-2.6	-6.0	29.5	48.5	78.0	173.7	-27.0	0.0	COMMUNITIES OF FAITH RRG INC
6.1	3.9	22.5	35.3	-13.0	-35.0	28.7	36.0	64.7	164.7	10.7	0.0	COMMUNITY BLOOD CENTERS
0.1	0.1	79.4	368.9	55.8	-4.9	188.6	19.4	208.0	115.2	-0.3	0.0	COMMUNITY HEALTH ALLIANCE RECIP
2.6	2.0	49.0	153.1	-8.2	-20.0	70.8	15.5	86.3	164.1	14.8	0.0	COMMUNITY HOSPITAL ALTERNATIVE
4.0	3.6	N/A	N/A	N/A	N/A	N/A	N/A	N/A	-23.3	100.0	0.0	COMMUNITY INS CORP
1.6	1.4	-50.8	1.6	-94.3	-75.7	999 +	-48.0	999 +	-54.5	-334.0	4.0	COMMUNITY MUTUAL INS CO
1.0	0.8	98.4	52.2	-0.7	7.8	56.0	29.9	85.9	147.3	57.5	0.0	COMP OPTIONS INS CO INC
N/A	N/A	N/A	N/A	N/A	N/A	N/A	N/A	N/A	N/A	0.0	0.0	COMPANION CAPTIVE INS CO
22.3	20.1	N/A	N/A	N/A	N/A	N/A	N/A	N/A	33.5	0.0	0.0	COMPANION COMMERCIAL INS CO
4.5	3.0	14.0	36.2	-22.2	-18.4	62.9	133.5	196.4	33.4	-83.2	0.0	COMPANION INC
1.0	0.6	85.5	124.9	15.4	18.4	94.2	34.5	128.7	90.5	-38.2	11.1 ●	COMPANION PROPERTY & CASUALTY
121.9	54.0	N/A	N/A	N/A	N/A	N/A	N/A	N/A	658.5	0.0	0.0	COMPANION SPECIALTY INS CO
N/A	N/A	N/A	17.8	2.4	6.2	N/A	N/A	N/A	N/A	0.0	0.0	COMPASS INS CO
N/A	N/A	--	--	--	--	--	--	--	--	--	--	COMPSOURCE OKLAHOMA
2.1	1.6	42.7	72.1	-14.2	-24.9	49.4	43.2	92.6	120.8	23.2	0.0	COMPTRUST AGC MUT CAPTIVE INS CO
N/A	N/A	N/A	N/A	N/A	-0.1	N/A	N/A	N/A	N/A	0.0	0.0	COMPUTER INS CO
6.4	5.1	25.5	31.4	1.3	1.9	66.0	24.7	90.7	-24.5	-31.1	0.0	COMPWEST INS CO
2.5	1.6	77.7	35.5	-4.4	-9.0	67.4	32.6	100.0	100.8	6.2	5.9 ●	CONCORD GENERAL MUTUAL INS CO
2.6	1.6	43.6	17.4	-2.3	-5.3	41.9	56.9	98.8	91.1	5.1	0.0	CONEMAUGH VALLEY MUTUAL INS CO
0.5	0.3	150.9	74.5	-8.1	-12.5	67.4	41.9	109.3	121.2	104.0	0.0	CONIFER INS CO
1.7	1.5	13.6	53.5	-10.8	-23.9	58.6	28.5	87.1	141.7	5.0	0.0 ●	CONNECTICUT MEDICAL INS CO
1.3	1.2	57.4	6.1	-2.1	-4.1	7.6	117.0	124.6	77.8	-12.1	0.0	CONSOLIDATED INS ASN
24.2	21.8	N/A	N/A	N/A	N/A	N/A	N/A	N/A	87.4	0.0	0.0	CONSOLIDATED INS CO
4.3	2.8	5.0	2.8	-2.2	-2.8	38.9	214.1	253.0	39.9	-49.3	0.0	CONSOLIDATED LLOYDS
N/A	N/A	1.7	157.1	54.2	95.9	999 +	616.0	999 +	7.0	0.0	0.0	CONSTELLATION REINSURANCE CO
10.6	6.2	30.8	N/A	N/A	N/A	N/A	30.0	30.0	131.5	N/A	0.0	CONSTITUTION INS CO
2.3	1.6	14.9	49.3	-3.1	-7.2	45.3	100.9	146.2	137.8	21.9	0.0	CONSUMER SPECIALTIES INS CO RRG
0.2	0.2	N/A	N/A	N/A	N/A	N/A	N/A	N/A	98.4	0.0	0.0	CONSUMERS COUNTY MUTUAL INS CO
1.0	0.7	181.2	87.0	-6.4	12.5	72.3	28.1	100.4	86.0	-9.7	0.0	CONSUMERS INS USA INC
N/A	N/A	1.5	0.4	-0.5	1.5	21.7	112.9	134.6	70.6	-75.8	0.0	CONTINENTAL AMERICAN INS CO
2.0	1.5	56.1	167.5	-0.9	3.1	87.8	24.2	112.0	87.2	1.4	11.6 ●	CONTINENTAL CASUALTY CO
11.1	10.0	N/A	4.5	N/A	N/A	N/A	N/A	N/A	80.2	0.0	0.0	CONTINENTAL DIVIDE INS CO
7.1	5.9	19.1	0.5	-0.2	-0.4	0.3	60.0	60.3	153.2	23.4	0.0	CONTINENTAL HERITAGE INS CO
3.1	1.7	72.8	53.4	0.3	-13.0	35.3	26.3	61.6	828.0	53.4	0.0	CONTINENTAL INDEMNITY CO
5.1	2.7	N/A	69.0	13.6	16.4	N/A	N/A	N/A	50.0	0.0	7.8 ●	CONTINENTAL INS CO
55.2	23.9	N/A	N/A	N/A	N/A	N/A	N/A	N/A	N/A	0.0	0.0	CONTINENTAL INS CO OF NJ
0.8	0.7	150.6	14.9	3.7	0.2	26.8	70.5	97.3	108.5	2.9	0.0	CONTINENTAL MUTUAL INS CO
N/A	N/A	N/A	N/A	N/A	N/A	N/A	N/A	N/A	N/A	0.0	0.0	CONTINENTAL RISK UNDERWRITERS
9.9	8.9	N/A	N/A	N/A	N/A	N/A	N/A	N/A	-920.9	0.0	0.0	CONTINENTAL WESTERN INS CO
1.5	1.2	113.0	0.5	-3.2	-14.9	77.2	29.3	106.5	136.3	18.1	0.0	CONTINUING CARE RRG INC
6.1	5.0	44.9	41.2	-8.2	-20.2	22.0	56.4	78.4	112.4	2.8	0.0	CONTRACTORS BONDING & INS CO

999 + Denotes number greater than 999.9%
999 - Denotes number less than -999.99%
● Bullets denote a more detailed analysis is available in Section II.

INSURANCE COMPANY NAME	DOM. STATE	RATING	TOTAL ASSETS ($MIL)	CAPITAL & SURPLUS ($MIL)	ANNUAL NET PREMIUM ($MIL)	NET INCOME ($MIL)	CAPITAL-IZATION INDEX (PTS)	RESERVE ADQ INDEX (PTS)	PROFIT-ABILITY INDEX (PTS)	LIQUIDITY INDEX (PTS)	STAB. INDEX (PTS)	STABILITY FACTORS
CONTRACTORS INS CO OF NORTH AMER	HI	E	43.3	18.5	2.5	0.5	7.1	4.6	3.0	10.0	0.1	DF
CONTROLLED RISK INS CO OF VT RRG	VT	C	61.9	35.5	16.5	1.7	9.0	9.1	8.5	7.1	3.7	R
CONVENTUS INTER INS EXCHANGE	NJ	C (3)	0.0	0.0	9.0	2.2	10.0	9.6	8.8	8.1	4.3	DRT
COOP OF AMER PHYS INS CO RRG	HI	C+(5)	0.0	0.0	6.4	0.0	7.3	3.6	5.8	7.9	4.6	DFGT
COOPERATIVA D SEGUROS MULTIPLES D	PR	C+	498.9	164.8	161.8	3.1	8.0	5.9	2.8	7.0	4.6	R
COPIC A RRG	DC	U	0.9	0.8	0.0	-0.1	N/A	N/A	2.4	7.0	1.7	FT
COPIC INS CO	CO	A-	548.6	262.7	82.0	6.6	9.9	9.6	8.9	7.4	6.9	F
COPPERPOINT AMERICAN INS CO	AZ	C+	7.5	5.3	0.0	-0.1	10.0	N/A	2.8	9.7	3.0	DFT
COPPERPOINT CASUALTY INS CO	AZ	C+	7.4	4.9	0.0	-0.2	10.0	3.6	2.9	9.2	3.1	DT
COPPERPOINT GENERAL INS CO	AZ	B-	16.1	10.1	0.0	-0.7	10.0	3.6	3.1	7.0	3.5	DFT
COPPERPOINT INDEMNITY INS CO	AZ	C-	11.3	7.6	0.0	-0.2	10.0	N/A	2.3	9.5	2.5	DFT
COPPERPOINT MUTUAL INS CO	AZ	A+	3,581.2	1,235.1	222.5	48.7	7.6	4.9	5.0	6.8	7.7	FG
COPPERPOINT NATIONAL INS CO	AZ	C	7.4	4.9	0.0	-0.1	10.0	N/A	2.6	9.1	2.6	DFT
COPPERPOINT PREMIER INS CO	AZ	C-	20.4	20.0	0.0	0.0	10.0	4.6	3.3	7.0	3.0	DFGT
COPPERPOINT WESTERN INS CO	AZ	B-	8.3	5.1	0.0	-0.2	10.0	3.6	3.3	7.0	3.6	DF
COREPOINT INS CO	MI	C+	207.1	135.7	49.0	2.8	8.0	9.3	3.9	7.0	3.7	GRT
CORNERSTONE MUTUAL INS CO	GA	U (5)	0.0	0.0	7.9	0.0	N/A	3.2	0.8	0.1	0.3	CDFL
CORNERSTONE NATIONAL INS CO	MO	C	38.4	11.1	36.3	-0.1	4.5	6.9	2.4	3.7	3.1	DFLR
COUNTRY CASUALTY INS CO	IL	B+	78.1	67.7	0.0	0.8	10.0	N/A	6.7	10.0	6.3	
COUNTRY MUTUAL INS CO	IL	A-	4,306.5	1,924.7	2,051.7	87.3	9.3	7.8	6.0	6.2	7.3	
COUNTRY PREFERRED INS CO	IL	B	199.7	65.2	0.0	1.4	10.0	N/A	8.5	10.0	5.9	T
COUNTRYWAY INS CO	NY	C	26.0	22.5	0.0	0.3	10.0	4.9	5.5	7.0	3.8	DF
COUNTRYWIDE INS CO	NY	D-	228.2	44.2	75.4	1.7	2.8	0.5	4.8	5.9	0.9	R
COURTESY INS CO	FL	B	718.2	331.9	124.9	24.2	10.0	6.2	8.9	7.5	5.1	
COVENANT INS CO	CT	C	82.2	25.8	36.0	1.1	7.5	8.5	4.6	6.5	3.7	T
COVENTRY INSURANCE CO	RI	U	1.9	1.9	0.0	0.1	N/A	N/A	4.4	7.0	2.3	T
COVERYS RRG INC	DC	D	6.8	4.5	0.1	-0.4	10.0	N/A	3.2	8.6	2.1	DGT
COVINGTON SPECIALTY INS CO	NH	B	99.8	47.8	13.2	0.8	10.0	5.0	6.8	8.5	4.2	GT
CPA MUTUAL INS CO OF AMERICA RRG	VT	C-	23.7	8.8	3.0	-0.3	7.1	7.0	2.3	6.9	2.9	DFR
CRESTBROOK INS CO	OH	B	99.8	94.4	0.0	2.4	10.0	N/A	4.9	10.0	4.5	ADT
CROSSFIT RRG INC	MT	C+	4.2	2.2	1.8	0.1	5.4	4.7	3.1	9.2	3.1	DGT
CROWN CAPTIVE INS CO	GA	D	1.3	0.7	0.3	0.0	8.0	6.9	4.8	9.2	1.1	DT
CROWN CAPTIVE INS CO INC	DC	E+	5.5	1.9	3.1	-0.1	4.7	4.4	4.7	3.3	0.5	DFLT
CRUDEN BAY RRG INC	VT	D-	11.7	4.4	2.5	0.3	6.4	10.0	2.2	7.1	0.6	D
CRUM & FORSTER INDEMNITY CO	DE	D+	46.6	16.2	12.8	0.4	7.2	5.9	5.9	8.1	2.7	DRT
CRUM & FORSTER INS CO	NJ	D+(3)	0.0	0.0	12.8	2.1	7.4	5.9	6.2	8.3	2.7	D
CRUM & FORSTER SPECIALTY INS CO	AZ	D+	61.9	47.1	0.0	0.5	10.0	4.1	5.9	7.0	2.7	R
CRUSADER INS CO	CA	B-	120.0	63.0	26.1	1.6	10.0	9.3	5.0	9.1	5.0	F
CRYSTAL RUN RECIPROCAL RRG	VT	C-	16.9	3.7	3.8	1.0	7.1	4.7	4.8	9.1	2.0	D
CSAA AFFINITY INS CO	PA	C+	210.5	150.9	43.3	2.4	9.7	7.6	5.5	6.8	4.2	R
CSAA FIRE & CASUALTY INS CO	IN	C	77.1	41.4	14.4	1.4	10.0	8.2	6.0	6.5	3.9	T
CSAA GENERAL INS CO	IN	C	254.1	144.4	86.6	5.7	10.0	7.6	6.7	6.6	4.2	T
CSAA INS EXCHANGE	CA	A-	6,956.8	3,916.7	2,714.9	86.3	9.5	7.6	6.6	6.4	5.5	
CSAA MID-ATLANTIC INS CO	PA	C-	36.7	23.7	8.7	0.7	10.0	7.6	5.3	6.8	3.2	DR
CSAA MID-ATLANTIC INS CO OF NJ	NJ	C	48.5	25.8	17.3	0.8	10.0	7.6	5.8	6.7	3.4	T
CSE SAFEGUARD INS CO	CA	C+	100.7	39.7	45.9	1.2	7.8	7.0	4.8	6.9	4.5	R
CTLIC RRG INC	DC	E (5)	0.0	0.0	0.3	0.0	0.8	N/A	2.5	9.2	0.1	CDGT
CUMBERLAND INS CO INC	NJ	B-	104.0	48.9	22.4	1.9	8.1	9.3	7.0	7.2	4.8	R
CUMBERLAND MUTUAL FIRE INS CO	NJ	B-	258.5	140.6	91.0	5.6	8.3	6.9	4.9	6.7	4.8	R
CUMIS INS SOCIETY INC	IA	B	2,309.5	686.2	621.0	53.8	9.9	6.9	4.8	6.5	5.7	
CUMIS MORTGAGE REINS CO	WI	U	9.9	9.8	0.0	0.0	N/A	0.0	4.6	0.0	0.0	LT
CUMIS SPECIALTY INS CO INC	IA	B	147.6	69.8	69.0	4.9	10.0	4.6	6.6	6.6	6.1	

See Page 27 for explanation of footnotes and Page 28 for explanation of stability factors.

Arrows denote recent upgrades ▲ or downgrades ▼ (see Section VII for explanations)

www.weissratings.com

RISK ADJ. CAPITAL RATIO #1	RATIO #2	PREMIUM TO SURPLUS (%)	RESV. TO SURPLUS (%)	RESV. DEVELOP. 1 YEAR (%)	RESV. DEVELOP. 2 YEAR (%)	LOSS RATIO (%)	EXP. RATIO (%)	COMB RATIO (%)	CASH FROM UNDER- WRITING (%)	NET PREMIUM GROWTH (%)	INVEST. IN AFFIL (%)	INSURANCE COMPANY NAME
1.6	1.4	13.6	117.0	-5.0	-10.8	14.0	34.1	48.1	31.1	40.4	0.0	CONTRACTORS INS CO OF NORTH
3.1	2.6	49.0	46.8	-3.2	-10.9	36.4	55.7	92.1	102.5	2.3	0.0	CONTROLLED RISK INS CO OF VT RRG
4.3	3.6	23.6	79.0	-19.9	-23.2	42.9	49.9	92.8	117.8	-44.3	0.0	CONVENTUS INTER INS EXCHANGE
1.9	1.3	29.5	48.5	-6.2	N/A	63.2	22.6	85.8	90.8	0.0	0.0	COOP OF AMER PHYS INS CO RRG
2.2	1.8	90.2	20.2	-0.7	0.5	68.6	27.7	96.3	100.6	2.5	14.3	COOPERATIVA D SEGUROS MULTIPLES
N/A	N/A	N/A	N/A	N/A	N/A	N/A	N/A	N/A	N/A	0.0	0.0	COPIC A RRG
4.6	3.1	31.5	70.9	-8.5	-18.0	59.4	23.5	82.9	109.6	-6.9	0.0 ●	COPIC INS CO
7.0	6.3	N/A	N/A	N/A	N/A	N/A	N/A	N/A	40.7	0.0	0.0	COPPERPOINT AMERICAN INS CO
5.8	5.2	N/A	N/A	N/A	N/A	N/A	N/A	N/A	135.4	0.0	0.0	COPPERPOINT CASUALTY INS CO
5.9	5.3	N/A	N/A	N/A	N/A	N/A	N/A	N/A	237.9	0.0	0.0	COPPERPOINT GENERAL INS CO
6.6	5.9	N/A	N/A	N/A	N/A	N/A	N/A	N/A	81.9	0.0	0.0	COPPERPOINT INDEMNITY INS CO
2.3	1.5	18.8	184.3	-0.8	0.3	89.2	26.7	115.9	35.6	0.0	1.7 ●	COPPERPOINT MUTUAL INS CO
5.7	5.1	N/A	N/A	N/A	N/A	N/A	N/A	N/A	57.9	0.0	0.0	COPPERPOINT NATIONAL INS CO
3.0	1.9	N/A	N/A	N/A	N/A	N/A	N/A	N/A	174.2	0.0	4.7	COPPERPOINT PREMIER INS CO
4.8	4.3	N/A	N/A	N/A	N/A	N/A	N/A	N/A	73.2	0.0	0.0	COPPERPOINT WESTERN INS CO
3.0	2.0	36.6	23.2	-1.6	-5.9	62.0	47.9	109.9	101.2	16.3	0.3	COREPOINT INS CO
N/A	N/A	172.5	213.5	6.7	29.5	76.4	86.4	162.8	67.9	-17.7	0.0	CORNERSTONE MUTUAL INS CO
0.8	0.7	337.9	153.2	-8.7	-8.9	71.7	29.1	100.8	90.4	1.9	0.0	CORNERSTONE NATIONAL INS CO
27.3	24.6	N/A	N/A	N/A	N/A	N/A	N/A	N/A	3.2	0.0	0.0 ●	COUNTRY CASUALTY INS CO
3.6	2.6	112.4	62.1	-2.9	-2.9	69.3	29.6	98.9	102.8	3.6	5.0 ●	COUNTRY MUTUAL INS CO
7.0	6.3	N/A	N/A	N/A	N/A	N/A	N/A	N/A	550.9	0.0	0.0	COUNTRY PREFERRED INS CO
21.1	19.0	N/A	N/A	N/A	N/A	N/A	N/A	N/A	-82.7	0.0	0.0	COUNTRYWAY INS CO
0.5	0.5	180.7	266.8	30.1	63.1	97.7	10.8	108.5	88.9	-0.7	1.7	COUNTRYWIDE INS CO
9.1	5.2	40.5	2.2	0.4	-0.6	52.7	17.2	69.9	171.2	-9.9	0.0 ●	COURTESY INS CO
1.9	1.3	145.3	71.0	-3.2	-8.3	64.5	33.0	97.5	105.6	6.8	0.0	COVENANT INS CO
N/A	N/A	N/A	N/A	N/A	N/A	N/A	N/A	N/A	N/A	0.0	0.0	COVENTRY INSURANCE CO
5.5	5.0	1.7	1.1	N/A	N/A	176.3	43.7	220.0	-556.4	N/A	0.0	COVERYS RRG INC
5.7	3.4	28.0	9.3	0.4	0.4	66.4	26.4	92.8	281.9	475.2	0.0	COVINGTON SPECIALTY INS CO
1.1	0.9	31.3	94.8	-21.2	-9.2	139.4	48.7	188.1	75.5	-29.7	0.0	CPA MUTUAL INS CO OF AMERICA RRG
58.9	27.4	N/A	N/A	N/A	N/A	N/A	N/A	N/A	63.9	0.0	0.0	CRESTBROOK INS CO
1.8	1.0	116.3	36.8	9.4	0.7	29.7	37.0	66.7	227.9	67.8	0.0	CROSSFIT RRG INC
2.1	1.2	38.8	40.1	1.9	-8.0	67.3	37.9	105.2	167.2	29.3	0.0	CROWN CAPTIVE INS CO
0.8	0.5	158.4	123.8	6.0	0.4	74.7	30.6	105.3	94.8	3.5	0.0	CROWN CAPTIVE INS CO INC
1.6	1.3	27.6	62.0	-63.7	-161.8	30.4	9.1	39.5	133.0	-19.4	0.0	CRUDEN BAY RRG INC
1.6	1.1	81.3	144.5	0.9	6.1	71.4	31.7	103.1	129.7	20.0	0.0	CRUM & FORSTER INDEMNITY CO
1.8	1.2	72.1	128.2	0.8	5.8	71.4	31.7	103.1	129.7	20.0	0.0	CRUM & FORSTER INS CO
15.7	14.1	N/A	N/A	N/A	N/A	N/A	N/A	N/A	-24.6	0.0	0.0	CRUM & FORSTER SPECIALTY INS CO
4.3	3.7	42.5	64.2	-7.8	-14.7	59.4	30.3	89.7	93.2	-4.7	0.0	CRUSADER INS CO
1.3	1.2	136.7	138.5	-0.2	-1.1	57.4	16.0	73.4	319.9	-9.7	0.0	CRYSTAL RUN RECIPROCAL RRG
3.2	3.1	29.5	12.4	0.2	-0.4	74.0	30.9	104.9	95.1	2.9	25.6	CSAA AFFINITY INS CO
7.9	5.7	35.1	14.7	0.3	-1.1	74.0	21.4	95.4	109.8	2.9	0.0	CSAA FIRE & CASUALTY INS CO
7.8	5.8	62.1	26.0	0.5	-1.1	74.0	24.4	98.4	91.3	2.9	0.0	CSAA GENERAL INS CO
3.7	2.5	70.9	29.7	0.6	-1.0	74.0	31.3	105.3	97.2	2.9	7.2 ●	CSAA INS EXCHANGE
8.5	6.3	37.6	15.8	0.3	-0.5	74.0	24.6	98.6	108.9	2.9	0.0	CSAA MID-ATLANTIC INS CO
4.6	3.4	69.4	29.1	0.5	-1.0	74.0	27.4	101.4	144.1	2.9	0.0	CSAA MID-ATLANTIC INS CO OF NJ
2.6	1.9	118.9	66.9	N/A	1.9	67.1	34.9	102.0	97.6	5.9	0.0	CSE SAFEGUARD INS CO
0.3	0.2	40.8	336.8	N/A	N/A	70.2	-3.0	67.2	-127.4	0.0	0.0	CTLIC RRG INC
4.7	2.3	47.3	83.2	-7.4	-6.0	54.5	34.2	88.7	97.9	2.0	0.0	CUMBERLAND INS CO INC
2.3	1.8	66.9	38.9	-1.0	-4.1	66.4	36.1	102.5	103.5	10.3	20.3	CUMBERLAND MUTUAL FIRE INS CO
4.4	3.0	99.9	54.2	-4.4	-6.2	63.8	30.4	94.2	108.1	12.3	5.7 ●	CUMIS INS SOCIETY INC
N/A	N/A	N/A	N/A	N/A	N/A	N/A	N/A	N/A	N/A	0.0	0.0	CUMIS MORTGAGE REINS CO
4.9	3.3	106.7	58.0	-4.7	-5.3	63.8	29.7	93.5	112.5	12.3	0.0	CUMIS SPECIALTY INS CO INC

999 + Denotes number greater than 999.9%
999 - Denotes number less than -999.99%
● Bullets denote a more detailed analysis is available in Section II.

INSURANCE COMPANY NAME	DOM. STATE	RATING	TOTAL ASSETS ($MIL)	CAPITAL & SURPLUS ($MIL)	ANNUAL NET PREMIUM ($MIL)	NET INCOME ($MIL)	CAPITAL- IZATION INDEX (PTS)	RESERVE ADQ INDEX (PTS)	PROFIT- ABILITY INDEX (PTS)	LIQUIDITY INDEX (PTS)	STAB. INDEX (PTS)	STABILITY FACTORS
CYPRESS INS CO	CA	C	1,184.6	285.0	271.9	10.7	6.5	5.8	4.8	9.4	4.2	FT
CYPRESS PROPERTY & CASUALTY INS CO	FL	C-	105.3	30.3	48.8	-0.4	5.0	9.4	2.5	6.9	3.1	F
CYPRESS TEXAS LLOYDS	TX	C-	46.2	15.9	22.7	1.3	4.5	8.8	2.8	6.7	2.9	D
DAILY UNDERWRITERS OF AMERICA	PA	C	36.6	25.4	10.6	0.5	7.6	3.4	7.7	6.5	4.2	DF
DAIRYLAND COUNTY MUTUAL INS CO OF TX	TX	B	13.8	12.5	0.0	0.0	10.0	N/A	4.2	7.6	4.9	D
DAIRYLAND INS CO	WI	A+	1,212.4	503.2	318.1	21.5	10.0	8.6	6.0	6.9	7.9	
DAKOTA FIRE INS CO	ND	C	210.0	55.5	87.8	1.1	7.8	9.3	6.0	6.3	4.2	T
DAKOTA TRUCK UNDERWRITERS	SD	C+	108.1	41.7	29.8	2.8	7.4	5.6	8.6	6.7	4.4	R
DANBURY INS CO	MA	C	12.0	7.0	4.3	0.2	7.8	7.0	3.1	6.5	3.7	DFRT
DANIELSON NATIONAL INS CO	CA	C-	9.7	5.6	1.1	-0.1	8.5	4.4	2.0	8.6	2.6	DFRT
DARWIN NATIONAL ASR CO	DE	B-	777.1	370.6	98.5	8.7	9.0	8.5	8.4	7.1	5.0	T
DE SMET FARM MUTUAL INS CO OF SD	SD	C	26.8	14.5	20.2	2.1	6.8	5.7	2.3	2.8	3.4	DLR
DE SMET INS CO OF SD	SD	C-	13.5	7.2	3.5	-0.3	10.0	6.7	2.6	6.5	3.0	DR
DEALERS ASR CO	OH	B-	88.0	54.6	14.2	3.9	10.0	4.6	8.8	9.1	4.7	R
DEALERS CHOICE MUTUAL INS INC	NC	C-	26.3	6.1	6.0	-1.0	3.3	9.6	1.6	5.5	2.7	CDF
DEERFIELD INS CO	IL	C-	114.2	62.7	17.0	0.2	8.3	8.1	4.8	7.5	2.9	DRT
DELAWARE GRANGE MUTUAL FIRE INS CO	DE	D	1.5	1.2	0.2	0.0	8.7	6.1	6.1	8.8	1.1	DRT
DELAWARE PROFESSIONAL INS CO	DE	E+	7.3	2.3	1.2	-0.4	1.0	10.0	1.2	7.0	0.4	CDF
DELPHI CASUALTY CO	IL	D	7.1	1.9	4.1	-0.5	6.6	4.0	1.9	6.5	2.2	DT
DELTA FIRE & CAS INS CO	GA	C-	6.6	5.0	1.8	0.1	7.9	8.2	3.1	6.7	2.9	DFR
DELTA LLOYDS INS CO OF HOUSTON	TX	D	10.7	7.0	3.0	-0.6	8.2	7.9	3.6	6.9	1.7	DFRT
DENTISTS BENEFITS INS CO	OR	C	18.4	11.9	4.5	-0.1	8.9	6.4	4.7	7.2	3.6	D
DENTISTS INS CO	CA	B	332.8	178.1	54.4	5.7	9.3	9.0	6.8	7.1	5.5	T
DEPOSITORS INS CO	IA	B-	278.0	36.6	0.0	0.3	10.0	N/A	6.5	7.0	5.1	
DEVELOPERS SURETY & INDEMNITY CO	IA	B-	137.5	79.5	41.8	3.0	8.3	8.0	3.6	7.2	4.5	R
DIAMOND INS CO	IL	D-	46.0	7.3	17.7	-0.3	1.5	5.0	5.4	6.7	1.3	CDRT
DIAMOND STATE INS CO	IN	C-	124.5	58.9	17.3	-0.7	8.0	7.6	2.0	8.2	3.2	GR
DIRECT AUTO INS CO	IL	C	29.6	6.3	13.6	-0.6	3.2	7.1	5.7	6.9	2.5	CD
DIRECT GENERAL INS CO	IN	C+	399.1	117.3	308.4	7.9	6.7	3.2	5.3	0.8	4.2	FLR
DIRECT GENERAL INS CO OF LA	LA	C-	33.2	12.7	20.9	0.6	7.2	7.9	3.0	3.2	3.0	DFLR
DIRECT GENERAL INS CO OF MS	MS	C	33.8	12.5	23.1	0.8	7.4	6.7	3.4	2.9	3.4	DFLR
DIRECT INS CO	TN	C	79.3	27.3	54.6	2.3	6.3	6.7	6.0	2.7	4.0	FLR
DIRECT NATIONAL INS CO	AR	C+	17.1	7.2	11.5	0.5	7.1	5.9	3.9	4.3	3.9	DFLR
DISCOVER PROPERTY & CASUALTY INS CO	CT	C+	140.8	68.1	28.2	3.7	10.0	7.9	7.1	7.4	4.7	T
DISCOVER SPECIALTY INS CO	CT	C+	110.9	42.0	28.2	3.2	8.6	8.3	7.4	6.9	4.7	T
DISCOVERY INS CO	NC	D	25.3	10.7	14.3	0.5	2.5	7.0	3.2	1.8	2.0	DFL
DIST-CO INS CO INC RRG	HI	D	2.2	2.0	0.1	-0.1	10.0	3.6	3.6	10.0	0.6	DGT
DISTRIBUTORS INS CO	TN	C- (5)	0.0	0.0	2.9	0.0	7.5	6.9	4.7	7.0	3.2	DGT
DISTRICTS MUTUAL INS	WI	E+	23.8	14.0	5.1	1.6	8.2	9.5	8.8	7.3	0.7	D
▼DOCTORS & SURGEONS NATL RRG INC	KY	D-	11.0	1.2	5.3	-1.1	1.6	3.0	1.1	7.1	1.0	CDT
DOCTORS CO AN INTERINSURANCE EXCH	CA	B-	3,490.5	1,794.2	675.7	19.9	7.6	9.4	8.4	7.4	4.7	R
DOCTORS DIRECT INS INC	IL	C	14.0	6.4	2.4	0.2	7.9	9.4	6.7	7.0	2.5	DFR
DONEGAL MUTUAL INS CO	PA	B-	389.9	199.5	97.8	-0.7	6.8	5.1	6.8	6.6	4.7	
DONGBU INS CO LTD	HI	D	194.9	56.7	95.8	-14.1	5.0	4.8	2.8	6.4	1.8	GRT
DONGBU INS CO LTD US GUAM BRANCH	GU	B-	51.4	31.8	18.0	4.7	7.4	5.7	8.9	7.3	5.2	T
DORCHESTER INS CO LTD	VI	C	20.0	11.1	3.1	0.5	10.0	9.6	7.2	7.1	3.5	DR
DORCHESTER MUTUAL INS CO	MA	C	73.1	37.4	23.5	-1.0	8.3	6.2	6.2	6.8	4.2	R
DORINCO REINSURANCE CO	MI	D+	1,586.7	536.2	196.8	62.6	6.8	6.5	4.6	6.5	2.6	T
DR INS CO	KY	U (5)	0.0	0.0	0.0	0.0	N/A	0.0	0.0	0.0	0.0	
DRIVE NEW JERSEY INS CO	NJ	C+(3)	0.0	0.0	27.8	3.6	9.1	5.3	4.2	7.1	4.3	R
DRIVERS INS CO	NY	E- (2)	4.3	-0.2	3.1	-0.2	0.0	0.6	0.3	0.0	0.0	CDLR
DRYDEN MUTUAL INS CO	NY	C+	174.1	111.9	51.5	8.3	10.0	6.7	8.8	7.0	4.6	R

See Page 27 for explanation of footnotes and
Page 28 for explanation of stability factors.
Arrows denote recent upgrades ▲ or downgrades ▼   (see Section VII for explanations)

58

www.weissratings.com

RISK ADJ. CAPITAL RATIO #1	CAPITAL RATIO #2	PREMIUM TO SURPLUS (%)	RESV. TO SURPLUS (%)	RESV. DEVELOP. 1 YEAR (%)	RESV. DEVELOP. 2 YEAR (%)	LOSS RATIO (%)	EXP. RATIO (%)	COMB RATIO (%)	CASH FROM UNDER-WRITING (%)	NET PREMIUM GROWTH (%)	INVEST. IN AFFIL (%)	INSURANCE COMPANY NAME
1.3	0.9	102.8	211.9	-6.5	-2.5	78.9	8.6	87.5	76.0	2.4	0.0 ●	CYPRESS INS CO
1.0	0.7	156.8	59.9	-21.1	-36.6	39.0	57.5	96.5	91.0	-4.4	0.0	CYPRESS PROPERTY & CASUALTY INS
1.0	0.6	154.5	50.3	-11.6	-10.5	50.0	45.5	95.5	97.9	11.6	0.0	CYPRESS TEXAS LLOYDS
2.5	1.7	42.4	22.8	7.9	18.1	60.7	31.5	92.2	90.1	-7.8	0.0	DAILY UNDERWRITERS OF AMERICA
24.5	22.0	N/A	N/A	N/A	N/A	N/A	N/A	N/A	34.0	0.0	0.0	DAIRYLAND COUNTY MUTUAL INS CO OF
5.0	3.3	67.4	102.5	-2.7	-4.9	76.3	24.8	101.1	102.7	5.2	0.0 ●	DAIRYLAND INS CO
2.0	1.4	162.4	162.6	-2.1	-8.5	67.2	32.9	100.1	107.5	9.1	0.0	DAKOTA FIRE INS CO
2.2	1.7	76.2	104.7	2.6	5.4	73.9	20.8	94.7	97.2	-16.1	7.0	DAKOTA TRUCK UNDERWRITERS
2.1	1.4	62.9	24.1	-4.0	-10.9	52.8	51.3	104.1	89.1	5.7	0.0	DANBURY INS CO
4.3	3.8	20.0	29.3	-10.4	-3.4	72.9	88.8	161.7	30.9	-71.7	0.0	DANIELSON NATIONAL INS CO
2.9	2.2	27.0	49.1	-0.3	-3.6	67.8	24.8	92.6	121.7	-0.2	17.8 ●	DARWIN NATIONAL ASR CO
1.3	1.2	168.7	25.2	-1.7	2.7	76.6	27.3	103.9	105.2	2.0	29.8	DE SMET FARM MUTUAL INS CO OF SD
2.7	2.1	46.6	28.2	-3.4	-4.6	103.9	16.4	120.3	95.8	-7.9	0.0	DE SMET INS CO OF SD
11.0	7.2	27.9	0.1	-0.1	-1.1	8.2	33.7	41.9	259.8	21.8	0.0	DEALERS ASR CO
0.6	0.4	80.5	272.9	-13.7	-14.0	119.4	35.5	154.9	57.7	-1.3	0.0	DEALERS CHOICE MUTUAL INS INC
3.2	1.9	28.2	21.9	-7.6	-7.0	32.4	56.1	88.5	101.5	-21.6	0.0	DEERFIELD INS CO
3.4	2.1	19.7	1.8	-0.3	-0.3	29.9	33.9	63.8	156.4	-1.0	0.0	DELAWARE GRANGE MUTUAL FIRE INS
0.2	0.2	43.9	193.7	-17.0	-62.0	225.7	55.6	281.3	45.4	29.4	0.0	DELAWARE PROFESSIONAL INS CO
1.0	0.9	170.8	97.3	19.1	24.3	77.5	17.8	95.3	99.7	-12.1	0.0	DELPHI CASUALTY CO
1.8	1.6	34.3	7.2	-6.4	-5.0	26.1	92.5	118.6	79.6	-10.4	27.5	DELTA FIRE & CAS INS CO
3.2	2.0	37.1	10.6	1.4	-3.8	96.6	37.6	134.2	77.8	10.9	0.0	DELTA LLOYDS INS CO OF HOUSTON
3.1	2.1	38.0	29.3	-10.7	-6.3	34.5	49.5	84.0	113.7	-6.9	0.0	DENTISTS BENEFITS INS CO
4.1	2.5	31.3	41.5	-6.2	-9.1	73.8	26.9	100.7	111.5	8.3	0.0	DENTISTS INS CO
3.5	3.2	N/A	N/A	N/A	N/A	N/A	N/A	N/A	241.1	0.0	5.5	DEPOSITORS INS CO
2.5	1.8	55.1	22.7	-1.8	-2.5	28.7	64.3	93.0	103.8	7.6	17.1	DEVELOPERS SURETY & INDEMNITY CO
0.3	0.2	224.3	282.6	-10.3	-21.5	67.6	23.9	91.5	121.0	29.0	0.0	DIAMOND INS CO
3.2	2.3	33.5	74.6	0.3	-0.6	72.2	4.5	76.7	351.8	104.0	14.2	DIAMOND STATE INS CO
0.7	0.4	215.4	194.4	-68.5	-53.1	54.3	39.7	94.0	146.8	14.7	0.0	DIRECT AUTO INS CO
1.0	1.0	290.2	88.8	11.5	20.7	78.1	19.1	97.2	86.9	13.8	13.5	DIRECT GENERAL INS CO
1.4	1.2	173.8	82.2	3.2	-1.0	99.3	8.7	108.0	81.4	-11.5	0.0	DIRECT GENERAL INS CO OF LA
1.5	1.3	196.5	64.6	-11.0	-6.5	73.3	25.6	98.9	86.0	6.0	0.0	DIRECT GENERAL INS CO OF MS
1.2	1.1	219.1	67.8	-11.0	-6.2	66.3	26.1	92.4	78.7	7.0	0.0	DIRECT INS CO
1.6	1.3	168.7	57.5	-14.8	-15.1	66.6	29.9	96.5	84.7	-11.3	0.0	DIRECT NATIONAL INS CO
6.0	3.8	43.8	78.8	-1.1	-2.5	60.9	30.6	91.5	165.4	3.0	0.0	DISCOVER PROPERTY & CASUALTY INS
3.7	2.3	72.6	130.6	-1.8	-4.4	60.9	29.6	90.5	110.8	3.0	0.0	DISCOVER SPECIALTY INS CO
0.8	0.6	146.4	88.1	-14.6	-19.0	81.1	20.1	101.2	72.1	17.1	0.0	DISCOVERY INS CO
16.8	10.6	6.7	1.2	-0.1	N/A	18.4	147.0	165.4	124.6	257.0	0.0	DIST-CO INS CO INC RRG
2.6	1.4	25.2	43.3	N/A	-1.9	80.6	39.2	119.8	99.2	7.7	0.0	DISTRIBUTORS INS CO
3.7	2.4	41.0	50.1	-13.3	-26.7	72.3	27.6	99.9	111.4	22.4	0.0	DISTRICTS MUTUAL INS
0.2	0.1	250.0	232.1	11.0	21.6	73.5	41.2	114.7	120.3	8.4	0.0	DOCTORS & SURGEONS NATL RRG INC
1.8	1.4	39.0	68.0	-3.9	-8.2	75.1	21.1	96.2	133.7	13.3	23.3 ●	DOCTORS CO AN INTERINSURANCE
2.0	1.5	39.1	74.6	-14.4	-30.8	46.3	56.0	102.3	69.3	-4.7	0.0	DOCTORS DIRECT INS INC
1.0	0.9	47.8	23.8	0.7	0.8	59.2	26.4	85.6	144.1	15.4	65.8 ●	DONEGAL MUTUAL INS CO
0.9	0.7	175.1	63.7	21.1	8.7	69.3	30.1	99.4	140.3	44.9	0.0	DONGBU INS CO LTD
3.0	1.9	62.8	17.9	-2.8	-8.7	34.3	39.8	74.1	148.5	-1.0	0.0	DONGBU INS CO LTD US GUAM BRANCH
4.8	3.1	27.2	49.6	-11.4	-22.3	39.6	56.2	95.8	87.3	-7.0	0.0	DORCHESTER INS CO LTD
2.5	1.8	61.8	34.7	0.1	-0.1	59.7	37.4	97.1	103.4	6.2	8.4	DORCHESTER MUTUAL INS CO
1.3	1.1	37.2	157.2	-3.7	-0.7	72.9	15.0	87.9	165.0	-5.5	0.0 ●	DORINCO REINSURANCE CO
N/A	N/A	N/A	N/A	N/A	N/A	N/A	N/A	N/A	N/A	0.0	0.0	DR INS CO
2.9	2.4	84.9	65.4	-1.5	0.5	68.3	19.7	88.0	237.9	11.0	0.0	DRIVE NEW JERSEY INS CO
-0.0	-0.0	999 +	999 +	97.8	125.2	102.0	19.5	121.5	87.1	-7.2	0.0	DRIVERS INS CO
7.0	4.9	50.7	25.8	-2.0	-5.0	39.0	36.1	75.1	140.0	11.0	0.0	DRYDEN MUTUAL INS CO

999 + Denotes number greater than 999.9%
999 − Denotes number less than -999.99%
● Bullets denote a more detailed analysis is available in Section II.

INSURANCE COMPANY NAME	DOM. STATE	RATING	TOTAL ASSETS ($MIL)	CAPITAL & SURPLUS ($MIL)	ANNUAL NET PREMIUM ($MIL)	NET INCOME ($MIL)	CAPITAL-IZATION INDEX (PTS)	RESERVE ADQ INDEX (PTS)	PROFIT-ABILITY INDEX (PTS)	LIQUIDITY INDEX (PTS)	STAB. INDEX (PTS)	STABILITY FACTORS
DTRIC INS CO LTD	HI	C	103.3	25.7	41.4	-1.2	7.2	9.4	2.1	5.5	3.5	R
DTRIC INS UNDERWRITERS LTD	HI	C-	19.2	4.2	0.0	0.1	7.9	N/A	8.4	7.0	3.3	DRT
DUBOIS MEDICAL RRG	DC	D	11.4	8.3	1.1	0.5	8.4	6.0	9.0	9.2	2.3	D
EAGLE WEST INS CO	CA	C+	120.1	47.1	61.4	0.7	7.6	6.0	6.6	6.0	4.6	T
EAGLESTONE REINS CO	PA	B	5,539.9	1,993.2	0.5	55.9	7.7	4.7	7.6	7.8	4.4	FGT
EASTERN ADVANTAGE ASR CO	PA	C	40.9	12.1	16.0	0.6	5.0	4.5	8.8	6.6	3.4	CD
EASTERN ALLIANCE INS CO	PA	D	246.5	85.8	92.3	5.1	7.7	4.7	8.9	6.7	1.9	GR
EASTERN ATLANTIC INS CO	PA	C-	65.1	30.4	16.2	-2.5	8.3	9.1	3.2	8.7	3.2	DT
EASTERN DENTISTS INS CO RRG	VT	C-	51.9	21.5	10.4	1.3	7.4	10.0	8.7	7.3	3.2	D
EASTERN MUTUAL INS CO	NY	C	22.1	13.2	5.1	0.4	10.0	9.4	8.6	7.0	3.9	D
EASTGUARD INS CO	PA	D+	93.6	32.5	12.5	1.3	3.6	10.0	8.5	5.9	2.6	CGRT
ECHELON PROP & CAS INS CO	IL	D+	11.5	5.9	5.3	0.0	8.0	4.7	3.7	6.8	2.5	DGRT
ECOLE INS CO	AZ	B-	9.5	7.1	0.6	0.0	7.9	4.6	5.1	7.7	3.5	DT
ECONOMY FIRE & CAS CO	IL	B-	472.1	375.1	0.0	11.8	10.0	N/A	6.3	7.0	5.1	
ECONOMY PREFERRED INS CO	IL	B	32.8	10.4	0.0	0.2	9.6	N/A	7.9	7.0	4.9	DGT
ECONOMY PREMIER ASR CO	IL	B	85.1	45.5	0.0	1.2	10.0	N/A	8.1	7.0	5.7	
EDISON INS CO	FL	U	20.6	20.0	0.0	-0.3	N/A	1.3	2.6	10.0	2.0	FT
ELECTRIC INS CO	MA	C+	1,533.4	527.2	353.3	11.1	7.9	6.7	6.6	6.7	3.4	R
ELEMENTS PROPERTY INS CO	FL	B-	38.8	25.1	7.8	0.8	10.0	N/A	3.8	9.8	3.8	DT
ELEPHANT INS CO	VA	C	106.4	45.4	19.3	-13.2	7.7	4.6	2.3	9.0	3.4	FGT
ELITE TRANSPORTATION RRG INC	AZ	U	10.4	2.0	0.0	0.0	N/A	4.1	4.7	6.4	0.0	T
ELIZABETHTOWN INS CO	DE	U	3.8	3.5	0.0	0.0	N/A	6.9	3.8	10.0	4.2	FRT
ELLINGTON MUTUAL INS CO	WI	D+	5.5	3.0	2.0	-0.2	7.2	6.0	1.4	5.2	2.0	DFR
EMC PROPERTY & CASUALTY CO	IA	B-	160.0	77.1	47.3	1.6	10.0	8.2	6.6	6.8	4.8	T
EMC REINSURANCE CO	IA	C+	420.9	166.8	129.0	3.9	7.6	9.4	6.9	6.7	4.8	T
EMCASCO INS CO	IA	B-	443.0	118.8	182.3	2.8	7.8	9.3	5.9	6.4	4.8	T
EMERGENCY CAP MGMT LLC A RRG	DE	D	4.2	2.1	0.7	0.1	5.5	3.6	8.0	8.0	1.6	DT
EMERGENCY MEDICINE PROFESSIONAL	NV	D	23.9	7.5	4.6	0.4	5.7	6.0	5.6	7.8	2.0	DR
EMERGENCY MEDICINE RRG INC	SC	D-	8.5	4.4	2.4	0.1	3.0	6.0	2.7	6.9	0.9	T
EMERGENCY PHYSICIANS INS CO RRG	NV	D	35.0	10.7	5.1	0.3	2.1	4.6	6.3	8.3	1.9	DRT
EMPIRE BONDING & INS CO	NY	B-	2.6	1.8	0.5	0.1	10.0	3.6	7.0	9.9	3.5	DT
EMPIRE FIRE & MARINE INS CO	NE	C	94.2	48.8	0.0	0.5	10.0	N/A	3.8	7.0	4.1	FR
EMPIRE INDEMNITY INS CO	OK	C+	56.8	49.7	0.0	0.4	10.0	N/A	7.6	7.0	4.5	R
EMPIRE INS CO	NY	U	27.4	10.1	0.0	-0.7	N/A	8.3	1.4	10.0	1.6	CFRT
EMPLOYERS ASSURANCE CO	FL	C	598.0	199.7	67.8	3.5	8.6	9.2	6.7	7.1	3.3	R
EMPLOYERS COMPENSATION INS CO	CA	B	1,812.7	304.3	183.2	9.5	7.3	8.8	5.8	7.8	5.8	T
EMPLOYERS FIRE INS CO	PA	C	19.5	19.4	0.0	0.1	10.0	4.8	2.2	7.0	3.4	DFRT
EMPLOYERS INS CO OF NEVADA INC	NV	C	2,299.8	343.7	359.6	23.2	3.1	9.4	6.4	3.7	3.9	CFLR
EMPLOYERS INS OF WAUSAU	WI	B-	5,248.3	1,304.3	2,427.2	28.7	7.4	5.6	4.6	6.8	4.9	AG
EMPLOYERS MUTUAL CAS CO	IA	B-	2,711.2	1,151.9	845.0	14.9	7.9	8.6	6.3	6.6	4.8	R
EMPLOYERS PREFERRED INS CO	FL	C	717.9	257.6	67.8	1.7	7.3	8.4	6.7	7.0	3.3	RT
ENCOMPASS FLORIDIAN INDEMNITY CO	IL	C-	4.7	4.6	0.0	0.1	10.0	N/A	3.4	7.0	2.7	DFT
ENCOMPASS FLORIDIAN INS CO	IL	C-	4.7	4.6	0.0	0.1	10.0	N/A	3.4	10.0	2.9	DFT
ENCOMPASS HOME & AUTO INS CO	IL	B-	13.8	13.2	0.0	0.1	10.0	N/A	7.4	10.0	4.5	DGT
ENCOMPASS INDEMNITY CO	IL	B	27.7	25.2	0.0	0.3	10.0	N/A	6.3	10.0	5.5	D
ENCOMPASS INDEPENDENT INS CO	IL	B-	7.7	7.6	0.0	0.2	10.0	N/A	7.5	10.0	4.1	D
ENCOMPASS INS CO	IL	C	11.1	11.0	0.0	0.3	10.0	4.6	3.7	7.0	2.9	DT
ENCOMPASS INS CO OF AMERICA	IL	C	22.5	21.6	0.0	0.7	10.0	N/A	6.3	10.0	3.9	D
ENCOMPASS INS CO OF MA	MA	C-	6.9	6.8	0.0	0.1	10.0	N/A	7.1	10.0	2.9	D
ENCOMPASS INS CO OF NJ	IL	C	31.7	31.4	0.0	0.5	10.0	N/A	7.8	10.0	4.2	
ENCOMPASS PROP & CAS INS CO OF NJ	IL	C	14.2	14.0	0.0	0.3	10.0	N/A	7.8	10.0	3.4	D
ENCOMPASS PROPERTY & CASUALTY CO	IL	C+	11.3	10.4	0.0	0.3	10.0	N/A	4.7	7.0	4.4	D

See Page 27 for explanation of footnotes and Page 28 for explanation of stability factors.

60

www.weissratings.com

Arrows denote recent upgrades ▲ or downgrades ▼   (see Section VII for explanations)

RISK ADJ. CAPITAL RATIO #1	RATIO #2	PREMIUM TO SURPLUS (%)	RESV. TO SURPLUS (%)	RESV. DEVELOP. 1 YEAR (%)	2 YEAR (%)	LOSS RATIO (%)	EXP. RATIO (%)	COMB RATIO (%)	CASH FROM UNDER-WRITING (%)	NET PREMIUM GROWTH (%)	INVEST. IN AFFIL (%)	INSURANCE COMPANY NAME
1.6	1.0	155.8	124.9	-6.9	-15.6	81.0	35.5	116.5	99.6	22.9	6.1	DTRIC INS CO LTD
1.4	1.2	N/A	N/A	N/A	N/A	N/A	N/A	N/A	-44.0	0.0	0.0	DTRIC INS UNDERWRITERS LTD
6.9	4.2	13.6	21.1	-7.9	-34.7	26.2	19.7	45.9	240.5	-2.0	0.0	DUBOIS MEDICAL RRG
2.2	1.4	132.8	76.8	-3.8	1.1	65.1	32.6	97.7	108.3	11.0	0.0	EAGLE WEST INS CO
2.4	1.5	N/A	248.3	21.2	20.9	-198.0	999 +	999 +	N/A	-99.9	0.0 ●	EAGLESTONE REINS CO
0.9	0.5	139.9	96.1	6.3	12.2	70.8	23.1	93.9	99.1	6.1	0.0	EASTERN ADVANTAGE ASR CO
1.7	1.4	115.0	78.7	5.7	10.3	70.8	23.1	93.9	116.7	29.5	0.0	EASTERN ALLIANCE INS CO
2.3	1.4	51.1	45.5	-3.7	-10.8	58.6	33.4	92.0	124.5	36.8	0.0	EASTERN ATLANTIC INS CO
1.7	1.4	52.7	104.9	-15.9	-33.9	36.9	45.9	82.8	118.6	16.1	0.0	EASTERN DENTISTS INS CO RRG
4.3	3.1	39.9	31.2	-10.6	-9.8	35.3	38.5	73.8	130.3	1.5	0.4	EASTERN MUTUAL INS CO
0.5	0.4	38.1	87.8	-3.2	-62.0	66.3	24.4	90.7	159.2	368.4	2.8	EASTGUARD INS CO
1.4	1.1	90.8	24.3	2.2	-?.?	61.3	31.0	92.3	127.2	182.0	1.9	ECHELON PROP & CAS INS CO
1.8	1.5	8.9	4.7	2.3	-0.4	89.4	47.5	136.9	226.0	-30.9	0.0	ECOLE INS CO
6.9	6.2	N/A	N/A	N/A	N/A	N/A	N/A	N/A	-894.4	0.0	14.1 ●	ECONOMY FIRE & CAS CO
2.7	2.4	N/A	N/A	N/A	N/A	N/A	N/A	N/A	999 +	0.0	0.0	ECONOMY PREFERRED INS CO
8.0	7.2	N/A	N/A	N/A	N/A	N/A	N/A	N/A	N/A	0.0	0.0	ECONOMY PREMIER ASR CO
N/A	N/A	N/A	28.9	29.9	68.7	N/A	N/A	N/A	N/A	0.0	0.0	EDISON INS CO
3.1	1.8	67.6	153.3	-12.9	-21.3	79.8	19.0	98.8	93.8	-3.7	2.2 ●	ELECTRIC INS CO
4.2	3.1	32.4	0.6	N/A	N/A	26.2	20.4	46.6	528.0	0.0	0.0	ELEMENTS PROPERTY INS CO
1.3	1.0	37.8	13.0	0.4	-0.1	96.3	91.8	188.1	59.6	22.1	0.0	ELEPHANT INS CO
N/A	N/A	N/A	N/A	N/A	N/A	N/A	N/A	N/A	N/A	-100.0	0.0	ELITE TRANSPORTATION RRG INC
N/A	N/A	N/A	6.7	-5.9	-8.3	N/A	N/A	N/A	N/A	100.0	0.0	ELIZABETHTOWN INS CO
1.6	1.0	74.3	13.2	-4.8	1.7	97.5	46.0	143.5	67.7	14.7	0.0	ELLINGTON MUTUAL INS CO
5.4	3.7	63.0	63.1	-0.8	-3.1	67.2	32.9	100.1	107.5	9.1	0.0	EMC PROPERTY & CASUALTY CO
1.9	1.3	80.4	111.6	-4.5	-14.0	59.0	23.6	82.6	135.5	20.3	0.0	EMC REINSURANCE CO
2.1	1.4	158.8	159.0	-2.1	-8.7	67.2	32.9	100.1	107.5	9.1	0.0	EMCASCO INS CO
1.2	0.8	35.2	69.0	-7.3	N/A	81.6	10.8	92.4	522.9	-33.4	0.0	EMERGENCY CAP MGMT LLC A RRG
1.4	1.0	67.8	102.8	-46.3	-47.3	0.9	56.4	57.3	278.0	24.2	0.0	EMERGENCY MEDICINE PROFESSIONAL
0.5	0.4	50.1	91.9	19.2	10.4	72.5	28.7	101.2	100.6	39.1	0.0	EMERGENCY MEDICINE RRG INC
1.1	0.8	51.2	232.2	-36.2	-24.6	56.8	12.0	68.8	77.4	-49.6	0.0	EMERGENCY PHYSICIANS INS CO RRG
4.8	3.9	28.8	2.3	N/A	-0.3	5.3	52.5	57.8	188.8	6.9	0.0	EMPIRE BONDING & INS CO
7.8	7.0	N/A	N/A	N/A	N/A	N/A	N/A	N/A	125.3	0.0	0.0	EMPIRE FIRE & MARINE INS CO
25.8	23.2	N/A	N/A	N/A	N/A	N/A	N/A	N/A	999 +	0.0	0.0	EMPIRE INDEMNITY INS CO
N/A	N/A	N/A	148.5	-2.5	-4.1	999 +	999 +	999 +	N/A	-100.4	0.0	EMPIRE INS CO
3.9	2.9	34.5	80.7	0.5	-12.1	73.8	31.6	105.4	117.5	19.1	0.0 ●	EMPLOYERS ASSURANCE CO
2.2	1.6	61.3	143.4	0.6	-9.6	73.8	37.4	111.2	112.7	19.1	0.0 ●	EMPLOYERS COMPENSATION INS CO
152.6	76.3	N/A	N/A	N/A	N/A	N/A	N/A	N/A	N/A	-100.0	0.0	EMPLOYERS FIRE INS CO
0.8	0.7	114.3	267.3	1.2	-20.5	73.8	27.6	101.4	136.7	19.1	41.1 ●	EMPLOYERS INS CO OF NEVADA INC
1.8	1.2	189.1	215.7	5.3	5.7	73.5	25.8	99.3	215.4	132.4	3.5 ●	EMPLOYERS INS OF WAUSAU
2.0	1.6	75.3	77.3	-0.9	-4.3	66.7	32.4	99.1	102.9	9.3	21.2 ●	EMPLOYERS MUTUAL CAS CO
1.4	1.3	26.7	62.5	0.3	-7.2	73.8	33.5	107.3	121.0	19.1	39.4 ●	EMPLOYERS PREFERRED INS CO
252.0	159.4	N/A	N/A	N/A	N/A	N/A	N/A	N/A	N/A	0.0	0.0	ENCOMPASS FLORIDIAN INDEMNITY CO
240.4	120.3	N/A	N/A	N/A	N/A	N/A	N/A	N/A	N/A	0.0	0.0	ENCOMPASS FLORIDIAN INS CO
44.4	40.0	N/A	N/A	N/A	N/A	N/A	N/A	N/A	-33.6	0.0	0.0	ENCOMPASS HOME & AUTO INS CO
29.1	26.2	N/A	N/A	N/A	N/A	N/A	N/A	N/A	999 +	0.0	0.0	ENCOMPASS INDEMNITY CO
166.3	126.4	N/A	N/A	N/A	N/A	N/A	N/A	N/A	-187.7	0.0	0.0	ENCOMPASS INDEPENDENT INS CO
161.3	80.7	N/A	N/A	N/A	N/A	N/A	N/A	N/A	N/A	100.0	0.0	ENCOMPASS INS CO
48.0	43.2	N/A	N/A	N/A	N/A	N/A	N/A	N/A	-89.7	0.0	0.0	ENCOMPASS INS CO OF AMERICA
148.8	132.0	N/A	N/A	N/A	N/A	N/A	N/A	N/A	-240.4	0.0	0.0	ENCOMPASS INS CO OF MA
115.7	56.7	N/A	N/A	N/A	N/A	N/A	N/A	N/A	76.3	0.0	0.0	ENCOMPASS INS CO OF NJ
103.2	51.6	N/A	N/A	N/A	N/A	N/A	N/A	N/A	127.7	0.0	0.0	ENCOMPASS PROP & CAS INS CO OF NJ
27.8	25.0	N/A	N/A	N/A	N/A	N/A	N/A	N/A	-3.6	0.0	0.0	ENCOMPASS PROPERTY & CASUALTY

999 + Denotes number greater than 999.9%
999 - Denotes number less than -999.99%
● Bullets denote a more detailed analysis is available in Section II.

INSURANCE COMPANY NAME	DOM. STATE	RATING	TOTAL ASSETS ($MIL)	CAPITAL & SURPLUS ($MIL)	ANNUAL NET PREMIUM ($MIL)	NET INCOME ($MIL)	CAPITAL-IZATION INDEX (PTS)	RESERVE ADQ INDEX (PTS)	PROFIT-ABILITY INDEX (PTS)	LIQUIDITY INDEX (PTS)	STAB. INDEX (PTS)	STABILITY FACTORS
ENDEAVOUR INS CO	MA	C	5.7	5.7	0.0	0.1	10.0	N/A	7.9	7.0	3.6	DR
ENDURANCE AMERICAN INS CO	DE	C-	1,896.0	241.0	362.2	-3.9	5.0	6.3	2.8	2.0	2.9	FLR
ENDURANCE AMERICAN SPECIALTY INS CO	DE	C-	485.9	90.9	184.5	-1.7	4.9	6.3	2.6	1.3	2.9	FLR
ENDURANCE REINS CORP OF AMERICA	DE	B	1,568.6	648.9	263.2	13.3	7.7	7.9	4.5	7.0	5.5	A
ENDURANCE RISK SOLUTIONS ASR CO	DE	D+	337.9	61.2	136.7	-1.4	3.3	6.3	2.6	1.2	2.4	FLR
ENUMCLAW PROP & CAS INS CO	WA	C	8.3	7.8	0.0	0.1	10.0	N/A	6.5	7.6	2.8	DT
EQUITABLE LIABILITY INS CO	DC	D-	3.5	1.3	1.1	0.0	7.5	10.0	3.4	9.1	1.0	DFT
EQUITY INS CO	TX	C	77.2	30.0	41.9	0.1	7.8	6.4	4.3	6.5	3.2	R
ERIE & NIAGARA INS ASSOC	NY	C	174.6	114.3	57.3	7.5	10.0	6.0	8.8	6.9	3.6	R
ERIE INS CO	PA	B-	837.4	297.4	252.3	2.5	10.0	8.7	6.6	6.6	4.9	T
ERIE INS CO OF NY	NY	B	90.1	22.3	25.2	-0.3	8.3	8.9	4.7	6.5	5.1	D
ERIE INS EXCHANGE	PA	B	13,233.4	6,601.6	4,767.7	161.1	9.3	8.6	6.6	6.5	5.1	T
ERIE INS PROPERTY & CASUALTY CO	PA	B	96.1	11.7	0.0	0.2	7.5	N/A	7.8	7.0	4.6	D
ESSENT GUARANTY INC	PA	A-	767.9	456.7	169.8	81.4	10.0	3.6	3.9	9.1	5.7	GT
ESSENT GUARANTY OF PA INC	PA	B-	68.5	41.7	16.4	9.3	10.0	3.6	8.2	9.1	3.6	DGT
ESSENTIA INS CO	MO	C	60.3	30.1	0.0	0.1	10.0	4.6	1.4	9.5	3.5	AGRT
ESSEX INS CO	DE	C	1,353.3	453.4	414.7	50.8	6.1	9.7	8.1	6.8	3.8	AR
ESURANCE INS CO	WI	C	206.6	189.0	0.0	1.1	10.0	4.6	3.6	10.0	3.9	RT
ESURANCE INS CO OF NEW JERSEY	WI	D	14.8	11.5	0.0	0.0	10.0	4.6	3.2	7.0	1.4	DRT
ESURANCE PROP & CAS INS CO	CA	D-	91.4	29.2	0.0	0.3	10.0	4.6	2.0	6.5	1.1	RT
ETHIO AMERICAN INS CO	GA	E+	7.9	3.1	3.8	-1.0	8.4	4.6	2.8	8.1	0.4	D
EULER HERMES AMERICAN CREDIT IND CO	MD	B	428.5	152.3	88.6	25.5	9.3	4.8	3.8	6.9	5.4	R
EVANSTON INS CO	IL	C	2,395.2	628.8	642.2	40.0	6.2	9.7	5.4	7.1	3.8	AR
EVER-GREENE MUTUAL INS CO	PA	C	5.2	5.0	0.3	0.2	10.0	7.3	8.9	9.0	2.1	D
EVEREADY INS CO	NY	E- (3)	0.0	0.0	15.0	-0.8	0.0	0.5	0.2	0.0	0.0	CFLT
EVEREST INDEMNITY INS CO	DE	C	130.5	56.7	9.9	2.1	8.7	4.8	7.1	7.0	3.8	R
EVEREST NATIONAL INS CO	DE	C	992.6	130.9	79.5	22.8	8.6	3.4	2.3	6.1	4.0	FRT
EVEREST REINSURANCE CO	DE	C+	10,434.6	3,103.7	2,024.4	257.3	6.3	4.9	5.9	6.9	4.7	R
EVEREST SECURITY INS CO	GA	C	32.7	22.5	3.2	2.0	10.0	6.1	3.9	6.9	3.7	DR
EVERETT CASH MUTUAL INS CO	PA	C	104.8	52.3	48.4	5.3	7.9	8.9	8.8	6.4	4.2	R
EVERGREEN NATIONAL INDEMNITY CO	OH	C	46.6	32.9	12.4	0.4	9.8	8.6	6.4	9.1	3.1	FR
EVERGREEN USA RRG INC	VT	D+	14.7	6.3	4.0	-0.3	7.1	5.9	4.1	8.1	2.6	DR
EVERSPAN FINANCIAL GUARANTEE CORP	WI	U	219.8	216.6	0.0	3.2	N/A	7.3	7.9	7.0	5.9	T
EXACT PROPERTY & CASUALTY CO INC	CA	C+	271.2	112.2	136.4	14.3	8.6	8.2	6.3	6.3	4.7	FR
EXCALIBUR REINS CORP	PA	E-	18.6	0.1	0.7	-0.1	0.0	4.0	0.9	0.0	0.1	CDFL
EXCELA RECIPROCAL RRG	VT	U	4.3	2.1	0.0	0.1	N/A	N/A	4.9	7.0	2.6	T
EXCELSIOR INS CO	NH	C	37.3	34.5	0.0	0.6	10.0	N/A	2.9	5.3	4.2	FRT
EXCESS SHARE INS CORP	OH	C	50.6	20.7	1.4	0.1	10.0	8.6	5.2	9.4	3.1	D
EXECUTIVE INS CO	NY	U	2.3	2.2	0.0	-0.3	N/A	4.6	1.7	7.0	2.9	FT
EXECUTIVE RISK INDEMNITY INC	DE	B+	3,025.1	1,241.6	721.2	121.4	8.8	8.9	8.6	6.9	5.6	
EXECUTIVE RISK SPECIALTY INS CO	CT	B-	276.8	150.2	45.1	9.3	10.0	8.3	8.8	7.1	4.9	T
EXPLORER AMERICAN INS CO	CA	U	2.6	2.6	0.0	0.0	N/A	3.6	5.8	7.0	4.0	T
EXPLORER INS CO	CA	C	248.1	75.9	92.5	10.9	6.3	4.3	6.7	6.2	3.7	GR
FACILITY INS CORP	TX	U	115.8	92.8	0.0	1.7	N/A	N/A	5.0	8.0	5.4	FRT
FACTORY MUTUAL INS CO	RI	C	15,135.4	9,945.8	2,824.5	467.8	8.3	6.5	7.4	6.7	3.4	R
FAIR AMERICAN INS & REINS CO	NY	B	257.2	235.4	3.6	3.7	10.0	6.1	5.1	10.0	5.2	T
FAIR AMERICAN SELECT INS CO	DE	U	49.0	46.9	0.0	0.6	N/A	N/A	4.9	7.0	5.4	T
FAIRMONT FARMERS MUTUAL INS CO	MN	C	25.5	13.5	12.1	0.5	8.7	7.9	6.1	6.6	3.4	D
FAIRMONT INS CO	CA	U	26.6	14.1	0.0	0.4	N/A	4.4	3.8	9.0	3.8	FT
FAIRMONT PREMIER INS CO	CA	U	133.0	113.4	0.0	0.5	N/A	5.9	5.3	7.5	6.2	FT
FAIRMONT SPECIALTY INS CO	CA	U	151.2	86.2	0.0	3.2	N/A	4.5	4.4	9.7	6.1	FT
FAIRWAY PHYSICIANS INS CO RRG	DC	D-	25.3	5.5	11.2	0.1	1.0	1.1	3.3	6.0	0.9	CDR

See Page 27 for explanation of footnotes and Page 28 for explanation of stability factors.
Arrows denote recent upgrades ▲ or downgrades ▼   (see Section VII for explanations)

62

www.weissratings.com

RISK ADJ. RATIO #1	CAPITAL RATIO #2	PREMIUM TO SURPLUS (%)	RESV. TO SURPLUS (%)	RESV. DEVELOP. 1 YEAR (%)	RESV. DEVELOP. 2 YEAR (%)	LOSS RATIO (%)	EXP. RATIO (%)	COMB RATIO (%)	CASH FROM UNDER- WRITING (%)	NET PREMIUM GROWTH (%)	INVEST. IN AFFIL (%)	INSURANCE COMPANY NAME
75.8	33.9	N/A	N/A	N/A	N/A	N/A	N/A	N/A	N/A	0.0	0.0	ENDEAVOUR INS CO
1.2	0.8	146.3	89.0	0.3	-0.3	94.4	18.5	112.9	87.5	1.2	20.1 •	ENDURANCE AMERICAN INS CO
0.9	0.5	198.8	120.9	0.4	-0.4	94.4	18.3	112.7	83.9	1.2	0.0	ENDURANCE AMERICAN SPECIALTY INS
1.9	1.6	41.8	83.4	-4.0	-2.1	51.2	41.2	92.4	92.6	9.8	26.2 •	ENDURANCE REINS CORP OF AMERICA
0.8	0.5	217.5	132.3	0.5	-0.4	94.4	18.5	112.9	87.0	1.2	0.0	ENDURANCE RISK SOLUTIONS ASR CO
35.0	31.5	N/A	N/A	N/A	N/A	N/A	N/A	N/A	62.5	0.0	0.0	ENUMCLAW PROP & CAS INS CO
1.8	1.6	88.6	162.6	-19.5	-57.4	64.6	33.0	97.6	90.9	-6.2	0.0	EQUITABLE LIABILITY INS CO
1.6	1.4	140.8	62.9	-1.6	1.7	89.3	13.1	102.4	89.8	10.9	0.0	EQUITY INS CO
6.7	4.5	53.8	16.6	-1.1	-1.7	39.2	39.7	78.9	132.2	6.3	0.1	ERIE & NIAGARA INS ASSOC
4.8	3.2	85.7	61.0	-0.7	-2.7	69.4	28.2	97.6	107.5	9.6	4.2 •	ERIE INS CO
2.6	1.7	114.6	83.5	-0.9	-3.5	69.4	28.2	97.6	107.6	9.6	0.0	ERIE INS CO OF NY
3.7	2.5	73.7	52.5	0.6	-2.0	69.4	28.2	97.6	106.9	9.6	5.5 •	ERIE INS EXCHANGE
1.4	1.2	N/A	N/A	N/A	N/A	N/A	N/A	N/A	N/A	0.0	0.0	ERIE INS PROPERTY & CASUALTY CO
8.1	5.4	49.0	0.8	-0.4	N/A	1.9	37.9	39.8	272.0	154.1	0.1 •	ESSENT GUARANTY INC
7.7	4.5	47.4	0.9	-0.5	N/A	2.0	23.5	25.5	401.2	180.6	0.0	ESSENT GUARANTY OF PA INC
6.5	5.8	N/A	N/A	N/A	N/A	N/A	N/A	N/A	-36.1	100.0	0.0	ESSENTIA INS CO
1.4	0.9	107.6	147.9	-26.7	-44.7	36.5	39.9	76.4	118.4	16.3	0.0 •	ESSEX INS CO
5.0	4.8	N/A	N/A	N/A	N/A	N/A	N/A	N/A	-57.2	100.0	24.8	ESURANCE INS CO
10.7	9.6	N/A	N/A	N/A	N/A	N/A	N/A	N/A	N/A	0.0	0.0	ESURANCE INS CO OF NEW JERSEY
4.0	3.6	N/A	N/A	N/A	N/A	N/A	N/A	N/A	459.5	0.0	0.0	ESURANCE PROP & CAS INS CO
2.1	1.6	92.1	67.6	4.9	0.2	75.0	33.8	108.8	99.4	14.9	0.0	ETHIO AMERICAN INS CO
4.0	3.0	64.4	44.9	-5.3	-17.2	48.1	38.0	86.1	129.6	2.7	0.0	EULER HERMES AMERICAN CREDIT IND
1.2	0.8	111.9	193.0	-13.2	-24.6	48.7	42.5	91.2	116.6	42.4	0.0 •	EVANSTON INS CO
54.0	29.6	6.4	0.4	-0.4	-0.4	3.0	10.9	13.9	687.1	0.8	0.0	EVER-GREENE MUTUAL INS CO
0.0	0.0	999 +	999 +	343.8	111.8	73.6	30.1	103.7	91.3	0.3	0.0	EVEREADY INS CO
7.2	6.5	18.2	N/A	0.9	7.0	43.3	75.2	118.5	167.3	-50.3	0.0	EVEREST INDEMNITY INS CO
7.9	7.0	74.1	N/A	14.7	17.8	98.5	33.3	131.8	47.1	-9.5	0.0	EVEREST NATIONAL INS CO
1.1	0.9	71.9	151.5	3.5	5.7	59.5	24.6	84.1	106.0	28.0	30.3 •	EVEREST REINSURANCE CO
9.1	8.2	15.5	N/A	1.6	-0.3	82.3	-21.6	60.7	108.6	-14.9	0.0	EVEREST SECURITY INS CO
2.2	1.6	100.9	42.0	1.2	-3.6	54.7	30.2	84.9	135.5	17.2	9.7	EVERETT CASH MUTUAL INS CO
3.0	2.4	36.5	10.2	-5.5	-7.2	-1.4	72.6	71.2	93.4	3.9	0.0	EVERGREEN NATIONAL INDEMNITY CO
1.2	1.0	59.7	97.3	-4.6	-9.4	58.4	47.8	106.2	121.9	8.8	0.0	EVERGREEN USA RRG INC
N/A	N/A	N/A	N/A	-0.1	-0.1	-25.0	999 +	999 +	-2.1	84.3	0.0	EVERSPAN FINANCIAL GUARANTEE
4.0	2.9	126.6	73.7	0.2	-1.0	67.1	34.1	101.2	97.7	-1.6	0.0	EXACT PROPERTY & CASUALTY CO INC
0.0	0.0	301.2	999 +	318.2	-223.9	730.1	-254.5	475.6	7.0	-20.6	0.0	EXCALIBUR REINS CORP
N/A	N/A	N/A	N/A	N/A	N/A	N/A	N/A	N/A	N/A	0.0	0.0	EXCELA RECIPROCAL RRG
36.6	33.0	N/A	N/A	N/A	N/A	N/A	N/A	N/A	87.4	0.0	0.0	EXCELSIOR INS CO
4.6	4.1	6.6	10.1	-5.7	-7.6	6.2	105.7	111.9	92.3	4.5	0.0	EXCESS SHARE INS CORP
N/A	N/A	N/A	N/A	N/A	N/A	N/A	N/A	N/A	N/A	0.0	0.0	EXECUTIVE INS CO
3.3	2.3	59.2	106.2	-3.9	-6.5	52.7	29.9	82.6	110.9	3.9	5.2 •	EXECUTIVE RISK INDEMNITY INC
5.3	3.4	31.9	57.3	-2.1	-3.7	52.7	29.9	82.6	107.6	3.9	0.0	EXECUTIVE RISK SPECIALTY INS CO
N/A	N/A	N/A	N/A	N/A	N/A	N/A	N/A	N/A	N/A	0.0	0.0	EXPLORER AMERICAN INS CO
1.3	0.9	148.3	171.0	-4.0	8.3	61.1	23.1	84.2	165.5	40.1	0.0	EXPLORER INS CO
N/A	N/A	N/A	30.0	N/A	N/A	999 +	999 +	999 +	0.1	-30.5	0.0	FACILITY INS CORP
2.5	1.9	30.9	21.0	2.2	0.1	50.6	27.6	78.2	123.0	-1.1	17.8 •	FACTORY MUTUAL INS CO
5.4	5.1	1.6	0.6	N/A	0.7	78.6	72.1	150.7	154.6	-94.6	19.7 •	FAIR AMERICAN INS & REINS CO
N/A	N/A	N/A	N/A	N/A	N/A	N/A	N/A	N/A	N/A	0.0	0.0	FAIR AMERICAN SELECT INS CO
2.8	2.0	94.4	18.0	-5.2	-5.6	61.7	34.5	96.2	115.5	13.3	0.0	FAIRMONT FARMERS MUTUAL INS CO
N/A	N/A	N/A	87.8	-5.1	-3.3	999 +	999 +	999 +	1.7	99.8	3.8	FAIRMONT INS CO
N/A	N/A	N/A	17.6	-1.0	-0.7	999 +	999 +	999 +	1.7	99.8	76.2	FAIRMONT PREMIER INS CO
N/A	N/A	N/A	78.3	-4.4	-3.0	999 +	999 +	999 +	1.7	99.8	8.7	FAIRMONT SPECIALTY INS CO
0.4	0.3	212.8	292.2	-5.0	-47.3	92.4	29.6	122.0	92.7	8.0	0.0	FAIRWAY PHYSICIANS INS CO RRG

999 + Denotes number greater than 999.9%
999 - Denotes number less than -999.99%
• Bullets denote a more detailed analysis is available in Section II.

INSURANCE COMPANY NAME	DOM. STATE	RATING	TOTAL ASSETS ($MIL)	CAPITAL & SURPLUS ($MIL)	ANNUAL NET PREMIUM ($MIL)	NET INCOME ($MIL)	CAPITAL-IZATION INDEX (PTS)	RESERVE ADQ INDEX (PTS)	PROFIT-ABILITY INDEX (PTS)	LIQUIDITY INDEX (PTS)	STAB. INDEX (PTS)	STABILITY FACTORS
FAITH AFFILIATED RRG INC	VT	E+	9.6	5.3	1.2	0.2	2.5	3.9	3.7	7.5	0.5	D
FALCON INS CO	IL	D+	12.9	7.3	2.2	-0.7	9.7	N/A	2.9	8.9	2.7	DGT
FALLS LAKE GENERAL INS CO	OH	C	6.0	4.1	0.7	0.0	10.0	7.8	7.2	6.9	2.9	DFGT
FALLS LAKE NATIONAL INS CO	OH	C	252.5	49.2	9.2	0.2	7.3	6.0	4.7	0.0	3.4	FGLT
FAMILY SECURITY INS CO	HI	D+	20.9	7.6	5.7	-1.4	7.1	N/A	2.5	8.1	2.7	DGT
FARM BU TOWN & COUNTRY INS CO OF MO	MO	B	330.8	138.4	168.4	7.7	8.2	6.5	6.2	5.1	6.0	L
FARM BUREAU CNTY MUTUAL INS CO OF	TX	C	19.7	5.8	0.0	0.0	8.3	N/A	3.6	7.0	3.6	D
FARM BUREAU GENERAL INS CO OF MI	MI	B	536.3	168.9	286.4	-2.3	8.8	6.2	4.6	5.6	6.3	G
FARM BUREAU INS OF NC INC	NC	B	9.4	9.1	0.0	0.1	10.0	N/A	7.1	7.0	4.5	D
FARM BUREAU MUTUAL INS CO OF AR	AR	C+	351.2	180.4	194.5	6.9	8.5	6.7	5.9	5.8	4.5	T
FARM BUREAU MUTUAL INS CO OF ID	ID	B+	431.4	236.4	151.7	2.3	9.6	6.0	4.5	6.5	5.0	
FARM BUREAU MUTUAL INS CO OF MI	MI	B-	650.9	275.7	286.9	10.5	8.7	6.6	4.7	5.8	5.0	
FARM BUREAU NEW HORIZONS INS CO MO	MO	D	39.7	16.4	25.7	0.6	5.7	7.9	3.4	6.1	1.8	DGT
FARM BUREAU PROP & CAS INS CO	IA	A-	2,012.0	801.5	1,127.9	-4.1	9.2	8.2	6.8	5.7	7.2	
FARM CREDIT SYS ASSOC CAPTIVE INS CO	CO	B-	103.1	80.7	15.7	11.8	10.0	9.3	8.9	7.9	5.2	D
FARM FAMILY CASUALTY INS CO	NY	B+	1,067.1	359.7	371.1	13.4	9.0	9.4	6.0	6.7	6.7	
FARMERS & MECH MU I ASN OF CECIL CTY	MD	D	1.1	0.5	0.4	-0.1	7.3	7.5	1.4	6.9	1.0	DFRT
FARMERS & MECH MUTUAL INS CO	PA	B	5.2	4.2	0.3	0.1	8.4	4.6	5.7	8.2	4.5	AD
FARMERS & MECHANICS FIRE & CAS INS	WV	D	10.5	3.7	5.2	0.5	4.4	4.1	3.4	5.8	1.6	DR
FARMERS & MECHANICS MUTUAL IC OF WV	WV	B-	58.4	41.3	20.1	1.9	9.9	4.8	8.8	6.8	4.9	DR
FARMERS & MERCHANTS MUTUAL FIRE I C	MI	C	26.6	21.1	3.5	0.5	9.5	6.2	6.6	7.0	4.0	DFR
FARMERS ALLIANCE MUTUAL INS CO	KS	C	281.3	144.0	123.7	1.0	10.0	7.9	4.0	6.5	4.2	R
FARMERS AUTOMOBILE INS ASN	IL	B+	1,172.9	487.8	428.5	-10.9	8.6	9.3	4.5	6.5	6.0	
FARMERS FIRE INS CO	PA	C	25.4	13.1	13.1	-0.6	7.4	6.0	2.5	6.8	3.4	DR
FARMERS INS CO INC	KS	C+	284.2	102.9	102.3	1.5	10.0	6.4	4.4	6.5	4.7	R
FARMERS INS CO OF AZ	AZ	C+	40.1	4.0	0.0	-0.1	5.2	N/A	3.5	2.0	3.3	CDFL
FARMERS INS CO OF FLEMINGTON	NJ	C+(3)	0.0	0.0	20.1	3.1	6.8	6.0	5.0	6.9	4.4	DF
FARMERS INS CO OF ID	ID	C+	188.6	69.0	102.3	0.7	9.0	8.2	4.4	6.4	4.8	R
FARMERS INS CO OF OR	OR	B	1,602.5	503.5	954.6	12.2	8.2	6.8	3.7	5.9	5.4	R
FARMERS INS CO OF WA	WA	B-	520.7	193.0	272.7	3.6	9.1	8.1	5.2	6.3	4.9	R
FARMERS INS EXCHANGE	CA	C	15,807.4	3,822.9	7,057.1	-31.1	5.7	6.5	3.8	3.8	3.4	FLR
FARMERS INS HAWAII INC	HI	B	92.0	83.9	0.0	1.1	10.0	6.0	8.0	10.0	5.6	F
FARMERS INS OF COLUMBUS INC	OH	B-	256.4	96.7	136.4	1.3	9.2	8.1	4.8	6.4	4.9	R
FARMERS MUTUAL F I C OF BRANCH CTY	MI	E+	1.5	1.0	0.8	-0.1	7.1	6.5	3.4	6.7	0.5	DFRT
FARMERS MUTUAL F I C OF MCCANDLESS	PA	C-	8.9	4.5	4.4	0.4	7.1	6.8	8.2	7.2	2.2	DR
FARMERS MUTUAL F I C OF OKARCHE OK	OK	C	17.1	11.3	9.0	2.6	8.1	5.9	3.4	5.7	2.8	DF
FARMERS MUTUAL F I C OF SALEM CTY	NJ	C	131.0	62.5	33.4	1.4	9.5	9.4	8.7	6.9	4.0	R
FARMERS MUTUAL FIRE INS CO OF	PA	C-	27.1	16.7	8.2	1.0	8.2	9.3	8.8	7.0	3.3	DR
FARMERS MUTUAL HAIL INS CO OF IA	IA	B-	844.6	311.5	431.1	-40.4	7.4	6.3	3.7	5.5	4.6	R
FARMERS MUTUAL INS CO	WV	C	13.7	9.0	5.2	0.7	10.0	4.6	8.7	7.5	2.8	DR
FARMERS MUTUAL INS CO OF ELLINWOOD	KS	E	3.1	1.1	2.3	0.0	4.5	4.8	1.1	0.7	0.1	DFLR
FARMERS MUTUAL INS CO OF NE	NE	B	506.0	281.5	264.9	-15.6	10.0	8.1	4.4	6.7	6.2	
FARMERS MUTUAL OF TENNESSEE	TN	C	21.5	12.9	9.1	-0.2	7.7	6.0	3.4	6.9	3.4	DR
FARMERS NEW CENTURY INS CO	IL	C+	185.3	69.0	102.3	0.7	9.0	8.2	4.7	6.4	4.7	R
FARMERS REINS CO	CA	B-	1,445.7	980.3	517.6	30.3	10.0	4.7	3.7	6.7	4.9	FT
FARMERS SPECIALTY INS CO	MI	B-	16.4	16.4	0.0	0.0	10.0	N/A	6.3	10.0	3.9	DFT
FARMERS TEXAS COUNTY MUTUAL INS CO	TX	C+	139.3	42.9	0.0	2.1	10.0	N/A	8.9	6.2	4.6	FR
FARMERS UNION MUTUAL INS CO	MT	C+	50.3	30.3	17.0	0.5	8.9	6.0	4.0	6.7	4.5	DFR
FARMERS UNION MUTUAL INS CO	ND	C	97.6	54.7	54.0	3.2	9.9	8.0	8.8	6.6	4.1	R
FARMERS UNION MUTUAL INS CO	AR	E	3.6	1.4	2.6	-0.7	3.1	6.0	0.5	6.4	0.3	DGT
FARMINGTON CASUALTY CO	CT	B	1,040.3	319.3	298.1	31.8	7.8	8.8	7.4	6.8	6.0	T
FARMINGTON MUTUAL INS CO	WI	D	6.8	5.9	1.1	0.0	8.9	6.4	6.2	8.0	1.9	DR

See Page 27 for explanation of footnotes and Page 28 for explanation of stability factors.

Arrows denote recent upgrades ▲ or downgrades ▼   (see Section VII for explanations)

64

www.weissratings.com

RISK ADJ. CAPITAL RATIO #1	RATIO #2	PREMIUM TO SURPLUS (%)	RESV. TO SURPLUS (%)	RESV. DEVELOP. 1 YEAR (%)	2 YEAR (%)	LOSS RATIO (%)	EXP. RATIO (%)	COMB RATIO (%)	CASH FROM UNDER-WRITING (%)	NET PREMIUM GROWTH (%)	INVEST. IN AFFIL (%)	INSURANCE COMPANY NAME
0.8	0.5	24.4	74.4	1.6	-3.0	100.4	25.1	125.5	130.1	5.9	0.0	FAITH AFFILIATED RRG INC
3.0	2.1	27.2	5.1	N/A	N/A	69.3	41.1	110.4	129.8	0.0	0.0	FALCON INS CO
4.8	3.4	17.5	35.3	-4.9	-7.1	36.7	28.9	65.6	107.4	0.0	0.0	FALLS LAKE GENERAL INS CO
1.2	1.1	19.4	39.2	-5.9	-44.5	36.7	28.9	65.6	5.1	0.0	83.9	FALLS LAKE NATIONAL INS CO
1.4	0.9	75.1	4.9	N/A	N/A	60.7	40.7	101.4	199.3	0.0	0.0	FAMILY SECURITY INS CO
2.7	1.8	128.6	49.3	3.2	-2.1	68.8	21.4	90.2	116.7	1.4	3.1	FARM BU TOWN & COUNTRY INS CO OF
2.0	1.8	N/A	N/A	N/A	N/A	N/A	N/A	N/A	N/A	0.0	0.0	FARM BUREAU CNTY MUTUAL INS CO OF
2.9	2.1	168.2	75.9	-1.7	1.0	74.8	24.3	99.1	121.0	56.9	0.0	FARM BUREAU GENERAL INS CO OF MI
83.1	51.6	N/A	N/A	N/A	N/A	N/A	N/A	N/A	N/A	0.0	0.0	FARM BUREAU INS OF NC INC
4.0	2.7	112.6	16.6	-5.2	-1.2	55.3	19.6	74.9	129.6	4.2	0.4	FARM BUREAU MUTUAL INS CO OF AR
3.2	2.6	65.1	29.5	0.6	2.3	78.2	25.2	103.4	98.7	10.4	16.0 ●	FARM BUREAU MUTUAL INS CO OF ID
3.8	2.5	109.1	80.3	-2.7	-2.5	69.8	31.4	101.2	94.6	-15.1	0.0 ●	FARM BUREAU MUTUAL INS CO OF MI
1.4	0.8	163.3	32.8	-17.8	-3.1	30.7	42.2	72.9	129.1	-25.1	0.0	FARM BUREAU NEW HORIZONS INS CO
3.3	2.5	140.6	61.5	-2.2	-2.5	70.2	25.4	95.6	108.1	7.1	5.1 ●	FARM BUREAU PROP & CAS INS CO
18.9	11.5	21.0	32.7	-5.8	-11.0	50.7	6.6	57.3	187.6	0.9	0.0	FARM CREDIT SYS ASSOC CAPTIVE INS
3.5	2.3	106.9	133.1	-5.9	-9.3	72.1	28.5	100.6	104.6	5.2	0.0 ●	FARM FAMILY CASUALTY INS CO
1.7	1.1	71.3	17.2	-3.6	-1.7	60.1	68.6	128.7	74.9	-4.8	0.0	FARMERS & MECH MU I ASN OF CECIL
3.1	1.9	6.6	2.3	-0.2	N/A	83.2	21.0	104.2	93.3	-1.4	0.0	FARMERS & MECH MUTUAL INS CO
0.8	0.6	158.3	68.0	11.9	11.1	84.3	33.0	117.3	100.2	10.7	0.0	FARMERS & MECHANICS FIRE & CAS INS
3.9	2.9	51.5	10.6	0.7	2.3	50.9	34.3	85.2	128.8	4.2	6.5	FARMERS & MECHANICS MUTUAL IC OF
4.3	2.6	17.1	2.8	-0.4	-1.0	47.2	50.4	97.6	93.0	5.7	0.0	FARMERS & MERCHANTS MUTUAL FIRE I
4.3	3.4	85.9	31.8	-4.8	-3.4	69.4	30.8	100.2	97.6	2.7	6.2	FARMERS ALLIANCE MUTUAL INS CO
2.2	1.9	86.1	66.1	-4.3	-10.2	75.4	27.9	103.3	104.4	6.6	21.5 ●	FARMERS AUTOMOBILE INS ASN
1.7	1.1	92.1	24.2	-1.8	-2.0	51.1	41.5	92.6	108.9	13.9	0.0	FARMERS FIRE INS CO
4.7	3.4	100.9	61.7	N/A	0.4	66.9	34.4	101.3	99.2	-1.6	0.0	FARMERS INS CO INC
0.7	0.6	N/A	N/A	N/A	N/A	N/A	N/A	N/A	130.8	0.0	0.0	FARMERS INS CO OF AZ
1.8	1.1	82.6	87.3	-36.1	-46.1	55.1	38.4	93.5	94.1	-5.3	0.0	FARMERS INS CO OF FLEMINGTON
3.3	2.4	149.7	87.1	0.2	-0.9	67.1	34.1	101.2	101.0	-1.6	0.0	FARMERS INS CO OF ID
2.5	1.8	194.7	117.5	-0.2	0.1	66.8	34.1	100.9	97.3	-1.6	0.0 ●	FARMERS INS CO OF OR
3.4	2.5	144.0	83.9	-0.1	-1.0	66.9	34.1	101.0	99.3	-1.6	0.0	FARMERS INS CO OF WA
0.8	0.8	181.9	114.3	-0.1	1.8	66.8	34.4	101.2	95.7	-1.6	42.8 ●	FARMERS INS EXCHANGE
7.8	7.3	N/A	3.8	0.4	1.9	N/A	N/A	N/A	0.2	0.0	12.3	FARMERS INS HAWAII INC
3.5	2.5	142.9	83.2	0.2	-0.9	67.1	34.1	101.2	99.7	-1.6	0.0	FARMERS INS OF COLUMBUS INC
1.2	0.9	67.6	0.9	2.8	1.4	50.4	47.2	97.6	72.0	25.8	0.0	FARMERS MUTUAL F I C OF BRANCH
1.7	1.1	110.1	25.3	-2.1	-6.7	36.5	32.4	68.9	140.4	6.9	0.0	FARMERS MUTUAL F I C OF
3.5	2.2	102.3	7.6	-2.3	1.4	67.9	35.2	103.1	89.8	17.8	0.0	FARMERS MUTUAL F I C OF OKARCHE
4.1	2.6	55.3	59.7	-8.8	-11.4	48.8	34.5	83.3	123.7	20.2	0.1	FARMERS MUTUAL F I C OF SALEM CTY
3.0	1.9	50.7	16.2	-5.5	-10.8	41.1	32.8	73.9	130.0	4.1	0.0	FARMERS MUTUAL FIRE INS CO OF
1.4	0.9	120.3	80.7	-4.2	-1.7	85.9	16.7	102.6	109.7	-8.4	3.2 ●	FARMERS MUTUAL HAIL INS CO OF IA
4.8	3.2	62.0	5.9	0.3	N/A	28.1	52.9	81.0	138.3	0.5	0.0	FARMERS MUTUAL INS CO
0.8	0.6	224.1	8.1	15.6	20.5	66.2	44.5	110.7	80.0	7.5	11.5	FARMERS MUTUAL INS CO OF
4.4	3.2	90.3	19.9	-2.6	-6.1	67.1	26.3	93.4	114.7	18.0	0.0 ●	FARMERS MUTUAL INS CO OF NE
1.9	1.2	68.0	8.2	-1.4	2.3	53.4	35.7	89.1	108.9	26.5	0.3	FARMERS MUTUAL OF TENNESSEE
3.3	2.4	149.7	87.1	-0.1	-0.9	66.9	34.1	101.0	102.5	-1.6	0.0	FARMERS NEW CENTURY INS CO
14.3	9.6	54.5	28.4	0.1	N/A	68.9	31.7	100.6	86.3	-34.5	0.0 ●	FARMERS REINS CO
222.3	111.2	N/A	N/A	N/A	N/A	N/A	N/A	N/A	-136.0	0.0	0.0	FARMERS SPECIALTY INS CO
4.8	4.3	N/A	N/A	N/A	N/A	N/A	N/A	N/A	-301.5	0.0	0.0	FARMERS TEXAS COUNTY MUTUAL INS
3.6	2.3	57.4	32.4	-2.9	-0.4	70.0	35.8	105.8	93.8	10.2	2.7	FARMERS UNION MUTUAL INS CO
3.6	3.1	101.8	21.3	-3.3	-4.6	69.1	24.9	94.0	114.2	8.9	0.0	FARMERS UNION MUTUAL INS CO
0.5	0.4	136.8	14.1	12.4	-83.0	109.0	34.7	143.7	84.1	49.9	0.0	FARMERS UNION MUTUAL INS CO
2.7	1.7	103.7	186.6	-2.7	-6.2	60.9	29.7	90.6	114.5	3.0	0.1 ●	FARMINGTON CASUALTY CO
3.7	2.3	20.9	1.0	-0.7	-1.9	30.1	37.2	67.3	138.5	0.3	0.0	FARMINGTON MUTUAL INS CO

999 + Denotes number greater than 999.9%
999 - Denotes number less than -999.99%
● Bullets denote a more detailed analysis is available in Section II.

INSURANCE COMPANY NAME	DOM. STATE	RATING	TOTAL ASSETS ($MIL)	CAPITAL & SURPLUS ($MIL)	ANNUAL NET PREMIUM ($MIL)	NET INCOME ($MIL)	CAPITAL-IZATION INDEX (PTS)	RESERVE ADQ INDEX (PTS)	PROFIT-ABILITY INDEX (PTS)	LIQUIDITY INDEX (PTS)	STAB. INDEX (PTS)	STABILITY FACTORS
FARMLAND MUTUAL INS CO	IA	B	504.2	166.5	176.8	-0.2	10.0	7.8	5.1	6.8	5.9	A
FB INS CO	KY	U	1.3	1.3	0.0	0.0	N/A	4.7	2.7	7.0	2.7	T
FCCI ADVANTAGE INS CO	FL	C+	6.9	6.1	0.0	0.1	10.0	N/A	6.2	9.5	3.8	DR
FCCI COMMERCIAL INS CO	FL	C-	14.0	16.9	0.0	0.1	10.0	N/A	5.7	8.8	3.2	DR
FCCI INS CO	FL	C+	1,712.2	560.6	559.1	14.3	8.3	9.6	6.8	6.7	4.2	R
FD INS CO	FL	C	81.5	23.2	23.7	1.3	4.4	7.0	6.1	7.1	3.5	CD
FDM PREFERRED INS CO	NY	D	7.0	1.6	1.7	0.1	4.1	5.9	5.8	7.4	2.0	CDT
FEDERAL INS CO	IN	B+	32,714.5	15,034.0	6,844.9	1,306.4	7.5	8.4	7.5	6.9	6.4	
FEDERATED MUTUAL INS CO	MN	A-	4,726.6	2,681.8	1,083.5	132.5	10.0	8.9	6.9	6.9	5.5	
FEDERATED NATIONAL INS CO	FL	D	331.9	98.5	166.8	24.8	1.6	4.9	2.9	3.3	2.0	CGLR
FEDERATED RURAL ELECTRIC INS EXCH	KS	C+	483.0	170.8	113.3	26.1	8.3	5.9	9.0	6.9	4.5	R
FEDERATED SERVICE INS CO	MN	B	422.2	197.0	120.4	13.8	10.0	9.3	6.9	6.9	5.4	T
FFVA MUTUAL INS CO	FL	C-	303.4	132.0	99.1	11.4	7.9	4.7	4.5	6.6	3.1	R
FHM INS CO	FL	C	97.5	39.5	35.5	-4.9	7.9	4.8	1.7	6.4	3.8	FR
FIDELITY & DEPOSIT CO OF MARYLAND	MD	C	228.2	171.4	0.0	2.0	10.0	N/A	3.7	10.0	3.9	R
FIDELITY & GUARANTY INS CO	IA	C+	20.5	19.6	0.0	0.3	10.0	N/A	6.0	9.4	4.7	DF
FIDELITY & GUARANTY INS UDWRS INC	WI	C+	167.8	104.6	20.1	4.5	10.0	7.6	6.3	10.0	4.7	T
FIDELITY FIRE & CASUALTY CO	FL	C-	79.8	23.3	28.3	0.7	5.3	5.8	4.2	6.7	2.9	DR
FIDELITY MOHAWK INS CO	NJ	C+(3)	0.0	0.0	0.0	0.2	8.7	N/A	6.9	7.0	4.6	DF
▼FIDUCIARY INS CO OF AMERICA	NY	E-	100.2	-3.2	44.6	-10.9	0.0	0.3	0.4	2.7	0.0	CDLR
FINANCIAL AMERICAN PROP & CAS INS CO	TX	D+	13.2	9.9	0.8	-0.4	10.0	4.6	3.4	7.0	2.4	DFRT
FINANCIAL CASUALTY & SURETY INC	TX	C-	20.8	13.5	13.7	1.1	6.6	3.9	6.6	7.5	3.0	D
FINANCIAL GUARANTY INS CO	NY	D	2,539.9	66.4	46.6	11.0	0.0	1.6	0.0	6.9	1.4	CRT
FINANCIAL INDEMNITY CO	IL	B-	82.7	26.9	0.0	1.5	10.0	3.7	3.5	7.0	5.2	F
FINANCIAL PACIFIC INS CO	CA	B-	213.5	82.9	57.8	1.3	8.3	6.8	5.9	7.0	5.3	T
FINGER LAKES FIRE & CASUALTY CO	NY	C	35.5	23.3	8.8	0.8	9.5	7.8	8.4	7.0	3.9	DR
FINIAL REINS CO	CT	D+	1,240.9	835.3	-2.2	13.6	10.0	8.6	9.0	10.0	2.5	FRT
FIRE DISTRICTS INS CO	NY	D	10.7	2.6	2.5	0.2	4.2	5.9	6.5	7.3	2.2	CD
FIRE DISTRICTS OF NY MUT INS CO INC	NY	C	69.3	19.8	12.5	2.2	5.2	7.0	6.7	7.4	3.5	DR
FIRE INS EXCHANGE	CA	C+	2,270.3	745.4	1,022.8	2.9	5.2	6.4	4.8	4.4	4.8	LR
FIREMANS FUND INDEMNITY CORP	NJ	B- (3)	0.0	0.0	0.0	-0.5	10.0	N/A	4.1	7.0	4.9	D
FIREMANS FUND INS CO	CA	C	9,903.6	2,089.7	2,577.7	-344.2	6.4	2.5	1.8	5.2	3.6	FR
FIREMANS FUND INS CO OF HI INC	HI	B-	11.3	9.0	0.0	0.1	10.0	N/A	6.8	9.3	4.3	DFR
FIREMANS FUND INS CO OF OH	OH	C	50.2	48.8	0.0	0.7	10.0	4.6	6.8	7.0	3.9	DRT
FIREMENS INS CO OF WASHINGTON DC	DE	C	101.1	31.1	0.0	0.6	10.0	N/A	6.1	7.0	4.2	
FIRST ACCEPTANCE INS CO INC	TX	D+	215.4	96.0	132.6	0.0	8.2	5.9	2.4	5.9	2.5	R
FIRST ACCEPTANCE INS CO OF GEORGIA	GA	C-	67.3	21.5	52.2	0.0	6.0	5.8	2.5	6.1	3.0	DR
FIRST ACCEPTANCE INS CO OF TN INC	TN	D+	24.5	10.2	16.1	0.0	5.7	5.9	1.7	6.4	2.7	DR
FIRST AMERICAN HOME BUYERS PRO	CA	U (5)	0.0	0.0	179.3	0.0	N/A	N/A	8.9	0.9	5.4	L
FIRST AMERICAN PROP & CAS INS CO	CA	C	97.6	43.7	56.6	2.3	7.1	6.9	6.4	5.8	3.6	R
FIRST AMERICAN SPECIALTY INS CO	CA	C	103.6	46.4	61.5	2.4	6.8	6.0	5.8	5.2	3.6	R
FIRST BENEFITS INS MUTUAL INC	NC	D-	35.4	7.3	15.8	0.3	0.9	7.1	5.6	7.1	1.2	CDGT
FIRST CHICAGO INS CO	IL	D	43.9	8.9	22.7	1.3	1.8	4.7	5.8	6.8	1.8	CDR
FIRST CHOICE CASUALTY INS CO	NV	U	5.5	2.7	0.0	-0.3	N/A	N/A	2.8	10.0	3.6	T
FIRST COLONIAL INS CO	FL	B+	355.0	156.0	64.5	5.1	10.0	6.8	6.6	7.1	6.5	
FIRST COMMUNITY INS CO	FL	D+	132.6	39.4	77.6	16.9	5.2	6.3	2.9	7.2	2.4	DGR
FIRST DAKOTA INDEMNITY CO	SD	C	42.3	11.9	13.4	0.7	5.1	4.8	8.6	6.7	4.1	DFR
FIRST FINANCIAL INS CO	IL	C-	536.8	406.7	30.5	5.4	7.3	6.9	7.5	8.1	2.6	R
FIRST FIRE & CASUALTY INS OF HI INC	HI	C	8.9	8.6	0.0	-0.9	10.0	N/A	3.1	7.0	2.5	DR
FIRST FLORIDIAN AUTO & HOME INS CO	FL	B	282.9	195.2	73.8	8.7	10.0	6.2	6.7	7.0	5.1	
FIRST FOUNDERS ASR CO	NJ	D (3)	0.0	0.0	0.4	0.3	10.0	5.2	8.4	9.1	2.1	D
FIRST GUARD INS CO	AZ	B-	20.6	19.5	7.7	1.2	10.0	7.3	8.9	6.9	4.1	D

See Page 27 for explanation of footnotes and
Page 28 for explanation of stability factors.
Arrows denote recent upgrades ▲ or downgrades ▼   (see Section VII for explanations)

RISK ADJ. CAPITAL RATIO #1	RATIO #2	PREMIUM TO SURPLUS (%)	RESV. TO SURPLUS (%)	RESV. DEVELOP. 1 YEAR (%)	2 YEAR (%)	LOSS RATIO (%)	EXP. RATIO (%)	COMB RATIO (%)	CASH FROM UNDER-WRITING (%)	NET PREMIUM GROWTH (%)	INVEST. IN AFFIL (%)	INSURANCE COMPANY NAME
4.0	2.8	106.5	70.2	-1.0	-2.0	66.2	33.0	99.2	115.3	18.1	0.0	FARMLAND MUTUAL INS CO
N/A	N/A	N/A	N/A	N/A	N/A	N/A	N/A	N/A	N/A	0.0	0.0	FB INS CO
17.5	15.7	N/A	N/A	N/A	N/A	N/A	N/A	N/A	123.0	0.0	0.0	FCCI ADVANTAGE INS CO
466.7	233.7	N/A	N/A	N/A	N/A	N/A	N/A	N/A	-341.8	0.0	0.0	FCCI COMMERCIAL INS CO
2.5	1.8	101.3	111.7	-7.0	-15.7	66.0	32.9	98.9	104.5	13.6	8.5 ●	FCCI INS CO
1.2	0.8	104.7	192.2	-12.0	-30.7	61.6	39.4	101.0	99.8	1.0	0.0	FD INS CO
0.8	0.3	109.5	218.8	-3.2	-13.3	80.8	19.5	100.3	235.4	2.3	0.0	FDM PREFERRED INS CO
1.4	1.3	46.4	82.1	-2.9	-4.7	51.7	30.6	82.3	111.6	3.9	37.8 ●	FEDERAL INS CO
3.7	3.0	43.0	53.6	-5.1	-7.3	69.6	28.8	98.4	107.2	15.0	14.4 ●	FEDERATED MUTUAL INS CO
0.4	0.3	217.0	70.2	-3.7	-7.4	54.2	30.2	84.4	167.9	137.1	0.0	FEDERATED NATIONAL INS CO
3.1	2.2	73.9	153.2	-8.8	-10.8	71.9	14.3	86.2	129.8	-0.2	0.0	FEDERATED RURAL ELECTRIC INS EXCH
5.3	3.4	65.4	81.5	-7.9	-10.9	69.6	29.1	98.7	100.8	15.0	0.0	FEDERATED SERVICE INS CO
2.3	1.8	80.5	100.5	-3.0	-1.9	69.5	26.3	95.8	103.4	6.8	0.0	FFVA MUTUAL INS CO
1.9	1.4	80.3	110.4	-5.7	N/A	73.6	35.3	108.9	76.6	-13.3	0.0	FHM INS CO
7.9	7.2	N/A	N/A	N/A	N/A	N/A	N/A	N/A	999 +	0.0	12.7	FIDELITY & DEPOSIT CO OF MARYLAND
45.5	41.0	N/A	N/A	N/A	N/A	N/A	N/A	N/A	-89.1	0.0	0.0	FIDELITY & GUARANTY INS CO
12.7	8.0	19.9	35.9	-0.5	-1.1	60.9	30.8	91.7	-173.5	3.0	0.0	FIDELITY & GUARANTY INS UDWRS INC
1.6	1.0	124.2	45.6	7.0	4.5	54.4	40.9	95.3	145.1	-1.6	0.0	FIDELITY FIRE & CASUALTY CO
3.5	2.1	N/A	N/A	N/A	N/A	N/A	N/A	N/A	N/A	0.0	0.0	FIDELITY MOHAWK INS CO
-0.0	-0.0	604.0	638.8	98.2	152.5	84.0	28.2	112.2	114.9	27.6	0.0	FIDUCIARY INS CO OF AMERICA
7.0	4.9	8.0	1.2	-0.6	-0.3	39.2	151.2	190.4	73.4	-11.0	0.0	FINANCIAL AMERICAN PROP & CAS INS
1.0	0.9	105.9	19.7	-9.0	-0.6	10.5	77.7	88.2	113.4	7.1	0.0	FINANCIAL CASUALTY & SURETY INC
0.2	0.1	70.1	999 +	112.5	140.6	999 +	58.8	999 +	40.0	0.0	0.8	FINANCIAL GUARANTY INS CO
3.8	3.4	N/A	N/A	N/A	N/A	N/A	N/A	N/A	-11.5	0.0	0.0	FINANCIAL INDEMNITY CO
2.7	1.7	71.2	85.9	-4.8	-7.1	63.3	28.6	91.9	128.9	10.3	0.0	FINANCIAL PACIFIC INS CO
3.9	2.5	39.6	16.3	0.9	-0.3	52.6	36.4	89.0	116.1	5.5	0.0	FINGER LAKES FIRE & CASUALTY CO
7.3	4.4	-0.3	46.0	-4.3	-9.1	999 +	-87.4	999 +	-3.9	N/A	0.0 ●	FINIAL REINS CO
0.9	0.3	100.7	201.2	-3.0	-12.5	80.8	16.9	97.7	183.0	2.3	0.0	FIRE DISTRICTS INS CO
1.3	0.9	66.4	196.6	2.2	4.5	91.2	15.1	106.3	138.0	2.3	6.7	FIRE DISTRICTS OF NY MUT INS CO INC
0.8	0.7	141.8	88.9	N/A	1.4	66.9	33.7	100.6	116.5	-1.6	54.3 ●	FIRE INS EXCHANGE
22.0	19.8	N/A	N/A	N/A	N/A	N/A	N/A	N/A	-9.8	0.0	0.0	FIREMANS FUND INDEMNITY CORP
1.1	0.7	104.0	232.9	0.2	21.2	68.6	36.5	105.1	79.3	-29.1	12.8 ●	FIREMANS FUND INS CO
11.5	10.3	N/A	N/A	N/A	N/A	N/A	N/A	N/A	24.8	0.0	0.0	FIREMANS FUND INS CO OF HI INC
87.5	64.2	N/A	N/A	N/A	N/A	N/A	N/A	N/A	0.1	100.0	0.0	FIREMANS FUND INS CO OF OH
4.0	3.6	N/A	N/A	N/A	N/A	N/A	N/A	N/A	999 +	0.0	0.0	FIREMENS INS CO OF WASHINGTON DC
1.9	1.6	139.8	58.4	-2.3	3.8	71.4	29.0	100.4	94.7	5.6	17.4	FIRST ACCEPTANCE INS CO INC
0.9	0.8	244.6	102.2	-4.0	6.8	71.4	29.0	100.4	95.6	5.6	0.0	FIRST ACCEPTANCE INS CO OF
1.4	1.2	258.8	108.2	-4.2	5.6	71.4	29.0	100.4	95.5	5.6	0.0	FIRST ACCEPTANCE INS CO OF TN INC
N/A	N/A	138.2	6.8	N/A	N/A	61.4	26.4	87.8	116.2	17.7	0.0	FIRST AMERICAN HOME BUYERS PRO
1.6	1.0	130.1	30.3	-3.6	-5.8	52.1	39.6	91.7	117.9	11.8	0.0	FIRST AMERICAN PROP & CAS INS CO
1.5	0.9	133.1	32.5	5.5	4.1	58.3	33.9	92.2	119.3	5.0	0.0	FIRST AMERICAN SPECIALTY INS CO
0.3	0.2	238.2	230.8	-24.2	-54.8	71.1	22.6	93.7	136.0	86.3	0.0	FIRST BENEFITS INS MUTUAL INC
0.5	0.4	294.7	255.8	-8.1	-4.7	63.2	30.0	93.2	113.1	13.4	0.0	FIRST CHICAGO INS CO
N/A	N/A	N/A	N/A	N/A	N/A	N/A	N/A	N/A	999 +	0.0	0.0	FIRST CHOICE CASUALTY INS CO
6.7	5.3	33.3	3.5	-1.9	-4.1	34.0	44.2	78.2	162.3	-0.1	0.0 ●	FIRST COLONIAL INS CO
1.7	1.4	340.8	63.2	0.5	-6.4	41.3	36.2	77.5	172.9	142.1	0.0	FIRST COMMUNITY INS CO
1.1	0.8	118.0	163.0	4.0	7.8	73.9	20.6	94.5	88.7	-16.1	0.0	FIRST DAKOTA INDEMNITY CO
1.2	1.1	7.8	19.2	-2.8	-6.3	36.2	38.8	75.0	103.0	-5.6	78.9 ●	FIRST FINANCIAL INS CO
63.1	48.6	N/A	N/A	N/A	N/A	N/A	N/A	N/A	N/A	0.0	0.0	FIRST FIRE & CASUALTY INS OF HI INC
10.9	8.5	36.6	23.5	-0.8	0.4	57.6	24.0	81.6	111.0	-9.0	0.0 ●	FIRST FLORIDIAN AUTO & HOME INS CO
8.1	5.6	10.2	7.5	0.1	-0.4	20.2	66.7	86.9	142.3	-6.3	0.0	FIRST FOUNDERS ASR CO
20.5	10.9	42.2	1.5	-0.3	-0.5	61.2	15.2	76.4	131.9	18.7	0.0	FIRST GUARD INS CO

999 + Denotes number greater than 999.9%
999 - Denotes number less than -999.99%
● Bullets denote a more detailed analysis is available in Section II.

INSURANCE COMPANY NAME	DOM. STATE	RATING	TOTAL ASSETS ($MIL)	CAPITAL & SURPLUS ($MIL)	ANNUAL NET PREMIUM ($MIL)	NET INCOME ($MIL)	CAPITAL- IZATION INDEX (PTS)	RESERVE ADQ INDEX (PTS)	PROFIT- ABILITY INDEX (PTS)	LIQUIDITY INDEX (PTS)	STAB. INDEX (PTS)	STABILITY FACTORS
FIRST INDEMNITY INS OF HI INC	HI	C	7.3	7.2	0.0	0.1	10.0	N/A	3.9	7.0	2.5	DRT
FIRST INDEMNITY OF AMERICA INS CO	NJ	D-	7.9	6.1	7.2	0.5	7.3	1.6	6.0	6.1	1.0	DR
FIRST INS CO OF HI LTD	HI	C	652.6	306.7	171.8	16.4	10.0	9.6	8.6	6.9	4.3	R
FIRST JERSEY CASUALTY INS CO INC	NJ	D (3)	0.0	0.0	2.1	0.0	2.2	1.6	2.9	5.9	1.4	CDFR
▼FIRST KEYSTONE RRG INC	SC	F (1)	13.6	2.4	7.8	0.1	0.9	0.2	1.7	1.1	0.0	CDFL
FIRST LIBERTY INS CORP	IL	C+	22.6	22.1	-5.4	0.1	10.0	4.6	3.5	4.0	4.3	ADFL
FIRST MEDICAL INS CO RRG	VT	C-	103.3	54.1	10.6	4.5	9.1	9.7	5.9	7.1	2.9	D
FIRST MERCURY INS CO	IL	D	146.1	56.7	0.0	-0.1	10.0	3.6	1.9	0.2	1.4	AGLR
FIRST MORTGAGE INS CO	NC	U	8.2	8.2	0.0	0.1	N/A	N/A	5.8	7.0	5.1	T
FIRST MUTUAL INS CO	NC	D	5.5	4.2	1.0	0.0	10.0	7.5	4.4	9.2	1.5	DR
FIRST NATIONAL INS CO OF AMERICA	NH	B-	55.7	54.0	-41.8	1.1	10.0	4.8	6.3	1.3	5.1	AFLT
FIRST NET INS CO	GU	E+	17.9	10.2	5.7	-1.9	10.0	7.6	4.5	6.9	0.5	D
FIRST NONPROFIT INS CO	DE	C-	142.2	37.1	-83.8	0.0	8.6	7.0	1.7	9.0	2.9	FRT
FIRST PROFESSIONALS INS CO INC	FL	C+	397.2	180.8	-3.8	11.6	8.1	9.3	3.3	7.6	4.2	FRT
FIRST PROTECTIVE INS CO	FL	D+	88.8	27.7	32.3	1.0	6.4	6.8	6.2	6.9	2.5	T
FIRST SECURITY INS OF HI INC	HI	C	5.4	5.4	0.0	0.0	10.0	N/A	4.8	7.0	2.5	DR
FIRST SPECIALTY INS CORP	MO	C	224.4	67.7	5.1	5.9	2.4	5.8	3.3	9.2	4.1	CFRT
FIRST STATE INS CO	CT	U	370.9	28.3	0.0	-3.9	N/A	0.1	2.4	6.4	0.0	ACFT
FIRST SURETY CORP	WV	D+	10.2	5.9	0.8	0.1	10.0	N/A	5.8	10.0	2.5	DGR
FIRST WASHINGTON INS CO INC	DC	U	2.0	2.0	0.0	0.0	N/A	3.9	2.8	10.0	2.9	T
FIRSTCOMP INS CO	NE	C+	301.6	127.3	45.0	9.1	7.4	3.9	4.5	8.0	4.4	FR
FIRSTLINE NATIONAL INS CO	MD	C+	76.7	43.6	29.3	-0.1	8.5	9.4	5.6	6.9	4.5	F
FITCHBURG MUTUAL INS CO	MA	C	98.2	52.3	31.9	-1.4	8.6	6.2	6.3	6.9	3.4	R
FLAGSHIP CITY INS CO	PA	B-	46.1	11.9	0.0	0.2	9.0	N/A	7.7	7.0	4.6	D
FLORIDA FAMILY INS CO	FL	C	108.3	54.0	46.3	2.7	8.3	7.5	8.5	6.9	3.9	T
FLORIDA FARM BU CASUALTY INS CO	FL	B-	530.4	261.3	235.5	14.5	8.5	7.8	7.3	6.3	4.8	T
FLORIDA FARM BUREAU GENERAL INS CO	FL	B	9.5	9.5	0.0	0.2	10.0	N/A	6.7	7.0	4.9	D
FLORIDA LAWYERS MUTUAL INS CO	FL	C	73.2	38.1	9.1	-0.3	9.1	9.4	6.9	9.0	4.2	DR
FLORIDA PENINSULA INS CO	FL	D	338.2	97.7	148.0	11.2	4.6	2.7	4.7	6.8	1.9	T
FLORIDA SELECT INS CO	FL	F (5)	0.0	0.0	-0.3	0.0	0.0	5.0	1.9	7.0	0.0	CDFT
FLORISTS INS CO	IL	C	7.6	6.4	0.0	0.1	10.0	6.2	3.6	8.2	3.6	DR
FLORISTS MUTUAL INS CO	IL	C	152.5	43.7	57.7	1.3	7.4	4.1	2.4	6.0	3.9	
FMH INS CO OF IOWA	IA	U	6.7	6.5	0.0	0.1	N/A	N/A	4.9	7.0	4.8	T
FMI INS CO	NJ	C+(3)	0.0	0.0	0.0	0.6	7.2	N/A	6.9	7.0	4.6	G
FOREMOST COUNTY MUTUAL INS CO	TX	C+	90.2	3.8	0.0	0.3	2.2	N/A	7.6	0.9	3.2	CDL
FOREMOST INS CO	MI	B	2,120.7	1,050.1	0.0	18.6	10.0	6.1	7.7	9.0	5.6	
FOREMOST LLOYDS OF TEXAS	TX	C+	62.5	4.3	0.0	0.2	3.3	N/A	8.2	2.1	3.3	CDFL
FOREMOST PROPERTY & CASUALTY INS	MI	C	76.6	17.4	0.0	0.2	9.1	N/A	6.3	7.0	4.2	D
FOREMOST SIGNATURE INS CO	MI	C+	103.7	19.4	0.0	0.1	9.7	N/A	5.8	9.5	4.6	DG
FORESTRY MUTUAL INS CO	NC	C-	51.8	14.2	15.4	0.1	6.8	9.7	4.4	6.4	3.3	DR
FORT WAYNE MEDICAL ASR CO RRG	AZ	D	4.6	2.4	1.0	0.1	9.6	7.0	8.0	9.7	2.0	DT
FORTRESS INS CO	IL	C+	137.4	60.8	16.6	1.0	5.5	6.0	4.4	7.0	4.4	G
FORTUITY INS CO	MI	B	38.0	14.5	15.8	0.4	9.0	6.9	5.5	6.6	4.9	DR
FOUNDERS INS CO	IL	D+	166.7	69.0	83.2	4.8	4.4	3.0	1.5	5.5	2.6	FR
FOUNDERS INS CO	NJ	C (3)	0.0	0.0	0.0	-0.2	10.0	N/A	3.8	7.0	3.8	DF
FOUNDERS INS CO OF MICHIGAN	MI	U	6.1	5.8	0.0	0.0	N/A	6.8	4.5	7.0	4.6	FT
FRANDISCO PROPERTY & CAS INS CO	GA	C+	91.0	61.0	33.5	4.6	9.5	6.1	8.7	6.9	4.5	T
FRANK WINSTON CRUM INS CO	FL	D	47.8	14.7	12.8	0.3	2.1	9.4	3.8	7.1	2.3	DGRT
FRANKENMUTH MUTUAL INS CO	MI	A	1,096.8	456.9	410.9	9.2	8.9	9.0	6.2	6.5	7.4	
FRANKLIN CASUALTY INS CO RRG	VT	E+	42.6	3.2	3.4	0.0	1.5	5.0	6.6	2.2	0.6	CDFL
FRANKLIN HOMEOWNERS ASR CO	DE	C	91.9	87.2	0.9	4.7	9.5	3.6	4.8	10.0	4.3	DFT
FRANKLIN INS CO	PA	C	25.6	10.9	7.2	0.2	7.6	6.7	6.5	6.9	3.7	DR

See Page 27 for explanation of footnotes and
Page 28 for explanation of stability factors.
Arrows denote recent upgrades ▲ or downgrades ▼   (see Section VII for explanations)

68

www.weissratings.com

RISK ADJ. CAPITAL RATIO #1	RATIO #2	PREMIUM TO SURPLUS (%)	RESV. TO SURPLUS (%)	RESV. DEVELOP. 1 YEAR (%)	2 YEAR (%)	LOSS RATIO (%)	EXP. RATIO (%)	COMB RATIO (%)	CASH FROM UNDER-WRITING (%)	NET PREMIUM GROWTH (%)	INVEST. IN AFFIL (%)	INSURANCE COMPANY NAME
109.0	54.5	N/A	N/A	N/A	N/A	N/A	N/A	N/A	N/A	0.0	0.0	FIRST INDEMNITY INS OF HI INC
1.3	1.0	130.9	-45.3	13.5	23.6	35.1	59.4	94.5	125.5	28.8	0.0	FIRST INDEMNITY OF AMERICA INS CO
5.5	3.8	60.0	81.3	-5.6	-29.3	59.2	33.3	92.5	108.5	15.6	3.6 ●	FIRST INS CO OF HI LTD
0.6	0.5	38.7	45.2	40.1	6.1	105.6	6.4	112.0	51.2	-36.7	0.0	FIRST JERSEY CASUALTY INS CO INC
0.2	0.2	282.8	269.6	135.5	171.9	93.9	26.7	120.6	84.1	0.5	0.0	FIRST KEYSTONE RRG INC
63.7	31.8	-24.3	N/A	N/A	N/A	N/A	-0.4	N/A	-1.0	-141.2	0.0	FIRST LIBERTY INS CORP
2.4	2.0	14.7	54.2	-5.0	-16.4	62.5	4.6	67.1	157.5	-4.7	0.0	FIRST MEDICAL INS CO RRG
5.9	5.3	N/A	N/A	N/A	N/A	N/A	N/A	N/A	92.9	0.0	0.0	FIRST MERCURY INS CO
N/A	N/A	N/A	N/A	N/A	N/A	N/A	N/A	N/A	N/A	0.0	0.0	FIRST MORTGAGE INS CO
6.2	4.5	25.2	1.8	-1.0	-1.4	47.0	34.8	81.8	123.3	-2.9	0.0	FIRST MUTUAL INS CO
85.3	72.8	-78.8	N/A	N/A	N/A	N/A	N/A	N/A	-11.7	-147.8	0.0	FIRST NATIONAL INS CO OF AMERICA
4.0	2.5	47.0	17.0	2.1	-1.4	10.0	45.3	94.3	121.9	-4.3	0.0	FIRST NET INS CO
4.6	4.2	-236.7	N/A	-107.8	-59.3	84.7	-15.0	69.7	-607.2	-249.4	0.0	FIRST NONPROFIT INS CO
2.7	2.4	-2.1	151.3	-17.1	-20.0	28.7	-186.0	-157.3	49.9	-103.5	12.2	FIRST PROFESSIONALS INS CO INC
2.0	1.7	119.8	43.4	7.5	-3.3	56.2	40.1	96.3	114.0	2.6	0.0	FIRST PROTECTIVE INS CO
137.7	68.8	N/A	N/A	N/A	N/A	N/A	N/A	N/A	N/A	0.0	0.0	FIRST SECURITY INS OF HI INC
0.7	0.5	8.0	93.0	9.9	9.5	124.6	-9.0	115.6	55.5	-81.4	0.0	FIRST SPECIALTY INS CORP
N/A	N/A	0.1	999 +	34.2	110.9	999 +	999 +	999 +	0.1	649.4	21.0	FIRST STATE INS CO
4.4	3.3	12.5	21.6	N/A	N/A	22.6	59.6	82.2	161.1	18.4	0.0	FIRST SURETY CORP
N/A	N/A	N/A	N/A	N/A	N/A	N/A	N/A	N/A	N/A	0.0	0.0	FIRST WASHINGTON INS CO INC
2.6	1.7	38.9	117.9	-11.5	-7.3	40.9	31.5	72.4	81.8	-9.4	0.0	FIRSTCOMP INS CO
2.8	1.8	67.4	56.8	-4.2	-10.0	55.6	37.7	93.3	95.4	12.2	0.0	FIRSTLINE NATIONAL INS CO
2.9	2.1	59.9	34.0	N/A	-0.4	59.4	37.5	96.9	123.6	6.2	7.0	FITCHBURG MUTUAL INS CO
2.3	2.1	N/A	N/A	N/A	N/A	N/A	N/A	N/A	N/A	0.0	0.0	FLAGSHIP CITY INS CO
2.5	2.3	91.2	13.9	-3.2	-2.6	42.3	39.4	81.7	128.0	16.1	15.2	FLORIDA FAMILY INS CO
3.1	2.1	95.6	42.4	-0.9	-0.4	73.3	21.5	94.8	108.9	4.1	2.6 ●	FLORIDA FARM BU CASUALTY INS CO
93.3	46.6	N/A	N/A	N/A	N/A	N/A	N/A	N/A	N/A	0.0	0.0	FLORIDA FARM BUREAU GENERAL INS
3.6	2.2	24.1	55.0	-7.8	-17.2	66.4	27.0	93.4	104.2	-0.8	0.0	FLORIDA LAWYERS MUTUAL INS CO
1.2	0.9	207.9	113.7	1.5	13.8	51.1	29.9	81.0	147.0	37.8	1.7	FLORIDA PENINSULA INS CO
-1.9	-1.7	2.3	-16.5	8.4	0.3	537.6	-780.2	-242.6	28.4	0.0	0.0	FLORIDA SELECT INS CO
12.8	11.5	N/A	6.5	-0.8	-0.5	N/A	N/A	N/A	303.7	0.0	0.0	FLORISTS INS CO
1.9	1.2	133.4	186.3	7.7	13.6	76.3	32.9	109.2	93.8	-5.5	6.5	FLORISTS MUTUAL INS CO
N/A	N/A	N/A	N/A	N/A	N/A	N/A	N/A	N/A	N/A	0.0	0.0	FMH INS CO OF IOWA
1.8	1.1	N/A	N/A	N/A	N/A	N/A	N/A	N/A	N/A	0.0	0.0	FMI INS CO
0.4	0.4	N/A	N/A	N/A	N/A	N/A	N/A	N/A	492.6	0.0	0.0	FOREMOST COUNTY MUTUAL INS CO
8.5	5.9	N/A	2.5	-0.5	-2.1	N/A	N/A	N/A	85.5	0.0	6.7 ●	FOREMOST INS CO
0.6	0.5	N/A	N/A	N/A	N/A	N/A	N/A	N/A	-8.3	0.0	0.0	FOREMOST LLOYDS OF TEXAS
2.4	2.1	N/A	N/A	N/A	N/A	N/A	N/A	N/A	75.8	0.0	0.0	FOREMOST PROPERTY & CASUALTY INS
2.3	2.1	N/A	N/A	N/A	N/A	N/A	N/A	N/A	-25.9	0.0	0.0	FOREMOST SIGNATURE INS CO
1.0	0.7	104.4	119.7	-12.4	-17.4	64.3	34.2	98.5	100.8	-0.6	2.2	FORESTRY MUTUAL INS CO
3.0	2.7	42.2	47.3	-3.4	-22.6	19.5	37.9	57.4	239.8	-18.5	0.0	FORT WAYNE MEDICAL ASR CO RRG
1.0	0.7	27.7	95.4	-4.4	-2.0	130.2	11.4	141.6	-40.6	337.9	0.0	FORTRESS INS CO
3.0	2.2	112.1	83.2	-10.6	-13.7	63.2	29.3	92.5	108.7	3.6	0.0	FORTUITY INS CO
2.0	1.5	164.7	267.3	41.3	48.0	109.1	35.6	144.7	70.7	-5.0	3.2	FOUNDERS INS CO
95.1	46.3	N/A	N/A	N/A	N/A	N/A	N/A	N/A	302.4	0.0	0.0	FOUNDERS INS CO
N/A	N/A	N/A	2.9	-2.6	-7.3	N/A	N/A	N/A	N/A	0.0	0.0	FOUNDERS INS CO OF MICHIGAN
3.5	3.1	59.4	1.8	-0.6	-0.8	12.8	69.6	82.4	122.1	6.6	0.0	FRANDISCO PROPERTY & CAS INS CO
0.9	0.5	89.2	100.2	-4.5	-9.5	55.8	39.9	95.7	122.4	68.1	0.0	FRANK WINSTON CRUM INS CO
3.0	2.4	92.3	68.5	-9.0	-11.9	63.2	29.3	92.5	103.2	3.6	12.6 ●	FRANKENMUTH MUTUAL INS CO
0.4	0.3	105.7	201.4	-2.5	-34.0	48.5	37.6	86.1	76.7	-1.6	0.0	FRANKLIN CASUALTY INS CO RRG
4.6	2.8	0.9	N/A	N/A	N/A	64.9	358.7	423.6	23.1	18.8	0.0	FRANKLIN HOMEOWNERS ASR CO
1.9	1.2	62.2	75.1	-4.6	-6.5	63.3	30.5	93.8	114.6	10.3	0.0	FRANKLIN INS CO

999 + Denotes number greater than 999.9%
999 - Denotes number less than -999.99%
● Bullets denote a more detailed analysis is available in Section II.

INSURANCE COMPANY NAME	DOM. STATE	RATING	TOTAL ASSETS ($MIL)	CAPITAL & SURPLUS ($MIL)	ANNUAL NET PREMIUM ($MIL)	NET INCOME ($MIL)	CAPITAL-IZATION INDEX (PTS)	RESERVE ADQ INDEX (PTS)	PROFIT-ABILITY INDEX (PTS)	LIQUIDITY INDEX (PTS)	STAB. INDEX (PTS)	STABILITY FACTORS
FRANKLIN MUTUAL INS CO	NJ	B (3)	0.0	0.0	104.2	35.3	8.1	8.8	8.2	8.5	5.6	T
FREDERICK MUTUAL INS CO	MD	B-	54.7	27.3	23.5	-1.7	8.5	5.7	3.7	6.9	4.9	
FREDERICKSBURG PROFESSIONAL RISK	VT	D	19.5	11.9	2.2	0.3	8.0	9.4	5.2	7.3	1.7	DFR
FREEDOM ADVANTAGE INS CO	PA	D	11.3	2.6	4.4	-0.5	3.6	7.0	2.2	6.6	2.1	DR
FREEDOM SPECIALTY INS CO	OH	B	26.0	12.3	0.0	0.2	10.0	N/A	6.9	7.7	4.3	DT
FREESTONE INS CO	DE	F (4)	0.0	0.0	96.7	0.3	0.4	2.7	1.6	7.1	0.0	CRT
FREMONT INS CO	MI	D	137.3	39.6	54.8	-1.4	8.8	4.4	3.3	6.2	1.7	RT
FRIENDS COVE MUTUAL INS CO	PA	C-	5.0	2.6	2.9	-0.4	7.3	7.7	2.9	6.8	2.1	DR
FRONTLINE INS UNLIMITED CO	IL	U	25.3	25.1	0.0	0.1	N/A	N/A	3.2	7.0	4.0	FT
FULMONT MUTUAL INS CO	NY	D-	5.4	1.7	3.3	-0.1	6.2	3.9	2.8	6.9	0.9	DFRT
GABLES RRG INC	VT	E (2)	8.0	2.6	2.5	-0.2	7.1	3.6	2.9	9.0	0.0	DGT
GALEN INS CO	MO	D-	16.1	6.8	4.5	0.2	6.0	9.8	5.7	7.3	1.3	DFR
GARRISON PROPERTY & CASUALTY INS CO	TX	B	1,435.4	543.6	710.0	28.7	8.3	6.5	6.1	5.9	4.9	RT
GATEWAY INS CO	MO	D-	43.5	12.0	13.1	0.6	1.6	3.3	1.4	1.4	1.0	CDFL
GEICO ADVANTAGE CO	NE	C+	713.8	447.2	215.6	-32.1	10.0	3.6	2.8	8.4	4.5	FGT
GEICO CASUALTY CO	MD	D-	2,376.6	990.7	2,209.4	-0.8	7.6	9.4	2.6	6.5	1.3	GT
GEICO CHOICE INS CO	NE	A-	388.0	227.4	163.6	-6.6	9.7	3.6	2.9	7.5	5.6	FGT
GEICO COUNTY MUTUAL INS CO	TX	U	31.9	5.0	0.0	0.0	N/A	N/A	3.9	7.0	4.2	FRT
GEICO GENERAL INS CO	MD	B+	215.7	130.9	0.0	0.2	10.0	N/A	7.4	10.0	5.3	
GEICO INDEMNITY CO	MD	B+	6,922.7	3,891.3	4,411.5	349.7	7.6	9.4	8.5	5.6	5.3	
GEICO SECURE INSURANCE CO	NE	A-	338.5	263.0	82.7	-0.2	10.0	3.6	3.6	9.1	5.9	GT
GEISINGER INS CORP RRG	VT	E	21.7	11.3	1.1	-0.1	10.0	3.6	3.9	7.8	0.3	DFR
GEM STATE INS CO	ID	C-	10.1	7.8	2.9	0.3	10.0	6.3	8.7	6.8	2.7	D
GEMINI INS CO	DE	C	117.3	54.8	0.0	1.0	10.0	N/A	5.7	7.0	3.9	RT
GENERAL AUTOMOBILE INS CO	OH	C	49.3	25.7	24.7	0.2	7.2	4.1	3.9	5.7	4.0	DFG
GENERAL CASUALTY CO OF IL	WI	C-	89.3	18.7	34.7	-0.6	5.0	3.9	1.6	6.8	3.0	DFRT
GENERAL CASUALTY CO OF WI	WI	C	893.2	297.7	312.2	-0.1	7.3	4.7	2.4	6.7	3.6	FR
GENERAL FIDELITY INS CO	SC	U	406.5	325.8	0.0	3.6	N/A	4.8	3.7	7.1	6.1	FGT
GENERAL INS CO OF AMERICA	NH	C	105.0	102.0	-480.6	-1.9	10.0	4.9	1.9	0.0	4.1	AFLR
GENERAL REINSURANCE CORP	DE	B-	16,162.6	11,698.4	543.0	393.7	7.4	7.9	8.2	8.6	4.9	R
GENERAL SECURITY IND CO OF AZ	AZ	D	181.6	49.2	5.9	-1.0	8.1	4.7	2.9	9.6	1.4	R
GENERAL SECURITY NATIONAL INS CO	NY	C-	264.3	96.9	7.5	-1.3	7.1	4.5	2.6	6.5	3.1	FRT
GENERAL STAR INDEMNITY CO	DE	B-	827.5	597.3	70.3	3.4	10.0	9.3	5.7	10.0	4.9	R
GENERAL STAR NATIONAL INS CO	DE	B	241.7	180.6	9.6	-0.6	10.0	9.1	5.0	10.0	5.2	F
GENERALI - US BRANCH	NY	D	78.0	28.0	35.4	2.1	2.1	3.4	5.0	3.6	1.9	CLRT
GENESEE PATRONS COOP INS	NY	D-	8.8	4.8	3.5	0.2	7.8	6.5	6.5	6.7	1.0	DR
GENESIS INS CO	CT	C	197.4	130.8	11.0	1.9	10.0	9.4	7.2	10.0	3.9	DR
GENEVA INS CO	IN	D+	3.9	1.9	2.5	0.1	7.4	4.1	2.1	5.2	1.5	DFT
GENWORTH FINANCIAL ASR CORP	NC	U	14.3	14.3	0.0	0.7	N/A	7.0	1.2	7.0	2.4	T
GENWORTH MORTGAGE INS CORP	NC	C-	2,609.6	1,261.2	463.1	132.2	3.0	0.8	2.6	5.2	3.1	CFR
GENWORTH MORTGAGE REINS CORP	NC	B-	13.1	10.7	1.5	1.1	10.0	3.6	3.2	10.0	3.5	ADGT
GENWORTH MTG INS CORP OF NC	NC	C-	332.9	126.3	50.5	8.8	5.4	4.3	2.3	5.7	3.1	FT
GENWORTH RESIDENTIAL MTG INS CORP	NC	C	220.6	80.5	39.0	1.2	7.0	6.8	2.0	6.7	4.0	AR
GEORGIA CASUALTY & SURETY CO	GA	C	42.0	18.6	15.8	0.8	7.7	5.8	3.8	6.4	3.8	D
GEORGIA DEALERS INS CO	GA	D	9.9	3.1	2.2	-0.5	2.7	4.6	0.7	6.7	2.0	CDFT
GEORGIA FARM BUREAU CASUALTY INS CO	GA	B	3.6	3.5	0.0	0.0	10.0	N/A	3.2	9.7	4.6	D
GEORGIA FARM BUREAU MUTUAL INS CO	GA	C	638.1	264.8	401.4	5.7	7.6	6.1	3.3	5.1	3.9	F
GEORGIA MUNICIPAL CAPTIVE INS CO	GA	D	7.6	2.4	2.6	0.0	6.1	3.6	4.6	7.1	1.9	DGT
GEORGIA MUTUAL INS CO	GA	F (4)	0.0	0.0	5.8	-1.2	3.2	3.8	0.2	7.2	0.0	CDGR
GEORGIA TRANSPORTATION CAPTIVE INS	GA	D	2.5	1.3	0.6	0.3	7.4	9.5	7.8	8.2	1.0	DT
GEOVERA INS CO	CA	D	92.8	32.7	26.3	6.4	1.4	6.4	5.0	6.0	1.4	CR
GEOVERA SPECIALTY INS CO	DE	C	108.4	22.3	12.3	3.2	2.8	6.2	6.4	6.4	3.6	CDGR

See Page 27 for explanation of footnotes and Page 28 for explanation of stability factors.

70

www.weissratings.com

Arrows denote recent upgrades ▲ or downgrades ▼ (see Section VII for explanations)

RISK ADJ. CAPITAL RATIO #1	RATIO #2	PREMIUM TO SURPLUS (%)	RESV. TO SURPLUS (%)	RESV. DEVELOP. 1 YEAR (%)	RESV. DEVELOP. 2 YEAR (%)	LOSS RATIO (%)	EXP. RATIO (%)	COMB RATIO (%)	CASH FROM UNDER- WRITING (%)	NET PREMIUM GROWTH (%)	INVEST. IN AFFIL (%)	INSURANCE COMPANY NAME
2.6	1.7	20.1	20.0	-3.8	-7.1	39.8	28.5	68.3	137.6	8.1	6.5	FRANKLIN MUTUAL INS CO
2.6	1.8	79.5	27.2	1.8	-0.9	57.2	40.0	97.2	108.0	14.0	0.0	FREDERICK MUTUAL INS CO
2.6	1.6	18.7	53.5	-14.0	-25.4	32.6	10.5	43.1	97.9	3.2	0.0	FREDERICKSBURG PROFESSIONAL RISK
0.6	0.5	142.1	223.1	-5.1	4.8	75.5	30.6	106.1	97.9	5.8	0.0	FREEDOM ADVANTAGE INS CO
4.3	3.9	N/A	N/A	N/A	N/A	N/A	N/A	N/A	956.3	0.0	0.0	FREEDOM SPECIALTY INS CO
0.4	0.2	167.9	351.9	20.6	27.5	83.6	29.0	112.6	96.6	-14.7	0.0	FREESTONE INS CO
2.7	2.1	132.8	96.3	3.3	13.0	73.4	30.1	103.5	99.2	44.5	0.0	FREMONT INS CO
1.5	1.0	95.8	20.0	-1.5	-2.7	51.2	45.7	96.9	130.6	3.9	0.0	FRIENDS COVE MUTUAL INS CO
N/A	N/A	N/A	N/A	N/A	N/A	N/A	N/A	N/A	N/A	0.0	0.0	FRONTLINE INS UNLIMITED CO
1.0	0.8	215.1	80.6	3.3	5.0	73.9	31.6	105.5	93.5	12.1	3.8	FULMONT MUTUAL INS CO
1.9	1.2	88.9	92.0	-24.8	N/A	85.0	11.2	96.2	265.1	37.5	0.0	GABLES RRG INC
0.9	0.7	62.0	65.2	-2.5	-43.4	41.3	55.7	97.0	100.7	12.8	0.0	GALEN INS CO
2.3	1.7	140.2	66.0	-5.9	-7.3	77.3	13.5	90.8	115.9	14.9	0.0 •	GARRISON PROPERTY & CASUALTY INS
0.4	0.3	116.7	158.5	0.2	6.7	63.9	35.5	99.4	54.9	-34.6	0.0	GATEWAY INS CO
3.7	2.6	44.5	12.0	0.2	N/A	107.4	52.9	160.3	75.9	386.6	0.0 •	GEICO ADVANTAGE CO
2.4	1.7	220.7	86.0	-6.3	-23.8	90.8	31.3	122.1	96.1	59.9	0.0 •	GEICO CASUALTY CO
3.5	2.3	69.1	18.4	0.5	N/A	99.3	34.3	133.6	93.9	308.2	0.0 •	GEICO CHOICE INS CO
N/A	N/A	N/A	N/A	N/A	N/A	N/A	N/A	N/A	67.4	0.0	0.0	GEICO COUNTY MUTUAL INS CO
15.7	14.1	N/A	N/A	N/A	N/A	N/A	N/A	N/A	N/A	0.0	0.0 •	GEICO GENERAL INS CO
2.1	1.6	121.3	64.4	-6.5	-20.6	73.2	15.0	88.2	116.2	4.9	14.6 •	GEICO INDEMNITY CO
6.6	4.2	31.0	8.4	0.1	N/A	91.7	30.9	122.6	105.1	291.9	0.0 •	GEICO SECURE INSURANCE CO
4.5	4.1	9.7	4.3	0.9	N/A	46.0	45.7	91.7	65.7	3.6	0.0	GEISINGER INS CORP RRG
4.7	3.2	39.9	5.1	-2.2	-2.3	56.2	33.2	89.4	115.8	4.5	0.0	GEM STATE INS CO
7.5	6.7	N/A	N/A	N/A	N/A	N/A	N/A	N/A	28.3	0.0	0.0	GEMINI INS CO
2.2	2.0	129.8	43.7	2.3	3.1	70.7	28.3	99.0	74.1	12.7	0.0	GENERAL AUTOMOBILE INS CO
1.0	0.6	176.7	172.0	8.4	17.2	75.2	35.6	110.8	78.4	-13.1	0.0	GENERAL CASUALTY CO OF IL
1.3	1.1	99.8	91.8	4.4	8.9	75.2	33.6	108.8	91.8	11.4	35.6 •	GENERAL CASUALTY CO OF WI
N/A	N/A	N/A	30.2	-19.8	-34.8	-485.8	999 +	999 +	6.1	110.6	29.1	GENERAL FIDELITY INS CO
8.5	8.0	-459.7	N/A	N/A	N/A	N/A	N/A	N/A	-13.6	-147.8	33.3	GENERAL INS CO OF AMERICA
1.5	1.3	4.7	27.2	-2.3	-4.2	30.7	44.4	75.1	71.1	-4.3	45.1 •	GENERAL REINSURANCE CORP
1.7	1.1	11.6	37.0	4.4	5.1	64.9	1.2	66.1	-34.4	40.7	0.0	GENERAL SECURITY IND CO OF AZ
1.7	1.0	7.5	103.1	-8.8	-5.0	54.8	164.8	219.6	26.5	-93.6	0.0	GENERAL SECURITY NATIONAL INS CO
5.5	3.4	10.9	19.5	-4.5	-9.7	39.8	47.0	86.8	113.9	19.9	0.0 •	GENERAL STAR INDEMNITY CO
9.0	6.2	4.9	23.3	-6.7	-13.4	-33.8	56.9	23.1	50.0	5.0	0.0 •	GENERAL STAR NATIONAL INS CO
0.5	0.4	120.4	66.8	13.7	24.0	67.4	31.5	98.9	138.2	-3.3	0.3	GENERALI - US BRANCH
2.5	1.6	79.4	24.1	-0.3	2.2	57.5	34.1	91.6	123.3	0.6	0.0	GENESEE PATRONS COOP INS
7.2	5.5	7.7	34.4	-1.9	-10.0	73.0	30.1	103.1	131.2	28.1	0.0	GENESIS INS CO
1.3	1.2	140.7	48.8	10.5	12.3	73.7	42.0	115.7	81.2	1.2	0.0	GENEVA INS CO
N/A	N/A	N/A	N/A	-0.2	-2.8	999 +	N/A	N/A	N/A	-100.0	0.0	GENWORTH FINANCIAL ASR CORP
1.2	1.0	48.2	119.4	-8.6	3.5	79.2	29.8	109.0	50.2	1.7	30.7 •	GENWORTH MORTGAGE INS CORP
12.8	11.5	6.7	0.3	0.1	N/A	4.7	15.7	20.4	540.3	88.4	0.0	GENWORTH MORTGAGE REINS CORP
1.2	0.9	40.9	153.3	-14.6	-38.7	64.3	N/A	64.3	50.1	-2.1	17.8	GENWORTH MTG INS CORP OF NC
1.2	0.9	48.9	134.1	-7.9	-5.1	59.9	24.4	84.3	102.0	-1.9	1.2	GENWORTH RESIDENTIAL MTG INS
3.6	2.3	91.7	81.3	0.9	7.2	74.2	27.4	101.6	99.8	-13.4	0.0	GEORGIA CASUALTY & SURETY CO
0.3	0.3	63.3	89.1	0.3	6.8	194.7	46.3	241.0	70.0	-40.3	0.0	GEORGIA DEALERS INS CO
100.3	49.9	N/A	N/A	N/A	N/A	N/A	N/A	N/A	N/A	0.0	0.0	GEORGIA FARM BUREAU CASUALTY INS
2.1	1.4	155.5	47.8	0.5	-0.7	74.3	31.7	106.0	92.0	5.4	1.7 •	GEORGIA FARM BUREAU MUTUAL INS
1.4	0.6	109.6	139.6	-3.8	N/A	85.3	20.2	105.5	175.6	3.1	0.0	GEORGIA MUNICIPAL CAPTIVE INS CO
0.1	0.1	368.8	141.1	3.6	8.0	93.4	22.7	116.1	102.7	94.5	0.0	GEORGIA MUTUAL INS CO
2.5	1.4	61.7	96.9	3.0	-19.3	76.5	27.5	104.0	119.0	0.7	0.0	GEORGIA TRANSPORTATION CAPTIVE
0.4	0.3	90.7	19.9	-1.2	-3.2	27.2	22.7	49.9	210.8	7.0	0.0	GEOVERA INS CO
0.7	0.4	54.9	12.1	-0.8	-1.9	27.2	22.7	49.9	390.5	7.0	0.0	GEOVERA SPECIALTY INS CO

999 + Denotes number greater than 999.9%
999 - Denotes number less than -999.99%
• Bullets denote a more detailed analysis is available in Section II.

INSURANCE COMPANY NAME	DOM. STATE	RATING	TOTAL ASSETS ($MIL)	CAPITAL & SURPLUS ($MIL)	ANNUAL NET PREMIUM ($MIL)	NET INCOME ($MIL)	CAPITAL-IZATION INDEX (PTS)	RESERVE ADQ INDEX (PTS)	PROFIT-ABILITY INDEX (PTS)	LIQUIDITY INDEX (PTS)	STAB. INDEX (PTS)	STABILITY FACTORS
GERMAN AMERICAN FARM MUTUAL	TX	B-	4.1	3.2	0.5	0.1	10.0	4.6	8.4	9.5	3.5	D
GERMAN MUTUAL INS CO	OH	E	34.0	9.4	18.1	0.2	5.3	5.8	1.4	2.9	0.1	DFLR
GERMANIA FARM MUTUAL INS ASN	TX	D	397.6	179.7	202.7	4.2	6.8	6.2	3.2	1.7	1.8	FLR
GERMANIA FIRE & CASUALTY CO	TX	C	30.2	14.3	17.8	0.4	8.4	8.8	4.2	5.9	4.0	DR
GERMANIA INS CO	TX	C+	74.1	39.2	30.4	3.9	8.9	6.2	7.4	6.8	4.6	R
GERMANIA SELECT INS CO	TX	B	188.2	79.7	125.1	1.5	9.5	5.7	8.2	5.9	6.0	
GERMANTOWN INS CO	PA	C+	86.2	41.3	29.9	-0.7	9.3	6.8	5.6	6.8	4.7	T
GERMANTOWN MUTUAL INS CO	WI	B-	91.6	42.4	39.9	-0.1	9.9	9.3	6.7	6.0	4.9	R
GHS INS CO	OK	E	19.7	8.7	3.0	-1.3	1.9	3.7	0.5	6.9	0.1	CDFR
GLOBAL HAWK INS CO RRG	VT	D-	34.5	7.3	14.9	0.6	1.9	4.8	8.4	8.4	1.3	DGRT
GLOBAL HAWK PROPERTY CAS INS CO	DE	U	5.0	5.0	0.0	0.0	N/A	0.0	4.9	0.0	0.0	CLT
GLOBAL INS CO	GA	U	3.5	3.5	0.0	0.2	N/A	5.2	5.0	10.0	4.2	ORT
GLOBAL LIBERTY INS CO OF NY	NY	D-	54.9	15.1	35.5	0.9	7.3	9.4	4.9	6.4	1.3	DGR
GLOBAL REINS CORP OF AMERICA	NY	D+	415.1	134.2	0.2	-5.1	2.6	9.5	2.5	10.0	2.6	CFRT
GNY CUSTOM INS CO	AZ	B+	55.8	50.3	2.3	0.9	10.0	4.6	6.8	9.2	6.5	D
GOAUTO INS CO	LA	D	25.9	7.4	11.6	-0.2	2.7	3.5	2.9	6.2	2.2	DFGR
GOLDEN BEAR INS CO	CA	D+	114.6	46.6	9.1	2.4	7.4	9.3	8.8	7.6	2.8	GR
GOLDEN EAGLE INS CORP	NH	C	64.5	53.3	-156.7	-0.4	10.0	4.8	1.9	0.0	3.5	FLRT
GOLDEN INS CO RRG	NV	D	8.5	3.1	2.8	0.4	2.0	1.9	5.7	7.7	1.8	CDGR
GOLDSTREET INS CO	NY	U	5.9	4.6	0.0	0.3	N/A	7.0	3.2	10.0	4.3	FRT
GOOD SHEPHERD RECIPROCAL RRG	SC	E+	6.8	3.3	1.9	0.5	1.0	0.4	3.7	7.3	0.0	CDGT
▲GOODVILLE MUTUAL CAS CO	PA	B-	215.3	115.0	100.5	2.9	9.4	7.5	8.3	6.8	5.1	T
GOTHAM INS CO	NY	B-	203.2	76.4	50.7	3.0	8.1	8.8	6.0	7.7	4.7	G
GOVERNMENT EMPLOYEES INS CO	MD	B+	22,729.4	13,358.4	11,644.8	1,263.8	8.0	9.3	8.5	6.3	5.3	G
GOVERNMENT ENTITIES MUTUAL INC	DC	D (2)	74.0	30.0	8.0	1.2	4.8	5.8	6.7	7.9	1.5	DR
GOVERNMENTAL INTERINSURANCE	IL	B	68.9	46.4	7.0	0.1	10.0	8.4	5.5	7.4	5.5	D
GOVT TECHNOLOGY INS CO RRG INC	NV	B-	1.0	0.6	0.5	0.0	7.1	N/A	3.3	4.8	3.5	DFGL
GRACO RRG INC	SC	U	1.0	0.6	0.0	0.1	N/A	N/A	3.2	10.0	0.0	T
GRAIN DEALERS MUTUAL INS CO	IN	C-	8.6	6.5	0.0	0.0	10.0	4.7	2.9	9.6	2.9	DFR
GRANADA INS CO	FL	E+	33.9	8.2	15.9	-0.4	0.2	2.2	2.7	1.0	0.6	CDFL
GRANGE INDEMNITY INS CO	OH	C	94.0	46.0	45.6	2.2	9.4	8.1	6.7	6.5	4.3	T
GRANGE INS ASN	WA	C+	269.9	140.4	132.7	0.9	9.6	6.2	6.7	6.4	4.4	R
GRANGE INS CO OF MI	OH	C	66.3	37.1	28.5	1.5	9.8	8.0	6.8	6.6	4.2	T
GRANGE MUTUAL CAS CO	OH	B+	2,088.9	1,042.4	957.4	22.9	8.6	8.1	6.7	6.2	5.0	
GRANGE MUTUAL FIRE INS CO	PA	D+	4.0	3.1	0.8	0.1	9.3	7.5	7.8	8.5	2.1	DR
GRANGE PROPERTY & CASUALTY INS CO	OH	C	58.8	32.1	22.8	2.8	9.7	8.1	6.8	6.7	3.9	T
GRANITE MUTUAL INS CO	VT	C+	4.3	4.3	0.0	0.0	10.0	N/A	6.5	7.0	3.4	DR
GRANITE RE INC	OK	C-	39.6	18.9	21.7	1.7	5.0	10.0	8.4	6.9	3.3	DR
GRANITE STATE INS CO	PA	B-	32.9	30.5	0.0	0.6	10.0	N/A	6.4	7.0	5.3	T
GRAPHIC ARTS MUTUAL INS CO	NY	C+	139.7	53.4	32.6	0.4	9.5	4.4	5.6	6.8	4.4	
GRAY CASUALTY & SURETY CO	LA	C	16.7	14.7	3.1	0.1	10.0	3.6	3.8	9.4	3.1	DR
GRAY INS CO	LA	C+	290.6	111.7	63.2	4.1	7.3	6.6	6.8	6.8	4.6	FR
GREAT AMERICAN ALLIANCE INS CO	OH	C	29.0	29.0	0.0	0.5	10.0	N/A	6.8	7.0	4.3	ART
GREAT AMERICAN ASR CO	OH	C+	19.1	19.1	0.0	0.2	10.0	N/A	4.9	7.0	4.4	ADR
GREAT AMERICAN CASUALTY INS CO	OH	U	12.7	12.7	0.0	0.2	N/A	N/A	6.9	7.0	5.4	AT
GREAT AMERICAN CONTEMPORARY INS CO	OH	U	10.3	10.3	0.0	0.1	N/A	N/A	6.1	7.0	5.4	ART
GREAT AMERICAN E & S INS CO	DE	C	45.8	45.8	0.0	0.5	10.0	N/A	7.4	7.0	4.0	AR
GREAT AMERICAN FIDELITY INS CO	DE	C	45.8	45.8	0.0	0.5	10.0	N/A	7.5	7.0	3.9	ADRT
GREAT AMERICAN INS CO	OH	B-	5,734.6	1,355.5	2,100.1	146.6	7.5	9.3	5.1	6.7	5.0	A
GREAT AMERICAN INS CO OF NEW YORK	NY	C	47.0	46.9	0.0	0.6	10.0	N/A	3.9	7.0	4.3	AR
GREAT AMERICAN LLOYDS INS CO	TX	C	1.4	1.5	0.0	0.0	10.0	N/A	6.5	10.0	2.9	DRT
GREAT AMERICAN PROTECTION INS CO	OH	C	25.9	25.9	0.0	0.4	10.0	N/A	6.8	7.0	3.7	ADRT

See Page 27 for explanation of footnotes and Page 28 for explanation of stability factors.

72

www.weissratings.com

Arrows denote recent upgrades ▲ or downgrades ▼   (see Section VII for explanations)

RISK ADJ. CAPITAL RATIO #1	CAPITAL RATIO #2	PREMIUM TO SURPLUS (%)	RESV. TO SURPLUS (%)	RESV. DEVELOP. 1 YEAR (%)	RESV. DEVELOP. 2 YEAR (%)	LOSS RATIO (%)	EXP. RATIO (%)	COMB RATIO (%)	CASH FROM UNDER-WRITING (%)	NET PREMIUM GROWTH (%)	INVEST. IN AFFIL (%)	INSURANCE COMPANY NAME
8.3	7.4	15.1	5.7	-1.7	-2.2	85.8	-13.6	72.2	135.7	17.6	0.0	GERMAN AMERICAN FARM MUTUAL
1.2	0.7	188.8	62.0	0.5	0.7	72.5	44.7	117.2	80.9	1.5	0.0	GERMAN MUTUAL INS CO
1.0	0.9	114.7	11.4	3.0	-1.6	82.5	29.7	112.2	89.8	1.6	53.0	GERMANIA FARM MUTUAL INS ASN
2.6	2.2	128.4	42.0	-4.2	-6.7	75.3	24.6	99.9	100.3	4.2	0.0	GERMANIA FIRE & CASUALTY CO
3.2	2.6	79.4	38.0	-4.4	-3.6	52.8	23.0	75.8	122.2	3.7	0.0	GERMANIA INS CO
3.1	2.6	151.2	39.2	-4.4	-6.2	68.3	25.8	94.1	107.9	7.6	1.4	GERMANIA SELECT INS CO
3.7	2.8	71.0	42.6	-6.3	-8.3	60.4	25.9	86.3	130.6	8.0	0.0	GERMANTOWN INS CO
4.4	3.1	93.7	45.3	-5.8	-9.9	65.8	30.0	95.8	105.7	5.8	0.0	GERMANTOWN MUTUAL INS CO
0.7	0.5	30.9	136.4	28.2	6.3	147.4	113.9	261.3	32.8	-82.1	0.0	GHS INS CO
0.6	0.4	224.1	132.3	15.0	2.2	76.6	18.3	94.9	205.9	82.6	0.0	GLOBAL HAWK INS CO RRG
N/A	N/A	N/A	N/A	N/A	N/A	N/A	N/A	N/A	N/A	0.0	0.0	GLOBAL HAWK PROPERTY CAS INS CO
N/A	N/A	N/A	N/A	-0.6	-0.4	-688.9	999 +	999 +	-22.6	97.6	0.0	GLOBAL INS CO
1.5	1.0	250.9	116.5	5.6	-5.2	65.5	32.3	97.8	118.3	91.4	0.0	GLOBAL LIBERTY INS CO OF NY
0.6	0.4	0.1	108.7	-8.8	-36.7	999 +	999 +	999 +	0.2	167.7	0.0 •	GLOBAL REINS CORP OF AMERICA
24.1	17.3	4.7	7.4	N/A	N/A	61.1	33.3	94.4	97.1	9.7	0.0 •	GNY CUSTOM INS CO
0.7	0.4	148.4	74.4	-0.9	N/A	115.8	16.4	132.2	100.4	213.6	0.0	GOAUTO INS CO
1.9	1.2	20.5	109.7	-7.9	-15.1	62.1	4.1	66.2	245.9	29.2	0.0	GOLDEN BEAR INS CO
22.9	20.6	-292.0	N/A	N/A	N/A	N/A	N/A	N/A	-8.8	-147.8	0.0	GOLDEN EAGLE INS CORP
0.6	0.4	116.0	42.3	21.2	26.0	62.9	23.8	86.7	134.2	61.1	0.0	GOLDEN INS CO RRG
N/A	N/A	N/A	42.8	N/A	-17.9	N/A	N/A	N/A	N/A	100.0	0.0	GOLDSTREET INS CO
0.3	0.2	69.3	77.0	22.9	65.3	72.3	9.8	82.1	214.2	70.6	0.0	GOOD SHEPHERD RECIPROCAL RRG
3.7	2.5	88.8	29.7	0.3	-0.1	69.4	27.1	96.5	119.2	22.7	0.0	GOODVILLE MUTUAL CAS CO
2.5	1.5	69.8	90.6	-2.1	-6.2	58.5	35.7	94.2	147.5	36.8	0.0	GOTHAM INS CO
3.4	2.1	96.3	65.4	-5.6	-11.5	77.2	11.2	88.4	117.0	4.7	0.5 •	GOVERNMENT EMPLOYEES INS CO
1.1	0.8	28.3	141.5	-3.7	-8.6	65.0	21.6	86.6	177.6	4.6	0.0	GOVERNMENT ENTITIES MUTUAL INC
4.7	3.4	15.1	30.7	-5.9	-6.8	68.7	45.5	114.2	88.4	7.8	0.0	GOVERNMENTAL INTERINSURANCE
1.2	1.0	98.3	N/A	N/A	N/A	2.7	62.3	65.0	96.7	52.0	0.0	GOVT TECHNOLOGY INS CO RRG INC
N/A	N/A	N/A	N/A	N/A	N/A	N/A	N/A	N/A	-84.5	-100.0	0.0	GRACO RRG INC
8.8	7.9	N/A	N/A	N/A	N/A	N/A	N/A	N/A	18.4	0.0	0.0	GRAIN DEALERS MUTUAL INS CO
0.1	0.1	187.3	158.0	21.2	36.2	63.4	34.0	97.4	72.7	-1.8	0.0	GRANADA INS CO
4.3	3.0	104.3	49.9	-0.5	-2.7	66.9	29.1	96.0	105.7	7.7	0.0	GRANGE INDEMNITY INS CO
3.3	2.5	96.2	40.3	-1.6	-1.9	67.6	28.9	96.5	107.6	5.9	8.3	GRANGE INS ASN
4.6	3.2	80.4	38.5	-0.4	-2.1	66.9	25.9	92.8	98.1	7.7	0.0	GRANGE INS CO OF MI
3.1	2.2	94.8	45.4	-0.5	-2.6	66.9	31.2	98.1	106.6	7.7	11.3 •	GRANGE MUTUAL CAS CO
4.1	2.5	29.0	5.3	-0.4	-1.2	56.3	46.9	103.2	97.1	2.3	0.0	GRANGE MUTUAL FIRE INS CO
4.8	3.3	78.0	37.4	-0.4	-2.3	66.9	15.6	82.5	110.9	7.7	0.0	GRANGE PROPERTY & CASUALTY INS
80.6	41.4	N/A	N/A	N/A	N/A	N/A	N/A	N/A	N/A	0.0	0.0	GRANITE MUTUAL INS CO
1.0	0.8	127.3	78.7	-21.3	-48.6	22.3	69.1	91.4	126.1	4.1	0.0	GRANITE RE INC
24.4	20.2	N/A	N/A	N/A	N/A	N/A	N/A	N/A	N/A	0.0	2.7	GRANITE STATE INS CO
3.9	2.5	62.4	104.7	-0.7	-2.5	65.5	36.3	101.8	96.6	8.9	2.7	GRAPHIC ARTS MUTUAL INS CO
10.6	8.0	21.4	10.2	N/A	N/A	35.3	50.7	86.0	118.4	10.9	0.0	GRAY CASUALTY & SURETY CO
2.0	1.5	56.8	146.8	N/A	-3.5	57.4	42.4	99.8	87.5	0.2	9.0	GRAY INS CO
99.1	49.5	N/A	N/A	N/A	N/A	N/A	N/A	N/A	N/A	0.0	0.0	GREAT AMERICAN ALLIANCE INS CO
112.8	55.1	N/A	N/A	N/A	N/A	N/A	N/A	N/A	N/A	0.0	0.0	GREAT AMERICAN ASR CO
N/A	N/A	N/A	N/A	N/A	N/A	N/A	N/A	N/A	N/A	0.0	0.0	GREAT AMERICAN CASUALTY INS CO
N/A	N/A	N/A	N/A	N/A	N/A	N/A	N/A	N/A	N/A	0.0	0.0	GREAT AMERICAN CONTEMPORARY INS
100.9	51.9	N/A	N/A	N/A	N/A	N/A	N/A	N/A	N/A	0.0	0.0	GREAT AMERICAN E & S INS CO
104.7	53.5	N/A	N/A	N/A	N/A	N/A	N/A	N/A	N/A	0.0	0.0	GREAT AMERICAN FIDELITY INS CO
1.6	1.1	149.7	173.1	-4.0	-6.0	59.1	33.8	92.9	115.4	12.8	11.6 •	GREAT AMERICAN INS CO
71.1	38.2	N/A	N/A	N/A	N/A	N/A	N/A	N/A	N/A	0.0	0.0	GREAT AMERICAN INS CO OF NEW
126.2	63.0	N/A	N/A	N/A	N/A	N/A	N/A	N/A	N/A	0.0	0.0	GREAT AMERICAN LLOYDS INS CO
75.5	38.7	N/A	N/A	N/A	N/A	N/A	N/A	N/A	N/A	0.0	0.0	GREAT AMERICAN PROTECTION INS CO

999 + Denotes number greater than 999.9%
999 - Denotes number less than -999.99%
• Bullets denote a more detailed analysis is available in Section II.

INSURANCE COMPANY NAME	DOM. STATE	RATING	TOTAL ASSETS ($MIL)	CAPITAL & SURPLUS ($MIL)	ANNUAL NET PREMIUM ($MIL)	NET INCOME ($MIL)	CAPITAL-IZATION INDEX (PTS)	RESERVE ADQ INDEX (PTS)	PROFIT-ABILITY INDEX (PTS)	LIQUIDITY INDEX (PTS)	STAB. INDEX (PTS)	STABILITY FACTORS
GREAT AMERICAN SECURITY INS CO	OH	C	17.9	17.9	0.0	0.2	10.0	N/A	6.6	7.0	3.7	ADRT
GREAT AMERICAN SPIRIT INS CO	OH	C	19.9	19.9	0.0	0.3	10.0	N/A	6.8	7.0	4.3	ADRT
GREAT CENTRAL FIRE INS CO	LA	D+ (3)	0.0	0.0	3.7	0.2	5.2	7.5	5.6	6.6	2.5	D
GREAT DIVIDE INS CO	ND	C	199.0	66.7	-20.6	1.5	10.0	4.7	5.3	3.4	3.9	FLRT
GREAT FALLS INS CO	ME	D	6.8	2.0	1.3	-0.1	1.2	3.6	0.9	3.8	1.5	CDFG
GREAT LAKES CASUALTY INS CO	MI	D	16.6	16.6	0.0	0.3	10.0	0.9	7.5	7.0	2.1	DT
GREAT LAKES MUTUAL INS CO	MI	D	9.4	5.6	4.0	0.7	8.4	9.1	7.9	7.0	2.3	D
GREAT MIDWEST INS CO	TX	B-	156.1	65.9	63.0	2.8	7.9	7.9	4.7	7.2	3.9	GT
GREAT NORTHERN INS CO	IN	B	1,661.0	472.9	360.6	58.4	8.2	9.2	8.2	6.9	4.9	T
GREAT NORTHWEST INS CO	MN	C-	21.4	6.7	0.0	0.4	8.3	3.2	2.9	10.0	3.3	DFR
GREAT PLAINS CASUALTY INC	IA	C	16.0	13.4	5.3	0.6	10.0	7.5	4.0	6.9	3.0	DT
GREAT WEST CASUALTY CO	NE	A-	1,829.1	566.4	712.5	73.6	9.5	9.5	8.9	6.6	7.1	A
GREATER NEW YORK MUTUAL INS CO	NY	B-	887.9	426.4	196.7	7.9	8.5	7.7	5.1	6.9	4.7	R
GREEN HILLS INS CO RRG	VT	E	11.8	4.7	4.5	0.7	7.6	9.7	1.9	6.9	0.0	D
GREEN MOUNTAIN INS CO INC	VT	B	11.2	10.8	0.0	0.2	10.0	N/A	7.7	7.0	4.0	DT
GREEN TREE PERPETUAL ASR CO	PA	U	0.2	0.2	0.0	-0.1	N/A	N/A	1.8	7.0	0.6	FT
GREENPATH INS CO	CA	U	11.7	10.4	0.0	-0.7	N/A	N/A	3.0	10.0	4.1	FT
GREENVILLE CASUALTY INS CO INC	SC	D-	14.6	5.6	19.2	-1.9	2.0	6.9	1.1	0.8	1.0	DGLT
GREENWICH INS CO	DE	C	1,036.8	384.4	159.7	31.7	7.7	6.2	5.1	6.8	3.5	AFR
GRINNELL MUTUAL REINSURANCE CO	IA	B-	910.5	420.4	451.7	31.6	8.6	9.1	6.7	6.1	4.7	R
GRINNELL SELECT INS CO	IA	C	40.5	27.4	0.0	0.6	10.0	3.8	6.2	10.0	4.1	F
GROWERS AUTOMOBILE INS ASN	IN	D (2)	5.9	4.6	0.1	0.0	7.4	N/A	4.2	10.0	2.2	DT
GUARANTEE CO OF NORTH AMERICA USA	MI	C+	191.5	162.0	30.9	8.6	10.0	6.0	6.9	9.6	4.6	R
GUARANTEE INS CO	FL	E+	424.4	84.6	67.3	-4.6	1.1	0.1	2.7	3.8	0.5	CLR
GUARDIAN INS CO INC	VI	C	35.2	17.0	18.9	1.1	8.0	8.1	3.6	6.3	2.9	DT
GUARDIAN RRG INC	MT	D-	5.8	3.5	1.1	0.1	7.0	5.0	4.4	7.1	1.3	D
GUIDEONE AMERICA INS CO	IA	B-	11.6	10.4	0.0	0.1	10.0	N/A	6.8	7.0	4.2	DRT
GUIDEONE ELITE INS CO	IA	C+	28.7	21.0	0.0	0.3	10.0	N/A	7.1	7.0	4.4	DR
GUIDEONE LLOYDS INS CO	TX	B-	3.5	3.2	0.0	0.0	10.0	N/A	6.9	7.0	3.9	DFR
GUIDEONE MUTUAL INS CO	IA	B-	2,459.2	449.4	334.8	10.6	7.3	9.3	5.2	6.4	4.6	FGRT
GUIDEONE NATIONAL INS CO	IA	C	49.9	45.3	0.0	0.3	10.0	N/A	4.9	9.5	3.6	DFGT
GUIDEONE PROPERTY & CASUALTY INS CO	IA	B	684.5	243.1	104.6	2.8	8.8	8.7	6.8	6.7	5.5	F
GUIDEONE SPECIALTY MUTUAL INS CO	IA	B	590.7	94.0	83.7	1.2	7.7	9.4	6.6	5.8	4.3	FGRT
GUILDERLAND REINSURANCE CO	NY	U	3.3	3.0	0.0	0.0	N/A	4.6	2.8	10.0	4.0	FGT
GUILFORD INS CO	IL	C-	392.7	274.1	40.7	5.8	7.8	8.3	8.3	7.8	2.6	R
GULF BUILDERS RRG INC	SC	F (5)	0.0	0.0	-0.1	0.0	3.0	4.6	0.8	10.0	0.0	FGT
GULF GUARANTY INS CO	MS	C	4.7	3.8	1.2	0.0	10.0	6.1	2.7	7.0	2.8	DF
GULF UNDERWRITERS INS CO	CT	U	55.9	48.7	0.0	1.0	N/A	N/A	6.6	7.0	5.4	T
GULFSTREAM PROP & CAS INS CO	FL	C	112.4	32.0	52.8	3.1	5.2	7.0	4.1	7.5	4.0	G
GUTHRIE RRG	SC	D	54.2	20.0	7.7	3.2	7.7	9.8	3.9	9.0	1.3	D
HALIFAX MUTUAL INS CO	NC	E	6.4	2.7	3.2	0.2	6.0	8.3	3.0	6.3	0.1	DRT
HALLMARK COUNTY MUTUAL INS CO	TX	C	5.2	5.5	0.0	0.0	10.0	N/A	3.9	7.0	2.4	DRT
HALLMARK INS CO	AZ	D	238.5	79.8	98.5	5.0	7.7	4.6	5.9	6.5	1.4	R
HALLMARK NATIONAL INS CO	OH	C	89.8	22.3	45.4	1.3	7.0	4.2	4.3	6.9	3.2	DR
HALLMARK SPECIALTY INS CO	OK	C	235.2	56.7	109.3	4.0	6.9	3.8	5.0	6.6	4.0	R
HAMDEN ASR RRG INC	VT	U	94.5	1.6	0.0	0.0	N/A	N/A	6.0	10.0	0.5	CT
HAMILTON MUTUAL INS CO	IA	C	78.8	31.4	27.0	0.3	9.0	8.6	5.2	6.7	3.9	T
HANNAHSTOWN MUTUAL INS CO	PA	D	3.5	2.2	1.0	0.1	7.9	6.6	6.0	7.3	1.7	DRT
HANOVER AMERICAN INS CO	NH	C	29.1	29.0	0.0	0.5	10.0	N/A	7.7	7.0	4.3	R
HANOVER FIRE & CASUALTY INS CO	PA	D+	4.3	3.0	3.4	0.2	6.1	5.9	5.1	6.8	2.0	DR
HANOVER INS CO	NH	B	6,424.6	1,993.9	2,759.4	111.0	7.3	5.5	5.3	5.9	5.2	A
HANOVER LLOYDS INS CO	TX	C+	5.8	5.8	0.0	0.1	10.0	N/A	7.6	7.0	3.6	DR

See Page 27 for explanation of footnotes and Page 28 for explanation of stability factors.
Arrows denote recent upgrades ▲ or downgrades ▼ (see Section VII for explanations)

74

www.weissratings.com

RISK ADJ. CAPITAL RATIO #1	RATIO #2	PREMIUM TO SURPLUS (%)	RESV. TO SURPLUS (%)	RESV. DEVELOP. 1 YEAR (%)	2 YEAR (%)	LOSS RATIO (%)	EXP. RATIO (%)	COMB RATIO (%)	CASH FROM UNDER- WRITING (%)	NET PREMIUM GROWTH (%)	INVEST. IN AFFIL (%)	INSURANCE COMPANY NAME
113.3	56.6	N/A	N/A	N/A	N/A	N/A	N/A	N/A	N/A	0.0	0.0	GREAT AMERICAN SECURITY INS CO
82.1	44.1	N/A	N/A	N/A	N/A	N/A	N/A	N/A	N/A	0.0	0.0	GREAT AMERICAN SPIRIT INS CO
1.0	0.8	126.5	8.1	-0.5	-1.0	23.0	76.0	99.0	100.2	-9.0	0.0	GREAT CENTRAL FIRE INS CO
7.2	6.4	-31.4	N/A	N/A	N/A	N/A	N/A	N/A	49.5	-138.8	0.0	GREAT DIVIDE INS CO
0.2	0.2	64.0	38.6	-2.1	2.4	84.2	61.9	146.1	75.0	70.5	0.0	GREAT FALLS INS CO
102.3	51.1	N/A	N/A	N/A	N/A	N/A	N/A	N/A	N/A	0.0	0.0	GREAT LAKES CASUALTY INS CO
4.1	2.5	81.5	18.3	-5.9	-9.2	32.8	32.3	65.1	155.2	14.1	0.0	GREAT LAKES MUTUAL INS CO
2.0	1.3	112.4	53.7	-1.5	-3.3	64.3	31.2	95.5	176.0	145.7	0.0	GREAT MIDWEST INS CO
2.8	1.8	75.3	135.1	-4.9	-8.1	52.7	29.9	82.6	110.7	3.9	0.0 •	GREAT NORTHERN INS CO
2.2	2.0	N/A	18.8	11.5	24.1	N/A	N/A	N/A	-64.9	0.0	0.0	GREAT NORTHWEST INS CO
5.9	3.5	41.5	9.2	-5.7	-1.9	72.3	15.4	87.7	134.4	27.6	0.0	GREAT PLAINS CASUALTY INC
3.9	2.4	130.3	124.0	-8.6	-17.8	71.3	22.1	93.4	111.6	6.5	0.0 •	GREAT WEST CASUALTY CO
2.4	1.9	47.4	73.8	-0.1	-0.3	61.1	33.3	94.4	97.1	9.7	16.9 •	GREATER NEW YORK MUTUAL INS CO
1.4	0.8	26.8	32.6	-0.3	-29.4	-18.0	18.3	0.3	471.0	1.1	0.0	GREEN HILLS INS CO RRG
5.2	3.1	N/A	N/A	N/A	N/A	N/A	N/A	N/A	N/A	0.0	0.0	GREEN MOUNTAIN INS CO INC
N/A	N/A	N/A	7.0	N/A	N/A	N/A	N/A	N/A	N/A	0.0	0.0	GREEN TREE PERPETUAL ASR CO
N/A	N/A	0.4	N/A	N/A	N/A	61.7	499.1	560.8	1.7	0.0	0.0	GREENPATH INS CO
0.6	0.5	422.4	105.9	4.6	0.8	85.4	28.7	114.1	106.5	149.9	29.2	GREENVILLE CASUALTY INS CO INC
1.5	1.3	38.3	97.4	-0.5	-1.2	65.3	35.3	100.6	99.8	2.9	28.5 •	GREENWICH INS CO
2.9	2.0	112.9	63.9	-5.5	-5.8	65.9	29.1	95.0	108.4	10.0	4.9 •	GRINNELL MUTUAL REINSURANCE CO
9.9	8.9	N/A	N/A	N/A	N/A	N/A	N/A	N/A	4.2	0.0	0.0	GRINNELL SELECT INS CO
2.1	1.2	3.3	2.6	N/A	N/A	139.9	96.4	236.3	146.8	0.0	0.0	GROWERS AUTOMOBILE INS ASN
7.4	5.1	19.8	5.1	-2.0	1.6	22.1	66.4	88.5	109.0	18.4	0.0	GUARANTEE CO OF NORTH AMERICA
0.7	0.4	116.6	192.1	0.4	118.5	111.2	17.1	128.3	98.2	-37.1	0.0	GUARANTEE INS CO
1.7	1.5	114.0	19.8	1.7	-2.5	59.9	36.4	96.3	107.2	42.5	20.8	GUARDIAN INS CO INC
1.4	1.1	32.4	65.6	-1.2	-3.9	89.4	20.5	109.9	91.5	-0.5	0.0	GUARDIAN RRG INC
20.2	18.2	N/A	N/A	N/A	N/A	N/A	N/A	N/A	-25.6	0.0	0.0	GUIDEONE AMERICA INS CO
10.4	9.3	N/A	N/A	N/A	N/A	N/A	N/A	N/A	-0.7	0.0	0.0	GUIDEONE ELITE INS CO
23.3	20.9	N/A	N/A	N/A	N/A	N/A	N/A	N/A	349.7	0.0	0.0	GUIDEONE LLOYDS INS CO
1.7	1.4	72.8	78.1	-3.4	-11.7	70.5	37.6	108.1	93.6	13.2	23.5 •	GUIDEONE MUTUAL INS CO
31.8	28.6	N/A	N/A	N/A	N/A	N/A	N/A	N/A	39.3	0.0	0.0	GUIDEONE NATIONAL INS CO
3.0	2.4	43.3	46.5	-1.9	-6.7	70.5	33.7	104.2	85.0	13.2	15.3 •	GUIDEONE PROPERTY & CASUALTY INS
2.5	1.8	89.7	96.2	-4.0	-14.0	70.5	33.7	104.2	69.9	13.2	8.1	GUIDEONE SPECIALTY MUTUAL INS CO
N/A	N/A	N/A	N/A	N/A	N/A	N/A	N/A	N/A	N/A	0.0	0.0	GUILDERLAND REINSURANCE CO
1.6	1.5	15.2	36.3	-3.0	-4.9	50.6	38.6	89.2	104.3	-5.6	47.2 •	GUILFORD INS CO
0.5	0.5	-52.9	20.2	-3.2	-0.7	27.2	-79.2	-52.0	1.0	-167.1	0.0	GULF BUILDERS RRG INC
3.5	3.0	32.3	3.9	-1.1	0.4	40.5	80.0	120.5	73.0	-8.9	2.0	GULF GUARANTY INS CO
N/A	N/A	N/A	N/A	N/A	N/A	N/A	N/A	N/A	286.3	0.0	0.0	GULF UNDERWRITERS INS CO
1.4	1.0	179.2	45.3	-5.3	-25.3	52.5	33.8	86.3	130.5	32.8	0.0	GULFSTREAM PROP & CAS INS CO
2.0	1.5	33.9	114.3	-16.7	-15.4	64.6	4.0	68.6	220.1	-0.6	0.0	GUTHRIE RRG
1.3	0.8	130.8	15.0	-7.4	-6.8	62.6	30.8	93.4	91.6	5.5	0.0	HALIFAX MUTUAL INS CO
72.0	29.0	N/A	N/A	N/A	N/A	N/A	N/A	N/A	N/A	0.0	0.0	HALLMARK COUNTY MUTUAL INS CO
2.1	1.4	130.4	111.2	2.3	N/A	72.4	31.2	103.6	98.6	21.0	13.7	HALLMARK INS CO
1.8	1.1	218.9	189.6	3.6	-2.5	72.4	32.9	105.3	117.6	-10.7	0.0	HALLMARK NATIONAL INS CO
2.2	1.3	196.6	167.6	3.5	N/A	72.4	34.2	106.6	106.0	5.3	0.0	HALLMARK SPECIALTY INS CO
N/A	N/A	N/A	N/A	N/A	N/A	N/A	N/A	N/A	N/A	0.0	0.0	HAMDEN ASR RRG INC
3.2	2.2	86.9	87.1	-1.1	-4.2	67.2	32.9	100.1	107.5	9.1	0.0	HAMILTON MUTUAL INS CO
2.7	1.6	47.0	11.7	2.1	-5.8	50.4	40.4	90.8	104.6	8.1	0.0	HANNAHSTOWN MUTUAL INS CO
86.1	41.3	N/A	N/A	N/A	N/A	N/A	N/A	N/A	N/A	0.0	0.0	HANOVER AMERICAN INS CO
1.2	1.0	120.9	16.2	-4.9	0.2	21.1	74.4	95.5	104.8	-3.4	0.0	HANOVER FIRE & CASUALTY INS CO
1.4	1.2	150.8	123.7	2.4	9.5	64.8	36.1	100.9	100.1	3.7	22.7 •	HANOVER INS CO
78.1	35.8	N/A	N/A	N/A	N/A	N/A	N/A	N/A	N/A	0.0	0.0	HANOVER LLOYDS INS CO

999 + Denotes number greater than 999.9%
999 - Denotes number less than -999.99%
• Bullets denote a more detailed analysis is available in Section II.

INSURANCE COMPANY NAME	DOM. STATE	RATING	TOTAL ASSETS ($MIL)	CAPITAL & SURPLUS ($MIL)	ANNUAL NET PREMIUM ($MIL)	NET INCOME ($MIL)	CAPITAL- IZATION INDEX (PTS)	RESERVE ADQ INDEX (PTS)	PROFIT- ABILITY INDEX (PTS)	LIQUIDITY INDEX (PTS)	STAB. INDEX (PTS)	STABILITY FACTORS
HANOVER NATIONAL INS CO	NH	U	12.0	11.9	0.0	0.2	N/A	N/A	7.7	7.0	5.4	OT
HANOVER NJ INS CO	NH	U	30.6	30.6	0.0	0.5	N/A	N/A	7.7	7.0	5.4	RT
HARBOR INS CO	OK	D+	13.9	3.3	5.4	-0.1	7.5	8.3	2.4	8.1	2.1	D
HARCO NATIONAL INS CO	IL	B-	344.2	178.1	76.4	7.7	7.1	4.6	5.4	5.9	4.7	GR
HARFORD MUTUAL INS CO	MD	B-	363.1	185.0	95.3	1.2	8.6	9.3	6.8	7.0	4.7	R
HARLEYSVILLE INS CO	PA	C	113.8	25.1	-23.4	0.8	9.1	4.9	3.7	6.5	3.8	AT
HARLEYSVILLE INS CO OF NEW YORK	PA	C	76.3	22.6	-11.7	0.6	10.0	4.9	4.4	6.9	3.8	RT
HARLEYSVILLE INS CO OF NJ	NJ	C-	93.8	42.8	-134.5	13.3	10.0	5.0	1.9	6.5	3.1	AFT
▼HARLEYSVILLE LAKE STATES INS CO	MI	C-	66.1	31.7	-52.6	4.4	10.0	5.0	1.9	6.5	3.1	AFT
▼HARLEYSVILLE PREFERRED INS CO	PA	C-	139.2	42.6	-134.5	13.5	10.0	5.0	1.9	6.6	3.1	AT
▼HARLEYSVILLE WORCESTER INS CO	PA	C-	160.8	52.0	-152.1	16.6	10.0	4.9	1.9	6.6	3.1	AT
HARTFORD ACCIDENT & INDEMNITY CO	CT	B	11,637.2	3,543.3	3,252.5	283.6	7.9	6.3	6.9	6.6	5.6	A
HARTFORD CASUALTY INS CO	IN	B	2,314.7	975.6	547.2	67.4	10.0	6.2	5.1	6.8	5.9	A
HARTFORD FIRE INS CO	CT	B	25,686.8	13,433.1	4,129.1	447.6	7.8	4.6	6.9	6.9	5.9	A
HARTFORD INS CO OF IL	IL	B	3,895.9	1,423.9	1,004.9	113.9	9.4	6.2	5.9	6.7	5.7	A
HARTFORD INS CO OF THE MIDWEST	IN	B	567.5	447.5	49.7	15.7	10.0	4.6	6.9	7.6	5.8	A
HARTFORD INS CO OF THE SOUTHEAST	CT	B	182.4	61.5	49.7	5.7	8.7	6.2	6.0	6.7	5.8	A
HARTFORD LLOYDS INS CO	TX	B	68.5	66.1	1.0	1.7	10.0	3.6	8.1	10.0	5.6	A
HARTFORD SM BOIL INSPECTION & INS	CT	B	1,348.6	617.8	727.6	69.7	8.6	9.3	5.9	7.0	6.1	
HARTFORD SM BOIL INSPECTION IC OF CT	CT	B	93.5	45.2	32.1	11.1	10.0	8.3	8.1	7.7	5.6	T
HARTFORD UNDERWRITERS INS CO	CT	B+	1,566.0	600.8	398.0	48.8	10.0	6.2	5.3	6.8	6.4	A
HARTLAND MUT INS CO	ND	D+	11.9	7.3	5.4	1.0	7.9	6.3	5.5	7.7	2.5	D
HASTINGS MUTUAL INS CO	MI	A-	777.9	346.3	354.9	9.4	10.0	6.7	4.8	6.6	7.3	
HAULERS INS CO INC	TN	C	70.7	37.2	33.6	1.3	10.0	7.4	4.4	6.5	4.3	
HAWAII EMPLOYERS MUTUAL INS CO	HI	C-	337.7	216.6	45.5	12.2	10.0	8.4	6.9	7.1	3.1	R
HAWAIIAN INS & GUARANTY CO LTD	HI	C+	24.6	12.1	10.4	0.4	7.5	5.9	5.4	7.0	4.4	DGR
HAWKEYE-SECURITY INS CO	WI	C+	14.5	12.9	0.0	0.1	10.0	N/A	5.9	7.4	4.4	DRT
HAY CREEK MUTUAL INS CO	MN	D	4.4	1.9	2.3	0.1	8.0	5.9	4.2	6.6	1.5	DT
HCC SPECIALTY INS CO	OK	C+	20.7	16.1	0.0	0.2	10.0	N/A	6.2	6.9	4.4	DFR
HDI-GERLING AMERICA INS CO	IL	C	305.0	129.5	7.1	7.0	10.0	6.9	8.7	7.7	3.6	FGRT
HEALTH CARE CASUALTY RRG INC	DC	D-	16.4	2.0	3.3	0.2	3.2	10.0	6.8	10.0	1.0	DFRT
HEALTH CARE INDEMNITY INC	CO	C-	537.4	137.1	48.2	4.8	6.1	9.5	2.1	7.4	2.9	FGR
HEALTH CARE INDUSTRY LIAB RECIP INS	DC	D-	44.6	15.6	3.4	0.3	5.7	4.1	8.9	7.4	1.3	DR
HEALTH CARE INS RECIPROCAL	MN	D	23.2	5.8	5.6	-1.1	6.1	9.5	2.5	7.0	1.8	DR
HEALTH CARE MUT CAPTIVE INS CO	GA	E	11.8	2.8	5.4	0.4	1.9	5.8	2.1	5.4	0.1	DFRT
HEALTH PROVIDERS INS RECIPROCAL RRG	HI	C+	75.1	54.6	6.5	5.4	8.9	9.5	8.8	7.1	4.5	DFRT
HEALTHCARE PROFESSIONAL INS CO INC	NY	D	294.6	34.8	37.1	-6.2	1.4	4.9	3.8	6.4	1.4	CDR
HEALTHCARE PROVIDERS INS CO RRG	SC	D	75.6	41.6	8.0	0.7	9.3	9.4	7.8	9.0	2.2	DR
HEALTHCARE PROVIDERS INS EXCH	PA	C-	85.3	25.2	33.0	-2.8	6.6	2.5	2.6	6.8	3.0	FR
HEALTHCARE UNDERWRITERS GROUP OF	KY	D+	23.1	8.9	3.1	-1.2	7.3	9.3	3.4	7.7	2.8	DFR
HEALTHCARE UNDERWRITERS GRP MUT	OH	D+	27.5	13.8	5.9	-0.1	8.6	9.6	7.1	8.8	2.7	DR
HEALTHCARE UNDERWRITERS GRP OF FL	FL	D	43.1	23.6	6.3	-0.1	9.4	9.4	6.9	8.3	1.7	DR
HEALTHCARE UNDERWRITING CO RRG	VT	D-	131.2	22.6	41.9	-3.0	0.7	3.5	2.6	7.7	0.8	CDGT
HEARTLAND HEALTHCARE RECIPROCAL	VT	D	14.8	8.7	2.8	-0.2	9.2	9.4	6.3	9.1	1.4	DT
HEARTLAND MUTUAL INS CO	MN	E	4.9	2.5	3.1	-0.3	9.0	6.7	3.9	6.8	0.1	D
HEREFORD INS CO	NY	D+	150.1	21.8	64.7	0.7	5.1	7.0	3.2	6.8	2.5	DR
HERITAGE CASUALTY INS CO	KS	U	61.2	61.0	0.0	0.7	N/A	5.8	3.7	7.0	5.9	T
▼HERITAGE INDEMNITY CO	CA	C	150.5	50.2	45.5	3.9	10.0	4.6	2.9	7.0	4.2	R
HERITAGE PROPERTY & CASUALTY INS CO	FL	C	347.1	124.7	139.6	3.4	3.8	3.6	7.3	7.0	3.2	GT
HERITAGE WARRANTY INS RRG INC	SC	U	0.6	0.5	0.0	0.0	N/A	6.9	1.1	10.0	1.7	FT
HERMITAGE INS CO	NY	E-	142.4	5.2	168.1	6.6	7.4	5.6	1.9	6.3	0.0	CFRT
HIGH POINT PREFERRED INS CO	NJ	C+(3)	0.0	0.0	82.5	22.5	7.4	6.9	4.3	6.6	4.5	

See Page 27 for explanation of footnotes and
Page 28 for explanation of stability factors.
Arrows denote recent upgrades ▲ or downgrades ▼   (see Section VII for explanations)

76

www.weissratings.com

RISK ADJ. CAPITAL RATIO #1	CAPITAL RATIO #2	PREMIUM TO SURPLUS (%)	RESV. TO SURPLUS (%)	RESV. DEVELOP. 1 YEAR (%)	DEVELOP. 2 YEAR (%)	LOSS RATIO (%)	EXP. RATIO (%)	COMB RATIO (%)	CASH FROM UNDER- WRITING (%)	NET PREMIUM GROWTH (%)	INVEST. IN AFFIL (%)	INSURANCE COMPANY NAME
N/A	N/A	N/A	N/A	N/A	N/A	N/A	N/A	N/A	N/A	0.0	0.0	HANOVER NATIONAL INS CO
N/A	N/A	N/A	N/A	N/A	N/A	N/A	N/A	N/A	N/A	0.0	0.0	HANOVER NJ INS CO
1.3	1.2	154.4	67.9	-8.3	-6.9	70.0	31.4	101.4	103.0	8.6	0.0	HARBOR INS CO
1.5	1.1	45.1	58.7	-0.8	1.7	67.0	33.4	100.4	103.5	31.4	10.1	HARCO NATIONAL INS CO
2.5	1.9	50.8	39.6	-2.9	-7.0	55.6	35.1	90.7	109.8	16.6	14.0	HARFORD MUTUAL INS CO
3.1	2.8	-67.4	N/A	N/A	N/A	N/A	20.0	N/A	132.9	-149.6	0.0	HARLEYSVILLE INS CO
3.3	3.0	-42.2	N/A	N/A	N/A	N/A	20.0	N/A	239.5	-149.6	0.0	HARLEYSVILLE INS CO OF NEW YORK
7.5	6.8	-70.5	N/A	N/A	N/A	N/A	20.0	N/A	85.2	-149.0	0.0 •	HARLEYSVILLE INS CO OF NJ
6.9	6.2	-70.6	N/A	N/A	N/A	N/A	20.0	N/A	78.6	-149.6	0.0	HARLEYSVILLE LAKE STATES INS CO
5.7	5.1	-68.7	N/A	N/A	N/A	N/A	20.0	N/A	96.9	-149.0	0.0 •	HARLEYSVILLE PREFERRED INS CO
6.4	5.8	-64.6	N/A	N/A	N/A	N/A	20.0	N/A	95.9	-148.8	0.0 •	HARLEYSVILLE WORCESTER INS CO
2.2	1.6	00.4	178.0	1.1	-0.2	00.0	29.1	97.9	103.1	1.1	9.4 •	HARTFORD ACCIDENT & INDEMNITY CO
5.2	3.3	60.4	108.2	0.6	-0.1	68.8	27.3	96.1	103.1	1.1	0.0 •	HARTFORD CASUALTY INS CO
2.0	1.4	29.3	52.5	0.3	N/A	68.8	32.1	100.9	106.9	1.1	26.0 •	HARTFORD FIRE INS CO
4.2	2.7	76.8	137.4	0.8	-0.1	68.8	29.1	97.9	103.1	1.1	0.0 •	HARTFORD INS CO OF IL
25.2	16.4	11.5	20.6	0.1	N/A	68.8	15.0	83.8	103.1	1.1	0.0 •	HARTFORD INS CO OF THE MIDWEST
3.4	2.3	89.9	160.9	1.0	-0.1	68.8	28.0	96.8	103.1	1.1	0.0	HARTFORD INS CO OF THE SOUTHEAST
67.5	32.3	1.5	2.8	N/A	N/A	68.8	-41.1	27.7	103.1	1.1	0.0	HARTFORD LLOYDS INS CO
2.1	1.8	113.5	30.2	-6.5	-10.4	26.8	57.6	84.4	124.5	8.9	15.1 •	HARTFORD SM BOIL INSPECTION & INS
3.1	2.9	62.7	14.5	-2.4	-3.8	27.4	14.0	41.4	247.7	7.4	3.0	HARTFORD SM BOIL INSPECTION IC OF
4.3	2.8	65.1	116.6	0.7	-0.1	68.8	27.3	96.1	103.1	1.1	0.0 •	HARTFORD UNDERWRITERS INS CO
3.1	2.1	85.1	8.7	-1.0	-1.9	47.5	33.3	80.8	128.3	2.8	3.3	HARTLAND MUT INS CO
4.6	3.3	105.8	68.6	-0.1	-2.9	76.8	27.8	104.6	111.3	8.0	0.0 •	HASTINGS MUTUAL INS CO
3.9	3.0	94.1	48.9	1.9	-0.1	80.8	24.9	105.7	106.0	13.3	0.0	HAULERS INS CO INC
5.4	3.8	21.7	36.1	-0.1	-1.9	72.0	26.3	98.3	109.4	35.3	0.0 •	HAWAII EMPLOYERS MUTUAL INS CO
2.4	1.5	88.7	22.4	-1.4	2.1	39.3	46.9	86.2	145.5	-28.2	0.0	HAWAIIAN INS & GUARANTY CO LTD
21.1	19.0	N/A	N/A	N/A	N/A	N/A	N/A	N/A	131.9	0.0	0.0	HAWKEYE-SECURITY INS CO
2.0	1.6	126.3	10.4	N/A	0.5	58.3	39.2	97.5	111.6	2.4	0.0	HAY CREEK MUTUAL INS CO
11.1	10.0	N/A	N/A	N/A	N/A	N/A	N/A	N/A	-72.5	0.0	0.0	HCC SPECIALTY INS CO
8.0	5.1	5.3	30.7	-1.9	-8.5	110.9	-150.7	-39.8	-41.1	41.1	3.0	HDI-GERLING AMERICA INS CO
0.8	0.6	173.1	357.9	-69.7	-119.3	64.3	30.2	94.5	-194.7	27.0	0.0	HEALTH CARE CASUALTY RRG INC
1.0	0.8	36.4	262.2	-16.4	-13.9	78.3	-4.8	73.5	64.5	59.9	0.0	HEALTH CARE INDEMNITY INC
2.4	1.6	22.4	60.8	-3.5	4.7	75.4	-1.0	74.4	278.4	-8.8	0.0	HEALTH CARE INDUSTRY LIAB RECIP
0.9	0.6	83.0	185.4	-22.4	-21.7	79.1	23.2	102.3	122.0	23.2	0.0	HEALTH CARE INS RECIPROCAL
0.6	0.4	236.7	231.4	-20.8	-4.2	70.0	32.1	102.1	90.3	8.9	0.0	HEALTH CARE MUT CAPTIVE INS CO
7.2	4.7	12.8	44.4	-5.4	-14.4	54.6	32.1	86.7	73.4	-45.9	0.0	HEALTH PROVIDERS INS RECIPROCAL
0.3	0.2	87.3	466.3	-19.9	-12.2	69.4	13.6	83.0	126.9	11.0	0.0	HEALTHCARE PROFESSIONAL INS CO
3.4	2.1	18.5	46.1	-9.5	-17.3	31.2	28.8	60.0	166.8	5.9	0.0	HEALTHCARE PROVIDERS INS CO RRG
0.9	0.7	101.4	141.7	39.3	42.1	80.7	35.6	116.3	91.0	18.0	0.0	HEALTHCARE PROVIDERS INS EXCH
1.8	1.5	31.8	112.0	-10.2	-22.0	76.4	58.0	134.4	66.7	-7.3	0.0	HEALTHCARE UNDERWRITERS GROUP
2.6	1.9	41.9	79.7	-14.2	-23.4	62.4	48.3	110.7	125.4	10.2	0.0	HEALTHCARE UNDERWRITERS GRP
3.8	3.0	26.6	69.0	-10.1	-13.8	70.6	40.3	110.9	93.4	4.9	0.0	HEALTHCARE UNDERWRITERS GRP OF
0.3	0.2	158.8	228.1	1.2	23.2	94.0	5.3	99.3	254.7	53.9	0.0	HEALTHCARE UNDERWRITING CO RRG
3.8	2.4	31.1	63.5	-15.5	-7.0	68.8	30.4	99.2	95.2	-31.7	0.0	HEARTLAND HEALTHCARE RECIPROCAL
3.0	2.0	109.8	12.2	-1.5	-2.3	58.0	37.8	95.8	114.7	25.5	0.0	HEARTLAND MUTUAL INS CO
1.0	0.6	299.9	364.2	7.6	-3.6	92.6	17.3	109.9	120.7	12.4	0.0	HEREFORD INS CO
N/A	N/A	N/A	N/A	N/A	0.3	N/A	N/A	N/A	N/A	-100.0	0.0	HERITAGE CASUALTY INS CO
5.5	5.0	40.4	1.0	0.1	N/A	70.3	24.8	95.1	94.2	-4.0	0.0	HERITAGE INDEMNITY CO
1.3	1.0	221.3	29.4	-1.8	N/A	44.4	10.2	54.6	264.6	208.5	0.0	HERITAGE PROPERTY & CASUALTY INS
N/A	N/A	N/A	1.0	-1.5	-10.3	65.4	999 +	999 +	N/A	88.4	0.0	HERITAGE WARRANTY INS RRG INC
0.2	0.2	999 +	999 +	60.5	62.8	105.8	50.4	156.2	52.8	24.2	13.1	HERMITAGE INS CO
2.2	1.6	76.6	61.9	-12.1	-8.8	53.4	17.9	71.3	126.2	2.0	5.4	HIGH POINT PREFERRED INS CO

999 + Denotes number greater than 999.9%
999 - Denotes number less than -999.99%
• Bullets denote a more detailed analysis is available in Section II.

INSURANCE COMPANY NAME	DOM. STATE	RATING	TOTAL ASSETS ($MIL)	CAPITAL & SURPLUS ($MIL)	ANNUAL NET PREMIUM ($MIL)	NET INCOME ($MIL)	CAPITAL-IZATION INDEX (PTS)	RESERVE ADQ INDEX (PTS)	PROFIT-ABILITY INDEX (PTS)	LIQUIDITY INDEX (PTS)	STAB. INDEX (PTS)	STABILITY FACTORS
HIGH POINT PROPERTY & CASUALTY INS	NJ	B (3)	0.0	0.0	0.0	1.0	8.4	3.9	4.4	7.0	5.5	FT
HIGH POINT SAFETY & INS CO	NJ	C+ (3)	0.0	0.0	0.0	1.1	10.0	N/A	7.5	7.0	4.6	
HIGHLANDS INS CO	TX	F (5)	0.0	0.0	40.8	0.0	0.0	0.7	0.0	1.9	0.0	CDFL
HIGHMARK CASUALTY INS CO	PA	C	428.0	162.5	290.7	1.7	5.7	9.4	8.7	5.6	4.0	RT
HILLSTAR INS CO	IN	C	5.4	4.1	1.3	0.0	10.0	6.1	3.4	7.0	3.3	ADT
HINGHAM MUTUAL FIRE INS CO	MA	C+	63.4	38.3	20.8	1.1	7.6	7.0	4.5	6.5	4.6	FR
HISCOX INS CO INC	IL	B-	141.6	54.2	25.8	-0.9	7.2	5.9	3.8	7.8	3.7	GRT
HM CASUALTY INS CO	PA	B-	29.5	8.3	0.0	1.4	8.7	3.7	9.7	9.2	3.5	DT
HOCHHEIM PRAIRIE CASUALTY INS CO	TX	C	80.3	29.6	50.4	4.3	7.0	6.9	5.0	5.3	3.5	R
HOCHHEIM PRAIRIE FARM MUT INS ASN	TX	E	153.8	48.5	109.1	-10.6	6.1	6.4	1.4	1.3	0.1	FLR
HOLYOKE MUTUAL INS CO IN SALEM	MA	B+	224.3	92.9	102.6	2.8	9.5	7.8	5.7	6.4	6.4	
HOME & FARM INS CO	IN	C-	6.1	3.1	2.3	-0.1	9.7	6.5	3.8	6.8	2.4	DRT
HOME CONSTRUCTION INS CO RRG	NV	U	6.1	2.5	0.0	0.1	N/A	6.0	4.7	10.0	3.0	CFRT
HOME STATE COUNTY MUTUAL INS CO	TX	C	299.9	6.1	3.1	0.3	3.1	9.1	6.6	7.6	3.2	CFR
HOME VALUE INS CO	OH	F (5)	0.0	0.0	0.0	0.0	8.4	N/A	0.9	10.0	0.0	DFGT
HOME-OWNERS INS CO	MI	A-	2,165.7	837.2	1,045.3	37.2	9.1	5.8	6.8	6.5	7.3	
HOMELAND INS CO OF DE	DE	B	52.9	50.7	0.0	0.5	10.0	N/A	4.9	7.0	4.3	T
HOMELAND INS CO OF NEW YORK	NY	C	112.8	109.1	0.0	0.2	9.1	4.8	3.5	7.0	3.9	RT
HOMEOWNERS CHOICE ASR CO INC	AL	U	2.0	1.9	0.0	0.0	N/A	N/A	3.5	7.0	3.4	FT
HOMEOWNERS CHOICE PROP & CAS INS	FL	D	387.2	149.4	218.8	28.8	4.1	5.9	6.4	7.1	2.3	GT
HOMEOWNERS OF AMERICA INS CO	TX	D-	29.0	12.1	5.2	3.1	8.4	6.1	5.0	9.6	1.1	DFR
HOMESHIELD FIRE & CASUALTY INS CO	OK	U	1.1	1.1	0.0	0.0	N/A	N/A	3.8	7.0	2.6	T
HOMESITE INDEMNITY CO	KS	C	53.1	39.0	54.2	6.6	7.1	6.5	5.6	6.1	3.6	R
HOMESITE INS CO	CT	C	129.8	84.1	117.5	14.2	7.7	6.5	5.9	6.3	3.8	R
HOMESITE INS CO OF CA	CA	C	45.0	36.1	49.7	5.3	7.2	6.4	5.3	6.1	3.5	R
HOMESITE INS CO OF FL	IL	C	11.0	10.9	18.1	1.2	6.9	6.2	4.0	6.1	2.9	RT
HOMESITE INS CO OF GEORGIA	GA	C	14.3	11.6	18.1	2.0	6.3	6.5	5.5	6.1	3.5	DR
HOMESITE INS CO OF IL	IL	C	12.9	9.1	13.6	0.8	7.0	6.6	5.3	6.1	3.5	DR
HOMESITE INS CO OF NY	NY	C	24.8	15.7	22.6	2.6	6.8	6.4	5.4	6.4	3.5	DR
HOMESITE INS CO OF THE MIDWEST	ND	C	340.0	98.9	144.6	20.1	7.6	6.6	5.6	5.6	4.0	FR
HOMESITE LLOYDS OF TEXAS	TX	D	15.1	10.6	13.6	0.9	7.2	6.4	3.9	6.3	1.4	DR
HOMESTEAD INS CO	PA	U	6.5	5.0	0.0	-0.2	N/A	8.3	4.3	10.0	3.3	FRT
HOMESURE OF VIRGINIA INC	VA	U (5)	0.0	0.0	13.6	0.0	N/A	9.3	4.3	7.0	3.7	DGT
HOOSIER INS CO	IN	C-	91.4	20.0	28.7	-0.4	6.0	4.0	1.9	6.8	3.2	DFRT
HOOSIER MOTOR MUTUAL INS CO	IN	C+	12.5	11.9	0.6	0.8	10.0	5.0	4.1	8.3	3.2	DF
HORACE MANN INS CO	IL	B	444.4	181.6	232.7	12.8	6.5	8.6	6.8	5.3	4.4	ACT
HORACE MANN LLOYDS	TX	C	4.6	2.8	0.0	0.0	10.0	N/A	6.9	10.0	3.0	DF
HORACE MANN PROP & CAS INS CO	IL	B	282.7	121.3	149.9	8.7	6.3	8.3	8.4	5.5	4.4	ACRT
HORIZON MIDWEST CASUALTY CO	KS	U	2.5	2.5	0.0	0.0	N/A	N/A	4.8	7.0	4.0	T
HOSPITALITY INS CO	MA	D+	8.3	7.4	0.0	0.0	10.0	N/A	4.9	7.0	2.7	DFT
HOSPITALITY MUT CAPT INS CO	GA	U (5)	0.0	0.0	2.5	0.0	N/A	5.8	2.5	0.0	0.0	CDFG
HOSPITALITY MUTUAL INS CO	MA	B-	52.7	27.3	10.8	-0.3	5.3	9.4	5.3	8.1	3.9	CDGT
HOSPITALS INS CO INC	NY	D (3)	0.0	0.0	234.1	76.5	2.2	5.0	6.3	6.8	1.5	CR
HOUSING & REDEVELOPMENT INS EXCH	PA	C-	40.2	12.5	20.5	0.6	4.2	9.9	4.0	5.9	3.2	DFR
HOUSING AUTHORITY PROP A MUTUAL CO	VT	C+	165.8	118.1	35.2	3.8	10.0	9.3	8.6	6.9	4.8	R
HOUSING AUTHORITY RISK RET GROUP	VT	C	315.1	199.6	28.3	7.3	10.0	9.7	8.7	7.8	3.6	FR
HOUSING ENTERPRISE INS CO	VT	C	62.5	32.6	16.4	-0.1	3.0	6.8	2.8	6.6	3.5	CF
HOUSING SPECIALTY INS CO	VT	U	15.8	15.8	0.0	-0.3	N/A	0.0	3.4	0.0	0.0	LT
HOUSTON CASUALTY CO	TX	B-	3,216.5	2,124.4	301.7	81.7	8.1	7.8	8.8	7.7	4.9	R
HOUSTON GENERAL INS EXCH	TX	U	2.4	2.4	0.0	0.0	N/A	7.2	0.9	7.0	2.1	FRT
HOUSTON SPECIALTY INS CO	TX	B	438.6	234.6	110.3	15.4	4.6	4.9	5.4	5.7	4.8	CGT
HOW INS CO A RRG	VA	U	122.6	110.0	0.0	0.5	N/A	0.8	3.8	7.0	1.2	T

See Page 27 for explanation of footnotes and Page 28 for explanation of stability factors.
Arrows denote recent upgrades ▲ or downgrades ▼   (see Section VII for explanations)

78

www.weissratings.com

RISK ADJ. CAPITAL RATIO #1	RATIO #2	PREMIUM TO SURPLUS (%)	RESV. TO SURPLUS (%)	RESV. DEVELOP. 1 YEAR (%)	2 YEAR (%)	LOSS RATIO (%)	EXP. RATIO (%)	COMB RATIO (%)	CASH FROM UNDER- WRITING (%)	NET PREMIUM GROWTH (%)	INVEST. IN AFFIL (%)	INSURANCE COMPANY NAME
1.9	1.9	N/A	N/A	N/A	N/A	N/A	N/A	N/A	N/A	0.0	51.9	HIGH POINT PROPERTY & CASUALTY
9.0	5.2	N/A	N/A	N/A	N/A	N/A	N/A	N/A	N/A	0.0	0.0	HIGH POINT SAFETY & INS CO
-0.0	-0.0	196.4	999 +	74.9	99.7	109.3	70.8	180.1	41.8	-86.8	0.0	HIGHLANDS INS CO
1.5	1.0	180.6	107.6	-5.6	-19.7	75.7	19.5	95.2	115.1	14.9	0.0	HIGHMARK CASUALTY INS CO
7.1	6.2	33.1	15.7	0.2	0.3	78.2	19.5	97.7	-100.2	6.6	0.0	HILLSTAR INS CO
2.1	1.4	56.1	21.5	-3.6	-9.9	52.8	49.7	102.5	91.3	5.7	13.7	HINGHAM MUTUAL FIRE INS CO
1.2	0.9	46.7	36.7	-1.9	0.3	65.1	27.6	92.7	187.5	56.9	0.0	HISCOX INS CO INC
2.3	2.0	N/A	N/A	N/A	N/A	N/A	N/A	N/A	-406.1	0.0	0.0	HM CASUALTY INS CO
1.8	1.3	199.0	96.6	-13.1	-19.7	71.7	23.0	94.7	104.2	-0.5	0.9	HOCHHEIM PRAIRIE CASUALTY INS CO
0.9	0.7	198.8	35.0	6.7	-2.6	98.9	27.1	126.0	84.3	4.3	24.5	HOCHHEIM PRAIRIE FARM MUT INS ASN
3.9	2.6	114.1	63.0	-2.9	-2.8	69.3	29.4	98.7	101.1	-1.5	0.7 •	HOLYOKE MUTUAL INS CO IN SALEM
3.2	2.8	72.0	22.3	-2.4	-4.1	67.2	35.7	102.9	114.7	-14.8	0.1	HOME & FARM INS CO
N/A	N/A	0.6	130.2	17.1	10.2	370.1	999 +	999 +	-15.7	-96.9	0.0	HOME CONSTRUCTION INS CO RRG
0.5	0.5	53.1	30.2	-4.9	-4.8	71.3	8.3	79.6	103.7	-1.6	0.0	HOME STATE COUNTY MUTUAL INS CO
0.4	0.4	0.3	N/A	N/A	N/A	999 +	999 +	999 +	0.2	0.0	0.0	HOME VALUE INS CO
3.9	2.6	130.8	74.5	2.3	3.4	69.3	26.1	95.4	109.9	6.6	0.0 •	HOME-OWNERS INS CO
64.4	58.0	N/A	N/A	N/A	N/A	N/A	N/A	N/A	N/A	0.0	0.0	HOMELAND INS CO OF DE
2.4	2.4	N/A	N/A	N/A	N/A	N/A	N/A	N/A	N/A	-100.0	46.0	HOMELAND INS CO OF NEW YORK
N/A	N/A	N/A	N/A	N/A	N/A	N/A	N/A	N/A	N/A	0.0	0.0	HOMEOWNERS CHOICE ASR CO INC
1.4	0.9	187.2	37.4	-4.4	0.6	33.5	37.7	71.2	135.0	24.2	0.0	HOMEOWNERS CHOICE PROP & CAS INS
3.8	3.4	58.1	8.9	-5.4	0.4	46.9	-12.5	34.4	-33.1	-5.4	0.0	HOMEOWNERS OF AMERICA INS CO
N/A	N/A	N/A	N/A	N/A	N/A	N/A	N/A	N/A	N/A	0.0	0.0	HOMESHIELD FIRE & CASUALTY INS CO
6.1	5.9	144.3	41.7	-3.2	3.4	60.2	20.3	80.5	127.9	15.8	0.0	HOMESITE INDEMNITY CO
6.9	6.6	144.8	41.8	-3.1	3.2	60.2	20.5	80.7	151.3	12.8	0.0	HOMESITE INS CO
6.2	6.1	142.1	41.1	-2.7	3.3	60.2	20.4	80.6	121.4	49.4	0.0	HOMESITE INS CO OF CA
5.1	4.9	169.1	48.9	-4.2	3.8	60.2	20.5	80.7	135.6	-27.4	0.0	HOMESITE INS CO OF FL
5.5	5.4	162.5	46.9	-3.5	3.5	60.2	20.6	80.8	121.8	10.3	0.0	HOMESITE INS CO OF GEORGIA
5.7	5.6	150.5	43.5	-3.0	2.8	60.2	21.8	82.0	120.2	10.3	0.0	HOMESITE INS CO OF IL
5.8	5.6	146.2	42.3	-3.0	3.2	60.2	19.9	80.1	158.9	24.6	0.0	HOMESITE INS CO OF NY
7.9	7.1	151.6	43.8	-3.4	3.2	60.2	20.1	80.3	95.7	2.9	0.0	HOMESITE INS CO OF THE MIDWEST
6.6	6.3	130.0	37.6	-2.6	2.5	60.2	20.2	80.4	116.5	10.3	0.0	HOMESITE LLOYDS OF TEXAS
N/A	N/A	N/A	33.1	-1.4	-3.7	N/A	N/A	N/A	N/A	0.0	0.0	HOMESTEAD INS CO
N/A	N/A	167.2	16.9	N/A	-7.9	55.2	41.8	97.0	104.3	0.4	0.0	HOMESURE OF VIRGINIA INC
1.1	0.7	139.0	136.3	8.2	16.5	75.2	35.9	111.1	77.0	-14.6	0.0	HOOSIER INS CO
5.8	3.1	5.5	0.2	0.2	-0.5	12.8	46.3	59.1	127.9	-0.2	0.0	HOOSIER MOTOR MUTUAL INS CO
1.8	1.1	131.5	60.6	-3.9	-7.3	69.0	27.3	96.3	104.3	4.5	0.0	HORACE MANN INS CO
4.0	3.6	N/A	N/A	N/A	N/A	N/A	N/A	N/A	190.6	0.0	0.0	HORACE MANN LLOYDS
1.7	1.1	130.2	60.0	-4.1	-7.3	69.0	27.3	96.3	105.8	2.5	0.0	HORACE MANN PROP & CAS INS CO
N/A	N/A	N/A	N/A	N/A	N/A	N/A	N/A	N/A	N/A	0.0	0.0	HORIZON MIDWEST CASUALTY CO
19.2	17.3	N/A	N/A	N/A	N/A	N/A	N/A	N/A	999 +	0.0	0.0	HOSPITALITY INS CO
N/A	N/A	408.3	213.6	77.4	0.4	85.4	54.4	139.8	89.5	84.7	0.0	HOSPITALITY MUT CAPT INS CO
1.0	0.8	39.2	56.2	-9.0	-12.0	48.5	44.7	93.2	144.1	56.0	16.7	HOSPITALITY MUTUAL INS CO
0.6	0.5	73.5	317.1	-66.2	-90.9	55.3	7.8	63.1	151.1	5.7	0.0	HOSPITALS INS CO INC
1.2	0.8	181.0	170.4	-24.5	-34.0	76.4	29.8	106.2	90.5	-3.5	0.0	HOUSING & REDEVELOPMENT INS EXCH
4.2	3.4	30.0	21.5	-6.6	-10.0	46.6	33.2	79.8	109.6	6.0	13.9	HOUSING AUTHORITY PROP A MUTUAL
4.4	3.5	14.5	41.6	-8.5	-19.5	43.6	31.5	75.1	99.3	-0.6	9.6 •	HOUSING AUTHORITY RISK RET GROUP
0.8	0.5	59.2	68.5	6.3	4.7	102.9	41.9	144.8	81.6	6.4	0.0	HOUSING ENTERPRISE INS CO
N/A	N/A	N/A	N/A	N/A	N/A	N/A	N/A	N/A	N/A	0.0	0.0	HOUSING SPECIALTY INS CO
2.0	1.8	15.8	38.6	-2.5	-3.4	40.5	26.2	66.7	122.3	-9.1	36.4 •	HOUSTON CASUALTY CO
N/A	N/A	N/A	0.1	N/A	-0.2	999 +	999 +	999 +	N/A	-54.9	0.0	HOUSTON GENERAL INS EXCH
0.8	0.7	58.7	22.7	-1.0	1.2	51.1	22.5	73.6	193.3	63.2	49.7	HOUSTON SPECIALTY INS CO
N/A	N/A	N/A	1.4	26.4	50.2	N/A	N/A	N/A	N/A	0.0	0.0	HOW INS CO A RRG

999 + Denotes number greater than 999.9%
999 - Denotes number less than -999.99%
• Bullets denote a more detailed analysis is available in Section II.

INSURANCE COMPANY NAME	DOM. STATE	RATING	TOTAL ASSETS ($MIL)	CAPITAL & SURPLUS ($MIL)	ANNUAL NET PREMIUM ($MIL)	NET INCOME ($MIL)	CAPITAL-IZATION INDEX (PTS)	RESERVE ADQ INDEX (PTS)	PROFIT-ABILITY INDEX (PTS)	LIQUIDITY INDEX (PTS)	STAB. INDEX (PTS)	STABILITY FACTORS
HSB SPECIALTY INS CO	CT	B	50.5	49.6	0.0	-0.2	10.0	N/A	3.9	10.0	5.4	DT
HUDSON EXCESS INS CO	DE	B	58.8	49.1	0.0	2.2	10.0	N/A	4.9	10.0	5.5	DT
HUDSON INS CO	DE	C-	1,014.1	439.7	129.6	10.3	8.7	5.7	6.6	7.6	3.1	FR
HUDSON SPECIALTY INS CO	NY	D+	371.6	177.7	50.5	18.7	8.9	7.8	8.9	7.3	2.6	R
HUTTERIAN BRETHREN MUTUAL INS CORP	IL	U	2.2	1.9	0.0	0.0	N/A	0.0	3.8	0.0	0.0	LT
HYUNDAI MARINE & FIRE INS CO LTD	CA	B-	81.2	50.2	12.7	-0.3	9.5	6.6	3.9	9.3	5.3	DFG
ICI MUTUAL INS CO RRG	VT	A-	330.9	251.2	29.2	11.7	10.0	9.3	8.5	8.4	6.3	
ICM INS CO	NY	F (5)	0.0	0.0	1.9	0.0	0.4	3.3	0.0	7.4	0.0	CDFG
ID COUNTIES RISK MGMT PROGRAM UNDW	ID	D	58.3	26.8	16.5	0.6	7.8	9.4	5.2	7.0	2.3	DR
IDAHO STATE INS FUND	ID	U (5)	0.0	0.0	121.2	0.0	N/A	6.0	9.7	7.2	3.7	
IDS PROPERTY CASUALTY INS CO	WI	B	1,438.0	584.3	883.7	-2.6	8.7	5.4	6.0	4.3	5.5	L
IFA INS CO	NJ	D	63.0	13.5	43.6	-3.5	1.9	1.9	1.4	2.1	2.2	CDFL
IL STATE BAR ASSOC MUTUAL INS CO	IL	C+	71.6	35.1	13.2	2.0	8.3	9.4	8.6	7.3	4.5	DR
ILLINOIS CASUALTY CO	IL	C	89.9	24.5	34.2	0.9	7.2	9.4	3.7	6.5	3.9	DR
ILLINOIS EMCASCO INS CO	IA	C+	326.2	90.3	135.0	1.9	7.9	9.3	6.1	6.4	4.6	T
ILLINOIS FARMERS INS CO	IL	C+	240.7	85.4	102.3	0.2	7.3	6.5	4.0	6.3	4.6	FR
ILLINOIS INS CO	IA	C-	33.7	21.6	13.0	2.9	8.4	9.4	7.1	9.0	3.0	DGT
ILLINOIS NATIONAL INS CO	IL	B-	39.3	36.8	0.0	2.2	10.0	N/A	3.6	7.0	5.3	T
ILLINOIS UNION INS CO	IL	C	356.7	158.5	0.0	2.1	10.0	N/A	7.9	9.2	3.5	FR
IMPERIAL FIRE & CASUALTY INS CO	LA	C	109.8	45.8	89.2	1.0	7.0	4.0	3.7	6.1	3.9	R
IMPERIUM INS CO	TX	C-	377.1	153.7	111.9	6.6	5.2	2.3	2.0	7.0	3.0	FR
IMT INS CO	IA	B	300.9	129.9	168.6	2.5	9.2	7.5	5.7	6.1	5.5	
INDEMNITY CO OF CA	CA	C	23.9	20.7	6.1	1.7	10.0	7.9	8.6	8.2	3.6	DR
INDEMNITY INS CO OF NORTH AMERICA	PA	C	410.3	109.5	87.1	3.8	8.2	8.0	4.5	7.2	4.1	R
INDEMNITY INS CORP RRG	DE	F (5)	0.0	0.0	35.2	1.8	1.0	1.7	5.1	7.2	0.0	CDGR
INDEMNITY NATIONAL INS CO	MS	C	18.4	12.0	2.2	0.8	9.0	8.4	4.4	9.1	3.2	DR
INDEPENDENCE AMERICAN INS CO	DE	C	101.3	60.9	128.8	3.7	7.6	6.4	8.8	2.1	4.2	GLR
INDEPENDENCE CASUALTY & SURETY CO	TX	C	44.6	29.4	9.2	1.3	9.0	5.9	8.1	8.4	3.7	DGR
INDEPENDENCE CASUALTY INS CO	MA	E+	4.4	4.3	0.0	0.1	10.0	N/A	7.9	7.0	0.8	DR
INDEPENDENT MUTUAL FIRE INS CO	IL	C+	42.1	36.2	3.6	0.1	7.9	5.1	6.8	7.5	4.7	D
INDEPENDENT TRUCKERS INS CO	IA	U (5)	0.0	0.0	0.4	0.0	N/A	7.3	6.0	7.6	3.3	DGR
INDIAN HARBOR INS CO	DE	C-	207.2	45.1	26.6	1.7	8.4	6.3	3.2	8.7	3.0	AR
INDIANA FARMERS MUTUAL INS CO	IN	B+	351.6	154.0	169.5	17.4	7.8	6.5	5.0	5.3	6.5	L
INDIANA HEALTHCARE RECIPROCAL RRG	VT	D	30.6	16.6	5.1	0.7	8.1	9.8	8.6	8.5	2.0	D
INDIANA INS CO	IN	C-	69.8	61.8	-250.8	-0.2	9.5	4.9	1.9	0.0	3.2	FLRT
INDIANA LUMBERMENS MUTUAL INS CO	IN	D	66.3	16.4	23.6	-1.8	2.8	1.8	1.1	0.5	2.3	DFLR
INDIANA OLD NATIONAL INS CO	VT	C-	2,068.3	2,067.2	1.2	36.9	10.0	N/A	8.1	10.0	3.0	GR
INFINITY ASSURANCE INS CO	OH	B-	7.2	5.8	1.3	0.1	10.0	6.1	4.5	7.0	3.5	ADT
INFINITY AUTO INS CO	OH	C	9.9	8.0	1.3	0.1	10.0	6.1	3.5	7.0	4.1	ADT
INFINITY CASUALTY INS CO	OH	B-	7.7	6.3	1.3	0.1	10.0	6.1	3.8	7.5	3.5	ADT
INFINITY COUNTY MUTUAL INS CO	TX	C	32.8	5.1	0.0	0.0	7.2	N/A	6.1	10.0	3.5	D
INFINITY INDEMNITY INS CO	IN	C	7.2	5.8	1.3	0.0	10.0	6.2	5.5	7.0	3.6	ADT
INFINITY INS CO	IN	B	2,031.5	659.1	1,316.0	34.6	7.8	7.0	6.2	5.1	5.3	A
INFINITY PREFERRED INS CO	OH	C	5.3	3.9	1.3	0.0	10.0	6.2	5.3	6.8	3.3	AD
INFINITY SAFEGUARD INS CO	OH	C+	5.6	4.2	1.3	0.1	10.0	6.2	3.6	6.8	3.3	ADT
INFINITY SECURITY INS CO	IN	C	6.1	4.7	1.3	0.0	10.0	6.1	3.0	8.9	3.5	ADT
INFINITY SELECT INS CO	IN	B-	6.7	5.3	1.3	0.1	10.0	6.1	3.7	7.0	3.5	ADT
INFINITY STANDARD INS CO	IN	C	7.0	5.6	1.3	0.1	10.0	6.1	3.5	8.3	3.6	ADT
INLAND INS CO	NE	C	258.7	192.9	0.4	5.5	8.1	6.1	8.2	10.0	3.7	R
INLAND MUTUAL INS CO	WV	C-	6.5	6.1	0.5	0.1	9.3	7.7	6.6	9.0	2.1	DGRT
INNOVATIVE PHYSICIAN SOLUTIONS RRG	AZ	D	5.2	1.9	1.3	0.2	1.2	3.9	2.5	2.9	1.5	CDLT
INS CO OF GREATER NY	NY	C+	110.7	56.9	23.4	1.3	10.0	7.7	5.4	6.9	4.7	T

See Page 27 for explanation of footnotes and Page 28 for explanation of stability factors.
Arrows denote recent upgrades ▲ or downgrades ▼ (see Section VII for explanations)

80

www.weissratings.com

RISK ADJ. CAPITAL		PREMIUM TO SURPLUS (%)	RESV. TO SURPLUS (%)	RESV. DEVELOP.		LOSS RATIO (%)	EXP. RATIO (%)	COMB RATIO (%)	CASH FROM UNDER-WRITING (%)	NET PREMIUM GROWTH (%)	INVEST. IN AFFIL (%)	INSURANCE COMPANY NAME
RATIO #1	RATIO #2			1 YEAR (%)	2 YEAR (%)							
118.4	66.5	N/A	N/A	N/A	N/A	N/A	N/A	N/A	588.6	0.0	0.0	HSB SPECIALTY INS CO
20.6	18.6	N/A	N/A	N/A	N/A	N/A	N/A	N/A	999 +	0.0	0.0	HUDSON EXCESS INS CO
2.3	2.0	31.3	36.9	-0.7	-0.4	86.0	25.6	111.6	61.3	19.5	30.2 ●	HUDSON INS CO
2.8	2.2	32.0	44.5	N/A	-1.3	68.7	12.2	80.9	231.8	44.1	19.3	HUDSON SPECIALTY INS CO
N/A	N/A	N/A	N/A	N/A	N/A	N/A	N/A	N/A	N/A	0.0	0.0	HUTTERIAN BRETHREN MUTUAL INS
8.3	5.6	25.3	28.6	-0.9	-9.5	65.0	37.1	102.1	83.4	4.4	0.0	HYUNDAI MARINE & FIRE INS CO LTD
11.4	7.1	12.4	23.5	-5.3	-8.0	17.7	40.2	57.9	208.7	3.0	0.4 ●	ICI MUTUAL INS CO RRG
-0.0	-0.0	178.6	506.6	39.6	41.4	130.5	109.6	240.1	28.0	-63.4	0.0	ICM INS CO
1.9	1.8	63.9	83.8	-12.9	-14.4	72.3	27.0	99.3	102.4	-4.2	0.0	ID COUNTIES RISK MGMT PROGRAM
N/A	N/A	80.7	93.2	-7.4	-6.1	47.5	8.7	56.2	150.6	-6.8	0.0	IDAHO STATE INS FUND
2.7	2.1	166.5	76.2	5.5	7.4	88.2	16.3	104.5	103.8	10.3	3.9 ●	IDS PROPERTY CASUALTY INS CO
0.4	0.3	282.0	266.1	17.9	37.8	86.3	24.0	110.3	79.3	0.0	0.0	IFA INS CO
3.6	2.1	40.2	81.7	-10.7	-18.2	64.1	30.3	94.4	110.9	2.5	0.0	IL STATE BAR ASSOC MUTUAL INS CO
1.4	1.0	142.0	150.9	-10.2	-16.4	67.0	35.3	102.3	106.5	18.3	0.0	ILLINOIS CASUALTY CO
2.1	1.4	154.3	154.5	-2.0	-8.1	67.2	32.9	100.1	107.5	9.1	0.0	ILLINOIS EMCASCO INS CO
1.2	1.2	120.9	73.7	N/A	0.4	66.9	34.3	101.2	91.2	-1.6	38.7	ILLINOIS FARMERS INS CO
2.2	1.8	70.7	51.9	0.3	-12.3	35.3	28.2	63.5	461.7	53.1	0.0	ILLINOIS INS CO
24.8	20.8	N/A	N/A	N/A	N/A	N/A	N/A	N/A	N/A	0.0	1.9	ILLINOIS NATIONAL INS CO
16.0	9.8	N/A	19.1	N/A	N/A	N/A	N/A	N/A	46.9	0.0	0.0	ILLINOIS UNION INS CO
2.2	1.9	203.7	64.6	17.2	22.8	71.2	24.8	96.0	106.5	49.2	0.0	IMPERIAL FIRE & CASUALTY INS CO
1.4	0.9	83.0	123.9	24.5	35.4	98.4	31.8	130.2	61.4	152.6	19.1	IMPERIUM INS CO
3.7	2.4	125.8	37.7	-0.1	-1.8	61.2	32.5	93.7	107.5	12.9	0.7	IMT INS CO
14.6	8.8	31.6	8.1	-2.1	-1.4	8.3	74.4	82.7	105.3	7.6	0.0	INDEMNITY CO OF CA
2.8	1.8	82.7	146.1	-6.0	-4.3	72.2	19.2	91.4	105.2	-2.8	0.0	INDEMNITY INS CO OF NORTH AMERICA
0.2	0.1	152.7	64.2	8.2	1.6	25.4	46.8	72.2	140.4	61.7	0.0	INDEMNITY INS CORP RRG
3.5	2.2	19.0	33.2	-7.0	-6.8	30.3	39.9	70.2	242.5	-4.5	0.0	INDEMNITY NATIONAL INS CO
2.5	1.5	222.6	60.0	-0.5	-0.2	68.7	29.2	97.9	110.9	50.2	0.0	INDEPENDENCE AMERICAN INS CO
3.2	2.1	33.0	38.0	-0.7	1.5	61.1	23.1	84.2	166.4	40.1	0.0	INDEPENDENCE CASUALTY & SURETY
86.9	39.7	N/A	N/A	N/A	N/A	N/A	N/A	N/A	N/A	0.0	0.0	INDEPENDENCE CASUALTY INS CO
2.4	1.4	10.4	0.6	-0.1	-0.2	24.7	83.9	108.6	92.5	-6.0	0.0	INDEPENDENT MUTUAL FIRE INS CO
N/A	N/A	7.4	0.7	-0.9	-0.3	28.6	79.9	108.5	94.0	-28.1	0.0	INDEPENDENT TRUCKERS INS CO
2.8	1.8	56.2	142.8	-0.5	-1.3	65.3	35.0	100.3	99.8	2.9	0.0	INDIAN HARBOR INS CO
2.6	1.5	121.6	57.3	-11.6	4.6	67.3	28.8	96.1	107.1	10.7	0.0 ●	INDIANA FARMERS MUTUAL INS CO
2.3	1.5	30.1	68.5	-3.0	-12.7	69.2	23.1	92.3	114.7	-1.7	0.0	INDIANA HEALTHCARE RECIPROCAL
5.6	5.3	-399.8	N/A	N/A	N/A	N/A	N/A	N/A	-12.5	-147.8	42.8	INDIANA INS CO
0.6	0.5	123.4	71.0	-2.9	4.5	63.6	61.9	125.5	39.8	-30.3	19.9	INDIANA LUMBERMENS MUTUAL INS CO
76.2	29.4	0.1	N/A	N/A	N/A	11.2	30.6	41.8	120.7	24.2	0.0 ●	INDIANA OLD NATIONAL INS CO
10.2	8.9	23.1	11.0	0.2	0.3	78.2	19.5	97.7	-79.1	6.6	0.0	INFINITY ASSURANCE INS CO
11.2	10.1	16.9	8.0	0.1	0.2	78.2	19.5	97.7	-5.7	6.6	0.0	INFINITY AUTO INS CO
11.0	9.6	21.3	10.1	0.1	0.2	78.2	19.5	97.7	269.2	6.6	0.0	INFINITY CASUALTY INS CO
1.1	1.0	N/A	N/A	N/A	N/A	N/A	N/A	N/A	N/A	0.0	0.0	INFINITY COUNTY MUTUAL INS CO
10.2	8.9	23.1	11.0	0.2	0.3	78.2	19.5	97.7	-36.7	6.6	0.0	INFINITY INDEMNITY INS CO
1.7	1.4	197.4	93.9	1.4	2.8	78.2	19.5	97.7	98.9	6.7	3.5 ●	INFINITY INS CO
6.7	5.9	34.9	16.6	0.2	0.4	78.2	19.5	97.7	109.2	6.6	0.0	INFINITY PREFERRED INS CO
7.5	6.6	32.0	15.2	0.2	0.3	78.2	19.5	97.7	133.5	6.6	1.0	INFINITY SAFEGUARD INS CO
8.2	7.2	28.6	13.6	0.1	0.2	78.2	19.5	97.7	103.8	6.6	0.0	INFINITY SECURITY INS CO
9.3	8.1	25.3	12.0	0.2	0.3	78.2	19.5	97.7	-50.9	6.6	0.0	INFINITY SELECT INS CO
3.3	3.1	24.2	11.5	0.2	0.3	78.2	19.5	97.7	999 +	6.6	26.5	INFINITY STANDARD INS CO
2.9	1.7	0.2	1.4	N/A	-0.1	14.8	74.6	89.4	67.9	0.6	0.0 ●	INLAND INS CO
4.3	2.6	8.3	4.3	-0.7	-2.7	25.1	53.1	78.2	115.2	3.0	0.0	INLAND MUTUAL INS CO
0.4	0.2	69.7	128.1	26.9	32.8	84.6	35.6	120.2	97.6	9.0	0.0	INNOVATIVE PHYSICIAN SOLUTIONS
4.0	2.9	42.1	65.5	-0.1	-0.2	61.1	33.3	94.4	97.1	9.7	0.0	INS CO OF GREATER NY

999 + Denotes number greater than 999.9%
999 - Denotes number less than -999.99%
● Bullets denote a more detailed analysis is available in Section II.

INSURANCE COMPANY NAME	DOM. STATE	RATING	TOTAL ASSETS ($MIL)	CAPITAL & SURPLUS ($MIL)	ANNUAL NET PREMIUM ($MIL)	NET INCOME ($MIL)	CAPITAL-IZATION INDEX (PTS)	RESERVE ADQ INDEX (PTS)	PROFIT-ABILITY INDEX (PTS)	LIQUIDITY INDEX (PTS)	STAB. INDEX (PTS)	STABILITY FACTORS
INS CO OF ILLINOIS	IL	C+	21.3	20.3	0.0	0.3	10.0	N/A	2.0	10.0	3.4	ADT
INS CO OF NORTH AMERICA	PA	C	818.3	168.7	217.7	-14.9	7.4	8.3	3.5	6.5	4.3	R
INS CO OF THE AMERICAS	FL	U	11.0	5.2	0.0	-2.3	N/A	10.0	1.6	9.2	1.8	CFRT
INS CO OF THE STATE OF PA	PA	D	315.2	112.0	713.5	87.5	7.4	3.9	1.9	6.6	0.0	A
INS CO OF THE WEST	CA	C	1,565.5	628.6	514.8	58.1	7.3	4.5	7.4	6.4	3.7	GR
INS PLACEMENT FACILITY OF PA	PA	E (3)	0.0	0.0	8.3	-0.9	1.5	9.4	0.9	7.6	0.0	CDFT
INSURANCE CO OF THE SOUTH	GA	C	21.4	11.1	15.3	1.6	7.3	6.7	6.7	6.7	3.4	D
INSUREMAX INS CO	IN	D+	11.7	4.7	13.5	-0.6	4.4	4.6	1.4	1.7	2.4	DFL
INSURORS INDEMNITY CO	TX	D	22.5	12.1	7.0	0.8	8.3	9.3	8.4	8.2	2.0	D
INSURORS INDEMNITY LLOYDS	TX	D	4.1	2.6	0.0	0.0	10.0	N/A	3.8	10.0	2.0	DRT
INTEGON CASUALTY INS CO	NC	C	48.2	11.3	0.0	0.2	7.9	3.1	3.8	6.9	2.9	DRT
INTEGON GENERAL INS CORP	NC	C-	28.3	11.2	0.0	0.3	10.0	2.7	1.9	10.0	2.9	DRT
INTEGON INDEMNITY CORP	NC	C-	53.5	35.2	0.0	1.0	8.9	2.4	2.8	7.0	3.3	RT
INTEGON NATIONAL INS CO	NC	D+	1,720.3	295.6	349.1	21.4	6.7	2.8	3.3	2.5	2.5	FLRT
INTEGON PREFERRED INS CO	NC	C	55.3	9.2	0.0	0.0	7.9	3.0	3.6	10.0	2.8	DGRT
INTEGRA INS INC	MN	D	2.0	2.0	2.7	0.1	4.4	N/A	6.5	6.8	1.6	DFT
INTEGRAND ASR CO	PR	C+	152.6	86.3	38.8	3.6	8.3	6.4	3.6	6.9	4.5	R
INTEGRITY MUTUAL INS CO	WI	B-	87.5	44.5	37.6	1.0	8.0	8.0	6.8	6.7	5.2	T
INTEGRITY PROP & CAS INS CO	WI	D-	20.3	10.8	8.0	0.7	9.7	8.0	6.8	6.1	1.2	D
INTERBORO MUTUAL INDEMNITY INS CO	NY	D-	90.5	30.9	36.6	0.7	7.1	9.6	5.4	6.2	1.3	R
INTERINS EXCH OF THE AUTOMOBILE CLUB	CA	A+	8,447.5	5,380.4	2,752.1	168.0	10.0	7.5	8.7	6.6	6.5	
INTERMED INS CO	MO	U	27.2	18.0	0.0	1.2	N/A	9.6	1.9	7.0	3.1	FRT
INTERMODAL INS CO RRG	DC	D- (5)	0.0	0.0	3.3	0.0	4.4	9.8	5.9	2.5	1.3	DFLT
INTERNATIONAL FIDELITY INS CO	NJ	C	213.5	87.0	113.2	5.3	7.5	9.1	6.8	7.3	3.1	FR
INTERSTATE BANKERS CASUALTY CO	IL	F (3)	0.0	0.0	11.3	-1.7	0.6	3.2	0.7	2.2	0.0	CDFL
INTERSTATE FIRE & CAS CO	IL	C	184.0	156.1	0.0	2.5	10.0	4.1	5.0	7.0	4.2	RT
INTREPID INS CO	MI	U	33.2	29.1	0.0	0.3	N/A	7.3	5.8	7.0	5.2	T
IOWA AMERICAN INS CO	IA	B	22.5	9.0	6.8	0.0	8.7	7.9	5.0	6.6	4.3	DF
IOWA MUTUAL INS CO	IA	B	101.6	32.5	23.8	0.7	7.6	7.8	5.6	6.5	5.5	D
IQS INS RRG INC	VT	D	1.6	1.2	0.4	0.1	9.0	N/A	5.9	7.8	0.6	DT
IRONSHORE INDEMNITY INC	MN	B-	322.6	155.5	51.2	1.9	8.7	5.5	4.7	8.4	3.7	FGRT
IRONSHORE RRG INC	DE	D	2.3	1.0	0.1	-0.1	8.1	3.6	2.8	7.7	1.0	DGT
IRONSHORE SPECIALTY INS CO	AZ	C	935.9	314.3	119.2	17.6	7.9	4.9	7.1	7.2	3.7	R
ISLAND HOME INS CO	GU	E+	26.4	15.6	28.3	4.1	7.7	0.5	9.2	4.8	0.8	DLT
ISLAND INS CO LTD	HI	B-	328.2	117.2	95.3	7.2	8.6	9.3	5.4	6.8	4.8	R
ISLAND PREMIER INS CO LTD	HI	C-	9.8	5.4	0.0	0.1	10.0	N/A	7.7	10.0	3.0	D
ISMIE INDEMNITY CO	IL	U	16.8	16.7	0.0	0.1	N/A	N/A	5.7	7.0	5.4	T
ISMIE MUTUAL INS CO	IL	B-	1,679.1	604.0	229.6	-12.8	9.2	9.6	6.9	7.4	4.6	R
IU HEALTH RRG INC	SC	D-	9.3	2.9	0.0	0.2	9.7	N/A	1.9	7.0	1.2	DR
JAMES RIVER CASUALTY CO	VA	C	29.4	15.5	3.5	0.2	9.3	3.9	7.1	6.9	2.8	DFGT
JAMES RIVER INS CO	OH	C	505.0	168.7	35.9	6.9	8.4	9.3	3.2	5.8	4.0	FR
JEFFERSON INS CO	NY	C	71.9	43.7	62.6	4.8	6.6	6.2	8.6	6.5	3.5	R
JEWELERS MUTUAL INS CO	WI	A-	329.0	202.5	143.8	13.4	10.0	6.2	8.5	6.7	6.7	
JM WOODWORTH RRG INC	NV	E+	14.6	1.5	5.4	-1.5	0.2	1.8	0.6	5.7	0.4	CDFR
JOHN DEERE INS CO	IA	C-	639.0	107.1	160.9	-14.0	5.2	7.0	2.9	1.1	2.9	FLRT
JOLIET AREA RRG CAPTIVE INS CO	GA	D- (5)	0.0	0.0	1.5	0.0	2.0	7.0	3.6	6.3	1.3	DGT
JUNIATA MUTUAL INS CO	PA	D+	7.9	4.7	4.7	-0.3	8.0	8.3	5.3	6.9	2.3	DR
KANSAS MEDICAL MUTUAL INS CO	KS	B-	158.2	113.1	21.6	0.4	10.0	9.6	8.7	7.7	5.0	D
KANSAS MUTUAL INS CO	KS	C- (3)	0.0	0.0	4.5	0.1	10.0	6.4	4.1	6.8	2.5	DF
KEMPER INDEPENDENCE INS CO	IL	B-	98.5	9.6	0.0	0.4	6.7	4.7	3.4	10.0	4.3	DR
KENSINGTON INS CO	NY	E+	14.9	3.6	9.9	-1.1	1.1	7.1	2.3	6.8	0.5	CDF
KENTUCKIANA MEDICAL RRG & INS CO INC	KY	E	51.4	32.0	9.3	-1.9	8.9	9.7	5.5	7.3	0.0	GR

See Page 27 for explanation of footnotes and Page 28 for explanation of stability factors.
Arrows denote recent upgrades ▲ or downgrades ▼ (see Section VII for explanations)

82

www.weissratings.com

RISK ADJ. CAPITAL		PREMIUM TO SURPLUS (%)	RESV. TO SURPLUS (%)	RESV. DEVELOP.		LOSS RATIO (%)	EXP. RATIO (%)	COMB RATIO (%)	CASH FROM UNDER- WRITING (%)	NET PREMIUM GROWTH (%)	INVEST. IN AFFIL (%)	INSURANCE COMPANY NAME
RATIO #1	RATIO #2			1 YEAR (%)	2 YEAR (%)							
48.2	43.4	N/A	N/A	N/A	N/A	N/A	N/A	N/A	-31.6	0.0	0.0	INS CO OF ILLINOIS
1.6	1.0	119.1	210.4	-7.3	-5.6	72.2	28.4	100.6	91.2	-2.8	0.0	INS CO OF NORTH AMERICA
N/A	N/A	N/A	122.4	-55.6	-67.7	N/A	N/A	N/A	N/A	0.0	0.0	INS CO OF THE AMERICAS
1.6	1.1	95.7	222.6	3.4	3.7	76.6	32.8	109.4	95.9	16.0	0.3 ●	INS CO OF THE STATE OF PA
1.7	1.2	96.5	111.2	-2.5	5.6	61.1	23.1	84.2	164.5	40.1	8.9 ●	INS CO OF THE WEST
0.3	0.3	661.3	72.3	-1.8	-13.4	58.1	52.4	110.5	86.4	0.8	0.0	INS PLACEMENT FACILITY OF PA
2.0	1.6	157.8	7.9	0.1	-3.5	33.5	52.1	85.6	115.0	5.0	0.0	INSURANCE CO OF THE SOUTH
0.7	0.7	242.9	112.2	1.7	-0.7	86.4	29.8	116.2	81.0	-4.5	0.0	INSUREMAX INS CO
2.2	1.6	59.8	33.4	-10.4	-15.0	34.4	50.6	85.0	129.5	27.3	13.1	INSURORS INDEMNITY CO
4.2	3.8	N/A	N/A	N/A	N/A	N/A	N/A	N/A	39.9	0.0	0.0	INSURORS INDEMNITY LLOYDS
2.0	1.8	N/A	N/A	N/A	N/A	N/A	N/A	N/A	469.8	100.0	0.0	INTEGON CASUALTY INS CO
3.2	2.8	N/A	N/A	N/A	N/A	N/A	N/A	N/A	-584.6	100.0	0.0	INTEGON GENERAL INS CORP
2.5	2.2	N/A	N/A	N/A	N/A	N/A	N/A	N/A	-129.8	100.0	31.6	INTEGON INDEMNITY CORP
1.7	1.2	218.6	146.2	6.7	-25.5	87.6	23.0	110.6	71.2	-59.8	0.0	INTEGON NATIONAL INS CO
1.3	1.2	N/A	N/A	N/A	N/A	N/A	N/A	N/A	-102.7	100.0	0.0	INTEGON PREFERRED INS CO
0.7	0.7	141.2	N/A	N/A	N/A	N/A	91.7	91.7	94.8	-0.4	0.0	INTEGRA INS INC
4.0	2.4	56.6	42.2	-1.2	1.3	62.6	29.2	91.8	86.2	-9.6	0.2	INTEGRAND ASR CO
2.0	1.7	87.4	41.8	-0.4	-2.4	66.9	30.6	97.5	106.8	7.7	28.1	INTEGRITY MUTUAL INS CO
4.6	3.2	79.4	38.0	-0.4	-2.2	66.9	21.2	88.1	111.6	7.7	0.0	INTEGRITY PROP & CAS INS CO
1.9	1.5	120.6	69.4	-4.2	-2.7	49.0	37.0	86.0	94.2	-1.9	0.0	INTERBORO MUTUAL INDEMNITY INS CO
5.3	3.2	52.8	18.5	-0.5	-1.0	71.1	21.9	93.0	108.9	5.3	0.7 ●	INTERINS EXCH OF THE AUTOMOBILE
N/A	N/A	N/A	67.8	-2.7	-36.1	-408.9	999 +	999 +	-5.7	-100.0	0.0	INTERMED INS CO
0.9	0.5	120.8	140.6	-21.9	-44.0	85.6	4.2	89.8	65.8	15.9	0.0	INTERMODAL INS CO RRG
1.5	1.3	106.0	9.3	-3.3	-9.3	19.2	71.1	90.3	103.0	2.9	12.9	INTERNATIONAL FIDELITY INS CO
0.2	0.1	419.9	488.2	70.8	45.7	92.2	36.2	128.4	90.7	-16.0	0.0	INTERSTATE BANKERS CASUALTY CO
35.4	31.9	N/A	N/A	N/A	N/A	N/A	N/A	N/A	-4.1	100.0	0.0	INTERSTATE FIRE & CAS CO
N/A	N/A	N/A	N/A	N/A	-0.1	N/A	N/A	N/A	N/A	0.0	0.0	INTREPID INS CO
3.2	2.3	76.0	59.0	-0.8	-1.5	66.8	34.9	101.7	90.6	4.8	0.0	IOWA AMERICAN INS CO
1.9	1.4	73.4	56.9	-0.8	-1.6	66.8	34.9	101.7	101.4	4.8	15.2	IOWA MUTUAL INS CO
4.3	2.6	40.8	9.6	N/A	N/A	31.2	36.0	67.2	239.2	0.0	0.0	IQS INS RRG INC
3.1	2.0	42.5	41.4	2.4	-3.1	73.7	33.3	107.0	48.5	61.2	0.0	IRONSHORE INDEMNITY INC
1.9	1.7	11.9	10.8	0.2	N/A	70.8	73.3	144.1	166.6	63.5	0.0	IRONSHORE RRG INC
2.2	1.3	39.7	55.0	-1.9	0.1	68.3	23.4	91.7	104.6	17.5	0.0 ●	IRONSHORE SPECIALTY INS CO
2.9	1.6	198.4	32.1	111.4	238.5	73.4	19.6	93.0	107.2	2.2	0.0	ISLAND HOME INS CO
3.0	1.9	79.5	110.6	-4.4	-12.3	65.8	29.5	95.3	105.7	4.5	4.9	ISLAND INS CO LTD
3.9	3.5	N/A	N/A	N/A	N/A	N/A	N/A	N/A	N/A	0.0	0.0	ISLAND PREMIER INS CO LTD
N/A	N/A	N/A	N/A	N/A	N/A	N/A	N/A	N/A	N/A	0.0	0.0	ISMIE INDEMNITY CO
3.3	2.7	37.6	112.7	-18.7	-37.8	37.6	2.9	40.5	175.4	-5.2	1.9 ●	ISMIE MUTUAL INS CO
1.6	1.4	N/A	N/A	N/A	N/A	N/A	N/A	N/A	N/A	0.0	0.0	IU HEALTH RRG INC
3.2	2.2	22.5	46.3	-6.3	-9.2	36.7	29.3	66.0	85.1	N/A	0.0	JAMES RIVER CASUALTY CO
3.2	1.9	22.4	67.2	-6.7	-9.7	36.7	43.9	80.6	31.8	-17.9	5.2	JAMES RIVER INS CO
1.4	1.2	161.9	12.1	-0.8	-2.6	32.6	54.0	86.6	122.8	19.8	0.0	JEFFERSON INS CO
5.2	3.2	78.7	11.6	-3.6	-0.7	43.5	41.4	84.9	117.5	7.8	0.1 ●	JEWELERS MUTUAL INS CO
0.0	0.0	178.2	382.0	15.8	3.9	95.2	41.8	137.0	60.5	-39.0	0.0	JM WOODWORTH RRG INC
0.9	0.7	131.2	49.0	-3.6	-21.5	98.9	24.9	123.8	70.6	21.1	0.0	JOHN DEERE INS CO
0.8	0.6	90.0	327.4	-22.4	-36.2	27.0	90.4	117.4	312.8	15.9	0.0	JOLIET AREA RRG CAPTIVE INS CO
2.6	1.9	95.7	8.8	-1.3	-7.1	40.2	40.8	81.0	118.2	12.7	0.0	JUNIATA MUTUAL INS CO
13.0	8.5	19.3	28.6	-6.7	-13.4	40.6	37.4	78.0	107.7	-6.7	0.0	KANSAS MEDICAL MUTUAL INS CO
4.1	3.3	72.0	6.3	-3.3	-2.6	72.8	27.6	100.4	91.2	13.9	0.0	KANSAS MUTUAL INS CO
1.1	1.0	N/A	N/A	N/A	N/A	N/A	N/A	N/A	203.2	0.0	0.0	KEMPER INDEPENDENCE INS CO
0.4	0.2	259.2	151.5	-17.5	-32.9	57.0	48.7	105.7	83.0	68.2	0.0	KENSINGTON INS CO
3.5	2.7	27.8	52.7	-4.6	-25.3	66.0	10.1	76.1	99.2	187.4	0.0	KENTUCKIANA MEDICAL RRG & INS CO

999 + Denotes number greater than 999.9%
999 - Denotes number less than -999.99%
● Bullets denote a more detailed analysis is available in Section II.

INSURANCE COMPANY NAME	DOM. STATE	RATING	TOTAL ASSETS ($MIL)	CAPITAL & SURPLUS ($MIL)	ANNUAL NET PREMIUM ($MIL)	NET INCOME ($MIL)	CAPITAL-IZATION INDEX (PTS)	RESERVE ADQ INDEX (PTS)	PROFIT-ABILITY INDEX (PTS)	LIQUIDITY INDEX (PTS)	STAB. INDEX (PTS)	STABILITY FACTORS
KENTUCKY EMPLOYERS MUTUAL INS	KY	C+	881.2	202.9	142.8	7.5	6.4	4.9	5.7	7.2	4.3	R
KENTUCKY FARM BUREAU MUTUAL INS CO	KY	A-	2,214.4	1,152.7	845.5	87.6	9.9	6.2	6.3	6.0	5.5	
KENTUCKY HOSPITAL INS CO RRG	KY	D-	20.5	8.7	2.2	0.5	7.6	9.5	2.2	7.0	0.9	DR
KENTUCKY NATIONAL INS CO	KY	E+	27.9	8.0	23.8	-0.6	1.3	2.7	3.3	0.4	0.6	DLRT
KESWICK GUARANTY INC	VI	B-	4.6	4.5	0.3	0.3	8.9	3.6	6.5	8.0	3.5	D
KEY INS CO	KS	D+	25.3	6.9	33.5	0.3	1.5	4.9	6.3	0.5	2.4	CL
KEY RISK INS CO	NC	C	50.6	29.2	0.0	0.6	10.0	N/A	5.9	10.0	4.2	R
KEYSTONE MUTUAL INS CO	MO	E	2.1	0.1	1.3	-0.1	0.0	5.1	0.0	7.6	0.0	CDT
KEYSTONE NATIONAL INS CO	PA	C	13.1	7.5	1.3	0.2	10.0	8.3	5.9	9.0	4.0	DR
KINGSTONE INS CO	NY	C	82.7	32.8	24.8	1.5	7.1	3.3	8.8	6.6	3.9	GR
KINSALE INS CO	AR	B	290.2	100.6	44.4	8.2	7.2	4.7	5.7	7.4	4.0	GT
KNIGHT SPECIALTY INS CO	DE	U	23.6	22.2	0.0	0.4	N/A	N/A	4.9	7.0	5.4	T
KNIGHTBROOK INS CO	DE	C	221.9	66.6	35.0	-3.5	5.0	4.9	4.4	7.3	3.5	RT
LACKAWANNA AMERICAN INS CO	PA	C	77.7	35.4	19.6	1.3	8.2	9.3	8.8	7.0	4.3	R
LACKAWANNA CASUALTY CO	PA	B-	213.5	84.8	68.9	2.5	7.2	9.1	3.6	6.3	4.5	R
LACKAWANNA NATIONAL INS CO	PA	C	29.6	12.2	9.8	0.5	5.8	8.7	8.9	6.8	4.1	DR
LAFAYETTE INS CO	LA	B-	174.8	75.2	50.6	1.3	8.3	6.9	6.7	7.0	5.0	T
LAKE STREET RRG INC	VT	D-	2.9	1.5	0.3	-0.1	7.3	7.0	3.6	10.0	1.1	DFT
LAKEVIEW INS CO	FL	C	34.9	16.2	15.4	0.8	8.6	5.4	8.7	6.8	3.6	D
LAMMICO	LA	C+	395.1	202.2	49.4	8.5	10.0	9.3	8.9	9.0	4.5	R
LAMMICO RRG INC	DC	U	6.1	5.8	0.0	0.1	N/A	3.6	3.5	10.0	2.1	FGT
LANCER INDEMNITY CO	NY	C	21.2	10.1	5.2	-0.4	9.8	9.3	4.9	7.0	3.8	DR
LANCER INS CO	IL	C+	576.6	180.6	218.3	6.4	9.0	7.0	6.9	6.7	4.6	R
LANCET IND RRG INC	NV	D	20.1	5.6	8.7	0.0	1.5	1.2	3.1	7.7	1.7	CDT
LANDCAR CASUALTY CO	UT	C-	36.2	19.0	8.1	1.6	8.0	7.7	7.4	7.6	3.0	DGT
LANDMARK AMERICAN INS CO	OK	C	381.9	219.9	48.9	12.1	10.0	7.9	8.6	7.7	4.2	AR
LAUNDRY OWNERS MUTUAL LIAB INS ASN	PA	D	15.1	5.4	5.0	1.1	3.7	4.2	3.3	7.5	1.8	DR
LAWYERS MUTUAL INS CO	CA	C	307.0	191.0	35.7	11.3	10.0	9.5	8.9	7.7	4.0	R
LAWYERS MUTUAL INS CO OF KENTUCKY	KY	C	22.8	7.9	4.3	0.4	7.2	9.6	6.2	7.3	2.7	DR
LAWYERS MUTUAL LIAB INS CO OF NC	NC	B-	94.0	66.3	14.4	8.8	8.6	7.0	6.4	7.1	5.0	D
LE MARS INS CO	IA	B-	64.2	26.5	29.7	-1.2	8.5	7.9	3.8	6.4	5.2	
LEADING INS GROUP INS CO LTD US BR	NY	E	225.0	34.4	72.9	-38.5	0.0	3.1	0.1	0.6	0.1	CDLR
LEAGUE OF WI MUNICIPALITIES MUT INS	WI	C	57.8	20.4	21.7	-1.9	6.8	7.1	3.9	6.8	4.0	DR
LEATHERSTOCKING COOP INS CO	NY	D+	24.0	14.0	8.4	1.0	9.2	9.4	8.8	6.9	2.5	DR
LEBANON VALLEY INS CO	PA	C-	23.7	11.3	7.7	-0.5	8.5	7.0	4.4	7.2	3.3	DR
LEGAL MUTUAL LIAB INS SOCIETY OF MD	MD	U (1)	0.5	0.0	0.0	-0.1	N/A	6.1	0.0	7.2	0.0	FRT
LEMIC INS CO	LA	F (3)	0.0	0.0	15.4	-10.4	0.0	1.6	0.1	7.0	0.0	CDFR
LENDERS PROTECTION ASR CO RRG	NE	D	2.4	2.4	0.0	0.0	10.0	N/A	4.0	10.0	1.9	DFT
LEON HIX INS CO	SC	U	3.4	3.4	0.0	0.1	N/A	N/A	4.9	7.0	3.4	T
LEXINGTON INS CO	DE	C+	26,043.5	6,843.7	3,755.8	745.1	8.2	8.0	4.6	6.9	4.4	R
LEXINGTON NATIONAL INS CORP	MD	D-	53.4	19.6	12.6	4.0	8.3	5.9	8.4	7.6	1.0	DR
LEXON INS CO	TX	C-	144.1	44.3	51.6	1.0	7.4	0.5	4.9	6.7	2.9	FR
LIBERTY AMERICAN INS CO	FL	U	8.5	8.2	0.0	0.7	N/A	4.3	1.9	10.0	3.1	T
▼LIBERTY AMERICAN SELECT INS CO	FL	C-	8.5	8.0	0.0	0.6	10.0	4.2	1.9	7.0	3.1	DT
LIBERTY COUNTY MUTUAL INS CO	TX	C-	8.2	5.6	0.0	-0.2	10.0	N/A	3.2	7.0	2.9	D
LIBERTY FIRST RRG INS CO	UT	F (5)	0.0	0.0	2.5	-0.5	0.2	0.5	1.9	8.5	0.0	CDGR
LIBERTY INS CORP	IL	D	225.6	215.2	-215.2	0.0	10.0	4.1	2.7	0.0	1.9	AFLT
LIBERTY INS UNDERWRITERS INC	IL	C	163.3	123.3	-5.4	3.4	10.0	4.6	6.8	7.0	4.3	AFRT
LIBERTY LLOYDS OF TX INS CO	TX	B	7.0	6.3	0.0	0.0	10.0	N/A	6.3	7.0	4.4	D
LIBERTY MUTUAL FIRE INS CO	WI	C+	5,274.8	1,224.8	2,163.5	49.3	7.1	4.2	3.8	5.3	4.5	A
LIBERTY MUTUAL INS CO	MA	B	42,150.7	15,587.3	13,889.2	331.1	7.6	5.7	6.1	6.2	4.4	ART
LIBERTY MUTUAL MID ATLANTIC INS CO	MA	C	19.6	18.6	0.0	0.4	10.0	N/A	8.0	7.0	4.3	D

See Page 27 for explanation of footnotes and Page 28 for explanation of stability factors.

Arrows denote recent upgrades ▲ or downgrades ▼ (see Section VII for explanations)

www.weissratings.com

RISK ADJ. CAPITAL RATIO #1	CAPITAL RATIO #2	PREMIUM TO SURPLUS (%)	RESV. TO SURPLUS (%)	RESV. DEVELOP. 1 YEAR (%)	RESV. DEVELOP. 2 YEAR (%)	LOSS RATIO (%)	EXP. RATIO (%)	COMB RATIO (%)	CASH FROM UNDER- WRITING (%)	NET PREMIUM GROWTH (%)	INVEST. IN AFFIL (%)	INSURANCE COMPANY NAME
1.4	0.9	72.7	270.5	-5.1	-7.9	80.9	24.0	104.9	135.5	15.0	0.0 ●	KENTUCKY EMPLOYERS MUTUAL INS
5.5	3.5	79.3	37.5	-2.5	-1.8	67.2	21.5	88.7	124.2	-0.6	0.1 ●	KENTUCKY FARM BUREAU MUTUAL INS
1.6	1.3	27.2	118.9	-10.2	-6.7	138.5	30.9	169.4	90.9	-29.2	0.0	KENTUCKY HOSPITAL INS CO RRG
0.4	0.3	301.2	93.2	-2.0	22.9	72.3	31.2	103.5	104.9	26.4	16.0	KENTUCKY NATIONAL INS CO
3.6	2.1	6.9	1.5	-0.8	N/A	-2.4	17.7	15.3	428.9	0.0	0.0	KESWICK GUARANTY INC
0.3	0.2	523.7	210.5	5.5	-19.7	72.8	25.2	98.0	113.8	35.8	0.0	KEY INS CO
7.9	7.1	N/A	N/A	N/A	N/A	N/A	N/A	N/A	-619.5	0.0	0.0	KEY RISK INS CO
0.0	0.0	811.8	491.7	-92.1	-30.8	36.2	63.9	100.1	120.6	8.2	0.0	KEYSTONE MUTUAL INS CO
4.6	4.1	17.4	2.9	-1.0	-0.1	24.7	39.4	64.1	202.4	24.6	0.0	KEYSTONE NATIONAL INS CO
2.0	1.3	78.0	53.8	16.1	21.8	60.9	22.7	83.6	140.2	27.0	3.2	KINGSTONE INS CO
2.3	1.3	54.5	69.5	-5.8	-2.7	64.0	15.0	79.0	214.9	-23.5	0.0	KINSALE INS CO
N/A	N/A	N/A	N/A	N/A	N/A	N/A	N/A	N/A	N/A	0.0	0.0	KNIGHT SPECIALTY INS CO
1.4	0.9	73.8	42.2	10.2	23.1	69.9	32.3	102.2	113.7	20.1	2.1	KNIGHTBROOK INS CO
2.4	1.9	57.6	62.2	-4.0	-10.8	71.6	17.6	89.2	124.9	5.2	0.0	LACKAWANNA AMERICAN INS CO
1.2	1.0	77.2	90.5	-5.8	-10.1	70.9	18.7	89.6	121.4	5.1	25.8	LACKAWANNA CASUALTY CO
1.4	0.7	84.3	86.7	-3.7	-7.5	74.1	17.2	91.3	125.9	5.3	0.0	LACKAWANNA NATIONAL INS CO
2.7	1.7	69.0	83.4	-5.3	-7.3	63.3	31.6	94.9	112.7	10.3	0.0	LAFAYETTE INS CO
1.6	1.3	18.7	69.5	-18.6	0.8	61.3	46.6	107.9	95.3	-70.4	0.0	LAKE STREET RRG INC
2.2	2.0	99.9	15.2	-3.3	-1.6	42.3	39.4	81.7	128.0	16.1	0.0	LAKEVIEW INS CO
4.9	3.8	25.5	83.6	-5.8	-8.2	57.6	25.3	82.9	112.7	-9.9	0.1 ●	LAMMICO
N/A	N/A	0.6	2.1	-3.4	N/A	999 +	212.4	999 +	56.1	146.0	0.0	LAMMICO RRG INC
2.2	1.9	51.0	34.1	0.7	-4.3	51.3	31.1	82.4	166.6	51.0	0.0	LANCER INDEMNITY CO
3.2	2.0	127.1	132.8	6.2	1.9	73.7	29.2	102.9	114.6	29.5	0.0	LANCER INS CO
0.7	0.5	192.6	168.8	32.7	78.7	85.1	40.9	126.0	99.3	-4.9	6.5	LANCET IND RRG INC
2.3	1.7	45.6	2.2	0.5	-2.3	32.5	10.3	42.8	374.8	37.2	0.0	LANDCAR CASUALTY CO
12.6	7.9	23.5	34.1	0.4	-2.0	43.7	26.5	70.2	127.2	-4.8	0.0 ●	LANDMARK AMERICAN INS CO
1.1	0.7	112.4	138.0	-22.9	-31.6	56.4	32.4	88.8	137.6	18.3	0.0	LAUNDRY OWNERS MUTUAL LIAB INS
7.5	4.8	19.5	49.3	-10.6	-18.9	53.6	14.8	68.4	108.5	-1.2	0.1	LAWYERS MUTUAL INS CO
1.6	1.2	58.6	138.7	-23.8	-28.2	85.3	21.5	106.8	114.2	-9.1	0.0	LAWYERS MUTUAL INS CO OF
3.9	2.9	24.3	34.1	-11.4	-24.7	28.6	23.3	51.9	111.5	2.8	3.1	LAWYERS MUTUAL LIAB INS CO OF NC
2.8	1.9	107.5	47.0	-1.3	-4.3	70.8	29.6	100.4	103.5	9.2	0.0	LE MARS INS CO
0.4	0.2	999 +	999 +	80.7	62.6	120.5	33.9	154.4	100.8	-28.1	0.0	LEADING INS GROUP INS CO LTD US BR
1.5	1.1	97.3	122.5	-36.4	-59.6	58.3	17.3	75.6	134.3	10.8	0.0	LEAGUE OF WI MUNICIPALITIES MUT INS
3.3	2.4	65.9	23.1	-11.0	-10.8	42.0	32.1	74.1	135.9	19.4	0.0	LEATHERSTOCKING COOP INS CO
2.8	1.9	65.1	48.7	-13.5	-17.1	47.5	45.8	93.3	97.2	3.8	0.0	LEBANON VALLEY INS CO
N/A	N/A	-11.4	373.3	-16.7	-9.0	-823.1	-175.2	-998.3	-90.6	94.5	0.0	LEGAL MUTUAL LIAB INS SOCIETY OF
-0.0	-0.0	-739.3	999 +	53.8	50.0	121.0	52.5	173.5	71.1	-29.6	0.0	LEMIC INS CO
73.8	36.2	N/A	N/A	N/A	N/A	N/A	N/A	N/A	2.0	0.0	0.0	LENDERS PROTECTION ASR CO RRG
N/A	N/A	N/A	N/A	N/A	N/A	N/A	N/A	N/A	N/A	0.0	0.0	LEON HIX INS CO
2.2	1.4	52.0	153.8	-4.6	-3.4	69.4	20.8	90.2	84.4	3.7	0.4 ●	LEXINGTON INS CO
2.1	1.7	63.6	1.3	2.1	2.9	-0.8	67.0	66.2	147.6	19.6	0.0	LEXINGTON NATIONAL INS CORP
1.6	1.1	117.3	53.9	17.1	42.6	47.7	51.6	99.3	72.1	-15.2	2.4	LEXON INS CO
N/A	N/A	N/A	0.6	-0.2	-2.1	N/A	N/A	N/A	115.8	-100.0	0.0	LIBERTY AMERICAN INS CO
30.3	27.3	N/A	0.7	-0.2	-2.4	N/A	N/A	N/A	67.7	-100.0	0.0	LIBERTY AMERICAN SELECT INS CO
6.3	5.6	N/A	N/A	N/A	N/A	N/A	N/A	N/A	N/A	0.0	0.0	LIBERTY COUNTY MUTUAL INS CO
-0.3	-0.2	149.9	267.7	21.4	98.2	41.3	11.6	52.9	222.4	-50.3	0.0	LIBERTY FIRST RRG INS CO
84.1	59.0	-99.9	N/A	N/A	N/A	N/A	N/A	N/A	-1.0	-141.2	0.0 ●	LIBERTY INS CORP
21.6	19.4	-4.5	N/A	N/A	N/A	N/A	4.9	N/A	355.7	-141.2	0.0	LIBERTY INS UNDERWRITERS INC
22.0	19.8	N/A	N/A	N/A	N/A	N/A	N/A	N/A	N/A	0.0	0.0	LIBERTY LLOYDS OF TX INS CO
1.7	1.1	177.9	227.6	6.9	6.6	73.5	29.0	102.5	94.7	28.5	4.2 ●	LIBERTY MUTUAL FIRE INS CO
1.6	1.4	91.8	114.4	2.8	3.2	73.5	28.7	102.2	106.6	44.1	23.8 ●	LIBERTY MUTUAL INS CO
39.5	20.9	N/A	N/A	N/A	N/A	N/A	N/A	N/A	N/A	0.0	0.0	LIBERTY MUTUAL MID ATLANTIC INS CO

999 + Denotes number greater than 999.9%
999 - Denotes number less than -999.99%
● Bullets denote a more detailed analysis is available in Section II.

INSURANCE COMPANY NAME	DOM. STATE	RATING	TOTAL ASSETS ($MIL)	CAPITAL & SURPLUS ($MIL)	ANNUAL NET PREMIUM ($MIL)	NET INCOME ($MIL)	CAPITAL-IZATION INDEX (PTS)	RESERVE ADQ INDEX (PTS)	PROFIT-ABILITY INDEX (PTS)	LIQUIDITY INDEX (PTS)	STAB. INDEX (PTS)	STABILITY FACTORS
LIBERTY MUTUAL PERSONAL INS CO	MA	B	6.8	6.8	0.0	0.0	10.0	N/A	7.1	7.0	4.0	DT
LIBERTY NORTHWEST INS CORP	OR	C	74.5	60.2	0.0	-0.7	10.0	N/A	2.7	10.0	3.5	FRT
LIBERTY PERSONAL INS CO	NH	C	16.9	15.7	0.0	0.4	10.0	N/A	1.9	7.0	4.0	DT
LIBERTY SURPLUS INS CORP	NH	C	136.5	93.4	0.0	1.0	10.0	N/A	7.4	7.0	3.5	AFT
LIGHTHOUSE CASUALTY CO	IL	D	9.0	1.8	2.3	0.0	5.5	N/A	2.4	7.8	1.6	DT
LIGHTHOUSE PROPERTY INS CORP	LA	C-	54.3	15.2	21.4	2.1	2.6	5.5	5.6	7.6	2.5	CDT
LIGHTNING ROD MUTUAL INS CO	OH	B-	250.8	145.6	102.2	8.1	9.9	7.7	5.1	6.8	4.7	
LINCOLN GENERAL INS CO	PA	E+	83.4	1.3	0.9	-0.4	0.0	4.0	0.0	9.2	0.0	CDFR
LION INS CO	NY	F (5)	0.0	0.0	0.0	0.0	10.0	5.7	2.9	10.0	0.0	FRT
LION INS CO	FL	B	220.6	76.9	21.6	4.3	9.0	8.1	8.6	9.7	4.5	R
LITITZ MUTUAL INS CO	PA	B-	223.7	140.4	64.2	-3.0	7.5	6.1	4.1	5.7	4.7	AR
LITTLE BLACK MUTUAL INS CO	WI	D-	4.6	1.7	2.2	-0.4	5.6	6.4	1.5	5.6	1.3	DRT
LITTLE RIVER INS CO	DE	U	3.2	3.2	0.0	0.0	N/A	4.7	2.9	7.0	4.1	T
LIVINGSTON MUTUAL INS CO	PA	C	3.1	1.5	0.5	0.0	8.5	6.2	2.6	6.5	2.3	DFT
LM GENERAL INS CO	IL	B-	10.5	9.6	-5.4	0.0	10.0	4.4	2.9	0.5	3.8	DFLT
LM INS CORP	IL	C	118.4	113.9	-10.8	2.9	10.0	4.7	5.6	6.6	4.3	AFT
LM PROPERTY & CASUALTY INS CO	IN	U	63.0	25.8	0.0	0.1	N/A	5.9	3.1	7.0	4.4	GT
LOCUST MUTUAL FIRE INS CO	PA	U (3)	0.0	0.0	0.0	-0.1	N/A	N/A	2.7	9.2	1.8	FT
LONE STAR ALLIANCE INC A RRG	DC	U	1.3	0.8	0.0	0.0	N/A	N/A	2.7	10.0	2.6	T
LONE STAR NATIONAL INS CO	IN	D-	6.0	3.7	0.8	-0.2	9.4	4.4	3.7	7.0	1.0	DGRT
LOUISIANA FARM BUREAU CAS INS CO	LA	B	10.4	10.4	0.0	0.2	10.0	N/A	7.8	10.0	4.8	D
LOUISIANA FARM BUREAU MUTUAL INS CO	LA	B	197.9	106.8	74.6	10.8	10.0	6.5	8.6	6.8	5.7	T
LOUISIANA WORKERS COMPENSATION	LA	A- (5)	1,576.2	883.4	138.0	0.0	1.6	4.8	6.9	6.9	5.5	CT
LOYA CASUALTY INS CO	CA	D	101.5	39.8	116.7	1.5	5.2	5.9	4.6	1.7	1.6	L
LOYA INS CO	TX	D	261.8	123.2	314.3	-7.2	7.2	4.8	3.6	1.5	2.1	L
LR INS INC	DE	U	8.7	7.7	0.0	1.6	N/A	N/A	6.2	10.0	3.5	G
LUBA CASUALTY INS CO	LA	B	217.0	74.7	78.8	2.8	7.7	9.3	6.5	6.8	6.2	T
LUMBER MUTUAL INS CO	MA	F (5)	0.0	0.0	0.0	0.0	0.3	2.4	1.8	9.1	0.0	CFGR
LUMBERMENS UNDERWRITING ALLIANCE	MO	C	316.6	71.2	83.6	-0.1	5.3	5.9	1.3	6.2	3.4	R
LUTHERAN MUTUAL FIRE INS CO	IL	C	10.3	10.1	0.3	0.4	10.0	4.6	6.1	9.3	3.0	DF
LVHN RRG	SC	U	60.3	5.0	0.0	0.0	N/A	0.2	3.8	0.0	0.0	LT
LYNDON PROPERTY INS CO	MO	B-	371.1	154.8	77.7	9.1	10.0	4.7	3.4	6.8	4.9	R
LYNDON SOUTHERN INS CO	DE	B-	87.6	38.5	53.3	7.7	6.9	4.7	8.6	6.6	4.9	GR
MACHINERY INS INC AN ASSESSABLE MUT	FL	D-	2.8	2.4	0.1	0.0	10.0	N/A	6.8	10.0	0.0	DT
MADA INS EXCHANGE	MN	U	0.5	0.0	0.0	-0.3	N/A	0.1	0.9	9.2	0.0	CFRT
MADISON INS CO	SC	D	73.5	6.0	15.3	1.8	0.0	2.6	5.8	9.5	2.3	CDG
MADISON MUTUAL INS CO	IL	B-	64.6	40.7	30.5	-1.3	8.7	6.0	3.6	6.1	5.0	F
MADISON MUTUAL INS CO	NY	C+	12.8	8.3	3.1	-0.3	10.0	7.6	4.6	7.1	3.0	DR
MAG MUTUAL INS CO	GA	B-	1,640.8	760.9	197.5	32.9	10.0	9.6	8.7	8.1	4.7	R
MAIDEN RE NORTH AMERICA INC	MO	B-	1,233.1	271.9	391.8	5.5	6.0	5.6	3.8	6.9	5.3	C
MAIDEN SPECIALTY INS CO	NC	C+	83.3	51.4	-1.5	2.6	10.0	5.9	7.8	10.0	4.1	FRT
MAIDSTONE INS CO	NY	C-	14.5	4.5	3.7	-0.6	7.4	5.2	1.7	6.1	3.1	FRT
MAIN STREET AMER PROTECTION INS CO	FL	U	14.9	14.7	0.0	0.5	N/A	N/A	7.9	7.0	5.4	T
MAIN STREET AMERICA ASR CO	FL	C	37.6	36.2	0.0	0.9	10.0	N/A	3.9	10.0	3.7	
MAINE EMPLOYERS MUTUAL INS CO	ME	B+(5)	813.8	377.7	117.5	0.0	5.3	4.1	6.9	7.0	5.0	CT
MAISON INS CO	LA	C-	27.4	10.2	12.8	2.2	7.5	3.6	3.4	8.3	2.8	DGT
MAKE TRANSPORTATION INS INC RRG	DE	E+	4.4	1.5	1.1	-0.1	8.5	9.4	5.2	7.6	0.8	DRT
MANAGED CARE MUT CAPTIVE INS CO	GA	U (5)	0.0	0.0	1.5	0.0	N/A	1.4	0.7	5.1	0.6	CFGT
MANHATTAN RE-INS CO	DE	F (5)	0.0	0.0	0.0	0.0	5.6	9.8	0.8	9.2	2.0	FRT
MANUFACTURERS ALLIANCE INS CO	PA	C-	179.8	64.2	45.2	0.0	8.3	2.2	3.4	6.8	3.3	AR
MANUFACTURING TECHNOLOGY MUT INS	MI	C	44.6	13.8	16.1	1.8	2.9	7.0	5.3	6.4	3.3	CDR
MAPFRE INS CO OF FLORIDA	FL	C-	79.3	35.1	38.9	-0.1	9.0	5.8	4.9	6.5	2.9	T

See Page 27 for explanation of footnotes and Page 28 for explanation of stability factors.
Arrows denote recent upgrades ▲ or downgrades ▼ (see Section VII for explanations)

86

www.weissratings.com

RISK ADJ. CAPITAL RATIO #1	CAPITAL RATIO #2	PREMIUM TO SURPLUS (%)	RESV. TO SURPLUS (%)	RESV. DEVELOP. 1 YEAR (%)	RESV. DEVELOP. 2 YEAR (%)	LOSS RATIO (%)	EXP. RATIO (%)	COMB RATIO (%)	CASH FROM UNDER-WRITING (%)	NET PREMIUM GROWTH (%)	INVEST. IN AFFIL (%)	INSURANCE COMPANY NAME
203.6	101.8	N/A	N/A	N/A	N/A	N/A	N/A	N/A	N/A	0.0	0.0	LIBERTY MUTUAL PERSONAL INS CO
4.0	3.7	N/A	N/A	N/A	N/A	N/A	N/A	N/A	999 +	0.0	24.8	LIBERTY NORTHWEST INS CORP
30.3	27.3	N/A	N/A	N/A	N/A	N/A	N/A	N/A	N/A	0.0	0.0	LIBERTY PERSONAL INS CO
15.5	13.9	N/A	N/A	N/A	N/A	N/A	N/A	N/A	169.4	0.0	0.0	LIBERTY SURPLUS INS CORP
0.8	0.6	146.8	30.6	N/A	N/A	76.6	37.3	113.9	144.3	0.0	0.0	LIGHTHOUSE CASUALTY CO
0.8	0.5	163.6	18.4	4.8	0.8	55.6	49.1	104.7	121.8	21.0	0.0	LIGHTHOUSE PROPERTY INS CORP
4.6	2.9	74.2	28.1	-2.3	-1.5	64.2	31.8	96.0	113.3	6.3	0.1	LIGHTNING ROD MUTUAL INS CO
0.0	0.0	55.9	999 +	-815.9	-783.5	-321.0	642.3	321.3	0.3	540.9	0.0	LINCOLN GENERAL INS CO
6.9	6.2	N/A	30.4	-8.2	-0.5	999 +	N/A	N/A	8.2	100.0	0.0	LION INS CO
4.9	3.2	29.9	53.1	-4.4	-2.5	45.9	40.7	86.6	136.4	1.1	0.0	LION INS CO
1.9	1.2	45.5	14.0	-2.0	-2.4	61.1	43.7	104.8	96.1	10.5	0.0	LITITZ MUTUAL INS CO
1.2	0.7	149.3	19.1	1.3	0.3	60.4	35.5	95.9	91.0	-1.8	0.0	LITTLE BLACK MUTUAL INS CO
N/A	N/A	N/A	N/A	-0.2	N/A	N/A	N/A	N/A	N/A	0.0	0.0	LITTLE RIVER INS CO
2.3	2.1	33.4	23.0	2.6	1.2	92.8	34.8	127.6	89.7	-0.4	0.0	LIVINGSTON MUTUAL INS CO
22.3	20.1	-56.0	5.3	-0.1	-0.1	N/A	N/A	N/A	-1.1	-141.2	0.0	LM GENERAL INS CO
82.8	64.4	-9.7	N/A	N/A	N/A	N/A	-0.1	N/A	-1.0	-105.4	0.0	LM INS CORP
N/A	N/A	N/A	113.1	1.7	1.4	999 +	999 +	999 +	N/A	0.0	0.0	LM PROPERTY & CASUALTY INS CO
N/A	N/A	2.3	N/A	N/A	N/A	200.5	155.1	355.6	27.9	21.3	0.0	LOCUST MUTUAL FIRE INS CO
N/A	N/A	0.1	N/A	N/A	N/A	N/A	999 +	999 +	-56.0	0.0	0.0	LONE STAR ALLIANCE INC A RRG
2.6	1.9	21.5	19.8	16.3	14.0	68.3	8.7	77.0	12.5	N/A	0.0	LONE STAR NATIONAL INS CO
94.7	47.4	N/A	N/A	N/A	N/A	N/A	N/A	N/A	N/A	0.0	0.0	LOUISIANA FARM BUREAU CAS INS CO
4.7	4.2	75.1	16.4	-3.5	-7.1	51.2	25.9	77.1	122.3	2.7	3.6	LOUISIANA FARM BUREAU MUTUAL INS
5.4	3.6	20.1	70.9	-0.7	-3.1	84.8	37.0	121.8	105.8	-17.8	0.0	LOUISIANA WORKERS COMPENSATION
1.1	0.8	305.6	112.9	-10.1	-13.3	62.6	35.7	98.3	102.8	9.8	0.0	LOYA CASUALTY INS CO
1.2	1.1	242.1	82.2	2.6	10.2	66.5	36.7	103.2	102.1	3.5	25.3	LOYA INS CO
N/A	N/A	N/A	N/A	N/A	N/A	N/A	999 +	999 +	0.3	0.0	0.0	LR INS INC
1.8	1.4	106.4	122.6	-5.8	-13.1	59.4	31.6	91.0	107.7	4.8	0.0	LUBA CASUALTY INS CO
0.1	0.1	0.7	407.0	33.1	32.6	999 +	999 +	999 +	0.4	146.2	54.4	LUMBER MUTUAL INS CO
1.7	1.1	165.4	285.5	6.8	5.3	75.1	39.5	114.6	106.9	40.7	0.0	LUMBERMENS UNDERWRITING
11.9	8.8	2.7	1.5	-0.8	N/A	192.5	95.3	287.8	33.5	8.6	0.0	LUTHERAN MUTUAL FIRE INS CO
N/A	N/A	N/A	N/A	123.9	81.4	N/A	N/A	N/A	142.2	0.0	0.0	LVHN RRG
4.8	3.5	53.0	10.0	2.2	0.2	75.6	22.1	97.7	114.2	4.1	0.0	LYNDON PROPERTY INS CO
1.9	1.2	172.1	12.4	3.0	N/A	34.1	53.2	87.3	122.2	22.8	0.0	LYNDON SOUTHERN INS CO
9.0	7.2	5.7	1.3	N/A	N/A	-17.3	94.0	76.7	86.2	-22.7	0.0	MACHINERY INS INC AN ASSESSABLE
N/A	N/A	N/A	999 +	772.7	660.5	N/A	N/A	N/A	N/A	0.0	0.0	MADA INS EXCHANGE
0.3	0.2	268.7	736.9	106.8	77.1	74.5	30.2	104.7	-57.7	648.5	0.0	MADISON INS CO
2.9	1.9	69.6	20.3	0.7	0.6	80.1	27.2	107.3	88.2	9.3	0.0	MADISON MUTUAL INS CO
6.1	4.0	35.9	18.3	-2.4	-0.6	61.8	38.1	99.9	103.2	0.8	0.0	MADISON MUTUAL INS CO
4.9	3.3	26.7	71.6	-12.8	-20.5	64.5	26.2	90.7	97.8	0.1	1.2 ●	MAG MUTUAL INS CO
1.3	0.7	145.3	130.0	-0.3	-3.6	75.6	29.0	104.6	169.5	13.2	5.1 ●	MAIDEN RE NORTH AMERICA INC
10.5	9.5	-3.0	7.8	8.5	3.7	55.9	-193.6	-137.7	-41.2	-109.1	0.0	MAIDEN SPECIALTY INS CO
1.9	1.4	80.0	142.1	-2.7	0.7	87.5	24.3	111.8	28.2	-24.4	0.0	MAIDSTONE INS CO
N/A	N/A	N/A	N/A	N/A	N/A	N/A	N/A	N/A	N/A	0.0	0.0	MAIN STREET AMER PROTECTION INS
36.4	18.1	N/A	N/A	N/A	N/A	N/A	N/A	N/A	N/A	0.0	0.0	MAIN STREET AMERICA ASR CO
2.4	1.8	41.1	114.4	-7.6	-8.1	57.3	22.0	79.3	104.6	-6.1	9.0	MAINE EMPLOYERS MUTUAL INS CO
1.8	1.4	165.7	4.6	-0.1	N/A	58.8	35.9	94.7	150.8	429.8	0.0	MAISON INS CO
1.7	1.5	67.3	68.1	-10.8	-17.7	58.9	22.7	81.6	132.6	17.0	0.0	MAKE TRANSPORTATION INS INC RRG
N/A	N/A	275.5	293.7	114.2	41.3	51.0	36.6	87.6	43.3	34.3	0.0	MANAGED CARE MUT CAPTIVE INS CO
2.4	0.9	-0.2	102.5	-76.7	-71.0	999 +	999 +	999 +	0.9	-120.0	0.0	MANHATTAN RE-INS CO
2.0	1.5	67.7	106.7	10.1	18.9	79.9	25.4	105.3	102.0	-5.3	5.3	MANUFACTURERS ALLIANCE INS CO
0.7	0.3	131.6	188.2	-10.9	-22.8	76.4	16.2	92.6	135.0	16.8	0.0	MANUFACTURING TECHNOLOGY MUT
2.8	2.1	108.0	44.4	3.8	6.8	73.5	27.8	101.3	103.0	3.5	0.0	MAPFRE INS CO OF FLORIDA

999 + Denotes number greater than 999.9%
999 - Denotes number less than -999.99%
● Bullets denote a more detailed analysis is available in Section II.

INSURANCE COMPANY NAME	DOM. STATE	RATING	TOTAL ASSETS ($MIL)	CAPITAL & SURPLUS ($MIL)	ANNUAL NET PREMIUM ($MIL)	NET INCOME ($MIL)	CAPITAL-IZATION INDEX (PTS)	RESERVE ADQ INDEX (PTS)	PROFIT-ABILITY INDEX (PTS)	LIQUIDITY INDEX (PTS)	STAB. INDEX (PTS)	STABILITY FACTORS
MAPFRE INS CO OF NEW YORK	NY	C+	139.9	51.3	72.3	0.7	9.5	5.7	3.9	6.0	4.7	
MAPFRE INSURANCE CO	NJ	C	63.9	24.9	31.5	0.2	5.6	4.7	2.4	5.2	3.4	DFRT
MAPFRE PAN AMERICAN INS CO	PR	C	14.7	10.2	0.9	0.1	10.0	7.4	6.1	9.5	3.8	DF
MAPFRE PRAICO INS CO	PR	D+	386.8	149.5	146.6	10.7	6.8	8.3	3.2	6.1	1.0	D
MAPFRE PREFERRED RISK INS CO	PR	C	78.0	25.7	10.0	-0.9	10.0	7.5	5.7	8.0	3.9	F
MAPLE VALLEY MUTUAL INS CO	WI	C	12.2	7.9	4.8	0.5	9.3	6.5	5.1	6.7	2.6	DFR
MARATHON FINANCIAL INS INC RRG	DE	D	7.4	2.2	0.0	0.1	7.1	8.9	3.3	9.1	1.7	DRT
MARKEL AMERICAN INS CO	VA	C	329.8	145.9	119.1	18.6	7.6	9.7	6.8	7.6	3.8	AR
MARKEL INS CO	IL	C	1,345.1	379.7	493.9	4.2	6.5	6.0	5.0	7.0	3.8	AR
MARYLAND CASUALTY CO	MD	C	166.8	149.0	0.0	1.0	10.0	N/A	3.7	7.0	3.5	FRT
MARYSVILLE MUTUAL INS CO	KS	C	37.9	20.5	17.6	0.9	8.9	6.1	6.7	6.1	3.9	DR
MASSACHUSETTS BAY INS CO	NH	C+	62.3	62.3	0.0	1.2	10.0	N/A	7.7	7.0	4.7	R
MASSACHUSETTS EMPLOYERS INS CO	MA	C	4.4	3.6	0.0	0.0	10.0	N/A	6.7	10.0	3.2	DR
MASSACHUSETTS HOMELAND INS CO	MA	C	9.9	8.7	0.0	0.1	10.0	N/A	5.4	6.4	2.5	DRT
MAXUM CASUALTY INS CO	DE	D+	56.0	16.7	13.3	0.3	7.1	6.0	5.3	7.1	2.5	DFRT
MAXUM INDEMNITY CO	DE	C	285.3	108.1	69.9	1.9	7.6	9.3	6.8	7.0	4.1	R
MAYA ASR CO	NY	E+	14.3	2.3	6.4	0.0	0.9	0.3	3.9	1.0	0.8	CDGL
MBIA INS CORP	NY	D	933.4	546.2	133.5	-27.0	3.1	2.3	0.5	7.0	1.4	CT
MCMILLAN WARNER MUTUAL INS CO	WI	C	14.5	7.7	7.1	-1.1	7.8	7.3	3.4	6.9	2.8	DR
MD RRG INC	MT	D-	17.7	11.2	3.9	1.0	8.7	5.1	9.2	9.3	1.3	DR
MDADVANTAGE INS CO OF NJ	NJ	C (3)	0.0	0.0	39.5	3.3	7.8	9.4	8.5	7.0	3.5	T
MDOW INS CO	TX	B-	8.8	5.1	0.0	0.2	10.0	N/A	8.6	7.9	3.5	DFT
MED MAL RRG INC	TN	D	5.1	2.3	0.5	0.2	7.5	N/A	3.4	8.9	1.6	DT
MEDICAL ALLIANCE INS CO	IL	D	9.0	4.8	2.2	0.1	8.9	N/A	8.1	9.3	2.1	DFR
MEDICAL INS EXCHANGE OF CALIFORNIA	CA	B	401.5	186.4	54.8	2.5	10.0	9.3	8.2	7.6	5.5	F
MEDICAL LIABILITY ALLIANCE	MO	C+	71.0	48.9	11.2	2.1	10.0	9.4	8.9	7.9	4.6	DR
MEDICAL LIABILITY MUTUAL INS CO	NY	D+	6,271.6	1,677.1	533.9	167.0	5.7	9.7	6.7	7.5	2.4	R
MEDICAL MUTUAL INS CO OF MAINE	ME	B-	263.7	154.0	33.9	6.3	10.0	9.5	8.8	8.5	5.3	T
MEDICAL MUTUAL INS CO OF NC	NC	B-	481.0	220.5	75.4	29.1	10.0	9.5	4.8	7.8	4.5	R
MEDICAL MUTUAL LIAB INS SOC OF MD	MD	B-	790.0	360.9	120.7	12.0	10.0	9.6	7.8	7.5	4.6	R
MEDICAL PROFESSIONAL MUTUAL INS CO	MA	B-	3,054.0	1,422.0	277.0	67.7	8.2	9.6	8.7	7.0	4.5	R
MEDICAL PROTECTIVE CO	IN	B	2,672.6	1,530.7	366.9	112.1	8.1	9.4	8.9	9.2	5.5	T
MEDICAL PROVIDERS MUTUAL INS CO RRG	DC	D	7.3	3.0	1.4	0.0	8.5	10.0	8.5	9.1	2.1	DFR
MEDICAL SECURITY INS CO	NC	C+	29.7	16.1	0.3	0.2	10.0	7.0	7.6	9.1	3.3	DFGR
MEDICUS INS CO	TX	C	82.4	33.3	0.0	0.7	10.0	5.1	6.5	7.7	3.4	R
MEDMAL DIRECT INS CO	FL	B-	26.3	11.0	10.5	0.5	5.1	4.8	4.1	7.4	3.5	CDGT
MEDMARC CASUALTY INS CO	VT	C	274.3	192.6	18.6	6.1	8.2	9.4	6.8	6.9	3.4	FGRT
MEDPRO RRG	DC	D+	27.2	3.8	1.5	0.7	5.7	5.3	6.7	9.2	2.4	DGT
MEDSTAR LIABILITY LTD INS CO INC RRG	DC	D-	3.7	1.0	0.7	-0.1	4.1	10.0	2.4	9.3	1.1	DFRT
MEEMIC INS CO	MI	C	251.2	67.4	91.3	-2.1	8.9	3.8	2.4	6.1	4.0	FT
MEMBERS INS CO	NC	E+	21.1	10.7	8.1	0.2	7.6	7.9	3.9	7.0	0.6	D
MEMBERSELECT INS CO	MI	B-	498.8	131.8	164.3	-3.7	9.0	4.1	3.1	6.4	4.9	F
MEMIC CASUALTY CO	VT	C	27.0	19.0	2.9	0.1	10.0	3.6	3.9	9.3	3.3	DGT
MEMIC INDEMNITY CO	NH	C	300.2	111.2	91.2	4.4	7.4	9.3	5.5	6.7	3.2	R
MENDAKOTA INS CO	MN	B	14.7	9.2	0.0	0.1	10.0	4.6	5.2	7.0	4.4	DR
MENDOTA INS CO	MN	D+	123.1	35.4	94.9	-0.8	0.0	1.9	3.5	0.0	2.6	CFLR
MENNONITE MUTUAL INS CO	OH	C-	21.8	12.1	10.5	0.7	9.2	8.1	8.1	7.0	3.2	D
MENTAL HEALTH RISK RETENTION GROUP	VT	C-	28.1	13.9	4.1	0.8	8.7	10.0	8.9	8.1	3.1	D
MERASTAR INS CO	IL	B-	25.8	8.5	0.0	0.4	8.7	N/A	3.8	10.0	4.3	DR
MERCED PROPERTY & CASUALTY CO	CA	C	21.1	17.0	3.9	0.6	8.5	8.0	6.8	6.9	4.3	DFR
MERCER INS CO	PA	C	230.5	94.8	65.1	1.7	7.6	6.8	6.7	6.7	4.3	R
MERCER INS CO OF NJ INC	NJ	C	74.3	27.9	21.7	0.3	7.3	6.9	6.4	8.6	3.7	R

See Page 27 for explanation of footnotes and Page 28 for explanation of stability factors.

88

www.weissratings.com

Arrows denote recent upgrades ▲ or downgrades ▼ (see Section VII for explanations)

RISK ADJ. CAPITAL RATIO #1	RATIO #2	PREMIUM TO SURPLUS (%)	RESV. TO SURPLUS (%)	RESV. DEVELOP. 1 YEAR (%)	2 YEAR (%)	LOSS RATIO (%)	EXP. RATIO (%)	COMB RATIO (%)	CASH FROM UNDER-WRITING (%)	NET PREMIUM GROWTH (%)	INVEST. IN AFFIL (%)	INSURANCE COMPANY NAME
3.1	2.4	135.1	55.6	4.3	7.2	73.5	27.0	100.5	110.4	-8.7	0.0	MAPFRE INS CO OF NEW YORK
1.3	1.0	167.9	69.1	5.0	7.7	73.5	27.6	101.1	84.3	-27.2	0.0	MAPFRE INSURANCE CO
7.3	6.6	8.3	1.6	-0.9	-0.7	66.9	62.7	129.6	-19.0	-19.8	0.0	MAPFRE PAN AMERICAN INS CO
1.4	0.9	98.6	55.9	-1.9	-3.9	52.7	30.1	82.8	100.8	2.6	8.0	MAPFRE PRAICO INS CO
3.7	3.4	37.1	6.8	-0.9	-1.4	83.4	-12.2	71.2	39.5	21.4	0.0	MAPFRE PREFERRED RISK INS CO
3.5	2.6	66.3	8.6	-2.1	-1.9	77.5	32.8	110.3	87.6	9.1	0.0	MAPLE VALLEY MUTUAL INS CO
1.4	1.2	N/A	1.7	-1.4	-3.2	63.7	N/A	N/A	N/A	0.0	0.0	MARATHON FINANCIAL INS INC RRG
3.5	2.3	87.7	152.9	-21.8	-27.5	43.8	39.6	83.4	111.6	8.8	0.0	MARKEL AMERICAN INS CO
1.7	1.0	142.2	172.5	-14.0	-31.3	61.3	39.1	100.4	125.4	18.5	5.3 ●	MARKEL INS CO
3.3	3.2	N/A	N/A	N/A	N/A	N/A	N/A	N/A	130.3	0.0	31.2	MARYLAND CASUALTY CO
2.5	2.2	90.3	5.9	-1.0	0.3	50.0	29.8	79.8	127.6	6.8	0.0	MARYSVILLE MUTUAL INS CO
86.5	40.4	N/A	N/A	N/A	N/A	N/A	N/A	N/A	N/A	0.0	0.0	MASSACHUSETTS BAY INS CO
9.1	8.2	N/A	N/A	N/A	N/A	N/A	N/A	N/A	N/A	0.0	0.0	MASSACHUSETTS EMPLOYERS INS CO
16.8	15.1	N/A	N/A	N/A	N/A	N/A	N/A	N/A	N/A	0.0	0.0	MASSACHUSETTS HOMELAND INS CO
1.8	1.1	81.9	126.0	1.4	-8.2	68.1	31.9	100.0	82.3	-3.6	0.0	MAXUM CASUALTY INS CO
2.5	1.7	65.9	101.4	1.2	-6.9	68.1	32.1	100.2	116.6	-3.6	6.3	MAXUM INDEMNITY CO
0.3	0.2	278.1	299.2	59.4	176.4	115.8	-15.1	100.7	98.4	14.0	0.0	MAYA ASR CO
0.8	0.2	33.1	9.9	10.5	-26.6	378.6	32.2	410.8	-7.4	-34.6	24.2 ●	MBIA INS CORP
1.9	1.4	83.9	10.7	-0.6	-0.2	54.5	36.4	90.9	120.0	0.0	0.0	MCMILLAN WARNER MUTUAL INS CO
3.4	2.1	37.9	61.2	-25.6	-60.7	35.1	12.2	47.3	318.4	-4.1	0.0	MD RRG INC
1.9	1.6	32.1	122.9	-4.5	-9.4	69.5	35.6	105.1	92.5	-3.8	0.0	MDADVANTAGE INS CO OF NJ
4.3	3.9	N/A	N/A	N/A	N/A	N/A	N/A	N/A	-474.2	0.0	0.0	MDOW INS CO
2.5	2.2	23.6	16.1	N/A	N/A	68.7	58.1	126.8	999 +	0.0	0.0	MED MAL RRG INC
3.1	2.7	48.0	N/A	N/A	N/A	16.5	73.9	90.4	79.3	0.1	0.0	MEDICAL ALLIANCE INS CO
4.3	3.1	29.8	67.8	-6.0	-11.0	81.9	17.9	99.8	110.5	4.7	3.4	MEDICAL INS EXCHANGE OF
9.4	6.8	24.0	31.6	-2.2	-8.6	33.4	16.0	49.4	205.5	-1.2	0.0	MEDICAL LIABILITY ALLIANCE
1.3	1.1	34.7	235.2	-10.2	-17.8	93.4	6.8	100.2	85.8	-2.9	0.3 ●	MEDICAL LIABILITY MUTUAL INS CO
6.5	4.5	23.1	57.0	-16.7	-24.1	14.9	30.2	45.1	114.2	-4.7	0.0	MEDICAL MUTUAL INS CO OF MAINE
4.8	3.6	22.5	47.3	-7.2	-13.4	54.7	12.0	66.7	137.0	4.4	2.8 ●	MEDICAL MUTUAL INS CO OF NC
3.4	3.0	35.5	67.2	-11.3	-19.3	50.3	19.8	70.1	117.3	-6.4	12.2 ●	MEDICAL MUTUAL LIAB INS SOC OF MD
2.2	1.8	19.5	88.0	-8.2	-15.6	60.1	22.6	82.7	111.5	-1.2	13.5 ●	MEDICAL PROFESSIONAL MUTUAL INS
4.2	3.0	26.1	109.0	-13.2	-3.9	51.3	20.7	72.0	115.7	-43.0	0.0 ●	MEDICAL PROTECTIVE CO
2.7	2.5	47.9	94.8	-26.5	-46.1	44.4	23.4	67.8	106.9	-4.5	0.0	MEDICAL PROVIDERS MUTUAL INS CO
5.7	5.1	2.0	11.3	0.9	-7.2	70.7	14.6	85.3	71.7	-81.5	0.0	MEDICAL SECURITY INS CO
5.7	5.2	N/A	20.9	N/A	N/A	N/A	N/A	N/A	-938.7	0.0	0.0	MEDICUS INS CO
1.2	0.8	100.6	72.6	-7.0	-8.7	59.5	35.7	95.2	180.8	34.4	0.0	MEDMAL DIRECT INS CO
2.7	2.2	9.9	34.4	-3.2	-5.5	60.4	56.0	116.4	32.9	145.7	21.8	MEDMARC CASUALTY INS CO
0.9	0.8	47.4	67.1	-1.9	-1.5	83.6	-17.4	66.2	94.2	41.7	0.0	MEDPRO RRG
0.7	0.5	58.5	194.5	6.5	-100.8	125.3	54.0	179.3	74.5	6.0	0.0	MEDSTAR LIABILITY LTD INS CO INC
2.8	2.1	130.5	94.6	3.1	12.1	73.4	30.3	103.7	88.0	-21.6	0.0	MEEMIC INS CO
1.5	1.0	88.0	21.0	-0.9	-2.9	68.0	30.7	98.7	125.0	43.5	0.0	MEMBERS INS CO
2.8	2.2	121.3	99.7	2.7	13.2	73.9	30.3	104.2	77.0	-9.7	0.0	MEMBERSELECT INS CO
5.5	3.0	15.5	6.6	-0.7	N/A	79.9	25.6	105.5	354.4	558.3	0.0	MEMIC CASUALTY CO
1.5	1.1	86.0	103.1	-0.1	-15.0	76.0	25.1	101.1	135.7	27.5	0.0	MEMIC INDEMNITY CO
5.5	4.9	N/A	N/A	N/A	N/A	N/A	N/A	N/A	-18.3	0.0	0.0	MENDAKOTA INS CO
0.1	0.1	316.6	150.5	8.6	20.0	79.4	29.9	109.3	90.2	12.4	34.1	MENDOTA INS CO
3.4	2.2	90.3	15.5	-0.2	-2.5	57.8	37.7	95.5	108.4	8.9	0.0	MENNONITE MUTUAL INS CO
3.4	2.3	31.1	75.0	-18.1	-37.3	36.6	10.0	46.6	258.7	-5.3	0.0	MENTAL HEALTH RISK RETENTION
2.6	2.3	N/A	N/A	N/A	N/A	N/A	N/A	N/A	9.1	0.0	0.0	MERASTAR INS CO
5.1	3.0	23.5	7.9	-1.4	-2.0	45.6	57.8	103.4	99.4	-0.7	0.0	MERCED PROPERTY & CASUALTY CO
1.7	1.3	68.4	82.6	-5.1	-7.2	63.3	31.4	94.7	96.7	10.3	18.7	MERCER INS CO
1.7	1.1	80.5	97.3	-6.1	-8.1	63.3	29.3	92.6	388.1	10.3	0.0	MERCER INS CO OF NJ INC

999 + Denotes number greater than 999.9%
999 - Denotes number less than -999.99%
● Bullets denote a more detailed analysis is available in Section II.

INSURANCE COMPANY NAME	DOM. STATE	RATING	TOTAL ASSETS ($MIL)	CAPITAL & SURPLUS ($MIL)	ANNUAL NET PREMIUM ($MIL)	NET INCOME ($MIL)	CAPITAL- IZATION INDEX (PTS)	RESERVE ADQ INDEX (PTS)	PROFIT- ABILITY INDEX (PTS)	LIQUIDITY INDEX (PTS)	STAB. INDEX (PTS)	STABILITY FACTORS
MERCHANTS BONDING CO (MUTUAL)	IA	C+	140.9	92.1	50.7	5.9	8.9	6.8	8.7	6.9	4.4	R
MERCHANTS MUTUAL INS CO	NY	B-	471.0	158.2	147.9	6.7	8.7	6.4	4.5	6.9	4.6	R
MERCHANTS NATIONAL BONDING INC	IA	D+	20.4	11.5	5.6	0.7	8.6	4.1	8.7	7.7	2.5	DRT
MERCHANTS NATIONAL INS CO	NH	C	109.5	36.4	42.3	2.0	6.8	5.6	3.8	6.7	4.3	R
MERCHANTS PREFERRED INS CO	NY	C+	65.2	25.5	21.1	1.1	7.9	5.8	4.4	7.3	4.4	DR
MERCHANTS PROPERTY INS CO OF IN	IN	U	72.7	55.8	0.0	1.4	N/A	3.6	6.8	7.0	5.4	T
MERCURY CASUALTY CO	CA	B+	1,993.8	1,063.6	738.1	85.4	7.6	5.9	6.4	6.8	6.7	
MERCURY COUNTY MUTUAL INS CO	TX	C	9.5	4.3	0.0	0.0	9.5	N/A	3.5	10.0	3.3	DF
MERCURY INDEMNITY CO OF AMERICA	FL	D-	54.8	37.7	0.0	0.3	10.0	N/A	6.9	7.0	1.0	F
MERCURY INDEMNITY CO OF GEORGIA	GA	B	13.4	10.3	0.0	0.1	10.0	3.6	6.7	10.0	4.9	D
MERCURY INS CO	CA	A-	1,591.4	683.4	1,350.1	65.5	8.2	5.6	5.1	5.4	7.0	L
MERCURY INS CO OF FL	FL	C-	46.8	40.0	0.0	0.5	10.0	N/A	6.2	9.5	3.3	T
MERCURY INS CO OF GA	GA	B	19.8	16.8	0.0	0.3	10.0	3.6	7.3	10.0	4.9	DT
MERCURY INS CO OF IL	IL	B	32.6	31.4	0.0	0.2	8.4	3.6	6.9	7.0	5.7	DT
MERCURY NATIONAL INS CO	IL	B	16.3	14.8	0.0	0.2	10.0	4.5	6.8	10.0	5.0	DF
MERIDIAN SECURITY INS CO	IN	C	117.1	68.3	0.0	1.2	10.0	N/A	7.8	7.0	3.4	R
MERITPLAN INS CO	CA	C	81.2	77.7	-0.1	0.1	10.0	6.1	3.1	7.0	2.9	DFGT
MERRIMACK MUTUAL FIRE INS CO	MA	B	1,305.5	832.1	246.4	34.4	7.9	6.2	6.5	7.0	4.8	
MESA UNDERWRITERS SPECIALTY INS CO	NJ	C-	286.4	66.9	90.6	4.3	7.3	6.7	5.5	6.8	3.1	RT
METROPOLITAN CASUALTY INS CO	RI	B	198.2	52.6	0.0	1.4	10.0	N/A	8.0	7.0	5.6	
METROPOLITAN DIRECT PROP & CAS INS	RI	B	115.9	30.8	0.0	0.9	10.0	N/A	7.1	7.0	5.9	D
METROPOLITAN GENERAL INS CO	RI	B	40.7	35.8	0.0	0.9	10.0	N/A	8.1	7.0	5.8	DT
METROPOLITAN GROUP PROP & CAS INS	RI	B	616.7	361.5	0.0	17.3	10.0	5.7	6.8	6.9	6.3	
METROPOLITAN LLOYDS INS CO TEXAS	TX	B	91.5	16.6	0.0	0.4	8.4	N/A	7.2	7.0	5.2	D
METROPOLITAN PROPERTY & CAS INS CO	RI	B	5,740.1	2,464.4	3,372.1	150.0	7.8	9.0	8.1	3.6	5.7	L
MFS MUTUAL INS CO	IA	C-	3.5	2.6	0.8	-0.1	6.0	6.1	1.8	6.1	2.0	DFRT
MGA INS CO INC	TX	C	240.6	103.0	191.3	8.1	7.8	3.5	6.7	5.5	3.9	R
MGIC ASSURANCE CORP	WI	U	10.5	10.2	0.1	0.0	N/A	5.9	5.2	10.0	5.4	T
MGIC CREDIT ASR CORP	WI	D+	44.4	44.0	0.2	0.9	10.0	7.7	5.1	10.0	2.7	DT
MGIC INDEMNITY CORP	WI	D+	496.0	466.2	21.4	8.1	10.0	N/A	7.6	9.1	2.4	AGT
MGIC MORTGAGE REINSURANCE CORP	WI	D+	13.4	8.4	0.3	0.8	7.0	2.6	1.3	8.8	2.4	DFT
MGIC REINSURANCE CORP	WI	D+	167.6	48.1	22.6	1.8	4.2	5.0	1.6	6.4	2.4	DFR
MGIC REINSURANCE CORP OF WI	WI	E	363.6	15.1	78.0	0.5	0.0	3.9	0.3	2.3	-0.5	CFLT
MGIC RESIDENTIAL REINSURANCE CORP	WI	D+	12.7	7.7	0.3	0.8	6.4	2.5	1.3	8.0	2.4	DFT
MHA INS CO	MI	B	539.0	267.3	68.2	0.0	10.0	9.4	7.3	8.6	4.7	R
MIAMI MUTUAL INS CO	OH	B	52.1	21.5	29.7	0.5	7.5	8.6	5.7	6.0	5.4	DR
MIC GENERAL INS CORP	MI	C-	37.3	19.7	0.0	0.2	10.0	3.0	5.4	6.9	3.3	DRT
MIC PROPERTY & CASUALTY INS CORP	MI	C	92.5	53.9	0.0	0.1	10.0	N/A	4.2	7.0	3.8	RT
MIC REINS CORP	WI	D	4.3	3.3	0.7	0.1	10.0	N/A	4.7	9.0	2.1	DGT
MIC REINS CORP OF WISCONSIN	WI	D	7.0	5.3	1.0	0.2	10.0	3.6	4.9	9.2	2.3	DGT
MICA RRG INC	DC	U	1.0	1.0	0.0	0.0	N/A	0.0	3.3	0.0	0.0	LT
MICHIGAN AUTO INS PLACEMENT FACILITY	MI	U	--	--	--	--	N/A	--	--	--	--	Z
MICHIGAN BASIC PROPERTY INS ASN	MI	U (5)	0.0	0.0	55.1	0.0	N/A	0.5	0.9	7.0	0.0	CDFT
MICHIGAN COMMERCIAL INS MUTUAL	MI	C-	90.7	24.5	44.3	-2.7	5.5	5.2	1.8	5.7	2.9	FR
MICHIGAN INS CO	MI	C+	113.9	41.0	42.4	-1.3	9.2	7.8	5.4	6.6	4.4	T
MICHIGAN MILLERS MUTUAL INS CO	MI	B-	186.7	71.7	107.0	-7.9	8.7	6.9	2.9	6.0	5.0	F
MICHIGAN PROFESSIONAL INS EXCHANGE	MI	C	102.2	53.4	13.0	3.8	8.6	9.6	8.8	7.3	4.3	DR
MICO INS CO	OH	B	13.2	13.0	0.0	0.3	10.0	N/A	3.7	7.0	4.3	DT
MID AMERICAN FIRE & CAS CO	NH	B	8.2	8.2	0.0	0.1	10.0	N/A	6.4	10.0	4.0	DFRT
MID-CENTURY INS CO	CA	C	3,719.4	951.2	2,181.9	32.0	7.4	9.3	6.1	5.4	4.3	R
MID-CENTURY INS CO OF TEXAS	TX	B-	37.8	35.0	0.0	0.3	10.0	N/A	7.4	7.0	3.8	DRT
MID-CONTINENT CAS CO	OH	C	485.0	136.5	137.8	12.2	5.7	9.4	2.8	7.2	4.0	R

See Page 27 for explanation of footnotes and
Page 28 for explanation of stability factors.
Arrows denote recent upgrades ▲ or downgrades ▼   (see Section VII for explanations)

90

www.weissratings.com

RISK ADJ. CAPITAL RATIO #1	RATIO #2	PREMIUM TO SURPLUS (%)	RESV. TO SURPLUS (%)	RESV. DEVELOP. 1 YEAR (%)	2 YEAR (%)	LOSS RATIO (%)	EXP. RATIO (%)	COMB RATIO (%)	CASH FROM UNDER-WRITING (%)	NET PREMIUM GROWTH (%)	INVEST. IN AFFIL (%)	INSURANCE COMPANY NAME
3.3	2.5	59.0	18.5	-2.8	-6.7	17.7	67.3	85.0	121.9	5.6	5.4	MERCHANTS BONDING CO (MUTUAL)
2.7	2.0	98.4	127.1	5.6	5.5	75.5	31.7	107.2	104.5	10.8	9.8	MERCHANTS MUTUAL INS CO
2.4	1.9	53.4	16.8	-2.5	7.5	17.7	67.4	85.1	144.6	4.4	0.0	MERCHANTS NATIONAL BONDING INC
1.3	0.9	124.1	133.8	6.8	7.5	75.5	31.8	107.3	106.3	10.8	29.0	MERCHANTS NATIONAL INS CO
2.9	1.5	86.4	93.1	4.9	5.4	75.5	31.8	107.3	107.6	10.8	0.0	MERCHANTS PREFERRED INS CO
N/A	N/A	N/A	N/A	N/A	N/A	N/A	N/A	N/A	N/A	0.0	0.0	MERCHANTS PROPERTY INS CO OF IN
1.6	1.4	64.1	34.5	-0.8	2.1	69.4	26.8	96.2	95.1	-17.0	35.0 •	MERCURY CASUALTY CO
2.7	2.4	N/A	N/A	N/A	N/A	N/A	N/A	N/A	120.6	0.0	0.0	MERCURY COUNTY MUTUAL INS CO
11.7	10.6	N/A	N/A	N/A	N/A	N/A	N/A	N/A	999 +	0.0	0.0	MERCURY INDEMNITY CO OF AMERICA
10.1	9.0	N/A	N/A	N/A	N/A	N/A	N/A	N/A	528.3	0.0	0.0	MERCURY INDEMNITY CO OF GEORGIA
2.0	1.8	206.9	71.2	1.6	6.3	75.2	25.5	100.7	100.8	4.8	0.0 •	MERCURY INS CO
21.7	19.5	N/A	N/A	N/A	N/A	N/A	N/A	N/A	113.1	0.0	0.0	MERCURY INS CO OF FL
16.9	15.2	N/A	N/A	N/A	N/A	N/A	N/A	N/A	-115.1	0.0	0.0	MERCURY INS CO OF GA
2.0	1.9	N/A	N/A	N/A	N/A	N/A	N/A	N/A	-22.6	0.0	48.8	MERCURY INS CO OF IL
25.8	21.1	N/A	N/A	N/A	N/A	N/A	N/A	N/A	999 +	0.0	0.0	MERCURY NATIONAL INS CO
10.3	9.2	N/A	N/A	N/A	N/A	N/A	N/A	N/A	158.1	0.0	0.0	MERIDIAN SECURITY INS CO
67.8	61.0	-0.2	1.0	0.2	0.3	-94.5	96.0	1.5	96.2	68.6	0.0	MERITPLAN INS CO
2.0	1.6	31.4	20.2	-1.2	-2.0	43.3	39.5	82.8	112.3	2.8	22.7 •	MERRIMACK MUTUAL FIRE INS CO
1.8	1.2	145.4	224.6	-3.4	-9.6	64.5	32.7	97.2	111.1	-25.3	0.0	MESA UNDERWRITERS SPECIALTY INS
5.5	5.0	N/A	N/A	N/A	N/A	N/A	N/A	N/A	999 +	0.0	0.0	METROPOLITAN CASUALTY INS CO
3.6	3.3	N/A	N/A	N/A	N/A	N/A	N/A	N/A	N/A	0.0	0.0	METROPOLITAN DIRECT PROP & CAS
24.2	21.7	N/A	N/A	N/A	N/A	N/A	N/A	N/A	999 +	0.0	0.0	METROPOLITAN GENERAL INS CO
16.1	8.6	N/A	19.6	1.8	4.7	N/A	N/A	N/A	-77.2	0.0	2.9 •	METROPOLITAN GROUP PROP & CAS
2.1	1.9	N/A	N/A	N/A	N/A	N/A	N/A	N/A	132.3	0.0	0.0	METROPOLITAN LLOYDS INS CO TEXAS
2.2	1.7	151.6	69.8	-2.1	-7.4	68.8	26.2	95.0	105.6	6.2	20.3 •	METROPOLITAN PROPERTY & CAS INS
1.1	0.7	31.0	7.2	-1.5	-0.9	93.1	55.8	148.9	73.6	14.8	0.0	MFS MUTUAL INS CO
1.6	1.5	186.3	70.7	-0.8	21.5	73.8	25.6	99.4	97.9	1.9	0.0	MGA INS CO INC
N/A	N/A	0.6	3.1	0.8	1.0	156.6	208.7	365.3	17.0	-36.4	0.0	MGIC ASSURANCE CORP
49.6	32.7	0.4	1.5	-1.3	-2.2	145.3	251.6	396.9	17.3	-22.4	0.0	MGIC CREDIT ASR CORP
18.5	16.5	4.7	0.1	N/A	N/A	2.3	70.8	73.1	483.7	188.2	1.1 •	MGIC INDEMNITY CORP
3.2	2.3	4.5	96.8	-9.4	7.0	234.1	40.0	274.1	7.9	-35.6	0.0	MGIC MORTGAGE REINSURANCE CORP
1.0	0.8	48.8	248.2	-39.3	-2.8	77.7	26.8	104.5	34.7	-13.8	0.0	MGIC REINSURANCE CORP
0.1	0.1	534.4	999 +	-145.5	22.4	98.1	18.6	116.7	38.1	-8.7	0.0	MGIC REINSURANCE CORP OF WI
2.9	2.1	4.9	106.6	-10.2	7.6	234.1	40.0	274.1	7.9	-35.6	0.0	MGIC RESIDENTIAL REINSURANCE
5.4	4.0	24.6	66.4	-0.4	-4.2	84.5	20.9	105.4	226.3	10.2	0.4 •	MHA INS CO
2.2	1.4	142.2	52.4	-2.8	-6.1	67.1	30.8	97.9	105.9	-1.6	0.0	MIAMI MUTUAL INS CO
5.9	5.3	N/A	N/A	N/A	N/A	N/A	N/A	N/A	133.7	100.0	0.0	MIC GENERAL INS CORP
9.7	8.8	N/A	N/A	N/A	N/A	N/A	N/A	N/A	-16.0	0.0	0.0	MIC PROPERTY & CASUALTY INS CORP
4.8	4.2	21.5	0.7	N/A	N/A	3.7	68.6	72.3	383.5	681.2	0.0	MIC REINS CORP
6.9	5.8	19.1	1.1	-0.2	N/A	6.5	58.4	64.9	432.3	508.9	0.0	MIC REINS CORP OF WISCONSIN
N/A	N/A	N/A	N/A	N/A	N/A	N/A	N/A	N/A	N/A	0.0	0.0	MICA RRG INC
N/A	N/A	--	--	--	--	--	--	--	--	--	--	MICHIGAN AUTO INS PLACEMENT
N/A	N/A	999 +	-653.6	80.0	44.5	154.3	21.9	176.2	59.0	5.6	0.0	MICHIGAN BASIC PROPERTY INS ASN
0.9	0.7	167.0	187.5	-0.1	12.6	76.4	35.6	112.0	86.2	-6.6	0.0	MICHIGAN COMMERCIAL INS MUTUAL
3.0	2.1	102.0	75.3	-0.3	-4.4	74.5	24.4	98.9	101.9	13.0	0.0	MICHIGAN INS CO
3.0	2.1	133.6	57.6	3.5	-0.4	69.2	34.4	103.6	90.9	15.1	0.0	MICHIGAN MILLERS MUTUAL INS CO
3.1	2.6	24.6	76.3	-8.9	-31.6	61.2	17.6	78.8	110.3	-0.1	0.0	MICHIGAN PROFESSIONAL INS
11.2	6.5	N/A	N/A	N/A	N/A	N/A	N/A	N/A	138.4	0.0	0.0	MICO INS CO
234.0	117.0	N/A	N/A	N/A	N/A	N/A	N/A	N/A	0.6	0.0	0.0	MID AMERICAN FIRE & CAS CO
1.8	1.4	236.8	150.4	1.2	-1.8	67.2	34.1	101.3	97.4	-1.6	8.8 •	MID-CENTURY INS CO
36.8	33.1	N/A	N/A	N/A	N/A	N/A	N/A	N/A	-5.3	0.0	0.0	MID-CENTURY INS CO OF TEXAS
1.1	0.8	104.4	193.5	3.6	-14.5	58.5	37.0	95.5	109.2	6.1	13.7	MID-CONTINENT CAS CO

999 + Denotes number greater than 999.9%
999 - Denotes number less than -999.99%
• Bullets denote a more detailed analysis is available in Section II.

INSURANCE COMPANY NAME	DOM. STATE	RATING	TOTAL ASSETS ($MIL)	CAPITAL & SURPLUS ($MIL)	ANNUAL NET PREMIUM ($MIL)	NET INCOME ($MIL)	CAPITAL-IZATION INDEX (PTS)	RESERVE ADQ INDEX (PTS)	PROFIT-ABILITY INDEX (PTS)	LIQUIDITY INDEX (PTS)	STAB. INDEX (PTS)	STABILITY FACTORS
MID-CONTINENT EXCESS & SURPLUS INS	DE	C	17.0	17.0	0.0	0.3	10.0	N/A	4.9	7.0	3.3	DT
MID-CONTINENT INS CO	OH	C	33.3	22.6	4.4	0.5	9.2	8.7	7.8	9.0	4.3	DR
MID-HUDSON CO-OPERTIVE INS CO	NY	C	19.9	11.3	6.3	0.2	8.3	8.5	8.5	7.0	3.1	DR
MIDDLE STATES INS CO INC	OK	D+	5.7	5.0	3.0	0.0	8.9	7.4	3.9	6.9	2.3	DG
MIDDLESEX INS CO	WI	B	679.5	256.9	181.8	9.8	9.7	8.7	5.9	6.8	5.4	
MIDDLESEX MUTUAL ASR CO	CT	B	250.8	85.5	75.8	1.5	9.4	7.8	3.9	6.5	6.0	
MIDROX INS CO	NY	D+	7.3	3.4	2.8	-0.1	8.0	9.3	5.5	6.9	2.1	DR
MIDSOUTH MUTUAL INS CO	TN	D+	14.0	6.0	3.1	-0.2	7.3	N/A	3.0	7.7	2.5	DT
MIDSTATE MUTUAL INS CO	NY	C+	40.4	23.0	11.8	0.1	8.6	6.6	4.3	6.7	4.7	DR
MIDSTATES REINSURANCE CORP	IL	U	85.8	34.5	0.0	0.4	N/A	5.6	2.7	7.1	3.9	CFRT
MIDVALE INDEMNITY CO	IL	U	13.2	12.5	0.0	0.4	N/A	9.1	7.8	10.0	5.0	FT
MIDWEST BUILDERS CASUALTY MUTUAL	KS	B	77.7	41.2	19.7	1.0	7.3	4.6	6.1	6.9	5.6	D
MIDWEST EMPLOYERS CAS CO	DE	C+	129.4	98.1	-4.5	4.1	10.0	4.6	2.8	1.0	4.3	FLRT
MIDWEST FAMILY MUTUAL INS CO	IA	C	174.7	46.7	94.1	2.2	7.4	5.8	5.0	5.9	4.3	R
MIDWEST INS CO	IL	C-	78.6	26.3	22.2	3.0	5.2	2.6	5.9	6.7	3.3	DR
MIDWEST INS GROUP INC RRG	VT	D	6.6	1.7	1.1	0.1	1.5	9.9	4.2	7.7	1.4	CDRT
MIDWEST PROVIDER INS CO RRG INC	AZ	E (1)	4.2	0.6	-0.6	0.0	1.6	3.4	0.4	9.0	0.1	CDFT
MIDWESTERN EQUITY TITLE INS CO	IN	D+	3.3	2.8	0.1	0.1	9.8	3.6	7.9	10.0	2.0	DR
MIDWESTERN INDEMNITY CO	NH	C	30.0	27.1	0.0	0.1	10.0	N/A	6.0	7.3	4.3	DFRT
MILBANK INS CO	IA	C	534.3	135.6	228.7	4.5	7.1	8.5	3.9	6.0	3.5	AR
MILLBROOK NMF RRG INC	SC	D	3.2	1.1	1.7	0.0	5.2	3.6	8.9	8.4	0.8	DGT
MILLERS CAPITAL INS CO	PA	C+	133.4	64.4	42.6	-1.7	9.7	9.6	5.8	6.8	4.5	R
MILLERS CLASSIFIED INS CO	IL	E	2.7	0.0	-0.4	-0.5	2.4	7.0	0.1	5.1	0.0	CFRT
MILLERS FIRST INS CO	IL	F	7.8	-4.0	0.0	0.3	0.0	4.8	0.1	7.0	0.0	CDRT
MILLVILLE INS CO OF NEW YORK	NY	C-	2.8	2.6	0.0	0.0	10.0	4.6	3.6	7.0	2.3	DFT
MILLVILLE MUTUAL INS CO	PA	C	71.4	45.6	25.4	1.3	9.6	8.4	8.8	7.0	4.3	T
MILWAUKEE CASUALTY INS CO	WI	B	48.0	16.7	4.3	2.3	10.0	5.0	8.9	9.3	4.1	DFGR
MINNESOTA LAWYERS MUTUAL INS CO	MN	B	157.8	74.6	31.5	0.5	8.8	5.5	6.0	6.8	6.3	
MISSISSIPPI FARM BU MUTUAL INS CO	MS	U (4)	0.0	0.0	0.0	13.1	N/A	5.1	1.9	9.5	0.0	CFGT
MISSISSIPPI FARM BUREAU CAS INS CO	MS	B	371.1	219.5	159.2	6.6	10.0	7.6	5.9	6.6	4.8	
MISSOURI DOCTORS MUTUAL INS CO	MO	E	7.0	0.3	4.3	0.0	0.0	1.1	0.1	2.5	0.0	CDFL
MISSOURI HOSPITAL PLAN	MO	C+	194.6	137.3	19.2	-4.6	9.1	6.3	3.6	8.0	4.5	R
MISSOURI PHYSICIANS ASSOCIATES	MO	U	1.8	1.7	0.0	0.0	N/A	5.8	3.4	7.0	0.0	RT
MISSOURI PROFESSIONALS MUTUAL INS	MO	E	17.7	3.0	-0.8	-0.2	1.7	3.9	0.1	9.0	0.1	CDFR
MISSOURI VALLEY MUTUAL INS CO	SD	D	5.6	2.8	3.5	0.4	8.1	6.9	4.2	5.4	1.5	DRT
MITSUI SUMITOMO INS CO OF AMER	NY	B+	883.6	324.2	182.7	13.1	9.4	9.4	6.7	7.0	6.5	
MITSUI SUMITOMO INS USA INC	NY	C	122.6	61.2	20.3	0.4	10.0	8.8	6.4	7.7	3.6	T
MMG INS CO	ME	C+	229.3	88.4	135.6	1.8	9.3	6.9	8.4	6.5	4.4	R
MMIC INS INC	MN	A-	701.8	289.8	110.4	17.1	7.6	9.5	8.9	7.1	7.1	
MMIC RRG INC	DC	U	0.7	0.6	0.0	0.0	N/A	N/A	2.9	10.0	2.1	FGT
MO EMPLOYERS MUTUAL INS CO	MO	C	552.5	202.5	166.1	6.2	7.8	9.3	5.4	6.6	4.2	R
MODERN SERVICE INS CO	IL	B	28.3	27.5	0.0	0.3	10.0	4.6	6.3	10.0	4.3	DT
MODERN USA INS CO	FL	C	37.9	15.5	21.9	1.5	5.1	4.5	5.1	6.5	3.9	CD
MONROE GUARANTY INS CO	IN	C	47.8	50.6	0.0	0.8	10.0	N/A	6.6	10.0	3.4	RT
MONTEREY INS CO	CA	C+	82.3	32.2	42.2	0.3	7.2	6.0	6.6	5.9	4.4	T
MONTGOMERY MUTUAL INS CO	MA	C	51.0	49.5	0.0	1.0	10.0	N/A	7.2	7.8	4.3	DR
MONTOUR MUTUAL INS CO	PA	D	1.0	0.6	0.2	-0.1	8.0	6.5	2.9	6.7	1.1	DT
MORTGAGE GUARANTY INS CORP	WI	D+	4,175.5	1,479.0	793.5	-43.1	3.8	2.3	1.3	6.4	2.4	AFR
MOSAIC INS CO	DE	U	21.7	19.9	0.0	1.4	N/A	N/A	2.1	10.0	3.3	FR
MOTOR CLUB INS CO	RI	U	47.8	45.9	0.0	0.4	N/A	6.2	8.4	10.0	6.5	T
MOTORISTS COMMERCIAL MUTUAL INS CO	OH	B	342.1	142.6	126.0	2.6	8.6	7.9	5.6	6.4	6.2	
MOTORISTS MUTUAL INS CO	OH	A-	1,354.2	558.2	480.0	12.9	8.8	7.9	5.2	6.4	7.2	

See Page 27 for explanation of footnotes and Page 28 for explanation of stability factors.

Arrows denote recent upgrades ▲ or downgrades ▼ (see Section VII for explanations)

92

www.weissratings.com

RISK ADJ. CAPITAL RATIO #1	CAPITAL RATIO #2	PREMIUM TO SURPLUS (%)	RESV. TO SURPLUS (%)	RESV. DEVELOP. 1 YEAR (%)	RESV. DEVELOP. 2 YEAR (%)	LOSS RATIO (%)	EXP. RATIO (%)	COMB. RATIO (%)	CASH FROM UNDER-WRITING (%)	NET PREMIUM GROWTH (%)	INVEST. IN AFFIL (%)	INSURANCE COMPANY NAME
82.7	40.7	N/A	N/A	N/A	N/A	N/A	N/A	N/A	N/A	0.0	0.0	MID-CONTINENT EXCESS & SURPLUS
4.5	2.9	20.0	36.0	0.5	-4.5	57.1	35.5	92.6	109.5	6.1	0.0	MID-CONTINENT INS CO
3.0	1.9	57.3	24.4	0.7	-2.3	52.7	35.3	88.0	128.2	12.0	0.0	MID-HUDSON CO-OPERTIVE INS CO
3.6	2.4	59.8	17.4	-0.4	-0.1	62.9	34.6	97.5	108.5	52.4	0.0	MIDDLE STATES INS CO INC
4.0	2.8	74.9	113.8	-3.0	-5.4	76.3	24.8	101.1	97.8	5.2	4.7 ●	MIDDLESEX INS CO
3.9	2.7	90.7	50.1	-1.7	-1.8	69.3	29.6	98.9	121.0	18.5	4.5	MIDDLESEX MUTUAL ASR CO
2.9	2.0	82.5	29.3	-7.8	-13.3	46.7	36.2	82.9	115.2	5.1	0.2	MIDROX INS CO
1.7	1.0	51.7	23.2	N/A	N/A	78.0	30.1	108.1	191.5	0.0	0.0	MIDSOUTH MUTUAL INS CO
3.0	2.1	51.3	38.5	-2.0	-4.3	62.7	38.2	100.9	101.9	-1.3	0.0	MIDSTATE MUTUAL INS CO
N/A	N/A	N/A	139.7	0.5	6.8	N/A	N/A	N/A	0.1	-100.0	0.0	MIDSTATES REINSURANCE CORP
N/A	N/A	N/A	N/A	0.3	-7.3	N/A	N/A	N/A	-106.0	-100.0	0.0	MIDVALE INDEMNITY CO
2.3	1.1	47.6	75.1	1.4	1.9	75.7	28.7	104.4	111.2	19.1	10.9	MIDWEST BUILDERS CASUALTY MUTUAL
7.1	6.7	-4.8	N/A	N/A	N/A	N/A	N/A	N/A	15.1	-129.6	0.0	MIDWEST EMPLOYERS CAS CO
2.0	1.3	211.7	130.8	-10.4	8.1	73.6	24.3	97.9	106.6	9.0	0.0	MIDWEST FAMILY MUTUAL INS CO
1.5	0.9	95.9	146.0	17.4	24.7	79.4	26.9	106.3	103.0	-1.3	0.0	MIDWEST INS CO
0.4	0.3	62.0	206.2	-31.7	-48.9	63.2	54.7	117.9	91.8	-40.4	0.0	MIDWEST INS GROUP INC RRG
0.4	0.2	-102.5	149.6	19.4	23.2	-526.5	-99.8	-626.3	57.0	-151.1	0.0	MIDWEST PROVIDER INS CO RRG INC
3.9	2.3	3.0	N/A	N/A	-0.3	N/A	30.9	30.9	369.8	8.6	0.0	MIDWESTERN EQUITY TITLE INS CO
3.6	3.5	N/A	N/A	N/A	N/A	N/A	N/A	N/A	52.5	0.0	30.0	MIDWESTERN INDEMNITY CO
1.8	1.1	176.5	157.9	-4.6	-6.3	68.5	34.5	103.0	98.7	0.6	0.0	MILBANK INS CO
1.2	0.8	159.2	47.8	-6.0	N/A	41.9	21.9	63.8	363.1	558.9	0.0	MILLBROOK NMF RRG INC
3.3	2.7	64.4	57.1	-6.1	-22.0	60.5	38.4	98.9	99.4	-0.9	0.0	MILLERS CAPITAL INS CO
0.1	0.1	-78.8	746.7	-6.6	-14.0	357.3	-361.7	-4.4	-3.5	-106.7	0.0	MILLERS CLASSIFIED INS CO
-1.5	-1.3	N/A	N/A	N/A	N/A	N/A	N/A	N/A	N/A	-100.0	0.0	MILLERS FIRST INS CO
24.5	22.0	N/A	N/A	N/A	N/A	N/A	N/A	N/A	523.0	0.0	0.0	MILLVILLE INS CO OF NEW YORK
4.0	2.9	57.8	14.9	-0.2	-4.2	50.4	28.3	78.7	127.2	5.0	4.7	MILLVILLE MUTUAL INS CO
3.5	3.1	28.9	21.8	3.4	1.0	79.1	-32.1	47.0	-8.7	55.5	0.0	MILWAUKEE CASUALTY INS CO
3.6	2.4	43.2	71.1	-7.3	-8.2	69.6	25.0	94.6	121.1	3.3	0.0	MINNESOTA LAWYERS MUTUAL INS CO
N/A	N/A	0.2	67.9	999 +	999 +	999 +	999 +	999 +	0.6	35.0	0.0	MISSISSIPPI FARM BU MUTUAL INS CO
4.6	3.8	75.1	13.1	-1.1	-2.5	70.4	22.2	92.6	106.4	5.2	0.0 ●	MISSISSIPPI FARM BUREAU CAS INS CO
0.0	0.0	999 +	999 +	44.4	128.5	51.6	57.2	108.8	71.9	-4.0	0.0	MISSOURI DOCTORS MUTUAL INS CO
2.6	2.3	13.8	28.9	1.7	1.8	73.5	4.7	78.2	171.5	0.9	24.4	MISSOURI HOSPITAL PLAN
N/A	N/A	N/A	7.2	-0.9	-1.8	N/A	N/A	N/A	N/A	0.0	0.0	MISSOURI PHYSICIANS ASSOCIATES
0.3	0.2	-22.1	109.5	27.1	-36.9	N/A	-314.7	N/A	-17.9	88.3	48.1	MISSOURI PROFESSIONALS MUTUAL INS
3.1	2.2	141.2	14.8	-1.4	-6.6	64.1	35.7	99.8	97.8	-1.0	0.0	MISSOURI VALLEY MUTUAL INS CO
3.8	2.5	57.2	123.0	-5.2	-12.3	73.5	28.8	102.3	109.3	16.7	0.0 ●	MITSUI SUMITOMO INS CO OF AMER
6.9	4.7	33.5	72.0	-2.9	-6.6	73.5	28.9	102.4	109.2	16.7	0.0	MITSUI SUMITOMO INS USA INC
3.5	2.4	154.6	51.1	1.7	0.6	61.1	34.5	95.6	112.2	14.8	0.0	MMG INS CO
1.7	1.4	40.4	88.6	-10.4	-15.8	72.9	22.8	95.7	108.4	-4.7	20.6 ●	MMIC INS INC
N/A	N/A	0.2	N/A	N/A	N/A	N/A	999 +	999 +	1.9	62.7	0.0	MMIC RRG INC
1.8	1.4	85.4	108.3	-7.9	-3.9	72.3	29.5	101.8	119.0	21.1	0.1 ●	MO EMPLOYERS MUTUAL INS CO
77.4	38.8	N/A	N/A	N/A	N/A	N/A	N/A	N/A	-124.0	0.0	0.0	MODERN SERVICE INS CO
1.1	0.7	156.2	26.2	-5.4	14.5	28.1	46.5	74.6	127.7	16.3	0.0	MODERN USA INS CO
97.5	46.7	N/A	N/A	N/A	N/A	N/A	N/A	N/A	865.0	0.0	0.0	MONROE GUARANTY INS CO
1.7	1.0	133.1	76.9	-3.8	1.1	65.1	32.6	97.7	108.3	11.0	0.0	MONTEREY INS CO
83.0	50.7	N/A	N/A	N/A	N/A	N/A	N/A	N/A	128.2	0.0	0.0	MONTGOMERY MUTUAL INS CO
2.5	1.5	28.3	4.0	-2.0	-0.2	52.5	70.6	123.1	116.1	6.9	0.0	MONTOUR MUTUAL INS CO
1.1	0.9	52.2	166.0	-2.2	52.5	91.1	19.7	110.8	49.2	-12.2	14.2 ●	MORTGAGE GUARANTY INS CORP
N/A	N/A	N/A	N/A	N/A	N/A	N/A	N/A	N/A	-3.7	0.0	0.0	MOSAIC INS CO
N/A	N/A	N/A	N/A	0.6	0.8	N/A	N/A	N/A	N/A	0.0	0.0	MOTOR CLUB INS CO
3.1	2.2	89.4	69.4	-1.0	-2.0	66.8	34.9	101.7	98.3	4.8	6.3	MOTORISTS COMMERCIAL MUTUAL INS
3.4	2.3	84.4	65.5	-1.1	-2.0	66.8	33.9	100.7	96.6	4.8	5.0 ●	MOTORISTS MUTUAL INS CO

999 + Denotes number greater than 999.9%
999 - Denotes number less than -999.99%
● Bullets denote a more detailed analysis is available in Section II.

INSURANCE COMPANY NAME	DOM. STATE	RATING	TOTAL ASSETS ($MIL)	CAPITAL & SURPLUS ($MIL)	ANNUAL NET PREMIUM ($MIL)	NET INCOME ($MIL)	CAPITAL-IZATION INDEX (PTS)	RESERVE ADQ INDEX (PTS)	PROFIT-ABILITY INDEX (PTS)	LIQUIDITY INDEX (PTS)	STAB. INDEX (PTS)	STABILITY FACTORS
MOTORS INS CORP	MI	C	2,494.6	1,071.0	462.9	17.9	9.6	8.0	3.1	7.0	3.8	R
MOUND PRAIRIE MUTUAL INS CO	MN	D	5.6	2.6	3.4	0.4	7.3	6.2	2.1	4.3	1.8	DFLT
MOUNT BEACON INS CO	FL	U	25.0	25.0	0.0	0.0	N/A	0.0	4.9	0.0	0.0	LT
MOUNT CARROLL MUTUAL INS CO	IL	D	6.0	3.8	2.2	0.1	7.6	6.9	6.7	6.6	1.8	DR
MOUNT VERNON FIRE INS CO	PA	C+	562.4	377.0	63.0	12.9	7.7	9.3	8.6	7.5	4.5	R
MOUNT VERNON SPECIALTY INS CO	PA	U	19.7	19.6	0.0	0.0	N/A	N/A	4.9	10.0	5.4	T
MOUNTAIN LAKE RRG INC	VT	B-	2.3	1.6	0.3	0.2	8.8	5.1	5.5	7.6	3.5	DT
MOUNTAIN LAUREL ASR CO	OH	C	127.9	50.2	121.8	9.0	7.0	6.9	9.2	1.7	3.5	LR
MOUNTAIN LAUREL RRG INC	VT	E+	26.6	10.3	5.6	1.2	1.9	9.5	5.0	5.9	0.7	D
MOUNTAIN STATES HEALTHCARE RECIP	MT	D-	116.0	54.8	23.4	8.7	8.6	9.9	8.8	6.9	1.1	T
MOUNTAIN STATES INDEMNITY CO	NM	C	55.4	34.0	9.0	1.1	7.8	6.1	3.0	6.8	4.3	DFR
MOUNTAIN STATES MUTUAL CAS CO	NM	B-	161.2	87.1	33.0	0.3	7.7	4.7	4.9	6.9	4.7	FR
MOUNTAIN VALLEY INDEMNITY CO	NH	D	31.2	16.3	12.2	-1.1	7.2	6.9	4.4	7.0	1.7	RT
MOUNTAIN WEST FARM BU MUTUAL INS CO	WY	C	365.6	136.1	157.2	-7.2	7.4	9.3	2.0	4.2	4.1	FL
MOUNTAINEER FREEDOM RRG INC	WV	D-	34.2	19.4	6.2	1.5	8.4	9.9	8.8	8.4	1.3	DG
MOUNTAINPOINT INS CO	AZ	U	11.8	11.8	0.0	0.0	N/A	4.6	1.8	9.2	3.0	FRT
MOWER COUNTY FARMERS MUT INS CO	MN	D	4.4	3.0	1.4	0.0	10.0	7.5	8.6	7.2	2.1	D
MPM INS CO OF KANSAS	KS	E+	21.2	3.6	8.6	0.0	1.0	0.2	1.7	9.1	0.5	CDT
MSA INS CO	SC	B-	18.0	17.7	0.0	0.2	10.0	N/A	7.4	7.0	4.9	D
MT HAWLEY INS CO	IL	C	818.9	404.1	202.9	83.3	8.5	9.4	3.8	6.9	4.0	AR
MT MCKINLEY INS CO	DE	U	24.4	20.2	0.0	-0.1	N/A	N/A	3.8	7.0	5.0	T
MT MORRIS MUTUAL INS CO	WI	D	28.1	10.9	16.4	-0.4	7.2	7.0	5.3	5.2	1.9	DR
MT WASHINGTON ASR CORP	NH	C	5.5	3.1	0.0	0.0	10.0	N/A	5.7	9.6	3.2	DR
MULTINATIONAL INS CO	PR	C-	30.2	13.4	11.3	-0.5	5.2	3.6	2.0	5.7	2.9	DFT
MUNICH REINSURANCE AMERICA INC	DE	C+	16,639.8	5,142.3	3,195.8	484.6	7.3	9.3	7.8	6.9	4.4	R
MUNICIPAL ASR CORP	NY	A+	1,528.4	541.6	709.9	59.1	8.9	N/A	8.9	7.0	6.5	GT
MUNICIPAL MUTUAL INS CO	WV	C	33.0	20.7	11.4	-1.4	8.7	8.0	3.8	6.9	4.1	D
MUTUAL BENEFIT INS CO	PA	B-	194.1	78.8	82.7	-0.5	8.7	9.3	5.9	6.5	4.7	R
MUTUAL FIRE INS CO OF S BEND TOWNSHP	PA	D+(3)	0.0	0.0	0.1	0.0	10.0	4.6	7.1	10.0	2.1	D
MUTUAL INS CO OF AZ	AZ	A	1,011.0	560.3	109.5	21.0	10.0	9.6	8.8	8.3	7.1	
MUTUAL INS CO OF LEHIGH CTY	PA	D	3.1	1.4	1.6	0.0	7.3	5.0	2.1	6.9	1.3	DRT
MUTUAL OF ENUMCLAW INS CO	WA	B	663.7	296.8	331.0	6.6	9.6	6.9	6.5	6.5	6.1	T
MUTUAL OF WAUSAU INS CORP	WI	C-	21.2	12.7	8.8	-0.1	7.6	6.2	3.5	6.7	2.5	DFT
MUTUAL RRG INC	HI	C	90.3	40.7	16.8	1.9	9.7	9.6	8.9	7.4	4.2	DR
MUTUAL SAVINGS FIRE INS CO	AL	D	6.8	6.0	0.0	0.1	10.0	3.6	6.9	7.0	2.2	DR
MUTUALAID EXCHANGE	KS	C	25.3	14.9	10.5	-0.5	7.5	8.1	2.3	6.8	3.4	DR
NAMIC INS CO INC	IN	C+	54.4	26.3	4.6	3.3	8.3	8.9	6.8	7.7	4.5	D
NARRAGANSETT BAY INS CO	RI	E	135.9	45.5	55.2	2.8	3.9	6.0	2.6	7.4	0.1	FRT
NASW RISK RETENTION GROUP INC	DC	D	2.7	1.2	0.2	-0.1	8.0	3.6	1.8	7.6	1.2	DGT
NATIONAL AMERICAN INS CO	OK	C+	175.1	62.6	81.8	4.1	8.4	5.0	8.6	6.2	4.1	R
NATIONAL AMERICAN INS CO OF CA	CA	D	40.3	16.7	1.1	-0.6	5.4	0.4	2.6	7.6	1.5	DFRT
NATIONAL ASSISTED LIVING RRG INC	DC	D	8.7	3.8	1.7	0.1	5.5	9.7	8.3	7.0	1.4	D
NATIONAL AUTOMOTIVE INS	LA	E	23.7	6.0	21.1	1.4	2.3	4.0	1.3	0.7	0.1	DGLR
NATIONAL BUILDERS & CONTRACTORS INS	NV	E	3.5	0.7	0.4	0.0	1.0	4.6	0.8	9.3	0.0	CDFR
NATIONAL BUILDING MATERIAL ASR CO	IN	C	6.5	3.6	0.8	-0.1	8.8	4.5	3.8	7.0	3.3	DGRT
NATIONAL CASUALTY CO	WI	B+	273.8	128.7	0.0	2.1	10.0	3.6	7.5	6.4	6.4	T
NATIONAL CATHOLIC RRG	VT	D-	69.9	17.7	11.4	-0.3	1.2	2.9	3.7	5.9	1.0	CDFR
NATIONAL CONTINENTAL INS CO	NY	C	176.3	55.5	18.7	7.0	7.5	5.9	5.7	6.7	3.5	FT
NATIONAL CONTRACTORS INS CO INC RRG	MT	E	5.3	1.8	0.9	-0.6	2.4	2.2	0.6	5.6	0.1	DFRT
NATIONAL DIRECT INS CO	NV	D	4.7	1.8	4.3	0.1	3.2	4.6	3.1	1.4	1.5	DGLT
NATIONAL FARMERS UNION PROP & CAS	WI	C-	192.9	40.2	76.5	-1.0	7.0	3.9	1.6	6.8	3.0	FRT
NATIONAL FIRE & CASUALTY CO	IL	C	7.5	4.6	1.3	0.3	7.9	9.1	3.6	6.9	3.5	DR

See Page 27 for explanation of footnotes and
Page 28 for explanation of stability factors.

Arrows denote recent upgrades ▲ or downgrades ▼   (see Section VII for explanations)

94

www.weissratings.com

RISK ADJ. CAPITAL RATIO #1	CAPITAL RATIO #2	PREMIUM TO SURPLUS (%)	RESV. TO SURPLUS (%)	RESV. DEVELOP. 1 YEAR (%)	RESV. DEVELOP. 2 YEAR (%)	LOSS RATIO (%)	EXP. RATIO (%)	COMB RATIO (%)	CASH FROM UNDER-WRITING (%)	NET PREMIUM GROWTH (%)	INVEST. IN AFFIL (%)	INSURANCE COMPANY NAME
4.9	3.1	42.3	19.2	-1.5	-2.0	66.9	43.2	110.1	88.6	-3.5	2.9 ●	MOTORS INS CORP
1.8	1.3	158.1	15.1	4.6	0.3	84.6	35.3	119.9	87.1	8.5	0.0	MOUND PRAIRIE MUTUAL INS CO
N/A	N/A	N/A	N/A	N/A	N/A	N/A	N/A	N/A	N/A	0.0	0.0	MOUNT BEACON INS CO
1.8	1.1	58.5	5.9	-2.3	-10.7	39.8	30.6	70.4	140.0	23.1	0.5	MOUNT CARROLL MUTUAL INS CO
1.9	1.5	18.1	28.6	-6.0	-10.4	33.5	39.7	73.2	123.8	5.9	27.0 ●	MOUNT VERNON FIRE INS CO
N/A	N/A	N/A	N/A	N/A	N/A	N/A	N/A	N/A	82.1	0.0	0.0	MOUNT VERNON SPECIALTY INS CO
3.7	2.8	20.6	31.0	-20.2	-15.1	-7.3	96.8	89.5	124.9	-43.5	0.0	MOUNTAIN LAKE RRG INC
1.5	1.3	298.4	77.4	-4.5	-5.8	75.3	22.9	98.2	102.5	9.8	0.0	MOUNTAIN LAUREL ASR CO
0.9	0.6	62.6	112.5	-44.5	-45.2	7.8	46.2	54.0	135.7	3.6	0.0	MOUNTAIN LAUREL RRG INC
3.4	2.3	50.7	108.6	-10.5	-24.1	81.3	10.8	92.1	133.8	-5.2	0.0	MOUNTAIN STATES HEALTHCARE RECIP
3.0	1.8	27.5	56.7	5.0	-1.7	90.3	36.9	127.2	73.3	-18.2	0.0	MOUNTAIN STATES INDEMNITY CO
2.1	1.7	38.4	56.2	1.1	1.8	66.3	38.4	104.7	74.7	28.8	24.5	MOUNTAIN STATES MUTUAL CAS CO
3.0	1.9	69.9	36.9	-1.5	-3.0	68.1	44.0	112.1	93.1	423.1	0.0	MOUNTAIN VALLEY INDEMNITY CO
1.8	1.2	111.6	76.5	-5.9	-12.5	101.6	25.4	127.0	87.3	4.3	7.2	MOUNTAIN WEST FARM BU MUTUAL INS
4.7	3.2	34.8	79.1	-14.9	-31.1	49.9	12.9	62.8	482.1	-3.9	0.0	MOUNTAINEER FREEDOM RRG INC
N/A	N/A	N/A	N/A	N/A	N/A	N/A	N/A	N/A	N/A	0.0	0.0	MOUNTAINPOINT INS CO
5.5	4.0	48.6	3.0	-0.3	-3.2	38.0	42.4	80.4	129.3	4.7	0.0	MOWER COUNTY FARMERS MUT INS CO
0.1	0.1	101.4	258.6	-29.5	60.1	85.4	43.3	128.7	105.9	-46.5	0.0	MPM INS CO OF KANSAS
82.2	38.7	N/A	N/A	N/A	N/A	N/A	N/A	N/A	N/A	0.0	0.0	MSA INS CO
2.1	1.6	38.8	54.7	-7.3	-11.1	26.0	36.7	62.7	119.3	21.5	12.0 ●	MT HAWLEY INS CO
N/A	N/A	N/A	N/A	N/A	N/A	N/A	N/A	N/A	N/A	0.0	0.0	MT MCKINLEY INS CO
1.4	1.0	148.3	31.1	-6.5	-1.5	62.3	33.1	95.4	107.6	16.7	0.0	MT MORRIS MUTUAL INS CO
3.8	3.4	N/A	N/A	N/A	N/A	N/A	N/A	N/A	97.5	0.0	0.0	MT WASHINGTON ASR CORP
0.9	0.5	71.0	18.6	-3.3	-0.6	42.4	82.7	125.1	82.9	-18.0	14.3	MULTINATIONAL INS CO
2.1	1.2	60.4	105.9	-4.8	-12.7	57.1	33.4	90.5	107.1	2.7	0.0 ●	MUNICH REINSURANCE AMERICA INC
4.7	2.6	138.0	N/A	N/A	N/A	N/A	1.8	1.8	999 +	0.0	0.0 ●	MUNICIPAL ASR CORP
3.0	2.0	51.8	12.4	-3.8	-5.4	67.3	31.0	98.3	97.7	-10.3	0.0	MUNICIPAL MUTUAL INS CO
3.0	2.2	101.4	73.7	-9.3	-13.1	63.4	31.7	95.1	102.9	-1.7	8.6	MUTUAL BENEFIT INS CO
167.6	115.1	3.4	0.1	N/A	N/A	54.8	37.9	92.7	107.4	-5.0	0.0	MUTUAL FIRE INS CO OF S BEND
6.6	4.6	20.4	56.3	-5.3	-16.5	63.3	18.3	81.6	125.0	-3.4	0.0 ●	MUTUAL INS CO OF AZ
1.9	1.2	115.5	34.3	-2.9	-15.3	60.3	43.8	104.1	101.7	0.7	1.3	MUTUAL INS CO OF LEHIGH CTY
4.0	2.9	115.4	59.7	-3.0	-8.1	68.4	31.6	100.0	100.5	7.1	5.0 ●	MUTUAL OF ENUMCLAW INS CO
2.1	1.3	69.2	9.5	-2.0	-2.0	64.1	46.9	111.0	97.1	1.0	0.0	MUTUAL OF WAUSAU INS CORP
3.8	2.9	44.2	79.6	-16.4	-22.5	67.3	9.3	76.6	173.2	17.5	0.2	MUTUAL RRG INC
16.2	14.6	N/A	N/A	N/A	N/A	N/A	N/A	N/A	170.1	0.0	0.0	MUTUAL SAVINGS FIRE INS CO
1.4	1.2	69.6	16.2	-2.8	-3.4	74.3	42.7	117.0	96.4	13.4	43.7	MUTUALAID EXCHANGE
2.7	1.9	18.3	24.4	-8.5	-7.8	59.0	32.1	91.1	113.0	6.2	0.0	NAMIC INS CO INC
1.1	0.7	131.8	30.8	10.9	4.2	64.1	27.9	92.0	60.4	10.4	0.0	NARRAGANSETT BAY INS CO
1.2	1.0	15.1	4.1	-0.2	N/A	50.5	150.6	201.1	999 +	363.5	0.0	NASW RISK RETENTION GROUP INC
2.6	1.8	134.3	88.5	-0.6	-4.3	59.5	31.5	91.0	122.0	25.4	0.0	NATIONAL AMERICAN INS CO
1.8	0.9	6.5	121.7	-0.3	43.5	114.7	109.4	224.1	19.8	-71.7	13.7	NATIONAL AMERICAN INS CO OF CA
1.2	0.7	44.6	76.3	-20.0	-34.8	31.1	44.7	75.8	145.2	17.9	0.0	NATIONAL ASSISTED LIVING RRG INC
1.1	1.0	404.9	125.4	73.3	25.8	101.6	13.3	114.9	88.3	63.5	0.0	NATIONAL AUTOMOTIVE INS
0.2	0.1	35.3	245.0	-11.0	-11.4	130.9	53.2	184.1	13.6	16.4	0.0	NATIONAL BUILDERS & CONTRACTORS
2.4	1.5	22.2	20.4	12.6	9.9	77.6	8.2	85.8	21.3	N/A	0.0	NATIONAL BUILDING MATERIAL ASR CO
13.6	12.3	N/A	N/A	N/A	N/A	N/A	N/A	N/A	841.6	0.0	0.0 ●	NATIONAL CASUALTY CO
0.4	0.2	63.5	218.2	16.7	29.6	102.1	26.7	128.8	68.9	5.9	0.0	NATIONAL CATHOLIC RRG
3.6	2.6	38.1	200.5	3.0	-8.4	72.8	-0.2	72.6	61.4	-81.0	0.0	NATIONAL CONTINENTAL INS CO
0.6	0.3	39.7	127.0	30.0	49.2	160.5	156.9	317.4	22.3	-11.2	0.0	NATIONAL CONTRACTORS INS CO INC
0.6	0.5	253.4	129.2	-0.8	-6.5	78.9	18.2	97.1	101.5	32.5	0.0	NATIONAL DIRECT INS CO
1.3	0.9	183.7	175.5	8.1	17.0	75.2	35.0	110.2	82.3	-5.0	0.0	NATIONAL FARMERS UNION PROP &
2.5	1.5	28.4	26.3	-6.8	-9.1	39.5	47.8	87.3	113.7	7.6	0.0	NATIONAL FIRE & CASUALTY CO

999 + Denotes number greater than 999.9%
999 - Denotes number less than -999.99%
● Bullets denote a more detailed analysis is available in Section II.

INSURANCE COMPANY NAME	DOM. STATE	RATING	TOTAL ASSETS ($MIL)	CAPITAL & SURPLUS ($MIL)	ANNUAL NET PREMIUM ($MIL)	NET INCOME ($MIL)	CAPITAL-IZATION INDEX (PTS)	RESERVE ADQ INDEX (PTS)	PROFIT-ABILITY INDEX (PTS)	LIQUIDITY INDEX (PTS)	STAB. INDEX (PTS)	STABILITY FACTORS
NATIONAL FIRE & INDEMNITY EXCHANGE	MO	C-	11.0	6.1	3.2	0.1	8.3	4.0	7.7	7.0	2.5	DFR
NATIONAL FIRE & MARINE INS CO	NE	C	8,030.5	5,368.4	316.5	576.9	8.1	6.1	8.1	9.2	4.1	GRT
NATIONAL FIRE INS CO OF HARTFORD	IL	C	120.0	119.9	0.0	3.4	10.0	N/A	6.3	8.8	3.8	AR
NATIONAL GENERAL ASR CO	MO	C	41.3	17.2	0.0	0.4	10.0	3.3	3.0	10.0	3.2	DRT
NATIONAL GENERAL INS CO	MO	C	60.8	27.6	0.0	0.7	10.0	4.6	2.2	7.0	3.4	RT
NATIONAL GENERAL INS ONLINE INC	MO	C-	30.9	10.7	0.0	0.0	10.0	3.1	4.8	10.0	2.9	DRT
NATIONAL GUARDIAN RRG INC	HI	D	18.3	6.4	2.0	0.4	2.8	9.9	8.6	8.4	1.9	DFR
NATIONAL HERITAGE INS CO	IL	D+	3.9	2.1	2.6	-0.3	7.9	5.9	1.6	7.7	1.9	DFT
NATIONAL HOME INS CO RRG	CO	U	35.5	10.3	-1.1	-0.3	N/A	1.5	2.4	7.0	2.3	RT
NATIONAL INDEMNITY CO	NE	B-	171,496.5	98,685.6	5,650.4	3,789.8	8.3	7.5	8.6	7.8	5.3	T
NATIONAL INDEMNITY CO OF MID-AMERICA	IA	B-	230.4	164.5	5.7	16.9	8.2	7.9	8.5	10.0	4.9	DGR
NATIONAL INDEMNITY CO OF THE SOUTH	FL	C+	305.0	177.6	33.0	2.4	8.4	8.7	8.0	9.1	4.3	GRT
NATIONAL INDEPENDENT TRUCKERS IC	SC	D+	11.5	6.3	2.5	-0.1	9.7	6.9	5.3	7.0	2.5	DR
NATIONAL INS ASN	IN	U	13.1	13.1	0.0	0.1	N/A	N/A	6.6	7.0	5.4	T
NATIONAL INS CO	PR	F (5)	0.0	0.0	0.0	0.0	5.7	3.8	0.7	5.7	0.0	DT
NATIONAL INS CO OF WISCONSIN INC	WI	C	43.6	19.0	10.9	1.2	7.2	9.7	8.0	6.9	4.0	D
NATIONAL INTERSTATE INS CO	OH	C+	1,100.3	287.9	277.6	3.5	7.4	8.3	6.7	6.6	4.7	R
NATIONAL INTERSTATE INS CO OF HAWAII	OH	D	46.1	11.8	7.9	0.1	8.9	7.8	5.6	7.2	1.5	DFR
▼NATIONAL LIABILITY & FIRE INS CO	CT	B	2,144.3	938.6	388.3	-14.8	9.1	8.5	5.4	9.1	5.3	
NATIONAL LLOYDS INS CO	TX	B-	217.2	106.5	138.9	7.4	9.6	6.3	5.1	6.7	4.8	R
NATIONAL MEDICAL PROFESSIONAL RRG	SC	D	6.2	3.0	0.0	-0.4	9.6	N/A	3.7	9.7	2.0	DFR
NATIONAL MERIT INS CO	IL	C	6.6	6.6	0.0	0.1	10.0	3.4	2.4	7.0	3.1	DRT
NATIONAL MORTGAGE INS CORP	WI	A-	264.6	234.3	3.3	-36.0	10.0	N/A	0.2	9.3	5.8	DFT
NATIONAL MORTGAGE RE INC ONE	WI	C-	11.3	9.2	0.2	-0.2	10.0	N/A	2.6	10.0	2.9	DFT
NATIONAL MUTUAL INS CO	OH	C	70.1	25.2	33.7	0.8	7.5	8.6	5.9	5.9	4.1	DR
NATIONAL PUBLIC FINANCE GUAR CORP	NY	B	5,398.3	2,311.4	12.1	169.6	10.0	3.4	3.2	10.0	4.0	AFT
NATIONAL SECURITY FIRE & CAS CO	AL	C+	72.8	29.6	47.2	3.5	7.6	6.8	4.2	5.1	4.4	R
NATIONAL SERVICE CONTRACT INS CO	DC	C	12.6	10.8	0.8	0.0	10.0	5.6	4.0	9.8	3.1	DFR
NATIONAL SPECIALTY INS CO	TX	C	68.7	42.8	18.7	0.5	9.8	6.3	7.8	7.0	4.3	R
NATIONAL SURETY CORP	IL	C	157.1	128.7	0.0	2.3	10.0	3.7	3.8	10.0	3.5	RT
NATIONAL TRUST INS CO	IN	C-	35.1	36.1	0.0	0.7	10.0	N/A	6.2	7.3	2.9	R
NATIONAL UNION FIRE INS CO OF PITTSB	PA	C	26,204.5	6,495.4	5,422.5	548.3	7.6	3.7	1.9	6.6	4.2	ART
NATIONAL UNITY INS CO	TX	D	67.4	19.7	60.6	-1.0	1.7	9.4	5.6	3.4	2.0	CDGL
NATIONS INS CO	CA	C-	26.5	11.6	15.0	0.2	7.3	4.5	5.7	7.1	3.1	D
NATIONWIDE AFFINITY INS CO OF AMER	OH	B	376.1	12.9	0.0	0.2	7.0	3.6	4.8	0.4	4.8	L
NATIONWIDE AGRIBUSINESS INS CO	IA	B-	456.3	68.0	0.0	1.4	10.0	N/A	7.5	6.0	5.2	A
NATIONWIDE ASR CO	WI	B-	146.2	60.1	0.0	0.2	10.0	N/A	6.0	10.0	5.2	AF
NATIONWIDE GENERAL INS CO	OH	B-	225.4	22.2	0.0	0.3	8.6	N/A	6.2	6.9	5.3	AD
NATIONWIDE INDEMNITY CO	OH	B-	3,181.4	1,025.3	0.2	-32.8	6.8	3.1	3.6	9.2	4.9	FT
NATIONWIDE INS CO OF AMERICA	WI	B-	499.8	152.0	0.0	1.6	10.0	N/A	7.7	7.5	5.2	
NATIONWIDE INS CO OF FLORIDA	OH	C+	338.6	282.9	33.8	8.1	10.0	4.6	4.2	6.9	3.6	
NATIONWIDE LLOYDS	TX	B	44.2	27.8	0.0	0.3	10.0	N/A	5.9	7.0	5.7	DF
NATIONWIDE MUTUAL FIRE INS CO	OH	B+	5,632.7	2,524.9	2,162.4	40.4	10.0	7.7	6.4	6.6	6.4	A
NATIONWIDE MUTUAL INS CO	OH	B	33,915.9	12,380.0	14,630.9	577.7	7.5	5.6	5.7	5.2	6.1	AL
NATIONWIDE PROPERTY & CAS INS CO	OH	B-	612.6	56.4	0.0	0.6	10.0	N/A	7.4	7.1	5.2	A
NAU COUNTRY INS CO	MN	C	1,195.0	271.4	444.3	-3.3	7.1	3.6	2.9	7.5	3.4	FRT
NAUTILUS INS CO	AZ	C-	256.7	151.6	-261.7	1.2	10.0	5.0	1.9	0.0	3.1	FLRT
NAVIGATORS INS CO	NY	B	2,434.8	874.3	680.0	54.4	8.1	6.4	6.9	6.9	5.6	
NAVIGATORS SPECIALTY INS CO	NY	C+	162.7	132.3	0.0	2.6	10.0	N/A	7.1	7.0	4.5	
NAZARETH MUTUAL INS CO	PA	D+	12.3	5.7	5.3	-0.2	7.2	5.8	4.3	6.7	2.4	DR
NCMIC INS CO	IA	B	645.6	249.4	102.2	10.5	8.1	9.7	8.9	7.8	5.5	T
NCMIC RRG INC	VT	D	6.0	3.9	0.6	0.1	10.0	N/A	3.6	10.0	1.9	DGT

See Page 27 for explanation of footnotes and Page 28 for explanation of stability factors.

Arrows denote recent upgrades ▲ or downgrades ▼   (see Section VII for explanations)

96

www.weissratings.com

RISK ADJ. CAPITAL RATIO #1	CAPITAL RATIO #2	PREMIUM TO SURPLUS (%)	RESV. TO SURPLUS (%)	RESV. DEVELOP. 1 YEAR (%)	DEVELOP. 2 YEAR (%)	LOSS RATIO (%)	EXP. RATIO (%)	COMB RATIO (%)	CASH FROM UNDER-WRITING (%)	NET PREMIUM GROWTH (%)	INVEST. IN AFFIL (%)	INSURANCE COMPANY NAME
2.7	2.4	51.6	45.6	-10.5	-8.9	21.7	53.4	75.1	101.9	-2.7	0.0	NATIONAL FIRE & INDEMNITY
2.4	1.5	6.3	15.2	1.3	0.5	69.8	24.7	94.5	132.1	140.9	7.0 ●	NATIONAL FIRE & MARINE INS CO
89.6	38.8	N/A	N/A	N/A	N/A	N/A	N/A	N/A	N/A	0.0	0.0	NATIONAL FIRE INS CO OF HARTFORD
4.2	3.7	N/A	N/A	N/A	N/A	N/A	N/A	N/A	-123.6	100.0	0.0	NATIONAL GENERAL ASR CO
5.5	4.9	N/A	N/A	N/A	N/A	N/A	N/A	N/A	-44.5	100.0	0.0	NATIONAL GENERAL INS CO
2.9	2.6	N/A	N/A	N/A	N/A	N/A	N/A	N/A	-64.6	100.0	0.0	NATIONAL GENERAL INS ONLINE INC
0.7	0.6	33.4	149.5	-9.1	-16.4	99.1	7.6	106.7	-79.8	-20.3	0.0	NATIONAL GUARDIAN RRG INC
1.6	1.3	107.6	10.3	2.5	0.9	60.5	50.5	111.0	93.4	1.3	0.0	NATIONAL HERITAGE INS CO
N/A	N/A	-6.5	48.1	104.1	97.5	407.6	-62.9	344.7	16.3	-6.8	0.0	NATIONAL HOME INS CO RRG
2.2	1.8	5.8	16.2	-1.2	-1.3	49.2	39.3	88.5	133.0	-25.6	23.4 ●	NATIONAL INDEMNITY CO
2.8	1.7	3.4	7.0	-2.4	-3.6	2.5	26.2	28.7	131.1	59.7	0.0	NATIONAL INDEMNITY CO OF
3.1	1.9	19.7	16.5	-0.7	-6.3	55.2	25.3	80.5	175.0	72.3	0.0	NATIONAL INDEMNITY CO OF THE
3.7	2.4	40.7	31.7	-4.4	1.7	32.4	45.1	77.5	121.3	30.6	0.0	NATIONAL INDEPENDENT TRUCKERS IC
N/A	N/A	N/A	N/A	N/A	N/A	N/A	N/A	N/A	N/A	0.0	0.0	NATIONAL INS ASN
1.7	0.8	N/A	N/A	N/A	N/A	N/A	N/A	N/A	N/A	-100.0	0.0	NATIONAL INS CO
2.1	1.3	55.2	120.4	-19.1	-36.7	58.7	28.1	86.8	104.5	-0.7	0.0	NATIONAL INS CO OF WISCONSIN INC
1.5	1.2	98.0	118.3	0.7	-2.1	70.8	28.6	99.4	102.9	6.5	19.3 ●	NATIONAL INTERSTATE INS CO
2.3	2.1	70.3	84.9	0.5	-1.6	70.8	28.4	99.2	79.0	6.5	0.0	NATIONAL INTERSTATE INS CO OF
3.6	2.2	43.2	56.1	-5.2	-7.5	64.8	23.5	88.3	131.4	13.2	0.0 ●	NATIONAL LIABILITY & FIRE INS CO
3.3	2.8	140.9	19.3	-0.1	-1.3	70.5	28.7	99.2	104.1	9.2	0.0	NATIONAL LLOYDS INS CO
2.8	2.5	N/A	N/A	N/A	N/A	N/A	N/A	N/A	-7.0	0.0	0.0	NATIONAL MEDICAL PROFESSIONAL
90.6	45.3	N/A	N/A	N/A	N/A	N/A	N/A	N/A	999 +	0.0	0.0	NATIONAL MERIT INS CO
4.3	4.2	1.8	N/A	N/A	N/A	N/A	999 +	999 +	10.7	0.0	0.0 ●	NATIONAL MORTGAGE INS CORP
5.1	4.9	2.5	N/A	N/A	N/A	N/A	345.7	345.7	8.4	0.0	0.0	NATIONAL MORTGAGE RE INC ONE
2.2	1.4	140.4	51.8	-2.8	-6.1	67.1	30.8	97.9	102.9	-1.6	0.2	NATIONAL MUTUAL INS CO
12.5	5.3	0.6	-4.2	3.7	-5.3	18.3	631.6	649.9	10.0	349.2	0.0 ●	NATIONAL PUBLIC FINANCE GUAR CORP
2.2	1.6	179.5	26.6	-1.1	-2.6	60.7	34.8	95.5	99.8	6.8	12.0	NATIONAL SECURITY FIRE & CAS CO
13.8	9.0	7.2	N/A	-0.2	-0.3	0.9	100.9	101.8	62.2	-9.3	0.0	NATIONAL SERVICE CONTRACT INS CO
4.9	3.6	59.4	6.2	-0.7	0.1	40.3	51.7	92.0	102.0	-5.4	0.0	NATIONAL SPECIALTY INS CO
28.7	25.8	N/A	N/A	N/A	N/A	N/A	N/A	N/A	-144.7	100.0	0.0	NATIONAL SURETY CORP
160.4	80.2	N/A	N/A	N/A	N/A	N/A	N/A	N/A	76.5	0.0	0.0	NATIONAL TRUST INS CO
2.0	1.4	92.9	216.0	1.7	4.4	76.7	32.7	109.4	82.2	16.0	0.8 ●	NATIONAL UNION FIRE INS CO OF
0.4	0.3	285.6	102.6	-5.9	-9.7	64.2	31.0	95.2	121.6	110.1	2.7	NATIONAL UNITY INS CO
1.7	1.2	132.8	57.0	1.9	9.8	75.9	21.2	97.1	98.6	4.3	0.0	NATIONS INS CO
1.1	0.9	N/A	N/A	N/A	N/A	N/A	N/A	N/A	153.6	0.0	0.0	NATIONWIDE AFFINITY INS CO OF AMER
5.8	5.2	N/A	N/A	N/A	N/A	N/A	N/A	N/A	150.2	0.0	0.0	NATIONWIDE AGRIBUSINESS INS CO
7.1	6.4	N/A	N/A	N/A	N/A	N/A	N/A	N/A	-237.4	0.0	0.0	NATIONWIDE ASR CO
2.2	2.0	N/A	N/A	N/A	N/A	N/A	N/A	N/A	-309.4	0.0	0.0	NATIONWIDE GENERAL INS CO
2.1	0.8	N/A	198.2	13.5	23.9	999 +	999 +	999 +	-0.8	-84.5	0.0 ●	NATIONWIDE INDEMNITY CO
13.5	12.1	N/A	N/A	N/A	N/A	N/A	N/A	N/A	999 +	0.0	0.0	NATIONWIDE INS CO OF AMERICA
5.9	4.3	12.4	8.4	-1.0	N/A	52.1	39.0	91.1	75.8	0.7	0.0 ●	NATIONWIDE INS CO OF FLORIDA
8.8	7.9	N/A	N/A	N/A	N/A	N/A	N/A	N/A	337.9	0.0	0.0	NATIONWIDE LLOYDS
4.8	3.4	88.4	57.2	-0.4	-1.3	66.2	32.7	98.9	121.8	27.8	4.2 ●	NATIONWIDE MUTUAL FIRE INS CO
1.5	1.3	124.1	82.1	-1.3	-2.2	66.2	33.0	99.2	96.2	17.1	30.3 ●	NATIONWIDE MUTUAL INS CO
4.3	2.8	N/A	N/A	N/A	N/A	N/A	N/A	N/A	-254.4	0.0	0.0	NATIONWIDE PROPERTY & CAS INS CO
1.5	1.0	161.7	154.6	8.8	16.7	75.2	34.1	109.3	82.2	-36.0	0.0 ●	NAU COUNTRY INS CO
14.1	13.9	-173.9	N/A	N/A	N/A	N/A	-0.7	N/A	-21.1	-144.9	0.0	NAUTILUS INS CO
2.3	1.7	84.6	112.3	-0.1	2.6	65.0	30.6	95.6	113.5	9.2	6.8 ●	NAVIGATORS INS CO
28.5	25.7	N/A	N/A	N/A	N/A	N/A	N/A	N/A	N/A	0.0	0.0	NAVIGATORS SPECIALTY INS CO
1.7	1.1	91.8	24.8	-2.5	-2.2	55.0	46.1	101.1	104.2	6.2	0.0	NAZARETH MUTUAL INS CO
2.5	1.9	42.3	99.7	-14.5	-33.3	50.2	22.7	72.9	152.9	1.5	1.7 ●	NCMIC INS CO
4.9	3.8	35.0	18.8	N/A	N/A	79.6	-53.9	25.7	93.7	0.0	0.0	NCMIC RRG INC

999 + Denotes number greater than 999.9%
999 - Denotes number less than -999.99%
● Bullets denote a more detailed analysis is available in Section II.

INSURANCE COMPANY NAME	DOM. STATE	RATING	TOTAL ASSETS ($MIL)	CAPITAL & SURPLUS ($MIL)	ANNUAL NET PREMIUM ($MIL)	NET INCOME ($MIL)	CAPITAL-IZATION INDEX (PTS)	RESERVE ADQ INDEX (PTS)	PROFIT-ABILITY INDEX (PTS)	LIQUIDITY INDEX (PTS)	STAB. INDEX (PTS)	STABILITY FACTORS
NEIGHBORHOOD SPIRIT PROP & CAS CO	CA	C+	275.0	114.7	136.4	13.7	8.7	8.2	6.3	6.4	4.6	FR
NETHERLANDS INS CO	NH	C	95.5	84.9	-94.0	1.6	10.0	4.9	2.4	0.2	3.6	FLRT
NEVADA CAPITAL INS CO	NV	C	105.3	50.6	46.0	0.8	8.1	6.0	6.7	6.0	4.2	T
NEVADA DOCS MEDICAL RRG INC	NV	E	2.1	0.5	1.7	0.0	0.7	4.0	1.4	2.5	0.0	CFLR
NEVADA GENERAL INS CO	NV	C	22.0	14.2	13.3	-0.4	8.5	6.6	2.4	6.6	3.6	DF
NEVADA MUTUAL INS CO INC	NV	D-	27.5	7.5	7.9	0.5	1.6	1.6	1.5	6.6	1.2	DFR
NEW CENTURY INS CO	TX	C	8.4	5.1	2.0	0.2	9.5	8.0	5.8	7.5	2.9	DRT
NEW ENGLAND GUARANTY INS CO INC	VT	C+	40.5	39.4	0.0	1.0	10.0	N/A	7.9	7.0	4.5	DT
NEW ENGLAND INS CO	CT	U	37.6	34.0	0.0	1.7	N/A	6.0	1.9	10.0	3.1	AFT
NEW ENGLAND MUTUAL INS CO	MA	C+	69.5	33.0	9.5	-3.6	9.1	4.6	3.2	6.9	3.8	DGT
NEW ENGLAND REINSURANCE CORP	CT	U	38.3	34.6	0.0	1.2	N/A	6.0	1.9	10.0	3.1	AFT
NEW HAMPSHIRE EMPLOYERS INS CO	NH	B-	3.8	3.4	0.0	0.0	10.0	N/A	6.9	10.0	3.5	DT
▼NEW HAMPSHIRE INS CO	PA	D+	272.1	138.9	713.5	223.4	7.1	3.3	1.9	6.6	2.4	AC
NEW HOME WARRANTY INS CO RRG	DC	B-	15.5	5.6	2.6	-0.2	7.2	4.6	3.3	8.1	3.5	DT
NEW JERSEY CAR RRG	DC	U (5)	0.0	0.0	0.1	0.0	N/A	N/A	3.8	9.1	1.2	T
NEW JERSEY CASUALTY INS CO	NJ	C (3)	0.0	0.0	84.1	13.9	7.3	2.9	6.3	7.1	3.5	
NEW JERSEY INDEMNITY INS CO	NJ	C+(3)	0.0	0.0	10.1	1.9	10.0	6.4	6.9	8.8	4.8	D
NEW JERSEY MANUFACTURERS INS CO	NJ	B-	6,565.0	2,456.2	1,597.6	135.5	8.2	5.9	3.9	6.8	5.3	
NEW JERSEY PHYS UNITED RECIP EXCH	NJ	D+(1)	40.7	15.4	10.1	-0.2	0.3	2.2	3.0	6.8	2.8	CD
NEW JERSEY RE-INS CO	NJ	B	559.6	376.2	37.1	7.4	8.2	6.9	8.5	8.4	5.7	T
NEW JERSEY SKYLANDS INS ASSN	NJ	C- (3)	0.0	0.0	26.5	-2.3	6.2	7.0	2.8	5.5	3.3	DF
NEW JERSEY SKYLANDS INS CO	NJ	C (3)	0.0	0.0	14.3	-0.8	7.2	7.0	3.9	5.9	3.8	DF
NEW LONDON COUNTY MUTUAL INS CO	CT	B-	112.9	63.2	35.9	2.0	8.1	9.0	3.5	6.6	4.7	R
NEW MEXICO ASR CO	NM	C-	5.4	1.5	0.0	-0.2	7.5	N/A	2.7	9.2	2.0	DGT
NEW MEXICO EMPLOYERS ASR CO	NM	B-	7.5	1.9	0.0	0.1	7.2	N/A	3.9	8.1	3.5	DGT
NEW MEXICO FOUNDATION INS CO	NM	C-	23.0	16.4	0.0	0.2	10.0	4.6	6.8	10.0	3.2	DR
NEW MEXICO MUTUAL CASUALTY CO	NM	C+	328.2	112.4	86.4	3.8	7.1	5.1	6.6	6.8	4.2	T
NEW MEXICO PREMIER INS CO	NM	C+	2.2	1.2	0.0	0.2	10.0	N/A	3.6	10.0	3.2	DFT
NEW MEXICO PROPERTY & CASUALTY CO	NM	D-	2.4	1.0	0.0	0.0	3.3	5.1	2.8	5.8	1.0	DFRT
NEW MEXICO SAFETY CASUALTY CO	NM	U	2.8	1.5	0.0	0.0	N/A	N/A	3.9	7.0	3.0	FT
NEW MEXICO SECURITY INS CO	NM	U	2.1	1.6	0.0	0.1	N/A	N/A	4.8	7.0	3.0	FT
NEW MEXICO SOUTHWEST CASUALTY CO	NM	C-	18.4	11.0	0.0	0.1	8.9	N/A	3.1	10.0	3.3	DR
NEW SOUTH INS CO	NC	C	74.8	17.4	0.0	0.3	8.2	2.4	3.2	7.0	3.2	DRT
NEW YORK CENTRAL MUTUAL FIRE INS CO	NY	B-	1,014.9	462.4	421.8	-4.2	9.8	7.8	5.9	6.6	4.7	R
NEW YORK HEALTHCARE INS CO INC RRG	DC	E+	23.4	4.6	7.9	0.1	0.4	0.5	5.5	7.9	0.5	CDR
NEW YORK MARINE & GENERAL INS CO	NY	B-	1,046.5	303.4	270.9	-0.1	6.0	9.2	4.2	7.1	4.7	GRT
NEW YORK MUNICIPAL INS RECIPROCAL	NY	C	140.9	50.9	38.4	-4.1	9.0	9.4	5.0	6.9	3.5	R
NEW YORK SCHOOLS INS RECIPROCAL	NY	B	288.9	140.3	51.3	2.2	9.9	8.4	8.5	6.9	5.9	T
NEW YORK TRANSPORTATION INS CORP	NY	U (3)	0.0	0.0	0.0	-0.3	N/A	4.1	1.9	10.0	1.8	FT
NEWPORT BONDING & SURETY CO	PR	E	5.8	2.1	1.8	0.0	2.7	1.3	2.4	4.2	0.3	DFGL
NEWPORT INS CO	AZ	C	47.8	45.9	-0.1	0.4	10.0	6.1	2.5	10.0	2.3	DT
NGM INS CO	FL	B-	2,281.1	961.2	1,018.2	34.4	8.4	8.3	6.7	6.2	4.6	R
NHRMA MUTUAL INS CO	IL	D	39.4	9.6	9.2	1.2	2.5	6.0	3.1	5.5	2.3	DGR
NIPPONKOA INS CO LTD (GUAM)	GU	D (3)	0.0	0.0	0.9	0.0	5.0	6.0	4.7	9.7	0.6	DGT
NLC MUTUAL INS CO	VT	B-	310.1	115.7	12.7	7.1	5.7	4.0	6.5	9.3	4.9	R
NODAK MUTUAL INS CO	ND	B-	236.5	110.9	136.3	3.2	8.8	8.8	5.8	5.8	4.7	T
NOETIC SPECIALTY INS CO	VT	C	119.4	61.5	12.4	2.4	9.0	9.3	8.3	7.0	3.5	RT
NORCAL MUTUAL INS CO	CA	B-	1,359.9	638.2	212.3	5.8	7.8	9.4	6.9	6.9	4.6	FR
NORFOLK & DEDHAM MUTUAL FIRE INS CO	MA	C+	357.0	173.3	112.5	-3.8	9.4	5.3	6.1	6.8	4.3	R
NORGUARD INS CO	PA	C	479.7	152.7	62.6	5.6	4.9	10.0	8.6	5.8	3.4	CGR
NORMANDY HARBOR INS CO INC	FL	D+	29.6	9.7	14.5	0.6	1.9	7.0	3.9	7.6	2.3	CDT
NORTH AMERICAN CAPACITY INS CO	NH	C	113.7	50.3	0.0	0.2	10.0	4.6	5.8	9.3	4.0	FRT

See Page 27 for explanation of footnotes and
Page 28 for explanation of stability factors.
Arrows denote recent upgrades ▲ or downgrades ▼   (see Section VII for explanations)

www.weissratings.com

RISK ADJ. CAPITAL RATIO #1	RATIO #2	PREMIUM TO SURPLUS (%)	RESV. TO SURPLUS (%)	RESV. DEVELOP. 1 YEAR (%)	2 YEAR (%)	LOSS RATIO (%)	EXP. RATIO (%)	COMB RATIO (%)	CASH FROM UNDER- WRITING (%)	NET PREMIUM GROWTH (%)	INVEST. IN AFFIL (%)	INSURANCE COMPANY NAME
4.1	3.0	123.9	72.1	0.2	-1.0	67.1	34.1	101.2	98.1	-1.6	0.0	NEIGHBORHOOD SPIRIT PROP & CAS CO
35.3	31.7	-112.9	N/A	N/A	N/A	N/A	0.1	N/A	0.7	-147.8	0.0	NETHERLANDS INS CO
2.9	1.8	92.9	53.7	-2.6	0.8	65.1	32.6	97.7	108.3	11.0	1.8	NEVADA CAPITAL INS CO
0.2	0.2	319.4	237.8	212.4	112.1	87.9	18.3	106.2	22.0	618.1	0.0	NEVADA DOCS MEDICAL RRG INC
2.1	1.9	89.0	42.0	-0.2	-3.9	71.2	46.9	118.1	87.8	13.2	0.0	NEVADA GENERAL INS CO
0.5	0.4	106.7	204.7	-18.7	-50.5	61.0	54.9	115.9	85.5	-14.2	16.0	NEVADA MUTUAL INS CO INC
2.9	2.1	43.0	4.8	-2.0	-2.3	49.1	40.8	89.9	123.4	10.8	0.0	NEW CENTURY INS CO
8.5	4.9	N/A	N/A	N/A	N/A	N/A	N/A	N/A	N/A	0.0	0.0	NEW ENGLAND GUARANTY INS CO INC
N/A	N/A	N/A	10.4	0.2	0.2	999 +	999 +	999 +	N/A	647.0	0.0	NEW ENGLAND INS CO
2.0	1.2	26.0	9.8	-0.2	N/A	90.4	43.5	133.9	103.5	-11.8	0.0	NEW ENGLAND MUTUAL INS CO
N/A	N/A	N/A	10.2	0.2	0.4	999 +	999 +	999 +	N/A	647.0	0.0	NEW ENGLAND REINSURANCE CORP
17.3	15.6	N/A	N/A	N/A	N/A	N/A	N/A	N/A	N/A	0.0	0.0	NEW HAMPSHIRE EMPLOYERS INS CO
0.4	0.4	97.5	226.8	3.5	9.1	76.6	31.7	108.3	94.4	16.0	7.7 ●	NEW HAMPSHIRE INS CO
1.1	0.9	47.6	9.5	-0.2	0.4	77.2	20.1	97.3	224.0	19.6	0.0	NEW HOME WARRANTY INS CO RRG
N/A	N/A	18.0	N/A	N/A	N/A	17.0	85.9	102.9	121.8	23.7	0.0	NEW JERSEY CAR RRG
2.3	1.1	46.5	149.5	2.4	7.1	74.8	12.5	87.3	148.4	21.5	0.0	NEW JERSEY CASUALTY INS CO
9.2	8.4	17.0	30.4	-6.9	-4.4	75.5	21.6	97.1	138.0	-6.7	0.0	NEW JERSEY INDEMNITY INS CO
2.5	1.8	70.3	133.4	-0.4	0.5	83.1	13.6	96.7	106.4	9.5	11.8 ●	NEW JERSEY MANUFACTURERS INS CO
0.1	0.1	64.8	121.5	5.1	25.0	66.6	44.1	110.7	104.2	14.6	0.0	NEW JERSEY PHYS UNITED RECIP EXCH
3.1	1.8	10.2	46.7	-3.7	-4.5	47.4	17.6	65.0	80.8	-9.9	0.0 ●	NEW JERSEY RE-INS CO
1.3	1.1	122.4	82.3	4.5	4.3	73.8	39.3	113.1	73.9	-5.8	27.3	NEW JERSEY SKYLANDS INS ASSN
2.2	1.5	105.6	71.0	4.2	3.5	73.8	39.3	113.1	73.9	-5.8	0.0	NEW JERSEY SKYLANDS INS CO
2.3	1.7	58.8	22.5	-3.8	-10.5	52.8	46.9	99.7	92.4	5.7	18.0	NEW LONDON COUNTY MUTUAL INS CO
1.1	1.0	N/A	52.2	N/A	N/A	N/A	N/A	N/A	47.2	0.0	0.0	NEW MEXICO ASR CO
1.1	1.0	N/A	66.9	N/A	N/A	N/A	N/A	N/A	28.1	0.0	0.0	NEW MEXICO EMPLOYERS ASR CO
9.0	4.0	N/A	21.8	N/A	N/A	N/A	N/A	N/A	38.4	0.0	0.0	NEW MEXICO FOUNDATION INS CO
1.3	1.0	79.6	165.0	4.7	2.8	66.5	34.5	101.0	116.7	18.2	12.2	NEW MEXICO MUTUAL CASUALTY CO
2.7	2.4	N/A	1.8	N/A	N/A	N/A	N/A	N/A	-32.7	0.0	0.0	NEW MEXICO PREMIER INS CO
2.0	0.8	-0.1	185.3	-66.5	-80.5	-4.7	999 +	999 +	51.4	-100.1	0.0	NEW MEXICO PROPERTY & CASUALTY
N/A	N/A	N/A	N/A	N/A	N/A	N/A	N/A	N/A	N/A	0.0	0.0	NEW MEXICO SAFETY CASUALTY CO
N/A	N/A	N/A	N/A	N/A	N/A	N/A	N/A	N/A	N/A	0.0	0.0	NEW MEXICO SECURITY INS CO
5.6	2.1	N/A	43.4	N/A	N/A	N/A	N/A	N/A	28.9	0.0	0.0	NEW MEXICO SOUTHWEST CASUALTY
2.3	2.1	N/A	N/A	N/A	N/A	N/A	N/A	N/A	-27.9	100.0	0.0	NEW SOUTH INS CO
3.8	2.9	90.4	61.9	-0.8	-2.0	67.9	30.1	98.0	99.3	1.7	4.4 ●	NEW YORK CENTRAL MUTUAL FIRE INS
0.2	0.1	184.9	331.4	23.4	80.6	65.2	36.6	101.8	116.8	-6.0	0.0	NEW YORK HEALTHCARE INS CO INC
1.3	0.9	112.8	158.2	-0.9	-7.8	60.6	38.5	99.1	144.6	36.9	14.5 ●	NEW YORK MARINE & GENERAL INS CO
2.1	1.6	67.8	99.3	0.3	-7.9	67.8	32.6	100.4	106.8	16.9	0.0	NEW YORK MUNICIPAL INS RECIPROCAL
4.0	3.0	37.5	64.6	-3.2	-4.8	75.4	19.0	94.4	109.5	-3.8	0.0	NEW YORK SCHOOLS INS RECIPROCAL
N/A	N/A	N/A	42.3	N/A	N/A	N/A	N/A	N/A	N/A	0.0	0.0	NEW YORK TRANSPORTATION INS
0.7	0.6	86.9	44.5	722.7	999 +	25.1	80.4	105.5	73.2	-18.1	0.0	NEWPORT BONDING & SURETY CO
67.1	41.6	-0.3	1.6	0.4	0.4	-94.5	96.0	1.5	-112.2	68.6	0.0	NEWPORT INS CO
3.0	2.3	108.7	76.5	-2.5	-3.4	68.2	31.4	99.6	106.2	3.7	10.4 ●	NGM INS CO
0.9	0.6	105.5	211.5	-28.8	-38.7	85.8	-2.1	83.7	109.4	38.0	13.8	NHRMA MUTUAL INS CO
1.0	0.7	76.6	7.4	-0.2	-0.2	37.5	33.4	70.9	157.4	160.3	0.0	NIPPONKOA INS CO LTD (GUAM)
1.5	0.9	11.7	162.0	7.2	11.1	136.9	19.0	155.9	184.5	6.9	0.0	NLC MUTUAL INS CO
3.2	2.1	128.1	38.7	-3.2	-4.2	73.6	19.2	92.8	122.9	20.6	6.4	NODAK MUTUAL INS CO
4.9	3.4	21.0	72.9	-11.1	-8.7	5.6	30.7	36.3	-131.9	63.9	0.0	NOETIC SPECIALTY INS CO
1.9	1.6	33.5	76.8	-3.2	-9.9	79.3	26.5	105.8	87.1	1.3	22.8 ●	NORCAL MUTUAL INS CO
3.6	2.4	63.0	35.7	N/A	-0.4	59.5	36.8	96.3	103.0	6.2	3.4	NORFOLK & DEDHAM MUTUAL FIRE INS
0.8	0.6	41.4	93.3	-3.3	-65.6	66.9	24.4	91.3	143.4	250.2	2.8	NORGUARD INS CO
0.6	0.3	156.4	81.3	-1.7	-37.5	55.3	34.8	90.1	116.9	13.5	0.0	NORMANDY HARBOR INS CO INC
6.8	6.1	N/A	3.5	N/A	N/A	N/A	N/A	N/A	-3.5	0.0	0.0	NORTH AMERICAN CAPACITY INS CO

999 + Denotes number greater than 999.9%
999 - Denotes number less than -999.99%
● Bullets denote a more detailed analysis is available in Section II.

INSURANCE COMPANY NAME	DOM. STATE	RATING	TOTAL ASSETS ($MIL)	CAPITAL & SURPLUS ($MIL)	ANNUAL NET PREMIUM ($MIL)	NET INCOME ($MIL)	CAPITAL-IZATION INDEX (PTS)	RESERVE ADQ INDEX (PTS)	PROFIT-ABILITY INDEX (PTS)	LIQUIDITY INDEX (PTS)	STAB. INDEX (PTS)	STABILITY FACTORS
NORTH AMERICAN ELITE INS CO	NH	C	110.5	35.0	0.0	1.5	10.0	N/A	6.7	8.5	3.7	FGRT
NORTH AMERICAN SPECIALTY INS CO	NH	C	544.5	379.2	11.4	4.4	10.0	8.3	7.8	10.0	3.7	R
NORTH CAROLINA FARM BU MUTUAL INS	NC	B-	1,735.1	997.6	737.3	60.1	9.4	8.3	4.4	5.9	4.9	
NORTH CAROLINA GRANGE MUTUAL INS	NC	E+	25.2	11.4	14.5	1.7	4.9	9.4	3.0	4.8	0.8	DL
NORTH COUNTRY INS CO	NY	C-	24.1	14.7	7.1	0.6	10.0	8.1	8.8	7.1	3.1	D
NORTH EAST INS CO	ME	D	72.7	13.8	24.3	-0.1	6.7	4.4	4.4	5.8	1.6	DFRT
NORTH LIGHT SPECIALTY INS CO	IL	B-	48.1	47.6	0.0	0.6	10.0	N/A	6.9	10.0	3.9	T
NORTH PACIFIC INS CO	OR	C+	17.7	7.7	0.0	0.1	10.0	N/A	6.4	7.0	4.1	DR
NORTH POINTE INS CO	PA	C-	105.3	25.4	34.1	1.9	3.7	3.7	1.9	6.7	2.9	DR
NORTH RIVER INS CO	NJ	C-	946.2	270.9	281.3	6.7	6.1	5.7	3.2	7.7	3.2	AR
NORTH SHORE LIJ PHYSICIANS INS RRG	VT	D	15.6	2.4	4.0	0.1	0.9	6.9	3.9	8.0	1.6	CDGT
NORTH STAR GENERAL INS CO	MN	U	4.3	4.3	0.0	0.0	N/A	N/A	3.8	7.0	4.3	T
NORTH STAR MUTUAL INS CO	MN	B-	548.9	290.1	288.7	11.0	10.0	7.5	8.2	6.7	4.7	R
NORTHERN INS CO OF NY	NY	C	38.7	29.9	0.0	0.4	10.0	N/A	6.2	9.8	4.3	FR
NORTHERN MUTUAL INS CO	MI	C	30.6	19.0	14.3	0.6	8.7	6.0	5.1	6.6	4.1	DR
NORTHERN SECURITY INS CO INC	VT	C	8.2	8.1	0.0	0.1	10.0	N/A	6.3	7.0	3.7	DR
NORTHFIELD INS CO	IA	C+	396.0	136.4	104.7	10.7	7.9	8.5	6.9	6.8	4.8	T
NORTHLAND CASUALTY CO	CT	B	109.2	37.0	28.2	2.9	8.1	8.4	6.2	6.8	5.8	D
NORTHLAND INS CO	CT	B	1,210.2	577.0	245.7	29.8	9.1	7.8	5.0	6.9	6.0	
NORTHSTONE INS CO	PA	D+	52.1	10.9	6.5	-0.1	4.2	6.1	3.5	7.1	2.2	CDT
NORTHWEST DENTISTS INS CO	WA	C	21.1	10.2	6.1	0.6	7.3	7.0	6.0	7.4	3.7	D
NORTHWEST GF MUTUAL INS CO	SD	E	15.1	5.8	9.3	1.5	7.0	8.9	3.0	6.2	0.3	D
NORTHWESTERN NATL INS CO SEG ACCNT	WI	D-	31.8	6.5	0.5	-0.9	1.3	N/A	2.9	6.9	1.3	DF
NORTHWESTERN NTL INS CO MILWAUKEE	WI	F	32.1	6.5	0.0	0.0	7.7	N/A	4.8	7.0	0.0	DRT
NOVA CASUALTY CO	NY	C	98.7	92.9	0.0	3.5	8.4	3.6	5.8	9.2	3.5	R
NOVANT HEALTH RRG INC	SC	E	11.7	4.5	2.2	0.1	3.0	2.3	4.8	10.0	0.0	DR
NUCLEAR ELECTRIC INS LTD	DE	D- (3)	0.0	0.0	205.2	178.5	9.0	3.5	4.4	6.8	1.1	F
NUTMEG INS CO	CT	C-	403.3	235.6	69.6	8.3	10.0	4.6	6.7	7.1	2.9	A
OAK RIVER INS CO	NE	C	563.0	183.1	111.9	6.7	7.1	6.7	4.9	8.2	4.3	R
OAKWOOD INS CO	TN	U	50.7	30.4	0.0	-0.1	N/A	5.0	1.9	10.0	3.1	FT
OASIS RECIPROCAL RRG	VT	B-	12.0	3.3	2.9	0.7	6.5	6.1	7.8	9.2	3.5	DG
OBI NATIONAL INS CO	PA	C	13.1	13.0	0.0	0.1	10.0	N/A	3.9	7.0	3.4	DT
OBSTETRICIANS & GYNECOLOGISTS RRG	MT	U	0.8	0.4	-0.3	-0.1	N/A	2.4	0.7	1.2	0.0	FLRT
OCCIDENTAL FIRE & CAS CO OF NC	NC	C-	444.7	158.2	121.8	-0.8	6.9	6.1	4.9	5.8	2.7	FRT
OCEAN HARBOR CASUALTY INS CO	FL	C	213.1	46.4	133.0	0.5	5.5	9.4	5.2	6.4	4.1	RT
OCEAN MARINE INDEMNITY INS CO	LA	C-	12.6	7.3	1.1	0.3	9.7	4.1	2.4	6.9	2.6	DR
OCEANUS INS CO A RRG	SC	C	71.5	16.9	27.1	-1.0	5.1	4.1	3.7	6.7	4.3	CDFR
ODYSSEY REINSURANCE CO	CT	C	7,784.8	3,397.4	1,267.5	152.9	7.3	9.3	4.2	6.9	3.6	AFRT
OGLESBY REINSURANCE CO	IL	A+	3,196.5	3,034.1	155.3	108.7	10.0	N/A	8.8	9.4	8.4	
OHA INS SOLUTIONS	OH	C-	43.5	23.3	4.0	-0.7	9.3	9.1	4.0	7.7	2.5	DFR
OHIC INS CO	OH	U	102.4	45.4	0.0	1.6	N/A	2.5	1.0	7.0	1.1	CRT
OHIO BAR LIABILITY INS CO	OH	B-	36.5	26.1	5.7	0.9	10.0	7.8	7.0	7.1	5.0	D
OHIO CASUALTY INS CO	NH	C	5,392.1	1,456.5	1,791.9	50.7	7.6	6.8	6.3	6.7	3.8	AR
OHIO FAIR PLAN UNDERWRITING ASN	OH	U (5)	0.0	0.0	5.9	0.0	N/A	1.8	1.9	7.0	0.0	CDFT
OHIO FARMERS INS CO	OH	B-	2,470.1	1,863.6	318.3	26.3	7.3	7.6	4.5	6.9	4.6	
OHIO INDEMNITY CO	OH	C	149.0	52.1	53.5	7.0	8.7	9.1	5.9	6.9	3.7	T
OHIO MUTUAL INS ASSOC	OH	B-	236.9	184.5	49.4	1.1	7.5	7.9	6.9	6.9	4.7	T
OHIO SECURITY INS CO	NH	C-	16.7	15.2	0.0	0.1	8.3	N/A	6.4	0.7	3.1	ADGL
OKLAHOMA ATTORNEYS MUTUAL INS CO	OK	B	54.8	37.2	5.4	1.1	10.0	6.6	5.9	9.2	5.3	D
OKLAHOMA FARM BUREAU MUTUAL INS CO	OK	C	298.4	89.8	149.4	10.4	7.1	7.0	2.9	3.3	3.5	FL
OKLAHOMA PROPERTY & CAS INS CO	OK	E+	3.6	2.9	0.3	0.0	10.0	10.0	4.9	6.9	0.6	DF
OKLAHOMA SPECIALTY INS CO	OK	C	43.6	16.8	0.0	0.3	10.0	N/A	7.0	10.0	3.3	DT

See Page 27 for explanation of footnotes and
Page 28 for explanation of stability factors.

100

www.weissratings.com

Arrows denote recent upgrades ▲ or downgrades ▼   (see Section VII for explanations)

RISK ADJ. CAPITAL RATIO #1	RATIO #2	PREMIUM TO SURPLUS (%)	RESV. TO SURPLUS (%)	RESV. DEVELOP. 1 YEAR (%)	2 YEAR (%)	LOSS RATIO (%)	EXP. RATIO (%)	COMB RATIO (%)	CASH FROM UNDER- WRITING (%)	NET PREMIUM GROWTH (%)	INVEST. IN AFFIL (%)	INSURANCE COMPANY NAME
4.4	3.9	N/A	2.4	N/A	N/A	999 +	999 +	999 +	-372.1	0.0	0.0	NORTH AMERICAN ELITE INS CO
5.3	4.7	3.0	6.9	-1.2	-3.2	8.4	50.0	58.4	999 +	9.6	15.9 ●	NORTH AMERICAN SPECIALTY INS CO
4.3	2.9	79.0	35.5	-4.8	-8.1	68.5	24.9	93.4	105.8	5.1	0.6 ●	NORTH CAROLINA FARM BU MUTUAL INS
1.4	1.0	155.7	23.6	3.1	-33.7	58.4	29.8	88.2	113.6	6.6	0.0	NORTH CAROLINA GRANGE MUTUAL INS
4.8	3.8	50.6	33.5	-2.7	-6.2	44.0	38.0	82.0	125.5	1.4	3.9	NORTH COUNTRY INS CO
1.6	1.4	172.7	306.6	40.2	42.1	105.8	60.8	166.6	55.9	-41.7	0.0	NORTH EAST INS CO
196.8	119.7	N/A	N/A	N/A	N/A	N/A	N/A	N/A	-565.6	0.0	0.0	NORTH LIGHT SPECIALTY INS CO
3.1	2.8	N/A	N/A	N/A	N/A	N/A	N/A	N/A	20.3	0.0	0.0	NORTH PACIFIC INS CO
1.0	0.7	162.3	147.4	8.3	17.3	75.2	33.2	108.4	95.3	-27.8	0.0	NORTH POINTE INS CO
1.1	0.8	106.9	190.1	1.0	6.6	71.4	31.7	103.1	106.2	20.0	21.0 ●	NORTH RIVER INS CO
0.3	0.2	179.2	368.7	11.0	-17.7	86.2	16.8	103.0	416.5	37.9	0.0	NORTH SHORE LIJ PHYSICIANS INS RRG
N/A	N/A	N/A	N/A	N/A	N/A	N/A	N/A	N/A	N/A	0.0	0.0	NORTH STAR GENERAL INS CO
4.4	3.0	103.1	32.0	1.2	-0.3	64.3	27.4	91.7	118.8	14.8	0.9 ●	NORTH STAR MUTUAL INS CO
13.5	12.2	N/A	N/A	N/A	N/A	N/A	N/A	N/A	999 +	0.0	0.0	NORTHERN INS CO OF NY
3.2	2.1	78.8	13.5	-7.9	-1.0	61.0	35.4	96.4	110.2	7.3	0.0	NORTHERN MUTUAL INS CO
81.6	38.4	N/A	N/A	N/A	N/A	N/A	N/A	N/A	N/A	0.0	0.0	NORTHERN SECURITY INS CO INC
2.7	1.7	83.3	149.8	-2.1	-4.9	60.9	29.6	90.5	108.0	3.0	0.0	NORTHFIELD INS CO
3.0	1.9	82.5	148.5	-2.1	-4.6	60.9	29.6	90.5	107.1	3.0	0.0	NORTHLAND CASUALTY CO
3.1	2.5	46.1	82.9	-1.1	-2.5	60.9	29.6	90.5	109.0	3.0	15.4 ●	NORTHLAND INS CO
1.2	0.4	60.1	192.4	-11.2	-200.1	75.1	22.2	97.3	104.0	-12.3	0.0	NORTHSTONE INS CO
1.4	1.1	63.0	73.0	-15.7	-26.9	55.3	33.9	89.2	110.8	4.2	0.0	NORTHWEST DENTISTS INS CO
2.1	1.5	223.4	44.7	-1.8	-5.5	69.9	34.2	104.1	98.0	-2.0	0.0	NORTHWEST GF MUTUAL INS CO
0.5	0.4	7.2	243.5	N/A	N/A	-213.8	210.2	-3.6	7.7	-21.1	33.1	NORTHWESTERN NATL INS CO SEG
1.5	1.4	N/A	N/A	N/A	N/A	N/A	N/A	N/A	N/A	0.0	0.0	NORTHWESTERN NTL INS CO
2.0	1.9	N/A	N/A	N/A	N/A	N/A	N/A	N/A	-201.6	0.0	56.4	NOVA CASUALTY CO
0.5	0.4	50.1	66.5	-2.9	24.4	46.3	31.1	77.4	999 +	-33.2	0.0	NOVANT HEALTH RRG INC
3.4	2.4	5.3	9.3	0.8	14.4	100.2	16.0	116.2	26.0	22.9	1.6	NUCLEAR ELECTRIC INS LTD
24.5	22.0	27.1	48.6	0.3	N/A	68.8	29.2	98.0	103.1	1.1	15.9 ●	NUTMEG INS CO
1.6	1.0	65.4	163.3	-10.3	-7.9	66.3	26.0	92.3	139.2	11.6	0.0	OAK RIVER INS CO
N/A	N/A	N/A	43.9	-0.5	-4.6	999 +	999 +	999 +	N/A	0.0	0.0	OAKWOOD INS CO
1.5	1.0	95.0	139.0	-45.8	-105.8	42.4	26.1	68.5	292.8	74.6	0.0	OASIS RECIPROCAL RRG
134.0	67.0	N/A	N/A	N/A	N/A	N/A	N/A	N/A	N/A	0.0	0.0	OBI NATIONAL INS CO
N/A	N/A	-50.1	113.3	-11.2	8.5	-40.4	-140.2	-180.6	25.0	-128.8	0.0	OBSTETRICIANS & GYNECOLOGISTS
1.1	0.9	78.6	48.7	-3.2	-3.1	64.9	30.6	95.5	82.1	27.3	43.1	OCCIDENTAL FIRE & CAS CO OF NC
0.9	0.8	299.7	162.4	-5.8	-6.6	65.1	35.0	100.1	124.2	-4.4	12.3	OCEAN HARBOR CASUALTY INS CO
4.0	3.0	15.5	68.8	16.2	17.4	214.8	42.5	257.3	75.0	18.9	0.0	OCEAN MARINE INDEMNITY INS CO
0.9	0.6	129.7	189.8	-6.1	23.0	73.1	42.2	115.3	88.8	-25.8	0.0	OCEANUS INS CO A RRG
1.6	1.1	40.9	105.7	-23.4	-24.5	29.2	43.7	72.9	72.8	-40.5	20.7 ●	ODYSSEY REINSURANCE CO
60.0	52.4	5.3	N/A	N/A	N/A	N/A	0.5	0.5	999 +	-22.1	0.0 ●	OGLESBY REINSURANCE CO
3.2	2.7	16.6	53.5	-9.0	-14.9	59.2	59.5	118.7	52.7	-2.5	0.0	OHA INS SOLUTIONS
N/A	N/A	N/A	142.0	25.0	81.3	N/A	N/A	N/A	N/A	-100.0	0.0	OHIC INS CO
4.1	2.9	21.8	23.0	-2.0	-2.9	51.9	36.8	88.7	101.1	16.3	6.0	OHIO BAR LIABILITY INS CO
2.4	1.5	129.5	200.0	5.1	6.5	73.5	35.0	108.5	119.9	-19.6	2.2 ●	OHIO CASUALTY INS CO
N/A	N/A	-126.2	-50.6	4.3	10.4	107.0	-5.3	101.7	84.2	27.4	0.0	OHIO FAIR PLAN UNDERWRITING ASN
1.2	1.2	17.6	15.7	-1.2	-2.1	59.8	34.7	94.5	101.6	4.3	68.8 ●	OHIO FARMERS INS CO
3.1	2.2	118.4	25.1	-11.4	-12.2	26.2	48.5	74.7	153.1	-10.4	0.0	OHIO INDEMNITY CO
1.3	1.3	27.8	13.4	-1.8	-3.0	65.8	30.6	96.4	106.1	9.1	67.1	OHIO MUTUAL INS ASSOC
25.9	23.3	N/A	N/A	N/A	N/A	N/A	N/A	N/A	435.5	0.0	0.0	OHIO SECURITY INS CO
4.7	3.1	14.8	24.7	-4.0	-3.7	69.5	26.7	96.2	118.9	-19.4	0.0	OKLAHOMA ATTORNEYS MUTUAL INS
1.6	1.2	172.4	69.5	-2.4	-4.2	83.6	16.1	99.7	93.2	-4.0	14.1	OKLAHOMA FARM BUREAU MUTUAL INS
10.3	9.3	11.9	31.4	-32.9	-68.0	49.9	80.3	130.2	36.6	-35.4	0.0	OKLAHOMA PROPERTY & CAS INS CO
3.9	3.5	N/A	N/A	N/A	N/A	N/A	N/A	N/A	111.9	0.0	0.0	OKLAHOMA SPECIALTY INS CO

999 + Denotes number greater than 999.9%
999 - Denotes number less than -999.99%
● Bullets denote a more detailed analysis is available in Section II.

INSURANCE COMPANY NAME	DOM. STATE	RATING	TOTAL ASSETS ($MIL)	CAPITAL & SURPLUS ($MIL)	ANNUAL NET PREMIUM ($MIL)	NET INCOME ($MIL)	CAPITAL-IZATION INDEX (PTS)	RESERVE ADQ INDEX (PTS)	PROFIT-ABILITY INDEX (PTS)	LIQUIDITY INDEX (PTS)	STAB. INDEX (PTS)	STABILITY FACTORS
OKLAHOMA SURETY CO	OH	C	28.9	18.1	4.4	0.5	8.5	9.0	7.5	8.8	4.3	DR
OKLAHOMA TRANSIT INS CO	OK	U (5)	0.0	0.0	0.0	0.0	N/A	N/A	3.2	7.0	2.7	FT
OLD AMERICAN CTY MUTUAL FIRE INS CO	TX	E+	66.6	5.0	58.7	0.0	0.0	7.4	5.1	0.1	0.7	CDLR
OLD AMERICAN INDEMNITY CO	KY	B-	9.3	4.6	2.0	-0.4	10.0	3.6	2.9	8.5	3.5	DFRT
OLD DOMINION INS CO	FL	B-	33.0	32.4	0.0	0.7	10.0	N/A	7.8	7.0	4.6	
OLD ELIZABETH MUTUAL FIRE INS CO	PA	U (3)	0.0	0.0	0.0	0.0	N/A	4.6	2.3	10.0	1.7	FGT
OLD GLORY INS CO	TX	D	21.9	9.1	8.0	0.1	6.1	5.8	3.0	6.4	1.4	DR
OLD GUARD INS CO	OH	C+	405.7	171.5	150.8	6.2	8.5	9.3	6.6	6.3	4.5	T
OLD RELIABLE CAS CO	MO	C-	6.0	5.0	0.0	0.1	10.0	N/A	3.1	10.0	3.3	DFRT
OLD REPUBLIC GENERAL INS CORP	IL	A-	1,829.0	434.3	286.3	52.7	7.6	6.7	8.4	7.0	7.1	
OLD REPUBLIC INS CO	PA	A-	2,580.9	931.8	365.4	78.7	9.0	5.6	7.7	7.5	7.2	A
OLD REPUBLIC LLOYDS OF TX	TX	B	1.9	0.7	0.6	0.0	7.5	9.3	3.9	8.9	4.9	DT
OLD REPUBLIC SECURITY ASR CO	AZ	U	6.5	6.5	0.0	0.0	N/A	4.7	1.9	7.0	3.1	FRT
OLD REPUBLIC SURETY CO	WI	B+	110.0	52.2	38.1	3.6	7.8	9.4	8.6	6.9	5.9	
OLD REPUBLIC UNION INS CO	IL	B	56.1	49.8	0.0	1.2	10.0	5.8	6.7	10.0	6.1	DG
OLD UNITED CAS CO	KS	B-	648.3	325.6	119.9	22.6	10.0	6.2	8.9	7.5	4.7	R
OLYMPUS INS CO	FL	D+	58.6	25.2	-19.2	3.3	8.0	3.3	2.9	7.3	2.5	DGR
OMAHA INDEMNITY CO	WI	U	14.6	12.5	0.0	0.1	N/A	9.1	3.7	10.0	4.9	T
OMEGA INS CO	FL	D	39.1	14.7	9.5	1.5	4.3	6.5	5.3	8.1	2.3	DFRT
OMEGA ONE INS CO	AL	U	10.1	9.3	-0.1	0.3	N/A	6.9	4.1	9.0	4.9	FRT
OMNI INDEMNITY CO	IL	B-	70.5	25.7	35.2	-2.3	7.7	4.5	3.3	5.3	4.9	FR
OMNI INS CO	IL	B	208.6	78.0	103.4	-6.7	8.0	4.5	4.3	4.3	5.9	L
OMS NATIONAL INS CO RRG	IL	B-	374.2	208.6	69.9	3.1	8.5	9.4	8.8	6.9	4.7	FR
ONEBEACON AMERICA INS CO	PA	C	96.1	88.9	0.0	0.2	10.0	4.8	1.9	7.0	3.5	DFRT
ONEBEACON INS CO	PA	C	1,074.1	898.5	0.0	4.0	7.2	6.2	3.6	9.4	4.0	CFRT
ONECIS INS CO	IL	U	24.3	20.7	0.0	3.0	N/A	N/A	7.5	7.0	5.1	GT
ONTARIO INS CO	NY	C-	16.0	11.2	3.6	0.3	10.0	6.7	8.4	8.4	3.1	DR
ONTARIO REINS CO LTD	GA	D	27.8	19.9	0.5	0.1	7.2	7.6	5.9	9.1	1.9	DF
ONYX INS CO INC A RRG	TN	D	16.5	4.0	2.2	0.0	7.6	N/A	2.8	9.6	2.0	DT
OOIDA RISK RETENTION GROUP INC	VT	D	84.5	14.7	17.9	-2.6	4.8	9.7	2.2	9.1	2.3	DGRT
OPHTHALMIC MUTUAL INS CO RRG	VT	B	267.0	177.5	39.9	14.4	10.0	9.3	8.9	7.7	5.6	T
ORANGE COUNTY MEDICAL RECIP INS RRG	AZ	D-	7.4	5.5	1.0	-0.2	10.0	10.0	7.4	9.2	1.3	D
ORDINARY MUTUAL A RRG CORP	VT	U	8.7	5.2	0.0	0.1	N/A	9.4	1.9	8.3	3.1	FRT
OREGON AUTOMOBILE INS CO	OR	C	8.7	7.7	0.0	0.1	10.0	N/A	6.2	10.0	3.9	DFR
OREGON MUTUAL INS CO	OR	B-	247.3	95.0	156.2	5.0	8.6	8.2	4.9	6.2	4.5	R
ORISKA INS CO	NY	E+	71.7	7.3	0.6	1.5	0.3	0.8	4.4	9.5	0.5	CDGR
ORTHOFORUM INS CO RRG	SC	D-	15.5	3.7	5.4	0.5	0.9	3.6	2.1	7.3	1.2	CDGT
OSWEGO COUNTY MUTUAL INS CO	NY	C-	22.0	12.7	5.9	0.2	8.6	9.3	8.4	6.8	3.2	D
OTSEGO COUNTY PATRONS CO-OP F R	NY	D	1.8	0.6	0.5	0.0	7.3	8.3	3.2	6.8	1.0	DGRT
OTSEGO MUTUAL FIRE INS CO	NY	A-	110.3	93.3	4.3	4.3	10.0	7.5	8.1	7.5	6.7	D
OWNERS INS CO	OH	A+	3,686.6	1,343.8	1,617.0	47.3	8.7	9.3	6.9	6.5	7.9	
PACE RRG INC	VT	E+	13.2	3.3	0.3	0.0	0.2	0.4	2.9	7.0	0.4	CDRT
PACIFIC COMPENSATION INS CO	CA	C-	243.4	94.0	40.7	-4.9	5.5	2.5	1.6	6.4	2.9	FGRT
PACIFIC EMPLOYERS INS CO	PA	B-	3,430.5	1,192.1	774.9	45.4	8.6	8.3	8.3	6.8	4.9	R
PACIFIC INDEMNITY CO	WI	B+	6,857.3	2,843.7	1,568.7	313.5	9.2	8.9	8.8	6.9	5.8	
PACIFIC INDEMNITY INS CO	GU	C-	30.0	18.9	8.5	1.9	8.4	9.0	8.6	8.2	3.1	DR
PACIFIC INS CO LTD	CT	B	645.3	237.9	169.1	18.6	9.3	6.2	4.9	6.7	5.8	A
PACIFIC PIONEER INSURANCE CO	CA	D+	26.2	9.0	6.9	-3.2	5.9	6.4	2.5	6.8	2.2	DFRT
PACIFIC PROPERTY & CASUALTY CO	CA	B	75.1	40.5	33.7	1.8	7.6	7.9	8.9	6.3	6.0	D
PACIFIC SPECIALTY INS CO	CA	C+	311.0	132.1	176.1	12.7	6.7	5.8	4.7	5.1	4.5	R
PACIFIC SPECIALTY PROPERTY & CAS CO	TX	E	4.6	4.1	0.6	0.0	10.0	6.0	6.7	9.2	0.0	DR
PACIFIC STAR INS CO	WI	C	9.6	6.6	1.8	0.0	10.0	4.3	2.8	6.9	3.6	DFR

See Page 27 for explanation of footnotes and
Page 28 for explanation of stability factors.

102

www.weissratings.com

Arrows denote recent upgrades ▲ or downgrades ▼   (see Section VII for explanations)

RISK ADJ. CAPITAL RATIO #1	RATIO #2	PREMIUM TO SURPLUS (%)	RESV. TO SURPLUS (%)	RESV. DEVELOP. 1 YEAR (%)	RESV. DEVELOP. 2 YEAR (%)	LOSS RATIO (%)	EXP. RATIO (%)	COMB RATIO (%)	CASH FROM UNDER-WRITING (%)	NET PREMIUM GROWTH (%)	INVEST. IN AFFIL (%)	INSURANCE COMPANY NAME
3.6	2.4	25.0	45.0	0.6	-5.6	57.1	35.5	92.6	109.5	6.1	0.0	OKLAHOMA SURETY CO
N/A	N/A	N/A	N/A	N/A	N/A	N/A	N/A	N/A	N/A	0.0	0.0	OKLAHOMA TRANSIT INS CO
0.1	0.0	999 +	0.7	-0.2	-0.4	N/A	99.4	99.4	104.7	-18.6	0.0	OLD AMERICAN CTY MUTUAL FIRE INS
3.1	2.8	42.6	27.2	2.6	1.0	100.6	35.9	136.5	88.8	50.2	0.0	OLD AMERICAN INDEMNITY CO
60.4	30.2	N/A	N/A	N/A	N/A	N/A	N/A	N/A	N/A	0.0	0.0	OLD DOMINION INS CO
N/A	N/A	5.7	0.4	-0.4	-0.3	2.7	201.9	204.6	63.9	123.1	0.0	OLD ELIZABETH MUTUAL FIRE INS CO
1.2	0.9	100.5	104.1	4.3	5.3	70.7	38.2	108.9	100.6	9.0	0.0	OLD GLORY INS CO
3.3	2.1	91.7	81.7	-6.4	-11.3	59.8	34.9	94.7	107.1	4.3	0.0	OLD GUARD INS CO
10.8	9.7	N/A	N/A	N/A	N/A	N/A	N/A	N/A	-8.4	0.0	0.0	OLD RELIABLE CAS CO
2.4	1.4	66.3	212.2	-4.6	-6.2	83.2	5.7	88.9	179.1	2.8	0.6 •	OLD REPUBLIC GENERAL INS CORP
3.7	2.3	39.0	100.8	-1.7	-4.2	52.2	32.3	84.5	120.7	1.7	1.6 •	OLD REPUBLIC INS CO
1.4	1.2	80.0	121.1	-8.5	-16.4	57.0	45.7	102.7	104.0	13.5	0.0	OLD REPUBLIC LLOYDS OF TX
N/A	N/A	N/A	N/A	N/A	-15.7	N/A	N/A	N/A	N/A	-100.0	0.0	OLD REPUBLIC SECURITY ASR CO
1.8	1.4	73.5	39.0	-16.7	-19.1	11.3	76.4	87.7	113.3	6.1	0.2 •	OLD REPUBLIC SURETY CO
3.5	2.0	N/A	11.4	1.5	1.5	999 +	999 +	999 +	2.1	12.9	0.0	OLD REPUBLIC UNION INS CO
8.2	4.3	39.6	3.4	-0.9	-1.1	44.7	23.6	68.3	171.2	10.2	0.0 •	OLD UNITED CAS CO
2.2	1.8	-88.9	30.7	40.0	36.2	-49.4	216.2	166.8	77.8	24.0	0.0	OLYMPUS INS CO
N/A	N/A	N/A	16.3	-3.4	-8.1	N/A	N/A	N/A	N/A	0.0	0.0	OMAHA INDEMNITY CO
0.9	0.6	69.9	20.5	-0.3	6.7	74.6	27.4	102.0	77.8	45.5	0.0	OMEGA INS CO
N/A	N/A	-0.6	10.5	-4.1	-15.1	-18.3	-163.1	-181.4	-2.7	-105.2	0.0	OMEGA ONE INS CO
1.6	1.5	130.5	74.4	11.6	14.3	77.5	20.1	97.6	89.6	-12.1	0.0	OMNI INDEMNITY CO
1.6	1.5	120.6	68.7	11.1	14.4	77.5	20.2	97.7	88.5	-12.1	25.2	OMNI INS CO
2.3	1.8	36.5	50.5	-7.3	-17.8	51.3	29.6	80.9	57.9	-9.6	18.8 •	OMS NATIONAL INS CO RRG
51.6	46.5	N/A	N/A	N/A	N/A	N/A	N/A	N/A	N/A	-100.0	0.0	ONEBEACON AMERICA INS CO
1.2	1.1	N/A	21.8	5.6	6.6	999 +	999 +	999 +	2.9	-100.0	74.9 •	ONEBEACON INS CO
N/A	N/A	N/A	N/A	N/A	N/A	N/A	999 +	999 +	N/A	0.0	0.0	ONECIS INS CO
6.5	4.1	33.3	16.3	-1.7	-2.5	52.5	32.9	85.4	113.5	4.0	0.0	ONTARIO INS CO
2.1	1.3	2.9	4.2	0.2	-0.2	66.8	47.9	114.7	88.3	-7.5	0.0	ONTARIO REINS CO LTD
1.4	1.3	88.5	14.8	N/A	N/A	95.2	11.9	107.1	517.3	0.0	0.0	ONYX INS CO INC A RRG
0.9	0.7	103.7	132.8	-11.6	-21.9	84.7	28.5	113.2	131.8	74.9	0.0	OOIDA RISK RETENTION GROUP INC
11.7	8.0	24.4	31.4	-6.4	-8.6	30.3	23.1	53.4	152.8	3.0	0.0	OPHTHALMIC MUTUAL INS CO RRG
7.7	5.2	16.9	16.8	-14.9	-50.0	2.4	13.5	15.9	291.7	-14.3	0.0	ORANGE COUNTY MEDICAL RECIP INS
N/A	N/A	N/A	69.5	-8.2	-25.7	N/A	N/A	N/A	N/A	0.0	0.0	ORDINARY MUTUAL A RRG CORP
17.9	16.1	N/A	N/A	N/A	N/A	N/A	N/A	N/A	-62.6	0.0	0.0	OREGON AUTOMOBILE INS CO
3.1	2.2	169.8	78.6	-3.7	-10.1	70.0	32.9	102.9	106.5	34.5	4.4	OREGON MUTUAL INS CO
0.2	0.1	8.4	199.4	60.0	87.9	999 +	-823.6	228.0	76.9	317.3	0.0	ORISKA INS CO
0.4	0.3	181.4	179.7	18.0	N/A	102.5	22.6	125.1	307.6	49.3	0.0	ORTHOFORUM INS CO RRG
3.1	2.0	48.3	37.1	-6.6	-15.1	60.4	34.1	94.5	117.4	13.2	0.0	OSWEGO COUNTY MUTUAL INS CO
1.2	1.1	82.4	24.5	-4.1	-6.8	76.1	20.4	96.5	104.9	53.1	0.0	OTSEGO COUNTY PATRONS CO-OP F R
6.0	3.5	4.9	3.5	-1.4	-1.2	26.3	22.8	49.1	230.0	-2.4	0.0 •	OTSEGO MUTUAL FIRE INS CO
3.7	2.4	125.2	86.7	-0.2	-7.0	67.5	28.2	95.7	109.9	6.5	0.0 •	OWNERS INS CO
0.3	0.2	9.8	115.8	-47.0	24.3	-260.8	146.6	-114.2	-29.3	-10.3	0.0	PACE RRG INC
0.9	0.5	41.0	127.8	N/A	4.8	86.7	69.0	155.7	63.5	113.8	0.0	PACIFIC COMPENSATION INS CO
3.2	2.2	67.9	120.0	-4.7	-3.4	72.2	22.0	94.2	98.1	-2.8	5.9 •	PACIFIC EMPLOYERS INS CO
4.1	2.6	56.6	102.5	-4.2	-7.0	52.5	29.3	81.8	113.0	4.2	0.4 •	PACIFIC INDEMNITY CO
4.1	2.5	49.7	20.3	2.2	-5.3	40.4	45.3	85.7	126.7	-0.9	0.0	PACIFIC INDEMNITY INS CO
3.9	2.6	77.4	138.6	0.8	-0.1	68.8	29.1	97.9	103.1	1.1	0.0 •	PACIFIC INS CO LTD
1.0	0.6	59.7	51.1	0.5	-4.1	97.8	26.8	124.6	61.4	26.2	0.0	PACIFIC PIONEER INSURANCE CO
2.5	1.5	87.3	41.7	-8.1	-5.3	68.3	21.5	89.8	112.7	6.7	0.0	PACIFIC PROPERTY & CASUALTY CO
1.0	0.6	85.5	28.0	1.7	2.9	53.9	42.0	95.9	111.5	9.2	1.2 •	PACIFIC SPECIALTY INS CO
18.3	12.2	14.8	5.7	-0.7	0.4	53.2	34.9	88.1	100.7	-25.2	0.0	PACIFIC SPECIALTY PROPERTY & CAS
4.5	3.6	27.3	21.1	5.8	7.3	88.8	30.0	118.8	71.4	-27.7	0.0	PACIFIC STAR INS CO

999 + Denotes number greater than 999.9%
999 - Denotes number less than -999.99%
• Bullets denote a more detailed analysis is available in Section II.

INSURANCE COMPANY NAME	DOM. STATE	RATING	TOTAL ASSETS ($MIL)	CAPITAL & SURPLUS ($MIL)	ANNUAL NET PREMIUM ($MIL)	NET INCOME ($MIL)	CAPITAL-IZATION INDEX (PTS)	RESERVE ADQ INDEX (PTS)	PROFIT-ABILITY INDEX (PTS)	LIQUIDITY INDEX (PTS)	STAB. INDEX (PTS)	STABILITY FACTORS
PACO ASR CO INC	IL	D+	74.4	35.4	11.3	1.6	3.0	7.0	5.3	7.8	2.5	DR
PAFCO GENERAL INS CO	IN	F (5)	0.0	0.0	6.3	0.0	1.5	4.9	0.3	2.9	0.0	CDFL
PALADIN REINSURANCE CORP	NY	U	1.5	0.6	0.0	0.0	N/A	4.0	1.0	10.0	1.8	FT
PALISADES INS CO	NJ	D+ (3)	0.0	0.0	0.0	0.1	10.0	4.1	6.4	7.0	2.5	D
PALISADES PROPERTY & CASUALTY INS	NJ	D (3)	0.0	0.0	0.0	0.5	10.0	4.1	2.6	6.9	1.5	DT
PALISADES SAFETY & INS ASSOC	NJ	C (3)	0.0	0.0	545.3	17.0	3.6	4.3	3.2	3.0	3.5	CFLT
PALLADIUM RRG INC	VT	U	21.8	2.4	-0.7	0.0	N/A	N/A	2.9	7.0	2.9	FT
PALMETTO CASUALTY INS CO	SC	C	6.8	6.7	0.0	0.1	10.0	N/A	7.3	7.0	3.8	D
PALMETTO SURETY CORP	SC	B-	10.2	3.5	3.3	0.5	7.0	9.3	6.3	7.8	3.5	DG
PALOMAR SPECIALTY INS CO	OR	U	80.3	70.1	0.0	-3.7	N/A	N/A	4.0	7.0	4.7	T
PANHANDLE FARMERS MUT INS CO OF WV	WV	C-	4.4	2.2	2.5	-0.2	7.4	7.6	3.1	6.3	2.0	DRT
PARAMOUNT INS CO	MD	D-	6.9	2.3	5.6	-0.2	4.7	1.9	4.8	5.6	1.3	DFRT
PARAMOUNT INS CO	NY	C-	53.7	16.3	19.4	-0.2	6.3	3.6	1.8	6.8	3.2	DR
PARATRANSIT INS CO A MUTUAL RRG	TN	D	24.1	12.2	3.3	0.4	9.1	9.9	8.6	7.4	2.2	DFR
PARK INS CO	NY	E	27.1	3.6	12.4	-0.4	0.0	0.3	2.5	0.7	0.1	CDFL
PARTNER REINSURANCE CO OF THE US	NY	C-	4,984.4	1,345.2	1,139.4	155.4	7.1	9.6	8.5	6.9	3.2	R
PARTNERRE AMERICA INS CO	DE	C	301.8	133.4	-0.2	4.8	10.0	7.0	6.1	7.0	4.0	DFRT
PARTNERRE INS CO OF NEW YORK	NY	C	135.6	117.1	0.1	1.1	8.3	4.8	6.2	9.1	4.0	DGRT
PARTNERS MUTUAL INS CO	WI	D	42.9	8.8	12.9	-0.2	7.0	4.1	2.9	6.5	2.2	DR
PASSPORT INS CO	ND	U (3)	0.0	0.0	0.0	0.0	N/A	N/A	3.9	7.0	2.1	T
PATRIOT GENERAL INS CO	WI	B	27.4	26.1	0.0	0.5	10.0	N/A	7.5	10.0	4.9	D
PATRIOT INS CO	ME	C	101.6	28.8	42.1	0.8	7.9	7.0	4.6	6.3	3.7	T
PATRONS MUTUAL FIRE INS CO OF IN PA	PA	D+ (3)	0.0	0.0	0.4	0.2	10.0	6.9	6.0	9.9	1.9	DT
PATRONS MUTUAL INS CO OF CT	CT	C	51.9	20.5	8.2	0.3	10.0	7.5	4.5	6.9	3.5	DR
PATRONS-OXFORD INS CO	ME	C	18.7	7.2	0.0	0.1	10.0	7.4	4.1	6.0	2.7	DFT
PAWTUCKET INS CO	RI	U	4.2	0.1	0.0	-0.1	N/A	0.3	0.4	9.9	0.0	CFRT
PCH MUTUAL INS CO INC RRG	DC	E+	9.7	3.0	1.0	-0.1	1.2	4.0	2.9	5.7	0.5	CDFR
PEACE CHURCH RRG INC	VT	D-	22.5	15.7	2.9	1.2	10.0	9.7	8.9	8.1	0.9	DFR
PEACHTREE CASUALTY INS CO	FL	D+	29.1	6.4	15.8	-3.5	4.0	1.8	1.6	4.2	2.4	CDFL
PEAK PROP & CAS INS CORP	WI	B	51.2	40.0	0.0	0.9	10.0	N/A	8.8	9.2	4.2	FR
PEERLESS INDEMNITY INS CO	IL	C+	192.5	182.6	-156.7	6.4	10.0	4.9	3.4	0.8	4.4	FLRT
PEERLESS INS CO	NH	B-	12,749.4	2,946.3	5,827.5	122.2	7.1	5.6	6.2	7.7	5.0	G
PEKIN INS CO	IL	B+	286.1	116.1	107.1	-0.5	10.0	9.3	6.2	6.6	6.0	
PELICAN INS RRG	VT	D-	18.6	15.2	2.6	0.7	7.9	9.3	7.5	7.0	1.3	DR
PEMCO MUTUAL INS CO	WA	B-	660.8	239.1	346.0	2.8	9.0	6.1	3.1	6.4	4.7	R
PENINSULA INDEMNITY CO	MD	C	10.9	9.3	0.0	0.2	10.0	N/A	7.3	7.0	3.9	DRT
PENINSULA INS CO	MD	C	82.9	40.9	40.9	1.8	8.6	6.3	5.5	6.3	4.2	T
PENINSULAR SURETY CO	FL	D+	2.3	1.9	0.4	0.4	6.5	5.5	1.3	7.7	2.1	DFT
PENN CHARTER MUTUAL INS CO	PA	C	12.5	10.0	0.0	0.2	7.4	7.2	6.9	10.0	3.7	D
PENN MILLERS INS CO	PA	C	153.5	84.1	0.0	2.5	10.0	9.0	6.3	7.0	3.8	FRT
PENN NATIONAL SECURITY INS CO	PA	B-	879.0	283.7	315.8	6.0	8.6	5.5	5.9	6.4	4.7	T
PENN PATRIOT INS CO	VA	C-	38.2	20.4	5.1	0.1	3.6	8.0	1.9	8.3	3.1	DFR
PENN RESERVE INS CO LTD	PA	D	1.8	1.6	0.1	0.0	10.0	N/A	4.5	10.0	1.4	DT
PENN-AMERICA INS CO	PA	C-	190.6	82.8	25.6	-0.6	8.2	7.8	1.9	7.0	3.1	FR
PENN-STAR INS CO	PA	C-	94.9	48.8	10.2	0.0	8.2	7.8	1.9	8.1	3.1	DR
PENNSYLVANIA INS CO	IA	C	28.6	16.6	21.7	2.8	5.5	8.5	1.9	8.0	3.1	DGRT
PENNSYLVANIA LUMBERMENS MUTUAL INS	PA	B	462.2	116.5	120.8	-10.4	7.2	5.0	3.3	6.5	6.0	
PENNSYLVANIA MANUFACTURERS ASN INS	PA	C	810.9	217.7	135.6	1.7	8.7	2.4	3.6	7.0	4.0	AR
PENNSYLVANIA MANUFACTURERS IND CO	PA	C	192.6	74.8	45.2	0.3	8.8	2.5	3.6	6.8	4.1	AR
PENNSYLVANIA NTL MUTUAL CAS INS CO	PA	B-	1,171.8	546.7	315.8	5.7	7.6	4.3	5.3	6.7	4.7	R
PENNSYLVANIA PHYSICIANS RECIP INS	PA	E+	13.9	6.4	4.6	0.8	3.3	5.8	4.9	6.8	0.0	DFR
PENNSYLVANIA PROFESSIONAL LIAB JUA	PA	U (5)	279.4	236.7	1.2	0.0	N/A	9.4	6.8	9.7	2.7	DFT

See Page 27 for explanation of footnotes and Page 28 for explanation of stability factors.

Arrows denote recent upgrades ▲ or downgrades ▼ (see Section VII for explanations)

104

www.weissratings.com

RISK ADJ. CAPITAL RATIO #1	CAPITAL RATIO #2	PREMIUM TO SURPLUS (%)	RESV. TO SURPLUS (%)	RESV. DEVELOP. 1 YEAR (%)	RESV. DEVELOP. 2 YEAR (%)	LOSS RATIO (%)	EXP. RATIO (%)	COMB RATIO (%)	CASH FROM UNDER-WRITING (%)	NET PREMIUM GROWTH (%)	INVEST. IN AFFIL (%)	INSURANCE COMPANY NAME
1.0	0.6	33.5	90.6	-7.8	-11.7	51.1	28.4	79.5	103.9	-5.3	0.0	PACO ASR CO INC
0.4	0.3	196.2	297.0	7.1	-17.7	95.7	39.4	135.1	51.3	-17.6	0.0	PAFCO GENERAL INS CO
N/A	N/A	-0.4	87.8	-10.4	-103.3	999 +	999 +	999 +	2.6	85.4	0.0	PALADIN REINSURANCE CORP
5.3	4.8	N/A	N/A	N/A	N/A	N/A	N/A	N/A	N/A	0.0	0.0	PALISADES INS CO
13.5	12.2	N/A	N/A	N/A	N/A	N/A	N/A	N/A	N/A	0.0	1.9	PALISADES PROPERTY & CASUALTY INS
0.6	0.5	158.4	154.5	-11.0	-5.1	73.3	30.3	103.6	94.9	7.7	33.8	PALISADES SAFETY & INS ASSOC
N/A	N/A	-30.7	N/A	N/A	N/A	N/A	39.0	39.0	-320.0	0.0	0.0	PALLADIUM RRG INC
93.4	46.7	N/A	N/A	N/A	N/A	N/A	N/A	N/A	N/A	0.0	0.0	PALMETTO CASUALTY INS CO
0.9	0.8	91.5	16.9	-5.7	-10.1	3.9	80.8	84.7	105.6	47.3	0.0	PALMETTO SURETY CORP
N/A	N/A	N/A	N/A	N/A	N/A	N/A	N/A	N/A	N/A	0.0	0.0	PALOMAR SPECIALTY INS CO
1.5	1.0	100.7	9.2	5.8	-1.8	47.2	38.6	85.8	118.9	7.0	0.0	PANHANDLE FARMERS MUT INS CO OF
1.0	0.9	218.5	106.3	-1.2	21.3	67.3	34.3	101.6	85.8	-24.2	0.0	PARAMOUNT INS CO
1.4	0.9	119.0	175.9	19.3	17.0	98.4	29.4	127.8	99.3	14.6	0.0	PARAMOUNT INS CO
3.8	2.4	28.4	62.7	-9.6	-39.7	49.0	27.4	76.4	90.1	13.1	0.0	PARATRANSIT INS CO A MUTUAL RRG
0.1	0.0	318.2	526.2	120.8	199.9	112.7	20.9	133.6	69.1	-31.4	0.0	PARK INS CO
1.6	1.0	85.5	201.9	-12.8	-28.1	66.6	29.7	96.3	94.6	23.5	3.1 ●	PARTNER REINSURANCE CO OF THE US
14.6	13.1	-0.1	1.1	N/A	-49.1	64.9	999 +	999 +	23.8	-107.4	0.0	PARTNERRE AMERICA INS CO
4.7	2.0	0.1	67.9	1.5	1.7	999 +	-823.2	999 +	57.6	41.3	0.0	PARTNERRE INS CO OF NEW YORK
1.4	1.0	142.9	145.7	0.8	11.3	65.5	33.7	99.2	105.2	85.2	0.0	PARTNERS MUTUAL INS CO
N/A	N/A	N/A	N/A	N/A	N/A	N/A	N/A	N/A	N/A	0.0	0.0	PASSPORT INS CO
50.7	45.6	N/A	N/A	N/A	N/A	N/A	N/A	N/A	78.0	0.0	0.0	PATRIOT GENERAL INS CO
2.6	1.9	150.1	111.4	-14.5	-19.0	63.2	29.3	92.5	107.1	3.6	0.0	PATRIOT INS CO
14.3	9.9	15.7	5.5	-2.5	-4.0	18.6	28.1	46.7	163.3	3.1	0.0	PATRONS MUTUAL FIRE INS CO OF IN
4.3	2.9	40.9	36.6	-0.9	-1.5	68.5	37.2	105.7	148.8	25.8	0.0	PATRONS MUTUAL INS CO OF CT
2.8	2.5	N/A	N/A	N/A	-1.0	N/A	N/A	N/A	17.2	0.0	0.0	PATRONS-OXFORD INS CO
N/A	N/A	N/A	164.4	20.5	317.2	N/A	N/A	N/A	N/A	0.0	0.0	PAWTUCKET INS CO
0.4	0.3	31.9	86.1	-20.0	-59.1	101.7	103.6	205.3	84.9	-60.9	0.0	PCH MUTUAL INS CO INC RRG
6.7	4.3	20.0	32.9	-11.6	-28.2	12.5	7.6	20.1	107.9	-1.4	0.0	PEACE CHURCH RRG INC
0.3	0.3	156.7	40.2	-4.1	4.9	65.0	39.3	104.3	89.3	11.5	0.0	PEACHTREE CASUALTY INS CO
15.5	14.0	N/A	N/A	N/A	N/A	N/A	N/A	N/A	394.9	0.0	0.0	PEAK PROP & CAS INS CORP
78.2	48.0	-89.0	N/A	N/A	N/A	N/A	0.1	N/A	-6.2	-147.8	0.0	PEERLESS INDEMNITY INS CO
1.6	1.1	209.1	248.4	8.6	9.8	73.5	26.9	100.4	999 +	111.8	5.9 ●	PEERLESS INS CO
4.5	3.1	91.5	70.2	-4.5	-10.9	75.4	27.9	103.3	105.8	6.6	3.6 ●	PEKIN INS CO
2.6	1.6	16.1	17.0	-2.0	-6.5	20.1	54.2	74.3	143.7	-22.5	0.0	PELICAN INS RRG
2.7	2.2	145.7	70.9	-2.8	-1.3	72.2	30.4	102.6	98.5	7.2	0.4 ●	PEMCO MUTUAL INS CO
15.3	13.8	N/A	N/A	N/A	N/A	N/A	N/A	N/A	124.9	0.0	0.0	PENINSULA INDEMNITY CO
3.0	2.4	97.6	49.3	3.7	4.3	71.8	28.3	100.1	97.3	0.0	14.8	PENINSULA INS CO
4.4	3.9	25.6	3.1	-4.1	2.4	16.1	297.4	313.5	31.7	-57.9	0.0	PENINSULAR SURETY CO
2.0	1.2	0.4	0.3	-0.2	-0.3	78.5	58.1	136.6	73.3	8.5	0.0	PENN CHARTER MUTUAL INS CO
11.3	10.2	N/A	51.1	-7.5	-9.1	N/A	N/A	N/A	-34.0	100.0	0.0	PENN MILLERS INS CO
2.9	2.0	112.0	114.1	0.6	8.3	65.5	35.4	100.9	99.4	2.1	0.0 ●	PENN NATIONAL SECURITY INS CO
3.3	2.2	109.4	274.9	0.3	-0.8	72.2	39.1	111.3	75.4	20.6	0.0	PENN PATRIOT INS CO
19.6	17.7	6.2	3.7	N/A	N/A	28.0	27.8	55.8	387.9	0.0	0.0	PENN RESERVE INS CO LTD
1.8	1.3	31.9	80.0	0.3	-0.6	72.2	37.8	110.0	73.2	20.6	15.9	PENN-AMERICA INS CO
4.7	3.1	42.8	107.5	0.3	-0.6	72.2	39.6	111.8	83.2	20.6	0.0	PENN-STAR INS CO
1.8	1.0	159.7	70.3	0.4	-1.3	61.0	16.9	77.9	426.9	141.0	0.0	PENNSYLVANIA INS CO
1.6	0.9	104.2	117.0	11.8	8.9	71.8	37.0	108.8	125.4	8.2	0.0	PENNSYLVANIA LUMBERMENS MUTUAL
2.4	1.7	60.4	95.1	9.0	17.5	79.9	26.6	106.5	144.6	-5.3	0.0 ●	PENNSYLVANIA MANUFACTURERS ASN
2.6	1.9	58.6	92.3	8.7	16.5	79.9	25.4	105.3	101.3	-5.3	0.0	PENNSYLVANIA MANUFACTURERS IND
1.6	1.4	58.4	59.5	0.3	4.6	65.5	33.5	99.0	101.5	13.0	33.1 ●	PENNSYLVANIA NTL MUTUAL CAS INS
1.1	0.8	79.3	136.7	-5.8	-20.0	60.8	39.5	100.3	96.1	0.8	0.0	PENNSYLVANIA PHYSICIANS RECIP INS
N/A	N/A	3.5	59.9	-15.0	-16.5	-106.3	46.2	-60.1	16.8	-26.4	0.0	PENNSYLVANIA PROFESSIONAL LIAB

999 + Denotes number greater than 999.9%
999 - Denotes number less than -999.99%
● Bullets denote a more detailed analysis is available in Section II.

INSURANCE COMPANY NAME	DOM. STATE	RATING	TOTAL ASSETS ($MIL)	CAPITAL & SURPLUS ($MIL)	ANNUAL NET PREMIUM ($MIL)	NET INCOME ($MIL)	CAPITAL-IZATION INDEX (PTS)	RESERVE ADQ INDEX (PTS)	PROFIT-ABILITY INDEX (PTS)	LIQUIDITY INDEX (PTS)	STAB. INDEX (PTS)	STABILITY FACTORS
PEOPLES TRUST INS CO	FL	D	242.8	62.7	131.8	0.2	2.8	1.7	3.9	6.7	2.1	GT
PERMANENT GEN ASR CORP OF OHIO	OH	C	162.0	66.1	101.9	2.1	7.8	5.0	4.7	5.5	3.7	R
PERMANENT GENERAL ASR CORP	OH	C	249.0	91.3	182.3	1.3	7.7	4.6	4.3	3.1	3.7	LR
PERSONAL EXPRESS INS CO	CA	C+	21.8	15.9	-5.2	0.7	9.0	5.9	8.6	8.6	4.6	DFRT
PERSONAL SERVICE INS CO	PA	C+	36.1	10.5	16.5	-1.1	7.4	4.5	2.8	4.5	4.4	DFLR
PETROLEUM CAS CO	TX	C-	33.2	24.8	4.0	0.9	6.8	5.7	8.0	10.0	3.3	D
PETROLEUM MARKETERS MGMT INS CO	IA	D	31.5	24.7	3.2	0.8	8.3	7.0	7.8	7.9	2.3	D
PHARMACISTS MUTUAL INS CO	IA	B	253.6	94.3	86.8	4.3	8.5	5.0	6.5	6.6	5.2	
PHENIX MUTUAL FIRE INS CO	NH	C+	62.3	22.1	23.8	0.4	7.4	8.1	6.1	6.3	4.6	D
PHILADELPHIA CBSP FOR INS OF HOUSES	PA	B-	320.6	236.4	35.8	2.7	7.1	6.2	6.6	6.6	4.7	FR
PHILADELPHIA CONTRIBUTIONSHIP INS CO	PA	B-	203.8	110.5	53.8	2.0	8.6	6.6	6.5	6.8	4.7	R
PHILADELPHIA INDEMNITY INS CO	PA	B	7,236.4	2,346.6	2,351.5	178.8	8.5	8.1	8.8	6.6	4.6	R
PHILADELPHIA REINSURANCE CORP	PA	U	214.3	130.0	0.0	3.0	N/A	4.6	5.6	10.0	6.5	T
PHOEBE RECIPROCAL RRG	SC	E	5.5	3.9	0.4	0.0	8.8	9.4	8.7	9.9	0.0	D
PHOENIX FUND INC	NC	F (5)	0.0	0.0	25.2	0.0	0.0	0.3	5.2	5.9	0.0	CDT
PHOENIX INS CO	CT	B	4,191.2	1,750.8	1,006.9	101.1	7.4	8.4	8.3	6.8	6.3	T
PHP RRG LTD	AZ	U	27.0	8.3	0.0	0.9	N/A	6.0	2.9	10.0	0.0	CFRT
PHYSICIANS CASUALTY RRG INC	NV	D+	6.9	1.3	2.0	0.1	3.8	4.0	4.1	9.1	1.0	DGT
PHYSICIANS IND RRG INC	NV	D-	7.8	1.6	2.0	0.9	1.2	9.7	0.9	6.2	1.0	DFT
PHYSICIANS INS A MUTUAL CO	WA	B-	470.6	217.7	72.9	7.8	10.0	9.6	8.3	7.4	4.7	R
PHYSICIANS INS CO	FL	D	13.0	5.6	0.4	-3.3	8.7	7.0	2.1	6.8	2.0	DFRT
PHYSICIANS INS EXCHANGE RESOURCE	VT	E	4.9	1.9	0.8	0.6	0.8	5.0	1.8	7.0	0.0	CDT
PHYSICIANS INS MUTUAL	MO	E+	4.9	1.6	0.9	0.1	5.6	4.1	4.6	6.6	0.5	DFT
PHYSICIANS INS PROGRAM RECIP EXCH	PA	D	26.4	10.2	4.2	-1.8	5.9	9.6	4.1	7.4	2.3	DFR
PHYSICIANS PROACTIVE PROTECTION INC	SC	D	62.9	19.1	9.0	2.1	7.3	9.9	8.2	8.0	2.3	DR
PHYSICIANS PROFESSIONAL IND ASSN	MO	E	10.9	0.8	3.5	-0.5	0.4	3.3	0.8	5.5	0.0	CDFR
PHYSICIANS PROFESSIONAL LIABILTY RRG	VT	C	40.2	19.8	4.9	0.4	9.0	9.8	6.7	7.6	4.2	DFR
PHYSICIANS RECIPROCAL INSURERS	NY	E-	1,447.3	-88.2	376.7	40.9	0.0	10.0	0.6	7.0	0.0	CFRT
PHYSICIANS REIMBURSEMENT FUND RRG	VT	D-	29.5	10.9	2.8	0.1	4.1	10.0	6.2	7.0	0.5	DR
PHYSICIANS RRG LLC	MT	U (5)	0.0	0.0	0.7	0.0	N/A	0.0	2.8	0.0	0.0	CDFG
PHYSICIANS SPECIALTY LTD RRG	SC	D-	14.2	4.2	1.4	0.3	2.8	9.6	2.5	10.0	1.0	DFR
PIA PROFESSIONAL LIABILITY INS RRG	MT	D	2.1	1.4	0.4	0.0	6.0	3.6	1.9	5.5	1.2	DFGT
PIEDMONT MUTUAL INS CO	NC	D	3.7	2.3	1.6	0.1	6.6	8.5	4.4	7.4	1.8	DFGR
PIH INS CO A RECIP RRG	HI	B-	13.2	7.1	3.4	0.5	7.4	6.1	9.5	6.9	3.5	D
PILGRIM INS CO	MA	C	59.6	15.9	25.1	-0.1	7.3	6.4	5.7	6.3	4.0	D
PINE TREE INS RECIPROCAL RRG	VT	D-	11.3	3.2	1.5	0.4	7.5	5.0	1.9	6.6	1.0	DFT
PINELANDS INS CO RRG INC	DC	E	3.4	0.7	1.4	-0.3	0.4	0.4	1.5	2.9	0.1	CDFL
PINNACLE CONSORTIUM OF HIGHER ED	VT	D	8.4	4.4	0.9	0.1	7.4	6.9	4.8	8.1	1.4	DFR
PINNACLEPOINT INS CO	WV	C-	54.5	10.0	9.3	0.3	4.5	N/A	3.1	7.0	3.3	CDT
PINNACOL ASR CO	CO	U (5)	2,094.0	641.4	372.8	0.0	N/A	4.8	0.4	7.0	0.0	CT
PIONEER SPECIALTY INS CO	MN	C-	56.9	23.0	20.5	1.3	8.4	8.6	8.4	6.6	3.3	DR
PIONEER STATE MUTUAL INS CO	MI	A	464.9	265.3	171.1	4.5	9.8	8.5	8.2	6.9	7.4	
PLANS LIABILITY INS CO	OH	C	81.2	38.6	2.5	-1.6	3.2	8.5	1.6	9.0	3.5	CDF
PLATEAU CASUALTY INS CO	TN	C	37.7	19.8	13.7	0.2	7.2	5.5	5.4	7.1	4.1	DR
PLATINUM UNDERWRITERS REINS CO	MD	B-	1,652.7	581.9	395.4	36.3	7.6	9.4	5.1	7.7	5.0	
PLATTE RIVER INS CO	NE	C	126.4	40.8	25.7	0.1	8.4	4.1	5.2	8.7	3.6	FR
PLAZA INS CO	IA	C	55.4	26.3	0.0	0.3	10.0	3.6	4.8	7.7	3.7	RT
PLICO INC	OK	D	152.1	60.5	33.7	4.5	7.7	10.0	8.4	7.0	2.3	FR
PLICO RRG INC	OK	U	1.6	1.6	0.0	0.0	N/A	N/A	3.6	10.0	3.1	FT
PLYMOUTH ROCK ASR CORP	MA	B-	485.6	160.0	288.7	29.0	8.0	8.2	6.7	4.8	4.7	LR
PMI INS CO	AZ	F	95.4	64.7	5.6	0.9	8.3	0.9	2.4	9.1	0.0	DRT
PMI MORTGAGE INS CO	AZ	F	1,370.8	-1,411.1	354.4	111.8	0.0	0.5	0.6	10.0	0.0	CRT

See Page 27 for explanation of footnotes and Page 28 for explanation of stability factors.

Arrows denote recent upgrades ▲ or downgrades ▼   (see Section VII for explanations)

106

www.weissratings.com

RISK ADJ. RATIO #1	CAPITAL RATIO #2	PREMIUM TO SURPLUS (%)	RESV. TO SURPLUS (%)	RESV. 1 YEAR (%)	DEVELOP. 2 YEAR (%)	LOSS RATIO (%)	EXP. RATIO (%)	COMB RATIO (%)	CASH FROM UNDER-WRITING (%)	NET PREMIUM GROWTH (%)	INVEST. IN AFFIL (%)	INSURANCE COMPANY NAME
0.6	0.4	215.1	53.9	9.5	42.8	40.1	33.2	73.3	189.0	136.9	0.0	PEOPLES TRUST INS CO
1.7	1.6	161.3	54.3	1.9	2.6	70.7	28.4	99.1	102.5	12.7	16.5	PERMANENT GEN ASR CORP OF OHIO
1.6	1.4	208.4	70.1	2.0	2.7	70.7	28.3	99.0	93.2	12.7	0.7	PERMANENT GENERAL ASR CORP
9.4	8.5	-35.1	2.9	-15.2	-2.5	41.4	16.7	58.1	-159.8	-138.3	2.1	PERSONAL EXPRESS INS CO
1.4	1.3	150.0	85.5	14.0	14.2	77.5	20.1	97.6	106.4	-12.1	0.0	PERSONAL SERVICE INS CO
1.5	0.9	16.8	33.3	0.1	0.6	31.3	29.1	60.4	133.9	-4.9	0.0	PETROLEUM CAS CO
3.2	1.9	12.4	17.2	-2.6	-5.5	22.6	44.5	67.1	156.4	-1.5	0.0	PETROLEUM MARKETERS MGMT INS CO
3.5	2.3	97.9	108.8	-8.5	-9.7	62.6	30.0	92.6	112.3	4.4	4.8	PHARMACISTS MUTUAL INS CO
2.1	1.4	109.8	85.2	-1.3	-2.4	66.8	34.9	101.7	103.3	4.8	0.0	PHENIX MUTUAL FIRE INS CO
1.3	1.1	15.2	10.1	-1.5	-2.0	63.0	32.5	95.5	93.6	8.1	47.7 •	PHILADELPHIA CBSP FOR INS OF
3.2	2.0	50.1	30.1	-4.9	-6.6	60.4	25.6	86.0	118.6	8.0	0.0	PHILADELPHIA CONTRIBUTIONSHIP INS
2.6	2.0	109.0	134.3	-1.1	-3.7	61.0	28.8	89.8	126.0	10.7	0.0 •	PHILADELPHIA INDEMNITY INS CO
N/A	N/A	N/A	55.2	N/A	-0.2	N/A	N/A	N/A	N/A	0.0	0.0	PHILADELPHIA REINSURANCE CORP
4.2	2.1	11.5	35.0	-9.3	-14.7	-3.4	31.3	27.9	273.1	5.7	0.0	PHOEBE RECIPROCAL RRG
0.1	0.1	378.0	273.0	49.1	32.3	71.3	27.2	98.5	133.5	0.0	0.0	PHOENIX FUND INC
1.6	1.4	63.8	114.7	-1.8	-4.2	60.9	29.7	90.6	110.9	3.0	29.2 •	PHOENIX INS CO
N/A	N/A	N/A	203.5	-12.3	-78.8	N/A	N/A	N/A	15.8	-100.0	0.0	PHP RRG LTD
0.8	0.6	202.8	64.4	-26.3	-17.1	32.8	27.0	59.8	220.6	214.3	0.0	PHYSICIANS CASUALTY RRG INC
0.8	0.6	316.3	567.7	-9.1	-24.6	81.7	53.2	134.9	80.2	-19.6	0.0	PHYSICIANS IND RRG INC
4.0	3.1	34.4	92.8	-10.3	-20.7	85.2	16.3	101.5	112.2	7.6	3.1 •	PHYSICIANS INS A MUTUAL CO
1.6	1.3	4.4	50.5	4.0	3.2	37.5	125.8	163.3	30.3	-89.9	0.0	PHYSICIANS INS CO
1.1	0.7	60.7	327.9	57.4	41.3	136.9	80.2	217.1	95.5	-42.9	0.0	PHYSICIANS INS EXCHANGE RESOURCE
1.3	0.9	58.2	171.5	-50.3	-43.4	10.0	14.4	24.4	110.8	-8.6	0.0	PHYSICIANS INS MUTUAL
1.3	0.8	35.0	114.7	-9.4	-17.5	54.3	46.5	100.8	83.1	-11.8	0.0	PHYSICIANS INS PROGRAM RECIP EXCH
2.3	1.5	53.2	99.9	-4.9	-37.0	47.9	16.0	63.9	189.6	-17.5	0.0	PHYSICIANS PROACTIVE PROTECTION
0.1	0.1	382.6	893.1	59.0	58.0	96.7	37.3	134.0	71.6	-21.6	0.0	PHYSICIANS PROFESSIONAL IND ASSN
3.1	2.6	25.6	63.7	-10.7	-25.7	52.2	66.7	118.9	65.0	-11.5	0.0	PHYSICIANS PROFESSIONAL LIABILTY
-0.0	-0.0	-319.1	999 +	-30.5	-42.4	81.8	21.8	103.6	88.4	3.0	0.0	PHYSICIANS RECIPROCAL INSURERS
0.7	0.6	25.7	151.6	-20.9	-55.6	73.8	55.3	129.1	93.1	-17.1	0.0	PHYSICIANS REIMBURSEMENT FUND
N/A	N/A	85.2	115.9	22.9	-10.0	104.8	24.8	129.6	81.5	10.9	0.0	PHYSICIANS RRG LLC
0.6	0.4	37.4	177.4	9.5	-27.1	154.8	-5.6	149.2	-48.1	-8.7	0.0	PHYSICIANS SPECIALTY LTD RRG
0.9	0.7	27.9	17.6	7.0	-0.1	116.0	78.1	194.1	74.6	65.8	0.0	PIA PROFESSIONAL LIABILITY INS RRG
1.4	1.0	74.6	10.3	-6.3	-2.6	41.0	48.7	89.7	90.1	23.9	0.2	PIEDMONT MUTUAL INS CO
1.8	1.1	52.9	59.2	2.7	-3.0	74.2	14.7	88.9	159.2	-14.7	0.0	PIH INS CO A RECIP RRG
1.2	0.9	170.9	65.8	1.8	-0.2	73.1	25.0	98.1	114.0	12.3	0.0	PILGRIM INS CO
0.8	0.6	22.3	56.8	6.8	-20.6	206.8	36.6	243.4	37.1	-39.5	0.0	PINE TREE INS RECIPROCAL RRG
0.1	0.1	207.6	260.1	74.4	71.0	147.0	5.6	152.6	52.8	17.9	0.0	PINELANDS INS CO RRG INC
1.9	1.2	21.8	43.5	-4.3	-10.3	41.9	54.7	96.6	50.8	-2.5	0.0	PINNACLE CONSORTIUM OF HIGHER ED
1.0	0.4	96.6	216.1	N/A	N/A	75.1	15.5	90.6	-46.3	0.0	0.0	PINNACLEPOINT INS CO
N/A	N/A	-384.1	-828.6	50.0	-14.1	90.8	13.0	103.8	82.3	N/A	0.0	PINNACOL ASR CO
2.7	1.9	94.2	74.4	-2.1	-4.0	68.7	26.6	95.3	106.2	9.7	0.0	PIONEER SPECIALTY INS CO
4.5	2.8	65.8	30.3	-4.2	-6.9	64.4	29.6	94.0	114.9	4.5	0.0 •	PIONEER STATE MUTUAL INS CO
0.6	0.5	6.4	80.4	15.8	-7.1	556.0	153.8	709.8	38.3	18.1	0.0	PLANS LIABILITY INS CO
1.4	1.1	75.0	5.8	-1.6	-2.1	38.3	51.2	89.5	117.4	16.3	38.0	PLATEAU CASUALTY INS CO
2.6	1.6	72.0	169.0	-14.0	-27.4	43.4	33.7	77.1	109.2	3.6	0.0 •	PLATINUM UNDERWRITERS REINS CO
3.0	1.7	62.2	67.2	11.2	16.3	67.8	51.2	119.0	92.7	14.9	0.0	PLATTE RIVER INS CO
5.8	5.2	N/A	N/A	N/A	N/A	N/A	N/A	N/A	-445.2	0.0	0.0	PLAZA INS CO
3.2	2.4	60.0	116.8	-14.9	-40.9	63.0	17.0	80.0	84.0	26.3	2.9	PLICO INC
N/A	N/A	0.3	0.3	N/A	N/A	90.0	451.7	541.7	4.5	0.0	0.0	PLICO RRG INC
1.7	1.2	188.9	72.8	2.0	-0.3	73.1	24.3	97.4	107.8	10.7	0.0	PLYMOUTH ROCK ASR CORP
5.5	4.1	8.7	33.8	-38.8	-48.9	-254.6	-4.9	-259.5	179.4	24.3	0.0	PMI INS CO
-0.9	-0.7	-22.9	-202.1	3.5	-11.9	103.3	-154.0	-50.7	-144.2	-2.4	9.8	PMI MORTGAGE INS CO

999 + Denotes number greater than 999.9%
999 - Denotes number less than -999.99%
• Bullets denote a more detailed analysis is available in Section II.

INSURANCE COMPANY NAME	DOM. STATE	RATING	TOTAL ASSETS ($MIL)	CAPITAL & SURPLUS ($MIL)	ANNUAL NET PREMIUM ($MIL)	NET INCOME ($MIL)	CAPITAL-IZATION INDEX (PTS)	RESERVE ADQ INDEX (PTS)	PROFIT-ABILITY INDEX (PTS)	LIQUIDITY INDEX (PTS)	STAB. INDEX (PTS)	STABILITY FACTORS
PMSLIC INS CO	PA	B-	467.5	223.8	78.5	1.5	10.0	9.4	6.8	7.4	4.6	T
PODIATRY INS CO OF AMERICA	IL	C+	335.7	122.7	75.0	6.2	6.9	9.3	7.9	7.3	4.6	A
POINT GUARD INS CO	PR	D	23.5	9.0	4.3	2.8	5.2	N/A	2.8	9.6	1.8	DFT
POLICYHOLDERS MUTUAL INS CO	WI	U	0.3	0.3	0.0	0.0	N/A	N/A	7.0	10.0	0.8	RT
PONCE DE LEON LTC RRG INC	FL	D	11.1	5.1	1.9	-0.1	7.1	5.0	1.5	6.5	1.4	DFR
POSITIVE PHYSICIANS INS EXCHANGE	PA	D	48.9	13.5	7.8	0.4	2.6	9.4	7.7	7.9	2.0	CDR
POTOMAC INS CO	PA	U	11.4	10.9	0.0	0.1	N/A	0.3	1.9	0.0	0.0	CFLR
PRAETORIAN INS CO	PA	C-	1,261.3	245.7	400.0	-3.9	7.2	4.1	1.9	7.0	3.1	FRT
PRE-PAID LEGAL CAS INC	OK	C	16.5	14.1	55.7	2.7	4.9	7.3	4.4	1.5	4.0	DLT
PREFERRED AUTO INS CO INC	TN	D-	7.5	2.9	2.1	0.2	8.9	9.3	5.1	8.9	0.9	DR
PREFERRED CONTRACTORS INS CO RRG	MT	E+	92.0	14.5	21.0	0.4	0.6	2.4	4.6	6.6	0.7	CDGR
PREFERRED EMPLOYERS INS CO	CA	C	89.8	44.1	-1.1	1.8	10.0	4.8	5.6	10.0	4.2	FRT
PREFERRED MANAGED RISK LTD	DC	U (5)	0.0	0.0	9.4	0.0	N/A	3.6	8.9	5.6	0.0	CDT
PREFERRED MUTUAL INS CO	NY	B	500.3	195.2	193.6	10.4	8.9	9.3	5.7	6.7	5.7	
PREFERRED PHYSICIANS MEDICAL RRG	MO	B-	202.8	114.7	26.0	5.0	10.0	9.5	8.9	7.8	5.3	T
PREFERRED PROFESSIONAL INS CO	NE	C+	300.7	138.6	45.3	6.5	10.0	9.4	5.0	8.4	4.4	FR
PREFERRED PROFESSIONAL RRG	DC	U	0.6	0.6	0.0	0.0	N/A	N/A	2.5	10.0	0.0	FT
PREMIER GROUP INS CO INC	TN	C-	54.2	32.9	14.1	2.5	9.0	9.1	8.8	7.1	3.2	DR
PREMIER INS CO OF MASSACHUSETTS	MA	B	361.7	228.8	132.1	9.4	10.0	4.7	5.8	6.7	5.8	F
PREMIER INS EXCHANGE RRG	VT	U (3)	0.0	0.0	0.0	-0.1	N/A	6.6	3.0	7.0	3.7	FT
PREMIER PHYSICIANS INS CO INC A RRG	NV	E+	11.8	3.3	4.4	-0.3	5.6	7.0	4.8	8.1	0.5	DF
PREPARED INS CO	FL	C-	54.5	16.6	24.6	0.0	3.5	4.6	3.6	6.9	3.3	DG
PRESERVER INS CO	NJ	D	146.4	8.5	53.6	-1.9	7.2	4.6	3.2	5.6	1.7	CDFR
PREVISOR INS CO	CO	U	5.3	5.2	0.0	-0.1	N/A	N/A	3.3	7.0	3.4	FT
PRIME INS CO	IL	D+	68.9	34.5	25.7	4.4	7.0	5.8	8.3	7.1	2.6	GR
PRIME P&C INS INC	IL	C-	18.6	11.4	7.1	1.2	10.0	N/A	4.8	9.0	3.0	DGT
▼PRIMEONE INS CO	MI	C-	16.7	9.0	6.4	-4.3	5.2	3.8	1.8	9.3	2.5	DFT
PRIMERO INS CO	NV	D	12.4	5.9	12.7	0.2	5.9	8.1	2.3	2.9	1.9	DFLR
PRINCETON EXCESS & SURPLUS LINES INS	DE	C	179.9	63.3	0.0	6.3	10.0	N/A	5.3	10.0	3.6	FR
PRINCETON INS CO	NJ	C	658.9	452.7	35.1	10.8	10.0	6.1	8.5	9.0	3.7	RT
PRIORITY ONE INS CO	TX	C	20.8	11.4	7.3	-0.6	8.3	8.1	2.3	6.5	3.6	DFR
PRIVILEGE UNDERWRITERS RECIP EXCH	FL	B-	208.2	64.7	74.4	-11.5	6.7	6.2	2.7	7.0	3.7	GT
PROAIR RRG INC	NV	U (1)	0.5	0.0	0.2	-0.4	N/A	6.5	0.1	2.6	0.0	LT
PROASSURANCE CASUALTY CO	MI	B-	1,291.9	513.6	166.0	56.3	9.3	9.9	7.6	7.5	4.6	AR
PROASSURANCE INDEMNTIY CO INC	AL	B-	1,737.4	633.8	240.0	78.5	10.0	9.8	7.1	7.4	4.6	AR
PROASSURANCE SPECIALTY INS CO INC	AL	C	40.2	29.4	0.0	0.0	10.0	N/A	6.8	9.9	4.3	D
PROBUILDERS SPECIALTY INS CO RRG	DC	U	36.8	13.2	0.0	-0.5	N/A	5.2	1.7	10.0	2.9	FRT
PROCENTURY INS CO	MI	B-	207.5	47.4	64.7	2.5	7.0	3.5	5.4	6.2	4.9	R
PRODUCERS AGRICULTURE INS CO	TX	U	432.2	61.5	0.1	4.7	N/A	4.3	5.4	7.0	6.3	T
PRODUCERS LLOYDS INS CO	TX	C	7.0	6.1	0.0	0.0	10.0	N/A	6.2	10.0	3.6	DFRT
PROFESSIONAL CASUALTY ASSN	PA	C-	52.8	12.8	12.3	-0.4	3.3	9.7	4.6	7.5	2.9	DR
▲PROFESSIONAL EXCHANGE ASR CO (A	HI	E+	4.2	1.2	1.4	0.0	0.3	N/A	5.9	7.2	0.4	CDGT
PROFESSIONAL INS EXCHANGE MUTUAL	UT	D	8.0	5.4	1.2	0.1	7.5	4.0	4.2	8.0	1.4	D
PROFESSIONAL LIAB INS CO OF AMERICA	NY	F (5)	0.0	0.0	11.4	0.0	2.4	1.6	3.0	6.7	0.0	CDFR
PROFESSIONAL QUALITY LIABILITY INS	VT	D	2.2	2.1	0.0	0.0	10.0	6.0	4.0	4.7	1.8	DFLR
PROFESSIONAL SECURITY INS CO	AZ	C	22.5	17.4	0.1	0.1	10.0	3.6	4.6	10.0	3.3	DFT
PROFESSIONAL SOLUTIONS INS CO	IA	D	21.1	9.1	2.9	-0.3	7.8	8.7	3.7	7.1	2.3	DR
PROFESSIONALS ADVOCATE INS CO	MD	B-	126.1	95.7	6.3	1.3	10.0	9.3	8.9	10.0	4.6	T
PROFESSIONALS DIRECT INS CO	MI	U	22.2	22.2	0.0	0.4	N/A	1.6	7.7	7.0	2.4	RT
PROFESSIONALS RRG INC	MT	D	3.4	1.3	0.5	-0.2	8.6	7.0	4.5	7.0	1.3	DT
PROGRESSIVE ADVANCED INS CO	OH	C	345.6	136.1	229.7	6.6	8.2	8.0	8.9	2.2	3.6	LR
PROGRESSIVE AMERICAN INS CO	OH	C	409.1	166.2	190.1	7.2	9.9	6.2	8.7	5.8	4.0	R

See Page 27 for explanation of footnotes and Page 28 for explanation of stability factors.

108

www.weissratings.com

Arrows denote recent upgrades ▲ or downgrades ▼ (see Section VII for explanations)

RISK ADJ. CAPITAL RATIO #1	RATIO #2	PREMIUM TO SURPLUS (%)	RESV. TO SURPLUS (%)	RESV. DEVELOP. 1 YEAR (%)	2 YEAR (%)	LOSS RATIO (%)	EXP. RATIO (%)	COMB RATIO (%)	CASH FROM UNDER-WRITING (%)	NET PREMIUM GROWTH (%)	INVEST. IN AFFIL (%)	INSURANCE COMPANY NAME
4.7	3.5	35.7	81.8	-3.2	-10.2	79.3	24.4	103.7	102.3	1.3	0.0 •	PMSLIC INS CO
2.1	1.5	65.7	144.2	-9.7	-10.0	66.8	23.3	90.1	105.4	-3.9	0.0	PODIATRY INS CO OF AMERICA
2.7	1.5	192.2	15.8	N/A	N/A	64.2	23.6	87.8	69.6	0.0	0.0	POINT GUARD INS CO
N/A	N/A	4.0	N/A	N/A	N/A	N/A	107.5	107.5	93.1	-5.0	0.0	POLICYHOLDERS MUTUAL INS CO
1.4	1.1	29.7	91.4	5.7	-0.3	177.4	75.6	253.0	47.2	-23.9	0.0	PONCE DE LEON LTC RRG INC
0.6	0.4	60.6	209.3	-18.7	-30.9	55.1	38.1	93.2	129.4	-1.3	0.0	POSITIVE PHYSICIANS INS EXCHANGE
N/A	N/A	0.1	999 +	N/A	N/A	999 +	33.4	999 +	N/A	N/A	0.0	POTOMAC INS CO
1.5	1.0	161.1	155.2	8.4	16.6	75.2	35.3	110.5	81.9	-26.6	0.0 •	PRAETORIAN INS CO
0.8	0.7	309.7	0.6	-0.4	-0.4	34.7	51.0	85.7	116.7	2.8	0.0	PRE-PAID LEGAL CAS INC
2.0	1.8	77.5	46.9	-6.9	-8.8	77.1	21.9	99.0	88.3	9.0	0.0	PREFERRED AUTO INS CO INC
0.4	0.2	164.4	256.4	7.1	33.5	61.1	36.8	97.9	139.5	35.4	0.0	PREFERRED CONTRACTORS INS CO
7.1	6.3	-2.6	N/A	N/A	N/A	N/A	N/A	N/A	-331.5	-113.8	0.0	PREFERRED EMPLOYERS INS CO
N/A	N/A	577.4	347.5	-19.0	N/A	62.0	25.8	87.8	238.6	0.0	0.0	PREFERRED MANAGED RISK LTD
3.4	2.2	104.5	81.2	-4.4	-9.8	65.5	30.1	95.6	113.1	6.1	0.1	PREFERRED MUTUAL INS CO
7.2	5.5	23.5	56.3	-6.7	-19.0	51.4	18.0	69.4	105.8	-11.6	0.0	PREFERRED PHYSICIANS MEDICAL RRG
4.5	3.2	22.0	60.0	-18.1	-26.8	26.5	6.8	33.3	98.0	-20.3	0.3 •	PREFERRED PROFESSIONAL INS CO
N/A	N/A	3.7	0.8	N/A	N/A	90.0	500.8	590.8	N/A	0.0	0.0	PREFERRED PROFESSIONAL RRG
2.9	2.4	45.6	50.8	-4.5	-4.3	48.5	7.3	55.8	130.7	-3.7	0.0	PREMIER GROUP INS CO INC
7.1	6.1	60.1	28.8	2.6	4.6	76.9	27.1	104.0	90.5	-13.9	0.0 •	PREMIER INS CO OF MASSACHUSETTS
N/A	N/A	N/A	4.6	0.1	0.2	N/A	N/A	N/A	N/A	0.0	0.0	PREMIER INS EXCHANGE RRG
1.0	0.7	121.6	98.2	13.8	-24.9	52.9	54.8	107.7	73.5	-18.2	0.0	PREMIER PHYSICIANS INS CO INC A
0.9	0.6	156.0	44.1	2.2	2.4	46.0	43.6	89.6	149.8	40.1	0.0	PREPARED INS CO
0.6	0.5	538.2	865.3	58.1	56.0	105.8	56.7	162.5	54.6	-26.4	3.0	PRESERVER INS CO
N/A	N/A	N/A	N/A	N/A	N/A	N/A	N/A	N/A	N/A	0.0	0.0	PREVISOR INS CO
1.5	1.0	89.2	51.9	3.8	5.5	51.8	22.0	73.8	137.8	48.2	24.5	PRIME INS CO
4.4	2.4	69.1	12.1	N/A	N/A	61.1	13.2	74.3	760.8	0.0	0.0	PRIME P&C INS INC
1.1	0.6	47.4	50.0	-3.9	-3.8	70.1	64.2	134.3	57.3	-17.2	0.0	PRIMEONE INS CO
1.2	1.1	219.6	102.5	-4.9	-2.3	82.1	24.8	106.9	87.2	1.3	0.0	PRIMERO INS CO
6.9	6.2	N/A	N/A	N/A	N/A	N/A	N/A	N/A	128.9	0.0	0.0	PRINCETON EXCESS & SURPLUS LINES
8.0	6.0	8.0	29.1	0.5	-132.4	104.5	14.4	118.9	134.4	107.0	0.0 •	PRINCETON INS CO
2.4	1.7	61.4	22.3	5.0	-7.6	87.5	41.0	128.5	79.0	1.9	7.8	PRIORITY ONE INS CO
1.7	1.0	123.8	25.6	2.0	-1.5	51.9	47.8	99.7	124.4	64.0	0.0	PRIVILEGE UNDERWRITERS RECIP
N/A	N/A	44.4	12.2	-1.6	-3.5	64.5	81.9	146.4	101.6	70.3	0.0	PROAIR RRG INC
3.7	2.8	31.7	127.3	-13.0	-37.7	52.4	27.9	80.3	95.0	-8.3	0.0 •	PROASSURANCE CASUALTY CO
4.2	3.2	31.8	100.1	-18.1	-35.6	26.8	20.3	47.1	105.8	-6.6	0.5 •	PROASSURANCE INDEMNTIY CO INC
11.7	10.5	N/A	11.5	N/A	N/A	N/A	N/A	N/A	184.0	0.0	0.0	PROASSURANCE SPECIALTY INS CO INC
N/A	N/A	N/A	175.7	-26.3	-12.3	N/A	N/A	N/A	0.2	0.0	0.0	PROBUILDERS SPECIALTY INS CO RRG
1.9	1.3	140.6	226.6	15.8	32.6	79.2	34.5	113.7	95.9	-14.0	0.0	PROCENTURY INS CO
N/A	N/A	0.1	10.3	0.3	2.5	999 +	999 +	999 +	41.7	-7.1	97.1	PRODUCERS AGRICULTURE INS CO
14.4	12.9	N/A	N/A	N/A	N/A	N/A	N/A	N/A	-2.4	0.0	0.0	PRODUCERS LLOYDS INS CO
1.1	0.8	93.2	223.2	-13.7	-14.5	52.0	41.4	93.4	120.3	1.5	0.0	PROFESSIONAL CASUALTY ASSN
0.3	0.2	213.3	143.9	N/A	N/A	68.8	25.4	94.2	426.2	0.0	0.0	PROFESSIONAL EXCHANGE ASR CO (A
1.6	1.2	23.9	29.8	0.3	10.3	60.8	43.9	104.7	103.9	-3.4	0.0	PROFESSIONAL INS EXCHANGE MUTUAL
0.5	0.4	50.2	89.5	11.6	40.3	85.3	94.2	179.5	73.0	-30.8	0.0	PROFESSIONAL LIAB INS CO OF
29.1	20.2	1.2	3.2	0.3	-0.5	98.3	193.1	291.4	17.1	-5.7	0.0	PROFESSIONAL QUALITY LIABILITY INS
7.3	4.9	0.8	0.9	N/A	N/A	999 +	415.0	999 +	-26.9	0.0	0.0	PROFESSIONAL SECURITY INS CO
1.8	1.3	31.2	52.6	-6.2	-12.1	66.7	33.1	99.8	101.9	11.2	0.0	PROFESSIONAL SOLUTIONS INS CO
19.9	16.1	6.6	16.0	-3.9	-8.6	14.8	-53.0	-38.2	-103.0	-5.9	0.0	PROFESSIONALS ADVOCATE INS CO
N/A	N/A	N/A	N/A	N/A	N/A	N/A	N/A	N/A	N/A	0.0	0.0	PROFESSIONALS DIRECT INS CO
1.8	1.6	31.9	19.7	-11.1	-7.8	-11.1	8.1	-3.0	162.8	24.1	0.0	PROFESSIONALS RRG INC
2.0	1.9	178.0	70.0	-1.1	-0.9	72.4	20.4	92.8	103.0	4.8	0.0	PROGRESSIVE ADVANCED INS CO
3.5	3.1	120.0	49.8	0.6	1.0	72.9	21.0	93.9	108.3	4.7	0.0	PROGRESSIVE AMERICAN INS CO

999 + Denotes number greater than 999.9%
999 - Denotes number less than -999.99%
• Bullets denote a more detailed analysis is available in Section II.

INSURANCE COMPANY NAME	DOM. STATE	RATING	TOTAL ASSETS ($MIL)	CAPITAL & SURPLUS ($MIL)	ANNUAL NET PREMIUM ($MIL)	NET INCOME ($MIL)	CAPITAL-IZATION INDEX (PTS)	RESERVE ADQ INDEX (PTS)	PROFIT-ABILITY INDEX (PTS)	LIQUIDITY INDEX (PTS)	STAB. INDEX (PTS)	STABILITY FACTORS
PROGRESSIVE BAYSIDE INS CO	OH	C	112.7	34.5	95.1	4.1	7.3	6.4	8.3	4.0	3.5	LR
PROGRESSIVE CASUALTY INS CO	OH	C+	6,444.3	1,629.6	4,657.8	223.4	5.1	6.5	9.4	1.2	4.5	LR
PROGRESSIVE CHOICE INS CO	OH	C	13.4	7.4	0.0	-0.6	9.7	6.4	1.9	7.0	2.9	DFRT
PROGRESSIVE CLASSIC INS CO	WI	C	349.6	104.2	285.2	12.0	7.3	6.5	9.1	4.9	4.3	LR
PROGRESSIVE COMMERCIAL CASUALTY	OH	U	9.4	9.4	0.0	0.1	N/A	N/A	6.4	7.0	5.3	OT
PROGRESSIVE COUNTY MUTUAL INS CO	TX	C-	434.1	5.0	0.0	0.0	2.7	N/A	3.9	7.0	3.2	CRT
PROGRESSIVE DIRECT INS CO	OH	C-	5,269.8	1,613.8	4,450.2	174.0	7.2	8.4	9.2	1.3	2.9	LR
PROGRESSIVE EXPRESS INS CO	OH	C	188.3	50.0	37.0	2.6	10.0	6.7	7.6	4.7	3.6	LR
PROGRESSIVE FREEDOM INS CO	NJ	C (3)	0.0	0.0	0.6	0.2	9.4	6.6	3.2	7.0	2.9	DRT
PROGRESSIVE GARDEN STATE INS CO	NJ	C+(3)	0.0	0.0	40.1	2.5	9.1	5.9	7.1	6.7	4.5	R
PROGRESSIVE GULF INS CO	OH	C	276.4	106.2	190.1	10.3	8.3	6.1	2.1	5.8	3.7	R
PROGRESSIVE HAWAII INS CORP	OH	C	168.8	59.3	130.1	15.1	7.3	8.8	9.6	4.5	3.6	LR
PROGRESSIVE MARATHON INS CO	MI	C	413.3	132.1	344.5	12.6	7.3	8.3	8.9	2.7	3.6	LR
PROGRESSIVE MAX INS CO	OH	C	385.1	121.1	344.5	11.3	7.1	8.4	8.9	2.6	3.7	LR
PROGRESSIVE MICHIGAN INS CO	MI	C	476.2	149.4	380.2	18.0	7.4	6.4	8.6	4.6	3.8	LR
PROGRESSIVE MOUNTAIN INS CO	OH	B-	228.7	67.1	95.1	6.0	9.0	6.3	7.7	5.7	4.5	R
PROGRESSIVE NORTHERN INS CO	WI	C+	1,437.1	436.1	1,140.7	59.2	7.2	6.5	9.3	1.8	4.4	LR
PROGRESSIVE NORTHWESTERN INS CO	OH	C+	1,391.0	433.9	1,140.7	62.8	7.2	6.5	9.3	2.9	4.5	LR
PROGRESSIVE PALOVERDE INS CO	IN	C	118.6	37.7	28.7	1.8	9.5	7.5	8.9	6.3	3.5	FR
PROGRESSIVE PREFERRED INS CO	OH	C	729.8	216.9	570.3	33.0	7.3	6.5	9.3	2.6	4.0	LR
PROGRESSIVE PREMIER INS CO OF IL	OH	B-	203.4	50.6	114.8	3.9	7.5	8.2	8.9	3.9	4.5	LR
PROGRESSIVE SECURITY INS CO	LA	C	255.5	48.6	39.2	3.6	10.0	5.9	8.6	6.6	3.9	R
PROGRESSIVE SELECT INS CO	OH	C	504.6	136.6	105.4	4.1	10.0	6.3	8.5	5.3	3.7	FR
PROGRESSIVE SOUTHEASTERN INS CO	IN	C+	157.5	57.5	95.1	4.9	7.8	6.3	8.9	2.8	4.5	LR
PROGRESSIVE SPECIALTY INS CO	OH	C	1,037.0	442.3	665.4	38.4	8.4	6.1	2.5	5.1	3.9	R
PROGRESSIVE UNIVERSAL INS CO	WI	C+	308.4	103.5	229.7	9.0	7.6	8.3	8.9	1.3	4.4	LR
PROGRESSIVE WEST INS CO	OH	C	139.0	34.6	29.4	1.2	9.8	6.2	6.8	7.0	3.6	R
PROPERTY & CASUALTY I CO OF	IN	B	236.5	115.3	49.7	9.8	10.0	6.2	6.1	6.9	5.8	A
PROPERTY-OWNERS INS CO	IN	A	217.0	104.6	70.0	0.0	8.2	8.1	7.0	6.7	7.6	
PROSELECT INS CO	MA	C	87.6	25.4	0.0	0.4	10.0	N/A	6.4	8.5	4.2	R
PROSELECT NATIONAL INS CO INC	AZ	U	15.3	12.8	0.0	0.1	N/A	N/A	6.3	7.0	5.4	RT
PROTECTION MUT INS CO	PA	U	0.7	0.5	0.0	0.0	N/A	7.4	2.2	9.3	1.5	FRT
PROTECTIVE INS CO	IN	A-	776.3	395.1	228.0	22.3	7.0	8.4	5.6	6.6	6.9	
PROTECTIVE SPECIALTY INS CO	IN	B	76.3	58.9	3.0	0.4	8.6	4.8	4.7	9.2	4.8	DFT
PROVIDENCE MUTUAL FIRE INS CO	RI	B-	194.6	101.4	64.1	5.0	8.4	6.2	3.2	6.4	4.7	R
PROVIDENCE PLANTATIONS INS CO	RI	U	1.2	1.2	0.0	0.0	N/A	N/A	3.8	7.0	0.0	CFT
PROVIDENCE WASHINGTON INS CO	RI	U	125.6	35.8	0.5	-0.4	N/A	9.4	1.5	10.0	2.9	FGT
PUBLIC SERVICE INS CO	IL	D+	515.2	136.4	175.0	5.6	7.2	3.6	1.4	6.8	2.6	FR
PUBLIC UTILITY MUTUAL INS CO RRG	VT	E	6.1	4.8	0.8	0.0	10.0	9.3	8.1	9.2	0.0	DR
PUERTO RICO MED DEFENSE MUT INS CO	PR	D+	13.5	3.0	4.3	0.1	2.0	7.0	5.5	7.1	1.9	CDGT
PURE INS CO	FL	B-	200.0	130.8	74.4	1.4	7.7	5.4	3.3	7.1	3.9	GT
PXRE REINSURANCE CO	CT	E	26.2	17.3	-0.2	0.0	9.9	7.0	1.8	6.8	0.0	FRT
PYMATUNING MUTUAL FIRE INS CO	PA	D+(3)	0.0	0.0	0.0	0.0	10.0	N/A	3.8	7.0	2.1	DT
QBE INS CORP	PA	C	2,576.0	685.5	750.5	-4.5	7.5	2.9	2.9	6.7	4.2	FRT
QBE OPTIMA INS CO	PR	D	65.7	12.6	24.3	-3.4	5.2	4.7	3.6	8.0	2.3	DR
QBE REINSURANCE CORP	PA	B	1,269.9	825.8	210.4	2.7	7.4	4.5	5.3	6.9	5.4	FRT
QBE SPECIALTY INS CO	ND	D	957.4	214.4	290.0	-4.1	7.3	3.3	3.7	6.6	2.0	FRT
QUALITAS INS CO	CA	U	15.9	15.3	0.0	-0.7	N/A	3.7	1.9	10.0	3.1	RT
QUALITY CASUALTY INS CO INC	AL	D	1.1	0.8	0.0	0.1	8.6	7.1	1.5	9.8	1.3	DGRT
QUANTA INDEMNITY CO	CO	D+	59.1	22.7	0.0	-0.5	0.0	9.1	2.2	7.6	2.5	CDFG
QUEEN CITY ASR INC	VT	A+	2,149.3	1,958.2	169.6	120.2	10.0	3.6	8.9	6.8	7.9	
QUINCY MUTUAL FIRE INS CO	MA	B	1,481.9	960.0	296.3	51.5	9.0	7.4	6.0	6.9	4.7	R

See Page 27 for explanation of footnotes and
Page 28 for explanation of stability factors.
Arrows denote recent upgrades ▲ or downgrades ▼   (see Section VII for explanations)

110

www.weissratings.com

RISK ADJ. CAPITAL RATIO #1	RATIO #2	PREMIUM TO SURPLUS (%)	RESV. TO SURPLUS (%)	RESV. DEVELOP. 1 YEAR (%)	2 YEAR (%)	LOSS RATIO (%)	EXP. RATIO (%)	COMB RATIO (%)	CASH FROM UNDER-WRITING (%)	NET PREMIUM GROWTH (%)	INVEST. IN AFFIL (%)	INSURANCE COMPANY NAME
1.5	1.3	313.5	130.2	1.5	2.1	72.9	20.7	93.6	111.0	4.7	0.0	PROGRESSIVE BAYSIDE INS CO
0.9	0.8	301.8	125.3	1.5	2.1	72.9	21.1	94.0	109.3	4.7	21.0 ●	PROGRESSIVE CASUALTY INS CO
4.4	4.0	-0.5	N/A	0.4	0.3	71.5	-233.7	-162.2	883.2	-100.1	0.0	PROGRESSIVE CHOICE INS CO
1.5	1.3	310.3	128.8	1.5	2.2	72.9	20.4	93.3	113.3	4.7	0.0	PROGRESSIVE CLASSIC INS CO
N/A	N/A	N/A	N/A	N/A	N/A	N/A	N/A	N/A	N/A	0.0	0.0	PROGRESSIVE COMMERCIAL CASUALTY
0.4	0.3	N/A	N/A	N/A	N/A	N/A	N/A	N/A	-17.5	0.0	0.0	PROGRESSIVE COUNTY MUTUAL INS CO
1.3	1.2	310.5	122.1	-1.8	-1.4	72.4	20.6	93.0	110.6	4.8	0.0 ●	PROGRESSIVE DIRECT INS CO
6.1	4.1	78.1	50.8	0.4	0.5	73.9	18.3	92.2	102.2	6.8	0.0	PROGRESSIVE EXPRESS INS CO
4.1	3.7	26.5	26.1	0.2	0.2	66.1	16.8	82.9	81.6	-18.4	0.0	PROGRESSIVE FREEDOM INS CO
2.8	2.3	90.3	54.8	N/A	1.9	79.1	15.7	94.8	179.1	22.8	0.0	PROGRESSIVE GARDEN STATE INS CO
2.2	2.0	108.6	82.6	0.7	0.7	72.9	19.4	92.3	110.2	4.7	0.0	PROGRESSIVE GULF INS CO
2.0	1.5	295.4	126.5	-4.8	-3.6	69.1	19.9	89.0	118.5	9.2	0.0	PROGRESSIVE HAWAII INS CORP
1.3	1.2	291.1	114.5	-1.7	-1.2	72.4	20.5	92.9	107.6	4.8	0.0	PROGRESSIVE MARATHON INS CO
1.2	1.1	316.3	124.4	-1.8	-1.4	72.4	20.6	93.0	110.6	4.8	0.0	PROGRESSIVE MAX INS CO
1.6	1.4	289.1	120.0	1.4	2.0	72.9	20.6	93.5	111.2	4.7	0.0	PROGRESSIVE MICHIGAN INS CO
2.8	2.4	156.8	65.1	0.7	1.0	72.9	18.6	91.5	112.0	4.7	0.0	PROGRESSIVE MOUNTAIN INS CO
1.5	1.3	307.7	127.8	1.5	2.2	72.9	19.8	92.7	111.1	4.7	0.0 ●	PROGRESSIVE NORTHERN INS CO
1.5	1.3	307.0	127.5	1.5	2.2	72.9	20.5	93.4	110.8	4.7	0.0 ●	PROGRESSIVE NORTHWESTERN INS CO
2.9	2.6	80.0	31.5	-0.5	-0.4	72.4	17.4	89.8	87.1	4.8	0.0	PROGRESSIVE PALOVERDE INS CO
1.5	1.3	310.4	128.9	1.5	2.2	72.9	19.9	92.8	111.4	4.7	0.0	PROGRESSIVE PREFERRED INS CO
1.5	1.4	248.7	97.8	-1.5	-1.2	72.4	21.1	93.5	103.4	4.8	0.0	PROGRESSIVE PREMIER INS CO OF IL
4.9	4.1	87.5	27.9	-0.2	2.7	80.5	18.4	98.9	120.5	3.6	0.0	PROGRESSIVE SECURITY INS CO
3.6	3.2	80.0	29.1	-1.4	0.7	67.7	17.8	85.5	90.5	21.6	0.0	PROGRESSIVE SELECT INS CO
1.9	1.6	181.0	75.2	0.9	1.3	72.9	18.0	90.9	104.8	4.7	0.0	PROGRESSIVE SOUTHEASTERN INS CO
2.6	2.2	172.3	71.5	0.7	0.7	72.9	19.4	92.3	107.3	4.7	0.0 ●	PROGRESSIVE SPECIALTY INS CO
1.5	1.4	244.5	96.2	-1.4	-1.1	72.4	18.4	90.8	105.2	4.8	0.0	PROGRESSIVE UNIVERSAL INS CO
3.3	2.8	88.3	31.6	2.1	1.3	83.8	20.8	104.6	102.8	3.0	0.0	PROGRESSIVE WEST INS CO
6.5	4.3	47.3	84.7	0.5	-0.1	68.8	14.9	83.7	103.1	1.1	0.0	PROPERTY & CASUALTY I CO OF
3.5	2.0	67.0	39.0	-2.8	-8.2	55.5	32.5	88.0	121.7	10.2	0.0 ●	PROPERTY-OWNERS INS CO
3.4	3.1	N/A	N/A	N/A	N/A	N/A	N/A	N/A	-815.8	0.0	0.0	PROSELECT INS CO
N/A	N/A	N/A	N/A	N/A	N/A	N/A	N/A	N/A	N/A	0.0	0.0	PROSELECT NATIONAL INS CO INC
N/A	N/A	6.2	2.7	-0.2	-0.7	49.7	174.8	224.5	38.1	-10.9	0.0	PROTECTION MUT INS CO
1.4	1.0	60.7	72.1	-4.0	-8.4	57.6	31.3	88.9	117.2	12.1	27.3 ●	PROTECTIVE INS CO
3.3	2.3	5.0	21.5	5.5	4.2	88.6	47.7	136.3	22.5	-73.4	0.0	PROTECTIVE SPECIALTY INS CO
2.8	1.9	63.9	41.0	-2.2	-0.7	69.9	39.7	109.6	93.0	12.2	0.7	PROVIDENCE MUTUAL FIRE INS CO
N/A	N/A	N/A	N/A	N/A	N/A	N/A	N/A	N/A	N/A	0.0	0.0	PROVIDENCE PLANTATIONS INS CO
N/A	N/A	1.8	179.2	7.3	-15.9	999 +	376.7	999 +	-0.3	131.4	7.8	PROVIDENCE WASHINGTON INS CO
1.9	1.2	128.7	214.9	24.9	18.2	103.6	31.0	134.6	98.0	14.5	0.0	PUBLIC SERVICE INS CO
5.9	4.1	17.0	16.4	-11.6	-15.2	4.7	61.0	65.7	136.1	-4.7	0.0	PUBLIC UTILITY MUTUAL INS CO RRG
0.6	0.4	161.0	137.6	-2.5	-11.8	52.0	46.0	98.0	186.0	-0.3	0.0	PUERTO RICO MED DEFENSE MUT INS
3.5	2.2	78.2	16.2	2.7	-1.9	51.4	47.5	98.9	114.2	64.0	0.0	PURE INS CO
5.0	3.3	-0.9	41.9	0.7	-48.1	-125.2	67.4	-57.8	2.4	72.1	0.0	PXRE REINSURANCE CO
38.6	36.1	0.5	0.4	N/A	N/A	255.5	263.7	519.2	443.7	-42.9	0.0	PYMATUNING MUTUAL FIRE INS CO
1.7	1.3	110.6	102.4	6.0	12.4	75.2	34.9	110.1	97.3	58.7	18.3 ●	QBE INS CORP
0.6	0.4	145.4	37.6	0.4	1.5	62.7	18.3	81.0	144.8	24.2	0.0	QBE OPTIMA INS CO
1.4	1.3	25.8	27.6	1.7	3.1	75.2	38.9	114.1	64.3	-36.9	60.7 ●	QBE REINSURANCE CORP
1.9	1.2	135.0	127.1	8.1	16.6	75.2	34.4	109.6	81.0	-23.3	0.0 ●	QBE SPECIALTY INS CO
N/A	N/A	N/A	N/A	N/A	N/A	N/A	N/A	N/A	9.4	0.0	0.0	QUALITAS INS CO
5.7	5.1	N/A	1.5	-12.9	-902.4	N/A	N/A	N/A	-125.1	0.0	0.0	QUALITY CASUALTY INS CO INC
0.0	0.0	N/A	55.6	-10.3	-15.1	-116.6	999 +	999 +	-3.1	100.1	0.0	QUANTA INDEMNITY CO
12.8	7.2	9.2	N/A	N/A	N/A	N/A	0.2	0.2	999 +	-0.3	0.0 ●	QUEEN CITY ASR INC
4.0	2.4	32.0	22.4	-3.0	-1.9	55.6	36.5	92.1	101.1	4.2	3.2 ●	QUINCY MUTUAL FIRE INS CO

999 + Denotes number greater than 999.9%
999 - Denotes number less than -999.99%
● Bullets denote a more detailed analysis is available in Section II.

INSURANCE COMPANY NAME	DOM. STATE	RATING	TOTAL ASSETS ($MIL)	CAPITAL & SURPLUS ($MIL)	ANNUAL NET PREMIUM ($MIL)	NET INCOME ($MIL)	CAPITAL-IZATION INDEX (PTS)	RESERVE ADQ INDEX (PTS)	PROFIT-ABILITY INDEX (PTS)	LIQUIDITY INDEX (PTS)	STAB. INDEX (PTS)	STABILITY FACTORS
R&Q REINS CO	PA	D	156.1	14.9	0.1	-2.0	0.0	1.1	0.5	9.3	1.4	CDFR
RADIAN ASSET ASR CO	NY	C	1,343.9	1,033.1	10.8	7.4	10.0	6.3	5.7	10.0	2.9	AFRT
RADIAN GUARANTY INC	PA	D	3,530.5	1,326.1	814.4	393.6	2.8	2.0	3.3	2.9	2.3	AFLR
RADIAN GUARANTY REINS INC	PA	E+	373.6	76.7	93.5	49.0	1.2	4.0	2.5	6.1	0.6	F
RADIAN INS INC	PA	C-	321.9	249.1	29.2	25.9	10.0	9.4	7.9	7.9	2.9	FT
RADIAN MORTGAGE ASR INC	PA	U	17.6	17.5	0.0	-0.4	N/A	0.4	2.9	7.0	0.7	AFT
RADIAN MORTGAGE INS INC	PA	D+	142.9	117.6	13.7	16.6	9.1	4.0	2.0	7.7	2.4	DFGT
RAINIER INS CO	AZ	C+	25.8	20.6	2.2	0.3	10.0	8.2	5.3	7.4	4.4	DF
RAM MUTUAL INS CO	MN	B-	88.6	45.3	45.2	5.5	7.7	9.4	6.7	7.2	5.0	T
RAMPART INS CO	NY	U	35.4	11.4	0.0	0.0	N/A	3.8	1.2	9.1	2.1	CFGT
RANCHERS & FARMERS INS CO	TX	C-	6.2	4.6	1.3	0.1	7.2	5.9	2.7	6.9	2.5	DFRT
RANCHERS & FARMERS MUTUAL INS CO	TX	D+	12.9	2.5	0.2	0.4	4.4	4.7	4.4	6.9	2.2	CDRT
REAL LEGACY ASR CO INC	PR	C	143.7	57.2	37.7	3.5	8.3	9.2	3.7	6.7	4.2	FR
REAMSTOWN MUTUAL INS CO	PA	D	8.0	3.1	5.3	-0.2	6.7	6.6	4.4	6.9	2.1	DR
RED CLAY RRG INC	SC	B-	6.9	3.5	1.5	0.3	8.8	7.0	7.5	9.5	3.5	D
RED ROCK INS CO	OK	F (2)	57.1	16.8	-3.7	-0.8	5.4	1.8	0.1	6.9	0.0	DFRT
RED ROCK RISK RETENTION GROUP INC	AZ	D+	6.7	5.0	0.9	-0.2	7.4	2.8	1.6	8.0	2.3	DFT
RED SHIELD INS CO	WA	B	41.8	20.8	11.3	0.2	9.0	8.5	6.0	7.6	4.9	DR
REDWOOD FIRE & CAS INS CO	NE	C	1,181.0	525.6	286.9	8.1	4.4	8.1	7.3	7.2	4.3	CGT
REGENT INS CO	WI	C-	144.0	28.7	45.4	-0.6	6.8	3.9	1.7	6.7	3.0	FRT
REGIS INS CO	PA	E	2.8	0.8	2.6	-1.3	1.2	5.5	0.0	0.9	0.0	CDFL
RELIABLE LLOYDS INS CO	TX	D+	15.4	10.3	0.0	0.6	10.0	N/A	8.9	9.9	2.5	DR
RELIAMAX INS CO	SD	D	9.8	1.3	6.5	0.4	3.4	4.1	1.9	6.8	1.5	CDGR
RELIAMAX SURETY CO	SD	D	55.5	21.0	23.7	0.1	7.3	7.5	8.7	8.1	2.3	DGT
REPUBLIC CREDIT INDEMNITY CO	IL	D	60.6	9.6	26.3	-1.3	2.4	3.9	2.8	7.3	1.9	CDFT
REPUBLIC FIRE & CASUALTY INS CO	OK	C+	8.3	8.1	0.0	0.1	10.0	N/A	3.9	10.0	4.1	DR
REPUBLIC INDEMNITY CO OF AMERICA	CA	C+	2,206.9	440.7	209.3	-29.8	7.4	8.2	3.6	7.0	4.6	AR
REPUBLIC INDEMNITY OF CA	CA	C	41.8	34.5	6.5	1.3	9.0	7.5	3.6	7.9	4.3	DR
REPUBLIC LLOYDS	TX	C	12.4	12.3	0.0	-0.1	10.0	N/A	3.8	10.0	2.1	DRT
REPUBLIC MORTGAGE INS CO	NC	F	845.6	27.9	227.9	87.4	0.9	0.3	0.4	7.0	0.0	CFRT
REPUBLIC MORTGAGE INS CO OF FLORIDA	FL	D	27.6	8.1	3.9	1.2	2.4	1.6	2.9	6.6	1.6	CDF
REPUBLIC MORTGAGE INS CO OF NC	NC	E	233.0	13.6	43.3	15.0	1.5	1.0	0.4	7.1	0.0	CFRT
REPUBLIC RRG	SC	U (3)	0.0	0.0	0.0	0.0	N/A	4.7	2.8	7.0	2.4	FT
REPUBLIC UNDERWRITERS INS CO	TX	C+	655.4	253.0	297.1	11.1	7.9	4.1	4.6	6.2	4.3	R
REPUBLIC VANGUARD INS CO	AZ	B-	27.9	24.7	0.0	0.5	10.0	N/A	6.7	10.0	4.5	DR
REPUBLIC-FRANKLIN INS CO	OH	C+	102.4	48.8	19.5	0.7	10.0	5.1	5.2	6.9	4.3	T
REPWEST INS CO	AZ	D-	298.7	145.5	32.3	16.5	1.1	1.7	3.0	7.8	1.0	CR
RESIDENCE MUTUAL INS CO	CA	C-	111.8	75.3	34.2	3.0	7.5	8.3	8.8	6.2	2.7	R
RESPONSE INDEMNITY CO OF CA	CA	U	6.3	4.3	0.0	0.0	N/A	4.6	3.1	7.0	0.0	RT
RESPONSE INS CO	IL	D	26.8	23.3	0.0	0.1	7.6	3.6	3.0	7.0	1.9	DRT
RESPONSE WORLDWIDE DIRECT AUTO INS	IL	C	6.7	6.6	0.0	0.1	10.0	2.6	2.7	7.0	2.9	DRT
RESPONSE WORLDWIDE INS CO	IL	C	10.7	10.5	0.0	0.2	10.0	2.7	2.9	6.9	3.1	DRT
RESPONSIVE AUTO INS CO	FL	C-	24.5	8.2	15.3	-0.7	3.9	2.1	3.9	6.6	2.9	D
RESTORATION RRG INC	VT	C-	63.4	20.8	10.7	2.1	5.4	9.7	8.8	8.3	3.3	DR
RETAILERS CASUALTY INS CO	LA	D+	73.5	30.1	21.1	1.1	7.5	4.7	6.4	6.6	2.5	DR
RETAILERS INS CO	MI	D-	19.7	9.5	5.7	-0.4	6.6	9.4	3.8	7.0	1.0	DR
RETAILFIRST INS CO	FL	A-	282.1	133.5	94.8	2.3	8.0	8.9	5.3	6.6	7.0	
▼RIDER INS CO	NJ	D	46.4	8.3	26.5	-4.9	4.8	7.0	0.9	3.1	2.1	DFLR
RISK MGMT INDEMNITY INC	DE	U (5)	0.0	0.0	4.8	0.0	N/A	6.0	6.2	8.9	3.4	DT
RIVERPORT INS CO	MN	B	107.6	38.0	0.0	0.7	10.0	4.9	5.3	7.0	4.1	FRT
RLI INDEMNITY CO	IL	B-	44.1	43.5	0.2	0.6	10.0	7.2	6.0	9.9	4.9	AD
RLI INS CO	IL	B	1,782.0	901.7	413.2	212.5	7.0	8.6	8.1	7.1	5.7	A

See Page 27 for explanation of footnotes and Page 28 for explanation of stability factors.
Arrows denote recent upgrades ▲ or downgrades ▼ (see Section VII for explanations)

112

www.weissratings.com

RISK ADJ. CAPITAL RATIO #1	RATIO #2	PREMIUM TO SURPLUS (%)	RESV. TO SURPLUS (%)	RESV. DEVELOP. 1 YEAR (%)	2 YEAR (%)	LOSS RATIO (%)	EXP. RATIO (%)	COMB RATIO (%)	CASH FROM UNDER- WRITING (%)	NET PREMIUM GROWTH (%)	INVEST. IN AFFIL (%)	INSURANCE COMPANY NAME
0.1	0.0	0.8	906.2	32.6	85.5	999 +	440.6	999 +	0.7	-54.0	0.0	R&Q REINS CO
21.9	20.1	0.9	-15.0	-0.8	-1.1	0.5	670.1	670.6	12.8	112.4	0.0 ●	RADIAN ASSET ASR CO
0.7	0.6	61.8	137.6	6.0	27.1	81.6	30.1	111.7	52.1	18.6	44.3 ●	RADIAN GUARANTY INC
0.8	0.6	157.8	419.9	-115.9	-197.9	26.4	1.0	27.4	84.0	19.2	0.0	RADIAN GUARANTY REINS INC
7.8	6.7	12.7	18.7	-6.8	-9.4	-11.1	54.7	43.6	64.0	-26.0	0.0 ●	RADIAN INS INC
N/A	N/A	N/A	N/A	N/A	N/A	N/A	N/A	N/A	N/A	0.0	0.0	RADIAN MORTGAGE ASR INC
9.8	8.0	14.0	29.3	-15.7	-64.4	-35.4	16.2	-19.2	71.6	860.5	0.0	RADIAN MORTGAGE INS INC
7.0	4.2	10.7	19.3	-2.2	-3.6	52.1	46.8	98.9	65.9	-7.2	0.0	RAINIER INS CO
2.7	1.8	114.3	49.0	-1.0	-14.2	53.3	28.5	81.8	133.2	10.8	0.0	RAM MUTUAL INS CO
N/A	N/A	0.2	233.5	5.1	9.7	999 +	999 +	999 +	2.3	587.7	0.0	RAMPART INS CO
3.1	2.1	26.8	8.3	9.0	2.2	76.2	91.8	168.0	68.1	-58.0	0.0	RANCHERS & FARMERS INS CO
1.0	0.9	8.2	3.5	2.4	-0.7	72.6	95.7	168.3	91.8	-82.0	0.0	RANCHERS & FARMERS MUTUAL INS CO
2.4	1.6	65.8	34.7	-6.9	-17.7	45.9	45.5	91.4	80.8	19.5	-8.3	REAL LEGACY ASR CO INC
1.5	1.0	162.5	32.2	-1.8	-1.5	44.0	37.3	81.3	118.3	2.5	0.0	REAMSTOWN MUTUAL INS CO
3.2	2.0	44.2	73.9	-15.9	-31.4	25.0	30.0	55.0	442.1	19.8	0.0	RED CLAY RRG INC
1.7	0.8	-17.3	156.7	999 +	21.5	-20.7	-127.8	-148.5	-9.3	47.0	0.0	RED ROCK INS CO
4.2	3.3	17.8	58.4	-0.9	19.2	42.7	49.1	91.8	15.2	-12.8	0.0	RED ROCK RISK RETENTION GROUP INC
3.5	2.2	55.5	36.2	0.3	-4.4	38.7	55.1	93.8	110.4	1.8	0.0	RED SHIELD INS CO
0.7	0.4	56.7	63.4	0.2	-0.4	66.9	28.6	95.5	188.8	193.5	0.0 ●	REDWOOD FIRE & CAS INS CO
1.2	0.8	145.9	144.5	8.2	16.8	75.2	36.2	111.4	74.9	-18.7	0.0	REGENT INS CO
0.2	0.1	123.7	149.8	13.7	14.0	112.0	111.9	223.9	41.7	-21.4	0.0	REGIS INS CO
6.7	6.0	N/A	N/A	N/A	N/A	N/A	N/A	N/A	-66.4	0.0	0.0	RELIABLE LLOYDS INS CO
0.1	0.1	67.1	33.7	2.1	7.2	54.0	18.2	72.2	132.5	47.3	65.2	RELIAMAX INS CO
4.1	2.9	111.1	2.0	-1.6	-1.2	23.2	26.8	50.0	210.2	37.7	0.0	RELIAMAX SURETY CO
0.4	0.3	241.2	271.3	-276.4	-757.1	102.2	7.6	109.8	80.1	-18.4	0.0	REPUBLIC CREDIT INDEMNITY CO
88.9	50.0	N/A	N/A	N/A	N/A	N/A	N/A	N/A	154.5	0.0	0.0	REPUBLIC FIRE & CASUALTY INS CO
1.3	0.8	83.0	213.8	-2.5	-2.3	68.6	28.1	96.7	111.9	32.2	2.7 ●	REPUBLIC INDEMNITY CO OF AMERICA
17.7	15.9	29.8	76.9	-0.9	-0.8	68.6	28.1	96.7	115.0	32.2	0.0	REPUBLIC INDEMNITY OF CA
141.3	70.8	N/A	N/A	N/A	N/A	N/A	N/A	N/A	32.8	0.0	0.0	REPUBLIC LLOYDS
0.1	0.0	61.7	395.3	-170.2	162.1	61.9	7.0	68.9	75.0	-21.7	0.1	REPUBLIC MORTGAGE INS CO
0.9	0.6	48.8	193.3	-38.0	16.7	61.6	16.9	78.5	39.7	-21.7	0.0	REPUBLIC MORTGAGE INS CO OF
0.2	0.1	63.5	422.0	-363.1	22.6	56.1	13.6	69.7	51.3	-21.1	0.0	REPUBLIC MORTGAGE INS CO OF NC
N/A	N/A	N/A	1.7	N/A	N/A	N/A	N/A	N/A	N/A	0.0	0.0	REPUBLIC RRG
2.3	1.9	120.7	78.7	-0.2	1.1	57.8	42.5	100.3	92.0	-4.0	16.7 ●	REPUBLIC UNDERWRITERS INS CO
23.7	21.3	N/A	N/A	N/A	N/A	N/A	N/A	N/A	N/A	0.0	0.0	REPUBLIC VANGUARD INS CO
5.5	3.4	41.0	68.8	-0.5	-1.7	65.5	35.2	100.7	96.1	8.9	0.0	REPUBLIC-FRANKLIN INS CO
0.3	0.3	25.5	119.2	1.4	5.8	24.5	50.5	75.0	144.3	10.4	0.0	REPWEST INS CO
2.2	1.4	47.5	15.3	-3.1	-3.8	60.4	27.3	87.7	119.0	4.3	8.6	RESIDENCE MUTUAL INS CO
N/A	N/A	N/A	N/A	N/A	0.1	N/A	N/A	N/A	N/A	0.0	0.0	RESPONSE INDEMNITY CO OF CA
1.4	1.4	N/A	N/A	N/A	N/A	N/A	N/A	N/A	180.1	0.0	73.6	RESPONSE INS CO
95.6	47.8	N/A	N/A	N/A	N/A	N/A	N/A	N/A	999 +	0.0	0.0	RESPONSE WORLDWIDE DIRECT AUTO
22.3	18.0	N/A	N/A	N/A	N/A	N/A	N/A	N/A	-202.0	0.0	2.6	RESPONSE WORLDWIDE INS CO
0.7	0.6	170.1	50.8	4.8	36.9	53.7	35.7	89.4	126.3	7.9	0.0	RESPONSIVE AUTO INS CO
1.1	0.6	54.2	138.5	-9.9	-29.7	74.5	22.3	96.8	169.2	-5.1	0.0	RESTORATION RRG INC
1.7	1.3	72.1	105.2	-5.2	-13.2	68.2	32.8	101.0	100.1	10.3	0.0	RETAILERS CASUALTY INS CO
1.8	0.8	57.5	68.4	-10.4	-27.2	64.9	36.4	101.3	111.2	24.6	0.0	RETAILERS INS CO
2.1	1.6	72.7	85.1	-0.2	-1.6	71.1	31.6	102.7	97.4	21.2	0.0 ●	RETAILFIRST INS CO
0.6	0.4	202.1	54.2	-3.8	3.7	65.0	48.0	113.0	81.8	3.2	0.0	RIDER INS CO
N/A	N/A	90.1	165.5	7.4	14.9	103.7	5.7	109.4	118.1	3.6	0.0	RISK MGMT INDEMNITY INC
5.3	4.8	N/A	N/A	N/A	N/A	N/A	N/A	N/A	185.2	100.0	0.0	RIVERPORT INS CO
55.9	39.0	0.5	0.3	-0.1	-0.2	-3.8	210.7	206.9	43.8	-0.3	0.0	RLI INDEMNITY CO
1.3	1.2	48.1	51.5	-3.7	-4.2	50.8	40.9	91.7	121.3	9.5	42.8 ●	RLI INS CO

999 + Denotes number greater than 999.9%
999 - Denotes number less than -999.99%
● Bullets denote a more detailed analysis is available in Section II.

INSURANCE COMPANY NAME	DOM. STATE	RATING	TOTAL ASSETS ($MIL)	CAPITAL & SURPLUS ($MIL)	ANNUAL NET PREMIUM ($MIL)	NET INCOME ($MIL)	CAPITAL-IZATION INDEX (PTS)	RESERVE ADQ INDEX (PTS)	PROFIT-ABILITY INDEX (PTS)	LIQUIDITY INDEX (PTS)	STAB. INDEX (PTS)	STABILITY FACTORS
ROAD CONTRACTORS MUTUAL INS CO	TN	C-	8.0	3.0	2.8	0.0	5.6	6.9	2.0	6.5	2.1	DF
ROCHDALE INS CO OF NEW YORK NY	NY	C-	262.4	67.3	77.0	7.6	6.7	4.5	8.5	6.5	3.2	R
ROCHE SURETY & CASUALTY INC	FL	D+	22.1	8.5	2.9	0.4	9.4	N/A	6.9	9.1	2.5	D
ROCKFORD MUTUAL INS CO	IL	C+	75.0	29.5	45.3	0.6	6.1	4.6	4.3	5.7	4.4	R
ROCKHILL INS CO	AZ	C	129.8	97.6	0.0	1.2	9.4	3.6	4.2	7.0	3.9	R
ROCKINGHAM CASUALTY CO	VA	C	32.9	27.9	0.0	0.3	10.0	5.1	6.9	7.8	4.2	DFR
ROCKINGHAM INS CO	VA	C+	111.0	59.9	36.4	1.7	5.7	6.3	4.0	5.8	4.5	R
ROCKWOOD CASUALTY INS CO	PA	C-	251.2	96.6	45.9	10.2	7.7	9.5	7.6	7.0	3.1	R
ROCKY MOUNTAIN FIRE & CAS CO	WA	C	22.6	19.4	4.0	0.3	10.0	6.4	8.4	7.0	4.0	DFR
RPX RRG INC	HI	D	5.5	3.7	1.6	0.4	5.8	3.6	2.0	9.2	0.8	DGT
RSUI INDEMNITY CO	NH	C+	3,367.6	1,526.2	765.1	151.7	8.2	8.3	8.8	7.0	4.5	AR
RURAL COMMUNITY INS CO	MN	B	7,691.1	593.1	491.5	-10.6	10.0	9.2	5.9	2.3	5.9	FL
RURAL MUTUAL INS CO	WI	C+	383.3	187.8	144.7	11.1	10.0	8.8	8.9	6.6	4.5	R
RURAL TRUST INS CO	TX	U	11.8	10.2	0.0	-0.3	N/A	6.1	3.8	10.0	4.1	FRT
RUTGERS CASUALTY INS CO	NJ	C-	25.2	10.5	4.6	-0.2	7.3	6.4	2.9	7.3	2.9	DFR
RUTGERS ENHANCED INS CO	NJ	D (3)	0.0	0.0	3.1	0.1	7.9	4.6	3.5	7.5	2.2	DFT
RVI AMERICA INS CO	CT	C	96.7	68.8	4.2	1.6	10.0	N/A	7.8	9.3	3.3	DGRT
RVOS FARM MUTUAL INS CO	TX	E+	73.3	18.7	55.7	-4.7	4.7	6.3	0.9	0.5	0.6	DFLR
SAFE AUTO INS CO	OH	C	385.4	147.7	286.4	17.3	7.5	8.8	2.2	4.1	3.5	L
SAFE HARBOR INS CO	FL	C-	61.9	21.4	39.2	4.8	4.2	5.2	9.0	6.5	2.9	DT
SAFE INS CO	WV	D-	9.7	7.5	2.9	0.5	10.0	8.6	8.7	7.6	1.0	DR
SAFECARD SERVICE INS CO	ND	D (3)	0.0	0.0	0.2	0.1	10.0	4.6	8.8	10.0	1.7	D
SAFECO INS CO OF AMERICA	NH	B-	4,416.2	1,252.5	1,349.1	63.6	7.5	6.9	6.4	6.7	4.9	AR
SAFECO INS CO OF ILLINOIS	IL	B	185.7	177.7	-104.5	1.5	9.4	4.8	3.7	1.7	5.5	AFLT
SAFECO INS CO OF INDIANA	IN	B-	14.7	14.7	0.0	0.2	10.0	N/A	6.6	7.0	3.9	DFRT
SAFECO INS CO OF OREGON	OR	B	13.7	13.1	0.0	0.2	10.0	N/A	7.9	7.0	4.8	DFRT
SAFECO LLOYDS INS CO	TX	B	12.8	12.8	0.0	0.2	10.0	N/A	6.6	7.0	4.7	DR
SAFECO NATIONAL INS CO	NH	B-	17.9	14.6	0.0	0.9	10.0	N/A	1.9	9.2	3.9	ADRT
SAFECO SURPLUS LINES INS CO	NH	U	42.1	40.4	0.0	0.7	N/A	N/A	7.6	7.0	5.4	RT
SAFEPOINT INS CO	FL	U	59.8	28.7	0.0	2.9	N/A	N/A	4.9	7.0	5.4	T
SAFETY FIRST INS CO	IL	C	18.3	14.4	1.7	0.1	10.0	5.5	7.0	8.7	4.0	DFR
SAFETY INDEMNITY INS CO	MA	C	115.7	55.9	48.8	2.3	10.0	9.0	8.0	6.8	3.4	T
SAFETY INS CO	MA	B+	1,429.1	622.4	627.8	40.7	9.6	9.0	7.7	6.6	5.0	
SAFETY NATIONAL CASUALTY CORP	MO	C	4,823.4	1,253.5	664.9	71.7	7.0	1.2	6.3	7.2	3.4	R
SAFETY PROPERTY & CASUALTY INS CO	MA	C	43.3	18.3	20.9	0.9	8.4	9.3	6.2	6.8	2.9	D
SAFEWAY COUNTY MUTUAL INS CO	TX	C	12.4	4.0	0.0	0.2	8.5	N/A	8.6	6.2	3.3	DFR
SAFEWAY INS CO	IL	B-	440.9	292.2	143.3	5.7	7.5	7.4	5.7	6.5	4.5	R
SAFEWAY INS CO OF AL	IL	C	62.3	31.1	41.4	1.2	7.8	7.7	3.4	6.4	4.1	R
SAFEWAY INS CO OF GEORGIA	GA	C	64.3	32.8	41.4	1.0	8.0	7.7	3.5	6.4	4.0	R
SAFEWAY INS CO OF LA	LA	C+	126.0	63.0	79.6	1.6	9.1	7.7	5.3	6.3	4.5	R
SAFEWAY PROPERTY INS CO	IL	C	52.3	30.9	16.9	1.9	8.1	7.3	8.7	8.0	4.0	R
SAGAMORE INS CO	IN	B-	155.7	123.6	21.6	-0.6	10.0	7.5	6.2	9.0	4.7	T
SAIF CORP	OR	A (5)	4,802.9	1,190.1	329.1	0.0	5.2	9.9	4.9	7.3	6.0	CFT
SAINT LUKES HEALTH SYSTEM RRG	SC	D	23.9	14.1	3.4	0.9	6.4	9.3	6.9	7.8	1.8	DFR
SALEM COUNTY MUTUAL FIRE INS CO	NJ	U (3)	0.0	0.0	0.0	-1.6	N/A	N/A	0.7	7.0	1.9	FT
SAMARITAN RRG INC	SC	D	29.7	16.6	8.4	1.4	8.1	7.0	8.9	7.8	1.8	D
▼SAMSUNG FIRE & MARINE INS CO LTD US	NY	B-	206.2	51.4	75.8	0.7	5.9	9.3	3.6	6.8	3.5	CGRT
SAN ANTONIO INDEMNITY CO	TX	F (5)	0.0	0.0	4.2	0.0	0.3	5.5	1.1	0.0	0.0	CDGL
SAN DIEGO INS CO	CA	U	66.2	62.8	0.0	1.2	N/A	N/A	6.3	7.0	5.4	T
SAN FRANCISCO REINSURANCE CO	CA	U	97.2	73.2	0.0	1.3	N/A	3.4	3.4	10.0	5.1	T
SANILAC MUTUAL INS CO	MI	U	0.8	0.5	0.4	0.0	N/A	3.6	1.4	5.7	1.5	FRT
SAUCON MUTUAL INS CO	PA	U (3)	0.0	0.0	-0.1	0.3	N/A	7.2	6.3	10.0	4.6	F

See Page 27 for explanation of footnotes and
Page 28 for explanation of stability factors.
Arrows denote recent upgrades ▲ or downgrades ▼   (see Section VII for explanations)

114

www.weissratings.com

RISK ADJ. CAPITAL RATIO #1	RATIO #2	PREMIUM TO SURPLUS (%)	RESV. TO SURPLUS (%)	RESV. DEVELOP. 1 YEAR (%)	2 YEAR (%)	LOSS RATIO (%)	EXP. RATIO (%)	COMB RATIO (%)	CASH FROM UNDER-WRITING (%)	NET PREMIUM GROWTH (%)	INVEST. IN AFFIL (%)	INSURANCE COMPANY NAME
1.4	0.6	92.6	126.0	-4.6	-10.7	121.2	5.6	126.8	64.7	-15.9	0.0	ROAD CONTRACTORS MUTUAL INS CO
1.4	0.9	130.8	140.1	-4.8	5.9	65.2	25.4	90.6	108.2	32.8	0.0	ROCHDALE INS CO OF NEW YORK NY
3.0	2.4	35.5	N/A	N/A	N/A	N/A	78.7	78.7	125.0	7.5	3.0	ROCHE SURETY & CASUALTY INC
1.3	0.8	147.6	64.0	-3.5	2.7	64.6	33.6	98.2	102.9	0.8	0.0	ROCKFORD MUTUAL INS CO
2.8	2.6	N/A	N/A	N/A	N/A	N/A	N/A	N/A	-990.5	0.0	30.9	ROCKHILL INS CO
20.7	18.6	N/A	N/A	N/A	N/A	N/A	N/A	N/A	69.9	0.0	0.0	ROCKINGHAM CASUALTY CO
1.0	0.9	62.2	28.2	-2.9	-7.6	69.0	35.1	104.1	101.6	10.3	29.3	ROCKINGHAM INS CO
2.0	1.6	54.5	114.9	-19.2	-27.8	30.0	30.8	60.8	133.0	2.3	15.0	ROCKWOOD CASUALTY INS CO
18.4	14.3	20.8	13.1	-1.3	-3.8	58.4	29.4	87.8	88.8	-34.5	0.0	ROCKY MOUNTAIN FIRE & CAS CO
0.9	0.7	48.8	17.7	-1.6	N/A	78.7	48.8	127.5	181.6	486.3	0.0	RPX RRG INC
2.6	1.8	51.3	81.9	-1.0	-2.1	53.4	26.6	80.0	127.4	15.7	8.4 •	RSUI INDEMNITY CO
4.0	2.4	81.9	10.7	-3.2	-3.1	92.9	2.0	94.9	52.6	17.2	0.0 •	RURAL COMMUNITY INS CO
5.6	3.9	81.9	50.0	-4.8	-8.5	59.7	25.4	85.1	119.0	6.4	0.0	RURAL MUTUAL INS CO
N/A	N/A	N/A	0.8	0.2	-0.5	N/A	N/A	N/A	N/A	0.0	0.0	RURAL TRUST INS CO
2.0	1.6	41.5	83.4	-0.4	1.6	64.3	37.8	102.1	69.5	-10.8	22.0	RUTGERS CASUALTY INS CO
2.0	1.5	67.8	136.4	-0.6	2.5	64.3	37.8	102.1	64.6	-10.8	0.0	RUTGERS ENHANCED INS CO
15.7	14.1	6.2	3.1	N/A	N/A	0.7	62.8	63.5	-573.4	0.0	0.0	RVI AMERICA INS CO
0.7	0.5	237.3	37.2	-3.6	2.4	87.0	33.6	120.6	83.3	2.9	30.2	RVOS FARM MUTUAL INS CO
1.6	1.4	221.3	112.1	-9.0	-2.5	73.4	26.6	100.0	93.0	0.9	0.0	SAFE AUTO INS CO
0.9	0.7	239.4	47.5	-0.4	8.0	44.8	34.9	79.7	130.0	41.7	0.0	SAFE HARBOR INS CO
4.9	3.1	42.5	12.3	-3.3	-5.2	42.5	39.0	81.5	120.5	2.3	0.0	SAFE INS CO
25.2	23.9	7.1	N/A	N/A	N/A	N/A	11.2	11.2	896.8	0.0	0.0	SAFECARD SERVICE INS CO
2.2	1.5	113.5	174.7	5.2	6.1	73.5	34.8	108.3	121.9	-18.7	6.2 •	SAFECO INS CO OF AMERICA
3.7	3.6	-59.6	N/A	N/A	N/A	N/A	N/A	N/A	-8.9	-147.8	30.9	SAFECO INS CO OF ILLINOIS
140.8	70.3	N/A	N/A	N/A	N/A	N/A	N/A	N/A	326.6	0.0	0.0	SAFECO INS CO OF INDIANA
47.2	42.5	N/A	N/A	N/A	N/A	N/A	N/A	N/A	279.3	0.0	0.0	SAFECO INS CO OF OREGON
222.5	111.3	N/A	N/A	N/A	N/A	N/A	N/A	N/A	72.0	0.0	0.0	SAFECO LLOYDS INS CO
13.9	12.5	N/A	N/A	N/A	N/A	N/A	N/A	N/A	617.4	0.0	0.0	SAFECO NATIONAL INS CO
N/A	N/A	N/A	N/A	N/A	N/A	N/A	N/A	N/A	N/A	0.0	0.0	SAFECO SURPLUS LINES INS CO
N/A	N/A	N/A	N/A	N/A	N/A	N/A	N/A	N/A	N/A	0.0	0.0	SAFEPOINT INS CO
9.4	6.9	11.7	17.6	1.9	-1.6	58.5	43.4	101.9	97.1	-5.4	0.0	SAFETY FIRST INS CO
5.0	3.5	90.2	51.0	-3.2	-5.3	65.7	28.2	93.9	107.2	5.1	0.0	SAFETY INDEMNITY INS CO
3.5	2.5	100.0	56.6	-3.5	-5.6	65.7	27.5	93.2	109.5	5.1	6.2 •	SAFETY INS CO
1.3	1.0	57.6	213.0	11.6	45.4	78.4	25.2	103.6	241.4	21.1	2.0 •	SAFETY NATIONAL CASUALTY CORP
2.7	1.9	119.3	67.5	-4.2	-7.1	65.7	30.0	95.7	107.7	5.1	0.0	SAFETY PROPERTY & CASUALTY INS CO
1.8	1.6	N/A	N/A	N/A	N/A	N/A	N/A	N/A	-95.4	0.0	0.0	SAFEWAY COUNTY MUTUAL INS CO
1.5	1.3	51.3	21.8	0.2	-0.5	79.1	22.7	101.8	102.3	23.9	53.1 •	SAFEWAY INS CO
1.7	1.5	138.3	58.7	0.5	-1.2	79.1	25.7	104.8	101.4	21.9	0.0	SAFEWAY INS CO OF AL
1.7	1.5	130.3	55.3	0.5	-1.2	79.1	26.1	105.2	106.3	23.0	0.0	SAFEWAY INS CO OF GEORGIA
2.5	2.3	130.3	55.3	0.5	-1.2	79.1	23.5	102.6	108.0	21.9	0.0	SAFEWAY INS CO OF LA
3.0	2.1	60.1	8.4	-0.1	-0.1	41.8	40.6	82.4	126.1	-3.0	0.0	SAFEWAY PROPERTY INS CO
16.3	9.7	17.4	8.0	0.1	-1.5	69.9	27.7	97.6	87.2	28.6	0.0	SAGAMORE INS CO
1.7	1.0	34.3	315.0	-4.8	-15.2	111.2	19.6	130.8	88.1	5.0	0.0	SAIF CORP
1.3	0.8	23.6	53.3	-10.6	-9.9	90.9	32.7	123.6	62.2	52.1	0.0	SAINT LUKES HEALTH SYSTEM RRG
N/A	N/A	-0.1	N/A	N/A	N/A	N/A	999 +	999 +	-0.5	0.0	0.0	SALEM COUNTY MUTUAL FIRE INS CO
2.8	1.7	55.3	36.4	0.2	3.6	69.9	12.8	82.7	220.7	4.5	0.0	SAMARITAN RRG INC
1.1	0.7	117.6	68.8	-0.9	-7.5	60.8	25.1	85.9	110.4	80.2	0.0	SAMSUNG FIRE & MARINE INS CO LTD
0.2	0.1	394.1	58.1	-14.1	1.3	76.0	26.0	102.0	99.2	75.3	0.0	SAN ANTONIO INDEMNITY CO
N/A	N/A	N/A	N/A	N/A	N/A	N/A	N/A	N/A	N/A	0.0	0.0	SAN DIEGO INS CO
N/A	N/A	N/A	31.5	3.1	13.9	N/A	N/A	N/A	N/A	0.0	0.0	SAN FRANCISCO REINSURANCE CO
N/A	N/A	89.6	3.8	N/A	N/A	51.5	74.8	126.3	75.7	-8.8	0.0	SANILAC MUTUAL INS CO
N/A	N/A	-0.5	0.4	-0.2	-0.7	-184.5	-910.3	999 +	-8.5	-1.5	0.0	SAUCON MUTUAL INS CO

999 + Denotes number greater than 999.9%
999 - Denotes number less than -999.99%
• Bullets denote a more detailed analysis is available in Section II.

INSURANCE COMPANY NAME	DOM. STATE	RATING	TOTAL ASSETS ($MIL)	CAPITAL & SURPLUS ($MIL)	ANNUAL NET PREMIUM ($MIL)	NET INCOME ($MIL)	CAPITAL- IZATION INDEX (PTS)	RESERVE ADQ INDEX (PTS)	PROFIT- ABILITY INDEX (PTS)	LIQUIDITY INDEX (PTS)	STAB. INDEX (PTS)	STABILITY FACTORS
SAUQUOIT VALLEY INS CO	NY	C-	4.8	3.8	0.7	-0.2	7.3	7.7	4.6	7.0	2.2	DFR
SAVERS PROPERTY & CASUALTY INS CO	MO	C	268.3	61.3	89.4	3.6	6.4	3.4	6.0	6.2	3.6	R
SAWGRASS MUTUAL INS CO	FL	D	27.4	10.6	5.8	-0.8	7.3	3.3	3.7	7.9	2.3	DT
SCHOOL BOARDS INS CO OF PA INC	PA	D	196.2	41.1	52.9	-1.3	5.4	4.1	2.0	6.8	2.0	FR
SCOR REINSURANCE CO	NY	D	2,254.6	692.7	755.6	41.5	5.2	5.7	5.5	6.3	2.2	R
SCOTTSDALE INDEMNITY CO	OH	B	77.3	37.2	0.0	0.1	10.0	N/A	7.0	7.7	5.6	DFT
SCOTTSDALE INS CO	OH	B-	2,197.2	764.3	707.1	0.6	8.5	4.7	5.3	6.4	4.9	A
SCOTTSDALE SURPLUS LINES INS CO	AZ	B	48.6	46.6	0.0	0.1	10.0	N/A	6.2	7.0	5.2	DF
SCRUBS MUTUAL ASR CO RRG	NV	C-	13.1	4.0	5.5	0.0	3.9	4.3	3.9	7.4	3.0	DR
SEABRIGHT INS CO	IL	D+	497.1	106.5	38.5	6.9	7.4	3.9	1.9	6.7	2.0	FRT
SEATON INS CO	RI	U	56.3	8.0	0.0	-0.1	N/A	1.4	2.8	10.0	0.0	CRT
SEAVIEW INS CO	CA	D+	20.4	10.0	8.0	2.0	7.4	5.1	6.9	8.5	2.2	DGT
SEAWAY MUTUAL INS CO	PA	U (3)	0.0	0.0	0.0	0.0	N/A	N/A	6.9	10.0	2.1	T
SEAWORTHY INS CO	MD	B-	106.6	52.0	37.4	-1.2	7.8	8.9	3.6	6.0	4.9	FRT
SECURA INS A MUTUAL CO	WI	B-	933.2	346.7	387.1	19.2	8.0	9.2	8.0	6.4	4.7	R
SECURA SUPREME INS CO	WI	C+	115.0	50.3	43.0	2.3	9.6	8.6	8.5	6.7	4.4	T
SECURIAN CASUALTY CO	MN	B	192.1	110.1	122.2	8.2	7.9	6.2	8.4	6.3	5.5	GT
SECURITY AMERICA RRG INC	VT	D	5.5	2.7	1.7	0.0	6.9	5.0	6.3	8.4	1.3	DR
SECURITY FIRST INS CO	FL	C	160.6	50.6	88.4	5.5	6.0	4.6	2.9	6.2	4.1	R
SECURITY MUTUAL INS CO	NY	C	96.5	46.9	33.5	2.1	9.0	5.9	8.0	7.0	3.9	R
SECURITY NATIONAL INS CO	DE	B-	642.6	111.1	44.7	20.1	9.4	5.0	9.5	9.2	4.3	FGRT
SECURITY NATIONAL INS CO	FL	D+	120.5	35.6	0.0	0.5	10.0	3.8	4.1	9.2	2.5	FR
SECURITY PLAN FIRE INS CO	LA	D	6.8	5.6	5.0	0.5	7.6	7.6	4.5	6.4	1.8	DR
SELECT INS CO	TX	U	73.3	73.0	0.0	1.7	N/A	N/A	7.9	10.0	5.4	T
SELECT MARKETS INS CO	IL	D	15.5	15.4	0.0	0.2	10.0	N/A	7.5	7.0	2.3	DRT
SELECT MD RRG INC	MT	D	2.2	0.8	0.3	-0.2	9.9	3.6	2.8	9.7	1.4	DFT
SELECT RISK INS CO	PA	C	37.6	13.8	14.6	0.1	8.0	9.3	6.3	6.5	4.2	D
SELECTIVE AUTO INS CO OF NJ	NJ	B-	329.7	71.2	108.7	5.3	7.5	9.1	6.6	6.9	5.1	A
SELECTIVE CASUALTY INS CO	NJ	B (3)	0.0	0.0	126.8	6.6	7.6	3.6	6.7	6.8	4.9	GT
SELECTIVE FIRE & CASUALTY INS CO	NJ	B- (3)	0.0	0.0	54.3	3.1	7.6	3.6	6.7	6.7	3.8	GT
SELECTIVE INS CO OF AMERICA	NJ	B-	2,040.8	492.8	579.7	55.8	7.7	8.8	5.6	6.8	5.1	A
SELECTIVE INS CO OF NEW ENGLAND	NJ	D	167.4	35.9	54.3	2.5	7.5	9.3	6.8	7.0	2.0	AGT
SELECTIVE INS CO OF NEW YORK	NY	B	377.5	83.0	126.8	5.9	7.5	9.1	6.6	6.7	5.4	A
SELECTIVE INS CO OF SC	IN	B	567.1	116.4	163.0	8.3	7.6	9.2	6.6	6.9	5.6	A
SELECTIVE INS CO OF THE SOUTHEAST	IN	B	438.2	86.1	126.8	6.2	7.5	9.2	6.6	7.0	5.5	A
SELECTIVE WAY INS CO	NJ	B	1,170.3	260.6	380.4	29.9	7.5	9.2	6.6	6.8	5.6	A
SENECA INS CO INC	DE	D+	192.9	133.7	-43.2	-0.2	9.2	9.3	3.8	2.5	2.8	LRT
SENECA SPECIALTY INS CO	AZ	C	48.5	48.2	0.0	0.7	10.0	4.6	7.6	10.0	3.5	RT
SENIOR AMERICAN INS CO	PA	E-	17.7	-2.2	2.9	-2.2	0.0	3.9	0.3	0.0	0.0	CDFL
SENTINEL ASR RRG INC	HI	D-	16.5	8.0	3.4	0.0	4.6	7.1	2.1	6.9	1.0	DFR
SENTINEL INS CO LTD	CT	B	220.3	148.4	29.8	13.7	10.0	4.6	6.7	7.2	5.8	A
SENTRUITY CASUALTY CO	TX	C+	130.5	42.2	4.5	0.9	10.0	5.1	8.9	10.0	3.3	FGRT
SENTRY CASUALTY CO	WI	B+	264.9	77.0	45.4	3.9	10.0	8.6	6.5	7.0	5.8	
SENTRY INS A MUTUAL CO	WI	A	6,922.0	4,306.8	999.7	153.5	8.3	7.8	6.7	7.0	7.5	
SENTRY LLOYDS OF TX	TX	B	6.8	6.6	0.0	0.1	10.0	N/A	7.8	10.0	4.9	D
SENTRY SELECT INS CO	WI	B+	676.5	243.3	181.8	12.1	9.7	8.8	6.0	6.7	6.5	
SEQUOIA INDEMNITY CO	NV	C	21.2	9.6	-1.5	-0.2	10.0	9.3	5.6	9.8	4.0	DFRT
SEQUOIA INS CO	CA	C+	250.9	78.1	-111.7	8.3	8.3	5.9	2.9	10.0	4.1	FRT
SERVICE INS CO	FL	B	48.3	31.7	8.6	4.1	9.0	6.6	5.5	7.2	5.5	DG
SERVICE INS CO INC	NJ	D-	12.1	6.1	1.5	0.2	9.9	7.0	7.5	9.1	1.1	DR
SERVICE LLOYDS INS CO	TX	B-	305.9	97.0	95.9	2.5	8.6	8.4	6.8	6.8	4.6	R
SEVEN SEAS INS CO INC	FL	C	22.6	14.2	17.2	5.6	9.0	7.7	3.4	8.6	3.8	DR

See Page 27 for explanation of footnotes and
Page 28 for explanation of stability factors.
Arrows denote recent upgrades ▲ or downgrades ▼   (see Section VII for explanations)

116   www.weissratings.com

RISK ADJ. RATIO #1	CAPITAL RATIO #2	PREMIUM TO SURPLUS (%)	RESV. TO SURPLUS (%)	RESV. DEVELOP. 1 YEAR (%)	RESV. DEVELOP. 2 YEAR (%)	LOSS RATIO (%)	EXP. RATIO (%)	COMB RATIO (%)	CASH FROM UNDER-WRITING (%)	NET PREMIUM GROWTH (%)	INVEST. IN AFFIL (%)	INSURANCE COMPANY NAME
2.0	1.2	16.8	6.0	-1.0	-1.8	61.8	39.7	101.5	86.2	-4.7	0.0	SAUQUOIT VALLEY INS CO
1.7	1.1	154.3	248.8	14.9	37.0	79.2	34.5	113.7	101.4	-14.0	0.0	SAVERS PROPERTY & CASUALTY INS
1.9	1.3	50.5	26.3	-0.7	15.4	57.4	22.3	79.7	107.3	27.7	0.0	SAWGRASS MUTUAL INS CO
1.5	0.9	125.4	285.0	-5.8	-14.2	69.6	37.6	107.2	87.0	-8.0	0.0	SCHOOL BOARDS INS CO OF PA INC
1.4	0.9	111.7	152.2	-4.4	0.6	62.3	34.6	96.9	101.5	6.5	0.0 ●	SCOR REINSURANCE CO
6.5	5.8	N/A	N/A	N/A	N/A	N/A	N/A	N/A	999 +	0.0	0.0	SCOTTSDALE INDEMNITY CO
2.4	1.9	98.7	65.1	-0.9	-1.8	66.2	33.0	99.2	122.7	18.1	18.0 ●	SCOTTSDALE INS CO
63.2	56.8	N/A	N/A	N/A	N/A	N/A	N/A	N/A	267.9	0.0	0.0	SCOTTSDALE SURPLUS LINES INS CO
0.8	0.5	143.4	140.2	-17.2	2.2	46.2	58.7	104.9	184.0	1.3	0.0	SCRUBS MUTUAL ASR CO RRG
1.7	1.0	17.0	189.1	10.4	7.8	120.7	74.0	194.7	50.4	-83.0	0.0 ●	SEABRIGHT INS CO
N/A	N/A	N/A	764.8	11.1	120.4	999 +	999 +	999 +	N/A	N/A	0.0	SEATON INS CO
2.0	1.5	99.4	4.6	-289.8	N/A	4.1	57.3	61.4	175.8	99.6	0.0	SEAVIEW INS CO
N/A	N/A	0.8	0.3	N/A	N/A	38.4	212.0	250.4	61.4	1.7	0.0	SEAWAY MUTUAL INS CO
2.4	1.6	72.3	18.3	-2.4	-12.5	66.8	34.1	100.9	40.4	45.0	0.0	SEAWORTHY INS CO
2.6	1.8	120.3	97.8	-10.9	-13.2	59.4	31.0	90.4	121.1	12.2	6.7 ●	SECURA INS A MUTUAL CO
4.7	3.5	90.1	73.2	-7.6	-8.7	59.4	29.5	88.9	117.1	12.2	0.0	SECURA SUPREME INS CO
2.7	2.1	120.9	17.6	-1.5	0.8	46.8	42.6	89.4	116.9	41.8	0.0	SECURIAN CASUALTY CO
1.3	0.9	62.6	43.9	1.9	-0.4	28.3	64.9	93.2	115.7	12.5	0.0	SECURITY AMERICA RRG INC
1.6	1.2	197.4	37.4	11.6	5.4	54.4	30.9	85.3	126.2	30.5	0.0	SECURITY FIRST INS CO
3.6	2.8	75.2	56.3	-5.2	-1.5	54.2	38.4	92.6	114.8	2.3	0.0	SECURITY MUTUAL INS CO
4.4	2.3	56.1	43.1	2.9	4.4	70.4	-19.3	51.1	-247.8	59.6	0.0	SECURITY NATIONAL INS CO
4.1	3.7	N/A	2.6	10.3	16.4	N/A	N/A	N/A	-43.8	0.0	0.0	SECURITY NATIONAL INS CO
1.8	1.5	97.2	9.5	-1.0	-2.7	40.6	63.5	104.1	95.9	-2.0	0.0	SECURITY PLAN FIRE INS CO
N/A	N/A	N/A	N/A	N/A	N/A	N/A	N/A	N/A	-43.9	0.0	0.0	SELECT INS CO
105.2	50.6	N/A	N/A	N/A	N/A	N/A	N/A	N/A	N/A	0.0	0.0	SELECT MARKETS INS CO
1.5	1.3	30.3	34.8	-9.2	N/A	35.8	42.0	77.8	93.2	-0.3	0.0	SELECT MD RRG INC
2.8	1.8	103.6	75.3	-9.5	-13.4	63.4	31.7	95.1	98.5	-1.7	0.0	SELECT RISK INS CO
2.0	1.3	159.7	246.7	-3.8	-7.6	64.5	32.7	97.2	120.2	8.7	0.0	SELECTIVE AUTO INS CO OF NJ
2.0	1.3	157.5	243.2	-3.5	N/A	64.5	32.7	97.2	124.1	9.5	0.0	SELECTIVE CASUALTY INS CO
2.1	1.3	155.3	239.9	-3.5	N/A	64.5	32.7	97.2	126.3	9.5	0.0	SELECTIVE FIRE & CASUALTY INS CO
2.4	1.5	125.1	193.2	-3.2	-4.8	64.5	32.7	97.2	115.5	16.7	0.0 ●	SELECTIVE INS CO OF AMERICA
1.9	1.3	155.9	240.7	-3.4	-16.1	64.5	32.7	97.2	118.6	9.3	0.0	SELECTIVE INS CO OF NEW ENGLAND
2.0	1.3	160.0	247.0	-3.5	-7.3	64.5	32.7	97.2	113.4	8.7	0.0	SELECTIVE INS CO OF NEW YORK
2.1	1.4	145.7	224.9	-3.6	-7.6	64.5	32.7	97.2	121.4	8.7	0.0	SELECTIVE INS CO OF SC
2.0	1.3	155.1	239.5	-3.7	-7.7	64.5	32.7	97.2	120.0	8.7	0.0	SELECTIVE INS CO OF THE SOUTHEAST
2.0	1.3	152.0	234.7	-3.6	-7.2	64.5	32.7	97.2	110.3	8.7	0.0 ●	SELECTIVE WAY INS CO
3.2	3.2	-32.5	N/A	N/A	-7.8	55.1	-41.6	13.5	125.7	-122.7	38.8	SENECA INS CO INC
98.3	49.1	N/A	N/A	N/A	N/A	N/A	N/A	N/A	N/A	0.0	0.0	SENECA SPECIALTY INS CO
-0.3	-0.2	999 +	999 +	999 +	999 +	138.3	20.3	158.6	51.7	-9.0	0.0	SENIOR AMERICAN INS CO
1.0	0.8	42.8	92.7	29.9	0.8	179.7	41.6	221.3	83.3	-13.5	0.0	SENTINEL ASR RRG INC
13.9	9.0	22.2	39.7	0.2	N/A	68.8	-15.6	53.2	103.1	1.1	0.0	SENTINEL INS CO LTD
4.9	4.4	10.9	0.8	-0.6	-0.1	29.3	-15.3	14.0	999 +	-79.4	0.0	SENTRUITY CASUALTY CO
5.2	3.4	62.2	94.6	-2.4	-4.5	76.3	24.8	101.1	104.9	5.2	0.0 ●	SENTRY CASUALTY CO
2.4	2.0	24.5	37.3	-1.1	-2.0	76.3	24.8	101.1	110.0	5.2	25.7 ●	SENTRY INS A MUTUAL CO
86.8	78.1	N/A	N/A	N/A	N/A	N/A	N/A	N/A	-201.6	0.0	0.0	SENTRY LLOYDS OF TX
4.2	2.8	79.9	121.4	-3.3	-5.8	76.3	24.8	101.1	102.6	5.2	0.0 ●	SENTRY SELECT INS CO
3.8	3.4	-15.7	N/A	-15.2	-18.6	120.2	13.4	133.6	-517.1	-271.7	0.0	SEQUOIA INDEMNITY CO
3.5	3.1	-150.0	16.4	-92.5	-35.6	90.1	-1.8	88.3	-664.3	-212.4	11.3	SEQUOIA INS CO
3.5	2.2	31.5	9.0	-1.6	0.4	35.8	28.7	64.5	144.8	-33.2	0.0	SERVICE INS CO
3.6	3.2	25.8	13.4	-5.4	-8.7	32.8	32.8	65.6	163.0	-8.1	0.0	SERVICE INS CO INC
2.9	2.0	100.2	74.4	0.2	-3.8	57.9	44.4	102.3	115.8	7.7	0.0	SERVICE LLOYDS INS CO
2.0	1.9	106.1	4.2	-0.9	-0.2	17.8	16.0	33.8	308.5	-0.7	0.6	SEVEN SEAS INS CO INC

999 + Denotes number greater than 999.9%
999 - Denotes number less than -999.99%
● Bullets denote a more detailed analysis is available in Section II.

INSURANCE COMPANY NAME	DOM. STATE	RATING	TOTAL ASSETS ($MIL)	CAPITAL & SURPLUS ($MIL)	ANNUAL NET PREMIUM ($MIL)	NET INCOME ($MIL)	CAPITAL-IZATION INDEX (PTS)	RESERVE ADQ INDEX (PTS)	PROFIT-ABILITY INDEX (PTS)	LIQUIDITY INDEX (PTS)	STAB. INDEX (PTS)	STABILITY FACTORS
SFM MUTUAL INS CO	MN	C+	499.5	108.0	141.2	6.2	5.9	6.0	6.5	6.4	4.8	T
SFM SELECT INS CO	MN	D-	4.8	3.5	0.0	0.0	10.0	4.6	5.8	10.0	1.3	DRT
SHAMOKIN TOWNSHIP MUTUAL FIRE INS	PA	U (3)	0.0	0.0	0.0	0.0	N/A	N/A	2.2	10.0	0.3	FT
SHEBOYGAN FALLS INS CO	WI	C+	28.1	11.9	14.6	-0.3	7.8	5.7	4.9	6.8	4.4	DR
SHELBY INS CO	TX	F (5)	0.0	0.0	0.0	0.0	10.0	N/A	2.6	7.0	0.0	
SHELTER GENERAL INS CO	MO	B-	156.9	85.8	88.0	6.6	10.0	9.3	3.6	5.9	5.0	F
SHELTER MUTUAL INS CO	MO	B	2,923.1	1,667.9	1,208.2	34.2	7.9	7.8	5.4	5.4	5.5	L
SHELTER REINSURANCE CO	MO	C	400.6	274.4	98.0	29.9	8.2	6.9	4.8	6.5	4.2	R
SIGMA RRG INC	DC	B-	14.3	6.1	2.5	0.2	6.5	7.0	8.9	9.1	3.5	CDT
SILVER OAK CASUALTY INC	NE	C+	223.8	91.5	51.7	4.5	7.7	9.2	8.9	7.2	4.5	R
SIMED	PR	D+	165.7	86.3	22.2	0.9	10.0	9.4	8.5	7.5	2.7	DR
SIRIUS AMERICA INS CO	NY	C+	1,553.2	604.8	252.8	38.4	7.2	5.0	3.7	7.0	4.5	FR
SLAVONIC INS CO OF TX	TX	U	4.1	4.0	0.0	0.1	N/A	7.2	6.8	10.0	4.3	R
SLAVONIC MUTUAL FIRE INS ASN	TX	C	28.4	27.9	0.9	0.8	10.0	6.2	6.9	9.2	3.9	DR
SOCIETY INS	WI	B-	360.9	124.8	143.1	10.2	8.2	8.6	6.1	6.5	5.1	T
SOMERSET CASUALTY INS CO	PA	D	32.8	19.3	6.0	0.5	10.0	9.4	8.8	7.7	2.3	DR
SOMPO JAPAN FIRE & MAR INS CO AMER	NY	C	76.1	74.0	0.1	0.5	10.0	3.6	5.8	7.0	3.6	DG
SOMPO JAPAN INS CO OF AMERICA	NY	B	1,244.3	541.1	124.4	5.8	8.3	9.3	6.8	7.1	5.8	T
SONNENBERG MUTUAL INS ASSOC	OH	C	22.7	13.3	9.3	0.8	8.5	7.8	5.5	6.8	4.0	D
SOUTH CAROLINA FARM BU MUTUAL INS	SC	C	112.1	47.6	52.3	-7.4	8.3	6.1	2.2	6.0	3.5	F
SOUTH CAROLINA FARM BUREAU INS	SC	U	3.1	3.1	0.0	0.0	N/A	N/A	4.9	7.0	4.2	T
SOUTHEAST EMPLOYERS MUT CAP INS CO	GA	U (5)	0.0	0.0	0.0	0.0	N/A	2.4	0.0	6.3	0.0	CFT
SOUTHERN COUNTY MUTUAL INS CO	TX	C	41.3	30.0	0.0	1.8	10.0	N/A	4.3	10.0	3.8	R
SOUTHERN FARM BUREAU CAS INS CO	MS	B-	2,041.1	1,265.2	825.8	36.4	8.6	8.0	6.9	6.4	4.8	T
SOUTHERN FARM BUREAU PROPERTY	MS	U	54.6	54.3	0.0	0.7	N/A	N/A	4.7	7.0	5.4	RT
SOUTHERN FIDELITY INS CO INC	FL	C+	195.2	78.5	111.1	6.9	7.3	9.3	7.9	5.9	4.6	R
SOUTHERN FIDELITY P&C INC	FL	C+	102.7	26.7	58.9	2.7	4.1	3.6	8.5	7.0	3.3	CDGT
SOUTHERN FIRE & CASUALTY CO	WI	C	19.1	5.5	6.0	0.0	7.3	3.9	2.3	7.7	3.5	DFRT
SOUTHERN GENERAL INS CO	GA	D	46.0	14.5	28.8	-0.6	6.4	4.1	1.5	0.7	2.3	DLR
SOUTHERN GUARANTY INS CO	WI	D+	126.5	22.9	46.6	-0.5	5.0	4.0	1.5	6.4	2.8	DFRT
SOUTHERN INS CO	TX	C	48.2	31.7	1.4	1.3	6.5	3.6	4.8	9.1	4.0	FRT
SOUTHERN INS CO OF VIRGINIA	VA	C+	133.1	61.5	58.9	0.6	9.7	6.0	3.8	6.1	4.7	FR
SOUTHERN MUTUAL CHURCH INS CO	SC	C	48.4	22.9	21.1	1.9	7.4	8.2	4.2	6.7	4.0	DR
SOUTHERN MUTUAL INS CO	GA	C	15.9	12.7	0.1	-0.2	10.0	6.0	4.2	10.0	4.1	DR
SOUTHERN OAK INS CO	FL	D+	118.0	37.5	71.4	6.4	5.1	3.7	6.2	6.5	2.5	T
SOUTHERN PILOT INS CO	WI	C	38.8	8.6	12.0	0.0	6.3	3.8	2.1	7.5	3.5	DFRT
SOUTHERN PIONEER PROP & CAS INS CO	AR	C-	29.4	14.8	15.1	0.0	8.2	7.9	5.3	7.1	2.9	DR
SOUTHERN STATES INS EXCHANGE	VA	C	45.3	19.1	13.9	2.8	7.7	9.3	7.1	6.4	3.9	DFR
SOUTHERN TRUST INS CO	GA	B-	43.5	22.5	25.7	0.9	8.2	7.6	4.4	6.0	4.6	DFR
SOUTHERN UNDERWRITERS INS CO	OK	C	5.4	5.4	0.0	0.1	10.0	N/A	5.4	10.0	2.4	DFRT
▼SOUTHERN VANGUARD INS CO	TX	C	20.0	10.0	0.0	0.4	10.0	N/A	7.0	10.0	2.9	DFR
SOUTHERN-OWNERS INS CO	MI	A	618.1	187.9	224.9	2.1	8.5	9.3	5.9	6.7	7.4	
SOUTHLAND LLOYDS INS CO	TX	U (3)	0.0	0.0	0.0	-0.1	N/A	6.4	1.3	9.9	2.5	FT
SOUTHWEST GENERAL INS CO	NM	D	3.0	1.6	0.9	-0.1	8.2	9.3	3.6	7.7	1.6	DFT
SOUTHWEST MARINE & GEN INS CO	AZ	B	117.6	51.9	26.0	1.5	7.3	4.3	4.7	7.5	4.7	T
SOUTHWEST PHYSICIANS RRG INC	SC	E+	79.9	19.9	16.7	5.3	0.9	4.6	5.0	6.6	0.5	CDR
SPARTA AMERICAN INS CO	CA	C	44.8	17.1	17.9	0.5	2.7	3.6	2.1	6.5	3.3	CDRT
SPARTA INS CO	CT	C-	418.8	186.7	163.1	3.7	6.0	4.0	2.0	6.6	3.2	R
SPARTA SPECIALTY INS CO	CT	C	103.2	47.4	42.4	1.3	5.9	2.4	3.1	6.8	3.7	T
SPARTAN INS CO	TX	D	5.8	4.9	2.8	0.6	9.8	4.7	5.8	7.9	2.2	DGR
SPARTAN PROPERTY INS CO	SC	C	51.9	25.4	37.5	6.4	7.1	6.1	8.2	7.9	4.3	T
SPECIALTY RISK OF AMERICA	IL	C-	9.9	3.4	4.5	-0.3	5.0	4.6	1.8	7.4	2.2	DG

See Page 27 for explanation of footnotes and
Page 28 for explanation of stability factors.

Arrows denote recent upgrades ▲ or downgrades ▼   (see Section VII for explanations)

118

www.weissratings.com

RISK ADJ. CAPITAL RATIO #1	CAPITAL RATIO #2	PREMIUM TO SURPLUS (%)	RESV. TO SURPLUS (%)	RESV. DEVELOP. 1 YEAR (%)	RESV. DEVELOP. 2 YEAR (%)	LOSS RATIO (%)	EXP. RATIO (%)	COMB RATIO (%)	CASH FROM UNDER-WRITING (%)	NET PREMIUM GROWTH (%)	INVEST. IN AFFIL (%)	INSURANCE COMPANY NAME
1.1	0.8	139.6	269.8	-2.1	-0.3	78.7	18.9	·97.6	123.1	4.5	1.4	SFM MUTUAL INS CO
6.3	5.7	N/A	1.0	-0.1	N/A	N/A	N/A	N/A	N/A	0.0	0.0	SFM SELECT INS CO
N/A	N/A	5.3	N/A	N/A	N/A	N/A	198.4	198.4	50.4	-20.3	0.0	SHAMOKIN TOWNSHIP MUTUAL FIRE INS
2.2	1.6	120.7	42.5	-2.0	5.3	60.8	31.0	91.8	113.7	13.5	0.0	SHEBOYGAN FALLS INS CO
19.5	17.2	N/A	N/A	N/A	N/A	N/A	N/A	N/A	1.9	0.0	0.0	SHELBY INS CO
5.3	4.4	110.6	68.1	-4.2	-9.3	79.9	26.1	106.0	92.5	-10.9	7.9	SHELTER GENERAL INS CO
2.1	1.6	77.1	25.5	-1.4	-2.8	74.2	28.0	102.2	100.8	5.5	24.7 ●	SHELTER MUTUAL INS CO
3.2	2.2	39.9	45.1	-15.8	-12.2	40.6	28.1	68.7	118.0	-4.1	0.0 ●	SHELTER REINSURANCE CO
1.1	0.7	45.1	114.8	-9.8	-17.5	74.1	12.1	86.2	300.8	8.6	0.0	SIGMA RRG INC
2.4	1.8	79.0	130.1	-3.5	-4.9	69.6	18.4	88.0	139.5	12.4	0.0	SILVER OAK CASUALTY INC
4.5	3.5	25.9	83.7	-6.7	-9.1	87.3	20.6	107.9	86.7	-12.9	0.0	SIMED
2.3	1.3	46.1	151.4	0.7	1.2	48.9	37.1	86.0	68.7	-6.8	0.0 ●	SIRIUS AMERICA INS CO
N/A	N/A	0.3	0.1	-0.2	-0.1	48.2	427.1	475.3	19.0	-29.8	0.0	SLAVONIC INS CO OF TX
7.1	6.7	3.2	N/A	N/A	-0.6	38.9	76.5	115.4	87.0	-9.1	14.8	SLAVONIC MUTUAL FIRE INS ASN
2.7	1.9	123.3	112.8	-1.3	-2.4	65.8	30.0	95.8	106.5	3.7	0.0	SOCIETY INS
3.9	3.0	32.1	40.7	-2.5	-17.7	55.1	19.0	74.1	238.5	21.5	0.0	SOMERSET CASUALTY INS CO
98.5	80.1	0.1	0.3	-0.1	N/A	267.9	244.8	512.7	999 +	78.8	0.0	SOMPO JAPAN FIRE & MAR INS CO
2.4	1.7	25.9	55.1	-4.8	-9.9	62.9	38.2	101.1	103.6	18.9	15.3 ●	SOMPO JAPAN INS CO OF AMERICA
3.2	2.0	74.2	28.1	-2.3	-1.6	64.2	31.8	96.0	113.3	6.3	0.0	SONNENBERG MUTUAL INS ASSOC
2.2	1.8	95.0	22.1	0.7	-0.9	69.1	32.4	101.5	91.6	-8.6	9.6	SOUTH CAROLINA FARM BU MUTUAL INS
N/A	N/A	N/A	N/A	N/A	N/A	N/A	N/A	N/A	N/A	0.0	0.0	SOUTH CAROLINA FARM BUREAU INS
N/A	N/A	-19.4	898.6	-0.7	27.8	14.3	-478.6	-464.3	10.3	-138.9	0.0	SOUTHEAST EMPLOYERS MUT CAP INS
11.6	10.5	N/A	N/A	N/A	N/A	N/A	N/A	N/A	-19.2	0.0	0.0	SOUTHERN COUNTY MUTUAL INS CO
2.3	2.0	66.8	28.8	-1.5	-4.0	80.3	17.7	98.0	101.8	2.8	28.4 ●	SOUTHERN FARM BUREAU CAS INS CO
N/A	N/A	N/A	N/A	N/A	N/A	N/A	N/A	N/A	N/A	0.0	0.0	SOUTHERN FARM BUREAU PROPERTY
2.1	1.4	154.1	26.7	-6.2	-7.3	35.6	51.9	87.5	100.1	7.8	0.0	SOUTHERN FIDELITY INS CO INC
1.1	0.7	241.3	50.1	-2.5	N/A	46.1	46.9	93.0	123.1	-9.6	0.0	SOUTHERN FIDELITY P&C INC
1.7	1.1	107.5	101.2	6.6	14.1	75.2	34.4	109.6	85.9	10.3	0.0	SOUTHERN FIRE & CASUALTY CO
0.8	0.7	222.6	70.7	10.3	9.9	75.6	37.9	113.5	108.0	17.9	0.0	SOUTHERN GENERAL INS CO
1.1	0.7	195.4	188.6	8.2	16.9	75.2	35.3	110.5	80.2	-10.5	0.0	SOUTHERN GUARANTY INS CO
1.8	1.1	4.7	46.0	3.3	6.3	121.1	-82.2	38.9	50.0	-8.3	0.0	SOUTHERN INS CO
4.9	3.2	94.0	51.4	2.9	2.8	69.2	31.9	101.1	86.0	-21.0	0.0	SOUTHERN INS CO OF VIRGINIA
1.8	1.2	101.1	31.4	-1.4	-10.0	51.0	38.4	89.4	113.1	4.9	0.0	SOUTHERN MUTUAL CHURCH INS CO
12.1	10.9	0.8	0.4	N/A	0.6	48.6	-715.3	-666.7	92.4	1.9	0.0	SOUTHERN MUTUAL INS CO
1.5	1.2	228.5	64.1	-7.4	-0.4	56.2	32.7	88.9	117.0	11.1	0.0	SOUTHERN OAK INS CO
1.3	0.8	138.2	130.0	7.2	15.5	75.2	34.4	109.6	85.9	6.0	0.0	SOUTHERN PILOT INS CO
2.5	1.5	103.0	27.9	4.3	-4.1	53.7	34.0	87.7	122.7	35.3	0.0	SOUTHERN PIONEER PROP & CAS INS
2.7	1.6	81.5	82.1	-15.2	-21.5	63.8	23.7	87.5	99.2	-3.8	0.0	SOUTHERN STATES INS EXCHANGE
2.9	1.9	118.7	27.0	0.4	-2.0	58.5	41.8	100.3	96.3	2.6	0.0	SOUTHERN TRUST INS CO
113.6	56.8	N/A	N/A	N/A	N/A	N/A	N/A	N/A	-50.2	0.0	0.0	SOUTHERN UNDERWRITERS INS CO
4.1	3.7	N/A	N/A	N/A	N/A	N/A	N/A	N/A	-256.8	0.0	0.0	SOUTHERN VANGUARD INS CO
2.5	1.8	121.9	128.9	-7.3	-15.8	74.0	25.4	99.4	108.9	10.1	0.0 ●	SOUTHERN-OWNERS INS CO
N/A	N/A	N/A	3.2	5.6	2.8	N/A	N/A	N/A	N/A	0.0	0.0	SOUTHLAND LLOYDS INS CO
2.7	2.1	54.0	20.8	-5.8	-13.6	44.3	72.4	116.7	81.7	-17.8	0.0	SOUTHWEST GENERAL INS CO
2.1	1.1	51.9	79.1	10.2	11.6	82.7	29.0	111.7	156.9	58.9	0.0	SOUTHWEST MARINE & GEN INS CO
0.6	0.4	98.4	283.9	-5.4	-43.7	86.6	2.1	88.7	247.1	-4.6	0.0	SOUTHWEST PHYSICIANS RRG INC
1.2	0.7	108.5	150.0	27.3	21.5	103.7	25.3	129.0	130.0	13.0	0.0	SPARTA AMERICAN INS CO
2.1	1.3	92.1	127.3	18.8	15.0	103.7	25.3	129.0	120.5	13.0	14.2	SPARTA INS CO
3.0	1.5	98.3	135.9	27.1	21.7	103.7	25.3	129.0	122.6	13.0	0.0	SPARTA SPECIALTY INS CO
2.9	2.9	63.3	4.6	-0.1	-0.6	3.9	55.0	58.9	136.9	39.9	0.0	SPARTAN INS CO
1.4	1.1	138.0	1.8	0.2	-0.2	4.6	59.1	63.7	157.6	24.0	0.0	SPARTAN PROPERTY INS CO
0.8	0.5	119.4	72.9	7.7	-6.2	54.5	56.3	110.8	94.1	42.7	0.0	SPECIALTY RISK OF AMERICA

999 + Denotes number greater than 999.9%
999 - Denotes number less than -999.99%
● Bullets denote a more detailed analysis is available in Section II.

INSURANCE COMPANY NAME	DOM. STATE	RATING	TOTAL ASSETS ($MIL)	CAPITAL & SURPLUS ($MIL)	ANNUAL NET PREMIUM ($MIL)	NET INCOME ($MIL)	CAPITAL-IZATION INDEX (PTS)	RESERVE ADQ INDEX (PTS)	PROFIT-ABILITY INDEX (PTS)	LIQUIDITY INDEX (PTS)	STAB. INDEX (PTS)	STABILITY FACTORS
SPECIALTY SURPLUS INS CO	IL	U	22.2	20.8	0.0	0.1	N/A	4.8	5.5	7.0	6.5	T
SPIRIT COMMERCIAL AUTO RRG INC	NV	D	48.5	10.8	17.3	0.0	2.4	3.6	3.3	7.8	1.4	CDGT
SPIRIT MOUNTAIN INS CO RRG INC	DC	D-	6.7	3.2	2.1	0.0	7.6	10.0	7.6	9.1	1.3	DR
SPRING VALLEY MUTUAL INS CO	MN	E+	3.9	3.9	0.0	0.1	10.0	6.0	2.7	7.0	0.6	DRT
SPRINGFIELD INS CO INC	CA	D+	94.2	19.9	23.9	-6.5	5.8	4.1	1.7	6.7	2.5	
ST CHARLES INS CO RRG	SC	E	13.7	9.5	1.2	0.7	8.7	6.1	8.9	9.3	0.0	D
ST CLAIR INS CO	NY	U	1.2	1.2	0.0	0.0	N/A	N/A	3.5	7.0	2.7	T
ST JOHNS INS CO INC	FL	D	123.8	49.9	29.3	1.9	3.0	6.9	3.9	1.3	1.8	CL
ST LUKES HEALTH NETWORK INS CO RRG	VT	E	57.0	13.3	11.5	-1.3	1.3	3.0	3.7	6.8	0.0	CD
ST PAUL FIRE & CAS INS CO	WI	U	16.7	16.3	0.0	0.4	N/A	N/A	6.0	7.0	5.4	T
ST PAUL FIRE & MARINE INS CO	CT	B	18,981.1	6,010.9	5,131.4	608.6	7.4	8.6	5.7	6.9	5.7	
ST PAUL GUARDIAN INS CO	CT	C+	78.3	28.4	20.1	2.2	7.9	8.3	6.1	6.9	4.7	T
ST PAUL MERCURY INS CO	CT	B-	358.8	140.8	80.6	10.1	9.4	8.6	7.5	6.9	4.9	T
ST PAUL PROTECTIVE INS CO	CT	B-	524.7	242.4	116.8	14.2	10.0	7.9	6.0	7.4	4.9	T
ST PAUL SURPLUS LINES INS CO	DE	C	643.9	212.2	177.2	18.7	7.3	8.6	7.6	7.0	4.0	T
STANDARD CASUALTY CO	TX	C	31.3	15.7	18.8	0.5	7.2	5.9	5.6	6.9	2.6	DGT
STANDARD FIRE INS CO	CT	B	3,617.4	1,223.8	974.8	118.7	7.8	8.3	6.9	6.9	5.5	T
STANDARD GUARANTY INS CO	DE	B-	443.0	156.6	237.7	3.8	10.0	6.6	9.3	6.7	4.5	GRT
STANDARD MUTUAL INS CO	IL	C	61.8	23.9	40.3	-4.0	8.3	8.6	2.4	5.9	4.1	FR
STAR & SHIELD INS EXCHANGE	FL	E+	21.8	5.8	15.3	-8.0	1.4	2.6	1.1	0.6	0.4	CDFG
STAR CASUALTY INS CO	FL	D+	18.1	9.4	12.4	0.9	6.7	2.1	3.9	7.1	2.5	D
STAR INS CO	MI	C	1,010.1	314.2	245.7	11.1	7.6	4.2	6.5	6.6	3.6	FR
STARNET INS CO	DE	C	216.7	110.6	0.0	1.6	10.0	3.6	4.5	9.2	3.4	R
STARR INDEMNITY & LIABILITY CO	TX	B-	3,725.1	1,818.1	847.3	20.8	7.2	4.4	4.2	7.0	4.9	GRT
STARR SURPLUS LINES INS CO	IL	B-	277.0	100.1	44.4	7.0	7.9	3.9	7.1	2.6	3.6	FGLT
STATE AUTO INS CO OF OHIO	OH	C-	32.7	16.4	0.0	0.5	10.0	3.8	6.7	7.0	3.2	ADRT
STATE AUTO INS CO OF WISCONSIN	WI	B	17.9	11.8	0.0	0.2	10.0	N/A	5.6	7.0	4.3	ADR
STATE AUTO PROPERTY & CASUALTY INS	IA	C-	2,108.4	612.8	833.3	17.5	7.4	8.5	5.0	6.3	2.9	AR
STATE AUTOMOBILE MUTUAL INS CO	OH	C+	2,298.3	862.6	555.6	-6.6	7.3	7.6	4.1	6.5	4.3	AF
STATE COMPENSATION INS FUND	CA	U (5)	19,387.8	6,382.0	972.9	0.0	N/A	5.8	5.6	7.7	3.6	F
STATE FARM CTY MUTUAL INS CO OF TX	TX	B-	196.8	38.2	29.1	-1.8	10.0	8.1	3.1	7.0	5.2	
STATE FARM FIRE & CAS CO	IL	B-	33,186.6	11,292.3	15,276.5	925.3	7.1	6.7	5.4	5.3	4.9	
STATE FARM FLORIDA INS CO	FL	C	1,895.7	868.9	575.4	124.0	5.1	5.8	2.9	6.3	3.4	
STATE FARM GENERAL INS CO	IL	B	6,749.8	3,756.9	1,919.0	295.8	9.3	6.3	8.8	6.7	6.3	
STATE FARM GUARANTY INS CO	IL	C-	32.4	13.3	0.0	0.0	10.0	N/A	6.2	9.2	3.1	DR
STATE FARM INDEMNITY CO	IL	B-	2,133.6	1,094.6	603.6	45.4	10.0	5.9	5.4	6.7	4.9	
STATE FARM LLOYDS	TX	B-	3,305.8	1,217.9	1,712.7	193.9	8.0	7.0	7.2	6.4	5.0	T
STATE FARM MUTUAL AUTOMOBILE INS CO	IL	B+	137,646.1	80,987.7	35,163.3	642.8	8.2	7.9	6.6	6.6	6.7	
STATE INS FUND	NY	U	--	--	--	--	N/A	--	--	--	--	Z
STATE INS FUND DISABILITY BENEFITS	NY	U	--	--	--	--	N/A	--	--	--	--	Z
STATE MUTUAL INS CO	ME	C	2.3	2.2	0.0	0.0	8.9	N/A	8.6	7.0	2.6	DT
STATE NATIONAL FIRE INS CO	LA	C	2.0	1.7	0.3	-0.2	10.0	7.4	2.3	7.6	2.2	DFT
STATE NATIONAL INS CO INC	TX	C+	285.5	213.4	42.0	1.9	8.2	4.6	7.8	7.0	4.5	FR
STATE VOLUNTEER MUTUAL INS CO	TN	A+	1,206.0	508.6	122.2	5.0	9.4	9.5	8.6	8.9	6.9	
STATE WORKERS INS FUND	PA	U (5)	0.0	0.0	471.1	0.0	N/A	7.9	1.5	7.0	0.0	CT
STATES SELF-INSURERS RISK RET GROUP	VT	D-	27.0	9.7	1.9	-0.3	1.4	4.4	5.2	7.5	1.3	CDR
STEADFAST INS CO	DE	C	553.3	436.6	0.0	4.5	10.0	N/A	4.2	7.1	3.5	FR
STEADPOINT INS CO	TN	C-	21.0	5.8	8.7	0.2	3.7	9.4	6.2	6.8	2.4	CDR
STERLING CAS INS CO	CA	E	15.6	3.4	13.3	0.6	2.8	4.8	1.2	0.0	0.1	DFL
STERLING INS CO	NY	C	148.3	87.1	49.3	3.1	10.0	9.4	8.7	7.1	3.6	R
STEWARD RRG	DC	U (5)	0.0	0.0	0.8	0.0	N/A	3.6	2.5	7.5	1.8	DGRT
STICO MUTUAL INS CO A RRG	VT	D	24.0	11.7	3.7	0.4	4.5	9.3	7.6	7.7	1.7	DR

See Page 27 for explanation of footnotes and
Page 28 for explanation of stability factors.
Arrows denote recent upgrades ▲ or downgrades ▼   (see Section VII for explanations)

120

www.weissratings.com

RISK ADJ. CAPITAL RATIO #1	RATIO #2	PREMIUM TO SURPLUS (%)	RESV. TO SURPLUS (%)	RESV. DEVELOP. 1 YEAR (%)	2 YEAR (%)	LOSS RATIO (%)	EXP. RATIO (%)	COMB RATIO (%)	CASH FROM UNDER-WRITING (%)	NET PREMIUM GROWTH (%)	INVEST. IN AFFIL (%)	INSURANCE COMPANY NAME
N/A	N/A	N/A	0.6	-2.5	-2.9	N/A	N/A	N/A	N/A	0.0	0.0	SPECIALTY SURPLUS INS CO
0.9	0.5	249.4	81.2	14.6	N/A	70.2	22.4	92.6	105.5	261.8	0.0	SPIRIT COMMERCIAL AUTO RRG INC
2.4	1.5	66.2	49.6	-43.0	-50.5	-12.4	58.7	46.3	232.4	-0.6	0.0	SPIRIT MOUNTAIN INS CO RRG INC
112.2	58.6	N/A	N/A	-0.2	-0.2	N/A	N/A	N/A	7.9	100.0	0.0	SPRING VALLEY MUTUAL INS CO
1.0	0.6	92.1	213.1	21.9	23.8	114.8	25.9	140.7	97.8	-2.2	0.0	SPRINGFIELD INS CO INC
4.9	2.7	14.0	32.0	-109.8	-91.9	-82.0	51.0	-31.0	229.2	34.0	0.0	ST CHARLES INS CO RRG
N/A	N/A	N/A	N/A	N/A	N/A	N/A	N/A	N/A	N/A	0.0	0.0	ST CLAIR INS CO
0.5	0.5	60.3	25.3	2.0	4.9	95.1	-16.0	79.1	257.1	28.5	0.0	ST JOHNS INS CO INC
0.3	0.2	79.3	260.3	61.1	40.5	128.9	13.3	142.2	109.2	4.3	0.0	ST LUKES HEALTH NETWORK INS CO
N/A	N/A	N/A	N/A	N/A	N/A	N/A	N/A	N/A	32.6	0.0	0.0	ST PAUL FIRE & CAS INS CO
1.5	1.2	86.8	158.4	-2.7	-6.1	60.5	30.1	90.6	107.2	2.5	21.0 ●	ST PAUL FIRE & MARINE INS CO
2.7	1.7	77.0	138.5	-1.9	-4.4	60.9	29.7	90.6	99.7	3.0	0.0	ST PAUL GUARDIAN INS CO
4.3	2.7	61.6	110.9	-1.5	-3.3	60.9	29.9	90.8	118.7	3.0	0.0	ST PAUL MERCURY INS CO
5.2	3.3	51.2	92.1	-1.3	-2.8	60.9	29.6	90.5	106.7	3.0	0.0 ●	ST PAUL PROTECTIVE INS CO
1.9	1.2	91.5	164.7	-2.4	-5.5	60.9	29.6	90.5	123.5	3.0	0.0 ●	ST PAUL SURPLUS LINES INS CO
1.9	1.2	125.0	6.6	2.3	2.1	50.2	42.0	92.2	115.8	39.0	0.0	STANDARD CASUALTY CO
1.9	1.5	78.9	142.0	-2.2	-5.2	60.9	26.2	87.1	109.2	3.0	16.5 ●	STANDARD FIRE INS CO
4.8	2.8	157.5	14.9	0.3	-3.1	41.5	27.2	68.7	299.8	95.9	0.0	STANDARD GUARANTY INS CO
2.1	1.6	144.6	49.7	-10.5	-8.1	68.7	36.3	105.0	91.6	0.7	0.0	STANDARD MUTUAL INS CO
0.4	0.3	168.4	150.3	63.6	30.1	127.4	32.1	159.5	96.3	-17.4	0.0	STAR & SHIELD INS EXCHANGE
1.5	1.3	139.9	32.0	26.7	37.1	79.2	8.8	88.0	111.4	26.6	0.0	STAR CASUALTY INS CO
2.1	1.7	79.4	127.9	8.5	19.3	79.2	34.2	113.4	81.3	-14.0	17.5 ●	STAR INS CO
12.1	10.9	N/A	N/A	N/A	N/A	N/A	N/A	N/A	-105.5	0.0	0.0	STARNET INS CO
1.3	1.1	45.4	40.5	1.9	8.5	81.6	20.6	102.2	170.4	35.5	36.3 ●	STARR INDEMNITY & LIABILITY CO
3.1	1.9	49.0	36.9	8.0	15.2	77.1	-11.9	65.2	86.9	50.6	0.0	STARR SURPLUS LINES INS CO
5.4	4.9	N/A	N/A	N/A	N/A	N/A	N/A	N/A	30.6	0.0	0.0	STATE AUTO INS CO OF OHIO
6.8	6.1	N/A	N/A	N/A	N/A	N/A	N/A	N/A	79.4	0.0	0.0	STATE AUTO INS CO OF WISCONSIN
2.1	1.3	137.1	122.7	-3.4	-4.7	68.5	34.5	103.0	100.1	0.6	0.0 ●	STATE AUTO PROPERTY & CASUALTY
1.3	1.1	64.7	58.0	-1.6	-2.1	68.5	34.9	103.4	92.6	0.6	48.3 ●	STATE AUTOMOBILE MUTUAL INS CO
N/A	N/A	59.2	275.2	-0.1	-15.9	111.8	21.4	133.2	71.3	-6.9	0.0	STATE COMPENSATION INS FUND
4.0	3.2	72.8	27.3	-2.5	-5.4	84.3	23.0	107.3	109.6	12.6	0.0	STATE FARM CTY MUTUAL INS CO OF TX
1.9	1.2	139.5	63.8	-4.2	-4.0	63.5	26.8	90.3	108.1	6.0	0.0 ●	STATE FARM FIRE & CAS CO
2.0	1.4	78.3	51.8	-6.8	-3.4	40.8	28.4	69.2	107.7	-3.7	0.0 ●	STATE FARM FLORIDA INS CO
5.8	3.7	55.6	36.5	-3.2	-0.3	55.5	28.6	84.1	117.1	-2.9	0.0 ●	STATE FARM GENERAL INS CO
3.9	3.5	N/A	N/A	N/A	N/A	N/A	N/A	N/A	999 +	0.0	0.0	STATE FARM GUARANTY INS CO
5.1	4.2	56.9	69.5	-7.6	-15.4	75.6	22.0	97.6	94.8	1.0	0.7 ●	STATE FARM INDEMNITY CO
2.2	2.1	154.9	33.3	-5.1	-12.5	53.5	28.6	82.1	124.6	15.4	0.0 ●	STATE FARM LLOYDS
2.2	1.9	46.5	34.9	-2.4	-5.0	79.9	25.6	105.5	96.7	4.3	23.1 ●	STATE FARM MUTUAL AUTOMOBILE INS
N/A	N/A	--	--	--	--	--	--	--	--	--	--	STATE INS FUND
N/A	N/A	--	--	--	--	--	--	--	--	--	--	STATE INS FUND DISABILITY BENEFITS
3.8	2.2	N/A	N/A	N/A	N/A	N/A	N/A	N/A	N/A	0.0	0.0	STATE MUTUAL INS CO
3.4	3.1	17.5	1.8	-0.5	-0.5	12.5	111.1	123.6	80.6	11.4	0.0	STATE NATIONAL FIRE INS CO
2.3	2.0	27.0	2.8	-0.3	N/A	40.3	51.7	92.0	89.0	38.4	46.2	STATE NATIONAL INS CO INC
3.6	2.7	24.6	110.5	-11.0	-20.1	89.0	17.4	106.4	89.9	-21.0	0.0 ●	STATE VOLUNTEER MUTUAL INS CO
N/A	N/A	445.0	999 +	-377.5	-101.2	87.6	7.4	95.0	132.6	35.6	0.0	STATE WORKERS INS FUND
0.4	0.2	19.2	109.7	3.7	7.8	116.3	-5.6	110.7	159.3	20.4	0.0	STATES SELF-INSURERS RISK RET
3.0	3.0	N/A	N/A	N/A	N/A	N/A	N/A	N/A	-6.9	0.0	34.5 ●	STEADFAST INS CO
0.8	0.4	150.8	138.5	-0.5	-14.9	68.0	31.1	99.1	127.5	20.0	0.0	STEADPOINT INS CO
0.6	0.5	435.7	152.9	9.9	20.9	70.3	35.5	105.8	70.6	7.2	0.0	STERLING CAS INS CO
6.1	4.6	58.5	26.4	-8.2	-15.9	37.9	39.6	77.5	125.1	5.2	0.5	STERLING INS CO
N/A	N/A	58.7	36.3	22.3	N/A	50.9	56.3	107.2	158.3	-0.8	0.0	STEWARD RRG
0.8	0.6	33.5	46.7	-1.9	-10.5	40.2	57.1	97.3	147.5	4.8	0.0	STICO MUTUAL INS CO A RRG

999 + Denotes number greater than 999.9%
999 - Denotes number less than -999.99%
● Bullets denote a more detailed analysis is available in Section II.

INSURANCE COMPANY NAME	DOM. STATE	RATING	TOTAL ASSETS ($MIL)	CAPITAL & SURPLUS ($MIL)	ANNUAL NET PREMIUM ($MIL)	NET INCOME ($MIL)	CAPITAL-IZATION INDEX (PTS)	RESERVE ADQ INDEX (PTS)	PROFIT-ABILITY INDEX (PTS)	LIQUIDITY INDEX (PTS)	STAB. INDEX (PTS)	STABILITY FACTORS
STILLWATER INS CO	CA	B-	303.2	154.2	154.4	12.2	6.2	8.1	5.4	2.9	4.5	LR
STILLWATER P&C INS CO	NY	C	120.0	112.1	1.7	5.4	10.0	6.3	8.7	10.0	4.1	T
STONE VALLEY MUTUAL FIRE INS CO	PA	U (3)	0.0	0.0	0.1	0.0	N/A	4.6	6.9	10.0	2.1	T
STONEGATE INS CO	IL	D	12.2	2.2	8.1	-0.4	1.6	2.3	2.5	6.1	1.5	CDFT
STONETRUST COMMERCIAL INS CO	LA	D+	115.9	28.6	59.5	2.3	2.6	9.4	7.2	6.9	2.6	RT
STONEWOOD INS CO	NC	C	79.9	35.6	3.1	1.0	8.4	8.2	3.6	6.4	4.0	FRT
STONINGTON INS CO	TX	E+	195.0	45.3	88.0	-0.8	1.3	5.6	2.2	8.7	0.7	GT
STRATFORD INS CO	NH	B-	180.0	71.4	25.2	0.4	9.6	8.3	6.6	8.0	4.7	R
STRATHMORE INS CO	NY	C	50.5	23.5	11.7	0.6	8.1	7.8	5.3	6.9	4.0	D
SU INS CO	WI	C	25.8	11.1	11.6	-1.0	10.0	6.3	4.1	6.9	3.3	D
SUBLIMITY INS CO	OR	C	34.1	14.5	22.9	0.4	7.9	8.2	6.8	5.3	3.6	DR
SUBURBAN HEALTH ORG RRG LLC	SC	U	0.9	0.7	0.0	0.1	N/A	N/A	3.0	10.0	1.8	FT
SUECIA INS CO	NY	U	46.9	20.5	0.0	0.3	N/A	5.3	3.8	10.0	4.9	RT
SUMMITPOINT INS CO	WV	C-	47.8	10.0	9.3	0.3	4.5	N/A	3.1	7.0	3.3	CDT
SUN SURETY INS CO	SD	D	17.5	8.4	3.1	0.5	8.4	N/A	8.5	7.2	1.4	D
SUNAPEE MUTUAL FIRE INS CO	NH	B	3.9	3.5	0.0	0.1	8.8	N/A	8.0	7.0	4.0	D
SUNDERLAND MARINE INS CO LTD	AK	D	10.2	2.6	2.2	0.0	7.3	6.9	1.1	8.3	1.7	DFR
SUNLAND RRG INC	DE	B-	5.8	1.2	0.5	0.0	7.4	3.8	7.3	7.5	3.5	DFGT
SUNSHINE STATE INS CO	FL	F (2)	22.9	7.2	-15.0	-1.5	9.6	6.0	1.5	3.4	0.0	DFLR
SUNZ INS CO	FL	E	66.2	10.6	24.6	2.1	0.0	3.5	1.6	0.4	0.1	CDGL
SUPERIOR GUARANTY INS CO	FL	U (5)	0.0	0.0	0.0	0.0	N/A	4.3	3.1	10.0	4.0	FRT
SUPERIOR INS CO	FL	U (5)	0.0	0.0	0.0	0.0	N/A	1.4	0.3	7.0	-1.0	CFT
SURETEC INDEMNITY CO	CA	C-	20.5	10.4	13.3	1.0	7.4	N/A	3.5	7.4	3.3	DT
SURETEC INS CO	TX	C	171.4	80.1	44.2	10.3	9.4	8.6	8.5	7.1	3.6	R
SURETY BONDING CO OF AMERICA	SD	C+	8.2	8.2	0.0	0.1	10.0	4.6	6.9	10.0	3.0	DRT
SUTTER INS CO	CA	B-	45.5	21.7	19.3	-1.0	9.3	8.1	3.8	6.6	4.7	DR
SWISS REINSURANCE AMERICA CORP	NY	B-	12,939.3	4,120.5	1,965.0	395.4	7.0	5.8	3.9	7.6	4.5	R
SYNCORA CAPITAL ASR INC	NY	E	523.7	117.0	22.2	-88.4	8.4	0.7	1.5	7.8	0.0	DF
SYNCORA GUARANTEE INC	NY	E-	1,210.4	972.1	23.7	84.6	10.0	4.0	5.3	7.0	0.0	GT
SYNERGY COMP INS CO	PA	D-	26.1	7.6	8.3	0.2	4.1	9.4	8.6	6.9	1.0	DR
SYNERGY INS CO	NC	D-	53.1	12.1	29.8	0.0	0.9	6.0	5.4	6.8	1.2	CDGR
SYSTEMS PROTECTION ASR RRG INC	MT	D- (5)	0.0	0.0	0.9	0.0	9.4	3.6	9.4	9.1	1.0	DGT
T H E INS CO	LA	C	201.2	59.6	57.8	2.7	7.5	9.4	6.7	6.8	4.3	R
TANK OWNER MEMBERS INS CO	TX	C-	27.3	13.7	6.1	1.7	7.6	8.8	3.9	7.2	3.2	DR
TDC SPECIALTY INS CO	DC	C	59.8	43.9	2.3	0.6	10.0	7.5	3.8	7.0	3.8	DF
TEACHERS AUTO INS CO	NJ	C (3)	0.0	0.0	0.0	0.6	10.0	6.2	8.1	10.0	4.2	D
TEACHERS INS CO	IL	B	339.9	145.0	185.0	10.0	6.5	8.4	6.6	5.4	4.9	ACT
TECHNOLOGY INS CO INC	NH	C	1,376.4	318.7	485.6	6.1	7.2	5.7	8.7	6.6	3.6	GR
TENNESSEE FARMERS ASR CO	TN	B+	1,133.1	710.2	555.8	78.2	8.4	7.7	5.1	5.7	6.1	
TENNESSEE FARMERS MUTUAL INS CO	TN	B+	2,369.1	1,782.9	559.4	89.2	8.0	7.5	5.2	6.4	6.1	
TERRA INS CO RRG	VT	C+	30.5	17.9	6.1	1.5	8.6	6.2	6.3	7.1	3.9	DFR
TERRAFIRMA RRG LLC	VT	D	5.6	4.5	1.0	0.2	10.0	N/A	4.9	9.1	0.9	DT
TEXAS BUILDERS INS CO	TX	U	12.7	9.1	0.1	1.1	N/A	9.7	4.8	10.0	4.8	FRT
TEXAS FAIR PLAN ASSN	TX	E-	103.1	2.8	84.1	16.1	0.0	5.0	0.3	7.0	0.0	CDGT
TEXAS FARM BUREAU CASUALTY INS CO	TX	A	1,123.7	655.9	583.4	9.2	10.0	8.3	6.5	5.8	7.4	
TEXAS FARM BUREAU MUTUAL INS CO	TX	D	682.4	287.4	343.1	-32.4	9.6	7.5	3.2	5.9	1.7	G
TEXAS FARM BUREAU UNDERWRITERS	TX	C	54.5	19.8	0.0	0.0	10.0	N/A	5.4	7.0	4.0	D
TEXAS FARMERS INS CO	TX	B-	282.6	84.6	136.4	1.4	8.7	6.6	4.1	6.5	4.9	FR
TEXAS GENERAL INDEMNITY CO	CO	U	26.1	14.7	0.0	0.3	N/A	5.5	5.0	10.0	6.0	FT
TEXAS HERITAGE INS CO	TX	C	24.6	18.7	5.0	0.6	10.0	6.1	4.5	7.4	3.5	DR
TEXAS HOSPITAL INS EXCHANGE	TX	D	33.3	12.3	6.8	0.4	7.2	9.9	7.2	6.9	2.1	DR
TEXAS INS CO	TX	C	5.4	5.4	0.1	0.1	10.0	6.2	7.9	10.0	3.3	DFT

See Page 27 for explanation of footnotes and Page 28 for explanation of stability factors.
Arrows denote recent upgrades ▲ or downgrades ▼   (see Section VII for explanations)

122

www.weissratings.com

RISK ADJ. CAPITAL		PREMIUM TO SURPLUS (%)	RESV. TO SURPLUS (%)	RESV. DEVELOP.		LOSS RATIO (%)	EXP. RATIO (%)	COMB RATIO (%)	CASH FROM UNDER- WRITING (%)	NET PREMIUM GROWTH (%)	INVEST. IN AFFIL (%)	INSURANCE COMPANY NAME
RATIO #1	RATIO #2			1 YEAR (%)	2 YEAR (%)							
1.1	0.8	99.4	32.5	-3.5	-5.2	56.8	34.3	91.1	105.9	7.6	40.3	STILLWATER INS CO
10.4	5.8	1.5	N/A	-0.1	-0.1	-0.1	0.9	0.8	-84.5	14.5	0.0	STILLWATER P&C INS CO
N/A	N/A	8.4	0.1	-0.1	-0.1	11.9	62.6	74.5	150.9	1.5	0.0	STONE VALLEY MUTUAL FIRE INS CO
0.3	0.2	293.5	111.0	7.7	20.6	53.9	45.4	99.3	98.5	-8.7	0.0	STONEGATE INS CO
0.7	0.5	212.2	150.9	10.4	-1.5	66.8	29.4	96.2	137.4	27.7	0.0	STONETRUST COMMERCIAL INS CO
5.4	3.4	9.1	25.1	-3.9	-5.3	36.7	57.7	94.4	5.8	-65.1	0.0	STONEWOOD INS CO
1.7	1.2	189.7	127.3	7.3	14.8	75.2	24.6	99.8	808.5	N/A	0.0	STONINGTON INS CO
3.3	2.5	35.5	85.9	-2.4	-4.8	68.9	31.9	100.8	117.8	30.1	0.0	STRATFORD INS CO
2.2	1.6	51.0	79.3	-0.1	-0.3	61.1	33.3	94.4	97.1	9.7	0.0	STRATHMORE INS CO
3.8	2.3	97.1	9.5	0.6	0.6	67.6	30.3	97.9	110.4	10.0	0.0	SU INS CO
1.9	1.5	164.7	34.2	-1.2	-1.1	66.1	33.2	99.3	103.3	9.0	0.1	SUBLIMITY INS CO
N/A	N/A	N/A	N/A	N/A	N/A	N/A	N/A	N/A	-1.3	0.0	0.0	SUBURBAN HEALTH ORG RRG LLC
N/A	N/A	N/A	87.8	-0.8	-1.2	999 +	999 +	999 +	-0.1	N/A	0.0	SUECIA INS CO
1.0	0.4	96.6	216.1	N/A	N/A	75.1	15.5	90.6	-46.1	0.0	0.0	SUMMITPOINT INS CO
2.3	1.9	40.2	N/A	N/A	N/A	4.8	80.3	85.1	120.4	23.6	26.8	SUN SURETY INS CO
3.6	2.1	N/A	N/A	N/A	N/A	N/A	N/A	N/A	N/A	0.0	0.0	SUNAPEE MUTUAL FIRE INS CO
0.8	0.7	61.4	44.3	-1.1	3.6	41.1	71.7	112.8	78.0	48.8	0.0	SUNDERLAND MARINE INS CO LTD
0.8	0.7	43.0	37.5	-4.0	-6.8	60.5	32.2	92.7	48.1	8.6	0.0	SUNLAND RRG INC
2.4	2.2	-172.6	68.6	6.5	13.9	-51.7	119.1	67.4	203.6	-14.6	7.3	SUNSHINE STATE INS CO
0.2	0.1	297.7	278.1	15.8	116.5	66.9	33.8	100.7	124.6	9.6	0.0	SUNZ INS CO
N/A	N/A	N/A	1.1	3.5	2.8	N/A	N/A	N/A	N/A	0.0	0.0	SUPERIOR GUARANTY INS CO
N/A	N/A	N/A	-3.7	-9.6	4.8	N/A	N/A	N/A	4.2	0.0	132.5	SUPERIOR INS CO
1.4	1.1	142.0	11.6	N/A	N/A	23.1	51.9	75.0	168.3	0.0	0.0	SURETEC INDEMNITY CO
3.6	2.1	56.6	14.5	-4.5	-2.2	17.4	58.9	76.3	130.8	-14.5	6.3	SURETEC INS CO
80.5	38.1	N/A	N/A	N/A	N/A	N/A	N/A	N/A	N/A	0.0	0.0	SURETY BONDING CO OF AMERICA
3.2	2.4	86.0	32.6	-1.8	-4.5	74.3	27.0	101.3	94.7	19.3	0.0	SUTTER INS CO
1.3	0.9	42.5	106.4	-6.8	-14.5	38.9	30.1	69.0	100.1	36.5	0.0 ●	SWISS REINSURANCE AMERICA CORP
1.8	1.0	11.9	37.6	122.5	165.3	256.8	5.6	262.4	17.3	-29.5	0.0	SYNCORA CAPITAL ASR INC
11.8	8.0	2.4	-26.6	-32.3	-103.0	-534.6	135.1	-399.5	-28.9	-14.3	5.7 ●	SYNCORA GUARANTEE INC
0.8	0.4	115.0	135.7	-23.8	-33.0	50.2	30.1	80.3	144.4	4.3	0.0	SYNERGY COMP INS CO
0.5	0.3	247.6	135.4	-8.4	2.2	61.7	11.1	72.8	298.9	399.4	0.0	SYNERGY INS CO
3.9	2.5	36.0	20.0	-7.2	N/A	25.3	14.9	40.2	439.5	298.3	0.0	SYSTEMS PROTECTION ASR RRG INC
1.5	1.2	93.0	161.4	-19.6	-19.1	57.7	32.0	89.7	114.8	14.1	0.0	T H E INS CO
2.0	1.2	52.4	70.9	-3.2	-6.1	38.1	11.7	49.8	205.5	6.4	2.1	TANK OWNER MEMBERS INS CO
8.5	7.3	5.2	11.8	-1.5	-1.4	142.9	54.1	197.0	-62.3	197.8	0.0	TDC SPECIALTY INS CO
4.2	3.8	N/A	1.6	-0.2	-0.1	N/A	N/A	N/A	N/A	0.0	0.0	TEACHERS AUTO INS CO
1.8	1.1	131.8	60.8	-4.0	-7.3	69.0	27.3	96.3	106.0	3.2	0.0	TEACHERS INS CO
1.6	1.0	205.3	150.9	5.2	3.2	67.1	22.7	89.8	122.7	57.5	0.0 ●	TECHNOLOGY INS CO INC
3.0	2.0	87.5	25.0	-3.2	-2.8	65.9	14.2	80.1	127.0	3.9	3.2 ●	TENNESSEE FARMERS ASR CO
1.8	1.7	33.9	12.8	-1.4	-1.5	66.8	14.7	81.5	121.4	3.6	47.6 ●	TENNESSEE FARMERS MUTUAL INS CO
3.3	2.4	36.0	10.6	-1.5	-2.9	4.9	62.6	67.5	85.3	1.5	0.0	TERRA INS CO RRG
5.9	3.5	23.5	7.6	N/A	N/A	39.0	41.6	80.6	250.8	0.0	0.0	TERRAFIRMA RRG LLC
N/A	N/A	1.1	61.7	-13.7	-18.5	-715.5	-261.5	-977.0	N/A	-91.6	0.9	TEXAS BUILDERS INS CO
0.1	0.0	-626.5	-192.8	30.9	27.8	52.3	26.8	79.1	138.5	27.1	0.0	TEXAS FAIR PLAN ASSN
4.7	3.6	90.4	30.7	-0.2	-2.6	81.5	19.2	100.7	99.1	6.8	0.0 ●	TEXAS FARM BUREAU CASUALTY INS
2.6	2.3	109.6	19.5	0.1	-1.4	82.6	24.2	106.8	99.9	12.7	1.4 ●	TEXAS FARM BUREAU MUTUAL INS CO
3.8	3.5	N/A	N/A	N/A	N/A	N/A	N/A	N/A	N/A	0.0	0.0	TEXAS FARM BUREAU UNDERWRITERS
2.9	2.1	163.7	101.0	N/A	1.0	66.9	32.9	99.8	95.6	-1.6	0.0	TEXAS FARMERS INS CO
N/A	N/A	N/A	35.2	-4.7	-7.9	N/A	N/A	N/A	N/A	0.0	0.0	TEXAS GENERAL INDEMNITY CO
9.6	7.3	27.3	2.4	-0.3	0.3	47.1	45.4	92.5	110.6	4.9	0.0	TEXAS HERITAGE INS CO
1.6	1.0	57.2	132.8	-28.7	-39.4	53.6	48.9	102.5	110.5	-7.3	0.0	TEXAS HOSPITAL INS EXCHANGE
181.8	118.0	2.7	8.1	-0.9	-1.1	39.7	45.4	85.1	71.9	-75.8	0.0	TEXAS INS CO

999 + Denotes number greater than 999.9%
999 - Denotes number less than -999.99%
● Bullets denote a more detailed analysis is available in Section II.

INSURANCE COMPANY NAME	DOM. STATE	RATING	TOTAL ASSETS ($MIL)	CAPITAL & SURPLUS ($MIL)	ANNUAL NET PREMIUM ($MIL)	NET INCOME ($MIL)	CAPITAL-IZATION INDEX (PTS)	RESERVE ADQ INDEX (PTS)	PROFIT-ABILITY INDEX (PTS)	LIQUIDITY INDEX (PTS)	STAB. INDEX (PTS)	STABILITY FACTORS
TEXAS LAWYERS INS EXCHANGE	TX	D+	88.2	53.2	14.5	6.4	10.0	9.4	8.9	7.8	2.6	DR
TEXAS MEDICAL INS CO	TX	D-	37.1	26.6	4.9	2.0	8.6	9.4	8.9	9.0	1.3	DR
TEXAS MEDICAL LIAB INS UNDWRG ASN	TX	U (5)	293.1	0.0	4.7	0.0	N/A	9.2	4.9	9.4	0.0	CDFT
TEXAS MUTUAL INS CO	TX	B+(5)	5,660.4	2,436.8	602.0	0.0	6.5	6.4	7.3	6.7	5.0	CT
TEXAS PACIFIC INDEMNITY CO	TX	B	7.6	7.3	0.0	0.1	10.0	N/A	7.7	7.0	4.5	D
TEXAS WINDSTORM INS ASN	TX	U (5)	0.0	0.0	0.0	0.0	N/A	9.1	0.0	7.4	0.0	CDFG
THAMES INS CO INC	CT	C	28.1	15.3	10.8	0.6	7.5	9.3	3.5	6.3	3.9	DF
THIRD COAST INS CO	IL	U	17.8	17.8	0.0	0.6	N/A	6.4	8.1	10.0	6.4	T
THOMSON SECURITY INS CO	DE	U (5)	0.0	0.0	0.0	0.0	N/A	N/A	4.9	7.0	0.5	FT
TIFT AREA CAPTIVE INS CO	GA	D (5)	0.0	0.0	1.2	0.0	7.5	7.1	6.9	7.0	2.1	DG
TIG INS CO	CA	D	2,315.8	1,000.6	1.0	9.6	1.5	2.8	2.5	7.0	1.5	CFGR
TITAN INDEMNITY CO	TX	B-	265.0	170.9	0.0	1.5	8.1	N/A	3.9	7.0	5.0	
TITAN INS CO	MI	C+	140.6	106.3	0.0	1.9	10.0	N/A	4.1	7.0	4.6	
TITAN INS CO INC RRG	SC	D	47.6	33.9	4.9	3.3	10.0	N/A	9.0	9.5	1.7	DRT
TITLE INDUSTRY ASR CO RRG	VT	D	6.2	3.7	0.7	0.2	9.0	7.0	5.5	10.0	2.1	DR
TITLE REINSURANCE CO	VT	D+(5)	0.0	0.0	2.8	0.0	6.8	7.0	2.6	8.9	2.3	DFGT
TM SPECIALTY INS CO	AZ	U	38.3	38.2	0.0	0.3	N/A	N/A	7.2	10.0	5.4	T
TNUS INS CO	NY	B-	83.0	53.5	0.0	0.8	10.0	6.1	5.5	10.0	4.0	FT
TOA-RE INS CO OF AMERICA	DE	B+	1,812.3	698.8	403.1	51.9	7.6	6.5	8.5	6.9	6.5	
TOKIO MARINE AMERICA INS CO	NY	A	1,387.9	530.9	275.0	22.6	8.3	4.9	4.9	6.8	6.0	FGT
TOKIO MARINE PACIFIC INS LTD	GU	B-	96.5	61.2	122.5	4.6	8.5	9.3	8.5	3.0	4.1	LT
TOKIO MARINE SPECIALTY INS CO	DE	C	455.3	167.8	123.8	9.2	9.2	7.9	8.8	6.9	4.1	T
TOKIO MILLENNIUM RE AG (US BRANCH)	NY	U	56.5	34.0	0.0	-8.4	N/A	0.0	1.7	0.0	0.0	LT
TOPA INS CO	CA	B-	175.1	74.0	81.4	0.1	8.6	8.9	3.7	6.3	4.5	R
TORUS NATIONAL INS CO	DE	C	169.0	78.6	30.6	6.2	8.2	4.6	3.7	7.3	3.3	GT
TORUS SPECIALTY INS CO	DE	C-	174.9	91.5	20.5	-0.6	5.7	4.8	1.6	6.2	3.2	FRT
TOWER BONDING & SURETY CO	PR	E+	4.0	2.7	2.3	0.1	4.8	6.0	5.3	5.7	0.5	DFT
TOWER HILL PREFERRED INS CO	FL	D	110.7	45.7	28.6	7.2	7.4	7.0	2.9	9.0	2.1	R
TOWER HILL PRIME INS CO	FL	D	144.0	52.7	40.4	9.9	7.3	4.2	2.9	8.6	1.6	RT
TOWER HILL SELECT INS CO	FL	D+	83.2	32.0	13.5	0.8	7.7	5.4	2.9	9.4	2.8	GR
TOWER HILL SIGNATURE INS CO	FL	D	134.7	50.7	39.4	11.5	3.4	3.9	3.2	6.9	1.6	GT
TOWER INS CO OF NEW YORK	NY	D-	426.2	125.6	57.3	-5.8	7.3	4.7	4.5	6.3	1.3	FRT
TOWER NATIONAL INS CO	MA	E+	33.3	6.2	12.1	0.1	5.1	4.5	3.1	6.1	0.4	DFRT
TOYOTA MOTOR INS CO	IA	C	450.5	207.2	65.6	11.1	10.0	6.1	8.8	7.7	3.5	R
TPA CAPTIVE INSURANCE CO INC	GA	C- (5)	0.0	0.0	1.2	0.0	6.4	9.2	2.7	10.0	2.3	DG
TRADERS INS CO	MO	D+	44.5	14.2	32.8	3.9	2.6	5.2	9.1	5.6	2.4	CDGR
TRADEWIND INS CO LTD	HI	C	15.5	7.8	0.0	0.1	10.0	N/A	7.8	10.0	3.8	DFT
TRANS CITY CASUALTY INS CO	AZ	C	17.3	11.0	2.5	0.3	10.0	9.4	5.4	9.4	3.6	DR
TRANS PACIFIC INS CO	NY	B	81.5	49.1	-0.4	1.3	10.0	6.3	4.0	10.0	5.9	FT
TRANSAMERICA CASUALTY INS CO	OH	B-	341.8	120.7	236.0	3.5	8.1	6.4	7.0	5.4	5.3	
TRANSATLANTIC REINSURANCE CO	NY	B	14,695.1	4,710.7	2,977.0	408.6	7.5	6.5	7.0	7.0	6.1	A
TRANSGUARD INS CO OF AMERICA INC	IL	B	256.9	136.1	56.4	7.1	7.9	9.4	8.4	7.0	5.5	T
TRANSIT GENERAL INS CO	IL	D	21.2	4.6	10.9	0.6	1.2	5.9	7.4	7.7	1.7	CDGT
TRANSIT MUTUAL INS CORP OF WI	WI	D	14.0	8.7	2.5	0.5	10.0	9.7	8.8	8.4	0.9	D
TRANSPORT INS CO	OH	U	36.7	10.0	0.0	-1.2	N/A	0.9	1.6	6.7	0.6	CFRT
TRANSPORTATION INS CO	IL	C	81.8	81.7	0.0	1.4	10.0	N/A	7.0	9.0	3.8	AR
TRAVCO INS CO	CT	B	222.6	74.9	54.4	5.4	8.6	8.4	6.9	7.1	5.8	T
TRAVEL AIR INS CO KANSAS	KS	U	5.4	4.8	0.0	0.1	N/A	6.6	3.7	10.0	3.3	T
TRAVELERS CASUALTY & SURETY CO	CT	A-	16,487.0	6,450.1	4,101.0	400.7	7.7	8.3	7.0	6.9	6.9	
TRAVELERS CASUALTY & SURETY CO OF	CT	C+	4,495.6	2,284.7	1,293.9	401.2	9.8	9.4	8.8	7.2	4.0	R
TRAVELERS CASUALTY CO	CT	C+	209.6	68.7	58.4	6.2	8.1	8.7	7.6	6.7	4.7	T
TRAVELERS CASUALTY CO OF	CT	B	330.8	103.6	94.7	9.3	7.9	8.8	7.8	6.9	5.9	T

See Page 27 for explanation of footnotes and Page 28 for explanation of stability factors.
Arrows denote recent upgrades ▲ or downgrades ▼ (see Section VII for explanations)

124

www.weissratings.com

RISK ADJ. CAPITAL RATIO #1	RATIO #2	PREMIUM TO SURPLUS (%)	RESV. TO SURPLUS (%)	RESV. DEVELOP. 1 YEAR (%)	2 YEAR (%)	LOSS RATIO (%)	EXP. RATIO (%)	COMB RATIO (%)	CASH FROM UNDER- WRITING (%)	NET PREMIUM GROWTH (%)	INVEST. IN AFFIL (%)	INSURANCE COMPANY NAME
7.5	5.0	30.9	62.2	-11.6	-20.4	55.0	10.6	65.6	195.7	3.5	0.1	TEXAS LAWYERS INS EXCHANGE
3.0	2.5	19.9	20.8	-6.7	-11.9	4.9	18.1	23.0	257.1	17.3	0.0	TEXAS MEDICAL INS CO
N/A	N/A	999 +	999 +	N/A	N/A	197.2	20.5	217.7	32.1	-46.2	0.0	TEXAS MEDICAL LIAB INS UNDWRG ASN
2.9	1.9	37.4	135.5	-12.3	-28.4	61.2	28.3	89.5	126.6	-5.5	0.0	TEXAS MUTUAL INS CO
52.0	46.8	N/A	N/A	N/A	N/A	N/A	N/A	N/A	N/A	0.0	0.0	TEXAS PACIFIC INDEMNITY CO
N/A	N/A	N/A	N/A	N/A	N/A	N/A	N/A	N/A	N/A	0.0	0.0	TEXAS WINDSTORM INS ASN
1.9	1.3	72.6	27.8	-4.7	-13.0	52.8	48.7	101.5	84.2	5.7	0.0	THAMES INS CO INC
N/A	N/A	N/A	0.7	-0.4	-4.0	N/A	N/A	N/A	N/A	0.0	0.0	THIRD COAST INS CO
N/A	N/A	N/A	N/A	N/A	N/A	N/A	N/A	N/A	N/A	0.0	0.0	THOMSON SECURITY INS CO
3.0	2.0	36.8	83.8	-25.8	-89.6	14.6	-6.5	8.1	-297.9	-3.0	0.0	TIFT AREA CAPTIVE INS CO
0.4	0.3	0.1	155.4	1.1	11.8	999 +	999 +	999 +	1.7	617.6	56.4 •	TIG INS CO
1.7	1.7	N/A	N/A	N/A	N/A	N/A	N/A	N/A	41.8	0.0	59.0	TITAN INDEMNITY CO
21.0	18.9	N/A	N/A	N/A	N/A	N/A	N/A	N/A	-3.0	0.0	0.0	TITAN INS CO
7.7	6.1	16.1	N/A	N/A	N/A	N/A	-28.2	-28.2	999 +	29.4	0.0	TITAN INS CO INC RRG
4.3	3.9	19.5	45.2	-15.2	-23.7	36.1	-70.7	-34.6	-587.6	-0.5	0.0	TITLE INDUSTRY ASR CO RRG
1.2	0.9	54.2	144.6	-27.5	-19.2	88.9	24.2	113.1	75.0	-9.8	0.0	TITLE REINSURANCE CO
N/A	N/A	N/A	0.1	N/A	N/A	N/A	N/A	N/A	528.5	0.0	0.0	TM SPECIALTY INS CO
11.8	10.6	N/A	3.3	N/A	-0.3	N/A	N/A	N/A	-463.2	0.0	0.0	TNUS INS CO
2.1	1.4	59.1	122.9	-1.9	-3.4	65.0	25.8	90.8	114.5	3.0	0.0 •	TOA-RE INS CO OF AMERICA
2.3	1.5	53.5	148.3	-5.9	-14.9	73.8	34.7	108.5	81.1	N/A	0.0 •	TOKIO MARINE AMERICA INS CO
3.3	1.9	202.3	27.3	-0.7	-0.7	80.3	14.8	95.1	104.1	-2.1	0.0	TOKIO MARINE PACIFIC INS LTD
3.2	2.4	78.7	96.9	-0.8	-2.9	61.0	28.8	89.8	146.6	10.7	0.0	TOKIO MARINE SPECIALTY INS CO
N/A	N/A	N/A	N/A	N/A	N/A	N/A	N/A	N/A	N/A	0.0	0.0	TOKIO MILLENNIUM RE AG (US BRANCH)
2.8	2.1	107.7	93.4	-3.8	-1.8	80.5	36.2	116.7	90.5	19.3	7.1	TOPA INS CO
2.5	1.3	41.9	39.6	0.6	0.1	79.1	40.2	119.3	141.6	35.4	0.0	TORUS NATIONAL INS CO
1.0	0.9	24.0	38.2	6.1	9.8	75.1	100.3	175.4	46.9	-37.8	51.6	TORUS SPECIALTY INS CO
1.1	1.0	89.7	29.5	-12.9	-21.2	12.9	103.0	115.9	82.1	-18.0	0.0	TOWER BONDING & SURETY CO
2.8	2.0	73.0	32.1	-0.1	9.3	53.6	15.9	69.5	148.7	25.7	0.0	TOWER HILL PREFERRED INS CO
2.4	1.6	92.4	40.7	2.5	24.9	70.8	16.4	87.2	136.7	21.7	0.0	TOWER HILL PRIME INS CO
2.9	2.4	43.1	33.9	-0.3	17.2	131.9	-45.4	86.5	556.1	155.8	0.0	TOWER HILL SELECT INS CO
0.7	0.5	93.3	38.8	2.1	2.2	50.6	19.1	69.7	177.1	108.3	0.0	TOWER HILL SIGNATURE INS CO
2.9	2.1	42.0	173.8	27.0	25.6	105.8	233.4	339.2	71.2	-85.1	6.1 •	TOWER INS CO OF NEW YORK
1.2	1.1	368.0	653.5	51.8	50.0	105.8	60.8	166.6	55.9	-41.7	0.0	TOWER NATIONAL INS CO
9.1	7.4	33.7	2.8	N/A	-0.4	38.0	27.3	65.3	182.3	26.1	0.0 •	TOYOTA MOTOR INS CO
1.6	1.0	25.2	99.7	0.7	-8.5	158.6	-4.7	153.9	-370.5	4.1	0.0	TPA CAPTIVE INSURANCE CO INC
0.6	0.5	300.5	127.0	-11.5	-10.7	68.8	15.2	84.0	129.0	26.3	0.0	TRADERS INS CO
3.8	3.4	N/A	N/A	N/A	N/A	N/A	N/A	N/A	N/A	0.0	3.6	TRADEWIND INS CO LTD
4.7	3.0	23.2	42.8	-8.3	-16.6	44.4	50.7	95.1	100.9	1.5	2.0	TRANS CITY CASUALTY INS CO
10.1	7.6	-0.8	26.2	0.6	-1.7	-238.7	35.7	-203.0	-222.6	-655.0	0.0	TRANS PACIFIC INS CO
2.3	1.5	199.8	59.7	7.1	-0.6	62.5	36.8	99.3	105.7	34.7	0.0	TRANSAMERICA CASUALTY INS CO
2.0	1.3	63.1	181.7	-6.0	-4.3	55.2	34.0	89.2	103.1	-3.2	7.4 •	TRANSATLANTIC REINSURANCE CO
3.1	1.8	43.8	62.2	-8.4	-15.0	54.1	33.3	87.4	109.7	1.8	0.0	TRANSGUARD INS CO OF AMERICA INC
0.5	0.3	270.1	223.2	-17.3	-20.8	85.7	9.5	95.2	200.9	95.3	0.0	TRANSIT GENERAL INS CO
5.9	5.3	30.6	46.8	-26.8	-38.8	13.1	31.1	44.2	195.1	-6.0	0.0	TRANSIT MUTUAL INS CORP OF WI
N/A	N/A	N/A	368.0	45.0	62.1	N/A	N/A	N/A	N/A	0.0	22.3	TRANSPORT INS CO
61.3	25.4	N/A	N/A	N/A	N/A	N/A	N/A	N/A	N/A	0.0	0.0	TRANSPORTATION INS CO
3.4	2.1	78.2	140.6	-2.0	-4.6	60.9	30.1	91.0	138.8	3.0	0.0	TRAVCO INS CO
N/A	N/A	N/A	0.7	-0.2	-9.0	N/A	N/A	N/A	N/A	0.0	0.0	TRAVEL AIR INS CO KANSAS
1.6	1.4	62.5	112.5	-1.9	-4.5	60.9	30.3	91.2	106.6	3.0	25.4 •	TRAVELERS CASUALTY & SURETY CO
5.8	3.9	68.8	67.5	-13.6	-23.7	13.9	39.2	53.1	144.7	5.8	0.0 •	TRAVELERS CASUALTY & SURETY CO
2.9	1.8	93.5	168.1	-2.4	-5.6	60.9	29.6	90.5	107.6	3.0	0.0	TRAVELERS CASUALTY CO
2.7	1.7	100.5	180.8	-2.6	-6.1	60.9	29.6	90.5	107.7	3.0	0.0	TRAVELERS CASUALTY CO OF

999 + Denotes number greater than 999.9%
999 - Denotes number less than -999.99%
• Bullets denote a more detailed analysis is available in Section II.

INSURANCE COMPANY NAME	DOM. STATE	RATING	TOTAL ASSETS ($MIL)	CAPITAL & SURPLUS ($MIL)	ANNUAL NET PREMIUM ($MIL)	NET INCOME ($MIL)	CAPITAL-IZATION INDEX (PTS)	RESERVE ADQ INDEX (PTS)	PROFIT-ABILITY INDEX (PTS)	LIQUIDITY INDEX (PTS)	STAB. INDEX (PTS)	STABILITY FACTORS
TRAVELERS CASUALTY INS CO OF	CT	B	1,972.9	614.0	549.8	66.2	7.9	8.8	7.8	6.7	6.1	T
TRAVELERS COMMERCIAL CASUALTY CO	CT	B	336.2	105.6	94.7	10.2	7.9	8.7	7.5	6.8	5.9	T
TRAVELERS COMMERCIAL INS CO	CT	B	352.9	102.6	94.7	9.1	7.9	8.8	7.4	6.7	5.9	T
TRAVELERS CONSTITUTION STATE INS CO	CT	C+	210.2	69.3	58.4	6.3	8.1	8.6	7.6	6.8	4.7	T
TRAVELERS EXCESS & SURPLUS LINES CO	CT	B	219.6	70.7	54.4	5.8	8.4	8.5	7.3	7.0	5.8	T
TRAVELERS HOME & MARINE INS CO	CT	B	410.9	134.7	54.4	5.7	10.0	8.2	8.2	8.2	5.9	T
TRAVELERS INDEMNITY CO	CT	B	20,782.1	6,559.3	4,531.6	547.8	7.8	8.1	3.8	6.8	6.3	
TRAVELERS INDEMNITY CO OF AMERICA	CT	B	639.2	212.4	155.1	15.3	8.4	8.7	7.9	7.2	5.9	T
TRAVELERS INDEMNITY CO OF CT	CT	B	1,161.8	413.4	275.9	41.9	8.6	8.4	7.8	6.9	6.0	T
TRAVELERS LLOYDS INS CO	TX	B-	30.3	20.0	0.0	1.2	10.0	N/A	5.9	10.0	4.9	DF
TRAVELERS LLOYDS OF TEXAS INS CO	TX	B	25.1	15.4	0.0	1.1	10.0	N/A	6.6	8.0	5.0	D
TRAVELERS PERSONAL INS CO	CT	B	202.9	69.9	54.4	5.5	8.3	8.5	7.0	6.8	5.8	T
TRAVELERS PERSONAL SECURITY INS CO	CT	B	212.0	71.9	54.4	5.1	8.5	8.4	7.0	6.8	5.8	T
TRAVELERS PROPERTY CAS OF AMERICA	CT	B	946.6	500.3	72.5	13.0	10.0	7.9	8.3	7.1	5.9	T
TRAVELERS PROPERTY CASUALTY INS CO	CT	B	239.5	76.6	60.4	6.1	8.3	8.5	7.0	7.0	5.8	T
TRENWICK AMERICA REINSURANCE CORP	CT	U	77.0	40.8	0.0	7.2	N/A	5.8	5.3	9.2	3.7	FT
TRI CENTURY INS CO	PA	C-	61.2	9.0	2.1	0.3	7.4	6.3	4.8	8.6	2.9	DR
TRI STATE INS CO OF MINNESOTA	MN	C	35.5	31.4	0.0	0.5	10.0	N/A	5.7	7.0	3.8	DT
TRI-STATE CONSUMER INS CO	NY	B	120.9	54.9	31.7	7.4	8.3	9.5	7.4	6.9	5.5	T
TRIAD GUARANTY ASR CORP	IL	F (5)	0.0	0.0	2.5	0.0	6.1	7.1	2.5	6.9	0.0	DFGT
TRIAD GUARANTY INS CORP	IL	F (5)	0.0	0.0	156.7	0.0	3.0	3.5	0.9	6.5	0.0	FT
TRIANGLE INS CO INC	OK	C	71.4	24.9	28.0	1.9	7.1	4.9	6.7	6.9	4.2	DR
TRINITY RISK SOLUTIONS RECIP INS RRG	DC	D	8.4	4.8	0.7	0.4	7.7	4.7	3.8	8.1	1.4	DRT
TRINITY UNIVERSAL INS CO	TX	B	2,323.6	948.6	1,435.7	16.8	7.6	9.0	6.1	3.3	5.8	AL
TRIPLE S PROPIEDAD INC	PR	C	283.7	140.7	94.6	8.7	7.8	6.4	6.8	6.1	3.9	R
TRITON INS CO	TX	C+	550.4	181.4	138.6	42.7	10.0	6.4	2.8	7.3	4.4	R
TRIUMPHE CASUALTY CO	OH	C	35.6	18.3	7.9	0.6	10.0	6.5	7.8	7.0	3.5	DR
TRUCK INS EXCHANGE	CA	C+	2,001.7	569.2	1,056.9	-6.2	5.4	6.5	3.6	3.4	4.8	FLR
TRUMBULL INS CO	CT	B	223.1	103.2	49.7	9.8	10.0	6.1	6.9	6.9	5.8	AT
TRUSTGARD INS CO	OH	B+	102.3	57.6	39.9	3.4	10.0	7.9	6.8	6.7	5.0	
TRUSTSTAR INS CO	MD	U	1.0	0.8	0.4	0.0	N/A	4.9	1.3	7.6	2.4	FT
TRYGG-HANSA INS CO LTD US BR	NY	U	2.4	2.3	0.0	-0.1	N/A	9.3	2.2	10.0	1.5	FRT
TUDOR INS CO	NH	C+	375.4	151.7	25.2	4.9	10.0	8.0	6.8	9.1	4.5	R
TUSCARORA WAYNE INS CO	PA	B+	91.3	54.3	34.0	2.6	9.8	8.4	8.5	7.0	5.0	T
TWIN CITY FIRE INS CO	IN	B	650.2	280.7	149.2	19.3	10.0	6.2	5.1	6.8	5.8	A
TWIN LIGHTS INS CO	NJ	D (3)	0.0	0.0	0.0	0.0	10.0	N/A	7.1	7.0	1.7	DT
U S LLOYDS INS CO	TX	D	23.6	7.5	20.3	-0.5	7.0	9.3	5.4	7.2	2.0	DR
UFB CASUALTY INS CO	IN	B	8.5	8.5	0.0	0.1	10.0	N/A	6.7	10.0	4.8	D
UMIA INS INC	OR	B	279.3	108.6	41.9	10.8	8.2	9.5	8.4	7.5	5.5	F
UMIALIK INS CO	AK	C+	49.3	20.4	17.1	1.3	8.0	8.7	8.0	6.7	3.9	DRT
UNDERWRITER FOR THE PROFESSIONS	OR	C	270.0	53.4	20.9	-0.6	7.6	5.8	3.6	7.6	4.3	T
UNDERWRITERS AT LLOYDS	KY	D	213.7	33.4	62.2	6.4	1.2	5.0	5.9	6.4	1.5	C
UNDERWRITERS AT LLOYDS LONDON	IL	D	369.8	176.6	61.0	-7.2	8.0	6.9	4.6	6.7	1.4	FRT
UNIGARD INDEMNITY CO	WI	C-	57.9	12.4	23.9	-0.4	4.9	3.9	1.6	7.5	3.3	DFRT
UNIGARD INS CO	WI	C	440.4	111.0	181.8	-0.7	7.3	4.0	2.2	7.0	3.5	RT
UNION AMERICAN INS CO	FL	F (5)	0.0	0.0	0.0	0.0	1.9	1.2	0.0	10.0	0.0	CDFG
UNION INS CO	IA	C	117.5	28.8	0.0	0.6	10.0	N/A	5.8	7.5	4.2	
UNION INS CO OF PROVIDENCE	IA	B-	114.5	54.7	33.8	1.3	10.0	8.2	6.6	6.8	4.8	T
UNION MUTUAL FIRE INS CO	VT	B-	186.0	70.4	83.9	-2.5	7.3	8.4	3.5	5.6	4.7	F
UNION MUTUAL INS CO	OK	F (4)	0.0	0.0	5.5	-1.2	4.3	6.0	0.7	0.8	0.0	CDGL
UNION NATIONAL FIRE INS CO	LA	B	9.5	6.4	0.0	0.2	10.0	N/A	3.9	10.0	4.1	DR
UNION STANDARD LLOYDS	TX	C	2.2	0.8	0.0	0.0	7.5	N/A	4.9	7.0	2.8	DT

See Page 27 for explanation of footnotes and
Page 28 for explanation of stability factors.
Arrows denote recent upgrades ▲ or downgrades ▼   (see Section VII for explanations)

126

www.weissratings.com

RISK ADJ. CAPITAL RATIO #1	RATIO #2	PREMIUM TO SURPLUS (%)	RESV. TO SURPLUS (%)	RESV. DEVELOP. 1 YEAR (%)	2 YEAR (%)	LOSS RATIO (%)	EXP. RATIO (%)	COMB RATIO (%)	CASH FROM UNDER-WRITING (%)	NET PREMIUM GROWTH (%)	INVEST. IN AFFIL (%)	INSURANCE COMPANY NAME
2.8	1.8	100.0	179.9	-2.6	-6.1	60.9	29.8	90.7	105.3	3.0	0.0 ●	TRAVELERS CASUALTY INS CO OF
2.8	1.7	99.3	178.6	-2.6	-6.0	60.9	29.6	90.5	107.6	3.0	0.0	TRAVELERS COMMERCIAL CASUALTY
2.7	1.7	101.2	182.1	-2.6	-6.1	60.9	30.0	90.9	111.6	3.0	0.0	TRAVELERS COMMERCIAL INS CO
3.0	1.9	92.7	166.8	-2.4	-5.6	60.9	29.6	90.5	107.5	3.0	0.0	TRAVELERS CONSTITUTION STATE INS
3.2	2.0	83.7	150.7	-2.2	-5.0	60.9	29.8	90.7	131.6	3.0	0.0	TRAVELERS EXCESS & SURPLUS LINES
5.9	3.7	42.2	75.9	-1.2	-2.7	60.9	33.9	94.8	257.8	3.0	0.0	TRAVELERS HOME & MARINE INS CO
1.7	1.4	67.6	126.0	-1.6	-3.6	60.9	29.5	90.4	97.4	-0.6	20.4 ●	TRAVELERS INDEMNITY CO
3.4	2.1	79.7	143.4	-2.1	-5.0	60.9	30.2	91.1	129.9	3.0	0.0 ●	TRAVELERS INDEMNITY CO OF AMERICA
3.7	2.3	75.5	135.8	-1.9	-4.5	60.9	29.9	90.8	116.6	3.0	0.0 ●	TRAVELERS INDEMNITY CO OF CT
8.0	7.2	N/A	N/A	N/A	N/A	N/A	N/A	N/A	118.3	0.0	0.0	TRAVELERS LLOYDS INS CO
6.5	5.8	N/A	N/A	N/A	N/A	N/A	N/A	N/A	26.8	0.0	0.0	TRAVELERS LLOYDS OF TEXAS INS CO
3.2	2.0	84.3	151.7	-2.2	-5.0	60.9	29.7	90.6	107.5	3.0	0.0	TRAVELERS PERSONAL INS CO
3.3	2.1	81.4	146.5	-2.1	-4.8	60.9	29.2	90.1	110.7	3.0	0.0	TRAVELERS PERSONAL SECURITY INS
16.0	9.9	14.9	26.8	-0.4	-0.9	60.9	34.6	95.5	259.8	3.0	0.0 ●	TRAVELERS PROPERTY CAS OF
3.1	2.0	85.7	154.2	-2.2	-5.1	60.9	30.0	90.9	114.7	3.0	0.0	TRAVELERS PROPERTY CASUALTY INS
N/A	N/A	N/A	112.9	-11.0	-15.8	999 +	999 +	999 +	0.3	-99.3	0.0	TRENWICK AMERICA REINSURANCE
1.3	1.1	24.5	89.9	-4.1	-3.2	79.3	24.1	103.4	98.8	-5.2	0.0	TRI CENTURY INS CO
24.7	22.2	N/A	N/A	N/A	N/A	N/A	N/A	N/A	5.1	0.0	0.0	TRI STATE INS CO OF MINNESOTA
3.5	2.1	65.1	92.1	-6.7	-16.7	50.6	29.3	79.9	122.1	2.2	0.0	TRI-STATE CONSUMER INS CO
1.6	1.3	29.6	92.6	-5.4	-76.8	122.9	39.9	162.8	47.9	-19.1	0.0	TRIAD GUARANTY ASR CORP
0.9	0.7	66.9	208.6	72.1	117.6	223.0	11.0	234.0	51.4	-20.7	1.1	TRIAD GUARANTY INS CORP
1.6	1.0	120.9	81.1	-8.3	-5.9	58.9	28.9	87.8	153.3	25.0	0.0	TRIANGLE INS CO INC
1.5	1.1	15.5	54.5	-0.8	N/A	72.2	57.5	129.7	220.5	-40.7	0.0	TRINITY RISK SOLUTIONS RECIP INS
2.2	1.6	145.9	79.3	-7.9	-8.6	66.7	29.8	96.5	95.0	-7.4	13.2 ●	TRINITY UNIVERSAL INS CO
2.7	1.8	72.6	55.9	2.9	3.0	59.4	32.7	92.1	104.7	-4.6	0.0	TRIPLE S PROPIEDAD INC
8.4	4.6	67.3	13.1	-1.1	-1.3	32.3	16.2	48.5	195.3	-5.9	0.0 ●	TRITON INS CO
5.6	3.8	45.0	55.2	0.1	-1.3	70.3	23.8	94.1	105.6	6.5	0.0	TRIUMPHE CASUALTY CO
0.8	0.7	187.6	117.7	-0.1	1.8	66.9	34.0	100.9	94.6	-1.6	43.3 ●	TRUCK INS EXCHANGE
5.9	3.8	53.5	95.7	0.6	-0.1	68.8	16.8	85.6	103.1	1.1	0.0	TRUMBULL INS CO
6.7	4.6	73.7	35.3	-0.4	-2.0	66.9	22.6	89.5	108.4	7.7	0.0 ●	TRUSTGARD INS CO
N/A	N/A	45.3	0.4	4.1	2.8	27.7	140.7	168.4	59.2	-4.6	0.0	TRUSTSTAR INS CO
N/A	N/A	N/A	221.9	-7.3	-13.4	689.1	999 +	999 +	2.8	-55.0	0.0	TRYGG-HANSA INS CO LTD US BR
5.4	3.9	17.3	57.0	-1.0	-2.3	68.9	32.9	101.8	135.1	29.7	0.0	TUDOR INS CO
3.9	2.9	62.8	20.8	-1.5	-2.6	48.5	41.0	89.5	124.0	8.9	8.9 ●	TUSCARORA WAYNE INS CO
5.3	3.5	51.8	92.7	0.5	-0.1	68.8	24.4	93.2	103.1	1.1	0.0 ●	TWIN CITY FIRE INS CO
16.2	14.5	N/A	N/A	N/A	N/A	N/A	N/A	N/A	N/A	0.0	0.0	TWIN LIGHTS INS CO
1.2	0.9	246.3	42.7	-8.3	-16.8	41.0	46.0	87.0	112.3	11.9	0.0	U S LLOYDS INS CO
97.3	48.6	N/A	N/A	N/A	N/A	N/A	N/A	N/A	N/A	0.0	0.0	UFB CASUALTY INS CO
2.1	1.6	40.8	130.8	-16.1	-35.1	61.0	26.0	87.0	99.3	-13.2	0.0	UMIA INS INC
2.9	2.1	88.3	69.7	-2.0	-3.8	68.7	26.5	95.2	110.7	9.7	0.0	UMIALIK INS CO
1.1	0.8	29.7	37.4	7.6	7.8	999 +	5.2	999 +	277.1	12.0	0.0	UNDERWRITER FOR THE PROFESSIONS
0.3	0.2	186.5	403.7	25.3	-11.0	61.5	24.3	85.8	115.7	-12.6	0.0	UNDERWRITERS AT LLOYDS
3.5	2.3	27.3	68.5	-13.4	-12.1	12.7	30.4	43.1	39.5	14.6	0.0 ●	UNDERWRITERS AT LLOYDS LONDON
1.0	0.7	184.7	173.8	8.6	17.9	75.2	34.4	109.6	85.9	0.0	0.0	UNIGARD INDEMNITY CO
1.7	1.2	162.6	145.9	7.2	16.6	75.2	33.0	108.2	98.7	29.3	5.2	UNIGARD INS CO
0.4	0.2	N/A	119.4	-23.4	-64.4	N/A	N/A	N/A	N/A	0.0	0.0	UNION AMERICAN INS CO
3.3	3.0	N/A	N/A	N/A	N/A	N/A	N/A	N/A	-254.3	0.0	0.0	UNION INS CO
5.5	3.8	63.3	63.4	-0.8	-3.1	67.2	32.9	100.1	107.5	9.1	0.0	UNION INS CO OF PROVIDENCE
1.4	1.1	116.9	51.0	-3.9	-4.0	61.1	36.9	98.0	95.2	0.9	28.7	UNION MUTUAL FIRE INS CO
-0.8	-0.7	428.9	37.2	2.4	-44.0	73.4	18.7	92.1	102.9	38.4	0.0	UNION MUTUAL INS CO
6.4	5.8	N/A	N/A	N/A	N/A	N/A	N/A	N/A	-54.2	0.0	0.0	UNION NATIONAL FIRE INS CO
1.5	1.3	N/A	N/A	N/A	N/A	N/A	N/A	N/A	97.6	0.0	0.0	UNION STANDARD LLOYDS

999 + Denotes number greater than 999.9%
999 - Denotes number less than -999.99%
● Bullets denote a more detailed analysis is available in Section II.

INSURANCE COMPANY NAME	DOM. STATE	RATING	TOTAL ASSETS ($MIL)	CAPITAL & SURPLUS ($MIL)	ANNUAL NET PREMIUM ($MIL)	NET INCOME ($MIL)	CAPITAL-IZATION INDEX (PTS)	RESERVE ADQ INDEX (PTS)	PROFIT-ABILITY INDEX (PTS)	LIQUIDITY INDEX (PTS)	STAB. INDEX (PTS)	STABILITY FACTORS
UNIONE ITALIANA REINS CO OF AMERICA	NY	U	69.8	31.8	0.0	0.5	N/A	4.1	3.9	10.0	5.3	FT
UNIQUE INS CO	IL	C-	69.5	13.4	39.4	1.6	2.4	5.4	6.2	5.1	2.9	CD
UNITED AMERICAS INS CO	NY	U	7.4	6.4	0.0	-0.1	N/A	3.3	3.5	7.3	3.5	CFRT
UNITED AUTOMOBILE INS CO	FL	D	347.1	74.3	209.1	-6.7	3.2	1.3	2.1	6.7	1.8	FR
UNITED BUSINESS INS CO	GA	D	6.3	1.0	4.0	-0.4	1.5	5.8	2.8	7.0	1.1	CDRT
UNITED CASUALTY & SURETY CO INC	MA	D	9.5	4.8	2.5	0.4	8.3	7.7	8.2	9.4	2.1	DR
UNITED CASUALTY INS CO OF AMERICA	IL	B	11.4	8.2	0.0	0.2	10.0	3.6	5.6	10.0	4.2	DR
UNITED CENTRAL PA RRG	VT	E	17.5	8.0	4.5	1.7	0.9	4.0	2.4	6.8	0.0	CDT
UNITED EDUCATORS INS A RECIP RRG	VT	C	814.2	270.4	123.7	16.9	7.5	7.0	6.9	8.2	3.9	R
UNITED EQUITABLE INS CO	IL	D+	21.4	4.5	13.8	-0.1	3.1	4.7	3.3	6.6	2.5	D
UNITED FARM FAMILY INS CO	NY	B	29.2	11.6	7.6	0.3	9.2	9.3	4.9	7.0	4.7	DF
UNITED FARM FAMILY MUTUAL INS CO	IN	B-	967.8	338.9	503.3	19.4	8.2	6.5	3.4	4.6	5.3	L
UNITED FINANCIAL CASUALTY CO	OH	C+	2,330.1	572.2	1,501.7	115.3	7.6	7.0	9.3	5.1	4.5	T
UNITED FIRE & CAS CO	IA	B	1,620.3	664.7	469.8	-0.6	7.0	6.9	5.8	6.8	5.5	
UNITED FIRE & INDEMNITY CO	TX	C+	46.2	16.2	14.5	0.0	6.2	5.8	3.3	7.2	4.5	D
UNITED FIRE LLOYDS	TX	C	26.3	7.4	7.2	0.0	3.2	5.9	2.9	7.0	3.3	D
UNITED FRONTIER MUTUAL INS CO	NY	C-	14.5	10.1	2.8	0.5	9.4	8.3	8.1	7.0	3.0	DR
UNITED GROUP CAPTIVE INS CO	GA	D	1.8	1.1	0.7	0.0	9.7	6.9	3.9	9.1	1.1	DT
UNITED GUAR RESIDENTIAL INS CO OF NC	NC	C	454.6	399.0	92.5	36.5	7.1	5.8	5.4	5.7	3.5	T
UNITED GUARANTY COML INS CO OF NC	NC	U	54.2	34.2	0.0	2.6	N/A	4.9	2.0	7.0	3.5	T
UNITED GUARANTY CREDIT INS CO	NC	B-	23.7	21.7	0.4	0.0	10.0	6.0	3.9	9.5	5.2	DT
UNITED GUARANTY INS CO	NC	C	148.3	53.6	35.7	2.1	7.3	4.2	3.1	6.3	3.9	
UNITED GUARANTY MORTGAGE INDEM CO	NC	C+	286.3	117.8	44.2	20.9	7.2	3.7	4.0	6.6	4.8	GR
UNITED GUARANTY MORTGAGE INS CO	NC	C	146.9	52.2	35.7	2.1	7.2	4.1	2.9	6.2	3.9	
UNITED GUARANTY MTG INS CO OF NC	NC	C	149.3	54.6	35.7	2.2	7.3	4.2	3.2	6.4	3.9	
UNITED GUARANTY RESIDENTIAL INS CO	NC	D+	3,230.8	1,404.0	799.9	197.0	8.1	3.0	5.6	6.7	2.4	GR
UNITED HERITAGE PROP & CAS CO	ID	D+	38.9	15.7	25.0	1.5	7.3	7.0	6.7	5.0	1.4	D
UNITED HOME INS CO	AR	D	28.2	8.0	19.3	1.5	3.4	4.7	3.9	4.9	2.2	DGLR
UNITED HOME INS CO A RRG	VT	U	2.3	1.5	0.0	0.1	N/A	N/A	3.1	7.0	0.0	FT
UNITED INS CO	UT	D+	27.3	9.1	19.3	1.5	3.2	6.7	8.4	2.4	2.5	DLR
UNITED INTERNATIONAL INS CO	NY	U	4.7	4.7	0.0	0.0	N/A	5.3	5.9	7.0	4.5	T
UNITED NATIONAL INS CO	PA	C	373.6	193.2	41.0	34.2	6.4	7.7	2.5	7.3	4.1	FR
UNITED NATIONAL SPECIALTY INS CO	WI	C	39.4	19.1	5.1	0.5	7.1	7.6	1.9	8.9	4.1	DFR
UNITED OHIO INS CO	OH	B-	280.2	137.1	118.9	6.8	10.0	9.3	6.9	6.7	4.7	T
UNITED PROPERTY & CASUALTY INS CO	FL	C	344.7	95.8	188.8	16.0	4.4	5.3	4.1	6.2	3.5	GT
UNITED SERVICES AUTOMOBILE ASN	TX	A+	30,759.0	22,619.2	6,189.3	443.6	7.6	7.6	7.8	6.8	7.9	
UNITED SPECIALTY INS CO	DE	B-	117.3	74.1	32.6	1.3	10.0	6.3	8.2	6.9	3.9	T
UNITED STATES FIDELITY & GUARANTY CO	CT	B	4,798.7	2,622.0	888.1	134.8	10.0	7.8	5.7	7.0	5.4	
UNITED STATES FIRE INS CO	DE	C	3,360.2	1,024.3	971.7	49.8	6.0	5.7	2.4	7.2	3.7	AR
UNITED STATES LIABILITY INS CO	PA	C	845.9	540.7	144.8	-3.9	7.4	9.2	6.5	7.7	4.3	R
UNITED STATES SURETY CO	MD	C+	55.7	35.3	22.2	2.8	8.4	9.0	7.1	6.9	4.5	DR
UNITED SURETY & INDEMNITY CO	PR	B	101.7	55.2	22.4	5.8	7.4	9.2	5.3	6.7	5.6	
UNITED WISCONSIN INS CO	WI	C+	358.8	85.4	67.9	10.7	7.7	3.4	5.5	6.5	4.4	R
UNITRIN ADVANTAGE INS CO	NY	E+	3.5	2.4	0.0	0.0	10.0	3.9	7.4	7.0	0.5	DFRT
UNITRIN AUTO & HOME INS CO	NY	D+	97.1	33.0	0.0	1.3	10.0	3.7	6.9	7.0	2.5	R
UNITRIN COUNTY MUTUAL INS CO	TX	B-	31.4	4.2	0.0	0.0	6.5	N/A	6.9	10.0	3.7	DR
UNITRIN DIRECT INS CO	IL	B	14.8	8.6	0.0	0.2	10.0	3.6	3.4	7.0	4.2	DRT
UNITRIN DIRECT PROPERTY & CAS CO	IL	B	17.6	9.5	0.0	0.3	10.0	3.6	4.2	7.0	4.3	DR
UNITRIN PREFERRED INS CO	NY	D+	26.8	9.6	0.0	0.9	8.9	3.8	3.7	10.0	2.4	DR
UNITRIN SAFEGUARD INS CO	WI	B	26.9	7.0	0.0	0.2	8.1	N/A	5.8	10.0	4.1	DRT
UNIVERSAL CASUALTY CO	IL	C-	30.8	20.2	0.1	5.2	4.7	3.6	2.8	9.1	2.9	DFT
UNIVERSAL FIRE & CASUALTY INS CO	IN	C-	14.0	6.6	2.9	0.1	8.3	N/A	5.5	6.9	2.5	D

See Page 27 for explanation of footnotes and
Page 28 for explanation of stability factors.

128

www.weissratings.com

Arrows denote recent upgrades ▲ or downgrades ▼   (see Section VII for explanations)

RISK ADJ. CAPITAL RATIO #1	RATIO #2	PREMIUM TO SURPLUS (%)	RESV. TO SURPLUS (%)	RESV. DEVELOP. 1 YEAR (%)	2 YEAR (%)	LOSS RATIO (%)	EXP. RATIO (%)	COMB RATIO (%)	CASH FROM UNDER-WRITING (%)	NET PREMIUM GROWTH (%)	INVEST. IN AFFIL (%)	INSURANCE COMPANY NAME
N/A	N/A	N/A	97.1	-0.1	-5.5	-643.3	999 +	999 +	-0.1	-19.3	0.0	UNIONE ITALIANA REINS CO OF
0.7	0.5	304.8	142.1	10.9	8.7	61.8	35.8	97.6	97.4	7.3	3.3	UNIQUE INS CO
N/A	N/A	N/A	199.8	-9.8	5.6	999 +	999 +	999 +	19.6	N/A	0.0	UNITED AMERICAS INS CO
0.7	0.6	259.9	155.7	24.8	61.6	76.0	19.1	95.1	87.2	-0.9	1.5	UNITED AUTOMOBILE INS CO
0.3	0.2	323.8	177.2	21.0	-10.1	70.7	32.9	103.6	117.6	29.2	0.0	UNITED BUSINESS INS CO
2.4	2.2	53.2	2.0	-2.4	-2.5	-0.7	80.9	80.2	124.3	-10.7	0.0	UNITED CASUALTY & SURETY CO INC
7.8	7.0	N/A	N/A	N/A	N/A	N/A	N/A	N/A	-106.4	0.0	0.0	UNITED CASUALTY INS CO OF AMERICA
0.3	0.3	72.5	143.1	23.8	29.5	102.7	7.5	110.2	98.8	16.5	0.0	UNITED CENTRAL PA RRG
1.6	1.3	48.6	151.0	N/A	-9.3	76.9	21.6	98.5	139.9	11.9	0.0 ●	UNITED EDUCATORS INS A RECIP RRG
0.6	0.5	297.2	198.9	-0.1	-21.0	60.1	42.2	102.3	110.9	8.9	0.0	UNITED EQUITABLE INS CO
3.6	2.6	66.9	83.4	-3.4	-7.0	72.1	28.4	100.5	43.2	5.2	0.0	UNITED FARM FAMILY INS CO
2.9	2.0	155.5	73.7	-7.4	-3.3	72.6	24.4	97.0	98.0	-3.4	3.8 ●	UNITED FARM FAMILY MUTUAL INS CO
2.1	1.5	305.2	180.2	5.6	6.7	75.3	20.2	95.5	119.0	28.0	0.0 ●	UNITED FINANCIAL CASUALTY CO
1.1	0.9	70.6	85.2	-5.7	-7.6	63.3	30.9	94.2	104.4	10.3	39.9 ●	UNITED FIRE & CAS CO
1.4	0.9	99.6	120.2	-6.7	-8.2	63.3	31.6	94.9	108.8	10.3	0.0	UNITED FIRE & INDEMNITY CO
1.2	0.8	179.9	217.3	-10.3	-12.4	63.3	31.6	94.9	106.0	10.3	0.0	UNITED FIRE LLOYDS
4.1	2.5	28.2	23.6	-0.5	-3.5	70.0	38.2	108.2	104.8	1.5	0.0	UNITED FRONTIER MUTUAL INS CO
3.6	3.0	61.3	58.1	-4.8	-6.6	62.8	24.3	87.1	122.8	-3.8	0.0	UNITED GROUP CAPTIVE INS CO
1.2	1.2	24.0	10.2	0.3	23.4	31.2	11.4	42.6	80.9	5.8	76.8 ●	UNITED GUAR RESIDENTIAL INS CO OF
N/A	N/A	N/A	50.5	-38.3	-2.9	-151.4	N/A	N/A	N/A	-100.0	0.0	UNITED GUARANTY COML INS CO OF NC
10.3	8.4	1.8	6.8	-5.9	1.5	-8.6	193.0	184.4	44.1	-25.6	0.0	UNITED GUARANTY CREDIT INS CO
1.1	0.9	57.2	82.2	1.4	37.2	73.9	24.8	98.7	75.3	24.0	0.0	UNITED GUARANTY INS CO
1.6	1.2	39.1	127.9	-20.4	-1.7	71.1	28.6	99.7	65.9	444.9	0.0	UNITED GUARANTY MORTGAGE INDEM
1.1	0.9	58.5	84.1	1.5	37.8	73.9	24.8	98.7	75.3	24.0	0.0	UNITED GUARANTY MORTGAGE INS CO
1.2	0.9	56.3	81.0	1.4	37.0	73.9	24.8	98.7	75.3	24.0	0.0	UNITED GUARANTY MTG INS CO OF NC
2.5	1.9	54.6	59.2	4.3	18.8	64.7	19.7	84.4	96.7	41.2	2.8 ●	UNITED GUARANTY RESIDENTIAL INS
1.5	1.3	180.4	44.9	-6.1	-12.3	72.5	30.9	103.4	106.5	20.9	0.0	UNITED HERITAGE PROP & CAS CO
0.7	0.7	299.0	30.3	-2.4	3.3	58.4	27.3	85.7	125.9	78.4	0.0	UNITED HOME INS CO
N/A	N/A	N/A	N/A	N/A	N/A	N/A	N/A	N/A	N/A	0.0	0.0	UNITED HOME INS CO A RRG
0.7	0.5	259.8	110.4	-29.6	-13.2	61.3	24.0	85.3	115.0	19.8	0.0	UNITED INS CO
N/A	N/A	N/A	N/A	-0.4	-0.6	N/A	N/A	N/A	N/A	0.0	0.0	UNITED INTERNATIONAL INS CO
1.9	1.6	20.9	52.4	0.2	-0.5	72.2	39.6	111.8	79.7	20.6	20.1 ●	UNITED NATIONAL INS CO
2.3	1.5	48.1	120.9	0.2	-0.4	72.2	39.1	111.3	62.9	20.6	0.0	UNITED NATIONAL SPECIALTY INS CO
6.9	4.9	89.8	43.3	-5.9	-9.7	65.8	31.1	96.9	108.4	9.1	0.0	UNITED OHIO INS CO
1.0	0.8	240.9	44.7	7.3	9.7	50.7	29.0	79.7	150.8	71.0	0.0	UNITED PROPERTY & CASUALTY INS CO
1.5	1.4	29.8	14.4	-1.6	-1.6	73.4	13.2	86.6	123.0	8.2	55.7 ●	UNITED SERVICES AUTOMOBILE ASN
6.7	4.9	60.6	6.3	-0.7	0.1	40.3	51.7	92.0	104.4	1.9	0.0	UNITED SPECIALTY INS CO
7.3	4.8	35.7	64.3	-0.8	-1.9	60.9	29.2	90.1	109.9	3.0	2.9 ●	UNITED STATES FIDELITY & GUARANTY
1.3	0.9	119.7	212.7	1.1	7.2	71.4	31.9	103.3	103.8	20.0	15.2 ●	UNITED STATES FIRE INS CO
1.4	1.3	26.9	27.1	-3.9	-8.4	47.9	43.1	91.0	135.4	22.2	46.8 ●	UNITED STATES LIABILITY INS CO
2.7	2.2	69.5	21.7	-6.3	-9.0	20.0	57.2	77.2	136.1	2.1	0.0	UNITED STATES SURETY CO
1.8	1.2	37.1	29.3	-4.5	-8.0	18.8	62.1	80.9	120.3	6.7	0.0	UNITED SURETY & INDEMNITY CO
1.9	1.5	91.8	113.3	2.2	5.9	61.5	30.9	92.4	131.9	27.0	0.0	UNITED WISCONSIN INS CO
5.1	4.6	N/A	N/A	N/A	N/A	N/A	N/A	N/A	-0.1	0.0	0.0	UNITRIN ADVANTAGE INS CO
4.4	4.0	N/A	N/A	N/A	N/A	N/A	N/A	N/A	61.1	0.0	0.0	UNITRIN AUTO & HOME INS CO
0.9	0.8	N/A	N/A	N/A	N/A	N/A	N/A	N/A	-7.9	0.0	0.0	UNITRIN COUNTY MUTUAL INS CO
5.0	4.5	N/A	N/A	N/A	N/A	N/A	N/A	N/A	128.0	0.0	0.0	UNITRIN DIRECT INS CO
4.5	4.1	N/A	N/A	N/A	N/A	N/A	N/A	N/A	72.8	0.0	0.0	UNITRIN DIRECT PROPERTY & CAS CO
2.9	2.6	N/A	N/A	N/A	N/A	N/A	N/A	N/A	191.6	0.0	0.0	UNITRIN PREFERRED INS CO
2.0	1.8	N/A	N/A	N/A	N/A	N/A	N/A	N/A	999 +	0.0	0.0	UNITRIN SAFEGUARD INS CO
4.3	2.9	0.8	89.3	-44.2	-55.2	999 +	976.4	999 +	0.7	455.7	0.0	UNIVERSAL CASUALTY CO
2.2	1.9	44.1	N/A	N/A	N/A	N/A	97.6	97.6	101.7	2.0	0.0	UNIVERSAL FIRE & CASUALTY INS CO

999 + Denotes number greater than 999.9%
999 - Denotes number less than -999.99%
● Bullets denote a more detailed analysis is available in Section II.

INSURANCE COMPANY NAME	DOM. STATE	RATING	TOTAL ASSETS ($MIL)	CAPITAL & SURPLUS ($MIL)	ANNUAL NET PREMIUM ($MIL)	NET INCOME ($MIL)	CAPITAL-IZATION INDEX (PTS)	RESERVE ADQ INDEX (PTS)	PROFIT-ABILITY INDEX (PTS)	LIQUIDITY INDEX (PTS)	STAB. INDEX (PTS)	STABILITY FACTORS
UNIVERSAL INS CO	PR	B-	823.2	250.0	202.7	15.0	8.9	7.9	6.1	6.9	4.7	R
UNIVERSAL INS CO	NC	E	25.2	8.4	10.5	0.2	5.8	4.0	2.6	7.1	0.1	D
UNIVERSAL INS CO OF NORTH AMERICA	FL	C-	126.0	39.9	32.7	-1.0	5.6	2.5	2.9	6.7	3.3	FOT
UNIVERSAL INS EXCHANGE	TX	U (5)	0.0	0.0	6.1	0.0	N/A	4.6	5.5	7.7	3.1	DRT
UNIVERSAL NORTH AMERICA INS CO	TX	C-	190.2	68.5	95.2	2.8	3.3	6.3	4.9	1.4	3.1	CLR
UNIVERSAL PROPERTY & CASUALTY INS	FL	E+	657.6	183.1	260.0	19.5	0.5	4.7	3.0	0.0	0.6	CLR
UNIVERSAL SURETY CO	NE	C	181.9	129.5	3.1	3.3	8.0	7.5	8.2	9.4	4.0	DR
UNIVERSAL SURETY OF AMERICA	SD	C	15.8	15.7	0.0	0.1	10.0	5.0	6.6	10.0	3.2	DRT
UNIVERSAL UNDERWRITERS INS CO	IL	C	390.3	341.8	0.0	4.5	10.0	N/A	5.1	10.0	3.5	R
UNIVERSAL UNDERWRITERS OF TX	IL	C+	14.1	10.0	0.0	0.1	10.0	N/A	6.7	9.9	4.4	DR
UPLAND MUTUAL INS INC	KS	C-	23.3	9.8	13.7	0.5	7.7	6.2	4.1	6.0	2.9	DR
UPMC HEALTH BENEFITS	PA	U	79.7	15.4	0.0	0.9	N/A	0.0	4.9	0.0	0.0	LT
UPMC WORK ALLIANCE INC	PA	D	2.3	1.2	0.5	0.1	7.3	N/A	3.9	7.0	1.2	DFT
UPPER HUDSON NATIONAL INS CO	NY	E	3.3	2.7	0.7	-0.8	8.6	6.0	1.0	9.1	0.1	DFT
URGENT CARE ASR CO RRG INC	NV	D	4.8	1.3	1.1	-0.3	7.6	5.9	2.9	9.2	1.4	DRT
US AGENCIES CASUALTY INS CO INC	LA	D+	35.3	26.9	0.0	0.1	10.0	6.1	2.9	2.5	2.4	FLRT
US COASTAL INS CO	NY	U	8.9	6.7	0.0	-0.5	N/A	N/A	2.9	7.0	3.6	FT
US INS CO OF AMERICA	IL	D-	5.9	2.2	1.4	0.0	0.7	5.5	3.3	6.7	1.0	CDRT
US LEGAL SERVICES INC	TN	D	2.0	1.9	1.1	0.2	7.7	4.9	8.4	7.8	1.5	DT
US SPECIALTY INS CO	TX	B-	2,023.8	651.7	440.5	85.1	7.7	5.1	8.7	6.9	4.9	R
US UNDERWRITERS INS CO	ND	C+	175.6	119.7	13.4	4.1	10.0	9.4	8.7	10.0	4.5	R
USA INS CO	MS	E+	14.9	7.2	10.7	-0.3	7.6	3.9	6.0	6.9	0.5	DR
USA UNDERWRITERS	MI	U	6.2	5.3	0.1	0.2	N/A	6.0	2.1	9.7	3.3	FT
USAA CASUALTY INS CO	TX	A+	8,886.5	4,527.2	4,756.9	354.4	8.8	8.1	8.8	6.1	7.5	
USAA COUNTY MUTUAL INS CO	TX	B	5.7	5.6	0.0	0.1	10.0	N/A	3.4	7.0	4.9	DT
USAA GENERAL INDEMNITY CO	TX	B+	2,785.3	931.9	1,633.0	84.7	7.8	9.4	8.8	5.3	5.0	GT
USAA TEXAS LLOYDS CO	TX	B+	575.9	258.3	275.0	11.1	8.8	7.9	8.8	6.4	6.5	
USAGENCIES DIRECT INS CO	NY	U	5.3	5.3	0.0	0.0	N/A	N/A	6.9	7.0	4.6	T
USPLATE GLASS INS CO	IL	C	25.4	19.8	9.5	2.1	8.2	6.1	8.0	7.4	3.9	DR
UTAH BUSINESS INS CO INC	UT	D-	17.1	4.4	13.4	0.0	0.9	4.3	4.6	4.4	1.3	CDFL
UTICA FIRST INS CO	NY	C	250.5	113.6	65.2	2.9	9.6	8.2	6.8	6.9	3.4	R
UTICA LLOYDS OF TX	TX	B	10.0	6.6	0.0	0.2	10.0	N/A	8.4	10.0	4.0	D
UTICA MUTUAL INS CO	NY	B-	2,254.6	791.6	579.5	13.5	8.0	4.3	4.3	6.7	4.9	R
UTICA NATIONAL ASR CO	NY	C	62.8	28.0	13.0	0.3	9.3	5.3	5.2	6.9	4.1	T
UTICA NATIONAL INS CO OF OHIO	OH	C-	14.5	11.1	0.0	0.9	10.0	N/A	4.3	9.3	1.6	DT
UTICA NATIONAL INS CO OF TX	TX	C+	32.9	15.2	6.5	0.3	9.7	5.5	5.7	6.9	4.4	D
UTICA SPECIALTY RISK INS CO	TX	C+	36.0	30.4	0.0	0.5	10.0	N/A	7.6	10.0	3.3	DFT
UV INS RRG INC	HI	D	1.1	0.5	0.3	-0.1	7.2	3.6	3.0	8.0	0.9	DT
VA FARM BUREAU TOWN & COUNTRY INS	VA	C	67.8	21.6	27.7	1.4	8.0	9.3	6.7	6.1	4.1	DR
VALIANT INS CO	DE	C	34.2	32.1	0.0	-0.8	10.0	6.5	2.0	6.5	3.8	DFRT
VALIANT SPECIALTY INS CO	DE	U	5.3	5.3	0.0	0.2	N/A	4.6	1.9	7.0	3.1	FT
VALLEY FORGE INS CO	PA	C	73.1	73.0	0.0	2.1	10.0	N/A	7.2	7.0	3.8	AR
VALLEY PROPERTY & CASUALTY INS CO	OR	B	12.1	7.2	0.0	0.2	10.0	N/A	3.7	7.0	4.1	DR
VANLINER INS CO	MO	B	336.2	124.9	103.1	2.7	10.0	9.3	7.1	6.7	5.5	FT
VANTAGE CASUALTY INS CO	IN	U	86.0	39.1	0.0	1.4	N/A	5.1	6.2	9.1	6.0	CFT
VANTAPRO SPECIALTY INS CO	AR	U	23.6	23.2	0.0	0.0	N/A	N/A	6.8	7.0	5.4	FGRT
VASA SPRING GARDEN MUTUAL INS CO	MN	D-	4.0	1.8	2.2	0.5	7.4	6.1	2.6	5.3	1.2	DT
VEHICULAR SERVICE INS CO RRG	OK	U	2.6	2.5	0.1	0.1	N/A	4.0	6.1	10.0	3.0	FT
VERLAN FIRE INS CO	NH	B-	25.3	25.2	0.0	0.5	10.0	3.7	7.3	7.0	5.0	T
VERMONT ACCIDENT INS CO INC	VT	B	7.9	7.4	0.0	0.1	9.4	N/A	7.7	7.0	4.5	D
VERMONT MUTUAL INS CO	VT	C+	733.7	353.0	313.7	29.1	9.4	9.2	8.5	6.7	4.7	R
VERSANT CASUALTY INS CO	MS	C	28.2	12.1	7.1	0.9	8.4	6.2	8.9	7.5	3.5	DT

See Page 27 for explanation of footnotes and Page 28 for explanation of stability factors.
Arrows denote recent upgrades ▲ or downgrades ▼   (see Section VII for explanations)

130   www.weissratings.com

RISK ADJ. RATIO #1	CAPITAL RATIO #2	PREMIUM TO SURPLUS (%)	RESV. TO SURPLUS (%)	RESV. DEVELOP. 1 YEAR (%)	2 YEAR (%)	LOSS RATIO (%)	EXP. RATIO (%)	COMB RATIO (%)	CASH FROM UNDER- WRITING (%)	NET PREMIUM GROWTH (%)	INVEST. IN AFFIL (%)	INSURANCE COMPANY NAME
3.2	2.1	80.1	26.3	N/A	-1.2	69.4	12.5	81.9	101.4	-2.8	5.7 •	UNIVERSAL INS CO
1.4	1.0	130.6	81.7	4.3	-1.7	69.5	30.8	100.3	90.9	7.2	0.0	UNIVERSAL INS CO
2.0	1.4	85.1	84.1	-1.5	12.7	71.1	27.7	98.8	66.6	-45.0	0.0	UNIVERSAL INS CO OF NORTH AMERICA
N/A	N/A	177.4	116.2	-13.0	26.8	55.0	37.7	92.7	111.4	9.9	0.3	UNIVERSAL INS EXCHANGE
0.7	0.4	141.7	38.4	0.4	-0.9	66.5	34.3	100.8	97.2	-2.0	0.0	UNIVERSAL NORTH AMERICA INS CO
0.2	0.2	160.7	55.5	-1.8	4.0	46.1	39.1	85.2	107.3	5.8	0.0	UNIVERSAL PROPERTY & CASUALTY INS
2.8	1.6	2.6	5.1	-1.2	-1.5	25.6	54.9	80.5	158.9	11.8	0.0	UNIVERSAL SURETY CO
101.8	50.8	N/A	N/A	N/A	N/A	N/A	N/A	N/A	N/A	0.0	0.0	UNIVERSAL SURETY OF AMERICA
10.8	9.8	N/A	N/A	N/A	N/A	N/A	N/A	N/A	-268.9	0.0	9.8 •	UNIVERSAL UNDERWRITERS INS CO
7.6	6.9	N/A	N/A	N/A	N/A	N/A	N/A	N/A	999 +	0.0	0.0	UNIVERSAL UNDERWRITERS OF TX
1.7	1.4	145.6	19.4	-1.0	0.5	68.0	30.0	98.0	102.2	-2.5	0.0	UPLAND MUTUAL INS INC
N/A	N/A	N/A	N/A	N/A	N/A	N/A	N/A	N/A	N/A	0.0	0.0	UPMC HEALTH BENEFITS
1.1	0.7	47.0	4.1	N/A	N/A	198.4	2.5	200.9	-2.7	0.0	0.0	UPMC WORK ALLIANCE INC
2.8	2.4	19.6	7.9	3.2	1.5	68.2	121.4	189.6	27.7	-45.5	0.0	UPPER HUDSON NATIONAL INS CO
1.1	0.9	68.9	57.5	-3.7	8.2	54.8	42.0	96.8	144.6	20.3	0.0	URGENT CARE ASR CO RRG INC
4.7	4.0	N/A	-0.1	N/A	0.1	N/A	N/A	N/A	89.0	0.0	27.0	US AGENCIES CASUALTY INS CO INC
N/A	N/A	N/A	N/A	N/A	N/A	N/A	N/A	N/A	N/A	0.0	0.0	US COASTAL INS CO
0.2	0.1	62.4	109.9	1.3	-9.7	91.5	28.0	119.5	97.2	-12.9	0.0	US INS CO OF AMERICA
2.0	1.7	63.5	5.0	N/A	-0.6	19.4	71.9	91.3	113.0	0.0	0.0	US LEGAL SERVICES INC
2.8	1.8	75.9	168.0	-6.6	-4.5	51.5	31.6	83.1	129.0	0.1	0.0 •	US SPECIALTY INS CO
6.6	4.7	11.6	38.3	-2.6	-9.9	36.4	38.7	75.1	108.5	-13.2	0.0	US UNDERWRITERS INS CO
1.8	1.6	143.2	57.4	1.3	-18.4	65.8	27.5	93.3	99.7	0.1	0.9	USA INS CO
N/A	N/A	1.1	18.8	3.3	3.8	999 +	265.2	999 +	1.4	0.0	0.0	USA UNDERWRITERS
3.1	2.3	114.1	53.7	-4.5	-5.0	77.3	12.8	90.1	115.4	8.5	7.0 •	USAA CASUALTY INS CO
198.6	145.6	N/A	N/A	N/A	N/A	N/A	N/A	N/A	N/A	0.0	0.0	USAA COUNTY MUTUAL INS CO
1.9	1.4	195.4	92.0	-9.8	-15.3	77.3	12.1	89.4	137.9	39.1	0.0 •	USAA GENERAL INDEMNITY CO
2.3	2.0	112.2	18.7	-5.4	-1.5	68.2	15.1	83.3	118.8	37.8	0.0 •	USAA TEXAS LLOYDS CO
N/A	N/A	N/A	N/A	N/A	N/A	N/A	N/A	N/A	-7.4	0.0	0.0	USAGENCIES DIRECT INS CO
2.9	2.2	46.2	0.5	N/A	-0.3	5.3	64.8	70.1	142.8	0.6	0.0	USPLATE GLASS INS CO
0.3	0.1	266.6	192.2	-11.5	8.5	62.3	39.4	101.7	95.3	-6.9	0.0	UTAH BUSINESS INS CO INC
3.3	2.6	58.6	69.7	-4.4	-8.8	67.0	27.2	94.2	108.1	13.1	0.0	UTICA FIRST INS CO
5.9	5.3	N/A	N/A	N/A	N/A	N/A	N/A	N/A	N/A	0.0	0.0	UTICA LLOYDS OF TX
2.1	1.5	74.8	125.3	-0.8	-2.9	65.5	38.8	104.3	96.4	8.9	11.4 •	UTICA MUTUAL INS CO
4.0	2.5	47.4	79.4	-0.5	-1.8	65.5	36.9	102.4	96.5	8.9	0.0	UTICA NATIONAL ASR CO
10.3	9.3	N/A	N/A	N/A	N/A	N/A	N/A	N/A	N/A	0.0	0.0	UTICA NATIONAL INS CO OF OHIO
4.3	2.8	44.0	73.7	-0.5	-1.7	65.5	33.5	99.0	96.4	8.9	0.0	UTICA NATIONAL INS CO OF TX
18.6	16.7	N/A	N/A	N/A	N/A	N/A	N/A	N/A	N/A	0.0	0.0	UTICA SPECIALTY RISK INS CO
1.1	0.8	54.1	47.8	-10.8	2.7	20.1	85.1	105.2	196.4	-29.1	0.0	UV INS RRG INC
2.3	1.9	139.5	76.2	-7.8	-13.5	68.7	27.8	96.5	102.7	-0.2	0.0	VA FARM BUREAU TOWN & COUNTRY
7.3	7.1	N/A	N/A	-13.4	-6.4	N/A	N/A	N/A	13.7	0.0	19.4	VALIANT INS CO
N/A	N/A	N/A	N/A	-0.9	N/A	N/A	N/A	N/A	-20.6	0.0	0.0	VALIANT SPECIALTY INS CO
60.4	25.5	N/A	N/A	N/A	N/A	N/A	N/A	N/A	N/A	0.0	0.0	VALLEY FORGE INS CO
4.8	4.3	N/A	N/A	N/A	N/A	N/A	N/A	N/A	-59.2	0.0	0.0	VALLEY PROPERTY & CASUALTY INS CO
4.6	2.9	84.6	102.2	0.7	-1.9	70.8	26.8	97.6	94.6	6.5	0.0	VANLINER INS CO
N/A	N/A	N/A	97.5	N/A	0.1	N/A	N/A	N/A	N/A	0.0	0.0	VANTAGE CASUALTY INS CO
N/A	N/A	N/A	N/A	N/A	N/A	N/A	N/A	N/A	N/A	0.0	0.0	VANTAPRO SPECIALTY INS CO
2.4	1.8	163.1	25.3	-0.2	-4.0	79.2	37.4	116.6	98.7	-2.2	0.0	VASA SPRING GARDEN MUTUAL INS CO
N/A	N/A	3.4	N/A	N/A	N/A	N/A	259.2	259.2	40.7	11.3	0.0	VEHICULAR SERVICE INS CO RRG
77.3	35.7	N/A	N/A	N/A	N/A	N/A	N/A	N/A	-50.0	0.0	0.0	VERLAN FIRE INS CO
4.2	2.5	N/A	N/A	N/A	N/A	N/A	N/A	N/A	N/A	0.0	0.0	VERMONT ACCIDENT INS CO INC
4.1	2.7	95.6	41.8	-5.6	-10.1	54.0	36.4	90.4	120.0	7.3	1.4 •	VERMONT MUTUAL INS CO
2.8	2.3	63.0	2.3	-0.5	-1.1	42.1	17.8	59.9	236.3	27.7	15.3	VERSANT CASUALTY INS CO

999 + Denotes number greater than 999.9%
999 - Denotes number less than -999.99%
• Bullets denote a more detailed analysis is available in Section II.

INSURANCE COMPANY NAME	DOM. STATE	RATING	TOTAL ASSETS ($MIL)	CAPITAL & SURPLUS ($MIL)	ANNUAL NET PREMIUM ($MIL)	NET INCOME ($MIL)	CAPITAL-IZATION INDEX (PTS)	RESERVE ADQ INDEX (PTS)	PROFIT-ABILITY INDEX (PTS)	LIQUIDITY INDEX (PTS)	STAB. INDEX (PTS)	STABILITY FACTORS
VESTA INS CORP	TX	F (5)	0.0	0.0	0.0	0.0	10.0	N/A	3.9	8.1	0.0	DGT
VETERINARY PET INS CO	CA	C	273.1	102.0	231.2	5.1	9.4	5.9	8.6	3.3	3.9	L
VFH CAPTIVE INS CO	GA	E+	6.3	1.9	3.2	-0.5	5.8	9.8	2.6	6.3	0.5	DF
VICTORIA AUTOMOBILE INS CO	OH	B	26.9	10.6	0.0	0.1	10.0	N/A	7.3	7.3	4.5	DFT
VICTORIA FIRE & CASUALTY CO	OH	B-	176.6	58.0	0.0	0.4	8.9	3.6	3.1	9.9	5.2	T
VICTORIA NATIONAL INS CO	OH	U	3.5	3.5	0.0	0.0	N/A	N/A	6.2	7.0	4.2	T
VICTORIA SELECT INS CO	OH	B-	38.3	8.3	0.0	0.1	8.1	N/A	6.7	7.0	4.2	D
VICTORIA SPECIALTY INSURANCE CO	OH	D	22.3	3.5	0.0	0.0	6.8	N/A	6.1	7.0	1.9	D
VICTORY INS CO INC	MT	D	14.3	5.0	8.9	0.4	3.5	2.7	3.0	7.3	2.0	DGRT
VIGILANT INS CO	NY	B	489.2	279.5	45.1	14.0	10.0	7.8	8.7	7.8	6.0	T
VIKING INS CO OF WI	WI	C	397.9	185.2	90.9	6.0	10.0	8.3	6.4	6.8	3.6	T
VININGS INS CO	DE	B	71.2	22.0	14.7	0.6	6.0	9.3	7.2	6.7	5.5	CD
VIRGINIA FARM BUREAU FIRE & CAS INS	VA	C	50.9	19.4	26.8	1.6	7.8	9.3	5.2	6.1	4.1	DR
VIRGINIA FARM BUREAU MUTUAL INS CO	VA	C	359.7	156.6	189.4	17.3	7.5	8.4	3.2	5.8	3.5	R
VIRGINIA PHYSICIANS RRG INC	MT	E+	1.7	0.9	0.3	0.0	7.2	3.8	3.1	10.0	0.5	DFT
VIRGINIA SENIOR CARE RRG	DC	B- (4)	0.0	0.0	0.7	0.0	10.0	3.6	6.5	10.0	3.5	DGT
VIRGINIA SURETY CO INC	IL	C+	1,059.2	334.4	341.8	37.3	8.6	4.8	8.1	6.9	4.7	R
VISION INS CO	TX	E	20.8	7.4	17.4	-3.4	2.2	6.8	1.9	0.6	0.3	CDFL
VOYAGER INDEMNITY INS CO	GA	C+	96.0	60.8	104.6	14.1	7.7	6.2	7.8	6.6	4.8	R
WACO FIRE & CAS INS CO	GA	D	26.8	15.7	3.3	0.6	7.9	9.7	3.8	7.5	1.9	DFR
WADENA INS CO	IA	C+	11.0	10.9	0.0	0.2	10.0	3.8	6.9	7.0	4.5	D
WALLROSE MUTUAL INS CO	PA	U	0.9	0.5	0.3	0.0	N/A	3.8	3.6	7.9	1.7	FT
WARNER INS CO	IL	D	11.7	11.5	0.0	0.1	8.2	3.6	2.7	7.0	2.0	DFRT
WARRANTY UNDERWRITERS INS CO	TX	D+	39.3	12.3	2.2	2.1	4.6	10.0	3.9	9.3	2.5	DFGR
WASHINGTON CASUALTY CO	WA	D	27.2	20.0	0.0	0.3	10.0	5.1	7.0	7.0	0.8	DFR
WASHINGTON COUNTY CO-OPERATIVE INS	NY	E+	7.3	5.4	1.5	0.2	10.0	5.3	7.4	7.0	0.5	D
WASHINGTON INTERNATIONAL INS CO	NH	C	110.5	74.1	3.7	1.1	10.0	7.6	8.2	10.0	3.5	DRT
WAUSAU BUSINESS INS CO	WI	C	38.7	25.3	-21.5	0.2	10.0	4.5	1.9	0.0	3.6	AFLR
WAUSAU GENERAL INS CO	WI	C	13.0	11.7	0.0	0.2	10.0	N/A	1.9	7.0	3.0	ADRT
WAUSAU UNDERWRITERS INS CO	WI	C	95.9	62.2	-21.5	1.1	10.0	4.6	2.6	2.8	3.8	AFLR
WAWANESA GENERAL INS CO	CA	C+	585.4	239.6	331.1	3.8	8.6	4.5	4.5	5.7	4.5	R
WAYNE COOPERATIVE INS CO	NY	C-	27.3	13.0	12.1	0.8	8.5	9.3	6.7	6.5	3.3	DR
WAYNE MUTUAL INS CO	OH	C	55.4	26.3	36.4	3.8	8.0	9.3	7.0	6.1	4.3	D
WEA PROPERTY & CASUALTY INS CO	WI	C-	16.7	4.8	10.3	-0.6	7.3	7.0	3.3	6.2	2.9	D
WELLINGTON INS CO	TX	C-	37.1	17.6	4.7	3.9	9.0	2.8	5.7	7.1	2.9	DFR
WELLSPAN RRG	VT	E+	25.2	6.9	6.8	1.3	7.7	10.0	6.5	7.3	0.6	D
WESCAP INS CO	CO	U	4.2	1.7	0.0	0.0	N/A	3.8	1.7	10.0	0.0	FT
WESCO INS CO	DE	C+	951.6	190.5	114.8	7.6	10.0	5.2	9.1	9.0	4.4	FGRT
WEST AMERICAN INSURANCE CO	IN	C-	77.2	49.0	0.0	1.2	10.0	N/A	1.9	7.0	3.1	ART
WEST BEND MUTUAL INS CO	WI	A-	2,162.6	801.6	814.3	24.9	8.7	6.6	7.9	6.4	7.2	
WEST BRANCH MUTUAL INS CO	PA	B-	1.1	0.8	0.4	0.0	7.5	5.4	4.9	7.3	3.5	DT
WEST VIRGINIA FARMERS MUT INS ASSOC	WV	C-	6.8	5.0	2.8	0.2	7.8	6.1	8.0	6.8	2.9	DGR
WEST VIRGINIA INS CO	WV	D	47.8	39.2	11.1	0.9	10.0	6.4	8.5	7.0	2.1	D
WEST VIRGINIA MUTUAL INS CO	WV	D-	179.0	106.0	22.3	1.6	10.0	9.7	8.5	9.0	1.3	FR
WEST VIRGINIA NATIONAL AUTO INS CO	WV	D	11.1	4.5	6.4	0.0	7.2	6.7	2.4	5.9	2.2	DFR
WESTCHESTER FIRE INS CO	PA	C	2,000.5	901.4	226.4	75.6	8.5	7.9	6.3	7.7	4.0	FR
WESTCHESTER SURPLUS LINES INS CO	GA	C	365.8	164.7	35.9	10.7	10.0	7.9	6.3	7.4	4.0	R
WESTERN AGRICULTURAL INS CO	IA	B+	178.2	70.8	98.1	-0.3	9.6	8.1	6.8	5.7	6.5	L
WESTERN BONDING CO	UT	U (3)	0.0	0.0	0.0	0.1	N/A	3.9	2.3	10.0	3.5	FT
WESTERN CATHOLIC INS CO RRG	VT	D-	7.1	1.6	2.2	0.3	0.0	1.2	5.0	7.9	0.0	CDT
WESTERN COMMUNITY INS CO	ID	B+	36.2	28.7	0.0	1.0	10.0	4.6	8.4	10.0	5.0	D
WESTERN GENERAL INS CO	CA	D+	53.1	20.7	34.0	-0.8	7.0	8.2	1.5	4.7	2.7	DLR

See Page 27 for explanation of footnotes and Page 28 for explanation of stability factors.

132

www.weissratings.com

Arrows denote recent upgrades ▲ or downgrades ▼ (see Section VII for explanations)

RISK ADJ. CAPITAL RATIO #1	RATIO #2	PREMIUM TO SURPLUS (%)	RESV. TO SURPLUS (%)	RESV. DEVELOP. 1 YEAR (%)	2 YEAR (%)	LOSS RATIO (%)	EXP. RATIO (%)	COMB RATIO (%)	CASH FROM UNDER-WRITING (%)	NET PREMIUM GROWTH (%)	INVEST. IN AFFIL (%)	INSURANCE COMPANY NAME
4.8	4.3	N/A	N/A	N/A	N/A	N/A	N/A	N/A	159.8	0.0	0.0	VESTA INS CORP
4.6	2.6	254.1	24.5	1.7	1.9	65.2	29.8	95.0	102.3	7.0	0.6	VETERINARY PET INS CO
0.7	0.6	126.6	109.5	5.3	-26.7	70.0	46.4	116.4	84.1	2.4	36.6	VFH CAPTIVE INS CO
3.4	3.0	N/A	N/A	N/A	N/A	N/A	N/A	N/A	83.4	0.0	0.0	VICTORIA AUTOMOBILE INS CO
2.3	2.1	N/A	N/A	N/A	N/A	N/A	N/A	N/A	181.7	0.0	40.7	VICTORIA FIRE & CASUALTY CO
N/A	N/A	N/A	N/A	N/A	N/A	N/A	N/A	N/A	-0.3	0.0	0.0	VICTORIA NATIONAL INS CO
1.8	1.6	N/A	N/A	N/A	N/A	N/A	N/A	N/A	-24.8	0.0	0.0	VICTORIA SELECT INS CO
1.0	0.9	N/A	N/A	N/A	N/A	N/A	N/A	N/A	-3.1	0.0	0.0	VICTORIA SPECIALTY INSURANCE CO
0.6	0.5	165.5	48.9	20.1	25.1	66.0	28.1	94.1	123.5	38.4	0.0	VICTORY INS CO INC
4.5	3.9	17.0	30.5	-1.1	-1.9	52.7	29.9	82.6	112.1	3.9	16.9 •	VIGILANT INS CO
4.5	3.4	61.0	77.5	-2.0	-3.7	76.3	24.8	101.1	102.4	5.2	8.7	VIKING INS CO OF WI
1.6	0.7	69.1	112.1	-3.5	-8.6	70.9	30.1	101.0	110.7	15.3	0.0	VININGS INS CO
2.1	1.7	150.8	85.1	-9.3	-14.6	68.7	29.8	98.5	101.3	-1.2	0.0	VIRGINIA FARM BUREAU FIRE & CAS INS
1.9	1.6	151.9	67.8	-8.6	-8.9	59.2	34.6	93.8	113.2	3.8	22.1	VIRGINIA FARM BUREAU MUTUAL INS CO
1.7	1.4	32.2	23.9	-44.5	-4.1	-80.0	45.1	-34.9	1.9	-5.8	0.0	VIRGINIA PHYSICIANS RRG INC
3.5	2.4	36.1	46.1	-0.2	-0.1	80.0	14.3	94.3	530.8	5.9	0.0	VIRGINIA SENIOR CARE RRG
3.2	2.7	110.5	29.0	-2.0	-2.5	55.3	23.8	79.1	124.0	4.4	2.0 •	VIRGINIA SURETY CO INC
0.4	0.3	304.4	133.5	2.0	8.8	83.2	37.3	120.5	84.3	0.4	0.0	VISION INS CO
2.4	1.7	184.5	22.3	-4.7	-0.8	29.2	40.4	69.6	132.3	3.7	0.0	VOYAGER INDEMNITY INS CO
3.0	1.8	22.0	76.2	-17.5	-19.2	62.2	54.4	116.6	69.5	-15.7	0.0	WACO FIRE & CAS INS CO
98.4	46.5	N/A	N/A	N/A	N/A	N/A	N/A	N/A	201.5	0.0	0.0	WADENA INS CO
N/A	N/A	55.3	8.0	0.6	5.0	37.8	66.1	103.9	48.4	-16.7	0.0	WALLROSE MUTUAL INS CO
1.8	1.8	N/A	N/A	N/A	N/A	N/A	N/A	N/A	-37.2	0.0	57.5	WARNER INS CO
1.7	1.2	18.7	97.9	-40.0	-83.2	62.9	-22.4	40.5	50.6	5.0	3.2	WARRANTY UNDERWRITERS INS CO
11.6	10.4	N/A	N/A	N/A	N/A	N/A	N/A	N/A	558.5	0.0	0.0	WASHINGTON CASUALTY CO
5.7	3.7	29.3	8.6	-1.4	-0.4	53.8	35.8	89.6	95.7	10.4	0.0	WASHINGTON COUNTY CO-OPERATIVE
14.1	11.6	5.1	7.5	-1.6	-1.0	1.9	95.3	97.2	-463.0	-14.3	0.0	WASHINGTON INTERNATIONAL INS CO
8.7	7.8	-85.7	N/A	N/A	N/A	N/A	-0.1	N/A	-9.1	-141.2	0.0	WAUSAU BUSINESS INS CO
22.6	20.3	N/A	N/A	N/A	N/A	N/A	N/A	N/A	173.6	0.0	0.0	WAUSAU GENERAL INS CO
12.3	11.0	-35.2	N/A	N/A	N/A	N/A	0.1	N/A	-43.0	-141.2	0.0	WAUSAU UNDERWRITERS INS CO
2.7	2.1	140.9	55.2	0.2	N/A	94.6	9.5	104.1	98.9	5.3	0.0 •	WAWANESA GENERAL INS CO
2.8	2.2	99.2	48.1	-9.1	-12.9	70.3	33.0	103.3	99.4	6.2	0.0	WAYNE COOPERATIVE INS CO
2.7	1.8	163.2	33.0	-3.6	-6.5	61.1	30.1	91.2	118.2	23.0	0.0	WAYNE MUTUAL INS CO
1.6	1.1	181.5	83.5	-1.2	-13.4	65.1	33.2	98.3	100.4	-2.8	0.0	WEA PROPERTY & CASUALTY INS CO
4.3	3.1	28.7	26.3	N/A	-9.6	84.5	26.5	111.0	86.5	-52.9	0.0	WELLINGTON INS CO
1.4	1.1	78.2	171.1	-36.9	-50.8	47.0	6.0	53.0	241.0	2.9	0.0	WELLSPAN RRG
N/A	N/A	N/A	174.4	-0.7	8.2	N/A	N/A	N/A	N/A	0.0	0.0	WESCAP INS CO
3.7	2.1	68.8	29.7	0.7	0.3	63.2	6.3	69.5	62.3	42.2	0.0	WESCO INS CO
11.1	10.0	N/A	N/A	N/A	N/A	N/A	N/A	N/A	51.9	0.0	0.0	WEST AMERICAN INSURANCE CO
3.4	2.2	117.9	105.6	-4.6	-6.0	61.1	30.2	91.3	115.8	12.0	0.0 •	WEST BEND MUTUAL INS CO
2.1	1.3	39.6	1.2	-0.2	-0.4	28.2	71.2	99.4	97.8	1.7	0.0	WEST BRANCH MUTUAL INS CO
2.0	1.5	58.3	2.2	-0.1	-0.4	34.6	42.2	76.8	162.8	357.4	0.0	WEST VIRGINIA FARMERS MUT INS
10.5	9.2	29.1	5.6	-2.3	-2.4	58.1	20.3	78.4	131.5	4.8	0.0	WEST VIRGINIA INS CO
7.6	5.5	21.2	44.8	-2.7	-18.0	69.1	33.3	102.4	91.4	-12.3	0.0	WEST VIRGINIA MUTUAL INS CO
1.4	1.3	142.1	63.2	-0.9	2.3	70.5	32.7	103.2	81.0	-21.2	0.0	WEST VIRGINIA NATIONAL AUTO INS CO
4.6	3.1	25.0	110.7	-7.3	-3.9	46.7	40.8	87.5	71.8	-41.9	0.0 •	WESTCHESTER FIRE INS CO
7.1	4.5	23.1	34.0	-1.7	-4.8	43.2	22.9	66.1	186.5	19.7	0.0	WESTCHESTER SURPLUS LINES INS CO
3.8	2.9	138.8	60.0	-2.1	-2.3	70.2	25.4	95.6	104.4	7.1	1.7 •	WESTERN AGRICULTURAL INS CO
N/A	N/A	N/A	N/A	N/A	3.9	999 +	N/A	N/A	N/A	-100.0	0.0	WESTERN BONDING CO
0.1	0.1	173.5	214.2	43.4	36.3	74.1	37.0	111.1	246.5	-3.9	0.0	WESTERN CATHOLIC INS CO RRG
14.6	13.1	N/A	N/A	N/A	N/A	N/A	N/A	N/A	16.5	0.0	0.0 •	WESTERN COMMUNITY INS CO
1.2	0.9	160.3	48.9	1.5	-1.6	61.9	53.1	115.0	99.5	-2.4	0.0	WESTERN GENERAL INS CO

999 + Denotes number greater than 999.9%
999 - Denotes number less than -999.99%
• Bullets denote a more detailed analysis is available in Section II.

INSURANCE COMPANY NAME	DOM. STATE	RATING	TOTAL ASSETS ($MIL)	CAPITAL & SURPLUS ($MIL)	ANNUAL NET PREMIUM ($MIL)	NET INCOME ($MIL)	CAPITAL- IZATION INDEX (PTS)	RESERVE ADQ INDEX (PTS)	PROFIT- ABILITY INDEX (PTS)	LIQUIDITY INDEX (PTS)	STAB. INDEX (PTS)	STABILITY FACTORS
WESTERN HERITAGE INS CO	AZ	B	144.1	106.6	0.0	1.4	10.0	N/A	7.5	7.9	5.4	R
WESTERN HOME INS CO	MN	C-	57.3	25.5	20.5	1.6	8.6	8.7	8.6	6.7	3.2	DRT
WESTERN INS RRG INC	AZ	U (5)	0.0	0.0	0.0	0.0	N/A	5.0	3.4	10.0	1.5	GT
WESTERN MUTUAL FIRE INS CO	MN	B-	6.4	4.2	2.6	0.4	10.0	3.9	8.4	7.5	3.5	D
WESTERN MUTUAL INS CO	CA	C-	73.4	49.0	22.6	2.0	7.1	8.3	8.8	6.2	2.7	R
WESTERN NATIONAL ASR CO	MN	C	56.3	23.6	20.5	1.5	8.4	8.8	8.6	6.4	3.8	DR
WESTERN NATIONAL MUTUAL INS CO	MN	B-	750.9	339.9	256.3	17.8	8.2	8.7	8.5	6.6	4.5	R
WESTERN PACIFIC MUT INS CO RISK RET	CO	C+	142.6	108.4	3.3	1.2	10.0	9.4	8.1	10.0	4.8	DFRT
WESTERN PROFESSIONAL INS CO	WA	U	13.8	13.6	0.0	0.3	N/A	N/A	6.1	7.0	5.4	T
WESTERN PROTECTORS INS CO	OR	C	11.4	8.8	0.2	0.1	10.0	4.6	5.3	9.7	3.5	DRT
WESTERN RESERVE MUTUAL CAS CO	OH	B-	180.7	105.6	74.3	5.8	9.9	7.7	5.2	6.5	4.7	
WESTERN SELECT INS CO	CA	C	16.2	15.4	0.2	0.3	10.0	3.6	6.9	10.0	3.2	DT
WESTERN SURETY CO	SD	C	2,003.0	1,333.9	418.4	128.6	10.0	9.4	8.6	7.0	4.3	R
WESTERN WORLD INS CO	NH	C	1,070.2	366.4	201.7	6.0	7.3	8.8	6.4	7.4	4.1	R
WESTFIELD INS CO	OH	B-	2,510.3	989.3	904.7	43.6	8.9	9.3	6.8	6.4	4.6	T
WESTFIELD NATIONAL INS CO	OH	B+	593.0	252.8	217.8	6.7	8.9	9.3	6.8	6.5	5.0	
WESTGUARD INS CO	PA	C	38.8	15.3	6.2	0.5	3.6	9.9	8.5	6.0	4.1	CDGR
WESTMINSTER AMERICAN INS CO	MD	C-	19.0	10.1	8.5	1.1	8.1	8.7	7.8	7.2	2.9	DR
WESTON INS CO	FL	B	48.3	42.4	-0.7	-1.5	10.0	N/A	3.6	9.8	4.7	T
WESTPORT INS CORP	MO	C+	5,352.8	1,605.0	580.1	133.6	5.8	6.8	4.9	7.2	4.5	GRT
WHITE PINE INS CO	MI	C-	46.6	30.2	7.9	-1.7	5.3	6.1	3.9	6.7	3.3	DFR
WHITECAP SURETY CO	MN	D-	1.3	1.1	3.4	0.1	1.4	N/A	7.2	1.6	1.0	CDLT
WI LAWYERS MUTUAL INS CO	WI	C	31.4	21.1	3.4	-0.2	10.0	8.5	4.5	9.0	3.9	DR
WILLIAMSBURG NATIONAL INS CO	MI	C-	144.9	32.9	46.1	1.8	6.9	3.3	5.9	6.2	3.1	R
WILMINGTON INS CO	DE	D	4.7	3.2	0.8	0.0	9.2	6.5	6.2	9.1	2.1	DG
WILSHIRE INS CO	NC	C-	217.3	104.6	53.1	1.9	7.4	6.3	5.6	6.8	2.7	R
WILSON MUTUAL INS CO	WI	B	98.6	23.0	20.4	0.0	7.6	8.0	4.9	6.3	5.5	D
WINDHAVEN INS CO	FL	D-	107.5	23.5	54.4	0.7	0.5	0.6	6.2	4.9	1.0	CDGL
WINDSOR MOUNT JOY MUTUAL INS CO	PA	C	64.2	40.7	19.4	0.9	10.0	8.9	8.6	8.0	4.2	R
WINTHROP PHYSICIANS RECIP RRG	VT	B-	3.0	2.3	0.4	-0.1	10.0	3.6	3.8	10.0	3.5	D
WISCONSIN COUNTY MUTUAL INS CORP	WI	C	79.7	32.6	18.5	-0.8	8.0	9.4	5.3	7.1	3.4	DR
WISCONSIN HEALTH CARE LIAB INS PLAN	WI	U (5)	0.0	0.0	2.7	0.0	N/A	5.6	4.5	9.2	1.0	CDFT
WISCONSIN MUNICIPAL MUTUAL INS CO	WI	C-	55.6	40.2	3.5	1.0	10.0	7.0	7.9	9.3	3.0	DR
WISCONSIN MUTUAL INS CO	WI	C+	131.0	61.2	64.8	0.9	9.3	4.4	6.0	6.4	4.8	R
WISCONSIN REINSURANCE CORP	WI	C-	82.8	39.9	49.5	2.1	5.6	6.9	5.1	6.2	3.2	R
WOLVERINE MUTUAL INS CO	MI	C	51.4	17.2	34.3	-0.9	7.5	8.9	4.8	6.1	4.0	D
WOODLANDS INS CO	TX	U	10.0	10.0	0.0	0.0	N/A	0.0	4.9	0.0	0.0	CLT
WOODRIDGE INS CO	IL	U	8.4	8.3	0.0	-0.1	N/A	6.1	3.6	10.0	4.8	FRT
WORK FIRST CASUALTY CO	DE	D-	41.1	10.0	15.9	0.8	0.7	2.4	2.8	5.0	0.9	CDFR
WORKERS COMPENSATION EXCHANGE	ID	E	8.4	0.7	2.0	0.0	0.1	4.0	3.9	6.6	0.3	CDFG
WORKERS COMPENSATION FUND OF UTAH	UT	B- (5)	1,701.1	702.7	151.5	0.0	6.0	3.9	6.8	7.1	3.5	CT
WORKMENS AUTO INS CO	CA	D-	30.5	7.8	33.0	-4.9	1.5	0.5	0.9	0.0	1.2	CDFL
WORTH CASUALTY CO	TX	C	11.2	7.2	0.0	-0.3	10.0	4.7	3.9	8.0	2.7	DFRT
WRIGHT NATIONAL FLOOD INS CO	TX	C-	18.4	9.4	2.4	0.9	10.0	3.6	1.9	6.8	3.1	DGT
▼WRIGHT SPECIALTY INS CO	NY	D+	24.9	13.5	2.8	-1.9	10.0	5.0	1.5	9.7	2.7	DT
X L INS CO OF NY	NY	D+	205.2	77.4	39.9	1.5	8.3	6.3	5.3	6.9	2.4	AFR
XL INS AMERICA INC	DE	C	707.9	225.0	133.1	12.1	7.1	6.3	5.9	7.1	3.8	FR
XL REINS AMERICA INC	NY	C	5,529.0	2,148.8	865.2	148.1	8.6	6.2	6.0	7.0	3.8	AR
XL SELECT INS CO	DE	D+	136.1	50.8	26.6	1.2	3.3	6.3	3.7	7.5	2.4	CR
XL SPECIALTY INS CO	DE	C	410.3	140.7	79.9	7.9	7.9	6.3	3.9	8.5	3.4	AR
YEL CO INS	FL	C-	15.7	10.9	1.2	0.7	10.0	9.3	8.4	10.0	3.0	D
YELLOWSTONE INS EXCH RRG	VT	D-	20.5	7.6	5.2	0.1	7.5	10.0	7.3	8.9	1.3	DR

See Page 27 for explanation of footnotes and Page 28 for explanation of stability factors.

Arrows denote recent upgrades ▲ or downgrades ▼ (see Section VII for explanations)

134

www.weissratings.com

RISK ADJ. RATIO #1	CAPITAL RATIO #2	PREMIUM TO SURPLUS (%)	RESV. TO SURPLUS (%)	RESV. DEVELOP. 1 YEAR (%)	RESV. DEVELOP. 2 YEAR (%)	LOSS RATIO (%)	EXP. RATIO (%)	COMB RATIO (%)	CASH FROM UNDER-WRITING (%)	NET PREMIUM GROWTH (%)	INVEST. IN AFFIL (%)	INSURANCE COMPANY NAME
19.7	17.7	N/A	N/A	N/A	N/A	N/A	N/A	N/A	999 +	0.0	0.0	WESTERN HERITAGE INS CO
3.0	2.1	85.8	67.8	-2.0	-3.8	68.7	26.7	95.4	111.4	9.7	0.0	WESTERN HOME INS CO
N/A	N/A	6.1	N/A	N/A	N/A	31.9	157.5	189.4	73.2	84.1	0.0	WESTERN INS RRG INC
5.3	4.8	68.6	8.6	-4.8	15.5	39.9	25.5	65.4	154.6	9.4	0.0	WESTERN MUTUAL FIRE INS CO
1.7	1.0	48.9	15.8	-3.2	-3.6	60.5	27.7	88.2	119.2	4.3	13.0	WESTERN MUTUAL INS CO
2.8	2.0	92.5	73.1	-2.1	-3.9	68.7	26.9	95.6	118.6	9.7	0.0	WESTERN NATIONAL ASR CO
2.2	1.8	81.6	64.4	-1.9	-3.6	68.7	26.2	94.9	114.6	9.7	20.0 ●	WESTERN NATIONAL MUTUAL INS CO
6.4	4.0	3.2	10.2	-8.7	-18.0	-62.9	124.5	61.6	47.2	25.9	0.0	WESTERN PACIFIC MUT INS CO RISK
N/A	N/A	N/A	N/A	N/A	N/A	N/A	N/A	N/A	N/A	0.0	0.0	WESTERN PROFESSIONAL INS CO
9.9	8.9	2.2	N/A	N/A	N/A	N/A	46.6	N/A	275.4	138.2	0.0	WESTERN PROTECTORS INS CO
4.6	2.8	70.1	27.6	2.3	-1.5	64.2	31.8	96.0	110.2	6.3	0.2	WESTERN RESERVE MUTUAL CAS CO
17.1	11.2	1.5	0.4	0.4	0.3	61.1	16.0	77.1	619.5	-8.1	0.0	WESTERN SELECT INS CO
6.3	4.8	34.7	30.4	-7.4	-15.3	9.2	52.8	62.0	148.2	1.6	1.3 ●	WESTERN SURETY CO
1.3	1.1	54.9	132.0	-3.6	-7.0	68.9	32.6	101.5	105.3	30.1	25.6 ●	WESTERN WORLD INS CO
3.8	2.5	91.3	81.3	-6.1	-10.3	59.8	33.2	93.0	107.1	4.3	0.0 ●	WESTFIELD INS CO
3.7	2.4	89.6	79.8	-6.1	-10.3	59.8	34.4	94.2	107.1	4.3	0.0 ●	WESTFIELD NATIONAL INS CO
0.7	0.5	42.3	88.5	-2.9	-54.4	67.8	24.4	92.2	102.3	101.4	0.0	WESTGUARD INS CO
1.6	1.4	92.9	11.1	-6.5	-4.7	26.5	40.3	66.8	125.8	16.2	0.0	WESTMINSTER AMERICAN INS CO
25.0	22.5	-1.3	0.2	N/A	N/A	-47.0	93.7	46.7	-239.1	0.0	0.0	WESTON INS CO
1.3	0.9	32.8	94.0	-6.9	-9.8	62.2	36.5	98.7	125.1	8.4	10.7 ●	WESTPORT INS CORP
1.7	1.1	68.2	53.5	-30.4	-64.5	21.9	69.0	90.9	76.1	-10.4	20.4	WHITE PINE INS CO
0.3	0.3	290.7	N/A	N/A	N/A	N/A	94.9	94.9	105.1	-2.2	0.0	WHITECAP SURETY CO
4.4	3.1	16.1	32.2	-0.7	-1.9	100.8	30.0	130.8	96.1	2.8	0.0	WI LAWYERS MUTUAL INS CO
1.9	1.3	147.0	236.9	14.2	38.9	79.2	34.4	113.6	102.6	-14.0	0.0	WILLIAMSBURG NATIONAL INS CO
3.0	2.1	24.9	6.7	-0.2	0.3	34.7	14.9	49.6	212.3	86.0	0.0	WILMINGTON INS CO
1.9	1.2	51.9	45.5	-5.0	-2.6	56.5	33.3	89.8	113.9	14.2	0.0	WILSHIRE INS CO
2.3	1.4	91.6	71.1	-1.0	-1.9	66.8	34.8	101.6	96.9	4.8	0.0	WILSON MUTUAL INS CO
0.1	0.1	246.5	98.6	47.6	118.4	67.0	18.9	85.9	178.2	169.8	0.0	WINDHAVEN INS CO
5.1	4.3	49.2	12.1	-4.1	-7.0	33.9	44.1	78.0	133.0	8.2	0.0	WINDSOR MOUNT JOY MUTUAL INS CO
5.1	4.0	14.3	6.7	N/A	N/A	11.6	73.2	84.8	140.3	14.8	0.0	WINTHROP PHYSICIANS RECIP RRG
2.1	1.5	55.6	88.9	-3.6	-12.5	69.7	31.6	101.3	125.9	12.5	7.7	WISCONSIN COUNTY MUTUAL INS CORP
N/A	N/A	13.1	652.0	-41.1	-119.2	64.4	29.0	93.4	45.6	-38.4	0.0	WISCONSIN HEALTH CARE LIAB INS
9.4	7.2	9.0	12.2	-3.9	-12.3	0.5	26.8	27.3	211.0	0.5	0.0	WISCONSIN MUNICIPAL MUTUAL INS CO
3.9	2.6	107.3	55.2	-2.8	-4.6	66.3	23.4	89.7	113.7	3.3	0.0	WISCONSIN MUTUAL INS CO
1.2	0.9	127.0	89.9	-3.3	0.3	69.0	17.9	86.9	134.7	12.5	15.3	WISCONSIN REINSURANCE CORP
1.7	1.2	195.4	68.7	-5.0	-2.7	65.0	31.1	96.1	108.5	7.5	0.0	WOLVERINE MUTUAL INS CO
N/A	N/A	N/A	N/A	N/A	N/A	N/A	N/A	N/A	N/A	0.0	0.0	WOODLANDS INS CO
N/A	N/A	N/A	N/A	0.1	-0.1	N/A	N/A	N/A	N/A	100.0	0.0	WOODRIDGE INS CO
0.6	0.2	154.7	312.1	-18.4	34.0	78.0	29.5	107.5	79.7	-27.9	0.0	WORK FIRST CASUALTY CO
0.2	0.1	283.9	999 +	-33.7	-121.1	99.5	12.4	111.9	73.0	59.5	0.0	WORKERS COMPENSATION EXCHANGE
3.0	1.9	25.2	139.5	-3.7	-4.7	79.1	29.2	108.3	85.1	-17.0	0.2	WORKERS COMPENSATION FUND OF
0.3	0.2	358.5	154.3	44.2	85.3	87.3	29.7	117.0	74.6	-3.5	0.0	WORKMENS AUTO INS CO
5.7	5.1	N/A	-0.1	N/A	N/A	N/A	N/A	N/A	-35.0	0.0	0.0	WORTH CASUALTY CO
4.2	3.7	16.4	3.0	0.1	N/A	509.6	-791.5	-281.9	-24.2	230.2	0.0	WRIGHT NATIONAL FLOOD INS CO
0.8	0.8	4.1	6.4	-0.6	0.3	53.9	99.9	153.8	88.0	-29.3	20.4	WRIGHT SPECIALTY INS CO
3.3	2.1	51.4	130.6	-0.6	-1.6	65.3	35.2	100.5	99.8	2.9	0.0	X L INS CO OF NY
1.2	0.9	53.9	137.0	-0.7	-1.8	65.3	27.9	93.2	99.8	2.9	20.2 ●	XL INS AMERICA INC
2.8	2.1	38.5	97.9	-0.5	-1.3	65.3	35.1	100.4	95.7	2.9	12.6 ●	XL REINS AMERICA INC
0.7	0.4	48.2	122.5	-0.6	-1.4	65.3	35.2	100.5	99.8	2.9	0.0	XL SELECT INS CO
2.2	1.6	50.4	128.1	-0.6	-1.5	65.3	36.1	101.4	99.8	2.9	12.0	XL SPECIALTY INS CO
7.4	6.6	11.7	43.2	-3.6	-11.5	30.5	4.6	35.1	917.0	0.0	0.0	YEL CO INS
2.1	1.6	70.0	80.7	-37.8	-74.7	13.0	44.1	57.1	127.6	29.0	0.0	YELLOWSTONE INS EXCH RRG

999 + Denotes number greater than 999.9%
999 - Denotes number less than -999.99%
● Bullets denote a more detailed analysis is available in Section II.

INSURANCE COMPANY NAME	DOM. STATE	RATING	TOTAL ASSETS ($MIL)	CAPITAL & SURPLUS ($MIL)	ANNUAL NET PREMIUM ($MIL)	NET INCOME ($MIL)	CAPITAL-IZATION INDEX (PTS)	RESERVE ADQ INDEX (PTS)	PROFIT-ABILITY INDEX (PTS)	LIQUIDITY INDEX (PTS)	STAB. INDEX (PTS)	STABILITY FACTORS
YORK INS CO	RI	U	17.0	9.5	0.1	0.1	N/A	9.3	2.1	10.0	3.3	FGT
YORK INS CO OF MAINE	ME	C	47.0	46.4	0.0	0.9	10.0	N/A	7.5	7.0	2.8	RT
YOSEMITE INS CO	IN	C	265.7	167.0	53.3	13.2	10.0	5.0	2.3	8.3	4.2	T
YOUNG AMERICA INS CO	TX	C	44.6	17.6	47.3	-3.4	5.3	5.8	2.7	2.1	3.6	DLRT
ZALE INDEMNITY CO	TX	C+	43.4	15.0	22.1	2.9	7.1	8.6	8.5	6.9	4.2	DRT
ZENITH INS CO	CA	C-	1,866.5	579.2	677.5	94.3	5.6	6.0	2.2	7.0	3.2	AR
ZEPHYR INS CO INC	HI	D-	84.2	55.7	14.9	7.4	10.0	N/A	9.8	9.0	1.2	DR
ZNAT INS CO	CA	C	69.1	26.4	13.8	1.2	7.8	6.0	3.5	9.4	3.4	AR
ZURICH AMERICAN INS CO	NY	C+	30,669.5	7,676.8	4,733.6	428.6	8.2	7.7	7.9	6.8	3.8	R
ZURICH AMERICAN INS CO OF IL	IL	C	47.0	34.6	0.0	0.6	10.0	N/A	3.9	7.0	3.4	RT

See Page 27 for explanation of footnotes and
Page 28 for explanation of stability factors.
Arrows denote recent upgrades ▲ or downgrades ▼   (see Section VII for explanations)

136

www.weissratings.com

RISK ADJ. RATIO #1	CAPITAL RATIO #2	PREMIUM TO SURPLUS (%)	RESV. TO SURPLUS (%)	RESV. 1 YEAR (%)	DEVELOP. 2 YEAR (%)	LOSS RATIO (%)	EXP. RATIO (%)	COMB RATIO (%)	CASH FROM UNDER- WRITING (%)	NET PREMIUM GROWTH (%)	INVEST. IN AFFIL (%)	INSURANCE COMPANY NAME
N/A	N/A	0.7	75.3	3.7	-7.2	999 +	460.9	999 +	4.4	131.4	0.0	YORK INS CO
79.6	50.5	N/A	N/A	N/A	N/A	N/A	N/A	N/A	N/A	0.0	0.0	YORK INS CO OF MAINE
18.2	8.2	34.7	18.4	-1.1	0.4	30.0	25.7	55.7	149.5	4.8	0.0	YOSEMITE INS CO
0.7	0.6	225.6	97.5	-3.1	3.9	69.5	39.4	108.9	96.5	-26.3	0.0	YOUNG AMERICA INS CO
1.5	1.2	138.4	12.7	-4.8	-7.8	16.4	32.4	48.8	164.9	4.1	41.5	ZALE INDEMNITY CO
1.1	0.8	131.3	220.6	-8.0	-0.2	62.4	33.4	95.8	114.9	13.5	2.4 ●	ZENITH INS CO
8.2	7.7	27.9	N/A	N/A	N/A	N/A	4.2	4.2	369.4	3.0	0.0	ZEPHYR INS CO INC
2.1	1.5	54.2	91.1	-2.9	-0.1	62.4	33.4	95.8	181.8	13.5	0.0	ZNAT INS CO
2.5	1.7	60.7	178.2	-1.2	-0.5	74.6	17.2	91.8	106.8	6.7	5.5 ●	ZURICH AMERICAN INS CO
12.8	11.5	N/A	N/A	N/A	N/A	N/A	N/A	N/A	599.5	0.0	0.0	ZURICH AMERICAN INS CO OF IL

999 + Denotes number greater than 999.9%
999 - Denotes number less than -999.99%
● Bullets denote a more detailed analysis is available in Section II.

Section II

Analysis of Largest Companies

A summary analysis of Weiss Recommended

U.S. Property and Casualty Insurers,

along with the largest companies based on capital and surplus.

Companies are listed in alphabetical order.

Section II Contents

This section contains rating factors, historical data and general information on each of the 450 largest property and casualty insurers in the U.S. that have the most recent quarterly financial information available.

1. **Financial Strength Rating** — The current rating appears to the right of the company name. Our ratings are designed to distinguish levels of insolvency risk and are measured on a scale from A (Excellent) to F (Failed). Highly-rated companies are, in our opinion, less likely to experience financial difficulties than lower-rated firms. See *About Weiss Financial Strength Ratings* for more information.

2. **Major Rating Factors** — A synopsis of the key indexes and sub-factors that have most influenced the rating of a particular insurer. Items are presented in the approximate order of their importance to the rating. There may be additional factors which have influenced the rating but do not appear due to space limitations or confidentiality agreements with insurers.

3. **Other Rating Factors** — A summary of those Weiss Ratings indexes that were not included as Major Rating Factors, but nevertheless, may have had some impact on the final grade.

4. **Principal Business** — The major types of policies written by an insurer along with the percentages for each line in relation to the entire book of business. Lines of business written by property and casualty insurers include personal and commercial insurance lines such as homeowners', auto, workers' compensation, commercial multiple peril, medical malpractice and product liability, among others.

5. **Principal Investments** — The major investments in an insurer's portfolio. These include cash, investment grade bonds, non investment grade bonds, common and preferred stock, and real estate.

6. **Investments in Affiliates** — The percentage of bonds, common and preferred stocks and other financial instruments an insurer has invested with affiliated companies.

7. **Group Affiliation** — The name of the group of companies to which a particular insurer belongs.

8. **Licensed in** — List of the states in which an insurer is licensed to conduct business.

9. **Commenced Business** — The month and year the company started its operations.

10. **Address** — The address of an insurer's corporate headquarters. This location may differ from the company's state of domicile.

11. **Phone** — The telephone number of an insurer's corporate headquarters.

12. Domicile State   The state that has primary regulatory responsibility for this company. You do not have to live in the domicile state to do business with this firm, provided it is registered to do business in your state.

13. NAIC Code   The identification number assigned to an insurer by the National Association of Insurance Commissioners (NAIC).

14. Historical Data   Five years of background data for Weiss Financial Strength Rating, risk-adjusted capital ratios (moderate and severe loss scenarios), total assets, capital, net premium, and net income. See the following page for more details on how to read the historical data table.

15. Customized Graph (or Table)   A graph or table depicting one of the company's major strengths or weaknesses.

How to Read the Historical Data Table

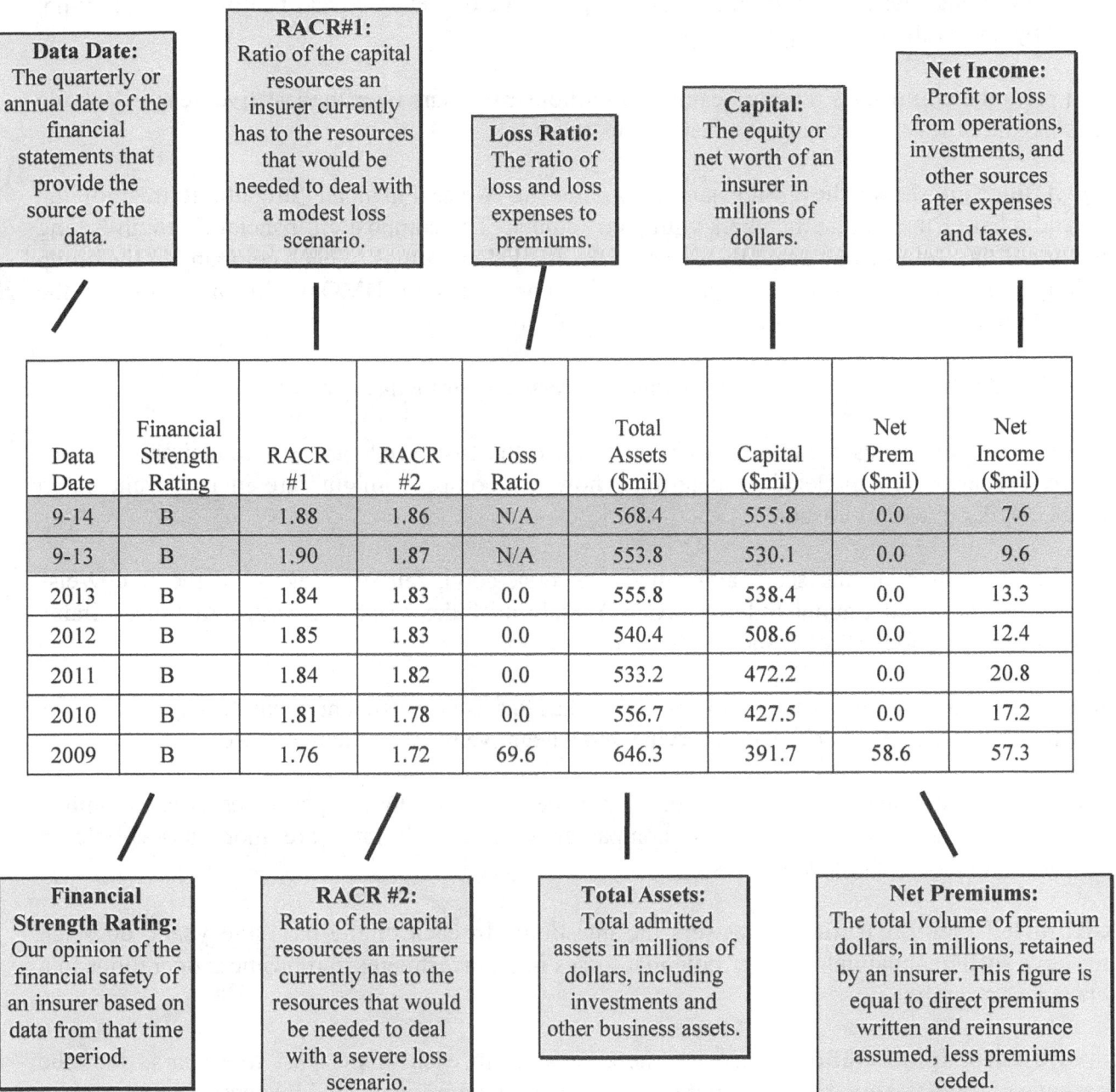

Data Date:
The quarterly or annual date of the financial statements that provide the source of the data.

RACR#1:
Ratio of the capital resources an insurer currently has to the resources that would be needed to deal with a modest loss scenario.

Loss Ratio:
The ratio of loss and loss expenses to premiums.

Capital:
The equity or net worth of an insurer in millions of dollars.

Net Income:
Profit or loss from operations, investments, and other sources after expenses and taxes.

Data Date	Financial Strength Rating	RACR #1	RACR #2	Loss Ratio	Total Assets ($mil)	Capital ($mil)	Net Prem ($mil)	Net Income ($mil)
9-14	B	1.88	1.86	N/A	568.4	555.8	0.0	7.6
9-13	B	1.90	1.87	N/A	553.8	530.1	0.0	9.6
2013	B	1.84	1.83	0.0	555.8	538.4	0.0	13.3
2012	B	1.85	1.83	0.0	540.4	508.6	0.0	12.4
2011	B	1.84	1.82	0.0	533.2	472.2	0.0	20.8
2010	B	1.81	1.78	0.0	556.7	427.5	0.0	17.2
2009	B	1.76	1.72	69.6	646.3	391.7	58.6	57.3

Financial Strength Rating:
Our opinion of the financial safety of an insurer based on data from that time period.

RACR #2:
Ratio of the capital resources an insurer currently has to the resources that would be needed to deal with a severe loss scenario.

Total Assets:
Total admitted assets in millions of dollars, including investments and other business assets.

Net Premiums:
The total volume of premium dollars, in millions, retained by an insurer. This figure is equal to direct premiums written and reinsurance assumed, less premiums ceded.

Row Descriptions:

Row 1 contains the most recent quarterly data as filed with state regulators and is presented on a year-to-date basis. For example, the figure for year-end premiums includes premiums received through the year-end. **Row 2** consists of data from the same quarter of the prior year so that you can compare current quarterly results to those of a year ago.

Row 3 contains data from the most recent annual statutory filing. **Rows 4-7** include data from year-end statements going back four years from the most recent annual filing so that you can compare current year-end results to those of the previous four years. With the exception of Total Assets and Capital, quarterly data are not comparable with annual data.

Customized Graphs

In the lower right-hand corner of each company section, a customized graph or text block highlights a key factor affecting that company's financial strength. One of eleven types of information is found, identified by one of the following headings:

Capital plots the company's reported capital in millions of dollars over the last five years. Volatile changes in capital levels may indicate unstable operations.

Group Affiliation shows the group name, a composite Weiss Financial Strength Rating for the group, and a list of the largest members with their ratings. The composite Financial Strength Rating is made up of the weighted average, by assets, of the individual ratings of each company in the group (including life/health companies, property/casualty companies or HMOs) plus a factor for the financial strength of the holding company, where applicable.

Income Trends shows underwriting and net income results over the last five years.

Liquidity Index evaluates a company's ability to raise the cash necessary to pay claims. Various cash flow scenarios are modeled to determine how the company might fare in the event of an unexpected spike in claims costs.

Rating Indexes illustrate the score and range -- strong, good, fair or weak -- on the five Weiss indexes: Risk-Adjusted Capital Index #2 (Cap2), Stability Index (Stab.), Reserve Adequacy Index (Res.), Profitability Index (Prof.), and Liquidity Index (Liq.).

Reserve Deficiency shows whether the company has set aside sufficient funds to pay claims. A positive number indicates insufficient reserving and a negative number adequate reserving.

Reserves to Capital analyzes the relationship between loss and loss expense reserves to capital. Operating results and capital levels for companies with a high ratio are more susceptible to fluctuations than those with lower ratios.

Risk-Adjusted Capital Ratio #1 answers the question: In each of the past five years, does the insurer have sufficient capital to cover potential losses in its investments and business operations in a *moderate* loss scenario?

Risk-Adjusted Capital Ratio #2 answers the question: In each of the past five years, does the insurer have sufficient capital to cover potential losses in its investments and business operations in a *severe* loss scenario?

21ST CENTURY CENTENNIAL INS CO   B   Good

Major Rating Factors: Good overall results on stability tests (5.8 on a scale of 0 to 10) despite negative cash flow from operations for 2013. Stability strengths include good operational trends and excellent risk diversification. History of adequate reserve strength (6.0) as reserves have been consistently at an acceptable level.

Other Rating Factors: Strong long-term capitalization index (8.3) based on excellent current risk adjusted capital (severe and moderate loss scenarios). Moreover, capital levels have been consistent in recent years. Excellent profitability (7.9) with operating gains in each of the last five years. Excellent liquidity (7.0) with ample operational cash flow and liquid investments.

Principal Business: Auto liability (70%) and auto physical damage (30%).

Principal Investments: Misc. investments (60%) and investment grade bonds (40%).

Investments in Affiliates: 59%

Group Affiliation: Farmers Insurance Group of Companies

Licensed in: All states except PR

Commenced Business: November 1977

Address: 500 Virginia Drive, Ft. Washington, PA 19034

Phone: (302) 252-2000   **Domicile State:** PA   **NAIC Code:** 34789

Data Date	Rating	RACR #1	RACR #2	Loss Ratio %	Total Assets ($mil)	Capital ($mil)	Net Premium ($mil)	Net Income ($mil)
9-14	B	1.88	1.86	N/A	568.4	555.8	0.0	7.6
9-13	B	1.90	1.87	N/A	553.8	530.1	0.0	9.6
2013	B	1.84	1.83	0.0	555.8	538.4	0.0	13.3
2012	B	1.85	1.83	0.0	540.4	508.6	0.0	12.4
2011	B	1.84	1.82	0.0	533.2	472.2	0.0	20.8
2010	B	1.81	1.78	0.0	556.7	427.5	0.0	17.2
2009	B	1.76	1.72	69.6	646.3	391.7	58.6	57.3

Farmers Insurance Group of Companies
Composite Group Rating: C

Largest Group Members	Assets ($mil)	Rating
FARMERS INS EXCHANGE	15557	C
MID-CENTURY INS CO	3715	C
FIRE INS EXCHANGE	2255	C+
FOREMOST INS CO	1939	B
TRUCK INS EXCHANGE	1933	C+

21ST CENTURY INS CO   B   Good

Major Rating Factors: History of adequate reserve strength (5.0 on a scale of 0 to 10) as reserves have been consistently at an acceptable level. Good overall profitability index (5.9). Fair expense controls. Return on equity has been low, averaging 3.7% over the past five years.

Other Rating Factors: Good overall results on stability tests (5.9). Stability strengths include good operational trends and excellent risk diversification. Strong long-term capitalization index (10.0) based on excellent current risk adjusted capital (severe and moderate loss scenarios), despite some fluctuation in capital levels. Superior liquidity (9.7) with ample operational cash flow and liquid investments.

Principal Business: Auto liability (57%) and auto physical damage (43%).

Principal Investments: Investment grade bonds (96%) and misc. investments (4%).

Investments in Affiliates: None

Group Affiliation: Farmers Insurance Group of Companies

Licensed in: All states except HI, LA, MA, NH, NM, RI, WY, PR

Commenced Business: December 1968

Address: 6301 Owensmouth Ave, Woodland Hills, CA 91367

Phone: (302) 252-2000   **Domicile State:** CA   **NAIC Code:** 12963

Data Date	Rating	RACR #1	RACR #2	Loss Ratio %	Total Assets ($mil)	Capital ($mil)	Net Premium ($mil)	Net Income ($mil)
9-14	B	76.45	41.31	N/A	889.9	878.1	0.0	15.9
9-13	B	53.84	32.66	N/A	935.7	855.0	0.0	11.3
2013	B	55.30	36.29	0.0	880.8	861.7	0.0	15.0
2012	B	33.35	26.04	0.0	931.9	897.4	0.0	13.1
2011	B	60.71	27.86	0.0	944.6	877.1	0.0	25.5
2010	B	46.42	27.87	0.0	985.8	848.0	0.0	42.4
2009	B	18.17	14.51	69.6	1,072.4	802.0	65.9	68.5

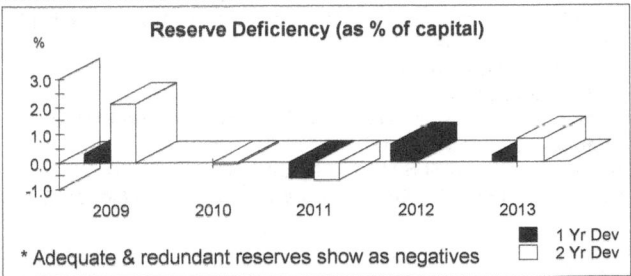

Reserve Deficiency (as % of capital)

* Adequate & redundant reserves show as negatives
■ 1 Yr Dev
□ 2 Yr Dev

21ST CENTURY NORTH AMERICA INS   B   Good

Major Rating Factors: History of adequate reserve strength (6.0 on a scale of 0 to 10) as reserves have been consistently at an acceptable level. Good overall results on stability tests (5.8). Stability strengths include good operational trends and excellent risk diversification.

Other Rating Factors: Strong long-term capitalization index (10.0) based on excellent current risk adjusted capital (severe and moderate loss scenarios). Moreover, capital levels have been consistent in recent years. Excellent profitability (8.2) with operating gains in each of the last five years. Superior liquidity (10.0) with ample operational cash flow and liquid investments.

Principal Business: Auto liability (66%) and auto physical damage (34%).

Principal Investments: Investment grade bonds (84%) and misc. investments (17%).

Investments in Affiliates: 18%

Group Affiliation: Farmers Insurance Group of Companies

Licensed in: All states except PR

Commenced Business: May 1975

Address: 505 Carr Rd, Wilmington, DE 19809

Phone: (302) 252-2000   **Domicile State:** NY   **NAIC Code:** 32220

Data Date	Rating	RACR #1	RACR #2	Loss Ratio %	Total Assets ($mil)	Capital ($mil)	Net Premium ($mil)	Net Income ($mil)
9-14	B	5.83	5.50	N/A	566.3	542.2	0.0	4.6
9-13	B	5.82	5.51	N/A	570.1	528.1	0.0	11.5
2013	B	5.76	5.47	0.0	572.0	532.6	0.0	15.2
2012	B	5.74	5.45	0.0	569.0	517.3	0.0	17.1
2011	B	5.57	5.24	0.0	617.4	489.3	0.0	25.3
2010	B	5.38	5.02	0.0	699.2	459.5	0.0	73.0
2009	B	4.60	3.94	69.6	1,780.7	461.3	50.7	84.4

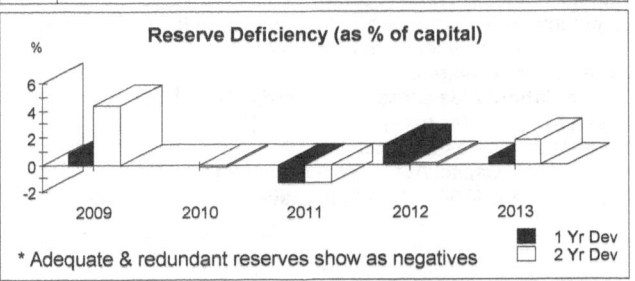

Reserve Deficiency (as % of capital)

* Adequate & redundant reserves show as negatives
■ 1 Yr Dev
□ 2 Yr Dev

21ST CENTURY PREMIER INS CO   B-   Good

Major Rating Factors: History of adequate reserve strength (6.0 on a scale of 0 to 10) as reserves have been consistently at an acceptable level. Good overall results on stability tests (5.2). Stability strengths include good operational trends and excellent risk diversification.

Other Rating Factors: Strong long-term capitalization index (10.0) based on excellent current risk adjusted capital (severe and moderate loss scenarios). Moreover, capital levels have been consistent in recent years. Excellent profitability (8.1) with operating gains in each of the last five years. Superior liquidity (10.0) with ample operational cash flow and liquid investments.

Principal Business: Auto liability (64%), auto physical damage (33%), homeowners multiple peril (2%), and group accident & health (1%).

Principal Investments: Investment grade bonds (75%) and misc. investments (25%).

Investments in Affiliates: 23%

Group Affiliation: Farmers Insurance Group of Companies

Licensed in: All states, the District of Columbia and Puerto Rico

Commenced Business: April 1866

Address: 500 Virginia Drive, Ft. Washington, PA 19034

Phone: (302) 252-2000   **Domicile State:** PA   **NAIC Code:** 20796

Data Date	Rating	RACR #1	RACR #2	Loss Ratio %	Total Assets ($mil)	Capital ($mil)	Net Premium ($mil)	Net Income ($mil)
9-14	B-	4.68	4.51	N/A	271.0	267.3	0.0	6.7
9-13	B-	4.85	4.63	N/A	264.3	253.2	0.0	8.3
2013	B-	4.58	4.46	0.0	264.5	257.9	0.0	11.3
2012	B-	4.74	4.60	0.0	256.4	240.6	0.0	10.9
2011	C+	4.94	4.75	0.0	252.1	221.5	0.0	15.4
2010	C+	5.06	4.79	0.0	263.9	200.0	0.0	13.0
2009	C+	0.71	0.69	69.6	308.9	182.1	0.2	39.2

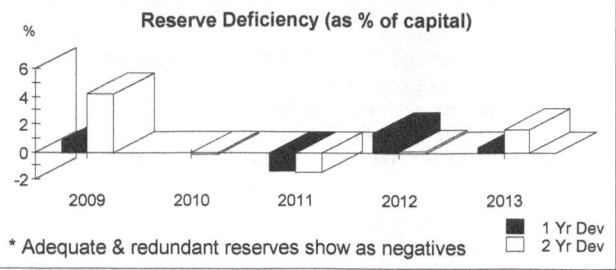

Reserve Deficiency (as % of capital)

* Adequate & redundant reserves show as negatives

ACA FINANCIAL GUARANTY CORP *   B+   Good

Major Rating Factors: History of adequate reserve strength (6.8 on a scale of 0 to 10) as reserves have been consistently at an acceptable level. Good overall results on stability tests (5.3) despite negative cash flow from operations for 2013. The largest net exposure for one risk is excessive at 199.9% of capital. Stability strengths include good operational trends and good risk diversification.

Other Rating Factors: Strong long-term capitalization index (7.6) based on excellent current risk adjusted capital (severe and moderate loss scenarios), despite some fluctuation in capital levels. Superior liquidity (9.4) with ample operational cash flow and liquid investments. Weak profitability index (1.6) with operating losses during 2010, 2011, 2012 and 2013. Average return on equity over the last five years has been poor at -1.9%.

Principal Business: Financial guaranty (100%).

Principal Investments: Investment grade bonds (102%), cash (2%), and non investment grade bonds (1%).

Investments in Affiliates: None

Group Affiliation: None

Licensed in: All states, the District of Columbia and Puerto Rico

Commenced Business: October 1986

Address: 7 Saint Paul St Suite 1660, Baltimore, MD 21202

Phone: (212) 375-2000   **Domicile State:** MD   **NAIC Code:** 22896

Data Date	Rating	RACR #1	RACR #2	Loss Ratio %	Total Assets ($mil)	Capital ($mil)	Net Premium ($mil)	Net Income ($mil)
9-14	B+	2.05	1.60	N/A	374.0	94.7	21.0	13.5
9-13	N/A	N/A	N/A	N/A	401.6	102.0	23.1	1.0
2013	B+	1.78	1.39	141.0	391.4	89.0	0.1	-9.2
2012	N/A	N/A	N/A	112.4	424.6	109.2	0.1	-6.0
2011	N/A	N/A	N/A	285.7	448.2	117.3	0.3	-26.3
2010	N/A	N/A	N/A	257.4	464.8	107.2	0.5	-24.0
2009	D-	6.50	4.93	98.2	463.5	137.5	0.9	48.8

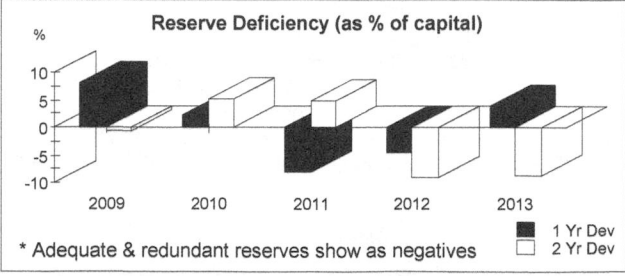

Reserve Deficiency (as % of capital)

* Adequate & redundant reserves show as negatives

ACCIDENT FUND INS CO OF AMERICA   C+   Fair

Major Rating Factors: Fair reserve development (3.3 on a scale of 0 to 10) as the level of reserves has at times been insufficient to cover claims. In 2010 and 2011 the two year reserve development was 16% and 18% deficient respectively. Fair overall results on stability tests (4.6) including negative cash flow from operations for 2013 and excessive premium growth.

Other Rating Factors: Good overall profitability index (5.2) despite operating losses during 2010 and 2011. Return on equity has been low, averaging 1.5% over the past five years. Good liquidity (6.4) with sufficient resources (cash flows and marketable investments) to handle a spike in claims. Strong long-term capitalization index (7.2) based on excellent current risk adjusted capital (severe and moderate loss scenarios), despite some fluctuation in capital levels.

Principal Business: Workers compensation (99%).

Principal Investments: Investment grade bonds (57%), misc. investments (41%), and non investment grade bonds (2%).

Investments in Affiliates: 16%

Group Affiliation: Blue Cross Blue Shield of Michigan

Licensed in: All states except PR

Commenced Business: December 1994

Address: 232 S Capitol Ave, Lansing, MI 48933

Phone: (517) 342-4200   **Domicile State:** MI   **NAIC Code:** 10166

Data Date	Rating	RACR #1	RACR #2	Loss Ratio %	Total Assets ($mil)	Capital ($mil)	Net Premium ($mil)	Net Income ($mil)
9-14	C+	1.43	1.15	N/A	2,514.9	734.6	514.3	42.6
9-13	C+	1.51	1.21	N/A	2,248.5	690.5	391.9	31.0
2013	C+	1.46	1.18	65.9	2,257.7	684.1	546.7	30.5
2012	C+	1.40	1.12	73.2	2,300.3	633.6	489.0	37.5
2011	C+	1.31	1.03	87.6	2,126.6	579.8	480.5	-26.6
2010	C+	1.35	1.06	92.9	2,199.0	648.2	574.3	-43.8
2009	C+	1.36	1.10	78.4	2,131.8	689.9	614.8	28.0

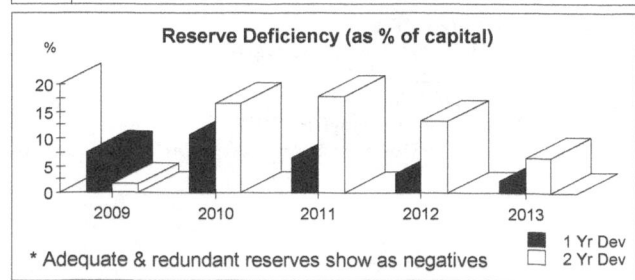

Reserve Deficiency (as % of capital)

* Adequate & redundant reserves show as negatives

ACE AMERICAN INS CO

B-   **Good**

Major Rating Factors: Fair overall results on stability tests (4.9 on a scale of 0 to 10) including potential drain of affiliation with ACE Ltd. Strong long-term capitalization index (7.1) based on excellent current risk adjusted capital (severe and moderate loss scenarios), despite some fluctuation in capital levels.

Other Rating Factors: Ample reserve history (8.2) that helps to protect the company against sharp claims increases. Excellent profitability (8.2) with operating gains in each of the last five years. Return on equity has been good over the last five years, averaging 14.0%. Excellent liquidity (7.1) with ample operational cash flow and liquid investments.

Principal Business: Other liability (36%), workers compensation (16%), group accident & health (13%), commercial multiple peril (11%), auto liability (6%), inland marine (3%), and other lines (15%).

Principal Investments: Investment grade bonds (54%), misc. investments (26%), non investment grade bonds (15%), cash (4%), and real estate (1%).

Investments in Affiliates: 21%

Group Affiliation: ACE Ltd

Licensed in: All states, the District of Columbia and Puerto Rico

Commenced Business: January 1946

Address: 1601 Chestnut St, Philadelphia, PA 19192

Phone: (215) 640-1000   **Domicile State:** PA   **NAIC Code:** 22667

Data Date	Rating	RACR #1	RACR #2	Loss Ratio %	Total Assets ($mil)	Capital ($mil)	Net Premium ($mil)	Net Income ($mil)
9-14	B-	1.50	1.22	N/A	12,524.0	2,988.0	1,240.0	131.4
9-13	B-	1.29	1.09	N/A	11,935.6	2,710.6	1,198.8	207.0
2013	B-	1.39	1.16	72.2	11,697.3	2,677.0	1,610.8	412.3
2012	B-	1.20	1.05	89.9	11,040.6	2,425.8	1,658.0	58.9
2011	B-	1.07	0.94	80.7	10,093.3	2,000.2	1,572.3	616.3
2010	B-	0.88	0.76	67.1	10,033.3	1,971.5	1,285.3	286.0
2009	B-	1.43	1.07	70.3	8,702.7	2,010.8	1,115.6	254.6

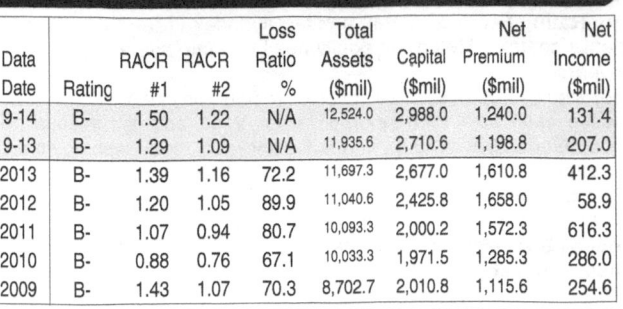

Capital

ACE PROPERTY & CASUALTY INS CO

C   **Fair**

Major Rating Factors: Fair overall results on stability tests (4.2 on a scale of 0 to 10) including fair financial strength of affiliated ACE Ltd. Good liquidity (6.8) with sufficient resources (cash flows and marketable investments) to handle a spike in claims.

Other Rating Factors: Strong long-term capitalization index (8.5) based on excellent current risk adjusted capital (severe and moderate loss scenarios), despite some fluctuation in capital levels. Ample reserve history (8.4) that helps to protect the company against sharp claims increases. Excellent profitability (7.6) with operating gains in each of the last five years.

Principal Business: Allied lines (80%), other liability (16%), auto liability (2%), and group accident & health (1%).

Principal Investments: Investment grade bonds (80%), misc. investments (11%), cash (6%), and non investment grade bonds (3%).

Investments in Affiliates: 3%

Group Affiliation: ACE Ltd

Licensed in: All states, the District of Columbia and Puerto Rico

Commenced Business: August 1819

Address: 1601 Chestnut St, Philadelphia, PA 19192

Phone: (215) 640-1000   **Domicile State:** PA   **NAIC Code:** 20699

Data Date	Rating	RACR #1	RACR #2	Loss Ratio %	Total Assets ($mil)	Capital ($mil)	Net Premium ($mil)	Net Income ($mil)
9-14	C	2.96	2.01	N/A	7,350.7	2,042.8	1,172.9	88.8
9-13	C	3.01	2.00	N/A	7,200.7	1,896.7	1,134.0	125.6
2013	C	2.95	2.01	72.2	7,214.1	1,920.5	1,523.8	165.6
2012	C	2.93	1.96	89.9	7,925.9	1,802.5	1,568.4	68.6
2011	C	2.74	1.82	80.7	6,425.0	1,620.8	1,489.5	128.9
2010	C	1.78	1.23	67.1	6,082.9	1,783.0	1,222.4	130.9
2009	C	1.77	1.18	69.6	5,360.9	1,569.0	1,061.0	87.2

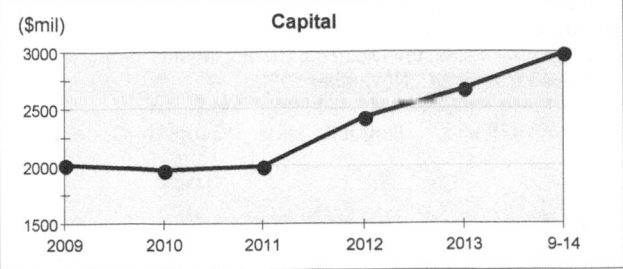

Rating Indexes

Ranges | Cap. 2 | Stab. | Res. | Prof. | Liq.
■ Weak   ■ Fair   ▢ Good   ▢ Strong

ACUITY A MUTUAL INS CO

B   **Good**

Major Rating Factors: Good liquidity (6.7 on a scale of 0 to 10) with sufficient resources (cash flows and marketable investments) to handle a spike in claims. Good overall results on stability tests (5.7).

Other Rating Factors: Strong long-term capitalization index (8.9) based on excellent current risk adjusted capital (severe and moderate loss scenarios). Moreover, capital levels have been consistent in recent years. Ample reserve history (9.3) that helps to protect the company against sharp claims increases. Excellent profitability (8.8) with operating gains in each of the last five years.

Principal Business: Workers compensation (26%), auto liability (22%), auto physical damage (13%), commercial multiple peril (11%), other liability (10%), homeowners multiple peril (9%), and other lines (9%).

Principal Investments: Investment grade bonds (59%), misc. investments (36%), non investment grade bonds (4%), and real estate (2%).

Investments in Affiliates: 0%

Group Affiliation: None

Licensed in: AL, AZ, AR, CO, DE, GA, ID, IL, IN, IA, KS, KY, ME, MI, MN, MS, MO, MT, NE, NV, NM, ND, OH, OK, OR, PA, SD, TN, TX, UT, VT, VA, WA, WV, WI, WY

Commenced Business: September 1925

Address: 2800 S Taylor Dr, Sheboygan, WI 53081-8470

Phone: (920) 458-9131   **Domicile State:** WI   **NAIC Code:** 14184

Data Date	Rating	RACR #1	RACR #2	Loss Ratio %	Total Assets ($mil)	Capital ($mil)	Net Premium ($mil)	Net Income ($mil)
9-14	B	3.80	2.34	N/A	3,017.8	1,283.5	842.7	71.0
9-13	B	4.04	2.50	N/A	2,754.0	1,150.8	746.8	81.4
2013	B	3.77	2.33	62.0	2,826.4	1,203.3	1,074.0	111.1
2012	B	3.85	2.40	63.2	2,475.2	994.3	937.8	95.4
2011	B	4.10	2.61	67.9	2,231.7	870.4	799.0	50.5
2010	B	4.13	2.63	68.3	2,126.0	825.8	736.9	57.7
2009	B	4.17	2.73	67.8	1,981.0	729.7	703.8	42.3

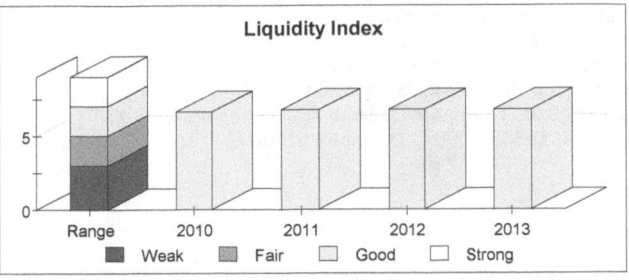

Liquidity Index

Range | 2010 | 2011 | 2012 | 2013
■ Weak   ■ Fair   ▢ Good   ▢ Strong

ADMIRAL INS CO   C-   Fair

Major Rating Factors: Weak profitability index (1.9 on a scale of 0 to 10). Fair expense controls. Return on equity has been fair, averaging 31.0% over the past five years.

Other Rating Factors: Fair overall results on stability tests (3.2) including negative cash flow from operations for 2013 and fair results on operational trends. Good liquidity (6.6) with sufficient resources (cash flows and marketable investments) to handle a spike in claims. Strong long-term capitalization index (7.6) based on excellent current risk adjusted capital (severe and moderate loss scenarios), despite some fluctuation in capital levels.

Principal Business: (Not applicable due to unusual reinsurance transactions.)

Principal Investments: Misc. investments (54%) and investment grade bonds (46%).

Investments in Affiliates: 52%

Group Affiliation: W R Berkley Corp

Licensed in: All states, the District of Columbia and Puerto Rico

Commenced Business: November 1952

Address: 1255 Orange Street, Wilmington, DE 19801

Phone: (856) 429-9200   **Domicile State:** DE   **NAIC Code:** 24856

Data Date	Rating	RACR #1	RACR #2	Loss Ratio %	Total Assets ($mil)	Capital ($mil)	Net Premium ($mil)	Net Income ($mil)
9-14	C-	1.79	1.82	N/A	682.0	605.3	0.0	4.1
9-13	C-	0.57	0.56	N/A	659.8	594.9	0.0	824.1
2013	C-	1.91	2.07	0.0	667.4	597.6	-255.7	826.2
2012	C	1.50	1.39	62.2	3,142.1	1,688.4	520.3	150.7
2011	C	1.35	1.24	59.6	3,018.2	1,481.0	499.0	170.1
2010	C	1.45	1.26	60.6	3,155.3	1,489.0	469.4	218.9
2009	C	1.22	0.95	75.1	3,308.4	1,340.2	563.0	56.2

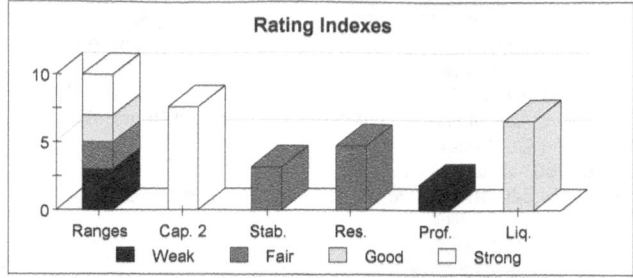

Rating Indexes

AFFILIATED FM INS CO   C   Fair

Major Rating Factors: Fair overall results on stability tests (3.9 on a scale of 0 to 10) including fair financial strength of affiliated FM Global. The largest net exposure for one risk is excessive at 7.6% of capital. History of adequate reserve strength (6.7) as reserves have been consistently at an acceptable level.

Other Rating Factors: Good liquidity (6.8) with sufficient resources (cash flows and marketable investments) to handle a spike in claims. Strong long-term capitalization index (8.3) based on excellent current risk adjusted capital (severe and moderate loss scenarios), despite some fluctuation in capital levels. Excellent profitability (7.0).

Principal Business: Fire (32%), inland marine (29%), allied lines (21%), commercial multiple peril (10%), boiler & machinery (6%), and ocean marine (2%).

Principal Investments: Investment grade bonds (51%) and misc. investments (49%).

Investments in Affiliates: None

Group Affiliation: FM Global

Licensed in: All states, the District of Columbia and Puerto Rico

Commenced Business: June 1950

Address: 1301 Atwood Avenue, Johnston, RI 02919-4908

Phone: (401) 275-3000   **Domicile State:** RI   **NAIC Code:** 10014

Data Date	Rating	RACR #1	RACR #2	Loss Ratio %	Total Assets ($mil)	Capital ($mil)	Net Premium ($mil)	Net Income ($mil)
9-14	C	3.82	2.40	N/A	2,524.3	1,343.1	284.7	78.6
9-13	C	3.24	2.10	N/A	2,312.4	1,194.4	293.8	110.2
2013	C	3.60	2.27	50.6	2,327.1	1,262.1	387.6	124.4
2012	C	2.70	1.77	59.7	2,302.2	1,034.1	444.2	86.0
2011	C	4.08	2.47	95.2	1,874.6	905.6	389.2	-23.7
2010	C	5.78	3.21	50.7	1,915.4	933.4	347.7	86.4
2009	C	7.20	3.72	41.8	1,621.7	828.2	381.8	115.4

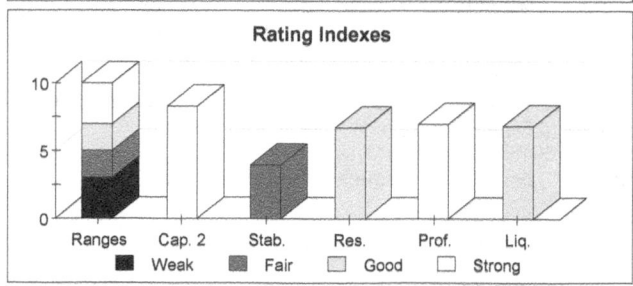

Rating Indexes

AGRI GENERAL INS CO   C-   Fair

Major Rating Factors: Weak profitability index (1.9 on a scale of 0 to 10). Fair expense controls. Return on equity has been fair, averaging 13.7% over the past five years. Fair overall results on stability tests (3.1) including fair results on operational trends.

Other Rating Factors: Strong long-term capitalization index (10.0) based on excellent current risk adjusted capital (severe and moderate loss scenarios), despite some fluctuation in capital levels. Ample reserve history (7.8) that can protect against increases in claims costs. Excellent liquidity (7.0) with ample operational cash flow and liquid investments.

Principal Business: (Not applicable due to unusual reinsurance transactions.)

Principal Investments: Investment grade bonds (91%) and misc. investments (9%).

Investments in Affiliates: None

Group Affiliation: ACE Ltd

Licensed in: All states except AK, DC, HI, NH, PR

Commenced Business: September 1983

Address: 9200 Northpark Dr Suite 350, Johnston, IA 50131

Phone: (515) 559-1000   **Domicile State:** IA   **NAIC Code:** 42757

Data Date	Rating	RACR #1	RACR #2	Loss Ratio %	Total Assets ($mil)	Capital ($mil)	Net Premium ($mil)	Net Income ($mil)
9-14	C-	82.92	40.72	N/A	254.6	253.8	0.0	4.0
9-13	C+	120.93	59.47	N/A	482.5	481.0	-0.5	9.9
2013	C-	77.53	38.13	170.5	254.1	249.0	-0.8	0.1
2012	C+	57.15	51.43	162.4	557.2	471.0	-2.1	92.0
2011	C	46.94	42.25	N/A	463.7	379.2	-16.6	48.1
2010	B	12.04	6.76	63.1	938.2	774.7	677.3	127.7
2009	B	3.71	2.32	56.5	980.8	683.4	819.0	195.2

Income Trends

AIG PROPERTY CASUALTY CO   C+   Fair

Major Rating Factors: Fair reserve development (3.6 on a scale of 0 to 10) as the level of reserves has at times been insufficient to cover claims. In 2011 and 2010 the two year reserve development was 17% and 25% deficient respectively. Fair profitability index (3.3) with operating losses during 2009 and 2010. Return on equity has been fair, averaging 13.5% over the past five years.

Other Rating Factors: Fair overall results on stability tests (4.8) including excessive premium growth. The largest net exposure for one risk is high at 3.5% of capital. Good liquidity (6.8) with sufficient resources (cash flows and marketable investments) to handle a spike in claims. Strong long-term capitalization index (7.7) based on excellent current risk adjusted capital (severe and moderate loss scenarios), despite some fluctuation in capital levels.

Principal Business: Homeowners multiple peril (51%), inland marine (11%), other liability (10%), auto physical damage (8%), auto liability (8%), earthquake (5%), and other lines (8%).

Principal Investments: Misc. investments (57%), investment grade bonds (41%), and cash (2%).

Investments in Affiliates: 0%

Group Affiliation: American International Group

Licensed in: All states except HI, PR

Commenced Business: August 1871

Address: 2595 Interstate Dr Suite 103, Harrisburg, PA 17110

Phone: (212) 770-7000   **Domicile State:** PA   **NAIC Code:** 19402

Data Date	Rating	RACR #1	RACR #2	Loss Ratio %	Total Assets ($mil)	Capital ($mil)	Net Premium ($mil)	Net Income ($mil)
9-14	C+	2.25	1.44	N/A	4,865.6	1,454.7	694.2	156.8
9-13	C+	2.18	1.40	N/A	3,454.9	1,072.9	482.5	99.3
2013	C+	2.30	1.46	76.6	3,656.5	1,166.3	713.5	124.6
2012	C+	2.27	1.47	87.1	3,429.8	1,080.2	615.3	668.0
2011	C+	1.77	1.42	83.9	4,068.2	1,700.5	626.7	27.8
2010	C+	1.75	1.31	108.8	4,407.7	1,693.6	619.6	-94.5
2009	C+	1.95	1.36	91.1	4,062.5	1,556.4	755.7	-25.5

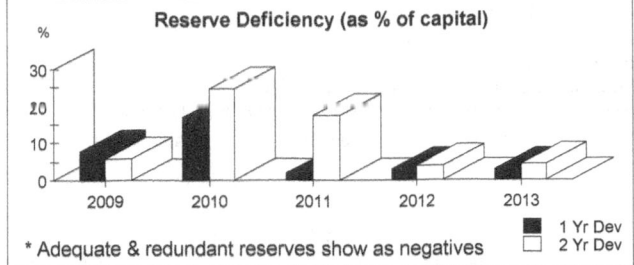

Reserve Deficiency (as % of capital)

* Adequate & redundant reserves show as negatives
■ 1 Yr Dev □ 2 Yr Dev

AIG SPECIALTY INS CO   C   Fair

Major Rating Factors: Weak overall results on stability tests (2.8 on a scale of 0 to 10). The largest net exposure for one risk is excessive at 19.4% of capital. Strengths include potentially strong support from affiliation with American International Group. Weak profitability index (1.9). Fair expense controls. Return on equity has been fair, averaging 24.8% over the past five years.

Other Rating Factors: History of adequate reserve strength (5.9) as reserves have been consistently at an acceptable level. Good liquidity (6.9) with sufficient resources (cash flows and marketable investments) to handle a spike in claims. Strong long-term capitalization index (7.7) based on excellent current risk adjusted capital (severe and moderate loss scenarios), despite some fluctuation in capital levels.

Principal Business: Other liability (92%), auto liability (3%), homeowners multiple peril (2%), burglary & theft (1%), and allied lines (1%).

Principal Investments: Investment grade bonds (626%), cash (58%), and non investment grade bonds (4%).

Investments in Affiliates: None

Group Affiliation: American International Group

Licensed in: All states, the District of Columbia and Puerto Rico

Commenced Business: July 1973

Address: 300 S Riverside Plaza Ste 2100, Chicago, IL 60606-6613

Phone: (212) 770-7000   **Domicile State:** IL   **NAIC Code:** 26883

Data Date	Rating	RACR #1	RACR #2	Loss Ratio %	Total Assets ($mil)	Capital ($mil)	Net Premium ($mil)	Net Income ($mil)
9-14	C	3.48	2.32	N/A	307.1	246.3	0.0	271.7
9-13	C+	2.08	1.39	N/A	2,608.6	734.6	329.9	120.7
2013	C+	2.07	1.40	69.4	2,579.6	741.8	417.3	158.8
2012	C+	2.15	1.44	100.0	2,808.8	807.8	402.4	40.1
2011	C+	2.07	1.35	94.7	3,025.1	854.5	490.3	8.6
2010	C+	1.61	1.07	86.2	2,722.0	722.3	402.8	6.9
2009	C	0.89	0.65	95.9	2,367.7	697.1	125.9	27.4

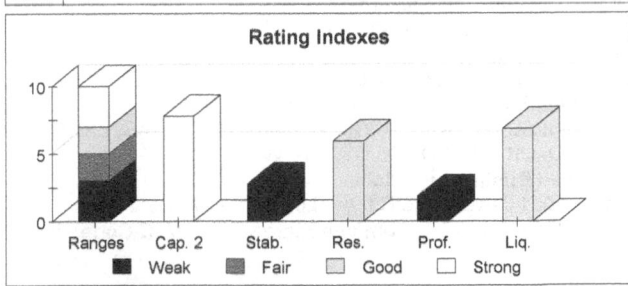

Rating Indexes

Ranges Cap. 2 Stab. Res. Prof. Liq.
■ Weak ■ Fair □ Good □ Strong

AIU INS CO   C   Fair

Major Rating Factors: Weak overall results on stability tests (2.8 on a scale of 0 to 10) including weak results on operational trends. The largest net exposure for one risk is excessive at 43.6% of capital. Strengths include potentially strong support from affiliation with American International Group. Weak profitability index (1.9) with operating losses during 2009, 2010, 2011 and 2012. Return on equity has been fair, averaging 9.0% over the past five years.

Other Rating Factors: History of adequate reserve strength (6.7) as reserves have been consistently at an acceptable level. Good liquidity (6.8) with sufficient resources (cash flows and marketable investments) to handle a spike in claims. Strong long-term capitalization index (8.2) based on excellent current risk adjusted capital (severe and moderate loss scenarios), despite some fluctuation in capital levels.

Principal Business: (Not applicable due to unusual reinsurance transactions.)

Principal Investments: Investment grade bonds (59%), misc. investments (29%), and cash (12%).

Investments in Affiliates: 37%

Group Affiliation: American International Group

Licensed in: All states except HI, WY, PR

Commenced Business: April 1851

Address: 70 Pine St, New York, NY 10270

Phone: (212) 770-7000   **Domicile State:** NY   **NAIC Code:** 19399

Data Date	Rating	RACR #1	RACR #2	Loss Ratio %	Total Assets ($mil)	Capital ($mil)	Net Premium ($mil)	Net Income ($mil)
9-14	C	2.77	2.69	N/A	243.7	238.7	0.0	2.9
9-13	C	2.29	2.01	N/A	290.8	225.9	-32.9	164.0
2013	C	2.69	2.64	438.2	285.1	224.9	-446.8	168.9
2012	C	2.62	1.70	64.2	2,412.1	622.1	689.8	-49.4
2011	C	2.66	1.77	76.8	2,638.0	595.6	715.1	-24.6
2010	C+	2.50	1.85	68.6	2,830.4	806.0	681.3	-9.2
2009	C	1.92	1.49	73.8	2,808.4	741.0	666.5	-86.5

American International Group Composite Group Rating: B Largest Group Members	Assets ($mil)	Rating
AMERICAN GENERAL LIFE INS CO	159157	B
VARIABLE ANNUITY LIFE INS CO	77174	B
UNITED STATES LIFE INS CO IN NYC	25538	B-
NATIONAL UNION FIRE INS CO OF PITTSB	24710	C
AMERICAN HOME ASR CO	23671	C

ALAMANCE INS CO
                                                                    C-   Fair

Major Rating Factors: Weak overall results on stability tests (2.6 on a scale of 0 to 10) including potential drain of affiliation with IFG Companies. Strong long-term capitalization index (7.6) based on excellent current risk adjusted capital (severe and moderate loss scenarios). Moreover, capital levels have been consistent in recent years.

Other Rating Factors: Ample reserve history (8.0) that helps to protect the company against sharp claims increases. Excellent profitability (8.3) with operating gains in each of the last five years. Excellent liquidity (7.8) with ample operational cash flow and liquid investments.

Principal Business: (This company is a reinsurer.)

Principal Investments: Misc. investments (60%) and investment grade bonds (40%).

Investments in Affiliates: 57%

Group Affiliation: IFG Companies

Licensed in: All states except CA, PR

Commenced Business: December 1998

Address: 238 International Road, Burlington, NC 27215

Phone: (336) 586-2500   **Domicile State:** IL   **NAIC Code:** 10957

Data Date	Rating	RACR #1	RACR #2	Loss Ratio %	Total Assets ($mil)	Capital ($mil)	Net Premium ($mil)	Net Income ($mil)
9-14	C-	1.48	1.44	N/A	486.7	368.4	28.4	7.0
9-13	C-	1.49	1.44	N/A	472.1	347.6	32.4	10.0
2013	C-	1.45	1.42	50.6	480.6	358.1	40.7	14.7
2012	C-	1.46	1.43	60.2	460.9	334.1	43.1	9.6
2011	C-	1.45	1.43	58.9	450.2	326.6	35.9	7.2
2010	C-	1.45	1.42	49.9	440.9	314.2	31.3	13.3
2009	C-	1.43	1.33	53.4	432.8	296.6	34.3	15.6

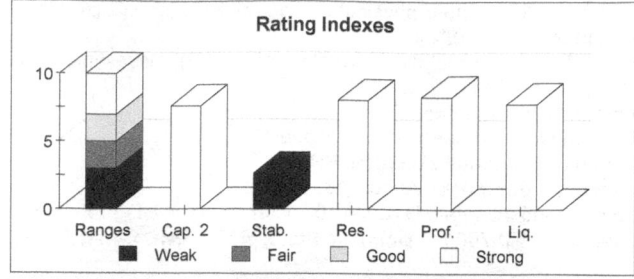

Rating Indexes

ALASKA NATIONAL INS CO
                                                                    B   Good

Major Rating Factors: Good overall results on stability tests (6.1 on a scale of 0 to 10). Strong long-term capitalization index (8.8) based on excellent current risk adjusted capital (severe and moderate loss scenarios), despite some fluctuation in capital levels.

Other Rating Factors: Ample reserve history (9.4) that helps to protect the company against sharp claims increases. Excellent profitability (8.0) with operating gains in each of the last five years. Return on equity has been good over the last five years, averaging 12.6%. Excellent liquidity (7.3) with ample operational cash flow and liquid investments.

Principal Business: Workers compensation (75%), commercial multiple peril (7%), other liability (6%), auto liability (6%), inland marine (2%), auto physical damage (1%), and other lines (3%).

Principal Investments: Investment grade bonds (74%), misc. investments (25%), and cash (1%).

Investments in Affiliates: None

Group Affiliation: Alaska National Corp

Licensed in: AL, AK, AZ, CA, CO, FL, HI, ID, IL, IA, KS, LA, MN, MS, MO, MT, NV, NM, ND, OK, OR, SD, TX, UT, WA, WY

Commenced Business: October 1980

Address: 7001 Jewell Lake Rd, Anchorage, AK 99502-2800

Phone: (907) 248-2642   **Domicile State:** AK   **NAIC Code:** 38733

Data Date	Rating	RACR #1	RACR #2	Loss Ratio %	Total Assets ($mil)	Capital ($mil)	Net Premium ($mil)	Net Income ($mil)
9-14	B	3.11	2.19	N/A	853.2	371.5	149.1	33.9
9-13	B	3.46	2.44	N/A	788.9	330.7	127.6	36.9
2013	B	3.18	2.20	51.3	830.4	352.2	200.6	50.3
2012	B	3.45	2.42	69.2	753.4	293.6	183.9	20.9
2011	B	4.67	3.19	55.8	691.5	303.6	135.2	33.9
2010	B	4.30	2.90	52.8	677.5	271.6	132.1	38.9
2009	B	4.31	2.55	51.2	700.4	293.0	142.3	47.4

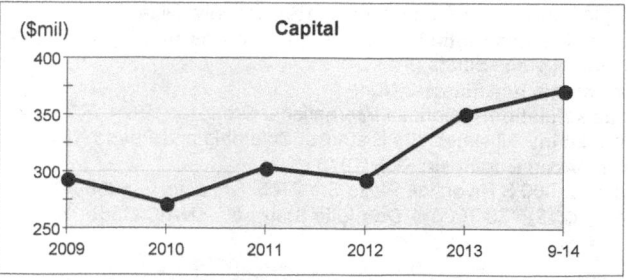

Capital

ALFA INS CORP *
                                                                    B+   Good

Major Rating Factors: Good overall profitability index (5.2 on a scale of 0 to 10) despite operating losses during 2011. Return on equity has been low, averaging 3.3% over the past five years. Good liquidity (6.8) with sufficient resources (cash flows and marketable investments) to handle a spike in claims.

Other Rating Factors: Good overall results on stability tests (6.5). Stability strengths include good operational trends and excellent risk diversification. The largest net exposure for one risk is conservative at 1.4% of capital. Strong long-term capitalization index (10.0) based on excellent current risk adjusted capital (severe and moderate loss scenarios), despite some fluctuation in capital levels. Ample reserve history (8.1) that helps to protect the company against sharp claims increases.

Principal Business: Auto liability (41%), auto physical damage (28%), homeowners multiple peril (25%), commercial multiple peril (3%), fire (1%), and inland marine (1%).

Principal Investments: Investment grade bonds (76%), misc. investments (18%), cash (5%), and non investment grade bonds (1%).

Investments in Affiliates: None

Group Affiliation: Alfa Ins Group

Licensed in: AL, GA, MS

Commenced Business: April 1945

Address: 2108 East South Blvd, Montgomery, AL 36116

Phone: (334) 288-3900   **Domicile State:** AL   **NAIC Code:** 22330

Data Date	Rating	RACR #1	RACR #2	Loss Ratio %	Total Assets ($mil)	Capital ($mil)	Net Premium ($mil)	Net Income ($mil)
9-14	B+	5.03	3.30	N/A	99.4	54.1	24.9	1.0
9-13	B+	6.15	4.12	N/A	98.7	57.4	24.0	1.9
2013	B+	6.01	4.11	65.6	98.3	59.2	32.7	3.4
2012	B+	6.76	4.71	65.8	97.6	60.3	31.1	4.2
2011	B	5.83	4.02	87.4	93.9	54.4	31.2	-0.9
2010	B	5.65	3.95	72.1	94.3	52.0	31.6	1.5
2009	B	6.22	4.37	79.8	106.1	54.2	30.2	1.7

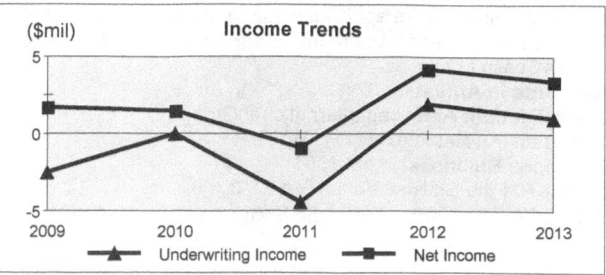

Income Trends

ALFA MUTUAL FIRE INS CO

B **Good**

Major Rating Factors: Good overall profitability index (5.2 on a scale of 0 to 10) despite operating losses during 2009, 2011 and the first nine months of 2014. Good liquidity (5.1) with sufficient resources (cash flows and marketable investments) to handle a spike in claims.

Other Rating Factors: Good overall results on stability tests (6.3). Strong long-term capitalization index (7.6) based on excellent current risk adjusted capital (severe and moderate loss scenarios), despite some fluctuation in capital levels. Ample reserve history (7.7) that can protect against increases in claims costs.

Principal Business: Fire (49%), allied lines (44%), and inland marine (7%).

Principal Investments: Investment grade bonds (54%), misc. investments (43%), cash (1%), non investment grade bonds (1%), and real estate (1%).

Investments in Affiliates: 38%

Group Affiliation: Alfa Ins Group

Licensed in: AL

Commenced Business: August 1946

Address: 2108 East South Blvd, Montgomery, AL 36116

Phone: (334) 288-3900   **Domicile State:** AL   **NAIC Code:** 19143

Data Date	Rating	RACR #1	RACR #2	Loss Ratio %	Total Assets ($mil)	Capital ($mil)	Net Premium ($mil)	Net Income ($mil)
9-14	B	1.90	1.42	N/A	687.7	399.2	249.2	-7.7
9-13	B	1.72	1.27	N/A	653.8	383.7	239.8	15.8
2013	B	1.96	1.48	68.6	659.5	399.3	327.1	25.7
2012	B	1.65	1.23	68.5	608.2	362.6	311.3	12.3
2011	B	1.50	1.12	90.5	604.8	339.0	311.6	-30.1
2010	B	1.60	1.18	74.6	614.4	362.7	316.2	19.5
2009	B	1.45	1.03	79.5	574.9	339.0	296.1	-20.8

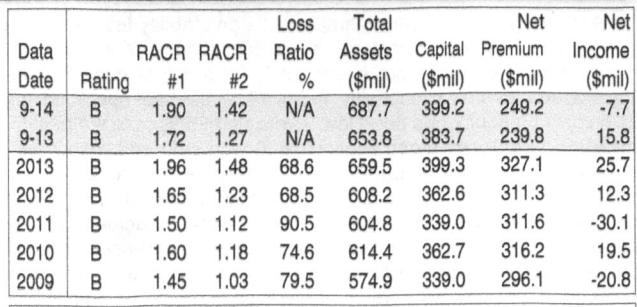

Income Trends

ALFA MUTUAL GENERAL INS CO *

B+ **Good**

Major Rating Factors: Good profitability index (5.0 on a scale of 0 to 10) despite operating losses during 2009 and 2011. Good liquidity (6.4) with sufficient resources (cash flows and marketable investments) to handle a spike in claims.

Other Rating Factors: Good overall results on stability tests (6.4). The largest net exposure for one risk is conservative at 1.3% of capital. Strong long-term capitalization index (7.7) based on excellent current risk adjusted capital (severe and moderate loss scenarios), despite some fluctuation in capital levels. Ample reserve history (7.5) that can protect against increases in claims costs.

Principal Business: Homeowners multiple peril (39%), auto liability (34%), auto physical damage (26%), and other liability (1%).

Principal Investments: Investment grade bonds (56%), misc. investments (37%), cash (6%), and non investment grade bonds (1%).

Investments in Affiliates: 1%

Group Affiliation: Alfa Ins Group

Licensed in: AL, GA, MS

Commenced Business: October 1955

Address: 2108 East South Blvd, Montgomery, AL 36116

Phone: (334) 288-3900   **Domicile State:** AL   **NAIC Code:** 19151

Data Date	Rating	RACR #1	RACR #2	Loss Ratio %	Total Assets ($mil)	Capital ($mil)	Net Premium ($mil)	Net Income ($mil)
9-14	B+	2.22	1.44	N/A	100.9	55.9	33.2	1.4
9-13	B	2.09	1.40	N/A	93.5	51.7	32.0	1.7
2013	B+	2.35	1.58	68.8	94.8	54.3	43.6	4.1
2012	B	1.89	1.28	69.0	86.8	48.3	41.5	3.2
2011	B	1.61	1.09	91.1	81.8	43.4	41.6	-5.9
2010	B+	1.83	1.24	75.3	86.3	50.1	42.2	3.0
2009	B	1.67	1.13	81.9	82.9	47.1	40.2	-3.1

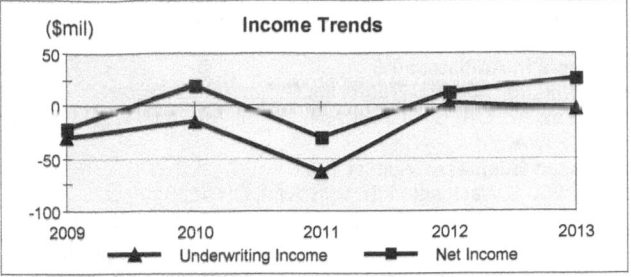

Income Trends

ALFA MUTUAL INS CO

B **Good**

Major Rating Factors: History of adequate reserve strength (6.2 on a scale of 0 to 10) as reserves have been consistently at an acceptable level. Good overall results on stability tests (6.0).

Other Rating Factors: Fair profitability index (4.0) with operating losses during 2009, 2011 and the first nine months of 2014. Strong long-term capitalization index (7.3) based on excellent current risk adjusted capital (severe and moderate loss scenarios), despite some fluctuation in capital levels. Vulnerable liquidity (2.2) as a spike in claims may stretch capacity.

Principal Business: Homeowners multiple peril (31%), auto liability (28%), auto physical damage (28%), farmowners multiple peril (8%), commercial multiple peril (3%), and inland marine (1%).

Principal Investments: Misc. investments (65%), investment grade bonds (28%), real estate (5%), and cash (2%).

Investments in Affiliates: 45%

Group Affiliation: Alfa Ins Group

Licensed in: AL, FL, GA, IL, IN, KY, NC, OH, PA, VA

Commenced Business: October 1947

Address: 2108 East South Blvd, Montgomery, AL 36116

Phone: (334) 288-3900   **Domicile State:** AL   **NAIC Code:** 19135

Data Date	Rating	RACR #1	RACR #2	Loss Ratio %	Total Assets ($mil)	Capital ($mil)	Net Premium ($mil)	Net Income ($mil)
9-14	B	1.48	1.15	N/A	1,293.2	570.5	431.9	-9.0
9-13	B	1.48	1.14	N/A	1,222.7	557.1	415.5	23.3
2013	B	1.59	1.25	68.7	1,231.2	580.4	566.7	48.5
2012	B	1.40	1.09	69.5	1,150.4	525.1	539.4	11.8
2011	B	1.29	1.00	91.4	1,125.1	482.4	539.8	-84.9
2010	B	1.65	1.28	75.8	1,208.3	641.9	548.0	17.9
2009	B	1.66	1.28	82.4	1,159.7	652.2	523.2	-44.9

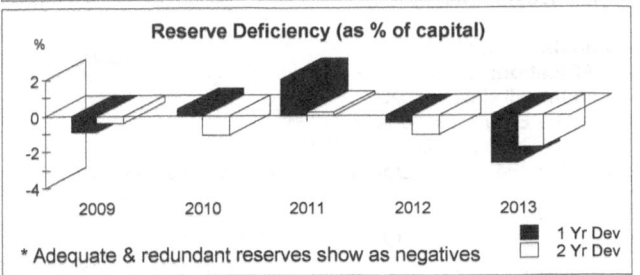

Reserve Deficiency (as % of capital)

* Adequate & redundant reserves show as negatives

ALL AMERICA INS CO *
B+   Good

Major Rating Factors: Good overall results on stability tests (6.4 on a scale of 0 to 10). Stability strengths include good operational trends and excellent risk diversification. The largest net exposure for one risk is conservative at 1.2% of capital. Good overall profitability index (6.4) despite operating losses during 2010. Return on equity has been low, averaging 2.2% over the past five years.

Other Rating Factors: Good liquidity (6.8) with sufficient resources (cash flows and marketable investments) to handle a spike in claims. Strong long-term capitalization index (10.0) based on excellent current risk adjusted capital (severe and moderate loss scenarios), despite some fluctuation in capital levels. Ample reserve history (7.0) that can protect against increases in claims costs.

Principal Business: Commercial multiple peril (56%), auto liability (21%), auto physical damage (8%), workers compensation (7%), and products liability (7%).

Principal Investments: Investment grade bonds (91%) and misc. investments (9%).

Investments in Affiliates: 0%

Group Affiliation: Central Mutual Ins Group

Licensed in: AZ, CA, CT, GA, IL, IN, IA, KY, MA, MI, NV, NJ, NY, NC, OH, OK, SC, TN, TX, VA, WI

Commenced Business: August 1961

Address: 800 S Washington St, Van Wert, OH 45891

Phone: (419) 238-1010   **Domicile State:** OH   **NAIC Code:** 20222

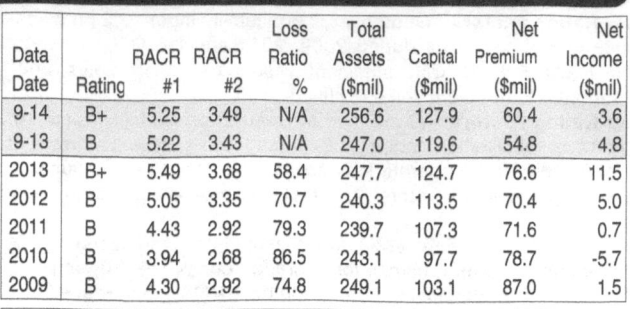

Data Date	Rating	RACR #1	RACR #2	Loss Ratio %	Total Assets ($mil)	Capital ($mil)	Net Premium ($mil)	Net Income ($mil)
9-14	B+	5.25	3.49	N/A	256.6	127.9	60.4	3.6
9-13	B	5.22	3.43	N/A	247.0	119.6	54.8	4.8
2013	B+	5.49	3.68	58.4	247.7	124.7	76.6	11.5
2012	B	5.05	3.35	70.7	240.3	113.5	70.4	5.0
2011	B	4.43	2.92	79.3	239.7	107.3	71.6	0.7
2010	B	3.94	2.68	86.5	243.1	97.7	78.7	-5.7
2009	B	4.30	2.92	74.8	249.1	103.1	87.0	1.5

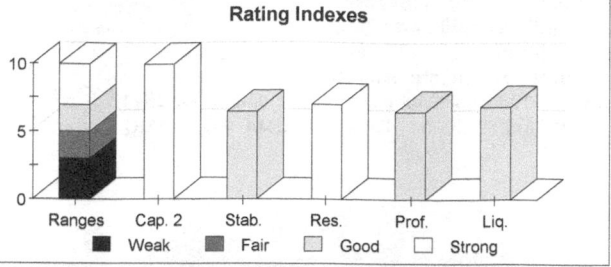

Rating Indexes

Ranges   Cap. 2   Stab.   Res.   Prof.   Liq.

■ Weak   ■ Fair   ▨ Good   □ Strong

ALLIANZ GLOBAL RISKS US INS CO
C-   Fair

Major Rating Factors: Poor long-term capitalization (2.7 on a scale of 0 to 10) based on weak current risk adjusted capital (moderate loss scenario), although results have slipped from the fair range over the last two years. Weak profitability index (1.9) with operating losses during 2012. Return on equity has been low, averaging 3.4% over the past five years.

Other Rating Factors: Fair overall results on stability tests (3.1) including negative cash flow from operations for 2013 and fair risk adjusted capital in prior years. The largest net exposure for one risk is excessive at 9.0% of capital. Good liquidity (6.2) with sufficient resources (cash flows and marketable investments) to handle a spike in claims. Ample reserve history (7.9) that can protect against increases in claims costs.

Principal Business: Fire (26%), aircraft (25%), products liability (11%), inland marine (9%), allied lines (8%), other liability (8%), and other lines (13%).

Principal Investments: Investment grade bonds (73%), misc. investments (26%), and cash (1%).

Investments in Affiliates: 9%

Group Affiliation: Allianz Ins Group

Licensed in: All states, the District of Columbia and Puerto Rico

Commenced Business: December 1977

Address: 225 W Washington St Suite 1800, Chicago, IL 60606-3484

Phone: (888) 466-7883   **Domicile State:** IL   **NAIC Code:** 35300

Data Date	Rating	RACR #1	RACR #2	Loss Ratio %	Total Assets ($mil)	Capital ($mil)	Net Premium ($mil)	Net Income ($mil)
9-14	C-	0.64	0.45	N/A	3,442.4	893.7	823.5	32.9
9-13	C-	0.70	0.50	N/A	3,182.7	865.4	668.5	12.1
2013	C-	0.74	0.52	79.5	3,176.9	867.3	868.2	10.0
2012	C-	0.75	0.54	82.8	3,099.8	866.9	916.0	-86.7
2011	C+	1.19	1.11	61.8	5,922.9	3,816.3	914.3	202.9
2010	C+	1.19	1.11	71.4	5,483.8	3,637.0	1,023.5	658.8
2009	C+	1.26	1.18	71.4	5,282.6	3,850.3	577.9	45.4

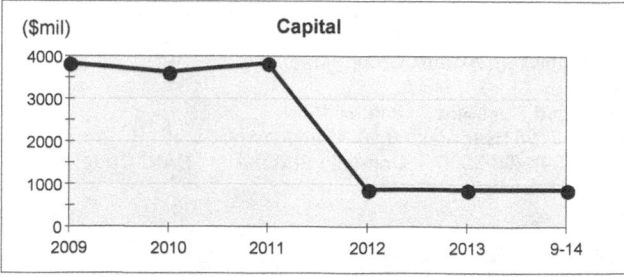

($mil)   Capital

ALLIED WORLD INS CO
C   Fair

Major Rating Factors: Fair overall results on stability tests (3.4 on a scale of 0 to 10) including potential drain of affiliation with Allied World Asr Holding Group and weak results on operational trends. History of adequate reserve strength (5.6) as reserves have been consistently at an acceptable level.

Other Rating Factors: Strong long-term capitalization index (7.7) based on excellent current risk adjusted capital (severe and moderate loss scenarios). Moreover, capital levels have been consistent in recent years. Excellent profitability (7.6) despite modest operating losses during 2012. Excellent liquidity (7.0) with ample operational cash flow and liquid investments.

Principal Business: Other liability (56%), surety (17%), ocean marine (13%), auto liability (8%), allied lines (4%), and fire (2%).

Principal Investments: Misc. investments (60%) and investment grade bonds (40%).

Investments in Affiliates: 47%

Group Affiliation: Allied World Asr Holding Group

Licensed in: All states except PR

Commenced Business: October 1986

Address: 14 Centre St, Concord, NH 03301

Phone: (646) 794-0500   **Domicile State:** NH   **NAIC Code:** 22730

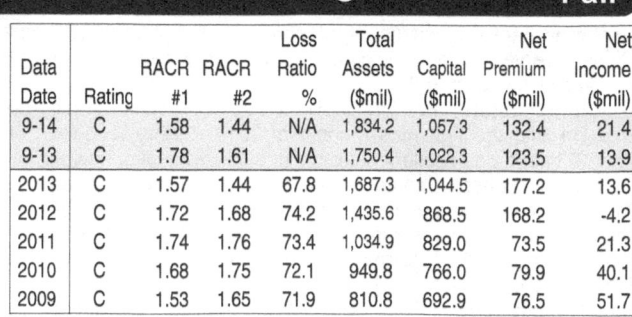

Data Date	Rating	RACR #1	RACR #2	Loss Ratio %	Total Assets ($mil)	Capital ($mil)	Net Premium ($mil)	Net Income ($mil)
9-14	C	1.58	1.44	N/A	1,834.2	1,057.3	132.4	21.4
9-13	C	1.78	1.61	N/A	1,750.4	1,022.3	123.5	13.9
2013	C	1.57	1.44	67.8	1,687.3	1,044.5	177.2	13.6
2012	C	1.72	1.68	74.2	1,435.6	868.5	168.2	-4.2
2011	C	1.74	1.76	73.4	1,034.9	829.0	73.5	21.3
2010	C	1.68	1.75	72.1	949.8	766.0	79.9	40.1
2009	C	1.53	1.65	71.9	810.8	692.9	76.5	51.7

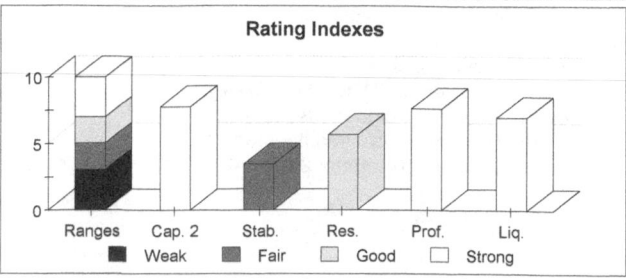

Rating Indexes

Ranges   Cap. 2   Stab.   Res.   Prof.   Liq.

■ Weak   ■ Fair   ▨ Good   □ Strong

ALLSTATE INS CO *   A-   Excellent

Major Rating Factors: Strong long-term capitalization index (8.0 on a scale of 0 to 10) based on excellent current risk adjusted capital (severe and moderate loss scenarios). Furthermore, this high level of risk adjusted capital has been consistently maintained in previous years. Excellent profitability (7.9) with operating gains in each of the last five years.

Other Rating Factors: Excellent overall results on stability tests (7.2). Stability strengths include excellent operational trends and excellent risk diversification. History of adequate reserve strength (5.6) as reserves have been consistently at an acceptable level. Good liquidity (5.9) with sufficient resources (cash flows and marketable investments) to handle a spike in claims.

Principal Business: Homeowners multiple peril (33%), auto liability (32%), auto physical damage (25%), allied lines (4%), commercial multiple peril (4%), other liability (1%), and inland marine (1%).

Principal Investments: Investment grade bonds (56%), misc. investments (34%), non investment grade bonds (10%), and real estate (1%).

Investments in Affiliates: 13%

Group Affiliation: Allstate Group

Licensed in: All states except NJ

Commenced Business: April 1931

Address: 2775 Sanders Rd, Northbrook, IL 60062-6127

Phone: (847) 402-5000   **Domicile State:** IL   **NAIC Code:** 19232

Data Date	Rating	RACR #1	RACR #2	Loss Ratio %	Total Assets ($mil)	Capital ($mil)	Net Premium ($mil)	Net Income ($mil)
9-14	A-	2.21	1.71	N/A	44,425.2	16,990.1	19,357.1	1,436.0
9-13	B+	2.03	1.57	N/A	42,662.5	16,271.1	18,453.3	1,596.6
2013	A-	2.21	1.72	66.4	43,733.3	17,254.7	25,108.5	2,465.5
2012	B+	2.07	1.62	69.4	42,133.1	16,260.9	24,193.4	1,950.4
2011	B+	1.78	1.42	78.4	41,023.0	15,126.7	23,547.7	223.0
2010	B+	1.84	1.45	73.3	40,786.1	15,383.8	23,483.4	1,029.1
2009	B+	1.95	1.54	71.7	40,828.5	15,026.1	23,832.9	1,285.0

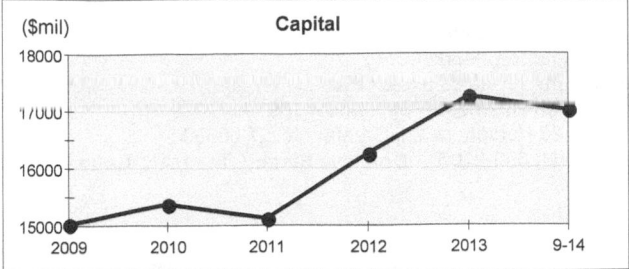

ALLSTATE NJ INS CO   B   Good

Major Rating Factors: Good overall profitability index (5.3 on a scale of 0 to 10) despite operating losses during 2011 and 2012. Return on equity has been low, averaging 4.2% over the past five years. Good liquidity (6.2) with sufficient resources (cash flows and marketable investments) to handle a spike in claims.

Other Rating Factors: Good overall results on stability tests (6.1). Fair reserve development (4.8) as reserves have generally been sufficient to cover claims. Strong long-term capitalization index (8.2) based on excellent current risk adjusted capital (severe and moderate loss scenarios), despite some fluctuation in capital levels.

Principal Business: Auto liability (46%), homeowners multiple peril (27%), auto physical damage (22%), allied lines (2%), other liability (2%), commercial multiple peril (1%), and inland marine (1%).

Principal Investments: Investment grade bonds (101%) and non investment grade bonds (1%).

Investments in Affiliates: 4%

Group Affiliation: Allstate Group

Licensed in: IL, NJ

Commenced Business: November 1997

Address: 721 U.S. Hwy 202/206,Ste 300, Bridgewater, NJ 08807-1759

Phone: (908) 252-5000   **Domicile State:** IL   **NAIC Code:** 10852

Data Date	Rating	RACR #1	RACR #2	Loss Ratio %	Total Assets ($mil)	Capital ($mil)	Net Premium ($mil)	Net Income ($mil)
9-14	B	2.56	1.91	N/A	2,569.7	896.6	890.9	117.0
9-13	B	2.47	1.82	N/A	2,674.4	887.9	898.5	119.6
2013	B	2.45	1.93	62.4	2,680.7	930.9	1,190.1	162.7
2012	B	1.97	1.53	91.5	2,647.6	767.5	1,199.4	-52.0
2011	B	2.23	1.85	86.9	2,658.2	813.4	1,158.3	-16.6
2010	B	2.41	2.02	84.3	2,550.4	826.3	1,114.6	16.8
2009	B	2.38	1.95	86.6	2,517.9	802.3	1,108.5	2.0

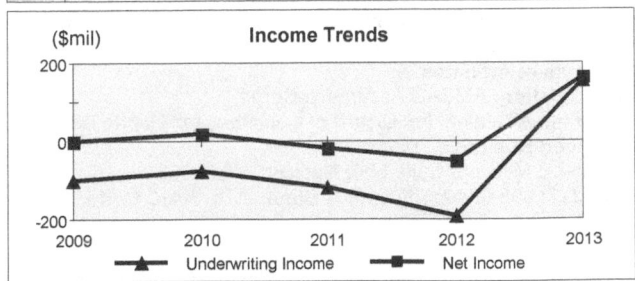

ALLSTATE PROPERTY & CASUALTY INS CO   B   Good

Major Rating Factors: Good overall results on stability tests (6.1 on a scale of 0 to 10). Strengths include potentially strong support from affiliation with Allstate Group, good operational trends and excellent risk diversification. Strong long-term capitalization index (10.0) based on excellent current risk adjusted capital (severe and moderate loss scenarios). Moreover, capital levels have been consistent in recent years.

Other Rating Factors: Excellent profitability (7.6) with operating gains in each of the last five years. Excellent expense controls. Superior liquidity (10.0) with ample operational cash flow and liquid investments.

Principal Business: Auto liability (41%), auto physical damage (29%), homeowners multiple peril (28%), and inland marine (1%).

Principal Investments: Investment grade bonds (97%), misc. investments (2%), and non investment grade bonds (1%).

Investments in Affiliates: None

Group Affiliation: Allstate Group

Licensed in: All states except HI, MA, NJ, PR

Commenced Business: April 1985

Address: 3075 Sanders Rd, Ste H1A, Northbrook, IL 60062-7127

Phone: (847) 402-5000   **Domicile State:** IL   **NAIC Code:** 17230

Data Date	Rating	RACR #1	RACR #2	Loss Ratio %	Total Assets ($mil)	Capital ($mil)	Net Premium ($mil)	Net Income ($mil)
9-14	B	74.80	57.02	N/A	218.3	205.4	0.0	1.7
9-13	B	72.12	61.82	N/A	216.5	202.9	0.0	4.3
2013	B	87.25	59.92	0.0	213.7	204.2	0.0	5.5
2012	B	109.24	64.02	0.0	204.4	197.8	0.0	4.6
2011	B	124.05	86.30	0.0	199.6	194.4	0.0	6.0
2010	B	146.78	73.39	0.0	167.6	164.4	0.0	5.4
2009	B	106.50	52.88	0.0	163.1	159.0	0.0	3.7

Allstate Group Composite Group Rating: B Largest Group Members	Assets ($mil)	Rating
ALLSTATE LIFE INS CO	47859	B
ALLSTATE INS CO	43733	A-
ALLSTATE LIFE INS CO OF NEW YORK	6742	B-
ALLSTATE NJ INS CO	2681	B
AMERICAN HERITAGE LIFE INS CO	1770	B

ALTERRA REINS USA INC *
B+   Good

Major Rating Factors: Good overall results on stability tests (6.5 on a scale of 0 to 10). Affiliation with Markel Corp is a strength. The largest net exposure for one risk is conservative at 1.3% of capital. History of adequate reserve strength (5.2) as reserves have been consistently at an acceptable level.

Other Rating Factors: Good overall profitability index (6.8) with small operating losses during 2010. Return on equity has been low, averaging 1.4% over the past five years. Strong long-term capitalization index (9.1) based on excellent current risk adjusted capital (severe and moderate loss scenarios), despite some fluctuation in capital levels. Excellent liquidity (8.2) with ample operational cash flow and liquid investments.

Principal Business: (This company is a reinsurer.)

Principal Investments: Investment grade bonds (71%) and misc. investments (29%).

Investments in Affiliates: 14%

Group Affiliation: Markel Corp

Licensed in: All states except PR

Commenced Business: September 1997

Address: 20 Horseneck Ln, Greenwich, CT 06830

Phone: (908) 630-2700   **Domicile State:** CT   **NAIC Code:** 10829

Data Date	Rating	RACR #1	RACR #2	Loss Ratio %	Total Assets ($mil)	Capital ($mil)	Net Premium ($mil)	Net Income ($mil)
9-14	B+	3.44	2.40	N/A	1,467.0	733.7	153.8	13.0
9-13	B+	4.36	2.84	N/A	1,309.2	672.0	142.7	11.2
2013	B+	3.62	2.60	68.0	1,364.7	715.0	186.9	19.6
2012	B+	5.26	3.44	73.5	1,299.2	671.6	201.7	9.7
2011	B	4.69	3.74	72.6	1,177.7	676.5	205.6	3.8
2010	B	3.60	2.82	71.2	1,058.7	661.4	171.1	-2.4
2009	B	11.01	6.90	69.2	810.5	530.3	66.4	11.0

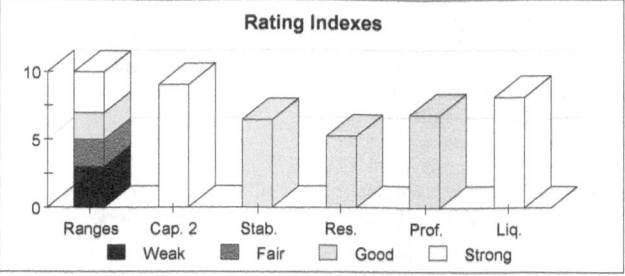

Rating Indexes

AMBAC ASSURANCE CORP
E   Very Weak

Major Rating Factors: Poor long-term capitalization index (0.7 on a scale of 0 to 10) based on weak current risk adjusted capital (severe and moderate loss scenarios). A history of deficient reserves (2.6). Underreserving can have an adverse impact on capital and profits. In 2012, the two year reserve development was 53% deficient.

Other Rating Factors: Weak profitability index (1.7) with operating losses during 2009, 2010, 2011 and 2013. Average return on equity over the last five years has been poor at -1.4%. overall results on stability tests (-0.5) including weak risk adjusted capital in prior years and weak results on operational trends. The largest net exposure for one risk is excessive at 527.8% of capital. Superior liquidity (10.0) with ample operational cash flow and liquid investments.

Principal Business: Financial guaranty (98%) and surety (2%).

Principal Investments: Investment grade bonds (62%), misc. investments (32%), and non investment grade bonds (6%).

Investments in Affiliates: 4%

Group Affiliation: AMBAC Assurance Corp

Licensed in: All states, the District of Columbia and Puerto Rico

Commenced Business: March 1970

Address: 2 E Mifflin St Suite 600, Madison, WI 53703

Phone: (212) 668-0340   **Domicile State:** WI   **NAIC Code:** 18708

Data Date	Rating	RACR #1	RACR #2	Loss Ratio %	Total Assets ($mil)	Capital ($mil)	Net Premium ($mil)	Net Income ($mil)
9-14	E	0.68	0.37	N/A	5,940.7	897.7	169.7	224.6
9-13	E	0.54	0.26	N/A	5,915.8	501.7	260.9	27.0
2013	E	0.60	0.30	145.2	5,793.6	840.3	90.3	-235.6
2012	E	0.30	0.14	157.6	5,216.2	100.0	104.0	616.1
2011	E	0.48	0.24	251.8	5,905.0	495.3	138.9	-835.8
2010	E	0.95	0.42	248.0	6,005.3	1,026.9	230.3	-1,471.9
2009	E	1.09	0.45	189.5	8,533.5	801.9	461.4	-2,479.6

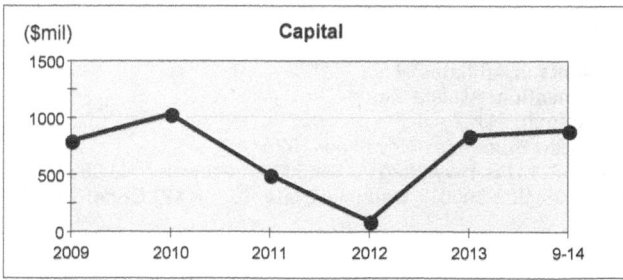

Capital

AMCO INS CO
C+   Fair

Major Rating Factors: Fair overall results on stability tests (4.5 on a scale of 0 to 10) including fair results on operational trends. Strengths include potentially strong support from affiliation with Nationwide Corp.

Other Rating Factors: Weak profitability index (1.9). Good expense controls. Return on equity has been fair, averaging 5.7% over the past five years. Strong long-term capitalization index (10.0) based on excellent current risk adjusted capital (severe and moderate loss scenarios), despite some fluctuation in capital levels. Superior liquidity (10.0) with ample operational cash flow and liquid investments.

Principal Business: Commercial multiple peril (25%), auto liability (22%), homeowners multiple peril (21%), auto physical damage (14%), other liability (6%), fire (3%), and other lines (9%).

Principal Investments: Investment grade bonds (153%).

Investments in Affiliates: 10%

Group Affiliation: Nationwide Corp

Licensed in: All states except AK, HI, LA, MA, NH, NJ, NY, OK, PR

Commenced Business: April 1959

Address: 1100 Locust St Dept 2007, Des Moines, IA 50391-2007

Phone: (515) 508-4211   **Domicile State:** IA   **NAIC Code:** 19100

Data Date	Rating	RACR #1	RACR #2	Loss Ratio %	Total Assets ($mil)	Capital ($mil)	Net Premium ($mil)	Net Income ($mil)
9-14	C+	4.63	3.96	N/A	971.4	205.0	0.0	31.5
9-13	B	7.96	6.91	N/A	1,082.8	395.6	0.0	7.0
2013	B	8.61	7.54	0.0	1,067.8	363.8	0.0	7.8
2012	B	8.97	7.99	0.0	1,057.5	429.2	0.0	15.6
2011	B	8.21	6.79	0.0	1,873.9	463.4	0.0	15.6
2010	B	6.57	5.65	0.0	1,764.8	459.5	0.0	15.6
2009	B	8.80	6.97	0.0	1,956.6	444.4	0.0	22.8

Nationwide Corp Composite Group Rating: B- Largest Group Members	Assets ($mil)	Rating
NATIONWIDE LIFE INS CO	120676	B-
NATIONWIDE MUTUAL INS CO	32676	B
NATIONWIDE LIFE ANNUITY INS CO	6902	B-
NATIONWIDE MUTUAL FIRE INS CO	5410	B+
NATIONWIDE INDEMNITY CO	3252	B-

www.weissratings.com

AMERICAN AGRICULTURAL INS CO

C+   **Fair**

Major Rating Factors: Fair overall results on stability tests (4.5 on a scale of 0 to 10). Good profitability index (5.0) despite operating losses during 2009, 2010 and 2011. Average return on equity over the last five years has been poor at -1.4%.

Other Rating Factors: Good liquidity (6.8) with sufficient resources (cash flows and marketable investments) to handle a spike in claims. Strong long-term capitalization index (7.5) based on excellent current risk adjusted capital (severe and moderate loss scenarios), despite some fluctuation in capital levels. Ample reserve history (7.0) that can protect against increases in claims costs.

Principal Business: Allied lines (100%).

Principal Investments: Investment grade bonds (74%), misc. investments (22%), and cash (4%).

Investments in Affiliates: 0%

Group Affiliation: None

Licensed in: All states except AK, CA, DC, HI, MN, NV, WV

Commenced Business: May 1948

Address: 225 South East sT, Indianapolis, IN 46202

Phone: (847) 969-2900   **Domicile State:** IN   **NAIC Code:** 10103

Data Date	Rating	RACR #1	RACR #2	Loss Ratio %	Total Assets ($mil)	Capital ($mil)	Net Premium ($mil)	Net Income ($mil)
9-14	C+	1.85	1.36	N/A	1,168.6	509.6	240.6	32.8
9-13	C	1.75	1.33	N/A	1,146.5	474.3	245.0	43.9
2013	C+	1.86	1.38	73.3	1,093.1	489.3	342.2	55.3
2012	C	1.74	1.35	86.3	1,041.0	440.1	283.6	10.0
2011	C	1.68	1.25	115.8	1,089.7	430.2	356.1	-86.5
2010	B	1.80	1.38	87.6	1,132.4	494.0	374.2	-3.1
2009	B	2.05	1.51	100.3	1,094.4	483.3	399.1	-36.5

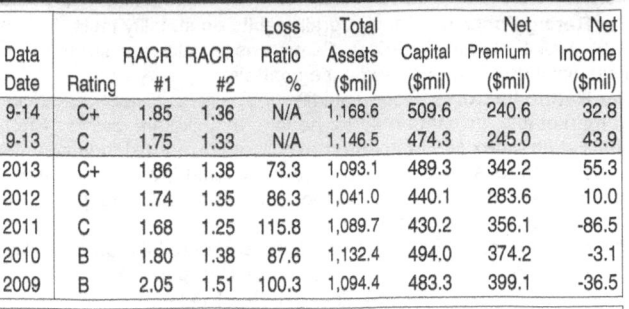

Rating Indexes

AMERICAN BANKERS INS CO OF FL

B   **Good**

Major Rating Factors: Good overall results on stability tests (5.5 on a scale of 0 to 10) despite potential drain of affiliation with Assurant Inc. History of adequate reserve strength (6.6) as reserves have been consistently at an acceptable level.

Other Rating Factors: Good liquidity (6.4) with sufficient resources (cash flows and marketable investments) to handle a spike in claims. Strong long-term capitalization index (7.7) based on excellent current risk adjusted capital (severe and moderate loss scenarios). Moreover, capital levels have been consistent in recent years. Excellent profitability (8.2) with operating gains in each of the last five years. Return on equity has been excellent over the last five years averaging 16.0%.

Principal Business: Other liability (24%), homeowners multiple peril (21%), allied lines (12%), credit (11%), credit accident & health (9%), inland marine (9%), and other lines (14%).

Principal Investments: Investment grade bonds (77%), misc. investments (13%), non investment grade bonds (7%), and cash (3%).

Investments in Affiliates: 1%

Group Affiliation: Assurant Inc

Licensed in: All states, the District of Columbia and Puerto Rico

Commenced Business: October 1947

Address: 11222 Quail Roost Dr, Miami, FL 33157

Phone: (305) 253-2244   **Domicile State:** FL   **NAIC Code:** 10111

Data Date	Rating	RACR #1	RACR #2	Loss Ratio %	Total Assets ($mil)	Capital ($mil)	Net Premium ($mil)	Net Income ($mil)
9-14	B	2.63	1.50	N/A	2,020.9	584.1	629.8	96.4
9-13	B	2.69	1.53	N/A	1,854.3	557.1	580.8	65.0
2013	B	2.62	1.49	40.1	1,844.9	542.1	884.0	96.5
2012	B	2.76	1.56	44.7	1,707.5	506.5	817.8	33.4
2011	B-	2.34	1.29	54.2	1,378.7	404.7	655.9	12.2
2010	B-	2.88	1.87	34.9	1,251.3	401.6	671.8	104.3
2009	B-	2.17	1.51	39.3	1,167.9	380.4	671.5	83.6

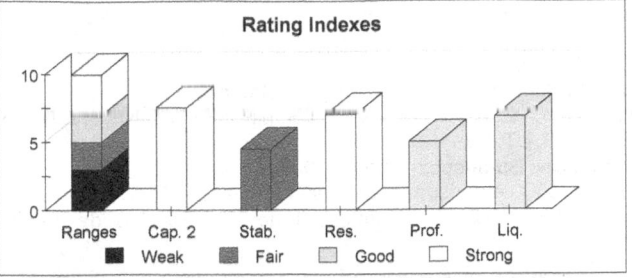

Rating Indexes

AMERICAN EXCESS INS EXCHANGE RRG

D   **Weak**

Major Rating Factors: Weak overall results on stability tests (2.2 on a scale of 0 to 10). The largest net exposure for one risk is excessive at 8.2% of capital. Strong long-term capitalization index (9.9) based on excellent current risk adjusted capital (severe and moderate loss scenarios), despite some fluctuation in capital levels.

Other Rating Factors: Ample reserve history (9.5) that helps to protect the company against sharp claims increases. Excellent profitability (8.4) with operating gains in each of the last five years. Return on equity has been excellent over the last five years averaging 18.3%. Superior liquidity (9.3) with ample operational cash flow and liquid investments.

Principal Business: Medical malpractice (95%) and other liability (5%).

Principal Investments: Investment grade bonds (69%), misc. investments (26%), and cash (5%).

Investments in Affiliates: None

Group Affiliation: None

Licensed in: AK, AZ, CA, CO, FL, HI, ID, IL, IN, IA, KS, KY, ME, MD, MA, MI, MN, MO, MT, NE, NV, NM, NY, ND, OH, OK, OR, PA, RI, SC, SD, TN, TX, VT, VA, WA, WV, WI

Commenced Business: April 1998

Address: 150 Dorset St #238, S Burlinton, VT 05403

Phone: (858) 481-2727   **Domicile State:** VT   **NAIC Code:** 10903

Data Date	Rating	RACR #1	RACR #2	Loss Ratio %	Total Assets ($mil)	Capital ($mil)	Net Premium ($mil)	Net Income ($mil)
9-14	D	4.78	3.14	N/A	388.5	236.0	17.6	24.9
9-13	D	6.25	3.99	N/A	404.6	239.9	17.4	31.3
2013	D	4.44	2.94	25.0	410.8	243.9	23.6	33.7
2012	D	6.09	3.91	4.1	406.9	237.9	23.4	39.1
2011	D	5.10	3.42	16.1	399.3	211.9	27.3	39.9
2010	D	4.62	2.86	N/A	418.0	214.2	26.7	47.0
2009	D	3.51	2.20	11.6	392.1	165.4	31.1	38.8

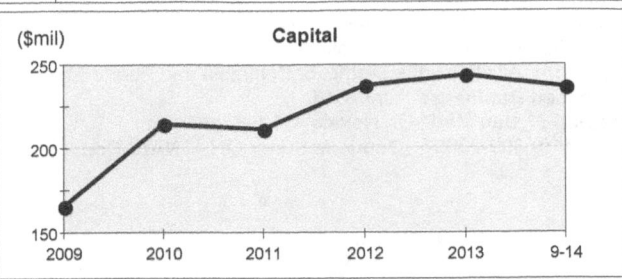

Capital

AMERICAN FAMILY MUT INS CO *

B+   Good

Major Rating Factors: Good overall results on stability tests (6.5 on a scale of 0 to 10). Affiliation with American Family Ins Group is a strength. Good overall profitability index (6.5). Fair expense controls.

Other Rating Factors: Good liquidity (5.9) with sufficient resources (cash flows and marketable investments) to handle a spike in claims. Strong long-term capitalization index (7.9) based on excellent current risk adjusted capital (severe and moderate loss scenarios). Moreover, capital levels have been consistent in recent years. Ample reserve history (9.1) that helps to protect the company against sharp claims increases.

Principal Business: Homeowners multiple peril (31%), auto liability (30%), auto physical damage (23%), commercial multiple peril (8%), other liability (3%), farmowners multiple peril (2%), and other lines (4%).

Principal Investments: Investment grade bonds (51%), misc. investments (44%), non investment grade bonds (3%), and real estate (2%).

Investments in Affiliates: 18%

Group Affiliation: American Family Ins Group

Licensed in: AZ, CO, ID, IL, IN, IA, KS, MN, MO, MT, NE, NV, NM, NC, ND, OH, OR, SC, SD, UT, WA, WI, WY

Commenced Business: October 1927

Address: 6000 American Pkwy, Madison, WI 53783-0001

Phone: (608) 249-2111   **Domicile State:** WI   **NAIC Code:** 19275

Data Date	Rating	RACR #1	RACR #2	Loss Ratio %	Total Assets ($mil)	Capital ($mil)	Net Premium ($mil)	Net Income ($mil)
9-14	B+	2.13	1.66	N/A	14,543.2	5,894.7	4,655.9	346.8
9-13	B	2.58	1.92	N/A	12,521.7	5,368.8	4,100.5	110.2
2013	B+	2.17	1.73	72.6	13,229.6	5,791.7	5,595.6	281.2
2012	B	2.56	1.94	73.0	12,038.9	5,165.0	5,435.1	323.7
2011	B	2.59	1.88	76.0	11,634.3	4,658.9	5,166.2	218.1
2010	B	2.53	1.81	72.0	11,577.0	4,570.8	5,324.3	423.2
2009	B	2.31	1.64	78.1	11,172.5	3,920.7	5,458.1	262.3

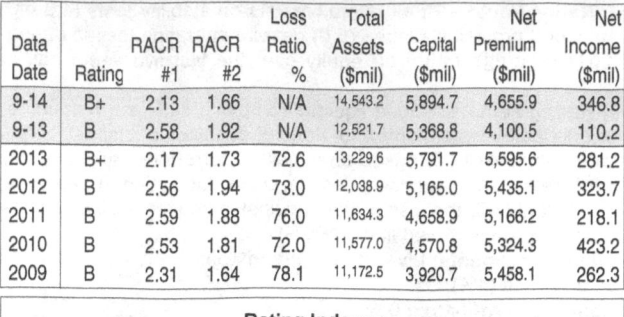

Rating Indexes

AMERICAN HOME ASR CO

C   Fair

Major Rating Factors: Fair profitability index (3.3 on a scale of 0 to 10) with operating losses during 2010. Return on equity has been low, averaging 4.9% over the past five years. Fair overall results on stability tests (4.2). The largest net exposure for one risk is excessive at 5.3% of capital.

Other Rating Factors: A history of deficient reserves (2.5). Underreserving can have an adverse impact on capital and profits. In 2011 and 2010 the two year reserve development was 33% and 50% deficient respectively. Good liquidity (6.5) with sufficient resources (cash flows and marketable investments) to handle a spike in claims. Strong long-term capitalization index (7.6) based on excellent current risk adjusted capital (severe and moderate loss scenarios), despite some fluctuation in capital levels.

Principal Business: Other accident & health (70%), auto liability (11%), other liability (6%), auto physical damage (4%), inland marine (4%), homeowners multiple peril (2%), and other lines (4%).

Principal Investments: Investment grade bonds (70%), misc. investments (24%), non investment grade bonds (5%), and cash (1%).

Investments in Affiliates: 0%

Group Affiliation: American International Group

Licensed in: All states except PR

Commenced Business: February 1899

Address: 175 Water St 18th Floor, New York, NY 10038

Phone: (212) 770-7000   **Domicile State:** NY   **NAIC Code:** 19380

Data Date	Rating	RACR #1	RACR #2	Loss Ratio %	Total Assets ($mil)	Capital ($mil)	Net Premium ($mil)	Net Income ($mil)
9-14	C	2.32	1.53	N/A	26,660.0	7,054.1	4,239.5	575.6
9-13	C	1.80	1.21	N/A	23,196.0	5,089.6	4,018.4	632.4
2013	C	1.77	1.17	70.0	23,671.1	5,091.7	5,852.4	703.0
2012	C	2.16	1.46	79.5	23,972.2	6,004.3	5,204.4	285.5
2011	C	2.02	1.37	80.0	23,900.3	5,667.3	5,308.9	494.6
2010	C	2.05	1.20	105.9	26,416.6	6,673.1	5,195.4	-776.5
2009	C	1.80	1.06	86.1	24,981.1	5,872.3	6,062.4	249.8

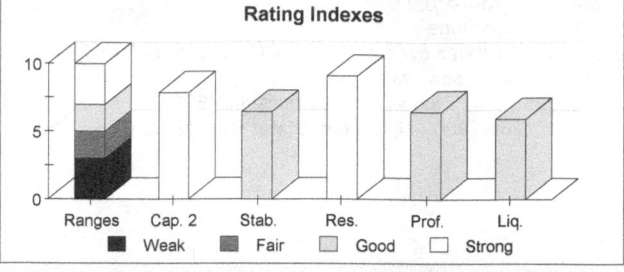

Income Trends

AMERICAN INS CO

C-   Fair

Major Rating Factors: Fair profitability index (3.6). Good expense controls. Return on equity has been fair, averaging 7.3% over the past five years.

Other Rating Factors: Fair overall results on stability tests (3.3) including weak results on operational trends. Strong long-term capitalization index (10.0) based on excellent current risk adjusted capital (severe and moderate loss scenarios), despite some fluctuation in capital levels. Excellent liquidity (7.0) with ample operational cash flow and liquid investments.

Principal Business: Commercial multiple peril (31%), homeowners multiple peril (22%), other liability (15%), workers compensation (10%), inland marine (7%), farmowners multiple peril (7%), and other lines (7%).

Principal Investments: Investment grade bonds (96%), misc. investments (3%), and cash (1%).

Investments in Affiliates: None

Group Affiliation: Allianz Ins Group

Licensed in: All states, the District of Columbia and Puerto Rico

Commenced Business: April 1846

Address: 777 San Marin Dr, Novato, CA 94998

Phone: (415) 899-2000   **Domicile State:** OH   **NAIC Code:** 21857

Data Date	Rating	RACR #1	RACR #2	Loss Ratio %	Total Assets ($mil)	Capital ($mil)	Net Premium ($mil)	Net Income ($mil)
9-14	C-	47.83	43.05	N/A	330.2	287.9	0.0	6.3
9-13	D+	56.70	43.38	N/A	350.9	313.2	0.0	2.7
2013	C-	47.36	42.62	0.0	325.5	283.5	0.0	4.8
2012	D+	43.16	38.84	0.0	370.1	312.3	-144.8	20.7
2011	C	1.14	0.78	88.2	1,308.3	314.0	407.4	4.7
2010	C	1.12	0.77	78.1	1,254.9	310.1	392.9	24.4
2009	C	1.16	0.80	70.8	1,354.1	369.6	461.3	82.3

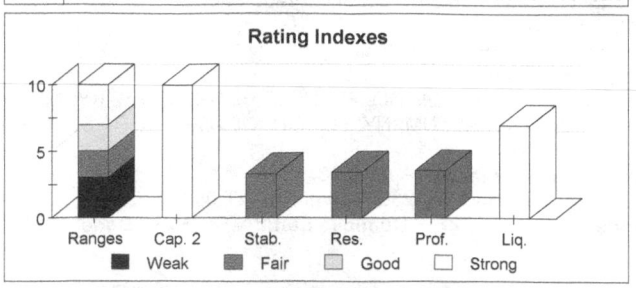

Rating Indexes

AMERICAN INTERSTATE INS CO   B-   Good

Major Rating Factors: Fair overall results on stability tests (4.6 on a scale of 0 to 10) including potential drain of affiliation with Amerisafe Inc. Strong long-term capitalization index (7.5) based on excellent current risk adjusted capital (severe and moderate loss scenarios), despite some fluctuation in capital levels.

Other Rating Factors: Ample reserve history (8.8) that helps to protect the company against sharp claims increases. Excellent profitability (8.7) with operating gains in each of the last five years. Excellent liquidity (7.3) with ample operational cash flow and liquid investments.

Principal Business: Workers compensation (100%).

Principal Investments: Investment grade bonds (75%), misc. investments (24%), and cash (1%).

Investments in Affiliates: 10%

Group Affiliation: Amerisafe Inc

Licensed in: All states except CT, NJ, OH, PR

Commenced Business: April 1974

Address: 13321 California St Suite 310, Omaha, NE 68154

Phone: (800) 256-9052   **Domicile State:** NE   **NAIC Code:** 31895

Data Date	Rating	RACR #1	RACR #2	Loss Ratio %	Total Assets ($mil)	Capital ($mil)	Net Premium ($mil)	Net Income ($mil)
9-14	B-	1.73	1.34	N/A	1,214.8	389.4	224.2	26.3
9-13	B-	1.91	1.50	N/A	1,079.9	338.8	195.7	22.0
2013	B-	1.74	1.35	69.4	1,093.7	354.3	284.8	35.3
2012	B-	2.02	1.60	75.7	1,001.8	323.9	251.2	25.4
2011	B-	2.23	1.75	75.6	922.6	314.4	206.5	22.3
2010	B-	2.60	2.01	72.1	915.4	320.4	166.9	24.8
2009	C+	2.42	1.89	65.2	935.8	323.5	190.0	46.3

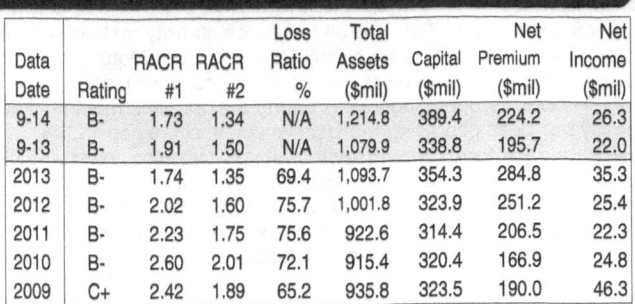

Capital ($mil)

AMERICAN MODERN HOME INS CO   C+   Fair

Major Rating Factors: Fair overall results on stability tests (4.3 on a scale of 0 to 10) including fair financial strength of affiliated Munich Re America Corp. Good overall profitability index (6.8). Weak expense controls. Return on equity has been fair, averaging 5.4% over the past five years.

Other Rating Factors: Good liquidity (6.5) with sufficient resources (cash flows and marketable investments) to handle a spike in claims. Strong long-term capitalization index (7.9) based on excellent current risk adjusted capital (severe and moderate loss scenarios), despite some fluctuation in capital levels. Ample reserve history (7.9) that can protect against increases in claims costs.

Principal Business: Homeowners multiple peril (34%), fire (21%), allied lines (14%), inland marine (13%), auto physical damage (5%), other liability (4%), and other lines (8%).

Principal Investments: Investment grade bonds (67%), misc. investments (22%), real estate (12%), and non investment grade bonds (2%).

Investments in Affiliates: 27%

Group Affiliation: Munich Re America Corp

Licensed in: All states, the District of Columbia and Puerto Rico

Commenced Business: September 1965

Address: 7000 Midland Blvd, Amelia, OH 45102-2607

Phone: (800) 543-2644   **Domicile State:** OH   **NAIC Code:** 23469

Data Date	Rating	RACR #1	RACR #2	Loss Ratio %	Total Assets ($mil)	Capital ($mil)	Net Premium ($mil)	Net Income ($mil)
9-14	C+	2.07	1.55	N/A	1,235.6	383.5	337.7	9.6
9-13	C+	2.45	1.86	N/A	1,211.0	397.2	292.7	3.1
2013	C+	2.17	1.66	43.8	1,256.4	373.6	431.7	5.8
2012	C+	2.52	1.95	50.3	1,156.6	389.8	361.7	5.6
2011	C+	2.51	2.06	56.5	1,097.1	357.6	323.6	11.3
2010	B+	2.54	2.01	45.0	1,067.2	350.4	398.3	37.0
2009	B+	2.48	1.96	51.6	974.6	315.1	368.0	37.0

Munich Re America Corp Composite Group Rating: C+ Largest Group Members	Assets ($mil)	Rating
MUNICH REINSURANCE AMERICA INC	16841	C+
MUNICH AMERICAN REASSURANCE CO	6981	B-
HARTFORD SM BOIL INSPECTION INS	1372	B
AMERICAN MODERN HOME INS CO	1256	C+
MUNICH AMERICAN LIFE REINS CO	1214	C+

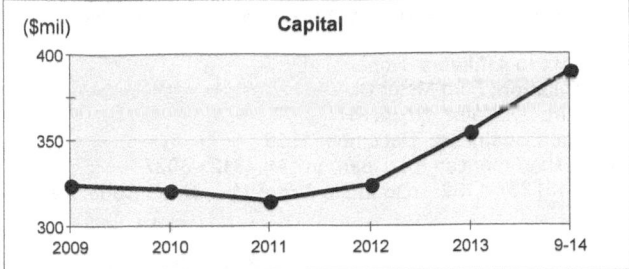

AMERICAN NATIONAL PROPERTY & CAS CO   B   Good

Major Rating Factors: Good overall profitability index (5.5 on a scale of 0 to 10) despite operating losses during 2009. Return on equity has been low, averaging 2.6% over the past five years. Good liquidity (6.4) with sufficient resources (cash flows and marketable investments) to handle a spike in claims.

Other Rating Factors: Good overall results on stability tests (6.3). Stability strengths include good operational trends and excellent risk diversification. Strong long-term capitalization index (7.6) based on excellent current risk adjusted capital (severe and moderate loss scenarios). Moreover, capital levels have been consistent in recent years. Ample reserve history (8.3) that helps to protect the company against sharp claims increases.

Principal Business: Auto liability (30%), homeowners multiple peril (29%), auto physical damage (16%), credit (10%), allied lines (7%), other liability (5%), and other lines (4%).

Principal Investments: Investment grade bonds (59%), misc. investments (40%), and real estate (1%).

Investments in Affiliates: 21%

Group Affiliation: American National Group Inc

Licensed in: All states except CT, HI, MA, NY

Commenced Business: January 1974

Address: 1949 E Sunshine, Springfield, MO 65899-0001

Phone: (417) 887-4990   **Domicile State:** MO   **NAIC Code:** 28401

Data Date	Rating	RACR #1	RACR #2	Loss Ratio %	Total Assets ($mil)	Capital ($mil)	Net Premium ($mil)	Net Income ($mil)
9-14	B	2.09	1.67	N/A	1,216.0	572.7	351.2	19.3
9-13	B	1.97	1.57	N/A	1,147.2	514.0	341.4	5.3
2013	B	2.02	1.65	75.2	1,155.6	537.5	468.0	25.4
2012	B	1.95	1.57	79.7	1,105.8	495.5	467.6	17.6
2011	B	1.67	1.27	82.4	1,019.2	383.6	485.0	14.0
2010	B	1.73	1.23	83.8	1,068.9	382.4	539.1	5.9
2009	B	1.63	1.13	86.8	1,062.5	374.3	558.7	-7.3

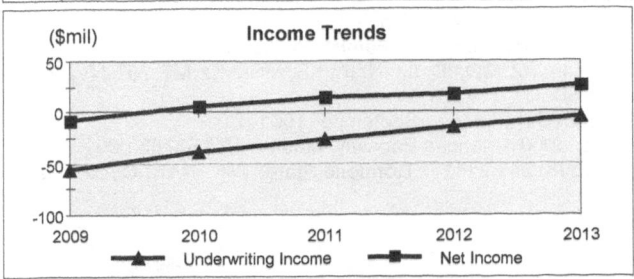

Income Trends ($mil)
Underwriting Income   Net Income

AMERICAN ROAD INS CO
C+   **Fair**

Major Rating Factors: Fair overall results on stability tests (4.4 on a scale of 0 to 10) including potential drain of affiliation with Ford Motor Co. The largest net exposure for one risk is excessive at 5.8% of capital. Good overall profitability index (6.1) despite operating losses during the first nine months of 2014. Return on equity has been good over the last five years, averaging 11.3%.

Other Rating Factors: Strong long-term capitalization index (10.0) based on excellent current risk adjusted capital (severe and moderate loss scenarios), despite some fluctuation in capital levels. Ample reserve history (7.5) that can protect against increases in claims costs. Excellent liquidity (7.2) with ample operational cash flow and liquid investments.

Principal Business: Aggregate write-ins for other lines of business (38%), inland marine (3%), and auto liability (1%).

Principal Investments: Investment grade bonds (98%), misc. investments (1%), and cash (1%).

Investments in Affiliates: None

Group Affiliation: Ford Motor Co

Licensed in: All states except PR

Commenced Business: December 1959

Address: The American Rd, Dearborn, MI 48121-6027

Phone: (313) 337-1102   **Domicile State:** MI   **NAIC Code:** 19631

Data Date	Rating	RACR #1	RACR #2	Loss Ratio %	Total Assets ($mil)	Capital ($mil)	Net Premium ($mil)	Net Income ($mil)
9-14	C+	23.20	11.65	N/A	589.2	263.8	94.1	-11.4
9-13	C	4.98	4.18	N/A	551.7	230.9	86.2	31.5
2013	C+	21.22	11.60	64.2	564.2	276.0	118.1	48.6
2012	C	4.82	4.11	77.5	482.8	214.0	99.5	19.9
2011	C	5.05	4.39	84.0	460.7	205.1	89.7	17.7
2010	C	6.77	5.86	47.3	528.5	274.4	81.0	55.4
2009	C	6.49	5.66	51.6	501.0	264.1	69.4	35.5

Rating Indexes

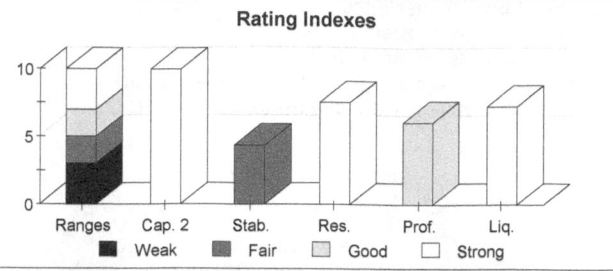

Ranges   Cap. 2   Stab.   Res.   Prof.   Liq.

■ Weak   ■ Fair   □ Good   □ Strong

AMERICAN SECURITY INS CO
B   **Good**

Major Rating Factors: Good overall results on stability tests (5.8 on a scale of 0 to 10) despite potential drain of affiliation with Assurant Inc. Stability strengths include good operational trends and excellent risk diversification. Good liquidity (6.5) with sufficient resources (cash flows and marketable investments) to handle a spike in claims.

Other Rating Factors: Strong long-term capitalization index (8.1) based on excellent current risk adjusted capital (severe and moderate loss scenarios), despite some fluctuation in capital levels. Ample reserve history (8.0) that helps to protect the company against sharp claims increases. Excellent profitability (8.6) with operating gains in each of the last five years. Return on equity has been excellent over the last five years averaging 42.2%.

Principal Business: Fire (62%), allied lines (26%), inland marine (5%), other liability (2%), homeowners multiple peril (2%), and credit (1%).

Principal Investments: Investment grade bonds (62%), misc. investments (33%), non investment grade bonds (7%), and real estate (1%).

Investments in Affiliates: 10%

Group Affiliation: Assurant Inc

Licensed in: All states except NH

Commenced Business: September 1938

Address: 260 Interstate N Circle NW, Atlanta, GA 30339-2111

Phone: (770) 763-1000   **Domicile State:** DE   **NAIC Code:** 42978

Data Date	Rating	RACR #1	RACR #2	Loss Ratio %	Total Assets ($mil)	Capital ($mil)	Net Premium ($mil)	Net Income ($mil)
9-14	B	2.45	1.73	N/A	2,104.9	790.8	1,217.9	208.2
9-13	B	4.17	2.59	N/A	1,884.6	791.9	1,029.1	237.1
2013	B	2.55	1.82	33.6	2,078.0	740.8	1,601.9	294.2
2012	B	3.84	2.39	43.1	1,949.3	703.1	1,496.0	279.8
2011	B	3.25	2.19	36.2	1,730.4	634.6	1,280.6	284.4
2010	B	2.78	2.01	28.5	1,738.1	674.0	1,217.1	340.6
2009	B	2.72	1.99	29.0	1,856.7	754.4	1,382.5	314.9

Rating Indexes

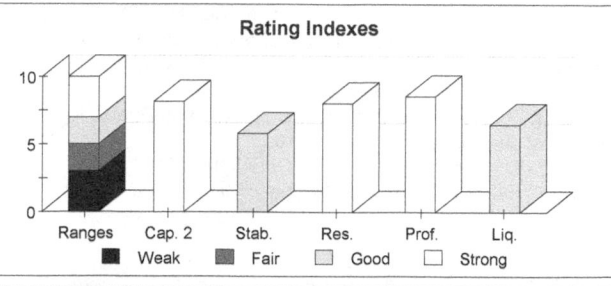

Ranges   Cap. 2   Stab.   Res.   Prof.   Liq.

■ Weak   ■ Fair   □ Good   □ Strong

AMERICAN STANDARD INS CO OF WI *
B+   **Good**

Major Rating Factors: Good overall results on stability tests (6.4 on a scale of 0 to 10). Strengths include potential support from affiliation with American Family Ins Group, good operational trends and excellent risk diversification. Strong long-term capitalization index (10.0) based on excellent current risk adjusted capital (severe and moderate loss scenarios), despite some fluctuation in capital levels.

Other Rating Factors: Excellent profitability (7.9) with operating gains in each of the last five years. Excellent expense controls. Superior liquidity (10.0) with ample operational cash flow and liquid investments.

Principal Business: Auto liability (66%) and auto physical damage (34%).

Principal Investments: Investment grade bonds (95%), cash (4%), and misc. investments (1%).

Investments in Affiliates: None

Group Affiliation: American Family Ins Group

Licensed in: AZ, CO, ID, IL, IN, IA, KS, MN, MO, MT, NE, NV, NM, NC, ND, OH, OR, SC, SD, UT, WA, WI, WY

Commenced Business: September 1961

Address: 6000 American Parkway, Madison, WI 53783-0001

Phone: (608) 249-2111   **Domicile State:** WI   **NAIC Code:** 19283

Data Date	Rating	RACR #1	RACR #2	Loss Ratio %	Total Assets ($mil)	Capital ($mil)	Net Premium ($mil)	Net Income ($mil)
9-14	B+	38.00	34.20	N/A	415.8	325.5	0.0	6.8
9-13	B+	38.48	34.63	N/A	400.0	316.9	0.0	6.3
2013	B+	40.40	36.36	0.0	393.9	318.6	0.0	8.0
2012	B+	39.71	35.74	0.0	384.6	310.7	0.0	11.7
2011	B+	41.26	37.14	0.0	360.0	299.0	0.0	10.8
2010	B+	37.57	33.81	0.0	358.9	288.3	0.0	14.1
2009	B+	33.24	29.91	0.0	357.8	274.4	0.0	11.5

American Family Ins Group Composite Group Rating: B+ Largest Group Members	Assets ($mil)	Rating
AMERICAN FAMILY MUT INS CO	13230	B+
AMERICAN FAMILY LIFE INS CO	5074	A+
AMERICAN STANDARD INS CO OF WI	394	B+
HOMESITE INS CO OF THE MIDWEST	315	C
HOMESITE INS CO	224	C

AMERICAN STRATEGIC INS CO

C+ **Fair**

Major Rating Factors: Fair overall results on stability tests (3.9 on a scale of 0 to 10) including potential drain of affiliation with ARX Holding Corp. Fair profitability index (4.7) with operating losses during 2012 and the first nine months of 2014. Return on equity has been low, averaging 4.1% over the past five years.

Other Rating Factors: Good liquidity (6.8) with sufficient resources (cash flows and marketable investments) to handle a spike in claims. Strong long-term capitalization index (8.1) based on excellent current risk adjusted capital (severe and moderate loss scenarios), despite some fluctuation in capital levels. Ample reserve history (9.2) that helps to protect the company against sharp claims increases.

Principal Business: Homeowners multiple peril (67%), allied lines (25%), fire (5%), and other liability (3%).

Principal Investments: Investment grade bonds (86%) and misc. investments (16%).

Investments in Affiliates: 1%

Group Affiliation: ARX Holding Corp

Licensed in: AL, AZ, CO, CT, DC, DE, FL, GA, IL, IA, MD, MA, MI, MN, NV, NJ, NC, OH, OR, PA, SC, TN, TX, UT, VA, WA, WI

Commenced Business: December 1997

Address: 805 Executive Cir Dr W #300, St Petersburg, FL 33702

Phone: (727) 821-8765   **Domicile State:** FL   **NAIC Code:** 10872

Data Date	Rating	RACR #1	RACR #2	Loss Ratio %	Total Assets ($mil)	Capital ($mil)	Net Premium ($mil)	Net Income ($mil)
9-14	C+	1.93	1.65	N/A	812.0	298.9	334.6	-9.4
9-13	B-	1.69	1.46	N/A	660.2	244.3	271.6	13.3
2013	B-	2.34	1.88	54.1	736.4	307.4	409.5	30.1
2012	B-	1.95	1.56	69.3	603.9	227.7	343.9	-15.9
2011	B	2.16	1.71	67.9	438.0	165.3	215.9	0.3
2010	B+	2.71	2.17	52.4	393.1	162.9	207.0	16.0
2009	B+	3.35	2.60	43.1	324.0	135.3	140.7	18.4

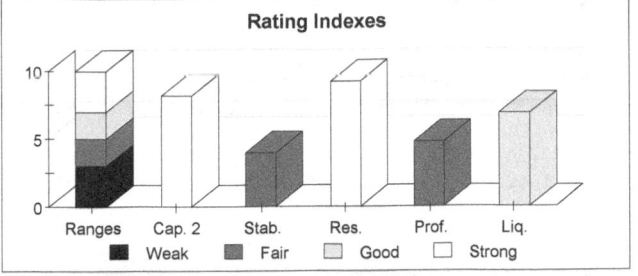

Rating Indexes

AMERISURE INS CO

B- **Good**

Major Rating Factors: Fair overall results on stability tests (4.7 on a scale of 0 to 10) including potential drain of affiliation with Amerisure Companies. Good overall profitability index (6.5). Fair expense controls. Return on equity has been low, averaging 2.8% over the past five years.

Other Rating Factors: Strong long-term capitalization index (8.0) based on excellent current risk adjusted capital (severe and moderate loss scenarios), despite some fluctuation in capital levels. Ample reserve history (8.6) that helps to protect the company against sharp claims increases. Excellent liquidity (7.0) with ample operational cash flow and liquid investments.

Principal Business: Workers compensation (54%), commercial multiple peril (18%), auto liability (15%), other liability (8%), auto physical damage (3%), and products liability (2%).

Principal Investments: Investment grade bonds (95%), misc. investments (2%), cash (2%), and non investment grade bonds (1%).

Investments in Affiliates: None

Group Affiliation: Amerisure Companies

Licensed in: All states except CA

Commenced Business: September 1968

Address: 26777 Halsted Road, Farmington Hills, MI 48331-3586

Phone: (248) 615-9000   **Domicile State:** MI   **NAIC Code:** 19488

Data Date	Rating	RACR #1	RACR #2	Loss Ratio %	Total Assets ($mil)	Capital ($mil)	Net Premium ($mil)	Net Income ($mil)
9-14	B-	2.43	1.65	N/A	745.1	217.0	154.2	2.8
9-13	B-	2.54	1.73	N/A	773.3	210.8	140.1	0.2
2013	B-	2.57	1.75	73.1	721.6	215.7	199.3	3.4
2012	B-	2.83	1.93	71.1	690.5	212.3	173.2	4.5
2011	B-	3.16	2.14	74.5	670.3	207.0	151.4	5.5
2010	B-	2.79	1.87	75.8	640.8	200.0	134.2	8.2
2009	B-	2.66	1.72	68.8	634.5	191.5	142.5	8.1

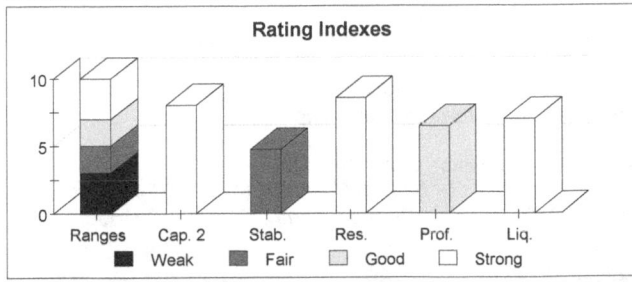

Rating Indexes

AMERISURE MUTUAL INS CO

B- **Good**

Major Rating Factors: Fair overall results on stability tests (4.7 on a scale of 0 to 10) including potential drain of affiliation with Amerisure Companies. Good overall profitability index (6.6). Fair expense controls. Return on equity has been low, averaging 4.3% over the past five years.

Other Rating Factors: Strong long-term capitalization index (8.0) based on excellent current risk adjusted capital (severe and moderate loss scenarios). Moreover, capital levels have been consistent in recent years. Ample reserve history (8.1) that helps to protect the company against sharp claims increases. Excellent liquidity (7.0) with ample operational cash flow and liquid investments.

Principal Business: Workers compensation (53%), commercial multiple peril (17%), other liability (13%), auto liability (9%), inland marine (2%), auto physical damage (2%), and other lines (3%).

Principal Investments: Investment grade bonds (56%), misc. investments (42%), non investment grade bonds (1%), and real estate (1%).

Investments in Affiliates: 15%

Group Affiliation: Amerisure Companies

Licensed in: All states, the District of Columbia and Puerto Rico

Commenced Business: September 1912

Address: 26777 Halsted Rd, Farmington Hills, MI 48331-3586

Phone: (248) 615-9000   **Domicile State:** MI   **NAIC Code:** 23396

Data Date	Rating	RACR #1	RACR #2	Loss Ratio %	Total Assets ($mil)	Capital ($mil)	Net Premium ($mil)	Net Income ($mil)
9-14	B-	2.14	1.66	N/A	2,027.5	818.4	344.4	33.2
9-13	B-	2.16	1.68	N/A	2,002.5	758.3	313.0	23.1
2013	B-	2.16	1.69	73.1	1,981.8	803.8	445.2	41.0
2012	B-	2.15	1.69	71.1	1,843.4	732.9	386.7	36.1
2011	B-	2.07	1.63	74.5	1,751.7	673.0	338.2	31.9
2010	B-	2.15	1.68	75.8	1,756.1	673.4	299.7	32.0
2009	C+	2.06	1.59	65.1	1,712.4	620.4	287.9	8.7

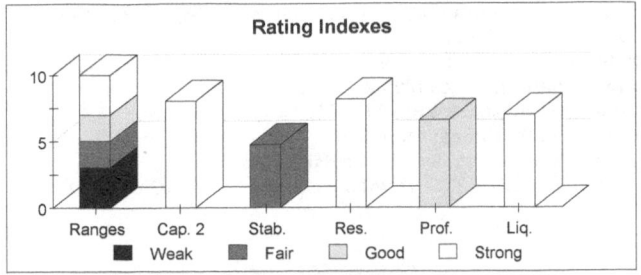

Rating Indexes

AMEX ASSURANCE CO
B   **Good**

Major Rating Factors: Good liquidity (6.8 on a scale of 0 to 10) with sufficient resources (cash flows and marketable investments) to handle a spike in claims. Good overall results on stability tests (5.9). Stability strengths include good operational trends and excellent risk diversification. The largest net exposure for one risk is acceptable at 2.9% of capital.

Other Rating Factors: Fair profitability index (4.9). Excellent expense controls. Return on equity has been fair, averaging 40.6% over the past five years. Strong long-term capitalization index (10.0) based on excellent current risk adjusted capital (severe and moderate loss scenarios), despite some fluctuation in capital levels. Ample reserve history (8.3) that helps to protect the company against sharp claims increases.

Principal Business: (Not applicable due to unusual reinsurance transactions.)

Principal Investments: Investment grade bonds (97%), misc. investments (2%), and non investment grade bonds (1%).

Investments in Affiliates: None

Group Affiliation: American Express Company

Licensed in: All states, the District of Columbia and Puerto Rico

Commenced Business: February 1973

Address: 227 W Monroe St Ste 3600, Chicago, IL 60606

Phone: (623) 492-3094   **Domicile State:** IL   **NAIC Code:** 27928

Data Date	Rating	RACR #1	RACR #2	Loss Ratio %	Total Assets ($mil)	Capital ($mil)	Net Premium ($mil)	Net Income ($mil)
9-14	B	9.82	5.70	N/A	299.7	205.8	142.1	53.7
9-13	B	9.83	5.77	N/A	317.3	214.8	124.9	62.7
2013	B	9.10	5.40	49.3	296.5	196.9	177.5	78.9
2012	B	7.41	4.31	42.8	269.2	196.7	244.3	78.9
2011	B	8.91	5.09	35.8	257.6	203.9	233.8	86.2
2010	B	8.55	4.94	32.6	266.9	206.5	227.0	88.7
2009	B-	7.93	4.62	35.0	268.5	205.1	228.2	86.6

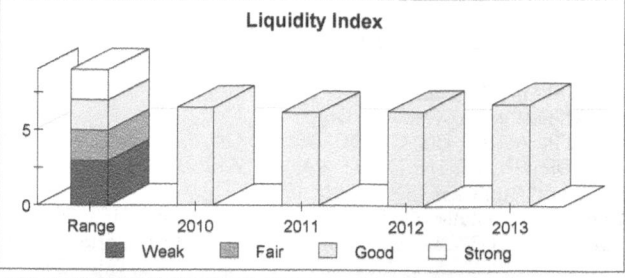

Liquidity Index

AMICA LLOYDS OF TEXAS *
A-   **Excellent**

Major Rating Factors: Strong long-term capitalization index (10.0 on a scale of 0 to 10) based on excellent current risk adjusted capital (severe and moderate loss scenarios). Furthermore, this high level of risk adjusted capital has been consistently maintained in previous years. Excellent profitability (8.3) with operating gains in each of the last five years.

Other Rating Factors: Excellent liquidity (7.4) with ample operational cash flow and liquid investments. Excellent overall results on stability tests (7.0). Stability strengths include excellent operational trends and excellent risk diversification. The largest net exposure for one risk is conservative at 1.1% of capital. History of adequate reserve strength (6.2) as reserves have been consistently at an acceptable level.

Principal Business: Homeowners multiple peril (94%), allied lines (4%), inland marine (1%), and fire (1%).

Principal Investments: Investment grade bonds (84%), misc. investments (11%), and non investment grade bonds (5%).

Investments in Affiliates: None

Group Affiliation: Amica Mutual Group

Licensed in: TX

Commenced Business: December 1998

Address: 2277 Plaza Dr Suite 400, Sugar Land, TX 77479-2643

Phone: (800) 242-6422   **Domicile State:** TX   **NAIC Code:** 10896

Data Date	Rating	RACR #1	RACR #2	Loss Ratio %	Total Assets ($mil)	Capital ($mil)	Net Premium ($mil)	Net Income ($mil)
9-14	A-	13.18	10.75	N/A	77.6	72.8	8.6	2.5
9-13	B+	9.95	7.86	N/A	92.7	70.4	11.8	2.2
2013	A-	9.76	8.04	49.1	93.0	71.7	17.7	3.7
2012	B+	10.74	8.54	45.3	86.3	67.8	14.9	3.9
2011	B+	8.56	6.11	60.1	79.9	63.6	13.2	2.0
2010	B+	4.30	3.13	46.0	76.0	61.4	12.1	2.8
2009	B+	5.41	3.93	74.3	71.3	58.5	10.1	1.6

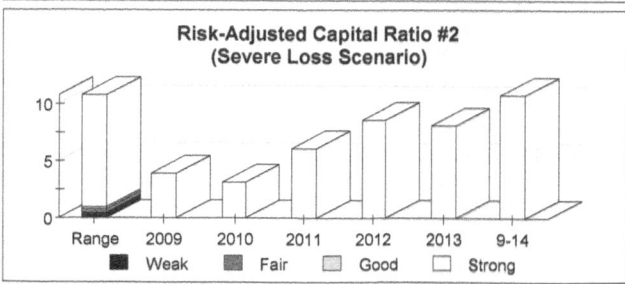

Risk-Adjusted Capital Ratio #2
(Severe Loss Scenario)

AMICA MUTUAL INS CO *
B+   **Good**

Major Rating Factors: Good liquidity (6.2 on a scale of 0 to 10) with sufficient resources (cash flows and marketable investments) to handle a spike in claims. Good overall results on stability tests (6.8). Affiliation with Amica Mutual Group is a strength.

Other Rating Factors: Strong long-term capitalization index (8.4) based on excellent current risk adjusted capital (severe and moderate loss scenarios), despite some fluctuation in capital levels. Ample reserve history (7.9) that can protect against increases in claims costs. Excellent profitability (8.1) with operating gains in each of the last five years.

Principal Business: Auto liability (39%), homeowners multiple peril (31%), auto physical damage (24%), other liability (3%), earthquake (1%), inland marine (1%), and allied lines (1%).

Principal Investments: Misc. investments (50%), investment grade bonds (50%), and real estate (1%).

Investments in Affiliates: 6%

Group Affiliation: Amica Mutual Group

Licensed in: All states except HI, PR

Commenced Business: April 1907

Address: 100 Amica Way, Lincoln, RI 02865

Phone: (800) 652-6422   **Domicile State:** RI   **NAIC Code:** 19976

Data Date	Rating	RACR #1	RACR #2	Loss Ratio %	Total Assets ($mil)	Capital ($mil)	Net Premium ($mil)	Net Income ($mil)
9-14	B+	3.00	1.95	N/A	5,054.3	2,733.6	1,325.9	103.0
9-13	B+	3.01	1.94	N/A	4,748.5	2,553.8	1,253.1	84.5
2013	B+	2.97	1.95	69.9	4,855.2	2,649.7	1,746.7	145.2
2012	B+	2.94	1.92	76.5	4,391.2	2,377.5	1,633.4	69.9
2011	B+	2.91	1.90	83.0	4,126.7	2,260.4	1,539.3	61.3
2010	B+	3.11	2.04	74.0	4,089.1	2,340.3	1,446.4	99.8
2009	B+	3.22	2.13	68.1	3,912.0	2,234.1	1,356.7	121.4

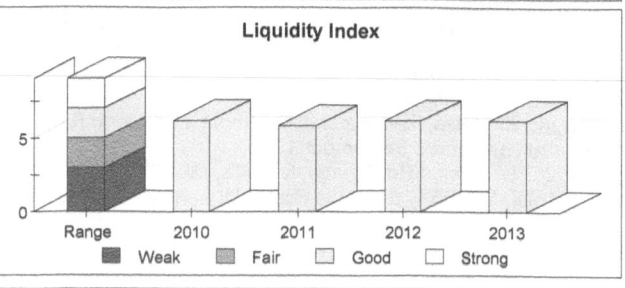

Liquidity Index

ARBELLA MUTUAL INS CO

C+   Fair

Major Rating Factors: Fair overall results on stability tests (4.3 on a scale of 0 to 10) including potential drain of affiliation with Arbella Ins Group. Fair profitability index (4.6) with operating losses during 2011.

Other Rating Factors: Good liquidity (6.3) with sufficient resources (cash flows and marketable investments) to handle a spike in claims. Strong long-term capitalization index (8.5) based on excellent current risk adjusted capital (severe and moderate loss scenarios), despite some fluctuation in capital levels. Ample reserve history (8.1) that helps to protect the company against sharp claims increases.

Principal Business: Auto liability (41%), auto physical damage (29%), homeowners multiple peril (27%), fire (1%), other liability (1%), allied lines (1%), and inland marine (1%).

Principal Investments: Investment grade bonds (66%), misc. investments (30%), cash (3%), and non investment grade bonds (1%).

Investments in Affiliates: 15%

Group Affiliation: Arbella Ins Group

Licensed in: MA

Commenced Business: October 1988

Address: 1100 Crown Colony Dr, Quincy, MA 02269

Phone: (617) 328-2800   **Domicile State:** MA   **NAIC Code:** 17000

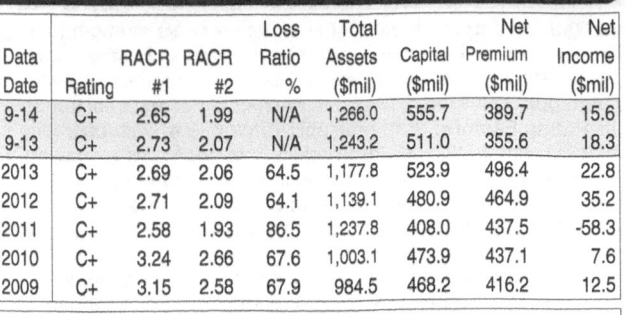

Data Date	Rating	RACR #1	RACR #2	Loss Ratio %	Total Assets ($mil)	Capital ($mil)	Net Premium ($mil)	Net Income ($mil)
9-14	C+	2.65	1.99	N/A	1,266.0	555.7	389.7	15.6
9-13	C+	2.73	2.07	N/A	1,243.2	511.0	355.6	18.3
2013	C+	2.69	2.06	64.5	1,177.8	523.9	496.4	22.8
2012	C+	2.71	2.09	64.1	1,139.1	480.9	464.9	35.2
2011	C+	2.58	1.93	86.5	1,237.8	408.0	437.5	-58.3
2010	C+	3.24	2.66	67.6	1,003.1	473.9	437.1	7.6
2009	C+	3.15	2.58	67.9	984.5	468.2	416.2	12.5

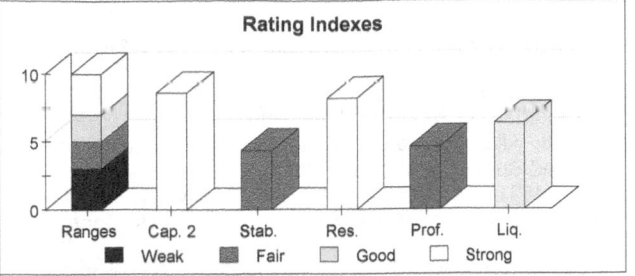

Rating Indexes

ARCH INS CO

C   Fair

Major Rating Factors: Fair overall results on stability tests (3.4 on a scale of 0 to 10) including potential drain of affiliation with Arch Capital Group Ltd. The largest net exposure for one risk is conservative at 1.1% of capital. Good overall profitability index (5.2) despite operating losses during 2011 and 2012. Return on equity has been low, averaging 0.9% over the past five years.

Other Rating Factors: Good liquidity (6.9) with sufficient resources (cash flows and marketable investments) to handle a spike in claims. Strong long-term capitalization index (7.1) based on excellent current risk adjusted capital (severe and moderate loss scenarios), despite some fluctuation in capital levels. Ample reserve history (7.8) that can protect against increases in claims costs.

Principal Business: Other liability (34%), workers compensation (20%), auto liability (11%), commercial multiple peril (8%), surety (5%), credit (5%), and other lines (16%).

Principal Investments: Investment grade bonds (70%), misc. investments (28%), and cash (2%).

Investments in Affiliates: 19%

Group Affiliation: Arch Capital Group Ltd

Licensed in: All states, the District of Columbia and Puerto Rico

Commenced Business: June 1980

Address: 3100 Broadway Suite 1000, Kansas City, MO 64111

Phone: (201) 743-4000   **Domicile State:** MO   **NAIC Code:** 11150

Data Date	Rating	RACR #1	RACR #2	Loss Ratio %	Total Assets ($mil)	Capital ($mil)	Net Premium ($mil)	Net Income ($mil)
9-14	C	1.38	1.04	N/A	3,201.7	777.2	551.3	28.3
9-13	C	1.31	0.95	N/A	2,710.7	642.2	502.5	12.5
2013	C	1.38	1.06	68.2	2,840.9	736.6	659.6	28.7
2012	C	1.21	0.88	75.6	2,696.9	563.5	750.0	-23.0
2011	C	0.70	0.54	73.8	2,318.1	569.7	618.5	-28.2
2010	C	0.95	0.77	72.7	1,928.0	615.8	304.7	5.2
2009	C	0.97	0.79	74.2	1,824.1	637.9	304.3	36.5

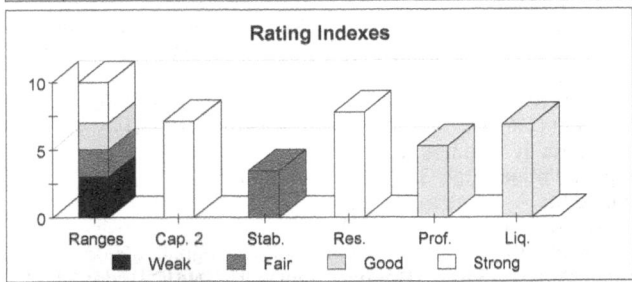

Rating Indexes

ARCH REINSURANCE CO

C-   Fair

Major Rating Factors: Weak overall results on stability tests (2.7 on a scale of 0 to 10) including potential drain of affiliation with Arch Capital Group Ltd. The largest net exposure for one risk is conservative at 1.3% of capital. Strong long-term capitalization index (7.7) based on excellent current risk adjusted capital (severe and moderate loss scenarios), despite some fluctuation in capital levels.

Other Rating Factors: Ample reserve history (7.9) that can protect against increases in claims costs. Excellent profitability (7.5) despite modest operating losses during 2011. Excellent liquidity (7.0) with ample operational cash flow and liquid investments.

Principal Business: (This company is a reinsurer.)

Principal Investments: Misc. investments (52%), investment grade bonds (44%), and cash (4%).

Investments in Affiliates: 50%

Group Affiliation: Arch Capital Group Ltd

Licensed in: All states except ME, NC, WI, WY, PR

Commenced Business: July 1995

Address: 1209 Orange St, Wilmington, DE 19801

Phone: (973) 898-9575   **Domicile State:** DE   **NAIC Code:** 10348

Data Date	Rating	RACR #1	RACR #2	Loss Ratio %	Total Assets ($mil)	Capital ($mil)	Net Premium ($mil)	Net Income ($mil)
9-14	C-	1.65	1.61	N/A	1,724.7	1,050.5	178.9	20.6
9-13	C-	1.84	1.76	N/A	1,444.0	919.4	134.2	31.9
2013	C-	1.61	1.58	46.8	1,547.9	1,013.2	204.0	33.0
2012	C-	1.71	1.67	65.1	1,315.9	822.6	190.0	7.2
2011	C-	1.69	1.66	74.0	1,223.5	822.9	145.3	-3.1
2010	C	1.65	1.61	58.1	1,207.6	870.6	61.5	16.9
2009	C	1.61	1.59	61.7	1,202.3	850.5	79.3	23.6

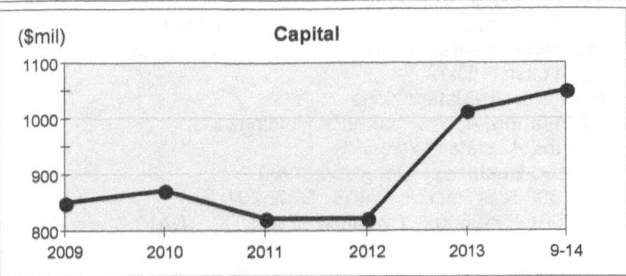

Capital

ARCH SPECIALTY INS CO | B | Good

Major Rating Factors: History of adequate reserve strength (5.0 on a scale of 0 to 10) as reserves have been consistently at an acceptable level. Good overall results on stability tests (5.5) despite excessive premium growth, negative cash flow from operations for 2013 and fair results on operational trends.

Other Rating Factors: Fair profitability index (3.4) with operating losses during 2010, 2011 and 2012. Return on equity has been low, averaging 0.8% over the past five years. Strong long-term capitalization index (10.0) based on excellent current risk adjusted capital (severe and moderate loss scenarios), despite some fluctuation in capital levels. Excellent liquidity (7.0) with ample operational cash flow and liquid investments.

Principal Business: Other liability (30%), fire (26%), allied lines (13%), medical malpractice (12%), earthquake (10%), commercial multiple peril (4%), and other lines (5%).

Principal Investments: Investment grade bonds (64%), misc. investments (33%), and cash (3%).

Investments in Affiliates: None

Group Affiliation: Arch Capital Group Ltd

Licensed in: All states, the District of Columbia and Puerto Rico

Commenced Business: January 1965

Address: 2345 Grand Blvd Suite 900, Kansas City, MO 64108

Phone: (201) 743-4000   **Domicile State:** MO   **NAIC Code:** 21199

Data Date	Rating	RACR #1	RACR #2	Loss Ratio %	Total Assets ($mil)	Capital ($mil)	Net Premium ($mil)	Net Income ($mil)
9-14	B	21.74	13.88	N/A	577.2	293.3	0.3	9.6
9-13	B	19.54	12.26	N/A	471.2	281.0	0.0	2.6
2013	B	21.66	13.74	N/A	473.5	283.5	0.0	5.6
2012	B	18.93	12.13	N/A	437.8	271.8	0.0	-6.8
2011	A-	16.52	9.72	N/A	462.5	315.1	0.0	-6.6
2010	A-	14.22	8.88	N/A	416.4	316.7	0.1	-0.8
2009	B+	10.99	6.68	N/A	418.1	315.0	0.0	12.4

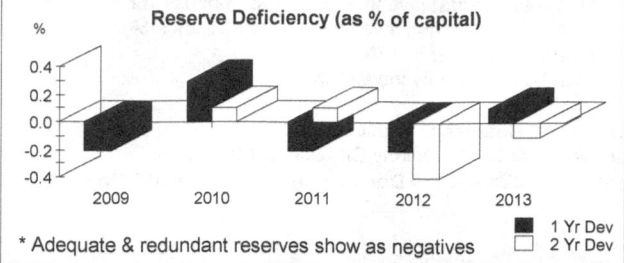

Reserve Deficiency (as % of capital)

* Adequate & redundant reserves show as negatives

■ 1 Yr Dev   □ 2 Yr Dev

ARGONAUT INS CO | C | Fair

Major Rating Factors: Fair overall results on stability tests (3.3 on a scale of 0 to 10) including potential drain of affiliation with Argo Group Intl Holdings Ltd and negative cash flow from operations for 2013. The largest net exposure for one risk is conservative at 1.3% of capital. Fair reserve development (3.3) as the level of reserves has at times been insufficient to cover claims. In 2012 and 2013 the two year reserve development was 16% and 18% deficient respectively.

Other Rating Factors: Good overall profitability index (5.8) despite operating losses during 2012. Return on equity has been fair, averaging 7.2% over the past five years. Strong long-term capitalization index (7.1) based on excellent current risk adjusted capital (severe and moderate loss scenarios), despite some fluctuation in capital levels. Excellent liquidity (7.2) with ample operational cash flow and liquid investments.

Principal Business: Other liability (29%), workers compensation (24%), surety (16%), commercial multiple peril (15%), auto liability (9%), auto physical damage (3%), and other lines (4%).

Principal Investments: Investment grade bonds (59%), misc. investments (37%), cash (2%), and non investment grade bonds (2%).

Investments in Affiliates: 9%

Group Affiliation: Argo Group Intl Holdings Ltd

Licensed in: All states except PR

Commenced Business: May 1957

Address: 225 W Washington St 6th Floor, Chicago, IL 60606

Phone: (210) 321-8400   **Domicile State:** IL   **NAIC Code:** 19801

Data Date	Rating	RACR #1	RACR #2	Loss Ratio %	Total Assets ($mil)	Capital ($mil)	Net Premium ($mil)	Net Income ($mil)
9-14	C	1.87	1.22	N/A	1,294.7	406.7	145.1	1.8
9-13	C	1.80	1.15	N/A	1,338.7	421.7	161.0	17.9
2013	C	1.86	1.21	82.8	1,308.9	409.4	196.9	49.8
2012	C	1.66	1.05	93.0	1,337.3	380.5	217.8	-13.8
2011	C	1.70	1.09	93.1	1,328.1	373.0	229.0	20.5
2010	C	1.47	0.97	68.2	1,383.3	378.9	228.2	38.1
2009	C	1.27	0.84	76.0	1,424.9	336.9	266.3	56.8

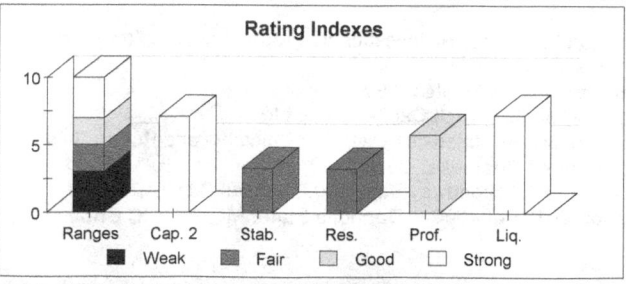

Rating Indexes

Ranges   Cap. 2   Stab.   Res.   Prof.   Liq.
■ Weak   ■ Fair   ▨ Good   □ Strong

ASPEN AMERICAN INS CO | C | Fair

Major Rating Factors: Fair overall results on stability tests (4.0 on a scale of 0 to 10) including excessive premium growth, weak results on operational trends and negative cash flow from operations for 2013. Weak profitability index (2.8) with operating losses during each of the last five years and the first nine months of 2014. Average return on equity over the last five years has been poor at -10.2%.

Other Rating Factors: Strong long-term capitalization index (10.0) based on excellent current risk adjusted capital (severe and moderate loss scenarios), despite some fluctuation in capital levels. Ample reserve history (9.4) that helps to protect the company against sharp claims increases. Excellent liquidity (7.1) with ample operational cash flow and liquid investments.

Principal Business: Commercial multiple peril (47%), other liability (20%), inland marine (10%), surety (8%), ocean marine (7%), fire (3%), and other lines (5%).

Principal Investments: Investment grade bonds (60%), misc. investments (25%), and cash (15%).

Investments in Affiliates: None

Group Affiliation: Aspen Insurance Holdings Ltd

Licensed in: All states except PR

Commenced Business: December 1990

Address: 350 N St Paul St, Dallas, TX 75201

Phone: (860) 258-3500   **Domicile State:** TX   **NAIC Code:** 43460

Data Date	Rating	RACR #1	RACR #2	Loss Ratio %	Total Assets ($mil)	Capital ($mil)	Net Premium ($mil)	Net Income ($mil)
9-14	C	4.36	2.93	N/A	481.1	233.2	30.3	-22.3
9-13	C	3.26	2.21	N/A	298.9	147.9	14.7	-20.3
2013	C	6.46	4.35	102.9	443.7	257.5	26.8	-27.4
2012	C	4.93	3.35	98.3	277.9	172.0	21.0	-34.6
2011	C-	8.75	6.60	275.0	143.2	103.0	5.5	-14.1
2010	C-	18.71	9.73	697.1	73.1	68.0	-0.3	-0.2
2009	C	5.60	3.33	N/A	250.8	155.3	0.1	-6.8

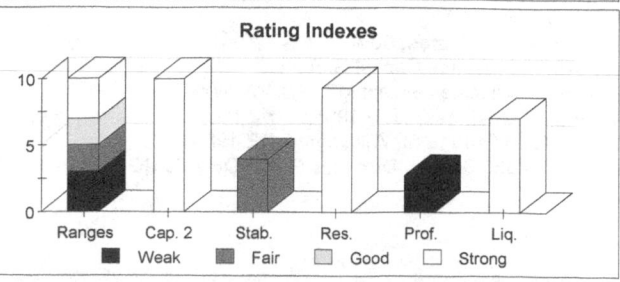

Rating Indexes

Ranges   Cap. 2   Stab.   Res.   Prof.   Liq.
■ Weak   ■ Fair   ▨ Good   □ Strong

ASSURED GUARANTY CORP　　　　　　　　　　D+　　　Weak

Major Rating Factors: Weak overall results on stability tests (1.1 on a scale of 0 to 10) including negative cash flow from operations for 2013. The largest net exposure for one risk is excessive at 28.9% of capital. Strengths include potentially strong support from affiliation with Assured Guaranty/Financial Sec Asr. Weak profitability index (1.9) with operating losses during 2009 and 2010. Return on equity has been low, averaging 5.0% over the past five years.

Other Rating Factors: Fair reserve development (4.8) as the level of reserves has at times been insufficient to cover claims. In 2009 and 2010 the one year reserve development was 16% and 18% deficient respectively. Strong long-term capitalization index (7.7) based on excellent current risk adjusted capital (severe and moderate loss scenarios), despite some fluctuation in capital levels. Superior liquidity (9.3) with ample operational cash flow and liquid investments.

Principal Business: Financial guaranty (100%).

Principal Investments: Investment grade bonds (80%), misc. investments (15%), non investment grade bonds (4%), and cash (1%).

Investments in Affiliates: 14%

Group Affiliation: Assured Guaranty/Financial Sec Asr

Licensed in: All states, the District of Columbia and Puerto Rico

Commenced Business: January 1988

Address: 1325 Ave Of The Americas 18 Fl, New York, NY 10019

Phone: (212) 974-0100　　**Domicile State:** MD　　**NAIC Code:** 30180

Data Date	Rating	RACR #1	RACR #2	Loss Ratio %	Total Assets ($mil)	Capital ($mil)	Net Premium ($mil)	Net Income ($mil)
9-14	D+	1.58	1.33	N/A	2,485.9	507.9	63.5	67.4
9-13	D+	2.84	2.22	N/A	2,509.5	708.4	81.8	152.4
2013	D+	2.15	1.82	N/A	2,504.4	692.6	-186.7	211.2
2012	D+	3.61	2.97	46.2	2,963.0	905.4	88.1	31.3
2011	C	3.81	3.13	N/A	3,010.4	1,021.5	92.7	229.9
2010	C-	2.21	1.83	181.8	2,999.6	854.1	146.4	-182.1
2009	C-	2.81	2.40	243.9	3,049.9	1,223.7	510.9	-243.1

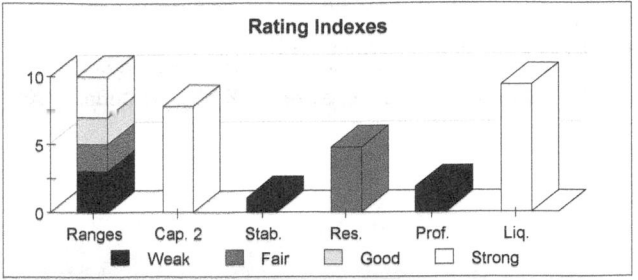

Rating Indexes

ASSURED GUARANTY MUNICIPAL CORP　　　　　D+　　　Weak

Major Rating Factors: Weak overall results on stability tests (2.4 on a scale of 0 to 10). The largest net exposure for one risk is excessive at 18.7% of capital. Strengths include potentially strong support from affiliation with Assured Guaranty/Financial Sec Asr. Strong long-term capitalization index (7.6) based on excellent current risk adjusted capital (severe and moderate loss scenarios), despite some fluctuation in capital levels.

Other Rating Factors: Fair reserve development (4.4) as reserves have generally been sufficient to cover claims. Excellent profitability (7.9) with operating gains in each of the last five years. Excellent expense controls. Return on equity has been excellent over the last five years averaging 21.7%. Excellent liquidity (7.0) with ample operational cash flow and liquid investments.

Principal Business: Financial guaranty (100%).

Principal Investments: Investment grade bonds (81%) and misc. investments (19%).

Investments in Affiliates: 10%

Group Affiliation: Assured Guaranty/Financial Sec Asr

Licensed in: All states, the District of Columbia and Puerto Rico

Commenced Business: September 1985

Address: 31 W 52nd St, New York, NY 10019

Phone: (212) 826-0100　　**Domicile State:** NY　　**NAIC Code:** 18287

Data Date	Rating	RACR #1	RACR #2	Loss Ratio %	Total Assets ($mil)	Capital ($mil)	Net Premium ($mil)	Net Income ($mil)
9-14	D+	2.50	1.64	N/A	5,751.6	1,610.0	149.1	198.0
9-13	D+	1.92	1.24	N/A	5,479.9	1,759.6	226.9	257.2
2013	D+	2.49	1.48	N/A	5,712.1	1,733.1	-191.3	339.6
2012	D+	2.07	1.42	65.6	4,498.5	1,780.1	196.1	203.3
2011	D+	1.61	0.98	N/A	4,385.6	1,209.3	150.8	398.5
2010	D+	1.43	0.79	47.4	4,237.3	927.0	157.2	250.3
2009	D+	1.13	0.61	16.5	4,429.0	854.2	194.9	183.3

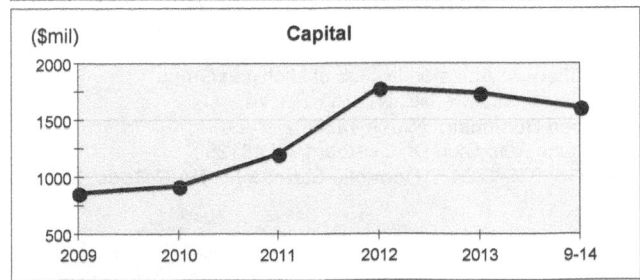

Capital

ATLANTIC SPECIALTY INS CO　　　　　　　　　C　　　Fair

Major Rating Factors: Fair overall results on stability tests (3.6 on a scale of 0 to 10) including fair financial strength of affiliated White Mountains Group and weak results on operational trends. The largest net exposure for one risk is conservative at 1.5% of capital. Good overall profitability index (5.6) despite operating losses during 2012. Return on equity has been low, averaging 3.4% over the past five years.

Other Rating Factors: Good liquidity (6.3) with sufficient resources (cash flows and marketable investments) to handle a spike in claims. Strong long-term capitalization (7.0) based on excellent current risk adjusted capital (severe and moderate loss scenarios) reflecting improvement over results in 2013. Ample reserve history (7.1) that can protect against increases in claims costs.

Principal Business: Other liability (27%), ocean marine (15%), group accident & health (11%), commercial multiple peril (11%), workers compensation (9%), inland marine (8%), and other lines (20%).

Principal Investments: Investment grade bonds (56%), misc. investments (38%), cash (2%), non investment grade bonds (2%), and real estate (2%).

Investments in Affiliates: 10%

Group Affiliation: White Mountains Group

Licensed in: All states except PR

Commenced Business: December 1986

Address: 140 Broadway, New York, NY 10005-1101

Phone: (781) 332-7000　　**Domicile State:** NY　　**NAIC Code:** 27154

Data Date	Rating	RACR #1	RACR #2	Loss Ratio %	Total Assets ($mil)	Capital ($mil)	Net Premium ($mil)	Net Income ($mil)
9-14	C	1.42	1.02	N/A	2,431.5	688.2	740.1	14.3
9-13	C	1.22	0.86	N/A	2,246.7	626.4	838.9	64.2
2013	C	1.33	0.96	54.6	2,258.8	665.8	969.2	116.3
2012	C	1.87	1.31	68.7	2,248.4	716.7	850.5	-72.8
2011	C	33.25	21.46	59.1	105.2	93.4	6.5	1.1
2010	C	12.59	8.65	62.0	59.1	47.3	6.0	2.6
2009	C	13.55	9.10	56.2	67.6	52.2	10.1	1.8

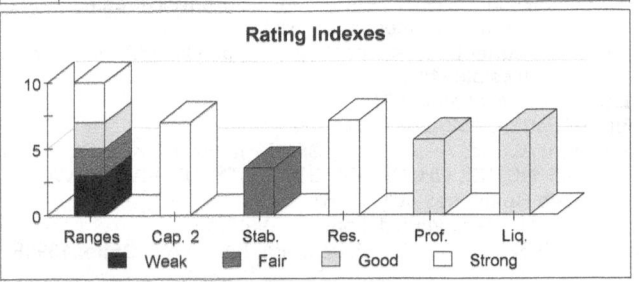

Rating Indexes

AUTO CLUB INDEMNITY CO *   B+   Good

Major Rating Factors: Good overall results on stability tests (5.0 on a scale of 0 to 10). Stability strengths include good operational trends and excellent risk diversification. Strong long-term capitalization index (7.8) based on excellent current risk adjusted capital (severe and moderate loss scenarios). Moreover, capital levels have been consistent in recent years.

Other Rating Factors: Excellent profitability (7.2) with operating gains in each of the last five years. Excellent expense controls. Superior liquidity (10.0) with ample operational cash flow and liquid investments.

Principal Business: Homeowners multiple peril (99%) and other liability (1%).

Principal Investments: Investment grade bonds (92%) and cash (8%).

Investments in Affiliates: None

Group Affiliation: Auto Club Enterprises Ins Group

Licensed in: TX

Commenced Business: December 1999

Address: 3333 Fairview Road, Costa Mesa, CA 92626-1698

Phone: (714) 850-5111   **Domicile State:** TX   **NAIC Code:** 11008

Data Date	Rating	RACR #1	RACR #2	Loss Ratio %	Total Assets ($mil)	Capital ($mil)	Net Premium ($mil)	Net Income ($mil)
9-14	B+	1.68	1.51	N/A	21.8	5.3	0.0	0.0
9-13	B+	1.79	1.61	N/A	19.7	5.2	0.0	0.0
2013	B+	1.92	1.72	0.0	18.0	5.2	0.0	0.0
2012	B+	2.00	1.80	0.0	16.7	5.2	0.0	0.0
2011	B+	2.36	2.13	0.0	13.7	5.1	0.0	0.0
2010	B+	2.73	2.46	0.0	11.9	5.1	0.0	0.0
2009	B+	1.15	1.04	0.0	12.2	2.7	0.0	0.0

Auto Club Enterprises Ins Group
Composite Group Rating: A+
Largest Group Members

	Assets ($mil)	Rating
INTERINS EXCH OF THE AUTOMOBILE CLUB	8106	A+
AUTOMOBILE CLUB OF SOUTHERN CA INS	747	B
AUTOMOBILE CLUB INTERINSURANCE EXCH	416	C
AUTO CLUB INS CO OF FL	281	C
AUTO CLUB FAMILY INS CO	95	C

AUTO CLUB INS ASSN   B   Good

Major Rating Factors: Good liquidity (6.1 on a scale of 0 to 10) with sufficient resources (cash flows and marketable investments) to handle a spike in claims. Fair overall results on stability tests (4.9) including potential drain of affiliation with Automobile Club of Michigan Group.

Other Rating Factors: Fair reserve development (4.4) as reserves have generally been sufficient to cover claims. Fair profitability index (3.7) with operating losses during 2011 and the first nine months of 2014. Strong long-term capitalization index (7.8) based on excellent current risk adjusted capital (severe and moderate loss scenarios), despite some fluctuation in capital levels.

Principal Business: Auto liability (43%), homeowners multiple peril (30%), auto physical damage (26%), and other liability (1%).

Principal Investments: Investment grade bonds (49%), misc. investments (44%), non investment grade bonds (7%), and real estate (2%).

Investments in Affiliates: 21%

Group Affiliation: Automobile Club of Michigan Group

Licensed in: IL, MI, MN, NE, NY, ND, PA, WI

Commenced Business: March 1922

Address: One Auto Club Dr, Dearborn, MI 48126

Phone: (313) 336-1234   **Domicile State:** MI   **NAIC Code:** 21202

Data Date	Rating	RACR #1	RACR #2	Loss Ratio %	Total Assets ($mil)	Capital ($mil)	Net Premium ($mil)	Net Income ($mil)
9-14	B	1.86	1.49	N/A	3,680.4	1,538.0	1,011.3	-14.7
9-13	B	1.90	1.54	N/A	3,644.9	1,558.4	1,001.4	52.0
2013	B	1.89	1.53	74.0	3,650.4	1,575.8	1,351.3	48.5
2012	B	1.89	1.57	86.3	3,350.4	1,526.3	1,229.1	18.2
2011	B	1.92	1.61	81.8	3,572.6	1,591.4	1,487.9	-24.5
2010	B	2.24	1.82	80.6	3,573.0	1,650.4	1,424.2	11.5
2009	B	2.26	1.83	75.8	3,300.5	1,553.8	1,359.1	80.6

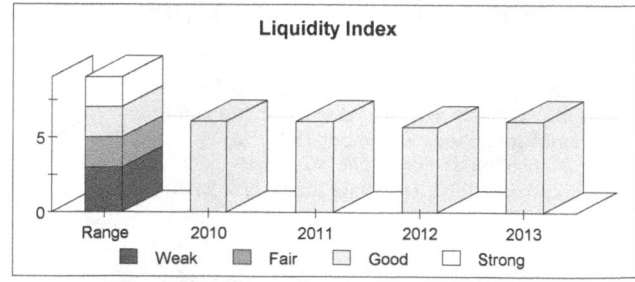

Liquidity Index
Range · 2010 · 2011 · 2012 · 2013
■ Weak ■ Fair □ Good □ Strong

AUTO-OWNERS INS CO *   A   Excellent

Major Rating Factors: Strong long-term capitalization index (8.4 on a scale of 0 to 10) based on excellent current risk adjusted capital (severe and moderate loss scenarios). Furthermore, this high level of risk adjusted capital has been consistently maintained in previous years. Excellent overall results on stability tests (7.7). Stability strengths include excellent operational trends and excellent risk diversification.

Other Rating Factors: History of adequate reserve strength (6.0) as reserves have been consistently at an acceptable level. Good overall profitability index (6.9). Fair expense controls. Good liquidity (6.9) with sufficient resources (cash flows and marketable investments) to handle a spike in claims.

Principal Business: Auto liability (21%), homeowners multiple peril (16%), fire (13%), commercial multiple peril (13%), auto physical damage (12%), workers compensation (9%), and other lines (15%).

Principal Investments: Investment grade bonds (52%), misc. investments (47%), and real estate (1%).

Investments in Affiliates: 26%

Group Affiliation: Auto-Owners Group

Licensed in: AL, AZ, AR, CO, FL, GA, ID, IL, IN, IA, KS, KY, MI, MN, MS, MO, NE, NV, NM, NC, ND, OH, OR, PA, SC, SD, TN, UT, VA, WA, WI

Commenced Business: July 1916

Address: 6101 Anacapri Blvd, Lansing, MI 48917

Phone: (517) 323-1200   **Domicile State:** MI   **NAIC Code:** 18988

Data Date	Rating	RACR #1	RACR #2	Loss Ratio %	Total Assets ($mil)	Capital ($mil)	Net Premium ($mil)	Net Income ($mil)
9-14	A	2.49	2.12	N/A	11,867.2	7,798.4	1,783.1	195.0
9-13	A	2.55	2.15	N/A	11,102.3	7,157.8	1,709.8	240.9
2013	A	2.42	2.08	60.9	11,392.8	7,510.8	2,325.4	340.3
2012	A	2.43	2.08	67.0	10,308.1	6,591.0	2,230.3	260.7
2011	A	2.47	2.11	89.9	9,767.0	6,062.2	2,173.7	14.7
2010	A	2.53	2.18	72.8	9,854.0	6,081.2	2,120.6	189.6
2009	A	2.61	2.24	70.0	9,428.1	5,702.7	2,114.1	222.5

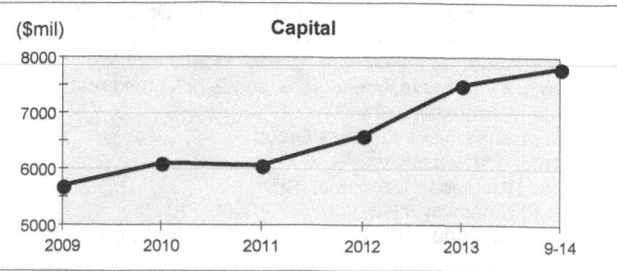

($mil)   Capital
2009 · 2010 · 2011 · 2012 · 2013 · 9-14

AUTOMOBILE CLUB INTERINSURANCE EXCH   C   Fair

Major Rating Factors: Fair overall results on stability tests (4.3 on a scale of 0 to 10) including fair financial strength of affiliated Auto Club Enterprises Ins Group. Good overall profitability index (5.2) despite operating losses during 2013.

Other Rating Factors: Good liquidity (6.7) with sufficient resources (cash flows and marketable investments) to handle a spike in claims. Strong long-term capitalization index (8.5) based on excellent current risk adjusted capital (severe and moderate loss scenarios). Moreover, capital levels have been consistent in recent years. Ample reserve history (7.5) that can protect against increases in claims costs.

Principal Business: Auto liability (55%) and auto physical damage (45%).

Principal Investments: Investment grade bonds (57%), misc. investments (43%), non investment grade bonds (4%), and real estate (1%).

Investments in Affiliates: 13%

Group Affiliation: Auto Club Enterprises Ins Group

Licensed in: AL, AR, CA, IL, IN, KS, LA, MS, MO, OH

Commenced Business: April 1927

Address: 12901 North Forty Dr, St Louis, MO 63141

Phone: (314) 523-7350   **Domicile State:** MO   **NAIC Code:** 15512

Data Date	Rating	RACR #1	RACR #2	Loss Ratio %	Total Assets ($mil)	Capital ($mil)	Net Premium ($mil)	Net Income ($mil)
9-14	C	2.92	2.21	N/A	400.5	202.9	87.9	9.3
9-13	C	3.06	2.27	N/A	400.9	203.6	84.7	8.1
2013	C	2.71	2.03	71.1	415.9	198.0	115.9	-5.3
2012	C	3.10	2.37	72.4	414.6	188.0	110.0	7.6
2011	C	3.24	2.50	73.7	386.7	175.4	105.9	4.2
2010	C	3.22	2.51	66.7	374.3	171.2	101.8	10.7
2009	C	3.64	2.95	61.7	300.3	154.3	98.6	10.1

Auto Club Enterprises Ins Group Composite Group Rating: A+ Largest Group Members	Assets ($mil)	Rating
INTERINS EXCH OF THE AUTOMOBILE CLUB	8106	A+
AUTOMOBILE CLUB OF SOUTHERN CA INS	747	B
AUTOMOBILE CLUB INTERINSURANCE EXCH	416	C
AUTO CLUB INS CO OF FL	281	C
AUTO CLUB FAMILY INS CO	95	C

AUTOMOBILE INS CO OF HARTFORD CT   B   Good

Major Rating Factors: Good overall results on stability tests (6.0 on a scale of 0 to 10). Affiliation with Travelers Companies Inc is a strength. Strong long-term capitalization index (8.3) based on excellent current risk adjusted capital (severe and moderate loss scenarios), despite some fluctuation in capital levels.

Other Rating Factors: Ample reserve history (8.6) that helps to protect the company against sharp claims increases. Excellent profitability (7.7) with operating gains in each of the last five years. Return on equity has been good over the last five years, averaging 12.3%. Excellent liquidity (7.0) with ample operational cash flow and liquid investments.

Principal Business: Homeowners multiple peril (56%), fire (14%), other liability (10%), allied lines (10%), auto liability (6%), auto physical damage (3%), and inland marine (1%).

Principal Investments: Investment grade bonds (92%) and misc. investments (8%).

Investments in Affiliates: None

Group Affiliation: Travelers Companies Inc

Licensed in: All states except CA, PR

Commenced Business: August 1968

Address: One Tower Square, Hartford, CT 06183

Phone: (860) 277-0111   **Domicile State:** CT   **NAIC Code:** 19062

Data Date	Rating	RACR #1	RACR #2	Loss Ratio %	Total Assets ($mil)	Capital ($mil)	Net Premium ($mil)	Net Income ($mil)
9-14	B	3.18	2.02	N/A	1,038.3	347.2	204.2	30.4
9-13	B	3.10	1.98	N/A	1,014.2	329.0	200.1	34.7
2013	B	2.99	1.90	60.9	1,002.2	317.3	275.9	47.3
2012	B	2.83	1.82	68.4	983.1	295.1	268.0	36.1
2011	B	2.69	1.73	76.9	959.4	282.5	262.4	16.2
2010	B	2.85	1.81	62.0	978.8	307.5	253.3	36.4
2009	B	2.66	1.74	58.3	986.3	298.1	248.3	51.8

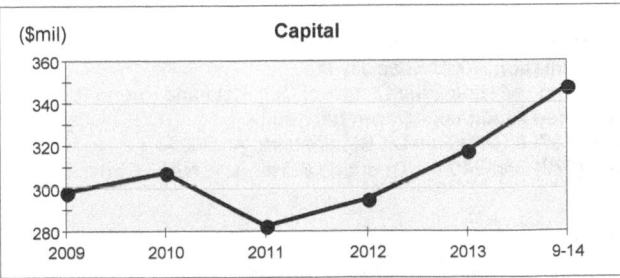

Capital ($mil)

AXIS INS CO   C+   Fair

Major Rating Factors: Fair overall results on stability tests (4.6 on a scale of 0 to 10) including potential drain of affiliation with AXIS Specialty Ltd. The largest net exposure for one risk is conservative at 1.8% of capital. Fair profitability index (3.8) with operating losses during 2012 and the first nine months of 2014. Return on equity has been low, averaging 1.0% over the past five years.

Other Rating Factors: History of adequate reserve strength (6.1) as reserves have been consistently at an acceptable level. Strong long-term capitalization index (7.2) based on excellent current risk adjusted capital (severe and moderate loss scenarios), despite some fluctuation in capital levels. Excellent liquidity (7.0) with ample operational cash flow and liquid investments.

Principal Business: Other liability (68%), fire (10%), allied lines (6%), group accident & health (4%), earthquake (3%), ocean marine (2%), and other lines (6%).

Principal Investments: Investment grade bonds (73%) and misc. investments (28%).

Investments in Affiliates: 22%

Group Affiliation: AXIS Specialty Ltd

Licensed in: All states except PR

Commenced Business: November 1979

Address: 3333 North Mayfair Rd, Wauwatosa, WI 53222

Phone: (678) 746-9400   **Domicile State:** IL   **NAIC Code:** 37273

Data Date	Rating	RACR #1	RACR #2	Loss Ratio %	Total Assets ($mil)	Capital ($mil)	Net Premium ($mil)	Net Income ($mil)
9-14	C+	1.71	1.13	N/A	1,462.3	536.1	221.5	-21.8
9-13	C+	1.73	1.26	N/A	1,333.8	509.5	191.6	-25.5
2013	C+	1.79	1.25	80.0	1,366.0	526.2	306.8	-10.1
2012	C+	1.94	1.52	80.0	1,196.5	538.9	227.4	-17.5
2011	C+	2.08	1.86	80.0	1,044.0	529.3	205.3	2.0
2010	C	1.84	1.72	59.3	868.7	471.2	176.7	36.7
2009	C	1.80	1.73	80.0	715.6	430.5	124.5	29.6

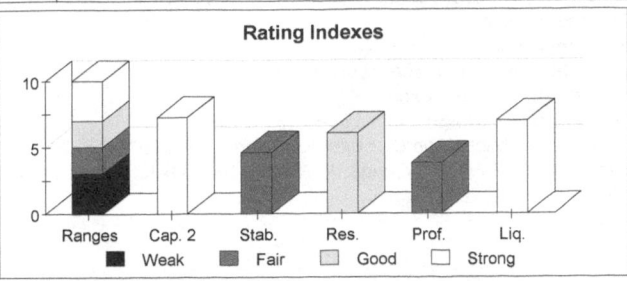

Rating Indexes

AXIS REINS CO
C+   **Fair**

Major Rating Factors: Fair overall results on stability tests (4.2 on a scale of 0 to 10) including potential drain of affiliation with AXIS Specialty Ltd. The largest net exposure for one risk is conservative at 1.8% of capital. Good overall profitability index (6.7). Weak expense controls. Return on equity has been fair, averaging 7.0% over the past five years.

Other Rating Factors: Strong long-term capitalization index (7.8) based on excellent current risk adjusted capital (severe and moderate loss scenarios), despite some fluctuation in capital levels. Ample reserve history (9.4) that helps to protect the company against sharp claims increases. Excellent liquidity (7.3) with ample operational cash flow and liquid investments.

Principal Business: Other liability (63%), fire (17%), earthquake (9%), fidelity (4%), allied lines (3%), boiler & machinery (2%), and ocean marine (2%).

Principal Investments: Investment grade bonds (90%), misc. investments (6%), cash (2%), and non investment grade bonds (2%).

Investments in Affiliates: None
Group Affiliation: AXIS Specialty Ltd
Licensed in: All states, the District of Columbia and Puerto Rico
Commenced Business: January 1992
Address: 430 Park Ave 4th Floor, New York, NY 10022
Phone: (678) 746-9400   **Domicile State:** NY   **NAIC Code:** 20370

Data Date	Rating	RACR #1	RACR #2	Loss Ratio %	Total Assets ($mil)	Capital ($mil)	Net Premium ($mil)	Net Income ($mil)
9-14	C+	2.43	1.51	N/A	2,884.6	809.3	380.3	2.7
9-13	C+	2.36	1.39	N/A	2,717.3	812.7	328.7	39.3
2013	C+	2.74	1.71	57.8	2,675.9	822.7	494.2	58.0
2012	C+	2.27	1.35	69.4	2,501.2	756.8	407.5	35.0
2011	C+	1.98	1.07	62.4	2,296.1	707.8	407.1	57.5
2010	C+	1.96	0.84	56.8	2,135.4	670.0	412.8	81.0
2009	C+	1.89	0.82	51.5	2,023.9	609.1	399.9	47.9

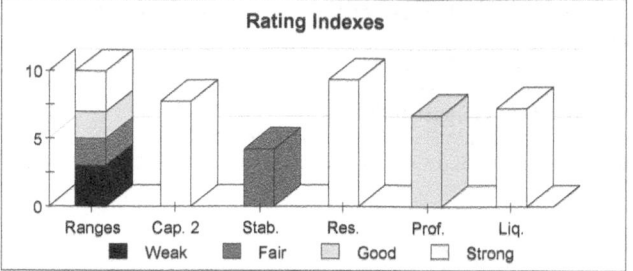

Rating Indexes

AXIS SURPLUS INS CO
C-   **Fair**

Major Rating Factors: Fair overall results on stability tests (3.0 on a scale of 0 to 10). The largest net exposure for one risk is excessive at 5.3% of capital. Strong long-term capitalization index (10.0) based on excellent current risk adjusted capital (severe and moderate loss scenarios), despite some fluctuation in capital levels.

Other Rating Factors: Ample reserve history (8.7) that helps to protect the company against sharp claims increases. Excellent profitability (8.1) with operating gains in each of the last five years. Excellent liquidity (7.0) with ample operational cash flow and liquid investments.

Principal Business: Other liability (62%), allied lines (18%), fire (13%), earthquake (6%), and homeowners multiple peril (1%).

Principal Investments: Investment grade bonds (95%), misc. investments (7%), and non investment grade bonds (1%).

Investments in Affiliates: None
Group Affiliation: AXIS Specialty Ltd
Licensed in: All states, the District of Columbia and Puerto Rico
Commenced Business: December 1983
Address: 3760 River Run Dr, Birmingham, AL 35243
Phone: (678) 746-9400   **Domicile State:** IL   **NAIC Code:** 26620

Data Date	Rating	RACR #1	RACR #2	Loss Ratio %	Total Assets ($mil)	Capital ($mil)	Net Premium ($mil)	Net Income ($mil)
9-14	C-	6.99	4.50	N/A	460.6	213.4	26.5	5.6
9-13	C-	7.55	4.56	N/A	436.8	219.8	23.2	6.3
2013	C-	7.27	4.71	31.1	428.4	206.2	33.4	14.1
2012	C-	6.64	4.03	64.4	443.1	209.0	29.6	6.8
2011	C-	1.65	1.29	70.6	401.1	197.4	37.9	7.9
2010	D+	1.30	0.97	53.9	370.5	153.7	42.4	10.3
2009	D	1.24	0.92	44.9	378.4	139.9	36.4	14.0

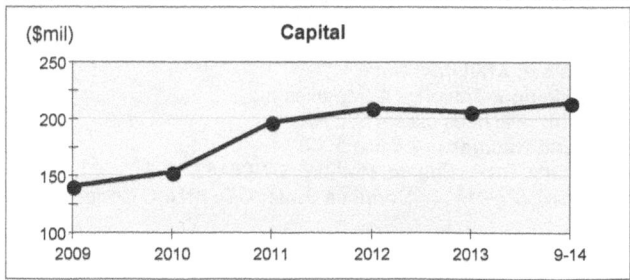

Capital

BALBOA INS CO
C-   **Fair**

Major Rating Factors: Weak profitability index (1.9 on a scale of 0 to 10). Weak expense controls. Return on equity has been fair, averaging 34.7% over the past five years. Fair overall results on stability tests (3.1) including weak results on operational trends and negative cash flow from operations for 2013. The largest net exposure for one risk is acceptable at 2.5% of capital.

Other Rating Factors: History of adequate reserve strength (6.1) as reserves have been consistently at an acceptable level. Strong long-term capitalization index (7.6) based on excellent current risk adjusted capital (severe and moderate loss scenarios), despite some fluctuation in capital levels. Excellent liquidity (7.0) with ample operational cash flow and liquid investments.

Principal Business: Credit (100%).

Principal Investments: Misc. investments (51%), investment grade bonds (45%), and cash (4%).

Investments in Affiliates: 50%
Group Affiliation: Bank of America Corp
Licensed in: All states except PR
Commenced Business: April 1948
Address: 3349 Michelson Dr Suite 200, Irvine, CA 92612-1627
Phone: (949) 222-8000   **Domicile State:** CA   **NAIC Code:** 24813

Data Date	Rating	RACR #1	RACR #2	Loss Ratio %	Total Assets ($mil)	Capital ($mil)	Net Premium ($mil)	Net Income ($mil)
9-14	C-	1.77	1.75	N/A	242.0	197.2	-0.9	2.6
9-13	C-	1.65	1.58	N/A	543.6	185.0	-2.3	3.5
2013	C-	1.75	1.72	N/A	297.5	194.5	-2.9	14.4
2012	C-	3.94	3.81	N/A	580.8	441.6	-9.3	281.1
2011	B	4.71	4.46	33.6	1,975.9	1,344.1	-441.7	672.8
2010	B	4.97	3.89	23.7	2,743.5	1,392.0	1,702.7	743.7
2009	B	6.17	4.46	37.0	3,120.7	1,741.5	1,660.9	408.6

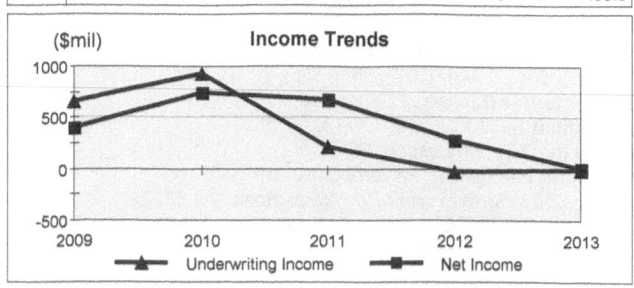

Income Trends

BAY STATE INS CO
B-   Good

Major Rating Factors: Fair overall results on stability tests (4.8 on a scale of 0 to 10) including potential drain of affiliation with Andover Group. History of adequate reserve strength (6.2) as reserves have been consistently at an acceptable level.

Other Rating Factors: Good overall profitability index (6.4) despite operating losses during 2011. Return on equity has been low, averaging 3.6% over the past five years. Strong long-term capitalization index (8.3) based on excellent current risk adjusted capital (severe and moderate loss scenarios), despite some fluctuation in capital levels. Excellent liquidity (7.4) with ample operational cash flow and liquid investments.

Principal Business: Homeowners multiple peril (89%), other liability (5%), inland marine (4%), and commercial multiple peril (2%).

Principal Investments: Misc. investments (67%), investment grade bonds (17%), and cash (16%).

Investments in Affiliates: None

Group Affiliation: Andover Group

Licensed in: CT, IL, ME, MA, NH, NJ, NY, RI

Commenced Business: July 1955

Address: 95 Old River Rd, Andover, MA 01810

Phone: (978) 475-3300   **Domicile State:** MA   **NAIC Code:** 19763

Data Date	Rating	RACR #1	RACR #2	Loss Ratio %	Total Assets ($mil)	Capital ($mil)	Net Premium ($mil)	Net Income ($mil)
9-14	B-	3.19	1.96	N/A	429.0	273.9	55.1	11.0
9-13	B-	3.31	2.06	N/A	382.3	242.4	51.8	11.8
2013	B-	3.33	2.06	43.3	412.6	260.3	73.9	16.6
2012	B-	3.36	2.13	64.9	361.4	217.4	71.9	5.9
2011	B-	3.36	2.16	90.4	326.4	200.1	67.3	-9.7
2010	B+	5.69	3.69	55.5	324.0	208.8	64.6	9.3
2009	B+	7.40	4.97	49.5	309.0	197.2	65.0	15.4

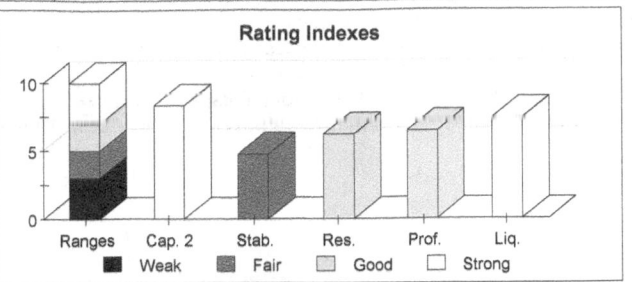
Rating Indexes

BERKLEY INS CO
C   Fair

Major Rating Factors: Fair overall results on stability tests (4.3 on a scale of 0 to 10) including weak results on operational trends. Strong long-term capitalization index (7.1) based on excellent current risk adjusted capital (severe and moderate loss scenarios), despite some fluctuation in capital levels.

Other Rating Factors: Ample reserve history (8.0) that helps to protect the company against sharp claims increases. Excellent profitability (8.3) with operating gains in each of the last five years. Return on equity has been good over the last five years, averaging 13.1%. Excellent liquidity (8.6) with ample operational cash flow and liquid investments.

Principal Business: Other liability (84%), surety (8%), commercial multiple peril (2%), auto liability (2%), ocean marine (2%), credit (1%), and other accident & health (1%).

Principal Investments: Investment grade bonds (56%), misc. investments (38%), cash (3%), non investment grade bonds (2%), and real estate (1%).

Investments in Affiliates: 17%

Group Affiliation: W R Berkley Corp

Licensed in: All states, the District of Columbia and Puerto Rico

Commenced Business: December 1975

Address: 100 Campus Drive, Florham Park, NJ 07932

Phone: (203) 542-3800   **Domicile State:** DE   **NAIC Code:** 32603

Data Date	Rating	RACR #1	RACR #2	Loss Ratio %	Total Assets ($mil)	Capital ($mil)	Net Premium ($mil)	Net Income ($mil)
9-14	C	1.38	1.08	N/A	16,852.4	5,125.2	3,577.2	431.0
9-13	C	1.38	1.15	N/A	16,021.1	4,877.4	3,214.6	1,423.4
2013	C	1.38	1.09	61.6	16,122.7	4,907.2	5,744.1	1,493.8
2012	C	1.44	1.31	67.3	10,223.8	4,656.3	1,719.3	294.5
2011	C	1.64	1.23	68.7	7,830.2	2,611.2	1,525.8	232.8
2010	C	1.62	1.07	69.0	7,517.5	2,623.7	1,327.2	323.6
2009	C	1.34	0.82	59.8	7,190.3	2,477.2	1,226.0	223.7

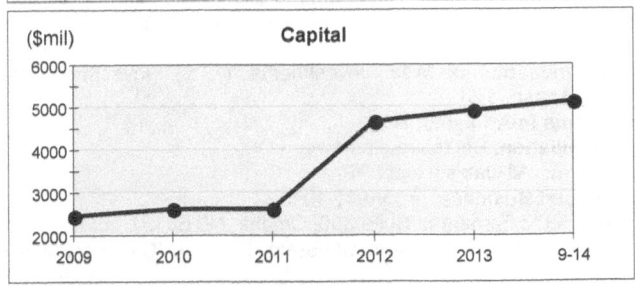
Capital

BERKLEY REGIONAL INS CO
C+   Fair

Major Rating Factors: Fair profitability index (3.9) with operating losses during the first nine months of 2014. Return on equity has been fair, averaging 14.2% over the past five years.

Other Rating Factors: Fair overall results on stability tests (4.4) including fair financial strength of affiliated W R Berkley Corp, weak results on operational trends and negative cash flow from operations for 2013. Vulnerable liquidity (0.7) as a spike in claims may stretch capacity. Strong long-term capitalization index (7.6) based on excellent current risk adjusted capital (severe and moderate loss scenarios), despite some fluctuation in capital levels.

Principal Business: (Not applicable due to unusual reinsurance transactions.)

Principal Investments: Misc. investments (53%) and investment grade bonds (47%).

Investments in Affiliates: 46%

Group Affiliation: W R Berkley Corp

Licensed in: All states except PR

Commenced Business: January 1987

Address: 1208 Orange St, Wilmington, DE 19801

Phone: (203) 629-3000   **Domicile State:** DE   **NAIC Code:** 29580

Data Date	Rating	RACR #1	RACR #2	Loss Ratio %	Total Assets ($mil)	Capital ($mil)	Net Premium ($mil)	Net Income ($mil)
9-14	C+	1.69	1.70	N/A	700.0	645.9	0.0	-7.0
9-13	B	1.56	1.53	N/A	678.7	637.7	0.0	130.7
2013	C+	1.89	2.08	0.0	681.2	643.2	-547.4	134.5
2012	B	1.39	1.17	58.7	2,700.8	717.3	1,185.6	127.2
2011	B	1.38	1.13	66.6	2,683.1	699.8	1,125.5	57.4
2010	B	1.46	1.17	59.7	2,687.6	689.9	1,099.2	137.7
2009	B	1.29	1.04	59.6	2,769.6	649.9	1,139.7	105.0

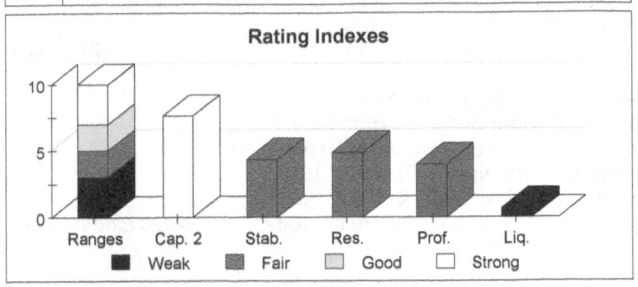
Rating Indexes

BERKSHIRE HATHAWAY ASR CORP *

A+ **Excellent**

Major Rating Factors: Strong long-term capitalization index (9.2 on a scale of 0 to 10) based on excellent current risk adjusted capital (severe and moderate loss scenarios). Furthermore, this high level of risk adjusted capital has been consistently maintained in previous years. Excellent profitability (8.8) with operating gains in each of the last five years.

Other Rating Factors: Superior liquidity (10.0) with ample operational cash flow and liquid investments. Excellent overall results on stability tests (7.6). Stability strengths include excellent risk diversification.

Principal Business: Financial guaranty (57%) and surety (43%).

Principal Investments: Misc. investments (54%), investment grade bonds (44%), and non investment grade bonds (2%).

Investments in Affiliates: None

Group Affiliation: Berkshire-Hathaway

Licensed in: All states, the District of Columbia and Puerto Rico

Commenced Business: December 2007

Address: Marine Air Terminal LaGuardia, Flushing, NY 11371

Phone: (402) 916-3000   **Domicile State:** NY   **NAIC Code:** 13070

Data Date	Rating	RACR #1	RACR #2	Loss Ratio %	Total Assets ($mil)	Capital ($mil)	Net Premium ($mil)	Net Income ($mil)
9-14	A+	4.07	2.42	N/A	2,246.2	1,432.0	24.1	74.1
9-13	A+	4.49	2.42	N/A	2,049.8	1,233.6	20.6	47.9
2013	A+	4.45	2.64	31.1	2,255.6	1,426.8	12.4	195.5
2012	A+	6.70	3.41	0.0	1,841.2	1,149.3	10.2	78.1
2011	A+	15.41	6.96	0.0	1,709.3	1,025.8	5.4	61.6
2010	N/A	N/A	N/A	0.0	1,681.6	1,018.8	6.5	52.1
2009	N/A	N/A	N/A	0.0	1,643.8	992.9	39.0	45.8

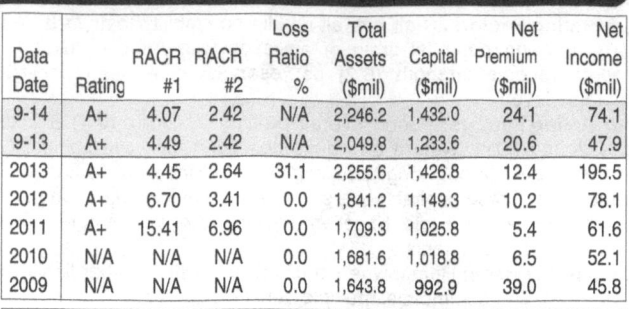

Risk-Adjusted Capital Ratio #2
(Severe Loss Scenario)

BERKSHIRE HATHAWAY HOMESTATE INS

C+ **Fair**

Major Rating Factors: Fair overall results on stability tests (4.4 on a scale of 0 to 10) including potential drain of affiliation with Berkshire-Hathaway, weak results on operational trends and excessive premium growth. Good long-term capitalization index (5.3) based on good current risk adjusted capital (moderate loss scenario). Moreover, capital levels have been consistent over the last several years.

Other Rating Factors: Good overall profitability index (6.8) despite operating losses during 2011. Return on equity has been low, averaging 2.6% over the past five years. Good liquidity (6.4) with sufficient resources (cash flows and marketable investments) to handle a spike in claims. Ample reserve history (7.6) that can protect against increases in claims costs.

Principal Business: Workers compensation (80%), auto liability (10%), auto physical damage (3%), other liability (2%), fidelity (1%), fire (1%), and other lines (2%).

Principal Investments: Misc. investments (77%), investment grade bonds (17%), and cash (6%).

Investments in Affiliates: None

Group Affiliation: Berkshire-Hathaway

Licensed in: All states except PR

Commenced Business: February 1970

Address: 3333 Farnam St Suite 300, Omaha, NE 68131

Phone: (402) 393-7255   **Domicile State:** NE   **NAIC Code:** 20044

Data Date	Rating	RACR #1	RACR #2	Loss Ratio %	Total Assets ($mil)	Capital ($mil)	Net Premium ($mil)	Net Income ($mil)
9-14	C+	1.18	0.78	N/A	1,860.9	1,089.3	229.7	136.3
9-13	C+	1.58	1.02	N/A	1,386.4	863.4	162.4	6.3
2013	C+	1.23	0.80	77.8	1,587.5	963.8	280.1	22.4
2012	C+	1.94	1.25	77.0	1,254.2	884.8	179.5	3.6
2011	C+	3.99	2.32	31.2	776.0	768.3	17.9	-42.0
2010	B+	3.82	2.22	24.7	805.0	664.9	26.2	18.9
2009	B+	3.84	2.22	58.7	751.2	594.7	50.7	14.5

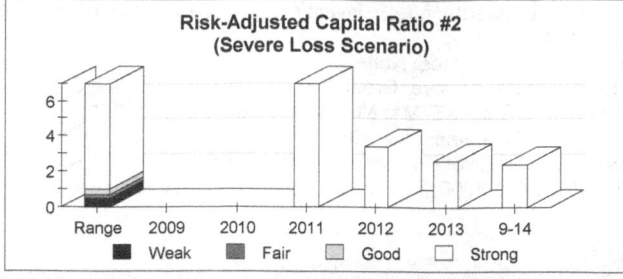

Rating Indexes

BERKSHIRE HATHAWAY SPECIALTY INS CO

C+ **Fair**

Major Rating Factors: Fair profitability index (4.5 on a scale of 0 to 10) with operating losses during 2009 and 2012. Return on equity has been low, averaging 1.4% over the past five years. Fair overall results on stability tests (4.4) including weak results on operational trends and negative cash flow from operations for 2013.

Other Rating Factors: A history of deficient reserves (2.9). Underreserving can have an adverse impact on capital and profits. Deficiencies in the two year reserve development occurred in three of the previous five years and ranged between 19% and 43%. Strong long-term capitalization index (8.4) based on excellent current risk adjusted capital (severe and moderate loss scenarios). Moreover, capital levels have been consistent in recent years. Superior liquidity (9.9) with ample operational cash flow and liquid investments.

Principal Business: Aircraft (100%).

Principal Investments: Misc. investments (97%), cash (2%), and investment grade bonds (1%).

Investments in Affiliates: None

Group Affiliation: Berkshire-Hathaway

Licensed in: All states except DC, HI, NH, PR

Commenced Business: February 1866

Address: 3024 Harney St, Omaha, NE 68131

Phone: (402) 916-3000   **Domicile State:** NE   **NAIC Code:** 22276

Data Date	Rating	RACR #1	RACR #2	Loss Ratio %	Total Assets ($mil)	Capital ($mil)	Net Premium ($mil)	Net Income ($mil)
9-14	C+	3.47	2.08	N/A	3,448.0	3,183.8	0.5	51.3
9-13	C+	1.81	0.91	N/A	90.4	76.5	1.8	-0.8
2013	C+	3.20	1.92	156.6	3,357.7	3,106.7	1.6	0.2
2012	C+	1.81	0.86	N/A	90.2	71.3	0.4	-0.5
2011	C+	2.09	0.88	0.0	95.1	68.8	0.0	2.0
2010	U	1.99	0.86	0.0	92.2	60.9	0.0	3.1
2009	U	2.39	1.01	0.0	88.5	58.5	0.0	-0.6

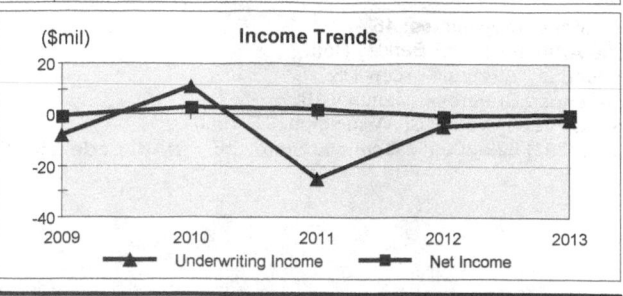

Income Trends

BITCO GENERAL INS CORP *   A-   Excellent

Major Rating Factors: Strong long-term capitalization index (8.9 on a scale of 0 to 10) based on excellent current risk adjusted capital (severe and moderate loss scenarios), despite some fluctuation in capital levels. Ample reserve history (9.3) that helps to protect the company against sharp claims increases.

Other Rating Factors: Excellent profitability (8.3) with operating gains in each of the last five years. Return on equity has been good over the last five years, averaging 12.9%. Excellent liquidity (7.1) with ample operational cash flow and liquid investments. Good overall results on stability tests (6.9). Affiliation with Old Republic Group is a strength.

Principal Business: Workers compensation (34%), commercial multiple peril (21%), auto liability (19%), other liability (13%), inland marine (7%), and auto physical damage (6%).

Principal Investments: Investment grade bonds (89%) and misc. investments (11%).

Investments in Affiliates: None
Group Affiliation: Old Republic Group
Licensed in: All states except HI, NH, PR
Commenced Business: August 1928
Address: 320 18th St, Rock Island, IL 61201
Phone: (309) 786-5401   **Domicile State:** IL   **NAIC Code:** 20095

Data Date	Rating	RACR #1	RACR #2	Loss Ratio %	Total Assets ($mil)	Capital ($mil)	Net Premium ($mil)	Net Income ($mil)
9-14	A-	3.49	2.23	N/A	796.8	286.0	164.3	35.2
9-13	A-	4.18	2.60	N/A	750.6	289.4	145.6	35.2
2013	A-	3.87	2.49	67.2	788.4	290.2	204.3	39.5
2012	A-	4.18	2.58	65.0	719.8	274.2	178.1	24.3
2011	A-	3.95	2.39	65.0	721.4	250.6	162.8	28.1
2010	A-	3.97	2.33	66.8	717.2	256.6	152.8	19.0
2009	A-	3.87	2.27	67.1	738.4	251.0	171.0	51.5

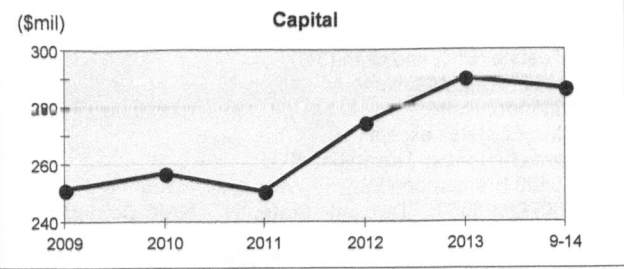

Capital

BITCO NATIONAL INS CO *   A-   Excellent

Major Rating Factors: Strong long-term capitalization index (8.4 on a scale of 0 to 10) based on excellent current risk adjusted capital (severe and moderate loss scenarios). Furthermore, this high level of risk adjusted capital has been consistently maintained in previous years. Ample reserve history (9.4) that helps to protect the company against sharp claims increases.

Other Rating Factors: Excellent profitability (8.0) with operating gains in each of the last five years. Return on equity has been good over the last five years, averaging 13.2%. Excellent overall results on stability tests (7.0). Stability strengths include excellent operational trends and excellent risk diversification. Good liquidity (6.9) with sufficient resources (cash flows and marketable investments) to handle a spike in claims.

Principal Business: Workers compensation (50%), commercial multiple peril (29%), auto liability (10%), inland marine (6%), auto physical damage (3%), and other liability (1%).

Principal Investments: Investment grade bonds (87%) and misc. investments (13%).

Investments in Affiliates: None
Group Affiliation: Old Republic Group
Licensed in: All states except AK, CT, HI, ME, ·NH, RI, VT, PR
Commenced Business: October 1942
Address: 320 18th St, Rock Island, IL 61201
Phone: (309) 732-0409   **Domicile State:** IL   **NAIC Code:** 20109

Data Date	Rating	RACR #1	RACR #2	Loss Ratio %	Total Assets ($mil)	Capital ($mil)	Net Premium ($mil)	Net Income ($mil)
9-14	A-	2.86	1.85	N/A	468.3	151.2	104.0	20.7
9-13	A-	3.21	2.04	N/A	464.7	156.6	91.3	18.0
2013	A-	3.19	2.05	64.2	465.0	157.0	128.8	21.9
2012	A-	3.25	2.06	60.7	450.6	150.6	113.6	15.3
2011	A-	3.18	1.99	60.1	456.1	145.3	104.0	18.8
2010	A-	3.09	1.90	60.9	464.2	140.9	97.3	19.6
2009	A-	2.65	1.65	68.0	476.2	126.5	107.3	14.6

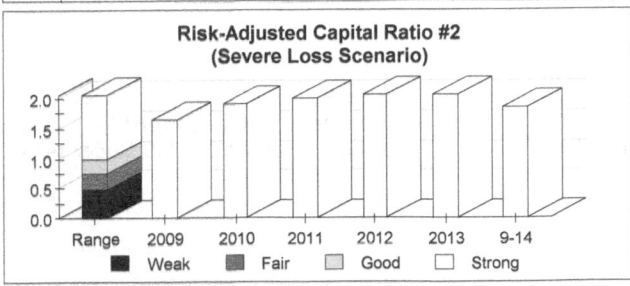

Risk-Adjusted Capital Ratio #2
(Severe Loss Scenario)

■ Weak   ■ Fair   □ Good   □ Strong

BRICKSTREET MUTUAL INS CO   C-   Fair

Major Rating Factors: Weak overall results on stability tests (2.9 on a scale of 0 to 10). Good long-term capitalization index (6.8) based on good current risk adjusted capital (severe loss scenario). Moreover, capital levels have been consistent over the last several years.

Other Rating Factors: Good overall profitability index (6.9). Fair expense controls. Ample reserve history (9.5) that helps to protect the company against sharp claims increases. Excellent liquidity (7.0) with ample operational cash flow and liquid investments.

Principal Business: Workers compensation (100%).

Principal Investments: Investment grade bonds (80%), misc. investments (17%), cash (2%), and real estate (1%).

Investments in Affiliates: 2%
Group Affiliation: BrickStreet Mutual Ins
Licensed in: AL, DC, GA, IL, IN, KY, MD, NC, PA, SC, TN, VA, WV
Commenced Business: January 2006
Address: 400 Quarrier St, Charleston, WV 25301
Phone: (304) 941-1000   **Domicile State:** WV   **NAIC Code:** 12372

Data Date	Rating	RACR #1	RACR #2	Loss Ratio %	Total Assets ($mil)	Capital ($mil)	Net Premium ($mil)	Net Income ($mil)
9-14	C-	2.32	0.86	N/A	1,873.7	634.8	231.7	31.3
9-13	C-	2.49	0.87	N/A	1,743.1	586.6	212.9	27.2
2013	C-	2.38	0.88	75.1	1,791.0	603.7	301.3	49.6
2012	C-	2.52	0.86	64.8	1,703.1	552.6	287.6	36.8
2011	D+	2.40	0.80	73.9	1,575.1	486.5	253.1	47.1
2010	D	2.31	0.77	77.8	1,499.3	447.4	244.3	52.8
2009	D	1.89	0.69	82.2	1,448.4	394.6	315.8	39.0

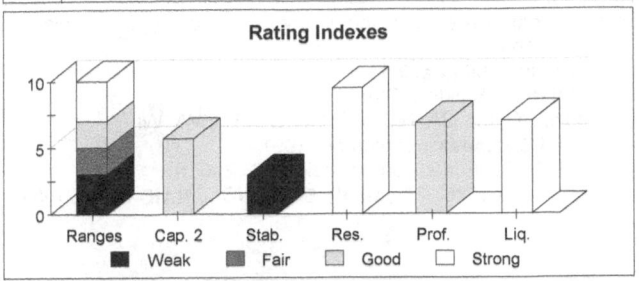

Rating Indexes

■ Weak   ■ Fair   □ Good   □ Strong

BROTHERHOOD MUTUAL INS CO *

A-   **Excellent**

Major Rating Factors: Strong long-term capitalization index (7.7 on a scale of 0 to 10) based on excellent current risk adjusted capital (severe and moderate loss scenarios). Furthermore, this high level of risk adjusted capital has been consistently maintained in previous years. Excellent overall results on stability tests (7.0). Stability strengths include excellent operational trends and excellent risk diversification.

Other Rating Factors: History of adequate reserve strength (5.8) as reserves have been consistently at an acceptable level. Good overall profitability index (5.2) despite operating losses during 2011. Good liquidity (5.7) with sufficient resources (cash flows and marketable investments) to handle a spike in claims.

Principal Business: Commercial multiple peril (71%), workers compensation (13%), auto liability (6%), other liability (4%), boiler & machinery (3%), and auto physical damage (2%).

Principal Investments: Investment grade bonds (47%), misc. investments (42%), real estate (8%), and cash (3%).

Investments in Affiliates: None

Group Affiliation: None

Licensed in: All states except PR

Commenced Business: November 1935

Address: 6400 Brotherhood Way, Ft Wayne, IN 46825

Phone: (260) 482-8668   **Domicile State:** IN   **NAIC Code:** 13528

Data Date	Rating	RACR #1	RACR #2	Loss Ratio %	Total Assets ($mil)	Capital ($mil)	Net Premium ($mil)	Net Income ($mil)
9-14	A-	1.93	1.48	N/A	443.2	181.0	195.4	0.2
9-13	A-	2.13	1.62	N/A	415.7	171.4	174.5	6.2
2013	A-	2.01	1.53	64.5	443.3	178.2	252.5	9.5
2012	A-	2.31	1.80	62.5	384.9	159.7	217.3	7.3
2011	A-	2.45	1.95	80.6	347.4	146.1	190.4	-15.8
2010	A-	2.87	2.22	69.1	337.8	149.6	170.6	2.6
2009	B+	2.89	2.27	64.0	327.5	143.5	163.7	5.4

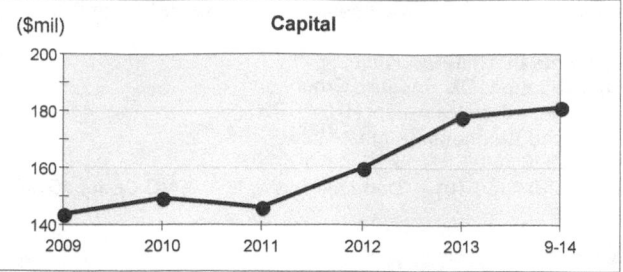

Capital

BUILD AMERICA MUTUAL ASR CO

D+   **Weak**

Major Rating Factors: Weak profitability index (2.7) with operating losses during 2012 and the first nine months of 2014.

Other Rating Factors: Weak overall results on stability tests (1.1) including excessive premium growth, weak results on operational trends and negative cash flow from operations for 2013. The largest net exposure for one risk is excessive at 50.0% of capital. Strong long-term capitalization index (10.0) based on excellent current risk adjusted capital (severe and moderate loss scenarios), despite some fluctuation in capital levels. Superior liquidity (10.0) with ample operational cash flow and liquid investments.

Principal Business: Financial guaranty (100%).

Principal Investments: Investment grade bonds (97%), misc. investments (2%), and cash (1%).

Investments in Affiliates: None

Group Affiliation: None

Licensed in: All states except PR

Commenced Business: July 2012

Address: One World Financial Center, New York, 10 281

Phone: (212) 235-2500   **Domicile State:** NY   **NAIC Code:** 14380

Data Date	Rating	RACR #1	RACR #2	Loss Ratio %	Total Assets ($mil)	Capital ($mil)	Net Premium ($mil)	Net Income ($mil)
9-14	D+	9.18	8.99	N/A	492.2	454.2	0.1	-23.7
9-13	A+	23.38	22.48	N/A	482.7	470.6	0.0	-22.5
2013	D+	14.08	13.68	0.0	486.5	469.0	3.0	-29.3
2012	A+	24.08	23.22	0.0	491.2	483.7	0.0	-18.2
2011	N/A	N/A	N/A	0.0	0.0	0.0	0.0	0.0
2010	N/A	N/A	N/A	0.0	0.0	0.0	0.0	0.0
2009	N/A	N/A	N/A	0.0	0.0	0.0	0.0	0.0

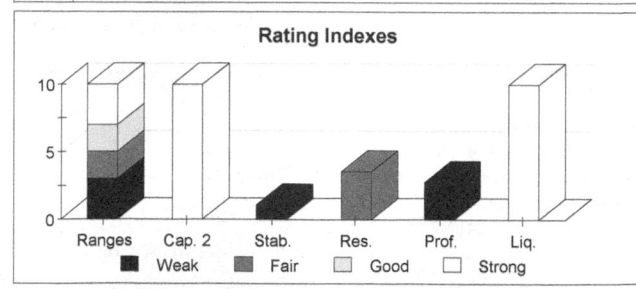

Rating Indexes

Ranges   Cap. 2   Stab.   Res.   Prof.   Liq.

■ Weak   ■ Fair   ☐ Good   ☐ Strong

BUILDERS MUTUAL INS CO *

B+   **Good**

Major Rating Factors: Good liquidity (6.8 on a scale of 0 to 10) with sufficient resources (cash flows and marketable investments) to handle a spike in claims. Good overall results on stability tests (6.5). Stability strengths include good operational trends and excellent risk diversification.

Other Rating Factors: Strong long-term capitalization index (7.8) based on excellent current risk adjusted capital (severe and moderate loss scenarios). Moreover, capital levels have been consistent in recent years. Ample reserve history (9.3) that helps to protect the company against sharp claims increases. Excellent profitability (7.7) with operating gains in each of the last five years.

Principal Business: Workers compensation (73%), commercial multiple peril (15%), products liability (5%), other liability (3%), inland marine (2%), and auto liability (2%).

Principal Investments: Investment grade bonds (75%), misc. investments (23%), and cash (2%).

Investments in Affiliates: 2%

Group Affiliation: Builders Group

Licensed in: DC, FL, GA, MD, MS, NC, SC, TN, VA, WI

Commenced Business: September 1997

Address: 6716 Six Forks Road, Raleigh, NC 27615

Phone: (919) 845-1976   **Domicile State:** NC   **NAIC Code:** 10844

Data Date	Rating	RACR #1	RACR #2	Loss Ratio %	Total Assets ($mil)	Capital ($mil)	Net Premium ($mil)	Net Income ($mil)
9-14	B+	2.14	1.49	N/A	625.9	258.2	151.4	14.1
9-13	B+	2.24	1.56	N/A	572.5	234.2	127.0	8.2
2013	B+	2.24	1.56	61.5	576.4	242.0	181.7	13.4
2012	B+	2.30	1.60	64.8	536.2	218.7	148.4	10.2
2011	B+	3.14	2.14	69.9	490.3	203.7	119.5	5.1
2010	B+	2.14	1.36	63.0	475.0	200.9	92.3	12.9
2009	B	2.00	1.28	59.2	470.9	197.1	81.0	10.4

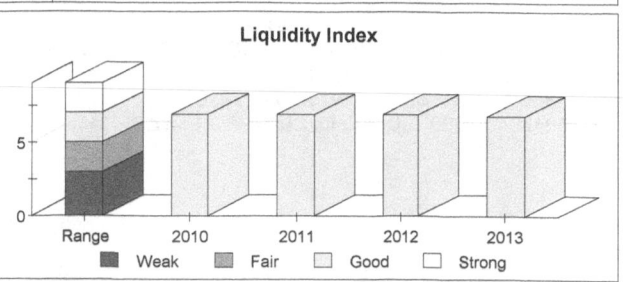

Liquidity Index

Range   2010   2011   2012   2013

■ Weak   ■ Fair   ☐ Good   ☐ Strong

CALIFORNIA CAPITAL INS CO   B-   Good

Major Rating Factors: Fair overall results on stability tests (4.7 on a scale of 0 to 10) including potential drain of affiliation with Capital Ins Group. History of adequate reserve strength (6.0) as reserves have been consistently at an acceptable level.

Other Rating Factors: Good overall profitability index (6.7). Fair expense controls. Return on equity has been low, averaging 2.6% over the past five years. Good liquidity (6.3) with sufficient resources (cash flows and marketable investments) to handle a spike in claims. Strong long-term capitalization index (8.1) based on excellent current risk adjusted capital (severe and moderate loss scenarios). Moreover, capital levels have been consistent in recent years.

Principal Business: Commercial multiple peril (40%), homeowners multiple peril (20%), auto liability (13%), auto physical damage (9%), farmowners multiple peril (5%), fire (5%), and other lines (10%).

Principal Investments: Investment grade bonds (68%), misc. investments (30%), and real estate (2%).

Investments in Affiliates: 25%

Group Affiliation: Capital Ins Group

Licensed in: AZ, CA, ID, MT, NV, OR, TX

Commenced Business: August 1898

Address: 2300 Garden Rd, Monterey, CA 93942-3110

Phone: (831) 233-5500   **Domicile State:** CA   **NAIC Code:** 13544

Data Date	Rating	RACR #1	RACR #2	Loss Ratio %	Total Assets ($mil)	Capital ($mil)	Net Premium ($mil)	Net Income ($mil)
9-14	B-	2.10	1.69	N/A	590.0	305.2	179.7	4.1
9-13	B-	2.18	1.75	N/A	563.4	299.0	163.5	7.7
2013	B-	2.15	1.76	65.1	569.5	303.3	234.0	9.2
2012	B-	2.18	1.79	67.2	536.6	289.7	210.8	6.6
2011	B-	2.19	1.79	70.3	508.1	281.3	191.0	1.8
2010	B-	2.41	1.94	62.0	483.3	276.2	181.6	9.2
2009	B-	2.40	1.94	60.2	454.5	258.6	168.7	10.4

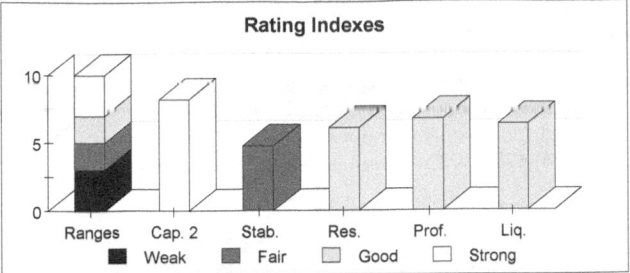

Rating Indexes

CALIFORNIA CASUALTY INDEMNITY EXCH   C+   Fair

Major Rating Factors: Fair overall results on stability tests (4.7 on a scale of 0 to 10) including potential drain of affiliation with California Casualty Ins Group and negative cash flow from operations for 2013. The largest net exposure for one risk is acceptable at 2.2% of capital. Fair profitability index (4.0) with operating losses during 2012 and the first nine months of 2014.

Other Rating Factors: Good liquidity (6.7) with sufficient resources (cash flows and marketable investments) to handle a spike in claims. Strong long-term capitalization index (8.3) based on excellent current risk adjusted capital (severe and moderate loss scenarios), despite some fluctuation in capital levels. Ample reserve history (7.8) that can protect against increases in claims costs.

Principal Business: Auto liability (37%), auto physical damage (33%), homeowners multiple peril (28%), and earthquake (1%).

Principal Investments: Misc. investments (53%) and investment grade bonds (49%).

Investments in Affiliates: 38%

Group Affiliation: California Casualty Ins Group

Licensed in: All states except MI, NJ, PR

Commenced Business: January 1914

Address: 1900 Alameda De Las Pulgas, San Mateo, CA 94403

Phone: (650) 574-4000   **Domicile State:** CA   **NAIC Code:** 20117

Data Date	Rating	RACR #1	RACR #2	Loss Ratio %	Total Assets ($mil)	Capital ($mil)	Net Premium ($mil)	Net Income ($mil)
9-14	C+	2.07	1.87	N/A	575.1	332.5	120.7	-2.2
9-13	C+	2.11	1.90	N/A	562.0	322.8	115.6	0.4
2013	C+	2.08	1.88	79.4	571.8	336.5	158.7	2.6
2012	C+	2.10	1.89	79.9	557.6	320.0	152.7	-1.8
2011	C+	2.10	1.92	76.8	623.4	325.1	150.0	4.3
2010	C+	2.06	1.87	76.0	566.6	340.2	150.7	4.6
2009	C+	2.03	1.86	76.1	559.5	327.1	153.0	5.8

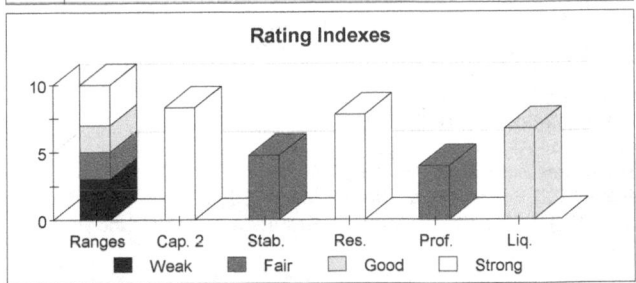

Rating Indexes

CALIFORNIA INS CO   B-   Good

Major Rating Factors: Fair overall results on stability tests (4.7 on a scale of 0 to 10) including weak results on operational trends and excessive premium growth. Strong long-term capitalization index (8.6) based on excellent current risk adjusted capital (severe and moderate loss scenarios). Moreover, capital levels have been consistent in recent years.

Other Rating Factors: Ample reserve history (9.4) that helps to protect the company against sharp claims increases. Excellent profitability (7.5). Return on equity has been good over the last five years, averaging 14.2%. Excellent liquidity (8.7) with ample operational cash flow and liquid investments.

Principal Business: Workers compensation (97%), surety (2%), aggregate write-ins for other lines of business (1%), and other liability (1%).

Principal Investments: Investment grade bonds (81%), misc. investments (11%), and cash (8%).

Investments in Affiliates: None

Group Affiliation: Berkshire-Hathaway

Licensed in: AK, AZ, CA, CT, GA, HI, ID, IL, IN, IA, KS, MD, MO, MT, NV, NJ, NY, NC, ND, OR, PA, TX, UT, VA, WA, WI

Commenced Business: June 1980

Address: 950 Tower Lane 14th Floor, Foster City, CA 94404

Phone: (402) 827-3424   **Domicile State:** CA   **NAIC Code:** 38865

Data Date	Rating	RACR #1	RACR #2	Loss Ratio %	Total Assets ($mil)	Capital ($mil)	Net Premium ($mil)	Net Income ($mil)
9-14	B-	3.65	2.04	N/A	614.3	365.6	174.9	44.5
9-13	B-	3.77	1.88	N/A	523.6	287.2	126.8	33.0
2013	B-	3.98	2.18	32.2	521.1	317.4	186.9	48.9
2012	B-	3.99	1.97	12.6	443.9	244.7	136.2	47.6
2011	B-	3.70	1.87	29.6	484.7	192.2	117.9	36.6
2010	B-	3.52	1.48	19.6	392.9	149.0	87.7	28.5
2009	C+	3.13	1.24	77.8	327.8	129.8	71.5	-4.4

Berkshire-Hathaway Composite Group Rating: B- Largest Group Members	Assets ($mil)	Rating
NATIONAL INDEMNITY CO	151912	B-
GOVERNMENT EMPLOYEES INS CO	25779	B+
COLUMBIA INS CO	19013	B-
GENERAL REINSURANCE CORP	16220	B-
BERKSHIRE HATHAWAY LIFE INS CO OF NE	13768	C+

CAMBRIDGE MUTUAL FIRE INS CO — B- — Good

Major Rating Factors: Fair overall results on stability tests (4.8 on a scale of 0 to 10) including potential drain of affiliation with Andover Group. History of adequate reserve strength (6.3) as reserves have been consistently at an acceptable level.

Other Rating Factors: Good overall profitability index (6.6) despite operating losses during 2011. Strong long-term capitalization index (8.3) based on excellent current risk adjusted capital (severe and moderate loss scenarios), despite some fluctuation in capital levels. Excellent liquidity (7.2) with ample operational cash flow and liquid investments.

Principal Business: Homeowners multiple peril (61%), commercial multiple peril (15%), fire (9%), allied lines (7%), other liability (6%), and inland marine (2%).

Principal Investments: Misc. investments (61%), investment grade bonds (21%), and cash (18%).

Investments in Affiliates: None

Group Affiliation: Andover Group

Licensed in: CT, IL, ME, MA, NH, NJ, NY, RI, VT

Commenced Business: January 1834

Address: 95 Old River Rd, Andover, MA 01810

Phone: (978) 475-3300   **Domicile State:** MA   **NAIC Code:** 19771

Data Date	Rating	RACR #1	RACR #2	Loss Ratio %	Total Assets ($mil)	Capital ($mil)	Net Premium ($mil)	Net Income ($mil)
9-14	B-	3.08	1.93	N/A	794.4	467.8	128.5	17.1
9-13	B-	3.17	2.05	N/A	693.7	398.8	121.0	40.4
2013	B-	3.15	2.01	43.3	738.7	421.9	172.5	51.3
2012	B-	3.02	2.01	64.9	679.7	352.6	167.8	11.9
2011	B-	2.94	1.97	90.4	631.2	331.6	157.1	-22.6
2010	B	4.96	3.39	55.5	603.2	335.4	150.6	19.9
2009	B	5.81	4.07	49.5	578.2	314.6	151.6	30.7

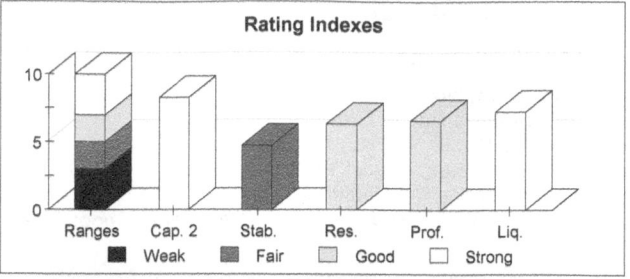

CANAL INS CO — B — Good

Major Rating Factors: Good overall results on stability tests (5.6 on a scale of 0 to 10) despite potential drain of affiliation with Canal Group and negative cash flow from operations for 2013. Stability strengths include good operational trends and excellent risk diversification. History of adequate reserve strength (5.0) as reserves have been consistently at an acceptable level.

Other Rating Factors: Good liquidity (6.8) with sufficient resources (cash flows and marketable investments) to handle a spike in claims. Fair profitability index (4.0) with operating losses during 2010. Average return on equity over the last five years has been poor at -0.2%. Strong long-term capitalization index (8.2) based on excellent current risk adjusted capital (severe and moderate loss scenarios), despite some fluctuation in capital levels.

Principal Business: Auto liability (74%), auto physical damage (19%), inland marine (6%), other liability (1%), and workers compensation (1%).

Principal Investments: Investment grade bonds (49%), misc. investments (48%), and non investment grade bonds (4%).

Investments in Affiliates: 5%

Group Affiliation: Canal Group

Licensed in: All states except AK, HI, PR

Commenced Business: March 1939

Address: 400 E Stone Ave, Greenville, SC 29601

Phone: (864) 242-5365   **Domicile State:** SC   **NAIC Code:** 10464

Data Date	Rating	RACR #1	RACR #2	Loss Ratio %	Total Assets ($mil)	Capital ($mil)	Net Premium ($mil)	Net Income ($mil)
9-14	B	2.75	1.94	N/A	858.0	460.8	134.7	6.4
9-13	B	2.63	1.88	N/A	853.1	451.1	150.6	6.8
2013	B	2.63	1.89	86.6	849.0	444.8	191.9	1.7
2012	B	2.60	1.89	79.1	831.0	421.3	200.1	6.2
2011	B-	2.53	1.80	93.7	850.3	401.9	189.3	2.7
2010	B-	2.12	1.50	105.7	912.1	409.2	197.5	-34.7
2009	B+	2.85	1.91	87.3	984.1	499.1	175.7	17.9

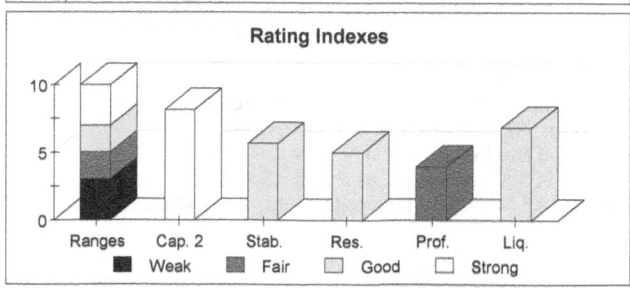

CATASTROPHE REINS CO — D- — Weak

Major Rating Factors: Weak overall results on stability tests (0.9 on a scale of 0 to 10). Fair reserve development (4.7) as reserves have generally been sufficient to cover claims.

Other Rating Factors: Good overall profitability index (6.6). Excellent expense controls. Return on equity has been good over the last five years, averaging 10.6%. Strong long-term capitalization index (10.0) based on excellent current risk adjusted capital (severe and moderate loss scenarios), despite some fluctuation in capital levels. Excellent liquidity (7.0) with ample operational cash flow and liquid investments.

Principal Business: (This company is a reinsurer.)

Principal Investments: Investment grade bonds (93%), misc. investments (4%), and non investment grade bonds (3%).

Investments in Affiliates: None

Group Affiliation: USAA Group

Licensed in: TX

Commenced Business: June 2006

Address: 9800 Fredericksburg Rd, San Antonio, TX 78288-0001

Phone: (210) 498-8000   **Domicile State:** TX   **NAIC Code:** 12578

Data Date	Rating	RACR #1	RACR #2	Loss Ratio %	Total Assets ($mil)	Capital ($mil)	Net Premium ($mil)	Net Income ($mil)
9-14	D-	9.52	5.99	N/A	1,979.8	1,784.8	207.7	204.1
9-13	D-	4.18	2.61	N/A	2,236.2	1,746.8	304.1	67.5
2013	D-	4.93	3.10	67.6	1,930.5	1,589.2	356.9	136.1
2012	D-	4.94	3.04	24.1	1,976.7	1,680.2	446.7	271.6
2011	E+	3.78	2.32	99.0	1,960.3	1,560.4	434.5	46.4
2010	E+	8.90	5.41	N/A	1,769.2	1,630.6	264.2	214.6
2009	E+	7.98	4.86	40.6	1,580.7	1,415.9	228.6	125.2

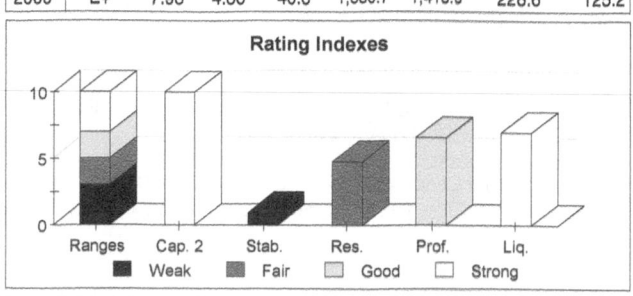

CATERPILLAR INS CO

B-   **Good**

Major Rating Factors: Good overall results on stability tests (5.3 on a scale of 0 to 10). Stability strengths include good operational trends and excellent risk diversification. Strong long-term capitalization index (8.6) based on excellent current risk adjusted capital (severe and moderate loss scenarios). Moreover, capital levels have been consistent in recent years.

Other Rating Factors: Ample reserve history (9.2) that helps to protect the company against sharp claims increases. Excellent profitability (8.9) with operating gains in each of the last five years. Return on equity has been good over the last five years, averaging 11.4%. Excellent liquidity (7.1) with ample operational cash flow and liquid investments.

Principal Business: Other liability (94%), aggregate write-ins for other lines of business (4%), and inland marine (2%).

Principal Investments: Investment grade bonds (69%), misc. investments (29%), and cash (2%).

Investments in Affiliates: None

Group Affiliation: Caterpillar Ins Holdings Inc

Licensed in: All states except PR

Commenced Business: February 1963

Address: 237 E High St, Jefferson City, MO 65101

Phone: (615) 341-8147   **Domicile State:** MO   **NAIC Code:** 11255

Data Date	Rating	RACR #1	RACR #2	Loss Ratio %	Total Assets ($mil)	Capital ($mil)	Net Premium ($mil)	Net Income ($mil)
9-14	B-	2.74	2.19	N/A	683.8	264.2	139.7	23.7
9-13	B-	2.27	1.87	N/A	654.2	233.3	139.4	23.4
2013	B-	2.62	2.16	55.2	639.6	243.4	214.6	33.2
2012	B-	2.26	1.87	51.0	575.6	203.9	199.2	41.5
2011	B-	2.14	1.88	79.5	474.0	151.6	164.4	3.9
2010	C+	2.92	2.60	71.8	401.8	141.0	118.2	11.5
2009	C+	3.04	2.50	68.3	349.4	126.2	104.0	14.7

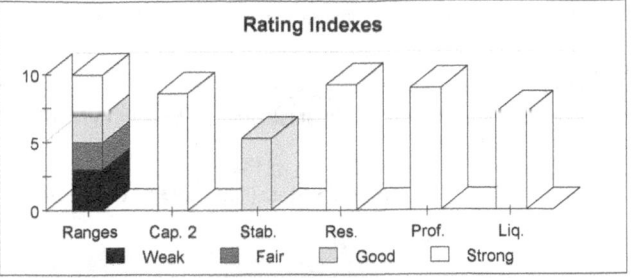

CATLIN SPECIALTY INS CO

C+   **Fair**

Major Rating Factors: Fair overall results on stability tests (4.3 on a scale of 0 to 10) including potential drain of affiliation with Catlin Group Ltd. The largest net exposure for one risk is high at 3.9% of capital. History of adequate reserve strength (5.9) as reserves have been consistently at an acceptable level.

Other Rating Factors: Strong long-term capitalization index (7.6) based on excellent current risk adjusted capital (severe and moderate loss scenarios), despite some fluctuation in capital levels. Excellent profitability (7.7) with operating gains in each of the last five years. Excellent liquidity (7.6) with ample operational cash flow and liquid investments.

Principal Business: Other liability (82%), products liability (8%), medical malpractice (5%), commercial multiple peril (2%), inland marine (2%), and allied lines (1%).

Principal Investments: Investment grade bonds (73%) and misc. investments (30%).

Investments in Affiliates: 23%

Group Affiliation: Catlin Group Ltd

Licensed in: All states except RI, PR

Commenced Business: January 1942

Address: 1209 Orange St, Wilmington, DE 19801

Phone: (404) 443-4910   **Domicile State:** DE   **NAIC Code:** 15989

Data Date	Rating	RACR #1	RACR #2	Loss Ratio %	Total Assets ($mil)	Capital ($mil)	Net Premium ($mil)	Net Income ($mil)
9-14	C+	2.02	1.56	N/A	628.7	201.2	56.4	1.9
9-13	C+	1.99	1.24	N/A	498.7	119.9	50.5	6.2
2013	C+	2.12	1.68	62.0	483.8	201.5	78.0	7.4
2012	C+	1.70	1.08	71.3	355.2	112.8	63.7	2.5
2011	C+	2.37	1.36	65.1	318.3	111.4	55.9	6.1
2010	C+	2.44	1.40	68.0	303.4	102.9	53.7	1.0
2009	C+	3.34	1.87	68.1	262.3	100.8	38.7	0.8

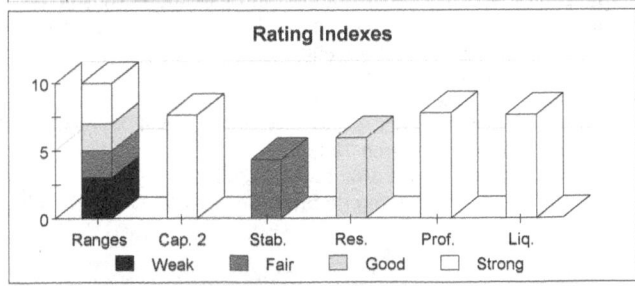

CENTRAL MUTUAL INS CO

B   **Good**

Major Rating Factors: Good overall profitability index (6.0 on a scale of 0 to 10) despite operating losses during 2009, 2010 and 2011. Good liquidity (6.7) with sufficient resources (cash flows and marketable investments) to handle a spike in claims.

Other Rating Factors: Good overall results on stability tests (5.9). Stability strengths include good operational trends and excellent risk diversification. Strong long-term capitalization index (8.3) based on excellent current risk adjusted capital (severe and moderate loss scenarios), despite some fluctuation in capital levels. Ample reserve history (7.0) that can protect against increases in claims costs.

Principal Business: Homeowners multiple peril (27%), auto liability (23%), commercial multiple peril (19%), auto physical damage (15%), other liability (5%), products liability (2%), and other lines (8%).

Principal Investments: Investment grade bonds (62%), misc. investments (35%), and real estate (4%).

Investments in Affiliates: 12%

Group Affiliation: Central Mutual Ins Group

Licensed in: AZ, CA, CO, CT, DE, GA, IL, IN, IA, KY, MA, MI, NV, NH, NJ, NM, NY, NC, OH, OK, PA, SC, TN, TX, VA, WI

Commenced Business: October 1876

Address: 800 S Washington St, Van Wert, OH 45891

Phone: (419) 238-1010   **Domicile State:** OH   **NAIC Code:** 20230

Data Date	Rating	RACR #1	RACR #2	Loss Ratio %	Total Assets ($mil)	Capital ($mil)	Net Premium ($mil)	Net Income ($mil)
9-14	B	2.82	2.05	N/A	1,330.2	638.5	317.0	13.8
9-13	B	2.75	1.98	N/A	1,246.2	562.9	287.8	21.0
2013	B	2.91	2.14	58.4	1,266.0	619.4	402.3	62.9
2012	B	2.63	1.92	70.7	1,184.2	510.5	369.9	23.0
2011	B-	2.38	1.72	79.3	1,163.1	457.8	375.9	-2.9
2010	B	2.42	1.74	86.5	1,240.4	467.7	413.0	-34.0
2009	B+	2.63	1.91	74.8	1,275.2	500.6	456.6	-5.3

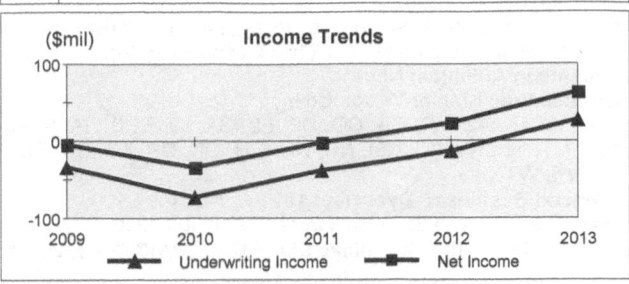

CENTRAL STATES INDEMNITY CO OF OMAHA *

B+ **Good**

Major Rating Factors: Good overall results on stability tests (5.3 on a scale of 0 to 10) despite potential drain of affiliation with Berkshire-Hathaway. Strong long-term capitalization index (9.7) based on excellent current risk adjusted capital (severe and moderate loss scenarios). Moreover, capital levels have been consistent in recent years.

Other Rating Factors: Ample reserve history (7.7) that can protect against increases in claims costs. Excellent profitability (8.1) with operating gains in each of the last five years. Superior liquidity (9.1) with ample operational cash flow and liquid investments.

Principal Business: Other accident & health (41%), inland marine (32%), aggregate write-ins for other lines of business (15%), credit accident & health (6%), aircraft (5%), and group accident & health (1%).

Principal Investments: Misc. investments (63%), investment grade bonds (36%), and cash (1%).

Investments in Affiliates: 4%

Group Affiliation: Berkshire-Hathaway

Licensed in: All states, the District of Columbia and Puerto Rico

Commenced Business: June 1977

Address: 1212 N 96th St, Omaha, NE 68114

Phone: (402) 997-8000   **Domicile State:** NE   **NAIC Code:** 34274

Data Date	Rating	RACR #1	RACR #2	Loss Ratio %	Total Assets ($mil)	Capital ($mil)	Net Premium ($mil)	Net Income ($mil)
9-14	B+	4.31	2.76	N/A	427.1	358.1	37.1	4.3
9-13	B+	4.17	2.58	N/A	372.9	315.8	31.1	8.6
2013	B+	4.34	2.79	36.2	412.3	346.0	43.0	17.7
2012	B+	4.34	2.69	18.3	335.1	285.5	32.2	13.1
2011	B+	4.37	2.58	10.3	287.0	249.6	29.8	12.8
2010	B+	4.38	2.57	20.2	272.9	235.2	33.6	9.7
2009	B+	4.14	2.45	29.9	252.4	216.5	40.7	8.4

Berkshire-Hathaway Composite Group Rating: B- Largest Group Members	Assets ($mil)	Rating
NATIONAL INDEMNITY CO	151912	B-
GOVERNMENT EMPLOYEES INS CO	25779	B+
COLUMBIA INS CO	19013	B-
GENERAL REINSURANCE CORP	16220	B-
BERKSHIRE HATHAWAY LIFE INS CO OF NE	13768	C+

CENTURION CASUALTY CO *

B+ **Good**

Major Rating Factors: Good overall results on stability tests (6.4 on a scale of 0 to 10). Strengths include potentially strong support from affiliation with Wells Fargo Group, good operational trends and excellent risk diversification. History of adequate reserve strength (6.1) as reserves have been consistently at an acceptable level.

Other Rating Factors: Strong long-term capitalization index (10.0) based on excellent current risk adjusted capital (severe and moderate loss scenarios), despite some fluctuation in capital levels. Superior liquidity (9.3) with ample operational cash flow and liquid investments. Fair profitability index (3.0). Good expense controls. Return on equity has been fair, averaging 11.9% over the past five years.

Principal Business: Aggregate write-ins for other lines of business (100%).

Principal Investments: Investment grade bonds (88%), misc. investments (5%), non investment grade bonds (5%), and cash (2%).

Investments in Affiliates: None

Group Affiliation: Wells Fargo Group

Licensed in: All states except AK, AR, DC, GA, MI, NH, NY, PA, VT, PR

Commenced Business: March 1983

Address: 800 Walnut St, Des Moines, IA 50309

Phone: (515) 557-7346   **Domicile State:** IA   **NAIC Code:** 42765

Data Date	Rating	RACR #1	RACR #2	Loss Ratio %	Total Assets ($mil)	Capital ($mil)	Net Premium ($mil)	Net Income ($mil)
9-14	B+	41.80	19.06	N/A	140.4	139.4	10.3	8.7
9-13	B+	38.57	16.65	N/A	129.7	127.9	11.6	9.7
2013	B+	42.92	21.18	6.9	131.9	130.8	15.1	12.6
2012	B+	32.85	14.27	5.8	121.6	118.3	17.6	13.5
2011	B+	20.87	14.19	2.4	194.7	142.7	20.8	40.1
2010	B+	57.90	28.27	18.0	467.9	410.5	27.0	26.6
2009	B	53.46	30.32	38.2	441.5	382.7	34.3	24.6

Wells Fargo Group Composite Group Rating: B Largest Group Members	Assets ($mil)	Rating
RURAL COMMUNITY INS CO	5245	B
CENTURION LIFE INS CO	1209	D
HERITAGE INDEMNITY CO	208	C
CENTURION CASUALTY CO	132	B+

CENTURY-NATIONAL INS CO

B **Good**

Major Rating Factors: Good overall profitability index (6.8 on a scale of 0 to 10). Weak expense controls. Return on equity has been fair, averaging 7.6% over the past five years. Good liquidity (6.8) with sufficient resources (cash flows and marketable investments) to handle a spike in claims.

Other Rating Factors: Good overall results on stability tests (5.5). Strong long-term capitalization index (8.6) based on excellent current risk adjusted capital (severe and moderate loss scenarios). Moreover, capital levels have been consistent in recent years. Ample reserve history (8.9) that helps to protect the company against sharp claims increases.

Principal Business: Homeowners multiple peril (35%), auto liability (26%), auto physical damage (11%), commercial multiple peril (10%), fire (7%), allied lines (6%), and earthquake (3%).

Principal Investments: Misc. investments (46%), investment grade bonds (43%), non investment grade bonds (10%), and cash (1%).

Investments in Affiliates: None

Group Affiliation: Kramer-Wilson Co Inc

Licensed in: AK, AZ, AR, CA, CO, DE, FL, GA, ID, IL, IN, IA, KY, LA, MD, MN, MS, MO, MT, NE, NV, NJ, NM, NC, ND, OH, OK, OR, PA, SC, SD, TN, TX, UT, VA, WA, WI, WY

Commenced Business: December 1956

Address: 12200 Sylvan St, N Hollywood, CA 91606-3216

Phone: (818) 760-0880   **Domicile State:** CA   **NAIC Code:** 26905

Data Date	Rating	RACR #1	RACR #2	Loss Ratio %	Total Assets ($mil)	Capital ($mil)	Net Premium ($mil)	Net Income ($mil)
9-14	B	3.58	2.23	N/A	615.6	395.0	97.7	20.0
9-13	B	3.63	2.28	N/A	579.2	383.9	90.8	6.1
2013	B	3.54	2.20	78.4	587.7	386.5	124.8	15.5
2012	B	3.52	2.21	66.6	531.6	336.9	117.4	9.7
2011	B-	3.61	2.27	52.7	513.3	326.8	110.5	20.9
2010	B-	3.37	2.20	50.9	529.9	324.4	117.0	38.1
2009	C+	2.97	2.04	38.8	524.7	288.6	127.6	39.3

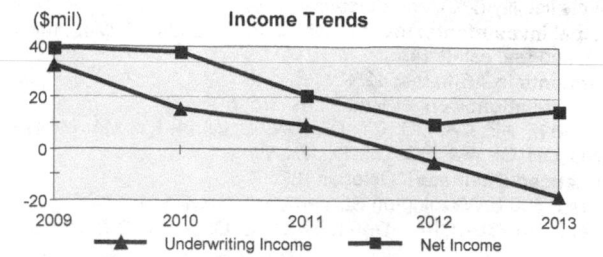

Income Trends

CHARTER OAK FIRE INS CO

B   Good

Major Rating Factors: Good liquidity (6.9 on a scale of 0 to 10) with sufficient resources (cash flows and marketable investments) to handle a spike in claims. Good overall results on stability tests (6.0). Affiliation with Travelers Companies Inc is a strength.

Other Rating Factors: Strong long-term capitalization index (7.9) based on excellent current risk adjusted capital (severe and moderate loss scenarios), despite some fluctuation in capital levels. Ample reserve history (8.8) that helps to protect the company against sharp claims increases. Excellent profitability (7.8) with operating gains in each of the last five years. Return on equity has been good over the last five years, averaging 14.6%.

Principal Business: Commercial multiple peril (31%), workers compensation (26%), auto liability (17%), homeowners multiple peril (10%), other liability (5%), auto physical damage (5%), and other lines (7%).

Principal Investments: Investment grade bonds (91%) and misc. investments (9%).

Investments in Affiliates: None

Group Affiliation: Travelers Companies Inc

Licensed in: All states except CA

Commenced Business: October 1935

Address: One Tower Square, Hartford, CT 06183

Phone: (860) 277-0111   **Domicile State:** CT   **NAIC Code:** 25615

Data Date	Rating	RACR #1	RACR #2	Loss Ratio %	Total Assets ($mil)	Capital ($mil)	Net Premium ($mil)	Net Income ($mil)
9-14	B	2.75	1.74	N/A	959.3	278.9	189.3	32.4
9-13	B	2.66	1.70	N/A	933.4	262.3	185.5	28.5
2013	B	2.50	1.59	60.9	916.9	245.9	255.8	42.6
2012	B	2.40	1.54	68.4	918.5	232.2	248.4	32.0
2011	B	2.27	1.47	76.9	877.5	221.6	243.2	13.8
2010	B	2.36	1.49	62.0	926.5	235.3	234.8	40.7
2009	B	2.20	1.44	58.3	952.5	228.6	230.2	40.0

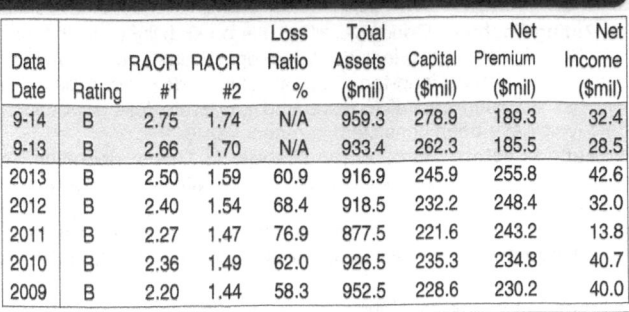

Liquidity Index

CHURCH MUTUAL INS CO *

A   Excellent

Major Rating Factors: Strong long-term capitalization index (8.2 on a scale of 0 to 10) based on excellent current risk adjusted capital (severe and moderate loss scenarios). Furthermore, this high level of risk adjusted capital has been consistently maintained in previous years. Ample reserve history (9.3) that helps to protect the company against sharp claims increases.

Other Rating Factors: Excellent overall results on stability tests (7.4). Stability strengths include excellent operational trends and excellent risk diversification. Good overall profitability index (6.0) despite operating losses during 2011 and 2013. Good liquidity (6.3) with sufficient resources (cash flows and marketable investments) to handle a spike in claims.

Principal Business: Commercial multiple peril (71%), workers compensation (17%), auto liability (5%), other liability (3%), auto physical damage (1%), allied lines (1%), and medical malpractice (1%).

Principal Investments: Investment grade bonds (78%), misc. investments (20%), cash (1%), and real estate (1%).

Investments in Affiliates: None

Group Affiliation: None

Licensed in: All states except PR

Commenced Business: June 1897

Address: 3000 Schuster Lane, Merrill, WI 54452

Phone: (715) 536-5577   **Domicile State:** WI   **NAIC Code:** 18767

Data Date	Rating	RACR #1	RACR #2	Loss Ratio %	Total Assets ($mil)	Capital ($mil)	Net Premium ($mil)	Net Income ($mil)
9-14	A	2.68	1.81	N/A	1,452.0	507.1	431.9	39.6
9-13	A	2.72	2.16	N/A	1,361.5	443.0	395.2	44.5
2013	A	2.71	1.83	63.6	1,357.7	473.2	557.3	-4.9
2012	A	2.76	2.22	66.4	1,229.7	415.3	492.5	78.1
2011	A-	2.57	1.98	87.3	1,176.7	376.2	466.6	-28.5
2010	A	2.59	2.16	79.2	1,224.1	413.7	481.5	26.2
2009	A	2.52	2.13	81.3	1,192.5	392.6	474.0	26.8

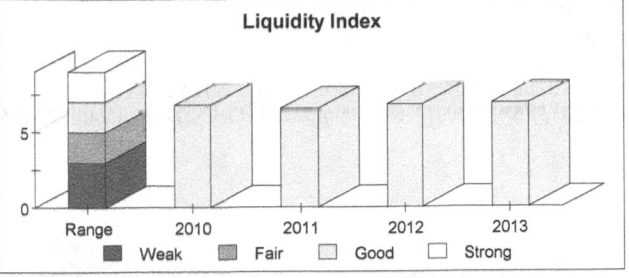

Capital

CIFG ASR NORTH AMERICA INC

E   Very Weak

Major Rating Factors: Weak profitability index (2.9 on a scale of 0 to 10) with operating losses during 2012. Return on equity has been fair, averaging 212.7% over the past five years. Weak overall results on stability tests (0.0) including negative cash flow from operations for 2013. The largest net exposure for one risk is excessive at 68.4% of capital.

Other Rating Factors: Fair reserve development (4.0) as the level of reserves has at times been insufficient to cover claims. In 2010 and 2009 the two year reserve development was 60% and 5004% deficient respectively. Strong long-term capitalization index (10.0) based on excellent current risk adjusted capital (severe and moderate loss scenarios), despite some fluctuation in capital levels. Excellent liquidity (8.1) with ample operational cash flow and liquid investments.

Principal Business: Financial guaranty (100%).

Principal Investments: Investment grade bonds (73%), misc. investments (18%), cash (6%), and non investment grade bonds (3%).

Investments in Affiliates: 8%

Group Affiliation: CIFG Holding Inc

Licensed in: All states except KS, OH

Commenced Business: April 2003

Address: 850 Third Ave, New York, NY 10022-7519

Phone: (212) 909-3939   **Domicile State:** NY   **NAIC Code:** 25771

Data Date	Rating	RACR #1	RACR #2	Loss Ratio %	Total Assets ($mil)	Capital ($mil)	Net Premium ($mil)	Net Income ($mil)
9-14	E	9.52	7.79	N/A	785.1	611.7	11.8	43.9
9-13	E	8.89	7.88	N/A	688.9	538.9	22.0	147.6
2013	E	9.81	8.52	N/A	685.9	552.4	19.4	157.9
2012	E	3.14	2.44	621.4	757.9	377.1	33.0	-212.2
2011	E	9.72	8.81	N/A	707.5	584.5	42.0	205.2
2010	E	5.21	4.32	N/A	620.7	394.2	31.1	166.9
2009	E-	8.83	6.20	N/A	218.6	248.8	-89.7	2,901.2

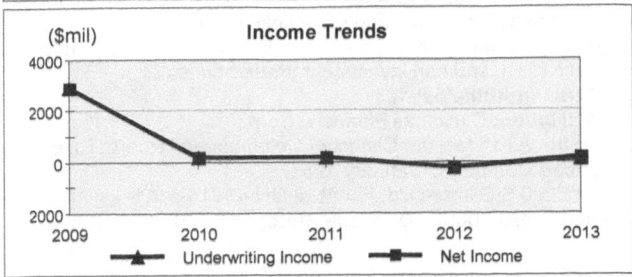

Income Trends

CINCINNATI CASUALTY CO

B **Good**

Major Rating Factors: Good overall results on stability tests (5.8 on a scale of 0 to 10). Stability strengths include good operational trends and excellent risk diversification. Strong long-term capitalization index (10.0) based on excellent current risk adjusted capital (severe and moderate loss scenarios). Moreover, capital levels have been consistent in recent years.

Other Rating Factors: Excellent profitability (8.1) with operating gains in each of the last five years. Superior liquidity (10.0) with ample operational cash flow and liquid investments.

Principal Business: (Not applicable due to unusual reinsurance transactions.)

Principal Investments: Investment grade bonds (70%), misc. investments (29%), and cash (1%).

Investments in Affiliates: None

Group Affiliation: Cincinnati Financial Corp

Licensed in: All states except PR

Commenced Business: March 1973

Address: 6200 S Gilmore Rd, Fairfield, OH 45014-5141

Phone: (513) 870-2000 **Domicile State:** OH **NAIC Code:** 28665

Data Date	Rating	RACR #1	RACR #2	Loss Ratio %	Total Assets ($mil)	Capital ($mil)	Net Premium ($mil)	Net Income ($mil)
9-14	B	10.74	6.20	N/A	362.0	326.0	0.0	8.6
9-13	B	11.10	6.41	N/A	363.6	309.7	0.0	7.4
2013	B	10.60	6.13	0.0	361.1	316.5	0.0	9.9
2012	B	12.67	7.29	0.0	329.3	292.6	0.0	9.8
2011	B	13.14	7.54	0.0	313.3	280.0	0.0	15.2
2010	B	12.65	7.38	0.0	293.2	268.5	0.0	9.9
2009	B	19.04	10.88	0.0	275.9	253.9	0.0	29.4

Cincinnati Financial Corp
Composite Group Rating: A
Largest Group Members

	Assets ($mil)	Rating
CINCINNATI INS CO	10560	A
CINCINNATI LIFE INS CO	3738	B
CINCINNATI SPECIALTY UNDERWRITER	453	B
CINCINNATI CASUALTY CO	361	B
CINCINNATI INDEMNITY CO	111	A-

CINCINNATI INDEMNITY CO *

A- **Excellent**

Major Rating Factors: Strong long-term capitalization index (10.0 on a scale of 0 to 10) based on excellent current risk adjusted capital (severe and moderate loss scenarios). Moreover, capital levels have been consistent in recent years. Excellent profitability (8.0) with operating gains in each of the last five years.

Other Rating Factors: Excellent liquidity (7.9) with ample operational cash flow and liquid investments. Good overall results on stability tests (5.5) despite weak results on operational trends. Strengths include potential support from affiliation with Cincinnati Financial Corp.

Principal Business: Workers compensation (33%), commercial multiple peril (23%), other liability (14%), auto liability (14%), auto physical damage (5%), allied lines (3%), and other lines (7%).

Principal Investments: Investment grade bonds (67%), misc. investments (27%), cash (4%), and non investment grade bonds (2%).

Investments in Affiliates: None

Group Affiliation: Cincinnati Financial Corp

Licensed in: All states except PR

Commenced Business: January 1989

Address: 6200 S Gilmore Rd, Fairfield, OH 45014-5141

Phone: (513) 870-2000 **Domicile State:** OH **NAIC Code:** 23280

Data Date	Rating	RACR #1	RACR #2	Loss Ratio %	Total Assets ($mil)	Capital ($mil)	Net Premium ($mil)	Net Income ($mil)
9-14	A-	9.99	5.69	N/A	115.5	84.6	0.0	2.3
9-13	A-	9.60	5.43	N/A	126.5	80.4	0.0	1.8
2013	A-	9.53	5.44	0.0	110.7	82.0	0.0	2.4
2012	A-	10.66	6.00	0.0	101.4	76.2	0.0	2.4
2011	A-	10.76	6.13	0.0	93.4	73.0	0.0	2.1
2010	A-	12.07	6.77	0.0	76.9	70.1	0.0	2.5
2009	A-	38.12	19.12	0.0	73.1	67.0	0.0	7.9

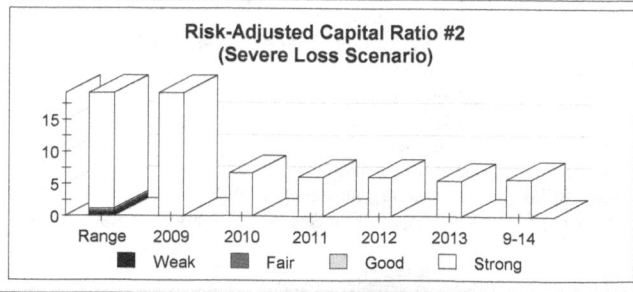

Risk-Adjusted Capital Ratio #2
(Severe Loss Scenario)

■ Weak ■ Fair ▨ Good □ Strong

CINCINNATI INS CO *

A **Excellent**

Major Rating Factors: Excellent overall results on stability tests (7.6 on a scale of 0 to 10). Stability strengths include excellent operational trends and excellent risk diversification. Strong long-term capitalization index (8.1) based on excellent current risk adjusted capital (severe and moderate loss scenarios). Furthermore, this high level of risk adjusted capital has been consistently maintained in previous years.

Other Rating Factors: Ample reserve history (9.3) that helps to protect the company against sharp claims increases. Excellent profitability (7.4) with operating gains in each of the last five years. Good liquidity (6.5) with sufficient resources (cash flows and marketable investments) to handle a spike in claims.

Principal Business: Commercial multiple peril (28%), auto liability (18%), other liability (16%), homeowners multiple peril (14%), auto physical damage (10%), workers compensation (3%), and other lines (12%).

Principal Investments: Investment grade bonds (53%), misc. investments (43%), cash (2%), and non investment grade bonds (2%).

Investments in Affiliates: 10%

Group Affiliation: Cincinnati Financial Corp

Licensed in: All states, the District of Columbia and Puerto Rico

Commenced Business: January 1951

Address: 6200 S Gilmore Rd, Fairfield, OH 45014-5141

Phone: (513) 870-2000 **Domicile State:** OH **NAIC Code:** 10677

Data Date	Rating	RACR #1	RACR #2	Loss Ratio %	Total Assets ($mil)	Capital ($mil)	Net Premium ($mil)	Net Income ($mil)
9-14	A	2.35	1.71	N/A	10,791.2	4,363.9	2,903.7	281.0
9-13	A	2.49	1.83	N/A	10,240.7	4,172.5	2,672.2	315.0
2013	A	2.41	1.76	62.1	10,559.8	4,325.7	3,769.2	417.7
2012	A	2.50	1.86	63.7	9,767.3	3,913.6	3,380.3	334.7
2011	A	2.50	1.86	77.4	9,501.8	3,746.8	3,021.6	120.2
2010	A-	2.54	1.86	68.6	9,343.0	3,777.2	2,907.4	318.0
2009	A-	2.57	1.90	71.6	9,144.9	3,647.8	2,874.2	338.9

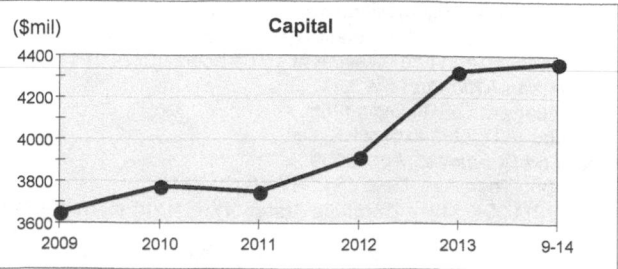

Capital

CINCINNATI SPECIALTY UNDERWRITER   B   Good

Major Rating Factors: History of adequate reserve strength (6.5 on a scale of 0 to 10) as reserves have been consistently at an acceptable level. Good overall profitability index (6.3) despite operating losses during 2009. Return on equity has been low, averaging 3.8% over the past five years.

Other Rating Factors: Good liquidity (6.8) with sufficient resources (cash flows and marketable investments) to handle a spike in claims. Good overall results on stability tests (5.5) despite excessive premium growth. Stability strengths include good operational trends and excellent risk diversification. Strong long-term capitalization index (7.6) based on excellent current risk adjusted capital (severe and moderate loss scenarios). Moreover, capital levels have been consistent in recent years.

Principal Business: Other liability (59%), products liability (25%), fire (9%), allied lines (6%), and medical malpractice (1%).

Principal Investments: Investment grade bonds (68%), misc. investments (27%), cash (4%), and non investment grade bonds (1%).

Investments in Affiliates: None

Group Affiliation: Cincinnati Financial Corp

Licensed in: All states except RI, PR

Commenced Business: November 2007

Address: 1807 N Market St, Wilmington, DE 19802-4810

Phone: (513) 870-2000   **Domicile State:** DE   **NAIC Code:** 13037

Data Date	Rating	RACR #1	RACR #2	Loss Ratio %	Total Assets ($mil)	Capital ($mil)	Net Premium ($mil)	Net Income ($mil)
9-14	B	2.71	1.37	N/A	531.6	253.2	109.3	22.7
9-13	B-	2.94	1.46	N/A	433.1	215.7	84.5	8.7
2013	B	2.96	1.50	56.7	453.5	228.4	127.7	18.2
2012	B-	3.33	1.65	69.3	377.7	199.1	105.0	5.7
2011	B-	4.45	2.24	60.4	308.9	186.0	79.4	11.1
2010	C+	5.22	2.65	83.7	263.4	171.7	58.0	0.7
2009	C	6.24	3.45	74.7	216.2	167.9	39.6	-6.7

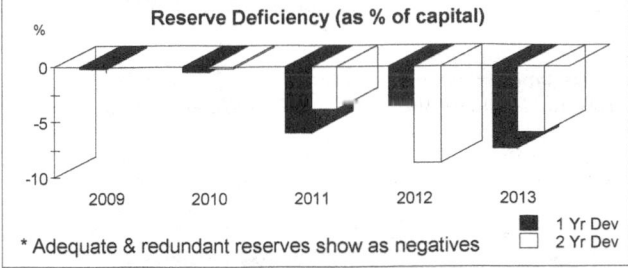

Reserve Deficiency (as % of capital)

* Adequate & redundant reserves show as negatives

■ 1 Yr Dev   □ 2 Yr Dev

CITIZENS INS CO OF AMERICA   B   Good

Major Rating Factors: Good overall results on stability tests (5.2 on a scale of 0 to 10) despite potential drain of affiliation with Hanover Ins Group Inc. The largest net exposure for one risk is conservative at 1.1% of capital. Good liquidity (6.1) with sufficient resources (cash flows and marketable investments) to handle a spike in claims.

Other Rating Factors: Fair profitability index (4.2). Fair expense controls. Return on equity has been fair, averaging 7.8% over the past five years. Strong long-term capitalization index (10.0) based on excellent current risk adjusted capital (severe and moderate loss scenarios), despite some fluctuation in capital levels. Ample reserve history (8.2) that helps to protect the company against sharp claims increases.

Principal Business: Homeowners multiple peril (34%), commercial multiple peril (26%), auto liability (18%), auto physical damage (12%), workers compensation (5%), other liability (2%), and other lines (3%).

Principal Investments: Investment grade bonds (80%), misc. investments (12%), non investment grade bonds (9%), and real estate (1%).

Investments in Affiliates: None

Group Affiliation: Hanover Ins Group Inc

Licensed in: All states except FL, KY, LA, OR, WY, PR

Commenced Business: August 1974

Address: 645 W Grand River, Howell, MI 48843

Phone: (517) 546-2160   **Domicile State:** MI   **NAIC Code:** 31534

Data Date	Rating	RACR #1	RACR #2	Loss Ratio %	Total Assets ($mil)	Capital ($mil)	Net Premium ($mil)	Net Income ($mil)
9-14	B	4.50	3.02	N/A	1,480.7	677.0	499.4	11.4
9-13	B	4.53	3.10	N/A	1,532.6	698.3	523.7	45.6
2013	B	4.35	3.04	67.1	1,476.6	662.2	679.8	67.9
2012	B	4.49	3.19	74.0	1,525.1	682.6	716.9	55.8
2011	B	4.95	3.49	68.7	1,515.7	701.7	687.3	60.0
2010	B	5.15	3.62	71.2	1,517.9	698.1	679.8	46.2
2009	B	5.39	3.87	66.4	1,535.2	703.1	680.5	67.4

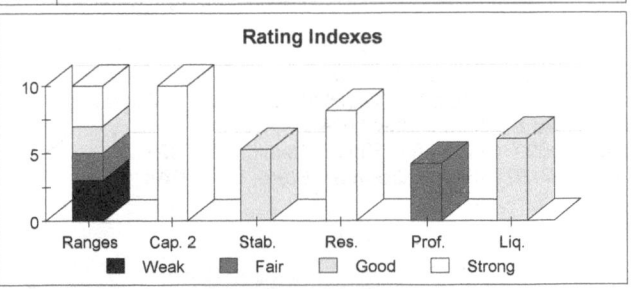

Rating Indexes

Ranges   Cap. 2   Stab.   Res.   Prof.   Liq.

■ Weak   ■ Fair   □ Good   □ Strong

CITIZENS PROPERTY INS CORP *   A+   Excellent

Major Rating Factors: Strong long-term capitalization index (10.0 on a scale of 0 to 10) based on excellent current risk adjusted capital (severe and moderate loss scenarios). Furthermore, this high level of risk adjusted capital has been consistently maintained in previous years. Excellent profitability (8.9) with operating gains in each of the last five years. Return on equity has been good over the last five years, averaging 11.7%.

Other Rating Factors: Excellent liquidity (8.4) with ample operational cash flow and liquid investments. Excellent overall results on stability tests (8.5). Stability strengths include excellent operational trends and excellent risk diversification. History of adequate reserve strength (5.9) as reserves have been consistently at an acceptable level.

Principal Business: Allied lines (49%), homeowners multiple peril (46%), and fire (5%).

Principal Investments: Investment grade bonds (100%) and non investment grade bonds (1%).

Investments in Affiliates: None

Group Affiliation: None

Licensed in: FL

Commenced Business: January 1993

Address: 2312 Killearn Ctr Blvd Bldg A, Tallahassee, FL 32309

Phone: (850) 513-3700   **Domicile State:** FL   **NAIC Code:** 10064

Data Date	Rating	RACR #1	RACR #2	Loss Ratio %	Total Assets ($mil)	Capital ($mil)	Net Premium ($mil)	Net Income ($mil)
9-14	A+	15.86	10.02	N/A	14,582.0	7,434.7	1,144.1	415.2
9-13	A+	8.83	5.84	N/A	15,191.1	6,808.6	1,473.0	492.0
2013	A+	13.10	8.46	39.9	14,766.6	7,008.2	1,702.1	665.3
2012	A+	7.50	5.03	47.8	15,443.2	6,295.2	2,109.5	664.8
2011	A+	6.14	4.20	60.2	13,414.2	5,588.1	2,473.1	448.7
2010	U	7.30	4.97	38.7	12,156.1	5,101.5	2,214.4	744.7
2009	U	4.33	3.14	34.0	8,788.9	3,993.0	1,571.3	763.8

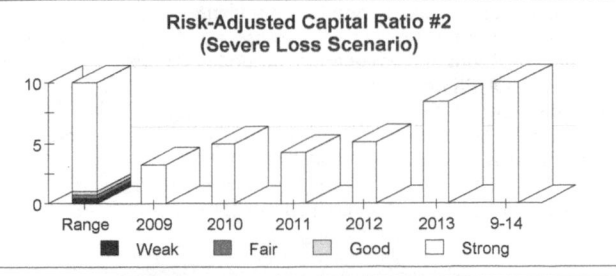

Risk-Adjusted Capital Ratio #2
(Severe Loss Scenario)

Range   2009   2010   2011   2012   2013   9-14

■ Weak   ■ Fair   □ Good   □ Strong

CLARENDON NATIONAL INS CO   C   Fair

Major Rating Factors: Fair overall results on stability tests (3.4 on a scale of 0 to 10) including weak results on operational trends, negative cash flow from operations for 2013 and fair risk adjusted capital in prior years. Poor long-term capitalization index (2.5) based on weak current risk adjusted capital (moderate loss scenario), although results have slipped from the fair range during the last year.

Other Rating Factors: Weak profitability index (2.4) with operating losses during 2009, 2010, 2011 and 2012. Average return on equity over the last five years has been poor at -5.9%. Ample reserve history (7.0) that can protect against increases in claims costs. Superior liquidity (10.0) with ample operational cash flow and liquid investments.

Principal Business: (Not applicable due to unusual reinsurance transactions.)

Principal Investments: Investment grade bonds (70%) and misc. investments (30%).

Investments in Affiliates: 27%

Group Affiliation: Enstar Group Ltd

Licensed in: All states, the District of Columbia and Puerto Rico

Commenced Business: November 1941

Address: 198 Princeton Highstown Rd 14A, Princeton Junction, NJ 08550

Phone: (212) 790-9700   **Domicile State:** IL   **NAIC Code:** 20532

Data Date	Rating	RACR #1	RACR #2	Loss Ratio %	Total Assets ($mil)	Capital ($mil)	Net Premium ($mil)	Net Income ($mil)
9-14	C	0.58	0.37	N/A	607.4	176.0	11.3	7.1
9-13	C-	0.74	0.47	N/A	628.3	226.9	-14.1	-27.1
2013	C	0.99	0.64	195.9	643.2	290.9	-12.8	11.6
2012	C-	0.90	0.57	308.3	656.0	260.3	-2.8	-7.1
2011	C-	0.73	0.46	N/A	682.1	247.9	0.5	-1.9
2010	C-	0.78	0.49	N/A	741.1	269.7	-2.7	-28.3
2009	C-	1.10	0.74	N/A	656.6	280.6	-1.6	-78.1

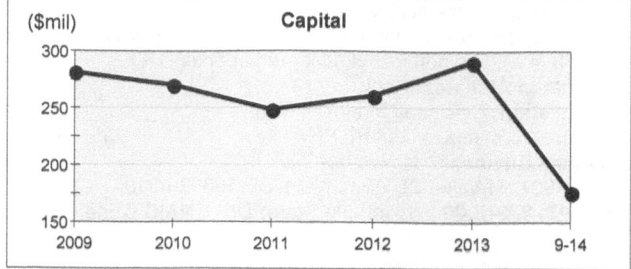

Capital ($mil)

CLEARWATER INS CO   D   Weak

Major Rating Factors: A history of deficient reserves (1.1 on a scale of 0 to 10) that places pressure on both capital and profits. In four of the last five years reserves (two year development) were between 16% and 66% deficient. Weak overall results on stability tests (1.9) including weak results on operational trends and negative cash flow from operations for 2013.

Other Rating Factors: Fair profitability index (3.0) with operating losses during 2012 and 2013. Average return on equity over the last five years has been poor at -4.2%. Good long-term capitalization index (6.2) based on good current risk adjusted capital (moderate loss scenario). Excellent liquidity (7.0) with ample operational cash flow and liquid investments.

Principal Business: (This company is a reinsurer.)

Principal Investments: Misc. investments (52%), investment grade bonds (41%), and cash (7%).

Investments in Affiliates: 10%

Group Affiliation: Fairfax Financial

Licensed in: All states, the District of Columbia and Puerto Rico

Commenced Business: July 1974

Address: 300 First Stamford Place, Stamford, CT 06902

Phone: (203) 977-8000   **Domicile State:** DE   **NAIC Code:** 25070

Data Date	Rating	RACR #1	RACR #2	Loss Ratio %	Total Assets ($mil)	Capital ($mil)	Net Premium ($mil)	Net Income ($mil)
9-14	D	1.34	0.97	N/A	1,197.0	410.7	0.1	9.3
9-13	D	1.05	0.68	N/A	1,133.5	360.0	0.1	-12.8
2013	D	1.22	0.89	N/A	1,304.1	380.1	0.1	-42.9
2012	D	0.93	0.60	N/A	1,200.7	348.9	0.2	-105.1
2011	D	1.09	0.67	N/A	1,239.7	381.4	-1.4	36.0
2010	D	0.39	0.31	N/A	1,318.5	287.0	-0.3	14.8
2009	D+	0.96	0.69	N/A	1,306.6	696.2	1.0	4.1

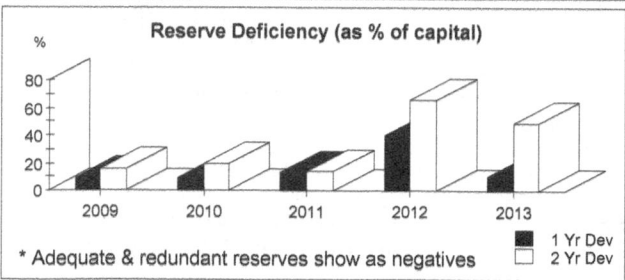

Reserve Deficiency (as % of capital)

* Adequate & redundant reserves show as negatives

CLEARWATER SELECT INS CO   D   Weak

Major Rating Factors: Poor long-term capitalization index (0.0 on a scale of 0 to 10) based on weak current risk adjusted capital (severe and moderate loss scenarios), although results have slipped from the excellent range over the last two years. A history of deficient reserves (0.9) that places pressure on both capital and profits. In 2013, the one year reserve development was 478% deficient.

Other Rating Factors: Vulnerable liquidity (0.0) as a spike in claims may stretch capacity. Weak overall results on stability tests (1.7) including weak risk adjusted capital in prior years and weak results on operational trends. The largest net exposure for one risk is excessive at 10.1% of capital. Strengths include potential support from affiliation with Fairfax Financial. Excellent profitability (8.1) with operating gains in each of the last five years. Excellent expense controls.

Principal Business: (This company is a reinsurer.)

Principal Investments: Investment grade bonds (87%), misc. investments (11%), cash (1%), and non investment grade bonds (1%).

Investments in Affiliates: 2%

Group Affiliation: Fairfax Financial

Licensed in: All states except CA, FL

Commenced Business: March 1994

Address: 300 First Stamford Place, Stamford, CT 06902

Phone: (203) 977-8000   **Domicile State:** CT   **NAIC Code:** 10019

Data Date	Rating	RACR #1	RACR #2	Loss Ratio %	Total Assets ($mil)	Capital ($mil)	Net Premium ($mil)	Net Income ($mil)
9-14	D	0.20	0.15	N/A	1,167.6	408.6	172.5	22.3
9-13	U	1.56	1.04	N/A	1,131.6	368.4	692.5	-6.2
2013	D	0.11	0.09	93.1	1,111.8	372.6	808.4	2.0
2012	U	43.36	27.71	N/A	118.6	111.3	0.0	6.0
2011	U	40.76	26.39	N/A	113.2	105.4	0.0	4.0
2010	U	35.99	23.09	N/A	108.0	99.4	0.0	3.6
2009	D-	21.93	10.08	123.4	105.2	96.0	2.7	5.0

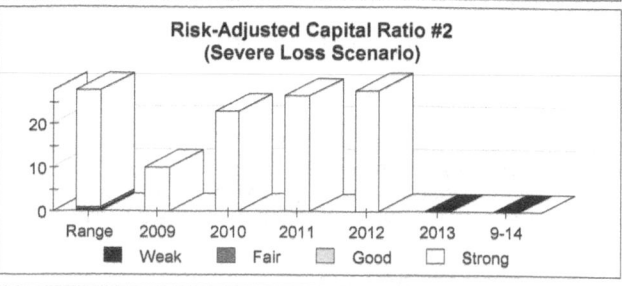

Risk-Adjusted Capital Ratio #2 (Severe Loss Scenario)

■ Weak   ■ Fair   ▨ Good   □ Strong

COAST NATIONAL INS CO   D+   Weak

Major Rating Factors: Weak overall results on stability tests (2.6 on a scale of 0 to 10) including potential drain of affiliation with Farmers Insurance Group of Companies. History of adequate reserve strength (6.0) as reserves have been consistently at an acceptable level.

Other Rating Factors: Good overall profitability index (6.8). Excellent expense controls. Return on equity has been low, averaging 1.9% over the past five years. Strong long-term capitalization index (10.0) based on excellent current risk adjusted capital (severe and moderate loss scenarios), despite some fluctuation in capital levels. Superior liquidity (10.0) with ample operational cash flow and liquid investments.

Principal Business: Auto liability (63%) and auto physical damage (37%).

Principal Investments: Investment grade bonds (84%) and misc. investments (16%).

Investments in Affiliates: 12%

Group Affiliation: Farmers Insurance Group of Companies

Licensed in: AZ, CA, FL, GA, MS, NV, OR, PA, TN, WA

Commenced Business: March 1987

Address: 333 S Anita Dr Suite 150, Orange, CA 92868

Phone: (954) 316-5200   **Domicile State:** CA   **NAIC Code:** 25089

Data Date	Rating	RACR #1	RACR #2	Loss Ratio %	Total Assets ($mil)	Capital ($mil)	Net Premium ($mil)	Net Income ($mil)
9-14	D+	7.88	7.20	N/A	613.8	410.5	0.0	4.9
9-13	D+	7.56	6.78	N/A	593.6	403.0	0.0	5.8
2013	D+	7.94	7.38	N/A	587.0	403.1	0.0	7.1
2012	D+	7.47	6.72	0.0	621.8	395.7	0.0	5.7
2011	D+	7.40	6.87	0.0	689.0	387.2	0.0	9.0
2010	D+	7.35	6.66	0.0	692.1	376.4	0.0	3.9
2009	D+	7.57	6.97	0.0	587.9	367.0	0.0	11.5

Farmers Insurance Group of Companies Composite Group Rating: C Largest Group Members	Assets ($mil)	Rating
FARMERS INS EXCHANGE	15557	C
MID-CENTURY INS CO	3715	C
FIRE INS EXCHANGE	2255	C+
FOREMOST INS CO	1939	B
TRUCK INS EXCHANGE	1933	C+

COLISEUM REINS CO   C   Fair

Major Rating Factors: Fair overall results on stability tests (3.2 on a scale of 0 to 10) including weak results on operational trends. The largest net exposure for one risk is high at 4.9% of capital. Weak profitability index (1.9). Excellent expense controls. Return on equity has been fair, averaging 8.5% over the past five years.

Other Rating Factors: History of adequate reserve strength (6.2) as reserves have been consistently at an acceptable level. Strong long-term capitalization index (10.0) based on excellent current risk adjusted capital (severe and moderate loss scenarios), despite some fluctuation in capital levels. Excellent liquidity (8.8) with ample operational cash flow and liquid investments.

Principal Business: (Not applicable due to unusual reinsurance transactions.)

Principal Investments: Misc. investments (62%), investment grade bonds (28%), and cash (10%).

Investments in Affiliates: 8%

Group Affiliation: AXA Ins Group

Licensed in: All states except PR

Commenced Business: December 1978

Address: 1209 Orange St, Wilmington, DE 19801

Phone: (212) 493-9300   **Domicile State:** DE   **NAIC Code:** 36552

Data Date	Rating	RACR #1	RACR #2	Loss Ratio %	Total Assets ($mil)	Capital ($mil)	Net Premium ($mil)	Net Income ($mil)
9-14	C	4.78	3.33	N/A	323.3	203.5	0.0	18.6
9-13	C	8.38	10.12	N/A	546.8	430.7	0.2	16.3
2013	C	4.68	3.24	19.5	320.7	203.0	0.1	30.6
2012	C	5.58	6.31	51.7	506.2	364.9	1.2	25.5
2011	C	11.71	6.49	N/A	585.1	437.5	3.1	26.9
2010	C	12.26	6.88	N/A	603.0	443.2	2.4	31.9
2009	C	3.48	2.61	N/A	775.8	601.6	0.0	26.5

AXA Ins Group Composite Group Rating: B Largest Group Members	Assets ($mil)	Rating
AXA EQUITABLE LIFE INS CO	158658	B
MONY LIFE INS CO OF AMERICA	2794	B-
AXA CORPORATE SOLUTIONS LIFE REINS	978	B-
US FINANCIAL LIFE INS CO	638	B
AXA EQUITABLE LIFE ANNUITY CO	465	B-

COLONY INS CO   C   Fair

Major Rating Factors: Fair overall results on stability tests (3.3 on a scale of 0 to 10) including potential drain of affiliation with Argo Group Intl Holdings Ltd and excessive premium growth. Fair profitability index (4.2). Weak expense controls. Return on equity has been fair, averaging 20.9% over the past five years.

Other Rating Factors: Strong long-term capitalization index (7.7) based on excellent current risk adjusted capital (severe and moderate loss scenarios), despite some fluctuation in capital levels. Ample reserve history (9.4) that helps to protect the company against sharp claims increases. Excellent liquidity (7.6) with ample operational cash flow and liquid investments.

Principal Business: Other liability (51%), products liability (15%), commercial multiple peril (12%), allied lines (10%), auto liability (4%), earthquake (4%), and other lines (5%).

Principal Investments: Investment grade bonds (61%), misc. investments (31%), and non investment grade bonds (8%).

Investments in Affiliates: 6%

Group Affiliation: Argo Group Intl Holdings Ltd

Licensed in: All states except PR

Commenced Business: July 1981

Address: 9201 Forest Hill Ave, Ste 200, Richmond, VA 23235-6865

Phone: (804) 560-2000   **Domicile State:** VA   **NAIC Code:** 39993

Data Date	Rating	RACR #1	RACR #2	Loss Ratio %	Total Assets ($mil)	Capital ($mil)	Net Premium ($mil)	Net Income ($mil)
9-14	C	2.10	1.48	N/A	1,367.1	369.0	158.7	38.0
9-13	C	2.08	1.44	N/A	1,354.8	377.2	123.6	33.6
2013	C	1.97	1.40	42.5	1,316.3	330.0	199.8	46.0
2012	C	1.87	1.31	46.1	1,277.1	328.0	175.7	39.6
2011	C	1.90	1.36	45.1	1,313.2	334.6	146.8	168.0
2010	C	1.71	1.35	52.6	1,426.5	378.6	146.4	59.0
2009	C	1.53	1.16	59.5	1,452.9	368.3	314.9	67.1

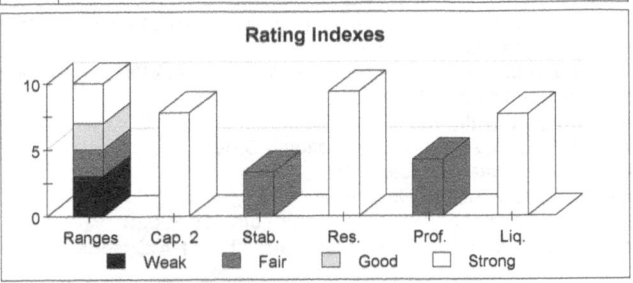

Rating Indexes

Ranges | Cap. 2 | Stab. | Res. | Prof. | Liq.

■ Weak   ▨ Fair   ▥ Good   □ Strong

COLUMBIA CASUALTY CO — C — Fair

Major Rating Factors: Fair overall results on stability tests (3.5 on a scale of 0 to 10) including fair financial strength of affiliated CNA Financial Corp.

Other Rating Factors: Good overall profitability index (5.4). Fair expense controls. Return on equity has been low, averaging 2.8% over the past five years. Strong long-term capitalization index (10.0) based on excellent current risk adjusted capital (severe and moderate loss scenarios), despite some fluctuation in capital levels. Superior liquidity (9.6) with ample operational cash flow and liquid investments.

Principal Business: Other liability (62%), medical malpractice (19%), products liability (13%), fire (3%), and allied lines (2%).

Principal Investments: Investment grade bonds (98%) and cash (2%).

Investments in Affiliates: None

Group Affiliation: CNA Financial Corp

Licensed in: All states, the District of Columbia and Puerto Rico

Commenced Business: March 1974

Address: CNA Center, Chicago, IL 60685

Phone: (312) 822-5000   **Domicile State:** IL   **NAIC Code:** 31127

Data Date	Rating	RACR #1	RACR #2	Loss Ratio %	Total Assets ($mil)	Capital ($mil)	Net Premium ($mil)	Net Income ($mil)
9-14	C	68.54	28.59	N/A	240.2	239.9	0.0	5.2
9-13	C	66.93	27.80	N/A	239.8	239.5	0.0	5.1
2013	C	67.97	28.36	0.0	235.2	234.9	0.0	6.8
2012	C	65.96	27.41	0.0	234.7	234.3	0.0	7.6
2011	C	68.66	28.71	0.0	235.1	234.9	0.0	7.4
2010	C	66.85	27.81	0.0	238.2	237.5	0.0	7.7
2009	C	96.19	41.43	0.0	250.2	249.5	0.0	3.4

CNA Financial Corp Composite Group Rating: C+ Largest Group Members	Assets ($mil)	Rating
CONTINENTAL CASUALTY CO	42642	C+
CONTINENTAL INS CO	2346	C
WESTERN SURETY CO	1856	C
COLUMBIA CASUALTY CO	235	C
AMERICAN CASUALTY CO OF READING	141	C

COLUMBIA INS CO — B- — Good

Major Rating Factors: Fair overall results on stability tests (4.9 on a scale of 0 to 10) including potential drain of affiliation with Berkshire-Hathaway. The largest net exposure for one risk is excessive at 5.2% of capital. Strong long-term capitalization index (7.6) based on excellent current risk adjusted capital (severe and moderate loss scenarios), despite some fluctuation in capital levels.

Other Rating Factors: Ample reserve history (7.6) that can protect against increases in claims costs. Excellent profitability (8.2) with operating gains in each of the last five years. Excellent liquidity (8.2) with ample operational cash flow and liquid investments.

Principal Business: Auto liability (51%), surety (33%), auto physical damage (13%), inland marine (1%), and aircraft (1%).

Principal Investments: Misc. investments (96%), investment grade bonds (3%), and cash (1%).

Investments in Affiliates: 22%

Group Affiliation: Berkshire-Hathaway

Licensed in: All states except GA, KS, MD, MI, NY, PR

Commenced Business: January 1970

Address: 3024 Harney St, Omaha, NE 68131-3580

Phone: (402) 916-3000   **Domicile State:** NE   **NAIC Code:** 27812

Data Date	Rating	RACR #1	RACR #2	Loss Ratio %	Total Assets ($mil)	Capital ($mil)	Net Premium ($mil)	Net Income ($mil)
9-14	B-	1.99	1.49	N/A	19,280.1	14,397.3	-481.1	534.7
9-13	C+	1.86	1.38	N/A	17,095.6	12,045.9	396.5	514.5
2013	B-	1.83	1.37	37.1	19,012.9	13,454.1	546.8	858.9
2012	C+	1.69	1.26	60.4	15,069.8	10,432.5	611.0	421.2
2011	C+	1.58	1.15	85.4	12,861.8	8,646.5	414.9	298.4
2010	C+	1.71	1.22	38.8	12,952.0	8,861.7	388.3	54.0
2009	C+	1.58	1.12	45.4	12,197.6	8,350.6	416.8	565.4

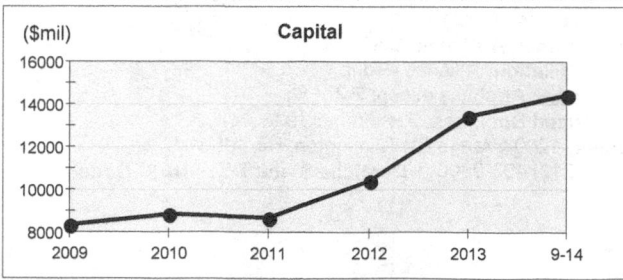

Capital ($mil)

COMMERCE & INDUSTRY INS CO — C — Fair

Major Rating Factors: Fair reserve development (3.1 on a scale of 0 to 10) as the level of reserves has at times been insufficient to cover claims. In 2011 and 2010 the two year reserve development was 21% and 30% deficient respectively. Fair profitability index (3.9) with operating losses during 2009 and 2010. Return on equity has been low, averaging 4.6% over the past five years.

Other Rating Factors: Fair overall results on stability tests (4.0). The largest net exposure for one risk is excessive at 7.4% of capital. Good liquidity (6.7) with sufficient resources (cash flows and marketable investments) to handle a spike in claims. Strong long-term capitalization index (7.8) based on excellent current risk adjusted capital (severe and moderate loss scenarios), despite some fluctuation in capital levels.

Principal Business: Workers compensation (54%), other liability (24%), aircraft (11%), auto liability (8%), homeowners multiple peril (1%), products liability (1%), and auto physical damage (1%).

Principal Investments: Investment grade bonds (121%), non investment grade bonds (1%), and cash (1%).

Investments in Affiliates: 1%

Group Affiliation: American International Group

Licensed in: All states except PR

Commenced Business: December 1957

Address: 175 Water St 18th Floor, New York, NY 10038

Phone: (212) 770-7000   **Domicile State:** NY   **NAIC Code:** 19410

Data Date	Rating	RACR #1	RACR #2	Loss Ratio %	Total Assets ($mil)	Capital ($mil)	Net Premium ($mil)	Net Income ($mil)
9-14	C	2.32	1.55	N/A	4,847.9	1,570.2	694.2	244.7
9-13	C	2.02	1.38	N/A	7,079.0	1,841.9	1,061.6	236.9
2013	C	2.05	1.37	73.0	7,339.2	1,905.6	1,569.7	309.1
2012	C	2.28	1.56	85.3	7,249.9	2,041.5	1,353.6	131.7
2011	C-	2.03	1.38	85.2	7,203.9	1,844.1	1,378.8	140.9
2010	C-	1.84	1.08	113.4	8,311.5	1,887.0	1,363.0	-347.5
2009	C+	2.67	1.58	90.3	8,391.4	2,750.5	1,662.6	-23.9

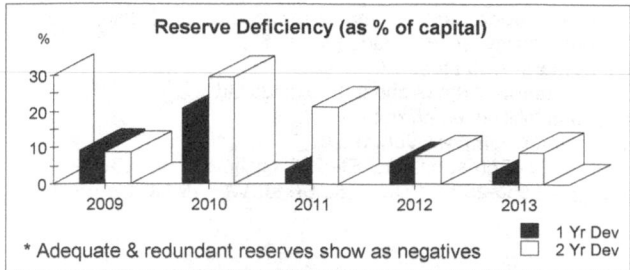

Reserve Deficiency (as % of capital)

* Adequate & redundant reserves show as negatives

■ 1 Yr Dev   □ 2 Yr Dev

COMMERCE INS CO   B-   Good

Major Rating Factors: Fair profitability index (3.4 on a scale of 0 to 10). Good expense controls. Return on equity has been fair, averaging 8.8% over the past five years. Fair overall results on stability tests (4.8).

Other Rating Factors: History of adequate reserve strength (5.7) as reserves have been consistently at an acceptable level. Good liquidity (5.4) with sufficient resources (cash flows and marketable investments) to handle a spike in claims. Strong long-term capitalization index (8.8) based on excellent current risk adjusted capital (severe and moderate loss scenarios), despite some fluctuation in capital levels.

Principal Business: Auto liability (53%), auto physical damage (37%), homeowners multiple peril (7%), commercial multiple peril (2%), and fire (1%).

Principal Investments: Investment grade bonds (78%), misc. investments (16%), non investment grade bonds (4%), and real estate (3%).

Investments in Affiliates: 4%

Group Affiliation: MAPFRE Ins Group

Licensed in: CA, CT, FL, ME, MA, NH, NY, OH, OR, RI, TX, VT

Commenced Business: May 1972

Address: 211 W Main St, Webster, MA 01570-0758

Phone: (508) 943-9000   **Domicile State:** MA   **NAIC Code:** 34754

Data Date	Rating	RACR #1	RACR #2	Loss Ratio %	Total Assets ($mil)	Capital ($mil)	Net Premium ($mil)	Net Income ($mil)
9-14	B-	2.76	2.11	N/A	2,349.1	803.8	999.6	35.2
9-13	B+	3.24	2.49	N/A	2,366.2	816.4	958.6	54.8
2013	B-	3.04	2.42	73.5	2,272.1	834.8	1,320.3	88.0
2012	B+	3.74	2.94	75.0	2,372.6	987.8	1,209.8	106.1
2011	B+	3.33	2.62	81.2	2,672.5	987.7	1,391.4	44.8
2010	B+	3.14	2.69	74.5	2,645.6	1,074.7	1,332.7	109.5
2009	B+	3.15	2.70	71.4	2,553.2	1,049.8	1,258.6	108.7

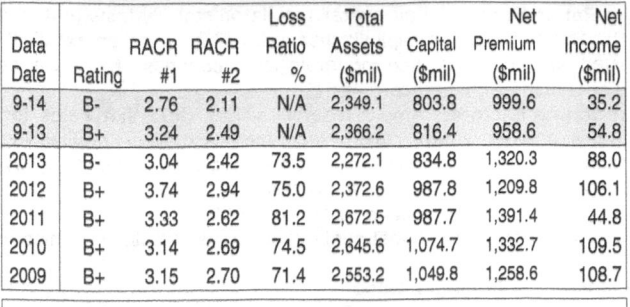

Income Trends

COMPANION PROPERTY & CASUALTY INS CO   C+   Fair

Major Rating Factors: Fair overall results on stability tests (4.5 on a scale of 0 to 10) including negative cash flow from operations for 2013. Strengths include potentially strong support from affiliation with Blue Cross Blue Shield of S Carolina. Fair reserve development (4.9) as reserves have generally been sufficient to cover claims. In 2013, the one year reserve development was 15% deficient.

Other Rating Factors: Good long-term capitalization index (5.3) based on good current risk adjusted capital (moderate loss scenario), despite some fluctuation in capital levels. Weak profitability index (2.7) with operating losses during 2011, 2012 and the first nine months of 2014. Average return on equity over the last five years has been poor at -11.0%. Excellent liquidity (7.1) with ample operational cash flow and liquid investments.

Principal Business: Workers compensation (66%), auto liability (8%), homeowners multiple peril (8%), auto physical damage (6%), commercial multiple peril (5%), other liability (2%), and other lines (5%).

Principal Investments: Investment grade bonds (63%), misc. investments (21%), cash (15%), and non investment grade bonds (1%).

Investments in Affiliates: 11%

Group Affiliation: Blue Cross Blue Shield of S Carolina

Licensed in: All states except NY, PR

Commenced Business: July 1984

Address: 51 Clemson Road, Columbia, SC 29223

Phone: (803) 735-0672   **Domicile State:** SC   **NAIC Code:** 12157

Data Date	Rating	RACR #1	RACR #2	Loss Ratio %	Total Assets ($mil)	Capital ($mil)	Net Premium ($mil)	Net Income ($mil)
9-14	C+	1.09	0.69	N/A	1,119.6	242.4	194.1	-86.5
9-13	B	1.21	0.90	N/A	980.4	222.1	212.2	-15.1
2013	B	1.50	1.07	94.3	998.6	250.8	214.4	-29.7
2012	B	1.12	0.82	86.3	863.3	241.9	347.2	-29.6
2011	B+	1.55	1.17	83.7	618.5	196.9	215.8	-20.3
2010	B+	2.52	2.09	54.2	564.7	216.5	132.8	8.9
2009	B	3.06	2.21	54.7	530.2	199.7	137.4	5.0

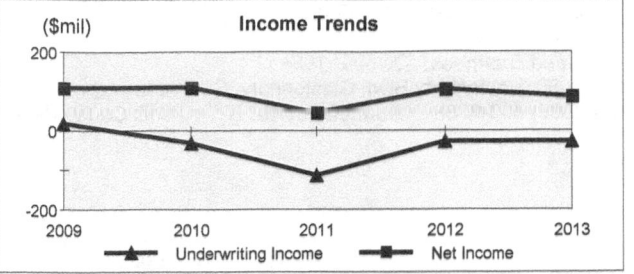

Rating Indexes

CONCORD GENERAL MUTUAL INS CO   B-   Good

Major Rating Factors: Fair overall results on stability tests (4.6 on a scale of 0 to 10) including potential drain of affiliation with Concord Group. Good overall profitability index (5.2) despite operating losses during 2011.

Other Rating Factors: Good liquidity (6.6) with sufficient resources (cash flows and marketable investments) to handle a spike in claims. Strong long-term capitalization index (8.0) based on excellent current risk adjusted capital (severe and moderate loss scenarios), despite some fluctuation in capital levels. Ample reserve history (9.1) that helps to protect the company against sharp claims increases.

Principal Business: Homeowners multiple peril (35%), auto liability (31%), auto physical damage (25%), other liability (4%), commercial multiple peril (3%), and inland marine (1%).

Principal Investments: Misc. investments (54%), investment grade bonds (43%), cash (2%), and real estate (1%).

Investments in Affiliates: 6%

Group Affiliation: Concord Group

Licensed in: ME, NH, SC, VT

Commenced Business: June 1928

Address: 4 Bouton St, Concord, NH 03301

Phone: (603) 224-4086   **Domicile State:** NH   **NAIC Code:** 20672

Data Date	Rating	RACR #1	RACR #2	Loss Ratio %	Total Assets ($mil)	Capital ($mil)	Net Premium ($mil)	Net Income ($mil)
9-14	B-	2.57	1.69	N/A	439.9	216.6	124.2	1.0
9-13	B-	2.65	1.71	N/A	409.2	197.3	117.9	2.5
2013	B-	2.60	1.72	67.4	426.1	211.9	164.6	10.1
2012	B-	2.88	1.90	68.8	373.6	187.2	155.0	7.9
2011	B-	2.73	1.81	84.6	348.4	171.8	144.7	-10.7
2010	B-	2.95	1.98	69.7	358.0	180.8	146.2	5.6
2009	B-	2.90	1.95	69.9	341.3	169.6	146.2	2.4

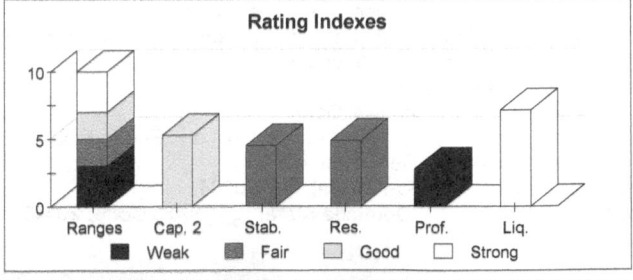

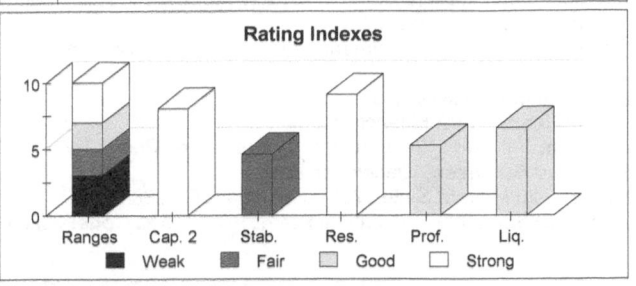

Rating Indexes

CONNECTICUT MEDICAL INS CO

C+   Fair

Major Rating Factors: Fair overall results on stability tests (4.8 on a scale of 0 to 10). Strong long-term capitalization index (7.7) based on excellent current risk adjusted capital (severe and moderate loss scenarios). Moreover, capital levels have been consistent in recent years.

Other Rating Factors: Ample reserve history (9.7) that helps to protect the company against sharp claims increases. Excellent profitability (8.8) with operating gains in each of the last five years. Excellent liquidity (8.2) with ample operational cash flow and liquid investments.

Principal Business: Medical malpractice (100%).

Principal Investments: Investment grade bonds (82%) and misc. investments (18%).

Investments in Affiliates: None

Group Affiliation: Connecticut Medical

Licensed in: CT, MA

Commenced Business: October 1984

Address: 80 Glastonbury Blvd, Glastonbury, CT 06033

Phone: (860) 633-7788   **Domicile State:** CT   **NAIC Code:** 15890

Data Date	Rating	RACR #1	RACR #2	Loss Ratio %	Total Assets ($mil)	Capital ($mil)	Net Premium ($mil)	Net Income ($mil)
9-14	C+	1.79	1.52	N/A	476.3	271.5	27.1	4.9
9-13	C+	7.26	5.16	N/A	460.5	256.7	25.9	7.4
2013	C+	1.73	1.48	58.6	468.6	264.4	35.9	11.2
2012	C+	7.50	5.50	24.7	440.8	243.7	34.1	21.0
2011	C+	6.37	4.83	35.2	422.1	218.2	32.7	17.2
2010	C+	5.69	4.42	9.2	417.7	202.8	33.3	27.5
2009	C+	4.01	3.32	3.9	405.1	170.9	33.2	28.7

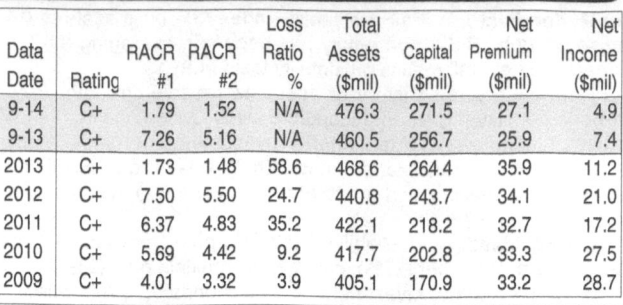

Rating Indexes

CONTINENTAL CASUALTY CO

C+   Fair

Major Rating Factors: Fair overall results on stability tests (4.1 on a scale of 0 to 10). The largest net exposure for one risk is excessive at 7.2% of capital. History of adequate reserve strength (6.5) as reserves have been consistently at an acceptable level.

Other Rating Factors: Good overall profitability index (5.8). Fair expense controls. Return on equity has been fair, averaging 5.7% over the past five years. Good liquidity (6.9) with sufficient resources (cash flows and marketable investments) to handle a spike in claims. Strong long-term capitalization index (7.8) based on excellent current risk adjusted capital (severe and moderate loss scenarios). Moreover, capital levels have been consistent in recent years.

Principal Business: Inland marine (36%), other liability (33%), other accident & health (6%), commercial multiple peril (5%), group accident & health (3%), workers compensation (3%), and other lines (14%).

Principal Investments: Investment grade bonds (72%), misc. investments (23%), and non investment grade bonds (5%).

Investments in Affiliates: 12%

Group Affiliation: CNA Financial Corp

Licensed in: All states, the District of Columbia and Puerto Rico

Commenced Business: December 1897

Address: 333 S Wabash Ave, Chicago, IL 60604

Phone: (312) 822-5000   **Domicile State:** IL   **NAIC Code:** 20443

Data Date	Rating	RACR #1	RACR #2	Loss Ratio %	Total Assets ($mil)	Capital ($mil)	Net Premium ($mil)	Net Income ($mil)
9-14	C+	2.06	1.59	N/A	43,193.4	11,404.5	4,204.8	760.7
9-13	C+	1.96	1.48	N/A	42,332.7	10,369.5	4,209.7	340.2
2013	C+	2.04	1.59	87.8	42,642.3	11,136.7	6,246.7	788.0
2012	C+	1.94	1.48	94.8	41,292.2	9,998.4	6,162.5	348.2
2011	C+	2.08	1.59	83.3	40,560.9	9,887.6	6,071.5	746.0
2010	C+	2.21	1.63	80.7	39,595.5	9,821.2	5,636.9	658.4
2009	C+	2.05	1.48	80.6	40,369.5	9,338.2	5,842.5	126.1

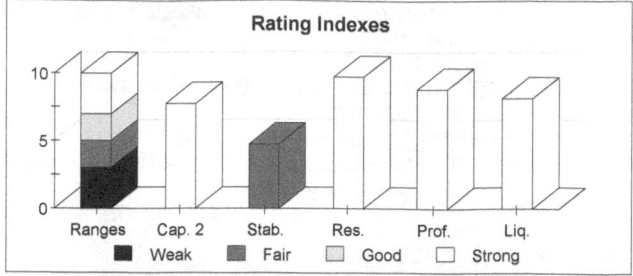

Rating Indexes

CONTINENTAL INS CO

C   Fair

Major Rating Factors: Fair reserve development (3.5 on a scale of 0 to 10) as reserves have generally been sufficient to cover claims. In 2013, the two year reserve development was 16% deficient. Fair profitability index (3.7) with operating losses during 2009 and 2010. Average return on equity over the last five years has been poor at -1.3%.

Other Rating Factors: Fair overall results on stability tests (4.0) including fair financial strength of affiliated CNA Financial Corp. Strong long-term capitalization index (9.4) based on excellent current risk adjusted capital (severe and moderate loss scenarios), despite some fluctuation in capital levels. Superior liquidity (10.0) with ample operational cash flow and liquid investments.

Principal Business: Commercial multiple peril (20%), workers compensation (20%), ocean marine (18%), auto liability (13%), medical malpractice (5%), fidelity (4%), and other lines (21%).

Principal Investments: Investment grade bonds (105%) and non investment grade bonds (1%).

Investments in Affiliates: 8%

Group Affiliation: CNA Financial Corp

Licensed in: All states, the District of Columbia and Puerto Rico

Commenced Business: December 1977

Address: 1320 Main St Suite 1700, Columbia, SC 29201

Phone: (312) 822-5000   **Domicile State:** PA   **NAIC Code:** 35289

Data Date	Rating	RACR #1	RACR #2	Loss Ratio %	Total Assets ($mil)	Capital ($mil)	Net Premium ($mil)	Net Income ($mil)
9-14	C	5.11	2.78	N/A	2,067.4	1,430.1	0.0	45.0
9-13	C	5.43	3.05	N/A	2,504.2	1,349.8	0.0	32.2
2013	C	4.78	2.58	0.0	2,345.5	1,366.9	0.0	121.8
2012	C	5.14	2.85	0.0	2,708.5	1,323.0	0.0	41.4
2011	C	4.88	2.58	0.0	2,668.5	1,240.6	0.0	202.1
2010	C-	3.46	2.21	0.0	2,658.2	1,146.5	0.0	-395.7
2009	C+	6.51	5.77	0.0	3,805.4	1,541.6	0.0	-64.2

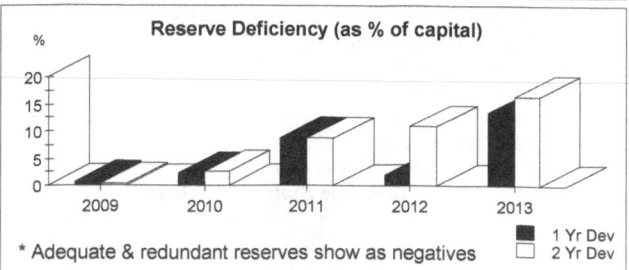

Reserve Deficiency (as % of capital)

* Adequate & redundant reserves show as negatives

www.weissratings.com

COPIC INS CO *

| A- | Excellent |

Major Rating Factors: Strong long-term capitalization index (9.4 on a scale of 0 to 10) based on excellent current risk adjusted capital (severe and moderate loss scenarios). Furthermore, this high level of risk adjusted capital has been consistently maintained in previous years. Ample reserve history (9.6) that helps to protect the company against sharp claims increases.

Other Rating Factors: Excellent profitability (8.9) with operating gains in each of the last five years. Return on equity has been good over the last five years, averaging 10.8%. Excellent liquidity (7.4) with ample operational cash flow and liquid investments. Good overall results on stability tests (6.9) despite negative cash flow from operations for 2013. Stability strengths include good operational trends and excellent risk diversification. The largest net exposure for one risk is conservative at 1.1% of capital.

Principal Business: Medical malpractice (94%), other liability (4%), and group accident & health (2%).

Principal Investments: Investment grade bonds (68%), misc. investments (29%), and cash (3%).

Investments in Affiliates: None

Group Affiliation: COPIC Trust

Licensed in: AZ, CO, ID, IA, KS, MT, NE, UT, WY

Commenced Business: September 1984

Address: 7800 E Dorado Pl Suite 200, Englewood, CO 80111

Phone: (720) 858-6000   **Domicile State:** CO   **NAIC Code:** 11860

Data Date	Rating	RACR #1	RACR #2	Loss Ratio %	Total Assets ($mil)	Capital ($mil)	Net Premium ($mil)	Net Income ($mil)
9-14	A-	4.60	3.10	N/A	548.6	262.7	62.8	6.6
9-13	A-	4.65	3.16	N/A	564.3	259.6	65.1	10.0
2013	A-	4.57	3.08	59.4	525.0	260.6	82.0	11.9
2012	A-	4.44	3.08	56.5	525.0	238.9	88.2	27.8
2011	A-	4.11	2.90	54.5	501.2	218.2	88.1	30.0
2010	A-	3.60	2.50	56.6	513.4	200.3	96.2	26.3
2009	A-	3.32	2.36	58.4	468.6	176.9	95.7	29.4

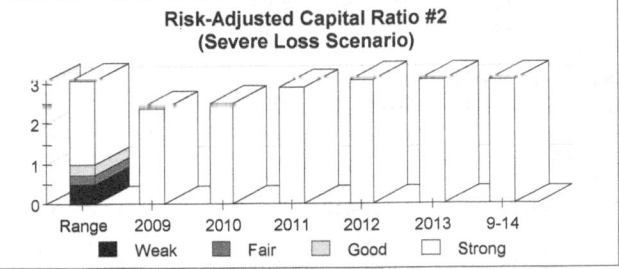

Risk-Adjusted Capital Ratio #2 (Severe Loss Scenario)

COPPERPOINT MUTUAL INS CO *

| A+ | Excellent |

Major Rating Factors: Strong long-term capitalization index (7.3 on a scale of 0 to 10) based on excellent current risk adjusted capital (severe and moderate loss scenarios). Furthermore, this high level of risk adjusted capital has been consistently maintained in previous years. Excellent overall results on stability tests (7.7). Stability strengths include good operational trends and excellent risk diversification.

Other Rating Factors: Good profitability index (5.0). Fair expense controls. Return on equity has been good over the last five years, averaging 10.4%. Good liquidity (6.8) with sufficient resources (cash flows and marketable investments) to handle a spike in claims. Fair reserve development (4.9) as reserves have generally been sufficient to cover claims. In 2009, the two year reserve development was 21% deficient.

Principal Business: Workers compensation (100%).

Principal Investments: Investment grade bonds (79%), misc. investments (20%), and real estate (1%).

Investments in Affiliates: 2%

Group Affiliation: CopperPoint Group

Licensed in: AZ

Commenced Business: January 2013

Address: 3030 N 3rd St, Phoenix, AZ 85012-3039

Phone: (602) 631-2240   **Domicile State:** AZ   **NAIC Code:** 14216

Data Date	Rating	RACR #1	RACR #2	Loss Ratio %	Total Assets ($mil)	Capital ($mil)	Net Premium ($mil)	Net Income ($mil)
9-14	A+	2.39	1.50	N/A	3,581.2	1,235.1	178.5	48.7
9-13	U	7.34	4.03	N/A	3,526.7	1,151.3	154.4	17.4
2013	A+	2.22	1.38	89.2	3,536.2	1,186.2	222.5	44.7
2012	U	266.05	133.00	101.8	3,729.6	1,066.6	183.5	287.6
2011	N/A	N/A	N/A	102.6	3,479.6	762.0	172.8	124.1
2010	N/A	N/A	N/A	124.1	3,448.3	655.5	158.9	46.7
2009	N/A	N/A	N/A	121.4	3,434.4	557.6	237.4	11.0

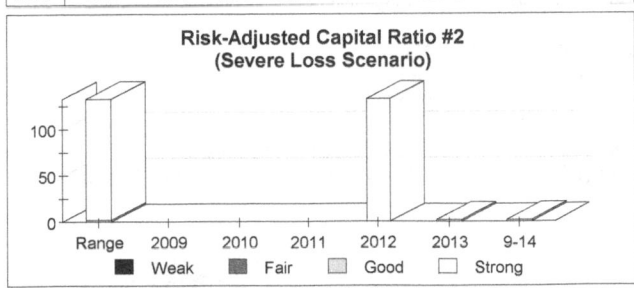

Risk-Adjusted Capital Ratio #2 (Severe Loss Scenario)

COUNTRY CASUALTY INS CO *

| B+ | Good |

Major Rating Factors: Good overall profitability index (6.7 on a scale of 0 to 10). Excellent expense controls. Return on equity has been low, averaging 1.8% over the past five years. Good overall results on stability tests (6.3). Strengths include potential support from affiliation with COUNTRY Financial, good operational trends and excellent risk diversification.

Other Rating Factors: Strong long-term capitalization index (10.0) based on excellent current risk adjusted capital (severe and moderate loss scenarios), despite some fluctuation in capital levels. Superior liquidity (10.0) with ample operational cash flow and liquid investments.

Principal Business: Homeowners multiple peril (45%), auto liability (37%), and auto physical damage (18%).

Principal Investments: Investment grade bonds (99%) and misc. investments (1%).

Investments in Affiliates: None

Group Affiliation: COUNTRY Financial

Licensed in: AL, AK, AZ, AR, CO, CT, DE, GA, ID, IL, IN, IA, KS, KY, ME, MD, MA, MI, MN, MO, MT, NE, NV, NM, ND, OH, OK, OR, PA, RI, SD, TN, TX, WA, WI, WY

Commenced Business: March 1964

Address: 1701 N. Towanda Ave, Bloomington, IL 61701

Phone: (309) 821-3000   **Domicile State:** IL   **NAIC Code:** 20982

Data Date	Rating	RACR #1	RACR #2	Loss Ratio %	Total Assets ($mil)	Capital ($mil)	Net Premium ($mil)	Net Income ($mil)
9-14	B+	27.34	24.61	N/A	78.1	67.7	0.0	0.8
9-13	B+	26.53	23.88	N/A	77.9	67.0	0.0	0.8
2013	B+	26.67	24.00	0.0	77.7	67.0	0.0	1.2
2012	B+	26.57	23.91	0.0	77.0	66.4	0.0	1.1
2011	B+	25.11	22.60	0.0	77.1	65.5	0.0	1.2
2010	B+	24.54	22.08	0.0	75.3	63.7	0.0	1.2
2009	B+	23.58	21.22	0.0	74.0	62.1	0.0	1.2

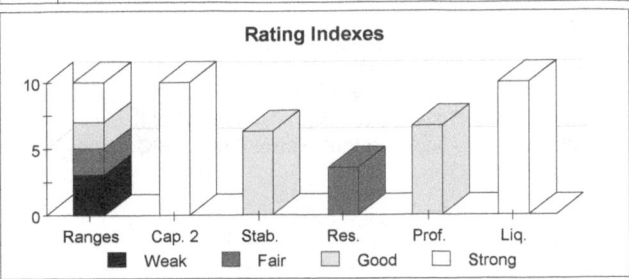

Rating Indexes

COUNTRY MUTUAL INS CO *

A-   Excellent

Major Rating Factors: Excellent overall results on stability tests (7.3 on a scale of 0 to 10). Stability strengths include excellent operational trends and excellent risk diversification. Strong long-term capitalization index (9.2) based on excellent current risk adjusted capital (severe and moderate loss scenarios). Furthermore, this high level of risk adjusted capital has been consistently maintained in previous years.

Other Rating Factors: Ample reserve history (7.8) that can protect against increases in claims costs. Good overall profitability index (6.0) despite operating losses during 2009 and 2011. Good liquidity (6.2) with sufficient resources (cash flows and marketable investments) to handle a spike in claims.

Principal Business: Homeowners multiple peril (41%), auto liability (17%), auto physical damage (12%), farmowners multiple peril (9%), allied lines (8%), commercial multiple peril (6%), and other lines (7%).

Principal Investments: Investment grade bonds (67%), misc. investments (31%), and non investment grade bonds (2%).

Investments in Affiliates: 5%

Group Affiliation: COUNTRY Financial

Licensed in: All states except DC, HI, LA, MD, MS, NJ, OH, SC, PR

Commenced Business: November 1925

Address: 1701 N. Towanda Ave, Bloomington, IL 61701

Phone: (309) 821-3000   **Domicile State:** IL   **NAIC Code:** 20990

Data Date	Rating	RACR #1	RACR #2	Loss Ratio %	Total Assets ($mil)	Capital ($mil)	Net Premium ($mil)	Net Income ($mil)
9-14	A-	3.68	2.62	N/A	4,306.5	1,924.7	1,566.0	87.3
9-13	B+	3.55	2.52	N/A	4,153.4	1,778.3	1,510.3	147.4
2013	A-	3.56	2.56	69.3	4,150.3	1,825.5	2,051.7	151.3
2012	B+	3.41	2.46	75.5	3,930.7	1,635.9	1,979.7	47.1
2011	B+	3.56	2.50	85.8	3,860.7	1,587.0	1,947.2	-140.8
2010	A	3.83	2.76	73.0	3,726.2	1,638.0	1,820.3	34.2
2009	A	3.87	2.79	75.6	3,533.6	1,558.2	1,788.8	-16.4

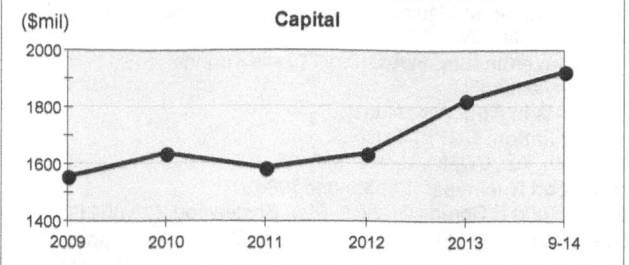

Capital ($mil)

COURTESY INS CO

B   Good

Major Rating Factors: Good overall results on stability tests (5.1 on a scale of 0 to 10) despite potential drain of affiliation with J M Family Enterprise Group. History of adequate reserve strength (6.2) as reserves have been consistently at an acceptable level.

Other Rating Factors: Strong long-term capitalization index (10.0) based on excellent current risk adjusted capital (severe and moderate loss scenarios). Moreover, capital levels have been consistent in recent years. Excellent profitability (8.9) with operating gains in each of the last five years. Return on equity has been good over the last five years, averaging 11.9%. Excellent liquidity (7.5) with ample operational cash flow and liquid investments.

Principal Business: Aggregate write-ins for other lines of business (28%).

Principal Investments: Investment grade bonds (86%) and misc. investments (14%).

Investments in Affiliates: None

Group Affiliation: J M Family Enterprise Group

Licensed in: All states except MI

Commenced Business: May 1988

Address: 100 NW 12th Ave, Deerfield Beach, FL 33442

Phone: (954) 429-2150   **Domicile State:** FL   **NAIC Code:** 26492

Data Date	Rating	RACR #1	RACR #2	Loss Ratio %	Total Assets ($mil)	Capital ($mil)	Net Premium ($mil)	Net Income ($mil)
9-14	B	9.10	5.22	N/A	718.2	331.9	81.2	24.2
9-13	B	8.46	4.84	N/A	672.2	295.2	78.3	28.2
2013	B	9.23	5.31	52.7	686.5	308.4	124.9	38.3
2012	B	8.81	5.04	45.1	627.2	265.0	138.6	29.8
2011	B	10.55	5.92	50.1	536.1	226.9	108.8	30.5
2010	B	9.19	5.17	57.5	490.3	202.4	95.2	31.2
2009	B-	8.44	4.75	69.5	448.8	161.9	84.7	14.3

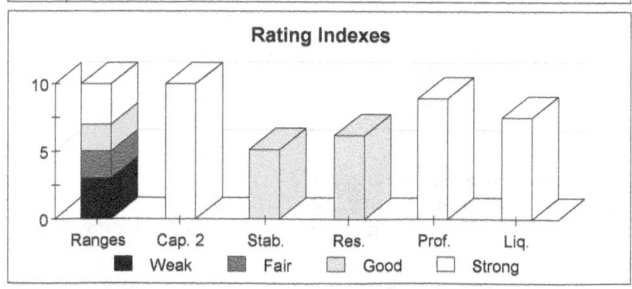

Rating Indexes

CSAA INS EXCHANGE *

A-   Excellent

Major Rating Factors: Strong long-term capitalization index (9.4 on a scale of 0 to 10) based on excellent current risk adjusted capital (severe and moderate loss scenarios). Moreover, capital levels have been consistent in recent years. Ample reserve history (7.6) that can protect against increases in claims costs.

Other Rating Factors: Good overall results on stability tests (5.5) despite potential drain of affiliation with CSAA Insurance Group. Good overall profitability index (6.6). Fair expense controls. Good liquidity (6.4) with sufficient resources (cash flows and marketable investments) to handle a spike in claims.

Principal Business: Auto liability (37%), auto physical damage (35%), homeowners multiple peril (25%), other liability (1%), and allied lines (1%).

Principal Investments: Investment grade bonds (50%), misc. investments (41%), non investment grade bonds (5%), and real estate (4%).

Investments in Affiliates: 7%

Group Affiliation: CSAA Insurance Group

Licensed in: CA, IN, NV, NY, UT, WY

Commenced Business: August 1914

Address: 3055 Oak Rd, Walnut Creek, CA 94597-2098

Phone: (800) 207-3618   **Domicile State:** CA   **NAIC Code:** 15539

Data Date	Rating	RACR #1	RACR #2	Loss Ratio %	Total Assets ($mil)	Capital ($mil)	Net Premium ($mil)	Net Income ($mil)
9-14	A-	3.73	2.59	N/A	6,956.8	3,916.7	2,057.4	86.3
9-13	A-	3.68	2.59	N/A	6,666.2	3,670.7	2,002.9	47.4
2013	A-	3.82	2.68	74.1	6,672.1	3,830.2	2,714.9	114.9
2012	A-	3.79	2.69	69.5	6,430.9	3,624.9	2,637.5	131.2
2011	A-	3.88	2.79	70.7	6,285.5	3,440.5	2,582.8	211.1
2010	A-	4.97	3.48	67.5	5,812.7	3,325.7	2,406.2	264.2
2009	A-	4.60	3.15	66.2	5,503.1	3,081.6	2,361.5	49.3

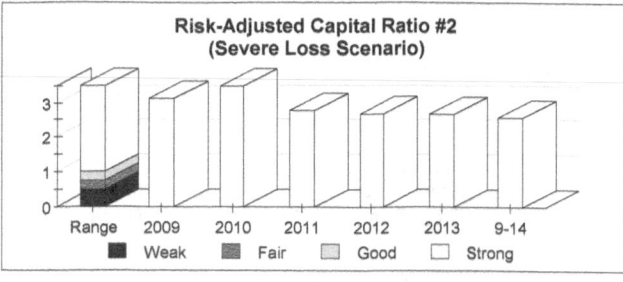

Risk-Adjusted Capital Ratio #2 (Severe Loss Scenario)

CUMIS INS SOCIETY INC

B   Good

Major Rating Factors: History of adequate reserve strength (6.9 on a scale of 0 to 10) as reserves have been consistently at an acceptable level. Good liquidity (6.5) with sufficient resources (cash flows and marketable investments) to handle a spike in claims.

Other Rating Factors: Good overall results on stability tests (5.7). Affiliation with CUNA Mutual Ins Group is a strength. The largest net exposure for one risk is conservative at 1.3% of capital. Fair profitability index (4.8) with operating losses during 2009. Return on equity has been low, averaging 1.4% over the past five years. Strong long-term capitalization index (10.0) based on excellent current risk adjusted capital (severe and moderate loss scenarios). Moreover, capital levels have been consistent in recent years.

Principal Business: Other liability (44%), allied lines (23%), fidelity (17%), commercial multiple peril (12%), auto physical damage (2%), auto liability (1%), and credit (1%).

Principal Investments: Investment grade bonds (73%), misc. investments (23%), non investment grade bonds (3%), and cash (1%).

Investments in Affiliates: 6%

Group Affiliation: CUNA Mutual Ins Group

Licensed in: All states, the District of Columbia and Puerto Rico

Commenced Business: June 1960

Address: 5910 Mineral Point Rd, Madison, WI 53705

Phone: (608) 238-5851   **Domicile State:** IA   **NAIC Code:** 10847

Data Date	Rating	RACR #1	RACR #2	Loss Ratio %	Total Assets ($mil)	Capital ($mil)	Net Premium ($mil)	Net Income ($mil)
9-14	B	4.42	3.04	N/A	2,309.5	686.2	475.8	53.8
9-13	B	4.55	3.13	N/A	2,021.8	592.4	436.4	32.4
2013	B	4.63	3.27	63.8	1,637.6	621.7	621.0	58.5
2012	B	4.67	3.28	63.5	1,636.9	562.0	553.1	29.1
2011	B	4.06	2.86	61.6	1,623.3	501.8	491.0	35.9
2010	B	3.24	2.18	65.6	1,529.4	470.4	479.7	12.5
2009	B-	2.24	1.49	70.9	1,254.4	422.2	528.7	-103.1

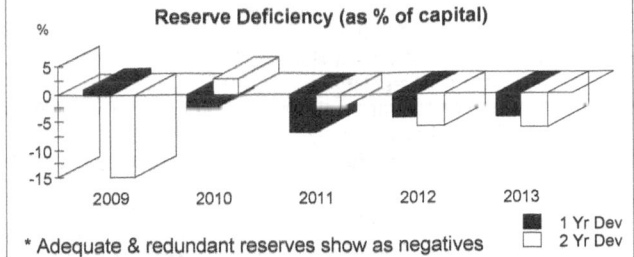

Reserve Deficiency (as % of capital)

* Adequate & redundant reserves show as negatives

■ 1 Yr Dev   □ 2 Yr Dev

CYPRESS INS CO

C   Fair

Major Rating Factors: Fair profitability index (4.8 on a scale of 0 to 10) with operating losses during 2009, 2010 and 2011. Average return on equity over the last five years has been poor at -2.4%. Fair overall results on stability tests (4.2) including negative cash flow from operations for 2013 and fair results on operational trends.

Other Rating Factors: Good long-term capitalization index (6.2) based on good current risk adjusted capital (moderate loss scenario), despite some fluctuation in capital levels. History of adequate reserve strength (5.8) as reserves have been consistently at an acceptable level. Superior liquidity (9.4) with ample operational cash flow and liquid investments.

Principal Business: Workers compensation (96%), auto liability (2%), and fire (1%).

Principal Investments: Investment grade bonds (64%), misc. investments (34%), and cash (2%).

Investments in Affiliates: None

Group Affiliation: Berkshire-Hathaway

Licensed in: AL, AR, CA, CO, DE, GA, HI, ID, IA, MS, NE, NM, OK, SC, TN, TX, VA

Commenced Business: March 1963

Address: 395 Oyster Point Blvd.,Ste 401, S.san Francisco, CA 94080

Phone: (650) 635-0444   **Domicile State:** CA   **NAIC Code:** 10855

Data Date	Rating	RACR #1	RACR #2	Loss Ratio %	Total Assets ($mil)	Capital ($mil)	Net Premium ($mil)	Net Income ($mil)
9-14	C	1.35	0.95	N/A	1,184.6	285.0	203.3	10.7
9-13	C	1.44	0.98	N/A	1,072.0	239.8	166.4	19.6
2013	C	1.45	1.01	78.9	1,140.2	264.4	271.9	25.3
2012	C	1.22	0.87	85.7	1,065.2	207.2	265.5	12.7
2011	C	1.04	0.76	88.5	897.9	187.4	297.8	-28.4
2010	C+	1.52	1.08	83.5	787.0	225.1	224.9	-17.2
2009	C+	1.63	1.17	90.7	691.9	226.5	216.0	-23.8

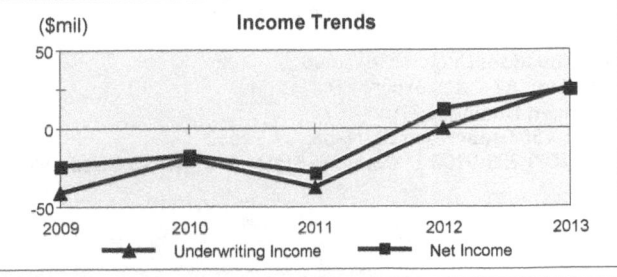

Income Trends

▲ Underwriting Income   ■ Net Income

DAIRYLAND INS CO *

A+   Excellent

Major Rating Factors: Strong long-term capitalization index (10.0 on a scale of 0 to 10) based on excellent current risk adjusted capital (severe and moderate loss scenarios). Furthermore, this high level of risk adjusted capital has been consistently maintained in previous years. Ample reserve history (8.6) that helps to protect the company against sharp claims increases.

Other Rating Factors: Excellent overall results on stability tests (7.9). Stability strengths include excellent operational trends and excellent risk diversification. Good overall profitability index (6.0). Fair expense controls. Return on equity has been fair, averaging 6.0% over the past five years. Good liquidity (6.9) with sufficient resources (cash flows and marketable investments) to handle a spike in claims.

Principal Business: Auto liability (73%) and auto physical damage (27%).

Principal Investments: Investment grade bonds (84%), misc. investments (15%), and non investment grade bonds (1%).

Investments in Affiliates: None

Group Affiliation: Sentry Ins Group

Licensed in: All states except CA, DC, HI, LA, NJ, OK, PR

Commenced Business: February 1953

Address: 1800 North Point Dr, Stevens Point, WI 54481

Phone: (715) 346-6000   **Domicile State:** WI   **NAIC Code:** 21164

Data Date	Rating	RACR #1	RACR #2	Loss Ratio %	Total Assets ($mil)	Capital ($mil)	Net Premium ($mil)	Net Income ($mil)
9-14	A+	5.04	3.36	N/A	1,212.4	503.2	235.6	21.5
9-13	A+	4.91	3.28	N/A	1,173.6	481.3	232.0	15.9
2013	A+	4.86	3.30	76.3	1,163.2	471.7	318.1	25.6
2012	A+	4.95	3.35	77.3	1,129.0	460.8	302.3	21.7
2011	A+	4.99	3.40	79.1	1,130.0	455.7	285.8	25.6
2010	A+	5.14	3.48	75.5	1,125.6	466.4	283.4	33.6
2009	A+	5.10	3.46	75.3	1,143.4	467.7	281.6	34.7

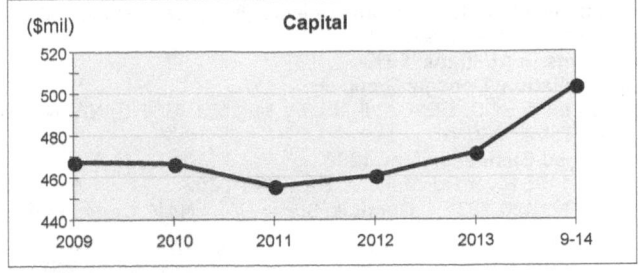

Capital

DARWIN NATIONAL ASR CO

B-   Good

Major Rating Factors: Good overall results on stability tests (5.0 on a scale of 0 to 10) despite fair results on operational trends. Strong long-term capitalization index (8.9) based on excellent current risk adjusted capital (severe and moderate loss scenarios), despite some fluctuation in capital levels.

Other Rating Factors: Ample reserve history (8.5) that helps to protect the company against sharp claims increases. Excellent profitability (8.4) with operating gains in each of the last five years. Excellent liquidity (7.1) with ample operational cash flow and liquid investments.

Principal Business: Other liability (66%), medical malpractice (15%), inland marine (7%), commercial multiple peril (4%), ocean marine (3%), surety (2%), and other lines (4%).

Principal Investments: Investment grade bonds (68%), misc. investments (30%), and cash (2%).

Investments in Affiliates: 18%

Group Affiliation: Allied World Asr Holding Group

Licensed in: All states except PR

Commenced Business: January 1972

Address: 10 Exchange Place, Jersey City, NJ 07302-3905

Phone: (860) 284-1300   **Domicile State:** DE   **NAIC Code:** 16624

Data Date	Rating	RACR #1	RACR #2	Loss Ratio %	Total Assets ($mil)	Capital ($mil)	Net Premium ($mil)	Net Income ($mil)
9-14	B-	2.91	2.27	N/A	777.1	370.6	73.6	8.7
9-13	B-	3.59	2.72	N/A	795.0	358.6	68.6	9.3
2013	B-	2.98	2.36	67.8	689.3	364.0	98.5	11.0
2012	B-	3.74	2.86	74.2	737.0	368.4	98.7	15.7
2011	C+	3.91	2.62	44.1	667.8	343.2	57.0	30.6
2010	C+	3.40	2.06	63.9	683.4	305.4	50.3	38.8
2009	C	2.68	1.61	33.0	700.8	283.3	80.9	58.9

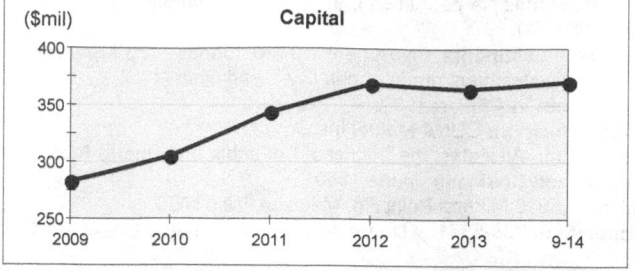

DOCTORS CO AN INTERINSURANCE EXCH

B-   Good

Major Rating Factors: Fair overall results on stability tests (4.7 on a scale of 0 to 10) including potential drain of affiliation with Doctors Co Group. Strong long-term capitalization index (7.6) based on excellent current risk adjusted capital (severe and moderate loss scenarios), despite some fluctuation in capital levels.

Other Rating Factors: Ample reserve history (9.4) that helps to protect the company against sharp claims increases. Excellent profitability (8.4) with operating gains in each of the last five years. Return on equity has been good over the last five years, averaging 11.2%. Excellent liquidity (7.4) with ample operational cash flow and liquid investments.

Principal Business: Medical malpractice (100%).

Principal Investments: Misc. investments (62%), investment grade bonds (36%), cash (1%), and non investment grade bonds (1%).

Investments in Affiliates: 23%

Group Affiliation: Doctors Co Group

Licensed in: All states except PR

Commenced Business: April 1976

Address: 185 Greenwood Dr, Napa, CA 94558

Phone: (707) 226-0100   **Domicile State:** CA   **NAIC Code:** 34495

Data Date	Rating	RACR #1	RACR #2	Loss Ratio %	Total Assets ($mil)	Capital ($mil)	Net Premium ($mil)	Net Income ($mil)
9-14	B-	1.82	1.46	N/A	3,490.5	1,794.2	498.7	19.9
9-13	B-	1.61	1.36	N/A	3,019.2	1,454.3	470.4	55.9
2013	B-	1.88	1.54	75.1	3,313.2	1,731.7	675.7	27.7
2012	B-	1.61	1.40	69.1	2,769.5	1,358.3	596.5	120.9
2011	B-	1.30	1.18	63.0	2,601.5	1,192.0	564.5	175.1
2010	B-	1.59	1.39	55.9	2,564.0	1,241.2	528.0	273.9
2009	B-	1.57	1.32	58.1	2,369.8	1,060.9	555.1	169.8

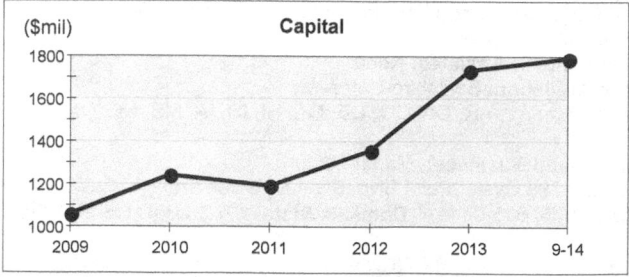

DONEGAL MUTUAL INS CO

B-   Good

Major Rating Factors: Fair overall results on stability tests (4.7 on a scale of 0 to 10) including potential drain of affiliation with Donegal Group Inc. Good long-term capitalization index (6.9) based on good current risk adjusted capital (moderate loss scenario), despite some fluctuation in capital levels.

Other Rating Factors: History of adequate reserve strength (5.1) as reserves have been consistently at an acceptable level. Good overall profitability index (6.8) despite modest operating losses during the first nine months of 2014. Good liquidity (6.6) with sufficient resources (cash flows and marketable investments) to handle a spike in claims.

Principal Business: Homeowners multiple peril (25%), auto liability (23%), auto physical damage (16%), commercial multiple peril (16%), workers compensation (10%), other liability (4%), and other lines (5%).

Principal Investments: Misc. investments (80%), real estate (10%), investment grade bonds (6%), and cash (4%).

Investments in Affiliates: 66%

Group Affiliation: Donegal Group Inc

Licensed in: AL, DC, DE, GA, IL, IN, IA, ME, MD, MI, NE, NH, NY, NC, OH, PA, SD, TN, VT, VA, WV, WI

Commenced Business: May 1889

Address: 1195 River Rd, Marietta, PA 17547-0302

Phone: (717) 426-1931   **Domicile State:** PA   **NAIC Code:** 13692

Data Date	Rating	RACR #1	RACR #2	Loss Ratio %	Total Assets ($mil)	Capital ($mil)	Net Premium ($mil)	Net Income ($mil)
9-14	B-	1.04	0.97	N/A	389.9	199.5	73.9	-0.7
9-13	B-	1.08	1.02	N/A	374.0	197.9	68.6	8.6
2013	B-	1.09	1.02	59.2	383.8	204.4	97.8	15.4
2012	B-	1.03	0.96	73.0	350.7	187.7	84.7	5.9
2011	B-	1.01	0.94	86.3	333.8	175.7	79.7	9.4
2010	B-	1.02	0.94	75.3	338.4	178.8	62.8	0.6
2009	C+	0.97	0.90	72.4	325.0	172.1	63.5	6.1

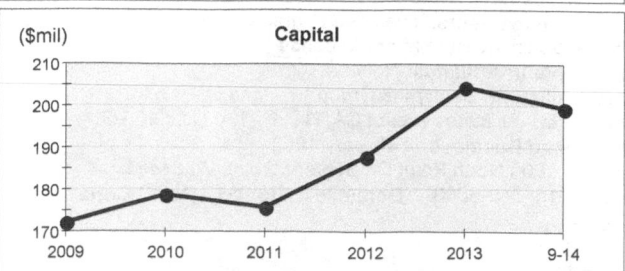

DORINCO REINSURANCE CO   D+   Weak

Major Rating Factors: Weak overall results on stability tests (2.6 on a scale of 0 to 10) including potential drain of affiliation with Dow Chemical Co. The largest net exposure for one risk is high at 4.6% of capital. Fair profitability index (4.6). Good expense controls. Return on equity has been fair, averaging 12.7% over the past five years.

Other Rating Factors: History of adequate reserve strength (6.5) as reserves have been consistently at an acceptable level. Good liquidity (6.5) with sufficient resources (cash flows and marketable investments) to handle a spike in claims. Strong long-term capitalization index (7.0) based on excellent current risk adjusted capital (severe and moderate loss scenarios), despite some fluctuation in capital levels.

Principal Business: Fire (56%) and other liability (44%).

Principal Investments: Investment grade bonds (56%), misc. investments (37%), and cash (7%).

Investments in Affiliates: None

Group Affiliation: Dow Chemical Co

Licensed in: AL, AZ, CA, CT, DE, FL, GA, ID, IL, IN, IA, KS, KY, I A, MD, MI, MN, MS, MO, NE, NH, NY, NC, ND, OH, OK, OR, PA, SC, SD, TX, UT, VT, VA, VV, WI, WY

Commenced Business: March 1977

Address: 1320 Waldo Rd #200, Midland, MI 48642

Phone: (989) 636-0047   **Domicile State:** MI   **NAIC Code:** 33499

Data Date	Rating	RACR #1	RACR #2	Loss Ratio %	Total Assets ($mil)	Capital ($mil)	Net Premium ($mil)	Net Income ($mil)
9-14	D+	1.39	1.10	N/A	1,586.7	536.2	130.4	62.6
9-13	D+	1.32	1.04	N/A	1,518.1	544.6	142.0	66.2
2013	D+	1.32	1.04	72.9	1,571.4	529.5	196.8	73.2
2012	D+	1.25	1.00	77.5	1,553.3	524.0	208.4	54.4
2011	D+	1.24	0.91	78.0	1,576.6	517.2	214.1	56.3
2010	D+	1.54	1.08	66.6	1,622.5	609.7	208.2	112.0
2009	D	0.71	0.48	70.3	1,741.2	604.4	225.5	47.5

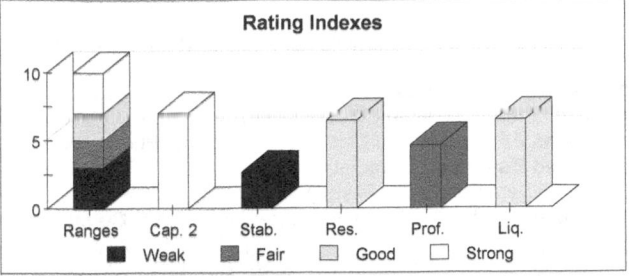

Rating Indexes

EAGLESTONE REINS CO   B   Good

Major Rating Factors: Fair overall results on stability tests (4.4 on a scale of 0 to 10) including weak results on operational trends and negative cash flow from operations for 2013. The largest net exposure for one risk is excessive at 7.4% of capital. Strengths include potentially strong support from affiliation with American International Group. Fair reserve development (4.7) as reserves have generally been sufficient to cover claims. In 2013, the one year reserve development was 21% deficient.

Other Rating Factors: Strong long-term capitalization index (7.2) based on excellent current risk adjusted capital (severe and moderate loss scenarios). Moreover, capital levels have been consistent in recent years. Excellent profitability (7.6) with operating gains in each of the last five years. Excellent expense controls. Return on equity has been good over the last five years, averaging 11.3%. Excellent liquidity (7.8) with ample operational cash flow and liquid investments.

Principal Business: (This company is a reinsurer.)

Principal Investments: Investment grade bonds (89%) and misc. investments (11%).

Investments in Affiliates: None

Group Affiliation: American International Group

Licensed in: (No states)

Commenced Business: April 1996

Address: 2595 Interstate Dr Suite 103, Harrisburg, PA 17110

Phone: (212) 770-7000   **Domicile State:** PA   **NAIC Code:** 10651

Data Date	Rating	RACR #1	RACR #2	Loss Ratio %	Total Assets ($mil)	Capital ($mil)	Net Premium ($mil)	Net Income ($mil)
9-14	B	2.49	1.56	N/A	5,539.9	1,993.2	33.5	55.9
9-13	B	1.49	0.98	N/A	5,749.5	1,454.4	47.0	94.2
2013	B	2.32	1.46	N/A	5,805.7	1,937.4	0.5	377.9
2012	B	1.41	0.91	223.5	6,199.7	1,358.8	539.9	49.8
2011	U	1.63	0.99	0.0	4,971.3	1,333.3	0.0	125.2
2010	B-	153.42	76.71	N/A	159.3	158.2	-10.1	35.8
2009	C+	2.83	2.12	96.9	302.3	129.1	55.5	9.3

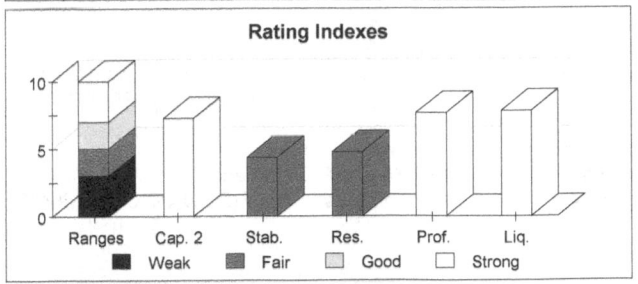

Rating Indexes

ECONOMY FIRE & CAS CO   B-   Good

Major Rating Factors: Good overall profitability index (6.3 on a scale of 0 to 10). Fair expense controls. Return on equity has been low, averaging 5.0% over the past five years. Good overall results on stability tests (5.1). Stability strengths include good operational trends and excellent risk diversification.

Other Rating Factors: Strong long-term capitalization index (10.0) based on excellent current risk adjusted capital (severe and moderate loss scenarios), despite some fluctuation in capital levels. Excellent liquidity (7.0) with ample operational cash flow and liquid investments.

Principal Business: Auto liability (36%), homeowners multiple peril (32%), auto physical damage (30%), inland marine (1%), and earthquake (1%).

Principal Investments: Investment grade bonds (81%), misc. investments (17%), non investment grade bonds (1%), and real estate (1%).

Investments in Affiliates: 14%

Group Affiliation: MetLife Inc

Licensed in: All states except DC, DE, HI, ME, MA, NH, NJ, RI, SC, VT, VA, PR

Commenced Business: January 1935

Address: 500 Economy Court, Freeport, IL 61032

Phone: (401) 827-2400   **Domicile State:** IL   **NAIC Code:** 22926

Data Date	Rating	RACR #1	RACR #2	Loss Ratio %	Total Assets ($mil)	Capital ($mil)	Net Premium ($mil)	Net Income ($mil)
9-14	B-	6.98	6.29	N/A	472.1	375.1	0.0	11.8
9-13	B-	7.30	6.57	N/A	468.8	377.6	0.0	13.2
2013	B-	6.85	6.23	0.0	456.3	362.8	0.0	17.4
2012	B-	7.15	6.50	0.0	450.6	364.1	0.0	18.2
2011	B-	7.41	6.69	0.0	447.7	364.0	0.0	18.4
2010	B-	7.42	6.71	0.0	423.5	350.4	0.0	17.5
2009	B-	7.61	6.76	0.0	424.8	346.8	0.0	19.1

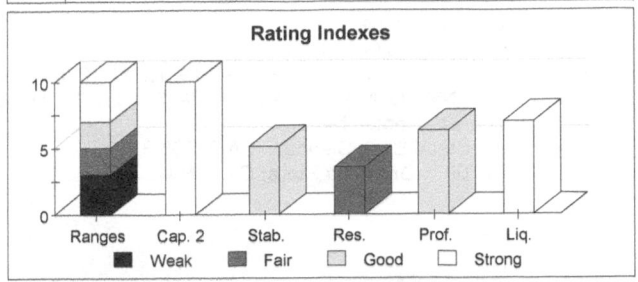

Rating Indexes

ELECTRIC INS CO

C+ Fair

Major Rating Factors: Fair overall results on stability tests (3.4 on a scale of 0 to 10) including potential drain of affiliation with Wilmington Trust. The largest net exposure for one risk is conservative at 1.4% of capital. History of adequate reserve strength (6.7) as reserves have been consistently at an acceptable level.

Other Rating Factors: Good overall profitability index (6.6). Good expense controls. Return on equity has been fair, averaging 5.4% over the past five years. Good liquidity (6.7) with sufficient resources (cash flows and marketable investments) to handle a spike in claims. Strong long-term capitalization index (8.1) based on excellent current risk adjusted capital (severe and moderate loss scenarios). Moreover, capital levels have been consistent in recent years.

Principal Business: Workers compensation (25%), products liability (22%), auto liability (19%), homeowners multiple peril (18%), auto physical damage (12%), and other liability (2%).

Principal Investments: Investment grade bonds (90%), misc. investments (10%), and real estate (1%).

Investments in Affiliates: 2%

Group Affiliation: Wilmington Trust

Licensed in: All states, the District of Columbia and Puerto Rico

Commenced Business: September 1966

Address: 75 Sam Fonzo Dr., Beverly, MA 01915

Phone: (978) 921-2080 **Domicile State:** MA **NAIC Code:** 21261

Data Date	Rating	RACR #1	RACR #2	Loss Ratio %	Total Assets ($mil)	Capital ($mil)	Net Premium ($mil)	Net Income ($mil)
9-14	C+	3.10	1.88	N/A	1,533.4	527.2	287.9	11.1
9-13	C+	2.67	1.64	N/A	1,540.6	502.7	290.7	18.4
2013	C+	3.16	1.92	79.8	1,448.7	522.6	353.3	33.6
2012	C+	2.64	1.63	85.5	1,442.4	481.7	367.0	25.6
2011	C+	2.46	1.46	88.2	1,444.6	460.2	377.1	22.6
2010	C+	2.09	1.10	86.5	1,406.6	447.8	400.5	26.5
2009	C+	1.83	0.97	85.9	1,329.1	407.1	398.2	25.5

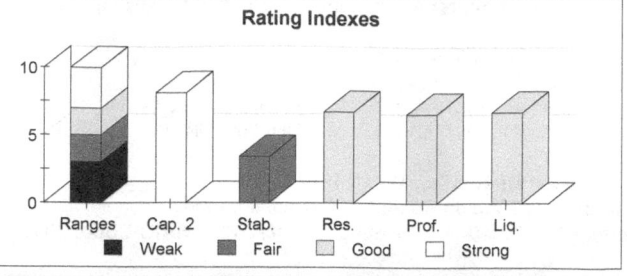

Rating Indexes

EMPLOYERS ASSURANCE CO

C Fair

Major Rating Factors: Fair overall results on stability tests (3.3 on a scale of 0 to 10) including potential drain of affiliation with Employers Group Inc. Good overall profitability index (6.7). Weak expense controls. Return on equity has been low, averaging 3.5% over the past five years.

Other Rating Factors: Strong long-term capitalization index (8.5) based on excellent current risk adjusted capital (severe and moderate loss scenarios), despite some fluctuation in capital levels. Ample reserve history (9.2) that helps to protect the company against sharp claims increases. Excellent liquidity (7.1) with ample operational cash flow and liquid investments.

Principal Business: Workers compensation (100%).

Principal Investments: Investment grade bonds (90%), cash (6%), and misc. investments (4%).

Investments in Affiliates: None

Group Affiliation: Employers Group Inc

Licensed in: AL, AZ, AR, CA, CO, DC, FL, GA, ID, IL, IN, IA, KS, KY, LA, MD, MI, MN, MS, MO, MT, NV, NJ, NM, NC, OH, OK, OR, PA, SC, TN, TX, UT, VA, WV, WI

Commenced Business: November 1979

Address: 851 Trafalgar Ct Suite 400E, Maitland, FL 32751

Phone: (775) 327-2700 **Domicile State:** FL **NAIC Code:** 25402

Data Date	Rating	RACR #1	RACR #2	Loss Ratio %	Total Assets ($mil)	Capital ($mil)	Net Premium ($mil)	Net Income ($mil)
9-14	C	3.97	2.90	N/A	598.0	199.7	51.2	3.5
9-13	C	3.63	2.63	N/A	539.7	196.6	47.2	2.6
2013	C	3.00	2.14	73.8	548.7	196.8	67.8	2.6
2012	C	3.26	2.34	57.4	474.3	152.9	57.0	1.6
2011	C	2.48	1.75	77.6	390.2	80.5	41.0	2.3
2010	C	3.19	2.17	66.2	419.1	92.2	31.3	4.8
2009	C	2.61	1.80	57.5	430.0	79.6	36.8	6.5

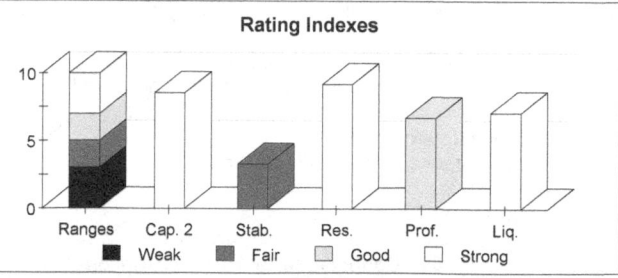

Rating Indexes

EMPLOYERS COMPENSATION INS CO

B Good

Major Rating Factors: Good overall profitability index (5.8 on a scale of 0 to 10). Weak expense controls. Return on equity has been low, averaging 4.4% over the past five years. Good overall results on stability tests (5.8). Stability strengths include good operational trends and excellent risk diversification.

Other Rating Factors: Strong long-term capitalization index (7.8) based on excellent current risk adjusted capital (severe and moderate loss scenarios), despite some fluctuation in capital levels. Ample reserve history (8.8) that helps to protect the company against sharp claims increases. Excellent liquidity (7.8) with ample operational cash flow and liquid investments.

Principal Business: Workers compensation (100%).

Principal Investments: Investment grade bonds (92%) and misc. investments (8%).

Investments in Affiliates: None

Group Affiliation: Employers Group Inc

Licensed in: AL, AZ, AR, CA, CO, DC, FL, GA, ID, IL, IN, IA, KS, KY, MD, MA, MI, MN, MS, MO, MT, NV, NJ, NM, NY, OK, OR, PA, SC, TN, TX, UT, VA, WI

Commenced Business: September 2002

Address: 500 North Brand Blvd, Glendale, CA 91203-3392

Phone: (775) 327-2700 **Domicile State:** CA **NAIC Code:** 11512

Data Date	Rating	RACR #1	RACR #2	Loss Ratio %	Total Assets ($mil)	Capital ($mil)	Net Premium ($mil)	Net Income ($mil)
9-14	B	2.23	1.61	N/A	1,812.7	304.3	138.2	9.5
9-13	B	2.08	1.43	N/A	1,641.8	304.8	127.5	9.1
2013	B	1.69	1.20	73.8	1,712.3	299.0	183.2	8.3
2012	B	2.32	1.59	57.4	1,477.8	292.9	153.8	5.8
2011	B-	3.11	2.19	77.6	1,283.9	274.6	110.7	11.5
2010	B-	3.83	2.61	66.2	1,216.1	299.4	84.5	16.4
2009	B-	3.79	2.63	57.5	1,254.5	317.1	99.4	23.8

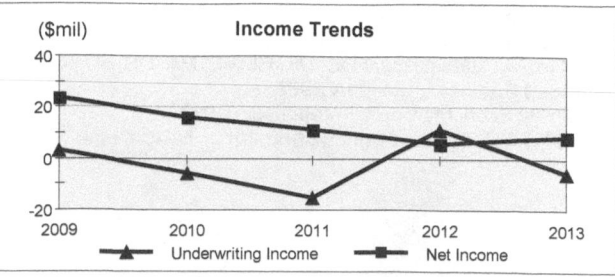

Income Trends

EMPLOYERS INS CO OF NEVADA INC   C   Fair

Major Rating Factors: Fair long-term capitalization index (4.3 on a scale of 0 to 10) based on fair current risk adjusted capital (moderate loss scenario). Fair liquidity (3.7) as cash resources may not be adequate to cover a spike in claims.
Other Rating Factors: Fair overall results on stability tests (3.9) including negative cash flow from operations for 2013 and fair risk adjusted capital in prior years. Good overall profitability index (6.4). Fair expense controls. Return on equity has been good over the last five years, averaging 11.5%. Ample reserve history (9.4) that helps to protect the company against sharp claims increases.
Principal Business: Workers compensation (100%).
Principal Investments: Misc. investments (55%) and investment grade bonds (45%).
Investments in Affiliates: 41%
Group Affiliation: Employers Group Inc
Licensed in: AZ, FL, ID, IL, MT, NV, OR, TX, UT
Commenced Business: January 2000
Address: 10375 Professional Circle, Reno, NV 89521-4802
Phone: (775) 327-2700   **Domicile State:** NV   **NAIC Code:** 10640

Data Date	Rating	RACR #1	RACR #2	Loss Ratio %	Total Assets ($mil)	Capital ($mil)	Net Premium ($mil)	Net Income ($mil)
9-14	C	0.86	0.71	N/A	2,299.8	343.7	271.3	23.2
9-13	C	0.78	0.63	N/A	2,142.1	324.8	250.3	9.4
2013	C	0.65	0.51	73.8	2,182.0	314.7	359.6	8.8
2012	C	0.76	0.62	57.4	1,968.8	295.5	301.9	6.3
2011	C-	0.79	0.67	77.6	1,759.8	251.8	217.3	30.6
2010	C-	0.93	0.79	66.2	1,757.5	299.3	165.9	66.0
2009	C+	1.51	1.30	57.5	2,058.9	512.1	195.2	103.5

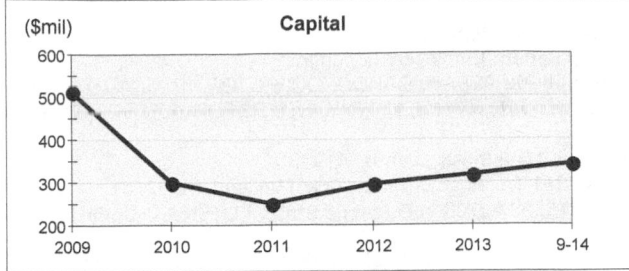

EMPLOYERS INS OF WAUSAU   B-   Good

Major Rating Factors: Fair overall results on stability tests (4.9 on a scale of 0 to 10) including potential drain of affiliation with Liberty Mutual Group. The largest net exposure for one risk is high at 4.7% of capital. Fair profitability index (4.6) with operating losses during 2011 and 2012. Return on equity has been low, averaging 1.9% over the past five years.
Other Rating Factors: History of adequate reserve strength (5.6) as reserves have been consistently at an acceptable level. Good liquidity (6.8) with sufficient resources (cash flows and marketable investments) to handle a spike in claims. Strong long-term capitalization index (7.4) based on excellent current risk adjusted capital (severe and moderate loss scenarios), despite some fluctuation in capital levels.
Principal Business: Workers compensation (77%), other liability (9%), auto liability (7%), commercial multiple peril (3%), auto physical damage (2%), and products liability (1%).
Principal Investments: Investment grade bonds (81%), misc. investments (14%), and non investment grade bonds (5%).
Investments in Affiliates: 4%
Group Affiliation: Liberty Mutual Group
Licensed in: All states, the District of Columbia and Puerto Rico
Commenced Business: September 1911
Address: 2000 Westwood Dr, Wausau, WI 54401
Phone: (617) 357-9500   **Domicile State:** WI   **NAIC Code:** 21458

Data Date	Rating	RACR #1	RACR #2	Loss Ratio %	Total Assets ($mil)	Capital ($mil)	Net Premium ($mil)	Net Income ($mil)
9-14	B-	1.85	1.26	N/A	5,248.3	1,304.3	1,469.2	28.7
9-13	B-	2.01	1.34	N/A	5,522.8	1,280.2	1,450.6	16.2
2013	B-	1.83	1.26	73.5	5,599.8	1,283.7	2,427.2	48.9
2012	B-	2.77	1.89	90.3	3,940.7	1,229.7	1,044.5	-47.7
2011	B-	2.77	1.85	90.1	3,795.7	1,228.8	915.9	-32.8
2010	B-	3.06	2.06	83.0	3,682.4	1,310.5	844.2	109.3
2009	B-	1.93	1.47	85.3	3,333.3	1,075.3	723.0	36.2

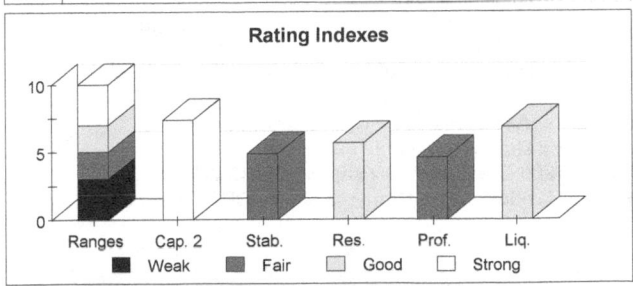

EMPLOYERS MUTUAL CAS CO   B-   Good

Major Rating Factors: Fair overall results on stability tests (4.8 on a scale of 0 to 10) including potential drain of affiliation with Employers Mutual Group. Good overall profitability index (6.3) despite operating losses during 2011.
Other Rating Factors: Good liquidity (6.6) with sufficient resources (cash flows and marketable investments) to handle a spike in claims. Strong long-term capitalization index (7.9) based on excellent current risk adjusted capital (severe and moderate loss scenarios), despite some fluctuation in capital levels. Ample reserve history (8.6) that helps to protect the company against sharp claims increases.
Principal Business: Other liability (24%), auto liability (19%), workers compensation (16%), allied lines (9%), auto physical damage (8%), inland marine (6%), and other lines (19%).
Principal Investments: Misc. investments (52%), investment grade bonds (45%), and real estate (5%).
Investments in Affiliates: 21%
Group Affiliation: Employers Mutual Group
Licensed in: All states except PR
Commenced Business: July 1913
Address: 717 Mulberry St, Des Moines, IA 50309-3872
Phone: (515) 280-2511   **Domicile State:** IA   **NAIC Code:** 21415

Data Date	Rating	RACR #1	RACR #2	Loss Ratio %	Total Assets ($mil)	Capital ($mil)	Net Premium ($mil)	Net Income ($mil)
9-14	B-	2.03	1.60	N/A	2,711.2	1,151.9	650.8	14.9
9-13	B-	2.05	1.60	N/A	2,520.7	1,041.9	605.9	23.2
2013	B-	2.06	1.65	66.7	2,538.0	1,121.9	845.0	56.1
2012	B-	1.99	1.57	66.4	2,308.9	963.0	772.9	36.1
2011	B-	2.02	1.59	80.3	2,200.5	892.4	695.8	-12.4
2010	B-	2.12	1.70	67.8	2,175.0	929.0	647.6	98.5
2009	B-	1.96	1.50	65.0	2,117.3	856.4	650.7	59.8

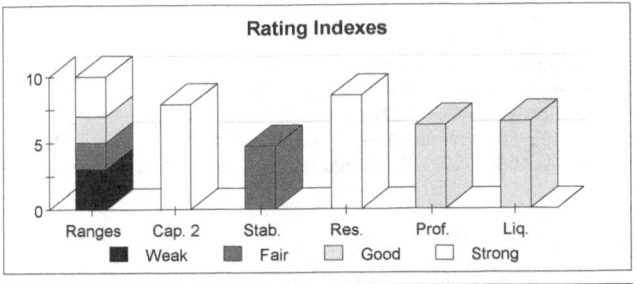

EMPLOYERS PREFERRED INS CO　　　　　　　　C　　　Fair

Major Rating Factors: Fair overall results on stability tests (3.3 on a scale of 0 to 10) including potential drain of affiliation with Employers Group Inc and weak results on operational trends. Good overall profitability index (6.7) despite modest operating losses during 2013. Return on equity has been low, averaging 3.6% over the past five years.

Other Rating Factors: Strong long-term capitalization index (7.3) based on excellent current risk adjusted capital (severe and moderate loss scenarios), despite some fluctuation in capital levels. Ample reserve history (8.4) that helps to protect the company against sharp claims increases. Excellent liquidity (7.0) with ample operational cash flow and liquid investments.

Principal Business: Workers compensation (100%).

Principal Investments: Investment grade bonds (54%) and misc. investments (46%).

Investments in Affiliates: 39%

Group Affiliation: Employers Group Inc

Licensed in: AL, AZ, AR, CA, CO, DC, FL, GA, ID, IL, IN, IA, KS, KY, MD, MI, MN, MS, MO, MT, NV, NJ, NM, NY, NC, OK, OR, PA, SC, SD, TN, TX, UT, VA, WI

Commenced Business: January 1982

Address: 851 Trafalgar Ct Suite 400e, Maitland, FL 32751

Phone: (775) 327-2700　**Domicile State:** FL　**NAIC Code:** 10346

Data Date	Rating	RACR #1	RACR #2	Loss Ratio %	Total Assets ($mil)	Capital ($mil)	Net Premium ($mil)	Net Income ($mil)
9-14	C	1.44	1.35	N/A	717.9	257.6	51.2	1.7
9-13	C	1.61	1.41	N/A	659.0	254.3	47.2	0.7
2013	C	1.30	1.18	73.8	673.1	254.0	67.8	-0.3
2012	C	1.45	1.33	57.4	580.6	206.2	57.0	-0.2
2011	C	1.92	1.70	77.6	432.6	136.1	41.0	8.5
2010	C	1.77	1.65	66.2	415.9	155.0	31.3	3.7
2009	C	1.93	1.76	57.5	413.9	149.2	36.8	17.7

Rating Indexes

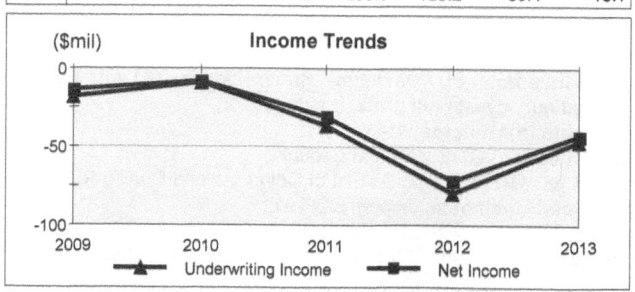

ENDURANCE AMERICAN INS CO　　　　　　　C-　　　Fair

Major Rating Factors: Weak profitability index (2.8 on a scale of 0 to 10) with operating losses during each of the last five years and the first nine months of 2014. Average return on equity over the last five years has been poor at -14.1%. Vulnerable liquidity (2.0) as a spike in claims may stretch capacity.

Other Rating Factors: Weak overall results on stability tests (2.9) including negative cash flow from operations for 2013. The largest net exposure for one risk is high at 3.3% of capital. Good long-term capitalization index (5.5) based on good current risk adjusted capital (moderate loss scenario). Over the last several years, capital levels have remained relatively consistent. History of adequate reserve strength (6.3) as reserves have been consistently at an acceptable level.

Principal Business: Other liability (71%), surety (11%), products liability (8%), ocean marine (5%), inland marine (3%), and commercial multiple peril (1%).

Principal Investments: Investment grade bonds (62%), misc. investments (31%), and cash (7%).

Investments in Affiliates: 20%

Group Affiliation: Endurance Specialty Holdings

Licensed in: All states except CA, FL, MN, PR

Commenced Business: April 1996

Address: 1209 Orange St, Wilmington, DE 19801

Phone: (914) 468-8000　**Domicile State:** DE　**NAIC Code:** 10641

Data Date	Rating	RACR #1	RACR #2	Loss Ratio %	Total Assets ($mil)	Capital ($mil)	Net Premium ($mil)	Net Income ($mil)
9-14	C-	1.20	0.80	N/A	1,896.0	241.0	228.8	-3.9
9-13	D	0.58	0.44	N/A	1,147.3	199.4	273.0	-21.7
2013	D+	1.27	0.87	94.4	1,313.8	247.5	362.2	-42.9
2012	D	0.73	0.56	103.1	1,305.2	231.0	358.0	-71.4
2011	C+	1.12	0.84	89.3	1,264.9	235.7	239.2	-30.7
2010	C	0.58	0.40	77.1	748.2	110.4	164.4	-8.5
2009	C	1.14	0.80	67.2	290.9	125.2	80.4	-13.1

Income Trends

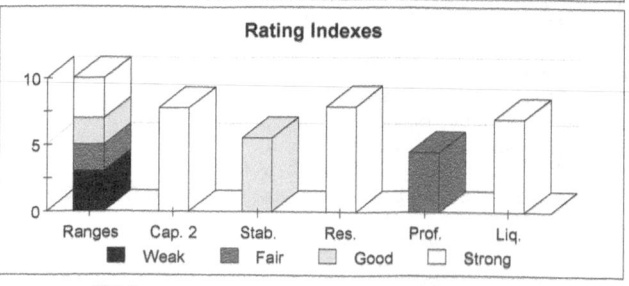

ENDURANCE REINS CORP OF AMERICA　　　　　B　　　Good

Major Rating Factors: Good overall results on stability tests (5.5 on a scale of 0 to 10). Stability strengths include good operational trends and excellent risk diversification. The largest net exposure for one risk is acceptable at 2.9% of capital. Fair profitability index (4.5) with operating losses during 2011 and 2012. Return on equity has been low, averaging 1.6% over the past five years.

Other Rating Factors: Strong long-term capitalization index (7.7) based on excellent current risk adjusted capital (severe and moderate loss scenarios), despite some fluctuation in capital levels. Ample reserve history (7.9) that can protect against increases in claims costs. Excellent liquidity (7.0) with ample operational cash flow and liquid investments.

Principal Business: Surety (90%) and allied lines (9%).

Principal Investments: Investment grade bonds (68%), misc. investments (25%), and cash (7%).

Investments in Affiliates: 26%

Group Affiliation: Endurance Specialty Holdings

Licensed in: All states, the District of Columbia and Puerto Rico

Commenced Business: December 2002

Address: 333 Westchester Ave, White Plains, NY 10604

Phone: (914) 468-8000　**Domicile State:** DE　**NAIC Code:** 11551

Data Date	Rating	RACR #1	RACR #2	Loss Ratio %	Total Assets ($mil)	Capital ($mil)	Net Premium ($mil)	Net Income ($mil)
9-14	B	1.97	1.65	N/A	1,568.6	648.9	182.5	13.3
9-13	B-	1.77	1.45	N/A	1,440.8	565.8	182.1	23.4
2013	B	1.92	1.61	51.2	1,489.7	629.0	263.2	28.4
2012	B-	1.84	1.50	81.6	1,466.6	587.4	239.8	-19.9
2011	B-	1.74	1.23	91.6	1,779.2	598.4	335.1	-24.3
2010	B-	2.50	1.51	64.2	1,649.6	628.3	317.5	40.5
2009	B-	2.14	1.31	75.0	1,850.8	608.0	352.7	22.4

Rating Indexes

ERIE INS CO — B-   Good

Major Rating Factors: Fair overall results on stability tests (4.9 on a scale of 0 to 10) including potential drain of affiliation with Erie Ins Group. Good overall profitability index (6.6). Fair expense controls. Return on equity has been fair, averaging 5.3% over the past five years.

Other Rating Factors: Good liquidity (6.6) with sufficient resources (cash flows and marketable investments) to handle a spike in claims. Strong long-term capitalization index (10.0) based on excellent current risk adjusted capital (severe and moderate loss scenarios). Moreover, capital levels have been consistent in recent years. Ample reserve history (8.7) that helps to protect the company against sharp claims increases.

Principal Business: Homeowners multiple peril (32%), auto liability (31%), auto physical damage (21%), commercial multiple peril (10%), workers compensation (4%), other liability (1%), and surety (1%).

Principal Investments: Investment grade bonds (88%), misc. investments (11%), and non investment grade bonds (1%).

Investments in Affiliates: 4%

Group Affiliation: Erie Ins Group

Licensed in: DC, IL, IN, KY, MD, MN, NY, NC, OH, PA, TN, VA, WV, WI

Commenced Business: January 1973

Address: 100 Erie Ins Place, Erie, PA 16530

Phone: (814) 870-2000   **Domicile State:** PA   **NAIC Code:** 26263

Data Date	Rating	RACR #1	RACR #2	Loss Ratio %	Total Assets ($mil)	Capital ($mil)	Net Premium ($mil)	Net Income ($mil)
9-14	B-	4.81	3.24	N/A	837.4	297.4	197.0	2.5
9-13	B-	5.10	3.46	N/A	774.1	290.0	180.7	12.6
2013	B-	5.04	3.48	69.4	771.8	294.4	252.3	17.1
2012	B-	5.16	3.57	76.0	713.3	276.4	230.1	13.8
2011	B-	5.13	3.56	80.3	667.0	260.0	212.7	9.4
2010	B	5.55	4.00	71.3	652.2	250.8	201.0	21.3
2009	B	5.02	3.64	69.3	625.1	231.5	193.1	16.0

Erie Ins Group
Composite Group Rating: B

Largest Group Members	Assets ($mil)	Rating
ERIE INS EXCHANGE	12592	B
ERIE FAMILY LIFE INS CO	2021	A-
ERIE INS CO	772	B-
ERIE INS PROPERTY CASUALTY CO	86	B
ERIE INS CO OF NY	81	B

ERIE INS EXCHANGE — B   Good

Major Rating Factors: Good overall results on stability tests (5.1 on a scale of 0 to 10) despite potential drain of affiliation with Erie Ins Group. Good overall profitability index (6.6) despite operating losses during 2009.

Other Rating Factors: Good liquidity (6.5) with sufficient resources (cash flows and marketable investments) to handle a spike in claims. Strong long-term capitalization index (9.2) based on excellent current risk adjusted capital (severe and moderate loss scenarios). Moreover, capital levels have been consistent in recent years. Ample reserve history (8.6) that helps to protect the company against sharp claims increases.

Principal Business: Auto liability (31%), homeowners multiple peril (24%), auto physical damage (21%), commercial multiple peril (15%), workers compensation (4%), other liability (3%), and fire (1%).

Principal Investments: Investment grade bonds (50%), misc. investments (49%), non investment grade bonds (1%), and real estate (1%).

Investments in Affiliates: 6%

Group Affiliation: Erie Ins Group

Licensed in: AL, CT, DC, DE, GA, IL, IN, IA, KY, ME, MD, MN, MO, MT, NE, NV, NH, NJ, NM, NY, NC, ND, OH, PA, RI, SC, SD, TN, TX, VT, VA, WV, WI, WY

Commenced Business: April 1925

Address: 100 Erie Ins Place, Erie, PA 16530

Phone: (814) 870-2000   **Domicile State:** PA   **NAIC Code:** 26271

Data Date	Rating	RACR #1	RACR #2	Loss Ratio %	Total Assets ($mil)	Capital ($mil)	Net Premium ($mil)	Net Income ($mil)
9-14	B	3.71	2.51	N/A	13,233.4	6,601.6	3,723.7	161.1
9-13	B	3.71	2.53	N/A	12,303.0	6,203.2	3,415.5	352.1
2013	B	3.68	2.51	69.4	12,591.7	6,467.0	4,767.7	478.8
2012	B	3.70	2.57	76.0	11,229.2	5,633.4	4,349.3	311.0
2011	B	3.62	2.50	80.3	10,382.3	5,166.0	4,020.7	182.4
2010	B	3.93	2.70	71.4	10,335.1	5,069.6	3,798.2	530.8
2009	B	4.66	3.04	69.3	9,548.0	4,517.6	3,648.8	-56.2

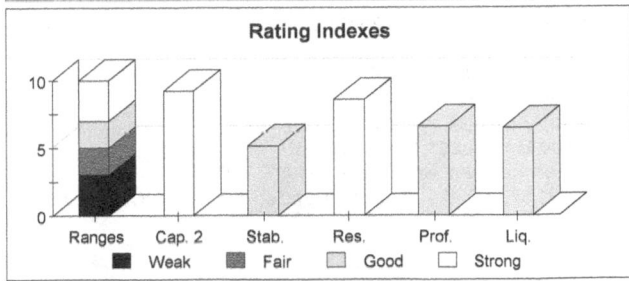

Rating Indexes

ESSENT GUARANTY INC * — A-   Excellent

Major Rating Factors: Strong long-term capitalization index (10.0 on a scale of 0 to 10) based on excellent current risk adjusted capital (severe and moderate loss scenarios). Furthermore, this high level of risk adjusted capital has been consistently maintained in previous years. Superior liquidity (9.1) with ample operational cash flow and liquid investments.

Other Rating Factors: Good overall results on stability tests (5.7) despite excessive premium growth and weak results on operational trends. Fair reserve development (3.6) as reserves have generally been sufficient to cover claims. Fair profitability index (3.9) with operating losses during 2009, 2010, 2011 and 2012. Average return on equity over the last five years has been poor at -3.8%.

Principal Business: Mortgage guaranty (100%).

Principal Investments: Misc. investments (58%), investment grade bonds (41%), and cash (1%).

Investments in Affiliates: 0%

Group Affiliation: Essent Group Ltd

Licensed in: All states except PR

Commenced Business: July 2009

Address: 201 King of Prussia Rd Ste 501, Radnor, PA 19087

Phone: (610) 230-0555   **Domicile State:** PA   **NAIC Code:** 13634

Data Date	Rating	RACR #1	RACR #2	Loss Ratio %	Total Assets ($mil)	Capital ($mil)	Net Premium ($mil)	Net Income ($mil)
9-14	A-	8.15	5.41	N/A	767.9	456.7	139.8	81.4
9-13	A-	4.10	3.53	N/A	451.4	281.4	76.4	33.1
2013	A-	6.30	4.22	1.9	546.8	346.4	169.8	49.8
2012	A-	3.11	2.58	3.4	246.2	163.8	66.8	-16.3
2011	A-	3.35	3.16	0.8	175.9	141.9	16.6	-34.1
2010	N/A	N/A	N/A	0.0	166.8	160.3	0.2	-25.8
2009	N/A	N/A	N/A	0.0	184.9	175.2	0.0	-6.8

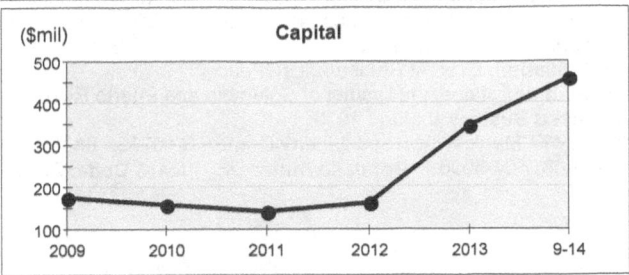

Capital

ESSEX INS CO

C   **Fair**

Major Rating Factors: Fair overall results on stability tests (3.8 on a scale of 0 to 10). The largest net exposure for one risk is conservative at 1.8% of capital. Good long-term capitalization index (6.5) based on good current risk adjusted capital (moderate loss scenario). Over the last several years, capital levels have remained relatively consistent.

Other Rating Factors: Good liquidity (6.8) with sufficient resources (cash flows and marketable investments) to handle a spike in claims. Ample reserve history (9.7) that helps to protect the company against sharp claims increases. Excellent profitability (8.1) with operating gains in each of the last five years. Return on equity has been good over the last five years, averaging 14.5%.

Principal Business: Other liability (37%), commercial multiple peril (20%), inland marine (10%), allied lines (8%), fire (5%), earthquake (5%), and other lines (15%).

Principal Investments: Investment grade bonds (52%) and misc. investments (49%).

Investments in Affiliates: None

Group Affiliation: Markel Corp

Licensed in: All states except PR

Commenced Business: October 1980

Address: 1209 Orange St, Wilmington, DE 19801

Phone: (804) 273-1400   **Domicile State:** DE   **NAIC Code:** 39020

Data Date	Rating	RACR #1	RACR #2	Loss Ratio %	Total Assets ($mil)	Capital ($mil)	Net Premium ($mil)	Net Income ($mil)
9-14	C	1.44	0.96	N/A	1,353.3	453.4	320.0	50.8
9-13	C	1.52	1.00	N/A	1,263.2	442.4	285.7	64.5
2013	C	1.33	0.89	36.5	1,210.7	385.3	414.7	87.9
2012	C	1.23	0.81	51.1	1,135.3	334.7	356.5	38.5
2011	C	1.43	1.00	50.6	1,109.4	345.5	317.7	34.4
2010	C	1.57	1.07	44.6	1,054.1	339.6	278.0	37.5
2009	C	1.63	1.11	41.5	1,046.8	343.6	236.5	57.5

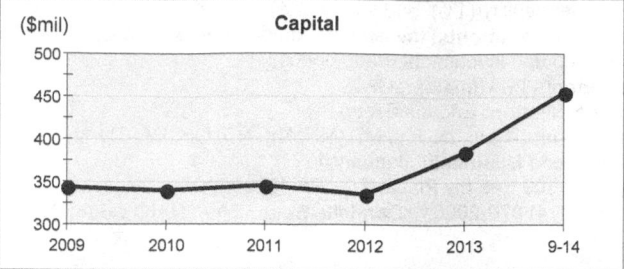

EVANSTON INS CO

C   **Fair**

Major Rating Factors: Fair overall results on stability tests (3.8 on a scale of 0 to 10) including excessive premium growth. The largest net exposure for one risk is conservative at 1.3% of capital. Good long-term capitalization index (6.0) based on good current risk adjusted capital (moderate loss scenario).

Other Rating Factors: Good overall profitability index (5.4). Weak expense controls. Return on equity has been good over the last five years, averaging 14.5%. Ample reserve history (9.7) that helps to protect the company against sharp claims increases. Excellent liquidity (7.1) with ample operational cash flow and liquid investments.

Principal Business: Other liability (55%), medical malpractice (23%), products liability (16%), fire (3%), allied lines (2%), commercial multiple peril (1%), and credit (1%).

Principal Investments: Investment grade bonds (56%) and misc. investments (44%).

Investments in Affiliates: None

Group Affiliation: Markel Corp

Licensed in: All states except NH

Commenced Business: December 1977

Address: Ten Parkway North, Deerfield, IL 60015

Phone: (847) 572-6000   **Domicile State:** IL   **NAIC Code:** 35378

Data Date	Rating	RACR #1	RACR #2	Loss Ratio %	Total Assets ($mil)	Capital ($mil)	Net Premium ($mil)	Net Income ($mil)
9-14	C	1.29	0.87	N/A	2,395.2	628.8	502.6	40.0
9-13	C	1.51	1.04	N/A	2,254.3	666.3	385.2	22.3
2013	C	1.34	0.90	48.7	2,152.3	574.2	642.2	82.0
2012	C	1.42	0.99	53.5	2,010.2	568.4	451.1	84.1
2011	C	1.20	0.93	45.2	2,073.6	611.3	477.4	117.9
2010	C	1.77	1.17	51.9	2,168.1	610.3	448.5	113.7
2009	C	1.17	0.80	57.4	2,230.5	531.1	509.6	53.6

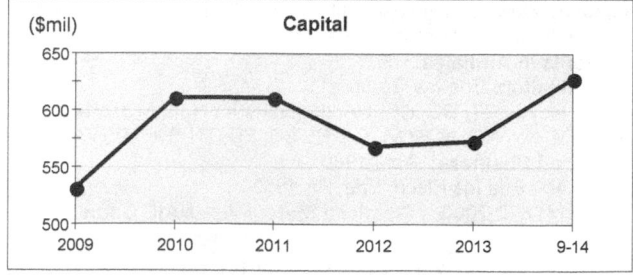

EVEREST REINSURANCE CO

C+   **Fair**

Major Rating Factors: Fair overall results on stability tests (4.7 on a scale of 0 to 10) including potential drain of affiliation with Everest Reinsurance Group. Fair reserve development (4.9) as reserves have generally been sufficient to cover claims.

Other Rating Factors: Good long-term capitalization index (6.6) based on good current risk adjusted capital (moderate loss scenario). Over the last several years, capital levels have remained relatively consistent. Good overall profitability index (5.9) despite operating losses during 2011. Return on equity has been fair, averaging 9.0% over the past five years. Good liquidity (6.9) with sufficient resources (cash flows and marketable investments) to handle a spike in claims.

Principal Business: Other liability (95%) and fidelity (5%).

Principal Investments: Investment grade bonds (56%), misc. investments (38%), non investment grade bonds (4%), and cash (2%).

Investments in Affiliates: 30%

Group Affiliation: Everest Reinsurance Group

Licensed in: All states, the District of Columbia and Puerto Rico

Commenced Business: June 1973

Address: 477 Martinsville Road, Liberty Corner, NJ 07938-0830

Phone: (908) 604-3000   **Domicile State:** DE   **NAIC Code:** 26921

Data Date	Rating	RACR #1	RACR #2	Loss Ratio %	Total Assets ($mil)	Capital ($mil)	Net Premium ($mil)	Net Income ($mil)
9-14	C+	1.18	0.96	N/A	10,434.6	3,103.7	1,565.2	257.3
9-13	C+	1.13	0.93	N/A	9,502.0	2,673.1	1,367.5	446.1
2013	C+	1.13	0.93	59.5	9,288.4	2,814.3	2,024.4	540.0
2012	C+	1.11	0.92	64.9	9,046.7	2,613.0	1,581.0	359.8
2011	C	0.98	0.80	106.4	8,610.6	2,322.1	1,653.4	-326.4
2010	C	1.44	1.00	81.1	8,178.8	2,527.5	1,702.9	218.5
2009	C	1.44	0.96	63.3	8,454.7	2,789.7	1,646.6	442.7

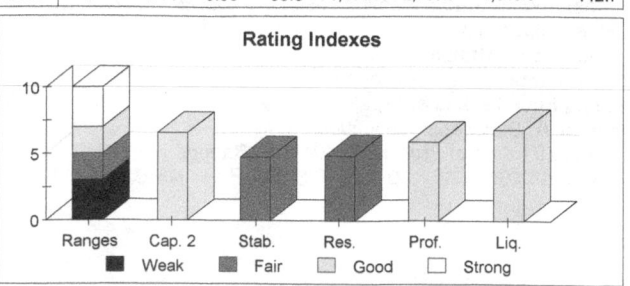

EXECUTIVE RISK INDEMNITY INC *   B+   Good

Major Rating Factors: Good liquidity (6.9 on a scale of 0 to 10) with sufficient resources (cash flows and marketable investments) to handle a spike in claims. Good overall results on stability tests (5.6). The largest net exposure for one risk is high at 4.1% of capital. Stability strengths include good operational trends and excellent risk diversification.

Other Rating Factors: Strong long-term capitalization index (8.9) based on excellent current risk adjusted capital (severe and moderate loss scenarios), despite some fluctuation in capital levels. Ample reserve history (8.9) that helps to protect the company against sharp claims increases. Excellent profitability (8.6) with operating gains in each of the last five years. Return on equity has been good over the last five years, averaging 12.8%.

Principal Business: Other liability (91%), commercial multiple peril (6%), fidelity (2%), and burglary & theft (1%).

Principal Investments: Investment grade bonds (84%), misc. investments (15%), and real estate (1%).

Investments in Affiliates: 5%

Group Affiliation: Chubb Corp

Licensed in: All states except PR

Commenced Business: January 1978

Address: 1209 Orange St, Wilmington, DE 19801-1120

Phone: (908) 903-2000   **Domicile State:** DE   **NAIC Code:** 35181

Data Date	Rating	RACR #1	RACR #2	Loss Ratio %	Total Assets ($mil)	Capital ($mil)	Net Premium ($mil)	Net Income ($mil)
9-14	B+	3.39	2.30	N/A	3,025.1	1,241.6	549.6	121.4
9-13	B+	3.39	2.27	N/A	2,995.7	1,207.6	533.0	124.3
2013	B+	3.43	2.34	52.7	2,977.3	1,218.6	721.2	174.1
2012	B+	3.17	2.12	67.3	2,899.9	1,100.6	694.2	115.4
2011	B+	3.19	2.15	68.4	2,832.4	1,076.9	682.0	105.2
2010	B	3.35	2.27	61.7	2,838.5	1,111.8	659.5	150.6
2009	B	3.22	2.17	55.7	2,807.6	1,078.7	665.3	169.4

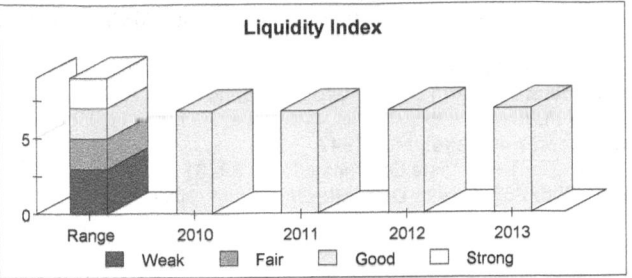

Liquidity Index

FACTORY MUTUAL INS CO   C   Fair

Major Rating Factors: Fair overall results on stability tests (3.4 on a scale of 0 to 10) including fair financial strength of affiliated FM Global. The largest net exposure for one risk is high at 4.3% of capital. History of adequate reserve strength (6.5) as reserves have been consistently at an acceptable level.

Other Rating Factors: Good liquidity (6.7) with sufficient resources (cash flows and marketable investments) to handle a spike in claims. Strong long-term capitalization index (8.0) based on excellent current risk adjusted capital (severe and moderate loss scenarios), despite some fluctuation in capital levels. Excellent profitability (7.4) despite modest operating losses during 2011.

Principal Business: Allied lines (37%), inland marine (32%), fire (18%), and boiler & machinery (12%).

Principal Investments: Misc. investments (73%), investment grade bonds (24%), non investment grade bonds (2%), and cash (1%).

Investments in Affiliates: 18%

Group Affiliation: FM Global

Licensed in: All states, the District of Columbia and Puerto Rico

Commenced Business: December 1835

Address: 1301 Atwood Avenue, Johnston, RI 02919-4908

Phone: (401) 275-3000   **Domicile State:** RI   **NAIC Code:** 21482

Data Date	Rating	RACR #1	RACR #2	Loss Ratio %	Total Assets ($mil)	Capital ($mil)	Net Premium ($mil)	Net Income ($mil)
9-14	C	2.58	1.95	N/A	15,135.4	9,945.8	2,024.5	467.8
9-13	C	2.67	2.01	N/A	13,403.1	8,770.6	2,103.6	682.9
2013	C	2.48	1.90	50.6	13,795.7	9,153.5	2,824.5	662.5
2012	C	2.47	1.89	59.8	12,239.9	7,525.1	2,855.3	612.1
2011	C	2.40	1.82	95.3	10,978.4	6,431.6	2,594.5	-5.6
2010	C	2.49	1.90	50.7	11,028.8	6,961.9	2,416.0	667.4
2009	C	2.04	1.63	41.9	10,015.4	6,203.6	2,585.3	899.2

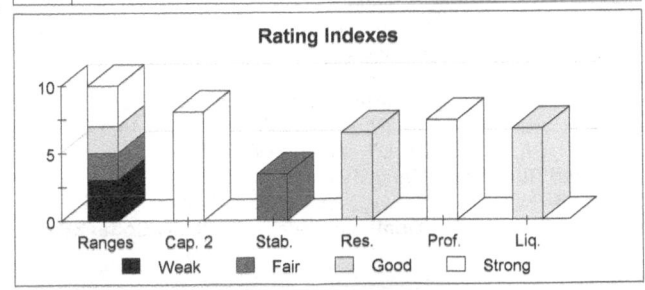

Rating Indexes

FAIR AMERICAN INS & REINS CO   B   Good

Major Rating Factors: Good overall profitability index (5.1). Weak expense controls. Return on equity has been fair, averaging 9.7% over the past five years.

Other Rating Factors: Good overall results on stability tests (5.2) despite excessive premium growth and weak results on operational trends. Affiliation with Alleghany Corp Group is a strength. Strong long-term capitalization index (10.0) based on excellent current risk adjusted capital (severe and moderate loss scenarios), despite some fluctuation in capital levels. Superior liquidity (10.0) with ample operational cash flow and liquid investments.

Principal Business: Medical malpractice (100%).

Principal Investments: Investment grade bonds (78%) and misc. investments (22%).

Investments in Affiliates: 20%

Group Affiliation: Alleghany Corp Group

Licensed in: All states except PR

Commenced Business: September 1985

Address: 80 Pine St, 7th Floor, New York, NY 10005

Phone: (212) 365-2200   **Domicile State:** NY   **NAIC Code:** 35157

Data Date	Rating	RACR #1	RACR #2	Loss Ratio %	Total Assets ($mil)	Capital ($mil)	Net Premium ($mil)	Net Income ($mil)
9-14	B	5.42	5.19	N/A	257.2	235.4	2.8	3.7
9-13	B	15.88	9.54	N/A	278.7	255.6	0.9	0.4
2013	B	5.35	5.15	78.6	254.8	230.6	3.6	0.3
2012	B	11.85	8.65	65.2	291.8	250.9	66.8	64.3
2011	B	2.08	1.34	85.7	750.1	233.1	173.2	3.6
2010	B-	2.18	1.35	67.9	693.5	226.6	170.9	24.1
2009	C+	1.52	0.90	64.4	649.0	203.5	179.5	33.1

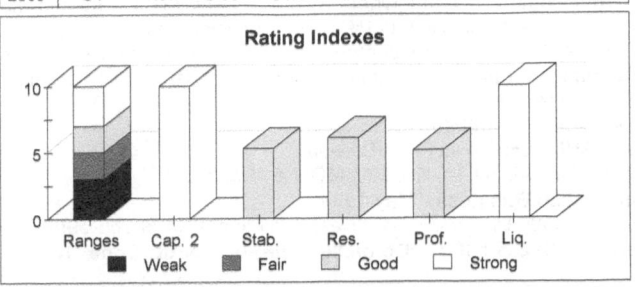

Rating Indexes

FARM BUREAU MUTUAL INS CO OF ID *

B+ **Good**

Major Rating Factors: Good overall results on stability tests (5.0 on a scale of 0 to 10) despite potential drain of affiliation with Farm Bureau Group of Idaho. History of adequate reserve strength (6.0) as reserves have been consistently at an acceptable level.

Other Rating Factors: Good liquidity (6.5) with sufficient resources (cash flows and marketable investments) to handle a spike in claims. Strong long-term capitalization index (9.5) based on excellent current risk adjusted capital (severe and moderate loss scenarios), despite some fluctuation in capital levels. Fair profitability index (4.5) with operating losses during 2012.

Principal Business: Auto liability (31%), auto physical damage (23%), farmowners multiple peril (19%), homeowners multiple peril (18%), allied lines (4%), inland marine (3%), and other liability (3%).

Principal Investments: Investment grade bonds (66%), misc. investments (31%), and real estate (3%).

Investments in Affiliates: 16%

Group Affiliation: Farm Bureau Group of Idaho

Licensed in: ID

Commenced Business: May 1947

Address: 275 Tierra Vista Dr, Pocatello, ID 83201

Phone: (208) 232-7914   **Domicile State:** ID   **NAIC Code:** 13765

Data Date	Rating	RACR #1	RACR #2	Loss Ratio %	Total Assets ($mil)	Capital ($mil)	Net Premium ($mil)	Net Income ($mil)
9-14	B+	3.27	2.64	N/A	431.4	236.4	115.1	2.3
9-13	B+	3.39	2.66	N/A	418.8	227.9	105.5	0.7
2013	B+	3.30	2.70	78.2	418.0	233.1	151.7	5.4
2012	B+	3.46	2.76	86.9	396.6	220.7	137.4	-8.9
2011	B+	3.68	2.98	76.0	388.5	224.4	134.8	4.5
2010	B+	3.89	3.13	68.0	373.7	223.0	131.1	14.7
2009	B+	4.00	3.15	69.7	363.3	210.1	129.5	15.5

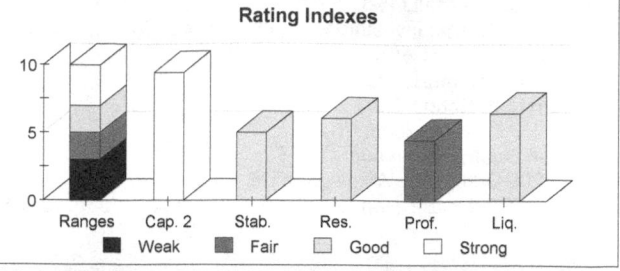

Rating Indexes

FARM BUREAU MUTUAL INS CO OF MI

B- **Good**

Major Rating Factors: Fair profitability index (4.7 on a scale of 0 to 10) with operating losses during 2009, 2010 and 2011. History of adequate reserve strength (6.6) as reserves have been consistently at an acceptable level.

Other Rating Factors: Good liquidity (5.8) with sufficient resources (cash flows and marketable investments) to handle a spike in claims. Good overall results on stability tests (5.0). The largest net exposure for one risk is conservative at 1.1% of capital. Strong long-term capitalization index (8.5) based on excellent current risk adjusted capital (severe and moderate loss scenarios), despite some fluctuation in capital levels.

Principal Business: Farmowners multiple peril (44%), auto liability (28%), auto physical damage (18%), workers compensation (5%), inland marine (2%), other liability (1%), and boiler & machinery (1%).

Principal Investments: Investment grade bonds (83%), misc. investments (17%), and non investment grade bonds (1%).

Investments in Affiliates: None

Group Affiliation: Michigan Farm Bureau

Licensed in: AL, CT, GA, IL, IN, IA, KS, KY, ME, MD, MA, MI, NE, NH, NJ, NC, ND, OH, OR, PA, RI, SD, TX, UT, VT, VA, WV, WI

Commenced Business: March 1949

Address: 7373 W Saginaw Hwy, Lansing, MI 48917

Phone: (517) 323-7000   **Domicile State:** MI   **NAIC Code:** 21555

Data Date	Rating	RACR #1	RACR #2	Loss Ratio %	Total Assets ($mil)	Capital ($mil)	Net Premium ($mil)	Net Income ($mil)
9-14	B-	3.89	2.56	N/A	650.9	275.7	235.8	10.5
9-13	C+	3.62	2.40	N/A	626.6	255.3	218.0	16.1
2013	B-	3.82	2.49	69.8	630.6	262.8	286.9	21.4
2012	C+	2.76	1.84	74.4	597.8	203.9	337.8	12.4
2011	C	2.63	1.77	86.8	567.2	189.4	324.9	-28.7
2010	B-	3.41	2.25	81.0	566.2	220.9	285.2	-0.1
2009	B-	3.38	2.22	78.7	577.1	230.6	310.7	-7.5

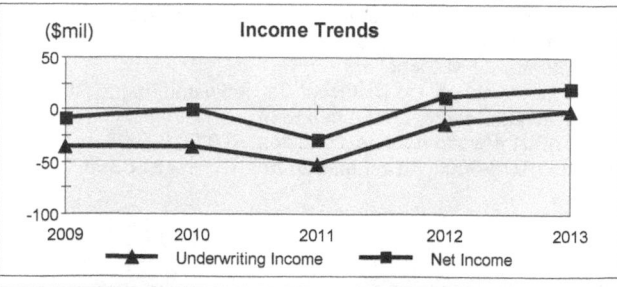

Income Trends

FARM BUREAU PROP & CAS INS CO *

A- **Excellent**

Major Rating Factors: Strong long-term capitalization index (9.2 on a scale of 0 to 10) based on excellent current risk adjusted capital (severe and moderate loss scenarios). Furthermore, this high level of risk adjusted capital has been consistently maintained in previous years. Ample reserve history (8.2) that helps to protect the company against sharp claims increases.

Other Rating Factors: Excellent overall results on stability tests (7.2). Stability strengths include excellent operational trends and excellent risk diversification. Good overall profitability index (6.8) despite modest operating losses during the first nine months of 2014. Return on equity has been fair, averaging 5.1% over the past five years. Good liquidity (5.7) with sufficient resources (cash flows and marketable investments) to handle a spike in claims.

Principal Business: Farmowners multiple peril (24%), homeowners multiple peril (23%), auto liability (21%), auto physical damage (21%), commercial multiple peril (5%), workers compensation (3%), and other liability (3%).

Principal Investments: Investment grade bonds (83%), misc. investments (17%), and real estate (2%).

Investments in Affiliates: 5%

Group Affiliation: Iowa Farm Bureau

Licensed in: AZ, ID, IA, KS, MN, MO, NE, NM, SD, UT, WI

Commenced Business: May 1939

Address: 5400 University Ave, West Des Moines, IA 50266-5997

Phone: (515) 225-5400   **Domicile State:** IA   **NAIC Code:** 13773

Data Date	Rating	RACR #1	RACR #2	Loss Ratio %	Total Assets ($mil)	Capital ($mil)	Net Premium ($mil)	Net Income ($mil)
9-14	A-	3.34	2.53	N/A	2,012.0	801.5	846.8	-4.1
9-13	A-	3.34	2.48	N/A	1,919.3	760.1	817.2	37.0
2013	A-	3.45	2.57	70.2	1,931.3	802.3	1,127.9	68.6
2012	A-	3.38	2.49	71.4	1,768.5	714.8	1,052.9	74.0
2011	A-	3.18	2.38	75.2	1,664.3	661.7	1,009.1	29.0
2010	A-	3.16	2.30	72.9	1,572.0	635.2	930.0	15.8
2009	A-	3.15	2.28	73.3	1,501.2	598.6	851.1	25.3

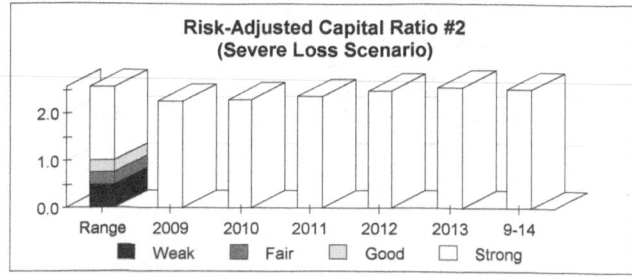

Risk-Adjusted Capital Ratio #2
(Severe Loss Scenario)

FARM FAMILY CASUALTY INS CO *

B+   **Good**

Major Rating Factors: Good overall results on stability tests (6.7 on a scale of 0 to 10). Affiliation with American National Group Inc is a strength. Good overall profitability index (6.0) despite operating losses during 2010. Return on equity has been low, averaging 4.3% over the past five years.

Other Rating Factors: Good liquidity (6.7) with sufficient resources (cash flows and marketable investments) to handle a spike in claims. Strong long-term capitalization index (8.9) based on excellent current risk adjusted capital (severe and moderate loss scenarios), despite some fluctuation in capital levels. Ample reserve history (9.4) that helps to protect the company against sharp claims increases.

Principal Business: Auto liability (24%), workers compensation (13%), other liability (11%), commercial multiple peril (10%), auto physical damage (10%), fire (10%), and other lines (22%).

Principal Investments: Investment grade bonds (85%), misc. investments (11%), cash (2%), and non investment grade bonds (2%).

Investments in Affiliates: None

Group Affiliation: American National Group Inc

Licensed in: CT, DE, ME, MD, MA, MO, NH, NJ, NY, RI, VT, VA, WV

Commenced Business: November 1956

Address: 344 Route 9W, Glenmont, NY 12077-2910

Phone: (518) 431-5000   **Domicile State:** NY   **NAIC Code:** 13803

Data Date	Rating	RACR #1	RACR #2	Loss Ratio %	Total Assets ($mil)	Capital ($mil)	Net Premium ($mil)	Net Income ($mil)
9-14	B+	3.54	2.34	N/A	1,067.1	359.7	287.7	13.4
9-13	B+	3.51	2.32	N/A	1,037.2	331.1	271.1	14.7
2013	B+	3.57	2.39	72.1	1,036.7	347.1	371.1	27.6
2012	B+	3.40	2.29	78.9	984.6	308.3	352.7	13.5
2011	B	3.24	2.19	81.4	966.6	293.2	354.9	14.6
2010	B	3.26	2.18	87.5	983.6	302.5	343.6	-3.9
2009	B	3.69	2.48	77.0	980.6	309.2	348.6	15.7

American National Group Inc Composite Group Rating: B Largest Group Members	Assets ($mil)	Rating
AMERICAN NATIONAL INS CO	18036	B
FARM FAMILY LIFE INS CO	1248	B
AMERICAN NATIONAL PROPERTY CAS CO	1156	B
FARM FAMILY CASUALTY INS CO	1037	B+
STANDARD LIFE ACCIDENT INS CO	528	A-

FARMERS AUTOMOBILE INS ASN *

B+   **Good**

Major Rating Factors: Good overall results on stability tests (6.0 on a scale of 0 to 10). Affiliation with Farmers Automobile Ins Assn is a strength. Good liquidity (6.5) with sufficient resources (cash flows and marketable investments) to handle a spike in claims.

Other Rating Factors: Strong long-term capitalization index (8.5) based on excellent current risk adjusted capital (severe and moderate loss scenarios), despite some fluctuation in capital levels. Ample reserve history (9.3) that helps to protect the company against sharp claims increases. Fair profitability index (4.5) with operating losses during the first nine months of 2014.

Principal Business: Homeowners multiple peril (32%), auto liability (32%), auto physical damage (29%), allied lines (3%), fire (2%), and inland marine (1%).

Principal Investments: Investment grade bonds (66%), misc. investments (31%), cash (2%), and real estate (1%).

Investments in Affiliates: 22%

Group Affiliation: Farmers Automobile Ins Assn

Licensed in: AZ, IL, IN, IA, MI, OH, WI

Commenced Business: April 1921

Address: 2505 Court St, Pekin, IL 61558

Phone: (309) 346-1161   **Domicile State:** IL   **NAIC Code:** 24201

Data Date	Rating	RACR #1	RACR #2	Loss Ratio %	Total Assets ($mil)	Capital ($mil)	Net Premium ($mil)	Net Income ($mil)
9-14	B+	2.27	1.95	N/A	1,172.9	487.8	327.7	-10.9
9-13	B+	2.38	2.05	N/A	1,141.5	492.6	307.6	13.2
2013	B+	2.36	2.06	75.4	1,153.5	497.8	428.5	10.2
2012	B+	2.35	2.07	75.1	1,079.7	471.3	402.0	22.8
2011	B+	2.35	2.06	83.5	1,031.5	447.4	368.5	5.0
2010	B+	2.32	2.00	75.9	998.6	417.8	361.8	9.4
2009	B+	2.35	2.05	74.6	872.9	398.2	327.0	13.0

Rating Indexes

Ranges Cap. 2 Stab. Res. Prof. Liq.
■ Weak   ■ Fair   □ Good   □ Strong

FARMERS INS CO OF OR

B   **Good**

Major Rating Factors: Good overall results on stability tests (5.4 on a scale of 0 to 10) despite potential drain of affiliation with Farmers Insurance Group of Companies. History of adequate reserve strength (6.8) as reserves have been consistently at an acceptable level.

Other Rating Factors: Good liquidity (5.9) with sufficient resources (cash flows and marketable investments) to handle a spike in claims. Fair profitability index (3.7) with operating losses during 2010 and 2011. Return on equity has been low, averaging 1.5% over the past five years. Strong long-term capitalization index (8.3) based on excellent current risk adjusted capital (severe and moderate loss scenarios), despite some fluctuation in capital levels.

Principal Business: Auto liability (60%), auto physical damage (20%), homeowners multiple peril (14%), commercial multiple peril (4%), allied lines (1%), and earthquake (1%).

Principal Investments: Investment grade bonds (98%), misc. investments (1%), and non investment grade bonds (1%).

Investments in Affiliates: None

Group Affiliation: Farmers Insurance Group of Companies

Licensed in: CA, MI, OR

Commenced Business: October 1970

Address: 13333 SW 68th Parkway, Tigard, OR 97223

Phone: (503) 372-2000   **Domicile State:** OR   **NAIC Code:** 21636

Data Date	Rating	RACR #1	RACR #2	Loss Ratio %	Total Assets ($mil)	Capital ($mil)	Net Premium ($mil)	Net Income ($mil)
9-14	B	2.58	1.89	N/A	1,602.5	503.5	710.3	12.2
9-13	B-	2.40	1.76	N/A	1,617.2	475.3	721.9	4.9
2013	B	2.48	1.81	66.8	1,614.9	490.3	954.6	21.9
2012	B-	2.36	1.73	72.3	1,600.3	470.2	969.9	6.4
2011	B-	2.28	1.66	73.2	1,577.2	458.7	990.9	-11.8
2010	B-	3.04	2.11	65.5	1,641.5	560.6	892.1	-18.2
2009	B-	3.53	2.45	66.4	1,469.1	557.8	679.1	35.4

Farmers Insurance Group of Companies Composite Group Rating: C Largest Group Members	Assets ($mil)	Rating
FARMERS INS EXCHANGE	15557	C
MID-CENTURY INS CO	3715	C
FIRE INS EXCHANGE	2255	C+
FOREMOST INS CO	1939	B
TRUCK INS EXCHANGE	1933	C+

FARMERS INS EXCHANGE

C   **Fair**

Major Rating Factors: Fair profitability index (3.8 on a scale of 0 to 10) with operating losses during 2010, 2011, 2012 and the first nine months of 2014. Fair liquidity (3.8) as cash resources may not be adequate to cover a spike in claims.

Other Rating Factors: Fair overall results on stability tests (3.4) including negative cash flow from operations for 2013. Good overall long-term capitalization (5.5) based on good current risk adjusted capital (severe and moderate loss scenarios). However, capital levels have fluctuated somewhat during past years. History of adequate reserve strength (6.5) as reserves have been consistently at an acceptable level.

Principal Business: Homeowners multiple peril (34%), auto liability (29%), auto physical damage (18%), commercial multiple peril (14%), other liability (2%), workers compensation (2%), and other lines (2%).

Principal Investments: Investment grade bonds (56%), misc. investments (45%), non investment grade bonds (1%), and real estate (1%).

Investments in Affiliates: 43%

Group Affiliation: Farmers Insurance Group of Companies

Licensed in: All states except AK, CT, HI, PR

Commenced Business: April 1928

Address: 4680 Wilshire Blvd, Los Angeles, CA 90010

Phone: (323) 932-3200   **Domicile State:** CA   **NAIC Code:** 21652

Data Date	Rating	RACR #1	RACR #2	Loss Ratio %	Total Assets ($mil)	Capital ($mil)	Net Premium ($mil)	Net Income ($mil)
9-14	C	0.86	0.80	N/A	15,807.4	3,822.9	5,251.5	-31.1
9-13	C	0.90	0.83	N/A	15,941.9	3,755.5	5,337.2	-42.3
2013	C	0.90	0.84	66.8	15,557.1	3,879.7	7,057.1	55.0
2012	C	0.91	0.85	73.4	15,530.2	3,750.8	7,170.1	-162.0
2011	C	0.96	0.89	73.2	15,237.4	3,820.2	7,325.7	-229.1
2010	C	0.96	0.88	66.1	15,066.8	3,678.8	6,594.8	-304.3
2009	C	1.07	0.99	67.5	15,016.6	3,699.2	5,020.8	57.8

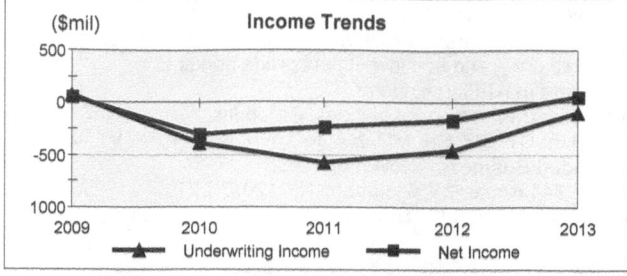

FARMERS MUTUAL HAIL INS CO OF IA

B-   **Good**

Major Rating Factors: Fair overall results on stability tests (4.6 on a scale of 0 to 10) including potential drain of affiliation with Farmers Mutual Hail Ins Co. The largest net exposure for one risk is high at 4.6% of capital. Fair profitability index (3.7) with operating losses during 2012 and the first nine months of 2014.

Other Rating Factors: History of adequate reserve strength (6.3) as reserves have been consistently at an acceptable level. Good liquidity (5.5) with sufficient resources (cash flows and marketable investments) to handle a spike in claims. Strong long-term capitalization index (7.0) based on good current risk adjusted capital (severe and moderate loss scenarios), although results have slipped from the excellent range during the last year.

Principal Business: Allied lines (97%), fire (1%), and auto liability (1%).

Principal Investments: Investment grade bonds (101%), non investment grade bonds (4%), and real estate (4%).

Investments in Affiliates: 3%

Group Affiliation: Farmers Mutual Hail Ins Co

Licensed in: All states except AK, DC, HI, LA, ME, NV, PR

Commenced Business: March 1893

Address: 6785 Westown Parkway, West Des Moines, IA 50266

Phone: (515) 282-9104   **Domicile State:** IA   **NAIC Code:** 13897

Data Date	Rating	RACR #1	RACR #2	Loss Ratio %	Total Assets ($mil)	Capital ($mil)	Net Premium ($mil)	Net Income ($mil)
9-14	B-	1.49	0.92	N/A	844.6	311.5	382.9	-40.4
9-13	B-	1.65	1.02	N/A	845.4	366.2	404.3	18.1
2013	B-	1.98	1.24	85.9	832.8	358.3	431.1	3.9
2012	B-	1.91	1.18	92.6	879.9	317.5	470.4	-15.1
2011	B-	2.64	1.63	79.4	679.4	360.0	405.2	19.9
2010	B-	2.58	1.67	63.7	505.5	345.7	369.2	41.8
2009	B-	1.88	1.23	69.2	453.5	287.5	306.3	21.5

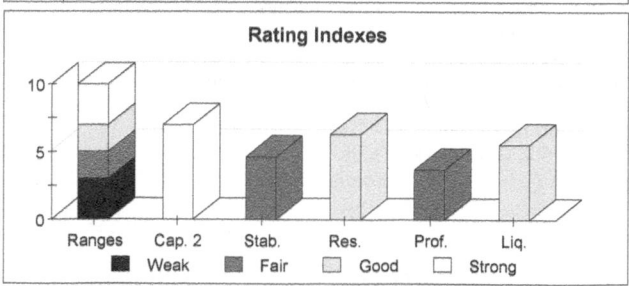

FARMERS MUTUAL INS CO OF NE

B   **Good**

Major Rating Factors: Good liquidity (6.7 on a scale of 0 to 10) with sufficient resources (cash flows and marketable investments) to handle a spike in claims. Good overall results on stability tests (6.2).

Other Rating Factors: Fair profitability index (4.4) with operating losses during 2010, 2011 and the first nine months of 2014. Strong long-term capitalization index (10.0) based on excellent current risk adjusted capital (severe and moderate loss scenarios), despite some fluctuation in capital levels. Ample reserve history (8.1) that helps to protect the company against sharp claims increases.

Principal Business: Farmowners multiple peril (29%), homeowners multiple peril (28%), auto physical damage (19%), auto liability (18%), allied lines (2%), fire (2%), and other liability (2%).

Principal Investments: Investment grade bonds (74%), misc. investments (16%), real estate (6%), and cash (4%).

Investments in Affiliates: None

Group Affiliation: None

Licensed in: IL, IN, IA, KS, NE, ND, SD

Commenced Business: November 1891

Address: 1220 Lincoln Mall, Lincoln, NE 68501

Phone: (402) 434-8300   **Domicile State:** NE   **NAIC Code:** 13889

Data Date	Rating	RACR #1	RACR #2	Loss Ratio %	Total Assets ($mil)	Capital ($mil)	Net Premium ($mil)	Net Income ($mil)
9-14	B	4.46	3.24	N/A	506.0	281.5	187.8	-15.6
9-13	B	4.68	3.39	N/A	496.9	279.9	185.3	7.8
2013	B	4.70	3.34	67.1	512.4	293.2	264.9	20.0
2012	B	5.08	3.60	70.0	461.8	269.7	224.5	18.2
2011	B	5.35	3.90	86.9	433.8	254.2	206.4	-10.5
2010	B	5.60	4.10	87.2	438.7	256.1	196.7	-0.6
2009	B	5.85	4.32	83.4	437.9	257.2	194.1	2.8

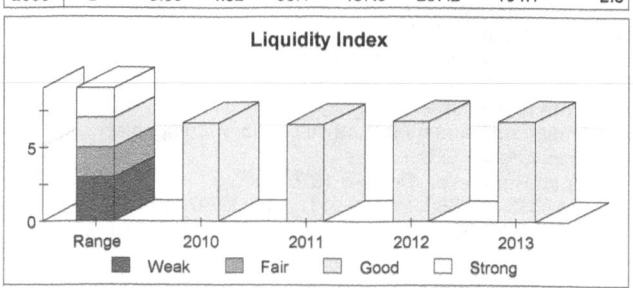

FARMERS REINS CO — B- — Good

Major Rating Factors: Fair reserve development (4.7 on a scale of 0 to 10) as reserves have generally been sufficient to cover claims. Fair profitability index (3.7) with operating losses during 2009. Return on equity has been low, averaging 4.3% over the past five years.

Other Rating Factors: Fair overall results on stability tests (4.9) including fair financial strength of affiliated Zurich Financial Services Group and negative cash flow from operations for 2013. Good liquidity (6.7) with sufficient resources (cash flows and marketable investments) to handle a spike in claims. Strong long-term capitalization index (10.0) based on excellent current risk adjusted capital (severe and moderate loss scenarios), despite some fluctuation in capital levels.

Principal Business: (This company is a reinsurer.)

Principal Investments: Investment grade bonds (91%) and misc. investments (9%).

Investments in Affiliates: None

Group Affiliation: Zurich Financial Services Group

Licensed in: CA

Commenced Business: August 1997

Address: 4680 Wilshire Blvd, Los Angeles, CA 90010

Phone: (323) 932-3200 **Domicile State:** CA **NAIC Code:** 10873

Data Date	Rating	RACR #1	RACR #2	Loss Ratio %	Total Assets ($mil)	Capital ($mil)	Net Premium ($mil)	Net Income ($mil)
9-14	B-	14.39	9.66	N/A	1,445.7	980.3	328.7	30.3
9-13	B-	11.97	8.10	N/A	1,557.3	1,026.8	416.0	24.5
2013	B-	11.88	8.08	68.9	1,400.2	949.7	517.6	48.3
2012	B-	8.83	6.05	72.4	1,606.1	1,015.5	790.5	31.9
2011	C+	9.54	5.40	70.5	1,602.0	974.1	705.8	13.4
2010	C+	7.48	4.39	66.5	1,725.0	1,042.8	838.8	142.4
2009	C+	5.15	3.24	68.2	1,958.3	1,019.4	1,323.0	-19.1

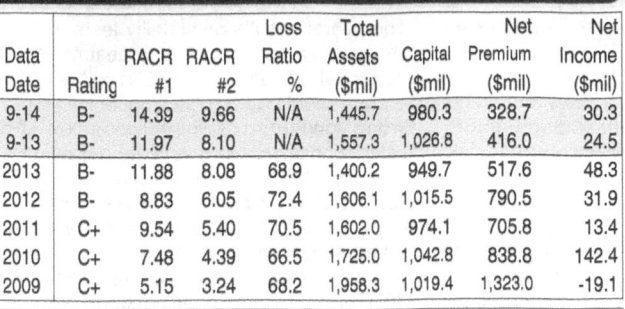

Rating Indexes

FARMINGTON CASUALTY CO — B — Good

Major Rating Factors: Good liquidity (6.8 on a scale of 0 to 10) with sufficient resources (cash flows and marketable investments) to handle a spike in claims. Good overall results on stability tests (6.0). Affiliation with Travelers Companies Inc is a strength.

Other Rating Factors: Strong long-term capitalization index (7.9) based on excellent current risk adjusted capital (severe and moderate loss scenarios), despite some fluctuation in capital levels. Ample reserve history (8.8) that helps to protect the company against sharp claims increases. Excellent profitability (7.4) with operating gains in each of the last five years. Return on equity has been good over the last five years, averaging 13.5%.

Principal Business: Workers compensation (50%), homeowners multiple peril (41%), and auto liability (8%).

Principal Investments: Investment grade bonds (93%) and misc. investments (7%).

Investments in Affiliates: 0%

Group Affiliation: Travelers Companies Inc

Licensed in: All states except PR

Commenced Business: October 1982

Address: One Tower Square, Hartford, CT 06183

Phone: (860) 277-0111 **Domicile State:** CT **NAIC Code:** 41483

Data Date	Rating	RACR #1	RACR #2	Loss Ratio %	Total Assets ($mil)	Capital ($mil)	Net Premium ($mil)	Net Income ($mil)
9-14	B	2.72	1.72	N/A	1,040.3	319.3	220.6	31.8
9-13	B	2.63	1.68	N/A	1,015.6	300.2	216.2	32.7
2013	B	2.52	1.60	60.9	1,000.6	287.4	298.1	45.9
2012	B	2.39	1.54	68.4	1,003.0	269.2	289.5	29.7
2011	B	2.31	1.49	76.9	974.4	261.2	283.4	16.9
2010	B	2.41	1.53	62.0	982.1	283.4	273.7	52.3
2009	B	2.23	1.46	58.3	984.4	271.7	268.3	43.5

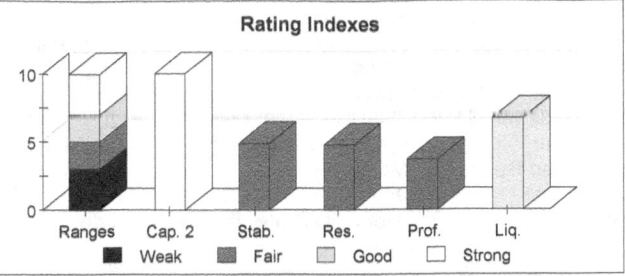

Liquidity Index

FCCI INS CO — C+ — Fair

Major Rating Factors: Fair overall results on stability tests (4.2 on a scale of 0 to 10) including potential drain of affiliation with FCCI Ins Group. Good overall profitability index (6.8). Fair expense controls. Return on equity has been fair, averaging 6.1% over the past five years.

Other Rating Factors: Good liquidity (6.7) with sufficient resources (cash flows and marketable investments) to handle a spike in claims. Strong long-term capitalization index (8.2) based on excellent current risk adjusted capital (severe and moderate loss scenarios). Moreover, capital levels have been consistent in recent years. Ample reserve history (9.6) that helps to protect the company against sharp claims increases.

Principal Business: Workers compensation (62%), commercial multiple peril (10%), auto liability (9%), other liability (5%), fire (3%), auto physical damage (3%), and other lines (8%).

Principal Investments: Investment grade bonds (69%), misc. investments (24%), non investment grade bonds (5%), and real estate (2%).

Investments in Affiliates: 9%

Group Affiliation: FCCI Ins Group

Licensed in: AL, AZ, AR, CO, FL, GA, IL, IN, IA, KS, KY, LA, MD, MI, MS, MO, NE, NC, OH, OK, PA, SC, TN, TX, VA

Commenced Business: April 1959

Address: 6300 University Parkway, Sarasota, FL 34240

Phone: (800) 226-3224 **Domicile State:** FL **NAIC Code:** 10178

Data Date	Rating	RACR #1	RACR #2	Loss Ratio %	Total Assets ($mil)	Capital ($mil)	Net Premium ($mil)	Net Income ($mil)
9-14	C+	2.51	1.80	N/A	1,712.2	560.6	444.1	14.3
9-13	C+	2.55	1.84	N/A	1,592.5	532.1	390.8	6.9
2013	C+	2.63	1.90	66.0	1,628.9	552.1	559.1	26.7
2012	C+	2.63	1.91	67.1	1,529.4	520.8	492.2	24.7
2011	C+	2.57	1.84	67.1	1,473.3	491.4	441.9	32.1
2010	C+	2.49	1.76	65.9	1,526.9	479.1	430.2	39.8
2009	C+	2.02	1.37	67.1	1,460.7	427.4	437.4	34.6

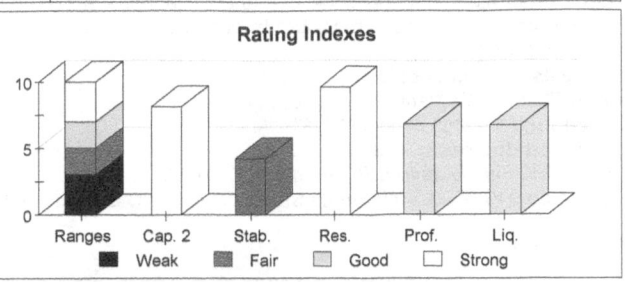

Rating Indexes

FEDERAL INS CO *   B+   Good

Major Rating Factors: Good overall results on stability tests (6.4 on a scale of 0 to 10). Affiliation with Chubb Corp is a strength. The largest net exposure for one risk is acceptable at 2.9% of capital. Good liquidity (6.9) with sufficient resources (cash flows and marketable investments) to handle a spike in claims.

Other Rating Factors: Strong long-term capitalization index (7.5) based on excellent current risk adjusted capital (severe and moderate loss scenarios), despite some fluctuation in capital levels. Ample reserve history (8.4) that helps to protect the company against sharp claims increases. Excellent profitability (7.5) with operating gains in each of the last five years. Return on equity has been good over the last five years, averaging 12.4%.

Principal Business: Other liability (33%), commercial multiple peril (17%), workers compensation (11%), homeowners multiple peril (9%), inland marine (6%), fidelity (4%), and other lines (19%).

Principal Investments: Misc. investments (50%), investment grade bonds (48%), and non investment grade bonds (2%).

Investments in Affiliates: 38%

Group Affiliation: Chubb Corp

Licensed in: All states, the District of Columbia and Puerto Rico

Commenced Business: March 1901

Address: 211 N Pennsylvania St #1350, Indianapolis, IN 46204-1927

Phone: (908) 903-2000   **Domicile State:** IN   **NAIC Code:** 20281

Data Date	Rating	RACR #1	RACR #2	Loss Ratio %	Total Assets ($mil)	Capital ($mil)	Net Premium ($mil)	Net Income ($mil)
9-14	B+	1.42	1.30	N/A	32,714.5	15,034.0	5,191.9	1,306.4
9-13	B+	1.41	1.30	N/A	31,868.2	14,520.9	5,060.9	1,455.6
2013	B+	1.42	1.31	51.7	31,761.3	14,741.3	6,844.9	2,021.9
2012	B+	1.36	1.25	64.8	31,246.7	13,841.0	6,586.4	1,564.7
2011	B+	1.39	1.28	65.0	30,726.6	13,707.5	6,473.8	1,760.6
2010	B+	1.48	1.36	60.8	31,062.6	14,317.3	6,309.1	2,002.6
2009	B+	1.54	1.41	54.9	30,688.1	14,321.5	6,325.8	1,541.2

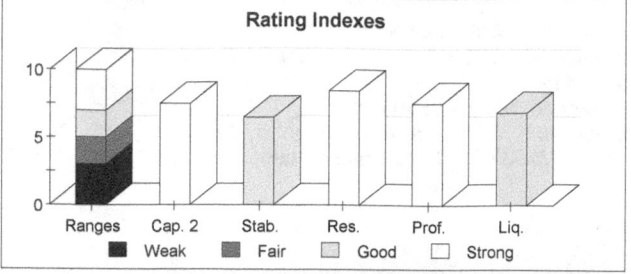

Rating Indexes

FEDERATED MUTUAL INS CO *   A-   Excellent

Major Rating Factors: Strong long-term capitalization index (10.0 on a scale of 0 to 10) based on excellent current risk adjusted capital (severe and moderate loss scenarios). Moreover, capital levels have been consistent in recent years. Ample reserve history (8.9) that helps to protect the company against sharp claims increases.

Other Rating Factors: Good overall results on stability tests (5.5) despite potential drain of affiliation with Federated Mutual Ins Group. Good overall profitability index (6.9). Fair expense controls. Good liquidity (6.9) with sufficient resources (cash flows and marketable investments) to handle a spike in claims.

Principal Business: Group accident & health (33%), workers compensation (17%), other liability (13%), auto liability (12%), commercial multiple peril (6%), auto physical damage (4%), and other lines (14%).

Principal Investments: Investment grade bonds (74%), misc. investments (26%), and real estate (1%).

Investments in Affiliates: 14%

Group Affiliation: Federated Mutual Ins Group

Licensed in: All states except HI, PR

Commenced Business: August 1904

Address: 121 E Park Square, Owatonna, MN 55060

Phone: (507) 455-5200   **Domicile State:** MN   **NAIC Code:** 13935

Data Date	Rating	RACR #1	RACR #2	Loss Ratio %	Total Assets ($mil)	Capital ($mil)	Net Premium ($mil)	Net Income ($mil)
9-14	A-	3.77	3.04	N/A	4,726.6	2,681.8	846.3	132.5
9-13	A-	3.83	3.09	N/A	4,483.6	2,479.4	749.9	93.4
2013	A-	3.67	3.00	69.6	4,523.5	2,518.3	1,083.5	127.9
2012	A-	3.86	3.19	74.6	4,233.8	2,365.4	942.3	106.1
2011	A-	3.71	3.03	79.6	4,075.1	2,237.2	875.9	52.5
2010	A-	3.83	3.12	65.8	4,019.4	2,190.9	784.6	152.3
2009	A-	3.61	2.90	64.8	3,944.9	2,017.8	809.2	137.1

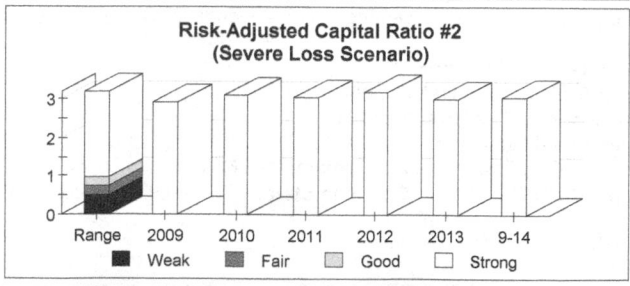

Risk-Adjusted Capital Ratio #2
(Severe Loss Scenario)

FINIAL REINS CO   D+   Weak

Major Rating Factors: Weak overall results on stability tests (2.5 on a scale of 0 to 10) including potential drain of affiliation with Berkshire-Hathaway, weak results on operational trends and negative cash flow from operations for 2013. The largest net exposure for one risk is conservative at 1.5% of capital. Strong long-term capitalization index (10.0) based on excellent current risk adjusted capital (severe and moderate loss scenarios). Moreover, capital levels have been consistent in recent years.

Other Rating Factors: Ample reserve history (8.6) that helps to protect the company against sharp claims increases. Excellent profitability (9.0) with operating gains in each of the last five years. Excellent expense controls. Superior liquidity (10.0) with ample operational cash flow and liquid investments.

Principal Business: (Not applicable due to unusual reinsurance transactions.)

Principal Investments: Investment grade bonds (71%), cash (19%), and misc. investments (10%).

Investments in Affiliates: None

Group Affiliation: Berkshire-Hathaway

Licensed in: All states except MS, PR

Commenced Business: February 1993

Address: 100 First Stamford Pl, Stamford, CT 06902

Phone: (402) 916-3000   **Domicile State:** CT   **NAIC Code:** 39136

Data Date	Rating	RACR #1	RACR #2	Loss Ratio %	Total Assets ($mil)	Capital ($mil)	Net Premium ($mil)	Net Income ($mil)
9-14	D+	7.38	4.42	N/A	1,240.9	835.3	0.7	13.6
9-13	U	6.83	4.03	N/A	1,219.8	748.7	-2.2	16.0
2013	D+	7.17	4.28	N/A	1,257.7	812.1	-2.2	59.1
2012	U	6.71	3.93	N/A	1,203.0	716.3	-0.1	47.1
2011	D+	5.97	3.37	N/A	1,168.8	609.7	-0.4	34.9
2010	D+	5.01	2.87	N/A	1,200.3	584.6	3.0	51.5
2009	D+	3.59	2.08	128.1	1,243.2	499.9	-6.3	53.9

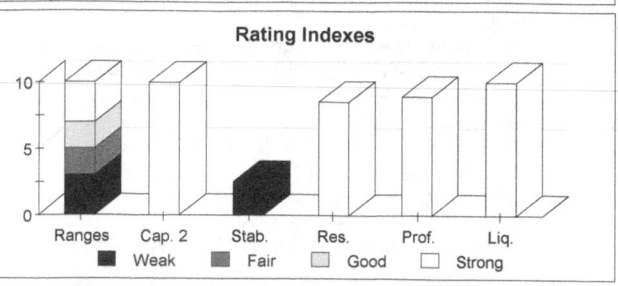

Rating Indexes

FIRE INS EXCHANGE   C+   Fair

Major Rating Factors: Fair profitability index (4.8 on a scale of 0 to 10) with operating losses during 2010, 2011 and 2012. Fair liquidity (4.4) as cash resources may not be adequate to cover a spike in claims.

Other Rating Factors: Fair overall results on stability tests (4.8) including fair financial strength of affiliated Farmers Insurance Group of Companies. Good long-term capitalization index (5.1) based on good current risk adjusted capital (severe and moderate loss scenarios). Over the last several years, capital levels have remained relatively consistent. History of adequate reserve strength (6.4) as reserves have been consistently at an acceptable level.

Principal Business: Homeowners multiple peril (65%), commercial multiple peril (15%), allied lines (10%), fire (8%), other liability (1%), and inland marine (1%).

Principal Investments: Misc. investments (63%), investment grade bonds (27%), and cash (10%).

Investments in Affiliates: 54%

Group Affiliation: Farmers Insurance Group of Companies

Licensed in: AL, AZ, AR, CA, CO, FL, GA, ID, IL, IN, IA, KS, MI, MN, MO, MT, NE, NV, NH, NJ, NM, NY, ND, OH, OK, OR, SD, TX, UT, WA, WI, WY

Commenced Business: November 1942

Address: 4680 Wilshire Blvd, Los Angeles, CA 90010

Phone: (323) 932-3200   **Domicile State:** CA   **NAIC Code:** 21660

Data Date	Rating	RACR #1	RACR #2	Loss Ratio %	Total Assets ($mil)	Capital ($mil)	Net Premium ($mil)	Net Income ($mil)
9-14	C+	0.84	0.79	N/A	2,270.3	745.4	761.1	2.9
9-13	C+	0.84	0.79	N/A	2,244.7	693.1	773.5	-6.2
2013	C+	0.83	0.78	66.9	2,254.8	721.3	1,022.8	12.7
2012	C+	0.83	0.78	73.3	2,204.0	662.2	1,039.1	-10.7
2011	C+	0.85	0.80	73.2	2,277.5	653.1	1,061.7	-26.2
2010	C	0.93	0.86	66.0	2,200.4	708.9	955.8	-36.7
2009	C	0.95	0.89	67.4	2,046.3	672.9	727.7	18.5

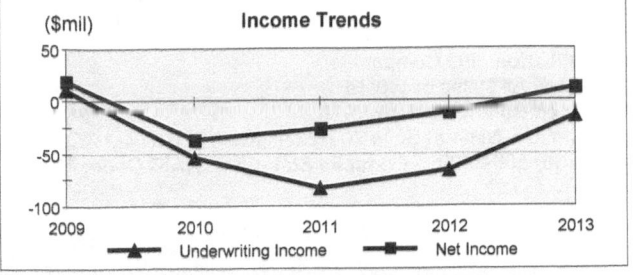

Income Trends

FIREMANS FUND INS CO   C   Fair

Major Rating Factors: Fair overall results on stability tests (3.6 on a scale of 0 to 10) including negative cash flow from operations for 2013. The largest net exposure for one risk is conservative at 1.6% of capital. A history of deficient reserves (2.5). Underreserving can have an adverse impact on capital and profits. In 2013 and 2012 the two year reserve development was 21% and 26% deficient respectively.

Other Rating Factors: Weak profitability index (1.8) with operating losses during 2011, 2012 and the first nine months of 2014. Average return on equity over the last five years has been poor at -1.0%. Good overall long-term capitalization (5.3) based on good current risk adjusted capital (moderate loss scenario). However, capital levels have fluctuated during prior years. Good liquidity (5.2) with sufficient resources to handle a spike in claims.

Principal Business: Homeowners multiple peril (29%), other liability (19%), commercial multiple peril (13%), inland marine (12%), auto liability (7%), auto physical damage (6%), and other lines (14%).

Principal Investments: Investment grade bonds (84%), misc. investments (14%), and non investment grade bonds (2%).

Investments in Affiliates: 13%

Group Affiliation: Allianz Ins Group

Licensed in: All states, the District of Columbia and Puerto Rico

Commenced Business: September 1864

Address: 777 San Marin Dr, Novato, CA 94998

Phone: (415) 899-2000   **Domicile State:** CA   **NAIC Code:** 21873

Data Date	Rating	RACR #1	RACR #2	Loss Ratio %	Total Assets ($mil)	Capital ($mil)	Net Premium ($mil)	Net Income ($mil)
9-14	C	1.14	0.75	N/A	9,903.6	2,089.7	1,893.7	-344.2
9-13	C	1.47	0.98	N/A	10,438.7	2,851.5	2,029.4	186.8
2013	C	1.39	0.92	68.6	9,843.7	2,478.7	2,577.7	237.4
2012	C	1.15	0.75	103.2	11,835.8	2,522.1	3,638.2	-814.8
2011	C	1.52	1.11	88.2	9,922.8	2,985.9	2,685.5	-42.9
2010	C	1.39	1.02	78.1	9,385.3	2,729.7	2,589.6	262.7
2009	C	1.31	0.98	70.8	10,000.7	3,047.7	3,055.6	771.8

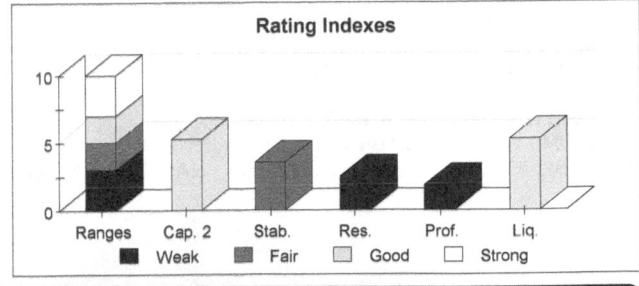

Rating Indexes

FIRST COLONIAL INS CO *   B+   Good

Major Rating Factors: History of adequate reserve strength (6.8 on a scale of 0 to 10) as reserves have been consistently at an acceptable level. Good overall profitability index (6.6). Weak expense controls. Return on equity has been good over the last five years, averaging 10.5%.

Other Rating Factors: Good overall results on stability tests (6.5). Stability strengths include good operational trends and excellent risk diversification. Strong long-term capitalization index (10.0) based on excellent current risk adjusted capital (severe and moderate loss scenarios), despite some fluctuation in capital levels. Excellent liquidity (7.1) with ample operational cash flow and liquid investments.

Principal Business: Credit (38%) and auto physical damage (1%).

Principal Investments: Investment grade bonds (105%) and non investment grade bonds (3%).

Investments in Affiliates: None

Group Affiliation: Allstate Group

Licensed in: All states except CA, PR

Commenced Business: April 1987

Address: 1776 American Heritage Life Dr, Jacksonville, FL 32224-6688

Phone: (904) 992-1776   **Domicile State:** FL   **NAIC Code:** 29980

Data Date	Rating	RACR #1	RACR #2	Loss Ratio %	Total Assets ($mil)	Capital ($mil)	Net Premium ($mil)	Net Income ($mil)
9-14	B+	6.77	5.35	N/A	355.0	156.0	45.6	5.1
9-13	B	6.38	5.38	N/A	375.0	190.3	46.0	10.2
2013	B+	8.50	6.78	34.0	380.8	193.8	64.5	17.8
2012	B	6.02	5.12	24.9	350.8	183.6	64.6	42.3
2011	B	2.01	1.87	22.6	349.7	150.4	72.3	1.1
2010	B	3.16	2.65	48.6	312.0	140.1	64.1	17.6
2009	B-	0.82	0.54	87.1	311.1	120.1	112.0	13.7

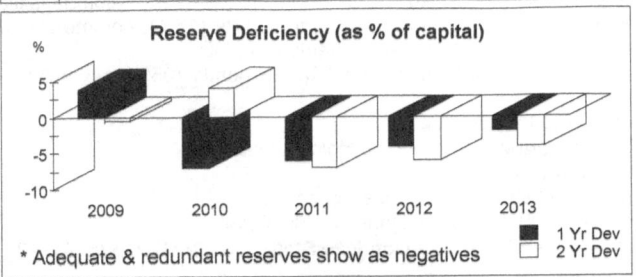

Reserve Deficiency (as % of capital)

* Adequate & redundant reserves show as negatives

FIRST FINANCIAL INS CO
C-   **Fair**

Major Rating Factors: Weak overall results on stability tests (2.6 on a scale of 0 to 10) including potential drain of affiliation with IFG Companies. History of adequate reserve strength (6.9) as reserves have been consistently at an acceptable level.

Other Rating Factors: Strong long-term capitalization index (7.3) based on excellent current risk adjusted capital (severe and moderate loss scenarios), despite some fluctuation in capital levels. Excellent profitability (7.5) with operating gains in each of the last five years. Excellent liquidity (8.1) with ample operational cash flow and liquid investments.

Principal Business: Other liability (83%), fire (7%), commercial multiple peril (5%), auto liability (3%), auto physical damage (1%), and allied lines (1%).

Principal Investments: Misc. investments (78%) and investment grade bonds (22%).

Investments in Affiliates: 79%
Group Affiliation: IFG Companies
Licensed in: All states except PR
Commenced Business: May 1970
Address: 400 S Ninth St Suite 200, Springfield, IL 62701-1822
Phone: (336) 586-2500   **Domicile State:** IL   **NAIC Code:** 11177

Data Date	Rating	RACR #1	RACR #2	Loss Ratio %	Total Assets ($mil)	Capital ($mil)	Net Premium ($mil)	Net Income ($mil)
9-14	C-	1.20	1.19	N/A	536.8	406.7	21.3	5.4
9-13	C-	1.18	1.17	N/A	517.0	375.9	24.3	10.1
2013	C-	1.18	1.17	36.2	533.6	393.5	30.5	16.3
2012	C-	1.13	1.13	26.2	507.2	354.7	32.3	18.8
2011	C-	1.20	1.20	33.8	519.7	365.4	27.0	12.9
2010	C-	1.23	1.22	48.8	518.2	356.2	23.4	14.3
2009	C-	1.20	1.19	103.2	508.1	331.2	25.7	11.9

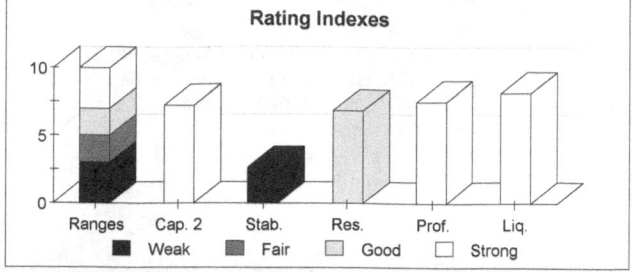

Rating Indexes

Weak   Fair   Good   Strong

FIRST FLORIDIAN AUTO & HOME INS CO
B   **Good**

Major Rating Factors: History of adequate reserve strength (6.2 on a scale of 0 to 10) as reserves have been consistently at an acceptable level. Good overall profitability index (6.7). Good expense controls. Return on equity has been good over the last five years, averaging 10.5%.

Other Rating Factors: Good overall results on stability tests (5.1). The largest net exposure for one risk is high at 4.8% of capital. Stability strengths include good operational trends and excellent risk diversification. Strong long-term capitalization index (10.0) based on excellent current risk adjusted capital (severe and moderate loss scenarios), despite some fluctuation in capital levels. Excellent liquidity (7.0) with ample operational cash flow and liquid investments.

Principal Business: Auto liability (48%), homeowners multiple peril (31%), auto physical damage (16%), and other liability (3%).

Principal Investments: Investment grade bonds (103%).

Investments in Affiliates: None
Group Affiliation: Travelers Companies Inc
Licensed in: FL
Commenced Business: June 1996
Address: 7840 Woodland Ctr Blvd, Tampa, FL 33614
Phone: (813) 890-4200   **Domicile State:** FL   **NAIC Code:** 10647

Data Date	Rating	RACR #1	RACR #2	Loss Ratio %	Total Assets ($mil)	Capital ($mil)	Net Premium ($mil)	Net Income ($mil)
9-14	B	10.97	8.58	N/A	282.9	195.2	52.8	8.7
9-13	B	11.19	8.39	N/A	297.7	207.6	58.0	15.2
2013	B	10.38	8.42	57.6	288.6	201.8	73.8	17.0
2012	B	9.29	7.20	75.3	287.6	192.6	81.1	9.2
2011	B	8.00	5.89	63.6	289.9	187.4	91.2	18.4
2010	B	7.47	5.86	59.9	307.1	194.8	102.6	26.3
2009	B	7.69	6.16	44.4	361.5	231.1	120.9	45.1

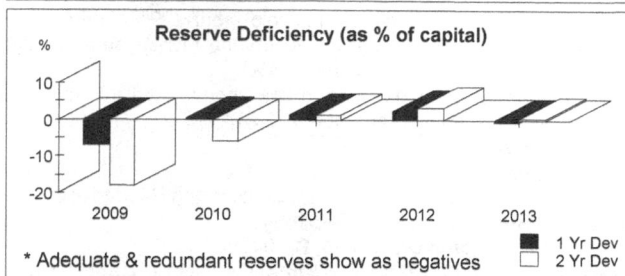

Reserve Deficiency (as % of capital)

* Adequate & redundant reserves show as negatives

1 Yr Dev   2 Yr Dev

FIRST INS CO OF HI LTD
C   **Fair**

Major Rating Factors: Fair overall results on stability tests (4.3 on a scale of 0 to 10) including fair financial strength of affiliated Tokio Marine Holdings Inc. The largest net exposure for one risk is conservative at 1.6% of capital. Good liquidity (6.9) with sufficient resources (cash flows and marketable investments) to handle a spike in claims.

Other Rating Factors: Strong long-term capitalization index (10.0) based on excellent current risk adjusted capital (severe and moderate loss scenarios), despite some fluctuation in capital levels. Ample reserve history (9.6) that helps to protect the company against sharp claims increases. Excellent profitability (8.6) with operating gains in each of the last five years. Return on equity has been good over the last five years, averaging 11.5%.

Principal Business: Allied lines (21%), workers compensation (19%), homeowners multiple peril (13%), auto liability (13%), commercial multiple peril (12%), other liability (11%), and other lines (10%).

Principal Investments: Investment grade bonds (95%) and misc. investments (6%).

Investments in Affiliates: 4%
Group Affiliation: Tokio Marine Holdings Inc
Licensed in: HI
Commenced Business: September 1982
Address: 1100 Ward Ave, Honolulu, HI 96814
Phone: (808) 527-7777   **Domicile State:** HI   **NAIC Code:** 41742

Data Date	Rating	RACR #1	RACR #2	Loss Ratio %	Total Assets ($mil)	Capital ($mil)	Net Premium ($mil)	Net Income ($mil)
9-14	C	5.53	3.85	N/A	652.6	306.7	130.5	16.4
9-13	C	5.73	3.73	N/A	642.6	276.5	125.5	9.6
2013	C	5.23	3.66	59.2	640.8	286.4	171.8	19.6
2012	C	6.38	4.14	41.1	646.9	286.9	148.7	50.8
2011	C	3.95	2.74	59.6	619.0	241.0	142.9	15.3
2010	C	3.93	2.70	45.3	606.8	238.2	135.4	33.5
2009	C	3.61	2.37	48.7	608.8	212.2	134.4	34.0

Tokio Marine Holdings Inc
Composite Group Rating: B
Largest Group Members

	Assets ($mil)	Rating
PHILADELPHIA INDEMNITY INS CO	6526	B
RELIANCE STANDARD LIFE INS CO	5980	B
SAFETY NATIONAL CASUALTY CORP	4184	C
TOKIO MARINE AMERICA INS CO	1384	A
RELIANCE STANDARD LIFE INS CO OF TX	746	U

FLORIDA FARM BU CASUALTY INS CO

B-   Good

Major Rating Factors: Fair overall results on stability tests (4.8 on a scale of 0 to 10) including potential drain of affiliation with Southern Farm Bureau Casualty. Good liquidity (6.3) with sufficient resources (cash flows and marketable investments) to handle a spike in claims.

Other Rating Factors: Strong long-term capitalization index (8.6) based on excellent current risk adjusted capital (severe and moderate loss scenarios). Moreover, capital levels have been consistent in recent years. Ample reserve history (7.8) that can protect against increases in claims costs. Excellent profitability (7.3) with operating gains in each of the last five years.

Principal Business: Homeowners multiple peril (77%), auto liability (17%), and auto physical damage (6%).

Principal Investments: Investment grade bonds (88%), misc. investments (7%), cash (3%), and real estate (2%).

Investments in Affiliates: 3%

Group Affiliation: Southern Farm Bureau Casualty

Licensed in: FL

Commenced Business: July 1974

Address: 5700 SW 34th St, Gainesville, FL 32608

Phone: (352) 378-8100   **Domicile State:** FL   **NAIC Code:** 31216

Data Date	Rating	RACR #1	RACR #2	Loss Ratio %	Total Assets ($mil)	Capital ($mil)	Net Premium ($mil)	Net Income ($mil)
9-14	B-	3.17	2.17	N/A	530.4	261.3	178.2	14.5
9-13	B-	3.07	2.09	N/A	506.3	240.0	173.3	11.6
2013	B-	3.02	2.11	73.4	502.8	246.3	235.5	19.9
2012	B-	3.00	2.08	74.6	474.0	227.5	226.3	14.8
2011	B-	2.59	1.80	78.2	444.1	212.3	217.0	9.0
2010	B-	2.80	1.92	81.2	438.7	201.7	196.2	3.5
2009	B-	3.38	2.28	85.2	420.1	199.2	175.0	0.5

Southern Farm Bureau Casualty Composite Group Rating: B- Largest Group Members	Assets ($mil)	Rating
SOUTHERN FARM BUREAU CAS INS CO	1998	B-
FLORIDA FARM BU CASUALTY INS CO	503	B-
MISSISSIPPI FARM BUREAU CAS INS CO	352	B
SOUTHERN FARM BUREAU PROPERTY	54	U
LOUISIANA FARM BUREAU CAS INS CO	11	B

FOREMOST INS CO

B   Good

Major Rating Factors: Good overall results on stability tests (5.6 on a scale of 0 to 10) despite potential drain of affiliation with Farmers Insurance Group of Companies. Stability strengths include good operational trends and excellent risk diversification. History of adequate reserve strength (6.1) as reserves have been consistently at an acceptable level.

Other Rating Factors: Strong long-term capitalization index (10.0) based on excellent current risk adjusted capital (severe and moderate loss scenarios). Moreover, capital levels have been consistent in recent years. Excellent profitability (7.7). Superior liquidity (9.0) with ample operational cash flow and liquid investments.

Principal Business: Homeowners multiple peril (48%), fire (19%), auto physical damage (9%), allied lines (9%), auto liability (7%), other liability (4%), and other lines (5%).

Principal Investments: Investment grade bonds (83%), misc. investments (9%), real estate (7%), and non investment grade bonds (1%).

Investments in Affiliates: 7%

Group Affiliation: Farmers Insurance Group of Companies

Licensed in: All states except PR

Commenced Business: June 1952

Address: 5600 Beech Tree Lane, Caledonia, MI 49316-0050

Phone: (616) 942-3000   **Domicile State:** MI   **NAIC Code:** 11185

Data Date	Rating	RACR #1	RACR #2	Loss Ratio %	Total Assets ($mil)	Capital ($mil)	Net Premium ($mil)	Net Income ($mil)
9-14	B	8.55	5.96	N/A	2,120.7	1,050.1	0.0	18.6
9-13	B	10.70	7.77	N/A	1,921.0	1,022.6	0.0	25.1
2013	B	10.90	7.99	0.0	1,938.6	1,029.9	0.0	38.5
2012	B	10.73	7.90	0.0	1,774.4	993.5	0.0	40.4
2011	B	8.18	6.59	0.0	1,691.6	948.4	0.0	50.4
2010	B	5.18	4.01	59.9	1,537.3	899.3	537.1	303.8
2009	B	1.96	1.58	62.2	2,036.0	632.6	1,405.2	-0.1

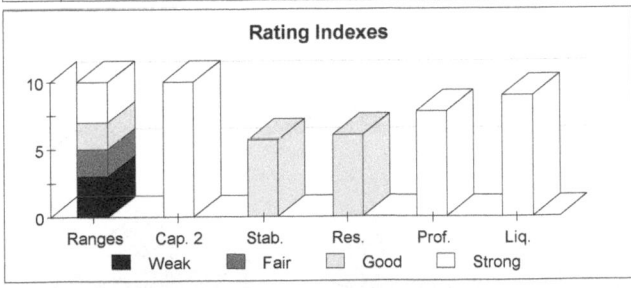

Rating Indexes

FRANKENMUTH MUTUAL INS CO *

A   Excellent

Major Rating Factors: Excellent overall results on stability tests (7.4 on a scale of 0 to 10). Stability strengths include excellent operational trends and excellent risk diversification. Strong long-term capitalization index (9.1) based on excellent current risk adjusted capital (severe and moderate loss scenarios). Furthermore, this high level of risk adjusted capital has been consistently maintained in previous years.

Other Rating Factors: Ample reserve history (9.0) that helps to protect the company against sharp claims increases. Good overall profitability index (6.2) despite operating losses during 2011. Good liquidity (6.5) with sufficient resources (cash flows and marketable investments) to handle a spike in claims.

Principal Business: Auto liability (27%), commercial multiple peril (19%), homeowners multiple peril (17%), auto physical damage (16%), workers compensation (13%), other liability (4%), and other lines (5%).

Principal Investments: Investment grade bonds (79%), misc. investments (20%), and real estate (3%).

Investments in Affiliates: 13%

Group Affiliation: Frankenmuth Mutual Group

Licensed in: All states except AK, CA, DC, HI, PR

Commenced Business: March 1922

Address: One Mutual Avenue, Frankenmuth, MI 48787-0001

Phone: (989) 652-6121   **Domicile State:** MI   **NAIC Code:** 13986

Data Date	Rating	RACR #1	RACR #2	Loss Ratio %	Total Assets ($mil)	Capital ($mil)	Net Premium ($mil)	Net Income ($mil)
9-14	A	3.05	2.41	N/A	1,096.8	456.9	310.8	9.2
9-13	A-	2.88	2.18	N/A	1,065.8	422.8	302.4	26.7
2013	A	3.13	2.51	63.2	1,069.3	445.0	410.9	40.1
2012	A-	2.81	2.16	70.2	1,015.6	389.8	396.8	29.2
2011	A-	2.68	2.05	84.4	955.0	356.0	399.2	-15.6
2010	A	2.95	2.27	72.3	927.0	383.3	316.0	27.7
2009	A	3.05	2.35	65.4	987.5	364.2	415.6	33.5

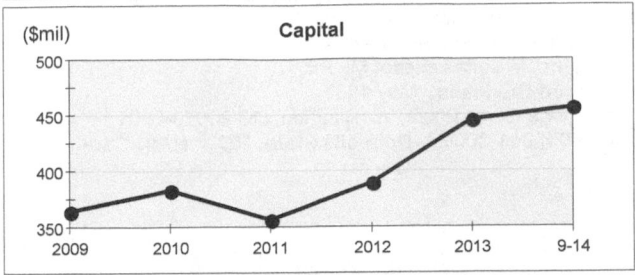

Capital

GARRISON PROPERTY & CASUALTY INS CO

B   Good

Major Rating Factors: History of adequate reserve strength (6.5 on a scale of 0 to 10) as reserves have been consistently at an acceptable level. Good overall profitability index (6.1) despite operating losses during 2009, 2010 and 2011. Average return on equity over the last five years has been poor at -0.1%.

Other Rating Factors: Good liquidity (5.9) with sufficient resources (cash flows and marketable investments) to handle a spike in claims. Fair overall results on stability tests (4.9) including weak results on operational trends and excessive premium growth. The largest net exposure for one risk is conservative at 1.5% of capital. Strong long-term capitalization index (8.1) based on excellent current risk adjusted capital (severe and moderate loss scenarios). Moreover, capital levels have been consistent in recent years.

Principal Business: Auto liability (48%), auto physical damage (36%), homeowners multiple peril (14%), inland marine (1%), allied lines (1%), and fire (1%).

Principal Investments: Investment grade bonds (81%), misc. investments (17%), and non investment grade bonds (2%).

Investments in Affiliates: None

Group Affiliation: USAA Group

Licensed in: All states except MA, PR

Commenced Business: December 1997

Address: 9800 Fredericksburg Rd, San Antonio, TX 78288-0344

Phone: (210) 498-8000   **Domicile State:** TX   **NAIC Code:** 21253

Data Date	Rating	RACR #1	RACR #2	Loss Ratio %	Total Assets ($mil)	Capital ($mil)	Net Premium ($mil)	Net Income ($mil)
9-14	B	2.32	1.75	N/A	1,435.4	543.6	744.4	28.7
9-13	B	2.78	2.12	N/A	1,195.9	454.7	503.0	34.8
2013	B	2.70	2.06	77.4	1,255.5	506.4	710.0	49.2
2012	B	2.69	2.10	83.6	1,107.9	417.8	617.7	22.9
2011	B	2.24	1.88	84.6	972.7	363.2	675.3	-1.3
2010	B	1.44	1.23	85.5	568.4	158.5	456.6	-8.3
2009	B	2.14	1.67	95.0	297.0	109.8	234.8	-16.8

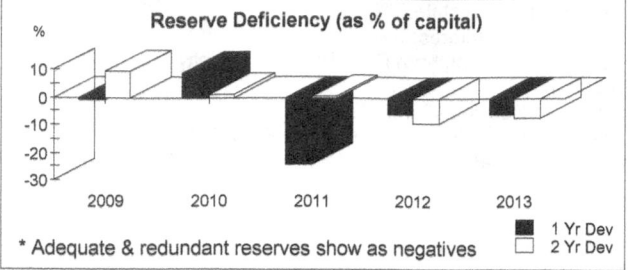

Reserve Deficiency (as % of capital)

* Adequate & redundant reserves show as negatives

■ 1 Yr Dev   □ 2 Yr Dev

GEICO ADVANTAGE CO

C+   Fair

Major Rating Factors: Fair overall results on stability tests (4.5) including weak results on operational trends and negative cash flow from operations for 2013.

Other Rating Factors: Weak profitability index (2.8) with operating losses during 2011, 2012 and the first nine months of 2014. Strong long-term capitalization index (9.8) based on excellent current risk adjusted capital (severe and moderate loss scenarios), despite some fluctuation in capital levels. Excellent liquidity (8.4) with ample operational cash flow and liquid investments.

Principal Business: Auto liability (59%) and auto physical damage (41%).

Principal Investments: Investment grade bonds (84%) and misc. investments (16%).

Investments in Affiliates: None

Group Affiliation: Berkshire-Hathaway

(No States listed)

Data Date	Rating	RACR #1	RACR #2	Loss Ratio %	Total Assets ($mil)	Capital ($mil)	Net Premium ($mil)	Net Income ($mil)
9-14	C+	3.76	2.64	N/A	713.8	447.2	113.5	-32.1
9-13	C	3.95	2.61	N/A	272.9	159.1	107.7	-56.9
2013	C+	4.75	3.61	107.4	629.6	484.6	215.6	-85.3
2012	A-	10.23	7.53	102.7	249.1	208.2	44.3	-17.1
2011	U	133.64	66.82	0.0	225.0	225.0	0.0	0.0
2010	N/A	N/A	N/A	0.0	0.0	0.0	0.0	0.0
2009	N/A	N/A	N/A	0.0	0.0	0.0	0.0	0.0

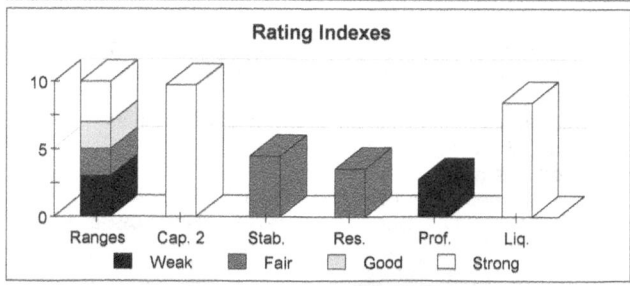

Rating Indexes

Ranges   Cap. 2   Stab.   Res.   Prof.   Liq.

■ Weak   ■ Fair   ▨ Good   □ Strong

GEICO CASUALTY CO

D-   Weak

Major Rating Factors: Weak profitability index (2.6 on a scale of 0 to 10) with operating losses during 2010, 2011, 2012 and 2013. Average return on equity over the last five years has been poor at -18.5%. Weak overall results on stability tests (1.3) including weak results on operational trends.

Other Rating Factors: Good liquidity (6.5) with sufficient resources (cash flows and marketable investments) to handle a spike in claims. Strong long-term capitalization index (7.7) based on excellent current risk adjusted capital (severe and moderate loss scenarios), despite some fluctuation in capital levels. Ample reserve history (9.4) that helps to protect the company against sharp claims increases.

Principal Business: Auto liability (62%) and auto physical damage (38%).

Principal Investments: Investment grade bonds (111%).

Investments in Affiliates: None

Group Affiliation: Berkshire-Hathaway

Licensed in: All states except MI, PR

Commenced Business: May 1983

Address: One Geico Plaza, Washington, DC 20076-0001

Phone: (800) 841-3000   **Domicile State:** MD   **NAIC Code:** 41491

Data Date	Rating	RACR #1	RACR #2	Loss Ratio %	Total Assets ($mil)	Capital ($mil)	Net Premium ($mil)	Net Income ($mil)
9-14	D-	2.47	1.74	N/A	2,376.6	990.7	544.7	-0.8
9-13	D-	1.58	1.30	N/A	2,471.1	899.6	1,440.0	-256.5
2013	D-	1.64	1.37	90.9	2,707.2	1,001.0	2,209.4	-342.5
2012	D-	1.73	1.48	87.7	1,712.6	661.8	1,381.8	-252.0
2011	D-	1.30	1.16	81.5	856.1	250.4	680.6	-84.5
2010	B-	1.95	1.83	72.5	830.6	366.7	664.6	-21.2
2009	B	8.33	5.88	71.6	306.7	145.6	47.7	7.6

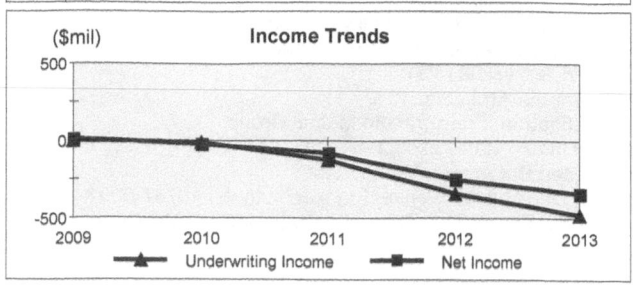

($mil)   **Income Trends**

◄— Underwriting Income   ■— Net Income

GEICO CHOICE INS CO *   A-   Excellent

Major Rating Factors: Strong long-term capitalization index (9.2 on a scale of 0 to 10) based on excellent current risk adjusted capital (severe and moderate loss scenarios). Furthermore, this high level of risk adjusted capital has been consistently maintained in previous years. Excellent liquidity (7.5) with ample operational cash flow and liquid investments.

Other Rating Factors: Good overall results on stability tests (5.6) despite weak results on operational trends and negative cash flow from operations for 2013. Weak profitability index (2.9) with operating losses during 2011, 2012 and the first nine months of 2014.

Principal Business: Auto liability (60%) and auto physical damage (40%).

Principal Investments: Investment grade bonds (73%) and misc. investments (27%).

Investments in Affiliates: None

Group Affiliation: Berkshire-Hathaway

(No States listed)

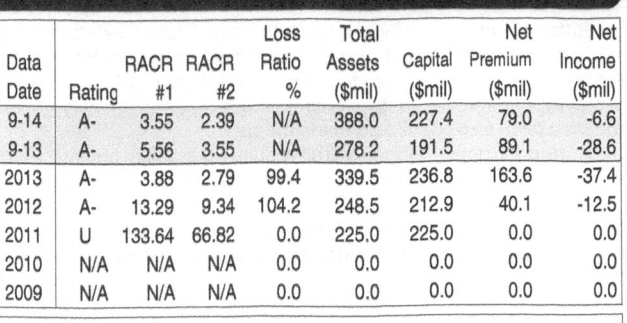

Data Date	Rating	RACR #1	RACR #2	Loss Ratio %	Total Assets ($mil)	Capital ($mil)	Net Premium ($mil)	Net Income ($mil)
9-14	A-	3.55	2.39	N/A	388.0	227.4	79.0	-6.6
9-13	A-	5.56	3.55	N/A	278.2	191.5	89.1	-28.6
2013	A-	3.88	2.79	99.4	339.5	236.8	163.6	-37.4
2012	A-	13.29	9.34	104.2	248.5	212.9	40.1	-12.5
2011	U	133.64	66.82	0.0	225.0	225.0	0.0	0.0
2010	N/A	N/A	N/A	0.0	0.0	0.0	0.0	0.0
2009	N/A	N/A	N/A	0.0	0.0	0.0	0.0	0.0

Risk-Adjusted Capital Ratio #2
(Severe Loss Scenario)

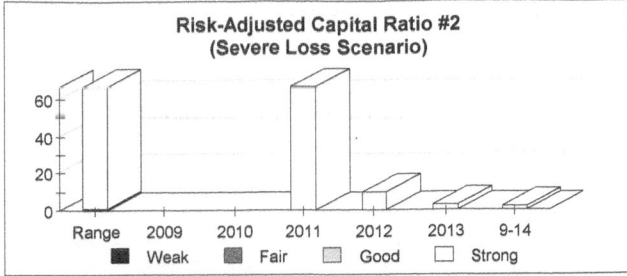

GEICO GENERAL INS CO *   B+   Good

Major Rating Factors: Good overall results on stability tests (5.3 on a scale of 0 to 10). Stability strengths include good operational trends and excellent risk diversification. Strong long-term capitalization index (10.0) based on excellent current risk adjusted capital (severe and moderate loss scenarios). Moreover, capital levels have been consistent in recent years.

Other Rating Factors: Excellent profitability (7.4) with operating gains in each of the last five years. Excellent expense controls. Superior liquidity (10.0) with ample operational cash flow and liquid investments.

Principal Business: Auto liability (63%) and auto physical damage (37%).

Principal Investments: Investment grade bonds (83%) and cash (17%).

Investments in Affiliates: None

Group Affiliation: Berkshire-Hathaway

Licensed in: All states except PR

Commenced Business: May 1934

Address: 5260 Western Avenue, Chevy Chase, MD 20815-3799

Phone: (800) 841-3000   **Domicile State:** MD   **NAIC Code:** 35882

Data Date	Rating	RACR #1	RACR #2	Loss Ratio %	Total Assets ($mil)	Capital ($mil)	Net Premium ($mil)	Net Income ($mil)
9-14	B+	15.74	14.17	N/A	215.7	130.9	0.0	0.2
9-13	B+	13.83	12.45	N/A	217.9	122.0	0.0	1.2
2013	B+	14.30	12.87	0.0	215.7	123.6	0.0	2.8
2012	B+	14.96	13.47	0.0	184.2	114.4	0.0	1.7
2011	B+	13.46	12.11	0.0	180.3	105.7	0.0	2.5
2010	B+	13.45	12.11	0.0	173.6	103.2	0.0	2.9
2009	B+	11.70	10.53	0.0	167.6	92.3	0.0	3.4

Berkshire-Hathaway Composite Group Rating: B- Largest Group Members	Assets ($mil)	Rating
NATIONAL INDEMNITY CO	151912	B-
GOVERNMENT EMPLOYEES INS CO	25779	B+
COLUMBIA INS CO	19013	B-
GENERAL REINSURANCE CORP	16220	B-
BERKSHIRE HATHAWAY LIFE INS CO OF NE	13768	C+

GEICO INDEMNITY CO *   B+   Good

Major Rating Factors: Good overall results on stability tests (5.3 on a scale of 0 to 10) despite potential drain of affiliation with Berkshire-Hathaway. Good liquidity (5.6) with sufficient resources (cash flows and marketable investments) to handle a spike in claims.

Other Rating Factors: Strong long-term capitalization index (7.2) based on excellent current risk adjusted capital (severe and moderate loss scenarios), despite some fluctuation in capital levels. Ample reserve history (9.4) that helps to protect the company against sharp claims increases. Excellent profitability (8.5) with operating gains in each of the last five years. Return on equity has been excellent over the last five years averaging 15.8%.

Principal Business: Auto liability (67%) and auto physical damage (33%).

Principal Investments: Misc. investments (57%), investment grade bonds (35%), non investment grade bonds (7%), and cash (1%).

Investments in Affiliates: 15%

Group Affiliation: Berkshire-Hathaway

Licensed in: All states except PR

Commenced Business: September 1961

Address: One Geico Plaza, Washington, DC 20076-0001

Phone: (800) 841-3000   **Domicile State:** MD   **NAIC Code:** 22055

Data Date	Rating	RACR #1	RACR #2	Loss Ratio %	Total Assets ($mil)	Capital ($mil)	Net Premium ($mil)	Net Income ($mil)
9-14	B+	2.18	1.65	N/A	6,922.7	3,891.3	526.3	349.7
9-13	B+	1.82	1.39	N/A	7,315.2	3,236.3	3,233.9	373.8
2013	B+	1.75	1.38	73.2	7,811.2	3,636.3	4,411.5	663.6
2012	B+	1.71	1.38	69.0	6,443.7	2,748.9	4,206.7	607.7
2011	B+	1.55	1.22	76.6	5,845.4	2,097.7	4,069.7	376.0
2010	B+	1.90	1.59	74.7	5,813.8	2,272.3	3,635.2	378.1
2009	B+	1.78	1.46	81.0	5,965.0	2,181.2	4,111.2	151.8

Rating Indexes

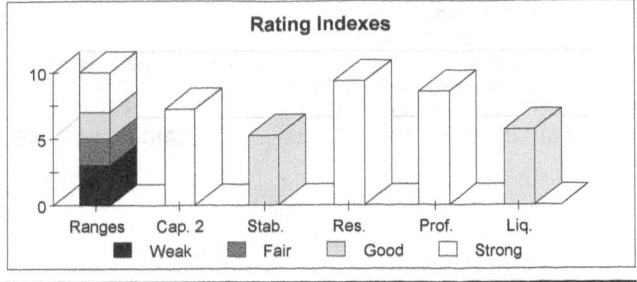

GEICO SECURE INSURANCE CO *
A-   Excellent

Major Rating Factors: Strong long-term capitalization index (10.0 on a scale of 0 to 10) based on excellent current risk adjusted capital (severe and moderate loss scenarios). Furthermore, this high level of risk adjusted capital has been consistently maintained in previous years. Superior liquidity (9.1) with ample operational cash flow and liquid investments.

Other Rating Factors: Good overall results on stability tests (5.9) despite weak results on operational trends. Fair profitability index (3.6) with operating losses during 2012 and 2013.

Principal Business: Auto liability (65%) and auto physical damage (35%).

Principal Investments: Investment grade bonds (78%) and misc. investments (22%).

Investments in Affiliates: None

Group Affiliation: Berkshire-Hathaway

(No States listed)

Data Date	Rating	RACR #1	RACR #2	Loss Ratio %	Total Assets ($mil)	Capital ($mil)	Net Premium ($mil)	Net Income ($mil)
9-14	A-	6.66	4.21	N/A	338.5	263.0	40.0	-0.2
9-13	A-	8.80	5.37	N/A	261.3	216.2	45.2	-10.2
2013	A-	7.75	5.16	91.7	322.2	266.6	82.7	-14.3
2012	A-	20.77	13.14	92.2	238.9	220.3	21.1	-5.1
2011	U	133.64	66.82	0.0	225.0	225.0	0.0	0.0
2010	N/A	N/A	N/A	0.0	0.0	0.0	0.0	0.0
2009	N/A	N/A	N/A	0.0	0.0	0.0	0.0	0.0

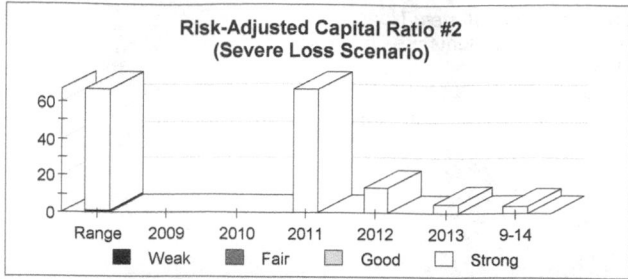

Risk-Adjusted Capital Ratio #2
(Severe Loss Scenario)

GENERAL CASUALTY CO OF WI
C   Fair

Major Rating Factors: Fair reserve development (4.7 on a scale of 0 to 10) as reserves have generally been sufficient to cover claims. Fair overall results on stability tests (3.6) including negative cash flow from operations for 2013.

Other Rating Factors: Weak profitability index (2.4) with operating losses during 2011, 2012 and 2013. Return on equity has been low, averaging 3.3% over the past five years. Good liquidity (6.7) with sufficient resources (cash flows and marketable investments) to handle a spike in claims. Strong long-term capitalization index (7.2) based on excellent current risk adjusted capital (severe and moderate loss scenarios), despite some fluctuation in capital levels.

Principal Business: Commercial multiple peril (34%), auto liability (18%), workers compensation (16%), homeowners multiple peril (10%), auto physical damage (9%), other liability (8%), and other lines (5%).

Principal Investments: Investment grade bonds (52%), misc. investments (41%), and real estate (7%).

Investments in Affiliates: 36%

Group Affiliation: QBE Ins Group Ltd

Licensed in: All states, the District of Columbia and Puerto Rico

Commenced Business: May 1925

Address: One General Dr, Sun Prairie, WI 53596

Phone: (608) 837-4440   **Domicile State:** WI   **NAIC Code:** 24414

Data Date	Rating	RACR #1	RACR #2	Loss Ratio %	Total Assets ($mil)	Capital ($mil)	Net Premium ($mil)	Net Income ($mil)
9-14	C	1.34	1.14	N/A	893.2	297.7	185.5	-0.1
9-13	B-	1.36	1.17	N/A	966.8	388.6	236.0	30.1
2013	C	1.41	1.20	75.2	866.6	312.7	312.2	0.0
2012	B-	1.57	1.36	73.5	1,025.0	448.1	280.2	-0.1
2011	B-	1.68	1.49	74.3	1,205.3	481.5	447.8	-21.9
2010	B-	1.75	1.67	66.4	965.1	523.3	227.4	48.1
2009	B-	1.55	1.43	65.1	1,218.1	556.3	349.0	80.2

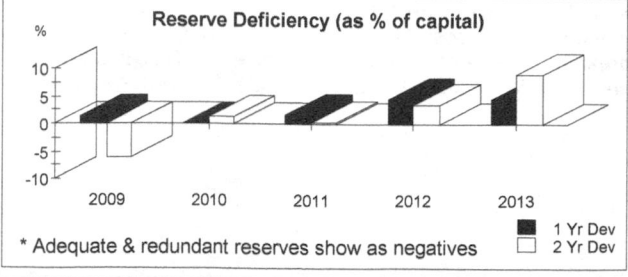

Reserve Deficiency (as % of capital)

* Adequate & redundant reserves show as negatives

GENERAL REINSURANCE CORP
B-   Good

Major Rating Factors: Fair overall results on stability tests (4.9 on a scale of 0 to 10) including potential drain of affiliation with Berkshire-Hathaway. The largest net exposure for one risk is conservative at 1.1% of capital. Strong long-term capitalization index (7.5) based on excellent current risk adjusted capital (severe and moderate loss scenarios), despite some fluctuation in capital levels.

Other Rating Factors: Ample reserve history (7.9) that can protect against increases in claims costs. Excellent profitability (8.2) with operating gains in each of the last five years. Excellent liquidity (8.6) with ample operational cash flow and liquid investments.

Principal Business: Aircraft (100%).

Principal Investments: Misc. investments (86%), investment grade bonds (12%), and non investment grade bonds (2%).

Investments in Affiliates: 45%

Group Affiliation: Berkshire-Hathaway

Licensed in: All states, the District of Columbia and Puerto Rico

Commenced Business: January 1973

Address: 695 E Main St, Stamford, CT 06904-2350

Phone: (203) 328-5000   **Domicile State:** DE   **NAIC Code:** 22039

Data Date	Rating	RACR #1	RACR #2	Loss Ratio %	Total Assets ($mil)	Capital ($mil)	Net Premium ($mil)	Net Income ($mil)
9-14	B-	1.55	1.38	N/A	16,162.6	11,698.4	430.9	393.7
9-13	B-	1.49	1.28	N/A	15,454.5	10,773.8	414.3	697.0
2013	B-	1.51	1.33	30.7	16,219.7	11,561.7	543.0	930.9
2012	B-	1.51	1.31	54.8	15,532.9	10,693.2	567.5	432.9
2011	B-	1.43	1.24	65.1	14,004.1	9,160.4	541.4	858.5
2010	B-	1.37	1.18	46.2	14,517.5	9,319.4	610.8	511.0
2009	B-	1.47	1.26	48.2	15,353.9	9,909.5	657.3	1,164.3

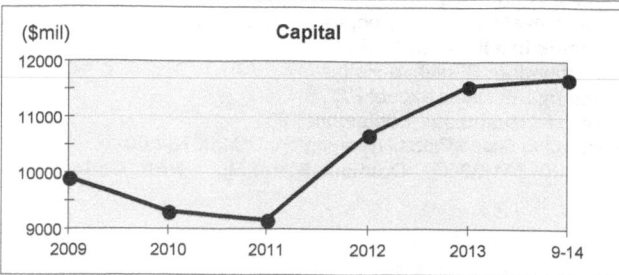

Capital

GENERAL STAR INDEMNITY CO
B-   Good

Major Rating Factors: Fair overall results on stability tests (4.9 on a scale of 0 to 10). The largest net exposure for one risk is conservative at 1.4% of capital. Good overall profitability index (5.7) despite operating losses during 2010. Return on equity has been low, averaging 4.1% over the past five years.

Other Rating Factors: Strong long-term capitalization index (10.0) based on excellent current risk adjusted capital (severe and moderate loss scenarios), despite some fluctuation in capital levels. Ample reserve history (9.3) that helps to protect the company against sharp claims increases. Superior liquidity (10.0) with ample operational cash flow and liquid investments.

Principal Business: Other liability (39%), allied lines (31%), fire (12%), medical malpractice (7%), products liability (7%), inland marine (2%), and earthquake (1%).

Principal Investments: Investment grade bonds (68%) and misc. investments (32%).

Investments in Affiliates: None

Group Affiliation: Berkshire-Hathaway

Licensed in: All states, the District of Columbia and Puerto Rico

Commenced Business: May 1979

Address: 1209 Orange St, Wilmington, DE 19801

Phone: (203) 328-5700   **Domicile State:** DE   **NAIC Code:** 37362

Data Date	Rating	RACR #1	RACR #2	Loss Ratio %	Total Assets ($mil)	Capital ($mil)	Net Premium ($mil)	Net Income ($mil)
9-14	B-	5.53	3.41	N/A	827.5	597.3	54.7	3.4
9-13	B-	6.43	3.95	N/A	822.1	618.5	47.4	11.0
2013	B-	6.24	3.84	39.8	859.4	645.8	70.3	47.6
2012	B-	7.17	4.49	27.6	748.4	566.4	58.6	14.0
2011	B-	7.74	4.99	15.1	696.6	508.7	47.7	43.2
2010	B-	5.95	3.87	1.7	758.8	533.4	44.4	-13.5
2009	B-	4.51	3.20	20.9	735.3	492.4	50.3	36.8

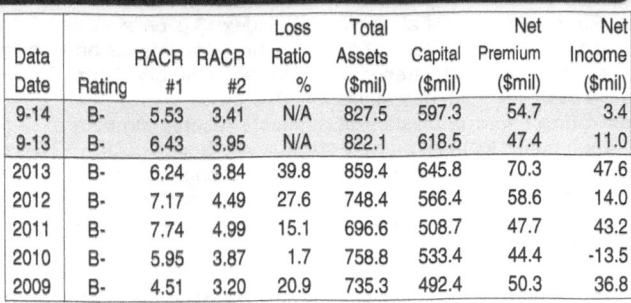

Rating Indexes

GENERAL STAR NATIONAL INS CO
B   Good

Major Rating Factors: Good profitability index (5.0 on a scale of 0 to 10) despite operating losses during 2009, 2010 and the first nine months of 2014. Return on equity has been low, averaging 2.3% over the past five years. Good overall results on stability tests (5.2) despite negative cash flow from operations for 2013. The largest net exposure for one risk is high at 4.0% of capital. Stability strengths include good operational trends and excellent risk diversification.

Other Rating Factors: Strong long-term capitalization index (10.0) based on excellent current risk adjusted capital (severe and moderate loss scenarios), despite some fluctuation in capital levels. Ample reserve history (9.1) that helps to protect the company against sharp claims increases. Superior liquidity (10.0) with ample operational cash flow and liquid investments.

Principal Business: Other liability (100%).

Principal Investments: Investment grade bonds (90%) and misc. investments (10%).

Investments in Affiliates: None

Group Affiliation: Berkshire-Hathaway

Licensed in: All states, the District of Columbia and Puerto Rico

Commenced Business: September 1864

Address: 471 E Broad St, Columbus, OH 43215

Phone: (203) 328-5700   **Domicile State:** DE   **NAIC Code:** 11967

Data Date	Rating	RACR #1	RACR #2	Loss Ratio %	Total Assets ($mil)	Capital ($mil)	Net Premium ($mil)	Net Income ($mil)
9-14	B	9.05	6.26	N/A	241.7	180.6	7.5	-0.6
9-13	B+	9.93	7.02	N/A	253.1	192.8	7.0	5.9
2013	B+	10.43	7.20	N/A	256.4	198.0	9.6	13.2
2012	B+	8.42	6.25	N/A	250.7	181.2	9.2	7.4
2011	B+	6.14	4.52	64.2	251.7	166.7	14.9	7.3
2010	B+	4.92	3.64	84.3	280.0	174.0	23.7	-0.5
2009	B+	4.44	3.34	98.8	268.0	165.1	25.2	-1.7

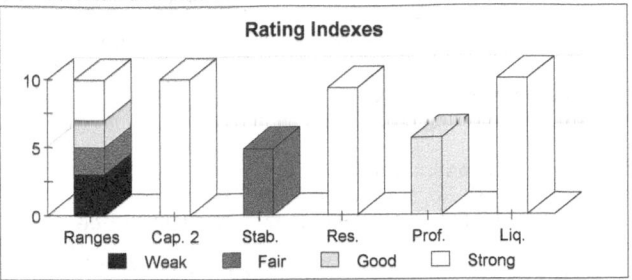

Income Trends

GENWORTH MORTGAGE INS CORP
C-   Fair

Major Rating Factors: A history of deficient reserves (0.8 on a scale of 0 to 10). Underreserving can have an adverse impact on capital and profits. In four of the last five years reserves (two year development) were between 43% and 138% deficient. Weak profitability index (2.6) with operating losses during 2009, 2010, 2011 and 2012. Average return on equity over the last five years has been poor at -63.0%.

Other Rating Factors: Fair overall results on stability tests (3.1) including negative cash flow from operations for 2013. Strengths include potentially strong support from affiliation with Genworth Financial. Fair long-term capitalization (3.6) based on excellent current risk adjusted capital (severe and moderate loss scenarios) reflecting improvement over results in 2013. Good liquidity (5.2) with sufficient resources (cash flows and marketable investments) to handle a spike in claims.

Principal Business: Mortgage guaranty (100%).

Principal Investments: Misc. investments (57%), investment grade bonds (41%), and non investment grade bonds (2%).

Investments in Affiliates: 31%

Group Affiliation: Genworth Financial

Licensed in: All states except PR

Commenced Business: May 1980

Address: 6601 Six Forks Road, Raleigh, NC 27615

Phone: (919) 846-4100   **Domicile State:** NC   **NAIC Code:** 38458

Data Date	Rating	RACR #1	RACR #2	Loss Ratio %	Total Assets ($mil)	Capital ($mil)	Net Premium ($mil)	Net Income ($mil)
9-14	C-	1.23	1.08	N/A	2,609.6	1,261.2	348.8	132.2
9-13	D+	0.73	0.59	N/A	2,271.9	752.7	337.8	48.9
2013	C-	0.88	0.77	79.2	2,373.5	960.3	463.1	70.0
2012	D+	0.41	0.32	139.4	2,247.3	485.6	455.3	-152.3
2011	D+	0.41	0.32	232.0	2,682.2	564.0	483.0	-604.5
2010	D+	0.70	0.55	244.9	2,655.4	739.3	523.5	-787.4
2009	C	0.45	0.36	211.7	2,736.4	407.5	542.5	-550.6

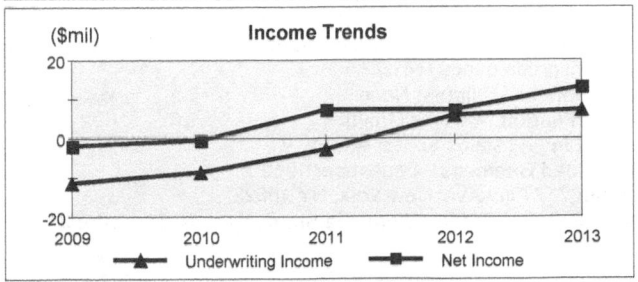

Reserve Deficiency (as % of capital)

GEORGIA FARM BUREAU MUTUAL INS CO

C — **Fair**

Major Rating Factors: Fair profitability index (3.3 on a scale of 0 to 10) with operating losses during 2009 and 2011. Fair overall results on stability tests (3.9) including fair financial strength of affiliated Georgia Farm Bureau Ins and negative cash flow from operations for 2013.

Other Rating Factors: History of adequate reserve strength (6.1) as reserves have been consistently at an acceptable level. Good liquidity (5.1) with sufficient resources (cash flows and marketable investments) to handle a spike in claims. Strong long-term capitalization index (7.6) based on excellent current risk adjusted capital (severe and moderate loss scenarios), despite some fluctuation in capital levels.

Principal Business: Homeowners multiple peril (30%), auto liability (28%), auto physical damage (19%), farmowners multiple peril (17%), commercial multiple peril (2%), allied lines (2%), and fire (1%).

Principal Investments: Investment grade bonds (71%), misc. investments (25%), and cash (4%).

Investments in Affiliates: 2%

Group Affiliation: Georgia Farm Bureau Ins

Licensed in: GA

Commenced Business: January 1959

Address: 1620 Bass Rd, Macon, GA 31210

Phone: (478) 474-8411   **Domicile State:** GA   **NAIC Code:** 14001

Data Date	Rating	RACR #1	RACR #2	Loss Ratio %	Total Assets ($mil)	Capital ($mil)	Net Premium ($mil)	Net Income ($mil)
9-14	C	2.12	1.43	N/A	638.1	264.8	310.2	5.7
9-13	C	1.99	1.33	N/A	621.6	237.8	295.0	-15.7
2013	C	2.07	1.41	74.3	620.6	258.1	401.4	2.6
2012	C	2.06	1.40	69.7	609.5	243.5	380.7	19.3
2011	C-	1.92	1.32	88.4	594.8	226.6	400.7	-49.7
2010	B-	2.48	1.69	76.6	700.4	314.2	436.3	20.7
2009	B	2.30	1.56	86.3	722.5	303.1	494.0	-36.6

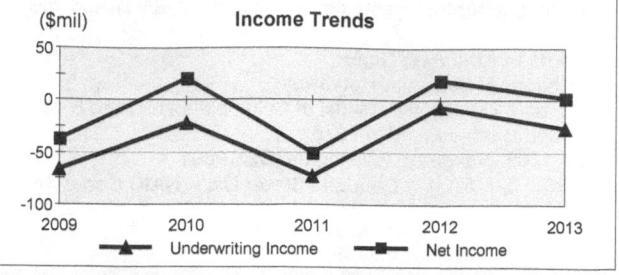

GLOBAL REINS CORP OF AMERICA

D+ — **Weak**

Major Rating Factors: Poor long-term capitalization index (2.7 on a scale of 0 to 10) based on weak current risk adjusted capital (moderate loss scenario), although results have slipped from the fair range during the last year. Weak profitability index (2.5) with operating losses during 2010 and the first nine months of 2014. Return on equity has been fair, averaging 11.9% over the past five years.

Other Rating Factors: Weak overall results on stability tests (2.6) including excessive premium growth, weak results on operational trends and negative cash flow from operations for 2013. The largest net exposure for one risk is high at 3.4% of capital. Ample reserve history (9.5) that helps to protect the company against sharp claims increases. Superior liquidity (10.0) with ample operational cash flow and liquid investments.

Principal Business: (This company is a reinsurer.)

Principal Investments: Investment grade bonds (75%), cash (24%), and non investment grade bonds (14%).

Investments in Affiliates: None

Group Affiliation: AXA Ins Group

Licensed in: All states except AK, FL, VT

Commenced Business: September 1940

Address: 717 Fifth Ave, New York, NY 10022

Phone: (212) 754-7500   **Domicile State:** NY   **NAIC Code:** 21032

Data Date	Rating	RACR #1	RACR #2	Loss Ratio %	Total Assets ($mil)	Capital ($mil)	Net Premium ($mil)	Net Income ($mil)
9-14	D+	0.65	0.42	N/A	415.1	134.2	0.4	-5.1
9-13	D+	0.74	0.49	N/A	436.0	185.6	0.1	23.9
2013	D+	0.88	0.57	N/A	432.8	197.2	0.2	31.4
2012	C	0.91	0.61	N/A	552.9	262.2	-0.4	63.9
2011	U	0.43	0.29	N/A	436.8	192.4	0.1	23.6
2010	U	0.31	0.21	N/A	448.5	162.3	0.0	-1.8
2009	D-	0.26	0.18	N/A	463.5	147.9	-1.0	30.8

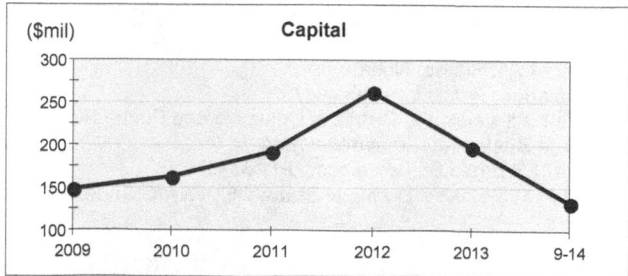

GNY CUSTOM INS CO *

B+ — **Good**

Major Rating Factors: Good overall profitability index (6.8 on a scale of 0 to 10). Fair expense controls. Return on equity has been low, averaging 2.7% over the past five years. Good overall results on stability tests (6.5). Stability strengths include good operational trends and excellent risk diversification.

Other Rating Factors: Strong long-term capitalization index (10.0) based on excellent current risk adjusted capital (severe and moderate loss scenarios), despite some fluctuation in capital levels. Superior liquidity (9.2) with ample operational cash flow and liquid investments. Fair reserve development (4.6) as reserves have generally been sufficient to cover claims.

Principal Business: Commercial multiple peril (92%), allied lines (4%), and fire (3%).

Principal Investments: Investment grade bonds (98%) and misc. investments (2%).

Investments in Affiliates: None

Group Affiliation: Greater New York Group

Licensed in: AZ, CT, DC, DE, IL, IN, MD, MA, MI, NJ, NY, NC, OH, PA, VT, VA

Commenced Business: June 2006

Address: 200 Madison Ave, New York, NY 10016-3903

Phone: (212) 683-9700   **Domicile State:** AZ   **NAIC Code:** 10814

Data Date	Rating	RACR #1	RACR #2	Loss Ratio %	Total Assets ($mil)	Capital ($mil)	Net Premium ($mil)	Net Income ($mil)
9-14	B+	24.19	17.37	N/A	55.8	50.3	1.8	0.9
9-13	B+	26.22	20.74	N/A	54.5	49.2	1.7	1.0
2013	B+	24.88	17.89	61.1	54.8	49.5	2.3	1.4
2012	B+	25.44	20.16	75.1	54.2	47.9	2.1	1.1
2011	B	25.31	18.58	94.2	52.5	46.8	2.0	1.0
2010	B	25.09	19.46	73.6	51.4	45.8	2.1	1.4
2009	B	25.30	20.38	63.8	49.9	44.4	2.2	1.5

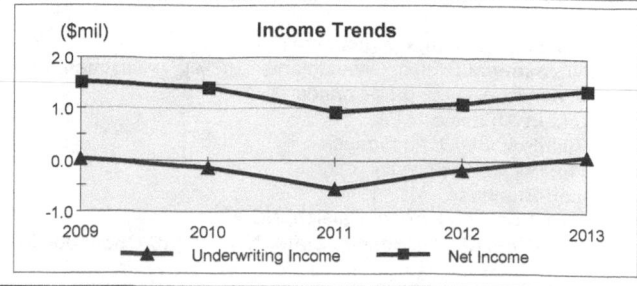

www.weissratings.com

GOVERNMENT EMPLOYEES INS CO *   B+   Good

Major Rating Factors: Good overall results on stability tests (5.3 on a scale of 0 to 10) despite potential drain of affiliation with Berkshire-Hathaway. Good liquidity (6.3) with sufficient resources (cash flows and marketable investments) to handle a spike in claims.

Other Rating Factors: Strong long-term capitalization index (7.6) based on excellent current risk adjusted capital (severe and moderate loss scenarios), despite some fluctuation in capital levels. Ample reserve history (9.3) that helps to protect the company against sharp claims increases. Excellent profitability (8.5) with operating gains in each of the last five years. Return on equity has been good over the last five years, averaging 14.3%.

Principal Business: Auto liability (60%), auto physical damage (38%), and other liability (2%).

Principal Investments: Misc. investments (56%), investment grade bonds (42%), non investment grade bonds (2%), and real estate (1%).

Investments in Affiliates: 1%

Group Affiliation: Berkshire-Hathaway

Licensed in: All states except PR

Commenced Business: December 1937

Address: One Geico Plaza, Washington, DC 20076-0001

Phone: (800) 841-3000   **Domicile State:** MD   **NAIC Code:** 22063

Data Date	Rating	RACR #1	RACR #2	Loss Ratio %	Total Assets ($mil)	Capital ($mil)	Net Premium ($mil)	Net Income ($mil)
9-14	B+	3.49	2.14	N/A	22,729.4	13,358.4	518.2	1,263.8
9-13	B+	2.49	1.66	N/A	23,007.8	10,464.5	8,546.6	1,089.2
2013	B+	2.67	1.81	77.3	25,778.8	12,089.8	11,644.8	2,010.1
2012	B+	2.14	1.52	80.2	19,089.6	8,017.6	11,118.7	1,026.0
2011	B+	1.91	1.40	81.3	16,974.9	6,132.3	10,628.3	901.7
2010	B+	2.45	1.94	76.6	16,462.9	6,464.5	9,958.6	1,282.1
2009	B+	2.21	1.61	77.2	15,302.9	6,118.2	9,391.9	552.5

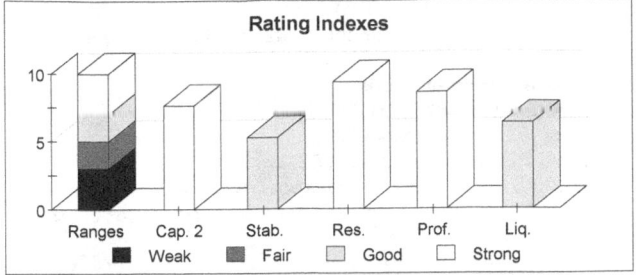

Rating Indexes

GRANGE MUTUAL CAS CO *   B+   Good

Major Rating Factors: Good overall results on stability tests (5.0 on a scale of 0 to 10) despite potential drain of affiliation with Grange Mutual Casualty Group. Good overall profitability index (6.7). Fair expense controls.

Other Rating Factors: Good liquidity (6.2) with sufficient resources (cash flows and marketable investments) to handle a spike in claims. Strong long-term capitalization index (8.6) based on excellent current risk adjusted capital (severe and moderate loss scenarios). Moreover, capital levels have been consistent in recent years. Ample reserve history (8.1) that helps to protect the company against sharp claims increases.

Principal Business: Auto liability (31%), auto physical damage (22%), homeowners multiple peril (18%), commercial multiple peril (17%), farmowners multiple peril (4%), other liability (3%), and other lines (6%).

Principal Investments: Investment grade bonds (50%), misc. investments (37%), real estate (6%), non investment grade bonds (5%), and cash (2%).

Investments in Affiliates: 11%

Group Affiliation: Grange Mutual Casualty Group

Licensed in: AL, GA, IL, IN, IA, KS, KY, MN, MO, OH, PA, SC, TN, VA, WI

Commenced Business: April 1935

Address: 650 S Front St, Columbus, OH 43206-1014

Phone: (614) 445-2900   **Domicile State:** OH   **NAIC Code:** 14060

Data Date	Rating	RACR #1	RACR #2	Loss Ratio %	Total Assets ($mil)	Capital ($mil)	Net Premium ($mil)	Net Income ($mil)
9-14	B+	3.11	2.25	N/A	2,088.9	1,042.4	736.2	22.9
9-13	B+	3.12	2.23	N/A	1,983.2	994.4	689.5	44.2
2013	B+	3.02	2.18	67.0	2,011.8	1,010.2	957.4	47.4
2012	B+	2.97	2.14	69.0	1,858.6	915.3	888.7	37.7
2011	B+	2.88	2.01	70.5	1,716.5	838.6	863.9	25.2
2010	A-	2.78	1.93	71.8	1,725.9	816.8	929.4	13.6
2009	A-	2.80	1.90	72.0	1,662.4	781.1	941.7	13.4

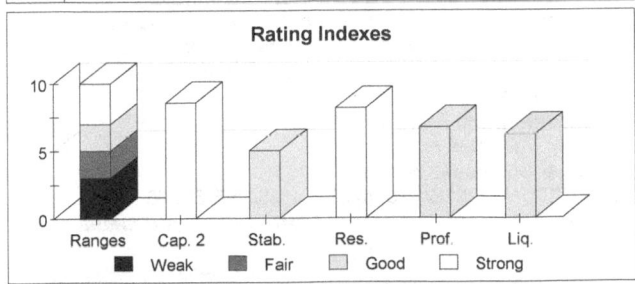

Rating Indexes

GREAT AMERICAN INS CO   B-   Good

Major Rating Factors: Good overall results on stability tests (5.0 on a scale of 0 to 10) despite potential drain of affiliation with American Financial Group Inc. The largest net exposure for one risk is acceptable at 2.3% of capital. Good overall profitability index (5.1). Fair expense controls. Return on equity has been excellent over the last five years averaging 21.8%.

Other Rating Factors: Good liquidity (6.7) with sufficient resources (cash flows and marketable investments) to handle a spike in claims. Strong long-term capitalization index (7.3) based on excellent current risk adjusted capital (severe and moderate loss scenarios), despite some fluctuation in capital levels. Ample reserve history (9.3) that helps to protect the company against sharp claims increases.

Principal Business: Allied lines (55%), other liability (20%), credit (5%), surety (5%), fidelity (5%), commercial multiple peril (3%), and other lines (8%).

Principal Investments: Investment grade bonds (65%), misc. investments (32%), non investment grade bonds (2%), and real estate (1%).

Investments in Affiliates: 12%

Group Affiliation: American Financial Group Inc

Licensed in: All states, the District of Columbia and Puerto Rico

Commenced Business: March 1872

Address: 580 Walnut St, Cincinnati, OH 45202

Phone: (513) 369-5000   **Domicile State:** OH   **NAIC Code:** 16691

Data Date	Rating	RACR #1	RACR #2	Loss Ratio %	Total Assets ($mil)	Capital ($mil)	Net Premium ($mil)	Net Income ($mil)
9-14	B-	1.65	1.19	N/A	5,734.6	1,355.5	1,579.6	146.6
9-13	C+	1.92	1.42	N/A	5,715.3	1,575.9	1,480.2	167.1
2013	B-	1.79	1.31	59.1	5,376.9	1,403.3	2,100.1	273.7
2012	C+	1.86	1.40	65.4	5,132.6	1,469.6	1,862.4	141.1
2011	C+	1.84	1.35	61.2	5,273.6	1,411.3	1,786.2	276.8
2010	C+	2.08	1.50	51.8	4,934.1	1,476.3	1,529.1	499.1
2009	C	1.87	1.29	44.8	5,353.0	1,433.1	1,500.1	458.0

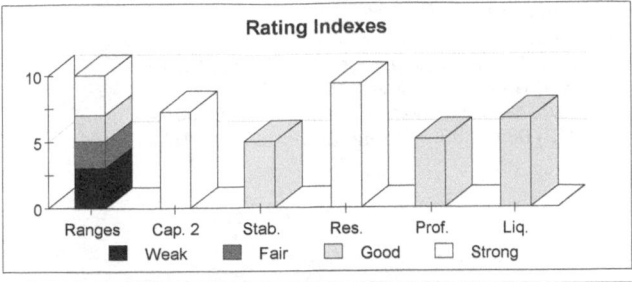

Rating Indexes

GREAT NORTHERN INS CO
B   **Good**

Major Rating Factors: Good liquidity (6.9 on a scale of 0 to 10) with sufficient resources (cash flows and marketable investments) to handle a spike in claims. Fair overall results on stability tests (4.9). The largest net exposure for one risk is excessive at 5.3% of capital.

Other Rating Factors: Strong long-term capitalization index (8.3) based on excellent current risk adjusted capital (severe and moderate loss scenarios), despite some fluctuation in capital levels. Ample reserve history (9.2) that helps to protect the company against sharp claims increases. Excellent profitability (8.2) with operating gains in each of the last five years. Return on equity has been excellent over the last five years averaging 15.7%.

Principal Business: Homeowners multiple peril (44%), commercial multiple peril (22%), inland marine (10%), auto liability (6%), other liability (5%), auto physical damage (4%), and other lines (9%).

Principal Investments: Investment grade bonds (92%) and misc. investments (8%).

Investments in Affiliates: None
Group Affiliation: Chubb Corp
Licensed in: All states except PR
Commenced Business: August 1952
Address: 100 S 5th St #1800, Minneapolis, MN 55402-1225
Phone: (908) 903-2000   **Domicile State:** IN   **NAIC Code:** 20303

Data Date	Rating	RACR #1	RACR #2	Loss Ratio %	Total Assets ($mil)	Capital ($mil)	Net Premium ($mil)	Net Income ($mil)
9-14	B	2.84	1.83	N/A	1,661.0	472.9	274.8	58.4
9-13	B	2.87	1.83	N/A	1,655.6	476.9	266.5	62.7
2013	B	2.97	1.92	52.7	1,653.1	478.8	360.6	83.4
2012	B	2.68	1.71	67.3	1,625.6	438.6	347.1	54.2
2011	B+	2.69	1.74	68.4	1,581.5	436.7	341.0	55.1
2010	B+	2.86	1.87	61.7	1,574.8	459.3	329.7	74.3
2009	B+	2.82	1.86	55.7	1,575.6	453.2	332.6	89.0

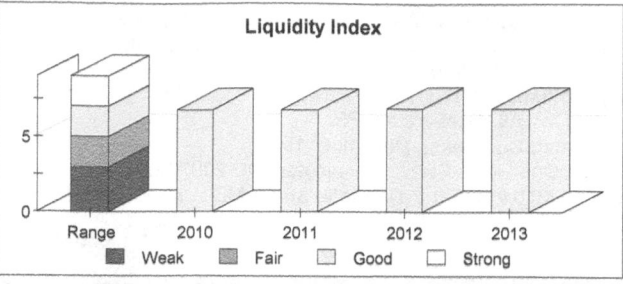

Liquidity Index

GREAT WEST CASUALTY CO *
A-   **Excellent**

Major Rating Factors: Strong long-term capitalization index (9.2 on a scale of 0 to 10) based on excellent current risk adjusted capital (severe and moderate loss scenarios). Furthermore, this high level of risk adjusted capital has been consistently maintained in previous years. Ample reserve history (9.5) that helps to protect the company against sharp claims increases.

Other Rating Factors: Excellent profitability (8.9) with operating gains in each of the last five years. Return on equity has been good over the last five years, averaging 13.6%. Excellent overall results on stability tests (7.1). Stability strengths include excellent operational trends and excellent risk diversification. Good liquidity (6.6) with sufficient resources (cash flows and marketable investments) to handle a spike in claims.

Principal Business: Auto liability (50%), auto physical damage (26%), workers compensation (12%), inland marine (9%), and other liability (4%).

Principal Investments: Investment grade bonds (83%), misc. investments (15%), cash (1%), and non investment grade bonds (1%).

Investments in Affiliates: None
Group Affiliation: Old Republic Group
Licensed in: All states except HI, PR
Commenced Business: April 1956
Address: 1100 W 29th St, South Sioux City, NE 68776
Phone: (402) 494-2411   **Domicile State:** NE   **NAIC Code:** 11371

Data Date	Rating	RACR #1	RACR #2	Loss Ratio %	Total Assets ($mil)	Capital ($mil)	Net Premium ($mil)	Net Income ($mil)
9-14	A-	3.94	2.42	N/A	1,829.1	566.4	555.8	73.6
9-13	A-	4.23	2.62	N/A	1,741.2	537.0	511.9	42.7
2013	A-	4.30	2.67	71.3	1,736.6	546.9	712.5	65.1
2012	A-	4.47	2.79	74.0	1,635.6	514.9	668.8	44.1
2011	A-	4.83	3.02	72.3	1,571.2	507.4	594.5	65.0
2010	A-	4.77	2.97	70.4	1,571.9	498.8	565.7	93.2
2009	A-	4.48	2.82	70.2	1,517.3	454.1	529.5	61.0

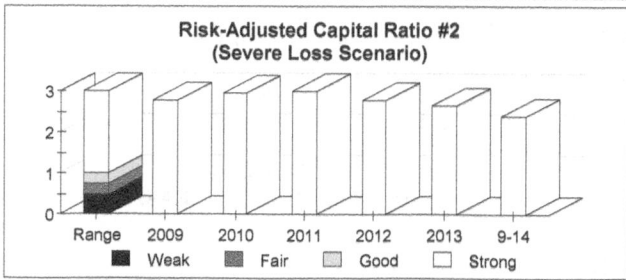

Risk-Adjusted Capital Ratio #2
(Severe Loss Scenario)

GREATER NEW YORK MUTUAL INS CO
B-   **Good**

Major Rating Factors: Fair overall results on stability tests (4.7 on a scale of 0 to 10) including potential drain of affiliation with Greater New York Group. Good overall profitability index (5.1) despite operating losses during 2011.

Other Rating Factors: Good liquidity (6.9) with sufficient resources (cash flows and marketable investments) to handle a spike in claims. Strong long-term capitalization index (8.5) based on excellent current risk adjusted capital (severe and moderate loss scenarios), despite some fluctuation in capital levels. Ample reserve history (7.7) that can protect against increases in claims costs.

Principal Business: Commercial multiple peril (95%), workers compensation (2%), other liability (1%), and auto liability (1%).

Principal Investments: Investment grade bonds (73%), misc. investments (24%), and cash (3%).

Investments in Affiliates: 17%
Group Affiliation: Greater New York Group
Licensed in: All states except AK, CA, FL, HI, ME, TX, PR
Commenced Business: November 1927
Address: 200 Madison Avenue, New York, NY 10016
Phone: (212) 683-9700   **Domicile State:** NY   **NAIC Code:** 22187

Data Date	Rating	RACR #1	RACR #2	Loss Ratio %	Total Assets ($mil)	Capital ($mil)	Net Premium ($mil)	Net Income ($mil)
9-14	B-	2.40	1.97	N/A	887.9	426.4	151.0	7.9
9-13	B-	2.51	2.20	N/A	856.3	404.5	139.4	13.0
2013	B-	2.41	2.00	61.1	863.7	414.5	196.7	18.0
2012	B-	2.53	2.26	75.1	859.6	388.6	179.2	2.9
2011	B	2.57	2.19	94.2	840.4	387.0	168.2	-19.0
2010	B	2.69	2.35	73.6	850.0	405.2	172.6	12.4
2009	B	2.68	2.40	63.8	840.8	390.9	180.8	21.2

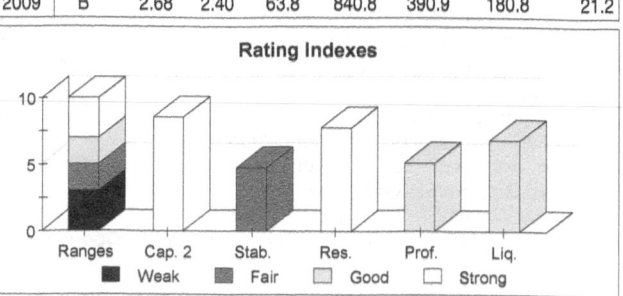

Rating Indexes

GREENWICH INS CO   C   Fair

Major Rating Factors: Fair overall results on stability tests (3.5 on a scale of 0 to 10) including potential drain of affiliation with XL Group plc and negative cash flow from operations for 2013. The largest net exposure for one risk is conservative at 1.3% of capital. History of adequate reserve strength (6.2) as reserves have been consistently at an acceptable level.

Other Rating Factors: Good overall profitability index (5.1). Fair expense controls. Return on equity has been fair, averaging 6.3% over the past five years. Good liquidity (6.8) with sufficient resources (cash flows and marketable investments) to handle a spike in claims. Strong long-term capitalization index (7.6) based on excellent current risk adjusted capital (severe and moderate loss scenarios), despite some fluctuation in capital levels.

Principal Business: Other liability (63%), allied lines (13%), auto liability (9%), workers compensation (4%), commercial multiple peril (4%), aggregate write-ins for other lines of business (3%), and other lines (3%).

Principal Investments: Investment grade bonds (67%), misc. investments (23%), and cash (10%).

Investments in Affiliates: 29%

Group Affiliation: XL Group plc

Licensed in: All states, the District of Columbia and Puerto Rico

Commenced Business: May 1946

Address: 1201 N Market St Suite 501, Wilmington, DE 19801

Phone: (203) 964-5200   **Domicile State:** DE   **NAIC Code:** 22322

Data Date	Rating	RACR #1	RACR #2	Loss Ratio %	Total Assets ($mil)	Capital ($mil)	Net Premium ($mil)	Net Income ($mil)
9-14	C	1.56	1.38	N/A	1,036.8	384.4	112.5	31.7
9-13	C	1.57	1.38	N/A	1,042.3	398.6	122.1	29.2
2013	C	1.69	1.51	65.3	1,053.3	416.6	159.7	30.8
2012	C	1.75	1.55	73.4	1,102.6	440.8	155.3	9.4
2011	C-	1.81	1.57	82.9	913.1	406.6	138.0	22.9
2010	C-	1.61	1.29	70.9	919.7	452.6	129.4	32.1
2009	D+	1.32	0.98	79.4	928.0	440.8	141.3	25.5

XL Group plc Composite Group Rating: C Largest Group Members	Assets ($mil)	Rating
XL REINS AMERICA INC	5528	C
GREENWICH INS CO	1053	C
XL INS AMERICA INC	734	C
XL SPECIALTY INS CO	441	C
X L INS CO OF NY	208	D+

GRINNELL MUTUAL REINSURANCE CO   B-   Good

Major Rating Factors: Fair overall results on stability tests (4.7 on a scale of 0 to 10) including potential drain of affiliation with Grinnell Mutual Group. Good overall profitability index (6.7) with small operating losses during 2012.

Other Rating Factors: Good liquidity (6.1) with sufficient resources (cash flows and marketable investments) to handle a spike in claims. Strong long-term capitalization index (8.6) based on excellent current risk adjusted capital (severe and moderate loss scenarios), despite some fluctuation in capital levels. Ample reserve history (9.1) that helps to protect the company against sharp claims increases.

Principal Business: Commercial multiple peril (19%), other liability (17%), workers compensation (16%), auto liability (15%), allied lines (14%), auto physical damage (13%), and other lines (7%).

Principal Investments: Investment grade bonds (78%), misc. investments (17%), cash (3%), non investment grade bonds (1%), and real estate (1%).

Investments in Affiliates: 5%

Group Affiliation: Grinnell Mutual Group

Licensed in: IL, IN, IA, MN, MO, NE, ND, OH, OK, PA, SD, WI

Commenced Business: April 1909

Address: 4211 Highway 146, Grinnell, IA 50112-0790

Phone: (641) 269-8000   **Domicile State:** IA   **NAIC Code:** 14117

Data Date	Rating	RACR #1	RACR #2	Loss Ratio %	Total Assets ($mil)	Capital ($mil)	Net Premium ($mil)	Net Income ($mil)
9-14	B-	2.90	2.06	N/A	910.5	420.4	353.6	31.6
9-13	B-	2.58	1.88	N/A	863.2	371.8	326.7	15.4
2013	B-	2.90	2.07	65.9	858.6	399.9	451.7	36.8
2012	B-	2.64	1.95	76.0	796.0	351.0	410.5	-2.1
2011	B-	2.78	2.04	75.7	742.9	336.5	375.1	1.1
2010	B-	3.00	2.19	74.6	754.5	342.9	368.7	5.2
2009	B-	2.97	2.18	66.9	737.6	327.4	369.1	25.0

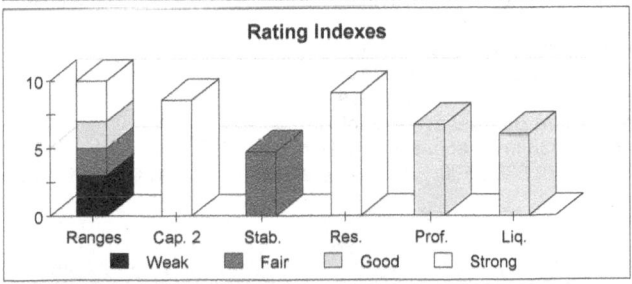

Rating Indexes

Ranges   Cap. 2   Stab.   Res.   Prof.   Liq.

■ Weak   ■ Fair   □ Good   □ Strong

GUIDEONE MUTUAL INS CO   B-   Good

Major Rating Factors: Fair overall results on stability tests (4.6 on a scale of 0 to 10) including potential drain of affiliation with GuideOne Group, weak results on operational trends and negative cash flow from operations for 2013. Good overall profitability index (5.2) despite operating losses during 2013.

Other Rating Factors: Good liquidity (6.4) with sufficient resources (cash flows and marketable investments) to handle a spike in claims. Strong long-term capitalization index (7.4) based on excellent current risk adjusted capital (severe and moderate loss scenarios), despite some fluctuation in capital levels. Ample reserve history (9.3) that helps to protect the company against sharp claims increases.

Principal Business: Allied lines (54%), commercial multiple peril (20%), auto liability (7%), workers compensation (7%), homeowners multiple peril (5%), auto physical damage (4%), and other liability (3%).

Principal Investments: Investment grade bonds (66%), misc. investments (35%), and real estate (1%).

Investments in Affiliates: 24%

Group Affiliation: GuideOne Group

Licensed in: All states except PR

Commenced Business: April 1947

Address: 1111 Ashworth Rd, West Des Moines, IA 50265-3538

Phone: (515) 267-5000   **Domicile State:** IA   **NAIC Code:** 15032

Data Date	Rating	RACR #1	RACR #2	Loss Ratio %	Total Assets ($mil)	Capital ($mil)	Net Premium ($mil)	Net Income ($mil)
9-14	B-	1.72	1.43	N/A	2,459.2	449.4	255.9	10.6
9-13	B-	1.81	1.54	N/A	1,177.4	422.0	226.0	-13.4
2013	B-	1.51	1.23	70.5	1,814.5	460.0	334.8	-9.4
2012	B-	1.90	1.66	59.8	1,134.8	423.4	295.7	24.4
2011	B-	1.99	1.75	72.4	1,074.1	408.4	282.3	10.9
2010	C+	2.03	1.78	64.6	1,047.2	411.3	282.5	24.7
2009	C+	1.88	1.62	63.0	1,026.9	377.6	298.0	28.3

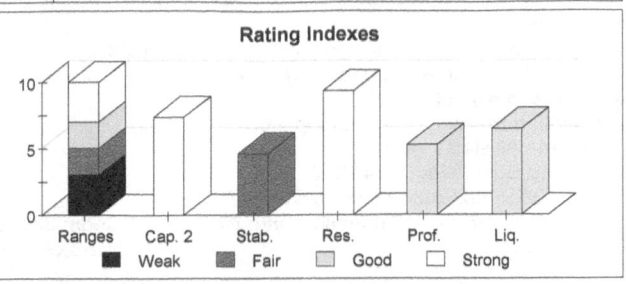

Rating Indexes

Ranges   Cap. 2   Stab.   Res.   Prof.   Liq.

■ Weak   ■ Fair   □ Good   □ Strong

GUIDEONE PROPERTY & CASUALTY INS CO | B | Good

Major Rating Factors: Good overall results on stability tests (5.5 on a scale of 0 to 10) despite potential drain of affiliation with GuideOne Group and negative cash flow from operations for 2013. Good overall profitability index (6.8). Fair expense controls. Return on equity has been low, averaging 3.2% over the past five years.

Other Rating Factors: Good liquidity (6.7) with sufficient resources (cash flows and marketable investments) to handle a spike in claims. Strong long-term capitalization index (8.9) based on excellent current risk adjusted capital (severe and moderate loss scenarios). Moreover, capital levels have been consistent in recent years. Ample reserve history (8.7) that helps to protect the company against sharp claims increases.

Principal Business: (This company is a reinsurer.)

Principal Investments: Investment grade bonds (74%) and misc. investments (26%).

Investments in Affiliates: 15%

Group Affiliation: GuideOne Group

Licensed in: IA

Commenced Business: December 1993

Address: 1111 Ashworth Rd, West Des Moines, IA 50265-3538

Phone: (515) 267-5000 **Domicile State:** IA **NAIC Code:** 13984

Data Date	Rating	RACR #1	RACR #2	Loss Ratio %	Total Assets ($mil)	Capital ($mil)	Net Premium ($mil)	Net Income ($mil)
9-14	B	3.08	2.43	N/A	684.5	243.1	80.0	2.8
9-13	B	3.90	3.14	N/A	430.2	238.1	70.6	0.4
2013	B	2.77	2.18	70.5	526.5	241.4	104.6	1.8
2012	B	4.07	3.34	59.8	417.1	234.9	92.4	9.2
2011	B	4.21	3.52	72.4	399.6	222.3	88.2	6.7
2010	B	5.16	4.09	64.6	390.0	216.5	88.3	9.1
2009	B	4.88	3.77	63.0	383.4	206.4	93.1	11.2

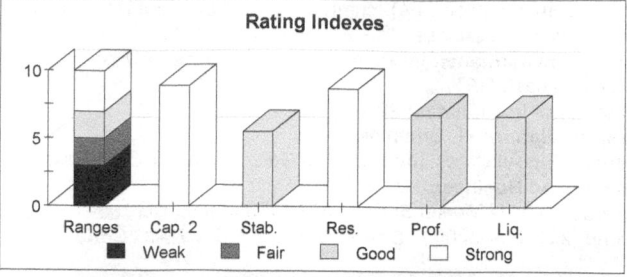

Rating Indexes

GUILFORD INS CO | C- | Fair

Major Rating Factors: Weak overall results on stability tests (2.6 on a scale of 0 to 10) including potential drain of affiliation with IFG Companies. Strong long-term capitalization index (7.9) based on excellent current risk adjusted capital (severe and moderate loss scenarios). Moreover, capital levels have been consistent in recent years.

Other Rating Factors: Ample reserve history (8.3) that helps to protect the company against sharp claims increases. Excellent profitability (8.3) with operating gains in each of the last five years. Excellent liquidity (7.8) with ample operational cash flow and liquid investments.

Principal Business: Other liability (84%), fire (9%), commercial multiple peril (6%), and allied lines (1%).

Principal Investments: Investment grade bonds (51%) and misc. investments (49%).

Investments in Affiliates: 47%

Group Affiliation: IFG Companies

Licensed in: All states except CA, CT, MS, NH, PR

Commenced Business: December 1998

Address: 238 International Road, Burlington, NC 27215

Phone: (336) 586-2500 **Domicile State:** IL **NAIC Code:** 10956

Data Date	Rating	RACR #1	RACR #2	Loss Ratio %	Total Assets ($mil)	Capital ($mil)	Net Premium ($mil)	Net Income ($mil)
9-14	C-	1.64	1.59	N/A	392.7	274.1	28.4	5.8
9-13	C-	1.64	1.59	N/A	384.5	259.7	32.4	8.2
2013	C-	1.61	1.57	50.6	390.3	267.5	40.7	12.3
2012	C-	1.61	1.57	60.2	377.8	250.7	43.1	7.6
2011	C-	1.59	1.55	58.9	369.8	246.0	35.9	5.6
2010	C-	1.58	1.54	49.9	363.9	237.4	31.3	10.7
2009	C-	1.55	1.35	53.4	361.1	224.9	34.3	13.1

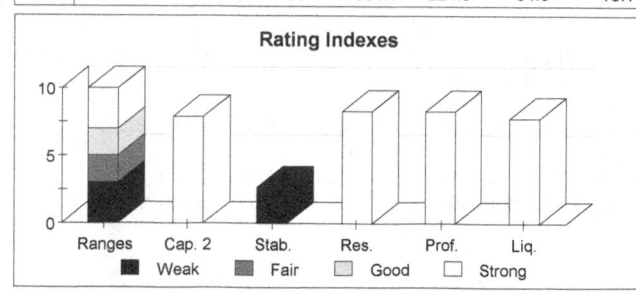

Rating Indexes

HANOVER INS CO | B | Good

Major Rating Factors: Good overall results on stability tests (5.2 on a scale of 0 to 10) despite potential drain of affiliation with Hanover Ins Group Inc. History of adequate reserve strength (5.5) as reserves have been consistently at an acceptable level.

Other Rating Factors: Good overall profitability index (5.3) despite operating losses during 2011 and 2012. Return on equity has been fair, averaging 5.0% over the past five years. Good liquidity (5.9) with sufficient resources (cash flows and marketable investments) to handle a spike in claims. Strong long-term capitalization index (7.3) based on excellent current risk adjusted capital (severe and moderate loss scenarios), despite some fluctuation in capital levels.

Principal Business: Other liability (23%), commercial multiple peril (20%), inland marine (15%), auto liability (9%), surety (7%), homeowners multiple peril (7%), and other lines (20%).

Principal Investments: Investment grade bonds (61%), misc. investments (34%), and non investment grade bonds (5%).

Investments in Affiliates: 23%

Group Affiliation: Hanover Ins Group Inc

Licensed in: All states except PR

Commenced Business: April 1852

Address: 100 North Parkway, Worcester, MA 01605

Phone: (508) 853-7200 **Domicile State:** NH **NAIC Code:** 22292

Data Date	Rating	RACR #1	RACR #2	Loss Ratio %	Total Assets ($mil)	Capital ($mil)	Net Premium ($mil)	Net Income ($mil)
9-14	B	1.49	1.24	N/A	6,424.6	1,993.9	2,107.9	111.0
9-13	B-	1.34	1.12	N/A	5,922.9	1,746.7	2,033.8	80.6
2013	B	1.42	1.21	64.8	6,047.1	1,829.7	2,759.4	184.3
2012	B-	1.21	1.03	76.1	5,696.5	1,518.9	2,661.5	-42.6
2011	B-	1.31	1.13	73.6	5,288.6	1,578.3	2,478.5	-7.1
2010	B-	1.47	1.27	64.0	5,253.5	1,742.8	2,375.3	113.0
2009	B-	1.60	1.41	63.9	5,035.0	1,737.1	1,987.5	174.3

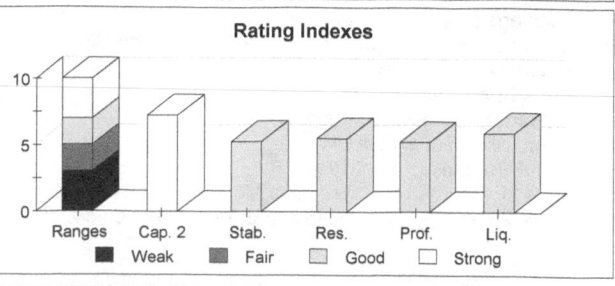

Rating Indexes

HARLEYSVILLE INS CO OF NJ   C-   Fair

Major Rating Factors: Weak profitability index (1.9 on a scale of 0 to 10) with operating losses during 2012. Return on equity has been fair, averaging 17.4% over the past five years. Fair overall results on stability tests (3.1) including weak results on operational trends and negative cash flow from operations for 2013.

Other Rating Factors: Good liquidity (6.5) with sufficient resources (cash flows and marketable investments) to handle a spike in claims. Strong long-term capitalization index (10.0) based on excellent current risk adjusted capital (severe and moderate loss scenarios), despite some fluctuation in capital levels.

Principal Business: (Not applicable due to unusual reinsurance transactions.)

Principal Investments: Investment grade bonds (361%).

Investments in Affiliates: None

Group Affiliation: Nationwide Corp

Licensed in: MA, MI, NJ, NC, PA

Commenced Business: May 1984

Address: 355 Maple Ave, Harleysville, PA 19438-2297

Phone: (215) 256-5000   **Domicile State:** NJ   **NAIC Code:** 42900

Data Date	Rating	RACR #1	RACR #2	Loss Ratio %	Total Assets ($mil)	Capital ($mil)	Net Premium ($mil)	Net Income ($mil)
9-14	C-	7.55	6.80	N/A	93.8	42.8	0.0	13.3
9-13	C	15.11	11.08	N/A	235.9	189.1	0.0	74.8
2013	C	30.17	27.15	0.0	239.3	190.7	-134.5	75.8
2012	C	1.65	1.15	72.1	814.3	143.8	274.5	-2.5
2011	B-	2.23	1.48	84.6	691.1	163.4	199.1	12.0
2010	B-	2.41	1.62	67.9	719.6	177.9	231.5	18.1
2009	B-	2.45	1.63	64.3	715.1	175.4	223.5	24.0

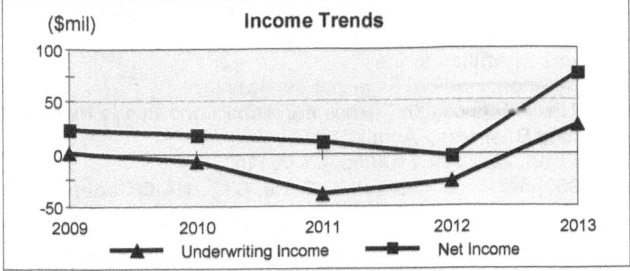

HARLEYSVILLE PREFERRED INS CO   C-   Fair

Major Rating Factors: Weak profitability index (1.9 on a scale of 0 to 10). Fair expense controls. Return on equity has been fair, averaging 19.4% over the past five years. Fair overall results on stability tests (3.1) including fair results on operational trends.

Other Rating Factors: Good liquidity (6.6) with sufficient resources (cash flows and marketable investments) to handle a spike in claims. Strong long-term capitalization index (10.0) based on excellent current risk adjusted capital (severe and moderate loss scenarios), despite some fluctuation in capital levels.

Principal Business: (Not applicable due to unusual reinsurance transactions.)

Principal Investments: Investment grade bonds (358%) and cash (1%).

Investments in Affiliates: None

Group Affiliation: Nationwide Corp

Licensed in: AL, AR, CT, DC, DE, FL, GA, IL, IN, IA, KS, KY, ME, MD, MA, MI, MN, MS, MO, NE, NH, NJ, NY, NC, ND, OH, PA, RI, SC, SD, TN, VT, VA, WV, WI

Commenced Business: May 1978

Address: 355 Maple Ave, Harleysville, PA 19438-2297

Phone: (215) 256-5000   **Domicile State:** PA   **NAIC Code:** 35696

Data Date	Rating	RACR #1	RACR #2	Loss Ratio %	Total Assets ($mil)	Capital ($mil)	Net Premium ($mil)	Net Income ($mil)
9-14	C-	5.77	5.19	N/A	139.2	42.6	0.0	13.5
9-13	B-	15.24	11.04	N/A	280.7	194.3	0.0	74.4
2013	B-	23.89	21.50	0.0	286.0	195.9	-134.5	75.6
2012	B-	1.79	1.24	72.1	830.8	156.8	274.5	3.6
2011	B-	2.16	1.44	84.6	691.6	158.2	199.1	18.1
2010	B-	2.34	1.56	67.9	743.5	176.0	231.5	21.2
2009	B-	2.42	1.61	64.3	747.4	173.5	223.5	26.7

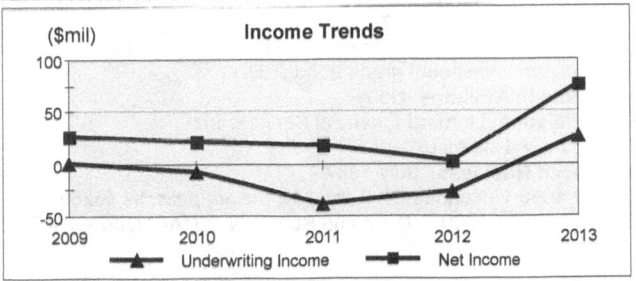

HARLEYSVILLE WORCESTER INS CO   C-   Fair

Major Rating Factors: Weak profitability index (1.9 on a scale of 0 to 10) with operating losses during 2012. Return on equity has been fair, averaging 15.8% over the past five years.

Other Rating Factors: Fair overall results on stability tests (3.1) including fair results on operational trends. Good liquidity (6.6) with sufficient resources (cash flows and marketable investments) to handle a spike in claims. Strong long-term capitalization index (10.0) based on excellent current risk adjusted capital (severe and moderate loss scenarios), despite some fluctuation in capital levels.

Principal Business: (Not applicable due to unusual reinsurance transactions.)

Principal Investments: Investment grade bonds (381%) and cash (1%).

Investments in Affiliates: None

Group Affiliation: Nationwide Corp

Licensed in: AL, AR, CT, DC, DE, FL, GA, IL, IN, IA, KS, KY, ME, MD, MA, MI, MN, MS, MO, NE, NH, NJ, NY, NC, ND, OH, PA, RI, SC, SD, TN, VT, VA, WV, WI

Commenced Business: May 1824

Address: 120 Front St, Suite 500, Worcester, MA 01608-1408

Phone: (215) 256-5000   **Domicile State:** PA   **NAIC Code:** 26182

Data Date	Rating	RACR #1	RACR #2	Loss Ratio %	Total Assets ($mil)	Capital ($mil)	Net Premium ($mil)	Net Income ($mil)
9-14	C-	6.48	5.83	N/A	160.8	52.0	0.0	16.6
9-13	C+	15.72	11.07	N/A	316.9	233.9	0.0	76.0
2013	C	28.06	25.25	0.0	327.6	235.6	-152.1	77.4
2012	C+	1.90	1.30	72.1	954.7	191.6	311.7	-2.3
2011	B-	2.28	1.52	84.6	763.5	184.6	218.1	10.4
2010	B-	2.41	1.61	67.9	808.4	208.5	253.6	18.5
2009	B-	2.52	1.68	64.3	582.7	137.0	170.3	17.5

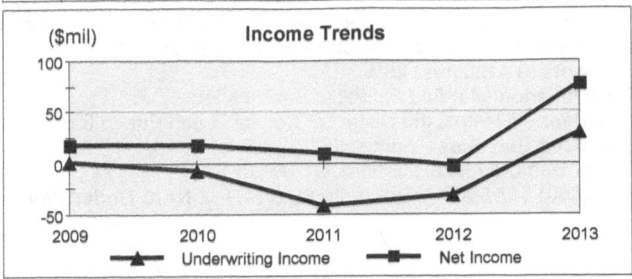

HARTFORD ACCIDENT & INDEMNITY CO

B **Good**

Major Rating Factors: History of adequate reserve strength (6.3 on a scale of 0 to 10) as reserves have been consistently at an acceptable level. Good overall profitability index (6.9). Fair expense controls. Return on equity has been good over the last five years, averaging 11.9%.

Other Rating Factors: Good liquidity (6.6) with sufficient resources (cash flows and marketable investments) to handle a spike in claims. Good overall results on stability tests (5.6). Strong long-term capitalization index (7.8) based on excellent current risk adjusted capital (severe and moderate loss scenarios), despite some fluctuation in capital levels.

Principal Business: Workers compensation (58%), auto liability (13%), homeowners multiple peril (7%), auto physical damage (7%), other liability (6%), commercial multiple peril (5%), and surety (2%).

Principal Investments: Investment grade bonds (68%), misc. investments (27%), and non investment grade bonds (5%).

Investments in Affiliates: 9%

Group Affiliation: Hartford Financial Services Inc

Licensed in: All states, the District of Columbia and Puerto Rico

Commenced Business: August 1913

Address: Hartford Plaza, Hartford, CT 06115

Phone: (860) 547-5000 **Domicile State:** CT **NAIC Code:** 22357

Data Date	Rating	RACR #1	RACR #2	Loss Ratio %	Total Assets ($mil)	Capital ($mil)	Net Premium ($mil)	Net Income ($mil)
9-14	B	2.29	1.66	N/A	11,637.2	3,543.3	2,457.3	283.6
9-13	B	2.34	1.72	N/A	11,295.7	3,467.9	2,414.2	267.6
2013	B	2.18	1.60	68.8	11,122.4	3,271.5	3,252.5	468.7
2012	B	2.17	1.60	72.7	11,063.3	3,107.6	3,218.3	362.2
2011	B-	2.03	1.52	78.5	10,631.4	2,823.1	3,219.4	269.3
2010	B-	2.24	1.73	67.3	10,744.5	3,183.0	3,167.2	599.2
2009	C+	2.04	1.57	64.4	10,570.3	2,938.0	3,191.0	182.4

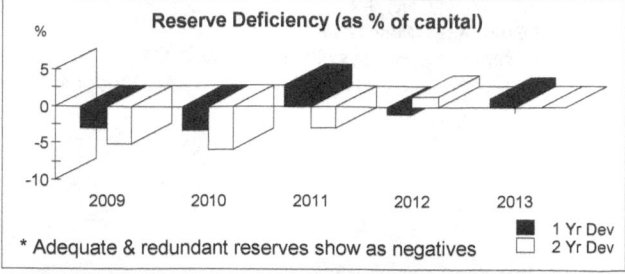

Reserve Deficiency (as % of capital)

* Adequate & redundant reserves show as negatives

1 Yr Dev / 2 Yr Dev

HARTFORD CASUALTY INS CO

B **Good**

Major Rating Factors: History of adequate reserve strength (6.2 on a scale of 0 to 10) as reserves have been consistently at an acceptable level. Good overall profitability index (5.1). Fair expense controls. Return on equity has been fair, averaging 8.2% over the past five years.

Other Rating Factors: Good liquidity (6.8) with sufficient resources (cash flows and marketable investments) to handle a spike in claims. Good overall results on stability tests (5.9). Stability strengths include good operational trends and excellent risk diversification. Strong long-term capitalization index (10.0) based on excellent current risk adjusted capital (severe and moderate loss scenarios), despite some fluctuation in capital levels.

Principal Business: Commercial multiple peril (33%), workers compensation (28%), other liability (13%), auto liability (13%), auto physical damage (6%), homeowners multiple peril (4%), and other lines (3%).

Principal Investments: Investment grade bonds (86%), misc. investments (11%), and non investment grade bonds (3%).

Investments in Affiliates: None

Group Affiliation: Hartford Financial Services Inc

Licensed in: All states except PR

Commenced Business: July 1987

Address: 4040 Vincennes Cir Suite 100, Indianapolis, IN 46268

Phone: (860) 547-5000 **Domicile State:** IN **NAIC Code:** 29424

Data Date	Rating	RACR #1	RACR #2	Loss Ratio %	Total Assets ($mil)	Capital ($mil)	Net Premium ($mil)	Net Income ($mil)
9-14	B	5.24	3.39	N/A	2,314.7	975.6	413.4	67.4
9-13	B	5.38	3.48	N/A	2,284.4	968.9	406.2	62.2
2013	B	5.01	3.28	68.8	2,207.0	905.8	547.2	83.6
2012	B	5.13	3.36	72.7	2,196.5	907.3	541.5	82.2
2011	B	5.32	3.55	78.5	2,192.4	895.5	541.6	48.0
2010	B	5.95	4.04	67.3	2,215.6	971.6	532.9	124.5
2009	B	5.62	3.81	64.4	2,250.4	981.3	536.9	38.6

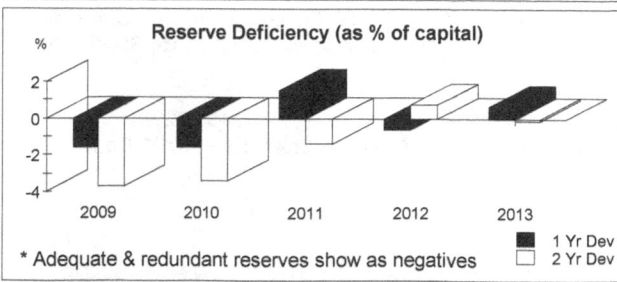

Reserve Deficiency (as % of capital)

* Adequate & redundant reserves show as negatives

1 Yr Dev / 2 Yr Dev

HARTFORD FIRE INS CO

B **Good**

Major Rating Factors: Good overall profitability index (6.9 on a scale of 0 to 10). Fair expense controls. Return on equity has been fair, averaging 6.6% over the past five years. Good liquidity (6.9) with sufficient resources (cash flows and marketable investments) to handle a spike in claims.

Other Rating Factors: Good overall results on stability tests (5.9). Fair reserve development (4.6) as reserves have generally been sufficient to cover claims. Strong long-term capitalization index (7.6) based on excellent current risk adjusted capital (severe and moderate loss scenarios), despite some fluctuation in capital levels.

Principal Business: Commercial multiple peril (31%), workers compensation (20%), inland marine (10%), auto liability (10%), other liability (9%), surety (8%), and other lines (12%).

Principal Investments: Non investment grade bonds (37%), misc. investments (32%), investment grade bonds (30%), and real estate (1%).

Investments in Affiliates: 26%

Group Affiliation: Hartford Financial Services Inc

Licensed in: All states, the District of Columbia and Puerto Rico

Commenced Business: August 1810

Address: Hartford Plaza, Hartford, CT 06115

Phone: (860) 547-5000 **Domicile State:** CT **NAIC Code:** 19682

Data Date	Rating	RACR #1	RACR #2	Loss Ratio %	Total Assets ($mil)	Capital ($mil)	Net Premium ($mil)	Net Income ($mil)
9-14	B	2.03	1.41	N/A	25,686.8	13,433.1	3,119.6	447.6
9-13	B	2.21	1.52	N/A	26,054.4	14,262.9	3,064.9	389.8
2013	B	2.16	1.50	68.8	25,684.8	14,081.4	4,129.1	1,006.6
2012	B	2.09	1.47	72.7	24,620.3	13,012.5	4,085.7	735.6
2011	B	2.56	2.31	78.5	24,140.3	12,594.3	4,087.0	987.6
2010	B+	2.63	2.41	67.3	25,075.7	13,958.9	4,020.8	958.0
2009	B+	2.62	2.43	64.4	24,542.9	13,190.2	4,051.0	906.3

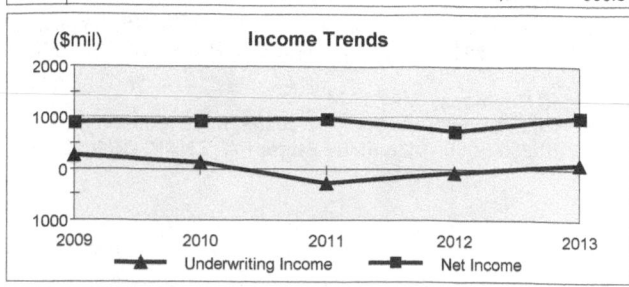

Income Trends

Underwriting Income / Net Income

HARTFORD INS CO OF IL
B   **Good**

Major Rating Factors: History of adequate reserve strength (6.2 on a scale of 0 to 10) as reserves have been consistently at an acceptable level. Good overall profitability index (5.9). Fair expense controls. Return on equity has been fair, averaging 9.4% over the past five years.

Other Rating Factors: Good liquidity (6.7) with sufficient resources (cash flows and marketable investments) to handle a spike in claims. Good overall results on stability tests (5.7). Stability strengths include good operational trends and excellent risk diversification. Strong long-term capitalization index (9.4) based on excellent current risk adjusted capital (severe and moderate loss scenarios), despite some fluctuation in capital levels.

Principal Business: Auto liability (46%), auto physical damage (21%), workers compensation (19%), homeowners multiple peril (10%), other liability (2%), and inland marine (1%).

Principal Investments: Investment grade bonds (83%), misc. investments (12%), and non investment grade bonds (5%).

Investments in Affiliates: None

Group Affiliation: Hartford Financial Services Inc

Licensed in: CT, HI, IL, MI, NY, PA

Commenced Business: January 1980

Address: 4245 Meridian Parkway, Aurora, IL 60504

Phone: (860) 547-5000   **Domicile State:** IL   **NAIC Code:** 38288

Data Date	Rating	RACR #1	RACR #2	Loss Ratio %	Total Assets ($mil)	Capital ($mil)	Net Premium ($mil)	Net Income ($mil)
9-14	B	4.21	2.72	N/A	3,895.9	1,423.9	759.2	113.9
9-13	B	4.27	2.78	N/A	3,788.7	1,389.6	745.9	83.1
2013	B	3.99	2.60	68.8	3,725.2	1,309.1	1,004.9	136.4
2012	B	4.06	2.67	72.7	3,698.8	1,301.0	994.3	123.1
2011	B	3.96	2.66	78.5	3,636.4	1,258.7	994.7	77.6
2010	B	4.37	2.96	67.3	3,650.2	1,330.5	978.6	158.1
2009	B	4.37	2.97	64.4	3,695.2	1,347.6	985.9	110.6

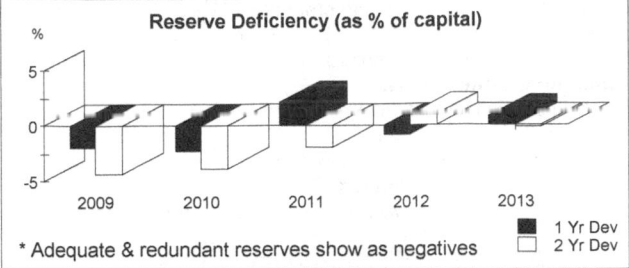

Reserve Deficiency (as % of capital)

* Adequate & redundant reserves show as negatives

■ 1 Yr Dev   □ 2 Yr Dev

HARTFORD INS CO OF THE MIDWEST
B   **Good**

Major Rating Factors: Good overall profitability index (6.9 on a scale of 0 to 10). Good expense controls. Return on equity has been fair, averaging 6.2% over the past five years. Good overall results on stability tests (5.8). Stability strengths include good operational trends and excellent risk diversification.

Other Rating Factors: Fair reserve development (4.6) as reserves have generally been sufficient to cover claims. Strong long-term capitalization index (10.0) based on excellent current risk adjusted capital (severe and moderate loss scenarios). Moreover, capital levels have been consistent in recent years. Excellent liquidity (7.6) with ample operational cash flow and liquid investments.

Principal Business: Workers compensation (27%), allied lines (23%), homeowners multiple peril (17%), auto liability (17%), auto physical damage (9%), commercial multiple peril (5%), and other liability (1%).

Principal Investments: Investment grade bonds (96%) and misc. investments (4%).

Investments in Affiliates: None

Group Affiliation: Hartford Financial Services Inc

Licensed in: All states except PR

Commenced Business: January 1980

Address: 4040 Vincennes Cir Suite 100, Indianapolis, IN 46268

Phone: (860) 547-5000   **Domicile State:** IN   **NAIC Code:** 37478

Data Date	Rating	RACR #1	RACR #2	Loss Ratio %	Total Assets ($mil)	Capital ($mil)	Net Premium ($mil)	Net Income ($mil)
9-14	B	25.21	16.43	N/A	567.5	447.5	37.6	15.7
9-13	B+	24.69	16.03	N/A	545.2	427.8	36.9	15.0
2013	B	25.12	16.51	68.8	550.1	432.1	49.7	19.2
2012	B+	20.83	13.70	72.7	470.1	352.7	49.2	21.0
2011	B+	19.50	12.97	78.5	451.5	330.0	49.2	19.7
2010	B+	18.73	12.55	67.3	422.7	309.6	48.4	23.4
2009	B+	15.88	10.70	64.4	383.0	264.7	48.8	21.7

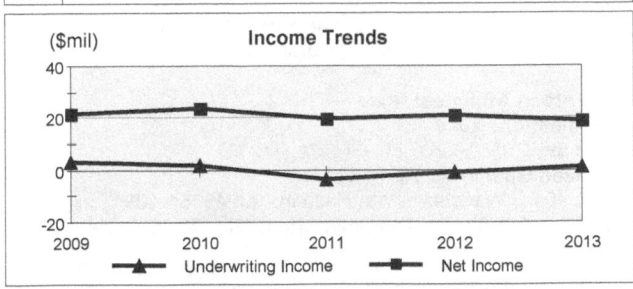

Income Trends

▲ Underwriting Income   ■ Net Income

HARTFORD SM BOIL INSPECTION & INS
B   **Good**

Major Rating Factors: Good overall profitability index (5.9 on a scale of 0 to 10). Weak expense controls. Return on equity has been excellent over the last five years averaging 20.4%. Good overall results on stability tests (6.1). Affiliation with Munich Re Group is a strength. The largest net exposure for one risk is conservative at 1.5% of capital.

Other Rating Factors: Strong long-term capitalization index (8.4) based on excellent current risk adjusted capital (severe and moderate loss scenarios), despite some fluctuation in capital levels. Ample reserve history (9.3) that helps to protect the company against sharp claims increases. Excellent liquidity (7.0) with ample operational cash flow and liquid investments.

Principal Business: Boiler & machinery (96%), inland marine (3%), and other liability (1%).

Principal Investments: Investment grade bonds (79%), misc. investments (16%), real estate (4%), and non investment grade bonds (1%).

Investments in Affiliates: 15%

Group Affiliation: Munich Re Group

Licensed in: All states, the District of Columbia and Puerto Rico

Commenced Business: October 1866

Address: One State St, Hartford, CT 06102-5024

Phone: (860) 722-1866   **Domicile State:** CT   **NAIC Code:** 11452

Data Date	Rating	RACR #1	RACR #2	Loss Ratio %	Total Assets ($mil)	Capital ($mil)	Net Premium ($mil)	Net Income ($mil)
9-14	B	2.11	1.87	N/A	1,348.6	617.8	555.7	69.7
9-13	B	2.10	1.90	N/A	1,339.6	589.3	519.3	52.3
2013	B	2.30	2.08	26.8	1,372.0	640.9	727.6	105.2
2012	B	2.40	2.19	26.8	1,353.9	649.2	668.4	128.0
2011	B	2.85	2.56	27.4	1,313.9	644.9	622.9	156.6
2010	B	2.85	2.57	30.9	1,340.6	654.6	631.9	169.4
2009	B	2.62	2.41	32.7	1,318.1	611.3	657.5	122.0

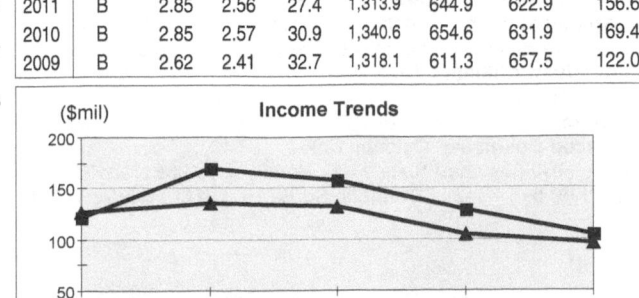

Income Trends

▲ Underwriting Income   ■ Net Income

HARTFORD UNDERWRITERS INS CO *

B+   Good

Major Rating Factors: History of adequate reserve strength (6.2 on a scale of 0 to 10) as reserves have been consistently at an acceptable level. Good overall profitability index (5.3). Fair expense controls. Return on equity has been fair, averaging 8.9% over the past five years.

Other Rating Factors: Good liquidity (6.8) with sufficient resources (cash flows and marketable investments) to handle a spike in claims. Good overall results on stability tests (6.4). Affiliation with Hartford Financial Services Inc is a strength. Strong long-term capitalization index (9.8) based on excellent current risk adjusted capital (severe and moderate loss scenarios), despite some fluctuation in capital levels.

Principal Business: Workers compensation (37%), auto liability (29%), auto physical damage (15%), homeowners multiple peril (11%), commercial multiple peril (3%), other liability (2%), and other lines (4%).

Principal Investments: Investment grade bonds (92%), misc. investments (5%), and non investment grade bonds (3%).

Investments in Affiliates: None

Group Affiliation: Hartford Financial Services Inc

Licensed in: All states except PR

Commenced Business: December 1987

Address: Hartford Plaza, Hartford, CT 06115

Phone: (860) 547-5000   **Domicile State:** CT   **NAIC Code:** 30104

Data Date	Rating	RACR #1	RACR #2	Loss Ratio %	Total Assets ($mil)	Capital ($mil)	Net Premium ($mil)	Net Income ($mil)
9-14	B+	4.32	2.82	N/A	1,566.0	600.8	300.7	48.8
9-13	B+	4.42	2.89	N/A	1,540.1	595.0	295.4	38.3
2013	B+	4.53	2.99	68.8	1,561.3	611.4	398.0	52.8
2012	B+	4.65	3.07	72.7	1,558.0	614.3	393.8	53.2
2011	B+	4.65	3.12	78.5	1,571.9	608.3	393.9	43.7
2010	B+	5.04	3.44	67.3	1,546.5	642.0	387.5	84.3
2009	B+	5.01	3.42	64.4	1,557.2	645.9	390.5	35.5

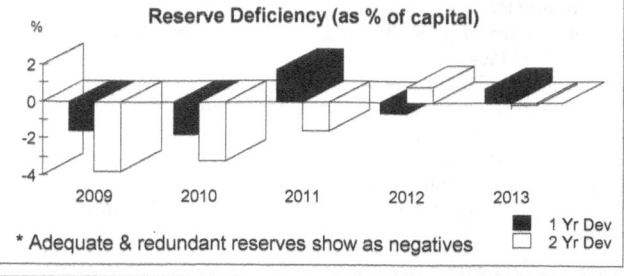

Reserve Deficiency (as % of capital)

* Adequate & redundant reserves show as negatives

■ 1 Yr Dev   □ 2 Yr Dev

HASTINGS MUTUAL INS CO *

A-   Excellent

Major Rating Factors: Strong long-term capitalization index (10.0 on a scale of 0 to 10) based on excellent current risk adjusted capital (severe and moderate loss scenarios). Furthermore, this high level of risk adjusted capital has been consistently maintained in previous years. Excellent overall results on stability tests (7.3). Stability strengths include excellent operational trends and excellent risk diversification.

Other Rating Factors: History of adequate reserve strength (6.7) as reserves have been consistently at an acceptable level. Good liquidity (6.6) with sufficient resources (cash flows and marketable investments) to handle a spike in claims. Fair profitability index (4.8) with operating losses during 2010.

Principal Business: Auto liability (20%), homeowners multiple peril (15%), workers compensation (15%), commercial multiple peril (15%), farmowners multiple peril (15%), auto physical damage (13%), and other lines (7%).

Principal Investments: Investment grade bonds (88%) and misc. investments (14%).

Investments in Affiliates: None

Group Affiliation: None

Licensed in: IL, IN, IA, KY, MI, OH, PA, TN, WI

Commenced Business: April 1885

Address: 404 E Woodlawn Ave, Hastings, MI 49058-1091

Phone: (800) 442-8277   **Domicile State:** MI   **NAIC Code:** 14176

Data Date	Rating	RACR #1	RACR #2	Loss Ratio %	Total Assets ($mil)	Capital ($mil)	Net Premium ($mil)	Net Income ($mil)
9-14	A-	4.67	3.31	N/A	777.9	346.3	274.2	9.4
9-13	A-	4.95	3.51	N/A	746.1	339.8	253.6	13.4
2013	A-	4.73	3.30	76.8	759.0	335.5	354.9	3.3
2012	A-	5.18	3.65	71.0	697.4	327.3	328.7	6.6
2011	A-	5.35	3.73	69.3	667.5	314.1	308.8	16.8
2010	A-	5.10	3.52	81.5	673.1	300.4	303.7	-12.8
2009	A+	5.94	4.05	74.3	646.7	307.4	280.8	1.9

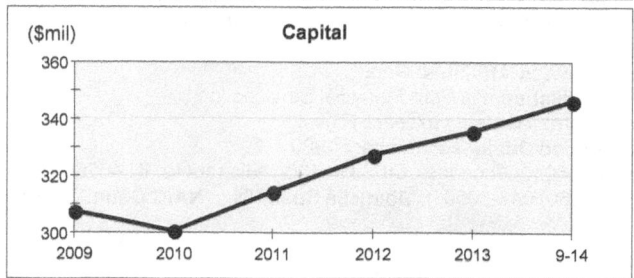

Capital ($mil)

HAWAII EMPLOYERS MUTUAL INS CO

C-   Fair

Major Rating Factors: Fair overall results on stability tests (3.1 on a scale of 0 to 10) including excessive premium growth. Good overall profitability index (6.9). Fair expense controls.

Other Rating Factors: Strong long-term capitalization index (10.0) based on excellent current risk adjusted capital (severe and moderate loss scenarios). Moreover, capital levels have been consistent in recent years. Ample reserve history (8.4) that helps to protect the company against sharp claims increases. Excellent liquidity (7.1) with ample operational cash flow and liquid investments.

Principal Business: Workers compensation (100%).

Principal Investments: Investment grade bonds (69%), misc. investments (22%), non investment grade bonds (4%), cash (3%), and real estate (2%).

Investments in Affiliates: None

Group Affiliation: None

Licensed in: HI

Commenced Business: October 1996

Address: 1100 Alakea St Suite 1400, Honolulu, HI 96813-3407

Phone: (808) 524-3642   **Domicile State:** HI   **NAIC Code:** 10781

Data Date	Rating	RACR #1	RACR #2	Loss Ratio %	Total Assets ($mil)	Capital ($mil)	Net Premium ($mil)	Net Income ($mil)
9-14	C-	5.49	3.86	N/A	337.7	216.6	40.8	12.2
9-13	C-	6.92	4.54	N/A	309.3	204.3	28.5	7.9
2013	C-	5.90	3.93	72.0	313.6	209.4	45.5	9.3
2012	C-	7.08	4.60	67.7	285.0	190.1	33.6	10.6
2011	C-	6.79	4.42	71.0	273.6	173.8	31.1	8.2
2010	C-	6.66	4.26	70.2	268.9	166.3	27.8	8.7
2009	D+	6.07	3.85	66.7	265.6	152.7	32.1	7.7

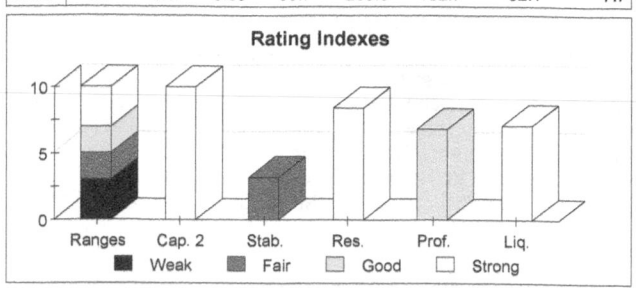

Rating Indexes

■ Weak   ▨ Fair   □ Good   □ Strong

HOLYOKE MUTUAL INS CO IN SALEM *   B+   Good

Major Rating Factors: Good overall profitability index (5.7 on a scale of 0 to 10) despite operating losses during 2011 and 2012. Good liquidity (6.4) with sufficient resources (cash flows and marketable investments) to handle a spike in claims.

Other Rating Factors: Good overall results on stability tests (6.4). Affiliation with COUNTRY Financial is a strength. Strong long-term capitalization index (9.5) based on excellent current risk adjusted capital (severe and moderate loss scenarios), despite some fluctuation in capital levels. Ample reserve history (7.8) that can protect against increases in claims costs.

Principal Business: Commercial multiple peril (71%), homeowners multiple peril (18%), allied lines (2%), auto liability (2%), other liability (2%), auto physical damage (2%), and other lines (3%).

Principal Investments: Investment grade bonds (77%), misc. investments (19%), non investment grade bonds (2%), and real estate (2%).

Investments in Affiliates: 1%

Group Affiliation: COUNTRY Financial

Licensed in: AZ, AR, CO, CT, GA, ID, IL, ME, MA, MN, MO, MT, NF, NV, NH, NJ, NM, NY, NC, ND, OR, RI, SC, SD, TX, UT, VT, WA, WY

Commenced Business: May 1843

Address: Holyoke Square, Salem, MA 01970-6506

Phone: (978) 744-6123   **Domicile State:** MA   **NAIC Code:** 14206

Data Date	Rating	RACR #1	RACR #2	Loss Ratio %	Total Assets ($mil)	Capital ($mil)	Net Premium ($mil)	Net Income ($mil)
9-14	B+	3.96	2.69	N/A	224.3	92.9	78.3	2.8
9-13	B	3.85	2.62	N/A	222.3	88.0	75.5	5.6
2013	B+	3.91	2.69	69.3	224.3	89.9	102.6	5.7
2012	B	3.71	2.58	75.5	216.6	81.7	104.1	-0.2
2011	B	4.34	2.92	85.8	200.8	82.4	83.8	-4.7
2010	B	4.76	3.30	73.0	200.3	87.3	82.3	1.3
2009	B	4.96	3.52	75.6	189.3	82.3	80.8	7.6

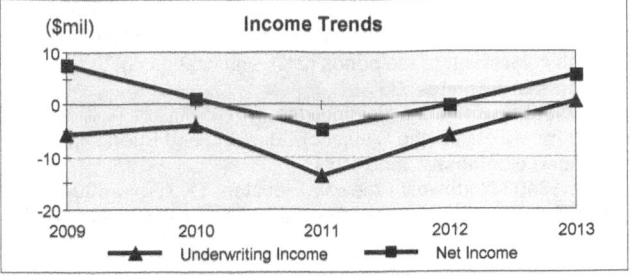

Income Trends

HOME-OWNERS INS CO *   A-   Excellent

Major Rating Factors: Strong long-term capitalization index (9.2 on a scale of 0 to 10) based on excellent current risk adjusted capital (severe and moderate loss scenarios). Furthermore, this high level of risk adjusted capital has been consistently maintained in previous years. Excellent overall results on stability tests (7.3). Stability strengths include excellent operational trends and excellent risk diversification.

Other Rating Factors: History of adequate reserve strength (5.8) as reserves have been consistently at an acceptable level. Good overall profitability index (6.8) with small operating losses during 2010. Return on equity has been low, averaging 4.8% over the past five years. Good liquidity (6.5) with sufficient resources (cash flows and marketable investments) to handle a spike in claims.

Principal Business: Auto liability (34%), homeowners multiple peril (30%), auto physical damage (23%), commercial multiple peril (7%), workers compensation (2%), other liability (1%), and inland marine (1%).

Principal Investments: Investment grade bonds (82%) and misc. investments (18%).

Investments in Affiliates: None

Group Affiliation: Auto-Owners Group

Licensed in: AL, AR, CO, GA, IL, IN, IA, KY, MI, MO, NE, NV, ND, OH, PA, SC, SD, UT, VA, WI

Commenced Business: May 1863

Address: 6101 Anacapri Blvd, Lansing, MI 48917-3999

Phone: (517) 323-1200   **Domicile State:** MI   **NAIC Code:** 26638

Data Date	Rating	RACR #1	RACR #2	Loss Ratio %	Total Assets ($mil)	Capital ($mil)	Net Premium ($mil)	Net Income ($mil)
9-14	A-	3.92	2.69	N/A	2,165.7	837.2	807.5	37.2
9-13	A-	3.81	2.58	N/A	2,016.1	783.3	755.2	69.7
2013	A-	3.77	2.62	69.3	2,069.7	799.4	1,045.3	73.7
2012	A-	3.32	2.29	73.3	1,854.4	684.9	980.9	46.6
2011	A-	3.28	2.27	81.4	1,716.2	612.4	921.8	10.0
2010	A-	3.49	2.36	84.6	1,645.3	617.3	860.0	-2.1
2009	A	3.39	2.22	80.9	1,456.9	537.4	811.4	30.7

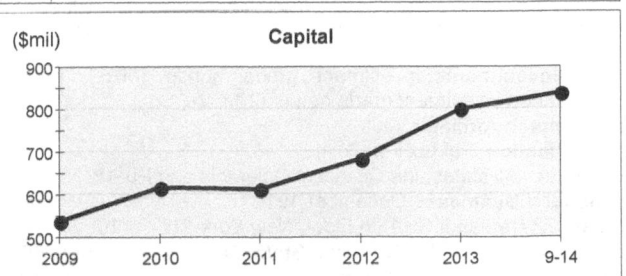

Capital

HOUSING AUTHORITY RISK RET GROUP INC   C   Fair

Major Rating Factors: Fair overall results on stability tests (3.6 on a scale of 0 to 10) including negative cash flow from operations for 2013. Strong long-term capitalization index (10.0) based on excellent current risk adjusted capital (severe and moderate loss scenarios). Moreover, capital levels have been consistent in recent years.

Other Rating Factors: Ample reserve history (9.7) that helps to protect the company against sharp claims increases. Excellent profitability (8.7) with operating gains in each of the last five years. Return on equity has been good over the last five years, averaging 11.6%. Excellent liquidity (7.8) with ample operational cash flow and liquid investments.

Principal Business: Other liability (88%) and auto liability (12%).

Principal Investments: Investment grade bonds (79%), misc. investments (16%), cash (3%), non investment grade bonds (1%), and real estate (1%).

Investments in Affiliates: 10%

Group Affiliation: Housing Investment Group Inc

Licensed in: All states except AK, PR

Commenced Business: June 1987

Address: 189 Commerce Court, Cheshire, CT 06410-0189

Phone: (203) 272-8220   **Domicile State:** VT   **NAIC Code:** 26797

Data Date	Rating	RACR #1	RACR #2	Loss Ratio %	Total Assets ($mil)	Capital ($mil)	Net Premium ($mil)	Net Income ($mil)
9-14	C	4.48	3.53	N/A	315.1	199.6	21.6	7.3
9-13	C	4.86	3.74	N/A	310.4	195.1	21.0	2.1
2013	C	4.68	3.75	43.6	314.8	194.7	28.3	7.0
2012	C	5.25	4.14	27.8	305.8	192.4	28.5	17.9
2011	C	4.55	3.71	N/A	307.1	179.3	28.6	26.8
2010	C	3.81	3.00	36.2	297.9	156.2	28.0	21.0
2009	C	3.30	2.65	N/A	282.2	136.9	30.8	30.2

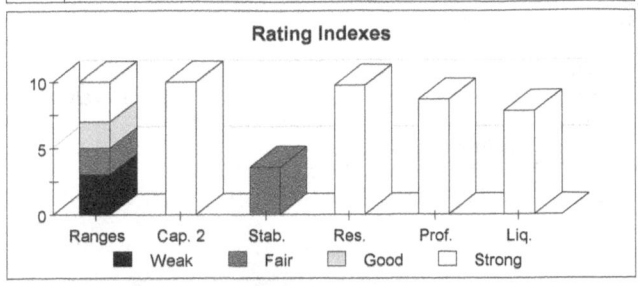

Rating Indexes

HOUSTON CASUALTY CO

B-   **Good**

Major Rating Factors: Fair overall results on stability tests (4.9 on a scale of 0 to 10). The largest net exposure for one risk is conservative at 1.0% of capital. Strong long-term capitalization index (8.1) based on excellent current risk adjusted capital (severe and moderate loss scenarios). Moreover, capital levels have been consistent in recent years.

Other Rating Factors: Ample reserve history (7.8) that can protect against increases in claims costs. Excellent profitability (8.8) with operating gains in each of the last five years. Return on equity has been good over the last five years, averaging 12.6%. Excellent liquidity (7.7) with ample operational cash flow and liquid investments.

Principal Business: Other liability (45%), ocean marine (22%), other accident & health (7%), fire (6%), earthquake (5%), inland marine (4%), and other lines (13%).

Principal Investments: Investment grade bonds (49%), misc. investments (48%), non investment grade bonds (2%), and cash (1%).

Investments in Affiliates: 36%

Group Affiliation: HCC Ins Holdings Inc

Licensed in: All states, the District of Columbia and Puerto Rico

Commenced Business: June 1981

Address: 13403 Northwest Freeway, Houston, TX 77040-6094

Phone: (713) 462-1000   **Domicile State:** TX   **NAIC Code:** 42374

Data Date	Rating	RACR #1	RACR #2	Loss Ratio %	Total Assets ($mil)	Capital ($mil)	Net Premium ($mil)	Net Income ($mil)
9-14	B-	2.04	1.83	N/A	3,216.5	2,124.4	228.2	81.7
9-13	B-	2.02	1.80	N/A	3,163.2	2,054.7	236.1	88.5
2013	B-	1.88	1.71	40.6	2,967.1	1,909.7	301.7	323.6
2012	B-	1.87	1.70	50.1	2,930.4	1,795.1	332.1	264.2
2011	B-	1.91	1.73	70.1	2,911.7	1,699.0	337.0	229.4
2010	B-	1.84	1.70	56.4	2,864.1	1,641.8	286.6	162.9
2009	B-	2.05	1.90	36.1	2,904.7	1,567.7	307.3	209.5

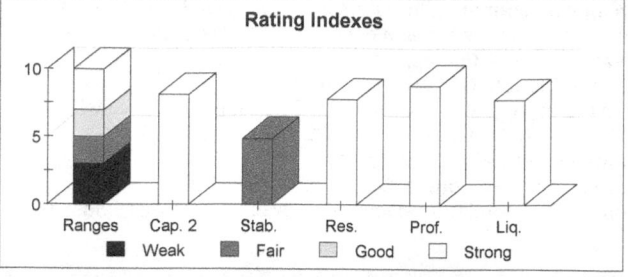

Rating Indexes

Ranges   Cap. 2   Stab.   Res.   Prof.   Liq.
■ Weak   ■ Fair   ▨ Good   □ Strong

HUDSON INS CO

C-   **Fair**

Major Rating Factors: Fair overall results on stability tests (3.1 on a scale of 0 to 10) including weak financial strength of affiliated Fairfax Financial and negative cash flow from operations for 2013. The largest net exposure for one risk is conservative at 1.1% of capital. History of adequate reserve strength (5.7) as reserves have been consistently at an acceptable level.

Other Rating Factors: Good overall profitability index (6.6). Fair expense controls. Return on equity has been low, averaging 4.2% over the past five years. Strong long-term capitalization index (8.6) based on excellent current risk adjusted capital (severe and moderate loss scenarios). Moreover, capital levels have been consistent in recent years. Excellent liquidity (7.6) with ample operational cash flow and liquid investments.

Principal Business: Allied lines (43%), other liability (37%), auto liability (5%), auto physical damage (5%), surety (5%), ocean marine (2%), and other lines (2%).

Principal Investments: Investment grade bonds (60%), misc. investments (38%), and non investment grade bonds (2%).

Investments in Affiliates: 30%

Group Affiliation: Fairfax Financial

Licensed in: All states, the District of Columbia and Puerto Rico

Commenced Business: December 1918

Address: 22 Cortlandt St. 18th Floor, New York, NY 10007

Phone: (212) 978-2800   **Domicile State:** DE   **NAIC Code:** 25054

Data Date	Rating	RACR #1	RACR #2	Loss Ratio %	Total Assets ($mil)	Capital ($mil)	Net Premium ($mil)	Net Income ($mil)
9-14	C-	2.36	2.00	N/A	1,014.1	439.7	117.9	10.3
9-13	C-	2.86	2.60	N/A	739.5	423.4	97.5	12.2
2013	C-	2.48	2.22	86.0	819.0	413.9	129.6	6.0
2012	C-	2.76	2.54	82.8	821.1	398.9	108.4	14.0
2011	C-	2.78	2.57	90.9	736.6	388.6	102.2	2.7
2010	D+	1.67	1.26	80.2	667.9	370.9	74.0	15.5
2009	D	0.77	0.64	65.1	538.7	227.1	79.5	26.6

Fairfax Financial Composite Group Rating: C Largest Group Members	Assets ($mil)	Rating
ODYSSEY REINSURANCE CO	7448	C
UNITED STATES FIRE INS CO	3155	C
TIG INS CO	2236	D
ZENITH INS CO	1784	C-
CLEARWATER INS CO	1304	D

ICI MUTUAL INS CO RRG *

A-   **Excellent**

Major Rating Factors: Strong long-term capitalization index (10.0 on a scale of 0 to 10) based on excellent current risk adjusted capital (severe and moderate loss scenarios). Furthermore, this high level of risk adjusted capital has been consistently maintained in previous years. Ample reserve history (9.3) that helps to protect the company against sharp claims increases.

Other Rating Factors: Excellent profitability (8.5) with operating gains in each of the last five years. Excellent liquidity (8.4) with ample operational cash flow and liquid investments. Good overall results on stability tests (6.3). The largest net exposure for one risk is high at 3.1% of capital. Stability strengths include good operational trends and excellent risk diversification.

Principal Business: Other liability (89%) and fidelity (11%).

Principal Investments: Investment grade bonds (77%), misc. investments (20%), and cash (3%).

Investments in Affiliates: 0%

Group Affiliation: None

Licensed in: AZ, CA, CO, CT, DC, FL, GA, IL, IA, KS, MD, MA, MI, MN, MO, NE, NJ, NY, ND, OH, PA, SC, TN, TX, VT, VA, WA, WI

Commenced Business: March 1988

Address: 40 Main St Suite 500, Burlington, VT 05401

Phone: (800) 643-4246   **Domicile State:** VT   **NAIC Code:** 11268

Data Date	Rating	RACR #1	RACR #2	Loss Ratio %	Total Assets ($mil)	Capital ($mil)	Net Premium ($mil)	Net Income ($mil)
9-14	A-	11.42	7.15	N/A	330.9	251.2	21.8	11.7
9-13	A-	11.02	6.82	N/A	313.7	231.2	21.6	10.4
2013	A-	10.76	6.82	17.7	322.1	235.8	29.2	12.5
2012	A-	11.83	7.43	45.3	314.0	224.6	28.3	9.4
2011	A-	13.07	8.27	38.3	304.6	213.1	31.7	10.2
2010	N/A	N/A	N/A	10.8	303.1	200.2	30.9	8.5
2009	N/A	N/A	N/A	24.9	303.1	194.0	30.9	15.8

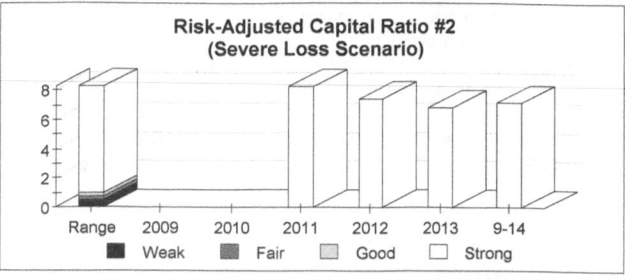

Risk-Adjusted Capital Ratio #2
(Severe Loss Scenario)

Range   2009   2010   2011   2012   2013   9-14
■ Weak   ■ Fair   ▨ Good   □ Strong

IDS PROPERTY CASUALTY INS CO | B | Good

Major Rating Factors: History of adequate reserve strength (5.4 on a scale of 0 to 10) as reserves have been consistently at an acceptable level. Good overall profitability index (6.0) despite modest operating losses during the first nine months of 2014. Return on equity has been fair, averaging 6.4% over the past five years.

Other Rating Factors: Good overall results on stability tests (5.5). Affiliation with Ameriprise Financial Group is a strength. Fair liquidity (4.3) as cash resources may not be adequate to cover a spike in claims. Strong long-term capitalization index (8.6) based on excellent current risk adjusted capital (severe and moderate loss scenarios). Moreover, capital levels have been consistent in recent years.

Principal Business: Auto liability (40%), homeowners multiple peril (30%), auto physical damage (29%), and other liability (1%).

Principal Investments: Investment grade bonds (85%), misc. investments (15%), and non investment grade bonds (1%).

Investments in Affiliates: 4%

Group Affiliation: Ameriprise Financial Group

Licensed in: All states except PR

Commenced Business: January 1973

Address: 3500 Packerland Dr, De Pere, WI 54115

Phone: (920) 330-5100   **Domicile State:** WI   **NAIC Code:** 29068

Data Date	Rating	RACR #1	RACR #2	Loss Ratio %	Total Assets ($mil)	Capital ($mil)	Net Premium ($mil)	Net Income ($mil)
9-14	B	2.72	2.19	N/A	1,438.0	584.3	701.7	-2.6
9-13	B	2.46	1.99	N/A	1,208.0	482.4	623.2	16.7
2013	B	2.57	2.13	88.2	1,268.3	530.7	883.7	11.3
2012	B	2.45	2.02	87.0	1,109.4	462.2	801.0	27.4
2011	B	2.50	2.12	88.1	1,039.9	431.0	741.7	22.5
2010	B	2.56	2.19	84.1	982.6	411.3	704.0	38.2
2009	B-	2.68	2.30	80.2	952.8	405.4	662.9	58.7

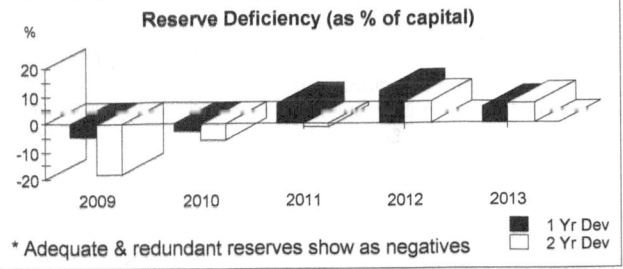

Reserve Deficiency (as % of capital)

* Adequate & redundant reserves show as negatives

■ 1 Yr Dev   □ 2 Yr Dev

INDIANA FARMERS MUTUAL INS CO * | B+ | Good

Major Rating Factors: History of adequate reserve strength (6.5 on a scale of 0 to 10) as reserves have been consistently at an acceptable level. Good profitability index (5.0) despite operating losses during 2012.

Other Rating Factors: Good liquidity (5.3) with sufficient resources (cash flows and marketable investments) to handle a spike in claims. Good overall results on stability tests (6.5). Strong long-term capitalization index (7.8) based on excellent current risk adjusted capital (severe and moderate loss scenarios), despite some fluctuation in capital levels.

Principal Business: Homeowners multiple peril (23%), auto liability (22%), auto physical damage (16%), farmowners multiple peril (15%), commercial multiple peril (10%), workers compensation (5%), and other lines (8%).

Principal Investments: Investment grade bonds (77%), misc. investments (22%), and cash (1%).

Investments in Affiliates: None

Group Affiliation: None

Licensed in: IN

Commenced Business: August 1877

Address: 10 W 106th St, Indianapolis, IN 46290

Phone: (317) 846-4211   **Domicile State:** IN   **NAIC Code:** 22624

Data Date	Rating	RACR #1	RACR #2	Loss Ratio %	Total Assets ($mil)	Capital ($mil)	Net Premium ($mil)	Net Income ($mil)
9-14	B+	2.61	1.56	N/A	351.6	154.0	129.8	17.4
9-13	B+	2.48	1.50	N/A	321.3	137.3	119.9	13.4
2013	B+	2.56	1.54	67.3	331.7	139.4	169.5	14.2
2012	B+	2.33	1.42	100.4	305.0	125.0	153.1	-22.0
2011	B+	3.37	2.00	65.6	294.4	140.8	145.5	13.6
2010	B	2.92	1.77	66.0	293.9	128.7	148.2	13.3
2009	B	2.70	1.75	71.8	275.3	110.5	161.0	8.6

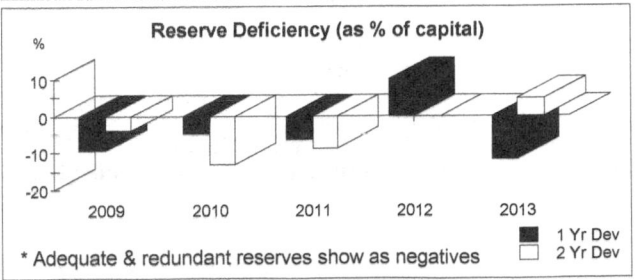

Reserve Deficiency (as % of capital)

* Adequate & redundant reserves show as negatives

■ 1 Yr Dev   □ 2 Yr Dev

INDIANA OLD NATIONAL INS CO | C- | Fair

Major Rating Factors: Fair reserve development (3.6 on a scale of 0 to 10) as reserves have generally been sufficient to cover claims. Fair overall results on stability tests (3.0). The largest net exposure for one risk is high at 4.8% of capital.

Other Rating Factors: Strong long-term capitalization index (10.0) based on excellent current risk adjusted capital (severe and moderate loss scenarios), despite some fluctuation in capital levels. Excellent profitability (8.1) with operating gains in each of the last five years. Superior liquidity (10.0) with ample operational cash flow and liquid investments.

Principal Business: Aggregate write-ins for other lines of business (58%), other liability (39%), earthquake (2%), and surety (1%).

Principal Investments: Investment grade bonds (60%), misc. investments (30%), and cash (10%).

Investments in Affiliates: None

Group Affiliation: Old National Bancorp

Licensed in: IN, VT

Commenced Business: March 1999

Address: 7 Burlington Square, 6th Floor, Burlington, VT 05401

Phone: (812) 464-1530   **Domicile State:** VT   **NAIC Code:** 11021

Data Date	Rating	RACR #1	RACR #2	Loss Ratio %	Total Assets ($mil)	Capital ($mil)	Net Premium ($mil)	Net Income ($mil)
9-14	C-	76.21	29.45	N/A	2,068.3	2,067.2	1.0	36.9
9-13	C-	68.58	26.65	N/A	2,025.9	2,021.7	0.8	21.0
2013	C-	66.31	24.93	11.2	2,037.5	2,030.9	1.2	30.2
2012	D+	144.54	72.04	29.3	1,026.5	1,023.1	0.9	12.2
2011	D+	164.74	82.07	30.1	1,012.7	1,010.2	1.1	10.1
2010	D	161.76	80.65	27.6	1,000.6	999.2	1.2	17.6
2009	D	145.10	72.04	9.2	1,045.0	1,029.9	1.7	55.0

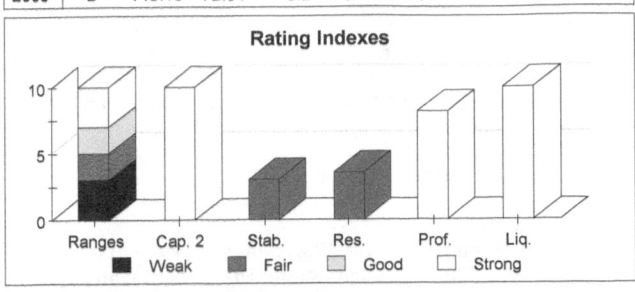

Rating Indexes

Ranges   Cap. 2   Stab.   Res.   Prof.   Liq.

■ Weak   ▨ Fair   ▤ Good   □ Strong

INFINITY INS CO
B   **Good**

Major Rating Factors: Good overall results on stability tests (5.3 on a scale of 0 to 10) despite potential drain of affiliation with Infinity Property & Casualty Group. Good overall profitability index (6.2). Good expense controls. Return on equity has been good over the last five years, averaging 12.0%.

Other Rating Factors: Good liquidity (5.1) with sufficient resources (cash flows and marketable investments) to handle a spike in claims. Strong long-term capitalization index (7.7) based on excellent current risk adjusted capital (severe and moderate loss scenarios), despite some fluctuation in capital levels. Ample reserve history (7.0) that can protect against increases in claims costs.

Principal Business: Auto liability (61%) and auto physical damage (39%).

Principal Investments: Investment grade bonds (83%), misc. investments (11%), non investment grade bonds (8%), and real estate (2%).

Investments in Affiliates: 4%

Group Affiliation: Infinity Property & Casualty Group

Licensed in: All states except KS, LA, NH, NJ, VT, WY, PR

Commenced Business: October 1978

Address: 2204 Lakeshore Dr, Suite 125, Birmingham, AL 35209-6787

Phone: (205) 870-4000   **Domicile State:** IN   **NAIC Code:** 22268

Data Date	Rating	RACR #1	RACR #2	Loss Ratio %	Total Assets ($mil)	Capital ($mil)	Net Premium ($mil)	Net Income ($mil)
9-14	B	1.73	1.48	N/A	2,031.5	659.1	983.7	34.6
9-13	B	1.62	1.37	N/A	1,957.8	642.7	966.1	26.3
2013	B	1.73	1.53	78.2	1,966.4	666.6	1,316.0	47.8
2012	B	1.60	1.39	79.7	1,860.6	605.7	1,233.1	33.8
2011	B	1.85	1.67	75.4	1,568.7	526.8	1,061.9	42.1
2010	B	1.84	1.66	67.0	1,419.4	475.4	933.6	95.7
2009	B-	1.94	1.73	66.5	1,412.5	466.3	832.1	107.3

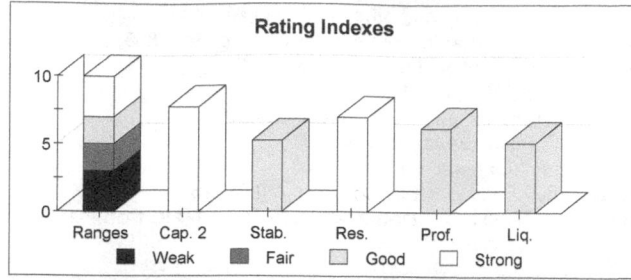

Rating Indexes

INLAND INS CO
C   **Fair**

Major Rating Factors: Fair overall results on stability tests (3.7 on a scale of 0 to 10) including fair financial strength of affiliated Universal Surety and excessive premium growth. The largest net exposure for one risk is excessive at 8.2% of capital. History of adequate reserve strength (6.1) as reserves have been consistently at an acceptable level.

Other Rating Factors: Strong long-term capitalization index (8.1) based on excellent current risk adjusted capital (severe and moderate loss scenarios). Moreover, capital levels have been consistent in recent years. Excellent profitability (8.2) with operating gains in each of the last five years. Superior liquidity (10.0) with ample operational cash flow and liquid investments.

Principal Business: Surety (100%).

Principal Investments: Misc. investments (90%), investment grade bonds (6%), and cash (4%).

Investments in Affiliates: None

Group Affiliation: Universal Surety

Licensed in: AZ, CO, IA, KS, MN, MO, MT, NE, ND, OK, SD, WY

Commenced Business: November 1958

Address: 601 South 12th Street, Lincoln, NE 68508

Phone: (402) 435-4302   **Domicile State:** NE   **NAIC Code:** 23264

Data Date	Rating	RACR #1	RACR #2	Loss Ratio %	Total Assets ($mil)	Capital ($mil)	Net Premium ($mil)	Net Income ($mil)
9-14	C	2.96	1.77	N/A	258.7	192.9	0.5	5.5
9-13	C	2.88	1.72	N/A	231.8	170.6	0.4	3.4
2013	C	2.93	1.75	14.8	254.7	190.0	0.4	9.7
2012	C	2.96	1.77	1.7	209.6	158.5	0.4	4.4
2011	C	2.98	1.78	1.1	188.3	143.5	0.5	3.4
2010	C	2.95	1.77	17.3	182.9	139.1	0.4	2.9
2009	C	2.96	1.77	50.0	169.5	129.2	0.6	3.1

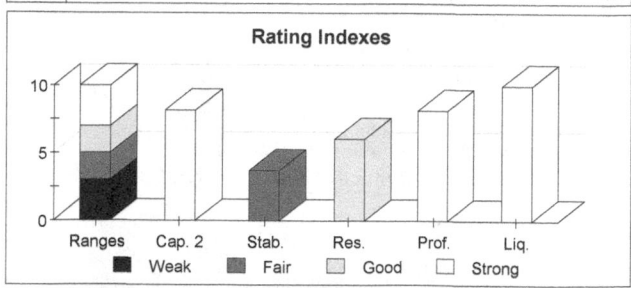

Rating Indexes

INS CO OF THE STATE OF PA
D   **Weak**

Major Rating Factors: Weak overall results on stability tests (0.0 on a scale of 0 to 10). The largest net exposure for one risk is excessive at 65.9% of capital. Strengths include potentially strong support from affiliation with American International Group. Weak profitability index (1.9) with operating losses during 2009 and 2010. Return on equity has been fair, averaging 40.8% over the past five years.

Other Rating Factors: Fair reserve development (3.9) as reserves have generally been sufficient to cover claims. In 2010, the two year reserve development was 18% deficient. Good liquidity (6.6) with sufficient resources (cash flows and marketable investments) to handle a spike in claims. Strong long-term capitalization index (7.3) based on excellent current risk adjusted capital (severe and moderate loss scenarios), despite some fluctuation in capital.

Principal Business: Workers compensation (69%), other liability (10%), auto liability (9%), fire (7%), surety (2%), commercial multiple peril (2%), and other lines (2%).

Principal Investments: Investment grade bonds (808%), non investment grade bonds (2%), and cash (2%).

Investments in Affiliates: 0%

Group Affiliation: American International Group

Licensed in: All states except PR

Commenced Business: April 1794

Address: 2595 Interstate Dr Suite 103, Harrisburg, PA 17110

Phone: (212) 770-7000   **Domicile State:** PA   **NAIC Code:** 19429

Data Date	Rating	RACR #1	RACR #2	Loss Ratio %	Total Assets ($mil)	Capital ($mil)	Net Premium ($mil)	Net Income ($mil)
9-14	D	1.61	1.14	N/A	315.2	112.0	0.0	87.5
9-13	C	1.96	1.34	N/A	3,212.9	776.8	482.5	96.8
2013	C	1.85	1.26	76.6	3,299.8	745.2	713.5	167.8
2012	C	2.45	1.69	87.1	3,347.4	952.0	615.3	1,291.4
2011	B-	1.51	1.41	83.9	4,418.7	2,004.8	626.7	28.6
2010	B-	1.60	1.42	108.8	4,641.7	2,070.9	619.6	-44.2
2009	B-	1.36	1.22	91.1	4,572.9	1,985.4	755.7	-20.2

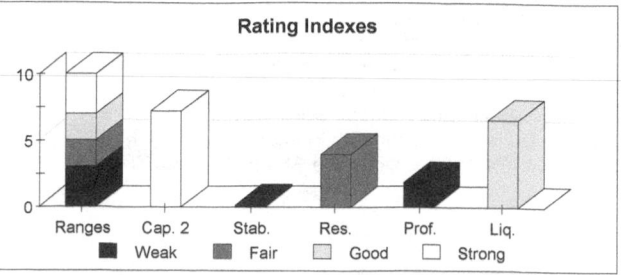

Rating Indexes

INS CO OF THE WEST — C — Fair

Major Rating Factors: Fair overall results on stability tests (3.7 on a scale of 0 to 10) including potential drain of affiliation with Western Insurance Holdings Inc and excessive premium growth. The largest net exposure for one risk is conservative at 1.6% of capital. Fair reserve development (4.5) as reserves have generally been sufficient to cover claims.

Other Rating Factors: Good liquidity (6.4) with sufficient resources (cash flows and marketable investments) to handle a spike in claims. Strong long-term capitalization index (7.3) based on excellent current risk adjusted capital (severe and moderate loss scenarios), despite some fluctuation in capital levels. Excellent profitability (7.4) despite modest operating losses during 2011.

Principal Business: Workers compensation (88%), earthquake (9%), and inland marine (2%).

Principal Investments: Misc. investments (49%), investment grade bonds (45%), and cash (6%).

Investments in Affiliates: 9%

Group Affiliation: Western Insurance Holdings Inc

Licensed in: All states except PR

Commenced Business: May 1972

Address: 11455 El Camino Real, San Diego, CA 92130-2045

Phone: (858) 350-2400 **Domicile State:** CA **NAIC Code:** 27847

Data Date	Rating	RACR #1	RACR #2	Loss Ratio %	Total Assets ($mil)	Capital ($mil)	Net Premium ($mil)	Net Income ($mil)
9-14	C	1.73	1.20	N/A	1,565.5	628.6	467.9	58.1
9-13	C	1.65	1.10	N/A	1,243.0	487.1	368.8	34.4
2013	C	1.72	1.21	61.1	1,314.5	533.5	514.8	68.8
2012	C	1.78	1.20	71.3	1,032.3	417.5	367.5	14.4
2011	C	1.80	1.20	79.1	875.6	350.4	284.7	-1.3
2010	C	2.17	1.43	69.0	869.9	375.0	319.6	13.7
2009	C	2.16	1.37	69.4	974.8	354.6	331.2	17.7

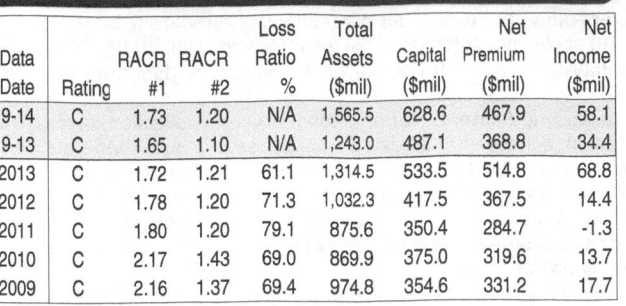

Rating Indexes

INTERINS EXCH OF THE AUTOMOBILE CLUB * — A+ — Excellent

Major Rating Factors: Strong long-term capitalization index (10.0 on a scale of 0 to 10) based on excellent current risk adjusted capital (severe and moderate loss scenarios). Furthermore, this high level of risk adjusted capital has been consistently maintained in previous years. Ample reserve history (7.5) that can protect against increases in claims costs.

Other Rating Factors: Excellent profitability (8.7) with operating gains in each of the last five years. Good overall results on stability tests (6.5) despite potential drain of affiliation with Auto Club Enterprises Ins Group. Good liquidity (6.6) with sufficient resources (cash flows and marketable investments) to handle a spike in claims.

Principal Business: Auto liability (45%), auto physical damage (35%), homeowners multiple peril (18%), fire (1%), and other liability (1%).

Principal Investments: Investment grade bonds (52%), misc. investments (41%), non investment grade bonds (6%), and real estate (2%).

Investments in Affiliates: 1%

Group Affiliation: Auto Club Enterprises Ins Group

Licensed in: CA, FL, HI, ME, MI, MO, NH, NM, OH, PA, TX, VT, VA

Commenced Business: October 1912

Address: 3333 Fairview Road, Costa Mesa, CA 92626

Phone: (714) 850-5111 **Domicile State:** CA **NAIC Code:** 15598

Data Date	Rating	RACR #1	RACR #2	Loss Ratio %	Total Assets ($mil)	Capital ($mil)	Net Premium ($mil)	Net Income ($mil)
9-14	A+	5.30	3.25	N/A	8,447.5	5,380.4	2,087.2	168.0
9-13	A+	5.44	3.36	N/A	7,881.3	4,988.1	2,012.5	138.7
2013	A+	5.26	3.26	71.1	8,106.5	5,214.6	2,752.1	269.8
2012	A+	5.69	3.60	72.4	7,254.0	4,609.7	2,612.8	220.0
2011	A+	5.78	3.72	73.7	6,733.5	4,265.3	2,514.2	188.5
2010	A+	5.75	3.75	66.7	6,510.7	4,077.9	2,417.5	256.8
2009	A+	6.03	4.06	61.7	5,898.3	3,691.0	2,341.8	346.7

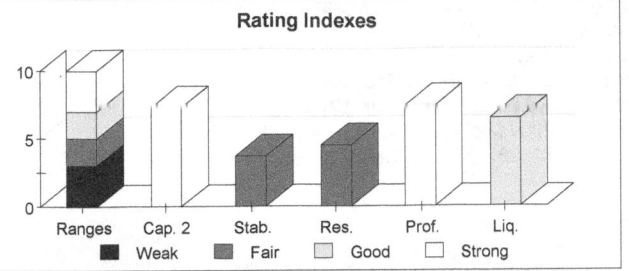

Risk-Adjusted Capital Ratio #2
(Severe Loss Scenario)

IRONSHORE SPECIALTY INS CO — C — Fair

Major Rating Factors: Fair overall results on stability tests (3.7 on a scale of 0 to 10) including potential drain of affiliation with Ironshore Holdings Inc. The largest net exposure for one risk is conservative at 1.6% of capital. Fair reserve development (4.9) as reserves have generally been sufficient to cover claims.

Other Rating Factors: Strong long-term capitalization index (7.6) based on excellent current risk adjusted capital (severe and moderate loss scenarios). Moreover, capital levels have been consistent in recent years. Excellent profitability (7.1). Excellent liquidity (7.2) with ample operational cash flow and liquid investments.

Principal Business: Other liability (62%), fire (11%), medical malpractice (10%), aircraft (6%), homeowners multiple peril (4%), products liability (4%), and other lines (3%).

Principal Investments: Investment grade bonds (62%), misc. investments (23%), non investment grade bonds (8%), and cash (7%).

Investments in Affiliates: None

Group Affiliation: Ironshore Holdings Inc

Licensed in: All states, the District of Columbia and Puerto Rico

Commenced Business: February 1953

Address: 650 California St 2nd Fl, San Francisco, CA 94108-2702

Phone: (646) 826-6600 **Domicile State:** AZ **NAIC Code:** 25445

Data Date	Rating	RACR #1	RACR #2	Loss Ratio %	Total Assets ($mil)	Capital ($mil)	Net Premium ($mil)	Net Income ($mil)
9-14	C	2.28	1.38	N/A	935.9	314.3	93.2	17.6
9-13	C	3.55	2.00	N/A	809.7	309.7	79.2	22.6
2013	C	2.59	1.58	68.3	832.9	300.3	119.2	21.4
2012	C	3.02	1.76	84.5	804.3	291.3	101.4	17.1
2011	C	3.21	1.93	85.0	698.0	282.2	90.4	6.2
2010	C	8.49	5.19	68.8	556.3	273.9	77.9	5.1
2009	C	8.46	5.17	56.3	306.7	165.3	57.3	-2.5

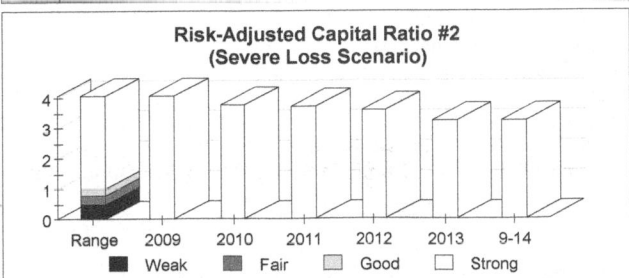

Rating Indexes

ISMIE MUTUAL INS CO

B-   Good

Major Rating Factors: Fair overall results on stability tests (4.6 on a scale of 0 to 10) including potential drain of affiliation with ISMIE Group. Good overall profitability index (6.9) despite operating losses during the first nine months of 2014.

Other Rating Factors: Strong long-term capitalization index (9.3) based on excellent current risk adjusted capital (severe and moderate loss scenarios), despite some fluctuation in capital levels. Ample reserve history (9.6) that helps to protect the company against sharp claims increases. Excellent liquidity (7.4) with ample operational cash flow and liquid investments.

Principal Business: Medical malpractice (99%) and aggregate write-ins for other lines of business (1%).

Principal Investments: Investment grade bonds (88%), misc. investments (5%), cash (4%), and non investment grade bonds (3%).

Investments in Affiliates: 2%

Group Affiliation: ISMIE Group

Licensed in: IL, IN, IA, MI, MO, WI

Commenced Business: June 1976

Address: 20 N Michigan Ave, Chicago, IL 60602-4811

Phone: (312) 782-2749   **Domicile State:** IL   **NAIC Code:** 32921

Data Date	Rating	RACR #1	RACR #2	Loss Ratio %	Total Assets ($mil)	Capital ($mil)	Net Premium ($mil)	Net Income ($mil)
9-14	B-	3.34	2.74	N/A	1,679.1	604.0	147.0	-12.8
9-13	B-	2.75	2.26	N/A	1,637.5	524.0	161.0	-5.5
2013	B-	3.66	2.98	37.6	1,616.4	609.9	229.6	80.1
2012	B-	2.99	2.47	52.9	1,544.7	522.9	242.2	57.0
2011	B-	2.63	2.18	53.0	1,492.8	461.0	236.5	47.1
2010	B-	2.21	1.84	69.4	1,487.3	417.7	200.0	29.3
2009	B-	1.82	1.54	73.4	1,449.7	384.6	215.8	14.9

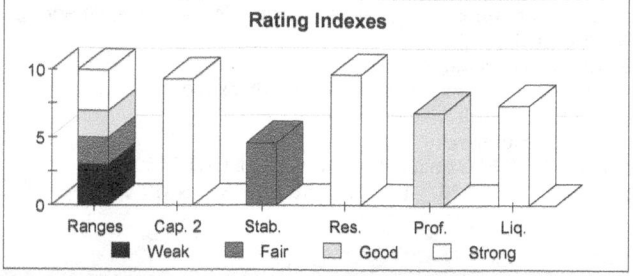

Rating Indexes

JEWELERS MUTUAL INS CO *

A-   Excellent

Major Rating Factors: Strong long-term capitalization index (10.0 on a scale of 0 to 10) based on excellent current risk adjusted capital (severe and moderate loss scenarios). Furthermore, this high level of risk adjusted capital has been consistently maintained in previous years. Excellent profitability (8.5) with operating gains in each of the last five years.

Other Rating Factors: History of adequate reserve strength (6.2) as reserves have been consistently at an acceptable level. Good liquidity (6.7) with sufficient resources (cash flows and marketable investments) to handle a spike in claims. Good overall results on stability tests (6.7). The largest net exposure for one risk is acceptable at 2.5% of capital.

Principal Business: Inland marine (84%) and commercial multiple peril (16%).

Principal Investments: Investment grade bonds (51%), misc. investments (42%), real estate (4%), and cash (3%).

Investments in Affiliates: 0%

Group Affiliation: None

Licensed in: All states except PR

Commenced Business: June 1914

Address: 24 Jewelers Park Dr, Neenah, WI 54957-3703

Phone: (920) 725-4326   **Domicile State:** WI   **NAIC Code:** 14354

Data Date	Rating	RACR #1	RACR #2	Loss Ratio %	Total Assets ($mil)	Capital ($mil)	Net Premium ($mil)	Net Income ($mil)
9-14	A-	5.26	3.25	N/A	329.0	202.5	110.4	13.4
9-13	A-	5.35	3.24	N/A	287.6	173.8	102.0	13.3
2013	A-	5.07	3.14	43.5	304.9	182.6	143.8	17.4
2012	A-	5.10	3.12	54.2	261.7	153.2	133.4	14.5
2011	A-	5.12	3.10	63.1	247.0	144.7	123.6	2.2
2010	A-	5.67	3.37	49.1	237.3	146.2	115.0	13.2
2009	A-	5.46	3.31	54.7	216.4	128.7	108.4	6.6

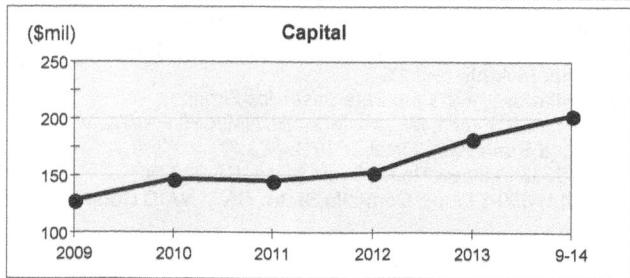

($mil)   Capital

KENTUCKY EMPLOYERS MUTUAL INS

C+   Fair

Major Rating Factors: Fair reserve development (4.9 on a scale of 0 to 10) as reserves have generally been sufficient to cover claims. Fair overall results on stability tests (4.3).

Other Rating Factors: Good overall profitability index (5.7) despite operating losses during 2010. Strong long-term capitalization index (7.0) based on good current risk adjusted capital (severe and moderate loss scenarios), although results have slipped from the excellent range during the last year. Excellent liquidity (7.2) with ample operational cash flow and liquid investments.

Principal Business: Workers compensation (100%).

Principal Investments: Investment grade bonds (85%), misc. investments (13%), and cash (2%).

Investments in Affiliates: None

Group Affiliation: None

Licensed in: KY

Commenced Business: September 1995

Address: 250 W Main Street, Ste 900, Lexington, KY 40507

Phone: (859) 425-7800   **Domicile State:** KY   **NAIC Code:** 10320

Data Date	Rating	RACR #1	RACR #2	Loss Ratio %	Total Assets ($mil)	Capital ($mil)	Net Premium ($mil)	Net Income ($mil)
9-14	C+	1.41	0.98	N/A	881.2	202.9	112.8	7.5
9-13	C+	1.48	1.02	N/A	787.9	184.8	96.8	7.8
2013	C+	1.51	1.04	80.9	816.2	196.4	142.8	16.8
2012	C+	1.51	1.04	89.1	747.9	173.1	124.2	9.0
2011	C+	1.47	0.78	105.3	709.5	159.6	112.8	12.9
2010	C+	1.50	0.75	91.6	653.3	143.7	102.9	-17.9
2009	C	1.25	0.66	87.9	648.2	154.0	119.5	16.1

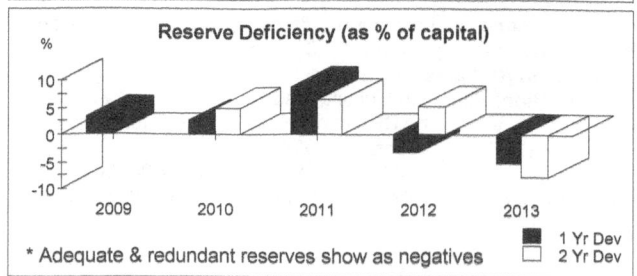

Reserve Deficiency (as % of capital)

* Adequate & redundant reserves show as negatives

KENTUCKY FARM BUREAU MUTUAL INS CO *   A-   Excellent

Major Rating Factors: Strong long-term capitalization index (10.0 on a scale of 0 to 10) based on excellent current risk adjusted capital (severe and moderate loss scenarios), despite some fluctuation in capital levels. Good overall results on stability tests (5.5) despite potential drain of affiliation with Kentucky Farm Bureau Group.

Other Rating Factors: History of adequate reserve strength (6.2) as reserves have been consistently at an acceptable level. Good overall profitability index (6.3) despite operating losses during 2009 and 2011. Good liquidity (6.0) with sufficient resources (cash flows and marketable investments) to handle a spike in claims.

Principal Business: Auto liability (35%), homeowners multiple peril (26%), auto physical damage (19%), farmowners multiple peril (12%), commercial multiple peril (7%), other liability (1%), and allied lines (1%).

Principal Investments: Investment grade bonds (73%) and misc. investments (27%).

Investments in Affiliates: 0%

Group Affiliation: Kentucky Farm Bureau Group

Licensed in: CA, CT, IL, IA, KY, MI, NC, VT, VA, WV, WI

Commenced Business: December 1943

Address: 9201 Bunsen Parkway, Louisville, KY 40220-3793

Phone: (502) 495-5000   **Domicile State:** KY   **NAIC Code:** 22993

Data Date	Rating	RACR #1	RACR #2	Loss Ratio %	Total Assets ($mil)	Capital ($mil)	Net Premium ($mil)	Net Income ($mil)
9-14	A-	5.51	3.56	N/A	2,214.4	1,152.7	631.4	87.6
9-13	A-	4.60	3.01	N/A	2,066.5	983.7	637.2	104.9
2013	A-	5.04	3.32	67.2	2,119.7	1,066.3	845.5	147.6
2012	A-	4.27	2.84	85.9	1,915.4	938.4	850.8	19.6
2011	A-	3.90	2.60	91.5	1,838.2	900.4	862.1	-26.7
2010	A-	4.05	2.76	79.3	1,801.2	927.1	814.7	59.0
2009	A-	3.97	2.70	99.6	1,639.1	852.6	734.4	-91.1

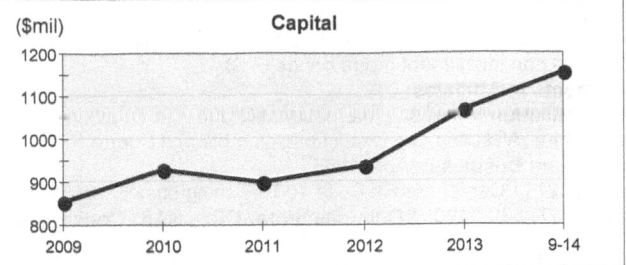

Capital

LAMMICO   C+   Fair

Major Rating Factors: Fair overall results on stability tests (4.5 on a scale of 0 to 10). The largest net exposure for one risk is conservative at 1.2% of capital. Strong long-term capitalization index (10.0) based on excellent current risk adjusted capital (severe and moderate loss scenarios). Moreover, capital levels have been consistent in recent years.

Other Rating Factors: Ample reserve history (9.3) that helps to protect the company against sharp claims increases. Excellent profitability (8.9) with operating gains in each of the last five years. Superior liquidity (9.0) with ample operational cash flow and liquid investments.

Principal Business: Medical malpractice (99%) and other liability (1%).

Principal Investments: Investment grade bonds (85%), misc. investments (14%), and cash (1%).

Investments in Affiliates: 0%

Group Affiliation: None

Licensed in: AR, LA, MS, TN, TX

Commenced Business: January 1982

Address: One Galleria Blvd Suite 700, Metairie, LA 70001

Phone: (504) 831-3756   **Domicile State:** LA   **NAIC Code:** 43656

Data Date	Rating	RACR #1	RACR #2	Loss Ratio %	Total Assets ($mil)	Capital ($mil)	Net Premium ($mil)	Net Income ($mil)
9-14	C+	4.95	3.81	N/A	395.1	202.2	34.5	8.5
9-13	C+	4.82	3.75	N/A	384.7	190.5	34.1	12.0
2013	C+	4.81	3.76	57.6	411.9	194.0	49.4	13.9
2012	C+	4.35	3.38	57.2	412.5	177.7	54.9	17.1
2011	C+	4.08	3.34	69.6	379.6	153.0	47.3	10.2
2010	C+	3.75	3.08	58.7	372.1	142.1	50.5	14.8
2009	C+	2.99	2.53	66.5	349.7	126.4	47.2	11.2

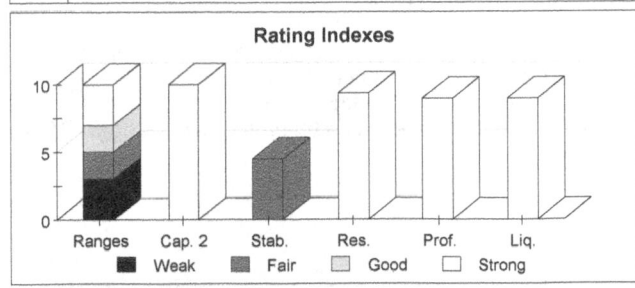

Rating Indexes

Ranges | Cap. 2 | Stab. | Res. | Prof. | Liq.
■ Weak   ■ Fair   ▨ Good   ☐ Strong

LANDMARK AMERICAN INS CO   C   Fair

Major Rating Factors: Fair overall results on stability tests (4.2 on a scale of 0 to 10) including potential drain of affiliation with Alleghany Corp Group. The largest net exposure for one risk is conservative at 1.1% of capital. Strong long-term capitalization index (10.0) based on excellent current risk adjusted capital (severe and moderate loss scenarios), despite some fluctuation in capital levels.

Other Rating Factors: Ample reserve history (7.9) that can protect against increases in claims costs. Excellent profitability (8.6) with operating gains in each of the last five years. Excellent liquidity (7.7) with ample operational cash flow and liquid investments.

Principal Business: Allied lines (34%), fire (23%), other liability (22%), medical malpractice (8%), inland marine (8%), products liability (3%), and earthquake (2%).

Principal Investments: Investment grade bonds (96%) and misc. investments (4%).

Investments in Affiliates: None

Group Affiliation: Alleghany Corp Group

Licensed in: All states, the District of Columbia and Puerto Rico

Commenced Business: April 1976

Address: 201 Robert S Kerr Ave Ste 600, Oklahoma City, OK 73102-4267

Phone: (404) 231-2366   **Domicile State:** OK   **NAIC Code:** 33138

Data Date	Rating	RACR #1	RACR #2	Loss Ratio %	Total Assets ($mil)	Capital ($mil)	Net Premium ($mil)	Net Income ($mil)
9-14	C	12.65	7.92	N/A	381.9	219.9	35.8	12.1
9-13	C	8.68	4.73	N/A	373.3	202.1	37.0	10.6
2013	C	12.07	7.60	43.7	397.2	208.1	48.9	16.5
2012	C	8.35	4.56	58.0	370.4	191.6	51.4	11.3
2011	C	9.29	4.54	45.4	367.0	195.0	46.9	14.1
2010	C	7.39	3.87	34.8	343.3	180.2	44.8	19.1
2009	C	5.01	2.85	34.8	328.6	161.3	51.1	17.0

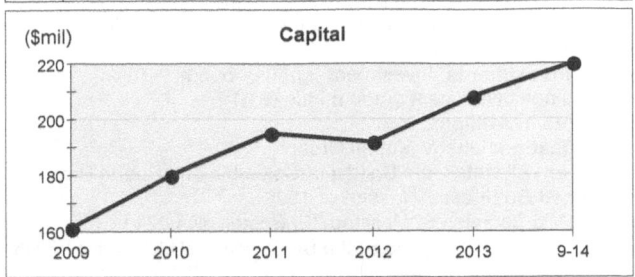

Capital

LEXINGTON INS CO

C+   Fair

Major Rating Factors: Fair profitability index (4.6 on a scale of 0 to 10). Good expense controls. Return on equity has been fair, averaging 11.0% over the past five years. Fair overall results on stability tests (4.4) including excessive premium growth. The largest net exposure for one risk is excessive at 6.5% of capital.

Other Rating Factors: Good liquidity (6.9) with sufficient resources (cash flows and marketable investments) to handle a spike in claims. Strong long-term capitalization index (7.9) based on excellent current risk adjusted capital (severe and moderate loss scenarios), despite some fluctuation in capital levels. Ample reserve history (8.0) that helps to protect the company against sharp claims increases.

Principal Business: Other liability (28%), fire (26%), allied lines (17%), medical malpractice (7%), inland marine (5%), homeowners multiple peril (4%), and other lines (12%).

Principal Investments: Investment grade bonds (75%), misc. investments (22%), and non investment grade bonds (3%).

Investments in Affiliates: 0%

Group Affiliation: American International Group

Licensed in: All states, the District of Columbia and Puerto Rico

Commenced Business: April 1965

Address: 2711 Centerville Rd Suite 400, Wilmington, DE 19808

Phone: (617) 330-1100   **Domicile State:** DE   **NAIC Code:** 19437

Data Date	Rating	RACR #1	RACR #2	Loss Ratio %	Total Assets ($mil)	Capital ($mil)	Net Premium ($mil)	Net Income ($mil)
9-14	C+	2.22	1.49	N/A	26,043.5	6,843.7	4,165.8	745.1
9-13	C+	3.09	2.09	N/A	23,112.5	7,929.7	2,969.5	1,455.3
2013	C+	2.85	1.92	69.4	22,120.5	7,224.1	3,755.8	1,660.2
2012	C+	2.87	1.94	100.0	24,296.4	7,925.6	3,621.9	409.0
2011	C+	2.71	1.75	94.7	24,208.4	7,797.9	4,314.5	517.6
2010	C+	2.54	1.66	86.0	23,872.7	7,374.0	4,699.7	455.7
2009	C+	2.19	1.36	75.4	20,119.5	6,913.6	3,776.6	805.2

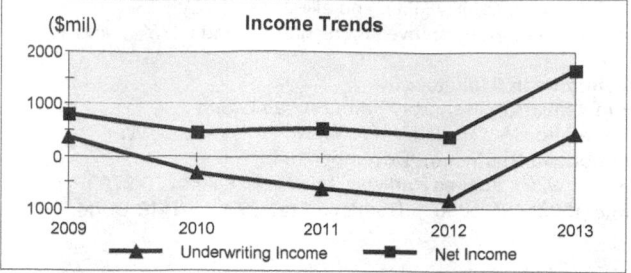

Income Trends

LIBERTY INS CORP

D   Weak

Major Rating Factors: Weak profitability index (2.7 on a scale of 0 to 10) with operating losses during 2009, 2011 and 2012. Average return on equity over the last five years has been poor at -3.3%. Vulnerable liquidity (0.0) as a spike in claims may stretch capacity.

Other Rating Factors: Weak overall results on stability tests (1.9) including negative cash flow from operations for 2013. Strong long-term capitalization index (10.0) based on excellent current risk adjusted capital (severe and moderate loss scenarios), despite some fluctuation in capital levels.

Principal Business: (Not applicable due to unusual reinsurance transactions.)

Principal Investments: Investment grade bonds (79%) and misc. investments (21%).

Investments in Affiliates: None

Group Affiliation: Liberty Mutual Group

Licensed in: All states, the District of Columbia and Puerto Rico

Commenced Business: November 1988

Address: 175 Berkeley St, Mailstop 3E, Boston, MA 02117

Phone: (617) 357-9500   **Domicile State:** IL   **NAIC Code:** 42404

Data Date	Rating	RACR #1	RACR #2	Loss Ratio %	Total Assets ($mil)	Capital ($mil)	Net Premium ($mil)	Net Income ($mil)
9-14	D	84.17	59.01	N/A	225.6	215.2	0.0	0.0
9-13	D	5.84	4.52	N/A	184.4	175.3	0.0	7.9
2013	D	135.89	66.60	0.0	218.6	215.4	-215.2	48.2
2012	D	0.80	0.53	90.3	1,449.7	168.7	522.2	-48.5
2011	C	1.18	0.76	90.1	1,428.3	245.0	458.0	-28.4
2010	C	1.41	0.90	83.0	1,421.2	276.2	461.1	1.8
2009	C	1.84	1.18	85.3	1,118.5	272.6	299.9	-4.4

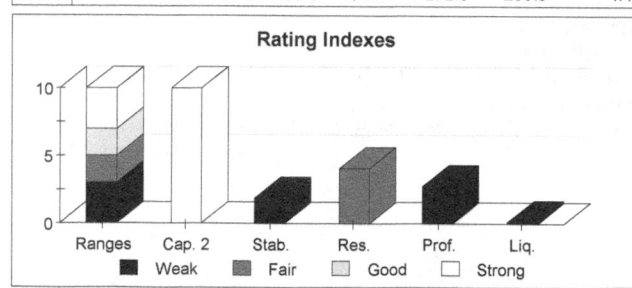

Rating Indexes

LIBERTY MUTUAL FIRE INS CO

C+   Fair

Major Rating Factors: Fair reserve development (4.2 on a scale of 0 to 10) as reserves have generally been sufficient to cover claims. Fair profitability index (3.8) with operating losses during 2009, 2011 and 2012. Average return on equity over the last five years has been poor at -1.4%.

Other Rating Factors: Fair overall results on stability tests (4.5) including fair financial strength of affiliated Liberty Mutual Group. The largest net exposure for one risk is excessive at 5.0% of capital. Good liquidity (5.3) with sufficient resources (cash flows and marketable investments) to handle a spike in claims. Strong long-term capitalization index (7.3) based on excellent current risk adjusted capital (severe and moderate loss scenarios), despite some fluctuation in capital levels.

Principal Business: Auto liability (29%), homeowners multiple peril (25%), auto physical damage (17%), workers compensation (9%), fire (7%), other liability (6%), and other lines (8%).

Principal Investments: Investment grade bonds (75%), misc. investments (19%), and non investment grade bonds (6%).

Investments in Affiliates: 4%

Group Affiliation: Liberty Mutual Group

Licensed in: All states, the District of Columbia and Puerto Rico

Commenced Business: November 1908

Address: 175 Berkeley St, Mailstop 3E, Boston, MA 02117

Phone: (617) 357-9500   **Domicile State:** WI   **NAIC Code:** 23035

Data Date	Rating	RACR #1	RACR #2	Loss Ratio %	Total Assets ($mil)	Capital ($mil)	Net Premium ($mil)	Net Income ($mil)
9-14	C+	1.74	1.19	N/A	5,274.8	1,224.8	1,469.2	49.3
9-13	C	1.56	1.06	N/A	5,451.2	1,149.0	1,450.6	16.6
2013	C+	1.75	1.20	73.5	5,561.6	1,216.3	2,163.5	87.5
2012	C	1.37	0.92	90.3	5,235.7	939.1	1,684.2	-130.8
2011	B-	1.57	1.04	90.1	4,876.8	1,073.0	1,476.9	-99.4
2010	B-	1.88	1.24	83.0	4,825.3	1,204.4	1,361.3	67.1
2009	B-	1.45	1.00	85.3	4,590.1	1,072.9	1,401.0	-15.3

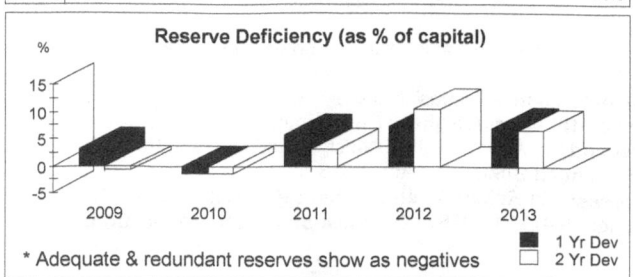

Reserve Deficiency (as % of capital)

* Adequate & redundant reserves show as negatives

LIBERTY MUTUAL INS CO   B   Good

Major Rating Factors: History of adequate reserve strength (5.7 on a scale of 0 to 10) as reserves have been consistently at an acceptable level. Good overall profitability index (6.1) despite operating losses during 2009 and 2011. Return on equity has been low, averaging 4.1% over the past five years.

Other Rating Factors: Good liquidity (6.2) with sufficient resources (cash flows and marketable investments) to handle a spike in claims. Fair overall results on stability tests (4.4) including potential drain of affiliation with Liberty Mutual Group and weak results on operational trends. The largest net exposure for one risk is acceptable at 2.4% of capital. Strong long-term capitalization index (7.6) based on excellent current risk adjusted capital (severe and moderate loss scenarios), despite some fluctuation in capital levels.

Principal Business: Inland marine (49%), surety (12%), other liability (12%), auto liability (10%), auto physical damage (7%), workers compensation (3%), and other lines (8%).

Principal Investments: Misc. investments (55%), investment grade bonds (39%), non investment grade bonds (4%), cash (1%), and real estate (1%).

Investments in Affiliates: 24%

Group Affiliation: Liberty Mutual Group

Licensed in: All states, the District of Columbia and Puerto Rico

Commenced Business: July 1912

Address: 175 Berkeley St,Mailstop 3E, Boston, MA 02117

Phone: (617) 357-9500   **Domicile State:** MA   **NAIC Code:** 23043

Data Date	Rating	RACR #1	RACR #2	Loss Ratio %	Total Assets ($mil)	Capital ($mil)	Net Premium ($mil)	Net Income ($mil)
9-14	B	1.66	1.41	N/A	42,150.7	15,587.3	9,182.8	331.1
9-13	B	1.63	1.34	N/A	44,397.2	14,707.1	9,066.1	-95.7
2013	B	1.63	1.39	73.5	44,475.8	15,126.4	13,889.2	507.4
2012	B	1.73	1.46	90.3	40,205.4	14,510.5	9,635.4	163.6
2011	B	1.61	1.36	90.1	37,394.8	13,596.4	8,449.3	-536.2
2010	B	1.65	1.40	83.0	36,701.5	13,763.3	7,740.8	2,921.7
2009	B	1.34	1.17	85.3	34,830.4	12,491.6	7,463.6	-65.1

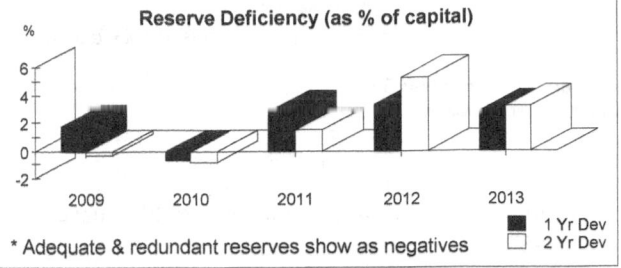

Reserve Deficiency (as % of capital)

* Adequate & redundant reserves show as negatives   ■ 1 Yr Dev   □ 2 Yr Dev

MAG MUTUAL INS CO   B-   Good

Major Rating Factors: Fair overall results on stability tests (4.7 on a scale of 0 to 10) including potential drain of affiliation with MAG Mutual Group. Strong long-term capitalization index (9.9) based on excellent current risk adjusted capital (severe and moderate loss scenarios). Moreover, capital levels have been consistent in recent years.

Other Rating Factors: Ample reserve history (9.6) that helps to protect the company against sharp claims increases. Excellent profitability (8.7) with operating gains in each of the last five years. Excellent liquidity (8.1) with ample operational cash flow and liquid investments.

Principal Business: Medical malpractice (96%), workers compensation (2%), and commercial multiple peril (1%).

Principal Investments: Investment grade bonds (71%), misc. investments (21%), and non investment grade bonds (8%).

Investments in Affiliates: 1%

Group Affiliation: MAG Mutual Group

Licensed in: AL, AZ, AR, FL, GA, IN, KY, MD, MS, NC, OH, SC, TN, VA, WV

Commenced Business: June 1982

Address: 3525 Piedmont Rd NE Bldg 8-600, Atlanta, GA 30305-1556

Phone: (404) 842-5600   **Domicile State:** GA   **NAIC Code:** 42617

Data Date	Rating	RACR #1	RACR #2	Loss Ratio %	Total Assets ($mil)	Capital ($mil)	Net Premium ($mil)	Net Income ($mil)
9-14	B-	4.97	3.38	N/A	1,640.8	760.9	147.2	32.9
9-13	B-	4.82	3.33	N/A	1,604.1	725.7	146.6	36.6
2013	B-	4.96	3.43	64.5	1,609.9	740.3	197.5	52.0
2012	B-	4.86	3.53	71.6	1,543.7	667.5	197.3	43.7
2011	B-	4.44	3.28	47.3	1,510.4	610.1	214.4	66.2
2010	B-	3.50	2.69	67.6	1,480.7	541.3	232.7	69.0
2009	B-	3.16	2.51	60.0	1,421.4	471.4	213.2	62.9

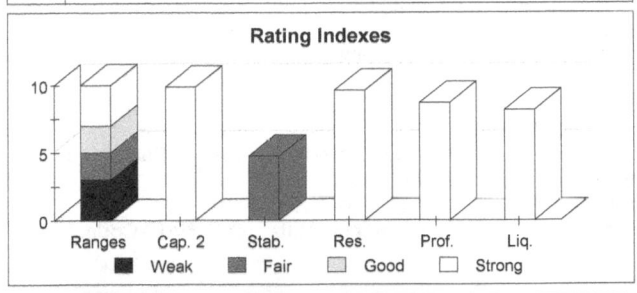

Rating Indexes

Ranges   Cap. 2   Stab.   Res.   Prof.   Liq.

■ Weak   ■ Fair   □ Good   □ Strong

MAIDEN RE NORTH AMERICA INC   B-   Good

Major Rating Factors: Fair profitability index (3.8 on a scale of 0 to 10) with operating losses during 2009, 2011, 2012 and 2013. Average return on equity over the last five years has been poor at -1.5%. Good long-term capitalization index (5.6) based on good current risk adjusted capital (severe loss scenario).

Other Rating Factors: History of adequate reserve strength (5.6) as reserves have been consistently at an acceptable level. Good liquidity (6.9) with sufficient resources (cash flows and marketable investments) to handle a spike in claims. Good overall results on stability tests (5.3). Stability strengths include good operational trends, good risk adjusted capital for prior years and excellent risk diversification. The largest net exposure for one risk is conservative at 1.9% of capital.

Principal Business: Auto liability (54%), auto physical damage (33%), and inland marine (15%).

Principal Investments: Investment grade bonds (85%), misc. investments (12%), non investment grade bonds (2%), and cash (1%).

Investments in Affiliates: 5%

Group Affiliation: Maiden Holdings Ltd

Licensed in: All states except PR

Commenced Business: August 2000

Address: 13736 Riverport Dr Suite 700, Maryland Heights, MO 63043

Phone: (856) 359-2400   **Domicile State:** MO   **NAIC Code:** 11054

Data Date	Rating	RACR #1	RACR #2	Loss Ratio %	Total Assets ($mil)	Capital ($mil)	Net Premium ($mil)	Net Income ($mil)
9-14	B-	1.36	0.75	N/A	1,233.1	271.9	331.2	5.5
9-13	B-	1.19	0.69	N/A	1,241.6	267.0	280.4	-3.8
2013	B-	1.55	0.87	75.6	1,159.6	269.6	391.8	-1.3
2012	B-	1.13	0.68	78.4	1,189.0	267.9	346.2	-19.2
2011	B-	1.48	0.91	74.6	1,115.3	268.1	196.3	-1.7
2010	B-	2.11	1.39	73.9	925.6	262.7	197.9	1.3
2009	U	4.68	3.55	72.9	639.5	258.6	77.5	-7.8

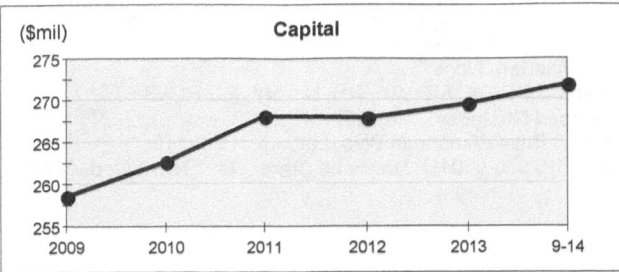

Capital

MARKEL INS CO
C — Fair

Major Rating Factors: Fair overall results on stability tests (3.8 on a scale of 0 to 10) including potential drain of affiliation with Markel Corp. The largest net exposure for one risk is acceptable at 2.1% of capital. History of adequate reserve strength (6.0) as reserves have been consistently at an acceptable level.

Other Rating Factors: Good profitability index (5.0) despite operating losses during 2011 and 2012. Return on equity has been low, averaging 0.5% over the past five years. Strong long-term capitalization index (7.1) based on excellent current risk adjusted capital (severe and moderate loss scenarios). Moreover, capital levels have been consistent in recent years. Excellent liquidity (7.0) with ample operational cash flow and liquid investments.

Principal Business: Workers compensation (34%), commercial multiple peril (21%), other liability (19%), auto liability (10%), inland marine (6%), other accident & health (5%), and other lines (6%).

Principal Investments: Investment grade bonds (64%) and misc. investments (36%).

Investments in Affiliates: 5%

Group Affiliation: Markel Corp

Licensed in: All states except PR

Commenced Business: December 1980

Address: Ten Parkway North, Deerfield, IL 60015

Phone: (800) 431-1270   **Domicile State:** IL   **NAIC Code:** 38970

Data Date	Rating	RACR #1	RACR #2	Loss Ratio %	Total Assets ($mil)	Capital ($mil)	Net Premium ($mil)	Net Income ($mil)
9-14	C	1.72	1.04	N/A	1,345.1	379.7	367.1	4.2
9-13	C	1.58	0.96	N/A	1,165.4	293.7	338.4	-8.8
2013	C	1.74	1.07	61.3	1,225.7	347.4	493.9	7.3
2012	C	1.80	1.10	64.6	1,019.5	272.8	416.6	-5.3
2011	C	0.71	0.49	73.3	839.7	206.4	332.6	-13.5
2010	C	1.38	0.96	67.0	732.5	194.1	235.8	10.1
2009	C	1.40	0.96	66.7	710.9	176.6	211.9	5.3

Markel Corp
Composite Group Rating: C

Largest Group Members	Assets ($mil)	Rating
EVANSTON INS CO	2152	C
ALTERRA REINS USA INC	1365	B+
MARKEL INS CO	1226	C
ESSEX INS CO	1211	C
MARKEL AMERICAN INS CO	441	C

MBIA INS CORP
D — Weak

Major Rating Factors: Weak overall results on stability tests (1.4 on a scale of 0 to 10) including weak risk adjusted capital in prior years. The largest net exposure for one risk is excessive at 24.8% of capital. Strengths include potentially strong support from affiliation with MBIA Inc. Fair long-term capitalization index (3.7) based on weak current risk adjusted capital (severe loss scenario).

Other Rating Factors: A history of deficient reserves (2.3) that places pressure on both capital and profits. In 2009, the one year reserve development was 22% deficient. Weak profitability index (0.5) with operating losses during each of the last five years and the first nine months of 2014. Average return on equity over the last five years has been poor at -55.4%. Excellent liquidity (7.0) with ample operational cash flow and liquid investments.

Principal Business: Financial guaranty (100%).

Principal Investments: Misc. investments (61%), investment grade bonds (29%), and cash (10%).

Investments in Affiliates: 24%

Group Affiliation: MBIA Inc

Licensed in: All states, the District of Columbia and Puerto Rico

Commenced Business: May 1968

Address: 113 King St, Armonk, NY 10504-1610

Phone: (914) 273-4545   **Domicile State:** NY   **NAIC Code:** 12041

Data Date	Rating	RACR #1	RACR #2	Loss Ratio %	Total Assets ($mil)	Capital ($mil)	Net Premium ($mil)	Net Income ($mil)
9-14	D	0.85	0.28	N/A	933.4	546.2	130.3	-27.0
9-13	D+	1.28	0.44	N/A	616.7	612.3	128.6	-358.0
2013	D	0.78	0.26	378.6	1,280.1	403.0	133.5	-494.0
2012	D+	1.20	0.41	338.8	1,012.7	965.1	204.2	-843.4
2011	D+	1.53	0.52	240.5	1,612.5	1,596.6	294.1	-477.2
2010	D+	0.99	0.35	256.2	3,458.4	1,074.7	358.7	-434.0
2009	D+	1.79	0.58	483.6	5,031.8	2,053.0	-3,136.7	-684.2

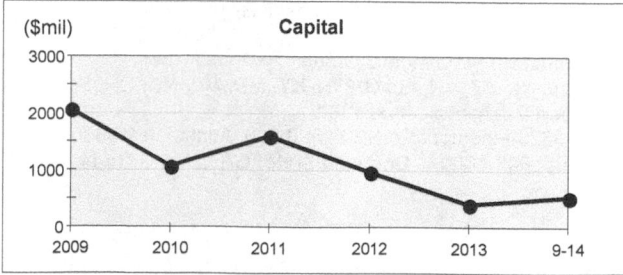

($mil) — Capital

MEDICAL LIABILITY MUTUAL INS CO
D+ — Weak

Major Rating Factors: Weak overall results on stability tests (2.4 on a scale of 0 to 10). The largest net exposure for one risk is conservative at 1.0% of capital. Good long-term capitalization index (6.0) based on good current risk adjusted capital (moderate loss scenario). Moreover, capital levels have been consistent in recent years.

Other Rating Factors: Good overall profitability index (6.7). Good expense controls. Return on equity has been excellent over the last five years averaging 22.0%. Ample reserve history (9.7) that helps to protect the company against sharp claims increases. Excellent liquidity (7.5) with ample operational cash flow and liquid investments.

Principal Business: (Not applicable due to unusual reinsurance transactions.)

Principal Investments: Investment grade bonds (73%), misc. investments (15%), non investment grade bonds (11%), and cash (1%).

Investments in Affiliates: 0%

Group Affiliation: None

Licensed in: CT, DE, ME, MA, NH, NJ, NY, PA, RI, VT

Commenced Business: May 1977

Address: 8 British American Blvd, Latham, NY 12110

Phone: (212) 576-9801   **Domicile State:** NY   **NAIC Code:** 34231

Data Date	Rating	RACR #1	RACR #2	Loss Ratio %	Total Assets ($mil)	Capital ($mil)	Net Premium ($mil)	Net Income ($mil)
9-14	D+	1.38	1.17	N/A	6,271.6	1,677.1	388.1	167.0
9-13	D+	1.09	0.91	N/A	6,058.6	1,342.3	407.4	85.9
2013	D+	1.27	1.08	93.4	5,777.6	1,538.8	533.9	172.2
2012	D+	1.04	0.89	106.5	5,567.8	1,271.0	550.1	94.5
2011	D+	0.91	0.76	107.9	5,889.0	1,164.6	552.9	466.5
2010	D+	0.61	0.51	84.4	5,214.1	838.0	598.4	301.1
2009	D+	0.35	0.29	81.4	5,073.2	491.2	564.5	107.1

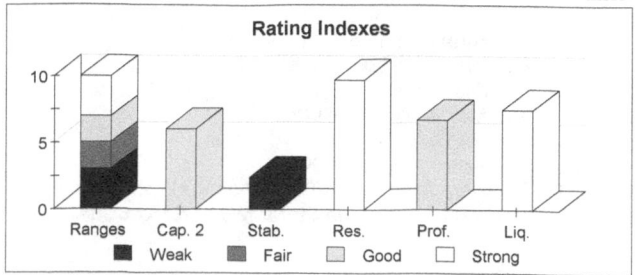

Rating Indexes

Ranges · Cap. 2 · Stab. · Res. · Prof. · Liq.

■ Weak ■ Fair □ Good □ Strong

MEDICAL MUTUAL INS CO OF NC   B-   Good

Major Rating Factors: Fair overall results on stability tests (4.5 on a scale of 0 to 10) including potential drain of affiliation with Medical Ins Group. Fair profitability index (4.8). Good expense controls.

Other Rating Factors: Strong long-term capitalization index (10.0) based on excellent current risk adjusted capital (severe and moderate loss scenarios), despite some fluctuation in capital levels. Ample reserve history (9.5) that helps to protect the company against sharp claims increases. Excellent liquidity (7.8) with ample operational cash flow and liquid investments.

Principal Business: Medical malpractice (100%).

Principal Investments: Investment grade bonds (87%), misc. investments (8%), cash (4%), and non investment grade bonds (1%).

Investments in Affiliates: 3%

Group Affiliation: Medical Ins Group

Licensed in: AL, AR, FL, GA, KY, MS, NC, SC, TN, VA, WV

Commenced Business: October 1975

Address: 700 Spring Forest Rd, Raleigh, NC 27609

Phone: (919) 872-7117   **Domicile State:** NC   **NAIC Code:** 32522

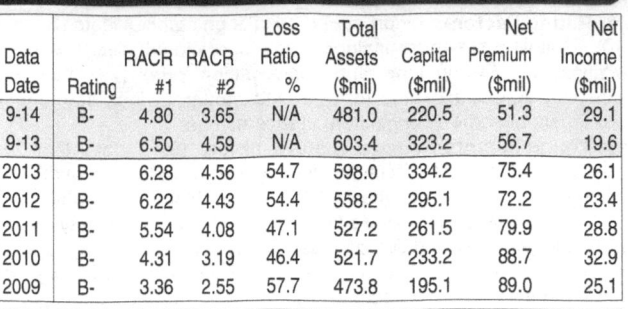

Data Date	Rating	RACR #1	RACR #2	Loss Ratio %	Total Assets ($mil)	Capital ($mil)	Net Premium ($mil)	Net Income ($mil)
9-14	B-	4.80	3.65	N/A	481.0	220.5	51.3	29.1
9-13	B-	6.50	4.59	N/A	603.4	323.2	56.7	19.6
2013	B-	6.28	4.56	54.7	598.0	334.2	75.4	26.1
2012	B-	6.22	4.43	54.4	558.2	295.1	72.2	23.4
2011	B-	5.54	4.08	47.1	527.2	261.5	79.9	28.8
2010	B-	4.31	3.19	46.4	521.7	233.2	88.7	32.9
2009	B-	3.36	2.55	57.7	473.8	195.1	89.0	25.1

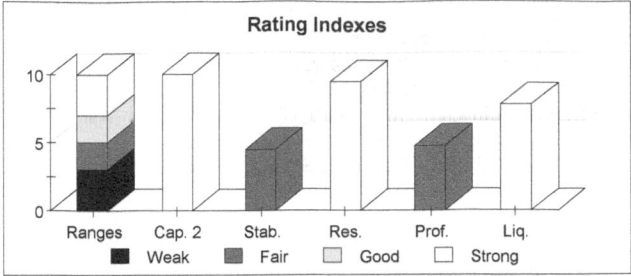

MEDICAL MUTUAL LIAB INS SOC OF MD   B-   Good

Major Rating Factors: Fair overall results on stability tests (4.6 on a scale of 0 to 10) including potential drain of affiliation with Medical Ins Group Of MD. Strong long-term capitalization index (9.6) based on excellent current risk adjusted capital (severe and moderate loss scenarios). Moreover, capital levels have been consistent in recent years.

Other Rating Factors: Ample reserve history (9.6) that helps to protect the company against sharp claims increases. Excellent profitability (7.8) with operating gains in each of the last five years. Excellent liquidity (7.5) with ample operational cash flow and liquid investments.

Principal Business: Medical malpractice (100%).

Principal Investments: Investment grade bonds (90%) and misc. investments (10%).

Investments in Affiliates: 12%

Group Affiliation: Medical Ins Group Of MD

Licensed in: MD, MI, NC, PA

Commenced Business: June 1975

Address: 225 International Cir, Hunt Valley, MD 21030

Phone: (410) 785-0050   **Domicile State:** MD   **NAIC Code:** 32328

Data Date	Rating	RACR #1	RACR #2	Loss Ratio %	Total Assets ($mil)	Capital ($mil)	Net Premium ($mil)	Net Income ($mil)
9-14	B-	3.42	3.03	N/A	790.0	360.9	89.9	12.0
9-13	B-	3.41	2.98	N/A	775.2	345.0	93.0	11.9
2013	B-	3.35	2.99	50.3	804.9	339.9	120.7	3.4
2012	B-	3.41	3.02	65.3	785.6	331.8	128.9	3.2
2011	B-	3.64	3.20	55.5	777.8	322.1	126.4	10.8
2010	B-	3.69	3.20	44.0	760.9	303.0	128.7	18.5
2009	B-	3.20	2.75	50.2	748.2	276.6	131.0	14.9

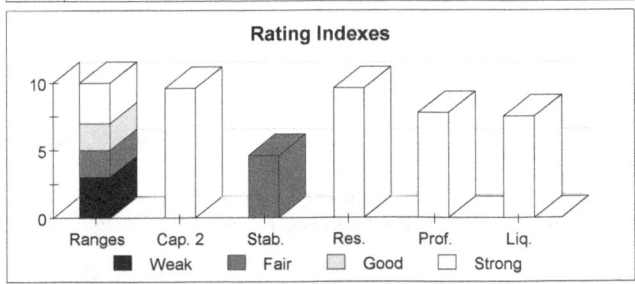

MEDICAL PROFESSIONAL MUTUAL INS CO   B-   Good

Major Rating Factors: Fair overall results on stability tests (4.5 on a scale of 0 to 10) including potential drain of affiliation with Medical Professional Mutual. The largest net exposure for one risk is acceptable at 2.3% of capital. Strong long-term capitalization index (8.0) based on excellent current risk adjusted capital (severe and moderate loss scenarios). Moreover, capital levels have been consistent in recent years.

Other Rating Factors: Ample reserve history (9.6) that helps to protect the company against sharp claims increases. Excellent profitability (8.7) with operating gains in each of the last five years. Return on equity has been good over the last five years, averaging 11.0%. Excellent liquidity (7.0) with ample operational cash flow and liquid investments.

Principal Business: Medical malpractice (99%) and other liability (1%).

Principal Investments: Investment grade bonds (63%), misc. investments (33%), cash (2%), and non investment grade bonds (2%).

Investments in Affiliates: 14%

Group Affiliation: Medical Professional Mutual

Licensed in: MA, NY, NC, VA

Commenced Business: July 1975

Address: 101 Arch St, Boston, MA 02110

Phone: (617) 330-1755   **Domicile State:** MA   **NAIC Code:** 10206

Data Date	Rating	RACR #1	RACR #2	Loss Ratio %	Total Assets ($mil)	Capital ($mil)	Net Premium ($mil)	Net Income ($mil)
9-14	B-	2.24	1.87	N/A	3,054.0	1,422.0	197.4	67.7
9-13	B-	2.25	1.91	N/A	3,158.6	1,341.5	217.7	55.1
2013	B-	2.36	2.01	60.1	3,151.4	1,423.4	277.0	135.3
2012	B-	2.23	1.92	72.0	3,103.7	1,282.8	280.3	87.5
2011	B-	2.04	1.79	46.1	2,955.2	1,132.2	291.6	146.3
2010	B-	1.68	1.47	64.8	2,799.7	977.5	303.0	117.1
2009	C+	1.42	1.24	45.6	2,425.1	792.4	301.9	138.1

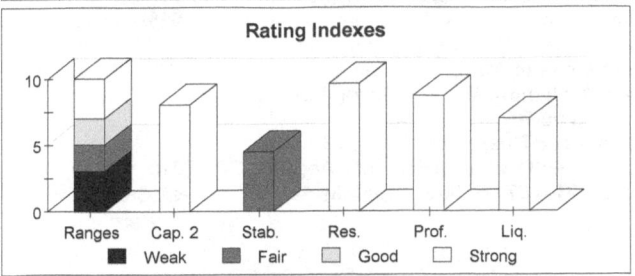

MEDICAL PROTECTIVE CO
B — **Good**

Major Rating Factors: Good overall results on stability tests (5.5 on a scale of 0 to 10). Stability strengths include good operational trends and excellent risk diversification. Strong long-term capitalization index (7.9) based on excellent current risk adjusted capital (severe and moderate loss scenarios). Moreover, capital levels have been consistent in recent years.

Other Rating Factors: Ample reserve history (9.4) that helps to protect the company against sharp claims increases. Excellent profitability (8.9) with operating gains in each of the last five years. Return on equity has been good over the last five years, averaging 11.0%. Superior liquidity (9.2) with ample operational cash flow and liquid investments.

Principal Business: Medical malpractice (99%) and other liability (1%).

Principal Investments: Investment grade bonds (75%), cash (13%), and misc. investments (12%).

Investments in Affiliates: None

Group Affiliation: Berkshire-Hathaway

Licensed in: All states except PR

Commenced Business: January 1910

Address: 5814 Reed Rd, Fort Wayne, IN 46835

Phone: (260) 485-9622 **Domicile State:** IN **NAIC Code:** 11843

Data Date	Rating	RACR #1	RACR #2	Loss Ratio %	Total Assets ($mil)	Capital ($mil)	Net Premium ($mil)	Net Income ($mil)
9-14	B	4.24	3.00	N/A	2,672.6	1,530.7	-627.3	112.1
9-13	B	2.40	1.86	N/A	3,215.6	1,292.0	278.9	124.5
2013	B	2.74	2.15	51.3	3,286.3	1,405.7	366.9	205.3
2012	B	1.79	1.45	71.7	3,013.5	1,075.4	643.8	133.3
2011	B	2.08	1.61	48.7	2,442.5	863.9	327.2	96.1
2010	B	1.84	1.41	59.2	2,271.2	755.7	334.7	53.7
2009	B	1.82	1.39	72.4	2,148.6	722.8	334.0	79.2

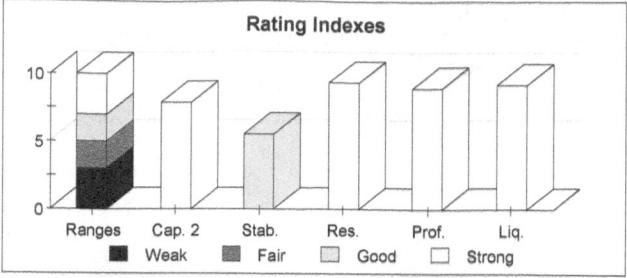

Rating Indexes

MERCURY CASUALTY CO *
B+ — **Good**

Major Rating Factors: History of adequate reserve strength (5.9 on a scale of 0 to 10) as reserves have been consistently at an acceptable level. Good overall profitability index (6.4). Fair expense controls. Return on equity has been good over the last five years, averaging 13.6%.

Other Rating Factors: Good liquidity (6.8) with sufficient resources (cash flows and marketable investments) to handle a spike in claims. Good overall results on stability tests (6.7). Stability strengths include good operational trends and excellent risk diversification. Strong long-term capitalization index (7.4) based on excellent current risk adjusted capital (severe and moderate loss scenarios), despite some fluctuation in capital levels.

Principal Business: Homeowners multiple peril (62%), auto liability (15%), commercial multiple peril (11%), auto physical damage (6%), fire (3%), and other liability (2%).

Principal Investments: Investment grade bonds (50%), misc. investments (42%), real estate (5%), cash (2%), and non investment grade bonds (1%).

Investments in Affiliates: 35%

Group Affiliation: Mercury General Group

Licensed in: AZ, CA, FL, GA, IL, MI, NV, NJ, NY, OK, PA, TX, VA, WA

Commenced Business: April 1962

Address: 4484 Wilshire Blvd, Los Angeles, CA 90010

Phone: (714) 671-6600 **Domicile State:** CA **NAIC Code:** 11908

Data Date	Rating	RACR #1	RACR #2	Loss Ratio %	Total Assets ($mil)	Capital ($mil)	Net Premium ($mil)	Net Income ($mil)
9-14	B+	1.60	1.46	N/A	1,993.8	1,063.6	540.7	85.4
9-13	B+	1.67	1.51	N/A	2,043.1	1,129.6	557.4	127.8
2013	B+	1.73	1.57	69.4	2,041.5	1,151.3	738.1	226.2
2012	B+	1.49	1.32	77.9	2,040.1	1,065.5	889.0	120.6
2011	B+	1.51	1.35	73.2	2,194.2	1,125.6	1,033.0	145.4
2010	B+	1.35	1.18	72.7	2,353.3	976.0	1,020.3	180.1
2009	A-	1.63	1.44	71.5	2,294.7	1,176.7	991.9	89.8

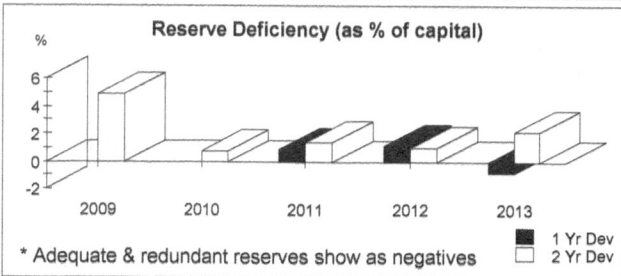

Reserve Deficiency (as % of capital)

* Adequate & redundant reserves show as negatives

MERCURY INS CO *
A- — **Excellent**

Major Rating Factors: Strong long-term capitalization index (8.2 on a scale of 0 to 10) based on excellent current risk adjusted capital (severe and moderate loss scenarios). Furthermore, this high level of risk adjusted capital has been consistently maintained in previous years. Excellent overall results on stability tests (7.0). Stability strengths include excellent operational trends and excellent risk diversification.

Other Rating Factors: History of adequate reserve strength (5.6) as reserves have been consistently at an acceptable level. Good overall profitability index (5.1). Fair expense controls. Return on equity has been good over the last five years, averaging 11.3%. Good liquidity (5.4) with sufficient resources (cash flows and marketable investments) to handle a spike in claims.

Principal Business: Auto liability (56%) and auto physical damage (44%).

Principal Investments: Investment grade bonds (93%), misc. investments (8%), and non investment grade bonds (1%).

Investments in Affiliates: None

Group Affiliation: Mercury General Group

Licensed in: CA

Commenced Business: July 1978

Address: 4484 Wilshire Blvd, Los Angeles, CA 90010

Phone: (714) 671-6600 **Domicile State:** CA **NAIC Code:** 27553

Data Date	Rating	RACR #1	RACR #2	Loss Ratio %	Total Assets ($mil)	Capital ($mil)	Net Premium ($mil)	Net Income ($mil)
9-14	A-	2.07	1.81	N/A	1,591.4	683.4	1,051.9	65.5
9-13	A-	2.05	1.79	N/A	1,546.8	656.1	996.6	35.8
2013	A-	1.99	1.81	75.2	1,532.9	652.6	1,350.1	66.5
2012	A-	2.05	1.84	77.1	1,476.2	645.4	1,287.8	24.2
2011	A-	2.34	2.12	71.8	1,416.8	688.5	1,225.6	75.4
2010	A-	2.23	2.01	70.6	1,375.0	642.2	1,201.5	78.4
2009	A-	2.26	2.03	65.8	1,394.1	661.2	1,217.1	119.8

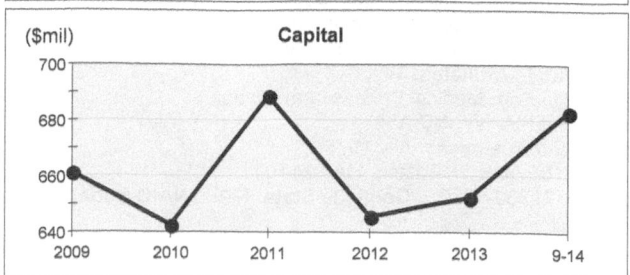

Capital

MERRIMACK MUTUAL FIRE INS CO　　　　　　　B　　　Good

Major Rating Factors: History of adequate reserve strength (6.2 on a scale of 0 to 10) as reserves have been consistently at an acceptable level. Good overall profitability index (6.5) despite operating losses during 2011.

Other Rating Factors: Fair overall results on stability tests (4.8) including potential drain of affiliation with Andover Group. Strong long-term capitalization index (7.7) based on excellent current risk adjusted capital (severe and moderate loss scenarios), despite some fluctuation in capital levels. Excellent liquidity (7.0) with ample operational cash flow and liquid investments.

Principal Business: Homeowners multiple peril (54%), commercial multiple peril (14%), fire (13%), allied lines (9%), other liability (8%), and inland marine (2%).

Principal Investments: Misc. investments (68%), investment grade bonds (17%), cash (14%), and real estate (1%).

Investments in Affiliates: 23%

Group Affiliation: Andover Group

Licensed in: CT, IL, ME, MA, NH, NJ, NY, RI, VT

Commenced Business: April 1828

Address: 95 Old River Rd, Andover, MA 01810

Phone: (978) 475-3300　**Domicile State:** MA　**NAIC Code:** 19798

Data Date	Rating	RACR #1	RACR #2	Loss Ratio %	Total Assets ($mil)	Capital ($mil)	Net Premium ($mil)	Net Income ($mil)
9-14	B	2.07	1.60	N/A	1,305.5	832.1	183.6	34.4
9-13	B	2.08	1.59	N/A	1,177.0	735.4	172.8	43.8
2013	B	2.02	1.58	43.3	1,251.0	785.2	246.4	60.1
2012	B	1.92	1.49	64.9	1,117.6	643.9	239.8	19.4
2011	B+	1.96	1.51	90.4	1,036.1	606.7	224.4	-35.5
2010	A	2.49	2.07	55.5	1,002.3	620.1	215.2	27.9
2009	A	2.87	2.51	49.5	956.8	579.0	216.5	41.4

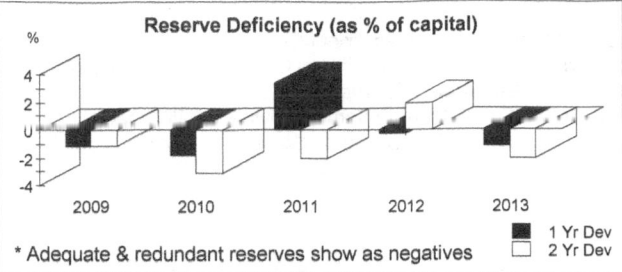

Reserve Deficiency (as % of capital)

* Adequate & redundant reserves show as negatives　■ 1 Yr Dev　□ 2 Yr Dev

METROPOLITAN GROUP PROP & CAS INS CO　　　B　　　Good

Major Rating Factors: History of adequate reserve strength (5.7 on a scale of 0 to 10) as reserves have been consistently at an acceptable level. Good overall profitability index (6.8). Good expense controls. Return on equity has been low, averaging 4.8% over the past five years.

Other Rating Factors: Good liquidity (6.9) with sufficient resources (cash flows and marketable investments) to handle a spike in claims. Good overall results on stability tests (6.3). Stability strengths include good operational trends and excellent risk diversification. Strong long-term capitalization index (10.0) based on excellent current risk adjusted capital (severe and moderate loss scenarios), despite some fluctuation in capital levels.

Principal Business: Auto liability (46%), auto physical damage (34%), homeowners multiple peril (19%), and inland marine (1%).

Principal Investments: Investment grade bonds (96%), misc. investments (3%), and non investment grade bonds (1%).

Investments in Affiliates: 3%

Group Affiliation: MetLife Inc

Licensed in: All states except HI, KY, ME, MN, NM, NC, OR, VA, WY, PR

Commenced Business: December 1977

Address: 700 Quaker Lane, Warwick, RI 02886

Phone: (401) 827-2400　**Domicile State:** RI　**NAIC Code:** 34339

Data Date	Rating	RACR #1	RACR #2	Loss Ratio %	Total Assets ($mil)	Capital ($mil)	Net Premium ($mil)	Net Income ($mil)
9-14	B	16.16	8.63	N/A	616.7	361.5	0.0	17.3
9-13	B	12.61	6.39	N/A	582.6	303.5	0.0	9.4
2013	B	16.98	8.60	0.0	582.5	344.9	0.0	13.0
2012	B	14.32	7.10	0.0	555.8	305.5	0.0	14.4
2011	B	15.56	7.44	0.0	550.2	316.0	0.0	13.2
2010	B	13.92	6.64	0.0	394.4	308.0	0.0	13.5
2009	B	12.74	9.86	0.0	390.0	298.4	0.0	17.2

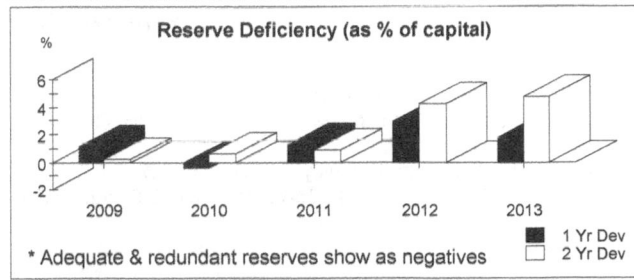

Reserve Deficiency (as % of capital)

* Adequate & redundant reserves show as negatives　■ 1 Yr Dev　□ 2 Yr Dev

METROPOLITAN PROPERTY & CAS INS CO　　　　B　　　Good

Major Rating Factors: Good overall results on stability tests (5.7 on a scale of 0 to 10). Fair liquidity (3.6) as cash resources may not be adequate to cover a spike in claims.

Other Rating Factors: Strong long-term capitalization index (7.9) based on excellent current risk adjusted capital (severe and moderate loss scenarios). Moreover, capital levels have been consistent in recent years. Ample reserve history (9.0) that helps to protect the company against sharp claims increases. Excellent profitability (8.1) with operating gains in each of the last five years. Return on equity has been good over the last five years, averaging 10.4%.

Principal Business: Homeowners multiple peril (48%), auto liability (26%), auto physical damage (19%), other liability (3%), inland marine (1%), other accident & health (1%), and other lines (2%).

Principal Investments: Investment grade bonds (71%), misc. investments (29%), and non investment grade bonds (2%).

Investments in Affiliates: 20%

Group Affiliation: MetLife Inc

Licensed in: All states except AK, CA, PR

Commenced Business: December 1972

Address: 700 Quaker Lane, Warwick, RI 02886

Phone: (401) 827-2400　**Domicile State:** RI　**NAIC Code:** 26298

Data Date	Rating	RACR #1	RACR #2	Loss Ratio %	Total Assets ($mil)	Capital ($mil)	Net Premium ($mil)	Net Income ($mil)
9-14	B	2.27	1.78	N/A	5,740.1	2,464.4	2,533.9	150.0
9-13	B	2.09	1.61	N/A	5,472.4	2,149.3	2,413.5	162.8
2013	B	2.07	1.65	68.8	5,499.7	2,224.9	3,372.1	265.8
2012	B	1.95	1.54	71.7	5,146.4	1,987.3	3,173.9	235.2
2011	B	1.83	1.42	78.9	4,967.4	1,857.3	3,055.4	2.2
2010	B	1.85	1.45	69.0	4,900.9	1,845.3	2,983.2	255.9
2009	B+	1.87	1.47	66.0	4,819.8	1,817.2	2,915.7	285.5

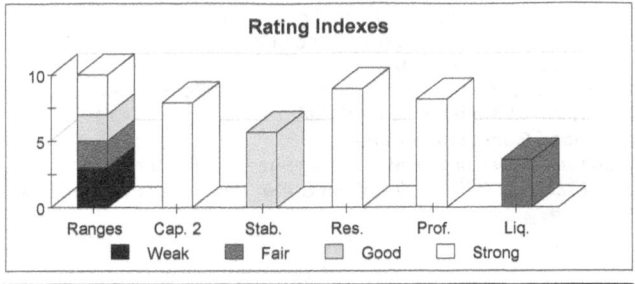

Rating Indexes

Ranges　Cap. 2　Stab.　Res.　Prof.　Liq.

■ Weak　▨ Fair　▤ Good　□ Strong

MGIC INDEMNITY CORP | D+ | Weak

Major Rating Factors: Fair reserve development (3.6 on a scale of 0 to 10) as reserves have generally been sufficient to cover claims. Weak overall results on stability tests (2.4) including weak financial strength of affiliated MGIC Investment Corp and weak results on operational trends.

Other Rating Factors: Strong long-term capitalization index (10.0) based on excellent current risk adjusted capital (severe and moderate loss scenarios). Moreover, capital levels have been consistent in recent years. Excellent profitability (7.6) with operating gains in each of the last five years. Superior liquidity (9.1) with ample operational cash flow and liquid investments.

Principal Business: Mortgage guaranty (100%).

Principal Investments: Investment grade bonds (96%) and misc. investments (4%).

Investments in Affiliates: 1%

Group Affiliation: MGIC Investment Corp

Licensed in: All states, the District of Columbia and Puerto Rico

Commenced Business: February 1957

Address: 250 East Kilbourn Avenue, Milwaukee, WI 53202

Phone: (800) 558-9900 **Domicile State:** WI **NAIC Code:** 18740

Data Date	Rating	RACR #1	RACR #2	Loss Ratio %	Total Assets ($mil)	Capital ($mil)	Net Premium ($mil)	Net Income ($mil)
9-14	D+	18.59	16.56	N/A	496.0	466.2	13.4	8.1
9-13	D+	30.03	25.40	N/A	476.4	455.2	15.0	6.4
2013	D+	17.16	15.54	2.3	481.0	458.1	21.4	9.5
2012	D+	39.79	32.74	1.4	458.8	448.3	7.4	13.0
2011	U	38.75	30.92	134.6	234.9	234.5	0.0	4.8
2010	U	39.84	32.83	N/A	230.2	229.7	0.0	4.8
2009	U	221.70	113.90	429.0	225.5	224.9	0.0	1.1

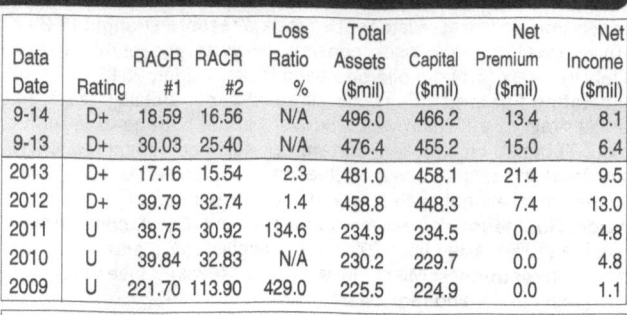

Rating Indexes

MHA INS CO | B | Good

Major Rating Factors: Fair overall results on stability tests (4.7 on a scale of 0 to 10). The largest net exposure for one risk is excessive at 5.9% of capital. Strong long-term capitalization index (10.0) based on excellent current risk adjusted capital (severe and moderate loss scenarios), despite some fluctuation in capital levels.

Other Rating Factors: Ample reserve history (9.4) that helps to protect the company against sharp claims increases. Excellent profitability (7.3) with operating gains in each of the last five years. Return on equity has been good over the last five years, averaging 11.7%. Excellent liquidity (8.6) with ample operational cash flow and liquid investments.

Principal Business: Medical malpractice (83%), workers compensation (13%), and other liability (5%).

Principal Investments: Investment grade bonds (92%), cash (5%), and misc. investments (3%).

Investments in Affiliates: 0%

Group Affiliation: Medical Professional Mutual

Licensed in: IL, IN, IA, KS, KY, MI, MN, MO, NE, ND, OH, OK, SD, WA, WI

Commenced Business: May 1976

Address: 6215 W St. Joseph Highway, Lansing, MI 48917

Phone: (517) 703-8500 **Domicile State:** MI **NAIC Code:** 33111

Data Date	Rating	RACR #1	RACR #2	Loss Ratio %	Total Assets ($mil)	Capital ($mil)	Net Premium ($mil)	Net Income ($mil)
9-14	B	5.44	4.09	N/A	539.0	267.3	54.4	0.0
9-13	B	5.90	4.60	N/A	506.4	272.3	47.1	3.8
2013	B	6.36	4.80	84.5	528.8	277.8	68.2	8.3
2012	B	6.63	5.19	91.4	482.7	269.1	61.9	5.2
2011	B	7.75	5.86	65.9	458.8	262.7	65.2	16.1
2010	B	8.77	6.87	24.3	409.9	247.7	49.3	31.0
2009	B	7.10	5.94	N/A	421.4	211.8	53.7	92.9

Medical Professional Mutual Composite Group Rating: C+ Largest Group Members	Assets ($mil)	Rating
MEDICAL PROFESSIONAL MUTUAL INS CO	3151	B-
MHA INS CO	529	B
PREFERRED PROFESSIONAL INS CO	409	C+
PROSELECT INS CO	71	C
OHA INS SOLUTIONS	44	C-

MID-CENTURY INS CO | C | Fair

Major Rating Factors: Fair overall results on stability tests (4.3 on a scale of 0 to 10). Good overall profitability index (6.1) with small operating losses during 2011. Return on equity has been fair, averaging 6.2% over the past five years.

Other Rating Factors: Good liquidity (5.4) with sufficient resources (cash flows and marketable investments) to handle a spike in claims. Strong long-term capitalization index (7.5) based on excellent current risk adjusted capital (severe and moderate loss scenarios), despite some fluctuation in capital levels. Ample reserve history (9.3) that helps to protect the company against sharp claims increases.

Principal Business: Auto liability (38%), auto physical damage (24%), homeowners multiple peril (23%), commercial multiple peril (10%), and workers compensation (5%).

Principal Investments: Investment grade bonds (89%), misc. investments (11%), and non investment grade bonds (1%).

Investments in Affiliates: 9%

Group Affiliation: Farmers Insurance Group of Companies

Licensed in: All states except AK, ME, PR

Commenced Business: February 1953

Address: 4680 Wilshire Blvd, Los Angeles, CA 90010

Phone: (323) 932-3200 **Domicile State:** CA **NAIC Code:** 21687

Data Date	Rating	RACR #1	RACR #2	Loss Ratio %	Total Assets ($mil)	Capital ($mil)	Net Premium ($mil)	Net Income ($mil)
9-14	C	1.84	1.40	N/A	3,719.4	951.2	1,623.6	32.0
9-13	C	1.77	1.34	N/A	3,810.4	887.9	1,650.1	18.9
2013	C	1.82	1.38	67.2	3,714.7	921.3	2,181.9	56.0
2012	C	1.70	1.28	70.9	3,657.5	854.4	2,216.8	37.2
2011	C	1.60	1.20	72.1	3,749.8	823.4	2,264.9	-5.7
2010	C	1.72	1.25	61.5	3,667.1	836.7	2,039.0	6.9
2009	C-	1.72	1.24	60.5	3,222.9	777.7	1,552.3	168.2

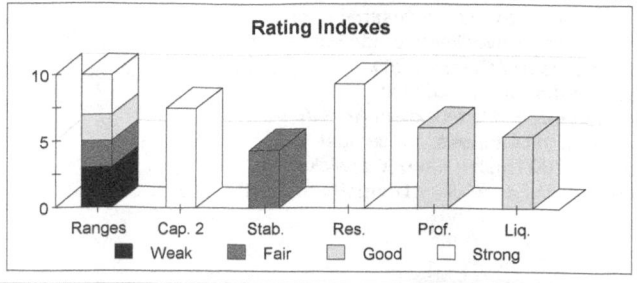

Rating Indexes

MIDDLESEX INS CO   B   Good

Major Rating Factors: Good overall profitability index (5.9 on a scale of 0 to 10). Fair expense controls. Return on equity has been fair, averaging 5.7% over the past five years. Good liquidity (6.8) with sufficient resources (cash flows and marketable investments) to handle a spike in claims.

Other Rating Factors: Good overall results on stability tests (5.4). The largest net exposure for one risk is conservative at 1.1% of capital. Strong long-term capitalization index (9.7) based on excellent current risk adjusted capital (severe and moderate loss scenarios), despite some fluctuation in capital levels. Ample reserve history (8.7) that helps to protect the company against sharp claims increases.

Principal Business: Workers compensation (51%), auto liability (35%), auto physical damage (5%), allied lines (4%), fire (3%), other liability (1%), and products liability (1%).

Principal Investments: Investment grade bonds (85%) and misc. investments (15%).

Investments in Affiliates: 5%

Group Affiliation: Sentry Ins Group

Licensed in: All states except PR

Commenced Business: March 1826

Address: 1800 N Point Dr, Stevens Point, WI 54481

Phone: (715) 346-6000   **Domicile State:** WI   **NAIC Code:** 23434

Data Date	Rating	RACR #1	RACR #2	Loss Ratio %	Total Assets ($mil)	Capital ($mil)	Net Premium ($mil)	Net Income ($mil)
9-14	B	4.03	2.80	N/A	679.5	256.9	134.6	9.8
9-13	B	3.99	2.77	N/A	654.6	248.4	132.6	7.0
2013	B	3.92	2.77	76.3	653.2	242.8	181.8	11.8
2012	B	4.00	2.81	77.3	628.2	237.4	172.7	10.3
2011	B	4.05	2.86	79.1	622.2	235.1	163.3	11.9
2010	B	4.21	2.96	75.5	617.6	238.3	161.9	16.3
2009	B	4.20	2.95	75.3	628.3	239.7	160.9	18.6

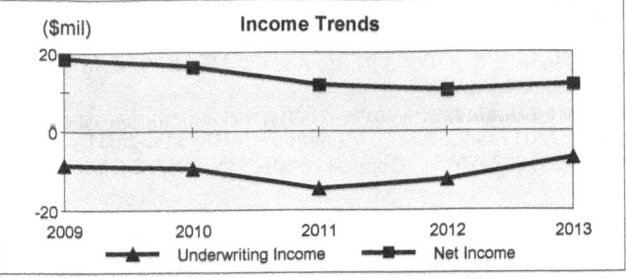

MISSISSIPPI FARM BUREAU CAS INS CO   B   Good

Major Rating Factors: Good overall profitability index (5.9 on a scale of 0 to 10) despite operating losses during 2011. Return on equity has been low, averaging 3.9% over the past five years. Good liquidity (6.6) with sufficient resources (cash flows and marketable investments) to handle a spike in claims.

Other Rating Factors: Fair overall results on stability tests (4.8) including potential drain of affiliation with Southern Farm Bureau Casualty. Strong long-term capitalization index (10.0) based on excellent current risk adjusted capital (severe and moderate loss scenarios), despite some fluctuation in capital levels. Ample reserve history (7.6) that can protect against increases in claims costs.

Principal Business: Homeowners multiple peril (39%), auto liability (26%), auto physical damage (22%), allied lines (4%), fire (3%), other liability (2%), and other lines (4%).

Principal Investments: Investment grade bonds (90%), misc. investments (6%), cash (3%), and non investment grade bonds (1%).

Investments in Affiliates: None

Group Affiliation: Southern Farm Bureau Casualty

Licensed in: FL, LA, MS, SC, TX

Commenced Business: September 1986

Address: 6310 I-55 North, Jackson, MS 39211

Phone: (601) 977-4301   **Domicile State:** MS   **NAIC Code:** 27669

Data Date	Rating	RACR #1	RACR #2	Loss Ratio %	Total Assets ($mil)	Capital ($mil)	Net Premium ($mil)	Net Income ($mil)
9-14	B	4.67	3.85	N/A	371.1	219.5	123.6	6.6
9-13	B	4.65	3.87	N/A	345.6	204.8	114.6	6.5
2013	B	4.81	3.70	70.4	351.8	212.0	159.2	15.7
2012	B	4.69	3.56	69.8	331.3	197.8	151.3	14.6
2011	B	4.66	3.54	86.4	303.1	181.0	140.5	-2.8
2010	B	4.50	2.93	83.3	304.0	186.8	137.3	0.1
2009	B	4.67	2.98	74.1	294.9	186.3	128.6	11.3

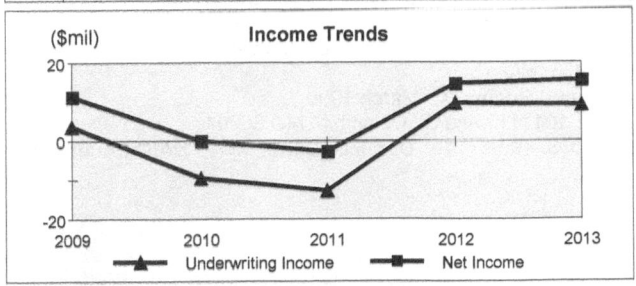

MITSUI SUMITOMO INS CO OF AMER *   B+   Good

Major Rating Factors: Good overall profitability index (6.7 on a scale of 0 to 10). Fair expense controls. Return on equity has been fair, averaging 6.7% over the past five years. Good overall results on stability tests (6.5). The largest net exposure for one risk is conservative at 1.0% of capital.

Other Rating Factors: Strong long-term capitalization index (9.3) based on excellent current risk adjusted capital (severe and moderate loss scenarios). Moreover, capital levels have been consistent in recent years. Ample reserve history (9.4) that helps to protect the company against sharp claims increases. Excellent liquidity (7.0) with ample operational cash flow and liquid investments.

Principal Business: Workers compensation (31%), commercial multiple peril (23%), other liability (13%), aircraft (9%), ocean marine (8%), allied lines (5%), and other lines (10%).

Principal Investments: Investment grade bonds (78%), misc. investments (15%), cash (4%), and real estate (3%).

Investments in Affiliates: None

Group Affiliation: MS & AD Ins Group Holdings Inc

Licensed in: All states, the District of Columbia and Puerto Rico

Commenced Business: January 1971

Address: 560 Lexington Ave 20th Floor, New York, NY 10022-6828

Phone: (908) 604-2900   **Domicile State:** NY   **NAIC Code:** 20362

Data Date	Rating	RACR #1	RACR #2	Loss Ratio %	Total Assets ($mil)	Capital ($mil)	Net Premium ($mil)	Net Income ($mil)
9-14	B+	3.81	2.50	N/A	883.6	324.2	134.6	13.1
9-13	B+	4.03	2.45	N/A	839.9	311.5	124.1	15.0
2013	B+	4.02	2.65	73.5	845.2	319.6	182.7	18.5
2012	B+	4.28	2.60	77.9	789.8	298.2	156.6	13.4
2011	B+	4.14	2.80	68.7	763.9	285.2	146.3	19.0
2010	B	3.78	2.54	68.7	744.8	275.2	136.6	21.3
2009	B	3.29	2.01	65.1	718.6	253.3	135.3	24.5

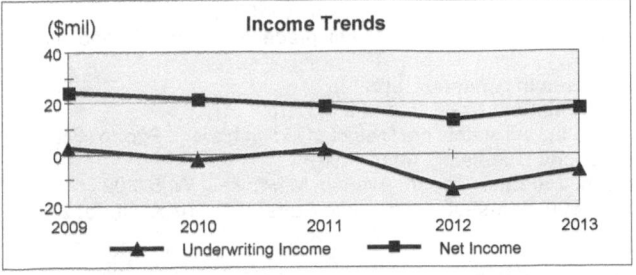

MMIC INS INC *

A- **Excellent**

Major Rating Factors: Strong long-term capitalization index (7.4 on a scale of 0 to 10) based on excellent current risk adjusted capital (severe and moderate loss scenarios). Furthermore, this high level of risk adjusted capital has been consistently maintained in previous years. Ample reserve history (9.5) that helps to protect the company against sharp claims increases.

Other Rating Factors: Excellent profitability (8.9) with operating gains in each of the last five years. Excellent liquidity (7.1) with ample operational cash flow and liquid investments. Excellent overall results on stability tests (7.1). Stability strengths include good operational trends and excellent risk diversification.

Principal Business: Medical malpractice (97%) and other liability (3%).

Principal Investments: Investment grade bonds (58%), misc. investments (40%), cash (1%), and non investment grade bonds (1%).

Investments in Affiliates: 21%

Group Affiliation: MMIC Group Inc

Licensed in: AR, CO, ID, IL, IN, IA, KS, KY, MI, MN, MO, MT, NE, ND, OH, OK, OR, SD, TN, UT, WI, WY

Commenced Business: October 1980

Address: 7701 France Ave S, Minneapolis, MN 55435-5981

Phone: (952) 838-6700   **Domicile State:** MN   **NAIC Code:** 16942

Data Date	Rating	RACR #1	RACR #2	Loss Ratio %	Total Assets ($mil)	Capital ($mil)	Net Premium ($mil)	Net Income ($mil)
9-14	A-	1.74	1.46	N/A	701.8	289.8	79.7	17.1
9-13	A-	2.70	1.73	N/A	696.2	252.6	83.3	9.6
2013	A-	1.66	1.40	72.9	708.2	273.6	110.4	14.4
2012	A-	3.78	2.64	72.0	554.2	257.0	115.9	27.0
2011	A-	3.85	2.91	64.2	525.5	234.3	117.6	25.1
2010	A-	3.63	2.76	71.1	504.8	220.4	110.8	20.0
2009	B+	3.19	2.38	63.5	483.4	198.0	104.9	18.6

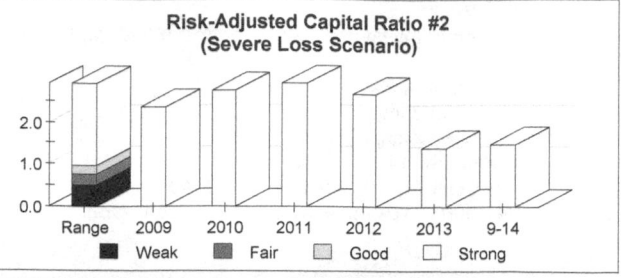

Risk-Adjusted Capital Ratio #2 (Severe Loss Scenario)

MO EMPLOYERS MUTUAL INS CO

C **Fair**

Major Rating Factors: Fair overall results on stability tests (4.2 on a scale of 0 to 10). Good overall profitability index (5.4) despite operating losses during 2012.

Other Rating Factors: Good liquidity (6.6) with sufficient resources (cash flows and marketable investments) to handle a spike in claims. Strong long-term capitalization index (7.7) based on excellent current risk adjusted capital (severe and moderate loss scenarios). Moreover, capital levels have been consistent in recent years. Ample reserve history (9.3) that helps to protect the company against sharp claims increases.

Principal Business: Workers compensation (100%).

Principal Investments: Investment grade bonds (72%), misc. investments (21%), non investment grade bonds (3%), real estate (3%), and cash (1%).

Investments in Affiliates: 0%

Group Affiliation: Missouri Employers Mutual

Licensed in: MO

Commenced Business: March 1995

Address: 101 N Keene St, Columbia, MO 65201

Phone: (573) 499-9714   **Domicile State:** MO   **NAIC Code:** 10191

Data Date	Rating	RACR #1	RACR #2	Loss Ratio %	Total Assets ($mil)	Capital ($mil)	Net Premium ($mil)	Net Income ($mil)
9-14	C	1.86	1.41	N/A	552.5	202.5	131.9	6.2
9-13	C	2.23	1.69	N/A	503.9	194.0	112.9	10.2
2013	C	2.01	1.51	72.3	508.8	194.4	166.1	5.9
2012	C	2.32	1.76	83.7	446.1	172.6	137.2	-1.9
2011	C	2.47	1.91	73.0	404.9	167.7	139.9	7.5
2010	C	2.82	2.15	72.7	364.0	163.1	108.1	10.0
2009	C	2.73	2.09	64.6	350.8	154.4	107.4	12.9

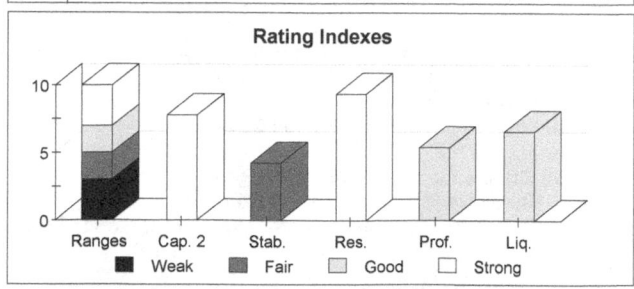

Rating Indexes

MORTGAGE GUARANTY INS CORP

D+ **Weak**

Major Rating Factors: A history of deficient reserves (2.3 on a scale of 0 to 10). Underreserving can have an adverse impact on capital and profits. In 2012 and 2013 the two year reserve development was 29% and 53% deficient respectively. Weak profitability index (1.3) with operating losses during 2011, 2012 and the first nine months of 2014. Average return on equity over the last five years has been poor at -18.6%.

Other Rating Factors: Weak overall results on stability tests (2.4) including negative cash flow from operations for 2013. Fair overall long-term capitalization (4.2) based on good current risk adjusted capital (moderate loss scenario). However, capital levels have fluctuated during prior years. Good liquidity (6.4) with sufficient resources (cash flows and marketable investments) to handle a spike in claims.

Principal Business: Mortgage guaranty (100%).

Principal Investments: Investment grade bonds (90%) and misc. investments (10%).

Investments in Affiliates: 14%

Group Affiliation: MGIC Investment Corp

Licensed in: All states, the District of Columbia and Puerto Rico

Commenced Business: March 1979

Address: 250 East Kilbourn Avenue, Milwaukee, WI 53202

Phone: (800) 558-9900   **Domicile State:** WI   **NAIC Code:** 29858

Data Date	Rating	RACR #1	RACR #2	Loss Ratio %	Total Assets ($mil)	Capital ($mil)	Net Premium ($mil)	Net Income ($mil)
9-14	D+	1.12	0.90	N/A	4,175.5	1,479.0	545.3	-43.1
9-13	D+	0.85	0.67	N/A	4,627.0	1,450.5	611.7	-82.3
2013	D+	0.99	0.79	91.1	4,406.2	1,520.6	793.5	-7.0
2012	D+	0.34	0.27	202.5	4,355.0	689.1	904.2	-808.5
2011	D+	0.87	0.68	152.6	5,528.9	1,568.8	957.7	-397.1
2010	D+	1.00	0.74	125.8	6,508.9	1,709.0	970.5	259.0
2009	D	0.73	0.52	234.2	7,214.6	1,429.0	1,056.0	341.2

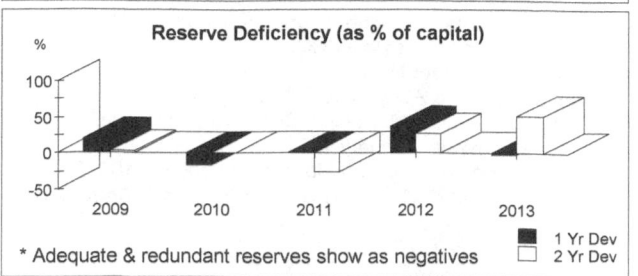

Reserve Deficiency (as % of capital)

* Adequate & redundant reserves show as negatives

MOTORISTS MUTUAL INS CO *

A-   Excellent

Major Rating Factors: Strong long-term capitalization index (8.9 on a scale of 0 to 10) based on excellent current risk adjusted capital (severe and moderate loss scenarios). Furthermore, this high level of risk adjusted capital has been consistently maintained in previous years. Ample reserve history (7.9) that can protect against increases in claims costs.

Other Rating Factors: Excellent overall results on stability tests (7.2). Stability strengths include good operational trends and excellent risk diversification. Good overall profitability index (5.2) despite operating losses during 2011. Good liquidity (6.4) with sufficient resources (cash flows and marketable investments) to handle a spike in claims.

Principal Business: Auto liability (29%), homeowners multiple peril (20%), auto physical damage (18%), other liability (11%), commercial multiple peril (10%), workers compensation (5%), and other lines (6%).

Principal Investments: Investment grade bonds (67%), misc. investments (31%), and real estate (3%).

Investments in Affiliates: 5%

Group Affiliation: The Motorists Group

Licensed in: CA, CT, IL, IN, IA, KY, MA, MI, MO, NH, NY, NC, OH, PA, RI, SD, VT, VA, WV, WI

Commenced Business: November 1928

Address: 471 E Broad St, Columbus, OH 43215

Phone: (614) 225-8211   **Domicile State:** OH   **NAIC Code:** 14621

Data Date	Rating	RACR #1	RACR #2	Loss Ratio %	Total Assets ($mil)	Capital ($mil)	Net Premium ($mil)	Net Income ($mil)
9-14	A-	3.42	2.39	N/A	1,354.2	558.2	355.8	12.9
9-13	B+	3.27	2.29	N/A	1,319.8	534.9	346.2	11.5
2013	A-	3.53	2.48	66.8	1,335.8	568.8	480.0	37.9
2012	B+	3.06	2.17	70.9	1,272.1	480.6	458.1	7.3
2011	B+	2.91	2.06	77.9	1,228.4	460.8	442.9	-20.8
2010	B+	2.96	2.01	73.5	1,292.8	503.3	487.0	0.7
2009	B+	2.80	1.86	73.2	1,255.0	487.5	475.3	1.2

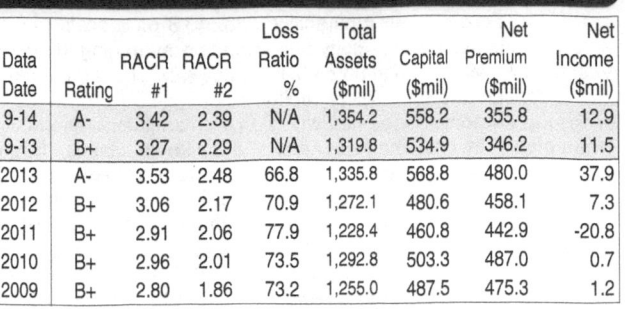

Capital

MOTORS INS CORP

C   Fair

Major Rating Factors: Fair profitability index (3.1 on a scale of 0 to 10). Weak expense controls. Return on equity has been fair, averaging 12.4% over the past five years. Fair overall results on stability tests (3.8) including fair financial strength of affiliated Ally Financial Inc.

Other Rating Factors: Strong long-term capitalization index (9.9) based on excellent current risk adjusted capital (severe and moderate loss scenarios), despite some fluctuation in capital levels. Ample reserve history (8.0) that helps to protect the company against sharp claims increases. Excellent liquidity (7.0) with ample operational cash flow and liquid investments.

Principal Business: Auto physical damage (55%).

Principal Investments: Investment grade bonds (67%), misc. investments (17%), non investment grade bonds (10%), and cash (6%).

Investments in Affiliates: 3%

Group Affiliation: Ally Financial Inc

Licensed in: All states except PR

Commenced Business: November 1939

Address: 300 Galleria Officentre, Southfield, MI 48034

Phone: (248) 263-6900   **Domicile State:** MI   **NAIC Code:** 22012

Data Date	Rating	RACR #1	RACR #2	Loss Ratio %	Total Assets ($mil)	Capital ($mil)	Net Premium ($mil)	Net Income ($mil)
9-14	C	4.92	3.10	N/A	2,494.6	1,071.0	382.9	17.9
9-13	C	2.25	1.46	N/A	2,785.3	1,051.8	409.1	80.6
2013	C	4.35	2.71	66.9	2,605.0	1,095.6	462.9	117.7
2012	C	2.49	1.63	73.2	2,770.1	1,183.2	479.8	93.0
2011	C	6.26	3.70	62.9	3,042.0	1,348.9	553.4	118.7
2010	C	5.74	3.30	62.1	3,406.8	1,406.9	340.6	478.3
2009	C+	4.03	2.76	68.1	5,374.3	1,908.3	1,428.1	152.7

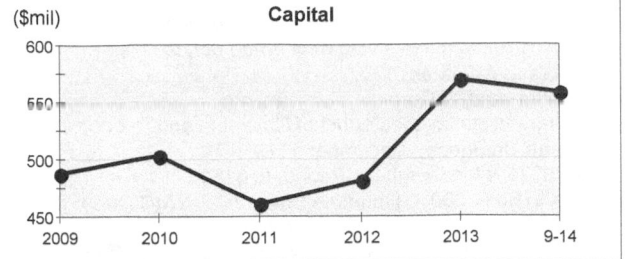

Income Trends

MOUNT VERNON FIRE INS CO

C+   Fair

Major Rating Factors: Fair overall results on stability tests (4.5 on a scale of 0 to 10). Strong long-term capitalization index (7.3) based on excellent current risk adjusted capital (severe and moderate loss scenarios). Moreover, capital levels have been consistent in recent years.

Other Rating Factors: Ample reserve history (9.3) that helps to protect the company against sharp claims increases. Excellent profitability (8.6) with operating gains in each of the last five years. Excellent liquidity (7.5) with ample operational cash flow and liquid investments.

Principal Business: Other liability (74%), fire (21%), products liability (2%), auto physical damage (2%), inland marine (1%), and auto liability (1%).

Principal Investments: Misc. investments (79%) and investment grade bonds (21%).

Investments in Affiliates: 27%

Group Affiliation: Berkshire-Hathaway

Licensed in: All states except PR

Commenced Business: December 1958

Address: 190 S. Warner Road, Wayne, PA 19087

Phone: (800) 523-5545   **Domicile State:** PA   **NAIC Code:** 26522

Data Date	Rating	RACR #1	RACR #2	Loss Ratio %	Total Assets ($mil)	Capital ($mil)	Net Premium ($mil)	Net Income ($mil)
9-14	C+	1.92	1.52	N/A	562.4	377.0	48.4	12.9
9-13	B-	1.86	1.42	N/A	484.0	313.1	45.5	11.5
2013	B-	1.84	1.48	33.5	526.4	348.2	63.0	24.1
2012	B-	1.80	1.41	43.7	433.8	273.7	59.4	15.6
2011	B-	1.80	1.44	47.2	379.5	226.3	57.3	10.3
2010	B-	1.87	1.46	41.5	368.0	210.3	59.7	12.0
2009	B-	1.70	1.26	41.3	343.2	172.9	64.0	14.0

Berkshire-Hathaway Composite Group Rating: B- Largest Group Members	Assets ($mil)	Rating
NATIONAL INDEMNITY CO	151912	B-
GOVERNMENT EMPLOYEES INS CO	25779	B+
COLUMBIA INS CO	19013	B-
GENERAL REINSURANCE CORP	16220	B-
BERKSHIRE HATHAWAY LIFE INS CO OF NE	13768	C+

MT HAWLEY INS CO
C   **Fair**

Major Rating Factors: Fair profitability index (3.8 on a scale of 0 to 10). Weak expense controls. Return on equity has been fair, averaging 16.4% over the past five years. Fair overall results on stability tests (4.0). The largest net exposure for one risk is conservative at 2.0% of capital.

Other Rating Factors: Good liquidity (6.9) with sufficient resources (cash flows and marketable investments) to handle a spike in claims. Strong long-term capitalization index (8.1) based on excellent current risk adjusted capital (severe and moderate loss scenarios), despite some fluctuation in capital levels. Ample reserve history (9.4) that helps to protect the company against sharp claims increases.

Principal Business: Other liability (45%), allied lines (18%), earthquake (10%), inland marine (10%), fire (9%), medical malpractice (6%), and products liability (1%).

Principal Investments: Investment grade bonds (79%), misc. investments (18%), cash (2%), and non investment grade bonds (1%).

Investments in Affiliates: 12%

Group Affiliation: RLI Corp

Licensed in: All states, the District of Columbia and Puerto Rico

Commenced Business: December 1979

Address: 9025 N Lindbergh Dr, Peoria, IL 61615

Phone: (309) 692-1000   **Domicile State:** IL   **NAIC Code:** 37974

Data Date	Rating	RACR #1	RACR #2	Loss Ratio %	Total Assets ($mil)	Capital ($mil)	Net Premium ($mil)	Net Income ($mil)
9-14	C	2.12	1.63	N/A	818.9	404.1	156.5	83.3
9-13	C	2.66	1.93	N/A	872.4	459.6	136.7	54.3
2013	C	2.63	2.01	26.0	925.3	523.0	202.9	76.0
2012	C	3.13	2.30	42.4	978.0	546.2	166.9	71.5
2011	C	3.17	2.34	21.4	1,032.9	574.5	157.3	91.6
2010	C	3.03	2.30	35.2	1,096.2	581.4	168.2	87.7
2009	C	2.83	2.14	34.8	1,097.6	565.6	186.8	86.2

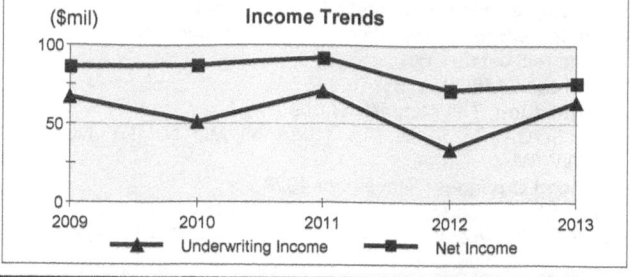

Income Trends

MUNICH REINSURANCE AMERICA INC
C+   **Fair**

Major Rating Factors: Fair overall results on stability tests (4.4 on a scale of 0 to 10) including potential drain of affiliation with Munich Re America Corp. The largest net exposure for one risk is acceptable at 2.4% of capital. Good liquidity (6.9) with sufficient resources (cash flows and marketable investments) to handle a spike in claims.

Other Rating Factors: Strong long-term capitalization index (7.4) based on excellent current risk adjusted capital (severe and moderate loss scenarios), despite some fluctuation in capital levels. Ample reserve history (9.3) that helps to protect the company against sharp claims increases. Excellent profitability (7.8) with operating gains in each of the last five years. Return on equity has been good over the last five years, averaging 10.5%.

Principal Business: (This company is a reinsurer.)

Principal Investments: Investment grade bonds (95%), non investment grade bonds (4%), and real estate (1%).

Investments in Affiliates: None

Group Affiliation: Munich Re America Corp

Licensed in: All states, the District of Columbia and Puerto Rico

Commenced Business: April 1917

Address: 555 College Rd E, Princeton, NJ 08543

Phone: (609) 243-4200   **Domicile State:** DE   **NAIC Code:** 10227

Data Date	Rating	RACR #1	RACR #2	Loss Ratio %	Total Assets ($mil)	Capital ($mil)	Net Premium ($mil)	Net Income ($mil)
9-14	C+	2.10	1.26	N/A	16,639.8	5,142.3	2,509.5	484.6
9-13	C+	1.77	1.10	N/A	17,056.7	4,617.9	2,259.8	190.2
2013	C+	2.31	1.40	57.1	16,840.8	5,288.0	3,195.8	806.1
2012	C+	1.80	1.12	66.4	17,362.6	4,624.8	3,113.0	378.2
2011	C+	1.65	1.02	66.9	16,096.5	4,262.0	3,101.6	576.9
2010	C	1.79	1.13	57.4	17,411.4	4,390.3	2,914.7	561.8
2009	C	1.58	1.01	67.2	16,030.3	3,824.6	2,804.3	46.7

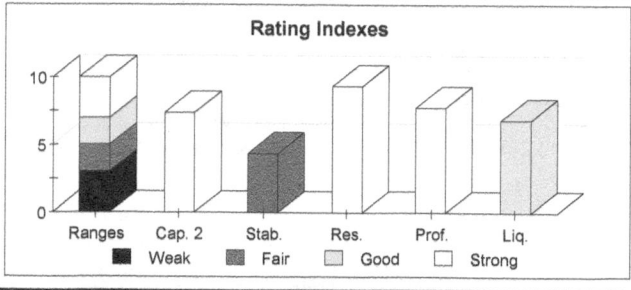

Rating Indexes

MUNICIPAL ASR CORP *
A+   **Excellent**

Major Rating Factors: Strong long-term capitalization index (9.0 on a scale of 0 to 10) based on excellent current risk adjusted capital (severe and moderate loss scenarios). Furthermore, this high level of risk adjusted capital has been consistently maintained in previous years. Excellent profitability (8.9) with operating gains in each of the last five years. Excellent expense controls.

Other Rating Factors: Excellent liquidity (7.0) with ample operational cash flow and liquid investments. Good overall results on stability tests (6.5) despite excessive premium growth and weak results on operational trends. The largest net exposure for one risk is excessive at 12.6% of capital.

Principal Business: Financial guaranty (100%).

Principal Investments: Investment grade bonds (98%) and misc. investments (2%).

Investments in Affiliates: None

Group Affiliation: Assured Guaranty Ltd

Licensed in: All states except AL, CA, NM, PR

Commenced Business: October 2008

Address: 31 W 52nd St, New York, NY 10019

Phone: (212) 974-0100   **Domicile State:** NY   **NAIC Code:** 13559

Data Date	Rating	RACR #1	RACR #2	Loss Ratio %	Total Assets ($mil)	Capital ($mil)	Net Premium ($mil)	Net Income ($mil)
9-14	A+	4.73	2.69	N/A	1,528.4	541.6	51.6	59.1
9-13	U	28.16	15.25	N/A	1,530.3	491.4	18.5	-7.1
2013	A+	3.74	2.27	0.0	1,516.2	514.4	709.9	25.7
2012	U	111.74	55.87	0.0	77.0	76.9	0.0	0.6
2011	U	107.24	53.62	0.0	75.1	75.1	0.0	0.0
2010	N/A	N/A	N/A	0.0	75.1	75.1	0.0	0.0
2009	N/A	N/A	N/A	0.0	75.1	75.1	0.0	0.0

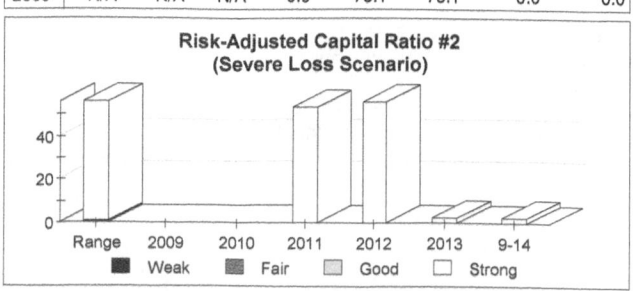

Risk-Adjusted Capital Ratio #2
(Severe Loss Scenario)

MUTUAL INS CO OF AZ * A Excellent

Major Rating Factors: Strong long-term capitalization index (10.0 on a scale of 0 to 10) based on excellent current risk adjusted capital (severe and moderate loss scenarios). Furthermore, this high level of risk adjusted capital has been consistently maintained in previous years. Ample reserve history (9.6) that helps to protect the company against sharp claims increases.

Other Rating Factors: Excellent profitability (8.8) with operating gains in each of the last five years. Excellent liquidity (8.3) with ample operational cash flow and liquid investments. Excellent overall results on stability tests (7.1). Stability strengths include good operational trends and excellent risk diversification.

Principal Business: (Not applicable due to unusual reinsurance transactions.)

Principal Investments: Investment grade bonds (88%), misc. investments (11%), and cash (1%).

Investments in Affiliates: None

Group Affiliation: None

Licensed in: AZ, CA, CO, NV, NM, UT

Commenced Business: March 1976

Address: 2602 East Thomas Rd, Phoenix, AZ 85016

Phone: (602) 956-5276   **Domicile State:** AZ   **NAIC Code:** 32832

Data Date	Rating	RACR #1	RACR #2	Loss Ratio %	Total Assets ($mil)	Capital ($mil)	Net Premium ($mil)	Net Income ($mil)
9-14	A	6.67	4.61	N/A	1,011.0	560.3	80.6	21.0
9-13	A	6.94	5.29	N/A	1,000.1	531.7	85.6	19.3
2013	A	6.77	4.81	63.3	1,008.0	536.5	109.5	20.9
2012	A	7.08	5.44	41.3	989.4	504.2	113.3	33.2
2011	A	6.19	4.77	26.1	982.2	463.6	116.8	44.4
2010	A	5.04	4.00	38.0	995.1	420.0	132.0	38.4
2009	A-	3.94	3.13	71.2	949.0	380.5	136.1	24.8

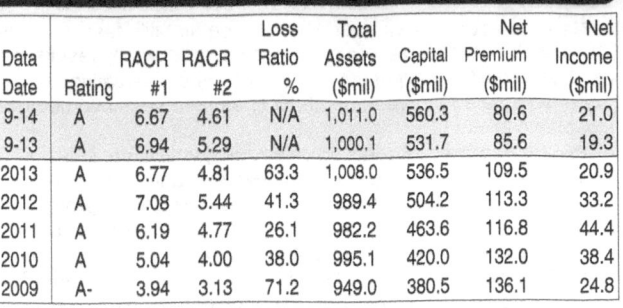

Risk-Adjusted Capital Ratio #2
(Severe Loss Scenario)

Range 2009 2010 2011 2012 2013 9-14
■ Weak ■ Fair □ Good □ Strong

MUTUAL OF ENUMCLAW INS CO B Good

Major Rating Factors: History of adequate reserve strength (6.9 on a scale of 0 to 10) as reserves have been consistently at an acceptable level. Good overall profitability index (6.5). Fair expense controls.

Other Rating Factors: Good liquidity (6.5) with sufficient resources (cash flows and marketable investments) to handle a spike in claims. Good overall results on stability tests (6.1). Strong long-term capitalization index (9.8) based on excellent current risk adjusted capital (severe and moderate loss scenarios). Moreover, capital levels have been consistent in recent years.

Principal Business: Auto liability (33%), homeowners multiple peril (21%), commercial multiple peril (15%), auto physical damage (15%), farmowners multiple peril (11%), other liability (3%), and other lines (3%).

Principal Investments: Investment grade bonds (79%), misc. investments (15%), cash (5%), and real estate (1%).

Investments in Affiliates: 5%

Group Affiliation: Enumclaw Ins Group

Licensed in: AK, AZ, CO, ID, MT, NV, OR, UT, WA

Commenced Business: March 1898

Address: 1460 Wells St, Enumclaw, WA 98022

Phone: (360) 825-2591   **Domicile State:** WA   **NAIC Code:** 14761

Data Date	Rating	RACR #1	RACR #2	Loss Ratio %	Total Assets ($mil)	Capital ($mil)	Net Premium ($mil)	Net Income ($mil)
9-14	B	4.07	2.99	N/A	663.7	296.8	252.0	6.6
9-13	B	3.91	2.90	N/A	634.4	279.5	239.7	3.8
2013	B	4.05	2.99	68.4	634.8	286.9	331.0	8.0
2012	B	3.90	2.89	68.0	598.9	266.3	309.1	18.2
2011	B	3.66	2.71	66.9	575.9	248.1	297.9	20.3
2010	B	3.07	2.21	71.3	570.1	230.3	313.0	11.5
2009	B	3.42	2.38	69.1	571.2	226.3	323.1	21.4

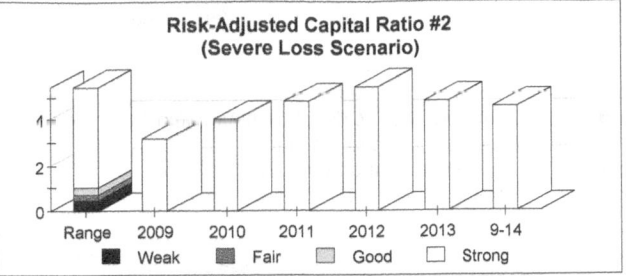

Reserve Deficiency (as % of capital)

2009 2010 2011 2012 2013
■ 1 Yr Dev □ 2 Yr Dev

* Adequate & redundant reserves show as negatives

NATIONAL CASUALTY CO * B+ Good

Major Rating Factors: Good liquidity (6.4 on a scale of 0 to 10) with sufficient resources (cash flows and marketable investments) to handle a spike in claims. Good overall results on stability tests (6.4). Strengths include potential support from affiliation with Nationwide Corp, good operational trends and excellent risk diversification.

Other Rating Factors: Strong long-term capitalization index (10.0) based on excellent current risk adjusted capital (severe and moderate loss scenarios), despite some fluctuation in capital levels. Excellent profitability (7.5) with operating gains in each of the last five years.

Principal Business: Auto liability (31%), inland marine (28%), other liability (15%), auto physical damage (10%), commercial multiple peril (7%), workers compensation (3%), and other lines (6%).

Principal Investments: Investment grade bonds (100%) and misc. investments (11%).

Investments in Affiliates: None

Group Affiliation: Nationwide Corp

Licensed in: All states except PR

Commenced Business: December 1904

Address: 8877 N Gainey Center Dr, Scottsdale, AZ 85258-2108

Phone: (480) 365-4000   **Domicile State:** WI   **NAIC Code:** 11991

Data Date	Rating	RACR #1	RACR #2	Loss Ratio %	Total Assets ($mil)	Capital ($mil)	Net Premium ($mil)	Net Income ($mil)
9-14	B+	13.68	12.31	N/A	273.8	128.7	0.0	2.1
9-13	B+	14.24	12.82	N/A	257.7	131.5	0.0	2.0
2013	B+	13.26	11.93	0.0	280.9	125.9	0.0	2.7
2012	B+	12.92	11.63	0.0	277.2	122.6	0.0	2.6
2011	B+	12.89	11.60	0.0	248.9	119.4	0.0	3.3
2010	B+	17.92	16.13	0.0	162.2	115.2	0.0	3.8
2009	B+	16.49	14.84	0.0	161.1	111.2	0.0	4.5

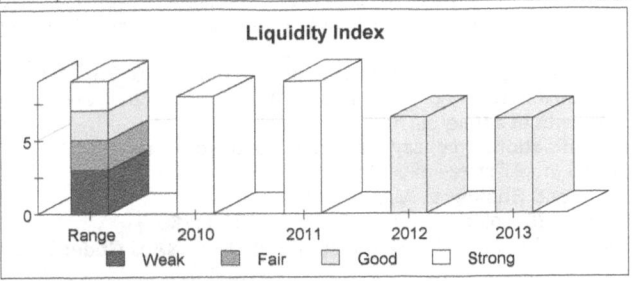

Liquidity Index

Range 2010 2011 2012 2013
■ Weak ■ Fair □ Good □ Strong

NATIONAL FIRE & MARINE INS CO — C — Fair

Major Rating Factors: Fair overall results on stability tests (4.1 on a scale of 0 to 10) including excessive premium growth and weak results on operational trends. The largest net exposure for one risk is conservative at 1.9% of capital. History of adequate reserve strength (6.1) as reserves have been consistently at an acceptable level.

Other Rating Factors: Strong long-term capitalization index (7.9) based on excellent current risk adjusted capital (severe and moderate loss scenarios), despite some fluctuation in capital levels. Excellent profitability (8.1) with operating gains in each of the last five years. Superior liquidity (9.2) with ample operational cash flow and liquid investments.

Principal Business: Other liability (45%), medical malpractice (13%), allied lines (12%), auto liability (10%), fire (5%), earthquake (4%), and other lines (11%).

Principal Investments: Misc. investments (94%) and investment grade bonds (6%).

Investments in Affiliates: 7%
Group Affiliation: Berkshire-Hathaway
Licensed in: All states, the District of Columbia and Puerto Rico
Commenced Business: January 1950
Address: 3024 Harney St, Omaha, NE 68131
Phone: (402) 916-3000   **Domicile State:** NE   **NAIC Code:** 20079

Data Date	Rating	RACR #1	RACR #2	Loss Ratio %	Total Assets ($mil)	Capital ($mil)	Net Premium ($mil)	Net Income ($mil)
9-14	C	2.41	1.58	N/A	8,030.5	5,368.4	340.0	576.9
9-13	C	2.80	1.83	N/A	6,601.2	4,509.1	157.0	136.0
2013	C	2.57	1.70	69.8	7,335.1	5,010.4	316.5	233.2
2012	C	2.80	1.86	54.6	5,597.0	3,857.6	131.4	279.5
2011	C	2.39	1.60	84.5	4,596.3	3,117.7	102.1	110.8
2010	C	2.57	1.72	46.2	4,985.5	3,357.7	98.4	64.4
2009	C	2.61	1.74	94.7	5,070.2	3,356.4	129.9	39.1

Rating Indexes

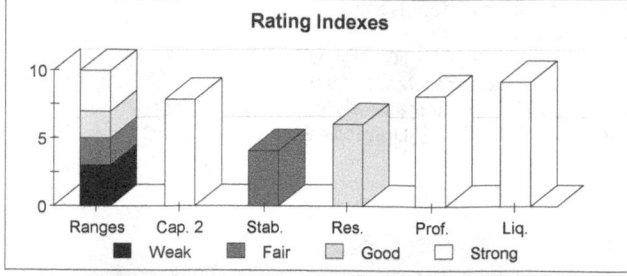

NATIONAL INDEMNITY CO — B- — Good

Major Rating Factors: Good overall results on stability tests (5.3 on a scale of 0 to 10) despite potential drain of affiliation with Berkshire-Hathaway and excessive premium growth. The largest net exposure for one risk is conservative at 1.8% of capital. Strong long-term capitalization index (8.3) based on excellent current risk adjusted capital (severe and moderate loss scenarios). Moreover, capital levels have been consistent in recent years.

Other Rating Factors: Ample reserve history (7.5) that can protect against increases in claims costs. Excellent profitability (8.6) with operating gains in each of the last five years. Excellent liquidity (7.8) with ample operational cash flow and liquid investments.

Principal Business: Auto liability (58%), aircraft (19%), auto physical damage (17%), inland marine (3%), surety (3%), and other liability (1%).

Principal Investments: Misc. investments (92%), investment grade bonds (4%), and cash (4%).

Investments in Affiliates: 23%
Group Affiliation: Berkshire-Hathaway
Licensed in: All states except PR
Commenced Business: May 1940
Address: 3024 Harney St, Omaha, NE 68131
Phone: (402) 916-3000   **Domicile State:** NE   **NAIC Code:** 20087

Data Date	Rating	RACR #1	RACR #2	Loss Ratio %	Total Assets ($mil)	Capital ($mil)	Net Premium ($mil)	Net Income ($mil)
9-14	B-	2.24	1.85	N/A	171,496.5	98,685.6	18,640.8	3,789.8
9-13	B-	2.63	2.09	N/A	140,976.2	88,175.2	4,472.8	4,896.2
2013	B-	2.24	1.87	49.2	151,911.7	97,226.1	5,650.4	8,390.8
2012	B-	2.48	2.01	62.8	128,202.6	79,408.9	7,469.8	5,489.3
2011	B-	2.58	2.05	83.2	118,802.0	72,576.9	5,859.3	5,324.6
2010	C+	2.57	2.08	57.3	111,645.0	68,437.1	4,422.8	6,079.3
2009	C	0.93	0.74	50.3	78,440.5	38,435.5	4,920.2	1,609.6

Rating Indexes

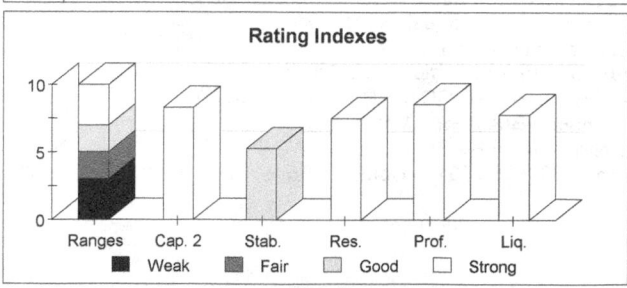

NATIONAL INTERSTATE INS CO — C+ — Fair

Major Rating Factors: Fair overall results on stability tests (4.7 on a scale of 0 to 10) including potential drain of affiliation with American Financial Group Inc. The largest net exposure for one risk is conservative at 1.2% of capital. Good overall profitability index (6.7). Fair expense controls. Return on equity has been good over the last five years, averaging 10.5%.

Other Rating Factors: Good liquidity (6.6) with sufficient resources (cash flows and marketable investments) to handle a spike in claims. Strong long-term capitalization index (7.4) based on excellent current risk adjusted capital (severe and moderate loss scenarios), despite some fluctuation in capital levels. Ample reserve history (8.3) that helps to protect the company against sharp claims increases.

Principal Business: Auto liability (51%), workers compensation (26%), auto physical damage (13%), other liability (7%), inland marine (1%), and allied lines (1%).

Principal Investments: Investment grade bonds (63%), misc. investments (31%), non investment grade bonds (3%), real estate (2%), and cash (1%).

Investments in Affiliates: 19%
Group Affiliation: American Financial Group Inc
Licensed in: All states except PR
Commenced Business: March 1989
Address: 3250 Interstate Drive, Richfield, OH 44286
Phone: (330) 659-8900   **Domicile State:** OH   **NAIC Code:** 32620

Data Date	Rating	RACR #1	RACR #2	Loss Ratio %	Total Assets ($mil)	Capital ($mil)	Net Premium ($mil)	Net Income ($mil)
9-14	C+	1.50	1.23	N/A	1,100.3	287.9	212.6	3.5
9-13	C+	1.57	1.29	N/A	1,038.9	278.8	203.5	12.9
2013	C+	1.52	1.26	70.8	1,054.1	283.4	277.6	21.9
2012	C+	1.61	1.36	62.3	1,017.5	269.7	260.7	52.9
2011	C+	1.65	1.37	63.6	994.7	293.6	251.5	31.0
2010	C+	1.74	1.53	60.6	799.6	273.6	230.3	19.9
2009	C+	4.93	3.26	53.1	696.3	238.4	205.2	33.2

American Financial Group Inc Composite Group Rating: B- Largest Group Members	Assets ($mil)	Rating
GREAT AMERICAN LIFE INS CO	20182	B-
GREAT AMERICAN INS CO	5377	B-
ANNUITY INVESTORS LIFE INS CO	2893	B
NATIONAL INTERSTATE INS CO	1054	C+
UNITED TEACHER ASSOCIATES INS CO	940	C

NATIONAL LIABILITY & FIRE INS CO
B   **Good**

Major Rating Factors: Good overall results on stability tests (5.3 on a scale of 0 to 10) despite potential drain of affiliation with Berkshire-Hathaway and excessive premium growth. Stability strengths include good operational trends and excellent risk diversification. Good overall profitability index (5.4) despite operating losses during the first nine months of 2014. Return on equity has been low, averaging 4.1% over the past five years.

Other Rating Factors: Strong long-term capitalization index (9.0) based on excellent current risk adjusted capital (severe and moderate loss scenarios), despite some fluctuation in capital levels. Ample reserve history (8.5) that helps to protect the company against sharp claims increases. Superior liquidity (9.1) with ample operational cash flow and liquid investments.

Principal Business: Auto liability (55%), ocean marine (13%), auto physical damage (11%), aircraft (10%), other liability (5%), inland marine (3%), and workers compensation (3%).

Principal Investments: Misc. investments (46%), investment grade bonds (37%), and cash (17%).

Investments in Affiliates: None

Group Affiliation: Berkshire-Hathaway

Licensed in: All states except PR

Commenced Business: December 1958

Address: 100 First Stamford Place, Stamford, CT 68131-3580

Phone: (402) 916-3000   **Domicile State:** CT   **NAIC Code:** 20052

Data Date	Rating	RACR #1	RACR #2	Loss Ratio %	Total Assets ($mil)	Capital ($mil)	Net Premium ($mil)	Net Income ($mil)
9-14	B	3.63	2.26	N/A	2,144.3	938.6	353.7	-14.8
9-13	B+	3.88	2.35	N/A	1,652.9	794.5	218.1	47.4
2013	B+	4.12	2.55	64.8	1,836.1	899.0	388.3	70.5
2012	B+	3.88	2.35	77.5	1,419.0	714.5	343.0	18.1
2011	B+	3.98	2.13	62.5	1,132.0	557.1	259.8	31.7
2010	A-	4.96	2.48	61.2	1,206.1	631.1	193.4	2.2
2009	A-	4.59	2.23	60.2	1,158.9	612.1	250.0	52.1

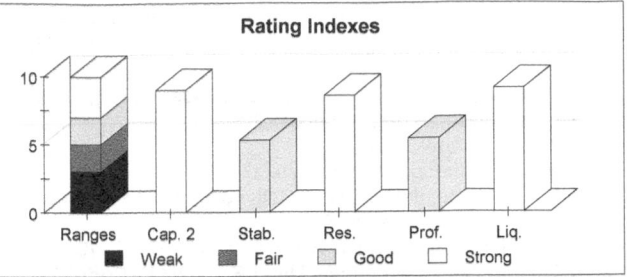

Rating Indexes

NATIONAL MORTGAGE INS CORP *
A-   **Excellent**

Major Rating Factors: Strong long-term capitalization index (10.0 on a scale of 0 to 10) based on excellent current risk adjusted capital (severe and moderate loss scenarios). Furthermore, this high level of risk adjusted capital has been consistently maintained in previous years. Superior liquidity (9.3) with ample operational cash flow and liquid investments.

Other Rating Factors: Good overall results on stability tests (5.8) despite excessive premium growth, negative cash flow from operations for 2013 and fair results on operational trends. Weak profitability index (0.2) with operating losses during 2010, 2011, 2012 and the first nine months of 2014.

Principal Business: Mortgage guaranty (100%).

Principal Investments: Investment grade bonds (71%), misc. investments (28%), and cash (1%).

Investments in Affiliates: None

Group Affiliation: NMI Holdings Inc

(No States listed)

Data Date	Rating	RACR #1	RACR #2	Loss Ratio %	Total Assets ($mil)	Capital ($mil)	Net Premium ($mil)	Net Income ($mil)
9-14	A-	4.30	4.25	N/A	264.6	234.3	7.3	-36.0
9-13	U	20.75	20.44	N/A	200.2	189.6	0.5	-23.4
2013	A-	4.93	4.85	0.0	194.2	180.3	3.3	-32.7
2012	U	23.24	23.15	0.0	210.0	210.0	0.0	0.0
2011	N/A	N/A	N/A	0.0	0.0	-1.4	0.0	-0.6
2010	N/A	N/A	N/A	0.0	0.2	-1.1	0.0	-2.4
2009	N/A	N/A	N/A	0.0	0.0	0.0	0.0	0.0

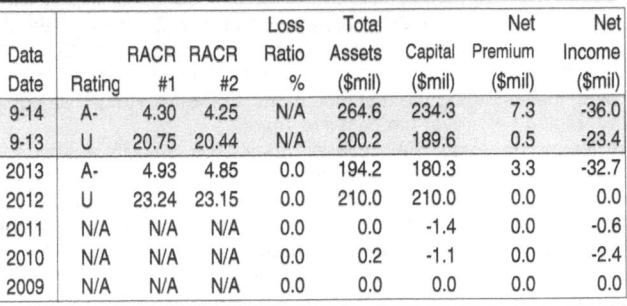

Risk-Adjusted Capital Ratio #2
(Severe Loss Scenario)

NATIONAL PUBLIC FINANCE GUAR CORP
B   **Good**

Major Rating Factors: Fair overall results on stability tests (4.0 on a scale of 0 to 10) including weak results on operational trends and negative cash flow from operations for 2013. The largest net exposure for one risk is excessive at 12.6% of capital. Strengths include potentially strong support from affiliation with MBIA Inc. Fair reserve development (3.4) as the level of reserves has at times been insufficient to cover claims. In 2009 and 2010 the two year reserve development was 96% and 119% deficient respectively.

Other Rating Factors: Fair profitability index (3.2) with operating losses during 2009. Return on equity has been fair, averaging 12.7% over the past five years. Strong long-term capitalization index (10.0) based on excellent current risk adjusted capital (severe and moderate loss scenarios). Moreover, capital levels have been consistent in recent years. Superior liquidity (10.0) with ample operational cash flow and liquid investments.

Principal Business: Financial guaranty (100%).

Principal Investments: Investment grade bonds (84%), non investment grade bonds (11%), and cash (5%).

Investments in Affiliates: None

Group Affiliation: MBIA Inc

Licensed in: All states, the District of Columbia and Puerto Rico

Commenced Business: March 1960

Address: 113 King St, Armonk, NY 10504-1610

Phone: (914) 273-4545   **Domicile State:** NY   **NAIC Code:** 23825

Data Date	Rating	RACR #1	RACR #2	Loss Ratio %	Total Assets ($mil)	Capital ($mil)	Net Premium ($mil)	Net Income ($mil)
9-14	B	12.58	5.35	N/A	5,398.3	2,311.4	231.7	169.6
9-13	B	21.60	11.28	N/A	5,695.7	2,162.3	276.4	153.1
2013	B	11.85	5.09	18.3	5,339.7	2,086.1	12.1	255.9
2012	B	12.49	6.44	5.5	5,726.2	1,998.5	-4.8	415.5
2011	B	8.76	4.49	1.3	6,656.1	1,423.7	-21.9	477.9
2010	B	7.02	3.97	14.5	7,290.0	907.7	109.6	408.8
2009	U	0.48	0.30	24.7	6,988.6	653.4	3,510.9	-299.1

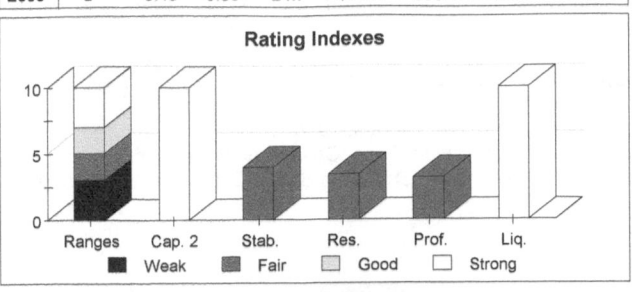

Rating Indexes

* Denotes a Weiss Ratings Recommended Company

NATIONAL UNION FIRE INS CO OF PITTSB | C | Fair

Major Rating Factors: Fair overall results on stability tests (4.2 on a scale of 0 to 10). The largest net exposure for one risk is excessive at 6.1% of capital. Strengths include potentially strong support from affiliation with American International Group. Fair reserve development (3.7) as the level of reserves has at times been insufficient to cover claims. In 2011 and 2010 the two year reserve development was 16% and 23% deficient respectively.

Other Rating Factors: Weak profitability index (1.9) with operating losses during 2010. Return on equity has been fair, averaging 27.9% over the past five years. Good liquidity (6.6) with sufficient resources (cash flows and marketable investments) to handle a spike in claims. Strong long-term capitalization index (7.6) based on excellent current risk adjusted capital (severe and moderate loss scenarios), despite some fluctuation in capital levels.

Principal Business: Other liability (35%), group accident & health (18%), ocean marine (13%), workers compensation (6%), auto liability (6%), commercial multiple peril (5%), and other lines (18%).

Principal Investments: Investment grade bonds (63%), misc. investments (35%), and non investment grade bonds (2%).

Investments in Affiliates: 1%

Group Affiliation: American International Group

Licensed in: All states, the District of Columbia and Puerto Rico

Commenced Business: March 1901

Address: 3595 Interstate Dr Suite 103, Harrisburg, PA 17110

Phone: (212) 458-7000 **Domicile State:** PA **NAIC Code:** 19445

Data Date	Rating	RACR #1	RACR #2	Loss Ratio %	Total Assets ($mil)	Capital ($mil)	Net Premium ($mil)	Net Income ($mil)
9-14	C	2.09	1.40	N/A	26,204.5	6,495.4	4,165.8	548.3
9-13	C	0.61	0.56	N/A	23,835.6	5,757.4	3,666.9	8,005.0
2013	C	2.03	1.38	76.7	24,709.6	5,836.5	5,422.5	8,102.0
2012	B-	1.60	1.46	87.1	32,282.9	14,398.9	4,676.2	1,039.0
2011	B-	1.74	1.55	84.1	30,962.5	12,774.8	4,861.3	604.4
2010	B	1.79	1.48	108.9	32,790.5	12,913.5	4,821.5	-676.9
2009	B	1.71	1.40	91.1	32,459.0	12,829.0	5,820.6	861.9

Rating Indexes

(Ranges, Cap. 2, Stab., Res., Prof., Liq.)
Weak · Fair · Good · Strong

NATIONWIDE INDEMNITY CO | B- | Good

Major Rating Factors: Fair reserve development (3.1 on a scale of 0 to 10) as reserves have generally been sufficient to cover claims. In 2013, the two year reserve development was 24% deficient. Fair profitability index (3.6) with operating losses during the first nine months of 2014. Return on equity has been fair, averaging 5.9% over the past five years.

Other Rating Factors: Fair overall results on stability tests (4.9) including negative cash flow from operations for 2013 and fair results on operational trends. Good long-term capitalization index (6.7) based on good current risk adjusted capital (severe loss scenario), although results have slipped from the excellent range over the last two years. Superior liquidity (9.2) with ample operational cash flow and liquid investments.

Principal Business: (This company is a reinsurer.)

Principal Investments: Investment grade bonds (94%), misc. investments (4%), and non investment grade bonds (2%).

Investments in Affiliates: None

Group Affiliation: Nationwide Corp

Licensed in: IL, IA, NY, OH, WI

Commenced Business: April 1994

Address: One Nationwide Plaza, Columbus, OH 43216

Phone: (614) 249-7111 **Domicile State:** OH **NAIC Code:** 10070

Data Date	Rating	RACR #1	RACR #2	Loss Ratio %	Total Assets ($mil)	Capital ($mil)	Net Premium ($mil)	Net Income ($mil)
9-14	B-	2.11	0.85	N/A	3,181.4	1,025.3	-0.8	-32.8
9-13	B-	2.58	0.99	N/A	3,362.9	1,110.6	-0.1	-30.1
2013	B-	2.21	0.89	N/A	3,251.9	1,069.4	0.2	-8.5
2012	B-	2.66	1.02	N/A	3,357.2	1,120.6	1.4	65.6
2011	C+	2.27	0.93	440.1	3,482.3	1,123.6	1.0	101.0
2010	C+	1.69	0.86	N/A	3,622.1	1,064.5	0.9	57.6
2009	C+	0.67	0.41	195.3	3,624.5	985.1	4.5	171.0

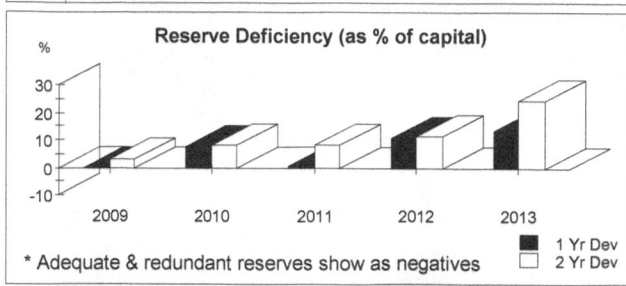

Reserve Deficiency (as % of capital)

(2009, 2010, 2011, 2012, 2013)
1 Yr Dev · 2 Yr Dev

* Adequate & redundant reserves show as negatives

NATIONWIDE INS CO OF FLORIDA | C+ | Fair

Major Rating Factors: Fair reserve development (4.6 on a scale of 0 to 10) as reserves have generally been sufficient to cover claims. Fair profitability index (4.2) with operating losses during 2010. Return on equity has been low, averaging 2.5% over the past five years.

Other Rating Factors: Fair overall results on stability tests (3.6). The largest net exposure for one risk is excessive at 8.5% of capital. Good liquidity (6.9) with sufficient resources (cash flows and marketable investments) to handle a spike in claims. Strong long-term capitalization index (10.0) based on excellent current risk adjusted capital (severe and moderate loss scenarios), despite some fluctuation in capital levels.

Principal Business: Homeowners multiple peril (98%) and inland marine (2%).

Principal Investments: Investment grade bonds (92%) and misc. investments (8%).

Investments in Affiliates: None

Group Affiliation: Nationwide Corp

Licensed in: FL, OH

Commenced Business: August 1998

Address: One Nationwide Plaza, Columbus, OH 43216

Phone: (614) 249-7111 **Domicile State:** OH **NAIC Code:** 10948

Data Date	Rating	RACR #1	RACR #2	Loss Ratio %	Total Assets ($mil)	Capital ($mil)	Net Premium ($mil)	Net Income ($mil)
9-14	C+	5.93	4.30	N/A	338.6	282.9	28.7	8.1
9-13	C+	5.73	4.13	N/A	327.1	268.4	25.9	7.8
2013	C+	6.12	4.44	52.1	325.4	272.9	33.8	12.4
2012	C+	5.32	3.82	80.8	330.1	257.8	33.6	5.3
2011	B-	4.41	3.17	88.9	368.1	278.2	32.4	5.1
2010	B-	2.28	1.65	104.5	393.5	267.9	66.2	-4.6
2009	C+	1.53	1.11	71.3	438.7	276.2	110.2	12.6

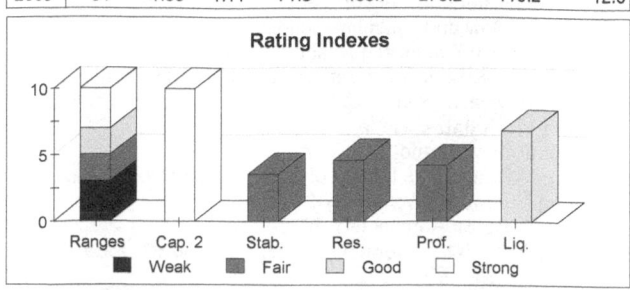

Rating Indexes

(Ranges, Cap. 2, Stab., Res., Prof., Liq.)
Weak · Fair · Good · Strong

NATIONWIDE MUTUAL FIRE INS CO *   B+   Good

Major Rating Factors: Good overall results on stability tests (6.4 on a scale of 0 to 10). Affiliation with Nationwide Corp is a strength. Good overall profitability index (6.4) with small operating losses during 2011.

Other Rating Factors: Good liquidity (6.6) with sufficient resources (cash flows and marketable investments) to handle a spike in claims. Strong long-term capitalization index (10.0) based on excellent current risk adjusted capital (severe and moderate loss scenarios). Moreover, capital levels have been consistent in recent years. Ample reserve history (7.7) that can protect against increases in claims costs.

Principal Business: Homeowners multiple peril (51%), auto liability (14%), allied lines (10%), auto physical damage (9%), commercial multiple peril (7%), other liability (3%), and other lines (6%).

Principal Investments: Investment grade bonds (76%), misc. investments (18%), and non investment grade bonds (6%).

Investments in Affiliates: 4%

Group Affiliation: Nationwide Corp

Licensed in: All states except PR

Commenced Business: April 1934

Address: One Nationwide Plaza, Columbus, OH 43216

Phone: (614) 249-7111   **Domicile State:** OH   **NAIC Code:** 23779

Data Date	Rating	RACR #1	RACR #2	Loss Ratio %	Total Assets ($mil)	Capital ($mil)	Net Premium ($mil)	Net Income ($mil)
9-14	B+	4.89	3.42	N/A	5,632.7	2,524.9	1,577.8	40.4
9-13	B+	5.06	3.56	N/A	5,356.2	2,405.2	1,488.9	52.1
2013	B+	4.96	3.51	66.2	5,410.1	2,445.1	2,162.4	73.7
2012	B+	5.59	4.02	71.9	4,729.7	2,317.4	1,691.9	33.9
2011	B+	5.53	3.97	77.0	4,553.4	2,243.2	1,617.1	-8.6
2010	B+	5.42	3.99	67.8	4,356.9	2,226.0	1,614.7	125.8
2009	B+	5.07	3.76	71.4	4,231.2	2,091.6	1,648.9	69.4

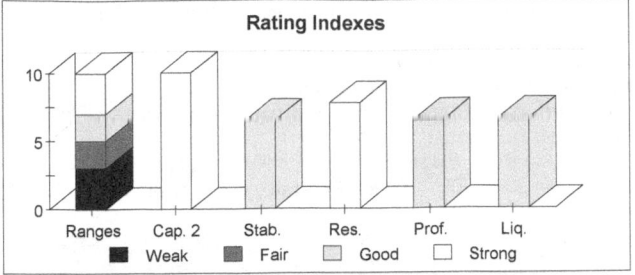

Rating Indexes

NATIONWIDE MUTUAL INS CO   B   Good

Major Rating Factors: History of adequate reserve strength (5.6 on a scale of 0 to 10) as reserves have been consistently at an acceptable level. Good overall profitability index (5.7) despite operating losses during 2011.

Other Rating Factors: Good liquidity (5.2) with sufficient resources (cash flows and marketable investments) to handle a spike in claims. Good overall results on stability tests (6.1). Affiliation with Nationwide Corp is a strength. Strong long-term capitalization index (7.5) based on excellent current risk adjusted capital (severe and moderate loss scenarios). Moreover, capital levels have been consistent in recent years.

Principal Business: Auto liability (40%), auto physical damage (25%), commercial multiple peril (9%), homeowners multiple peril (7%), farmowners multiple peril (5%), other liability (5%), and other lines (9%).

Principal Investments: Misc. investments (55%), investment grade bonds (40%), non investment grade bonds (3%), and real estate (3%).

Investments in Affiliates: 30%

Group Affiliation: Nationwide Corp

Licensed in: All states except PR

Commenced Business: April 1926

Address: One Nationwide Plaza, Columbus, OH 43216

Phone: (614) 249-7111   **Domicile State:** OH   **NAIC Code:** 23787

Data Date	Rating	RACR #1	RACR #2	Loss Ratio %	Total Assets ($mil)	Capital ($mil)	Net Premium ($mil)	Net Income ($mil)
9-14	B	1.54	1.34	N/A	33,915.9	12,380.0	10,913.1	577.7
9-13	B	1.44	1.26	N/A	32,483.4	11,691.9	10,298.4	317.6
2013	B	1.49	1.31	66.2	32,675.8	11,792.5	14,630.9	499.8
2012	B	1.44	1.28	71.9	29,551.8	11,344.0	12,492.6	21.7
2011	B	1.48	1.31	77.2	29,149.9	11,294.7	12,326.8	-894.5
2010	B	1.52	1.35	67.8	28,204.6	10,586.1	11,960.2	424.8
2009	B	1.49	1.30	71.4	27,262.0	9,475.0	12,213.7	55.2

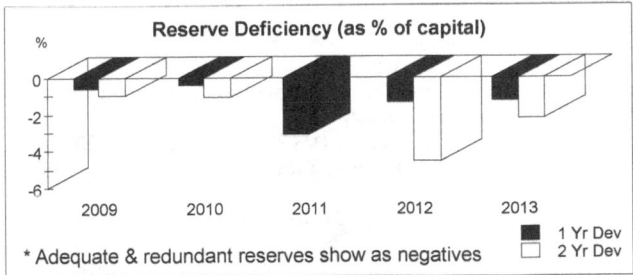

Reserve Deficiency (as % of capital)

* Adequate & redundant reserves show as negatives

NAU COUNTRY INS CO   C   Fair

Major Rating Factors: Fair reserve development (3.6 on a scale of 0 to 10) as reserves have generally been sufficient to cover claims. In 2013, the two year reserve development was 17% deficient. Fair overall results on stability tests (3.4) including fair financial strength of affiliated QBE Ins Group Ltd, weak results on operational trends and negative cash flow from operations for 2013.

Other Rating Factors: Weak profitability index (2.9) with operating losses during 2012 and the first nine months of 2014. Return on equity has been fair, averaging 9.7% over the past five years. Strong long-term capitalization index (7.0) based on excellent current risk adjusted capital (severe and moderate loss scenarios), despite some fluctuation in capital levels. Excellent liquidity (7.5) with ample operational cash flow and liquid investments.

Principal Business: Allied lines (100%).

Principal Investments: Investment grade bonds (235%) and cash (9%).

Investments in Affiliates: None

Group Affiliation: QBE Ins Group Ltd

Licensed in: All states except AK, DC, HI, ME, NY, RI, PR

Commenced Business: May 1919

Address: 7333 Sunwood Dr, Ramsey, MN 55303-5119

Phone: (763) 427-3770   **Domicile State:** MN   **NAIC Code:** 25240

Data Date	Rating	RACR #1	RACR #2	Loss Ratio %	Total Assets ($mil)	Capital ($mil)	Net Premium ($mil)	Net Income ($mil)
9-14	C	1.51	1.02	N/A	1,195.0	271.4	316.8	-3.3
9-13	C	1.43	1.00	N/A	1,191.6	341.6	349.3	0.2
2013	C	1.53	1.04	75.2	1,300.1	274.8	444.3	-29.0
2012	C	1.28	0.90	73.5	1,458.6	335.4	693.9	-23.7
2011	C-	2.66	1.61	90.2	1,346.0	379.8	811.2	45.8
2010	C	8.33	4.53	65.1	492.7	293.3	368.6	88.0
2009	C-	4.75	2.82	64.9	582.0	295.1	353.3	95.9

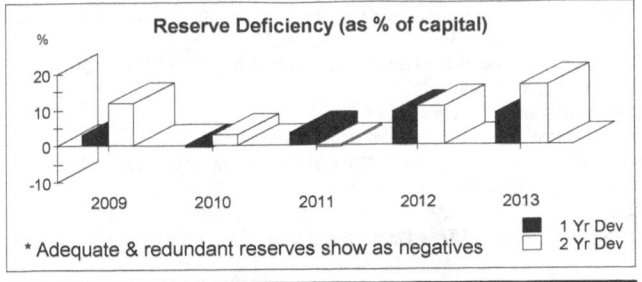

Reserve Deficiency (as % of capital)

* Adequate & redundant reserves show as negatives

NAVIGATORS INS CO

B   **Good**

Major Rating Factors: Good overall results on stability tests (5.6 on a scale of 0 to 10) despite potential drain of affiliation with Navigators Group Inc. The largest net exposure for one risk is acceptable at 2.3% of capital. History of adequate reserve strength (6.4) as reserves have been consistently at an acceptable level.
Other Rating Factors: Good overall profitability index (6.9). Fair expense controls. Return on equity has been fair, averaging 6.5% over the past five years. Good liquidity (6.9) with sufficient resources (cash flows and marketable investments) to handle a spike in claims. Strong long-term capitalization index (8.1) based on excellent current risk adjusted capital (severe and moderate loss scenarios), despite some fluctuation in capital levels.
Principal Business: Other liability (61%), ocean marine (33%), inland marine (3%), auto physical damage (1%), and international (1%).
Principal Investments: Investment grade bonds (75%), misc. investments (20%), and cash (5%).
Investments in Affiliates: 7%
Group Affiliation: Navigators Group Inc
Licensed in: All states, the District of Columbia and Puerto Rico
Commenced Business: March 1983
Address: One Penn Plaza, 55th Floor, New York, NY 10119
Phone: (914) 934-8999   **Domicile State:** NY   **NAIC Code:** 42307

Data Date	Rating	RACR #1	RACR #2	Loss Ratio %	Total Assets ($mil)	Capital ($mil)	Net Premium ($mil)	Net Income ($mil)
9-14	B	2.34	1.75	N/A	2,434.8	874.3	526.3	54.4
9-13	B	2.43	1.82	N/A	2,179.1	729.0	473.8	37.3
2013	B	2.26	1.70	65.0	2,215.0	804.1	680.0	56.6
2012	B	2.48	1.88	73.0	2,102.4	682.9	623.0	25.2
2011	B	2.51	1.96	72.3	1,903.9	662.2	542.4	13.0
2010	B	2.76	2.17	63.8	1,823.7	686.9	429.4	81.1
2009	B	2.57	1.98	63.6	1,789.1	645.8	477.7	42.9

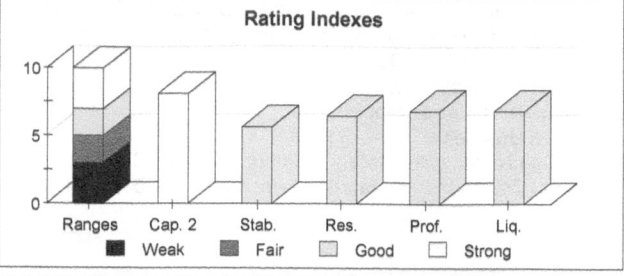

Rating Indexes

NCMIC INS CO

B   **Good**

Major Rating Factors: Good overall results on stability tests (5.5 on a scale of 0 to 10) despite potential drain of affiliation with NCMIC Group. Strong long-term capitalization index (8.3) based on excellent current risk adjusted capital (severe and moderate loss scenarios). Moreover, capital levels have been consistent in recent years.
Other Rating Factors: Ample reserve history (9.7) that helps to protect the company against sharp claims increases. Excellent profitability (8.9) with operating gains in each of the last five years. Return on equity has been good over the last five years, averaging 10.3%. Excellent liquidity (7.8) with ample operational cash flow and liquid investments.
Principal Business: Medical malpractice (100%).
Principal Investments: Investment grade bonds (71%), misc. investments (24%), and cash (5%).
Investments in Affiliates: 2%
Group Affiliation: NCMIC Group
Licensed in: All states, the District of Columbia and Puerto Rico
Commenced Business: January 1946
Address: 1452 29th St Ste 102, W Des Moines, IA 50266-1307
Phone: (515) 313-4500   **Domicile State:** IA   **NAIC Code:** 15865

Data Date	Rating	RACR #1	RACR #2	Loss Ratio %	Total Assets ($mil)	Capital ($mil)	Net Premium ($mil)	Net Income ($mil)
9-14	B	2.58	1.94	N/A	645.6	249.4	84.0	10.5
9-13	B	2.46	1.84	N/A	592.1	234.4	74.5	15.1
2013	B	2.68	2.02	50.2	593.9	241.5	102.2	27.2
2012	B	2.40	1.80	43.4	583.1	218.2	100.7	29.5
2011	B	2.11	1.56	55.0	570.5	197.9	96.0	17.9
2010	B	1.92	1.39	47.9	539.1	182.3	91.3	21.1
2009	B-	1.74	1.26	52.7	494.4	162.5	86.7	16.0

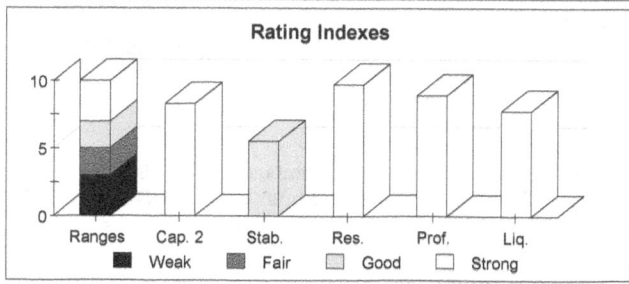

Rating Indexes

NEW HAMPSHIRE INS CO

D+   **Weak**

Major Rating Factors: Weak profitability index (1.9 on a scale of 0 to 10) with operating losses during 2009 and 2010. Return on equity has been fair, averaging 30.0% over the past five years. Fair long-term capitalization index (3.9) based on weak current risk adjusted capital (severe and moderate loss scenarios), although results have slipped from the excellent range during the last year.
Other Rating Factors: Fair reserve development (3.3) as the level of reserves has at times been insufficient to cover claims. In 2011 and 2010 the two year reserve development was 19% and 22% deficient respectively. Weak overall results on stability tests (2.4). Good liquidity (6.6) with sufficient resources (cash flows and marketable investments) to handle a spike in claims.
Principal Business: Workers compensation (53%), inland marine (17%), other liability (8%), commercial multiple peril (7%), auto liability (6%), ocean marine (2%), and other lines (9%).
Principal Investments: Investment grade bonds (830%), non investment grade bonds (42%), and cash (1%).
Investments in Affiliates: 8%
Group Affiliation: American International Group
Licensed in: All states, the District of Columbia and Puerto Rico
Commenced Business: April 1870
Address: 3595 Interstate Dr Suite 103, Harrisburg, PA 17110
Phone: (212) 770-7000   **Domicile State:** PA   **NAIC Code:** 23841

Data Date	Rating	RACR #1	RACR #2	Loss Ratio %	Total Assets ($mil)	Capital ($mil)	Net Premium ($mil)	Net Income ($mil)
9-14	D+	0.49	0.46	N/A	272.1	138.9	0.0	223.4
9-13	C	1.57	1.13	N/A	3,319.7	762.8	482.5	111.8
2013	C	1.50	1.07	76.6	3,271.4	731.4	713.5	129.3
2012	C	1.94	1.41	87.1	3,209.0	922.7	615.3	12.3
2011	C	1.74	1.26	83.9	3,162.4	808.9	626.7	61.6
2010	C	1.99	1.24	108.8	3,534.4	1,015.3	619.6	-130.8
2009	C+	1.65	1.26	91.1	4,014.1	1,409.4	755.7	-27.5

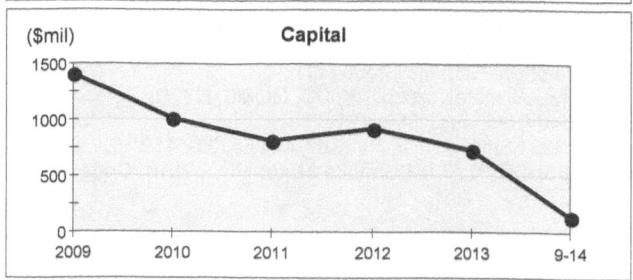

Capital

NEW JERSEY MANUFACTURERS INS CO   B-   Good

Major Rating Factors: Fair profitability index (3.9 on a scale of 0 to 10) with operating losses during 2011 and 2012. Return on equity has been low, averaging 2.4% over the past five years. History of adequate reserve strength (5.9) as reserves have been consistently at an acceptable level.

Other Rating Factors: Good liquidity (6.8) with sufficient resources (cash flows and marketable investments) to handle a spike in claims. Good overall results on stability tests (5.3) despite fair financial strength of affiliated NJ Manufacturers. Strong long-term capitalization index (8.3) based on excellent current risk adjusted capital (severe and moderate loss scenarios), despite some fluctuation in capital levels.

Principal Business: Auto liability (41%), workers compensation (28%), auto physical damage (19%), and homeowners multiple peril (12%).

Principal Investments: Investment grade bonds (76%), misc. investments (22%), and real estate (2%).

Investments in Affiliates: 12%

Group Affiliation: NJ Manufacturers

Licensed in: CT, DE, ME, NJ, NY, PA, RI

Commenced Business: July 1913

Address: 301 Sullivan Way, West Trenton, NJ 08628

Phone: (609) 883-1300   **Domicile State:** NJ   **NAIC Code:** 12122

Data Date	Rating	RACR #1	RACR #2	Loss Ratio %	Total Assets ($mil)	Capital ($mil)	Net Premium ($mil)	Net Income ($mil)
9-14	B-	2.53	1.89	N/A	6,565.0	2,456.2	1,160.0	135.5
9-13	C+	2.43	1.81	N/A	6,193.7	2,240.7	1,142.8	135.7
2013	B-	2.38	1.80	83.1	6,282.4	2,273.9	1,597.6	123.6
2012	C+	2.25	1.69	107.5	5,945.3	2,057.3	1,459.1	-289.4
2011	B	2.70	2.06	95.8	5,892.8	2,253.7	1,365.5	-134.0
2010	B	2.99	2.30	85.4	5,875.9	2,382.5	1,312.6	7.1
2009	B	3.12	2.39	96.1	5,715.6	2,291.3	1,265.9	515.4

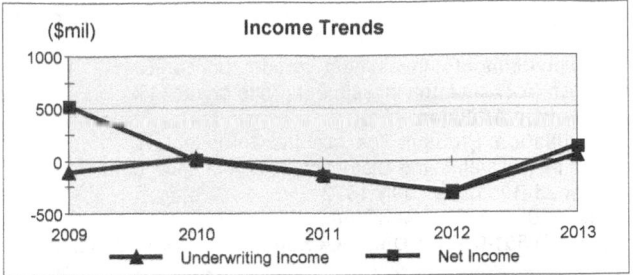

Income Trends

NEW JERSEY RE-INS CO   B   Good

Major Rating Factors: Good overall results on stability tests (5.7 on a scale of 0 to 10) despite potential drain of affiliation with NJ Manufacturers. Stability strengths include good operational trends and excellent risk diversification. History of adequate reserve strength (6.9) as reserves have been consistently at an acceptable level.

Other Rating Factors: Strong long-term capitalization index (8.0) based on excellent current risk adjusted capital (severe and moderate loss scenarios). Moreover, capital levels have been consistent in recent years. Excellent profitability (8.5) with operating gains in each of the last five years. Return on equity has been excellent over the last five years averaging 17.3%. Excellent liquidity (8.4) with ample operational cash flow and liquid investments.

Principal Business: Auto liability (32%), allied lines (24%), other liability (17%), workers compensation (11%), auto physical damage (11%), homeowners multiple peril (3%), and fire (2%).

Principal Investments: Investment grade bonds (98%), misc. investments (1%), and cash (1%).

Investments in Affiliates: None

Group Affiliation: NJ Manufacturers

Licensed in: All states except AR, CA, CO, DC, ID, KS, LA, NM, UT, WY, PR

Commenced Business: January 1978

Address: 301 Sullivan Way, West Trenton, NJ 08628

Phone: (609) 883-1300   **Domicile State:** NJ   **NAIC Code:** 35432

Data Date	Rating	RACR #1	RACR #2	Loss Ratio %	Total Assets ($mil)	Capital ($mil)	Net Premium ($mil)	Net Income ($mil)
9-14	B	3.15	1.89	N/A	559.6	376.2	25.7	7.4
9-13	B	2.92	1.75	N/A	554.1	359.2	29.2	19.4
2013	B	2.99	1.77	47.4	553.6	362.3	37.1	21.1
2012	B	2.52	1.49	92.5	546.8	330.4	41.2	12.0
2011	B-	11.40	6.81	88.5	550.3	313.0	44.4	14.2
2010	C+	10.57	6.34	63.9	539.5	298.7	50.8	26.3
2009	C+	8.14	4.95	N/A	569.7	273.9	56.8	204.2

NJ Manufacturers Composite Group Rating: B- Largest Group Members	Assets ($mil)	Rating
NEW JERSEY MANUFACTURERS INS CO	6282	B-
NEW JERSEY RE-INS CO	554	B
NEW JERSEY CASUALTY INS CO	481	C
NEW JERSEY INDEMNITY INS CO	83	C+

NEW YORK CENTRAL MUTUAL FIRE INS CO   B-   Good

Major Rating Factors: Fair overall results on stability tests (4.7 on a scale of 0 to 10) including potential drain of affiliation with Central Services Group. Good overall profitability index (5.9) despite operating losses during 2011 and the first nine months of 2014.

Other Rating Factors: Good liquidity (6.6) with sufficient resources (cash flows and marketable investments) to handle a spike in claims. Strong long-term capitalization index (9.6) based on excellent current risk adjusted capital (severe and moderate loss scenarios), despite some fluctuation in capital levels. Ample reserve history (7.8) that can protect against increases in claims costs.

Principal Business: Homeowners multiple peril (37%), auto liability (37%), auto physical damage (20%), commercial multiple peril (2%), fire (2%), other liability (1%), and allied lines (1%).

Principal Investments: Investment grade bonds (83%), misc. investments (16%), and real estate (1%).

Investments in Affiliates: 4%

Group Affiliation: Central Services Group

Licensed in: NY

Commenced Business: April 1899

Address: 1899 Central Plaza E, Edmeston, NY 13335

Phone: (607) 965-8321   **Domicile State:** NY   **NAIC Code:** 14834

Data Date	Rating	RACR #1	RACR #2	Loss Ratio %	Total Assets ($mil)	Capital ($mil)	Net Premium ($mil)	Net Income ($mil)
9-14	B-	3.88	2.91	N/A	1,014.9	462.4	315.0	-4.2
9-13	B-	3.71	2.81	N/A	1,010.5	440.3	314.1	11.7
2013	B-	3.82	2.93	67.9	1,010.8	466.4	421.8	30.7
2012	B-	3.60	2.83	70.7	980.7	423.9	414.7	18.6
2011	B-	3.71	2.86	82.8	960.7	407.0	418.1	-6.6
2010	B-	3.74	2.85	68.7	982.3	429.1	433.4	33.5
2009	B-	3.54	2.71	67.7	956.4	397.0	425.9	21.1

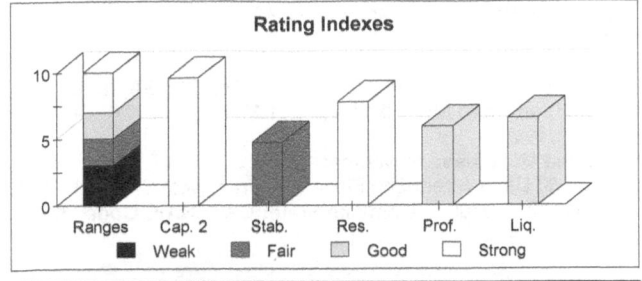

Rating Indexes

NEW YORK MARINE & GENERAL INS CO | B- | Good

Major Rating Factors: Fair overall results on stability tests (4.7 on a scale of 0 to 10) including potential drain of affiliation with ProSight Specialty Ins Group Inc, excessive premium growth and fair results on operational trends. The largest net exposure for one risk is conservative at 1.6% of capital. Fair profitability index (4.2) with operating losses during 2011. Return on equity has been low, averaging 2.3% over the past five years.

Other Rating Factors: Good long-term capitalization index (6.7) based on good current risk adjusted capital (moderate loss scenario). Over the last several years, capital levels have remained relatively consistent. Ample reserve history (9.2) that helps to protect the company against sharp claims increases. Excellent liquidity (7.1) with ample operational cash flow and liquid investments.

Principal Business: Auto liability (25%), other liability (18%), workers compensation (16%), ocean marine (15%), fire (4%), inland marine (3%), and other lines (21%).

Principal Investments: Investment grade bonds (64%), misc. investments (30%), cash (5%), and non investment grade bonds (1%).

Investments in Affiliates: 15%

Group Affiliation: ProSight Specialty Ins Group Inc

Licensed in: All states, the District of Columbia and Puerto Rico

Commenced Business: July 1972

Address: 919 Third Ave, New York, NY 10022

Phone: (212) 551-0600 **Domicile State:** NY **NAIC Code:** 16608

Data Date	Rating	RACR #1	RACR #2	Loss Ratio %	Total Assets ($mil)	Capital ($mil)	Net Premium ($mil)	Net Income ($mil)
9-14	B-	1.38	0.99	N/A	1,046.5	303.4	232.5	-0.1
9-13	B-	1.35	0.99	N/A	874.8	227.6	183.6	-3.4
2013	B-	1.21	0.88	60.6	891.7	240.1	270.9	1.8
2012	B	1.55	1.16	60.0	738.9	230.6	197.9	8.0
2011	B	1.82	1.50	65.8	666.1	216.0	128.9	-20.9
2010	B	1.82	1.49	83.8	622.2	185.5	138.3	13.9
2009	B	2.22	1.79	47.1	606.0	202.2	122.1	23.2

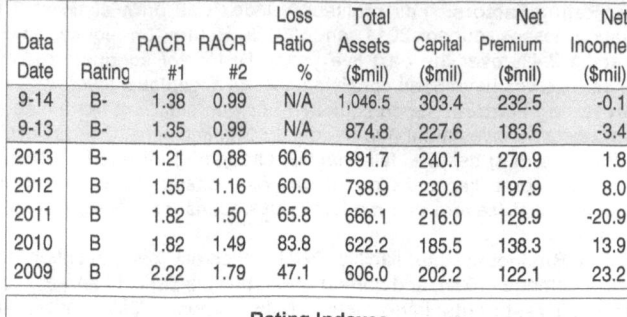

Rating Indexes

NGM INS CO | B- | Good

Major Rating Factors: Fair overall results on stability tests (4.6 on a scale of 0 to 10) including potential drain of affiliation with Main Street America Group Inc. Good overall profitability index (6.7). Fair expense controls. Return on equity has been fair, averaging 7.1% over the past five years.

Other Rating Factors: Good liquidity (6.2) with sufficient resources (cash flows and marketable investments) to handle a spike in claims. Strong long-term capitalization index (8.7) based on excellent current risk adjusted capital (severe and moderate loss scenarios). Moreover, capital levels have been consistent in recent years. Ample reserve history (8.3) that helps to protect the company against sharp claims increases.

Principal Business: Auto liability (34%), homeowners multiple peril (21%), auto physical damage (14%), workers compensation (13%), surety (6%), commercial multiple peril (4%), and other lines (8%).

Principal Investments: Investment grade bonds (72%), misc. investments (24%), non investment grade bonds (3%), and cash (1%).

Investments in Affiliates: 10%

Group Affiliation: Main Street America Group Inc

Licensed in: All states except AK, CA, HI, LA, MN, MS, PR

Commenced Business: July 1923

Address: 4601 Touchton Rd E Suite 3400, Jacksonville, FL 32245

Phone: (904) 380-7282 **Domicile State:** FL **NAIC Code:** 14788

Data Date	Rating	RACR #1	RACR #2	Loss Ratio %	Total Assets ($mil)	Capital ($mil)	Net Premium ($mil)	Net Income ($mil)
9-14	B-	3.07	2.32	N/A	2,281.1	961.2	736.7	34.4
9-13	B-	2.56	1.84	N/A	2,249.4	883.1	757.7	26.4
2013	B-	2.98	2.26	68.2	2,265.3	936.9	1,018.2	53.7
2012	B-	2.56	1.87	69.2	2,120.1	838.4	981.6	62.1
2011	B-	2.54	1.84	74.5	2,018.2	770.5	889.4	26.5
2010	B-	2.20	1.55	65.9	2,010.4	762.0	903.3	67.9
2009	B-	2.20	1.59	64.2	1,894.0	692.0	815.5	80.4

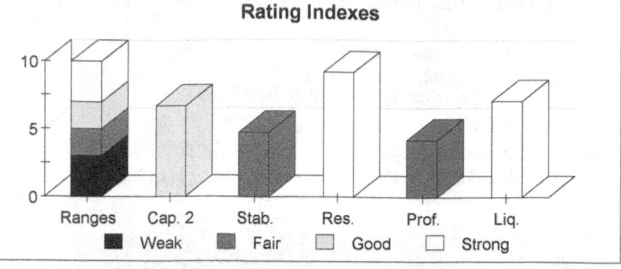

Rating Indexes

NORCAL MUTUAL INS CO | B- | Good

Major Rating Factors: Fair overall results on stability tests (4.6 on a scale of 0 to 10) including potential drain of affiliation with NORCAL Mutual and negative cash flow from operations for 2013. Good overall profitability index (6.9). Good expense controls.

Other Rating Factors: Good liquidity (6.9) with sufficient resources (cash flows and marketable investments) to handle a spike in claims. Strong long-term capitalization index (7.8) based on excellent current risk adjusted capital (severe and moderate loss scenarios), despite some fluctuation in capital levels. Ample reserve history (9.4) that helps to protect the company against sharp claims increases.

Principal Business: Medical malpractice (100%).

Principal Investments: Investment grade bonds (49%), misc. investments (47%), and non investment grade bonds (4%).

Investments in Affiliates: 23%

Group Affiliation: NORCAL Mutual

Licensed in: AL, AK, AZ, AR, CA, CT, DC, DE, FL, GA, IL, IN, IA, KS, KY, LA, MD, MA, MI, MN, MS, MO, NE, NV, NJ, NM, NC, OH, OK, OR, PA, RI, SC, TX, UT, VA, WA, WV

Commenced Business: November 1975

Address: 560 Davis Street 2nd Floor, San Francisco, CA 94111-1902

Phone: (415) 397-9700 **Domicile State:** CA **NAIC Code:** 33200

Data Date	Rating	RACR #1	RACR #2	Loss Ratio %	Total Assets ($mil)	Capital ($mil)	Net Premium ($mil)	Net Income ($mil)
9-14	B-	1.90	1.60	N/A	1,359.9	638.2	148.5	5.8
9-13	B-	1.84	1.54	N/A	1,348.8	621.6	162.8	25.0
2013	B-	1.86	1.56	79.3	1,323.3	634.2	212.3	31.6
2012	B-	1.75	1.46	71.9	1,323.6	607.6	209.6	29.8
2011	B-	1.74	1.45	76.8	1,304.6	579.5	231.9	32.7
2010	B-	2.13	1.71	65.3	1,225.5	582.4	170.6	49.5
2009	B-	1.92	1.55	57.1	1,163.7	506.3	177.7	42.9

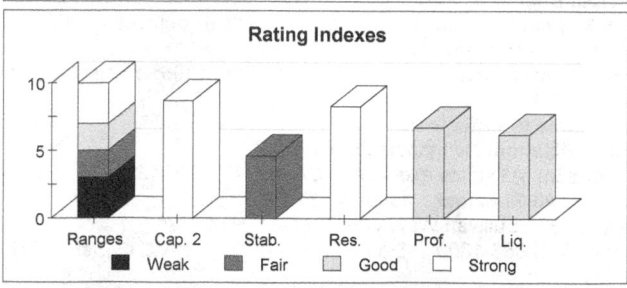

Rating Indexes

NORTH AMERICAN SPECIALTY INS CO   C   Fair

Major Rating Factors: Fair overall results on stability tests (3.7 on a scale of 0 to 10) including potential drain of affiliation with Swiss Reinsurance. The largest net exposure for one risk is acceptable at 2.2% of capital. Strong long-term capitalization index (10.0) based on excellent current risk adjusted capital (severe and moderate loss scenarios). Moreover, capital levels have been consistent in recent years.

Other Rating Factors: Ample reserve history (8.3) that helps to protect the company against sharp claims increases. Excellent profitability (7.8) with operating gains in each of the last five years. Superior liquidity (10.0) with ample operational cash flow and liquid investments.

Principal Business: Surety (32%), other liability (31%), inland marine (21%), aircraft (6%), ocean marine (5%), allied lines (2%), and other lines (3%).

Principal Investments: Investment grade bonds (77%), misc. investments (19%), cash (2%), and non investment grade bonds (2%).

Investments in Affiliates: 16%

Group Affiliation: Swiss Reinsurance

Licensed in: All states, the District of Columbia and Puerto Rico

Commenced Business: October 1974

Address: 650 Elm St, Manchester, NH 03101-2524

Phone: (603) 644-6600   **Domicile State:** NH   **NAIC Code:** 29874

Data Date	Rating	RACR #1	RACR #2	Loss Ratio %	Total Assets ($mil)	Capital ($mil)	Net Premium ($mil)	Net Income ($mil)
9-14	C	5.30	4.78	N/A	544.5	379.2	9.9	4.4
9-13	C	5.57	5.14	N/A	504.5	371.3	8.6	5.6
2013	C	5.38	4.98	8.4	514.2	373.0	11.4	4.6
2012	C	5.50	5.09	N/A	503.5	363.7	10.4	12.5
2011	C	5.23	4.96	N/A	472.1	344.6	10.7	23.4
2010	C	5.08	4.56	91.6	473.0	316.7	13.1	0.7
2009	C	5.37	4.89	N/A	501.7	316.7	10.3	33.2

Swiss Reinsurance
Composite Group Rating: C+

Largest Group Members	Assets ($mil)	Rating
SWISS REINSURANCE AMERICA CORP	11400	D
SWISS RE LIFE HEALTH AMER INC	9995	C+
WESTPORT INS CORP	5454	C+
AURORA NATIONAL LIFE ASR CO	3144	B
NORTH AMERICAN SPECIALTY INS CO	514	C

NORTH CAROLINA FARM BU MUTUAL INS CO   B-   Good

Major Rating Factors: Fair profitability index (4.4 on a scale of 0 to 10) with operating losses during 2011. Fair overall results on stability tests (4.9) including fair financial strength of affiliated NC Farm Bureau Ins.

Other Rating Factors: Good liquidity (5.9) with sufficient resources (cash flows and marketable investments) to handle a spike in claims. Strong long-term capitalization index (9.2) based on excellent current risk adjusted capital (severe and moderate loss scenarios), despite some fluctuation in capital levels. Ample reserve history (8.3) that helps to protect the company against sharp claims increases.

Principal Business: Auto liability (32%), homeowners multiple peril (30%), auto physical damage (21%), allied lines (4%), farmowners multiple peril (3%), fire (2%), and other lines (8%).

Principal Investments: Investment grade bonds (82%) and misc. investments (19%).

Investments in Affiliates: 1%

Group Affiliation: NC Farm Bureau Ins

Licensed in: NC

Commenced Business: October 1953

Address: 5301 Glenwood Ave, Raleigh, NC 27612

Phone: (919) 782-1705   **Domicile State:** NC   **NAIC Code:** 14842

Data Date	Rating	RACR #1	RACR #2	Loss Ratio %	Total Assets ($mil)	Capital ($mil)	Net Premium ($mil)	Net Income ($mil)
9-14	B-	4.37	2.91	N/A	1,735.1	997.6	527.6	60.1
9-13	C+	4.06	2.70	N/A	1,635.6	890.0	535.0	44.0
2013	B-	3.87	2.60	68.5	1,664.7	933.1	737.3	86.8
2012	C+	3.82	2.56	76.0	1,568.5	836.0	701.8	33.1
2011	C	2.83	1.91	111.0	1,535.8	762.3	813.0	-235.0
2010	A-	7.11	5.07	72.0	1,679.5	995.3	701.2	39.9
2009	A	6.32	4.71	78.0	1,674.1	944.4	713.7	15.4

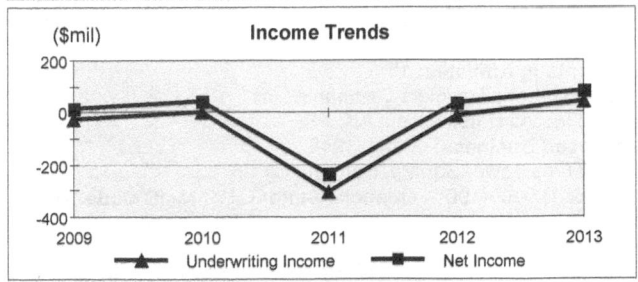

Income Trends ($mil) — Underwriting Income, Net Income (2009–2013)

NORTH RIVER INS CO   C-   Fair

Major Rating Factors: Fair profitability index (3.2 on a scale of 0 to 10) with operating losses during 2012. Return on equity has been fair, averaging 17.6% over the past five years. Fair overall results on stability tests (3.2) including weak financial strength of affiliated Fairfax Financial.

Other Rating Factors: Good overall long-term capitalization (6.0) based on good current risk adjusted capital (moderate loss scenario). However, capital levels have fluctuated during prior years. History of adequate reserve strength (5.7) as reserves have been consistently at an acceptable level. Excellent liquidity (7.7) with ample operational cash flow and liquid investments.

Principal Business: Other liability (53%), workers compensation (16%), auto liability (9%), products liability (9%), commercial multiple peril (8%), auto physical damage (3%), and surety (2%).

Principal Investments: Investment grade bonds (70%), misc. investments (27%), and non investment grade bonds (3%).

Investments in Affiliates: 21%

Group Affiliation: Fairfax Financial

Licensed in: All states except PR

Commenced Business: October 1972

Address: 305 Madison Avenue, Morristown, NJ 07960

Phone: (973) 490-6600   **Domicile State:** NJ   **NAIC Code:** 21105

Data Date	Rating	RACR #1	RACR #2	Loss Ratio %	Total Assets ($mil)	Capital ($mil)	Net Premium ($mil)	Net Income ($mil)
9-14	C-	1.11	0.87	N/A	946.2	270.9	212.2	6.7
9-13	C-	0.98	0.77	N/A	883.6	228.2	196.0	61.4
2013	C-	1.13	0.89	71.4	938.2	263.1	281.3	87.7
2012	C-	1.19	0.94	81.2	869.7	277.0	234.5	-17.2
2011	C-	1.52	1.13	81.0	816.8	282.3	201.8	68.3
2010	C-	1.74	1.38	79.5	880.5	399.9	133.9	114.1
2009	C	2.00	1.46	73.7	1,069.8	554.9	132.0	106.1

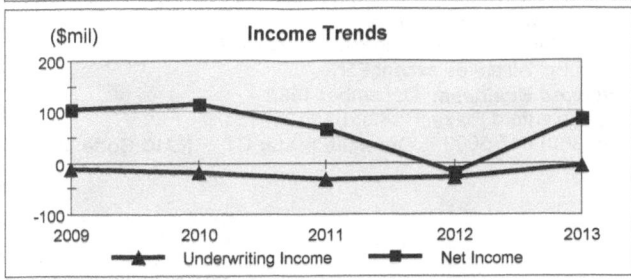

Income Trends ($mil) — Underwriting Income, Net Income (2009–2013)

NORTH STAR MUTUAL INS CO

B-   **Good**

Major Rating Factors: Fair overall results on stability tests (4.7 on a scale of 0 to 10) including potential drain of affiliation with North Star Companies. Good liquidity (6.7) with sufficient resources (cash flows and marketable investments) to handle a spike in claims.

Other Rating Factors: Strong long-term capitalization index (10.0) based on excellent current risk adjusted capital (severe and moderate loss scenarios). Moreover, capital levels have been consistent in recent years. Ample reserve history (7.5) that can protect against increases in claims costs. Excellent profitability (8.2) with operating gains in each of the last five years.

Principal Business: Homeowners multiple peril (24%), allied lines (24%), auto physical damage (13%), auto liability (13%), farmowners multiple peril (10%), other liability (6%), and other lines (10%).

Principal Investments: Investment grade bonds (85%) and misc. investments (18%).

Investments in Affiliates: 1%
Group Affiliation: North Star Companies
Licensed in: IA, MN, NE, ND, OK, SD, WI
Commenced Business: February 1920
Address: 269 Barstad Rd S, Cottonwood, MN 56229
Phone: (507) 423-6262   **Domicile State:** MN   **NAIC Code:** 14850

Data Date	Rating	RACR #1	RACR #2	Loss Ratio %	Total Assets ($mil)	Capital ($mil)	Net Premium ($mil)	Net Income ($mil)
9-14	B-	4.40	3.09	N/A	548.9	290.1	227.9	11.0
9-13	B-	4.64	3.29	N/A	504.1	262.6	201.1	3.9
2013	B-	4.61	3.18	64.3	520.2	280.0	288.7	20.9
2012	B-	5.17	3.63	70.9	460.3	253.3	251.5	11.5
2011	B	5.84	4.06	74.0	424.7	240.5	211.3	6.9
2010	B+	6.36	4.34	73.6	401.6	230.3	176.1	13.1
2009	B+	6.34	4.21	64.6	376.4	218.8	166.0	16.0

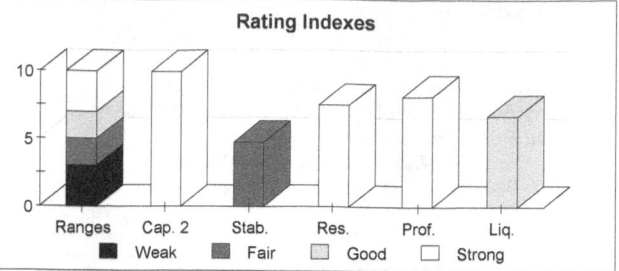

Rating Indexes

Ranges   Cap. 2   Stab.   Res.   Prof.   Liq.
■ Weak   ■ Fair   ▨ Good   □ Strong

NORTHLAND INS CO

B   **Good**

Major Rating Factors: Good profitability index (5.0 on a scale of 0 to 10). Fair expense controls. Return on equity has been fair, averaging 9.5% over the past five years. Good liquidity (6.9) with sufficient resources (cash flows and marketable investments) to handle a spike in claims.

Other Rating Factors: Good overall results on stability tests (6.0). Stability strengths include good operational trends and excellent risk diversification. Strong long-term capitalization index (9.2) based on excellent current risk adjusted capital (severe and moderate loss scenarios), despite some fluctuation in capital levels. Ample reserve history (7.8) that can protect against increases in claims costs.

Principal Business: Auto liability (58%), auto physical damage (27%), inland marine (10%), commercial multiple peril (2%), and other liability (2%).

Principal Investments: Investment grade bonds (80%) and misc. investments (21%).

Investments in Affiliates: 15%
Group Affiliation: Travelers Companies Inc
Licensed in: All states except AK, PR
Commenced Business: March 1948
Address: One Tower Square, Hartford, CT 06183
Phone: (651) 310-4100   **Domicile State:** CT   **NAIC Code:** 24015

Data Date	Rating	RACR #1	RACR #2	Loss Ratio %	Total Assets ($mil)	Capital ($mil)	Net Premium ($mil)	Net Income ($mil)
9-14	B	3.12	2.52	N/A	1,210.2	577.0	181.8	29.8
9-13	B	3.19	2.57	N/A	1,202.3	568.1	178.2	31.8
2013	B	2.97	2.43	60.9	1,157.6	533.3	245.7	56.8
2012	B	3.05	2.48	68.4	1,150.6	524.6	238.6	41.9
2011	B	3.15	2.56	76.9	1,158.0	535.1	233.6	36.7
2010	B	3.20	2.58	62.0	1,183.7	572.6	225.6	65.9
2009	B	3.17	2.58	58.3	1,199.9	577.3	221.2	72.1

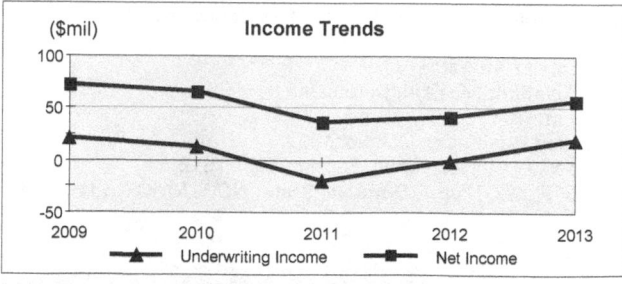

($mil)   Income Trends

▲ Underwriting Income   ■ Net Income

NUTMEG INS CO

C-   **Fair**

Major Rating Factors: Weak overall results on stability tests (2.9 on a scale of 0 to 10). Fair reserve development (4.6) as reserves have generally been sufficient to cover claims.

Other Rating Factors: Good overall profitability index (6.7). Fair expense controls. Return on equity has been low, averaging 4.9% over the past five years. Strong long-term capitalization index (10.0) based on excellent current risk adjusted capital (severe and moderate loss scenarios), despite some fluctuation in capital levels. Excellent liquidity (7.1) with ample operational cash flow and liquid investments.

Principal Business: N/A

Principal Investments: Investment grade bonds (61%), misc. investments (38%), and non investment grade bonds (1%).

Investments in Affiliates: 16%
Group Affiliation: Hartford Financial Services Inc
Licensed in: All states except PR
Commenced Business: December 1980
Address: Hartford Plaza, Hartford, CT 06115
Phone: (860) 547-5000   **Domicile State:** CT   **NAIC Code:** 39608

Data Date	Rating	RACR #1	RACR #2	Loss Ratio %	Total Assets ($mil)	Capital ($mil)	Net Premium ($mil)	Net Income ($mil)
9-14	C-	24.51	22.06	N/A	403.3	235.6	52.6	8.3
9-13	C-	24.22	21.80	N/A	397.0	231.9	51.7	26.1
2013	C-	26.77	24.09	68.8	421.7	256.6	69.6	28.3
2012	C-	23.82	21.44	72.7	392.0	227.9	68.9	8.9
2011	D+	0.05	0.03	78.5	416.5	246.1	68.9	11.4
2010	B-	1.09	0.76	67.3	412.4	254.2	67.8	10.5
2009	B-	3.16	2.22	64.4	369.1	209.7	68.3	1.5

Hartford Financial Services Inc Composite Group Rating: C+ Largest Group Members	Assets ($mil)	Rating
HARTFORD LIFE INS CO	128074	C+
HARTFORD LIFE ANNUITY INS CO	54557	B-
HARTFORD FIRE INS CO	25685	B
HARTFORD LIFE ACCIDENT INS CO	13891	C-
HARTFORD ACCIDENT INDEMNITY CO	11122	B

ODYSSEY REINSURANCE CO

C   **Fair**

Major Rating Factors: Fair profitability index (4.2 on a scale of 0 to 10) with operating losses during 2011. Return on equity has been fair, averaging 6.9% over the past five years. Fair overall results on stability tests (3.6) including excessive premium growth and negative cash flow from operations for 2013. The largest net exposure for one risk is excessive at 8.4% of capital.

Other Rating Factors: Good long-term capitalization index (6.9) based on good current risk adjusted capital (moderate loss scenario), despite some fluctuation in capital levels. Good liquidity (6.9) with sufficient resources (cash flows and marketable investments) to handle a spike in claims. Ample reserve history (9.3) that helps to protect the company against sharp claims increases.

Principal Business: (This company is a reinsurer.)

Principal Investments: Misc. investments (52%), investment grade bonds (41%), cash (4%), and non investment grade bonds (3%).

Investments in Affiliates: 21%

Group Affiliation: Fairfax Financial

Licensed in: All states, the District of Columbia and Puerto Rico

Commenced Business: September 1986

Address: 300 First Stamford Pl, Stamford, CT 06902

Phone: (203) 977-8000   **Domicile State:** CT   **NAIC Code:** 23680

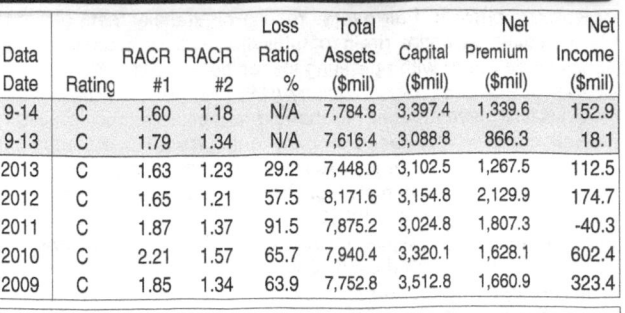

Data Date	Rating	RACR #1	RACR #2	Loss Ratio %	Total Assets ($mil)	Capital ($mil)	Net Premium ($mil)	Net Income ($mil)
9-14	C	1.60	1.18	N/A	7,784.8	3,397.4	1,339.6	152.9
9-13	C	1.79	1.34	N/A	7,616.4	3,088.8	866.3	18.1
2013	C	1.63	1.23	29.2	7,448.0	3,102.5	1,267.5	112.5
2012	C	1.65	1.21	57.5	8,171.6	3,154.8	2,129.9	174.7
2011	C	1.87	1.37	91.5	7,875.2	3,024.8	1,807.3	-40.3
2010	C	2.21	1.57	65.7	7,940.4	3,320.1	1,628.1	602.4
2009	C	1.85	1.34	63.9	7,752.8	3,512.8	1,660.9	323.4

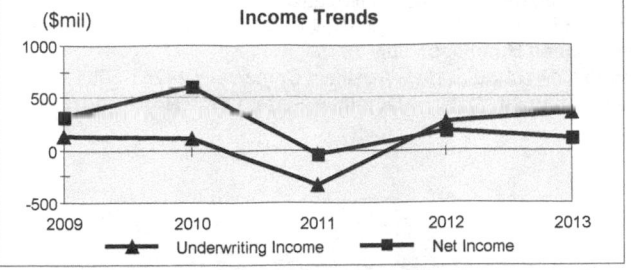

Income Trends

OGLESBY REINSURANCE CO *

A+   **Excellent**

Major Rating Factors: Strong long-term capitalization index (10.0 on a scale of 0 to 10) based on excellent current risk adjusted capital (severe and moderate loss scenarios). Furthermore, this high level of risk adjusted capital has been consistently maintained in previous years. Excellent profitability (8.8). Excellent expense controls.

Other Rating Factors: Superior liquidity (9.4) with ample operational cash flow and liquid investments. Excellent overall results on stability tests (8.4). Stability strengths include excellent risk diversification.

Principal Business: (This company is a reinsurer.)

Principal Investments: Investment grade bonds (95%) and misc. investments (5%).

Investments in Affiliates: None

Group Affiliation: State Farm Group

Licensed in: IL

Commenced Business: July 2011

Address: One State Farm Plaza, Bloomington, IL 61710-0001

Phone: (309) 766-2311   **Domicile State:** IL   **NAIC Code:** 14103

Data Date	Rating	RACR #1	RACR #2	Loss Ratio %	Total Assets ($mil)	Capital ($mil)	Net Premium ($mil)	Net Income ($mil)
9-14	A+	60.04	52.43	N/A	3,196.5	3,034.1	123.1	108.7
9-13	A+	39.73	35.86	N/A	3,043.8	2,888.3	142.3	126.0
2013	A+	52.33	46.32	0.0	3,022.7	2,923.9	155.3	161.7
2012	A+	39.07	35.40	0.0	2,930.5	2,775.3	199.3	165.2
2011	A+	37.91	34.29	0.0	2,761.6	2,609.9	178.2	78.0
2010	N/A	N/A	N/A	0.0	0.0	0.0	0.0	0.0
2009	N/A	N/A	N/A	0.0	0.0	0.0	0.0	0.0

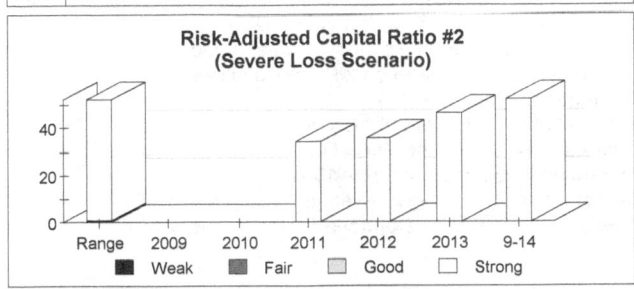

Risk-Adjusted Capital Ratio #2 (Severe Loss Scenario)

OHIO CASUALTY INS CO

C   **Fair**

Major Rating Factors: Fair overall results on stability tests (3.8 on a scale of 0 to 10) including potential drain of affiliation with Liberty Mutual Group. The largest net exposure for one risk is high at 4.1% of capital. History of adequate reserve strength (6.8) as reserves have been consistently at an acceptable level.

Other Rating Factors: Good overall profitability index (6.3). Fair expense controls. Return on equity has been good over the last five years, averaging 11.7%. Good liquidity (6.7) with sufficient resources (cash flows and marketable investments) to handle a spike in claims. Strong long-term capitalization index (7.4) based on excellent current risk adjusted capital (severe and moderate loss scenarios), despite some fluctuation in capital levels.

Principal Business: Other liability (35%), surety (22%), commercial multiple peril (16%), auto liability (7%), workers compensation (7%), inland marine (5%), and other lines (8%).

Principal Investments: Investment grade bonds (74%), misc. investments (20%), non investment grade bonds (5%), and real estate (1%).

Investments in Affiliates: 2%

Group Affiliation: Liberty Mutual Group

Licensed in: All states except PR

Commenced Business: March 1920

Address: 62 Maple Ave, Keene, NH 03431

Phone: (617) 357-9500   **Domicile State:** NH   **NAIC Code:** 24074

Data Date	Rating	RACR #1	RACR #2	Loss Ratio %	Total Assets ($mil)	Capital ($mil)	Net Premium ($mil)	Net Income ($mil)
9-14	C	2.43	1.56	N/A	5,392.1	1,456.5	1,469.2	50.7
9-13	C	2.24	1.57	N/A	5,754.3	1,536.6	1,450.6	9.4
2013	C	2.34	1.52	73.5	5,639.6	1,384.1	1,791.9	313.5
2012	C	1.97	1.41	66.7	5,100.5	1,274.6	2,227.3	112.0
2011	C	1.74	1.24	74.0	4,860.0	1,087.6	2,169.2	27.8
2010	C	1.84	1.32	67.8	4,842.0	1,117.2	2,150.7	164.7
2009	C	2.23	1.57	62.6	5,277.2	1,336.2	2,238.9	197.1

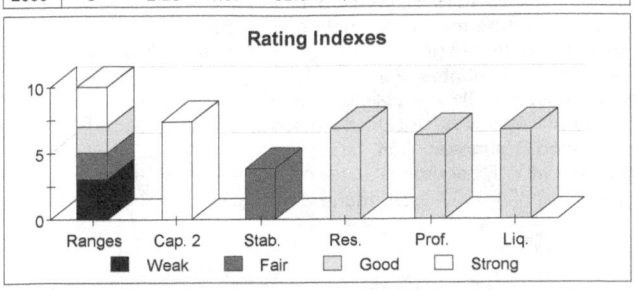

Rating Indexes

OHIO FARMERS INS CO

B-   Good

Major Rating Factors: Fair overall results on stability tests (4.6 on a scale of 0 to 10) including potential drain of affiliation with Westfield Companies. Fair profitability index (4.5) with operating losses during 2011.

Other Rating Factors: Good liquidity (6.9) with sufficient resources (cash flows and marketable investments) to handle a spike in claims. Strong long-term capitalization index (7.1) based on excellent current risk adjusted capital (severe and moderate loss scenarios), despite some fluctuation in capital levels. Ample reserve history (7.6) that can protect against increases in claims costs.

Principal Business: Surety (100%).

Principal Investments: Misc. investments (78%), investment grade bonds (17%), real estate (3%), and cash (2%).

Investments in Affiliates: 69%

Group Affiliation: Westfield Companies

Licensed in: All states except AK, CA, CT, HI, ID, ME, NH, OR, PR

Commenced Business: July 1848

Address: One Park Circle, Westfield Center, OH 44251-5001

Phone: (330) 887-0101   **Domicile State:** OH   **NAIC Code:** 24104

Data Date	Rating	RACR #1	RACR #2	Loss Ratio %	Total Assets ($mil)	Capital ($mil)	Net Premium ($mil)	Net Income ($mil)
9-14	B-	1.28	1.23	N/A	2,470.1	1,863.6	239.2	26.3
9-13	B-	1.31	1.24	N/A	2,323.4	1,691.4	231.8	11.8
2013	B-	1.25	1.21	59.8	2,404.6	1,808.7	318.3	21.1
2012	B-	1.22	1.18	64.9	2,131.9	1,525.6	305.3	36.9
2011	B-	1.24	1.19	79.3	1,915.6	1,361.7	363.0	-62.4
2010	B	1.29	1.26	66.5	1,661.1	1,382.9	133.0	68.5
2009	B	1.31	1.28	64.0	1,504.2	1,240.2	130.0	59.8

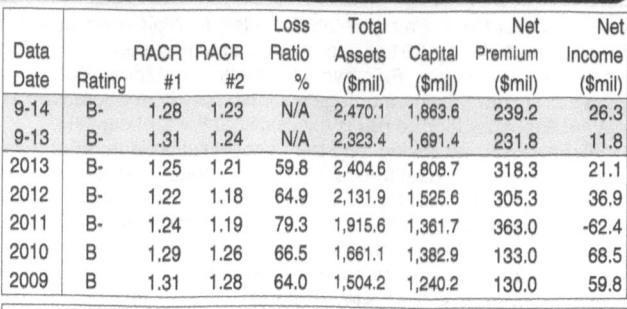

Rating Indexes

OLD REPUBLIC GENERAL INS CORP *

A-   Excellent

Major Rating Factors: Strong long-term capitalization index (7.7 on a scale of 0 to 10) based on excellent current risk adjusted capital (severe and moderate loss scenarios). Furthermore, this high level of risk adjusted capital has been consistently maintained in previous years. Excellent profitability (8.4) with operating gains in each of the last five years. Excellent expense controls.

Other Rating Factors: Excellent liquidity (7.0) with ample operational cash flow and liquid investments. Excellent overall results on stability tests (7.1). Stability strengths include good operational trends and excellent risk diversification. The largest net exposure for one risk is conservative at 1.1% of capital. History of adequate reserve strength (6.7) as reserves have been consistently at an acceptable level.

Principal Business: Workers compensation (63%), other liability (25%), auto liability (10%), and auto physical damage (2%).

Principal Investments: Investment grade bonds (81%), misc. investments (16%), non investment grade bonds (2%), and cash (1%).

Investments in Affiliates: 1%

Group Affiliation: Old Republic Group

Licensed in: All states, the District of Columbia and Puerto Rico

Commenced Business: January 1961

Address: 307 North Michigan Avenue, Chicago, IL 60601

Phone: (312) 346-8100   **Domicile State:** IL   **NAIC Code:** 24139

Data Date	Rating	RACR #1	RACR #2	Loss Ratio %	Total Assets ($mil)	Capital ($mil)	Net Premium ($mil)	Net Income ($mil)
9-14	A-	2.42	1.45	N/A	1,829.0	434.3	223.7	52.7
9-13	A-	2.26	1.08	N/A	1,637.0	369.8	212.5	40.5
2013	A-	2.74	1.63	83.2	1,730.6	431.7	286.3	54.2
2012	A-	2.22	1.06	88.0	1,507.9	332.6	278.6	33.4
2011	A-	2.52	1.32	89.1	1,290.8	308.0	263.8	35.5
2010	A-	2.90	1.44	110.6	1,127.3	302.7	182.1	5.0
2009	A-	2.79	1.40	96.0	1,038.3	302.3	157.9	22.9

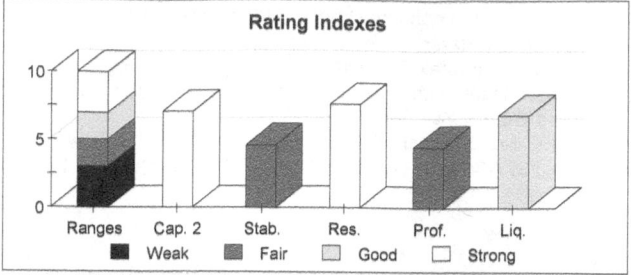

Risk-Adjusted Capital Ratio #2
(Severe Loss Scenario)

OLD REPUBLIC INS CO *

A-   Excellent

Major Rating Factors: Strong long-term capitalization index (9.1 on a scale of 0 to 10) based on excellent current risk adjusted capital (severe and moderate loss scenarios). Furthermore, this high level of risk adjusted capital has been consistently maintained in previous years. Excellent profitability (7.7) with operating gains in each of the last five years.

Other Rating Factors: Excellent liquidity (7.5) with ample operational cash flow and liquid investments. Excellent overall results on stability tests (7.2). Stability strengths include excellent operational trends and excellent risk diversification. History of adequate reserve strength (5.6) as reserves have been consistently at an acceptable level.

Principal Business: Workers compensation (31%), other liability (19%), inland marine (16%), aircraft (9%), credit (8%), auto liability (6%), and other lines (11%).

Principal Investments: Investment grade bonds (79%), misc. investments (16%), non investment grade bonds (3%), and cash (2%).

Investments in Affiliates: 2%

Group Affiliation: Old Republic Group

Licensed in: All states, the District of Columbia and Puerto Rico

Commenced Business: April 1935

Address: 414 W Pittsburgh St, Greensburg, PA 15601-0789

Phone: (724) 834-5000   **Domicile State:** PA   **NAIC Code:** 24147

Data Date	Rating	RACR #1	RACR #2	Loss Ratio %	Total Assets ($mil)	Capital ($mil)	Net Premium ($mil)	Net Income ($mil)
9-14	A-	3.78	2.34	N/A	2,580.9	931.8	298.1	78.7
9-13	A-	3.88	2.32	N/A	2,497.5	912.9	282.5	76.6
2013	A-	4.02	2.48	52.2	2,472.7	937.8	365.4	107.4
2012	A-	3.96	2.36	57.2	2,439.8	874.9	359.3	84.4
2011	A-	4.23	2.29	61.6	2,394.1	859.6	358.7	79.3
2010	A-	3.39	1.74	86.1	2,469.4	869.3	319.8	37.3
2009	A-	6.27	3.14	64.3	2,405.7	899.3	309.8	71.2

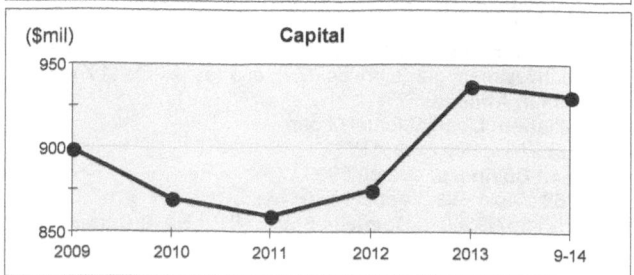

Capital

OLD REPUBLIC SURETY CO *   B+   Good

Major Rating Factors: Good liquidity (6.9 on a scale of 0 to 10) with sufficient resources (cash flows and marketable investments) to handle a spike in claims. Good overall results on stability tests (5.9). The largest net exposure for one risk is high at 3.6% of capital. Stability strengths include good operational trends and excellent risk diversification.

Other Rating Factors: Strong long-term capitalization index (7.8) based on excellent current risk adjusted capital (severe and moderate loss scenarios). Moreover, capital levels have been consistent in recent years. Ample reserve history (9.4) that helps to protect the company against sharp claims increases. Excellent profitability (8.6) with operating gains in each of the last five years. Return on equity has been good over the last five years, averaging 10.1%.

Principal Business: Surety (91%) and fidelity (9%).

Principal Investments: Investment grade bonds (76%), misc. investments (22%), and cash (2%).

Investments in Affiliates: 0%

Group Affiliation: Old Republic Group

Licensed in: AL, AZ, AR, CA, CO, DC, FL, GA, ID, IL, IN, IA, KS, MD, MN, MS, MO, MT, NE, NV, NM, NC, ND, OH, OK, OR, PA, SC, SD, TN, TX, UT, VA, WA, WV, WI, WY

Commenced Business: December 1981

Address: 445 S Moorland Rd Suite 301, Brookfield, WI 53005

Phone: (262) 797-2640   **Domicile State:** WI   **NAIC Code:** 40444

Data Date	Rating	RACR #1	RACR #2	Loss Ratio %	Total Assets ($mil)	Capital ($mil)	Net Premium ($mil)	Net Income ($mil)
9-14	B+	1.81	1.47	N/A	110.0	52.2	31.5	3.6
9-13	B+	1.98	1.59	N/A	104.3	49.0	26.0	1.3
2013	B+	2.06	1.68	11.3	105.7	51.9	38.1	4.8
2012	B+	1.86	1.52	21.9	98.9	48.7	35.9	4.8
2011	B+	1.84	1.52	19.4	101.0	48.1	39.5	6.6
2010	A-	1.70	1.41	20.1	102.4	45.8	42.7	5.6
2009	A-	1.58	1.32	24.7	98.6	43.3	43.4	2.8

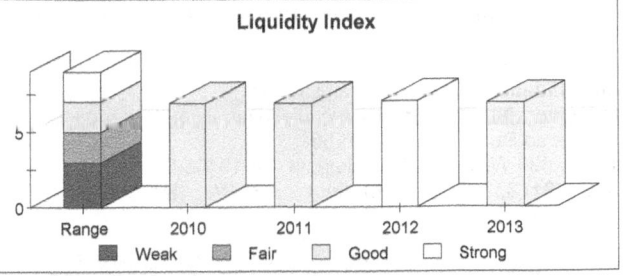

Liquidity Index

OLD UNITED CAS CO   B-   Good

Major Rating Factors: Fair overall results on stability tests (4.7 on a scale of 0 to 10) including potential drain of affiliation with Van Enterprises Group. History of adequate reserve strength (6.2) as reserves have been consistently at an acceptable level.

Other Rating Factors: Strong long-term capitalization index (10.0) based on excellent current risk adjusted capital (severe and moderate loss scenarios). Moreover, capital levels have been consistent in recent years. Excellent profitability (8.9) with operating gains in each of the last five years. Return on equity has been good over the last five years, averaging 10.8%. Excellent liquidity (7.5) with ample operational cash flow and liquid investments.

Principal Business: Credit (16%), aircraft (4%), and ocean marine (2%).

Principal Investments: Investment grade bonds (69%), misc. investments (22%), and non investment grade bonds (9%).

Investments in Affiliates: None

Group Affiliation: Van Enterprises Group

Licensed in: All states except PR

Commenced Business: April 1989

Address: 8500 Shawnee Mission Pkwy 200, Merriam, KS 66202

Phone: (913) 895-0200   **Domicile State:** KS   **NAIC Code:** 37060

Data Date	Rating	RACR #1	RACR #2	Loss Ratio %	Total Assets ($mil)	Capital ($mil)	Net Premium ($mil)	Net Income ($mil)
9-14	B-	8.25	4.39	N/A	648.3	325.6	69.2	22.6
9-13	B-	7.43	3.99	N/A	595.8	291.0	66.8	18.9
2013	B-	8.22	4.39	44.7	603.8	302.6	119.9	27.3
2012	B-	8.02	4.18	45.7	522.5	262.0	108.8	24.6
2011	B-	11.12	5.52	46.1	488.0	251.2	100.9	24.6
2010	B-	12.17	6.10	42.0	444.5	227.6	81.2	21.9
2009	B-	19.44	8.93	46.3	404.0	201.5	72.3	35.1

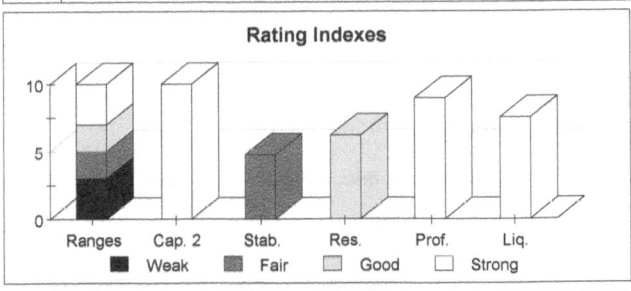

Rating Indexes

OMS NATIONAL INS CO RRG   B-   Good

Major Rating Factors: Fair overall results on stability tests (4.7 on a scale of 0 to 10) including potential drain of affiliation with National Group and negative cash flow from operations for 2013. The largest net exposure for one risk is conservative at 1.3% of capital. Good liquidity (6.9) with sufficient resources (cash flows and marketable investments) to handle a spike in claims.

Other Rating Factors: Strong long-term capitalization index (7.9) based on excellent current risk adjusted capital (severe and moderate loss scenarios). Moreover, capital levels have been consistent in recent years. Ample reserve history (9.4) that helps to protect the company against sharp claims increases. Excellent profitability (8.8) with operating gains in each of the last five years. Return on equity has been good over the last five years, averaging 10.5%.

Principal Business: Medical malpractice (100%).

Principal Investments: Investment grade bonds (50%), misc. investments (48%), and cash (2%).

Investments in Affiliates: 19%

Group Affiliation: National Group

Licensed in: All states except PR

Commenced Business: April 1988

Address: 6133 N River Rd Ste 650, Rosemont, IL 60018

Phone: (847) 384-0041   **Domicile State:** IL   **NAIC Code:** 44121

Data Date	Rating	RACR #1	RACR #2	Loss Ratio %	Total Assets ($mil)	Capital ($mil)	Net Premium ($mil)	Net Income ($mil)
9-14	B-	2.39	1.88	N/A	374.2	208.6	45.8	3.1
9-13	B-	2.63	1.94	N/A	406.1	176.3	58.7	2.7
2013	B-	2.43	1.98	51.3	342.9	191.5	69.9	21.4
2012	B-	2.88	2.19	55.1	383.0	166.6	77.3	15.6
2011	B-	2.53	1.93	53.3	357.3	146.6	76.9	17.1
2010	B-	2.54	1.93	59.0	333.3	131.6	78.1	18.3
2009	B-	2.27	1.75	62.6	305.0	107.4	64.9	13.7

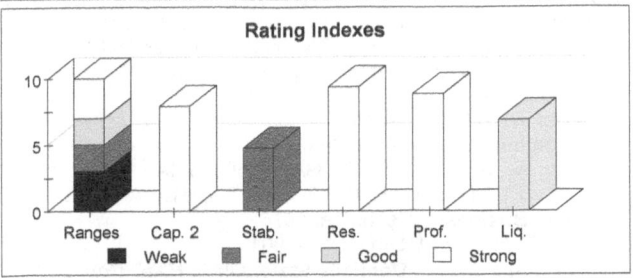

Rating Indexes

ONEBEACON INS CO

C   Fair

Major Rating Factors: Fair profitability index (3.6 on a scale of 0 to 10) with operating losses during 2013. Return on equity has been fair, averaging 13.1% over the past five years. Fair overall results on stability tests (4.0) including fair financial strength of affiliated White Mountains Group, weak results on operational trends and negative cash flow from operations for 2013. The largest net exposure for one risk is conservative at 1.1% of capital.

Other Rating Factors: Good long-term capitalization index (5.1) based on excellent current risk adjusted capital (severe and moderate loss scenarios), despite some fluctuation in capital levels. History of adequate reserve strength (6.2) as reserves have been consistently at an acceptable level. Superior liquidity (9.4) with ample operational cash flow and liquid investments.

Principal Business: Workers compensation (100%).

Principal Investments: Misc. investments (74%), investment grade bonds (24%), and cash (2%).

Investments in Affiliates: 75%

Group Affiliation: White Mountains Group

Licensed in: All states, the District of Columbia and Puerto Rico

Commenced Business: July 1956

Address: 436 Walnut St, Philadelphia, PA 19106-3786

Phone: (781) 332-7000   **Domicile State:** PA   **NAIC Code:** 21970

Data Date	Rating	RACR #1	RACR #2	Loss Ratio %	Total Assets ($mil)	Capital ($mil)	Net Premium ($mil)	Net Income ($mil)
9-14	C	1.26	1.19	N/A	1,074.1	898.5	0.1	4.0
9-13	C	0.97	0.96	N/A	1,055.9	826.7	0.3	14.4
2013	C	1.21	1.12	N/A	1,085.9	866.2	0.0	-36.9
2012	C	1.01	0.99	56.9	1,279.6	875.2	268.7	331.7
2011	C	1.19	1.08	59.1	2,077.6	942.7	609.3	38.8
2010	C+	1.54	1.34	62.0	2,351.8	922.0	542.9	263.1
2009	B-	1.45	1.33	56.2	3,053.3	1,353.8	906.1	117.8

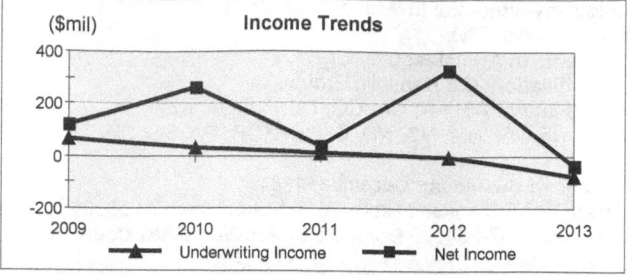

Income Trends

OTSEGO MUTUAL FIRE INS CO *

A-   Excellent

Major Rating Factors: Strong long-term capitalization index (10.0 on a scale of 0 to 10) based on excellent current risk adjusted capital (severe and moderate loss scenarios). Furthermore, this high level of risk adjusted capital has been consistently maintained in previous years. Ample reserve history (7.5) that can protect against increases in claims costs.

Other Rating Factors: Excellent profitability (8.1) with operating gains in each of the last five years. Excellent liquidity (7.5) with ample operational cash flow and liquid investments. Good overall results on stability tests (6.7). Stability strengths include good operational trends and good risk diversification.

Principal Business: Homeowners multiple peril (84%), fire (8%), allied lines (6%), and other liability (1%).

Principal Investments: Misc. investments (60%), investment grade bonds (39%), and cash (1%).

Investments in Affiliates: None

Group Affiliation: None

Licensed in: NY

Commenced Business: April 1897

Address: 143 Arnold Road, Burlington Flats, NY 13315-0040

Phone: (607) 965-8211   **Domicile State:** NY   **NAIC Code:** 14915

Data Date	Rating	RACR #1	RACR #2	Loss Ratio %	Total Assets ($mil)	Capital ($mil)	Net Premium ($mil)	Net Income ($mil)
9-14	A-	6.03	3.59	N/A	110.3	93.3	3.0	4.3
9-13	A-	5.82	3.48	N/A	100.4	85.4	3.0	2.7
2013	A-	5.68	3.39	26.3	104.6	88.7	4.3	3.8
2012	A-	5.54	3.32	107.9	93.3	79.0	4.4	1.1
2011	A-	5.67	3.39	61.9	89.4	76.6	4.7	2.4
2010	A-	5.45	3.25	61.0	85.5	73.3	4.4	2.6
2009	A-	5.24	3.11	46.7	80.8	69.9	4.3	3.6

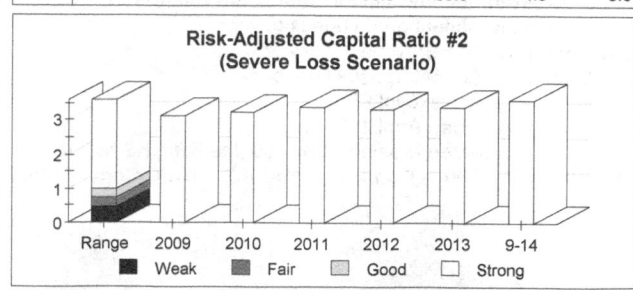

Risk-Adjusted Capital Ratio #2
(Severe Loss Scenario)

OWNERS INS CO *

A+   Excellent

Major Rating Factors: Strong long-term capitalization index (9.0 on a scale of 0 to 10) based on excellent current risk adjusted capital (severe and moderate loss scenarios). Furthermore, this high level of risk adjusted capital has been consistently maintained in previous years. Ample reserve history (9.3) that helps to protect the company against sharp claims increases.

Other Rating Factors: Excellent overall results on stability tests (7.9). Stability strengths include excellent operational trends and excellent risk diversification. Good overall profitability index (6.9). Fair expense controls. Return on equity has been fair, averaging 6.4% over the past five years. Good liquidity (6.5) with sufficient resources (cash flows and marketable investments) to handle a spike in claims.

Principal Business: Auto liability (25%), homeowners multiple peril (23%), commercial multiple peril (20%), auto physical damage (17%), workers compensation (8%), other liability (3%), and other lines (4%).

Principal Investments: Investment grade bonds (83%), misc. investments (16%), and cash (1%).

Investments in Affiliates: None

Group Affiliation: Auto-Owners Group

Licensed in: AL, AZ, AR, CO, FL, GA, ID, IL, IN, IA, KS, KY, MI, MN, MS, MO, NE, NV, NM, NC, ND, OH, OR, PA, SC, SD, TN, UT, VA, WA, WI

Commenced Business: December 1975

Address: 2325 N Cole St, Lima, OH 45801

Phone: (517) 323-1200   **Domicile State:** OH   **NAIC Code:** 32700

Data Date	Rating	RACR #1	RACR #2	Loss Ratio %	Total Assets ($mil)	Capital ($mil)	Net Premium ($mil)	Net Income ($mil)
9-14	A+	3.71	2.40	N/A	3,686.6	1,343.8	1,229.6	47.3
9-13	A	3.45	2.03	N/A	3,455.7	1,211.2	1,170.3	47.4
2013	A+	3.73	2.44	67.5	3,510.8	1,292.1	1,617.0	120.6
2012	A	3.48	2.08	70.3	3,191.7	1,139.3	1,518.7	92.5
2011	A	3.22	1.90	78.2	2,993.1	1,016.7	1,420.7	28.2
2010	A	3.28	1.94	74.1	2,838.4	990.8	1,289.4	73.8
2009	A	3.18	2.08	78.0	2,647.8	893.5	1,161.7	50.5

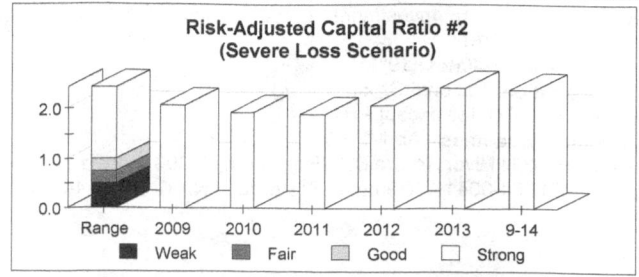

Risk-Adjusted Capital Ratio #2
(Severe Loss Scenario)

PACIFIC EMPLOYERS INS CO

B-   **Good**

Major Rating Factors: Fair overall results on stability tests (4.9 on a scale of 0 to 10) including potential drain of affiliation with ACE Ltd. Good liquidity (6.8) with sufficient resources (cash flows and marketable investments) to handle a spike in claims.

Other Rating Factors: Strong long-term capitalization index (8.9) based on excellent current risk adjusted capital (severe and moderate loss scenarios). Moreover, capital levels have been consistent in recent years. Ample reserve history (8.3) that helps to protect the company against sharp claims increases. Excellent profitability (8.3) with operating gains in each of the last five years.

Principal Business: Workers compensation (70%), surety (14%), fire (6%), allied lines (5%), inland marine (2%), other liability (2%), and other lines (2%).

Principal Investments: Investment grade bonds (89%), cash (6%), and misc. investments (5%).

Investments in Affiliates: 6%

Group Affiliation: ACE Ltd

Licensed in: All states except PR

Commenced Business: October 1923

Address: 1601 Chestnut St, Philadelphia, PA 19192

Phone: (215) 640-1000   **Domicile State:** PA   **NAIC Code:** 22748

Data Date	Rating	RACR #1	RACR #2	Loss Ratio %	Total Assets ($mil)	Capital ($mil)	Net Premium ($mil)	Net Income ($mil)
9-14	B-	3.25	2.27	N/A	3,430.5	1,192.1	596.5	45.4
9-13	B-	3.33	2.31	N/A	3,310.8	1,133.3	576.7	76.0
2013	B-	3.27	2.31	72.2	3,309.0	1,141.6	774.9	89.1
2012	B-	3.27	2.27	89.9	3,329.0	1,085.8	797.6	29.4
2011	B-	3.26	2.23	80.7	3,072.9	1,048.4	757.5	62.4
2010	B-	1.79	1.25	67.1	2,747.8	977.8	621.7	89.5
2009	C+	1.81	1.22	69.6	2,572.7	874.9	539.6	91.5

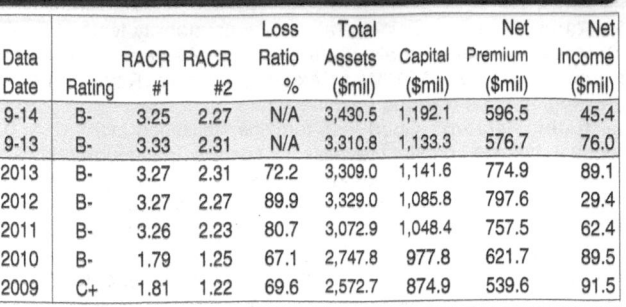

Rating Indexes

Ranges   Cap. 2   Stab.   Res.   Prof.   Liq.

■ Weak   ■ Fair   □ Good   □ Strong

PACIFIC INDEMNITY CO *

B+   **Good**

Major Rating Factors: Good liquidity (6.9 on a scale of 0 to 10) with sufficient resources (cash flows and marketable investments) to handle a spike in claims. Good overall results on stability tests (5.8). The largest net exposure for one risk is high at 3.8% of capital.

Other Rating Factors: Strong long-term capitalization index (9.4) based on excellent current risk adjusted capital (severe and moderate loss scenarios). Moreover, capital levels have been consistent in recent years. Ample reserve history (8.9) that helps to protect the company against sharp claims increases. Excellent profitability (8.8) with operating gains in each of the last five years. Return on equity has been good over the last five years, averaging 13.4%.

Principal Business: Homeowners multiple peril (45%), workers compensation (24%), inland marine (12%), commercial multiple peril (5%), other liability (4%), auto liability (3%), and other lines (7%).

Principal Investments: Investment grade bonds (81%) and misc. investments (19%).

Investments in Affiliates: 0%

Group Affiliation: Chubb Corp

Licensed in: All states except PR

Commenced Business: February 1926

Address: Two Plaza East Suite 1450, Milwaukee, WI 53202-3146

Phone: (908) 903-2000   **Domicile State:** WI   **NAIC Code:** 20346

Data Date	Rating	RACR #1	RACR #2	Loss Ratio %	Total Assets ($mil)	Capital ($mil)	Net Premium ($mil)	Net Income ($mil)
9-14	B+	4.17	2.69	N/A	6,857.3	2,843.7	1,192.2	313.5
9-13	B+	3.96	2.53	N/A	6,628.2	2,690.1	1,159.8	322.2
2013	B+	4.16	2.69	52.5	6,640.5	2,771.4	1,568.7	425.6
2012	B+	3.74	2.39	66.1	6,465.8	2,496.2	1,506.1	278.8
2011	A-	3.71	2.40	68.3	6,283.8	2,440.8	1,474.5	265.0
2010	B+	3.69	2.42	61.5	6,207.7	2,424.1	1,423.4	336.2
2009	B+	3.38	2.22	57.7	5,989.2	2,200.2	1,431.6	329.3

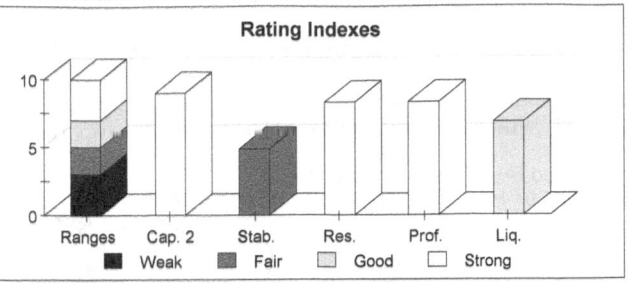

Liquidity Index

Range   2010   2011   2012   2013

■ Weak   ■ Fair   □ Good   □ Strong

PACIFIC INS CO LTD

B   **Good**

Major Rating Factors: History of adequate reserve strength (6.2 on a scale of 0 to 10) as reserves have been consistently at an acceptable level. Good liquidity (6.7) with sufficient resources (cash flows and marketable investments) to handle a spike in claims.

Other Rating Factors: Good overall results on stability tests (5.8). Stability strengths include good operational trends and excellent risk diversification. Fair profitability index (4.9). Fair expense controls. Return on equity has been fair, averaging 9.2% over the past five years. Strong long-term capitalization index (9.4) based on excellent current risk adjusted capital (severe and moderate loss scenarios), despite some fluctuation in capital levels.

Principal Business: Other liability (65%), workers compensation (30%), auto liability (3%), and auto physical damage (2%).

Principal Investments: Investment grade bonds (92%) and misc. investments (8%).

Investments in Affiliates: None

Group Affiliation: Hartford Financial Services Inc

Licensed in: All states, the District of Columbia and Puerto Rico

Commenced Business: January 1995

Address: Hartford Plaza, Hartford, CT 06115

Phone: (860) 547-5000   **Domicile State:** CT   **NAIC Code:** 10046

Data Date	Rating	RACR #1	RACR #2	Loss Ratio %	Total Assets ($mil)	Capital ($mil)	Net Premium ($mil)	Net Income ($mil)
9-14	B	3.97	2.62	N/A	645.3	237.9	127.8	18.6
9-13	B	4.01	2.65	N/A	646.5	233.7	125.5	14.9
2013	B	3.76	2.50	68.8	619.3	218.5	169.1	20.3
2012	B	3.86	2.57	72.7	618.7	220.2	167.4	17.2
2011	B	3.84	2.59	78.5	619.3	218.8	167.4	13.4
2010	B	4.33	2.96	67.3	621.9	237.7	164.7	30.7
2009	B	4.15	2.83	64.4	617.6	230.7	165.9	20.2

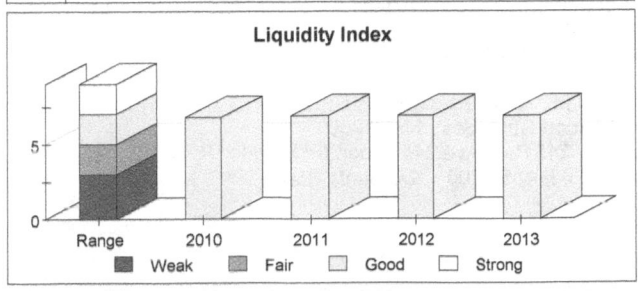

Reserve Deficiency (as % of capital)

2009   2010   2011   2012   2013

* Adequate & redundant reserves show as negatives

■ 1 Yr Dev   □ 2 Yr Dev

PACIFIC SPECIALTY INS CO

C+   Fair

Major Rating Factors: Fair overall results on stability tests (4.5 on a scale of 0 to 10) including potential drain of affiliation with Western Service Contract Group. Fair profitability index (4.7). Weak expense controls. Return on equity has been fair, averaging 9.8% over the past five years.

Other Rating Factors: Good long-term capitalization index (5.4) based on fair current risk adjusted capital (severe loss scenario), although results have slipped from the excellent range during the last year. History of adequate reserve strength (5.8) as reserves have been consistently at an acceptable level. Good liquidity (5.1) with sufficient resources (cash flows and marketable investments) to handle a spike in claims.

Principal Business: Homeowners multiple peril (80%), auto liability (5%), other liability (5%), auto physical damage (3%), commercial multiple peril (3%), earthquake (2%), and fire (1%).

Principal Investments: Investment grade bonds (78%), non investment grade bonds (21%), and cash (1%).

Investments in Affiliates: 1%

Group Affiliation: Western Service Contract Group

Licensed in: All states except PR

Commenced Business: January 1990

Address: 3601 Haven Avenue, Menlo Park, CA 94025-1010

Phone: (650) 780-4800   **Domicile State:** CA   **NAIC Code:** 37850

Data Date	Rating	RACR #1	RACR #2	Loss Ratio %	Total Assets ($mil)	Capital ($mil)	Net Premium ($mil)	Net Income ($mil)
9-14	C+	1.07	0.66	N/A	311.0	132.1	136.2	12.7
9-13	C	1.66	1.01	N/A	357.5	199.6	124.1	13.1
2013	C+	1.82	1.10	53.9	377.1	205.9	176.1	14.1
2012	C	1.61	0.97	60.2	334.2	184.8	161.2	13.5
2011	C	1.43	0.86	56.7	301.7	169.0	154.3	22.9
2010	C	1.15	0.78	60.1	283.5	153.8	144.1	12.3
2009	C	1.14	0.83	54.5	250.1	141.6	128.7	15.9

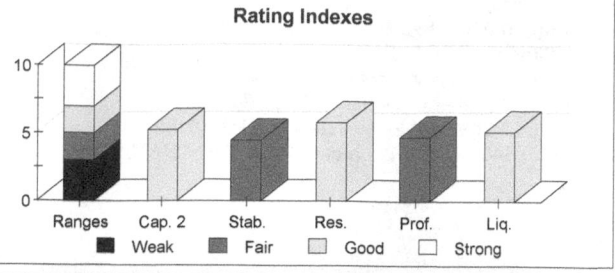

Rating Indexes

PARTNER REINSURANCE CO OF THE US

C-   Fair

Major Rating Factors: Fair overall results on stability tests (3.2 on a scale of 0 to 10). The largest net exposure for one risk is conservative at 1.2% of capital. Good liquidity (6.9) with sufficient resources (cash flows and marketable investments) to handle a spike in claims.

Other Rating Factors: Strong long-term capitalization index (7.1) based on excellent current risk adjusted capital (severe and moderate loss scenarios), despite some fluctuation in capital levels. Ample reserve history (9.6) that helps to protect the company against sharp claims increases. Excellent profitability (8.5) with operating gains in each of the last five years. Return on equity has been good over the last five years, averaging 11.8%.

Principal Business: (This company is a reinsurer.)

Principal Investments: Investment grade bonds (79%), misc. investments (19%), and cash (2%).

Investments in Affiliates: 3%

Group Affiliation: PartnerRe Ltd

Licensed in: All states except PR

Commenced Business: May 1980

Address: 245 Park Ave 24th Floor, New York, NY 10167

Phone: (203) 485-4200   **Domicile State:** NY   **NAIC Code:** 38636

Data Date	Rating	RACR #1	RACR #2	Loss Ratio %	Total Assets ($mil)	Capital ($mil)	Net Premium ($mil)	Net Income ($mil)
9-14	C-	1.67	1.09	N/A	4,984.4	1,345.2	902.3	155.4
9-13	C-	1.86	1.21	N/A	4,904.6	1,296.6	824.2	120.0
2013	C-	1.68	1.09	66.6	4,886.7	1,332.0	1,139.4	122.7
2012	C-	1.93	1.25	64.2	4,528.3	1,260.2	922.9	181.1
2011	D+	1.75	1.14	68.1	4,390.6	1,173.6	892.9	106.4
2010	D	1.91	1.26	56.1	3,682.9	1,197.0	632.5	146.6
2009	D	1.15	0.68	61.7	3,452.3	792.6	763.6	89.4

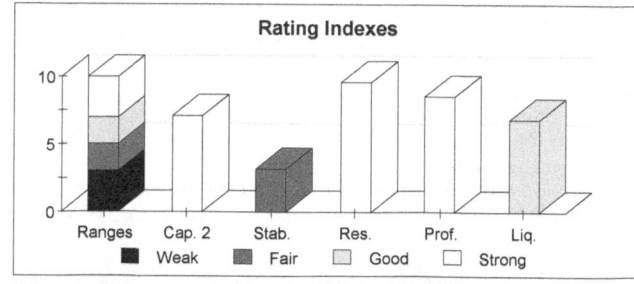

Rating Indexes

PEERLESS INS CO

B-   Good

Major Rating Factors: Good overall results on stability tests (5.0 on a scale of 0 to 10) despite potential drain of affiliation with Liberty Mutual Group. The largest net exposure for one risk is excessive at 5.1% of capital. Stability strengths include good operational trends and excellent risk diversification. History of adequate reserve strength (5.6) as reserves have been consistently at an acceptable level.

Other Rating Factors: Good overall profitability index (6.2). Fair expense controls. Return on equity has been fair, averaging 8.3% over the past five years. Strong long-term capitalization index (7.2) based on excellent current risk adjusted capital (severe and moderate loss scenarios), despite some fluctuation in capital levels. Excellent liquidity (7.7) with ample operational cash flow and liquid investments.

Principal Business: Commercial multiple peril (28%), auto liability (19%), workers compensation (11%), homeowners multiple peril (11%), auto physical damage (10%), other liability (8%), and other lines (12%).

Principal Investments: Investment grade bonds (76%), misc. investments (19%), and non investment grade bonds (5%).

Investments in Affiliates: 6%

Group Affiliation: Liberty Mutual Group

Licensed in: All states except HI, PR

Commenced Business: November 1903

Address: 62 Maple Ave, Keene, NH 03431

Phone: (617) 357-9500   **Domicile State:** NH   **NAIC Code:** 24198

Data Date	Rating	RACR #1	RACR #2	Loss Ratio %	Total Assets ($mil)	Capital ($mil)	Net Premium ($mil)	Net Income ($mil)
9-14	B-	1.67	1.14	N/A	12,749.4	2,946.3	3,673.1	122.2
9-13	B-	1.75	1.23	N/A	13,428.7	2,771.3	3,626.4	76.3
2013	B-	1.60	1.09	73.5	13,621.2	2,786.4	5,827.5	151.5
2012	B-	1.71	1.33	66.7	7,629.8	1,887.3	2,751.4	349.4
2011	B-	1.45	1.18	74.0	7,361.8	1,802.5	2,679.6	23.6
2010	C+	1.51	1.24	67.8	7,420.5	1,777.7	2,656.8	170.4
2009	C+	1.98	1.61	62.6	8,377.2	2,409.3	2,765.7	213.3

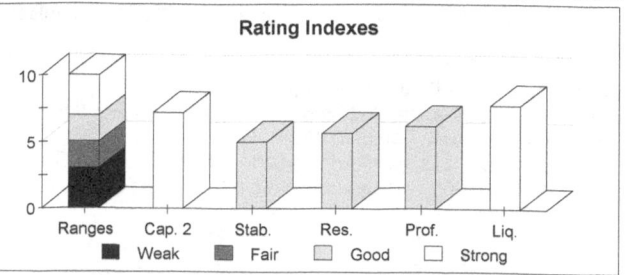

Rating Indexes

PEKIN INS CO *   B+   Good

Major Rating Factors: Good overall results on stability tests (6.0 on a scale of 0 to 10). Affiliation with Farmers Automobile Ins Assn is a strength. Good overall profitability index (6.2) despite modest operating losses during the first nine months of 2014. Return on equity has been low, averaging 3.7% over the past five years.

Other Rating Factors: Good liquidity (6.6) with sufficient resources (cash flows and marketable investments) to handle a spike in claims. Strong long-term capitalization index (10.0) based on excellent current risk adjusted capital (severe and moderate loss scenarios), despite some fluctuation in capital levels. Ample reserve history (9.3) that helps to protect the company against sharp claims increases.

Principal Business: Commercial multiple peril (28%), workers compensation (21%), auto liability (18%), homeowners multiple peril (13%), auto physical damage (13%), other liability (5%), and other lines (3%).

Principal Investments: Investment grade bonds (82%) and misc. investments (18%).

Investments in Affiliates: 4%

Group Affiliation: Farmers Automobile Ins Assn

Licensed in: AZ, IL, IN, IA, MI, OH, WI

Commenced Business: July 1961

Address: 2505 Court St, Pekin, IL 61558

Phone: (309) 346-1161   **Domicile State:** IL   **NAIC Code:** 24228

Data Date	Rating	RACR #1	RACR #2	Loss Ratio %	Total Assets ($mil)	Capital ($mil)	Net Premium ($mil)	Net Income ($mil)
9-14	B+	4.53	3.16	N/A	286.1	116.1	81.9	-0.5
9-13	B+	4.64	3.25	N/A	283.3	115.5	76.9	4.5
2013	B+	4.79	3.39	75.4	281.9	117.1	107.1	4.4
2012	B+	4.80	3.43	75.1	262.7	111.6	100.5	7.6
2011	B+	4.65	3.29	83.5	250.0	104.3	92.1	2.0
2010	B+	4.45	3.10	75.9	245.9	97.8	90.5	4.0
2009	B+	4.53	3.25	74.6	203.5	92.2	81.8	4.5

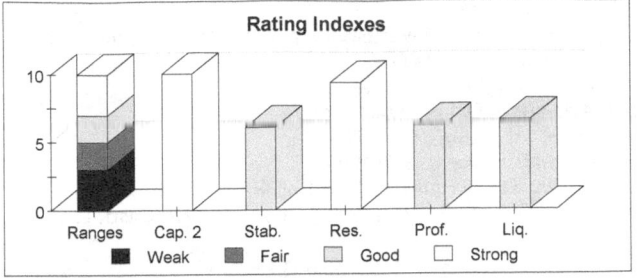

Rating Indexes

PEMCO MUTUAL INS CO   B-   Good

Major Rating Factors: Fair overall results on stability tests (4.7 on a scale of 0 to 10) including potential drain of affiliation with PEMCO Corp. Fair profitability index (3.1) with operating losses during 2010, 2012 and 2013.

Other Rating Factors: History of adequate reserve strength (6.1) as reserves have been consistently at an acceptable level. Good liquidity (6.4) with sufficient resources (cash flows and marketable investments) to handle a spike in claims. Strong long-term capitalization index (8.9) based on excellent current risk adjusted capital (severe and moderate loss scenarios), despite some fluctuation in capital levels.

Principal Business: Auto liability (47%), homeowners multiple peril (25%), auto physical damage (23%), fire (2%), other liability (2%), and inland marine (1%).

Principal Investments: Investment grade bonds (88%), cash (7%), and misc. investments (5%).

Investments in Affiliates: 0%

Group Affiliation: PEMCO Corp

Licensed in: ID, OR, WA

Commenced Business: February 1949

Address: 325 Eastlake Ave E, Seattle, WA 98109-5466

Phone: (206) 628-4290   **Domicile State:** WA   **NAIC Code:** 24341

Data Date	Rating	RACR #1	RACR #2	Loss Ratio %	Total Assets ($mil)	Capital ($mil)	Net Premium ($mil)	Net Income ($mil)
9-14	B-	2.79	2.27	N/A	660.8	239.1	265.7	2.8
9-13	B-	2.81	2.21	N/A	629.0	233.3	247.0	1.1
2013	B-	2.82	2.34	72.2	629.4	237.4	346.0	-3.3
2012	B-	2.77	2.23	79.3	611.4	232.7	322.6	-16.3
2011	B-	3.05	2.51	72.8	603.8	241.6	315.4	8.2
2010	B-	2.89	2.39	74.6	597.9	238.9	312.2	-6.0
2009	B	2.64	2.25	76.8	524.1	246.2	234.2	26.8

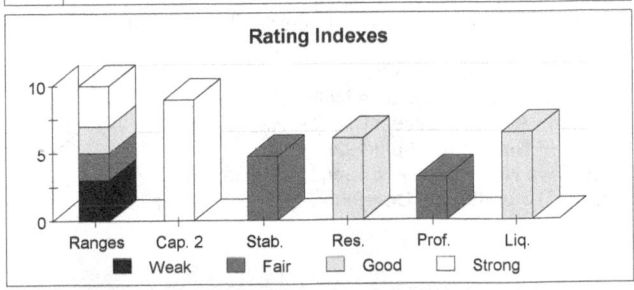

Rating Indexes

PENN NATIONAL SECURITY INS CO   B-   Good

Major Rating Factors: Fair overall results on stability tests (4.7 on a scale of 0 to 10) including potential drain of affiliation with Pennsylvania National Ins Group. History of adequate reserve strength (5.5) as reserves have been consistently at an acceptable level.

Other Rating Factors: Good overall profitability index (5.9) despite operating losses during 2011 and 2012. Return on equity has been low, averaging 3.0% over the past five years. Good liquidity (6.4) with sufficient resources (cash flows and marketable investments) to handle a spike in claims. Strong long-term capitalization index (8.6) based on excellent current risk adjusted capital (severe and moderate loss scenarios), despite some fluctuation in capital levels.

Principal Business: Workers compensation (32%), auto liability (20%), fire (12%), other liability (10%), commercial multiple peril (9%), products liability (7%), and other lines (9%).

Principal Investments: Investment grade bonds (91%), misc. investments (8%), and cash (1%).

Investments in Affiliates: None

Group Affiliation: Pennsylvania National Ins Group

Licensed in: AL, DC, DE, MD, NJ, NC, PA, SC, TN, VA

Commenced Business: January 1989

Address: Two North Second Street, Harrisburg, PA 17101

Phone: (717) 234-4941   **Domicile State:** PA   **NAIC Code:** 32441

Data Date	Rating	RACR #1	RACR #2	Loss Ratio %	Total Assets ($mil)	Capital ($mil)	Net Premium ($mil)	Net Income ($mil)
9-14	B-	2.99	2.03	N/A	879.0	283.7	238.1	6.0
9-13	B-	2.96	2.01	N/A	852.8	269.5	225.5	7.4
2013	B-	3.04	2.07	65.5	843.2	282.1	315.8	10.3
2012	B-	2.92	2.00	77.4	804.2	254.5	309.5	-1.6
2011	B-	3.80	2.49	78.9	699.0	251.8	226.2	-2.0
2010	C+	4.42	2.91	70.1	685.2	260.0	216.5	12.2
2009	C+	4.24	2.79	63.0	670.9	243.7	212.8	20.6

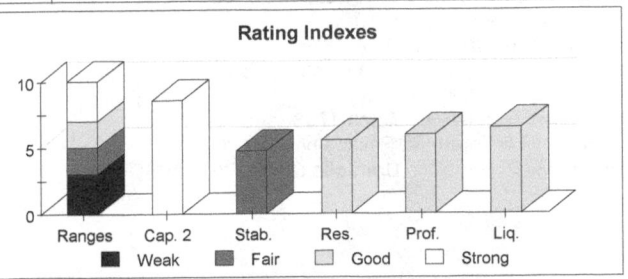

Rating Indexes

PENNSYLVANIA MANUFACTURERS ASN INS | C | Fair

Major Rating Factors: Fair profitability index (3.6 on a scale of 0 to 10) with operating losses during 2010. Return on equity has been low, averaging 4.0% over the past five years. Fair overall results on stability tests (4.0).

Other Rating Factors: A history of deficient reserves (2.4) that places pressure on both capital and profits. Deficiencies in the two year reserve development occurred in three of the previous five years and ranged between 18% and 34%. Strong long-term capitalization index (8.3) based on excellent current risk adjusted capital (severe and moderate loss scenarios), despite some fluctuation in capital levels. Excellent liquidity (7.0) with ample operational cash flow and liquid investments.

Principal Business: Workers compensation (75%), inland marine (15%), auto liability (4%), other liability (3%), commercial multiple peril (1%), and auto physical damage (1%).

Principal Investments: Investment grade bonds (86%), misc. investments (7%), cash (5%), and real estate (2%).

Investments in Affiliates: None

Group Affiliation: Old Republic Group

Licensed in: All states except PR

Commenced Business: July 1964

Address: 380 Sentry Parkway, Blue Bell, PA 19422-0754

Phone: (610) 397-5000　**Domicile State:** PA　**NAIC Code:** 12262

Data Date	Rating	RACR #1	RACR #2	Loss Ratio %	Total Assets ($mil)	Capital ($mil)	Net Premium ($mil)	Net Income ($mil)
9-14	C	2.47	1.77	N/A	810.9	217.7	113.1	1.7
9-13	C	2.90	2.18	N/A	754.8	223.2	106.5	15.7
2013	C	2.86	2.11	79.9	761.2	224.5	135.6	18.0
2012	C	2.91	2.22	79.3	730.6	225.4	143.1	1.0
2011	C	3.08	2.35	68.1	699.2	230.1	141.5	11.4
2010	C	2.89	2.20	102.4	715.3	238.8	159.2	-3.8
2009	C	2.46	1.93	66.1	774.5	256.7	232.7	26.5

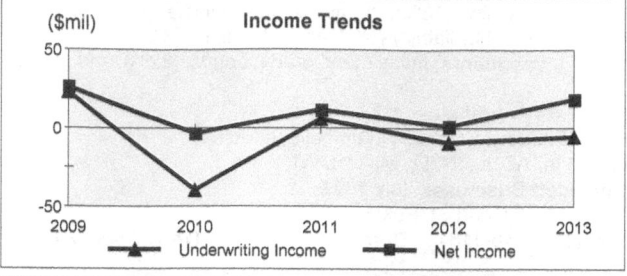

Income Trends

PENNSYLVANIA NTL MUTUAL CAS INS CO | B- | Good

Major Rating Factors: Fair overall results on stability tests (4.7 on a scale of 0 to 10) including potential drain of affiliation with Pennsylvania National Ins Group. Fair reserve development (4.3) as reserves have generally been sufficient to cover claims.

Other Rating Factors: Good overall profitability index (5.3) despite operating losses during 2010 and 2011. Good liquidity (6.7) with sufficient resources (cash flows and marketable investments) to handle a spike in claims. Strong long-term capitalization index (7.7) based on excellent current risk adjusted capital (severe and moderate loss scenarios), despite some fluctuation in capital levels.

Principal Business: Auto liability (25%), other liability (14%), homeowners multiple peril (14%), auto physical damage (14%), workers compensation (11%), commercial multiple peril (8%), and other lines (14%).

Principal Investments: Investment grade bonds (53%), misc. investments (44%), and cash (3%).

Investments in Affiliates: 33%

Group Affiliation: Pennsylvania National Ins Group

Licensed in: All states except CA, CT, HI, NV, NH, ND, WY, PR

Commenced Business: April 1920

Address: Two North Second Street, Harrisburg, PA 17101

Phone: (717) 234-4941　**Domicile State:** PA　**NAIC Code:** 14990

Data Date	Rating	RACR #1	RACR #2	Loss Ratio %	Total Assets ($mil)	Capital ($mil)	Net Premium ($mil)	Net Income ($mil)
9-14	B-	1.66	1.48	N/A	1,171.8	546.7	238.1	5.7
9-13	B-	1.69	1.49	N/A	1,117.3	514.0	225.5	16.9
2013	B-	1.65	1.47	65.5	1,126.1	541.2	315.8	22.4
2012	B-	1.59	1.42	77.4	1,036.8	473.7	279.4	13.9
2011	B-	1.49	1.32	80.5	1,071.1	451.2	291.5	-23.2
2010	B-	1.56	1.39	89.4	1,126.9	487.1	272.6	-23.3
2009	B-	1.71	1.53	68.6	1,083.5	484.8	268.3	8.5

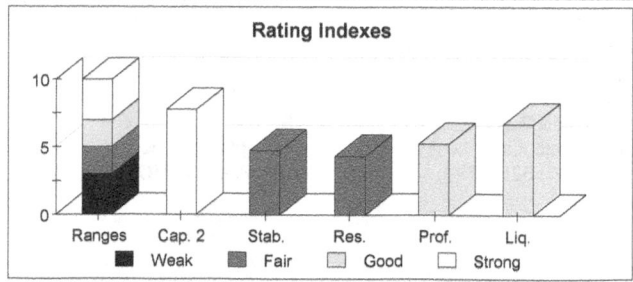

Rating Indexes

PHILADELPHIA CBSP FOR INS OF HOUSES | B- | Good

Major Rating Factors: Fair overall results on stability tests (4.7 on a scale of 0 to 10) including potential drain of affiliation with Philadelphia Contrib Group and negative cash flow from operations for 2013. History of adequate reserve strength (6.2) as reserves have been consistently at an acceptable level.

Other Rating Factors: Good overall profitability index (6.6) with small operating losses during 2011. Return on equity has been low, averaging 2.0% over the past five years. Good liquidity (6.6) with sufficient resources (cash flows and marketable investments) to handle a spike in claims. Strong long-term capitalization index (7.2) based on excellent current risk adjusted capital (severe and moderate loss scenarios), despite some fluctuation in capital levels.

Principal Business: (This company is a reinsurer.)

Principal Investments: Misc. investments (96%), investment grade bonds (2%), cash (1%), and real estate (1%).

Investments in Affiliates: 48%

Group Affiliation: Philadelphia Contrib Group

Licensed in: IL, NJ, NY, PA

Commenced Business: March 1753

Address: 212 S Fourth St, Philadelphia, PA 19106

Phone: (888) 627-1752　**Domicile State:** PA　**NAIC Code:** 17930

Data Date	Rating	RACR #1	RACR #2	Loss Ratio %	Total Assets ($mil)	Capital ($mil)	Net Premium ($mil)	Net Income ($mil)
9-14	B-	1.30	1.10	N/A	320.6	236.4	27.2	2.7
9-13	B-	1.36	1.12	N/A	296.8	215.1	26.1	3.9
2013	B-	1.30	1.10	63.0	316.6	234.8	35.8	6.0
2012	B-	1.27	1.08	87.8	266.3	187.5	33.1	1.1
2011	B-	1.26	1.08	97.7	254.9	181.0	32.0	-1.5
2010	B	1.30	1.11	82.0	271.2	194.4	31.6	9.2
2009	B	1.28	1.09	65.8	264.6	190.1	32.2	6.0

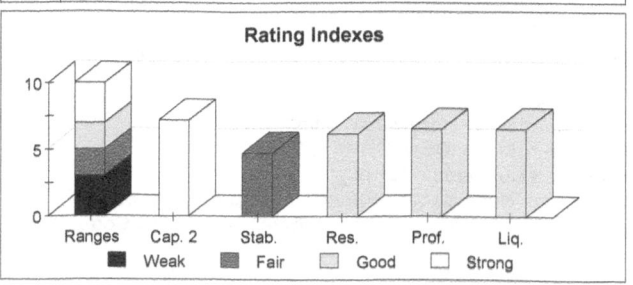

Rating Indexes

PHILADELPHIA INDEMNITY INS CO   B   Good

Major Rating Factors: Good liquidity (6.6 on a scale of 0 to 10) with sufficient resources (cash flows and marketable investments) to handle a spike in claims. Fair overall results on stability tests (4.6) including potential drain of affiliation with Tokio Marine Holdings Inc.

Other Rating Factors: Strong long-term capitalization index (8.5) based on excellent current risk adjusted capital (severe and moderate loss scenarios). Moreover, capital levels have been consistent in recent years. Ample reserve history (8.1) that helps to protect the company against sharp claims increases. Excellent profitability (8.8) with operating gains in each of the last five years. Return on equity has been good over the last five years, averaging 12.1%.

Principal Business: Commercial multiple peril (54%), other liability (22%), auto liability (14%), auto physical damage (5%), surety (2%), allied lines (1%), and inland marine (1%).

Principal Investments: Investment grade bonds (90%) and misc. investments (10%).

Investments in Affiliates: None

Group Affiliation: Tokio Marine Holdings Inc

Licensed in: All states except PR

Commenced Business: March 1927

Address: 1 Bala Plz #100, Bala Cynwyd, PA 19004-1401

Phone: (610) 617-7900   **Domicile State:** PA   **NAIC Code:** 18058

Data Date	Rating	RACR #1	RACR #2	Loss Ratio %	Total Assets ($mil)	Capital ($mil)	Net Premium ($mil)	Net Income ($mil)
9-14	B	2.67	2.01	N/A	7,236.4	2,346.6	1,828.8	178.8
9-13	B	2.85	2.18	N/A	6,457.3	2,080.2	1,679.4	202.6
2013	B	2.66	2.02	61.0	6,526.1	2,156.7	2,351.5	293.5
2012	B	3.01	2.32	62.8	6,047.3	2,017.2	2,124.8	229.6
2011	B	3.08	2.36	70.3	5,462.8	1,867.0	1,932.8	155.0
2010	B	3.17	2.47	60.0	5,004.5	1,806.3	1,870.9	250.4
2009	B	3.00	2.30	56.2	4,517.4	1,647.1	1,784.1	243.7

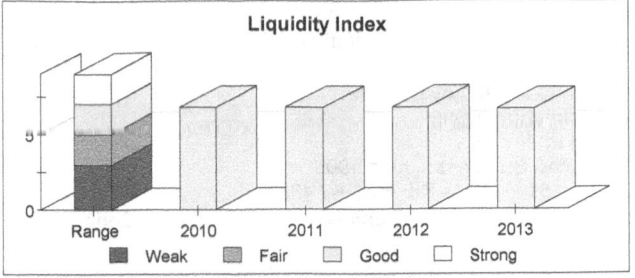

Liquidity Index

PHOENIX INS CO   B   Good

Major Rating Factors: Good liquidity (6.8 on a scale of 0 to 10) with sufficient resources (cash flows and marketable investments) to handle a spike in claims. Good overall results on stability tests (6.3). Affiliation with Travelers Companies Inc is a strength.

Other Rating Factors: Strong long-term capitalization index (7.4) based on excellent current risk adjusted capital (severe and moderate loss scenarios), despite some fluctuation in capital levels. Ample reserve history (8.4) that helps to protect the company against sharp claims increases. Excellent profitability (8.3) with operating gains in each of the last five years. Return on equity has been good over the last five years, averaging 11.5%.

Principal Business: Workers compensation (36%), commercial multiple peril (23%), auto liability (11%), homeowners multiple peril (11%), other liability (6%), inland marine (6%), and other lines (7%).

Principal Investments: Investment grade bonds (64%), misc. investments (35%), and non investment grade bonds (1%).

Investments in Affiliates: 29%

Group Affiliation: Travelers Companies Inc

Licensed in: All states except CA, PR

Commenced Business: July 1850

Address: One Tower Square, Hartford, CT 06183

Phone: (860) 277-0111   **Domicile State:** CT   **NAIC Code:** 25623

Data Date	Rating	RACR #1	RACR #2	Loss Ratio %	Total Assets ($mil)	Capital ($mil)	Net Premium ($mil)	Net Income ($mil)
9-14	B	1.65	1.46	N/A	4,191.2	1,750.8	745.3	101.1
9-13	B	1.56	1.37	N/A	3,994.0	1,555.6	730.3	98.4
2013	B	1.53	1.37	60.9	4,009.4	1,579.1	1,006.9	194.5
2012	B	1.43	1.27	68.4	3,860.1	1,390.6	978.0	98.5
2011	B	1.39	1.23	76.9	3,697.1	1,294.5	957.5	80.2
2010	B	1.29	1.13	62.0	3,605.2	1,201.1	924.6	185.2
2009	B	1.82	1.48	58.3	3,696.3	1,224.7	906.4	239.1

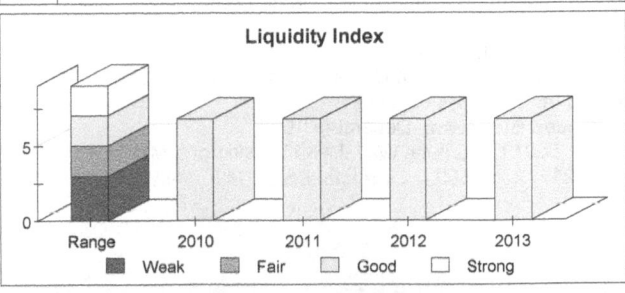

Liquidity Index

PHYSICIANS INS A MUTUAL CO   B-   Good

Major Rating Factors: Fair overall results on stability tests (4.7 on a scale of 0 to 10) including potential drain of affiliation with Washington State Health. The largest net exposure for one risk is conservative at 1.3% of capital. Strong long-term capitalization index (10.0) based on excellent current risk adjusted capital (severe and moderate loss scenarios). Moreover, capital levels have been consistent in recent years.

Other Rating Factors: Ample reserve history (9.6) that helps to protect the company against sharp claims increases. Excellent profitability (8.3) with operating gains in each of the last five years. Excellent liquidity (7.4) with ample operational cash flow and liquid investments.

Principal Business: Medical malpractice (87%) and aggregate write-ins for other lines of business (12%).

Principal Investments: Investment grade bonds (80%), misc. investments (17%), and cash (3%).

Investments in Affiliates: 3%

Group Affiliation: Washington State Health

Licensed in: AK, AZ, CA, CO, ID, MT, NV, OR, UT, WA, WY

Commenced Business: December 1981

Address: 1730 Minor Ave, Suite 1800, Seattle, WA 98101

Phone: (206) 343-7300   **Domicile State:** WA   **NAIC Code:** 40738

Data Date	Rating	RACR #1	RACR #2	Loss Ratio %	Total Assets ($mil)	Capital ($mil)	Net Premium ($mil)	Net Income ($mil)
9-14	B-	4.06	3.13	N/A	470.6	217.7	56.3	7.8
9-13	B-	4.04	3.16	N/A	453.4	206.3	51.2	3.7
2013	B-	4.11	3.20	85.2	454.0	211.9	72.9	5.6
2012	B-	4.03	3.21	80.1	428.5	195.4	67.8	8.2
2011	B-	3.76	3.01	82.7	421.0	186.0	73.3	8.4
2010	B-	3.66	2.93	70.9	398.6	180.0	69.7	13.3
2009	B-	3.46	2.79	66.3	377.8	161.2	71.2	16.5

Rating Indexes

PIONEER STATE MUTUAL INS CO *

A   **Excellent**

Major Rating Factors: Strong long-term capitalization index (9.6 on a scale of 0 to 10) based on excellent current risk adjusted capital (severe and moderate loss scenarios). Furthermore, this high level of risk adjusted capital has been consistently maintained in previous years. Ample reserve history (8.5) that helps to protect the company against sharp claims increases.

Other Rating Factors: Excellent profitability (8.2) with operating gains in each of the last five years. Excellent overall results on stability tests (7.4). Stability strengths include excellent operational trends and excellent risk diversification. Good liquidity (6.9) with sufficient resources (cash flows and marketable investments) to handle a spike in claims.

Principal Business: Auto liability (38%), homeowners multiple peril (28%), auto physical damage (24%), farmowners multiple peril (5%), inland marine (2%), fire (1%), and other lines (3%).

Principal Investments: Investment grade bonds (61%), misc. investments (39%), and real estate (1%).

Investments in Affiliates: None

Group Affiliation: None

Licensed in: IN, MI

Commenced Business: June 1908

Address: 1510 N Elms Rd, Flint, MI 48532

Phone: (810) 733-2300   **Domicile State:** MI   **NAIC Code:** 18309

Data Date	Rating	RACR #1	RACR #2	Loss Ratio %	Total Assets ($mil)	Capital ($mil)	Net Premium ($mil)	Net Income ($mil)
9-14	A	4.50	2.83	N/A	464.9	265.3	127.1	4.5
9-13	A	4.85	3.09	N/A	435.1	250.7	122.7	9.4
2013	A	4.51	2.84	64.4	448.4	260.0	171.1	13.6
2012	A	5.03	3.25	66.2	400.9	233.1	163.7	11.8
2011	A	5.36	3.53	73.5	363.8	215.4	150.5	8.5
2010	A	5.15	3.35	70.7	349.2	207.9	143.0	11.5
2009	A	5.35	3.52	75.4	324.5	191.9	131.6	5.1

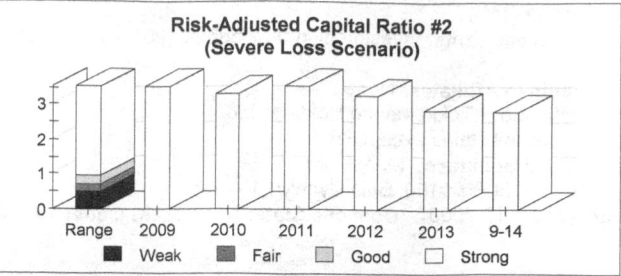

Risk-Adjusted Capital Ratio #2 (Severe Loss Scenario)

Range 2009 2010 2011 2012 2013 9-14
■ Weak ■ Fair ▨ Good □ Strong

PLATINUM UNDERWRITERS REINS CO

B-   **Good**

Major Rating Factors: Good overall profitability index (5.1 on a scale of 0 to 10). Fair expense controls. Return on equity has been good over the last five years, averaging 11.0%. Good overall results on stability tests (5.0). The largest net exposure for one risk is high at 4.9% of capital. Stability strengths include good operational trends and excellent risk diversification.

Other Rating Factors: Strong long-term capitalization index (7.8) based on excellent current risk adjusted capital (severe and moderate loss scenarios), despite some fluctuation in capital levels. Ample reserve history (9.4) that helps to protect the company against sharp claims increases. Excellent liquidity (7.7) with ample operational cash flow and liquid investments.

Principal Business: (This company is a reinsurer.)

Principal Investments: Investment grade bonds (97%), misc. investments (2%), and cash (1%).

Investments in Affiliates: None

Group Affiliation: Platinum Underwriters Holdings Ltd

Licensed in: All states except PR

Commenced Business: December 1995

Address: 5801 Centennial Way, LA303, Baltimore, MD 21209-3653

Phone: (212) 238-9600   **Domicile State:** MD   **NAIC Code:** 10357

Data Date	Rating	RACR #1	RACR #2	Loss Ratio %	Total Assets ($mil)	Capital ($mil)	Net Premium ($mil)	Net Income ($mil)
9-14	B-	2.61	1.61	N/A	1,652.7	581.9	257.5	36.3
9-13	B-	2.67	1.70	N/A	1,735.7	614.6	277.6	68.1
2013	B-	2.46	1.53	43.4	1,620.3	549.2	395.4	93.2
2012	B-	2.39	1.53	57.0	1,661.8	555.4	381.6	73.0
2011	C+	2.20	1.43	74.7	1,667.7	529.9	396.5	25.1
2010	C+	2.77	1.18	54.8	1,751.8	642.8	425.2	111.2
2009	C	2.34	1.04	76.8	1,773.6	586.3	570.9	28.6

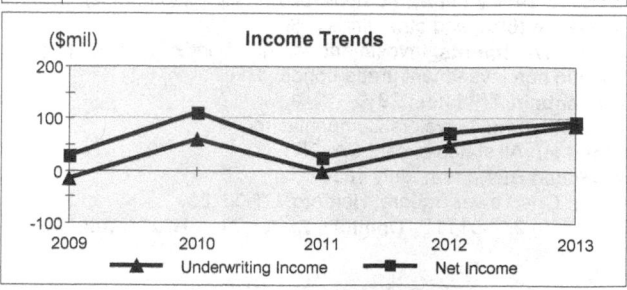

Income Trends ($mil)

2009 2010 2011 2012 2013
—▲— Underwriting Income   —■— Net Income

PMSLIC INS CO

B-   **Good**

Major Rating Factors: Fair overall results on stability tests (4.6 on a scale of 0 to 10) including potential drain of affiliation with NORCAL Mutual. Good overall profitability index (6.8). Good expense controls. Return on equity has been low, averaging 4.7% over the past five years.

Other Rating Factors: Strong long-term capitalization index (10.0) based on excellent current risk adjusted capital (severe and moderate loss scenarios), despite some fluctuation in capital levels. Ample reserve history (9.4) that helps to protect the company against sharp claims increases. Excellent liquidity (7.4) with ample operational cash flow and liquid investments.

Principal Business: Medical malpractice (100%).

Principal Investments: Investment grade bonds (80%), misc. investments (18%), cash (1%), and non investment grade bonds (1%).

Investments in Affiliates: None

Group Affiliation: NORCAL Mutual

Licensed in: CA, DE, NJ, OH, PA

Commenced Business: January 1978

Address: 777 E Park Dr, Harrisburg, PA 17111

Phone: (717) 791-1212   **Domicile State:** PA   **NAIC Code:** 35114

Data Date	Rating	RACR #1	RACR #2	Loss Ratio %	Total Assets ($mil)	Capital ($mil)	Net Premium ($mil)	Net Income ($mil)
9-14	B-	4.71	3.54	N/A	467.5	223.8	54.9	1.5
9-13	B-	4.68	3.51	N/A	467.7	221.9	60.2	1.7
2013	B-	4.66	3.53	79.3	472.1	220.1	78.5	3.5
2012	B-	4.79	3.63	71.9	476.4	220.8	77.5	10.7
2011	B-	4.36	3.24	76.8	452.6	207.2	85.8	3.6
2010	B-	5.07	4.04	65.3	434.7	199.8	63.1	18.2
2009	C+	4.32	3.53	57.1	433.9	183.7	65.7	16.1

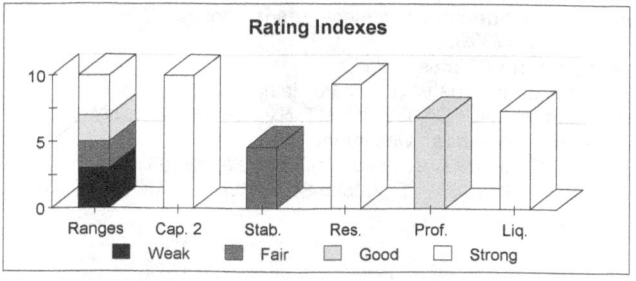

Rating Indexes

Ranges Cap. 2 Stab. Res. Prof. Liq.
■ Weak ■ Fair ▨ Good □ Strong

PRAETORIAN INS CO   C-   Fair

Major Rating Factors: Weak profitability index (1.9 on a scale of 0 to 10) with operating losses during 2010, 2011, 2012 and the first nine months of 2014. Average return on equity over the last five years has been poor at -4.0%. Fair reserve development (4.1) as reserves have generally been sufficient to cover claims. In 2013, the two year reserve development was 17% deficient.

Other Rating Factors: Fair overall results on stability tests (3.1) including weak results on operational trends and negative cash flow from operations for 2013. Strong long-term capitalization index (7.1) based on excellent current risk adjusted capital (severe and moderate loss scenarios), despite some fluctuation in capital levels. Excellent liquidity (7.0) with ample operational cash flow and liquid investments.

Principal Business: Workers compensation (27%), commercial multiple peril (17%), auto liability (14%), homeowners multiple peril (13%), auto physical damage (11%), inland marine (9%), and other lines (10%).

Principal Investments: Investment grade bonds (88%), cash (8%), and misc. investments (4%).

Investments in Affiliates: None

Group Affiliation: QBE Ins Group Ltd

Licensed in: All states, the District of Columbia and Puerto Rico

Commenced Business: August 1979

Address: 3435 Wilshire Blvd, Ste 700, Los Angeles, CA 90010

Phone: (212) 805-9700   **Domicile State:** PA   **NAIC Code:** 37257

Data Date	Rating	RACR #1	RACR #2	Loss Ratio %	Total Assets ($mil)	Capital ($mil)	Net Premium ($mil)	Net Income ($mil)
9-14	C-	1.55	1.04	N/A	1,261.3	245.7	308.5	-3.9
9-13	C	1.89	1.28	N/A	1,188.7	333.4	316.9	14.1
2013	C-	1.67	1.14	75.2	971.9	248.4	400.0	-28.2
2012	C	1.64	1.12	73.5	1,109.4	316.3	545.2	-13.5
2011	B-	1.59	1.00	77.2	991.8	346.3	287.0	-27.0
2010	B-	2.05	1.17	70.8	1,144.6	420.9	311.7	-0.5
2009	C+	1.70	0.99	69.3	1,130.2	453.2	329.8	9.1

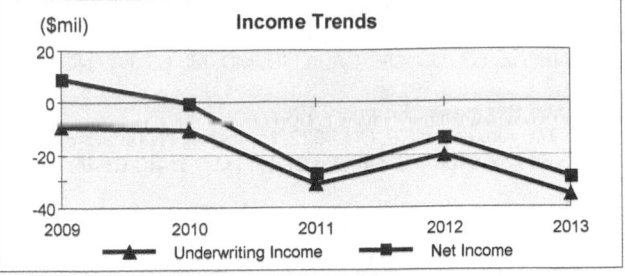

Income Trends

PREFERRED PROFESSIONAL INS CO   C+   Fair

Major Rating Factors: Fair overall results on stability tests (4.4 on a scale of 0 to 10) including negative cash flow from operations for 2013. Good profitability index (5.0). Excellent expense controls. Return on equity has been good over the last five years, averaging 10.5%.

Other Rating Factors: Strong long-term capitalization index (9.9) based on excellent current risk adjusted capital (severe and moderate loss scenarios), despite some fluctuation in capital levels. Ample reserve history (9.4) that helps to protect the company against sharp claims increases. Excellent liquidity (8.4) with ample operational cash flow and liquid investments.

Principal Business: Medical malpractice (79%), workers compensation (13%), other liability (4%), auto liability (4%), and auto physical damage (1%).

Principal Investments: Investment grade bonds (98%), non investment grade bonds (4%), and cash (3%).

Investments in Affiliates: 0%

Group Affiliation: Medical Professional Mutual

Licensed in: All states except PR

Commenced Business: July 1976

Address: 11605 Miracle Hills Dr #200, Omaha, NE 68154-4467

Phone: (402) 392-1566   **Domicile State:** NE   **NAIC Code:** 36234

Data Date	Rating	RACR #1	RACR #2	Loss Ratio %	Total Assets ($mil)	Capital ($mil)	Net Premium ($mil)	Net Income ($mil)
9-14	C+	4.53	3.23	N/A	300.7	138.6	30.6	6.5
9-13	C+	4.61	3.21	N/A	395.1	183.7	33.0	10.3
2013	C+	5.80	3.95	26.5	408.9	206.1	45.3	34.2
2012	C+	4.53	3.24	68.4	402.7	177.2	56.8	16.1
2011	C+	4.49	3.13	80.4	368.9	163.1	62.8	14.5
2010	C+	4.53	3.20	63.2	372.2	163.2	69.3	20.4
2009	C+	4.19	2.99	83.9	352.6	147.2	62.4	13.0

Medical Professional Mutual Composite Group Rating: C+ Largest Group Members	Assets ($mil)	Rating
MEDICAL PROFESSIONAL MUTUAL INS CO	3151	B-
MHA INS CO	529	B
PREFERRED PROFESSIONAL INS CO	409	C+
PROSELECT INS CO	71	C
OHA INS SOLUTIONS	44	C-

PREMIER INS CO OF MASSACHUSETTS   B   Good

Major Rating Factors: Good overall profitability index (5.8 on a scale of 0 to 10) with small operating losses during 2011. Return on equity has been low, averaging 3.3% over the past five years. Good liquidity (6.7) with sufficient resources (cash flows and marketable investments) to handle a spike in claims.

Other Rating Factors: Good overall results on stability tests (5.8) despite negative cash flow from operations for 2013. Stability strengths include good operational trends and excellent risk diversification. Fair reserve development (4.7) as reserves have generally been sufficient to cover claims. Strong long-term capitalization index (10.0) based on excellent current risk adjusted capital (severe and moderate loss scenarios), despite some fluctuation in capital levels.

Principal Business: Auto liability (61%) and auto physical damage (39%).

Principal Investments: Investment grade bonds (100%) and misc. investments (1%).

Investments in Affiliates: None

Group Affiliation: Travelers Companies Inc

Licensed in: MA

Commenced Business: July 1993

Address: One Research Dr Suite 315c, Westborough, MA 01581

Phone: (508) 616-6200   **Domicile State:** MA   **NAIC Code:** 12850

Data Date	Rating	RACR #1	RACR #2	Loss Ratio %	Total Assets ($mil)	Capital ($mil)	Net Premium ($mil)	Net Income ($mil)
9-14	B	7.11	6.17	N/A	361.7	228.8	91.8	9.4
9-13	B	6.13	5.37	N/A	372.7	226.0	107.8	7.5
2013	B	5.86	5.32	76.9	362.1	219.7	132.1	7.0
2012	B	5.06	4.61	75.6	375.0	218.6	153.4	12.2
2011	B	4.22	3.84	82.7	391.5	210.2	175.1	-0.6
2010	B	3.87	3.54	82.8	412.0	209.7	189.7	3.1
2009	B-	3.59	3.33	78.1	435.7	206.4	204.9	9.7

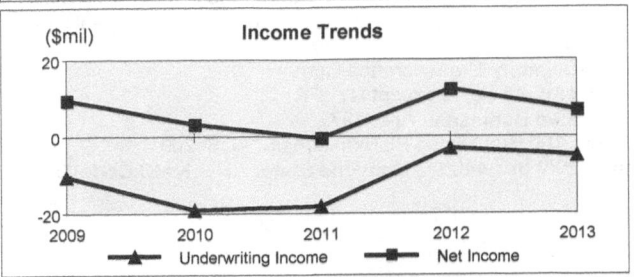

Income Trends

PRINCETON INS CO

C   Fair

Major Rating Factors: Fair overall results on stability tests (3.7 on a scale of 0 to 10) including fair financial strength of affiliated Berkshire Hathaway and weak results on operational trends. History of adequate reserve strength (6.1) as reserves have been consistently at an acceptable level.

Other Rating Factors: Strong long-term capitalization index (10.0) based on excellent current risk adjusted capital (severe and moderate loss scenarios), despite some fluctuation in capital levels. Excellent profitability (8.5) with operating gains in each of the last five years. Superior liquidity (9.0) with ample operational cash flow and liquid investments.

Principal Business: Medical malpractice (98%) and other liability (1%).

Principal Investments: Investment grade bonds (74%), cash (17%), misc. investments (7%), non investment grade bonds (1%), and real estate (1%).

Investments in Affiliates: None

Group Affiliation: Berkshire Hathaway

Licensed in: AZ, CT, DC, DE, GA, IL, IN, MD, MI, NJ, NY, NC, PA, SC, VA, WA, WV

Commenced Business: February 1982

Address: 746 Alexander Rd, CN-5322, Princeton, NJ 08543-5322

Phone: (609) 452-9404 **Domicile State:** NJ **NAIC Code:** 42226

Data Date	Rating	RACR #1	RACR #2	Loss Ratio %	Total Assets ($mil)	Capital ($mil)	Net Premium ($mil)	Net Income ($mil)
9-14	C	8.08	6.00	N/A	658.9	452.7	25.5	10.8
9-13	C	10.27	7.33	N/A	626.3	433.4	25.6	11.4
2013	C	8.15	6.06	104.5	628.5	438.8	35.1	12.6
2012	C	10.70	7.63	99.4	585.5	412.6	-502.9	79.6
2011	C-	1.58	1.33	74.8	1,037.4	350.4	135.4	37.9
2010	D+	1.52	1.28	76.4	1,073.4	353.7	145.0	38.3
2009	D+	1.30	1.05	74.7	1,022.1	313.3	151.0	27.7

Berkshire Hathaway
Composite Group Rating: B-

Largest Group Members	Assets ($mil)	Rating
NATIONAL INDEMNITY CO	151912	B-
GOVERNMENT EMPLOYEES INS CO	25779	B+
COLUMBIA INS CO	19013	B-
GENERAL REINSURANCE CORP	16220	B-
BERKSHIRE HATHAWAY LIFE INS CO OF NE	13768	C+

PROASSURANCE CASUALTY CO

B-   Good

Major Rating Factors: Fair overall results on stability tests (4.6 on a scale of 0 to 10) including potential drain of affiliation with ProAssurance Corp. Strong long-term capitalization index (9.5) based on excellent current risk adjusted capital (severe and moderate loss scenarios), despite some fluctuation in capital levels.

Other Rating Factors: Ample reserve history (9.9) that helps to protect the company against sharp claims increases. Excellent profitability (7.6) with operating gains in each of the last five years. Return on equity has been excellent over the last five years averaging 17.5%. Excellent liquidity (7.5) with ample operational cash flow and liquid investments.

Principal Business: Medical malpractice (89%) and other liability (11%).

Principal Investments: Investment grade bonds (79%), misc. investments (12%), non investment grade bonds (8%), and cash (1%).

Investments in Affiliates: None

Group Affiliation: ProAssurance Corp

Licensed in: AL, CA, CT, DE, FL, GA, IL, IN, IA, KS, KY, MD, MA, MI, MN, MS, MO, NE, NV, NJ, ND, OH, PA, SC, SD, TN, VT, VA, WV, WI

Commenced Business: June 1980

Address: 2600 Professionals Dr, Okemos, MI 48805-0150

Phone: (517) 349-6500 **Domicile State:** MI **NAIC Code:** 38954

Data Date	Rating	RACR #1	RACR #2	Loss Ratio %	Total Assets ($mil)	Capital ($mil)	Net Premium ($mil)	Net Income ($mil)
9-14	B-	3.71	2.81	N/A	1,291.9	513.6	123.9	56.3
9-13	B-	3.41	2.65	N/A	1,296.9	502.1	125.7	61.6
2013	B-	3.66	2.80	52.4	1,342.0	523.6	166.0	72.1
2012	B-	3.52	2.77	23.2	1,430.7	567.0	190.1	124.4
2011	B-	2.71	2.28	17.7	1,468.8	546.2	183.0	99.3
2010	B-	2.57	2.14	32.4	1,508.9	496.0	181.9	90.5
2009	B-	2.16	1.80	41.0	1,141.0	370.2	140.2	65.1

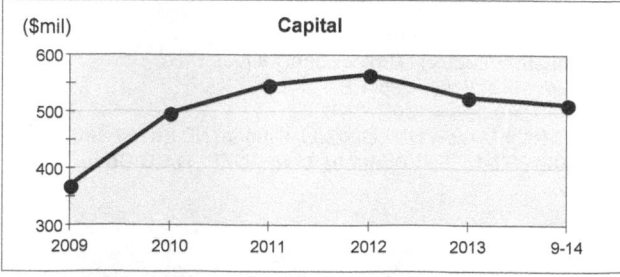

Capital ($mil)

PROASSURANCE INDEMNTIY CO INC

B-   Good

Major Rating Factors: Fair overall results on stability tests (4.6 on a scale of 0 to 10) including potential drain of affiliation with ProAssurance Corp. Strong long-term capitalization index (10.0) based on excellent current risk adjusted capital (severe and moderate loss scenarios), despite some fluctuation in capital levels.

Other Rating Factors: Ample reserve history (9.8) that helps to protect the company against sharp claims increases. Excellent profitability (7.1) with operating gains in each of the last five years. Return on equity has been excellent over the last five years averaging 21.5%. Excellent liquidity (7.4) with ample operational cash flow and liquid investments.

Principal Business: Medical malpractice (98%) and other liability (2%).

Principal Investments: Investment grade bonds (76%), misc. investments (16%), non investment grade bonds (6%), cash (1%), and real estate (1%).

Investments in Affiliates: 1%

Group Affiliation: ProAssurance Corp

Licensed in: All states except NY, PR

Commenced Business: April 1977

Address: 100 Brookwood Pl, Birmingham, AL 35209

Phone: (205) 877-4400 **Domicile State:** AL **NAIC Code:** 33391

Data Date	Rating	RACR #1	RACR #2	Loss Ratio %	Total Assets ($mil)	Capital ($mil)	Net Premium ($mil)	Net Income ($mil)
9-14	B-	4.21	3.20	N/A	1,737.4	633.8	164.9	78.5
9-13	B-	5.03	3.92	N/A	1,896.9	875.8	176.4	96.2
2013	B-	4.72	3.65	26.8	1,718.4	753.7	240.0	147.5
2012	B-	4.31	3.40	24.4	1,861.9	772.5	256.9	180.1
2011	B-	3.88	3.18	17.2	2,042.5	775.9	280.9	179.6
2010	B-	3.19	2.66	31.6	1,942.6	696.6	267.8	148.6
2009	B	2.97	2.49	25.6	1,770.9	603.3	226.6	145.3

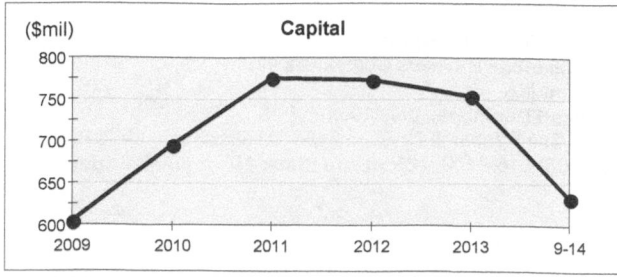

Capital ($mil)

PROGRESSIVE CASUALTY INS CO   C+   Fair

Major Rating Factors: Fair overall results on stability tests (4.5 on a scale of 0 to 10) including potential drain of affiliation with Progressive Group. Good long-term capitalization index (5.4) based on good current risk adjusted capital (severe and moderate loss scenarios). Over the last several years, capital levels have remained relatively consistent.

Other Rating Factors: History of adequate reserve strength (6.5) as reserves have been consistently at an acceptable level. Vulnerable liquidity (1.2) as a spike in claims may stretch capacity. Excellent profitability (9.4) with operating gains in each of the last five years. Return on equity has been excellent over the last five years averaging 27.4%.

Principal Business: Auto liability (64%), auto physical damage (30%), inland marine (3%), homeowners multiple peril (1%), and other liability (1%).

Principal Investments: Misc. investments (48%), investment grade bonds (38%), real estate (10%), non investment grade bonds (3%), and cash (1%).

Investments in Affiliates: 21%

Group Affiliation: Progressive Group

Licensed in: All states, the District of Columbia and Puerto Rico

Commenced Business: December 1956

Address: 6300 Wilson Mills Rd,W33, Mayfield Village, OH 44143-2182

Phone: (440) 461-5000   **Domicile State:** OH   **NAIC Code:** 24260

Data Date	Rating	RACR #1	RACR #2	Loss Ratio %	Total Assets ($mil)	Capital ($mil)	Net Premium ($mil)	Net Income ($mil)
9-14	C+	0.99	0.82	N/A	6,444.3	1,629.6	3,572.0	223.4
9-13	C+	0.96	0.80	N/A	6,208.2	1,624.9	3,445.2	175.7
2013	C+	0.94	0.80	72.9	5,772.4	1,543.1	4,657.8	501.3
2012	C+	0.90	0.78	75.1	5,332.1	1,448.5	4,447.9	406.7
2011	C+	0.84	0.73	72.0	5,129.9	1,359.9	4,151.1	556.8
2010	C+	0.74	0.66	70.3	4,800.5	1,333.5	4,005.2	279.5
2009	C+	0.82	0.73	70.1	4,881.0	1,361.7	3,959.7	289.9

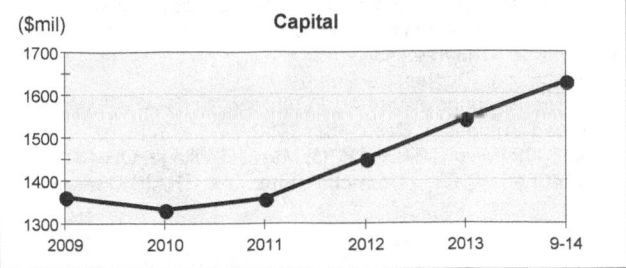

Capital

PROGRESSIVE DIRECT INS CO   C-   Fair

Major Rating Factors: Vulnerable liquidity (1.3 on a scale of 0 to 10) as a spike in claims may stretch capacity. Weak overall results on stability tests (2.9).

Other Rating Factors: Strong long-term capitalization index (7.2) based on excellent current risk adjusted capital (severe and moderate loss scenarios). Moreover, capital levels have been consistent in recent years. Ample reserve history (8.4) that helps to protect the company against sharp claims increases. Excellent profitability (9.2) with operating gains in each of the last five years. Return on equity has been excellent over the last five years averaging 17.2%.

Principal Business: Auto liability (64%), auto physical damage (34%), and inland marine (1%).

Principal Investments: Investment grade bonds (66%), misc. investments (28%), real estate (4%), and non investment grade bonds (2%).

Investments in Affiliates: None

Group Affiliation: Progressive Group

Licensed in: All states except TX, PR

Commenced Business: January 1987

Address: 6300 Wilson Mills Rd, Mayfield Village, OH 44143-2182

Phone: (440) 461-5000   **Domicile State:** OH   **NAIC Code:** 16322

Data Date	Rating	RACR #1	RACR #2	Loss Ratio %	Total Assets ($mil)	Capital ($mil)	Net Premium ($mil)	Net Income ($mil)
9-14	C-	1.39	1.22	N/A	5,269.8	1,613.8	3,525.9	174.0
9-13	C-	1.46	1.27	N/A	4,962.6	1,578.0	3,255.1	206.4
2013	C-	1.26	1.13	72.4	4,724.2	1,433.3	4,450.2	286.3
2012	C-	1.27	1.15	74.2	4,541.6	1,363.3	4,246.7	222.7
2011	C-	1.29	1.17	71.7	4,185.6	1,272.4	3,955.8	208.4
2010	C-	1.32	1.20	73.3	3,947.0	1,203.9	3,677.9	208.0
2009	C-	1.34	1.23	73.3	3,569.6	1,121.7	3,316.4	203.2

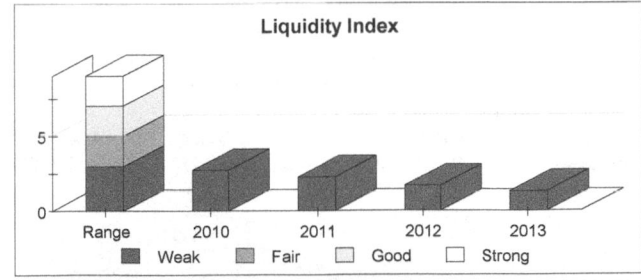

Liquidity Index

Range   2010   2011   2012   2013

■ Weak   ■ Fair   □ Good   □ Strong

PROGRESSIVE NORTHERN INS CO   C+   Fair

Major Rating Factors: Fair overall results on stability tests (4.4 on a scale of 0 to 10) including potential drain of affiliation with Progressive Group. History of adequate reserve strength (6.5) as reserves have been consistently at an acceptable level.

Other Rating Factors: Vulnerable liquidity (1.8) as a spike in claims may stretch capacity. Strong long-term capitalization index (7.2) based on excellent current risk adjusted capital (severe and moderate loss scenarios), despite some fluctuation in capital levels. Excellent profitability (9.3) with operating gains in each of the last five years. Return on equity has been excellent over the last five years averaging 23.4%.

Principal Business: Auto liability (60%), auto physical damage (36%), inland marine (2%), other liability (1%), and homeowners multiple peril (1%).

Principal Investments: Investment grade bonds (73%), misc. investments (24%), and non investment grade bonds (3%).

Investments in Affiliates: None

Group Affiliation: Progressive Group

Licensed in: All states except AL, AR, CA, FL, MA, MO, NJ, ND, TN, TX, PR

Commenced Business: March 1981

Address: 8025 Excelsior Dr Suite 200, Madison, WI 53717

Phone: (440) 461-5000   **Domicile State:** WI   **NAIC Code:** 38628

Data Date	Rating	RACR #1	RACR #2	Loss Ratio %	Total Assets ($mil)	Capital ($mil)	Net Premium ($mil)	Net Income ($mil)
9-14	C+	1.53	1.31	N/A	1,437.1	436.1	874.8	59.2
9-13	C+	1.53	1.30	N/A	1,395.6	418.3	843.7	55.5
2013	C+	1.30	1.15	72.9	1,305.4	370.7	1,140.7	78.6
2012	C+	1.30	1.16	75.1	1,245.7	347.5	1,089.3	51.9
2011	C+	1.33	1.20	72.0	1,167.3	329.7	1,016.6	63.7
2010	C+	1.32	1.20	70.3	1,135.5	315.7	980.9	95.9
2009	C+	1.38	1.25	70.0	1,176.6	326.9	984.3	115.8

Progressive Group
Composite Group Rating: C+
Largest Group Members

Largest Group Members	Assets ($mil)	Rating
PROGRESSIVE CASUALTY INS CO	5772	C+
PROGRESSIVE DIRECT INS CO	4724	C-
UNITED FINANCIAL CASUALTY CO	2138	C+
PROGRESSIVE NORTHERN INS CO	1305	C+
PROGRESSIVE NORTHWESTERN INS CO	1268	C+

PROGRESSIVE NORTHWESTERN INS CO

C+ Fair

Major Rating Factors: Fair overall results on stability tests (4.5 on a scale of 0 to 10) including potential drain of affiliation with Progressive Group. History of adequate reserve strength (6.5) as reserves have been consistently at an acceptable level.

Other Rating Factors: Vulnerable liquidity (2.9) as a spike in claims may stretch capacity. Strong long-term capitalization index (7.2) based on excellent current risk adjusted capital (severe and moderate loss scenarios), despite some fluctuation in capital levels. Excellent profitability (9.3) with operating gains in each of the last five years. Return on equity has been excellent over the last five years averaging 22.0%.

Principal Business: Auto liability (58%), auto physical damage (38%), inland marine (3%), and other liability (1%).

Principal Investments: Investment grade bonds (76%), misc. investments (23%), and non investment grade bonds (1%).

Investments in Affiliates: None

Group Affiliation: Progressive Group

Licensed in: All states except AL, FL, IL, MA, NH, PA, VT, WY, PR

Commenced Business: September 1983

Address: 6300 Wilson Mills Rd W33, Mayfield Village, OH 44143-2182

Phone: (440) 461-5000   **Domicile State:** OH   **NAIC Code:** 42919

Data Date	Rating	RACR #1	RACR #2	Loss Ratio %	Total Assets ($mil)	Capital ($mil)	Net Premium ($mil)	Net Income ($mil)
9-14	C+	1.52	1.30	N/A	1,391.0	433.9	874.8	62.8
9-13	C+	1.50	1.27	N/A	1,342.7	415.3	843.7	47.8
2013	C+	1.30	1.13	72.9	1,267.5	371.6	1,140.7	66.0
2012	C+	1.29	1.14	75.1	1,207.2	347.3	1,089.3	57.0
2011	C+	1.32	1.17	72.0	1,127.0	328.5	1,016.6	65.5
2010	C+	1.33	1.20	70.3	1,099.4	319.3	980.9	82.2
2009	C+	1.40	1.26	70.1	1,093.3	326.3	969.7	104.1

Progressive Group
Composite Group Rating: C+

Largest Group Members	Assets ($mil)	Rating
PROGRESSIVE CASUALTY INS CO	5772	C+
PROGRESSIVE DIRECT INS CO	4724	C-
UNITED FINANCIAL CASUALTY CO	2138	C+
PROGRESSIVE NORTHERN INS CO	1305	C+
PROGRESSIVE NORTHWESTERN INS CO	1268	C+

PROGRESSIVE SPECIALTY INS CO

C Fair

Major Rating Factors: Fair overall results on stability tests (3.9 on a scale of 0 to 10). Weak profitability index (2.5). Good expense controls. Return on equity has been fair, averaging 12.9% over the past five years.

Other Rating Factors: History of adequate reserve strength (6.1) as reserves have been consistently at an acceptable level. Good liquidity (5.1) with sufficient resources (cash flows and marketable investments) to handle a spike in claims. Strong long-term capitalization index (8.7) based on excellent current risk adjusted capital (severe and moderate loss scenarios), despite some fluctuation in capital levels.

Principal Business: Auto liability (64%), auto physical damage (35%), and inland marine (1%).

Principal Investments: Investment grade bonds (69%) and misc. investments (31%).

Investments in Affiliates: None

Group Affiliation: Progressive Group

Licensed in: All states except LA, MA, NH, NC, WY, PR

Commenced Business: May 1976

Address: 6300 Wilson Mills Rd,W33, Mayfield Village, OH 44143-2182

Phone: (440) 461-5000   **Domicile State:** OH   **NAIC Code:** 32786

Data Date	Rating	RACR #1	RACR #2	Loss Ratio %	Total Assets ($mil)	Capital ($mil)	Net Premium ($mil)	Net Income ($mil)
9-14	C	2.61	2.20	N/A	1,037.0	442.3	510.3	38.4
9-13	C	3.29	2.72	N/A	1,117.0	540.5	492.2	74.4
2013	C	2.27	1.96	72.9	941.3	386.2	665.4	87.0
2012	C	2.94	2.54	75.1	994.3	467.3	635.4	60.3
2011	C	3.90	3.38	72.0	1,065.8	574.7	593.0	64.0
2010	B	5.58	4.81	70.3	1,275.3	800.4	572.2	70.5
2009	B	5.23	4.67	70.1	1,189.7	719.9	565.7	70.7

Progressive Group
Composite Group Rating: C+

Largest Group Members	Assets ($mil)	Rating
PROGRESSIVE CASUALTY INS CO	5772	C+
PROGRESSIVE DIRECT INS CO	4724	C-
UNITED FINANCIAL CASUALTY CO	2138	C+
PROGRESSIVE NORTHERN INS CO	1305	C+
PROGRESSIVE NORTHWESTERN INS CO	1268	C+

PROPERTY-OWNERS INS CO *

A Excellent

Major Rating Factors: Strong long-term capitalization index (8.7 on a scale of 0 to 10) based on excellent current risk adjusted capital (severe and moderate loss scenarios). Furthermore, this high level of risk adjusted capital has been consistently maintained in previous years. Ample reserve history (8.1) that helps to protect the company against sharp claims increases.

Other Rating Factors: Excellent profitability (7.0) with operating gains in each of the last five years. Excellent overall results on stability tests (7.6). Stability strengths include excellent operational trends and excellent risk diversification. Good liquidity (6.7) with sufficient resources (cash flows and marketable investments) to handle a spike in claims.

Principal Business: Commercial multiple peril (39%), homeowners multiple peril (26%), workers compensation (10%), auto liability (9%), auto physical damage (6%), inland marine (4%), and other lines (7%).

Principal Investments: Investment grade bonds (87%), misc. investments (12%), and cash (1%).

Investments in Affiliates: None

Group Affiliation: Auto-Owners Group

Licensed in: AL, AR, GA, IL, IN, IA, KY, MI, MO, NE, NV, ND, SC, SD, UT, VA, WI

Commenced Business: September 1976

Address: 3950 W Delphi Pike, Marion, IN 46952-9266

Phone: (517) 323-1200   **Domicile State:** IN   **NAIC Code:** 32905

Data Date	Rating	RACR #1	RACR #2	Loss Ratio %	Total Assets ($mil)	Capital ($mil)	Net Premium ($mil)	Net Income ($mil)
9-14	A	3.57	2.07	N/A	217.0	104.6	52.2	0.0
9-13	A	3.35	1.79	N/A	206.6	100.0	48.7	5.2
2013	A	3.83	2.21	55.5	209.7	104.5	70.0	9.0
2012	A	3.32	1.77	61.3	193.9	93.5	63.5	7.5
2011	A	2.59	1.42	80.2	179.5	85.3	63.3	1.6
2010	A	2.84	1.53	72.4	173.0	83.8	61.7	4.6
2009	A	2.71	1.48	66.4	155.0	78.0	59.8	5.2

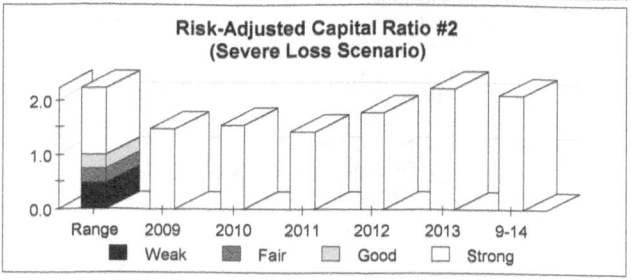

Risk-Adjusted Capital Ratio #2
(Severe Loss Scenario)

Range 2009 2010 2011 2012 2013 9-14

■ Weak   ▨ Fair   ▢ Good   □ Strong

PROTECTIVE INS CO *　　　　　　　　　　　　　　　　　　　　A-　　　Excellent

Major Rating Factors: Strong long-term capitalization index (7.1 on a scale of 0 to 10) based on excellent current risk adjusted capital (severe and moderate loss scenarios), despite some fluctuation in capital levels. Ample reserve history (8.4) that helps to protect the company against sharp claims increases.

Other Rating Factors: Good overall profitability index (5.6) despite operating losses during 2011. Return on equity has been low, averaging 3.7% over the past five years. Good liquidity (6.6) with sufficient resources (cash flows and marketable investments) to handle a spike in claims. Good overall results on stability tests (6.9).

Principal Business: Workers compensation (40%), other liability (22%), auto liability (19%), auto physical damage (16%), group accident & health (2%), and surety (1%).

Principal Investments: Misc. investments (62%), investment grade bonds (31%), non investment grade bonds (4%), and real estate (4%).

Investments in Affiliates: 27%

Group Affiliation: Protective Ins Group

Licensed in: All states except PR

Commenced Business: December 1954

Address: 1099 N Meridian St, Indianapolis, IN 46204

Phone: (317) 636-9800　　**Domicile State:** IN　　**NAIC Code:** 12416

Data Date	Rating	RACR #1	RACR #2	Loss Ratio %	Total Assets ($mil)	Capital ($mil)	Net Premium ($mil)	Net Income ($mil)
9-14	A-	1.46	1.05	N/A	776.3	395.1	172.8	22.3
9-13	A-	1.32	0.94	N/A	730.0	360.1	165.8	24.4
2013	A-	1.42	1.03	57.6	741.1	375.8	228.0	28.6
2012	A-	1.30	0.94	57.6	680.1	337.5	203.4	24.0
2011	A-	1.22	0.89	93.6	633.5	312.3	199.2	-23.0
2010	A	1.61	1.28	68.7	620.6	365.1	172.5	9.2
2009	A	1.62	1.30	53.5	590.0	355.3	151.2	20.8

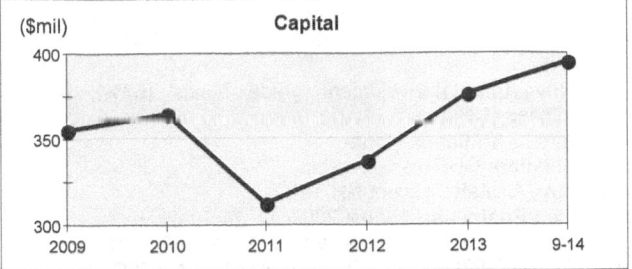

Capital

QBE INS CORP　　　　　　　　　　　　　　　　　　　　　　　C　　　Fair

Major Rating Factors: Fair overall results on stability tests (4.2 on a scale of 0 to 10) including weak results on operational trends and negative cash flow from operations for 2013. A history of deficient reserves (2.9) that places pressure on both capital and profits. In 2011, the two year reserve development was 24% deficient.

Other Rating Factors: Weak profitability index (2.9) with operating losses during each of the last five years and the first nine months of 2014. Average return on equity over the last five years has been poor at -9.2%. Good liquidity (6.7) with sufficient resources (cash flows and marketable investments) to handle a spike in claims. Strong long-term capitalization index (7.5) based on excellent current risk adjusted capital (severe and moderate loss scenarios), despite some fluctuation in capital levels.

Principal Business: Commercial multiple peril (33%), group accident & health (13%), workers compensation (10%), allied lines (10%), homeowners multiple peril (8%), credit (6%), and other lines (19%).

Principal Investments: Investment grade bonds (58%), misc. investments (33%), and cash (9%).

Investments in Affiliates: 18%

Group Affiliation: QBE Ins Group Ltd

Licensed in: All states except PR

Commenced Business: October 1980

Address: 1209 Orange St, Wilmington, DE 19801

Phone: (212) 805-9700　　**Domicile State:** PA　　**NAIC Code:** 39217

Data Date	Rating	RACR #1	RACR #2	Loss Ratio %	Total Assets ($mil)	Capital ($mil)	Net Premium ($mil)	Net Income ($mil)
9-14	C	1.76	1.31	N/A	2,576.0	685.5	552.3	-4.5
9-13	C	2.12	1.61	N/A	2,462.3	835.8	571.4	21.8
2013	C	1.95	1.49	75.2	2,138.2	678.7	750.5	-61.1
2012	C	2.04	1.55	73.5	2,188.1	802.4	473.1	-24.3
2011	C	1.77	1.16	50.9	2,424.9	840.8	1,600.7	-40.9
2010	B-	1.30	1.01	66.9	1,057.1	354.7	436.5	-40.0
2009	C+	0.94	0.63	74.6	769.4	238.1	369.4	-57.8

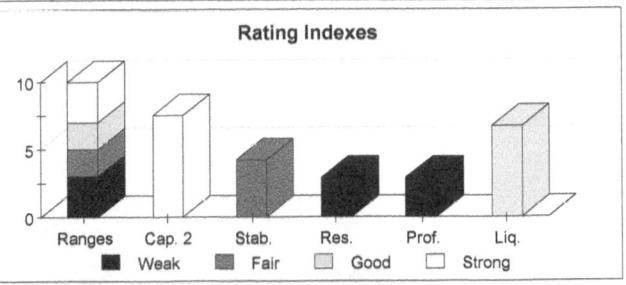

Rating Indexes

Ranges　Cap. 2　Stab.　Res.　Prof.　Liq.

■ Weak　▨ Fair　▤ Good　□ Strong

QBE REINSURANCE CORP　　　　　　　　　　　　　　　　　　B　　　Good

Major Rating Factors: Good overall results on stability tests (5.4 on a scale of 0 to 10) despite potential drain of affiliation with QBE Ins Group Ltd, negative cash flow from operations for 2013 and fair results on operational trends. Good overall profitability index (5.3). Fair expense controls. Return on equity has been low, averaging 3.2% over the past five years.

Other Rating Factors: Good liquidity (6.9) with sufficient resources (cash flows and marketable investments) to handle a spike in claims. Fair reserve development (4.5) as reserves have generally been sufficient to cover claims. Strong long-term capitalization index (7.1) based on excellent current risk adjusted capital (severe and moderate loss scenarios), despite some fluctuation in capital levels.

Principal Business: (This company is a reinsurer.)

Principal Investments: Misc. investments (70%), investment grade bonds (26%), and cash (4%).

Investments in Affiliates: 61%

Group Affiliation: QBE Ins Group Ltd

Licensed in: All states, the District of Columbia and Puerto Rico

Commenced Business: October 1964

Address: 88 Pine Street, 16th Floorr, New York, NY 10005

Phone: (212) 805-9700　　**Domicile State:** PA　　**NAIC Code:** 10219

Data Date	Rating	RACR #1	RACR #2	Loss Ratio %	Total Assets ($mil)	Capital ($mil)	Net Premium ($mil)	Net Income ($mil)
9-14	B	1.40	1.34	N/A	1,269.9	825.8	139.6	2.7
9-13	B	1.37	1.31	N/A	1,468.7	987.0	185.1	16.8
2013	B	1.40	1.36	75.2	1,232.9	814.7	210.4	0.0
2012	B	1.33	1.28	73.5	1,545.6	943.1	333.1	5.0
2011	B	1.39	1.30	64.6	1,750.9	1,080.5	369.6	11.7
2010	B-	1.36	1.20	61.1	1,168.0	587.3	357.3	27.7
2009	B-	1.48	1.07	58.2	1,091.4	580.5	185.0	67.1

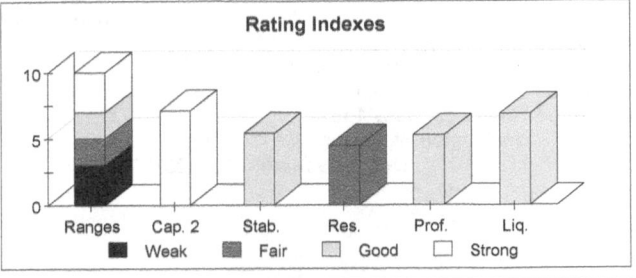

Rating Indexes

Ranges　Cap. 2　Stab.　Res.　Prof.　Liq.

■ Weak　▨ Fair　▤ Good　□ Strong

QBE SPECIALTY INS CO   D   Weak

Major Rating Factors: Weak overall results on stability tests (2.0 on a scale of 0 to 10) including weak results on operational trends and negative cash flow from operations for 2013. Fair reserve development (3.3) as reserves have generally been sufficient to cover claims. In 2013, the two year reserve development was 17% deficient.

Other Rating Factors: Fair profitability index (3.7) with operating losses during 2009, 2012 and the first nine months of 2014. Average return on equity over the last five years has been poor at -1.0%. Good liquidity (6.6) with sufficient resources (cash flows and marketable investments) to handle a spike in claims. Strong long-term capitalization index (7.4) based on excellent current risk adjusted capital (severe and moderate loss scenarios), despite some fluctuation in capital levels.

Principal Business: Commercial multiple peril (29%), allied lines (25%), inland marine (17%), fire (9%), homeowners multiple peril (8%), other liability (5%), and other lines (6%).

Principal Investments: Investment grade bonds (67%), misc. investments (20%), and cash (13%).

Investments in Affiliates: None
Group Affiliation: QBE Ins Group Ltd
Licensed in: All states except NH, PR
Commenced Business: August 2002
Address: 88 Pine St 4th Floor, New York, NY 10005-1801
Phone: (212) 805-9700   **Domicile State:** ND   **NAIC Code:** 11515

Data Date	Rating	RACR #1	RACR #2	Loss Ratio %	Total Assets ($mil)	Capital ($mil)	Net Premium ($mil)	Net Income ($mil)
9-14	D	1.90	1.26	N/A	957.4	214.4	218.8	-4.1
9-13	D	1.79	1.23	N/A	829.0	237.6	224.4	4.9
2013	D	2.05	1.39	75.2	709.1	214.8	290.0	-14.6
2012	D	1.65	1.14	73.5	750.8	232.6	378.0	-14.0
2011	D	1.14	0.87	35.9	555.1	245.6	228.4	22.3
2010	D-	2.01	1.30	36.1	520.2	225.7	264.2	9.9
2009	D-	2.22	1.37	40.6	343.4	139.9	270.7	-5.9

QBE Ins Group Ltd
Composite Group Rating: C
Largest Group Members

	Assets ($mil)	Rating
QBE INS CORP	2138	C
NAU COUNTRY INS CO	1300	C
QBE REINSURANCE CORP	1233	B
PRAETORIAN INS CO	972	C-
GENERAL CASUALTY CO OF WI	867	C

QUEEN CITY ASR INC *   A+   Excellent

Major Rating Factors: Strong long-term capitalization index (10.0 on a scale of 0 to 10) based on excellent current risk adjusted capital (severe and moderate loss scenarios). Furthermore, this high level of risk adjusted capital has been consistently maintained in previous years. Excellent profitability (8.9) with operating gains in each of the last five years. Excellent expense controls. Return on equity has been good over the last five years, averaging 11.4%.

Other Rating Factors: Excellent overall results on stability tests (7.9). Stability strengths include excellent risk diversification. Good liquidity (6.8) with sufficient resources (cash flows and marketable investments) to handle a spike in claims.

Principal Business: Aggregate write-ins for other lines of business (82%), earthquake (16%), fidelity (1%), and other liability (1%).

Principal Investments: Misc. investments (100%).

Investments in Affiliates: None
Group Affiliation: Kroger Co
(No States listed)

Data Date	Rating	RACR #1	RACR #2	Loss Ratio %	Total Assets ($mil)	Capital ($mil)	Net Premium ($mil)	Net Income ($mil)
9-14	A+	12.89	7.27	N/A	2,149.3	1,958.2	127.2	120.2
9-13	A+	12.20	6.96	N/A	1,987.9	1,796.8	127.5	122.9
2013	A+	11.78	6.77	0.0	2,001.9	1,838.0	169.6	164.1
2012	A+	11.11	6.45	0.0	1,830.9	1,673.9	170.0	162.8
2011	A+	12.17	6.96	0.0	1,686.8	1,511.1	28.9	160.4
2010	N/A	N/A	N/A	0.0	1,589.0	1,350.7	166.5	200.9
2009	N/A	N/A	N/A	N/A	1,385.2	1,149.8	195.8	176.6

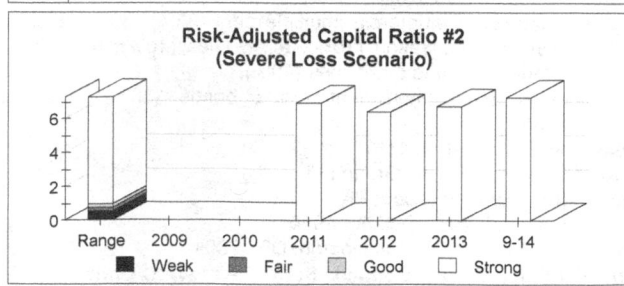

Risk-Adjusted Capital Ratio #2
(Severe Loss Scenario)

Range 2009 2010 2011 2012 2013 9-14
■ Weak   ■ Fair   ▨ Good   □ Strong

QUINCY MUTUAL FIRE INS CO   B   Good

Major Rating Factors: Good overall profitability index (6.0 on a scale of 0 to 10) despite operating losses during 2011. Good liquidity (6.9) with sufficient resources (cash flows and marketable investments) to handle a spike in claims.

Other Rating Factors: Fair overall results on stability tests (4.7) including potential drain of affiliation with Quincy Mutual Group. Strong long-term capitalization index (8.7) based on excellent current risk adjusted capital (severe and moderate loss scenarios), despite some fluctuation in capital levels. Ample reserve history (7.4) that can protect against increases in claims costs.

Principal Business: Homeowners multiple peril (34%), auto liability (27%), auto physical damage (19%), commercial multiple peril (14%), allied lines (3%), and fire (2%).

Principal Investments: Misc. investments (57%), investment grade bonds (36%), non investment grade bonds (5%), cash (1%), and real estate (1%).

Investments in Affiliates: 3%
Group Affiliation: Quincy Mutual Group
Licensed in: CT, ME, MA, NH, NJ, NY, PA, RI
Commenced Business: May 1851
Address: 57 Washington St, Quincy, MA 02169
Phone: (617) 770-5100   **Domicile State:** MA   **NAIC Code:** 15067

Data Date	Rating	RACR #1	RACR #2	Loss Ratio %	Total Assets ($mil)	Capital ($mil)	Net Premium ($mil)	Net Income ($mil)
9-14	B	4.02	2.48	N/A	1,481.9	960.0	199.8	51.5
9-13	B	3.57	2.25	N/A	1,430.3	870.7	214.9	21.9
2013	B	3.71	2.30	55.6	1,471.1	927.1	296.3	49.8
2012	B	3.72	2.36	61.7	1,310.9	796.7	284.3	47.8
2011	B	3.55	2.30	101.1	1,186.1	729.1	276.3	-12.9
2010	B	3.92	2.43	64.4	1,227.0	776.8	258.4	39.0
2009	B	3.72	2.32	63.9	1,161.8	709.1	253.4	44.0

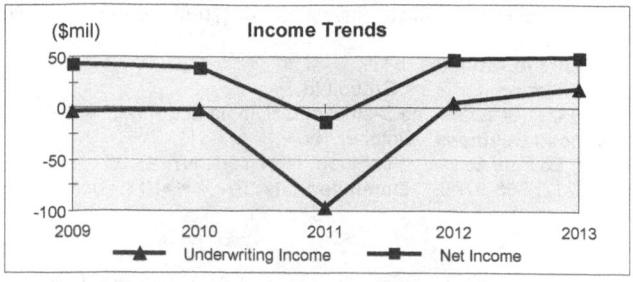

($mil)   Income Trends

2009 2010 2011 2012 2013
—▲— Underwriting Income   —■— Net Income

RADIAN ASSET ASR CO　　　　　　　C　　　Fair

Major Rating Factors: Weak overall results on stability tests (2.9 on a scale of 0 to 10) including weak results on operational trends and negative cash flow from operations for 2013. The largest net exposure for one risk is excessive at 6.4% of capital. History of adequate reserve strength (6.3) as reserves have been consistently at an acceptable level.

Other Rating Factors: Good overall profitability index (5.7). Weak expense controls. Return on equity has been low, averaging 5.0% over the past five years. Strong long-term capitalization index (10.0) based on excellent current risk adjusted capital (severe and moderate loss scenarios), despite some fluctuation in capital levels. Superior liquidity (10.0) with ample operational cash flow and liquid investments.

Principal Business: (Not applicable due to unusual reinsurance transactions.)
Principal Investments: Investment grade bonds (108%).
Investments in Affiliates: None
Group Affiliation: Radian Group Inc
Licensed in: All states, the District of Columbia and Puerto Rico
Commenced Business: April 1986
Address: 360 Madison Ave, 25th Floor, New York, NY 10017-4605
Phone: (212) 983-3100　**Domicile State:** NY　**NAIC Code:** 36250

Data Date	Rating	RACR #1	RACR #2	Loss Ratio %	Total Assets ($mil)	Capital ($mil)	Net Premium ($mil)	Net Income ($mil)
9-14	C	21.90	20.11	N/A	1,343.9	1,033.1	32.1	7.4
9-13	B-	61.39	25.06	N/A	1,513.6	1,203.2	57.7	21.1
2013	C	16.93	16.23	0.5	1,501.5	1,198.0	10.8	24.9
2012	B-	37.64	15.92	29.7	1,676.0	1,144.1	-87.7	103.3
2011	B-	5.62	4.48	91.0	2,049.1	973.9	43.2	69.1
2010	B-	6.23	5.32	35.5	2,188.6	1,048.6	49.3	58.0
2009	B-	5.80	4.90	127.0	2,175.4	1,059.1	13.2	42.8

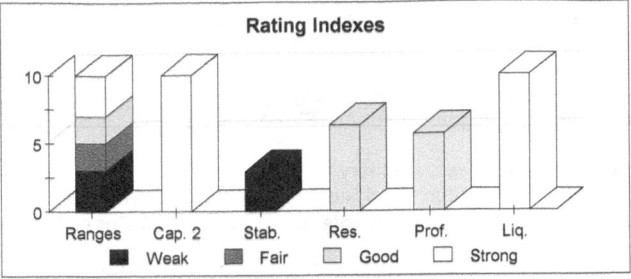

Rating Indexes

(Ranges, Cap. 2, Stab., Res., Prof., Liq.)
Weak | Fair | Good | Strong

RADIAN GUARANTY INC　　　　　　　D　　　Weak

Major Rating Factors: A history of deficient reserves (2.0 on a scale of 0 to 10) that places pressure on both capital and profits. Deficiencies in the two year reserve development occurred in three of the previous five years and ranged between 17% and 74%. Vulnerable liquidity (2.9) as a spike in claims may stretch capacity.

Other Rating Factors: Weak overall results on stability tests (2.3) including negative cash flow from operations for 2013. Fair long-term capitalization index (3.5) based on fair current risk adjusted capital (severe and moderate loss scenarios). Fair profitability index (3.3) with operating losses during each of the last five years. However, profits have turned positive in the first nine months of 2014. Average return on equity over the last five years has been poor at -21.9%.

Principal Business: Mortgage guaranty (100%).
Principal Investments: Misc. investments (52%) and investment grade bonds (48%).
Investments in Affiliates: 44%
Group Affiliation: Radian Group Inc
Licensed in: All states, the District of Columbia and Puerto Rico
Commenced Business: April 1977
Address: 1601 Market Street, 12th Floor, Philadelphia, PA 19103
Phone: (800) 523-1988　**Domicile State:** PA　**NAIC Code:** 33790

Data Date	Rating	RACR #1	RACR #2	Loss Ratio %	Total Assets ($mil)	Capital ($mil)	Net Premium ($mil)	Net Income ($mil)
9-14	D	0.71	0.65	N/A	3,530.5	1,326.1	536.8	393.6
9-13	D	0.64	0.56	N/A	3,661.4	1,239.1	504.2	10.7
2013	D	0.66	0.59	81.6	3,657.5	1,317.8	814.4	-23.8
2012	D	0.45	0.38	133.2	3,872.0	926.1	686.8	-175.9
2011	D	0.45	0.38	189.8	3,821.8	843.2	631.7	-545.1
2010	D+	0.68	0.57	202.0	4,313.7	1,295.7	620.8	-535.2
2009	D	0.45	0.38	156.0	4,216.7	741.4	559.7	-211.8

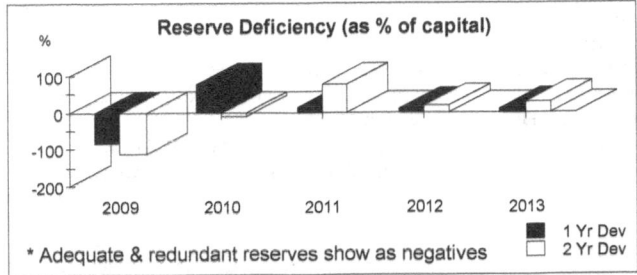

Reserve Deficiency (as % of capital)

(2009, 2010, 2011, 2012, 2013)
* Adequate & redundant reserves show as negatives
1 Yr Dev | 2 Yr Dev

RADIAN INS INC　　　　　　　　　C-　　　Fair

Major Rating Factors: Weak overall results on stability tests (2.9 on a scale of 0 to 10) including weak results on operational trends and negative cash flow from operations for 2013. The largest net exposure for one risk is high at 3.5% of capital. Strong long-term capitalization index (10.0) based on excellent current risk adjusted capital (severe and moderate loss scenarios). Moreover, capital levels have been consistent in recent years.

Other Rating Factors: Ample reserve history (9.4) that helps to protect the company against sharp claims increases. Excellent profitability (7.9) with operating gains in each of the last five years. Return on equity has been excellent over the last five years averaging 17.7%. Excellent liquidity (7.9) with ample operational cash flow and liquid investments.

Principal Business: Mortgage guaranty (61%) and financial guaranty (39%).
Principal Investments: Investment grade bonds (82%), misc. investments (10%), and cash (8%).
Investments in Affiliates: None
Group Affiliation: Radian Group Inc
Licensed in: PA
Commenced Business: January 1995
Address: 1601 Market St 12th Floor, Philadelphia, PA 19103
Phone: (800) 523-1988　**Domicile State:** PA　**NAIC Code:** 20720

Data Date	Rating	RACR #1	RACR #2	Loss Ratio %	Total Assets ($mil)	Capital ($mil)	Net Premium ($mil)	Net Income ($mil)
9-14	C-	7.84	6.76	N/A	321.9	249.1	17.5	25.9
9-13	C-	4.98	4.08	N/A	318.8	225.2	23.2	18.7
2013	C-	5.33	4.52	N/A	314.1	230.8	29.2	26.5
2012	C-	3.77	3.10	30.4	323.3	218.6	39.5	58.0
2011	C-	3.66	2.82	103.8	269.0	162.4	16.1	9.9
2010	D+	1.81	1.28	174.8	432.1	151.7	10.0	43.9
2009	C-	0.98	0.69	287.1	618.8	108.9	12.6	19.9

Radian Group Inc
Composite Group Rating: D
Largest Group Members

	Assets ($mil)	Rating
RADIAN GUARANTY INC	3658	D
RADIAN ASSET ASR CO	1501	C
RADIAN GUARANTY REINS INC	404	E+
RADIAN INS INC	314	C-
RADIAN MORTGAGE INS INC	137	D+

REDWOOD FIRE & CAS INS CO   C   Fair

Major Rating Factors: Fair long-term capitalization index (3.3 on a scale of 0 to 10) based on weak current risk adjusted capital (severe loss scenario), although results have slipped from the fair range during the last year. Fair overall results on stability tests (4.3) including weak results on operational trends, excessive premium growth and fair risk adjusted capital in prior years.
Other Rating Factors: Ample reserve history (8.1) that helps to protect the company against sharp claims increases. Excellent profitability (7.3) with operating gains in each of the last five years. Excellent liquidity (7.2) with ample operational cash flow and liquid investments.
Principal Business: Auto liability (69%), auto physical damage (19%), inland marine (4%), fire (2%), workers compensation (2%), commercial multiple peril (2%), and allied lines (1%).
Principal Investments: Investment grade bonds (51%), misc. investments (30%), and cash (19%).
Investments in Affiliates: None
Group Affiliation: Berkshire-Hathaway
Licensed in: All states except AL, FL, MA, NJ, NY, OH, OR, PA, RI, SD, WY, PR
Commenced Business: January 1970
Address: 9290 W Dodge Road,Ste 300, Omaha, NE 68114-3363
Phone: (402) 393-7255   **Domicile State:** NE   **NAIC Code:** 11673

Data Date	Rating	RACR #1	RACR #2	Loss Ratio %	Total Assets ($mil)	Capital ($mil)	Net Premium ($mil)	Net Income ($mil)
9-14	C	0.74	0.47	N/A	1,181.0	525.6	232.2	8.1
9-13	B-	1.09	0.68	N/A	928.0	452.7	172.0	15.4
2013	C	0.93	0.59	66.9	1,031.3	506.0	286.9	49.2
2012	B-	1.50	0.92	53.9	761.7	426.0	97.7	3.1
2011	B	6.13	2.65	N/A	747.3	452.7	15.1	38.8
2010	B	4.53	2.09	N/A	812.9	449.2	16.4	47.8
2009	B	5.32	2.45	47.6	862.2	422.3	23.6	35.7

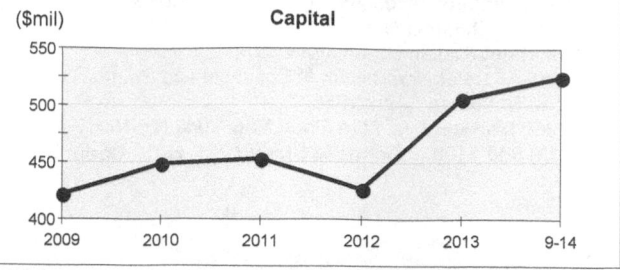

Capital ($mil)

REPUBLIC INDEMNITY CO OF AMERICA   C+   Fair

Major Rating Factors: Fair profitability index (3.6 on a scale of 0 to 10) with operating losses during the first nine months of 2014. Return on equity has been fair, averaging 5.1% over the past five years. Fair overall results on stability tests (4.6) including fair financial strength of affiliated American Financial Group Inc and excessive premium growth.
Other Rating Factors: Good long-term capitalization index (6.6) based on good current risk adjusted capital (moderate loss scenario), despite some fluctuation in capital levels. Ample reserve history (8.2) that helps to protect the company against sharp claims increases. Excellent liquidity (7.0) with ample operational cash flow and liquid investments.
Principal Business: Workers compensation (100%).
Principal Investments: Misc. investments (65%), investment grade bonds (34%), and cash (1%).
Investments in Affiliates: 3%
Group Affiliation: American Financial Group Inc
Licensed in: All states except CT, MA, MN, NH, NJ, NY, ND, PA, VT, WY, PR
Commenced Business: March 1973
Address: 15821 Ventura Blvd, Suite 370, Encino, CA 91436
Phone: (818) 990-9860   **Domicile State:** CA   **NAIC Code:** 22179

Data Date	Rating	RACR #1	RACR #2	Loss Ratio %	Total Assets ($mil)	Capital ($mil)	Net Premium ($mil)	Net Income ($mil)
9-14	C+	1.30	0.86	N/A	2,206.9	440.7	450.1	-29.8
9-13	B-	2.06	1.47	N/A	892.3	299.5	147.4	18.2
2013	C+	1.72	1.24	68.6	847.7	252.3	209.3	30.4
2012	B-	2.21	1.54	80.2	858.5	279.8	158.4	11.9
2011	B-	2.42	1.66	75.4	830.8	278.8	131.4	21.0
2010	B-	2.47	1.39	77.0	847.8	282.1	149.7	14.9
2009	B-	2.38	1.28	70.2	828.6	279.1	163.0	19.9

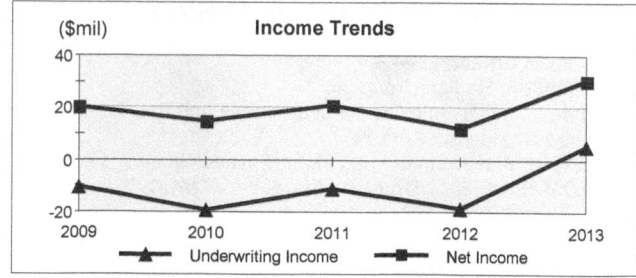

Income Trends ($mil) — Underwriting Income, Net Income

REPUBLIC UNDERWRITERS INS CO   C+   Fair

Major Rating Factors: Fair overall results on stability tests (4.3 on a scale of 0 to 10) including potential drain of affiliation with Delek Group Ltd. Fair reserve development (4.1) as reserves have generally been sufficient to cover claims.
Other Rating Factors: Fair profitability index (4.6) with operating losses during 2011. Return on equity has been low, averaging 1.5% over the past five years. Good liquidity (6.2) with sufficient resources (cash flows and marketable investments) to handle a spike in claims. Strong long-term capitalization index (7.9) based on excellent current risk adjusted capital (severe and moderate loss scenarios), despite some fluctuation in capital levels.
Principal Business: Workers compensation (73%), homeowners multiple peril (8%), commercial multiple peril (5%), auto liability (5%), auto physical damage (3%), other liability (2%), and other lines (3%).
Principal Investments: Investment grade bonds (76%), misc. investments (23%), and cash (1%).
Investments in Affiliates: 17%
Group Affiliation: Delek Group Ltd
Licensed in: AZ, AR, CA, CO, CT, KS, LA, MS, NV, NM, OK, TX, UT
Commenced Business: October 1965
Address: 2727 Turtle Creek Blvd, Dallas, TX 75219
Phone: (972) 788-6000   **Domicile State:** TX   **NAIC Code:** 24538

Data Date	Rating	RACR #1	RACR #2	Loss Ratio %	Total Assets ($mil)	Capital ($mil)	Net Premium ($mil)	Net Income ($mil)
9-14	C+	2.36	1.91	N/A	655.4	253.0	199.6	11.1
9-13	C+	2.07	1.63	N/A	690.5	237.2	235.8	9.7
2013	C+	2.24	1.80	57.9	678.6	246.1	297.1	23.8
2012	C+	1.99	1.57	67.9	658.1	228.4	309.6	10.3
2011	C+	1.81	1.44	78.6	671.0	219.1	354.0	-49.3
2010	B-	1.99	1.51	56.1	676.1	254.0	344.4	11.7
2009	B-	2.15	1.63	67.6	675.7	249.1	336.1	19.7

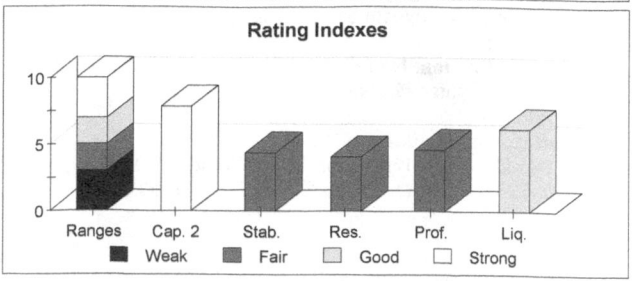

Rating Indexes — Ranges, Cap. 2, Stab., Res., Prof., Liq. — Weak, Fair, Good, Strong

RETAILFIRST INS CO *

A-   **Excellent**

Major Rating Factors: Strong long-term capitalization index (7.9 on a scale of 0 to 10) based on excellent current risk adjusted capital (severe and moderate loss scenarios). Furthermore, this high level of risk adjusted capital has been consistently maintained in previous years. Ample reserve history (8.9) that helps to protect the company against sharp claims increases.

Other Rating Factors: Excellent overall results on stability tests (7.0). Stability strengths include excellent operational trends and excellent risk diversification. Good overall profitability index (5.3). Fair expense controls. Return on equity has been low, averaging 4.4% over the past five years. Good liquidity (6.6) with sufficient resources (cash flows and marketable investments) to handle a spike in claims.

Principal Business: Workers compensation (100%).

Principal Investments: Investment grade bonds (78%), misc. investments (20%), and real estate (2%).

Investments in Affiliates: None

Group Affiliation: RetailFirst Mutual Holdings Inc

Licensed in: Fl

Commenced Business: January 1979

Address: 2310 Commerce Point Dr, Lakeland, FL 33801

Phone: (863) 665-6060   **Domicile State:** FL   **NAIC Code:** 10700

Data Date	Rating	RACR #1	RACR #2	Loss Ratio %	Total Assets ($mil)	Capital ($mil)	Net Premium ($mil)	Net Income ($mil)
9-14	A-	2.11	1.60	N/A	282.1	133.5	74.9	2.3
9-13	A-	2.71	2.11	N/A	263.2	128.0	69.1	3.0
2013	A-	2.22	1.68	71.1	265.2	130.4	94.8	2.9
2012	A-	2.92	2.24	72.6	252.9	121.9	78.2	2.9
2011	A-	3.21	2.42	71.8	240.9	115.5	66.0	3.9
2010	N/A	N/A	N/A	65.3	232.3	112.0	59.7	5.5
2009	N/A	N/A	N/A	48.4	263.7	123.5	72.5	12.9

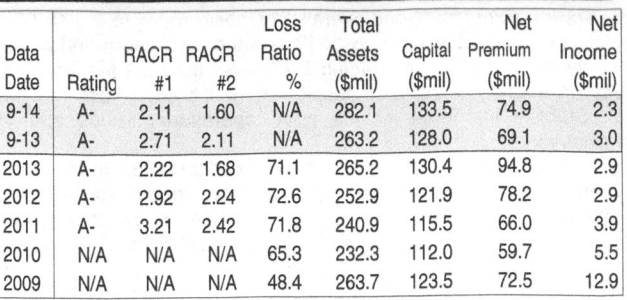

Capital

RLI INS CO

B   **Good**

Major Rating Factors: Good overall results on stability tests (5.7 on a scale of 0 to 10) despite potential drain of affiliation with RLI Corp. Strong long-term capitalization index (7.2) based on excellent current risk adjusted capital (severe and moderate loss scenarios), despite some fluctuation in capital levels.

Other Rating Factors: Ample reserve history (8.6) that helps to protect the company against sharp claims increases. Excellent profitability (8.1) with operating gains in each of the last five years. Return on equity has been excellent over the last five years averaging 18.6%. Excellent liquidity (7.1) with ample operational cash flow and liquid investments.

Principal Business: Other liability (42%), surety (20%), auto liability (14%), inland marine (6%), ocean marine (5%), auto physical damage (4%), and other lines (8%).

Principal Investments: Misc. investments (61%), investment grade bonds (35%), cash (2%), non investment grade bonds (1%), and real estate (1%).

Investments in Affiliates: 43%

Group Affiliation: RLI Corp

Licensed in: All states, the District of Columbia and Puerto Rico

Commenced Business: November 1960

Address: 9025 N Lindbergh Dr, Peoria, IL 61615

Phone: (309) 692-1000   **Domicile State:** IL   **NAIC Code:** 13056

Data Date	Rating	RACR #1	RACR #2	Loss Ratio %	Total Assets ($mil)	Capital ($mil)	Net Premium ($mil)	Net Income ($mil)
9-14	B	1.34	1.21	N/A	1,782.0	901.7	312.0	212.5
9-13	B	1.20	1.10	N/A	1,623.2	809.2	288.8	190.5
2013	B	1.25	1.12	50.8	1,679.4	859.2	413.2	205.9
2012	B	1.00	0.91	53.3	1,423.9	684.1	377.2	127.2
2011	B	1.05	0.95	44.7	1,467.2	710.2	362.4	139.0
2010	B	1.21	1.09	43.9	1,393.8	732.4	316.7	129.3
2009	B	1.33	1.20	46.4	1,426.8	784.2	282.9	28.9

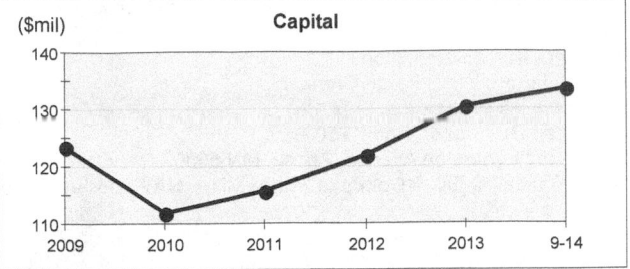

Capital

RSUI INDEMNITY CO

C+   **Fair**

Major Rating Factors: Fair overall results on stability tests (4.5 on a scale of 0 to 10) including potential drain of affiliation with Alleghany Corp Group. The largest net exposure for one risk is conservative at 1.2% of capital. Strong long-term capitalization index (8.3) based on excellent current risk adjusted capital (severe and moderate loss scenarios). Moreover, capital levels have been consistent in recent years.

Other Rating Factors: Ample reserve history (8.3) that helps to protect the company against sharp claims increases. Excellent profitability (8.8) with operating gains in each of the last five years. Return on equity has been good over the last five years, averaging 12.8%. Excellent liquidity (7.0) with ample operational cash flow and liquid investments.

Principal Business: Other liability (70%), allied lines (16%), fire (10%), inland marine (2%), and earthquake (2%).

Principal Investments: Investment grade bonds (63%), misc. investments (34%), non investment grade bonds (2%), and cash (1%).

Investments in Affiliates: 8%

Group Affiliation: Alleghany Corp Group

Licensed in: All states except PR

Commenced Business: December 1977

Address: 900 Elm St, Manchester, NH 03101

Phone: (404) 231-2366   **Domicile State:** NH   **NAIC Code:** 22314

Data Date	Rating	RACR #1	RACR #2	Loss Ratio %	Total Assets ($mil)	Capital ($mil)	Net Premium ($mil)	Net Income ($mil)
9-14	C+	2.63	1.86	N/A	3,367.6	1,526.2	573.7	151.7
9-13	C+	2.83	2.02	N/A	3,220.8	1,454.4	517.9	97.9
2013	C+	2.68	1.92	53.4	3,323.2	1,492.4	765.1	160.2
2012	C+	2.71	1.96	72.2	3,013.4	1,296.0	661.4	108.7
2011	C+	2.72	1.65	53.7	2,772.7	1,262.3	581.0	137.0
2010	C+	2.97	1.75	46.5	2,675.3	1,242.2	525.7	181.4
2009	C	2.70	1.56	44.0	2,635.5	1,119.7	569.9	211.7

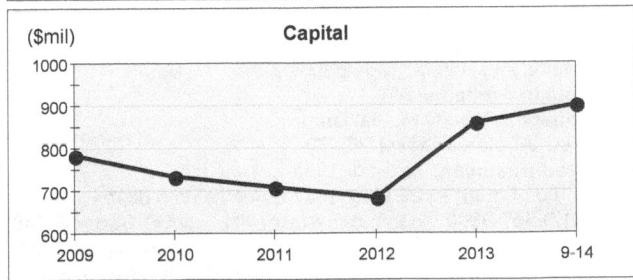

Rating Indexes

RURAL COMMUNITY INS CO

B   Good

Major Rating Factors: Good overall profitability index (5.9 on a scale of 0 to 10) despite operating losses during 2012 and the first nine months of 2014. Return on equity has been fair, averaging 8.7% over the past five years. Good overall results on stability tests (5.9) despite negative cash flow from operations for 2013. Stability strengths include good operational trends and excellent risk diversification.

Other Rating Factors: Strong long-term capitalization index (10.0) based on excellent current risk adjusted capital (severe and moderate loss scenarios), despite some fluctuation in capital levels. Ample reserve history (9.2) that helps to protect the company against sharp claims increases. Vulnerable liquidity (2.3) as a spike in claims may stretch capacity.

Principal Business: Allied lines (100%).

Principal Investments: Investment grade bonds (89%) and misc. investments (11%).

Investments in Affiliates: None

Group Affiliation: Wells Fargo Group

Licensed in: All states except PR

Commenced Business: April 1980

Address: 3501 Thurston Avenue, Anoka, MN 55303

Phone: (763) 427-0290   **Domicile State:** MN   **NAIC Code:** 39039

Data Date	Rating	RACR #1	RACR #2	Loss Ratio %	Total Assets ($mil)	Capital ($mil)	Net Premium ($mil)	Net Income ($mil)
9-14	B	4.05	2.42	N/A	7,691.1	593.1	312.9	-10.6
9-13	B	4.69	2.90	N/A	3,974.5	569.8	374.1	-17.0
2013	B	9.16	5.06	92.9	5,245.2	599.8	491.5	20.9
2012	B	11.70	6.36	100.9	5,421.1	580.3	419.4	-5.5
2011	B	11.06	5.76	89.6	6,023.7	585.4	443.8	25.7
2010	B	14.65	7.54	63.0	3,647.4	559.2	283.5	146.6
2009	B-	8.05	4.38	67.8	4,250.0	391.9	318.9	73.2

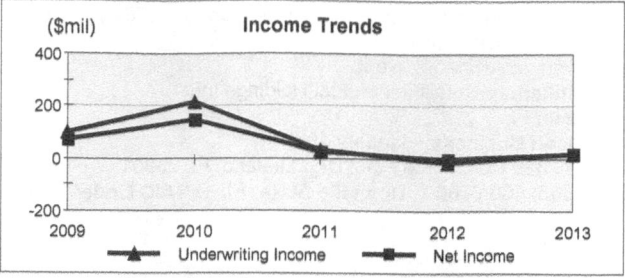

Income Trends

SAFECO INS CO OF AMERICA

B-   Good

Major Rating Factors: Fair overall results on stability tests (4.9 on a scale of 0 to 10). The largest net exposure for one risk is high at 3.6% of capital. History of adequate reserve strength (6.9) as reserves have been consistently at an acceptable level.

Other Rating Factors: Good overall profitability index (6.4). Fair expense controls. Return on equity has been good over the last five years, averaging 10.8%. Good liquidity (6.7) with sufficient resources (cash flows and marketable investments) to handle a spike in claims. Strong long-term capitalization index (7.2) based on excellent current risk adjusted capital (severe and moderate loss scenarios), despite some fluctuation in capital levels.

Principal Business: Homeowners multiple peril (42%), auto liability (19%), auto physical damage (15%), fire (7%), allied lines (6%), other liability (5%), and other lines (6%).

Principal Investments: Investment grade bonds (72%), misc. investments (21%), and non investment grade bonds (7%).

Investments in Affiliates: 6%

Group Affiliation: Liberty Mutual Group

Licensed in: All states except PR

Commenced Business: October 1953

Address: 1001 Fourth Ave Safeco Plaza, Seattle, WA 98154

Phone: (617) 357-9500   **Domicile State:** NH   **NAIC Code:** 24740

Data Date	Rating	RACR #1	RACR #2	Loss Ratio %	Total Assets ($mil)	Capital ($mil)	Net Premium ($mil)	Net Income ($mil)
9-14	B-	2.28	1.55	N/A	4,416.2	1,252.5	1,101.9	63.6
9-13	B-	2.18	1.52	N/A	4,849.3	1,200.6	1,087.9	45.8
2013	B-	2.18	1.48	73.5	4,747.1	1,188.7	1,349.1	154.8
2012	B-	1.79	1.28	66.7	4,029.8	945.1	1,659.6	193.5
2011	C+	1.55	1.14	74.0	3,854.2	870.8	1,616.3	29.2
2010	C+	1.60	1.19	67.8	3,838.0	844.9	1,602.5	93.3
2009	B	2.85	2.04	62.6	4,327.4	1,147.1	1,638.4	104.4

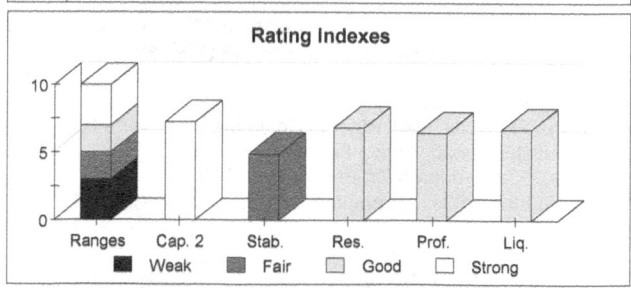

Rating Indexes

SAFETY INS CO *

B+   Good

Major Rating Factors: Good overall results on stability tests (5.0 on a scale of 0 to 10) despite potential drain of affiliation with Safety Group. Good liquidity (6.6) with sufficient resources (cash flows and marketable investments) to handle a spike in claims.

Other Rating Factors: Strong long-term capitalization index (9.4) based on excellent current risk adjusted capital (severe and moderate loss scenarios), despite some fluctuation in capital levels. Ample reserve history (9.0) that helps to protect the company against sharp claims increases. Excellent profitability (7.7) with operating gains in each of the last five years.

Principal Business: Auto liability (54%), auto physical damage (34%), homeowners multiple peril (7%), commercial multiple peril (3%), other liability (1%), fire (1%), and allied lines (1%).

Principal Investments: Investment grade bonds (77%), misc. investments (14%), and non investment grade bonds (10%).

Investments in Affiliates: 6%

Group Affiliation: Safety Group

Licensed in: MA, NH

Commenced Business: January 1980

Address: 20 Custom House St, Boston, MA 02110

Phone: (617) 951-0600   **Domicile State:** MA   **NAIC Code:** 39454

Data Date	Rating	RACR #1	RACR #2	Loss Ratio %	Total Assets ($mil)	Capital ($mil)	Net Premium ($mil)	Net Income ($mil)
9-14	B+	3.59	2.54	N/A	1,429.1	622.4	481.0	40.7
9-13	B+	3.88	2.82	N/A	1,387.1	617.1	457.4	42.1
2013	B+	3.72	2.71	65.7	1,396.8	628.0	627.8	53.1
2012	B+	3.97	2.99	65.7	1,319.7	599.0	597.5	52.4
2011	B+	4.22	3.37	78.0	1,235.4	570.5	558.3	9.0
2010	B+	4.62	3.89	65.4	1,230.7	582.4	519.1	51.6
2009	B+	4.59	3.88	65.1	1,208.3	556.6	479.4	47.0

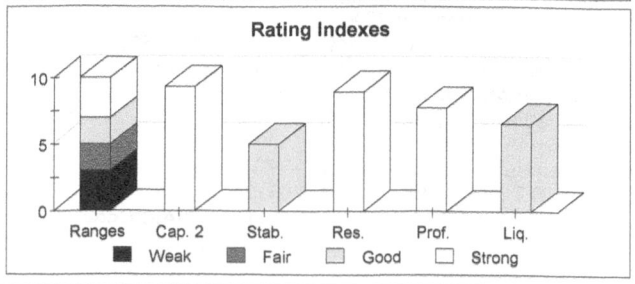

Rating Indexes

SAFETY NATIONAL CASUALTY CORP   C   Fair

Major Rating Factors: Fair overall results on stability tests (3.4 on a scale of 0 to 10). The largest net exposure for one risk is excessive at 5.8% of capital. Strengths include potentially strong support from affiliation with Tokio Marine Holdings Inc. A history of deficient reserves (1.2) that places pressure on both capital and profits. In the last five years, reserves (two year development) fluctuated between 47% and 28% deficeint.

Other Rating Factors: Good overall profitability index (6.3). Fair expense controls. Return on equity has been fair, averaging 8.1% over the past five years. Strong long-term capitalization index (7.1) based on excellent current risk adjusted capital (severe and moderate loss scenarios). Moreover, capital levels have been consistent in recent years. Excellent liquidity (7.2) with ample operational cash flow and liquid investments.

Principal Business: Workers compensation (16%), other liability (2%), auto liability (2%), and surety (1%).

Principal Investments: Investment grade bonds (67%), misc. investments (24%), and non investment grade bonds (9%).

Investments in Affiliates: 2%

Group Affiliation: Tokio Marine Holdings Inc

Licensed in: All states, the District of Columbia and Puerto Rico

Commenced Business: December 1942

Address: 1832 Schuetz Rd, St Louis, MO 63146-3540

Phone: (314) 995-5300   **Domicile State:** MO   **NAIC Code:** 15105

Data Date	Rating	RACR #1	RACR #2	Loss Ratio %	Total Assets ($mil)	Capital ($mil)	Net Premium ($mil)	Net Income ($mil)
9-14	C	1.35	1.03	N/A	4,823.4	1,253.5	491.7	71.7
9-13	C	1.48	1.15	N/A	4,105.0	1,124.7	460.6	91.0
2013	C	1.39	1.06	78.4	4,183.6	1,153.8	664.9	122.7
2012	C	1.36	1.06	101.1	3,544.1	960.8	549.0	36.8
2011	C	1.50	0.94	76.9	2,868.9	844.5	449.2	89.9
2010	C	1.59	1.00	67.4	2,471.4	728.9	369.4	94.0
2009	C	1.25	0.68	70.4	2,185.2	626.1	330.8	19.4

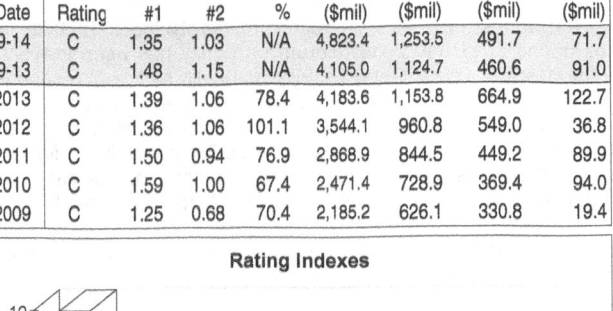

Rating Indexes — Ranges, Cap. 2, Stab., Res., Prof., Liq. — Weak, Fair, Good, Strong

SAFEWAY INS CO   B-   Good

Major Rating Factors: Fair overall results on stability tests (4.5 on a scale of 0 to 10) including potential drain of affiliation with Safeway Ins Group. Good overall profitability index (5.7) despite modest operating losses during 2013. Return on equity has been low, averaging 2.2% over the past five years.

Other Rating Factors: Good liquidity (6.5) with sufficient resources (cash flows and marketable investments) to handle a spike in claims. Strong long-term capitalization index (7.6) based on excellent current risk adjusted capital (severe and moderate loss scenarios), despite some fluctuation in capital levels. Ample reserve history (7.4) that can protect against increases in claims costs.

Principal Business: Auto liability (61%) and auto physical damage (38%).

Principal Investments: Misc. investments (72%), investment grade bonds (20%), cash (7%), and real estate (1%).

Investments in Affiliates: 53%

Group Affiliation: Safeway Ins Group

Licensed in: AL, AK, AZ, CA, CO, DC, DE, FL, GA, ID, IL, IN, IA, KS, LA, ME, MD, MA, MI, MN, MS, MO, MT, NE, NV, NJ, NM, ND, OK, OR, PA, SC, SD, TX, UT, WA, WV, WI, WY

Commenced Business: December 1962

Address: 790 Pasquinelli, Westmont, IL 60559

Phone: (630) 887-8300   **Domicile State:** IL   **NAIC Code:** 12521

Data Date	Rating	RACR #1	RACR #2	Loss Ratio %	Total Assets ($mil)	Capital ($mil)	Net Premium ($mil)	Net Income ($mil)
9-14	B-	1.51	1.38	N/A	440.9	292.2	123.6	5.7
9-13	B-	1.58	1.42	N/A	406.0	274.0	99.6	-1.3
2013	B-	1.47	1.35	79.1	408.1	279.3	143.3	-0.2
2012	B-	1.65	1.52	78.7	372.9	271.3	115.7	8.1
2011	B-	1.69	1.58	73.5	364.8	273.0	109.5	5.8
2010	B-	1.73	1.61	71.8	356.6	271.5	109.7	7.1
2009	B-	1.76	1.64	71.4	342.5	260.3	108.5	8.4

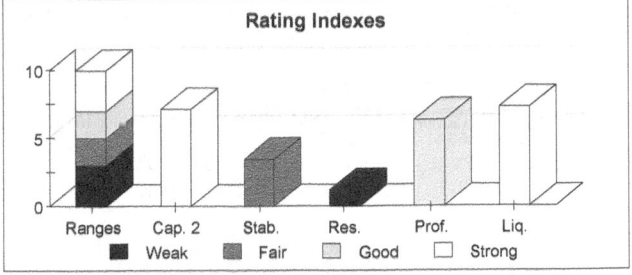

Rating Indexes — Ranges, Cap. 2, Stab., Res., Prof., Liq. — Weak, Fair, Good, Strong

SCOR REINSURANCE CO   D   Weak

Major Rating Factors: Weak overall results on stability tests (2.2 on a scale of 0 to 10). The largest net exposure for one risk is high at 3.3% of capital. Good long-term capitalization index (6.3) based on good current risk adjusted capital (moderate loss scenario). Over the last several years, capital levels have remained relatively consistent.

Other Rating Factors: History of adequate reserve strength (5.7) as reserves have been consistently at an acceptable level. Good overall profitability index (5.5) despite operating losses during 2012. Return on equity has been low, averaging 4.4% over the past five years. Good liquidity (6.3) with sufficient resources (cash flows and marketable investments) to handle a spike in claims.

Principal Business: (This company is a reinsurer.)

Principal Investments: Investment grade bonds (106%), non investment grade bonds (2%), and cash (1%).

Investments in Affiliates: None

Group Affiliation: SCOR Reinsurance Group

Licensed in: AL, AK, AZ, CA, DC, DE, HI, ID, IL, IN, IA, KY, LA, MI, MN, MS, MT, NE, NM, NY, NC, ND, OH, OK, OR, PA, RI, TN, TX, UT, WA, WI, PR

Commenced Business: September 1985

Address: 199 Water St, New York, NY 10038-3526

Phone: (212) 480-1900   **Domicile State:** NY   **NAIC Code:** 30058

Data Date	Rating	RACR #1	RACR #2	Loss Ratio %	Total Assets ($mil)	Capital ($mil)	Net Premium ($mil)	Net Income ($mil)
9-14	D	1.42	0.92	N/A	2,254.6	692.7	544.0	41.5
9-13	D	1.06	0.70	N/A	2,325.2	641.4	582.4	44.0
2013	D	1.39	0.90	62.3	2,364.7	676.4	755.6	66.6
2012	D	1.04	0.69	76.6	2,247.6	618.9	709.3	-89.2
2011	D	1.17	0.77	72.4	2,106.6	658.7	645.2	54.0
2010	D	1.04	0.67	70.4	2,032.5	619.0	617.1	52.4
2009	D	0.76	0.51	57.0	1,642.6	551.8	522.9	40.6

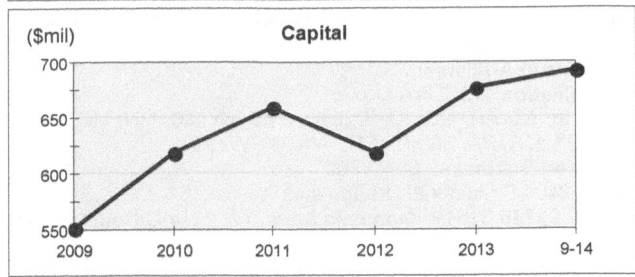

Capital ($mil) — 2009, 2010, 2011, 2012, 2013, 9-14

SCOTTSDALE INS CO

B- **Good**

Major Rating Factors: Fair reserve development (4.7 on a scale of 0 to 10) as reserves have generally been sufficient to cover claims. Fair overall results on stability tests (4.9).

Other Rating Factors: Good overall profitability index (5.3) despite operating losses during 2011 and 2012. Return on equity has been low, averaging 1.6% over the past five years. Good liquidity (6.4) with sufficient resources (cash flows and marketable investments) to handle a spike in claims. Strong long-term capitalization index (8.5) based on excellent current risk adjusted capital (severe and moderate loss scenarios), despite some fluctuation in capital levels.

Principal Business: Other liability (50%), commercial multiple peril (23%), allied lines (10%), homeowners multiple peril (6%), auto liability (4%), fire (4%), and other lines (4%).

Principal Investments: Investment grade bonds (80%), misc. investments (24%), and non investment grade bonds (1%).

Investments in Affiliates: 18%

Group Affiliation: Nationwide Corp

Licensed in: All states, the District of Columbia and Puerto Rico

Commenced Business: July 1982

Address: 8877 N. Gainey Center Dr, Scottsdale, AZ 85258

Phone: (480) 365-4000   **Domicile State:** OH   **NAIC Code:** 41297

Data Date	Rating	RACR #1	RACR #2	Loss Ratio %	Total Assets ($mil)	Capital ($mil)	Net Premium ($mil)	Net Income ($mil)
9-14	B-	2.44	1.97	N/A	2,197.2	764.3	525.9	0.6
9-13	B-	2.45	2.00	N/A	2,062.7	711.7	496.3	9.5
2013	B-	2.42	1.99	66.2	2,133.3	716.4	707.1	16.2
2012	B-	2.42	2.03	71.9	1,879.5	670.2	598.9	-2.3
2011	B-	2.66	2.16	0.0	1,747.5	678.8	572.4	-11.6
2010	B-	2.54	2.08	0.0	1,765.1	655.1	571.6	30.3
2009	B-	2.40	1.95	0.0	1,771.5	610.2	583.7	27.8

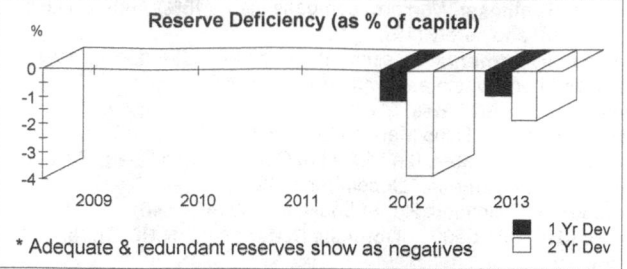

Reserve Deficiency (as % of capital)

* Adequate & redundant reserves show as negatives

■ 1 Yr Dev   □ 2 Yr Dev

SEABRIGHT INS CO

D+ **Weak**

Major Rating Factors: Weak overall results on stability tests (2.0 on a scale of 0 to 10) including potential drain of affiliation with Enstar Group Ltd and negative cash flow from operations for 2013. The largest net exposure for one risk is conservative at 1.2% of capital. Weak profitability index (1.9) with operating losses during 2013. Return on equity has been low, averaging 3.9% over the past five years.

Other Rating Factors: Fair reserve development (3.9) as reserves have generally been sufficient to cover claims. Good liquidity (6.7) with sufficient resources (cash flows and marketable investments) to handle a spike in claims. Strong long-term capitalization index (7.1) based on excellent current risk adjusted capital (severe and moderate loss scenarios), despite some fluctuation in capital levels.

Principal Business: Workers compensation (98%) and credit (2%).

Principal Investments: Investment grade bonds (127%), non investment grade bonds (8%), and cash (4%).

Investments in Affiliates: None

Group Affiliation: Enstar Group Ltd

Licensed in: All states except ND, PR

Commenced Business: January 1962

Address: 161 N Clark St Suite 3525, Chicago, IL 60601

Phone: (206) 269-8500   **Domicile State:** IL   **NAIC Code:** 15563

Data Date	Rating	RACR #1	RACR #2	Loss Ratio %	Total Assets ($mil)	Capital ($mil)	Net Premium ($mil)	Net Income ($mil)
9-14	D+	1.77	1.05	N/A	497.1	106.5	4.4	6.9
9-13	D+	1.99	1.22	N/A	726.5	241.8	118.6	-2.1
2013	D+	2.73	1.65	120.7	714.4	226.8	38.5	-30.6
2012	D+	2.23	1.42	66.9	904.3	309.6	252.2	38.0
2011	D+	1.91	0.99	0.0	960.7	356.8	264.2	16.1
2010	D+	1.00	0.60	0.0	1,099.9	504.8	265.9	21.4
2009	D+	1.18	0.72	0.0	1,118.8	553.4	311.2	44.8

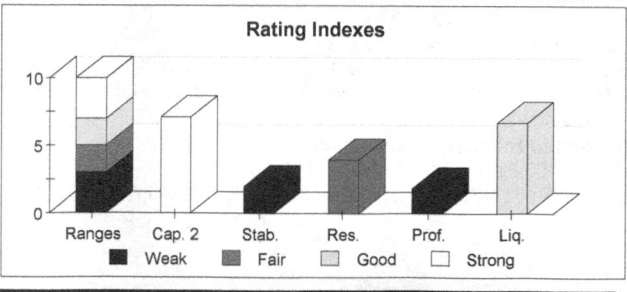

Rating Indexes

Ranges   Cap. 2   Stab.   Res.   Prof.   Liq.

■ Weak   ■ Fair   □ Good   □ Strong

SECURA INS A MUTUAL CO

B- **Good**

Major Rating Factors: Fair overall results on stability tests (4.7 on a scale of 0 to 10) including potential drain of affiliation with SECURA Group. Good liquidity (6.4) with sufficient resources (cash flows and marketable investments) to handle a spike in claims.

Other Rating Factors: Strong long-term capitalization index (8.2) based on excellent current risk adjusted capital (severe and moderate loss scenarios), despite some fluctuation in capital levels. Ample reserve history (9.2) that helps to protect the company against sharp claims increases. Excellent profitability (8.0) with operating gains in each of the last five years.

Principal Business: Workers compensation (28%), commercial multiple peril (27%), auto liability (16%), farmowners multiple peril (9%), other liability (7%), auto physical damage (6%), and other lines (7%).

Principal Investments: Investment grade bonds (65%), misc. investments (33%), and real estate (2%).

Investments in Affiliates: 7%

Group Affiliation: SECURA Group

Licensed in: AZ, AR, CO, ID, IL, IN, IA, KS, KY, MI, MN, MO, MT, NE, NV, NM, ND, OH, OK, OR, PA, SD, TN, UT, WA, WI, WY

Commenced Business: May 1900

Address: 2401 S Memorial Dr, Appleton, WI 54915

Phone: (920) 739-3161   **Domicile State:** WI   **NAIC Code:** 22543

Data Date	Rating	RACR #1	RACR #2	Loss Ratio %	Total Assets ($mil)	Capital ($mil)	Net Premium ($mil)	Net Income ($mil)
9-14	B-	2.61	1.88	N/A	933.2	346.7	301.0	19.2
9-13	B-	2.06	1.49	N/A	875.5	298.0	270.7	23.1
2013	B-	2.58	1.87	59.4	872.1	321.7	387.1	45.3
2012	B-	1.98	1.43	64.0	797.4	273.3	344.9	22.9
2011	B-	1.95	1.40	74.4	734.2	241.2	320.7	6.8
2010	B-	2.42	1.78	67.8	704.1	248.8	301.5	8.5
2009	B-	2.53	1.85	66.5	660.3	234.3	287.3	14.3

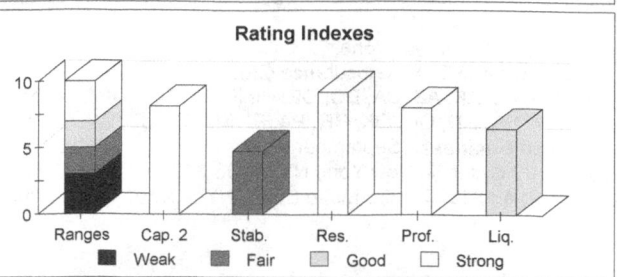

Rating Indexes

Ranges   Cap. 2   Stab.   Res.   Prof.   Liq.

■ Weak   ■ Fair   □ Good   □ Strong

SELECTIVE INS CO OF AMERICA   B-   Good

Major Rating Factors: Good overall profitability index (5.6 on a scale of 0 to 10). Fair expense controls. Return on equity has been fair, averaging 8.5% over the past five years. Good liquidity (6.8) with sufficient resources (cash flows and marketable investments) to handle a spike in claims.

Other Rating Factors: Good overall results on stability tests (5.1) despite fair financial strength of affiliated Selective Ins. Strong long-term capitalization index (7.8) based on excellent current risk adjusted capital (severe and moderate loss scenarios), despite some fluctuation in capital levels. Ample reserve history (8.8) that helps to protect the company against sharp claims increases.

Principal Business: Allied lines (22%), other liability (18%), workers compensation (16%), auto liability (13%), fire (6%), auto physical damage (4%), and other lines (20%).

Principal Investments: Investment grade bonds (81%), misc. investments (18%), and non investment grade bonds (1%).

Investments in Affiliates: None

Group Affiliation: Selective Ins

Licensed in: All states except AZ, CO, FL, ID, LA, NH, NM, OK, UT, VT, PR

Commenced Business: April 1926

Address: 40 Wantage Ave, Branchville, NJ 07890

Phone: (973) 948-3000   **Domicile State:** NJ   **NAIC Code:** 12572

Data Date	Rating	RACR #1	RACR #2	Loss Ratio %	Total Assets ($mil)	Capital ($mil)	Net Premium ($mil)	Net Income ($mil)
9-14	B-	2.46	1.58	N/A	2,040.8	492.8	442.5	55.8
9-13	C+	2.53	1.56	N/A	1,918.5	435.6	411.1	35.8
2013	B-	2.47	1.59	64.5	1,951.0	463.4	579.7	53.1
2012	C+	2.19	1.38	70.6	1,708.3	369.9	496.8	29.8
2011	B	2.18	1.42	74.7	2,400.8	507.4	735.2	15.2
2010	B	2.39	1.55	69.3	2,338.2	542.6	687.3	55.4
2009	B	1.99	1.28	68.1	2,296.6	489.1	708.7	24.7

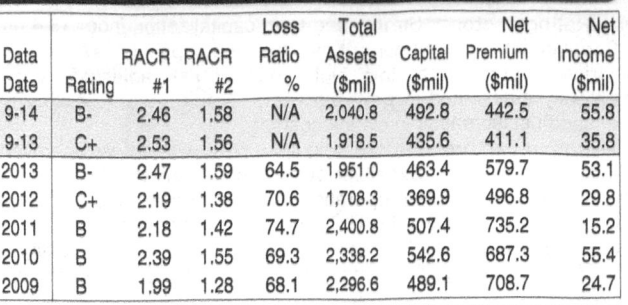

Income Trends

SELECTIVE WAY INS CO   B   Good

Major Rating Factors: Good overall results on stability tests (5.6 on a scale of 0 to 10) despite potential drain of affiliation with Selective Ins. Stability strengths include good operational trends and excellent risk diversification. Good overall profitability index (6.6). Fair expense controls. Return on equity has been fair, averaging 7.0% over the past five years.

Other Rating Factors: Good liquidity (6.8) with sufficient resources (cash flows and marketable investments) to handle a spike in claims. Strong long-term capitalization index (7.5) based on excellent current risk adjusted capital (severe and moderate loss scenarios), despite some fluctuation in capital levels. Ample reserve history (9.2) that helps to protect the company against sharp claims increases.

Principal Business: Other liability (24%), auto liability (19%), workers compensation (14%), fire (8%), allied lines (8%), products liability (6%), and other lines (22%).

Principal Investments: Investment grade bonds (86%), misc. investments (13%), and non investment grade bonds (1%).

Investments in Affiliates: None

Group Affiliation: Selective Ins

Licensed in: CA, DC, DE, GA, MD, MI, NJ, NY, NC, PA, SC, VA

Commenced Business: November 1973

Address: 40 Wantage Ave, Branchville, NJ 07890

Phone: (973) 948-3000   **Domicile State:** NJ   **NAIC Code:** 26301

Data Date	Rating	RACR #1	RACR #2	Loss Ratio %	Total Assets ($mil)	Capital ($mil)	Net Premium ($mil)	Net Income ($mil)
9-14	B	2.05	1.33	N/A	1,170.3	260.6	290.4	29.9
9-13	B	2.07	1.31	N/A	1,109.7	236.1	269.8	17.8
2013	B	2.09	1.36	64.5	1,124.5	250.3	380.4	27.5
2012	B	2.00	1.28	70.7	1,048.0	211.2	350.0	10.1
2011	B	2.22	1.45	74.7	1,021.1	221.6	311.9	7.8
2010	B	2.33	1.52	69.3	979.8	225.8	291.6	6.2
2009	B	1.91	1.23	68.1	956.5	199.8	300.7	13.8

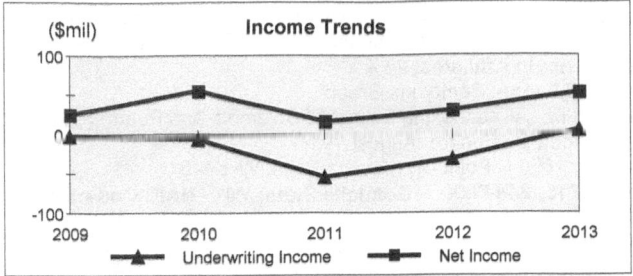

Rating Indexes

SENTRY CASUALTY CO *   B+   Good

Major Rating Factors: Good overall profitability index (6.5 on a scale of 0 to 10). Fair expense controls. Return on equity has been fair, averaging 6.1% over the past five years. Good overall results on stability tests (5.8). The largest net exposure for one risk is high at 3.8% of capital.

Other Rating Factors: Strong long-term capitalization index (10.0) based on excellent current risk adjusted capital (severe and moderate loss scenarios), despite some fluctuation in capital levels. Ample reserve history (8.6) that helps to protect the company against sharp claims increases. Excellent liquidity (7.0) with ample operational cash flow and liquid investments.

Principal Business: Workers compensation (92%), other liability (6%), and auto liability (2%).

Principal Investments: Investment grade bonds (90%) and misc. investments (10%).

Investments in Affiliates: None

Group Affiliation: Sentry Ins Group

Licensed in: All states except PR

Commenced Business: August 1973

Address: 3400 80th St, Moline, IL 61265

Phone: (715) 346-6000   **Domicile State:** WI   **NAIC Code:** 28460

Data Date	Rating	RACR #1	RACR #2	Loss Ratio %	Total Assets ($mil)	Capital ($mil)	Net Premium ($mil)	Net Income ($mil)
9-14	B+	5.20	3.43	N/A	264.9	77.0	33.7	3.9
9-13	B+	5.51	3.64	N/A	243.2	79.7	33.1	3.3
2013	B+	5.18	3.50	76.3	240.3	73.0	45.4	5.0
2012	B+	5.55	3.74	77.3	212.4	74.9	43.2	3.7
2011	B+	5.39	3.65	79.1	187.9	70.9	40.8	3.6
2010	B+	5.20	3.51	75.5	176.5	67.8	40.5	4.5
2009	B	4.85	3.29	75.3	169.6	63.5	40.2	4.1

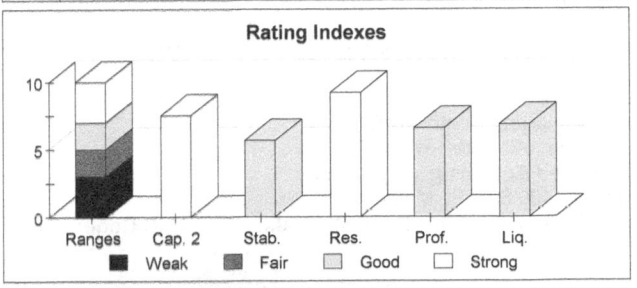

Income Trends

SENTRY INS A MUTUAL CO *

A   **Excellent**

Major Rating Factors: Strong long-term capitalization index (8.4 on a scale of 0 to 10) based on excellent current risk adjusted capital (severe and moderate loss scenarios). Furthermore, this high level of risk adjusted capital has been consistently maintained in previous years. Ample reserve history (7.8) that can protect against increases in claims costs.

Other Rating Factors: Excellent liquidity (7.0) with ample operational cash flow and liquid investments. Excellent overall results on stability tests (7.5). Stability strengths include excellent operational trends and excellent risk diversification. Good overall profitability index (6.7). Fair expense controls.

Principal Business: Workers compensation (36%), auto liability (24%), other liability (7%), auto physical damage (7%), homeowners multiple peril (6%), allied lines (5%), and other lines (15%).

Principal Investments: Misc. investments (59%), investment grade bonds (40%), non investment grade bonds (1%), and real estate (1%).

Investments in Affiliates: 26%

Group Affiliation: Sentry Ins Group

Licensed in: All states, the District of Columbia and Puerto Rico

Commenced Business: August 1914

Address: 1800 N Point Dr, Stevens Point, WI 54481

Phone: (715) 346-6000   **Domicile State:** WI   **NAIC Code:** 24988

Data Date	Rating	RACR #1	RACR #2	Loss Ratio %	Total Assets ($mil)	Capital ($mil)	Net Premium ($mil)	Net Income ($mil)
9-14	A	2.42	2.06	N/A	6,922.0	4,306.8	740.5	153.5
9-13	A	2.26	1.95	N/A	6,526.8	3,878.0	729.2	158.4
2013	A	2.34	2.01	76.3	6,632.0	4,075.3	999.7	308.4
2012	A	2.19	1.92	77.3	6,248.1	3,637.2	950.0	230.0
2011	A	2.07	1.83	79.1	5,891.4	3,417.2	898.3	206.7
2010	A	2.02	1.79	75.5	5,749.8	3,365.4	890.6	282.2
2009	A	1.90	1.69	75.3	5,578.2	3,114.1	885.0	124.8

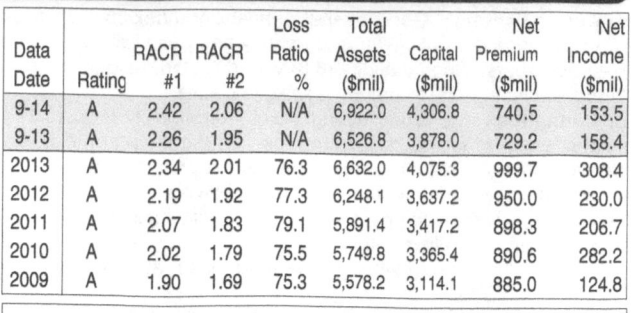

Risk-Adjusted Capital Ratio #2 (Severe Loss Scenario)

SENTRY SELECT INS CO *

B+   **Good**

Major Rating Factors: Good overall profitability index (6.0 on a scale of 0 to 10). Fair expense controls. Return on equity has been fair, averaging 6.6% over the past five years. Good liquidity (6.7) with sufficient resources (cash flows and marketable investments) to handle a spike in claims.

Other Rating Factors: Good overall results on stability tests (6.5). The largest net exposure for one risk is conservative at 1.2% of capital. Strong long-term capitalization index (9.8) based on excellent current risk adjusted capital (severe and moderate loss scenarios), despite some fluctuation in capital levels. Ample reserve history (8.8) that helps to protect the company against sharp claims increases.

Principal Business: Auto liability (39%), inland marine (19%), auto physical damage (13%), other liability (11%), workers compensation (7%), fire (4%), and other lines (7%).

Principal Investments: Investment grade bonds (86%) and misc. investments (14%).

Investments in Affiliates: None

Group Affiliation: Sentry Ins Group

Licensed in: All states except PR

Commenced Business: August 1929

Address: 3400 80th St, Moline, IL 61265

Phone: (715) 346-6000   **Domicile State:** WI   **NAIC Code:** 21180

Data Date	Rating	RACR #1	RACR #2	Loss Ratio %	Total Assets ($mil)	Capital ($mil)	Net Premium ($mil)	Net Income ($mil)
9-14	B+	4.27	2.86	N/A	676.5	243.3	134.6	12.1
9-13	B+	4.16	2.78	N/A	647.6	231.6	132.6	7.4
2013	B+	4.12	2.81	76.3	641.3	227.5	181.8	12.4
2012	B+	4.20	2.84	77.3	620.8	221.5	172.7	11.5
2011	B	4.25	2.89	79.1	616.9	220.3	163.3	12.8
2010	B	4.41	2.99	75.5	621.0	226.4	161.9	19.8
2009	B	4.34	2.95	75.3	635.1	225.1	160.9	17.2

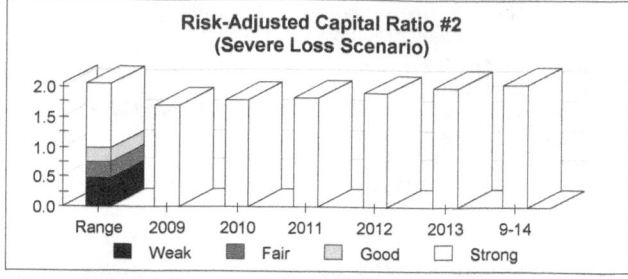

Income Trends

SHELTER MUTUAL INS CO

B   **Good**

Major Rating Factors: Good overall results on stability tests (5.5 on a scale of 0 to 10) despite potential drain of affiliation with Shelter Ins Companies. Good overall profitability index (5.4) despite operating losses during 2011.

Other Rating Factors: Good liquidity (5.4) with sufficient resources (cash flows and marketable investments) to handle a spike in claims. Strong long-term capitalization index (7.9) based on excellent current risk adjusted capital (severe and moderate loss scenarios), despite some fluctuation in capital levels. Ample reserve history (7.8) that can protect against increases in claims costs.

Principal Business: Homeowners multiple peril (30%), auto liability (30%), auto physical damage (22%), allied lines (6%), fire (4%), farmowners multiple peril (3%), and other lines (6%).

Principal Investments: Misc. investments (53%), investment grade bonds (45%), cash (1%), and real estate (1%).

Investments in Affiliates: 25%

Group Affiliation: Shelter Ins Companies

Licensed in: AL, AR, CO, DE, GA, ID, IL, IN, IA, KS, KY, LA, MD, MA, MN, MS, MO, MT, NE, NV, NH, NJ, NY, NC, OH, OK, OR, PA, SC, SD, TN, TX, VT, VA, WV, WI

Commenced Business: January 1946

Address: 1817 W Broadway, Columbia, MO 65218

Phone: (573) 445-8441   **Domicile State:** MO   **NAIC Code:** 23388

Data Date	Rating	RACR #1	RACR #2	Loss Ratio %	Total Assets ($mil)	Capital ($mil)	Net Premium ($mil)	Net Income ($mil)
9-14	B	2.11	1.66	N/A	2,923.1	1,667.9	955.7	34.2
9-13	B	2.09	1.60	N/A	2,691.9	1,484.4	879.9	21.3
2013	B	2.03	1.62	74.2	2,756.5	1,566.9	1,208.2	65.5
2012	B	2.06	1.60	75.1	2,490.3	1,397.9	1,144.8	70.1
2011	B	1.99	1.56	91.6	2,306.5	1,281.4	1,090.6	-28.8
2010	B	2.00	1.59	74.1	2,328.9	1,347.9	1,036.1	81.7
2009	B	1.90	1.52	82.8	2,187.5	1,250.9	966.7	49.3

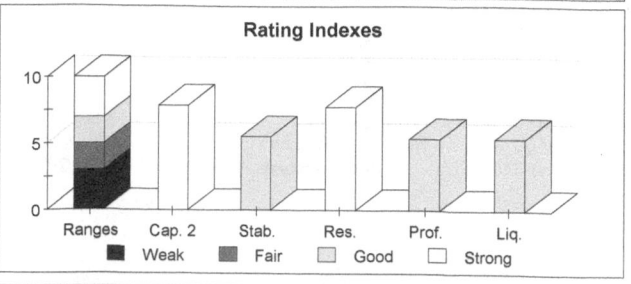

Rating Indexes

SHELTER REINSURANCE CO　　　　　　　　　　　　C　　　Fair

Major Rating Factors: Fair profitability index (4.8 on a scale of 0 to 10) with operating losses during 2011. Return on equity has been fair, averaging 6.0% over the past five years. Fair overall results on stability tests (4.2). The largest net exposure for one risk is high at 3.6% of capital.

Other Rating Factors: History of adequate reserve strength (6.9) as reserves have been consistently at an acceptable level. Good liquidity (6.5) with sufficient resources (cash flows and marketable investments) to handle a spike in claims. Strong long-term capitalization index (7.9) based on excellent current risk adjusted capital (severe and moderate loss scenarios), despite some fluctuation in capital levels.

Principal Business: Earthquake (100%).

Principal Investments: Investment grade bonds (94%), misc. investments (5%), and cash (1%).

Investments in Affiliates: None

Group Affiliation: Shelter Ins Companies

Licensed in: CA, IA, KS, MD, MI, MN, MO, ND, PA, SD, TN, WI

Commenced Business: November 1986

Address: 1817 West Broadway, Columbia, MO 65218

Phone: (573) 445-8441　　**Domicile State:** MO　　**NAIC Code:** 26557

Data Date	Rating	RACR #1	RACR #2	Loss Ratio %	Total Assets ($mil)	Capital ($mil)	Net Premium ($mil)	Net Income ($mil)
9-14	C	3.28	2.24	N/A	400.6	274.4	77.9	29.9
9-13	C	2.80	1.92	N/A	388.1	238.9	74.1	23.6
2013	C	2.94	2.00	40.6	383.0	245.4	98.0	30.5
2012	C	1.86	1.27	54.1	321.8	165.2	102.1	21.3
2011	C	1.43	1.04	140.8	294.1	143.2	101.7	-35.9
2010	B-	4.26	2.72	67.3	285.5	178.8	90.0	12.4
2009	B-	4.64	2.96	35.6	251.5	166.4	80.7	27.0

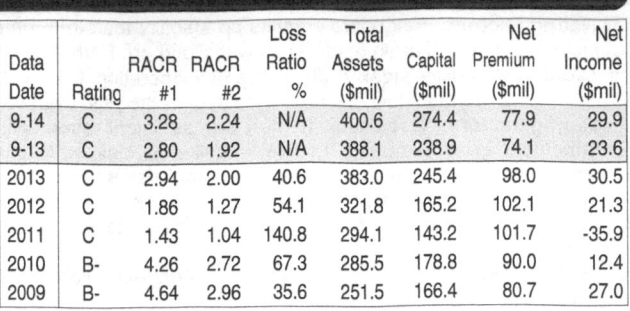

SIRIUS AMERICA INS CO　　　　　　　　　　　　　C+　　　Fair

Major Rating Factors: Fair overall results on stability tests (4.5 on a scale of 0 to 10) including potential drain of affiliation with White Mountains Group and negative cash flow from operations for 2013. The largest net exposure for one risk is high at 3.8% of capital. Fair profitability index (3.7). Fair expense controls. Return on equity has been fair, averaging 9.7% over the past five years.

Other Rating Factors: History of adequate reserve strength (5.0) as reserves have been consistently at an acceptable level. Strong long-term capitalization index (7.0) based on excellent current risk adjusted capital (severe and moderate loss scenarios), despite some fluctuation in capital levels. Excellent liquidity (7.0) with ample operational cash flow and liquid investments.

Principal Business: Group accident & health (71%), aggregate write-ins for other lines of business (23%), and inland marine (5%).

Principal Investments: Investment grade bonds (77%), misc. investments (20%), cash (2%), and non investment grade bonds (1%).

Investments in Affiliates: None

Group Affiliation: White Mountains Group

Licensed in: All states, the District of Columbia and Puerto Rico

Commenced Business: January 1980

Address: One Liberty Plaza, 19th Floor, New York, NY 10006

Phone: (212) 312-2500　　**Domicile State:** NY　　**NAIC Code:** 38776

Data Date	Rating	RACR #1	RACR #2	Loss Ratio %	Total Assets ($mil)	Capital ($mil)	Net Premium ($mil)	Net Income ($mil)
9-14	C+	2.39	1.37	N/A	1,553.2	604.8	196.7	38.4
9-13	C	2.03	1.27	N/A	1,635.4	596.8	174.8	38.5
2013	C+	2.14	1.21	48.9	1,559.4	548.4	252.8	55.9
2012	C	1.64	1.03	76.8	1,669.7	528.3	271.2	26.2
2011	C	1.50	0.95	71.7	1,807.7	533.7	485.3	101.4
2010	C	2.01	1.32	79.7	2,400.5	742.6	527.2	70.2
2009	C	2.23	1.51	68.6	2,438.1	832.0	489.1	46.9

White Mountains Group
Composite Group Rating: B+
Largest Group Members

	Assets ($mil)	Rating
SYMETRA LIFE INS CO	27220	B+
ATLANTIC SPECIALTY INS CO	2259	C
SIRIUS AMERICA INS CO	1559	C+
ONEBEACON INS CO	1086	C
FIRST SYMETRA NATL LIFE INS CO OF NY	813	A-

SOMPO JAPAN INS CO OF AMERICA　　　　　　　　B　　　Good

Major Rating Factors: Good overall profitability index (6.8 on a scale of 0 to 10). Weak expense controls. Return on equity has been low, averaging 3.5% over the past five years. Good overall results on stability tests (5.8) despite excessive premium growth.

Other Rating Factors: Strong long-term capitalization index (8.2) based on excellent current risk adjusted capital (severe and moderate loss scenarios), despite some fluctuation in capital levels. Ample reserve history (9.3) that helps to protect the company against sharp claims increases. Excellent liquidity (7.1) with ample operational cash flow and liquid investments.

Principal Business: Commercial multiple peril (27%), workers compensation (16%), fire (15%), products liability (9%), other liability (9%), ocean marine (8%), and other lines (15%).

Principal Investments: Misc. investments (53%), investment grade bonds (43%), and cash (4%).

Investments in Affiliates: 15%

Group Affiliation: NKSJ Holdings Inc

Licensed in: All states except PR

Commenced Business: January 1963

Address: 777 Third Ave 28th Floor, New York, NY 10017

Phone: (704) 759-2200　　**Domicile State:** NY　　**NAIC Code:** 11126

Data Date	Rating	RACR #1	RACR #2	Loss Ratio %	Total Assets ($mil)	Capital ($mil)	Net Premium ($mil)	Net Income ($mil)
9-14	B	2.44	1.77	N/A	1,244.3	541.1	146.3	5.8
9-13	B	3.09	2.20	N/A	940.0	488.8	89.1	12.4
2013	B	2.44	1.86	62.9	936.3	481.1	124.4	13.8
2012	B	3.41	2.47	59.2	911.0	494.2	104.7	19.2
2011	B	3.44	2.54	71.7	869.1	445.4	83.2	14.1
2010	B	3.50	2.61	61.8	839.6	436.6	63.6	14.0
2009	B-	3.57	2.66	50.5	814.4	415.6	56.5	25.2

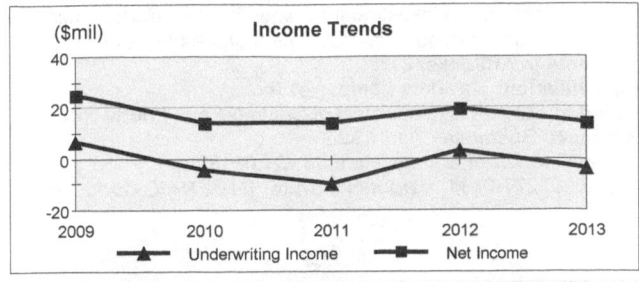

SOUTHERN FARM BUREAU CAS INS CO
B-   Good

Major Rating Factors: Fair overall results on stability tests (4.8 on a scale of 0 to 10) including potential drain of affiliation with Southern Farm Bureau Casualty. Good overall profitability index (6.9) with small operating losses during 2009. Return on equity has been low, averaging 2.7% over the past five years.

Other Rating Factors: Good liquidity (6.4) with sufficient resources (cash flows and marketable investments) to handle a spike in claims. Strong long-term capitalization index (8.5) based on excellent current risk adjusted capital (severe and moderate loss scenarios). Moreover, capital levels have been consistent in recent years. Ample reserve history (8.0) that helps to protect the company against sharp claims increases.

Principal Business: Auto physical damage (48%), auto liability (46%), other liability (5%), and allied lines (1%).

Principal Investments: Investment grade bonds (60%), misc. investments (41%), and real estate (1%).

Investments in Affiliates: 28%

Group Affiliation: Southern Farm Bureau Casualty

Licensed in: AR, CO, FL, LA, MS, SC, TX

Commenced Business: September 1947

Address: 1800 E County Line Rd, Ridgeland, MS 39157

Phone: (601) 957-7777   **Domicile State:** MS   **NAIC Code:** 18325

Data Date	Rating	RACR #1	RACR #2	Loss Ratio %	Total Assets ($mil)	Capital ($mil)	Net Premium ($mil)	Net Income ($mil)
9-14	B-	2.30	2.07	N/A	2,041.1	1,265.2	625.9	36.4
9-13	B-	2.44	2.17	N/A	1,955.2	1,238.3	611.6	52.1
2013	B-	2.29	2.09	80.3	1,998.3	1,235.9	825.8	36.4
2012	B-	2.34	2.12	74.3	1,899.2	1,161.1	803.0	70.8
2011	B-	2.28	2.04	85.0	1,804.8	1,064.3	794.0	10.3
2010	B	2.29	2.04	80.8	1,805.4	1,063.7	785.4	32.8
2009	B	2.28	2.05	86.5	1,767.4	1,036.7	791.6	-2.1

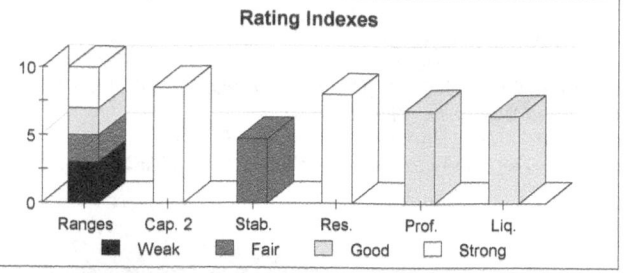

Rating Indexes

SOUTHERN-OWNERS INS CO *
A   Excellent

Major Rating Factors: Strong long-term capitalization index (8.4 on a scale of 0 to 10) based on excellent current risk adjusted capital (severe and moderate loss scenarios). Furthermore, this high level of risk adjusted capital has been consistently maintained in previous years. Ample reserve history (9.3) that helps to protect the company against sharp claims increases.

Other Rating Factors: Excellent overall results on stability tests (7.4). Stability strengths include excellent operational trends and excellent risk diversification. Good overall profitability index (5.9) despite operating losses during 2010. Return on equity has been low, averaging 1.8% over the past five years. Good liquidity (6.7) with sufficient resources (cash flows and marketable investments) to handle a spike in claims.

Principal Business: Auto liability (44%), other liability (22%), auto physical damage (16%), commercial multiple peril (9%), workers compensation (4%), homeowners multiple peril (3%), and inland marine (2%).

Principal Investments: Investment grade bonds (82%), misc. investments (17%), and cash (1%).

Investments in Affiliates: None

Group Affiliation: Auto-Owners Group

Licensed in: FL, MI

Commenced Business: June 1995

Address: 6101 Anacapri Blvd, Lansing, MI 48917-3968

Phone: (517) 323-1200   **Domicile State:** MI   **NAIC Code:** 10190

Data Date	Rating	RACR #1	RACR #2	Loss Ratio %	Total Assets ($mil)	Capital ($mil)	Net Premium ($mil)	Net Income ($mil)
9-14	A	2.54	1.87	N/A	618.1	187.9	178.7	2.1
9-13	A-	2.64	1.93	N/A	563.3	173.4	161.4	7.6
2013	A	2.73	2.04	74.0	573.8	184.6	224.9	13.5
2012	A-	2.59	1.93	80.4	537.8	161.5	204.4	2.2
2011	A-	2.73	1.80	82.0	497.2	156.3	186.5	0.4
2010	A-	2.81	1.77	95.5	456.4	161.0	153.7	-8.5
2009	A-	4.52	3.32	71.7	409.0	165.0	134.4	9.2

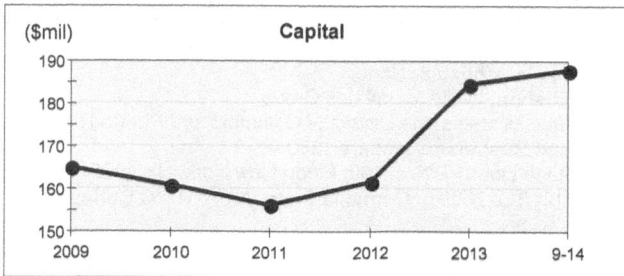

Capital

ST PAUL FIRE & MARINE INS CO
B   Good

Major Rating Factors: Good overall results on stability tests (5.7 on a scale of 0 to 10) despite potential drain of affiliation with Travelers Companies Inc. Good overall profitability index (5.7). Fair expense controls. Return on equity has been good over the last five years, averaging 11.9%.

Other Rating Factors: Good liquidity (6.9) with sufficient resources (cash flows and marketable investments) to handle a spike in claims. Strong long-term capitalization index (7.4) based on excellent current risk adjusted capital (severe and moderate loss scenarios), despite some fluctuation in capital levels. Ample reserve history (8.6) that helps to protect the company against sharp claims increases.

Principal Business: Other liability (62%), auto liability (10%), products liability (7%), fire (6%), ocean marine (4%), inland marine (4%), and other lines (8%).

Principal Investments: Investment grade bonds (63%), misc. investments (31%), real estate (5%), and non investment grade bonds (1%).

Investments in Affiliates: 21%

Group Affiliation: Travelers Companies Inc

Licensed in: All states, the District of Columbia and Puerto Rico

Commenced Business: April 1925

Address: One Tower Square, Hartford, CT 06183

Phone: (860) 277-0111   **Domicile State:** CT   **NAIC Code:** 24767

Data Date	Rating	RACR #1	RACR #2	Loss Ratio %	Total Assets ($mil)	Capital ($mil)	Net Premium ($mil)	Net Income ($mil)
9-14	B	1.55	1.26	N/A	18,981.1	6,010.9	3,791.0	608.6
9-13	B	1.54	1.26	N/A	18,596.6	5,919.4	3,734.1	559.4
2013	B	1.57	1.29	60.5	18,566.3	5,914.7	5,131.4	883.9
2012	B	1.59	1.32	67.7	18,761.8	6,000.7	5,006.4	594.8
2011	B	1.57	1.28	76.1	18,414.7	5,713.6	4,923.4	401.5
2010	B	1.58	1.28	61.9	18,356.9	5,820.9	4,776.4	912.5
2009	B	1.80	1.47	58.0	19,223.1	6,591.4	4,700.1	722.0

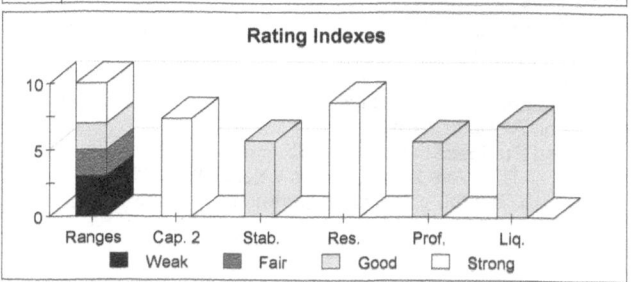

Rating Indexes

ST PAUL PROTECTIVE INS CO   B-   Good

Major Rating Factors: Fair overall results on stability tests (4.9 on a scale of 0 to 10) including fair financial strength of affiliated Travelers Companies Inc. Good overall profitability index (6.0). Fair expense controls. Return on equity has been fair, averaging 8.2% over the past five years.
Other Rating Factors: Strong long-term capitalization index (10.0) based on excellent current risk adjusted capital (severe and moderate loss scenarios), despite some fluctuation in capital levels. Ample reserve history (7.9) that can protect against increases in claims costs. Excellent liquidity (7.4) with ample operational cash flow and liquid investments.
Principal Business: Auto liability (32%), other liability (21%), auto physical damage (18%), fire (10%), allied lines (8%), commercial multiple peril (7%), and other lines (3%).
Principal Investments: Investment grade bonds (97%) and misc. investments (3%).
Investments in Affiliates: None
Group Affiliation: Travelers Companies Inc
Licensed in: All states, the District of Columbia and Puerto Rico
Commenced Business: February 1932
Address: One Tower Square, Hartford, CT 06183
Phone: (651) 310-7911   **Domicile State:** CT   **NAIC Code:** 19224

Data Date	Rating	RACR #1	RACR #2	Loss Ratio %	Total Assets ($mil)	Capital ($mil)	Net Premium ($mil)	Net Income ($mil)
9-14	B-	5.21	3.31	N/A	524.7	242.4	86.5	14.2
9-13	B-	5.30	3.38	N/A	524.9	239.9	84.7	16.2
2013	B-	5.04	3.21	60.9	510.1	228.2	116.8	22.8
2012	B-	5.02	3.23	68.4	506.8	224.2	113.4	16.3
2011	B-	4.92	3.18	76.9	500.4	221.6	111.1	9.7
2010	B-	5.07	3.22	62.0	506.2	234.4	107.3	21.3
2009	B-	4.97	3.24	58.3	517.1	237.8	105.1	24.8

Travelers Companies Inc Composite Group Rating: B Largest Group Members	Assets ($mil)	Rating
TRAVELERS INDEMNITY CO	20663	B
ST PAUL FIRE MARINE INS CO	18566	B
TRAVELERS CASUALTY SURETY CO	16464	A-
UNITED STATES FIDELITY GUARANTY CO	4654	B
TRAVELERS CASUALTY SURETY CO OF AM	4147	C+

ST PAUL SURPLUS LINES INS CO   C   Fair

Major Rating Factors: Fair overall results on stability tests (4.0 on a scale of 0 to 10). Strong long-term capitalization index (7.3) based on excellent current risk adjusted capital (severe and moderate loss scenarios), despite some fluctuation in capital levels.
Other Rating Factors: Ample reserve history (8.6) that helps to protect the company against sharp claims increases. Excellent profitability (7.6) with operating gains in each of the last five years. Return on equity has been good over the last five years, averaging 12.0%. Excellent liquidity (7.0) with ample operational cash flow and liquid investments.
Principal Business: Other liability (80%), fire (12%), allied lines (5%), inland marine (3%), and products liability (1%).
Principal Investments: Investment grade bonds (96%) and misc. investments (4%).
Investments in Affiliates: None
Group Affiliation: Travelers Companies Inc
Licensed in: All states, the District of Columbia and Puerto Rico
Commenced Business: December 1974
Address: 2711 Centerville Rd Suite 400, Wilmington, DE 19808
Phone: (651) 310-7911   **Domicile State:** DE   **NAIC Code:** 30481

Data Date	Rating	RACR #1	RACR #2	Loss Ratio %	Total Assets ($mil)	Capital ($mil)	Net Premium ($mil)	Net Income ($mil)
9-14	C	1.97	1.27	N/A	643.9	212.2	131.2	18.7
9-13	C	1.92	1.25	N/A	638.3	201.7	128.5	20.1
2013	C	1.83	1.18	60.9	619.0	193.6	177.2	28.7
2012	C	1.75	1.14	68.4	625.0	181.9	172.1	19.3
2011	C	1.91	1.24	76.9	603.5	173.1	168.5	8.6
2010	C	2.36	1.50	62.0	610.8	186.4	162.7	25.9
2009	C	2.35	1.54	58.3	636.6	189.6	159.5	30.2

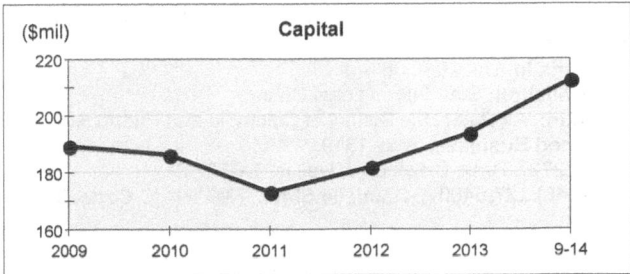
Capital

STANDARD FIRE INS CO   B   Good

Major Rating Factors: Good overall profitability index (6.9 on a scale of 0 to 10). Fair expense controls. Return on equity has been good over the last five years, averaging 15.0%. Good liquidity (6.9) with sufficient resources (cash flows and marketable investments) to handle a spike in claims.
Other Rating Factors: Good overall results on stability tests (5.5). Stability strengths include good operational trends and excellent risk diversification. Strong long-term capitalization index (7.8) based on excellent current risk adjusted capital (severe and moderate loss scenarios), despite some fluctuation in capital levels. Ample reserve history (8.3) that helps to protect the company against sharp claims increases.
Principal Business: Homeowners multiple peril (41%), allied lines (18%), auto liability (13%), workers compensation (11%), auto physical damage (9%), ocean marine (3%), and other lines (4%).
Principal Investments: Investment grade bonds (73%), misc. investments (24%), and non investment grade bonds (3%).
Investments in Affiliates: 17%
Group Affiliation: Travelers Companies Inc
Licensed in: All states, the District of Columbia and Puerto Rico
Commenced Business: March 1910
Address: One Tower Square, Hartford, CT 06183
Phone: (860) 277-0111   **Domicile State:** CT   **NAIC Code:** 19070

Data Date	Rating	RACR #1	RACR #2	Loss Ratio %	Total Assets ($mil)	Capital ($mil)	Net Premium ($mil)	Net Income ($mil)
9-14	B	1.94	1.52	N/A	3,617.4	1,223.8	721.4	118.7
9-13	B-	1.93	1.51	N/A	3,534.4	1,159.9	706.9	121.0
2013	B	2.02	1.60	60.9	3,605.3	1,234.8	974.8	217.9
2012	B-	1.82	1.43	68.4	3,440.2	1,057.8	946.7	130.7
2011	C+	1.78	1.39	76.9	3,374.0	1,009.9	926.9	94.6
2010	B	1.97	1.55	62.0	3,522.9	1,192.8	895.1	235.8
2009	B	2.13	1.72	58.3	3,763.0	1,376.0	877.4	237.1

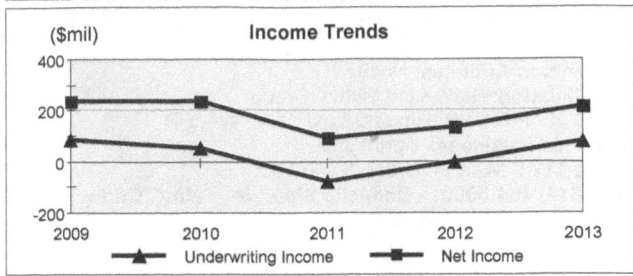
Income Trends

STAR INS CO
C   Fair

Major Rating Factors: Fair overall results on stability tests (3.6 on a scale of 0 to 10) including potential drain of affiliation with Meadowbrook Ins Group and negative cash flow from operations for 2013. Fair reserve development (4.2) as reserves have generally been sufficient to cover claims. In 2013, the two year reserve development was 19% deficient.

Other Rating Factors: Good overall profitability index (6.5). Fair expense controls. Return on equity has been fair, averaging 7.5% over the past five years. Good liquidity (6.6) with sufficient resources (cash flows and marketable investments) to handle a spike in claims. Strong long-term capitalization index (7.6) based on excellent current risk adjusted capital (severe and moderate loss scenarios). Moreover, capital levels have been consistent in recent years.

Principal Business: Workers compensation (63%), commercial multiple peril (10%), auto liability (7%), other liability (4%), inland marine (4%), auto physical damage (2%), and other lines (10%).

Principal Investments: Investment grade bonds (73%), misc. investments (25%), and cash (2%).

Investments in Affiliates: 18%

Group Affiliation: Meadowbrook Ins Group

Licensed in: All states except PR

Commenced Business: November 1985

Address: 26255 American Drive, Southfield, MI 48034-6112

Phone: (248) 358-1100   **Domicile State:** MI   **NAIC Code:** 18023

Data Date	Rating	RACR #1	RACR #2	Loss Ratio %	Total Assets ($mil)	Capital ($mil)	Net Premium ($mil)	Net Income ($mil)
9-14	C	2.11	1.73	N/A	1,010.1	314.2	172.5	11.1
9-13	C	2.04	1.62	N/A	1,050.6	320.2	188.1	0.3
2013	C	2.10	1.73	79.2	1,000.3	309.6	245.7	3.9
2012	C	1.73	1.39	79.3	956.8	263.1	285.7	5.8
2011	C	1.48	1.13	65.9	861.9	229.1	275.0	25.8
2010	C	1.58	1.23	60.5	795.2	226.4	248.5	28.6
2009	C	1.64	1.24	60.8	715.5	207.0	207.8	25.4

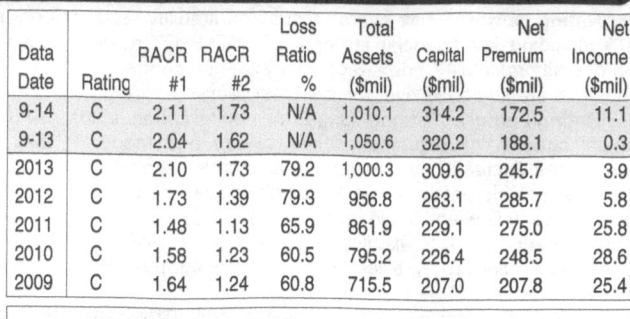

Rating Indexes

(Ranges, Cap. 2, Stab., Res., Prof., Liq. — Weak, Fair, Good, Strong)

STARR INDEMNITY & LIABILITY CO
B-   Good

Major Rating Factors: Fair reserve development (4.4 on a scale of 0 to 10) as reserves have generally been sufficient to cover claims. Fair profitability index (4.2) with operating losses during 2009. Average return on equity over the last five years has been poor at -0.1%.

Other Rating Factors: Fair overall results on stability tests (4.9) including weak results on operational trends. Strong long-term capitalization index (7.2) based on excellent current risk adjusted capital (severe and moderate loss scenarios), despite some fluctuation in capital levels. Excellent liquidity (7.0) with ample operational cash flow and liquid investments.

Principal Business: Other liability (37%), ocean marine (16%), workers compensation (11%), commercial multiple peril (11%), aircraft (10%), allied lines (3%), and other lines (11%).

Principal Investments: Misc. investments (50%), investment grade bonds (48%), and cash (2%).

Investments in Affiliates: 36%

Group Affiliation: Starr International Co Inc

Licensed in: All states, the District of Columbia and Puerto Rico

Commenced Business: May 1919

Address: 2727 Turtle Creek Blvd, Dallas, TX 75219

Phone: (646) 227-6400   **Domicile State:** TX   **NAIC Code:** 38318

Data Date	Rating	RACR #1	RACR #2	Loss Ratio %	Total Assets ($mil)	Capital ($mil)	Net Premium ($mil)	Net Income ($mil)
9-14	B-	1.34	1.11	N/A	3,725.1	1,818.1	636.5	20.8
9-13	B-	1.39	1.25	N/A	3,198.7	1,764.6	514.5	-3.3
2013	B-	1.35	1.13	81.6	3,467.4	1,865.1	847.3	13.2
2012	B-	1.38	1.22	76.7	2,904.1	1,871.3	625.3	14.9
2011	C+	1.85	1.20	79.5	1,158.3	539.0	402.5	1.7
2010	C+	3.26	2.16	68.1	913.1	523.6	239.7	3.4
2009	C	5.34	4.00	78.0	723.2	518.7	97.6	-22.9

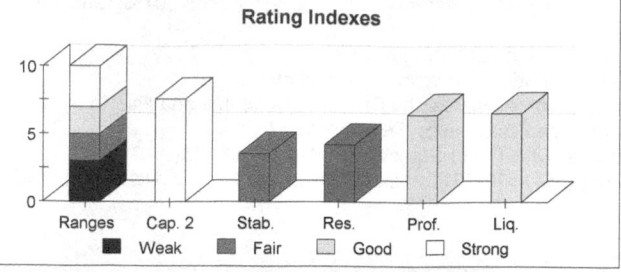

Reserve Deficiency (as % of capital)

(2009, 2010, 2011, 2012, 2013 — 1 Yr Dev, 2 Yr Dev)

* Adequate & redundant reserves show as negatives

STATE AUTO PROPERTY & CASUALTY INS
C-   Fair

Major Rating Factors: Weak overall results on stability tests (2.9 on a scale of 0 to 10). Good profitability index (5.0) despite operating losses during 2011. Return on equity has been low, averaging 0.6% over the past five years.

Other Rating Factors: Good liquidity (6.3) with sufficient resources (cash flows and marketable investments) to handle a spike in claims. Strong long-term capitalization index (7.3) based on excellent current risk adjusted capital (severe and moderate loss scenarios), despite some fluctuation in capital levels. Ample reserve history (8.5) that helps to protect the company against sharp claims increases.

Principal Business: Homeowners multiple peril (27%), auto liability (23%), commercial multiple peril (17%), auto physical damage (14%), other liability (5%), allied lines (4%), and other lines (10%).

Principal Investments: Investment grade bonds (74%), misc. investments (23%), and cash (3%).

Investments in Affiliates: None

Group Affiliation: State Auto Mutual Group

Licensed in: All states except CA, NH, NM, WA, PR

Commenced Business: April 1950

Address: 112 S Main St, Greer, SC 29650

Phone: (614) 464-5000   **Domicile State:** IA   **NAIC Code:** 25127

Data Date	Rating	RACR #1	RACR #2	Loss Ratio %	Total Assets ($mil)	Capital ($mil)	Net Premium ($mil)	Net Income ($mil)
9-14	C-	2.17	1.37	N/A	2,108.4	612.8	628.5	17.5
9-13	D+	2.03	1.31	N/A	2,036.2	553.7	620.4	26.8
2013	C-	2.19	1.40	68.5	2,066.5	607.7	833.3	39.6
2012	D+	1.92	1.26	74.8	1,889.0	505.5	828.0	3.5
2011	D	1.55	0.94	82.4	2,122.2	506.7	1,000.0	-48.7
2010	B-	2.35	1.50	70.3	2,001.1	572.8	983.8	10.0
2009	B	2.35	1.48	71.1	1,812.2	533.9	864.9	6.9

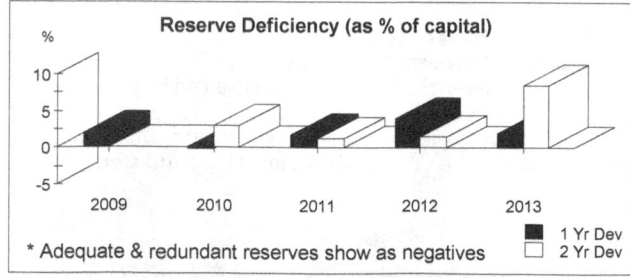

Rating Indexes

(Ranges, Cap. 2, Stab., Res., Prof., Liq. — Weak, Fair, Good, Strong)

STATE AUTOMOBILE MUTUAL INS CO   C+   Fair

Major Rating Factors: Fair overall results on stability tests (4.3 on a scale of 0 to 10) including potential drain of affiliation with State Auto Mutual Group and negative cash flow from operations for 2013. Fair profitability index (4.1) with operating losses during 2011, 2012 and the first nine months of 2014.

Other Rating Factors: Good liquidity (6.5) with sufficient resources (cash flows and marketable investments) to handle a spike in claims. Strong long-term capitalization index (7.3) based on excellent current risk adjusted capital (severe and moderate loss scenarios), despite some fluctuation in capital levels. Ample reserve history (7.6) that can protect against increases in claims costs.

Principal Business: Auto liability (26%), auto physical damage (15%), homeowners multiple peril (14%), other liability (11%), commercial multiple peril (10%), workers compensation (7%), and other lines (18%).

Principal Investments: Misc. investments (62%), investment grade bonds (31%), cash (5%), and real estate (2%).

Investments in Affiliates: 48%

Group Affiliation: State Auto Mutual Group

Licensed in: All states except PR

Commenced Business: September 1921

Address: 518 E Broad St, Columbus, OH 43215-3976

Phone: (614) 464-5000   **Domicile State:** OH   **NAIC Code:** 25135

Data Date	Rating	RACR #1	RACR #2	Loss Ratio %	Total Assets ($mil)	Capital ($mil)	Net Premium ($mil)	Net Income ($mil)
9-14	C+	1.31	1.19	N/A	2,298.3	862.6	425.1	-6.6
9-13	C	1.32	1.19	N/A	2,166.9	794.9	413.7	-4.7
2013	C+	1.33	1.22	68.5	2,196.1	858.1	555.6	-3.0
2012	C	1.28	1.17	74.6	2,093.8	748.7	552.0	-10.4
2011	C+	1.16	1.10	82.3	2,156.9	785.5	437.2	-42.5
2010	C+	1.35	1.33	69.6	1,929.3	1,033.3	316.0	7.5
2009	C+	1.35	1.33	69.4	1,721.8	924.6	279.4	5.2

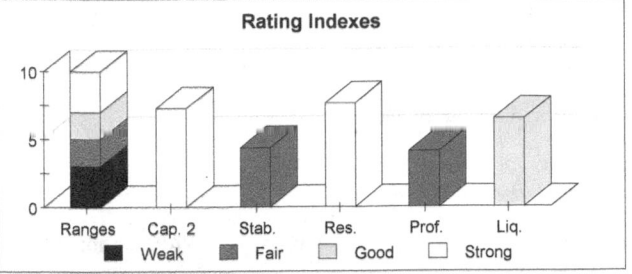

Rating Indexes

STATE FARM FIRE & CAS CO   B-   Good

Major Rating Factors: Fair overall results on stability tests (4.9 on a scale of 0 to 10). History of adequate reserve strength (6.7) as reserves have been consistently at an acceptable level.

Other Rating Factors: Good overall profitability index (5.4) despite operating losses during 2009 and 2011. Return on equity has been low, averaging 1.3% over the past five years. Good liquidity (5.3) with sufficient resources (cash flows and marketable investments) to handle a spike in claims. Strong long-term capitalization index (7.2) based on excellent current risk adjusted capital (severe and moderate loss scenarios), despite some fluctuation in capital levels.

Principal Business: Homeowners multiple peril (72%), auto liability (7%), commercial multiple peril (6%), auto physical damage (4%), other liability (3%), inland marine (3%), and other lines (4%).

Principal Investments: Investment grade bonds (74%) and misc. investments (26%).

Investments in Affiliates: None

Group Affiliation: State Farm Group

Licensed in: All states except PR

Commenced Business: June 1935

Address: One State Farm Plaza, Bloomington, IL 61710

Phone: (309) 766-2311   **Domicile State:** IL   **NAIC Code:** 25143

Data Date	Rating	RACR #1	RACR #2	Loss Ratio %	Total Assets ($mil)	Capital ($mil)	Net Premium ($mil)	Net Income ($mil)
9-14	B-	1.98	1.23	N/A	33,186.6	11,292.3	11,637.8	925.3
9-13	C+	1.77	1.09	N/A	30,901.7	9,825.2	11,070.4	959.9
2013	B-	1.99	1.23	63.5	31,460.7	10,951.2	15,276.5	1,803.8
2012	C+	1.64	1.01	77.4	28,999.1	8,805.4	14,409.5	317.2
2011	C	1.45	0.86	91.3	27,243.3	7,748.7	14,161.4	-1,465.1
2010	B	1.73	1.07	79.5	27,656.8	8,772.9	13,613.0	50.8
2009	B	1.70	1.04	80.8	26,422.2	8,540.9	13,025.5	-206.1

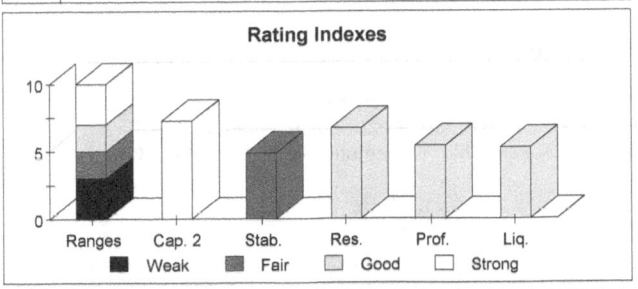

Rating Indexes

STATE FARM FLORIDA INS CO   C   Fair

Major Rating Factors: Fair overall results on stability tests (3.4 on a scale of 0 to 10). Weak profitability index (2.9) with operating losses during 2009 and 2010. Return on equity has been low, averaging 1.6% over the past five years.

Other Rating Factors: Good long-term capitalization index (5.8) based on good current risk adjusted capital (moderate loss scenario), despite some fluctuation in capital levels. History of adequate reserve strength (5.8) as reserves have been consistently at an acceptable level. Good liquidity (6.3) with sufficient resources (cash flows and marketable investments) to handle a spike in claims.

Principal Business: Homeowners multiple peril (86%), other liability (6%), inland marine (4%), and commercial multiple peril (4%).

Principal Investments: Investment grade bonds (93%) and misc. investments (7%).

Investments in Affiliates: None

Group Affiliation: State Farm Group

Licensed in: FL, IL

Commenced Business: December 1998

Address: One State Farm Plaza, Bloomington, IL 61710

Phone: (863) 318-3000   **Domicile State:** FL   **NAIC Code:** 10739

Data Date	Rating	RACR #1	RACR #2	Loss Ratio %	Total Assets ($mil)	Capital ($mil)	Net Premium ($mil)	Net Income ($mil)
9-14	C	2.02	1.43	N/A	1,895.7	868.9	423.1	124.0
9-13	C-	1.50	1.05	N/A	1,854.9	689.5	448.2	121.3
2013	C-	1.60	1.13	40.8	1,793.7	734.6	575.4	174.5
2012	D+	1.04	0.73	53.4	1,766.2	534.5	597.3	144.5
2011	D	0.55	0.39	72.1	1,744.1	368.1	699.4	50.8
2010	D	0.51	0.36	91.1	1,763.1	327.4	643.6	-66.2
2009	D	0.76	0.52	134.4	1,830.6	366.3	488.4	-180.4

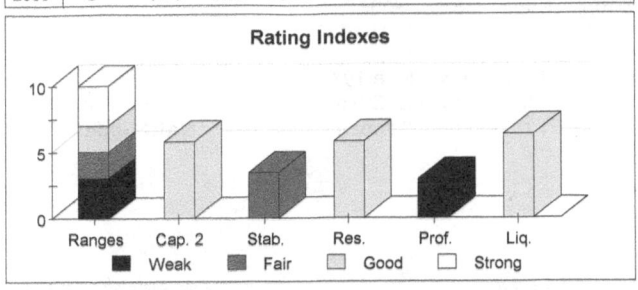

Rating Indexes

STATE FARM GENERAL INS CO   B   Good

Major Rating Factors: Good overall results on stability tests (6.3 on a scale of 0 to 10). Stability strengths include good operational trends and excellent risk diversification. History of adequate reserve strength (6.3) as reserves have been consistently at an acceptable level.

Other Rating Factors: Good liquidity (6.7) with sufficient resources (cash flows and marketable investments) to handle a spike in claims. Strong long-term capitalization index (9.9) based on excellent current risk adjusted capital (severe and moderate loss scenarios). Moreover, capital levels have been consistent in recent years. Excellent profitability (8.8) with operating gains in each of the last five years. Return on equity has been good over the last five years, averaging 11.1%.

Principal Business: Homeowners multiple peril (73%), commercial multiple peril (15%), other liability (7%), inland marine (3%), earthquake (1%), and farmowners multiple peril (1%).

Principal Investments: Investment grade bonds (92%) and misc. investments (8%).

Investments in Affiliates: None
Group Affiliation: State Farm Group
Licensed in: All states except CT, MA, RI, PR
Commenced Business: May 1962
Address: One State Farm Plaza, Bloomington, IL 61710
Phone: (309) 766-2311   **Domicile State:** IL   **NAIC Code:** 25151

Data Date	Rating	RACR #1	RACR #2	Loss Ratio %	Total Assets ($mil)	Capital ($mil)	Net Premium ($mil)	Net Income ($mil)
9-14	B	5.86	3.79	N/A	6,749.8	3,756.9	1,426.1	295.8
9-13	B	4.46	2.83	N/A	6,383.7	3,352.0	1,487.5	305.7
2013	B	5.25	3.31	55.5	6,388.1	3,452.6	1,919.0	379.9
2012	B	4.19	2.61	63.1	6,061.2	3,101.9	1,976.9	268.2
2011	B	3.07	1.87	55.1	5,685.5	2,817.9	1,958.9	346.1
2010	B	2.88	1.75	62.8	5,294.0	2,478.8	1,846.9	244.4
2009	B	2.45	1.49	55.7	4,969.3	2,234.7	1,803.8	312.4

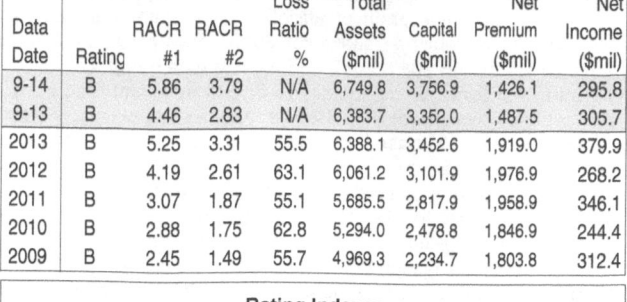

STATE FARM INDEMNITY CO   B-   Good

Major Rating Factors: Fair overall results on stability tests (4.9 on a scale of 0 to 10). History of adequate reserve strength (5.9) as reserves have been consistently at an acceptable level.

Other Rating Factors: Good overall profitability index (5.4) despite operating losses during 2009 and 2010. Return on equity has been low, averaging 1.6% over the past five years. Good liquidity (6.7) with sufficient resources (cash flows and marketable investments) to handle a spike in claims. Strong long-term capitalization index (10.0) based on excellent current risk adjusted capital (severe and moderate loss scenarios), despite some fluctuation in capital levels.

Principal Business: Auto liability (74%) and auto physical damage (26%).
Principal Investments: Investment grade bonds (97%) and misc. investments (3%).

Investments in Affiliates: 1%
Group Affiliation: State Farm Group
Licensed in: IL, NJ
Commenced Business: March 1991
Address: One State Farm Plaza, Bloomington, IL 61710
Phone: (973) 739-5000   **Domicile State:** IL   **NAIC Code:** 43796

Data Date	Rating	RACR #1	RACR #2	Loss Ratio %	Total Assets ($mil)	Capital ($mil)	Net Premium ($mil)	Net Income ($mil)
9-14	B-	5.12	4.23	N/A	2,133.6	1,094.6	457.9	45.4
9-13	B-	4.87	3.98	N/A	2,083.7	1,038.9	449.8	66.6
2013	B-	4.72	4.14	75.6	2,098.9	1,061.7	603.6	74.5
2012	B-	3.97	3.45	80.2	2,047.2	965.9	597.5	56.5
2011	C+	3.56	3.10	79.3	2,058.9	927.1	614.6	83.5
2010	C	3.05	2.53	104.4	1,976.3	828.6	610.5	-58.9
2009	C	3.82	3.14	109.7	1,914.6	889.5	573.7	-88.0

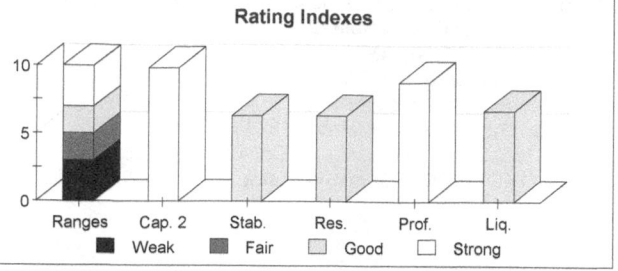

STATE FARM LLOYDS   B-   Good

Major Rating Factors: Good liquidity (6.4 on a scale of 0 to 10) with sufficient resources (cash flows and marketable investments) to handle a spike in claims. Good overall results on stability tests (5.0).

Other Rating Factors: Strong long-term capitalization index (8.4) based on excellent current risk adjusted capital (severe and moderate loss scenarios), despite some fluctuation in capital levels. Ample reserve history (7.0) that can protect against increases in claims costs. Excellent profitability (7.2).

Principal Business: Homeowners multiple peril (94%), commercial multiple peril (4%), and farmowners multiple peril (2%).

Principal Investments: Investment grade bonds (84%) and misc. investments (16%).

Investments in Affiliates: None
Group Affiliation: State Farm Group
Licensed in: TX
Commenced Business: June 1983
Address: 17301 Preston Rd, Dallas, TX 75252
Phone: (972) 732-5000   **Domicile State:** TX   **NAIC Code:** 43419

Data Date	Rating	RACR #1	RACR #2	Loss Ratio %	Total Assets ($mil)	Capital ($mil)	Net Premium ($mil)	Net Income ($mil)
9-14	B-	2.27	2.10	N/A	3,305.8	1,217.9	1,306.6	193.9
9-13	C+	2.46	2.27	N/A	3,077.1	1,087.5	1,172.6	109.5
2013	B-	2.26	1.93	53.5	3,075.5	1,105.4	1,712.7	215.2
2012	C+	2.39	2.03	59.8	2,927.0	1,073.3	1,484.6	153.4
2011	C	2.02	1.51	76.9	2,803.5	916.9	1,536.7	-32.0
2010	C	1.28	0.93	59.2	2,791.7	964.3	1,540.4	143.1
2009	C	1.17	0.85	74.3	2,695.5	944.4	1,496.6	-34.3

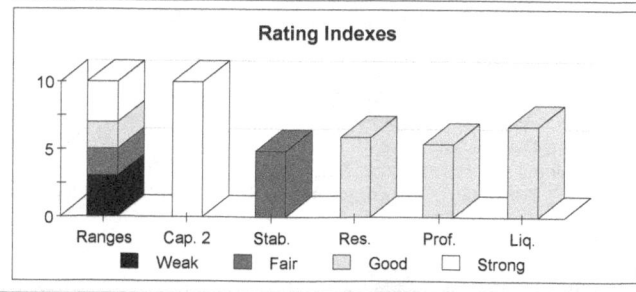

STATE FARM MUTUAL AUTOMOBILE INS CO *   B+   Good

Major Rating Factors: Good overall results on stability tests (6.7 on a scale of 0 to 10). Affiliation with State Farm Group is a strength. Good overall profitability index (6.6). Good expense controls.

Other Rating Factors: Good liquidity (6.6) with sufficient resources (cash flows and marketable investments) to handle a spike in claims. Strong long-term capitalization index (8.0) based on excellent current risk adjusted capital (severe and moderate loss scenarios), despite some fluctuation in capital levels. Ample reserve history (7.9) that can protect against increases in claims costs.

Principal Business: Auto liability (60%), auto physical damage (37%), other accident & health (2%), and group accident & health (1%).

Principal Investments: Misc. investments (66%) and investment grade bonds (34%).

Investments in Affiliates: 23%
Group Affiliation: State Farm Group
Licensed in: All states except PR
Commenced Business: June 1922
Address: One State Farm Plaza, Bloomington, IL 61710
Phone: (309) 766-2311   **Domicile State:** IL   **NAIC Code:** 25178

Data Date	Rating	RACR #1	RACR #2	Loss Ratio %	Total Assets ($mil)	Capital ($mil)	Net Premium ($mil)	Net Income ($mil)
9-14	B+	2.28	1.91	N/A	137,646.1	80,987.7	27,063.8	642.8
9-13	B+	2.22	1.85	N/A	124,091.8	69,633.0	25,853.7	1,322.0
2013	B+	2.18	1.84	79.9	129,337.9	75,678.9	35,163.3	1,836.5
2012	B+	2.14	1.81	78.1	114,933.2	65,241.9	33,697.9	1,525.0
2011	B+	2.17	1.83	82.4	108,097.4	60,791.0	32,844.2	1,088.2
2010	B+	2.15	1.82	83.5	106,988.0	61,222.1	32,527.6	950.8
2009	B+	2.16	1.82	83.5	100,680.6	58,180.3	32,168.0	570.2

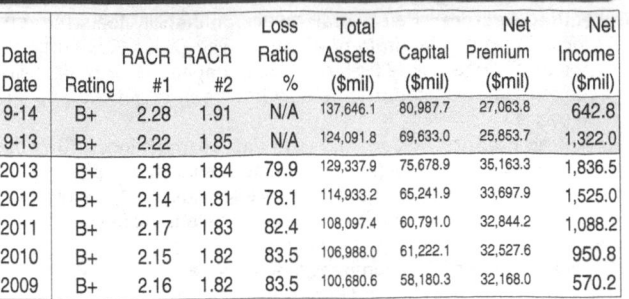

Rating Indexes

STATE VOLUNTEER MUTUAL INS CO *   A+   Excellent

Major Rating Factors: Strong long-term capitalization index (8.8 on a scale of 0 to 10) based on excellent current risk adjusted capital (severe and moderate loss scenarios). Furthermore, this high level of risk adjusted capital has been consistently maintained in previous years. Ample reserve history (9.5) that helps to protect the company against sharp claims increases.

Other Rating Factors: Excellent profitability (8.6) with operating gains in each of the last five years. Excellent liquidity (8.9) with ample operational cash flow and liquid investments. Good overall results on stability tests (6.9). Stability strengths include good operational trends and excellent risk diversification.

Principal Business: Medical malpractice (100%).

Principal Investments: Investment grade bonds (87%), misc. investments (12%), and cash (1%).

Investments in Affiliates: None
Group Affiliation: None
Licensed in: AL, AR, GA, IN, KY, MS, MO, NC, TN, VA
Commenced Business: May 1976
Address: 101 Westpark Dr Suite 300, Brentwood, TN 37024-1065
Phone: (615) 377-1999   **Domicile State:** TN   **NAIC Code:** 33049

Data Date	Rating	RACR #1	RACR #2	Loss Ratio %	Total Assets ($mil)	Capital ($mil)	Net Premium ($mil)	Net Income ($mil)
9-14	A+	3.66	2.70	N/A	1,206.0	508.6	83.9	5.0
9-13	A+	3.57	2.69	N/A	1,199.5	476.1	88.7	2.1
2013	A+	3.65	2.76	89.0	1,186.2	496.7	122.2	17.4
2012	A+	3.54	2.71	82.6	1,169.5	464.0	154.6	26.1
2011	A+	3.46	2.67	71.7	1,148.1	436.4	129.9	28.0
2010	A	3.06	2.34	52.5	1,211.3	430.6	198.0	66.7
2009	A-	2.65	1.99	60.8	1,092.4	354.7	256.7	70.1

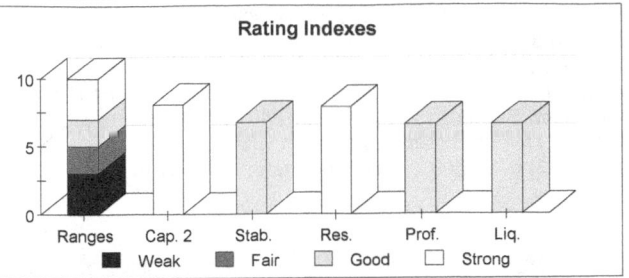

Risk-Adjusted Capital Ratio #2
(Severe Loss Scenario)

STEADFAST INS CO   C   Fair

Major Rating Factors: Fair profitability index (4.2 on a scale of 0 to 10). Good expense controls. Return on equity has been low, averaging 4.2% over the past five years. Fair overall results on stability tests (3.5) including negative cash flow from operations for 2013.

Other Rating Factors: Strong long-term capitalization index (10.0) based on excellent current risk adjusted capital (severe and moderate loss scenarios), despite some fluctuation in capital levels. Excellent liquidity (7.1) with ample operational cash flow and liquid investments.

Principal Business: Other liability (61%), commercial multiple peril (17%), medical malpractice (7%), allied lines (5%), fire (5%), products liability (2%), and other lines (4%).

Principal Investments: Investment grade bonds (61%), misc. investments (38%), and cash (1%).

Investments in Affiliates: 35%
Group Affiliation: Zurich Financial Services Group
Licensed in: All states, the District of Columbia and Puerto Rico
Commenced Business: May 1988
Address: 1400 American Lane, Schaumburg, IL 60196-1056
Phone: (847) 605-6000   **Domicile State:** DE   **NAIC Code:** 26387

Data Date	Rating	RACR #1	RACR #2	Loss Ratio %	Total Assets ($mil)	Capital ($mil)	Net Premium ($mil)	Net Income ($mil)
9-14	C	3.09	3.02	N/A	553.3	436.6	0.0	4.5
9-13	C	3.25	3.16	N/A	574.0	454.7	0.0	6.9
2013	C	3.06	3.00	0.0	602.2	430.0	0.0	5.1
2012	C	3.21	3.15	0.0	555.4	444.4	0.0	12.7
2011	C	3.37	3.28	0.0	568.8	442.3	0.0	24.6
2010	C	3.35	3.25	0.0	577.5	456.4	0.0	31.6
2009	C-	3.33	3.20	0.0	629.7	478.8	0.0	32.7

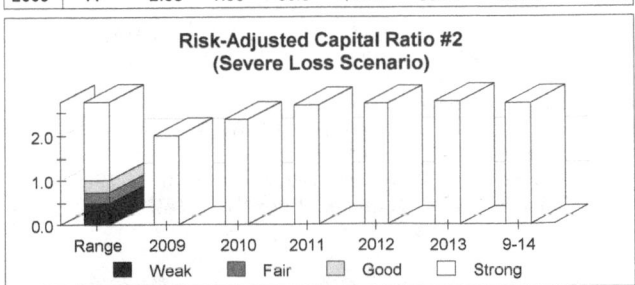

Rating Indexes

SWISS REINSURANCE AMERICA CORP

B- **Good**

Major Rating Factors: Fair overall results on stability tests (4.5 on a scale of 0 to 10) including potential drain of affiliation with Swiss Reinsurance. The largest net exposure for one risk is high at 3.4% of capital. Fair profitability index (3.9). Fair expense controls. Return on equity has been fair, averaging 11.4% over the past five years.

Other Rating Factors: Good long-term capitalization index (6.7) based on good current risk adjusted capital (moderate loss scenario), despite some fluctuation in capital levels. History of adequate reserve strength (5.8) as reserves have been consistently at an acceptable level. Excellent liquidity (7.6) with ample operational cash flow and liquid investments.

Principal Business: (This company is a reinsurer.)

Principal Investments: Investment grade bonds (69%), misc. investments (29%), and non investment grade bonds (2%).

Investments in Affiliates: None

Group Affiliation: Swiss Reinsurance

Licensed in: All states, the District of Columbia and Puerto Rico

Commenced Business: September 1940

Address: 175 King Street, Armonk, NY 10504

Phone: (913) 676-5200   **Domicile State:** NY   **NAIC Code:** 25364

Data Date	Rating	RACR #1	RACR #2	Loss Ratio %	Total Assets ($mil)	Capital ($mil)	Net Premium ($mil)	Net Income ($mil)
9-14	B-	1.38	0.94	N/A	12,939.3	4,120.5	1,396.9	395.4
9-13	B-	1.51	1.00	N/A	11,426.4	4,392.9	1,401.4	484.8
2013	B-	1.50	1.03	39.0	11,409.4	4,619.3	1,965.0	644.9
2012	B-	1.73	1.15	43.3	12,061.1	4,973.2	1,439.4	431.8
2011	C+	1.93	1.15	55.6	12,608.0	4,960.9	1,641.2	600.7
2010	C	1.55	1.02	61.6	13,230.7	5,039.3	1,585.3	367.4
2009	C	1.69	1.03	71.5	14,559.2	4,805.2	1,655.3	681.3

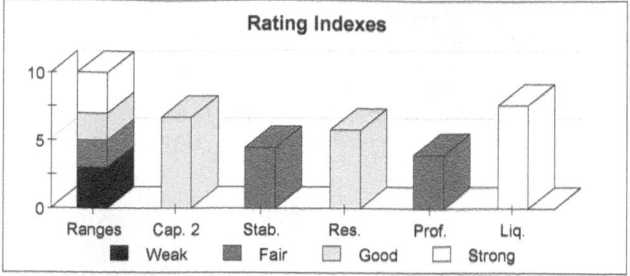

Rating Indexes

SYNCORA GUARANTEE INC

E- **Very Weak**

Major Rating Factors: Weak overall results on stability tests (0.0 on a scale of 0 to 10). The largest net exposure for one risk is excessive at 128.3% of capital. Fair reserve development (4.0) as the level of reserves has at times been insufficient to cover claims. In 2011 and 2009 the one year reserve development was 177% and 444% deficient respectively.

Other Rating Factors: Good overall profitability index (5.3) despite operating losses during 2011. Return on equity has been good over the last five years, averaging 367.1%. Strong long-term capitalization index (10.0) based on excellent current risk adjusted capital (severe and moderate loss scenarios), despite some fluctuation in capital levels. Excellent liquidity (7.0) with ample operational cash flow and liquid investments.

Principal Business: Financial guaranty (100%).

Principal Investments: Investment grade bonds (56%), misc. investments (38%), non investment grade bonds (5%), and cash (1%).

Investments in Affiliates: 6%

Group Affiliation: Syncora Holdings Ltd

Licensed in: All states except AK, FL, OH, TN, PR

Commenced Business: January 1872

Address: 250 Park Ave 19th Floor, New York, NY 10177-1999

Phone: (212) 478-3400   **Domicile State:** NY   **NAIC Code:** 20311

Data Date	Rating	RACR #1	RACR #2	Loss Ratio %	Total Assets ($mil)	Capital ($mil)	Net Premium ($mil)	Net Income ($mil)
9-14	E-	11.85	8.04	N/A	1,210.4	972.1	38.6	84.6
9-13	E-	4.24	3.08	N/A	1,105.3	556.4	56.3	-16.9
2013	E-	11.39	8.21	N/A	1,034.5	973.3	23.7	391.5
2012	E-	4.15	2.98	N/A	1,099.9	510.7	27.6	307.8
2011	E-	0.85	0.59	211.2	833.7	186.1	39.8	-30.4
2010	E-	0.99	0.78	49.9	764.5	132.6	51.0	15.4
2009	E-	0.60	0.41	N/A	1,145.1	99.7	-356.4	2,000.6

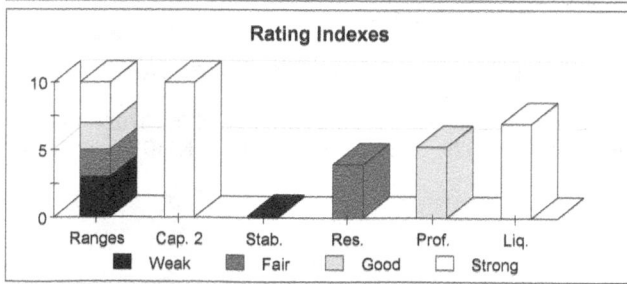

Rating Indexes

TECHNOLOGY INS CO INC

C **Fair**

Major Rating Factors: Fair overall results on stability tests (3.6 on a scale of 0 to 10) including potential drain of affiliation with AmTrust Financial Services Inc and excessive premium growth. History of adequate reserve strength (5.7) as reserves have been consistently at an acceptable level.

Other Rating Factors: Good liquidity (6.6) with sufficient resources (cash flows and marketable investments) to handle a spike in claims. Strong long-term capitalization index (7.1) based on excellent current risk adjusted capital (severe and moderate loss scenarios). Moreover, capital levels have been consistent in recent years. Excellent profitability (8.7) with operating gains in each of the last five years.

Principal Business: Workers compensation (86%), other liability (9%), auto liability (2%), commercial multiple peril (1%), inland marine (1%), and products liability (1%).

Principal Investments: Investment grade bonds (86%), misc. investments (6%), cash (5%), and non investment grade bonds (3%).

Investments in Affiliates: None

Group Affiliation: AmTrust Financial Services Inc

Licensed in: All states except PR

Commenced Business: July 1991

Address: 20 Trafalgar Square, Nashua, NH 03063

Phone: (212) 220-7120   **Domicile State:** NH   **NAIC Code:** 42376

Data Date	Rating	RACR #1	RACR #2	Loss Ratio %	Total Assets ($mil)	Capital ($mil)	Net Premium ($mil)	Net Income ($mil)
9-14	C	1.61	1.09	N/A	1,376.4	318.7	421.7	6.1
9-13	C	1.46	0.99	N/A	1,062.1	220.8	288.6	0.7
2013	C	1.62	1.11	67.1	1,132.6	236.5	485.6	16.6
2012	C	1.75	1.19	67.9	915.5	206.8	308.4	45.6
2011	C	1.93	1.36	77.8	845.8	193.0	226.9	1.7
2010	C	2.30	1.66	69.2	539.0	186.5	166.9	11.5
2009	C	2.84	1.70	64.9	601.3	167.3	131.2	15.3

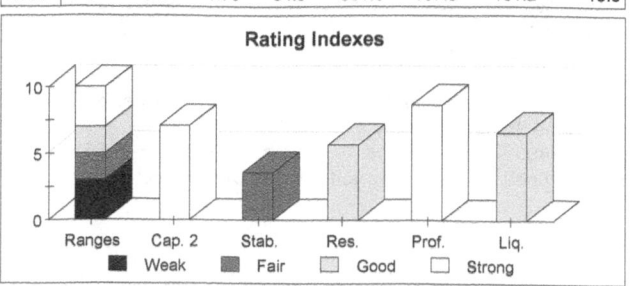

Rating Indexes

TENNESSEE FARMERS ASR CO *

B+   Good

Major Rating Factors: Good overall results on stability tests (6.1 on a scale of 0 to 10). Affiliation with Tennessee Farmers Mutual is a strength. Good overall profitability index (5.1) despite operating losses during 2011. Return on equity has been low, averaging 2.7% over the past five years.

Other Rating Factors: Good liquidity (5.7) with sufficient resources (cash flows and marketable investments) to handle a spike in claims. Strong long-term capitalization index (8.3) based on excellent current risk adjusted capital (severe and moderate loss scenarios), despite some fluctuation in capital levels. Ample reserve history (7.7) that can protect against increases in claims costs.

Principal Business: (This company is a reinsurer.)

Principal Investments: Investment grade bonds (79%), misc. investments (16%), and cash (5%).

Investments in Affiliates: 3%

Group Affiliation: Tennessee Farmers Mutual

Licensed in: TN

Commenced Business: August 1991

Address: 147 Bear Creek Pike, Columbia, TN 38401-2266

Phone: (931) 388-7872   **Domicile State:** TN   **NAIC Code:** 41220

Data Date	Rating	RACR #1	RACR #2	Loss Ratio %	Total Assets ($mil)	Capital ($mil)	Net Premium ($mil)	Net Income ($mil)
9-14	B+	3.04	2.09	N/A	1,133.1	710.2	422.6	78.2
9-13	B+	2.82	1.94	N/A	1,017.9	624.5	405.8	108.7
2013	B+	2.77	1.92	65.9	1,014.2	635.5	555.8	144.0
2012	B+	2.41	1.67	87.5	874.5	511.9	534.7	25.0
2011	B+	2.76	1.89	126.1	877.2	492.5	480.9	-157.9
2010	A-	7.46	5.30	84.6	919.0	620.3	461.1	25.6
2009	A	7.82	5.50	85.0	892.6	603.4	432.7	28.3

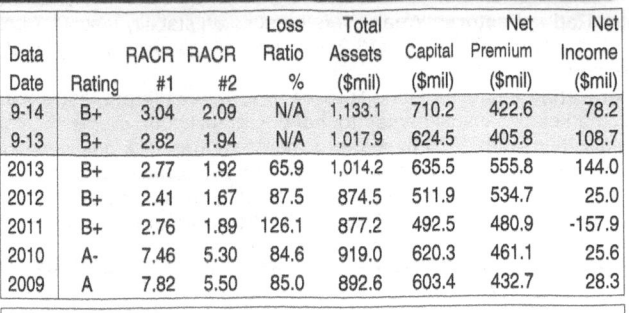

Rating Indexes

TENNESSEE FARMERS MUTUAL INS CO *

B+   Good

Major Rating Factors: Good overall results on stability tests (6.1 on a scale of 0 to 10). Affiliation with Tennessee Farmers Mutual is a strength. Good overall profitability index (5.2) despite operating losses during 2009 and 2011.

Other Rating Factors: Good liquidity (6.4) with sufficient resources (cash flows and marketable investments) to handle a spike in claims. Strong long-term capitalization index (8.0) based on excellent current risk adjusted capital (severe and moderate loss scenarios), despite some fluctuation in capital levels. Ample reserve history (7.5) that can protect against increases in claims costs.

Principal Business: Homeowners multiple peril (30%), auto liability (27%), auto physical damage (26%), farmowners multiple peril (10%), fire (5%), other liability (1%), and allied lines (1%).

Principal Investments: Misc. investments (56%), investment grade bonds (43%), and cash (1%).

Investments in Affiliates: 48%

Group Affiliation: Tennessee Farmers Mutual

Licensed in: TN

Commenced Business: December 1952

Address: 147 Bear Creek Pike, Columbia, TN 38401-2266

Phone: (931) 388-7872   **Domicile State:** TN   **NAIC Code:** 15245

Data Date	Rating	RACR #1	RACR #2	Loss Ratio %	Total Assets ($mil)	Capital ($mil)	Net Premium ($mil)	Net Income ($mil)
9-14	B+	1.88	1.73	N/A	2,369.1	1,782.9	425.1	89.2
9-13	B+	1.93	1.74	N/A	2,200.1	1,607.7	408.5	105.8
2013	B+	1.80	1.67	66.8	2,191.9	1,650.4	559.4	159.8
2012	B+	1.81	1.68	87.9	1,940.0	1,449.4	540.2	34.2
2011	B+	1.85	1.70	137.2	1,978.5	1,405.0	522.8	-146.0
2010	A-	1.98	1.87	92.4	2,137.0	1,654.7	502.6	22.2
2009	A-	2.04	1.92	97.2	2,064.5	1,627.8	474.2	-9.1

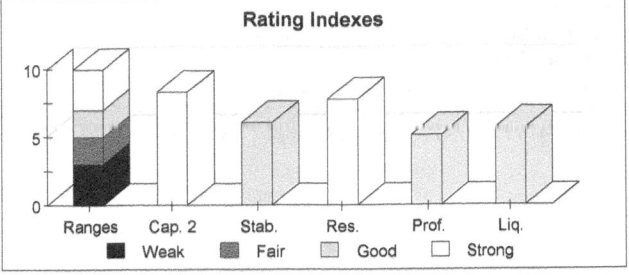

Rating Indexes

TEXAS FARM BUREAU CASUALTY INS CO *

A   Excellent

Major Rating Factors: Strong long-term capitalization index (10.0 on a scale of 0 to 10) based on excellent current risk adjusted capital (severe and moderate loss scenarios). Furthermore, this high level of risk adjusted capital has been consistently maintained in previous years. Ample reserve history (8.3) that helps to protect the company against sharp claims increases.

Other Rating Factors: Excellent overall results on stability tests (7.4). Stability strengths include excellent operational trends and excellent risk diversification. Good overall profitability index (6.5) with small operating losses during 2011. Return on equity has been low, averaging 2.8% over the past five years. Good liquidity (5.8) with sufficient resources (cash flows and marketable investments) to handle a spike in claims.

Principal Business: Auto liability (51%), auto physical damage (47%), and other liability (2%).

Principal Investments: Investment grade bonds (61%) and misc. investments (42%).

Investments in Affiliates: None

Group Affiliation: TX Farm Bureau Mutual

Licensed in: TX

Commenced Business: August 2007

Address: 7420 Fish Pond Rd, Waco, TX 76710

Phone: (254) 772-3030   **Domicile State:** TX   **NAIC Code:** 13004

Data Date	Rating	RACR #1	RACR #2	Loss Ratio %	Total Assets ($mil)	Capital ($mil)	Net Premium ($mil)	Net Income ($mil)
9-14	A	4.73	3.67	N/A	1,123.7	655.9	455.5	9.2
9-13	A	4.87	3.71	N/A	1,079.0	626.4	426.2	21.5
2013	A	4.80	3.83	81.5	1,099.9	645.0	583.4	28.0
2012	A	4.65	3.60	82.5	1,048.1	606.2	546.4	8.1
2011	A	2.60	1.86	89.7	1,014.1	589.1	563.0	-2.6
2010	N/A	N/A	N/A	75.2	975.3	605.3	538.7	44.3
2009	N/A	N/A	N/A	83.0	906.8	552.7	523.7	13.2

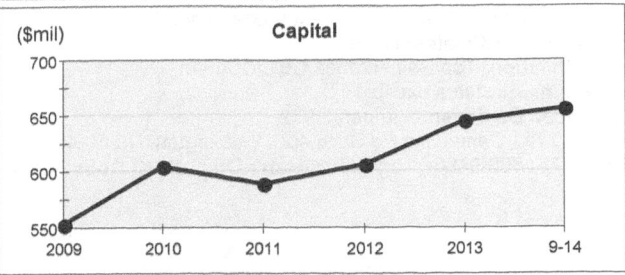

Capital

TEXAS FARM BUREAU MUTUAL INS CO

D **Weak**

Major Rating Factors: Weak overall results on stability tests (1.7 on a scale of 0 to 10). Fair profitability index (3.2) with operating losses during 2012 and the first nine months of 2014.

Other Rating Factors: Good liquidity (5.9) with sufficient resources (cash flows and marketable investments) to handle a spike in claims. Strong long-term capitalization index (9.2) based on excellent current risk adjusted capital (severe and moderate loss scenarios), despite some fluctuation in capital levels. Ample reserve history (7.5) that can protect against increases in claims costs.

Principal Business: Auto liability (36%), homeowners multiple peril (33%), auto physical damage (30%), and other liability (2%).

Principal Investments: Investment grade bonds (84%), misc. investments (15%), and cash (1%).

Investments in Affiliates: 1%

Group Affiliation: TX Farm Bureau Mutual

Licensed in: TX

Commenced Business: February 1950

Address: 7420 Fish Pond Road, Waco, TX 76710

Phone: (254) 772-3030 **Domicile State:** TX **NAIC Code:** 25380

Data Date	Rating	RACR #1	RACR #2	Loss Ratio %	Total Assets ($mil)	Capital ($mil)	Net Premium ($mil)	Net Income ($mil)
9-14	D	2.65	2.39	N/A	682.4	287.4	265.8	-32.4
9-13	D	2.62	2.39	N/A	635.3	295.4	228.4	-43.2
2013	D	3.28	2.75	82.6	659.9	313.0	343.1	-19.4
2012	B-	3.89	3.26	87.0	616.5	323.2	304.5	-39.1
2011	B-	2.73	2.08	82.7	349.5	152.8	141.2	3.9
2010	B-	4.15	3.38	82.8	329.5	145.8	128.9	6.4
2009	B-	4.23	3.39	87.0	313.1	140.5	122.1	3.0

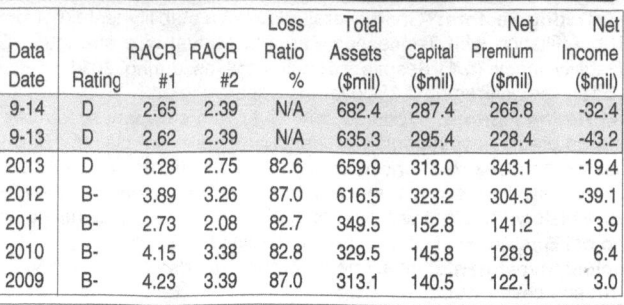

Rating Indexes

TIG INS CO

D **Weak**

Major Rating Factors: Poor long-term capitalization index (1.5 on a scale of 0 to 10) based on weak current risk adjusted capital (severe and moderate loss scenarios). A history of deficient reserves (2.8). Underreserving can have an adverse impact on capital and profits. In four of the last five years reserves (two year development) were between 16% and 26% deficient.

Other Rating Factors: Weak profitability index (2.5) with operating losses during 2009, 2012 and 2013. Average return on equity over the last five years has been poor at -6.4%. Weak overall results on stability tests (1.5) including weak risk adjusted capital in prior years, weak results on operational trends and negative cash flow from operations for 2013. Excellent liquidity (7.0) with ample operational cash flow and liquid investments.

Principal Business: Other liability (51%) and workers compensation (49%).

Principal Investments: Misc. investments (76%) and investment grade bonds (24%).

Investments in Affiliates: 56%

Group Affiliation: Fairfax Financial

Licensed in: All states except PR

Commenced Business: April 1915

Address: 5205 N OConnor Blvd,2nd Floor, Irving, TX 75015

Phone: (603) 656-2233 **Domicile State:** CA **NAIC Code:** 25534

Data Date	Rating	RACR #1	RACR #2	Loss Ratio %	Total Assets ($mil)	Capital ($mil)	Net Premium ($mil)	Net Income ($mil)
9-14	D	0.48	0.37	N/A	2,315.8	1,000.6	0.0	9.6
9-13	D	0.35	0.27	N/A	2,218.5	791.2	1.0	-117.1
2013	D	0.40	0.31	N/A	2,235.8	850.0	1.0	-140.5
2012	D	0.42	0.33	N/A	2,310.1	928.1	0.1	-128.2
2011	D	0.43	0.36	N/A	2,459.8	862.9	1.7	106.8
2010	D	0.45	0.38	N/A	2,478.3	942.2	1.7	46.7
2009	D-	0.37	0.31	N/A	2,202.7	786.6	-0.2	-195.1

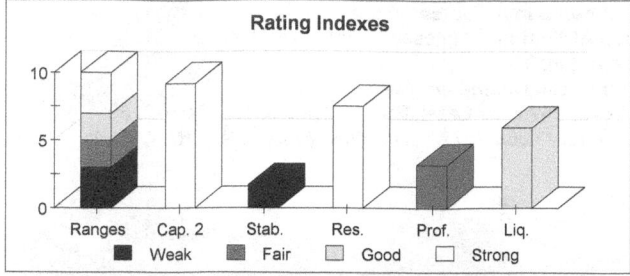

Capital

TOA-RE INS CO OF AMERICA *

B+ **Good**

Major Rating Factors: History of adequate reserve strength (6.5 on a scale of 0 to 10) as reserves have been consistently at an acceptable level. Good liquidity (6.9) with sufficient resources (cash flows and marketable investments) to handle a spike in claims.

Other Rating Factors: Good overall results on stability tests (6.5). The largest net exposure for one risk is conservative at 1.6% of capital. Strong long-term capitalization index (7.7) based on excellent current risk adjusted capital (severe and moderate loss scenarios). Moreover, capital levels have been consistent in recent years. Excellent profitability (8.5) with operating gains in each of the last five years.

Principal Business: (This company is a reinsurer.)

Principal Investments: Investment grade bonds (78%), misc. investments (19%), cash (2%), and non investment grade bonds (1%).

Investments in Affiliates: None

Group Affiliation: Toa Reinsurance Co Ltd Japan

Licensed in: All states except PR

Commenced Business: January 1972

Address: 2711 Centerville Rd Suite 400, Wilmington, DE 19808

Phone: (973) 898-9480 **Domicile State:** DE **NAIC Code:** 42439

Data Date	Rating	RACR #1	RACR #2	Loss Ratio %	Total Assets ($mil)	Capital ($mil)	Net Premium ($mil)	Net Income ($mil)
9-14	B+	2.19	1.45	N/A	1,812.3	698.8	271.3	51.9
9-13	B	1.87	1.25	N/A	1,793.4	650.9	295.7	38.1
2013	B+	2.14	1.43	65.1	1,779.4	682.4	403.1	70.7
2012	B	1.84	1.23	78.3	1,670.3	599.1	391.3	32.6
2011	B	2.32	1.53	67.6	1,577.6	586.9	293.7	63.7
2010	B	2.18	1.47	67.7	1,515.6	563.4	252.4	66.8
2009	B	1.91	1.28	74.5	1,414.4	476.0	231.8	33.3

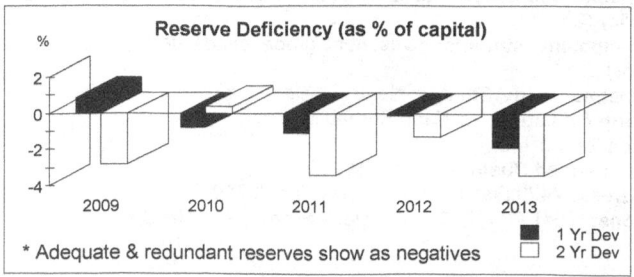

Reserve Deficiency (as % of capital)

* Adequate & redundant reserves show as negatives

TOKIO MARINE AMERICA INS CO *   A   Excellent

Major Rating Factors: Strong long-term capitalization index (8.0 on a scale of 0 to 10) based on excellent current risk adjusted capital (severe and moderate loss scenarios). Furthermore, this high level of risk adjusted capital has been consistently maintained in previous years. Good overall results on stability tests (6.0) despite weak results on operational trends and negative cash flow from operations for 2013. The largest net exposure for one risk is excessive at 5.1% of capital. Strengths include potentially strong support from affiliation with Tokio Marine Holdings Inc.

Other Rating Factors: Good liquidity (6.8) with sufficient resources (cash flows and marketable investments) to handle a spike in claims. Fair reserve development (4.9) as reserves have generally been sufficient to cover claims. Fair profitability index (4.9) with small operating losses during 2011. Return on equity has been low, averaging 2.0% over the past five years.

Principal Business: Ocean marine (15%), fire (12%), workers compensation (11%), auto liability (11%), other liability (10%), allied lines (8%), and other lines (32%).

Principal Investments: Investment grade bonds (100%) and cash (2%).

Investments in Affiliates: None

Group Affiliation: Tokio Marine Holdings Inc

Licensed in: All states except PR

Commenced Business: September 1999

Address: 230 Park Ave, New York, NY 10169-0005

Phone: (212) 297-6600   **Domicile State:** NY   **NAIC Code:** 10945

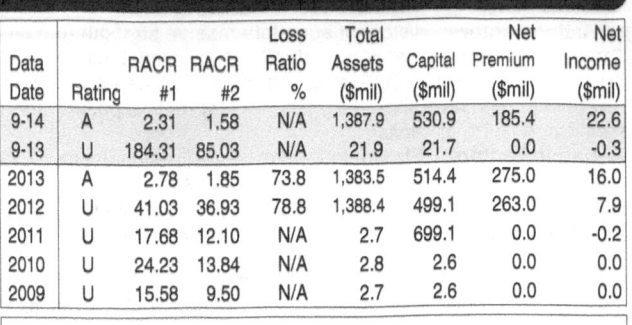

Data Date	Rating	RACR #1	RACR #2	Loss Ratio %	Total Assets ($mil)	Capital ($mil)	Net Premium ($mil)	Net Income ($mil)
9-14	A	2.31	1.58	N/A	1,387.9	530.9	185.4	22.6
9-13	U	184.31	85.03	N/A	21.9	21.7	0.0	-0.3
2013	A	2.78	1.85	73.8	1,383.5	514.4	275.0	16.0
2012	U	41.03	36.93	78.8	1,388.4	499.1	263.0	7.9
2011	U	17.68	12.10	N/A	2.7	699.1	0.0	-0.2
2010	U	24.23	13.84	N/A	2.8	2.6	0.0	0.0
2009	U	15.58	9.50	N/A	2.7	2.6	0.0	0.0

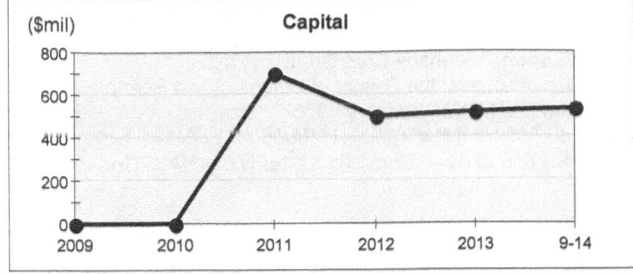

TOWER INS CO OF NEW YORK   D-   Weak

Major Rating Factors: Weak overall results on stability tests (1.3 on a scale of 0 to 10) including weak risk adjusted capital in prior years and negative cash flow from operations for 2013. Fair reserve development (4.7) as reserves have generally been sufficient to cover claims. In 2013, the one year reserve development was 27% deficient.

Other Rating Factors: Fair profitability index (4.5) with operating losses during 2012 and the first nine months of 2014. Good liquidity (6.3) with sufficient resources (cash flows and marketable investments) to handle a spike in claims. Strong long-term capitalization index (7.9) based on excellent current risk adjusted capital (severe and moderate loss scenarios).

Principal Business: Commercial multiple peril (29%), homeowners multiple peril (27%), workers compensation (21%), auto liability (12%), other liability (4%), auto physical damage (2%), and other lines (5%).

Principal Investments: Investment grade bonds (92%) and non investment grade bonds (10%).

Investments in Affiliates: 6%

Group Affiliation: ACP Re Holdings LLC

Licensed in: All states except WY, PR

Commenced Business: December 1990

Address: 120 Broadway 31st Floor, New York, NY 10271

Phone: (212) 655-2000   **Domicile State:** NY   **NAIC Code:** 44300

Data Date	Rating	RACR #1	RACR #2	Loss Ratio %	Total Assets ($mil)	Capital ($mil)	Net Premium ($mil)	Net Income ($mil)
9-14	D-	2.94	2.14	N/A	426.2	125.6	21.4	-5.8
9-13	C	N/A	N/A	N/A	N/A	N/A	N/A	N/A
2013	C	N/A	N/A	105.8	543.7	136.4	57.3	-127.1
2012	C	2.21	1.57	75.3	875.1	244.7	385.2	-10.5
2011	C	1.70	1.23	69.9	981.6	280.5	364.6	25.9
2010	C	1.37	0.95	62.0	902.2	266.4	302.7	51.4
2009	C	1.18	0.77	62.8	1,258.9	233.1	268.2	10.1

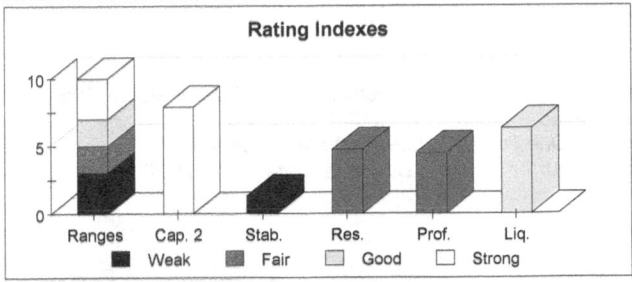

TOYOTA MOTOR INS CO   C   Fair

Major Rating Factors: Fair overall results on stability tests (3.5 on a scale of 0 to 10) including potential drain of affiliation with Toyota Motor Corp. History of adequate reserve strength (6.1) as reserves have been consistently at an acceptable level.

Other Rating Factors: Strong long-term capitalization index (10.0) based on excellent current risk adjusted capital (severe and moderate loss scenarios). Moreover, capital levels have been consistent in recent years. Excellent profitability (8.8) with operating gains in each of the last five years. Return on equity has been good over the last five years, averaging 10.8%. Excellent liquidity (7.7) with ample operational cash flow and liquid investments.

Principal Business: Other liability (71%), credit (8%), and aggregate write-ins for other lines of business (4%).

Principal Investments: Investment grade bonds (90%), misc. investments (4%), cash (3%), and non investment grade bonds (3%).

Investments in Affiliates: None

Group Affiliation: Toyota Motor Corp

Licensed in: All states except PR

Commenced Business: December 1909

Address: 19001 S.Western Ave TC22, Torrance, CA 90509

Phone: (310) 468-4019   **Domicile State:** IA   **NAIC Code:** 37621

Data Date	Rating	RACR #1	RACR #2	Loss Ratio %	Total Assets ($mil)	Capital ($mil)	Net Premium ($mil)	Net Income ($mil)
9-14	C	9.14	7.46	N/A	450.5	207.2	39.2	11.1
9-13	C	11.27	9.14	N/A	421.2	189.6	34.0	12.5
2013	C	9.87	8.12	38.0	420.0	194.9	65.6	17.1
2012	C	11.31	9.35	34.1	411.6	177.0	52.0	20.1
2011	C	11.79	8.87	33.7	422.8	157.3	43.7	18.6
2010	C	10.74	8.75	45.0	394.8	138.8	41.6	26.7
2009	C	9.95	8.02	71.2	351.2	112.5	32.6	6.5

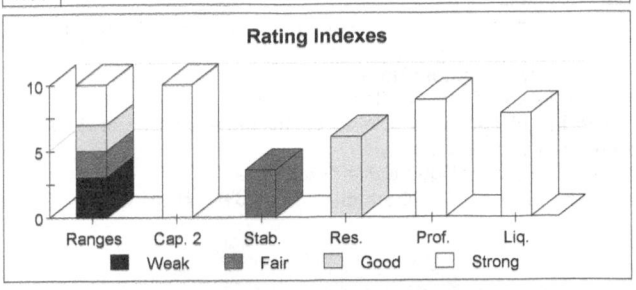

TRANSATLANTIC REINSURANCE CO

B   **Good**

Major Rating Factors: History of adequate reserve strength (6.5 on a scale of 0 to 10) as reserves have been consistently at an acceptable level. Good overall results on stability tests (6.1). Stability strengths include good operational trends and excellent risk diversification. The largest net exposure for one risk is conservative at 1.1% of capital.

Other Rating Factors: Strong long-term capitalization index (7.3) based on excellent current risk adjusted capital (severe and moderate loss scenarios), despite some fluctuation in capital levels. Excellent profitability (7.0) despite modest operating losses during 2011. Excellent liquidity (7.0) with ample operational cash flow and liquid investments.

Principal Business: (This company is a reinsurer.)

Principal Investments: Investment grade bonds (81%), misc. investments (16%), cash (2%), and non investment grade bonds (1%).

Investments in Affiliates: 7%

Group Affiliation: Alleghany Corp Group

Licensed in: All states, the District of Columbia and Puerto Rico

Commenced Business: January 1953

Address: 80 Pine St, New York, NY 10005

Phone: (212) 365-2200   **Domicile State:** NY   **NAIC Code:** 19453

Data Date	Rating	RACR #1	RACR #2	Loss Ratio %	Total Assets ($mil)	Capital ($mil)	Net Premium ($mil)	Net Income ($mil)
9-14	B	2.00	1.37	N/A	14,695.1	4,710.7	2,243.1	408.6
9-13	B	2.02	1.34	N/A	14,818.8	4,425.1	2,253.4	493.0
2013	B	2.02	1.39	55.2	15,013.0	4,718.9	2,977.0	770.4
2012	B	1.92	1.28	71.2	14,661.5	4,179.1	3,074.5	345.5
2011	B	1.90	1.26	85.7	13,307.8	3,843.8	3,291.5	-15.3
2010	B-	2.28	1.46	67.9	13,123.9	4,325.4	3,247.1	355.8
2009	C+	1.71	1.04	64.4	12,420.6	4,016.1	3,410.0	415.5

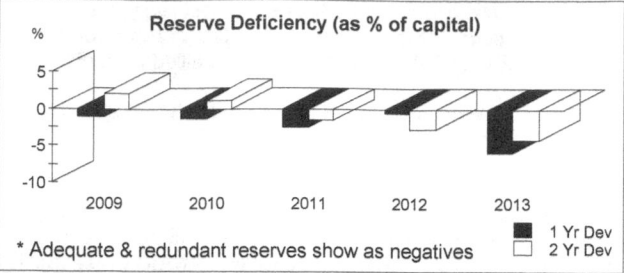

Reserve Deficiency (as % of capital)

* Adequate & redundant reserves show as negatives

■ 1 Yr Dev   □ 2 Yr Dev

TRAVELERS CASUALTY & SURETY CO *

A-   **Excellent**

Major Rating Factors: Strong long-term capitalization index (7.6 on a scale of 0 to 10) based on excellent current risk adjusted capital (severe and moderate loss scenarios), despite some fluctuation in capital levels. Ample reserve history (8.3) that helps to protect the company against sharp claims increases.

Other Rating Factors: Excellent profitability (7.0) with operating gains in each of the last five years. Return on equity has been excellent over the last five years averaging 15.7%. Good overall results on stability tests (6.9). Affiliation with Travelers Companies Inc is a strength. Good liquidity (6.9) with sufficient resources (cash flows and marketable investments) to handle a spike in claims.

Principal Business: Workers compensation (71%), surety (16%), homeowners multiple peril (10%), other liability (1%), fire (1%), and allied lines (1%).

Principal Investments: Investment grade bonds (67%), misc. investments (31%), and non investment grade bonds (2%).

Investments in Affiliates: 25%

Group Affiliation: Travelers Companies Inc

Licensed in: All states, the District of Columbia and Puerto Rico

Commenced Business: May 1907

Address: One Tower Square, Hartford, CT 06183

Phone: (860) 277-0111   **Domicile State:** CT   **NAIC Code:** 19038

Data Date	Rating	RACR #1	RACR #2	Loss Ratio %	Total Assets ($mil)	Capital ($mil)	Net Premium ($mil)	Net Income ($mil)
9-14	A-	1.66	1.43	N/A	16,487.0	6,450.1	3,034.8	400.7
9-13	B+	1.77	1.48	N/A	16,171.8	6,347.9	2,973.7	469.3
2013	A-	1.75	1.53	60.9	16,464.4	6,558.6	4,101.0	1,165.6
2012	B+	1.58	1.36	68.3	15,137.1	5,149.5	3,983.1	610.4
2011	B+	1.59	1.35	76.9	14,784.7	4,897.2	3,899.7	620.3
2010	B+	1.70	1.44	62.0	15,034.6	5,439.8	3,765.8	1,088.5
2009	B	1.72	1.50	58.3	15,965.4	6,197.9	3,691.5	1,335.5

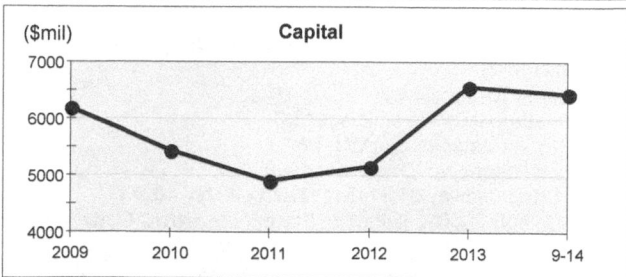

Capital

TRAVELERS CASUALTY & SURETY CO OF AM

C+   **Fair**

Major Rating Factors: Fair overall results on stability tests (4.0 on a scale of 0 to 10). The largest net exposure for one risk is excessive at 7.5% of capital. Strong long-term capitalization index (10.0) based on excellent current risk adjusted capital (severe and moderate loss scenarios), despite some fluctuation in capital levels.

Other Rating Factors: Ample reserve history (9.4) that helps to protect the company against sharp claims increases. Excellent profitability (8.8) with operating gains in each of the last five years. Return on equity has been excellent over the last five years averaging 23.7%. Excellent liquidity (7.2) with ample operational cash flow and liquid investments.

Principal Business: Other liability (46%), surety (41%), fidelity (10%), and burglary & theft (2%).

Principal Investments: Investment grade bonds (85%), misc. investments (15%), and non investment grade bonds (1%).

Investments in Affiliates: None

Group Affiliation: Travelers Companies Inc

Licensed in: All states, the District of Columbia and Puerto Rico

Commenced Business: July 1974

Address: One Tower Square, Hartford, CT 06183

Phone: (860) 277-0111   **Domicile State:** CT   **NAIC Code:** 31194

Data Date	Rating	RACR #1	RACR #2	Loss Ratio %	Total Assets ($mil)	Capital ($mil)	Net Premium ($mil)	Net Income ($mil)
9-14	C+	5.87	3.92	N/A	4,495.6	2,284.7	1,025.2	401.2
9-13	C+	4.93	3.33	N/A	4,514.0	2,150.8	946.8	338.5
2013	C+	4.75	3.18	13.9	4,147.5	1,881.7	1,293.9	500.5
2012	C+	3.99	2.70	26.4	4,339.6	1,780.5	1,223.0	417.0
2011	C+	3.81	2.54	27.2	4,256.4	1,652.1	1,245.3	416.2
2010	C+	4.28	2.86	35.3	4,238.3	1,802.2	1,244.9	385.1
2009	C+	4.80	3.16	30.5	4,334.3	1,836.8	1,262.7	403.3

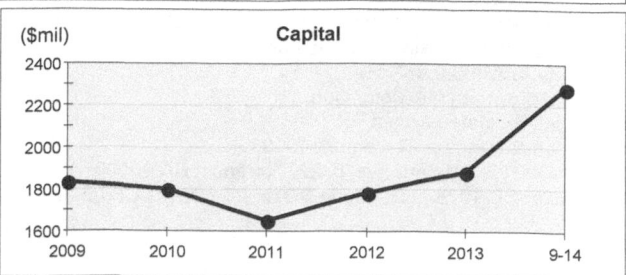

Capital

TRAVELERS CASUALTY INS CO OF AMERICA | B | Good

Major Rating Factors: Good liquidity (6.7 on a scale of 0 to 10) with sufficient resources (cash flows and marketable investments) to handle a spike in claims. Good overall results on stability tests (6.1). Affiliation with Travelers Companies Inc is a strength.

Other Rating Factors: Strong long-term capitalization index (8.0) based on excellent current risk adjusted capital (severe and moderate loss scenarios), despite some fluctuation in capital levels. Ample reserve history (8.8) that helps to protect the company against sharp claims increases. Excellent profitability (7.8) with operating gains in each of the last five years. Return on equity has been good over the last five years, averaging 13.0%.

Principal Business: Commercial multiple peril (68%), workers compensation (15%), auto liability (13%), and auto physical damage (4%).

Principal Investments: Investment grade bonds (90%) and misc. investments (10%).

Investments in Affiliates: None

Group Affiliation: Travelers Companies Inc

Licensed in: All states except PR

Commenced Business: October 1971

Address: One Tower Square, Hartford, CT 06183

Phone: (860) 277-0111   **Domicile State:** CT   **NAIC Code:** 19046

Data Date	Rating	RACR #1	RACR #2	Loss Ratio %	Total Assets ($mil)	Capital ($mil)	Net Premium ($mil)	Net Income ($mil)
9-14	B	2.85	1.80	N/A	1,972.9	614.0	406.9	66.2
9-13	B	2.70	1.73	N/A	1,920.9	569.2	398.7	63.6
2013	B	2.62	1.66	60.9	1,893.1	549.8	549.8	91.5
2012	B	2.45	1.57	68.4	1,841.4	506.6	534.0	59.7
2011	B	2.35	1.52	76.9	1,826.2	489.0	522.8	26.5
2010	B	2.41	1.53	62.0	1,822.6	514.4	504.8	59.8
2009	B	2.34	1.53	58.3	1,866.8	519.4	494.9	94.5

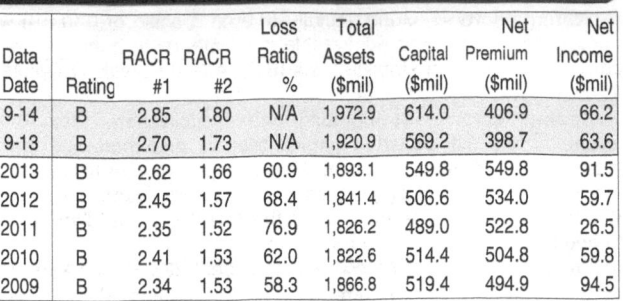

Liquidity Index

TRAVELERS INDEMNITY CO | B | Good

Major Rating Factors: Good liquidity (6.8 on a scale of 0 to 10) with sufficient resources (cash flows and marketable investments) to handle a spike in claims. Good overall results on stability tests (6.3).

Other Rating Factors: Fair profitability index (3.8). Fair expense controls. Return on equity has been fair, averaging 12.8% over the past five years. Strong long-term capitalization index (7.7) based on excellent current risk adjusted capital (severe and moderate loss scenarios), despite some fluctuation in capital levels. Ample reserve history (8.1) that helps to protect the company against sharp claims increases.

Principal Business: Workers compensation (23%), other liability (18%), commercial multiple peril (15%), allied lines (11%), auto liability (10%), fire (9%), and other lines (14%).

Principal Investments: Investment grade bonds (73%), misc. investments (24%), non investment grade bonds (4%), and real estate (1%).

Investments in Affiliates: 20%

Group Affiliation: Travelers Companies Inc

Licensed in: All states, the District of Columbia and Puerto Rico

Commenced Business: May 1906

Address: One Tower Square, Hartford, CT 06183

Phone: (860) 277-0111   **Domicile State:** CT   **NAIC Code:** 25658

Data Date	Rating	RACR #1	RACR #2	Loss Ratio %	Total Assets ($mil)	Capital ($mil)	Net Premium ($mil)	Net Income ($mil)
9-14	B	1.74	1.44	N/A	20,782.1	6,559.3	3,472.5	547.8
9-13	A-	1.93	1.61	N/A	21,349.1	7,336.1	3,402.6	622.6
2013	B	1.82	1.52	60.9	20,662.6	6,701.6	4,531.6	1,065.7
2012	A-	1.93	1.63	68.4	21,834.6	7,119.3	4,921.4	706.8
2011	A-	1.95	1.63	76.8	20,948.7	6,975.3	4,462.2	404.2
2010	A-	1.99	1.65	62.1	21,109.5	7,069.4	4,309.3	1,376.5
2009	A-	2.15	1.82	58.3	22,208.6	8,372.6	4,223.9	1,200.5

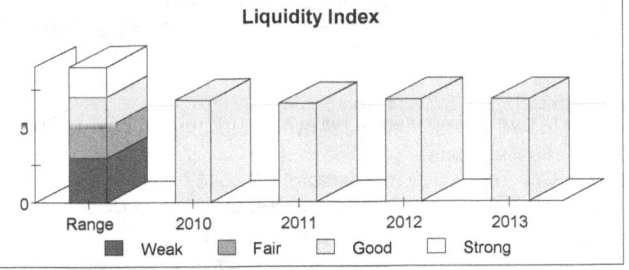

Liquidity Index

TRAVELERS INDEMNITY CO OF AMERICA | B | Good

Major Rating Factors: Good overall results on stability tests (5.9 on a scale of 0 to 10). Affiliation with Travelers Companies Inc is a strength. Strong long-term capitalization index (8.5) based on excellent current risk adjusted capital (severe and moderate loss scenarios), despite some fluctuation in capital levels.

Other Rating Factors: Ample reserve history (8.7) that helps to protect the company against sharp claims increases. Excellent profitability (7.9) with operating gains in each of the last five years. Return on equity has been good over the last five years, averaging 10.6%. Excellent liquidity (7.2) with ample operational cash flow and liquid investments.

Principal Business: Workers compensation (40%), commercial multiple peril (31%), auto liability (7%), homeowners multiple peril (6%), other liability (5%), farmowners multiple peril (4%), and other lines (7%).

Principal Investments: Investment grade bonds (94%) and misc. investments (6%).

Investments in Affiliates: None

Group Affiliation: Travelers Companies Inc

Licensed in: All states except CA, PR

Commenced Business: May 1946

Address: One Tower Square, Hartford, CT 06183

Phone: (860) 277-0111   **Domicile State:** CT   **NAIC Code:** 25666

Data Date	Rating	RACR #1	RACR #2	Loss Ratio %	Total Assets ($mil)	Capital ($mil)	Net Premium ($mil)	Net Income ($mil)
9-14	B	3.44	2.18	N/A	639.2	212.4	114.8	15.3
9-13	B	3.29	2.10	N/A	645.7	198.3	112.5	17.8
2013	B	3.24	2.07	60.9	628.0	194.5	155.1	25.1
2012	B	3.05	1.96	68.4	639.0	180.7	150.6	16.9
2011	B	2.78	1.80	76.9	602.7	165.7	147.5	1.6
2010	B	2.81	1.78	62.0	615.6	171.5	142.4	22.7
2009	B	2.38	1.55	58.3	650.1	150.4	139.6	26.4

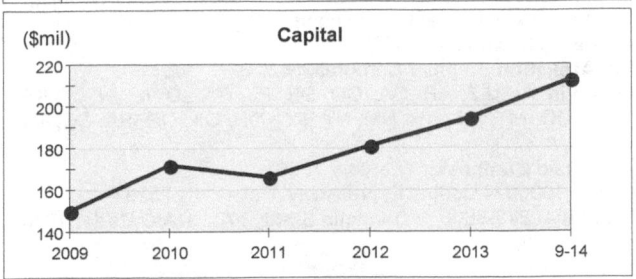

Capital

TRAVELERS INDEMNITY CO OF CT

B   Good

Major Rating Factors: Good liquidity (6.9 on a scale of 0 to 10) with sufficient resources (cash flows and marketable investments) to handle a spike in claims. Good overall results on stability tests (6.0). Affiliation with Travelers Companies Inc is a strength.

Other Rating Factors: Strong long-term capitalization index (8.8) based on excellent current risk adjusted capital (severe and moderate loss scenarios), despite some fluctuation in capital levels. Ample reserve history (8.4) that helps to protect the company against sharp claims increases. Excellent profitability (7.8) with operating gains in each of the last five years. Return on equity has been good over the last five years, averaging 10.8%.

Principal Business: Commercial multiple peril (33%), workers compensation (29%), auto liability (18%), other liability (9%), auto physical damage (5%), farmowners multiple peril (2%), and other lines (3%).

Principal Investments: Investment grade bonds (87%) and misc. investments (13%).

Investments in Affiliates: None

Group Affiliation: Travelers Companies Inc

Licensed in: All states, the District of Columbia and Puerto Rico

Commenced Business: September 1860

Address: One Tower Square, Hartford, CT 06183

Phone: (860) 277-0111   **Domicile State:** CT   **NAIC Code:** 25682

Data Date	Rating	RACR #1	RACR #2	Loss Ratio %	Total Assets ($mil)	Capital ($mil)	Net Premium ($mil)	Net Income ($mil)
9-14	B	3.76	2.38	N/A	1,161.8	413.4	204.2	41.9
9-13	B	3.56	2.27	N/A	1,110.5	380.9	200.1	38.6
2013	B	3.43	2.18	60.9	1,082.4	365.6	275.9	51.8
2012	B	3.33	2.14	68.4	1,065.2	350.1	268.0	33.9
2011	B	3.12	2.01	76.9	1,017.6	330.5	262.4	15.1
2010	B	3.16	2.00	62.0	1,017.0	342.3	253.3	36.3
2009	B	3.07	2.00	58.3	1,072.2	345.2	248.3	44.5

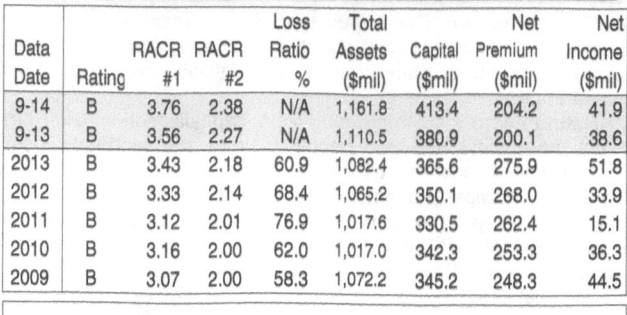

Liquidity Index

TRAVELERS PROPERTY CAS OF AMERICA

B   Good

Major Rating Factors: Good overall results on stability tests (5.9 on a scale of 0 to 10). Affiliation with Travelers Companies Inc is a strength. Strong long-term capitalization index (10.0) based on excellent current risk adjusted capital (severe and moderate loss scenarios). Moreover, capital levels have been consistent in recent years.

Other Rating Factors: Ample reserve history (7.9) that can protect against increases in claims costs. Excellent profitability (8.3) with operating gains in each of the last five years. Excellent liquidity (7.1) with ample operational cash flow and liquid investments.

Principal Business: Workers compensation (33%), commercial multiple peril (17%), other liability (12%), auto liability (10%), inland marine (9%), fire (4%), and other lines (15%).

Principal Investments: Investment grade bonds (95%) and misc. investments (5%).

Investments in Affiliates: None

Group Affiliation: Travelers Companies Inc

Licensed in: All states except PR

Commenced Business: August 1971

Address: One Tower Square, Hartford, CT 06183

Phone: (860) 277-0111   **Domicile State:** CT   **NAIC Code:** 25674

Data Date	Rating	RACR #1	RACR #2	Loss Ratio %	Total Assets ($mil)	Capital ($mil)	Net Premium ($mil)	Net Income ($mil)
9-14	B	16.01	9.98	N/A	946.6	500.3	53.7	13.0
9-13	B	15.38	9.66	N/A	855.9	463.8	52.6	13.7
2013	B	16.40	10.35	60.9	907.0	487.0	72.5	20.2
2012	B	15.37	9.74	68.4	841.7	450.1	70.4	16.0
2011	B	14.73	9.40	76.9	792.2	433.7	68.9	11.4
2010	B	14.03	8.86	62.0	768.1	421.8	66.6	10.4
2009	B	3.18	2.08	58.3	410.2	95.9	65.3	10.3

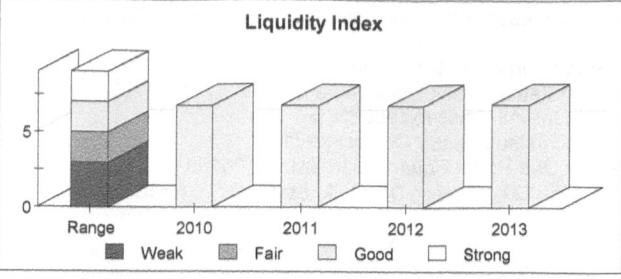

Travelers Companies Inc Composite Group Rating: B Largest Group Members	Assets ($mil)	Rating
TRAVELERS INDEMNITY CO	20663	B
ST PAUL FIRE MARINE INS CO	18566	B
TRAVELERS CASUALTY SURETY CO	16464	A-
UNITED STATES FIDELITY GUARANTY CO	4654	B
TRAVELERS CASUALTY SURETY CO OF AM	4147	C+

TRINITY UNIVERSAL INS CO

B   Good

Major Rating Factors: Good overall profitability index (6.1 on a scale of 0 to 10). Fair expense controls. Return on equity has been fair, averaging 8.0% over the past five years. Good overall results on stability tests (5.8). Stability strengths include good operational trends and excellent risk diversification.

Other Rating Factors: Fair liquidity (3.3) as cash resources may not be adequate to cover a spike in claims. Strong long-term capitalization index (7.6) based on excellent current risk adjusted capital (severe and moderate loss scenarios), despite some fluctuation in capital levels. Ample reserve history (9.0) that helps to protect the company against sharp claims increases.

Principal Business: Auto liability (38%), homeowners multiple peril (33%), auto physical damage (26%), other liability (2%), and inland marine (1%).

Principal Investments: Investment grade bonds (55%), misc. investments (43%), and non investment grade bonds (3%).

Investments in Affiliates: 13%

Group Affiliation: Kemper Corporation

Licensed in: AL, AZ, AR, CA, CO, DE, FL, GA, ID, IL, IN, IA, KS, KY, LA, MI, MN, MS, MO, MT, NE, NH, NM, NY, NC, OH, OK, OR, PA, SC, TN, TX, UT, VA, WA, WV, WI, WY

Commenced Business: February 1926

Address: 10000 N Central Expressway, Dallas, TX 75231

Phone: (904) 245-5600   **Domicile State:** TX   **NAIC Code:** 19887

Data Date	Rating	RACR #1	RACR #2	Loss Ratio %	Total Assets ($mil)	Capital ($mil)	Net Premium ($mil)	Net Income ($mil)
9-14	B	2.22	1.64	N/A	2,323.6	948.6	1,017.9	16.8
9-13	B	2.01	1.47	N/A	2,401.1	927.1	1,125.6	84.1
2013	B	2.19	1.62	66.7	2,380.9	984.1	1,435.7	138.5
2012	B	1.80	1.34	78.1	2,407.9	839.0	1,550.5	41.0
2011	B	1.69	1.29	79.6	2,452.5	824.0	1,614.5	31.3
2010	B	1.47	1.18	74.0	2,642.8	899.6	1,694.1	111.5
2009	B-	1.49	1.25	70.9	2,794.7	874.8	1,876.8	79.2

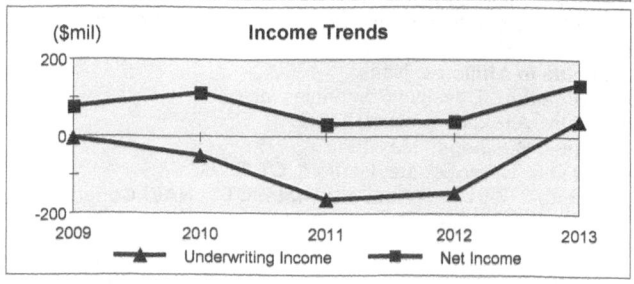

Income Trends

TRITON INS CO   C+   Fair

Major Rating Factors: Fair overall results on stability tests (4.4 on a scale of 0 to 10). History of adequate reserve strength (6.4) as reserves have been consistently at an acceptable level.

Other Rating Factors: Weak profitability index (2.8). Good expense controls. Return on equity has been fair, averaging 26.1% over the past five years. Strong long-term capitalization index (10.0) based on excellent current risk adjusted capital (severe and moderate loss scenarios), despite some fluctuation in capital levels. Excellent liquidity (7.3) with ample operational cash flow and liquid investments.

Principal Business: Aggregate write-ins for other lines of business (69%), credit accident & health (29%), and inland marine (2%).

Principal Investments: Investment grade bonds (86%), misc. investments (10%), cash (3%), and non investment grade bonds (1%).

Investments in Affiliates: None
Group Affiliation: Citigroup Inc
Licensed in: All states except PR
Commenced Business: July 1982
Address: 3001 Meacham Blvd Ste 200, Fort Worth, TX 76137-4615
Phone: (800) 316-5607   **Domicile State:** TX   **NAIC Code:** 41211

Data Date	Rating	RACR #1	RACR #2	Loss Ratio %	Total Assets ($mil)	Capital ($mil)	Net Premium ($mil)	Net Income ($mil)
9-14	C+	8.48	4.66	N/A	550.4	181.4	97.5	42.7
9-13	C+	9.05	5.00	N/A	517.4	190.8	104.4	47.5
2013	C+	10.15	5.58	32.3	527.8	205.9	138.6	64.0
2012	C+	10.46	5.85	30.9	554.4	219.4	147.3	74.9
2011	B	13.05	7.36	34.1	633.2	292.0	142.7	79.6
2010	B	12.95	7.41	36.2	677.7	311.4	117.5	94.0
2009	B	11.66	6.79	77.0	819.9	385.5	135.4	14.1

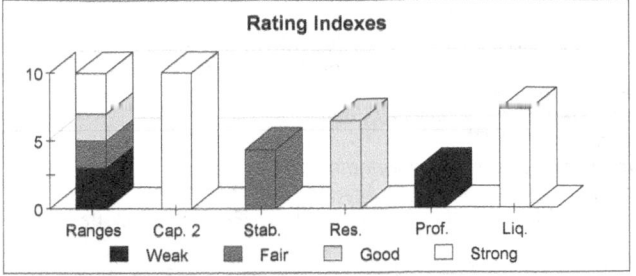

Rating Indexes: Ranges, Cap. 2, Stab., Res., Prof., Liq. — Weak, Fair, Good, Strong

TRUCK INS EXCHANGE   C+   Fair

Major Rating Factors: Fair profitability index (3.6 on a scale of 0 to 10) with operating losses during 2010, 2011, 2012 and the first nine months of 2014. Fair liquidity (3.4) as cash resources may not be adequate to cover a spike in claims.

Other Rating Factors: Fair overall results on stability tests (4.8) including negative cash flow from operations for 2013. Good overall long-term capitalization (5.3) based on good current risk adjusted capital (severe and moderate loss scenarios). However, capital levels have fluctuated somewhat during past years. History of adequate reserve strength (6.5) as reserves have been consistently at an acceptable level.

Principal Business: Commercial multiple peril (46%), workers compensation (21%), auto liability (12%), other liability (10%), homeowners multiple peril (6%), auto physical damage (4%), and medical malpractice (1%).

Principal Investments: Investment grade bonds (53%) and misc. investments (51%).

Investments in Affiliates: 43%
Group Affiliation: Farmers Insurance Group of Companies
Licensed in: All states except PR
Commenced Business: February 1935
Address: 4680 Wilshire Blvd, Los Angeles, CA 90010
Phone: (323) 932-3200   **Domicile State:** CA   **NAIC Code:** 21709

Data Date	Rating	RACR #1	RACR #2	Loss Ratio %	Total Assets ($mil)	Capital ($mil)	Net Premium ($mil)	Net Income ($mil)
9-14	C+	0.86	0.78	N/A	2,001.7	569.2	786.4	-6.2
9-13	C+	0.87	0.79	N/A	1,988.7	542.7	799.3	-9.7
2013	C+	0.86	0.80	66.9	1,933.4	563.5	1,056.9	1.5
2012	C+	0.87	0.80	73.3	1,963.0	535.0	1,073.8	-29.3
2011	C+	0.94	0.87	73.2	1,976.4	554.5	1,097.1	-23.4
2010	C	0.91	0.81	66.1	1,934.8	552.4	987.6	-49.7
2009	C	0.98	0.88	67.4	1,680.2	540.4	751.9	14.2

Income Trends ($mil): 2009, 2010, 2011, 2012, 2013 — Underwriting Income, Net Income

TRUSTGARD INS CO *   B+   Good

Major Rating Factors: Good overall results on stability tests (5.0 on a scale of 0 to 10) despite potential drain of affiliation with Grange Mutual Casualty Group. The largest net exposure for one risk is high at 3.5% of capital. Stability strengths include good operational trends and excellent risk diversification. Good overall profitability index (6.8). Good expense controls. Return on equity has been fair, averaging 9.4% over the past five years.

Other Rating Factors: Good liquidity (6.7) with sufficient resources (cash flows and marketable investments) to handle a spike in claims. Strong long-term capitalization index (10.0) based on excellent current risk adjusted capital. Moreover, capital levels have been consistent in recent years. Ample reserve history (7.9) that can protect against increases in claims costs.

Principal Business: Auto liability (39%), homeowners multiple peril (30%), auto physical damage (24%), fire (2%), workers compensation (2%), allied lines (1%), and other liability (1%).

Principal Investments: Investment grade bonds (93%), misc. investments (6%), and cash (1%).

Investments in Affiliates: None
Group Affiliation: Grange Mutual Casualty Group
Licensed in: CO, GA, IL, IN, IA, KS, KY, MN, MO, NE, ND, OH, OR, PA, SC, SD, TN, TX, VA, WA, WI
Commenced Business: November 1981
Address: 650 S Front St, Columbus, OH 43206
Phone: (614) 445-2900   **Domicile State:** OH   **NAIC Code:** 40118

Data Date	Rating	RACR #1	RACR #2	Loss Ratio %	Total Assets ($mil)	Capital ($mil)	Net Premium ($mil)	Net Income ($mil)
9-14	B+	6.70	4.64	N/A	102.3	57.6	30.7	3.4
9-13	B+	6.24	4.29	N/A	93.2	53.2	28.7	3.5
2013	B+	6.39	4.41	67.0	96.2	54.2	39.9	4.4
2012	B+	6.02	4.13	69.0	90.3	49.6	37.0	4.3
2011	B+	5.24	3.45	70.5	83.3	45.4	36.0	4.3
2010	B+	4.28	2.87	71.8	80.0	41.2	38.7	4.5
2009	B+	3.50	2.27	72.0	73.4	36.7	39.2	4.0

Grange Mutual Casualty Group
Composite Group Rating: B+
Largest Group Members

Largest Group Members	Assets ($mil)	Rating
GRANGE MUTUAL CAS CO	2012	B+
GRANGE LIFE INS CO	353	B-
TRUSTGARD INS CO	96	B+
GRANGE INDEMNITY INS CO	88	C
INTEGRITY MUTUAL INS CO	83	B-

TUSCARORA WAYNE INS CO *   B+   Good

Major Rating Factors: Good overall results on stability tests (5.0 on a scale of 0 to 10) despite potential drain of affiliation with Tuscarora Group. Stability strengths include excellent operational trends and good risk diversification. Strong long-term capitalization index (9.9) based on excellent current risk adjusted capital (severe and moderate loss scenarios). Moreover, capital levels have been consistent in recent years.

Other Rating Factors: Ample reserve history (8.4) that helps to protect the company against sharp claims increases. Excellent profitability (8.5) with operating gains in each of the last five years. Excellent liquidity (7.0) with ample operational cash flow and liquid investments.

Principal Business: Commercial multiple peril (33%), homeowners multiple peril (32%), fire (14%), farmowners multiple peril (10%), allied lines (6%), other liability (4%), and inland marine (2%).

Principal Investments: Investment grade bonds (73%), misc. investments (23%), non investment grade bonds (3%), and real estate (1%).

Investments in Affiliates: 9%

Group Affiliation: Tuscarora Group

Licensed in: OH, PA

Commenced Business: September 1874

Address: 601 State St, Wyalusing, PA 18853

Phone: (570) 746-1515   **Domicile State:** PA   **NAIC Code:** 17825

Data Date	Rating	RACR #1	RACR #2	Loss Ratio %	Total Assets ($mil)	Capital ($mil)	Net Premium ($mil)	Net Income ($mil)
9-14	B+	3.91	2.90	N/A	91.3	54.3	25.9	2.6
9-13	B+	3.80	2.80	N/A	86.4	51.2	24.0	1.5
2013	B+	4.05	2.98	48.5	89.8	54.1	34.0	3.4
2012	B+	3.88	2.85	56.3	79.6	48.9	31.2	1.9
2011	B+	3.91	2.84	61.2	73.6	45.9	29.2	1.8
2010	B+	4.00	2.86	48.3	73.8	43.7	29.4	3.8
2009	B+	4.10	2.87	42.9	67.6	38.5	24.0	5.2

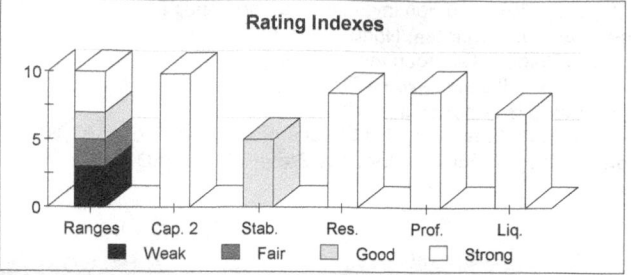

Rating Indexes

TWIN CITY FIRE INS CO   B   Good

Major Rating Factors: History of adequate reserve strength (6.2 on a scale of 0 to 10) as reserves have been consistently at an acceptable level. Good overall profitability index (5.1). Good expense controls. Return on equity has been fair, averaging 9.5% over the past five years.

Other Rating Factors: Good liquidity (6.8) with sufficient resources (cash flows and marketable investments) to handle a spike in claims. Good overall results on stability tests (5.8). Strong long-term capitalization index (10.0) based on excellent current risk adjusted capital (severe and moderate loss scenarios), despite some fluctuation in capital levels.

Principal Business: Workers compensation (56%), other liability (19%), auto liability (11%), auto physical damage (5%), products liability (4%), homeowners multiple peril (3%), and commercial multiple peril (2%).

Principal Investments: Investment grade bonds (98%), misc. investments (1%), and non investment grade bonds (1%).

Investments in Affiliates: None

Group Affiliation: Hartford Financial Services Inc

Licensed in: All states except PR

Commenced Business: July 1987

Address: 4040 Vincennes Cir Suite 100, Indianapolis, IN 46268

Phone: (860) 547-5000   **Domicile State:** IN   **NAIC Code:** 29459

Data Date	Rating	RACR #1	RACR #2	Loss Ratio %	Total Assets ($mil)	Capital ($mil)	Net Premium ($mil)	Net Income ($mil)
9-14	B	5.36	3.53	N/A	650.2	280.7	112.8	19.3
9-13	B	5.51	3.63	N/A	632.5	280.4	110.8	20.4
2013	B	5.67	3.77	68.8	641.7	288.1	149.2	27.7
2012	B	5.82	3.86	72.7	643.1	291.1	147.7	26.4
2011	B	5.81	3.90	78.5	647.6	290.2	147.7	18.9
2010	B	6.20	4.22	67.3	640.3	301.2	145.3	32.7
2009	B	6.20	4.22	64.4	647.4	305.2	146.4	36.2

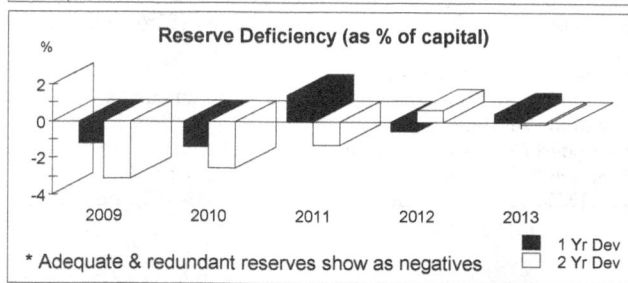

Reserve Deficiency (as % of capital)

* Adequate & redundant reserves show as negatives

UNDERWRITERS AT LLOYDS LONDON   D   Weak

Major Rating Factors: Weak overall results on stability tests (1.4 on a scale of 0 to 10) including negative cash flow from operations for 2013. Fair profitability index (4.6) with operating losses during the first nine months of 2014.

Other Rating Factors: History of adequate reserve strength (6.9) as reserves have been consistently at an acceptable level. Good liquidity (6.7) with sufficient resources (cash flows and marketable investments) to handle a spike in claims. Strong long-term capitalization index (9.3) based on excellent current risk adjusted capital (severe and moderate loss scenarios), despite some fluctuation in capital levels.

Principal Business: Other liability (76%), commercial multiple peril (15%), inland marine (3%), auto physical damage (3%), and surety (2%).

Principal Investments: Investment grade bonds (109%).

Investments in Affiliates: None

Group Affiliation: None

Licensed in: IL

Commenced Business: February 1929

Address: 115 S La Salle Street, Chicago, IL 60603

Phone: (312) 407-6200   **Domicile State:** IL   **NAIC Code:** 15792

Data Date	Rating	RACR #1	RACR #2	Loss Ratio %	Total Assets ($mil)	Capital ($mil)	Net Premium ($mil)	Net Income ($mil)
9-14	D	3.51	2.33	N/A	369.8	176.6	44.6	-7.2
9-13	D-	5.22	3.46	N/A	426.9	223.8	45.1	37.7
2013	D	4.79	3.18	12.7	399.7	223.2	61.0	37.6
2012	D-	2.64	1.79	54.6	514.4	187.1	53.3	11.6
2011	E+	0.48	0.35	66.0	542.6	195.9	62.2	12.9
2010	E+	0.70	0.53	56.4	605.6	223.1	64.0	21.2
2009	E+	0.40	0.30	43.6	663.5	241.6	77.6	44.2

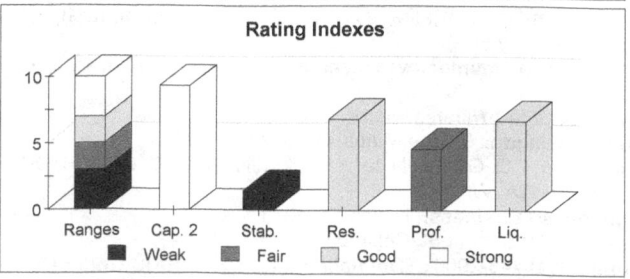

Rating Indexes

UNITED EDUCATORS INS A RECIP RRG — C — Fair

Major Rating Factors: Fair overall results on stability tests (3.9 on a scale of 0 to 10). The largest net exposure for one risk is high at 3.0% of capital. Good overall profitability index (6.9). Good expense controls. Return on equity has been good over the last five years, averaging 10.2%.

Other Rating Factors: Strong long-term capitalization index (7.5) based on excellent current risk adjusted capital (severe and moderate loss scenarios), despite some fluctuation in capital levels. Excellent liquidity (8.2) with ample operational cash flow and liquid investments.

Principal Business: Other liability (100%).

Principal Investments: Investment grade bonds (78%), misc. investments (21%), and non investment grade bonds (1%).

Investments in Affiliates: None

Group Affiliation: None

Licensed in: All states, the District of Columbia and Puerto Rico

Commenced Business: March 1987

Address: Two Wisconsin Circle, Ste 1040, Chevy Chase, MD 20815-9913

Phone: (301) 907-4908 **Domicile State:** VT **NAIC Code:** 10020

Data Date	Rating	RACR #1	RACR #2	Loss Ratio %	Total Assets ($mil)	Capital ($mil)	Net Premium ($mil)	Net Income ($mil)
9-14	C	1.66	1.33	N/A	814.2	270.4	96.0	16.9
9-13	C	1.70	1.36	N/A	751.3	253.2	85.6	34.0
2013	C	1.68	1.35	76.9	759.7	254.5	123.7	37.7
2012	C	1.81	1.47	83.6	727.9	253.3	110.6	19.7
2011	C	1.79	1.40	81.2	674.5	239.9	101.8	22.1
2010	C	1.82	1.48	85.6	650.5	226.5	96.7	19.1
2009	C	1.82	1.49	78.3	571.1	209.1	91.9	25.7

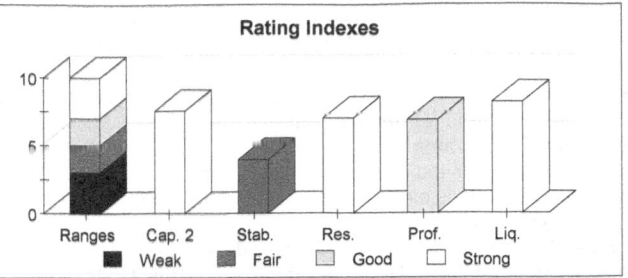

Rating Indexes

UNITED FARM FAMILY MUTUAL INS CO — B- — Good

Major Rating Factors: Fair profitability index (3.4 on a scale of 0 to 10) with operating losses during 2009, 2011 and 2012. Fair liquidity (4.6) as cash resources may not be adequate to cover a spike in claims.

Other Rating Factors: History of adequate reserve strength (6.5) as reserves have been consistently at an acceptable level. Good overall results on stability tests (5.3). Strong long-term capitalization index (8.3) based on excellent current risk adjusted capital (severe and moderate loss scenarios), despite some fluctuation in capital levels.

Principal Business: Auto liability (25%), homeowners multiple peril (24%), auto physical damage (21%), farmowners multiple peril (15%), allied lines (6%), commercial multiple peril (6%), and other lines (3%).

Principal Investments: Investment grade bonds (73%) and misc. investments (27%).

Investments in Affiliates: 4%

Group Affiliation: Indiana Farm Bureau Inc

Licensed in: IN, OH

Commenced Business: February 1935

Address: 225 South East St, Indianapolis, IN 46202-4056

Phone: (317) 692-7200 **Domicile State:** IN **NAIC Code:** 15288

Data Date	Rating	RACR #1	RACR #2	Loss Ratio %	Total Assets ($mil)	Capital ($mil)	Net Premium ($mil)	Net Income ($mil)
9-14	B-	2.99	2.03	N/A	967.8	338.9	379.1	19.4
9-13	C+	2.41	1.58	N/A	955.2	281.0	369.9	27.3
2013	B-	2.89	2.00	72.6	915.0	323.7	503.3	35.8
2012	C+	2.02	1.35	96.9	877.5	241.4	521.2	-56.2
2011	B	2.92	2.08	84.1	890.9	314.7	498.1	-10.6
2010	B	2.82	1.97	73.3	879.9	333.5	487.3	28.6
2009	B	2.54	1.79	83.2	873.0	298.6	486.0	-2.3

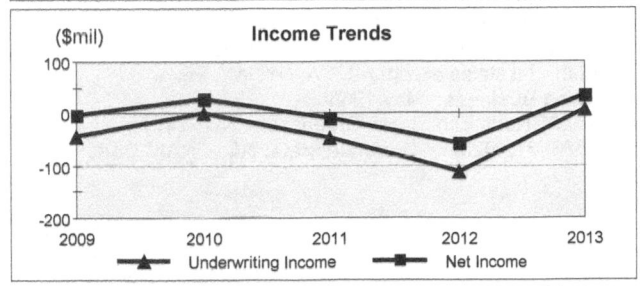

Income Trends

UNITED FINANCIAL CASUALTY CO — C+ — Fair

Major Rating Factors: Fair overall results on stability tests (4.5 on a scale of 0 to 10) including potential drain of affiliation with Progressive Group. Good liquidity (5.1) with sufficient resources (cash flows and marketable investments) to handle a spike in claims.

Other Rating Factors: Strong long-term capitalization index (7.8) based on excellent current risk adjusted capital (severe and moderate loss scenarios), despite some fluctuation in capital levels. Ample reserve history (7.0) that can protect against increases in claims costs. Excellent profitability (9.3) with operating gains in each of the last five years. Return on equity has been excellent over the last five years averaging 29.9%.

Principal Business: Auto liability (67%), auto physical damage (32%), and inland marine (1%).

Principal Investments: Investment grade bonds (74%), misc. investments (25%), and non investment grade bonds (1%).

Investments in Affiliates: None

Group Affiliation: Progressive Group

Licensed in: All states except PR

Commenced Business: August 1984

Address: 6300 Wilson Mills Rd W33, Mayfield Village, OH 44143-2182

Phone: (440) 461-5000 **Domicile State:** OH **NAIC Code:** 11770

Data Date	Rating	RACR #1	RACR #2	Loss Ratio %	Total Assets ($mil)	Capital ($mil)	Net Premium ($mil)	Net Income ($mil)
9-14	C+	2.18	1.56	N/A	2,330.1	572.2	1,154.3	115.3
9-13	C+	1.96	1.36	N/A	2,079.2	449.3	1,062.0	33.0
2013	C+	1.96	1.41	75.3	2,137.9	492.0	1,501.7	60.4
2012	C+	2.12	1.48	72.8	1,815.9	391.3	1,173.2	74.0
2011	C+	2.38	1.63	64.1	1,630.4	390.3	975.1	134.2
2010	C+	2.46	1.68	63.2	1,693.5	406.3	996.5	166.6
2009	C	1.14	0.83	63.9	1,790.4	405.4	1,086.9	183.8

Progressive Group
Composite Group Rating: C+
Largest Group Members

	Assets ($mil)	Rating
PROGRESSIVE CASUALTY INS CO	5772	C+
PROGRESSIVE DIRECT INS CO	4724	C-
UNITED FINANCIAL CASUALTY CO	2138	C+
PROGRESSIVE NORTHERN INS CO	1305	C+
PROGRESSIVE NORTHWESTERN INS CO	1268	C+

UNITED FIRE & CAS CO

B   Good

Major Rating Factors: Good overall results on stability tests (5.5 on a scale of 0 to 10) despite potential drain of affiliation with United Fire & Casualty Group. Stability strengths include good operational trends and excellent risk diversification. Good long-term capitalization index (6.9) based on good current risk adjusted capital (moderate loss scenario), despite some fluctuation in capital levels.

Other Rating Factors: History of adequate reserve strength (6.9) as reserves have been consistently at an acceptable level. Good overall profitability index (5.8) despite operating losses during 2009 and the first nine months of 2014. Return on equity has been low, averaging 3.6% over the past five years. Good liquidity (6.8) with sufficient resources (cash flows and marketable investments) to handle a spike in claims.

Principal Business: Other liability (19%), auto liability (18%), workers compensation (14%), products liability (8%), auto physical damage (8%), allied lines (7%), and other lines (25%).

Principal Investments: Misc. investments (56%), investment grade bonds (40%), cash (2%), and real estate (2%).

Investments in Affiliates: 40%

Group Affiliation: United Fire & Casualty Group

Licensed in: All states except HI, ME, MA, NH, VT, PR

Commenced Business: January 1947

Address: 118 Second Ave SE, Cedar Rapids, IA 52407

Phone: (319) 399-5700   **Domicile State:** IA   **NAIC Code:** 13021

Data Date	Rating	RACR #1	RACR #2	Loss Ratio %	Total Assets ($mil)	Capital ($mil)	Net Premium ($mil)	Net Income ($mil)
9-14	B	1.16	0.98	N/A	1,620.3	664.7	365.6	-0.6
9-13	B	1.19	1.07	N/A	1,535.7	629.0	332.7	30.0
2013	B	1.18	1.01	63.3	1,558.7	665.8	469.8	58.9
2012	B	1.14	1.04	70.5	1,434.1	586.0	426.0	19.0
2011	B-	1.14	1.03	75.3	1,309.7	565.8	371.0	19.6
2010	B-	1.76	1.46	68.9	1,260.7	594.3	344.4	43.9
2009	B-	1.70	1.43	83.9	1,238.7	556.3	352.6	-11.6

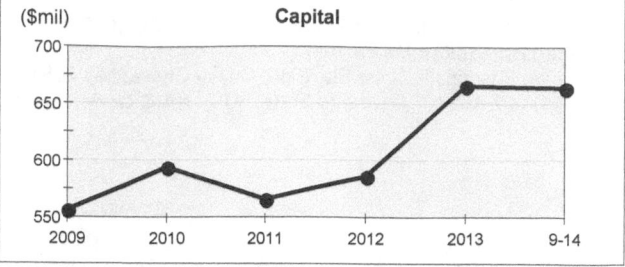

UNITED GUAR RESIDENTIAL INS CO OF NC

C   Fair

Major Rating Factors: Fair overall results on stability tests (3.5 on a scale of 0 to 10). Good long-term capitalization index (6.3) based on excellent current risk adjusted capital (severe and moderate loss scenarios), despite some fluctuation in capital levels.

Other Rating Factors: History of adequate reserve strength (5.8) as reserves have been consistently at an acceptable level. Good overall profitability index (5.4) despite operating losses during 2011 and 2012. Return on equity has been fair, averaging 6.1% over the past five years. Good liquidity (5.7) with sufficient resources (cash flows and marketable investments) to handle a spike in claims.

Principal Business: Credit (100%).

Principal Investments: Misc. investments (81%), investment grade bonds (17%), and cash (2%).

Investments in Affiliates: 77%

Group Affiliation: American International Group

Licensed in: All states except AZ, CA, NY, WY, PR

Commenced Business: May 1963

Address: 230 North Elm Street, Greensboro, NC 27401

Phone: (336) 373-0232   **Domicile State:** NC   **NAIC Code:** 16667

Data Date	Rating	RACR #1	RACR #2	Loss Ratio %	Total Assets ($mil)	Capital ($mil)	Net Premium ($mil)	Net Income ($mil)
9-14	C	1.29	1.27	N/A	454.6	399.0	44.0	36.5
9-13	C-	1.07	1.05	N/A	376.6	320.9	76.5	38.8
2013	C	1.23	1.21	31.2	448.5	385.6	92.5	47.7
2012	C-	1.06	1.02	174.2	472.2	319.8	97.2	-40.4
2011	D	1.13	1.08	97.5	417.2	257.8	135.0	-0.7
2010	D	1.04	0.95	98.0	819.1	296.1	203.4	3.1
2009	D-	0.51	0.42	236.3	792.9	234.5	170.1	59.2

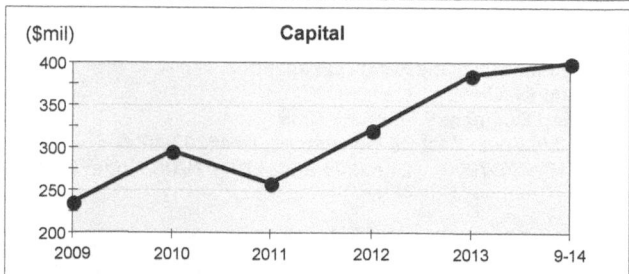

UNITED GUARANTY RESIDENTIAL INS CO

D+   Weak

Major Rating Factors: Weak overall results on stability tests (2.4 on a scale of 0 to 10). Fair reserve development (3.0) as the level of reserves has at times been insufficient to cover claims. Deficiencies in the two year reserve development occurred in three of the previous five years and ranged between 19% and 30%.

Other Rating Factors: Good overall profitability index (5.6) despite operating losses during 2012. Return on equity has been fair, averaging 7.1% over the past five years. Good liquidity (6.7) with sufficient resources (cash flows and marketable investments) to handle a spike in claims. Strong long-term capitalization index (8.5) based on excellent current risk adjusted capital (severe and moderate loss scenarios), despite some fluctuation in capital levels.

Principal Business: Mortgage guaranty (100%).

Principal Investments: Investment grade bonds (86%), misc. investments (10%), cash (2%), and non investment grade bonds (2%).

Investments in Affiliates: 3%

Group Affiliation: American International Group

Licensed in: All states, the District of Columbia and Puerto Rico

Commenced Business: December 1963

Address: 230 North Elm Street, Greensboro, NC 27401

Phone: (336) 373-0232   **Domicile State:** NC   **NAIC Code:** 15873

Data Date	Rating	RACR #1	RACR #2	Loss Ratio %	Total Assets ($mil)	Capital ($mil)	Net Premium ($mil)	Net Income ($mil)
9-14	D+	2.52	1.99	N/A	3,230.8	1,404.0	501.4	197.0
9-13	D+	1.47	1.23	N/A	2,946.9	1,229.6	433.3	64.4
2013	D+	2.58	2.01	64.7	3,059.3	1,465.7	799.9	88.4
2012	D+	1.82	1.46	116.6	2,930.3	1,383.0	576.6	-100.8
2011	D+	2.13	1.78	71.5	2,502.2	1,062.5	524.9	94.7
2010	D+	2.09	1.64	84.7	2,661.9	1,233.3	428.4	64.8
2009	D+	1.48	1.14	60.8	2,589.8	1,058.7	424.6	149.6

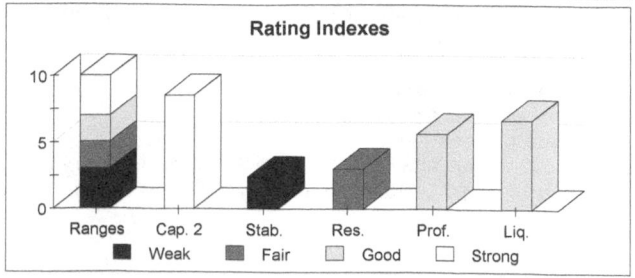

UNITED NATIONAL INS CO   C   Fair

Major Rating Factors: Fair overall results on stability tests (4.1 on a scale of 0 to 10) including negative cash flow from operations for 2013. Weak profitability index (2.5). Weak expense controls. Return on equity has been fair, averaging 20.2% over the past five years.

Other Rating Factors: Strong long-term capitalization (7.0) based on excellent current risk adjusted capital (severe and moderate loss scenarios) reflecting improvement over results in 2013. Ample reserve history (7.7) that can protect against increases in claims costs. Excellent liquidity (7.3) with ample operational cash flow and liquid investments.

Principal Business: Fire (33%), allied lines (30%), inland marine (14%), other liability (12%), commercial multiple peril (5%), earthquake (4%), and products liability (2%).

Principal Investments: Misc. investments (66%), investment grade bonds (33%), and cash (1%).

Investments in Affiliates: 20%

Group Affiliation: Fox Paine & Co LLC

Licensed in: All states except PR

Commenced Business: December 1960

Address: Three Bala Plaza E 300, Bala Cynwyd, PA 19004

Phone: (610) 664-1500   **Domicile State:** PA   **NAIC Code:** 13064

Data Date	Rating	RACR #1	RACR #2	Loss Ratio %	Total Assets ($mil)	Capital ($mil)	Net Premium ($mil)	Net Income ($mil)
9-14	C	1.91	1.60	N/A	373.6	193.2	30.0	34.2
9-13	C	1.51	1.23	N/A	535.8	328.3	27.3	16.1
2013	C	1.25	0.93	72.2	548.5	196.3	41.0	106.0
2012	C	1.38	1.13	75.6	502.2	301.5	34.0	20.6
2011	C	1.42	1.20	71.0	519.6	313.5	38.5	31.9
2010	C	1.55	1.33	33.1	568.0	337.0	37.5	42.4
2009	C	1.69	1.52	62.9	603.4	333.2	41.0	50.3

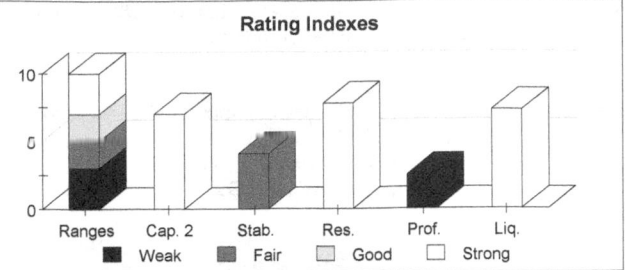

Rating Indexes

UNITED SERVICES AUTOMOBILE ASN *   A+   Excellent

Major Rating Factors: Strong long-term capitalization index (7.5 on a scale of 0 to 10) based on excellent current risk adjusted capital (severe and moderate loss scenarios). Furthermore, this high level of risk adjusted capital has been consistently maintained in previous years. Ample reserve history (7.6) that can protect against increases in claims costs.

Other Rating Factors: Excellent profitability (7.8) with operating gains in each of the last five years. Excellent overall results on stability tests (7.9). Stability strengths include excellent operational trends and excellent risk diversification. Good liquidity (6.8) with sufficient resources (cash flows and marketable investments) to handle a spike in claims.

Principal Business: Homeowners multiple peril (34%), auto liability (31%), auto physical damage (26%), allied lines (3%), fire (2%), other liability (2%), and inland marine (2%).

Principal Investments: Misc. investments (68%), investment grade bonds (28%), real estate (4%), and non investment grade bonds (1%).

Investments in Affiliates: 56%

Group Affiliation: USAA Group

Licensed in: All states, the District of Columbia and Puerto Rico

Commenced Business: June 1922

Address: 9800 Fredericksburg Rd, San Antonio, TX 78288

Phone: (210) 498-2211   **Domicile State:** TX   **NAIC Code:** 25941

Data Date	Rating	RACR #1	RACR #2	Loss Ratio %	Total Assets ($mil)	Capital ($mil)	Net Premium ($mil)	Net Income ($mil)
9-14	A+	1.56	1.45	N/A	30,759.0	22,619.2	4,810.3	443.6
9-13	A+	1.58	1.47	N/A	28,385.0	20,442.9	4,490.9	556.5
2013	A+	1.48	1.40	73.4	28,667.0	20,754.5	6,189.3	922.6
2012	A+	1.47	1.39	81.9	25,880.7	18,362.9	5,721.4	437.2
2011	A+	1.51	1.45	87.2	23,936.1	16,917.5	5,563.0	486.2
2010	A+	1.51	1.43	76.0	22,709.4	15,917.5	5,455.5	516.5
2009	A+	1.52	1.43	74.3	20,971.9	14,538.1	5,253.0	105.3

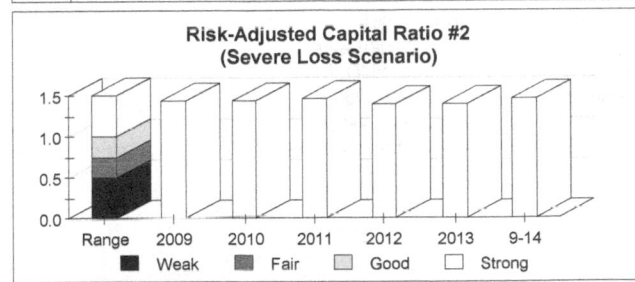

Risk-Adjusted Capital Ratio #2
(Severe Loss Scenario)

UNITED STATES FIDELITY & GUARANTY CO   B   Good

Major Rating Factors: Good overall results on stability tests (5.4 on a scale of 0 to 10) despite potential drain of affiliation with Travelers Companies Inc. Stability strengths include good operational trends and excellent risk diversification. Good overall profitability index (5.7). Fair expense controls. Return on equity has been fair, averaging 8.3% over the past five years.

Other Rating Factors: Strong long-term capitalization index (10.0) based on excellent current risk adjusted capital (severe and moderate loss scenarios), despite some fluctuation in capital levels. Ample reserve history (7.8) that can protect against increases in claims costs. Excellent liquidity (7.0) with ample operational cash flow and liquid investments.

Principal Business: Workers compensation (88%) and surety (2%).

Principal Investments: Investment grade bonds (94%), misc. investments (5%), and non investment grade bonds (1%).

Investments in Affiliates: 3%

Group Affiliation: Travelers Companies Inc

Licensed in: All states, the District of Columbia and Puerto Rico

Commenced Business: August 1896

Address: One Tower Square, Hartford, CT 06183

Phone: (860) 277-0111   **Domicile State:** CT   **NAIC Code:** 25887

Data Date	Rating	RACR #1	RACR #2	Loss Ratio %	Total Assets ($mil)	Capital ($mil)	Net Premium ($mil)	Net Income ($mil)
9-14	B	7.36	4.84	N/A	4,798.7	2,622.0	657.3	134.8
9-13	B	7.96	5.26	N/A	4,962.1	2,780.1	644.1	158.4
2013	B	7.16	4.72	60.9	4,653.9	2,484.4	888.1	224.2
2012	B	7.64	5.08	68.4	4,797.2	2,627.5	862.6	216.7
2011	B	7.20	4.79	76.9	4,646.8	2,488.7	844.5	103.2
2010	B	6.93	4.54	62.0	4,599.1	2,457.9	815.5	313.3
2009	B	6.59	4.34	58.3	4,627.1	2,465.8	799.4	212.3

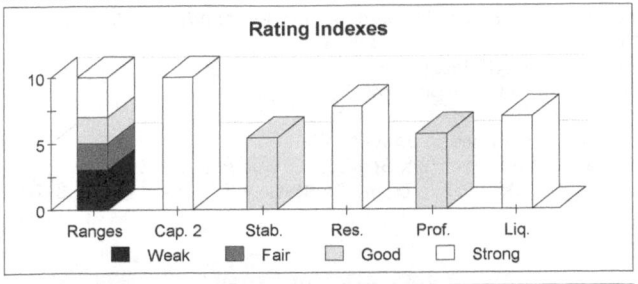

Rating Indexes

UNITED STATES FIRE INS CO

C   Fair

Major Rating Factors: Fair overall results on stability tests (3.7 on a scale of 0 to 10). Weak profitability index (2.4) with operating losses during 2010, 2011, 2012 and 2013. Average return on equity over the last five years has been poor at -2.4%.

Other Rating Factors: Good overall long-term capitalization (6.7) based on good current risk adjusted capital (moderate loss scenario). However, capital levels have fluctuated during prior years. History of adequate reserve strength (5.7) as reserves have been consistently at an acceptable level. Excellent liquidity (7.2) with ample operational cash flow and liquid investments.

Principal Business: Group accident & health (30%), inland marine (19%), workers compensation (15%), other liability (11%), ocean marine (8%), auto liability (6%), and other lines (11%).

Principal Investments: Investment grade bonds (58%), misc. investments (39%), cash (2%), and non investment grade bonds (1%).

Investments in Affiliates: 15%

Group Affiliation: Fairfax Financial

Licensed in: All states, the District of Columbia and Puerto Rico

Commenced Business: April 1824

Address: 305 Madison Avenue, Morristown, NJ 07960

Phone: (973) 490-6600   **Domicile State:** DE   **NAIC Code:** 21113

Data Date	Rating	RACR #1	RACR #2	Loss Ratio %	Total Assets ($mil)	Capital ($mil)	Net Premium ($mil)	Net Income ($mil)
9-14	C	1.32	0.99	N/A	3,360.2	1,024.3	733.1	49.8
9-13	C	1.33	0.98	N/A	3,097.3	850.0	677.1	-78.3
2013	C	1.14	0.87	71.4	3,154.5	812.1	971.7	-75.7
2012	C	1.42	1.07	81.2	2,924.1	881.7	810.0	-50.1
2011	C	1.39	1.06	81.0	2,722.9	894.8	697.3	-43.8
2010	C	1.34	1.03	79.5	2,511.8	901.2	462.7	-24.7
2009	C	1.44	1.03	73.7	2,743.4	1,055.5	456.0	41.3

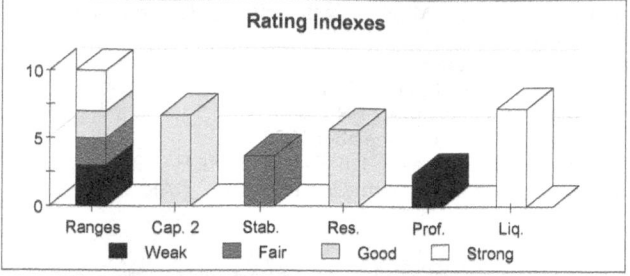

Rating Indexes

UNITED STATES LIABILITY INS CO

C   Fair

Major Rating Factors: Fair overall results on stability tests (4.3 on a scale of 0 to 10). Good overall profitability index (6.5) despite operating losses during 2010 and the first nine months of 2014. Return on equity has been fair, averaging 6.3% over the past five years.

Other Rating Factors: Strong long-term capitalization index (7.5) based on excellent current risk adjusted capital (severe and moderate loss scenarios). Moreover, capital levels have been consistent in recent years. Ample reserve history (9.2) that helps to protect the company against sharp claims increases. Excellent liquidity (7.7) with ample operational cash flow and liquid investments.

Principal Business: Other liability (82%), fire (16%), and products liability (1%).

Principal Investments: Misc. investments (70%) and investment grade bonds (30%).

Investments in Affiliates: 47%

Group Affiliation: Berkshire-Hathaway

Licensed in: All states except ND, PR

Commenced Business: May 1951

Address: 190 S. Warner Road, Wayne, PA 19087

Phone: (800) 523-5545   **Domicile State:** PA   **NAIC Code:** 25895

Data Date	Rating	RACR #1	RACR #2	Loss Ratio %	Total Assets ($mil)	Capital ($mil)	Net Premium ($mil)	Net Income ($mil)
9-14	C	1.49	1.33	N/A	845.9	540.7	116.5	-3.9
9-13	C	1.56	1.31	N/A	741.9	482.5	96.7	4.4
2013	C	1.50	1.35	47.9	811.3	537.5	144.8	25.0
2012	C	1.52	1.31	47.2	675.5	441.1	118.5	15.7
2011	C	1.45	1.22	38.8	577.8	372.4	85.9	11.0
2010	C	1.50	1.25	43.6	552.4	357.4	77.8	-1.7
2009	C	1.52	1.24	41.8	512.6	311.4	80.7	81.8

Berkshire-Hathaway Composite Group Rating: B- Largest Group Members	Assets ($mil)	Rating
NATIONAL INDEMNITY CO	151912	B-
GOVERNMENT EMPLOYEES INS CO	25779	B+
COLUMBIA INS CO	19013	B-
GENERAL REINSURANCE CORP	16220	B-
BERKSHIRE HATHAWAY LIFE INS CO OF NE	13768	C+

UNIVERSAL INS CO

B-   Good

Major Rating Factors: Fair overall results on stability tests (4.7 on a scale of 0 to 10) including potential drain of affiliation with Universal Ins Co Group. Good overall profitability index (6.1). Fair expense controls. Return on equity has been good over the last five years, averaging 11.9%.

Other Rating Factors: Good liquidity (6.9) with sufficient resources (cash flows and marketable investments) to handle a spike in claims. Strong long-term capitalization index (8.7) based on excellent current risk adjusted capital (severe and moderate loss scenarios), despite some fluctuation in capital levels. Ample reserve history (7.9) that can protect against increases in claims costs.

Principal Business: Auto physical damage (47%), commercial multiple peril (20%), homeowners multiple peril (11%), auto liability (10%), allied lines (4%), other liability (3%), and other lines (6%).

Principal Investments: Investment grade bonds (71%), misc. investments (20%), real estate (8%), and cash (1%).

Investments in Affiliates: 6%

Group Affiliation: Universal Ins Co Group

Licensed in: PR

Commenced Business: January 1972

Address: Metro Office Park St 1 Lot 10, Guaynabo, PR 00921

Phone: (787) 706-7155   **Domicile State:** PR   **NAIC Code:** 31704

Data Date	Rating	RACR #1	RACR #2	Loss Ratio %	Total Assets ($mil)	Capital ($mil)	Net Premium ($mil)	Net Income ($mil)
9-14	B-	3.22	2.10	N/A	823.2	250.0	151.0	15.0
9-13	B-	3.65	2.37	N/A	823.3	274.3	154.9	33.1
2013	B-	3.46	2.26	69.4	802.8	253.1	202.7	38.1
2012	B-	3.56	2.32	68.4	778.3	258.9	208.5	25.2
2011	B-	4.89	2.84	66.6	769.7	251.9	207.4	28.6
2010	B-	4.38	2.91	66.5	708.9	245.4	217.5	32.0
2009	B	1.91	1.64	67.2	742.9	233.0	229.7	31.1

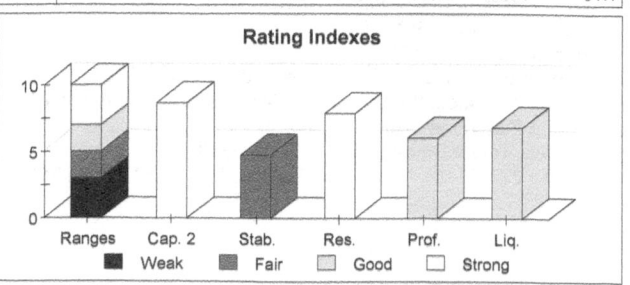

Rating Indexes

UNIVERSAL UNDERWRITERS INS CO　　　C　　Fair

Major Rating Factors: Fair overall results on stability tests (3.5 on a scale of 0 to 10).

Other Rating Factors: Good overall profitability index (5.1). Fair expense controls. Return on equity has been fair, averaging 5.3% over the past five years. Strong long-term capitalization index (10.0) based on excellent current risk adjusted capital (severe and moderate loss scenarios), despite some fluctuation in capital levels. Superior liquidity (10.0) with ample operational cash flow and liquid investments.

Principal Business: Auto physical damage (18%), other liability (17%), auto liability (16%), allied lines (4%), fire (3%), boiler & machinery (1%), and other lines (40%).

Principal Investments: Investment grade bonds (85%), misc. investments (11%), and cash (4%).

Investments in Affiliates: 10%

Group Affiliation: Zurich Financial Services Group

Licensed in: All states except PR

Commenced Business: January 1982

Address: 1400 American Lane, Schaumburg, IL 60196-1056

Phone: (047) 005-6000　**Domicile State:** IL　**NAIC Code:** 41181

Data Date	Rating	RACR #1	RACR #2	Loss Ratio %	Total Assets ($mil)	Capital ($mil)	Net Premium ($mil)	Net Income ($mil)
9-14	C	10.82	9.84	N/A	390.3	341.8	0.0	4.5
9-13	C	11.68	10.61	N/A	391.0	349.4	0.0	6.5
2013	C	10.82	9.95	0.0	386.2	336.1	0.0	5.2
2012	C	11.63	10.69	0.0	385.4	341.7	0.0	10.4
2011	C	13.23	12.02	0.0	376.0	341.8	0.0	47.2
2010	C	4.84	4.63	0.0	385.8	343.7	0.0	26.1
2009	C-	4.47	4.34	0.0	408.5	352.1	0.0	10.5

Zurich Financial Services Group
Composite Group Rating: C+

Largest Group Members	Assets ($mil)	Rating
ZURICH AMERICAN INS CO	30184	C+
ZURICH AMERICAN LIFE INS CO	12969	C
FARMERS NEW WORLD LIFE INS CO	7141	B-
CENTRE LIFE INS CO	1928	B-
FARMERS REINS CO	1400	B-

US SPECIALTY INS CO　　　B-　　Good

Major Rating Factors: Fair overall results on stability tests (4.9 on a scale of 0 to 10). The largest net exposure for one risk is high at 3.3% of capital. History of adequate reserve strength (5.1) as reserves have been consistently at an acceptable level.

Other Rating Factors: Good liquidity (6.9) with sufficient resources (cash flows and marketable investments) to handle a spike in claims. Strong long-term capitalization index (7.8) based on excellent current risk adjusted capital (severe and moderate loss scenarios), despite some fluctuation in capital levels. Excellent profitability (8.7) with operating gains in each of the last five years. Return on equity has been excellent over the last five years averaging 15.7%.

Principal Business: Other liability (62%), surety (11%), aircraft (8%), commercial multiple peril (6%), inland marine (2%), auto liability (2%), and other lines (9%).

Principal Investments: Investment grade bonds (82%), misc. investments (14%), and non investment grade bonds (4%).

Investments in Affiliates: None

Group Affiliation: HCC Ins Holdings Inc

Licensed in: All states except PR

Commenced Business: April 1987

Address: 13403 Northwest Freeway, Houston, TX 77040-6094

Phone: (713) 462-1000　**Domicile State:** TX　**NAIC Code:** 29599

Data Date	Rating	RACR #1	RACR #2	Loss Ratio %	Total Assets ($mil)	Capital ($mil)	Net Premium ($mil)	Net Income ($mil)
9-14	B-	2.88	1.86	N/A	2,023.8	651.7	325.7	85.1
9-13	B-	2.90	1.90	N/A	2,038.2	648.5	336.8	94.7
2013	B-	2.56	1.66	51.5	1,928.6	580.3	440.5	124.8
2012	B-	2.58	1.71	59.5	2,056.0	552.5	440.2	104.9
2011	B-	1.90	1.18	67.5	1,889.7	507.3	460.9	61.1
2010	B-	1.05	0.75	59.4	1,746.7	530.7	448.9	88.4
2009	B-	2.62	1.73	70.8	1,528.4	424.9	485.2	34.7

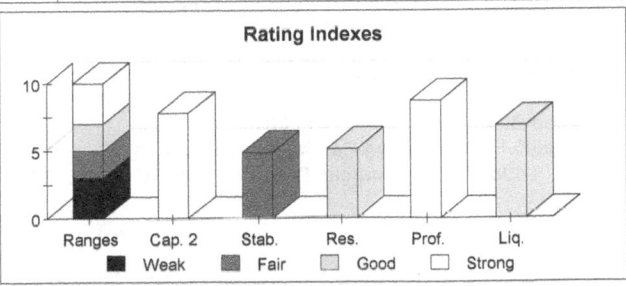

Rating Indexes

USAA CASUALTY INS CO *　　　A+　　Excellent

Major Rating Factors: Strong long-term capitalization index (8.9 on a scale of 0 to 10) based on excellent current risk adjusted capital (severe and moderate loss scenarios). Furthermore, this high level of risk adjusted capital has been consistently maintained in previous years. Ample reserve history (8.1) that helps to protect the company against sharp claims increases.

Other Rating Factors: Excellent profitability (8.8) with operating gains in each of the last five years. Excellent overall results on stability tests (7.5). Stability strengths include good operational trends and excellent risk diversification. Good liquidity (6.1) with sufficient resources (cash flows and marketable investments) to handle a spike in claims.

Principal Business: Auto liability (38%), auto physical damage (30%), homeowners multiple peril (28%), inland marine (2%), allied lines (1%), fire (1%), and other liability (1%).

Principal Investments: Investment grade bonds (65%), misc. investments (34%), and non investment grade bonds (1%).

Investments in Affiliates: 7%

Group Affiliation: USAA Group

Licensed in: All states except PR

Commenced Business: December 1990

Address: 9800 Fredericksburg Rd, San Antonio, TX 78288

Phone: (210) 498-8000　**Domicile State:** TX　**NAIC Code:** 25968

Data Date	Rating	RACR #1	RACR #2	Loss Ratio %	Total Assets ($mil)	Capital ($mil)	Net Premium ($mil)	Net Income ($mil)
9-14	A+	3.16	2.36	N/A	8,886.5	4,527.2	3,435.7	354.4
9-13	A+	3.25	2.45	N/A	8,389.0	4,116.3	3,370.0	324.0
2013	A+	2.90	2.20	77.4	8,445.8	4,168.8	4,756.9	319.9
2012	A+	2.98	2.29	83.6	7,773.4	3,673.3	4,385.4	151.9
2011	A+	3.79	2.99	84.5	7,294.9	3,570.8	3,848.9	224.9
2010	A+	4.95	4.02	78.5	7,241.9	3,660.8	3,696.8	303.8
2009	A+	4.96	4.04	73.1	6,816.5	3,533.1	3,652.1	395.2

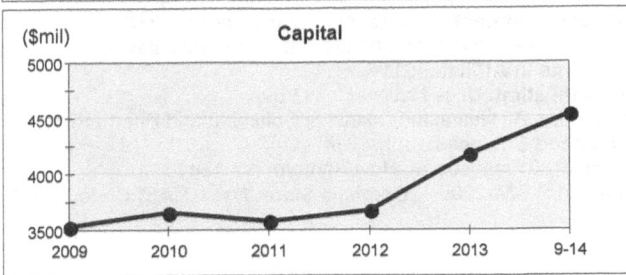

Capital

USAA GENERAL INDEMNITY CO *
B+   Good

Major Rating Factors: Good overall results on stability tests (5.0 on a scale of 0 to 10) despite weak results on operational trends and excessive premium growth. Strengths include potentially strong support from affiliation with USAA Group. The largest exposure for one risk is acceptable at 2.4% of capital. Good liquidity (5.3) with sufficient resources (cash flows and marketable investments) to handle a spike in claims.

Other Rating Factors: Strong long-term capitalization index (7.7) based on excellent current risk adjusted capital (severe and moderate loss scenarios). Moreover, capital levels have been consistent in recent years. Ample reserve history (9.4) that helps to protect the company against sharp claims increases. Excellent profitability (8.8) despite modest operating losses during 2010.

Principal Business: Auto liability (39%), auto physical damage (35%), homeowners multiple peril (16%), allied lines (9%), inland marine (1%), and fire (1%).

Principal Investments: Investment grade bonds (74%), misc. investments (24%), and non investment grade bonds (2%).

Investments in Affiliates: None

Group Affiliation: USAA Group

Licensed in: All states, the District of Columbia and Puerto Rico

Commenced Business: August 1972

Address: 9800 Fredericksburg Rd, San Antonio, TX 78288

Phone: (210) 498-8000   **Domicile State:** TX   **NAIC Code:** 18600

Data Date	Rating	RACR #1	RACR #2	Loss Ratio %	Total Assets ($mil)	Capital ($mil)	Net Premium ($mil)	Net Income ($mil)
9-14	B+	1.91	1.43	N/A	2,785.3	931.9	1,546.0	84.7
9-13	B+	1.95	1.51	N/A	2,068.2	674.2	1,156.9	80.8
2013	B+	1.99	1.53	77.3	2,256.6	835.6	1,633.0	117.0
2012	B+	2.01	1.59	83.2	1,676.2	580.8	1,173.6	42.8
2011	B+	2.35	1.78	87.0	1,099.6	401.3	828.8	4.5
2010	B+	2.11	1.69	85.0	803.1	279.3	648.1	-2.5
2009	B+	2.27	1.83	87.0	564.2	207.0	455.3	2.5

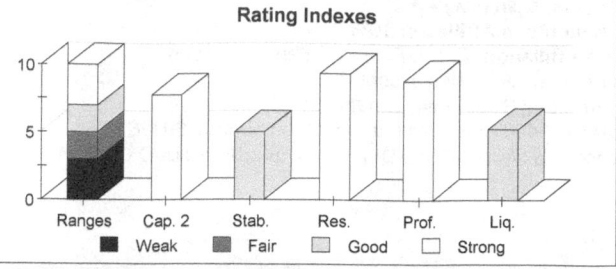

Rating Indexes

USAA TEXAS LLOYDS CO *
B+   Good

Major Rating Factors: Good liquidity (6.4 on a scale of 0 to 10) with sufficient resources (cash flows and marketable investments) to handle a spike in claims. Good overall results on stability tests (6.5) despite excessive premium growth. The largest net exposure for one risk is acceptable at 2.6% of capital.

Other Rating Factors: Strong long-term capitalization index (8.6) based on excellent current risk adjusted capital (severe and moderate loss scenarios). Moreover, capital levels have been consistent in recent years. Ample reserve history (7.9) that can protect against increases in claims costs. Excellent profitability (8.8) with operating gains in each of the last five years.

Principal Business: Homeowners multiple peril (93%), allied lines (5%), and fire (2%).

Principal Investments: Investment grade bonds (86%), misc. investments (12%), and non investment grade bonds (2%).

Investments in Affiliates: None

Group Affiliation: USAA Group

Licensed in: TX

Commenced Business: September 2001

Address: 9800 Fredericksburg Rd, San Antonio, TX 78288

Phone: (210) 498-8000   **Domicile State:** TX   **NAIC Code:** 11120

Data Date	Rating	RACR #1	RACR #2	Loss Ratio %	Total Assets ($mil)	Capital ($mil)	Net Premium ($mil)	Net Income ($mil)
9-14	B+	2.30	2.05	N/A	575.9	258.3	228.3	11.1
9-13	B	2.87	2.54	N/A	496.2	228.2	176.4	10.0
2013	B+	2.63	2.17	68.2	505.7	245.1	275.0	26.6
2012	B	3.14	2.56	79.0	462.9	216.9	199.6	3.0
2011	B	3.85	3.22	81.8	417.9	214.8	177.7	2.9
2010	B	4.21	3.58	60.3	385.4	210.8	158.3	27.0
2009	B+	3.29	2.46	79.2	358.3	181.2	169.0	5.4

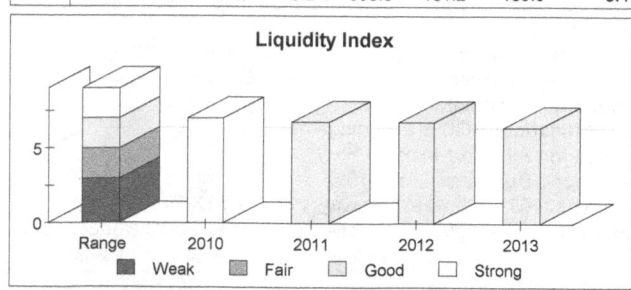

Liquidity Index

UTICA MUTUAL INS CO
B-   Good

Major Rating Factors: Fair overall results on stability tests (4.9 on a scale of 0 to 10) including potential drain of affiliation with Utica National Ins Group. The largest net exposure for one risk is conservative at 1.4% of capital. Fair reserve development (4.3) as reserves have generally been sufficient to cover claims.

Other Rating Factors: Fair profitability index (4.3) with operating losses during 2009, 2011 and 2012. Good liquidity (6.7) with sufficient resources (cash flows and marketable investments) to handle a spike in claims. Strong long-term capitalization index (7.9) based on excellent current risk adjusted capital (severe and moderate loss scenarios), despite some fluctuation in capital levels.

Principal Business: Other liability (35%), workers compensation (24%), commercial multiple peril (14%), auto liability (14%), auto physical damage (5%), homeowners multiple peril (4%), and other lines (3%).

Principal Investments: Investment grade bonds (66%), misc. investments (31%), non investment grade bonds (2%), and real estate (1%).

Investments in Affiliates: 11%

Group Affiliation: Utica National Ins Group

Licensed in: All states, the District of Columbia and Puerto Rico

Commenced Business: July 1914

Address: 180 Genesee St, New Hartford, NY 13413

Phone: (315) 734-2000   **Domicile State:** NY   **NAIC Code:** 25976

Data Date	Rating	RACR #1	RACR #2	Loss Ratio %	Total Assets ($mil)	Capital ($mil)	Net Premium ($mil)	Net Income ($mil)
9-14	B-	2.19	1.58	N/A	2,254.6	791.6	454.6	13.5
9-13	B-	2.09	1.54	N/A	2,147.0	738.4	410.5	1.9
2013	B-	2.27	1.65	65.5	2,130.1	775.1	579.5	29.9
2012	B-	2.46	1.85	70.5	2,110.6	742.7	532.3	-5.9
2011	B-	2.25	1.67	94.8	2,334.2	733.0	531.0	-45.9
2010	B-	2.36	1.80	67.6	2,284.5	767.1	522.4	43.5
2009	B-	2.87	1.95	86.6	2,229.2	720.5	518.9	-44.3

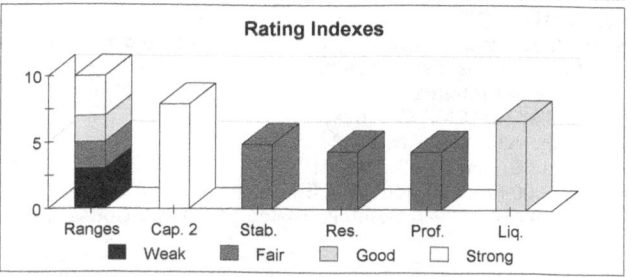

Rating Indexes

VERMONT MUTUAL INS CO   C+   Fair

Major Rating Factors: Fair overall results on stability tests (4.7 on a scale of 0 to 10) including potential drain of affiliation with Vermont Mutual Group. Good liquidity (6.7) with sufficient resources (cash flows and marketable investments) to handle a spike in claims.

Other Rating Factors: Strong long-term capitalization index (9.1) based on excellent current risk adjusted capital (severe and moderate loss scenarios). Moreover, capital levels have been consistent in recent years. Ample reserve history (9.2) that helps to protect the company against sharp claims increases. Excellent profitability (8.5) with operating gains in each of the last five years.

Principal Business: Homeowners multiple peril (41%), commercial multiple peril (21%), auto liability (13%), auto physical damage (12%), fire (5%), allied lines (4%), and other lines (4%).

Principal Investments: Investment grade bonds (64%), misc. investments (30%), cash (3%), non investment grade bonds (2%), and real estate (1%).

Investments in Affiliates: 1%

Group Affiliation: Vermont Mutual Group

Licensed in: CT, ME, MA, NH, NY, RI, VT

Commenced Business: March 1828

Address: 89 State St, Montpelier, VT 05602

Phone: (802) 223-2341   **Domicile State:** VT   **NAIC Code:** 26018

Data Date	Rating	RACR #1	RACR #2	Loss Ratio %	Total Assets ($mil)	Capital ($mil)	Net Premium ($mil)	Net Income ($mil)
9-14	C+	4.19	2.72	N/A	733.7	353.0	247.6	29.1
9-13	C+	4.19	2.79	N/A	679.5	308.3	216.0	16.0
2013	C+	4.12	2.64	54.0	690.7	328.2	313.7	25.9
2012	C+	4.19	2.77	51.0	614.2	283.8	292.3	35.0
2011	C+	3.79	2.56	68.3	557.2	239.8	280.6	8.7
2010	C+	3.75	2.50	58.9	540.2	230.8	257.1	24.4
2009	C+	3.60	2.45	56.1	477.6	207.1	236.6	18.8

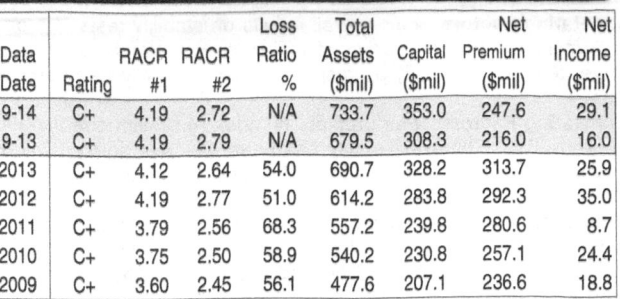

Rating Indexes — Ranges, Cap. 2, Stab., Res., Prof., Liq. (■ Weak ■ Fair □ Good □ Strong)

VIGILANT INS CO   B   Good

Major Rating Factors: Good overall results on stability tests (6.0 on a scale of 0 to 10). Stability strengths include good operational trends and excellent risk diversification. The largest net exposure for one risk is conservative at 1.2% of capital. Strong long-term capitalization index (10.0) based on excellent current risk adjusted capital (severe and moderate loss scenarios). Moreover, capital levels have been consistent in recent years.

Other Rating Factors: Ample reserve history (7.8) that can protect against increases in claims costs. Excellent profitability (8.7) with operating gains in each of the last five years. Excellent liquidity (7.8) with ample operational cash flow and liquid investments.

Principal Business: Homeowners multiple peril (46%), workers compensation (15%), commercial multiple peril (14%), inland marine (7%), other liability (7%), auto liability (3%), and other lines (8%).

Principal Investments: Investment grade bonds (84%), misc. investments (14%), and non investment grade bonds (2%).

Investments in Affiliates: 17%

Group Affiliation: Chubb Corp

Licensed in: All states except PR

Commenced Business: October 1939

Address: 55 Water St, New York, NY 10041

Phone: (212) 612-4000   **Domicile State:** NY   **NAIC Code:** 20397

Data Date	Rating	RACR #1	RACR #2	Loss Ratio %	Total Assets ($mil)	Capital ($mil)	Net Premium ($mil)	Net Income ($mil)
9-14	B	4.52	3.90	N/A	489.2	279.5	34.4	14.0
9-13	B	4.51	3.86	N/A	455.4	259.4	33.3	12.9
2013	B	5.10	4.72	52.7	467.9	264.9	45.1	16.7
2012	B	4.86	4.36	67.3	451.3	246.8	43.4	12.8
2011	B	5.29	4.51	68.4	440.4	233.6	42.6	15.8
2010	B	6.05	4.85	61.7	422.4	212.6	41.2	31.7
2009	B	4.52	3.88	55.7	395.9	176.6	41.6	16.0

Chubb Corp
Composite Group Rating: B+

Largest Group Members	Assets ($mil)	Rating
FEDERAL INS CO	31761	B+
PACIFIC INDEMNITY CO	6640	B+
EXECUTIVE RISK INDEMNITY INC	2977	B+
GREAT NORTHERN INS CO	1653	B
VIGILANT INS CO	468	B

VIRGINIA SURETY CO INC   C+   Fair

Major Rating Factors: Fair overall results on stability tests (4.7 on a scale of 0 to 10) including potential drain of affiliation with Onex Corp. Fair reserve development (4.8) as reserves have generally been sufficient to cover claims.

Other Rating Factors: Good liquidity (6.9) with sufficient resources (cash flows and marketable investments) to handle a spike in claims. Strong long-term capitalization index (9.4) based on excellent current risk adjusted capital (severe and moderate loss scenarios), despite some fluctuation in capital levels. Excellent profitability (8.1) with operating gains in each of the last five years. Return on equity has been excellent over the last five years averaging 20.1%.

Principal Business: Other liability (94%), inland marine (4%), and aggregate write-ins for other lines of business (1%).

Principal Investments: Investment grade bonds (87%), misc. investments (7%), cash (5%), and non investment grade bonds (1%).

Investments in Affiliates: 2%

Group Affiliation: Onex Corp

Licensed in: All states, the District of Columbia and Puerto Rico

Commenced Business: July 1982

Address: 175 W Jackson, Chicago, IL 60604

Phone: (312) 356-3000   **Domicile State:** IL   **NAIC Code:** 40827

Data Date	Rating	RACR #1	RACR #2	Loss Ratio %	Total Assets ($mil)	Capital ($mil)	Net Premium ($mil)	Net Income ($mil)
9-14	C+	3.21	2.76	N/A	1,059.2	334.4	226.5	37.3
9-13	C+	3.18	2.65	N/A	1,048.5	332.6	252.9	46.7
2013	C+	2.85	2.48	55.3	1,007.8	309.2	341.8	73.6
2012	C+	2.90	2.42	62.5	978.9	292.1	327.3	52.1
2011	C	2.20	1.64	46.7	970.1	286.3	292.2	72.2
2010	C	2.02	1.36	66.6	1,009.1	294.1	283.2	74.5
2009	C-	1.50	1.07	63.1	1,055.4	302.9	322.6	36.8

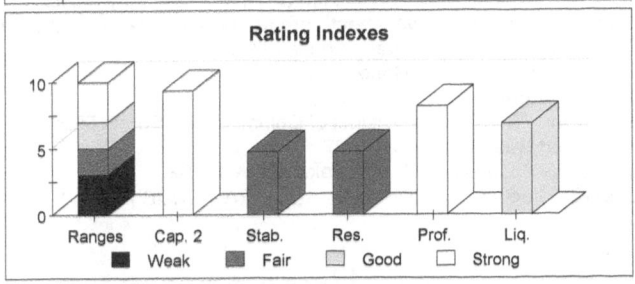

Rating Indexes — Ranges, Cap. 2, Stab., Res., Prof., Liq. (■ Weak ■ Fair □ Good □ Strong)

WAWANESA GENERAL INS CO

C+　　**Fair**

Major Rating Factors: Fair overall results on stability tests (4.5 on a scale of 0 to 10) including potential drain of affiliation with Wawanesa Ins Group. Fair reserve development (4.5) as reserves have generally been sufficient to cover claims.

Other Rating Factors: Fair profitability index (4.5) with operating losses during 2010 and 2013. Return on equity has been low, averaging 1.2% over the past five years. Good liquidity (5.7) with sufficient resources (cash flows and marketable investments) to handle a spike in claims. Strong long-term capitalization index (8.6) based on excellent current risk adjusted capital (severe and moderate loss scenarios), despite some fluctuation in capital levels.

Principal Business: Auto liability (53%), auto physical damage (39%), homeowners multiple peril (7%), and earthquake (1%).

Principal Investments: Investment grade bonds (94%), misc. investments (3%), and cash (3%).

Investments in Affiliates: None

Group Affiliation: Wawanesa Ins Group

Licensed in: CA, OR

Commenced Business: January 1997

Address: 9050 Friars Road,Suite 200, San Diego, CA 92108-5865

Phone: (858) 874-5440　　**Domicile State:** CA　　**NAIC Code:** 10683

Data Date	Rating	RACR #1	RACR #2	Loss Ratio %	Total Assets ($mil)	Capital ($mil)	Net Premium ($mil)	Net Income ($mil)
9-14	C+	2.73	2.10	N/A	585.4	239.6	252.8	3.8
9-13	C+	2.86	2.19	N/A	558.4	234.2	239.4	-2.8
2013	C+	2.73	2.17	94.6	558.2	235.1	331.1	-1.3
2012	C+	2.86	2.27	93.8	542.9	235.8	314.4	10.2
2011	C	2.96	2.32	96.7	534.1	228.0	290.9	2.1
2010	C	1.88	1.45	97.6	366.8	120.4	258.6	-0.9
2009	C	1.93	1.48	94.9	347.8	119.6	255.0	1.6

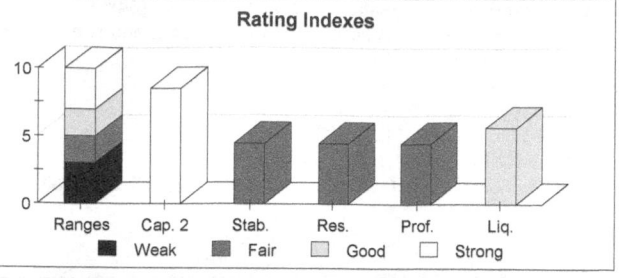

Rating Indexes

WEST BEND MUTUAL INS CO *

A-　　**Excellent**

Major Rating Factors: Strong long-term capitalization index (8.6 on a scale of 0 to 10) based on excellent current risk adjusted capital (severe and moderate loss scenarios). Furthermore, this high level of risk adjusted capital has been consistently maintained in previous years. Excellent profitability (7.9) with operating gains in each of the last five years.

Other Rating Factors: Excellent overall results on stability tests (7.2). Stability strengths include excellent operational trends and excellent risk diversification. History of adequate reserve strength (6.6) as reserves have been consistently at an acceptable level. Good liquidity (6.4) with sufficient resources (cash flows and marketable investments) to handle a spike in claims.

Principal Business: Workers compensation (25%), other liability (18%), auto liability (15%), homeowners multiple peril (11%), auto physical damage (10%), fire (7%), and other lines (13%).

Principal Investments: Investment grade bonds (66%), misc. investments (24%), non investment grade bonds (5%), real estate (4%), and cash (1%).

Investments in Affiliates: None

Group Affiliation: None

Licensed in: IL, IN, IA, KS, KY, MI, MN, MO, NE, OH, WI

Commenced Business: May 1894

Address: 1900 S 18th Ave, West Bend, WI 53095

Phone: (262) 334-5571　　**Domicile State:** WI　　**NAIC Code:** 15350

Data Date	Rating	RACR #1	RACR #2	Loss Ratio %	Total Assets ($mil)	Capital ($mil)	Net Premium ($mil)	Net Income ($mil)
9-14	A-	3.49	2.25	N/A	2,162.6	801.6	628.1	24.9
9-13	B+	3.34	2.17	N/A	1,930.6	670.4	569.2	45.8
2013	A-	3.27	2.11	61.1	1,975.4	690.7	814.3	62.8
2012	B+	3.34	2.20	62.3	1,786.2	613.5	726.7	60.3
2011	B+	3.10	2.09	74.1	1,666.6	547.6	656.2	20.1
2010	B+	3.28	2.14	72.1	1,650.1	542.0	668.1	33.9
2009	B+	2.88	1.90	67.8	1,559.8	489.8	667.7	5.6

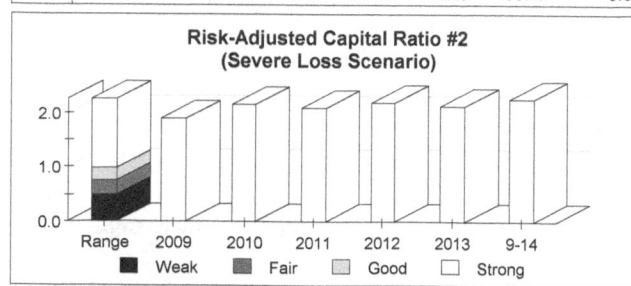

Risk-Adjusted Capital Ratio #2 (Severe Loss Scenario)

WESTCHESTER FIRE INS CO

C　　**Fair**

Major Rating Factors: Fair overall results on stability tests (4.0 on a scale of 0 to 10) including fair financial strength of affiliated ACE Ltd and negative cash flow from operations for 2013. Good overall profitability index (6.3). Fair expense controls. Return on equity has been good over the last five years, averaging 10.9%.

Other Rating Factors: Strong long-term capitalization index (9.3) based on excellent current risk adjusted capital (severe and moderate loss scenarios), despite some fluctuation in capital levels. Ample reserve history (7.9) that can protect against increases in claims costs. Excellent liquidity (7.7) with ample operational cash flow and liquid investments.

Principal Business: Other liability (55%), surety (25%), inland marine (7%), fidelity (4%), products liability (2%), fire (2%), and other lines (5%).

Principal Investments: Investment grade bonds (94%), misc. investments (15%), and non investment grade bonds (4%).

Investments in Affiliates: None

Group Affiliation: ACE Ltd

Licensed in: All states, the District of Columbia and Puerto Rico

Commenced Business: April 1967

Address: 1601 Chestnut St, Philadelphia, PA 19192

Phone: (215) 640-1000　　**Domicile State:** PA　　**NAIC Code:** 10030

Data Date	Rating	RACR #1	RACR #2	Loss Ratio %	Total Assets ($mil)	Capital ($mil)	Net Premium ($mil)	Net Income ($mil)
9-14	C	4.61	3.13	N/A	2,000.5	901.4	235.0	75.6
9-13	C	2.30	1.41	N/A	2,028.9	880.4	205.6	93.4
2013	C	4.31	2.96	46.7	2,056.1	906.6	226.4	114.1
2012	C	2.05	1.25	67.2	2,119.3	813.7	389.8	103.8
2011	C-	1.37	0.96	59.4	2,420.5	1,104.6	343.3	102.0
2010	C-	4.03	2.74	59.2	2,243.1	913.5	192.9	107.3
2009	C-	2.05	1.34	69.6	35.4	16.7	6.1	1.3

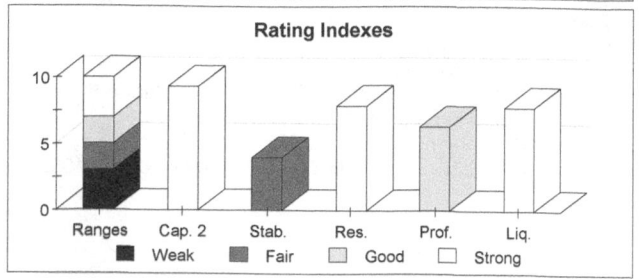

Rating Indexes

WESTERN AGRICULTURAL INS CO *   B+   Good

Major Rating Factors: Good overall profitability index (6.8 on a scale of 0 to 10) despite modest operating losses during the first nine months of 2014. Return on equity has been fair, averaging 5.5% over the past five years. Good liquidity (5.7) with sufficient resources (cash flows and marketable investments) to handle a spike in claims.

Other Rating Factors: Good overall results on stability tests (6.5). Affiliation with Iowa Farm Bureau is a strength. Strong long-term capitalization index (9.8) based on excellent current risk adjusted capital (severe and moderate loss scenarios). Moreover, capital levels have been consistent in recent years. Ample reserve history (8.1) that helps to protect the company against sharp claims increases.

Principal Business: Allied lines (64%), farmowners multiple peril (9%), auto liability (8%), auto physical damage (6%), homeowners multiple peril (5%), workers compensation (4%), and other lines (4%).

Principal Investments: Investment grade bonds (102%) and misc. investments (3%).

Investments in Affiliates: 2%
Group Affiliation: Iowa Farm Bureau
Licensed in: AL, AZ, AR, CO, ID, IL, IN, IA, KS, MI, MN, MO, MT, NE, NV, NM, ND, OH, OK, SC, SD, TN, TX, UT, VA, WI, WY
Commenced Business: January 1972
Address: 5400 University Ave, West Des Moines, IA 50266-5997
Phone: (515) 225-5400   **Domicile State:** IA   **NAIC Code:** 27871

Data Date	Rating	RACR #1	RACR #2	Loss Ratio %	Total Assets ($mil)	Capital ($mil)	Net Premium ($mil)	Net Income ($mil)
9-14	B+	3.81	2.92	N/A	178.2	70.8	73.6	-0.3
9-13	B+	3.89	2.92	N/A	171.6	67.9	71.1	3.5
2013	B+	3.93	2.92	70.2	171.2	70.7	98.1	6.4
2012	B+	3.87	2.83	71.5	163.5	63.9	91.6	7.7
2011	B+	3.48	2.60	75.4	148.8	58.3	87.8	2.9
2010	B+	3.66	2.58	73.1	142.8	57.1	80.9	1.7
2009	B+	3.17	2.08	73.4	255.3	53.7	74.0	1.5

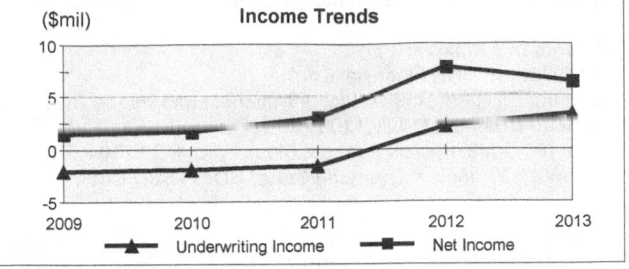

Income Trends

WESTERN COMMUNITY INS CO *   B+   Good

Major Rating Factors: Good overall results on stability tests (5.0 on a scale of 0 to 10). Stability strengths include good operational trends and excellent risk diversification. Strong long-term capitalization index (10.0) based on excellent current risk adjusted capital (severe and moderate loss scenarios). Moreover, capital levels have been consistent in recent years.

Other Rating Factors: Excellent profitability (8.4) with operating gains in each of the last five years. Excellent expense controls. Superior liquidity (10.0) with ample operational cash flow and liquid investments.

Principal Business: Commercial multiple peril (66%), auto liability (17%), auto physical damage (9%), inland marine (5%), and other liability (2%).

Principal Investments: Investment grade bonds (91%), misc. investments (8%), and cash (1%).

Investments in Affiliates: None
Group Affiliation: Farm Bureau Group of Idaho
Licensed in: ID, OR, WA
Commenced Business: July 1980
Address: 275 Tierra Vista Dr, Pocatello, ID 83201
Phone: (208) 232-7914   **Domicile State:** ID   **NAIC Code:** 39519

Data Date	Rating	RACR #1	RACR #2	Loss Ratio %	Total Assets ($mil)	Capital ($mil)	Net Premium ($mil)	Net Income ($mil)
9-14	B+	14.62	13.15	N/A	36.2	28.7	0.0	1.0
9-13	B+	14.38	12.94	N/A	34.3	27.3	0.0	1.0
2013	B+	15.54	13.99	0.0	34.1	27.7	0.0	1.3
2012	B+	15.82	14.24	0.0	31.8	26.2	0.0	1.3
2011	B+	14.84	13.35	0.0	30.7	24.9	0.0	1.2
2010	B+	12.58	11.32	77.4	30.6	23.7	0.0	1.1
2009	B+	10.73	9.65	35.3	30.6	22.5	0.1	1.3

Farm Bureau Group of Idaho Composite Group Rating: B+ Largest Group Members	Assets ($mil)	Rating
FARM BUREAU MUTUAL INS CO OF ID	418	B+
WESTERN COMMUNITY INS CO	34	B+

WESTERN NATIONAL MUTUAL INS CO   B-   Good

Major Rating Factors: Fair overall results on stability tests (4.5 on a scale of 0 to 10) including potential drain of affiliation with Western National Mutual. Good liquidity (6.6) with sufficient resources (cash flows and marketable investments) to handle a spike in claims.

Other Rating Factors: Strong long-term capitalization index (8.2) based on excellent current risk adjusted capital (severe and moderate loss scenarios). Moreover, capital levels have been consistent in recent years. Ample reserve history (8.7) that helps to protect the company against sharp claims increases. Excellent profitability (8.5) with operating gains in each of the last five years.

Principal Business: Workers compensation (23%), auto liability (20%), homeowners multiple peril (17%), auto physical damage (14%), other liability (10%), products liability (6%), and other lines (10%).

Principal Investments: Investment grade bonds (62%), misc. investments (35%), non investment grade bonds (2%), and real estate (2%).

Investments in Affiliates: 20%
Group Affiliation: Western National Mutual
Licensed in: AK, AZ, CO, ID, IL, IA, KS, MD, MI, MN, MO, MT, NE, NV, NJ, NM, ND, OH, OR, PA, RI, SD, TX, UT, WA, WI
Commenced Business: June 1915
Address: 5350 W 78th St, Minneapolis, MN 55439
Phone: (952) 835-5350   **Domicile State:** MN   **NAIC Code:** 15377

Data Date	Rating	RACR #1	RACR #2	Loss Ratio %	Total Assets ($mil)	Capital ($mil)	Net Premium ($mil)	Net Income ($mil)
9-14	B-	2.28	1.85	N/A	750.9	339.9	199.6	17.8
9-13	B-	2.25	1.86	N/A	691.5	309.1	184.1	10.9
2013	B-	2.16	1.78	68.7	696.0	314.2	256.3	15.7
2012	B-	2.23	1.88	70.0	647.0	292.4	233.7	12.4
2011	B-	2.28	1.84	72.1	593.9	269.6	196.8	11.7
2010	B-	2.25	1.74	73.2	563.2	252.8	173.0	11.4
2009	B-	2.17	1.51	67.2	513.0	235.1	158.5	15.4

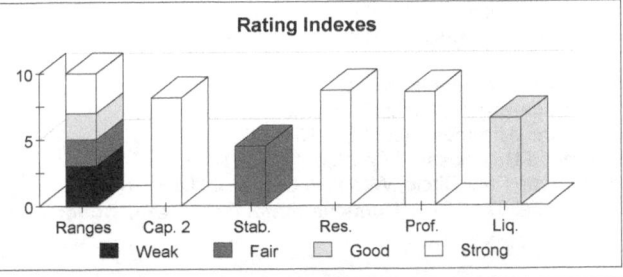

Rating Indexes

WESTERN SURETY CO

C **Fair**

Major Rating Factors: Fair overall results on stability tests (4.3 on a scale of 0 to 10) including fair financial strength of affiliated CNA Financial Corp. The largest net exposure for one risk is acceptable at 2.3% of capital. Strong long-term capitalization index (10.0) based on excellent current risk adjusted capital (severe and moderate loss scenarios). Moreover, capital levels have been consistent in recent years.

Other Rating Factors: Ample reserve history (9.4) that helps to protect the company against sharp claims increases. Excellent profitability (8.6) with operating gains in each of the last five years. Return on equity has been good over the last five years, averaging 14.0%. Excellent liquidity (7.0) with ample operational cash flow and liquid investments.

Principal Business: Surety (91%), fidelity (7%), and other liability (1%).

Principal Investments: Investment grade bonds (92%) and misc. investments (8%).

Investments in Affiliates: 1%

Group Affiliation: CNA Financial Corp

Licensed in: All states, the District of Columbia and Puerto Rico

Commenced Business: July 1900

Address: 101 South Phillips Avenue, Sioux Falls, SD 57104-6703

Phone: (605) 336-0850   **Domicile State:** SD   **NAIC Code:** 13188

Data Date	Rating	RACR #1	RACR #2	Loss Ratio %	Total Assets ($mil)	Capital ($mil)	Net Premium ($mil)	Net Income ($mil)
9-14	C	6.35	4.81	N/A	2,003.0	1,333.9	319.2	128.6
9-13	C	5.53	4.18	N/A	1,876.8	1,179.8	312.0	126.2
2013	C	5.67	4.30	9.2	1,856.4	1,205.6	418.4	152.7
2012	C	4.57	3.46	15.6	1,732.5	1,052.4	411.7	126.7
2011	C	3.96	2.99	26.6	1,587.1	889.5	419.6	96.2
2010	C	3.94	2.99	11.2	1,481.3	825.6	412.9	141.3
2009	C	3.11	2.37	16.3	1,342.0	679.3	407.4	123.6

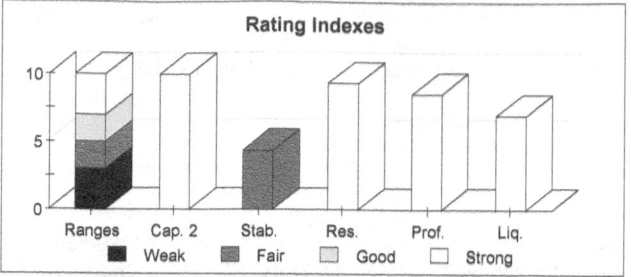

Rating Indexes

WESTERN WORLD INS CO

C **Fair**

Major Rating Factors: Fair overall results on stability tests (4.1 on a scale of 0 to 10) including excessive premium growth. Good overall profitability index (6.4). Fair expense controls. Return on equity has been low, averaging 3.0% over the past five years.

Other Rating Factors: Strong long-term capitalization index (7.2) based on excellent current risk adjusted capital (severe and moderate loss scenarios), despite some fluctuation in capital levels. Ample reserve history (8.8) that helps to protect the company against sharp claims increases. Excellent liquidity (7.4) with ample operational cash flow and liquid investments.

Principal Business: Other liability (58%), commercial multiple peril (26%), products liability (11%), medical malpractice (2%), auto liability (2%), and auto physical damage (1%).

Principal Investments: Investment grade bonds (68%), misc. investments (29%), cash (2%), and non investment grade bonds (1%).

Investments in Affiliates: 26%

Group Affiliation: Western World Group

Licensed in: All states except PR

Commenced Business: April 1964

Address: 50 Washington St, Keene, NH 03431

Phone: (201) 847-8600   **Domicile State:** NH   **NAIC Code:** 13196

Data Date	Rating	RACR #1	RACR #2	Loss Ratio %	Total Assets ($mil)	Capital ($mil)	Net Premium ($mil)	Net Income ($mil)
9-14	C	1.33	1.13	N/A	1,070.2	366.4	171.2	6.0
9-13	C	1.49	1.30	N/A	1,029.4	355.7	128.0	3.0
2013	C	1.39	1.19	68.9	1,047.0	367.7	201.7	7.8
2012	C	1.55	1.36	70.0	1,011.0	357.0	155.1	6.2
2011	C	1.60	1.42	72.0	993.3	351.8	132.2	5.8
2010	C	1.63	1.41	68.0	996.3	344.7	118.1	15.2
2009	C	1.61	1.33	66.0	1,005.1	332.6	134.9	18.2

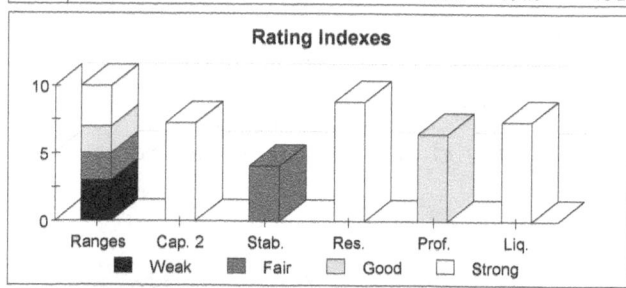

Rating Indexes

WESTFIELD INS CO

B- **Good**

Major Rating Factors: Fair overall results on stability tests (4.6 on a scale of 0 to 10) including potential drain of affiliation with Westfield Companies. Good overall profitability index (6.8). Fair expense controls. Return on equity has been fair, averaging 9.4% over the past five years.

Other Rating Factors: Good liquidity (6.4) with sufficient resources (cash flows and marketable investments) to handle a spike in claims. Strong long-term capitalization index (8.9) based on excellent current risk adjusted capital (severe and moderate loss scenarios), despite some fluctuation in capital levels. Ample reserve history (9.3) that helps to protect the company against sharp claims increases.

Principal Business: Commercial multiple peril (28%), auto liability (22%), auto physical damage (11%), other liability (10%), workers compensation (8%), homeowners multiple peril (7%), and other lines (15%).

Principal Investments: Investment grade bonds (67%) and misc. investments (33%).

Investments in Affiliates: None

Group Affiliation: Westfield Companies

Licensed in: All states except CA, NH, PR

Commenced Business: July 1929

Address: One Park Circle, Westfield Center, OH 44251-5001

Phone: (330) 887-0101   **Domicile State:** OH   **NAIC Code:** 24112

Data Date	Rating	RACR #1	RACR #2	Loss Ratio %	Total Assets ($mil)	Capital ($mil)	Net Premium ($mil)	Net Income ($mil)
9-14	B-	3.86	2.56	N/A	2,510.3	989.3	679.9	43.6
9-13	B-	3.53	2.34	N/A	2,399.6	942.8	658.9	87.4
2013	B-	3.76	2.50	59.8	2,450.5	991.2	904.7	127.7
2012	B-	3.33	2.22	64.9	2,243.1	853.6	867.8	89.6
2011	B-	3.25	2.13	79.3	2,128.8	774.3	757.9	29.5
2010	B-	2.92	1.97	66.5	2,231.6	746.3	945.7	83.8
2009	B-	2.79	1.94	64.0	2,090.4	654.6	924.1	72.6

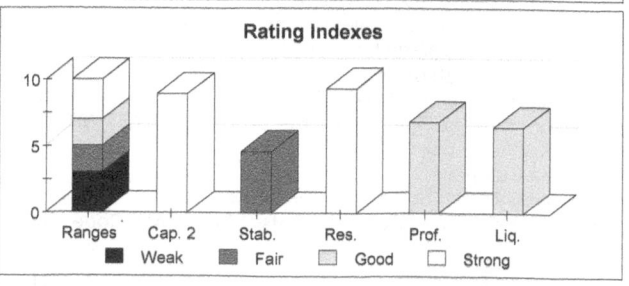

Rating Indexes

WESTFIELD NATIONAL INS CO *   B+   Good

Major Rating Factors: Good overall results on stability tests (5.0 on a scale of 0 to 10) despite potential drain of affiliation with Westfield Companies. The largest net exposure for one risk is conservative at 1.2% of capital. Good overall profitability index (6.8) with small operating losses during 2011. Return on equity has been fair, averaging 7.1% over the past five years.

Other Rating Factors: Good liquidity (6.5) with sufficient resources (cash flows and marketable investments) to handle a spike in claims. Strong long-term capitalization index (9.0) based on excellent current risk adjusted capital (severe and moderate loss scenarios), despite some fluctuation in capital levels. Ample reserve history (9.3) that helps to protect against sharp claims increases.

Principal Business: Homeowners multiple peril (38%), auto liability (26%), auto physical damage (23%), workers compensation (4%), other liability (4%), commercial multiple peril (2%), and inland marine (2%).

Principal Investments: Investment grade bonds (71%) and misc. investments (29%).

Investments in Affiliates: None

Group Affiliation: Westfield Companies

Licensed in: AL, AZ, AR, CA, CO, DC, DE, FL, GA, ID, IL, IN, IA, KS, KY, MD, MI, MN, MS, MO, MT, NE, NV, NM, NC, ND, OH, OK, PA, SC, SD, TN, TX, UT, VA, WA, WV, WI

Commenced Business: April 1968

Address: One Park Circle, Westfield Center, OH 44251

Phone: (330) 887-0101   **Domicile State:** OH   **NAIC Code:** 24120

Data Date	Rating	RACR #1	RACR #2	Loss Ratio %	Total Assets ($mil)	Capital ($mil)	Net Premium ($mil)	Net Income ($mil)
9-14	B+	3.70	2.45	N/A	593.0	252.8	163.7	6.7
9-13	B+	3.54	2.36	N/A	557.8	230.6	158.6	18.8
2013	B+	3.75	2.51	59.8	571.9	243.2	217.8	25.2
2012	B+	3.27	2.18	64.9	524.9	208.0	208.9	19.8
2011	B+	3.06	2.01	79.3	501.8	186.6	199.6	-1.7
2010	B+	3.49	2.32	66.5	489.3	193.2	192.1	15.8
2009	B+	3.46	2.36	64.0	459.1	176.6	187.7	19.4

Westfield Companies Composite Group Rating: B- Largest Group Members	Assets ($mil)	Rating
WESTFIELD INS CO	2451	B-
OHIO FARMERS INS CO	2405	B-
WESTFIELD NATIONAL INS CO	572	B+
OLD GUARD INS CO	392	C+
AMERICAN SELECT INS CO	220	C+

WESTPORT INS CORP   C+   Fair

Major Rating Factors: Fair profitability index (4.9 on a scale of 0 to 10). Weak expense controls. Return on equity has been fair, averaging 6.9% over the past five years. Fair overall results on stability tests (4.5) including fair results on operational trends. The largest net exposure for one risk is high at 3.4% of capital.

Other Rating Factors: Good long-term capitalization index (6.0) based on good current risk adjusted capital (moderate loss scenario). History of adequate reserve strength (6.8) as reserves have been consistently at an acceptable level. Excellent liquidity (7.2) with ample operational cash flow and liquid investments.

Principal Business: Allied lines (27%), other liability (21%), fire (20%), group accident & health (14%), earthquake (10%), boiler & machinery (5%), and aircraft (3%).

Principal Investments: Investment grade bonds (72%), misc. investments (27%), and non investment grade bonds (1%).

Investments in Affiliates: 11%

Group Affiliation: Swiss Reinsurance

Licensed in: All states, the District of Columbia and Puerto Rico

Commenced Business: September 1981

Address: 237 E High St, Jefferson City, MO 65101

Phone: (913) 676-5200   **Domicile State:** MO   **NAIC Code:** 39845

Data Date	Rating	RACR #1	RACR #2	Loss Ratio %	Total Assets ($mil)	Capital ($mil)	Net Premium ($mil)	Net Income ($mil)
9-14	C+	1.31	0.90	N/A	5,352.8	1,605.0	187.4	133.6
9-13	C	0.59	0.46	N/A	5,352.7	1,724.8	392.4	170.4
2013	C+	1.25	0.85	62.2	5,454.1	1,769.4	580.1	167.8
2012	C	0.57	0.44	64.9	5,331.3	1,726.5	535.1	108.0
2011	C+	1.17	0.80	112.0	5,349.6	1,940.9	99.6	135.3
2010	C	2.64	1.72	118.7	5,784.7	1,676.1	93.5	95.5
2009	C	1.84	1.10	169.5	7,251.7	1,961.5	104.2	56.1

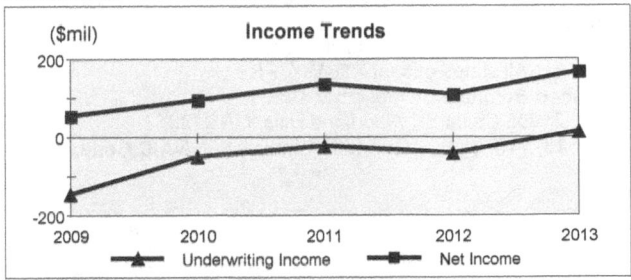

Income Trends — Underwriting Income ▲ — Net Income ■ (2009–2013)

XL INS AMERICA INC   C   Fair

Major Rating Factors: Fair overall results on stability tests (3.8 on a scale of 0 to 10) including potential drain of affiliation with XL Group plc and negative cash flow from operations for 2013. The largest net exposure for one risk is conservative at 1.8% of capital. History of adequate reserve strength (6.3) as reserves have been consistently at an acceptable level.

Other Rating Factors: Good overall profitability index (5.9). Fair expense controls. Return on equity has been fair, averaging 5.2% over the past five years. Strong long-term capitalization index (7.0) based on good current risk adjusted capital (severe and moderate loss scenarios), although results have slipped from the excellent range during the last year. Excellent liquidity (7.1) with ample operational cash flow and liquid investments.

Principal Business: Other liability (27%), fire (25%), allied lines (16%), workers compensation (8%), earthquake (7%), inland marine (5%), and other lines (12%).

Principal Investments: Investment grade bonds (76%), misc. investments (20%), and cash (4%).

Investments in Affiliates: 20%

Group Affiliation: XL Group plc

Licensed in: All states, the District of Columbia and Puerto Rico

Commenced Business: December 1945

Address: 1201 N Market St Suite 501, Wilmington, DE 19801

Phone: (203) 964-5200   **Domicile State:** DE   **NAIC Code:** 24554

Data Date	Rating	RACR #1	RACR #2	Loss Ratio %	Total Assets ($mil)	Capital ($mil)	Net Premium ($mil)	Net Income ($mil)
9-14	C	1.24	0.98	N/A	707.9	225.0	93.7	12.1
9-13	C	1.51	1.24	N/A	762.7	233.9	101.8	21.8
2013	C	1.35	1.07	65.3	734.2	246.8	133.1	26.0
2012	C	1.65	1.37	73.4	775.6	253.0	129.4	16.7
2011	C	1.54	1.25	82.9	686.3	223.4	115.0	6.0
2010	C	1.32	0.96	70.9	674.1	245.3	107.8	10.5
2009	C	0.97	0.68	79.4	663.0	234.1	117.8	1.3

XL Group plc Composite Group Rating: C Largest Group Members	Assets ($mil)	Rating
XL REINS AMERICA INC	5528	C
GREENWICH INS CO	1053	C
XL INS AMERICA INC	734	C
XL SPECIALTY INS CO	441	C
X L INS CO OF NY	208	D+

XL REINS AMERICA INC

| | | | | C | | Fair | |

Major Rating Factors: Fair overall results on stability tests (3.8 on a scale of 0 to 10) including potential drain of affiliation with XL Group plc. The largest net exposure for one risk is conservative at 1.2% of capital. History of adequate reserve strength (6.2) as reserves have been consistently at an acceptable level.

Other Rating Factors: Good overall profitability index (6.0). Fair expense controls. Return on equity has been fair, averaging 5.3% over the past five years. Strong long-term capitalization index (8.8) based on excellent current risk adjusted capital (severe and moderate loss scenarios), despite some fluctuation in capital levels. Excellent liquidity (7.0) with ample operational cash flow and liquid investments.

Principal Business: Other liability (100%).

Principal Investments: Investment grade bonds (80%), misc. investments (17%), and cash (3%).

Investments in Affiliates: 13%

Group Affiliation: XL Group plc

Licensed in: All states, the District of Columbia and Puerto Rico

Commenced Business: October 1929

Address: 111 Broadway Suite 1802, New York, NY 10006

Phone: (203) 964-5200   **Domicile State:** NY   **NAIC Code:** 20583

Data Date	Rating	RACR #1	RACR #2	Loss Ratio %	Total Assets ($mil)	Capital ($mil)	Net Premium ($mil)	Net Income ($mil)
9-14	C	2.83	2.17	N/A	5,529.0	2,148.8	609.2	148.1
9-13	C	2.70	2.06	N/A	5,561.6	2,160.9	661.5	125.3
2013	C	2.94	2.26	65.3	5,527.8	2,244.5	865.2	161.4
2012	C	2.93	2.25	73.4	5,413.0	2,237.8	841.2	65.5
2011	C	2.93	2.17	82.9	5,128.5	2,093.7	747.3	73.3
2010	C	2.18	1.53	70.9	5,219.0	2,273.7	700.9	137.5
2009	C	1.54	1.06	79.4	5,279.0	2,191.3	765.6	86.0

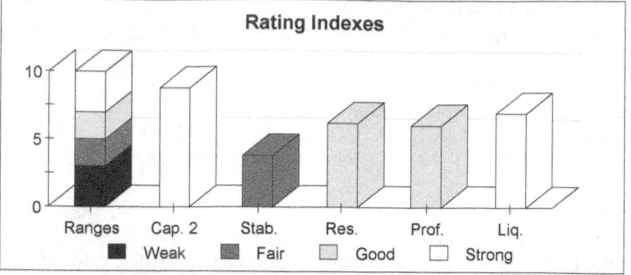

Rating Indexes

ZENITH INS CO

| | | | | C- | | Fair | |

Major Rating Factors: Weak profitability index (2.2 on a scale of 0 to 10) with operating losses during 2011, 2012 and 2013. Average return on equity over the last five years has been poor at -1.5%. Fair overall results on stability tests (3.2).

Other Rating Factors: Good overall long-term capitalization (5.7) based on good current risk adjusted capital (moderate loss scenario). However, capital levels have fluctuated during prior years. History of adequate reserve strength (6.0) as reserves have been consistently at an acceptable level. Excellent liquidity (7.0) with ample operational cash flow and liquid investments.

Principal Business: Workers compensation (95%), commercial multiple peril (2%), auto liability (1%), and other liability (1%).

Principal Investments: Investment grade bonds (65%), misc. investments (31%), cash (2%), non investment grade bonds (1%), and real estate (1%).

Investments in Affiliates: 2%

Group Affiliation: Fairfax Financial

Licensed in: All states except ND, WY, PR

Commenced Business: December 1950

Address: 21255 Califa St, Woodland Hills, CA 91367

Phone: (818) 713-1000   **Domicile State:** CA   **NAIC Code:** 13269

Data Date	Rating	RACR #1	RACR #2	Loss Ratio %	Total Assets ($mil)	Capital ($mil)	Net Premium ($mil)	Net Income ($mil)
9-14	C-	1.17	0.84	N/A	1,866.5	579.2	518.3	94.3
9-13	D+	1.22	0.90	N/A	1,763.2	491.4	483.8	-23.5
2013	C-	1.12	0.84	62.4	1,783.8	515.8	677.5	-18.1
2012	D+	1.21	0.89	77.8	1,646.3	443.7	596.7	-125.4
2011	C+	1.99	1.45	83.1	1,714.1	620.1	493.8	-4.0
2010	C+	2.65	1.90	83.7	1,703.5	690.2	417.2	20.8
2009	C+	3.56	2.49	69.1	1,995.2	979.2	443.0	44.5

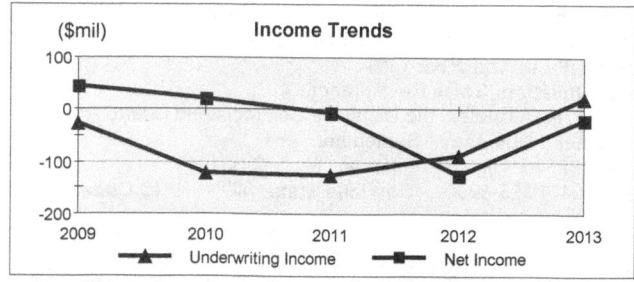

Income Trends

ZURICH AMERICAN INS CO

| | | | | C+ | | Fair | |

Major Rating Factors: Fair overall results on stability tests (3.8 on a scale of 0 to 10). The largest net exposure for one risk is excessive at 8.0% of capital. Good liquidity (6.8) with sufficient resources (cash flows and marketable investments) to handle a spike in claims.

Other Rating Factors: Strong long-term capitalization index (8.2) based on excellent current risk adjusted capital (severe and moderate loss scenarios), despite some fluctuation in capital levels. Ample reserve history (7.7) that can protect against increases in claims costs. Excellent profitability (7.9) with operating gains in each of the last five years. Return on equity has been good over the last five years, averaging 10.6%.

Principal Business: Workers compensation (26%), other liability (24%), commercial multiple peril (9%), auto liability (9%), allied lines (6%), fire (6%), and other lines (21%).

Principal Investments: Investment grade bonds (78%), misc. investments (21%), and cash (1%).

Investments in Affiliates: 6%

Group Affiliation: Zurich Financial Services Group

Licensed in: All states, the District of Columbia and Puerto Rico

Commenced Business: January 1913

Address: 165 Broadway, 28th Floor, New York, NY 10006

Phone: (847) 605-6000   **Domicile State:** NY   **NAIC Code:** 16535

Data Date	Rating	RACR #1	RACR #2	Loss Ratio %	Total Assets ($mil)	Capital ($mil)	Net Premium ($mil)	Net Income ($mil)
9-14	C+	2.55	1.74	N/A	30,669.5	7,676.8	3,383.9	428.6
9-13	C+	2.72	1.87	N/A	30,465.6	7,756.2	3,357.9	757.9
2013	C+	2.76	1.90	74.6	30,184.0	7,798.4	4,733.6	772.8
2012	C+	2.75	1.91	81.8	30,011.1	7,642.3	4,437.8	1,156.5
2011	C	2.57	1.72	78.8	28,729.2	7,018.8	4,155.8	960.4
2010	C	2.56	1.55	76.3	29,420.4	7,374.2	4,400.1	819.0
2009	C	1.98	1.14	77.2	29,935.7	7,417.2	4,382.8	426.6

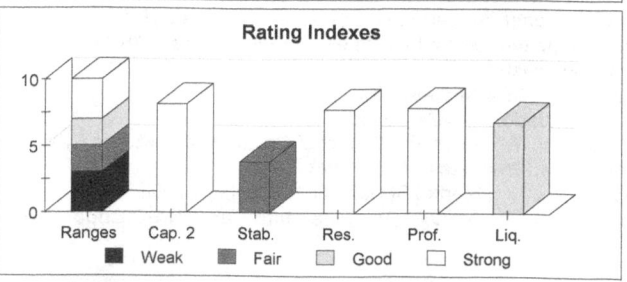

Rating Indexes

Section III

Weiss
Recommended Companies

A compilation of those

U.S. Property and Casualty Insurers

receiving a Weiss Financial Strength Rating

of A+, A, A- or B+.

Companies are listed in alphabetical order.

Section III Contents

This section provides a list of recommended carriers (based strictly on financial safety) along with additional information you should have when shopping for insurance. It contains all insurers receiving a Financial Strength Rating of A+, A, A- or B+. If an insurer is not on this list, it should not be automatically assumed that the firm is weak. Indeed, there are many firms that have not achieved a B+ or better rating but are in relatively good condition with adequate resources to cover their risk during an average recession. Not being included in this list should not be construed as a recommendation to cancel a policy.

Left Pages

1. **Financial Strength Rating**   Our rating is measured on a scale from A to F and considers a wide range of factors. Highly-rated companies are, in our opinion, less likely to experience financial difficulties than lower rated firms. See *About Weiss Financial Strength Ratings* for more information.

2. **Insurance Company Name**   The legally-registered name, which can sometimes differ from the name that the company uses for advertising. An insurer's name can be very similar to the name of other companies which may not be on our Recommended List, so make sure you note the exact name before contacting your agent.

3. **Address**   The address of the main office where you can contact the firm for additional financial data or for the location of local branches and/or registered agents.

4. **Telephone Number**   The number to call for additional financial data or for the phone numbers of local branches and/or registered agents.

Right Pages

The right-side pages present the percentage of the company's business that is involved in each type of insurance. Specifically, the numbers shown are the amounts of direct premium (received directly from policyholders) for each line of business as a percent of total premiums.

1. **Domicile State**   The state which has primary regulatory responsibility for the company. It may differ from the location of the company's corporate headquarters. You do not have to be living in the domicile state to purchase insurance from this firm, provided it is licensed to do business in your state.

2. **Auto**   Coverage for damage to a policyholder's own automobile and for the financial loss from auto-related bodily injury or property damage.

3. **Homeowners Multiple Peril**   Package policies for homeowners providing a broad spectrum of property and liability coverages.

4.	**Farmowners Multiple Peril**	Package policies for farm or ranch owners providing a broad spectrum of property and liability coverages.

4. Farmowners Multiple Peril — Package policies for farm or ranch owners providing a broad spectrum of property and liability coverages.

5. Commercial Multiple Peril — Package policies for businesses and other commercial establishments providing a broad spectrum of property and liability coverages.

6. Commercial Auto Liability — Coverage against financial loss because of auto related injuries or damages to third parties.

7. Other Liability — Encompasses all third-party liability coverages not included in other business areas. It can include among others: professional liability, environmental liability, product liability, umbrella liability, general liability.

8. Medical Malpractice — Errors and omissions liability coverages for persons engaged in the practice of medicine, surgery, dentistry, nursing, pharmacy, or other health care services. Also covers health care institutions.

9. Workers' Compensation — Liability coverage issued to employers which provides for the payment of medical care, disability income or possible additional liability amounts to employees who are injured on the job.

10. Accident and Health — This includes three categories: (1) group accident and health, which consists of medical and hospitalization insurance plans under which a number of persons and their dependents are insured under a single policy issued to an employer or a common associated entity; (2) credit accident and health, which makes certain debt payments, usually for car or home loans, in the case of accident or illness; and (3) other accident and health, issued to individuals, to pay health care benefits or loss of income due to accidental injury or death.

11. Other — Fire, allied lines, mortgage guaranty, ocean marine, inland marine, financial guaranty, product liability, aircraft, fidelity, surety, glass, burglary and theft, boiler and machinery, credit, international, reinsurance, aggregate write-ins for other lines of business and other miscellaneous types of insurance.

Weiss Financial Strength Ratings are not deemed to be a recommendation concerning the purchase or sale of the securities of any insurance company that is publicly owned.

RATING	INSURANCE COMPANY NAME	ADDRESS	CITY	STATE	ZIP	PHONE
B+	ACA FINANCIAL GUARANTY CORP	7 SAINT PAUL ST SUITE 1660	BALTIMORE	MD	21202	(212) 375-2000
B+	ALFA INS CORP	2108 EAST SOUTH BLVD	MONTGOMERY	AL	36116	(334) 288-3900
B+	ALFA MUTUAL GENERAL INS CO	2108 EAST SOUTH BLVD	MONTGOMERY	AL	36116	(334) 288-3900
B+	ALL AMERICA INS CO	800 S WASHINGTON ST	VAN WERT	OH	45891	(419) 238-1010
A-	ALLSTATE INS CO	2775 SANDERS RD	NORTHBROOK	IL	60062	(847) 402-5000
B+	ALTERRA REINS USA INC	20 HORSENECK LN	GREENWICH	CT	06830	(908) 630-2700
B+	AMERICAN FAMILY MUT INS CO	6000 AMERICAN PKWY	MADISON	WI	53783	(608) 249-2111
B+	AMERICAN STANDARD INS CO OF WI	6000 AMERICAN PARKWAY	MADISON	WI	53783	(608) 249-2111
A-	AMICA LLOYDS OF TEXAS	2277 PLAZA DR SUITE 400	SUGAR LAND	TX	77479	(800) 242-6422
B+	AMICA MUTUAL INS CO	100 AMICA WAY	LINCOLN	RI	02865	(800) 652-6422
B+	AUTO CLUB INDEMNITY CO	3333 FAIRVIEW ROAD	COSTA MESA	CA	92626	(714) 850-5111
A	AUTO-OWNERS INS CO	6101 ANACAPRI BLVD	LANSING	MI	48917	(517) 323-1200
A+	BERKSHIRE HATHAWAY ASR CORP	MARINE AIR TERMINAL LAGUARDIA	FLUSHING	NY	11371	(402) 916-3000
A-	BITCO GENERAL INS CORP	320 18TH ST	ROCK ISLAND	IL	61201	(309) 786-5401
A-	BITCO NATIONAL INS CO	320 18TH ST	ROCK ISLAND	IL	61201	(309) 732-0409
A-	BROTHERHOOD MUTUAL INS CO	6400 BROTHERHOOD WAY	FT WAYNE	IN	46825	(260) 482-8668
B+	BUILDERS MUTUAL INS CO	6716 SIX FORKS ROAD	RALEIGH	NC	27615	(919) 845-1976
B+	CENTRAL STATES INDEMNITY CO OF OMAHA	1212 N 96TH ST	OMAHA	NE	68114	(402) 997-8000
B+	CENTURION CASUALTY CO	800 WALNUT ST	DES MOINES	IA	50309	515-557-7346
A	CHURCH MUTUAL INS CO	3000 SCHUSTER LANE	MERRILL	WI	54452	(715) 536-5577
A-	CINCINNATI INDEMNITY CO	6200 S GILMORE RD	FAIRFIELD	OH	45014	(513) 870-2000
A	CINCINNATI INS CO	6200 S GILMORE RD	FAIRFIELD	OH	45014	(513) 870-2000
A+	CITIZENS PROPERTY INS CORP	2312 KILLEARN CTR BLVD BLDG A	TALLAHASSEE	FL	32309	(850) 513-3700
A-	COPIC INS CO	7800 E DORADO PL SUITE 200	ENGLEWOOD	CO	80111	(720) 858-6000
A+	COPPERPOINT MUTUAL INS CO	3030 N 3RD ST	PHOENIX	AZ	85012	(602) 631-2240
B+	COUNTRY CASUALTY INS CO	1701 N. TOWANDA AVE	BLOOMINGTON	IL	61701	(309) 821-3000
A-	COUNTRY MUTUAL INS CO	1701 N. TOWANDA AVE	BLOOMINGTON	IL	61701	(309) 821-3000
A-	CSAA INS EXCHANGE	3055 OAK RD	WALNUT CREEK	CA	94597	(800) 207-3618
A+	DAIRYLAND INS CO	1800 NORTH POINT DR	STEVENS POINT	WI	54481	(715) 346-6000
A-	ESSENT GUARANTY INC	201 KING OF PRUSSIA RD STE 501	RADNOR	PA	19087	(610) 230-0555
B+	EXECUTIVE RISK INDEMNITY INC	1209 ORANGE ST	WILMINGTON	DE	19801	(908) 903-2000
B+	FARM BUREAU MUTUAL INS CO OF ID	275 TIERRA VISTA DR	POCATELLO	ID	83201	(208) 232-7914
A-	FARM BUREAU PROP & CAS INS CO	5400 UNIVERSITY AVE	WEST DES MOINES	IA	50266	(515) 225-5400
B+	FARM FAMILY CASUALTY INS CO	344 ROUTE 9W	GLENMONT	NY	12077	(518) 431-5000
B+	FARMERS AUTOMOBILE INS ASN	2505 COURT ST	PEKIN	IL	61558	(309) 346-1161
B+	FEDERAL INS CO	211 N PENNSYLVANIA ST #1350	INDIANAPOLIS	IN	46204	(908) 903-2000
A-	FEDERATED MUTUAL INS CO	121 E PARK SQUARE	OWATONNA	MN	55060	(507) 455-5200
B+	FIRST COLONIAL INS CO	1776 AMERICAN HERITAGE LIFE DR	JACKSONVILLE	FL	32224	(904) 992-1776
A	FRANKENMUTH MUTUAL INS CO	ONE MUTUAL AVENUE	FRANKENMUTH	MI	48787	(989) 652-6121
A-	GEICO CHOICE INS CO	1440 KIEWIT PLAZA	OMAHA	NE	68131	(800) 841-3000
B+	GEICO GENERAL INS CO	5260 WESTERN AVENUE	CHEVY CHASE	MD	20815	(800) 841-3000
B+	GEICO INDEMNITY CO	ONE GEICO PLAZA	WASHINGTON	DC	20076	(800) 841-3000
A-	GEICO SECURE INSURANCE CO	1440 KIEWIT PLAZA	OMAHA	NE	68131	(800) 841-3000
B+	GNY CUSTOM INS CO	200 MADISON AVE	NEW YORK	NY	10016	(212) 683-9700
B+	GOVERNMENT EMPLOYEES INS CO	ONE GEICO PLAZA	WASHINGTON	DC	20076	(800) 841-3000
B+	GRANGE MUTUAL CAS CO	650 S FRONT ST	COLUMBUS	OH	43206	(614) 445-2900
A-	GREAT WEST CASUALTY CO	1100 W 29TH ST	SOUTH SIOUX CITY	NE	68776	(402) 494-2411
B+	HARTFORD UNDERWRITERS INS CO	HARTFORD PLAZA	HARTFORD	CT	06115	(860) 547-5000
A-	HASTINGS MUTUAL INS CO	404 E WOODLAWN AVE	HASTINGS	MI	49058	(800) 442-8277
B+	HOLYOKE MUTUAL INS CO IN SALEM	HOLYOKE SQUARE	SALEM	MA	01970	(978) 744-6123
A-	HOME-OWNERS INS CO	6101 ANACAPRI BLVD	LANSING	MI	48917	(517) 323-1200
A-	ICI MUTUAL INS CO RRG	40 MAIN ST SUITE 500	BURLINGTON	VT	05401	(800) 643-4246
B+	INDIANA FARMERS MUTUAL INS CO	10 W 106TH ST	INDIANAPOLIS	IN	46290	(317) 846-4211
A+	INTERINS EXCH OF THE AUTOMOBILE CLUB	3333 FAIRVIEW ROAD	COSTA MESA	CA	92626	(714) 850-5111
A-	JEWELERS MUTUAL INS CO	24 JEWELERS PARK DR	NEENAH	WI	54957	(920) 725-4326
A-	KENTUCKY FARM BUREAU MUTUAL INS CO	9201 BUNSEN PARKWAY	LOUISVILLE	KY	40220	(502) 495-5000

DOM. STATE	AUTO	HOME MULT. PERIL	FARM MULT. PERIL	COMM. MULT. PERIL	COMM. AUTO LIAB.	OTHER LIABILITY	MED MALPRAC.	WORK. COMP.	ACCID. & HEALTH	OTHER	INSURANCE COMPANY NAME
MD	0	0	0	0	0	0	0	0	0	100	ACA FINANCIAL GUARANTY CORP
AL	69	25	0	3	0	0	0	0	0	2	ALFA INS CORP
AL	60	39	0	0	0	1	0	0	0	0	ALFA MUTUAL GENERAL INS CO
OH	8	0	0	56	21	0	0	7	0	8	ALL AMERICA INS CO
IL	55	33	0	4	3	1	0	0	0	5	ALLSTATE INS CO
CT (*)	0	0	0	0	0	0	0	0	0	0	ALTERRA REINS USA INC
WI	53	31	2	8	1	3	0	1	2	1	AMERICAN FAMILY MUT INS CO
WI	100	0	0	0	0	0	0	0	0	0	AMERICAN STANDARD INS CO OF WI
TX	0	94	0	0	0	0	0	0	0	6	AMICA LLOYDS OF TEXAS
RI	63	31	0	0	0	3	0	0	0	3	AMICA MUTUAL INS CO
TX	0	99	0	0	0	1	0	0	0	0	AUTO CLUB INDEMNITY CO
MI	24	16	2	13	9	8	0	9	0	19	AUTO-OWNERS INS CO
NY	0	0	0	0	0	0	0	0	0	100	BERKSHIRE HATHAWAY ASR CORP
IL	6	0	0	21	19	13	0	34	0	7	BITCO GENERAL INS CORP
IL	3	0	0	29	10	1	0	50	0	6	BITCO NATIONAL INS CO
IN	2	0	0	71	6	4	0	13	0	3	BROTHERHOOD MUTUAL INS CO
NC	1	0	0	15	2	3	0	73	0	7	BUILDERS MUTUAL INS CO
NE	0	0	0	0	0	0	0	0	48	52	CENTRAL STATES INDEMNITY CO OF OMAHA
IA	0	0	0	0	0	0	0	0	0	100	CENTURION CASUALTY CO
WI	1	0	0	71	5	3	1	17	0	1	CHURCH MUTUAL INS CO
OH	5	0	0	23	14	14	0	33	0	10	CINCINNATI INDEMNITY CO
OH	18	14	0	28	10	16	1	3	0	11	CINCINNATI INS CO
FL	0	46	0	0	0	0	0	0	0	54	CITIZENS PROPERTY INS CORP
CO	0	0	0	0	0	4	94	0	2	0	COPIC INS CO
AZ	0	0	0	0	0	0	0	100	0	0	COPPERPOINT MUTUAL INS CO
IL	55	45	0	0	0	0	0	0	0	0	COUNTRY CASUALTY INS CO
IL	27	41	9	6	1	2	0	4	0	9	COUNTRY MUTUAL INS CO
CA	73	25	0	0	0	1	0	0	0	1	CSAA INS EXCHANGE
WI	100	0	0	0	0	0	0	0	0	0	DAIRYLAND INS CO
PA	0	0	0	0	0	0	0	0	0	100	ESSENT GUARANTY INC
DE	0	0	0	6	0	91	0	0	0	3	EXECUTIVE RISK INDEMNITY INC
ID	54	18	19	0	0	3	0	0	0	6	FARM BUREAU MUTUAL INS CO OF ID
IA	41	23	24	5	1	3	0	3	0	1	FARM BUREAU PROP & CAS INS CO
NY	21	8	0	10	13	11	0	13	0	24	FARM FAMILY CASUALTY INS CO
IL	61	32	0	0	0	0	0	0	0	6	FARMERS AUTOMOBILE INS ASN
IN	2	9	0	17	2	33	0	11	3	23	FEDERAL INS CO
MN	5	0	0	6	11	13	0	17	34	14	FEDERATED MUTUAL INS CO
FL	1	0	0	0	0	0	0	0	0	38	FIRST COLONIAL INS CO
MI	35	17	0	19	7	4	0	13	0	5	FRANKENMUTH MUTUAL INS CO
NE	100	0	0	0	0	0	0	0	0	0	GEICO CHOICE INS CO
MD	100	0	0	0	0	0	0	0	0	0	GEICO GENERAL INS CO
MD	100	0	0	0	0	0	0	0	0	0	GEICO INDEMNITY CO
NE	100	0	0	0	0	0	0	0	0	0	GEICO SECURE INSURANCE CO
AZ	0	0	0	92	0	0	0	0	0	8	GNY CUSTOM INS CO
MD	97	0	0	0	1	2	0	0	0	0	GOVERNMENT EMPLOYEES INS CO
OH	47	18	4	17	6	3	0	2	0	4	GRANGE MUTUAL CAS CO
NE	26	0	0	0	50	4	0	12	0	9	GREAT WEST CASUALTY CO
CT	41	11	0	3	3	2	0	37	0	4	HARTFORD UNDERWRITERS INS CO
MI	27	15	15	15	6	3	0	15	0	3	HASTINGS MUTUAL INS CO
MA	3	18	0	71	0	2	0	0	0	5	HOLYOKE MUTUAL INS CO IN SALEM
MI	55	30	0	7	2	1	0	2	0	2	HOME-OWNERS INS CO
VT	0	0	0	0	0	89	0	0	0	11	ICI MUTUAL INS CO RRG
IN	35	23	15	10	3	2	0	5	0	6	INDIANA FARMERS MUTUAL INS CO
CA	80	18	0	0	0	1	0	0	0	1	INTERINS EXCH OF THE AUTOMOBILE CLUB
WI	0	0	0	16	0	0	0	0	0	84	JEWELERS MUTUAL INS CO
KY	53	26	12	7	1	1	0	0	0	1	KENTUCKY FARM BUREAU MUTUAL INS CO

(*) Denotes reinsurers, companies that do not sell to consumers

RATING	INSURANCE COMPANY NAME	ADDRESS	CITY	STATE	ZIP	PHONE
A-	LOUISIANA WORKERS COMPENSATION CORP	2237 S. ACADIAN THRUWAY,#102	BATON ROUGE	LA	70808	(225) 924-7788
B+	MAINE EMPLOYERS MUTUAL INS CO	261 COMMERCIAL ST	PORTLAND	ME	04104	(207) 791-3300
B+	MERCURY CASUALTY CO	4484 WILSHIRE BLVD	LOS ANGELES	CA	90010	(714) 671-6600
A-	MERCURY INS CO	4484 WILSHIRE BLVD	LOS ANGELES	CA	90010	(714) 671-6600
B+	MITSUI SUMITOMO INS CO OF AMER	560 LEXINGTON AVE 20TH FLOOR	NEW YORK	NY	10022	(908) 604-2900
A-	MMIC INS INC	7701 FRANCE AVE S	MINNEAPOLIS	MN	55435	(952) 838-6700
A-	MOTORISTS MUTUAL INS CO	471 E BROAD ST	COLUMBUS	OH	43215	(614) 225-8211
A+	MUNICIPAL ASR CORP	31 W 52ND ST	NEW YORK	NY	10019	212-974-0100
A	MUTUAL INS CO OF AZ	2602 EAST THOMAS RD	PHOENIX	AZ	85016	(602) 956-5276
B+	NATIONAL CASUALTY CO	8877 N GAINEY CENTER DR	SCOTTSDALE	AZ	85258	(480) 365-4000
A-	NATIONAL MORTGAGE INS CORP	1834 STEVEN ST	SUN PRAIRIE	WI	53590	(925) 300-6375
B+	NATIONWIDE MUTUAL FIRE INS CO	ONE NATIONWIDE PLAZA	COLUMBUS	OH	43216	(614) 249-7111
A+	OGLESBY REINSURANCE CO	ONE STATE FARM PLAZA	BLOOMINGTON	IL	61710	(309) 766-2311
A-	OLD REPUBLIC GENERAL INS CORP	307 NORTH MICHIGAN AVENUE	CHICAGO	IL	60601	(312) 346-8100
A-	OLD REPUBLIC INS CO	414 W PITTSBURGH ST	GREENSBURG	PA	15601	(724) 834-5000
B+	OLD REPUBLIC SURETY CO	445 S MOORLAND RD SUITE 301	BROOKFIELD	WI	53005	(262) 797-2640
A-	OTSEGO MUTUAL FIRE INS CO	143 ARNOLD ROAD RD	BURLINGTON FLATS	NY	13315	(607) 965-8211
A+	OWNERS INS CO	2325 N COLE ST	LIMA	OH	45801	(517) 323-1200
B+	PACIFIC INDEMNITY CO	TWO PLAZA EAST SUITE 1450	MILWAUKEE	WI	53202	(908) 903-2000
B+	PEKIN INS CO	2505 COURT ST	PEKIN	IL	61558	(309) 346-1161
A	PIONEER STATE MUTUAL INS CO	1510 N ELMS RD	FLINT	MI	48532	(810) 733-2300
A	PROPERTY-OWNERS INS CO	3950 W DELPHI PIKE	MARION	IN	46952	(517) 323-1200
A-	PROTECTIVE INS CO	1099 N MERIDIAN ST	INDIANAPOLIS	IN	46204	(317) 636-9800
A+	QUEEN CITY ASR INC	76 SAINT PAUL ST SUITE 500	BURLINGTON	VT	05401	(802) 264-4577
A-	RETAILFIRST INS CO	2310 COMMERCE POINT DR	LAKELAND	FL	33801	863-665-6060
B+	SAFETY INS CO	20 CUSTOM HOUSE ST	BOSTON	MA	02110	(617) 951-0600
A	SAIF CORP	400 HIGH ST,SOUTHEAST	SALEM	OR	97312	(503) 373-8000
B+	SENTRY CASUALTY CO	3400 80TH ST	MOLINE	IL	61265	(715) 346-6000
A	SENTRY INS A MUTUAL CO	1800 N POINT DR	STEVENS POINT	WI	54481	(715) 346-6000
B+	SENTRY SELECT INS CO	3400 80TH ST	MOLINE	IL	61265	(715) 346-6000
A	SOUTHERN-OWNERS INS CO	6101 ANACAPRI BLVD	LANSING	MI	48917	(517) 323-1200
B+	STATE FARM MUTUAL AUTOMOBILE INS CO	ONE STATE FARM PLAZA	BLOOMINGTON	IL	61710	(309) 766-2311
A+	STATE VOLUNTEER MUTUAL INS CO	101 WESTPARK DR SUITE 300	BRENTWOOD	TN	37024	(615) 377-1999
B+	TENNESSEE FARMERS ASR CO	147 BEAR CREEK PIKE	COLUMBIA	TN	38401	(931) 388-7872
B+	TENNESSEE FARMERS MUTUAL INS CO	147 BEAR CREEK PIKE	COLUMBIA	TN	38401	(931) 388-7872
A	TEXAS FARM BUREAU CASUALTY INS CO	7420 FISH POND RD	WACO	TX	76710	(254) 772-3030
B+	TEXAS MUTUAL INS CO	221 W. SIXTH STREET, STE 300	AUSTIN	TX	78701	(512) 224-3800
B+	TOA-RE INS CO OF AMERICA	2711 CENTERVILLE RD SUITE 400	WILMINGTON	DE	19808	(973) 898-9480
A	TOKIO MARINE AMERICA INS CO	230 PARK AVE	NEW YORK	NY	10169	(212) 297-6600
A-	TRAVELERS CASUALTY & SURETY CO	ONE TOWER SQUARE	HARTFORD	CT	06183	(860) 277-0111
B+	TRUSTGARD INS CO	650 S FRONT ST	COLUMBUS	OH	43206	(614) 445-2900
B+	TUSCARORA WAYNE INS CO	601 STATE ST	WYALUSING	PA	18853	(570) 746-1515
A+	UNITED SERVICES AUTOMOBILE ASN	9800 FREDERICKSBURG RD	SAN ANTONIO	TX	78288	(210) 498-2211
A+	USAA CASUALTY INS CO	9800 FREDERICKSBURG RD	SAN ANTONIO	TX	78288	(210) 498-8000
B+	USAA GENERAL INDEMNITY CO	9800 FREDERICKSBURG RD	SAN ANTONIO	TX	78288	(210) 498-8000
B+	USAA TEXAS LLOYDS CO	9800 FREDERICKSBURG RD	SAN ANTONIO	TX	78288	(210) 498-8000
A-	WEST BEND MUTUAL INS CO	1900 S 18TH AVE	WEST BEND	WI	53095	262-334-5571
B+	WESTERN AGRICULTURAL INS CO	5400 UNIVERSITY AVE	WEST DES MOINES	IA	50266	(515) 225-5400
B+	WESTERN COMMUNITY INS CO	275 TIERRA VISTA DR	POCATELLO	ID	83201	(208) 232-7914
B+	WESTFIELD NATIONAL INS CO	ONE PARK CIRCLE	WESTFIELD CENTER	OH	44251	(330) 887-0101

DOM. STATE	AUTO	HOME MULT. PERIL	FARM MULT. PERIL	COMM. MULT. PERIL	COMM. AUTO LIAB.	OTHER LIABILITY	MED MALPRAC.	WORK. COMP.	ACCID. & HEALTH	OTHER	INSURANCE COMPANY NAME
LA	0	0	0	0	0	0	0	100	0	0	LOUISIANA WORKERS COMPENSATION CORP
ME	0	0	0	0	0	2	0	98	0	0	MAINE EMPLOYERS MUTUAL INS CO
CA	17	62	0	11	4	2	0	0	0	4	MERCURY CASUALTY CO
CA	100	0	0	0	0	0	0	0	0	0	MERCURY INS CO
NY	1	0	0	23	4	13	0	31	0	27	MITSUI SUMITOMO INS CO OF AMER
MN	0	0	0	0	0	3	97	0	0	0	MMIC INS INC
OH	37	20	0	10	10	11	0	5	0	6	MOTORISTS MUTUAL INS CO
NY	0	0	0	0	0	0	0	0	0	100	MUNICIPAL ASR CORP
AZ	0	0	0	0	0	0	100	0	0	0	MUTUAL INS CO OF AZ
WI	10	0	0	7	31	15	0	3	0	31	NATIONAL CASUALTY CO
WI	0	0	0	0	0	0	0	0	0	100	NATIONAL MORTGAGE INS CORP
OH	21	51	0	7	2	3	0	1	0	16	NATIONWIDE MUTUAL FIRE INS CO
IL (*)	0	0	0	0	0	0	0	0	0	0	OGLESBY REINSURANCE CO
IL	2	0	0	0	10	25	0	63	0	0	OLD REPUBLIC GENERAL INS CORP
PA	1	0	0	0	6	19	0	31	1	36	OLD REPUBLIC INS CO
WI	0	0	0	0	0	0	0	0	0	100	OLD REPUBLIC SURETY CO
NY	0	84	0	0	0	1	0	0	0	14	OTSEGO MUTUAL FIRE INS CO
OH	34	23	0	20	8	3	0	8	0	3	OWNERS INS CO
WI	6	45	0	5	0	4	0	24	0	16	PACIFIC INDEMNITY CO
IL	21	13	0	28	10	5	0	21	0	3	PEKIN INS CO
MI	61	28	5	1	1	0	0	1	0	3	PIONEER STATE MUTUAL INS CO
IN	6	26	2	39	9	3	0	10	0	6	PROPERTY-OWNERS INS CO
IN	16	0	0	0	19	22	0	40	2	1	PROTECTIVE INS CO
VT	0	0	0	0	0	1	0	0	0	99	QUEEN CITY ASR INC
FL	0	0	0	0	0	0	0	100	0	0	RETAILFIRST INS CO
MA	81	7	0	3	7	1	0	0	0	1	SAFETY INS CO
OR	0	0	0	0	0	0	0	100	0	0	SAIF CORP
WI	0	0	0	0	2	6	0	92	0	0	SENTRY CASUALTY CO
WI	21	6	0	2	10	7	0	36	1	17	SENTRY INS A MUTUAL CO
WI	13	0	0	0	39	11	0	7	1	29	SENTRY SELECT INS CO
MI	58	3	0	9	2	22	0	4	0	2	SOUTHERN-OWNERS INS CO
IL	96	0	0	0	1	0	0	0	3	0	STATE FARM MUTUAL AUTOMOBILE INS CO
TN	0	0	0	0	0	0	100	0	0	0	STATE VOLUNTEER MUTUAL INS CO
TN (*)	0	0	0	0	0	0	0	0	0	0	TENNESSEE FARMERS ASR CO
TN	52	30	10	1	1	1	0	0	0	6	TENNESSEE FARMERS MUTUAL INS CO
TX	96	0	0	0	2	2	0	0	0	0	TEXAS FARM BUREAU CASUALTY INS CO
TX	0	0	0	0	0	0	0	100	0	0	TEXAS MUTUAL INS CO
DE (*)	0	0	0	0	0	0	0	0	0	0	TOA-RE INS CO OF AMERICA
NY	6	3	0	8	10	10	0	11	0	52	TOKIO MARINE AMERICA INS CO
CT	0	10	0	0	0	1	0	71	0	17	TRAVELERS CASUALTY & SURETY CO
OH	58	30	0	0	5	1	0	2	0	4	TRUSTGARD INS CO
PA	0	32	10	33	0	4	0	0	0	22	TUSCARORA WAYNE INS CO
TX	57	34	0	0	0	2	0	0	0	7	UNITED SERVICES AUTOMOBILE ASN
TX	67	28	0	0	0	1	0	0	0	4	USAA CASUALTY INS CO
TX	74	16	0	0	0	0	0	0	0	10	USAA GENERAL INDEMNITY CO
TX	0	93	0	0	0	0	0	0	0	7	USAA TEXAS LLOYDS CO
WI	19	11	0	0	6	18	0	25	0	21	WEST BEND MUTUAL INS CO
IA	12	5	9	3	2	1	0	4	0	64	WESTERN AGRICULTURAL INS CO
ID	9	0	0	66	17	2	0	0	0	5	WESTERN COMMUNITY INS CO
OH	48	38	0	2	1	4	0	4	0	3	WESTFIELD NATIONAL INS CO

(*) Denotes reinsurers, companies that do not sell to consumers

Section IV

Weiss Recommended Companies by Type of Business

A compilation of those

U.S. Property and Casualty Insurers

receiving a Weiss Financial Strength Rating

of A+, A, A- or B+.

Companies are ranked by Financial Strength Rating
in each line of business where they have received
more than $1 million in direct premiums.

Section IV Contents

This section is broken into six subsections, each presenting a list of the recommended carriers receiving at least $1 million in direct premiums from a particular line of business: Auto, Commercial Multiple Peril, Fire and Allied, Homeowners Multiple Peril, Medical Malpractice, and Workers' Compensation. Recommended companies are those insurers receiving a Financial Strength Rating of A+, A, A- or B+. If an insurer is not on this list, it should not be automatically assumed that the firm is weak. Indeed, there are many firms that have not achieved a B+ or better rating but are in relatively good condition with adequate resources to cover their risk during an average recession. Not being included in this list should not be construed as a recommendation to cancel policies.

Companies are ranked within each line of business by their Financial Strength Rating. However, companies with the same rating should be viewed as having the same relative financial strength regardless of their ranking in these tables. While the specific order in which they appear on the page is based upon differences in our underlying indexes, you can assume that companies with the same rating have differences that are only minor and relatively inconsequential.

The six lines of business covered in this section are defined as follows:

Auto:	Coverage for auto physical damage and auto liability. Auto physical covers damage to the policyholder's own automobile. Auto liability covers against financial loss from lawsuits (and legal settlements) for auto-related bodily injuries or property damage caused by the insured.
Commercial Multiple Peril:	Package policies for business and other commercial establishments providing a broad spectrum of property and liability coverages.
Fire & Allied:	Coverage for losses caused by fire, lightning, sprinkler damage, windstorm, and water damage.
Homeowners Multiple Peril:	Package policies for homeowners providing a broad spectrum of property and liability coverages.
Medical Malpractice:	Errors and omissions liability coverages for persons engaged in the practice of medicine, surgery, dentistry, nursing, pharmacy, or other health care services. Also covers health care institutions.
Workers' Compensation:	Liability coverage issued to employers which provides for the payment of medical care, certain disability income benefits and possible additional liability amounts to employees who are injured on the job.

Column definitions are as follows:

1. **Insurance Company Name**

The legally-registered name, which can sometimes differ from the name that the company uses for advertising. An insurer's name can be very similar to the name of other companies which may not be on our Recommended List, so make sure you note the exact name before contacting your agent.

2. **Domicile State**

The state which has primary regulatory responsibility for the company. It may differ from the location of the company's corporate headquarters. You do not have to be living in the domicile state to purchase insurance from this firm, provided it is licensed to do business in your state.

3. **Total Premiums**

Total direct premiums received by the company during the year for all types of policies.

4. **Policy-Type Premium**

Direct premiums received by the company for a specific type of insurance coverage, such as Auto Premiums. Companies that have less than $1,000,000 in this type of premium are not listed.

5. **Maximum Benefit**

Conservative consumers may want to limit the size of their policy with this company to the amount shown. This figure is based on the view that a policy's maximum benefits per risk should not exceed 1% of the company's capital and surplus.

Weiss Financial Strength Ratings are not deemed to be a recommendation concerning the purchase or sale of the securities of any insurance company that is publicly owned.

Auto

INSURANCE COMPANY NAME	DOMICILE STATE	TOTAL PREMIUM ($)	AUTO PREMIUM ($)	MAXIMUM BENEFIT ($)
Rating: A+				
DAIRYLAND INS CO	WI	158,546,975	158,546,975	5,000,000
INTERINS EXCH OF THE AUTOMOBILE CLUB	CA	2,247,766,810	1,798,040,771	50,000,000
OWNERS INS CO	OH	1,793,066,156	755,172,401	10,000,000
UNITED SERVICES AUTOMOBILE ASN	TX	6,712,310,392	3,849,717,010	200,000,000
USAA CASUALTY INS CO	TX	4,610,619,666	3,095,832,889	40,000,000
Rating: A				
AUTO-OWNERS INS CO	MI	2,158,404,410	724,761,072	70,000,000
CHURCH MUTUAL INS CO	WI	618,618,944	38,490,762	5,000,000
CINCINNATI INS CO	OH	3,297,205,566	897,457,476	40,000,000
FRANKENMUTH MUTUAL INS CO	MI	521,119,431	220,033,073	4,000,000
PIONEER STATE MUTUAL INS CO	MI	196,832,212	120,787,270	3,000,000
PROPERTY-OWNERS INS CO	IN	93,550,956	13,853,358	1,000,000
SENTRY INS A MUTUAL CO	WI	469,388,089	146,629,385	40,000,000
SOUTHERN-OWNERS INS CO	MI	269,958,360	161,500,943	2,000,000
TEXAS FARM BUREAU CASUALTY INS CO	TX	254,398,795	249,217,403	6,000,000
TOKIO MARINE AMERICA INS CO	NY	386,036,085	59,161,583	5,000,000
Rating: A-				
ALLSTATE INS CO	IL	7,741,648,307	4,421,297,963	200,000,000
BITCO GENERAL INS CORP	IL	302,243,044	74,854,887	3,000,000
BITCO NATIONAL INS CO	IL	63,305,411	8,430,052	1,000,000
BROTHERHOOD MUTUAL INS CO	IN	326,485,247	25,318,265	2,000,000
CINCINNATI INDEMNITY CO	OH	342,347,553	64,927,120	800,000
COUNTRY MUTUAL INS CO	IL	1,497,594,626	430,724,419	20,000,000
CSAA INS EXCHANGE	CA	1,802,794,201	1,312,589,388	40,000,000
FARM BUREAU PROP & CAS INS CO	IA	1,054,471,542	442,214,958	8,000,000
FEDERATED MUTUAL INS CO	MN	1,042,477,300	166,510,613	20,000,000
GEICO CHOICE INS CO	NE	163,626,776	163,626,776	2,000,000
GEICO SECURE INSURANCE CO	NE	82,704,491	82,704,491	3,000,000
GREAT WEST CASUALTY CO	NE	885,743,535	667,101,250	5,000,000
HASTINGS MUTUAL INS CO	MI	393,644,135	130,042,720	3,000,000
HOME-OWNERS INS CO	MI	1,212,815,933	694,764,266	8,000,000
KENTUCKY FARM BUREAU MUTUAL INS CO	KY	901,260,790	483,939,631	10,000,000
MERCURY INS CO	CA	1,350,176,279	1,350,176,279	6,000,000
MOTORISTS MUTUAL INS CO	OH	426,507,756	202,927,079	6,000,000
OLD REPUBLIC GENERAL INS CORP	IL	365,567,174	41,559,951	4,000,000
OLD REPUBLIC INS CO	PA	872,137,244	59,996,263	9,000,000
PROTECTIVE INS CO	IN	316,545,506	110,316,832	4,000,000
WEST BEND MUTUAL INS CO	WI	901,376,156	228,324,696	7,000,000
Rating: B+				
ALFA INS CORP	AL	107,495,630	74,587,275	600,000
ALFA MUTUAL GENERAL INS CO	AL	66,900,125	39,996,344	500,000
ALL AMERICA INS CO	OH	33,677,094	9,776,764	1,000,000
AMERICAN FAMILY MUT INS CO	WI	5,180,129,721	2,757,094,117	60,000,000

Auto (Continued)

INSURANCE COMPANY NAME	DOMICILE STATE	TOTAL PREMIUM ($)	AUTO PREMIUM ($)	MAXIMUM BENEFIT ($)
Rating: **B+** **(Continued)**				
AMERICAN STANDARD INS CO OF WI	WI	252,291,645	252,291,645	3,000,000
AMICA MUTUAL INS CO	RI	1,648,111,004	1,031,124,727	30,000,000
BUILDERS MUTUAL INS CO	NC	171,411,873	4,616,962	2,000,000
COUNTRY CASUALTY INS CO	IL	35,087,364	19,251,255	700,000
FARM BUREAU MUTUAL INS CO OF ID	ID	138,151,008	74,718,978	2,000,000
FARM FAMILY CASUALTY INS CO	NY	382,409,328	130,837,959	3,000,000
FARMERS AUTOMOBILE INS ASN	IL	239,604,334	147,297,731	5,000,000
FEDERAL INS CO	IN	5,862,086,753	227,985,741	100,000,000
FIRST COLONIAL INS CO	FL	172,765,194	1,230,849	2,000,000
GEICO GENERAL INS CO	MD	6,994,505,522	6,994,505,522	1,000,000
GEICO INDEMNITY CO	MD	4,441,323,642	4,441,323,643	40,000,000
GOVERNMENT EMPLOYEES INS CO	MD	4,657,477,454	4,555,951,507	100,000,000
GRANGE MUTUAL CAS CO	OH	541,018,913	286,757,335	10,000,000
HARTFORD UNDERWRITERS INS CO	CT	1,364,082,197	599,505,209	6,000,000
HOLYOKE MUTUAL INS CO IN SALEM	MA	61,373,085	2,403,873	900,000
INDIANA FARMERS MUTUAL INS CO	IN	183,050,627	70,422,103	1,000,000
MERCURY CASUALTY CO	CA	454,714,809	96,309,719	10,000,000
MITSUI SUMITOMO INS CO OF AMER	NY	202,065,492	10,855,915	3,000,000
NATIONAL CASUALTY CO	WI	795,271,654	325,079,178	1,000,000
NATIONWIDE MUTUAL FIRE INS CO	OH	1,607,053,243	367,188,861	20,000,000
PACIFIC INDEMNITY CO	WI	670,120,553	42,329,629	30,000,000
PEKIN INS CO	IL	328,254,242	101,637,256	1,000,000
SAFETY INS CO	MA	591,184,494	517,892,202	6,000,000
SENTRY CASUALTY CO	WI	153,159,979	2,868,371	700,000
SENTRY SELECT INS CO	WI	398,701,634	207,104,616	2,000,000
STATE FARM MUTUAL AUTOMOBILE INS CO	IL	32,236,152,562	31,178,818,825	700,000,000
TENNESSEE FARMERS MUTUAL INS CO	TN	1,135,612,608	594,103,818	20,000,000
TRUSTGARD INS CO	OH	164,779,874	103,815,169	500,000
USAA GENERAL INDEMNITY CO	TX	1,818,233,213	1,339,974,115	8,000,000
WESTERN AGRICULTURAL INS CO	IA	288,886,744	41,249,816	700,000
WESTERN COMMUNITY INS CO	ID	23,409,444	6,163,089	300,000
WESTFIELD NATIONAL INS CO	OH	301,787,956	148,131,533	2,000,000

Commercial Multiple Peril

INSURANCE COMPANY NAME	DOMICILE STATE	TOTAL PREMIUM ($)	COMM. MULT. PERIL PREMIUM ($)	MAXIMUM BENEFIT ($)
Rating: A+				
INTERINS EXCH OF THE AUTOMOBILE CLUB	CA	2,247,766,810	13,803,542	50,000,000
OWNERS INS CO	OH	1,793,066,156	426,852,490	10,000,000
QUEEN CITY ASR INC	VT	169,565,434	1,250,000	20,000,000
UNITED SERVICES AUTOMOBILE ASN	TX	6,712,310,392	120,092,609	200,000,000
USAA CASUALTY INS CO	TX	4,610,619,666	43,216,729	40,000,000
Rating: A				
AUTO-OWNERS INS CO	MI	2,158,404,410	446,089,682	70,000,000
CHURCH MUTUAL INS CO	WI	618,618,944	460,071,587	5,000,000
CINCINNATI INS CO	OH	3,297,205,566	1,458,069,617	40,000,000
FRANKENMUTH MUTUAL INS CO	MI	521,119,431	118,971,982	4,000,000
PIONEER STATE MUTUAL INS CO	MI	196,832,212	2,770,066	3,000,000
PROPERTY-OWNERS INS CO	IN	93,550,956	39,044,869	1,000,000
SENTRY INS A MUTUAL CO	WI	469,388,089	40,687,831	40,000,000
SOUTHERN-OWNERS INS CO	MI	269,958,360	82,573,465	2,000,000
TEXAS FARM BUREAU CASUALTY INS CO	TX	254,398,795	5,181,392	6,000,000
TOKIO MARINE AMERICA INS CO	NY	386,036,085	71,223,994	5,000,000
Rating: A-				
ALLSTATE INS CO	IL	7,741,648,307	408,422,512	200,000,000
BITCO GENERAL INS CORP	IL	302,243,044	102,436,003	3,000,000
BITCO NATIONAL INS CO	IL	63,305,411	19,091,740	1,000,000
BROTHERHOOD MUTUAL INS CO	IN	326,485,247	246,273,836	2,000,000
CINCINNATI INDEMNITY CO	OH	342,347,553	127,044,198	800,000
COPIC INS CO	CO	88,013,765	3,158,450	3,000,000
COUNTRY MUTUAL INS CO	IL	1,497,594,626	127,927,994	20,000,000
CSAA INS EXCHANGE	CA	1,802,794,201	16,871,096	40,000,000
FARM BUREAU PROP & CAS INS CO	IA	1,054,471,542	75,927,896	8,000,000
FEDERATED MUTUAL INS CO	MN	1,042,477,300	202,342,823	20,000,000
GREAT WEST CASUALTY CO	NE	885,743,535	32,635,931	5,000,000
HASTINGS MUTUAL INS CO	MI	393,644,135	72,718,786	3,000,000
HOME-OWNERS INS CO	MI	1,212,815,933	99,792,565	8,000,000
ICI MUTUAL INS CO RRG	VT	87,506,584	77,635,048	2,000,000
JEWELERS MUTUAL INS CO	WI	151,646,412	23,758,347	2,000,000
KENTUCKY FARM BUREAU MUTUAL INS CO	KY	901,260,790	72,382,907	10,000,000
MMIC INS INC	MN	125,239,741	4,084,356	3,000,000
MOTORISTS MUTUAL INS CO	OH	426,507,756	89,838,228	6,000,000
OLD REPUBLIC GENERAL INS CORP	IL	365,567,174	92,292,438	4,000,000
OLD REPUBLIC INS CO	PA	872,137,244	169,373,583	9,000,000
PROTECTIVE INS CO	IN	316,545,506	69,582,325	4,000,000
TRAVELERS CASUALTY & SURETY CO	CT	339,576,876	3,450,478	60,000,000
WEST BEND MUTUAL INS CO	WI	901,376,156	164,699,183	7,000,000
Rating: B+				
ALFA INS CORP	AL	107,495,630	3,623,731	600,000
ALL AMERICA INS CO	OH	33,677,094	18,850,778	1,000,000
AMERICAN FAMILY MUT INS CO	WI	5,180,129,721	520,797,555	60,000,000
AMICA MUTUAL INS CO	RI	1,648,111,004	44,414,708	30,000,000

Commercial Multiple Peril (Continued)

INSURANCE COMPANY NAME	DOMICILE STATE	TOTAL PREMIUM ($)	COMM. MULT. PERIL PREMIUM ($)	MAXIMUM BENEFIT ($)
BUILDERS MUTUAL INS CO	NC	171,411,873	29,676,428	2,000,000
EXECUTIVE RISK INDEMNITY INC	DE	125,382,306	121,859,635	10,000,000
FARM BUREAU MUTUAL INS CO OF ID	ID	138,151,008	3,506,741	2,000,000
FARM FAMILY CASUALTY INS CO	NY	382,409,328	81,365,439	3,000,000
FEDERAL INS CO	IN	5,862,086,753	2,976,466,138	100,000,000
GOVERNMENT EMPLOYEES INS CO	MD	4,657,477,454	101,456,156	100,000,000
GRANGE MUTUAL CAS CO	OH	541,018,913	104,048,819	10,000,000
HARTFORD UNDERWRITERS INS CO	CT	1,364,082,197	69,029,718	6,000,000
HOLYOKE MUTUAL INS CO IN SALEM	MA	61,373,085	45,014,127	900,000
INDIANA FARMERS MUTUAL INS CO	IN	183,050,627	23,256,410	1,000,000
MAINE EMPLOYERS MUTUAL INS CO	ME	136,829,478	2,282,951	1,000,000
MERCURY CASUALTY CO	CA	454,714,809	56,796,831	10,000,000
MITSUI SUMITOMO INS CO OF AMER	NY	202,065,492	73,971,413	3,000,000
NATIONAL CASUALTY CO	WI	795,271,654	174,514,699	1,000,000
NATIONWIDE MUTUAL FIRE INS CO	OH	1,607,053,243	162,268,376	20,000,000
PACIFIC INDEMNITY CO	WI	670,120,553	62,924,185	30,000,000
PEKIN INS CO	IL	328,254,242	105,974,727	1,000,000
SAFETY INS CO	MA	591,184,494	22,425,659	6,000,000
SENTRY CASUALTY CO	WI	153,159,979	8,453,755	700,000
SENTRY SELECT INS CO	WI	398,701,634	44,331,729	2,000,000
STATE FARM MUTUAL AUTOMOBILE INS CO	IL	32,236,152,562	3,427,376	700,000,000
TENNESSEE FARMERS MUTUAL INS CO	TN	1,135,612,608	26,983,998	20,000,000
TRUSTGARD INS CO	OH	164,779,874	1,091,696	500,000
TUSCARORA WAYNE INS CO	PA	31,143,304	11,302,627	500,000
USAA GENERAL INDEMNITY CO	TX	1,818,233,213	5,668,058	8,000,000
WESTERN AGRICULTURAL INS CO	IA	288,886,744	10,616,643	700,000
WESTERN COMMUNITY INS CO	ID	23,409,444	15,988,100	300,000
WESTFIELD NATIONAL INS CO	OH	301,787,956	18,336,872	2,000,000

Fire & Allied

INSURANCE COMPANY NAME	DOMICILE STATE	TOTAL PREMIUM ($)	FIRE & ALLIED PREMIUM ($)	MAXIMUM BENEFIT ($)
Rating: **A+**				
CITIZENS PROPERTY INS CORP	FL	2,761,637,564	1,489,301,805	70,000,000
INTERINS EXCH OF THE AUTOMOBILE CLUB	CA	2,247,766,810	18,237,972	50,000,000
OWNERS INS CO	OH	1,793,066,156	8,963,912	10,000,000
UNITED SERVICES AUTOMOBILE ASN	TX	6,712,310,392	311,716,856	200,000,000
USAA CASUALTY INS CO	TX	4,610,619,666	103,118,476	40,000,000
Rating: **A**				
AUTO-OWNERS INS CO	MI	2,158,404,410	351,797,428	70,000,000
CHURCH MUTUAL INS CO	WI	618,618,944	7,250,111	5,000,000
CINCINNATI INS CO	OH	3,297,205,566	145,777,604	40,000,000
FRANKENMUTH MUTUAL INS CO	MI	521,119,431	4,843,382	4,000,000
PIONEER STATE MUTUAL INS CO	MI	196,832,212	3,009,961	3,000,000
SENTRY INS A MUTUAL CO	WI	469,388,089	49,275,140	40,000,000
TOKIO MARINE AMERICA INS CO	NY	386,036,085	77,680,412	5,000,000
Rating: **A-**				
ALLSTATE INS CO	IL	7,741,648,307	311,826,408	200,000,000
AMICA LLOYDS OF TEXAS	TX	93,106,464	4,019,543	700,000
CINCINNATI INDEMNITY CO	OH	342,347,553	23,183,189	800,000
COUNTRY MUTUAL INS CO	IL	1,497,594,626	124,773,164	20,000,000
CSAA INS EXCHANGE	CA	1,802,794,201	12,643,468	40,000,000
FEDERATED MUTUAL INS CO	MN	1,042,477,300	79,152,992	20,000,000
HASTINGS MUTUAL INS CO	MI	393,644,135	8,597,400	3,000,000
HOME-OWNERS INS CO	MI	1,212,815,933	2,371,589	8,000,000
KENTUCKY FARM BUREAU MUTUAL INS CO	KY	901,260,790	8,905,628	10,000,000
MOTORISTS MUTUAL INS CO	OH	426,507,756	6,470,394	6,000,000
OTSEGO MUTUAL FIRE INS CO	NY	16,613,872	2,368,479	900,000
TRAVELERS CASUALTY & SURETY CO	CT	339,576,876	4,579,465	60,000,000
WEST BEND MUTUAL INS CO	WI	901,376,156	121,766,883	7,000,000
Rating: **B+**				
ALFA INS CORP	AL	107,495,630	1,475,133	600,000
AMERICAN FAMILY MUT INS CO	WI	5,180,129,721	26,495,639	60,000,000
AMICA MUTUAL INS CO	RI	1,648,111,004	18,421,626	30,000,000
FARM BUREAU MUTUAL INS CO OF ID	ID	138,151,008	5,211,043	2,000,000
FARM FAMILY CASUALTY INS CO	NY	382,409,328	71,297,901	3,000,000
FARMERS AUTOMOBILE INS ASN	IL	239,604,334	11,695,144	5,000,000
FEDERAL INS CO	IN	5,862,086,753	36,180,957	100,000,000
GRANGE MUTUAL CAS CO	OH	541,018,913	16,957,377	10,000,000
HARTFORD UNDERWRITERS INS CO	CT	1,364,082,197	33,063,413	6,000,000
HOLYOKE MUTUAL INS CO IN SALEM	MA	61,373,085	2,420,845	900,000
INDIANA FARMERS MUTUAL INS CO	IN	183,050,627	4,149,947	1,000,000
MERCURY CASUALTY CO	CA	454,714,809	15,061,448	10,000,000
MITSUI SUMITOMO INS CO OF AMER	NY	202,065,492	11,968,257	3,000,000
NATIONAL CASUALTY CO	WI	795,271,654	13,331,999	1,000,000
NATIONWIDE MUTUAL FIRE INS CO	OH	1,607,053,243	216,934,358	20,000,000
PACIFIC INDEMNITY CO	WI	670,120,553	1,207,166	30,000,000

Fire & Allied (Continued)

INSURANCE COMPANY NAME	DOMICILE STATE	TOTAL PREMIUM ($)	FIRE & ALLIED PREMIUM ($)	MAXIMUM BENEFIT ($)
Rating:	**B+**	**(Continued)**		
PEKIN INS CO	IL	328,254,242	3,569,430	1,000,000
SAFETY INS CO	MA	591,184,494	6,811,222	6,000,000
SENTRY SELECT INS CO	WI	398,701,634	26,169,415	2,000,000
TENNESSEE FARMERS MUTUAL INS CO	TN	1,135,612,608	65,036,838	20,000,000
TRUSTGARD INS CO	OH	164,779,874	5,602,132	500,000
TUSCARORA WAYNE INS CO	PA	31,143,304	6,189,671	500,000
USAA GENERAL INDEMNITY CO	TX	1,818,233,213	170,649,458	8,000,000
USAA TEXAS LLOYDS CO	TX	362,652,216	24,212,310	2,000,000
WESTERN AGRICULTURAL INS CO	IA	288,886,744	183,594,185	700,000

Homeowners Multiple Peril

INSURANCE COMPANY NAME	DOMICILE STATE	TOTAL PREMIUM ($)	HOME OWNERS PREMIUM ($)	MAXIMUM BENEFIT ($)
Rating: A+				
CITIZENS PROPERTY INS CORP	FL	2,761,637,564	1,272,335,759	70,000,000
INTERINS EXCH OF THE AUTOMOBILE CLUB	CA	2,247,766,810	412,478,812	50,000,000
OWNERS INS CO	OH	1,793,066,156	408,817,729	10,000,000
UNITED SERVICES AUTOMOBILE ASN	TX	6,712,310,392	2,286,481,461	200,000,000
USAA CASUALTY INS CO	TX	4,610,619,666	1,270,986,696	40,000,000
Rating: A				
AUTO-OWNERS INS CO	MI	2,158,404,410	336,883,853	70,000,000
CHURCH MUTUAL INS CO	WI	618,618,944	1,393,364	5,000,000
CINCINNATI INS CO	OH	3,297,205,566	447,448,677	40,000,000
FRANKENMUTH MUTUAL INS CO	MI	521,119,431	87,487,900	4,000,000
PIONEER STATE MUTUAL INS CO	MI	196,832,212	54,855,745	3,000,000
PROPERTY-OWNERS INS CO	IN	93,550,956	23,979,960	1,000,000
SENTRY INS A MUTUAL CO	WI	469,388,089	29,030,649	40,000,000
SOUTHERN-OWNERS INS CO	MI	269,958,360	8,846,229	2,000,000
TOKIO MARINE AMERICA INS CO	NY	386,036,085	9,775,338	5,000,000
Rating: A-				
ALLSTATE INS CO	IL	7,741,648,307	2,522,179,955	200,000,000
AMICA LLOYDS OF TEXAS	TX	93,106,464	87,861,449	700,000
COUNTRY MUTUAL INS CO	IL	1,497,594,626	611,288,839	20,000,000
CSAA INS EXCHANGE	CA	1,802,794,201	452,486,738	40,000,000
FARM BUREAU PROP & CAS INS CO	IA	1,054,471,542	243,172,048	8,000,000
FEDERATED MUTUAL INS CO	MN	1,042,477,300	2,730,051	20,000,000
HASTINGS MUTUAL INS CO	MI	393,644,135	60,108,892	3,000,000
HOME-OWNERS INS CO	MI	1,212,815,933	368,101,285	8,000,000
KENTUCKY FARM BUREAU MUTUAL INS CO	KY	901,260,790	230,317,781	10,000,000
MOTORISTS MUTUAL INS CO	OH	426,507,756	84,952,982	6,000,000
OTSEGO MUTUAL FIRE INS CO	NY	16,613,872	14,008,711	900,000
TRAVELERS CASUALTY & SURETY CO	CT	339,576,876	34,302,400	60,000,000
WEST BEND MUTUAL INS CO	WI	901,376,156	96,281,326	7,000,000
Rating: B+				
ALFA INS CORP	AL	107,495,630	27,112,590	600,000
ALFA MUTUAL GENERAL INS CO	AL	66,900,125	26,422,401	500,000
AMERICAN FAMILY MUT INS CO	WI	5,180,129,721	1,609,365,207	60,000,000
AMICA MUTUAL INS CO	RI	1,648,111,004	517,586,457	30,000,000
AUTO CLUB INDEMNITY CO	TX	84,258,830	83,219,934	50,000
COUNTRY CASUALTY INS CO	IL	35,087,364	15,795,691	700,000
FARM BUREAU MUTUAL INS CO OF ID	ID	138,151,008	25,333,469	2,000,000
FARM FAMILY CASUALTY INS CO	NY	382,409,328	31,087,024	3,000,000
FARMERS AUTOMOBILE INS ASN	IL	239,604,334	77,741,882	5,000,000
FEDERAL INS CO	IN	5,862,086,753	500,251,818	100,000,000
GRANGE MUTUAL CAS CO	OH	541,018,913	98,096,275	10,000,000
HARTFORD UNDERWRITERS INS CO	CT	1,364,082,197	144,713,922	6,000,000

Homeowners Multiple Peril (Continued)

INSURANCE COMPANY NAME	DOMICILE STATE	TOTAL PREMIUM ($)	HOME OWNERS PREMIUM ($)	MAXIMUM BENEFIT ($)
Rating: **B+** **(Continued)**				
HOLYOKE MUTUAL INS CO IN SALEM	MA	61,373,085	10,857,636	900,000
INDIANA FARMERS MUTUAL INS CO	IN	183,050,627	42,139,265	1,000,000
MERCURY CASUALTY CO	CA	454,714,809	283,904,956	10,000,000
NATIONWIDE MUTUAL FIRE INS CO	OH	1,607,053,243	814,028,146	20,000,000
PACIFIC INDEMNITY CO	WI	670,120,553	300,022,708	30,000,000
PEKIN INS CO	IL	328,254,242	43,932,097	1,000,000
SAFETY INS CO	MA	591,184,494	42,416,253	6,000,000
TENNESSEE FARMERS MUTUAL INS CO	TN	1,135,612,608	337,046,824	20,000,000
TRUSTGARD INS CO	OH	164,779,874	50,102,381	500,000
TUSCARORA WAYNE INS CO	PA	31,143,304	9,922,271	500,000
USAA GENERAL INDEMNITY CO	TX	1,818,233,213	285,809,032	8,000,000
USAA TEXAS LLOYDS CO	TX	362,652,216	337,663,320	2,000,000
WESTERN AGRICULTURAL INS CO	IA	288,886,744	13,689,701	700,000
WESTFIELD NATIONAL INS CO	OH	301,787,956	113,246,491	2,000,000

Medical Malpractice

INSURANCE COMPANY NAME	DOMICILE STATE	TOTAL PREMIUM ($)	MEDICAL MALPRACTICE PREMIUM ($)	MAXIMUM BENEFIT ($)
Rating: A+				
STATE VOLUNTEER MUTUAL INS CO	TN	152,275,262	152,164,421	5,000,000
Rating: A				
CHURCH MUTUAL INS CO	WI	618,618,944	5,504,355	5,000,000
CINCINNATI INS CO	OH	3,297,205,566	29,738,711	40,000,000
MUTUAL INS CO OF AZ	AZ	118,845,683	118,845,683	5,000,000
Rating: A-				
CINCINNATI INDEMNITY CO	OH	342,347,553	1,113,037	800,000
COPIC INS CO	CO	88,013,765	83,145,618	3,000,000
MMIC INS INC	MN	125,239,741	121,155,385	3,000,000

Workers' Compensation

INSURANCE COMPANY NAME	DOMICILE STATE	TOTAL PREMIUM ($)	WORKERS' COMPENSATION PREMIUM ($)	MAXIMUM BENEFIT ($)
Rating: A+				
COPPERPOINT MUTUAL INS CO	AZ	70,971,035	70,971,035	10,000,000
OWNERS INS CO	OH	1,793,066,156	136,898,141	10,000,000
Rating: A				
AUTO-OWNERS INS CO	MI	2,158,404,410	198,047,546	70,000,000
CHURCH MUTUAL INS CO	WI	618,618,944	105,842,536	5,000,000
CINCINNATI INS CO	OH	3,297,205,566	102,052,518	40,000,000
FRANKENMUTH MUTUAL INS CO	MI	521,119,431	67,950,395	4,000,000
PIONEER STATE MUTUAL INS CO	MI	196,832,212	1,326,089	3,000,000
PROPERTY-OWNERS INS CO	IN	93,550,956	9,482,670	1,000,000
SAIF CORP	OR	436,159,631	436,159,631	4,000,000
SENTRY INS A MUTUAL CO	WI	469,388,089	167,959,949	40,000,000
SOUTHERN-OWNERS INS CO	MI	269,958,360	12,091,473	2,000,000
TOKIO MARINE AMERICA INS CO	NY	386,036,085	43,296,818	5,000,000
Rating: A-				
BITCO GENERAL INS CORP	IL	302,243,044	103,031,561	3,000,000
BITCO NATIONAL INS CO	IL	63,305,411	31,697,901	1,000,000
BROTHERHOOD MUTUAL INS CO	IN	326,485,247	43,856,394	2,000,000
CINCINNATI INDEMNITY CO	OH	342,347,553	114,127,685	800,000
COUNTRY MUTUAL INS CO	IL	1,497,594,626	59,401,051	20,000,000
FARM BUREAU PROP & CAS INS CO	IA	1,054,471,542	32,856,028	8,000,000
FEDERATED MUTUAL INS CO	MN	1,042,477,300	175,332,495	20,000,000
GREAT WEST CASUALTY CO	NE	885,743,535	108,749,474	5,000,000
HASTINGS MUTUAL INS CO	MI	393,644,135	59,394,884	3,000,000
HOME-OWNERS INS CO	MI	1,212,815,933	29,586,656	8,000,000
LOUISIANA WORKERS COMPENSATION CORP	LA	185,312,608	185,312,608	900,000
MOTORISTS MUTUAL INS CO	OH	426,507,756	22,088,664	6,000,000
OLD REPUBLIC GENERAL INS CORP	IL	365,567,174	231,239,496	4,000,000
OLD REPUBLIC INS CO	PA	872,137,244	269,521,042	9,000,000
PROTECTIVE INS CO	IN	316,545,506	125,362,077	4,000,000
RETAILFIRST INS CO	FL	82,947,816	82,947,816	1,000,000
TRAVELERS CASUALTY & SURETY CO	CT	339,576,876	242,403,330	60,000,000
WEST BEND MUTUAL INS CO	WI	901,376,156	225,148,908	7,000,000
Rating: B+				
ALL AMERICA INS CO	OH	33,677,094	2,431,615	1,000,000
AMERICAN FAMILY MUT INS CO	WI	5,180,129,721	48,594,307	60,000,000
BUILDERS MUTUAL INS CO	NC	171,411,873	124,568,681	2,000,000
FARM FAMILY CASUALTY INS CO	NY	382,409,328	48,480,949	3,000,000
FEDERAL INS CO	IN	5,862,086,753	637,593,400	100,000,000
GRANGE MUTUAL CAS CO	OH	541,018,913	9,066,667	10,000,000
HARTFORD UNDERWRITERS INS CO	CT	1,364,082,197	502,831,113	6,000,000
INDIANA FARMERS MUTUAL INS CO	IN	183,050,627	8,830,624	1,000,000
MAINE EMPLOYERS MUTUAL INS CO	ME	136,829,478	134,546,527	1,000,000
MITSUI SUMITOMO INS CO OF AMER	NY	202,065,492	62,242,200	3,000,000
NATIONAL CASUALTY CO	WI	795,271,654	26,288,068	1,000,000
NATIONWIDE MUTUAL FIRE INS CO	OH	1,607,053,243	13,112,144	20,000,000

Workers' Compensation (Continued)

INSURANCE COMPANY NAME	DOMICILE STATE	TOTAL PREMIUM ($)	WORKERS' COMPENSATION PREMIUM ($)	MAXIMUM BENEFIT ($)
PACIFIC INDEMNITY CO	WI	670,120,553	157,607,530	30,000,000
PEKIN INS CO	IL	328,254,242	67,800,304	1,000,000
SENTRY CASUALTY CO	WI	153,159,979	141,028,270	700,000
SENTRY SELECT INS CO	WI	398,701,634	28,422,875	2,000,000
TEXAS MUTUAL INS CO	TX	1,031,356,678	1,031,356,678	6,000,000
TRUSTGARD INS CO	OH	164,779,874	2,662,773	500,000
WESTERN AGRICULTURAL INS CO	IA	288,886,744	12,447,235	700,000
WESTFIELD NATIONAL INS CO	OH	301,787,956	12,502,823	2,000,000

Section V

Weiss Recommended Companies by State

A compilation of those

U.S. Property and Casualty Insurers

receiving a Weiss Financial Strength Rating

of A+, A, A- or B+.

Companies are ranked by Financial Strength Rating
in each state where they are licensed to do business.

Section V Contents

This section provides a list of the recommended carriers licensed to do business in each state. It contains all insurers receiving a Financial Strength Rating of A+, A, A- or B+. If an insurer is not on this list, it should not be automatically assumed that the firm is weak. Indeed, there are many firms that have not achieved a B+ or better rating but are in relatively good condition with adequate resources to cover their risk during an average recession. Not being included in this list should not be construed as a recommendation to cancel policies.

Companies are ranked within each state by their Financial Strength Rating. However, companies with the same rating should be viewed as having the same relative safety regardless of their ranking in this table. While the specific order in which they appear on the page is based upon differences in our underlying indexes, you can assume that companies with the same rating have differences that are only minor and relatively inconsequential.

1. **Insurance Company Name**   The legally-registered name, which can sometimes differ from the name that the company uses for advertising. An insurer's name can be very similar to the name of other companies which may not be on our Recommended List, so make sure you note the exact name before contacting your agent.

2. **Domicile State**   The state which has primary regulatory responsibility for the company. It may differ from the location of the company's corporate headquarters. You do not have to be living in the domicile state to purchase insurance from this firm, provided it is licensed to do business in your state.

3. **Total Assets**   All assets admitted by state insurance regulators in millions of dollars. This includes investments and current business assets such as receivables from agents and reinsurers.

Weiss Financial Strength Ratings are not deemed to be a recommendation concerning the purchase or sale of the securities of any insurance company that is publicly owned.

Alabama

INSURANCE COMPANY NAME	DOM. STATE	TOTAL ASSETS ($MIL)
Rating: A+		
BERKSHIRE HATHAWAY ASR CORP	NY	2,246.2
DAIRYLAND INS CO	WI	1,212.4
OWNERS INS CO	OH	3,686.6
QUEEN CITY ASR INC	VT	2,149.3
STATE VOLUNTEER MUTUAL INS CO	TN	1,206.0
UNITED SERVICES AUTOMOBILE ASN	TX	30,759.0
USAA CASUALTY INS CO	TX	8,886.5
Rating: A		
AUTO-OWNERS INS CO	MI	11,867.2
CHURCH MUTUAL INS CO	WI	1,452.0
CINCINNATI INS CO	OH	10,791.2
FRANKENMUTH MUTUAL INS CO	MI	1,096.8
PROPERTY-OWNERS INS CO	IN	217.0
SENTRY INS A MUTUAL CO	WI	6,922.0
TOKIO MARINE AMERICA INS CO	NY	1,387.9
Rating: A-		
ALLSTATE INS CO	IL	44,425.2
BITCO GENERAL INS CORP	IL	796.8
BITCO NATIONAL INS CO	IL	468.3
BROTHERHOOD MUTUAL INS CO	IN	443.2
CINCINNATI INDEMNITY CO	OH	115.5
COUNTRY MUTUAL INS CO	IL	4,306.5
ESSENT GUARANTY INC	PA	767.9
FEDERATED MUTUAL INS CO	MN	4,726.6
GEICO CHOICE INS CO	NE	388.0
GEICO SECURE INSURANCE CO	NE	338.5
GREAT WEST CASUALTY CO	NE	1,829.1
HOME-OWNERS INS CO	MI	2,165.7
JEWELERS MUTUAL INS CO	WI	329.0
NATIONAL MORTGAGE INS CORP	WI	264.6
OLD REPUBLIC GENERAL INS CORP	IL	1,829.0
OLD REPUBLIC INS CO	PA	2,580.9
PROTECTIVE INS CO	IN	776.3
TRAVELERS CASUALTY & SURETY CO	CT	16,487.0
Rating: B+		
ACA FINANCIAL GUARANTY CORP	MD	374.0
ALFA INS CORP	AL	99.4
ALFA MUTUAL GENERAL INS CO	AL	100.9
ALTERRA REINS USA INC	CT	1,467.0
AMICA MUTUAL INS CO	RI	5,054.3
CENTRAL STATES INDEMNITY CO OF OMAHA	NE	427.1
CENTURION CASUALTY CO	IA	140.4
COUNTRY CASUALTY INS CO	IL	78.1
EXECUTIVE RISK INDEMNITY INC	DE	3,025.1
FEDERAL INS CO	IN	32,714.5
FIRST COLONIAL INS CO	FL	355.0
GEICO GENERAL INS CO	MD	215.7
GEICO INDEMNITY CO	MD	6,922.7
GOVERNMENT EMPLOYEES INS CO	MD	22,729.4
GRANGE MUTUAL CAS CO	OH	2,088.9
HARTFORD UNDERWRITERS INS CO	CT	1,566.0
MITSUI SUMITOMO INS CO OF AMER	NY	883.6
NATIONAL CASUALTY CO	WI	273.8

INSURANCE COMPANY NAME	DOM. STATE	TOTAL ASSETS ($MIL)
NATIONWIDE MUTUAL FIRE INS CO	OH	5,632.7
OLD REPUBLIC SURETY CO	WI	110.0
PACIFIC INDEMNITY CO	WI	6,857.3
SENTRY CASUALTY CO	WI	264.9
SENTRY SELECT INS CO	WI	676.5
STATE FARM MUTUAL AUTOMOBILE INS CO	IL	137,646.1
TOA-RE INS CO OF AMERICA	DE	1,812.3
USAA GENERAL INDEMNITY CO	TX	2,785.3
WESTERN AGRICULTURAL INS CO	IA	178.2
WESTFIELD NATIONAL INS CO	OH	593.0

Alaska

INSURANCE COMPANY NAME	DOM. STATE	TOTAL ASSETS ($MIL)	INSURANCE COMPANY NAME	DOM. STATE	TOTAL ASSETS ($MIL)
Rating: A+					
BERKSHIRE HATHAWAY ASR CORP	NY	2,246.2			
DAIRYLAND INS CO	WI	1,212.4			
MUNICIPAL ASR CORP	NY	1,528.4			
QUEEN CITY ASR INC	VT	2,149.3			
UNITED SERVICES AUTOMOBILE ASN	TX	30,759.0			
USAA CASUALTY INS CO	TX	8,886.5			
Rating: A					
CHURCH MUTUAL INS CO	WI	1,452.0			
CINCINNATI INS CO	OH	10,791.2			
SENTRY INS A MUTUAL CO	WI	6,922.0			
TOKIO MARINE AMERICA INS CO	NY	1,387.9			
Rating: A-					
ALLSTATE INS CO	IL	44,425.2			
BITCO GENERAL INS CORP	IL	796.8			
BROTHERHOOD MUTUAL INS CO	IN	443.2			
CINCINNATI INDEMNITY CO	OH	115.5			
COUNTRY MUTUAL INS CO	IL	4,306.5			
ESSENT GUARANTY INC	PA	767.9			
FEDERATED MUTUAL INS CO	MN	4,726.6			
GEICO CHOICE INS CO	NE	388.0			
GEICO SECURE INSURANCE CO	NE	338.5			
GREAT WEST CASUALTY CO	NE	1,829.1			
JEWELERS MUTUAL INS CO	WI	329.0			
NATIONAL MORTGAGE INS CORP	WI	264.6			
OLD REPUBLIC GENERAL INS CORP	IL	1,829.0			
OLD REPUBLIC INS CO	PA	2,580.9			
PROTECTIVE INS CO	IN	776.3			
TRAVELERS CASUALTY & SURETY CO	CT	16,487.0			
Rating: B+					
ACA FINANCIAL GUARANTY CORP	MD	374.0			
ALTERRA REINS USA INC	CT	1,467.0			
AMICA MUTUAL INS CO	RI	5,054.3			
CENTRAL STATES INDEMNITY CO OF OMAHA	NE	427.1			
COUNTRY CASUALTY INS CO	IL	78.1			
EXECUTIVE RISK INDEMNITY INC	DE	3,025.1			
FEDERAL INS CO	IN	32,714.5			
FIRST COLONIAL INS CO	FL	355.0			
GEICO GENERAL INS CO	MD	215.7			
GEICO INDEMNITY CO	MD	6,922.7			
GOVERNMENT EMPLOYEES INS CO	MD	22,729.4			
HARTFORD UNDERWRITERS INS CO	CT	1,566.0			
MITSUI SUMITOMO INS CO OF AMER	NY	883.6			
NATIONAL CASUALTY CO	WI	273.8			
NATIONWIDE MUTUAL FIRE INS CO	OH	5,632.7			
PACIFIC INDEMNITY CO	WI	6,857.3			
SENTRY CASUALTY CO	WI	264.9			
SENTRY SELECT INS CO	WI	676.5			
STATE FARM MUTUAL AUTOMOBILE INS CO	IL	137,646.1			
TOA-RE INS CO OF AMERICA	DE	1,812.3			
USAA GENERAL INDEMNITY CO	TX	2,785.3			

Arizona

INSURANCE COMPANY NAME	DOM. STATE	TOTAL ASSETS ($MIL)
Rating: A+		
BERKSHIRE HATHAWAY ASR CORP	NY	2,246.2
COPPERPOINT MUTUAL INS CO	AZ	3,581.2
DAIRYLAND INS CO	WI	1,212.4
MUNICIPAL ASR CORP	NY	1,528.4
OWNERS INS CO	OH	3,686.6
QUEEN CITY ASR INC	VT	2,149.3
UNITED SERVICES AUTOMOBILE ASN	TX	30,759.0
USAA CASUALTY INS CO	TX	8,886.5
Rating: A		
AUTO-OWNERS INS CO	MI	11,867.2
CHURCH MUTUAL INS CO	WI	1,452.0
CINCINNATI INS CO	OH	10,791.2
FRANKENMUTH MUTUAL INS CO	MI	1,096.8
MUTUAL INS CO OF AZ	AZ	1,011.0
SENTRY INS A MUTUAL CO	WI	6,922.0
TOKIO MARINE AMERICA INS CO	NY	1,387.9
Rating: A-		
ALLSTATE INS CO	IL	44,425.2
BITCO GENERAL INS CORP	IL	796.8
BITCO NATIONAL INS CO	IL	468.3
BROTHERHOOD MUTUAL INS CO	IN	443.2
CINCINNATI INDEMNITY CO	OH	115.5
COPIC INS CO	CO	548.6
COUNTRY MUTUAL INS CO	IL	4,306.5
ESSENT GUARANTY INC	PA	767.9
FARM BUREAU PROP & CAS INS CO	IA	2,012.0
FEDERATED MUTUAL INS CO	MN	4,726.6
GEICO CHOICE INS CO	NE	388.0
GEICO SECURE INSURANCE CO	NE	338.5
GREAT WEST CASUALTY CO	NE	1,829.1
ICI MUTUAL INS CO RRG	VT	330.9
JEWELERS MUTUAL INS CO	WI	329.0
NATIONAL MORTGAGE INS CORP	WI	264.6
OLD REPUBLIC GENERAL INS CORP	IL	1,829.0
OLD REPUBLIC INS CO	PA	2,580.9
PROTECTIVE INS CO	IN	776.3
TRAVELERS CASUALTY & SURETY CO	CT	16,487.0
Rating: B+		
ACA FINANCIAL GUARANTY CORP	MD	374.0
ALL AMERICA INS CO	OH	256.6
ALTERRA REINS USA INC	CT	1,467.0
AMERICAN FAMILY MUT INS CO	WI	14,543.2
AMERICAN STANDARD INS CO OF WI	WI	415.8
AMICA MUTUAL INS CO	RI	5,054.3
CENTRAL STATES INDEMNITY CO OF OMAHA	NE	427.1
CENTURION CASUALTY CO	IA	140.4
COUNTRY CASUALTY INS CO	IL	78.1
EXECUTIVE RISK INDEMNITY INC	DE	3,025.1
FARMERS AUTOMOBILE INS ASN	IL	1,172.9
FEDERAL INS CO	IN	32,714.5
FIRST COLONIAL INS CO	FL	355.0
GEICO GENERAL INS CO	MD	215.7
GEICO INDEMNITY CO	MD	6,922.7

INSURANCE COMPANY NAME	DOM. STATE	TOTAL ASSETS ($MIL)
GNY CUSTOM INS CO	AZ	55.8
GOVERNMENT EMPLOYEES INS CO	MD	22,729.4
HARTFORD UNDERWRITERS INS CO	CT	1,566.0
HOLYOKE MUTUAL INS CO IN SALEM	MA	224.3
MERCURY CASUALTY CO	CA	1,993.8
MITSUI SUMITOMO INS CO OF AMER	NY	883.6
NATIONAL CASUALTY CO	WI	273.8
NATIONWIDE MUTUAL FIRE INS CO	OH	5,632.7
OLD REPUBLIC SURETY CO	WI	110.0
PACIFIC INDEMNITY CO	WI	6,857.3
PEKIN INS CO	IL	286.1
SENTRY CASUALTY CO	WI	264.9
SENTRY SELECT INS CO	WI	676.5
STATE FARM MUTUAL AUTOMOBILE INS CO	IL	137,646.1
TOA-RE INS CO OF AMERICA	DE	1,812.3
USAA GENERAL INDEMNITY CO	TX	2,785.3
WESTERN AGRICULTURAL INS CO	IA	178.2
WESTFIELD NATIONAL INS CO	OH	593.0

Arkansas

INSURANCE COMPANY NAME	DOM. STATE	TOTAL ASSETS ($MIL)
Rating: A+		
BERKSHIRE HATHAWAY ASR CORP	NY	2,246.2
DAIRYLAND INS CO	WI	1,212.4
MUNICIPAL ASR CORP	NY	1,528.4
OWNERS INS CO	OH	3,686.6
QUEEN CITY ASR INC	VT	2,149.3
STATE VOLUNTEER MUTUAL INS CO	TN	1,206.0
UNITED SERVICES AUTOMOBILE ASN	TX	30,759.0
USAA CASUALTY INS CO	TX	8,886.5
Rating: A		
AUTO-OWNERS INS CO	MI	11,867.2
CHURCH MUTUAL INS CO	WI	1,452.0
CINCINNATI INS CO	OH	10,791.2
FRANKENMUTH MUTUAL INS CO	MI	1,096.8
PROPERTY-OWNERS INS CO	IN	217.0
SENTRY INS A MUTUAL CO	WI	6,922.0
TOKIO MARINE AMERICA INS CO	NY	1,387.9
Rating: A-		
ALLSTATE INS CO	IL	44,425.2
BITCO GENERAL INS CORP	IL	796.8
BITCO NATIONAL INS CO	IL	468.3
BROTHERHOOD MUTUAL INS CO	IN	443.2
CINCINNATI INDEMNITY CO	OH	115.5
COUNTRY MUTUAL INS CO	IL	4,306.5
ESSENT GUARANTY INC	PA	767.9
FEDERATED MUTUAL INS CO	MN	4,726.6
GEICO CHOICE INS CO	NE	388.0
GEICO SECURE INSURANCE CO	NE	338.5
GREAT WEST CASUALTY CO	NE	1,829.1
HOME-OWNERS INS CO	MI	2,165.7
JEWELERS MUTUAL INS CO	WI	329.0
MMIC INS INC	MN	701.8
NATIONAL MORTGAGE INS CORP	WI	264.6
OLD REPUBLIC GENERAL INS CORP	IL	1,829.0
OLD REPUBLIC INS CO	PA	2,580.9
PROTECTIVE INS CO	IN	776.3
TRAVELERS CASUALTY & SURETY CO	CT	16,487.0
Rating: B+		
ACA FINANCIAL GUARANTY CORP	MD	374.0
ALTERRA REINS USA INC	CT	1,467.0
AMICA MUTUAL INS CO	RI	5,054.3
CENTRAL STATES INDEMNITY CO OF OMAHA	NE	427.1
COUNTRY CASUALTY INS CO	IL	78.1
EXECUTIVE RISK INDEMNITY INC	DE	3,025.1
FEDERAL INS CO	IN	32,714.5
FIRST COLONIAL INS CO	FL	355.0
GEICO GENERAL INS CO	MD	215.7
GEICO INDEMNITY CO	MD	6,922.7
GOVERNMENT EMPLOYEES INS CO	MD	22,729.4
HARTFORD UNDERWRITERS INS CO	CT	1,566.0
HOLYOKE MUTUAL INS CO IN SALEM	MA	224.3
MITSUI SUMITOMO INS CO OF AMER	NY	883.6
NATIONAL CASUALTY CO	WI	273.8
NATIONWIDE MUTUAL FIRE INS CO	OH	5,632.7

INSURANCE COMPANY NAME	DOM. STATE	TOTAL ASSETS ($MIL)
OLD REPUBLIC SURETY CO	WI	110.0
PACIFIC INDEMNITY CO	WI	6,857.3
SENTRY CASUALTY CO	WI	264.9
SENTRY SELECT INS CO	WI	676.5
STATE FARM MUTUAL AUTOMOBILE INS CO	IL	137,646.1
TOA-RE INS CO OF AMERICA	DE	1,812.3
USAA GENERAL INDEMNITY CO	TX	2,785.3
WESTERN AGRICULTURAL INS CO	IA	178.2
WESTFIELD NATIONAL INS CO	OH	593.0

California

INSURANCE COMPANY NAME	DOM. STATE	TOTAL ASSETS ($MIL)
Rating: A+		
BERKSHIRE HATHAWAY ASR CORP	NY	2,246.2
INTERINS EXCH OF THE AUTOMOBILE CLUB	CA	8,447.5
QUEEN CITY ASR INC	VT	2,149.3
UNITED SERVICES AUTOMOBILE ASN	TX	30,759.0
USAA CASUALTY INS CO	TX	8,886.5
Rating: A		
CHURCH MUTUAL INS CO	WI	1,452.0
CINCINNATI INS CO	OH	10,791.2
MUTUAL INS CO OF AZ	AZ	1,011.0
SENTRY INS A MUTUAL CO	WI	6,922.0
TOKIO MARINE AMERICA INS CO	NY	1,387.9
Rating: A-		
ALLSTATE INS CO	IL	44,425.2
BITCO GENERAL INS CORP	IL	796.8
BITCO NATIONAL INS CO	IL	468.3
BROTHERHOOD MUTUAL INS CO	IN	443.2
CINCINNATI INDEMNITY CO	OH	115.5
COUNTRY MUTUAL INS CO	IL	4,306.5
CSAA INS EXCHANGE	CA	6,956.8
ESSENT GUARANTY INC	PA	767.9
FEDERATED MUTUAL INS CO	MN	4,726.6
GEICO CHOICE INS CO	NE	388.0
GEICO SECURE INSURANCE CO	NE	338.5
GREAT WEST CASUALTY CO	NE	1,829.1
ICI MUTUAL INS CO RRG	VT	330.9
JEWELERS MUTUAL INS CO	WI	329.0
KENTUCKY FARM BUREAU MUTUAL INS CO	KY	2,214.4
MERCURY INS CO	CA	1,591.4
MOTORISTS MUTUAL INS CO	OH	1,354.2
NATIONAL MORTGAGE INS CORP	WI	264.6
OLD REPUBLIC GENERAL INS CORP	IL	1,829.0
OLD REPUBLIC INS CO	PA	2,580.9
PROTECTIVE INS CO	IN	776.3
TRAVELERS CASUALTY & SURETY CO	CT	16,487.0
Rating: B+		
ACA FINANCIAL GUARANTY CORP	MD	374.0
ALL AMERICA INS CO	OH	256.6
ALTERRA REINS USA INC	CT	1,467.0
AMICA MUTUAL INS CO	RI	5,054.3
CENTRAL STATES INDEMNITY CO OF OMAHA	NE	427.1
CENTURION CASUALTY CO	IA	140.4
EXECUTIVE RISK INDEMNITY INC	DE	3,025.1
FEDERAL INS CO	IN	32,714.5
GEICO GENERAL INS CO	MD	215.7
GEICO INDEMNITY CO	MD	6,922.7
GOVERNMENT EMPLOYEES INS CO	MD	22,729.4
HARTFORD UNDERWRITERS INS CO	CT	1,566.0
MERCURY CASUALTY CO	CA	1,993.8
MITSUI SUMITOMO INS CO OF AMER	NY	883.6
NATIONAL CASUALTY CO	WI	273.8
NATIONWIDE MUTUAL FIRE INS CO	OH	5,632.7
OLD REPUBLIC SURETY CO	WI	110.0
PACIFIC INDEMNITY CO	WI	6,857.3

INSURANCE COMPANY NAME	DOM. STATE	TOTAL ASSETS ($MIL)
SENTRY CASUALTY CO	WI	264.9
SENTRY SELECT INS CO	WI	676.5
STATE FARM MUTUAL AUTOMOBILE INS CO	IL	137,646.1
TOA-RE INS CO OF AMERICA	DE	1,812.3
USAA GENERAL INDEMNITY CO	TX	2,785.3
WESTFIELD NATIONAL INS CO	OH	593.0

Colorado

INSURANCE COMPANY NAME	DOM. STATE	TOTAL ASSETS ($MIL)
Rating: A+		
BERKSHIRE HATHAWAY ASR CORP	NY	2,246.2
DAIRYLAND INS CO	WI	1,212.4
MUNICIPAL ASR CORP	NY	1,528.4
OWNERS INS CO	OH	3,686.6
QUEEN CITY ASR INC	VT	2,149.3
UNITED SERVICES AUTOMOBILE ASN	TX	30,759.0
USAA CASUALTY INS CO	TX	8,886.5
Rating: A		
AUTO-OWNERS INS CO	MI	11,867.2
CHURCH MUTUAL INS CO	WI	1,452.0
CINCINNATI INS CO	OH	10,791.2
FRANKENMUTH MUTUAL INS CO	MI	1,096.8
MUTUAL INS CO OF AZ	AZ	1,011.0
SENTRY INS A MUTUAL CO	WI	6,922.0
TOKIO MARINE AMERICA INS CO	NY	1,387.9
Rating: A-		
ALLSTATE INS CO	IL	44,425.2
BITCO GENERAL INS CORP	IL	796.8
BITCO NATIONAL INS CO	IL	468.3
BROTHERHOOD MUTUAL INS CO	IN	443.2
CINCINNATI INDEMNITY CO	OH	115.5
COPIC INS CO	CO	548.6
COUNTRY MUTUAL INS CO	IL	4,306.5
ESSENT GUARANTY INC	PA	767.9
FEDERATED MUTUAL INS CO	MN	4,726.6
GEICO CHOICE INS CO	NE	388.0
GEICO SECURE INSURANCE CO	NE	338.5
GREAT WEST CASUALTY CO	NE	1,829.1
HOME-OWNERS INS CO	MI	2,165.7
ICI MUTUAL INS CO RRG	VT	330.9
JEWELERS MUTUAL INS CO	WI	329.0
MMIC INS INC	MN	701.8
NATIONAL MORTGAGE INS CORP	WI	264.6
OLD REPUBLIC GENERAL INS CORP	IL	1,829.0
OLD REPUBLIC INS CO	PA	2,580.9
PROTECTIVE INS CO	IN	776.3
TRAVELERS CASUALTY & SURETY CO	CT	16,487.0
Rating: B+		
ACA FINANCIAL GUARANTY CORP	MD	374.0
ALTERRA REINS USA INC	CT	1,467.0
AMERICAN FAMILY MUT INS CO	WI	14,543.2
AMERICAN STANDARD INS CO OF WI	WI	415.8
AMICA MUTUAL INS CO	RI	5,054.3
CENTRAL STATES INDEMNITY CO OF OMAHA	NE	427.1
CENTURION CASUALTY CO	IA	140.4
COUNTRY CASUALTY INS CO	IL	78.1
EXECUTIVE RISK INDEMNITY INC	DE	3,025.1
FEDERAL INS CO	IN	32,714.5
FIRST COLONIAL INS CO	FL	355.0
GEICO GENERAL INS CO	MD	215.7
GEICO INDEMNITY CO	MD	6,922.7
GOVERNMENT EMPLOYEES INS CO	MD	22,729.4
HARTFORD UNDERWRITERS INS CO	CT	1,566.0

INSURANCE COMPANY NAME	DOM. STATE	TOTAL ASSETS ($MIL)
HOLYOKE MUTUAL INS CO IN SALEM	MA	224.3
MITSUI SUMITOMO INS CO OF AMER	NY	883.6
NATIONAL CASUALTY CO	WI	273.8
NATIONWIDE MUTUAL FIRE INS CO	OH	5,632.7
OLD REPUBLIC SURETY CO	WI	110.0
PACIFIC INDEMNITY CO	WI	6,857.3
SENTRY CASUALTY CO	WI	264.9
SENTRY SELECT INS CO	WI	676.5
STATE FARM MUTUAL AUTOMOBILE INS CO	IL	137,646.1
TOA-RE INS CO OF AMERICA	DE	1,812.3
TRUSTGARD INS CO	OH	102.3
USAA GENERAL INDEMNITY CO	TX	2,785.3
WESTERN AGRICULTURAL INS CO	IA	178.2
WESTFIELD NATIONAL INS CO	OH	593.0

Connecticut

INSURANCE COMPANY NAME	DOM. STATE	TOTAL ASSETS ($MIL)
Rating: A+		
BERKSHIRE HATHAWAY ASR CORP	NY	2,246.2
DAIRYLAND INS CO	WI	1,212.4
MUNICIPAL ASR CORP	NY	1,528.4
QUEEN CITY ASR INC	VT	2,149.3
UNITED SERVICES AUTOMOBILE ASN	TX	30,759.0
USAA CASUALTY INS CO	TX	8,886.5
Rating: A		
CHURCH MUTUAL INS CO	WI	1,452.0
CINCINNATI INS CO	OH	10,791.2
FRANKENMUTH MUTUAL INS CO	MI	1,096.8
SENTRY INS A MUTUAL CO	WI	6,922.0
TOKIO MARINE AMERICA INS CO	NY	1,387.9
Rating: A-		
ALLSTATE INS CO	IL	44,425.2
BITCO GENERAL INS CORP	IL	796.8
BROTHERHOOD MUTUAL INS CO	IN	443.2
CINCINNATI INDEMNITY CO	OH	115.5
COUNTRY MUTUAL INS CO	IL	4,306.5
ESSENT GUARANTY INC	PA	767.9
FEDERATED MUTUAL INS CO	MN	4,726.6
GEICO CHOICE INS CO	NE	388.0
GEICO SECURE INSURANCE CO	NE	338.5
GREAT WEST CASUALTY CO	NE	1,829.1
ICI MUTUAL INS CO RRG	VT	330.9
JEWELERS MUTUAL INS CO	WI	329.0
KENTUCKY FARM BUREAU MUTUAL INS CO	KY	2,214.4
MOTORISTS MUTUAL INS CO	OH	1,354.2
NATIONAL MORTGAGE INS CORP	WI	264.6
OLD REPUBLIC GENERAL INS CORP	IL	1,829.0
OLD REPUBLIC INS CO	PA	2,580.9
PROTECTIVE INS CO	IN	776.3
TRAVELERS CASUALTY & SURETY CO	CT	16,487.0
Rating: B+		
ACA FINANCIAL GUARANTY CORP	MD	374.0
ALL AMERICA INS CO	OH	256.6
ALTERRA REINS USA INC	CT	1,467.0
AMICA MUTUAL INS CO	RI	5,054.3
CENTRAL STATES INDEMNITY CO OF OMAHA	NE	427.1
CENTURION CASUALTY CO	IA	140.4
COUNTRY CASUALTY INS CO	IL	78.1
EXECUTIVE RISK INDEMNITY INC	DE	3,025.1
FARM FAMILY CASUALTY INS CO	NY	1,067.1
FEDERAL INS CO	IN	32,714.5
FIRST COLONIAL INS CO	FL	355.0
GEICO GENERAL INS CO	MD	215.7
GEICO INDEMNITY CO	MD	6,922.7
GNY CUSTOM INS CO	AZ	55.8
GOVERNMENT EMPLOYEES INS CO	MD	22,729.4
HARTFORD UNDERWRITERS INS CO	CT	1,566.0
HOLYOKE MUTUAL INS CO IN SALEM	MA	224.3
MAINE EMPLOYERS MUTUAL INS CO	ME	813.8
MITSUI SUMITOMO INS CO OF AMER	NY	883.6
NATIONAL CASUALTY CO	WI	273.8

INSURANCE COMPANY NAME	DOM. STATE	TOTAL ASSETS ($MIL)
NATIONWIDE MUTUAL FIRE INS CO	OH	5,632.7
PACIFIC INDEMNITY CO	WI	6,857.3
SENTRY CASUALTY CO	WI	264.9
SENTRY SELECT INS CO	WI	676.5
STATE FARM MUTUAL AUTOMOBILE INS CO	IL	137,646.1
TOA-RE INS CO OF AMERICA	DE	1,812.3
USAA GENERAL INDEMNITY CO	TX	2,785.3

Delaware

INSURANCE COMPANY NAME	DOM. STATE	TOTAL ASSETS ($MIL)
Rating: A+		
BERKSHIRE HATHAWAY ASR CORP	NY	2,246.2
DAIRYLAND INS CO	WI	1,212.4
MUNICIPAL ASR CORP	NY	1,528.4
QUEEN CITY ASR INC	VT	2,149.3
UNITED SERVICES AUTOMOBILE ASN	TX	30,759.0
USAA CASUALTY INS CO	TX	8,886.5
Rating: A		
CHURCH MUTUAL INS CO	WI	1,452.0
CINCINNATI INS CO	OH	10,791.2
FRANKENMUTH MUTUAL INS CO	MI	1,096.8
SENTRY INS A MUTUAL CO	WI	6,922.0
TOKIO MARINE AMERICA INS CO	NY	1,387.9
Rating: A-		
ALLSTATE INS CO	IL	44,425.2
BITCO GENERAL INS CORP	IL	796.8
BITCO NATIONAL INS CO	IL	468.3
BROTHERHOOD MUTUAL INS CO	IN	443.2
CINCINNATI INDEMNITY CO	OH	115.5
COUNTRY MUTUAL INS CO	IL	4,306.5
ESSENT GUARANTY INC	PA	767.9
FEDERATED MUTUAL INS CO	MN	4,726.6
GEICO CHOICE INS CO	NE	388.0
GEICO SECURE INSURANCE CO	NE	338.5
GREAT WEST CASUALTY CO	NE	1,829.1
JEWELERS MUTUAL INS CO	WI	329.0
NATIONAL MORTGAGE INS CORP	WI	264.6
OLD REPUBLIC GENERAL INS CORP	IL	1,829.0
OLD REPUBLIC INS CO	PA	2,580.9
PROTECTIVE INS CO	IN	776.3
TRAVELERS CASUALTY & SURETY CO	CT	16,487.0
Rating: B+		
ACA FINANCIAL GUARANTY CORP	MD	374.0
ALTERRA REINS USA INC	CT	1,467.0
AMICA MUTUAL INS CO	RI	5,054.3
CENTRAL STATES INDEMNITY CO OF OMAHA	NE	427.1
CENTURION CASUALTY CO	IA	140.4
COUNTRY CASUALTY INS CO	IL	78.1
EXECUTIVE RISK INDEMNITY INC	DE	3,025.1
FARM FAMILY CASUALTY INS CO	NY	1,067.1
FEDERAL INS CO	IN	32,714.5
FIRST COLONIAL INS CO	FL	355.0
GEICO GENERAL INS CO	MD	215.7
GEICO INDEMNITY CO	MD	6,922.7
GNY CUSTOM INS CO	AZ	55.8
GOVERNMENT EMPLOYEES INS CO	MD	22,729.4
HARTFORD UNDERWRITERS INS CO	CT	1,566.0
MAINE EMPLOYERS MUTUAL INS CO	ME	813.8
MITSUI SUMITOMO INS CO OF AMER	NY	883.6
NATIONAL CASUALTY CO	WI	273.8
NATIONWIDE MUTUAL FIRE INS CO	OH	5,632.7
PACIFIC INDEMNITY CO	WI	6,857.3
SENTRY CASUALTY CO	WI	264.9
SENTRY SELECT INS CO	WI	676.5

INSURANCE COMPANY NAME	DOM. STATE	TOTAL ASSETS ($MIL)
STATE FARM MUTUAL AUTOMOBILE INS CO	IL	137,646.1
TOA-RE INS CO OF AMERICA	DE	1,812.3
USAA GENERAL INDEMNITY CO	TX	2,785.3
WESTFIELD NATIONAL INS CO	OH	593.0

District Of Columbia

INSURANCE COMPANY NAME	DOM. STATE	TOTAL ASSETS ($MIL)
Rating: A+		
BERKSHIRE HATHAWAY ASR CORP	NY	2,246.2
MUNICIPAL ASR CORP	NY	1,528.4
QUEEN CITY ASR INC	VT	2,149.3
UNITED SERVICES AUTOMOBILE ASN	TX	30,759.0
USAA CASUALTY INS CO	TX	8,886.5
Rating: A		
CHURCH MUTUAL INS CO	WI	1,452.0
CINCINNATI INS CO	OH	10,791.2
SENTRY INS A MUTUAL CO	WI	6,922.0
TOKIO MARINE AMERICA INS CO	NY	1,387.9
Rating: A-		
ALLSTATE INS CO	IL	44,425.2
BITCO GENERAL INS CORP	IL	796.8
BITCO NATIONAL INS CO	IL	468.3
BROTHERHOOD MUTUAL INS CO	IN	443.2
CINCINNATI INDEMNITY CO	OH	115.5
ESSENT GUARANTY INC	PA	767.9
FEDERATED MUTUAL INS CO	MN	4,726.6
GEICO CHOICE INS CO	NE	388.0
GEICO SECURE INSURANCE CO	NE	338.5
GREAT WEST CASUALTY CO	NE	1,829.1
ICI MUTUAL INS CO RRG	VT	330.9
JEWELERS MUTUAL INS CO	WI	329.0
NATIONAL MORTGAGE INS CORP	WI	264.6
OLD REPUBLIC GENERAL INS CORP	IL	1,829.0
OLD REPUBLIC INS CO	PA	2,580.9
PROTECTIVE INS CO	IN	776.3
TRAVELERS CASUALTY & SURETY CO	CT	16,487.0
Rating: B+		
ACA FINANCIAL GUARANTY CORP	MD	374.0
ALTERRA REINS USA INC	CT	1,467.0
AMICA MUTUAL INS CO	RI	5,054.3
BUILDERS MUTUAL INS CO	NC	625.9
CENTRAL STATES INDEMNITY CO OF OMAHA	NE	427.1
EXECUTIVE RISK INDEMNITY INC	DE	3,025.1
FEDERAL INS CO	IN	32,714.5
FIRST COLONIAL INS CO	FL	355.0
GEICO GENERAL INS CO	MD	215.7
GEICO INDEMNITY CO	MD	6,922.7
GNY CUSTOM INS CO	AZ	55.8
GOVERNMENT EMPLOYEES INS CO	MD	22,729.4
HARTFORD UNDERWRITERS INS CO	CT	1,566.0
MITSUI SUMITOMO INS CO OF AMER	NY	883.6
NATIONAL CASUALTY CO	WI	273.8
NATIONWIDE MUTUAL FIRE INS CO	OH	5,632.7
OLD REPUBLIC SURETY CO	WI	110.0
PACIFIC INDEMNITY CO	WI	6,857.3
SENTRY CASUALTY CO	WI	264.9
SENTRY SELECT INS CO	WI	676.5
STATE FARM MUTUAL AUTOMOBILE INS CO	IL	137,646.1
TOA-RE INS CO OF AMERICA	DE	1,812.3
USAA GENERAL INDEMNITY CO	TX	2,785.3
WESTFIELD NATIONAL INS CO	OH	593.0

Florida

INSURANCE COMPANY NAME	DOM. STATE	TOTAL ASSETS ($MIL)
Rating:	**A+**	
BERKSHIRE HATHAWAY ASR CORP	NY	2,246.2
CITIZENS PROPERTY INS CORP	FL	14,582.0
DAIRYLAND INS CO	WI	1,212.4
INTERINS EXCH OF THE AUTOMOBILE CLUB	CA	8,447.5
MUNICIPAL ASR CORP	NY	1,528.4
OWNERS INS CO	OH	3,686.6
QUEEN CITY ASR INC	VT	2,149.3
UNITED SERVICES AUTOMOBILE ASN	TX	30,759.0
USAA CASUALTY INS CO	TX	8,886.5
Rating:	**A**	
AUTO-OWNERS INS CO	MI	11,867.2
CHURCH MUTUAL INS CO	WI	1,452.0
CINCINNATI INS CO	OH	10,791.2
FRANKENMUTH MUTUAL INS CO	MI	1,096.8
SENTRY INS A MUTUAL CO	WI	6,922.0
SOUTHERN-OWNERS INS CO	MI	618.1
TOKIO MARINE AMERICA INS CO	NY	1,387.9
Rating:	**A-**	
ALLSTATE INS CO	IL	44,425.2
BITCO GENERAL INS CORP	IL	796.8
BITCO NATIONAL INS CO	IL	468.3
BROTHERHOOD MUTUAL INS CO	IN	443.2
CINCINNATI INDEMNITY CO	OH	115.5
COUNTRY MUTUAL INS CO	IL	4,306.5
ESSENT GUARANTY INC	PA	767.9
FEDERATED MUTUAL INS CO	MN	4,726.6
GEICO CHOICE INS CO	NE	388.0
GEICO SECURE INSURANCE CO	NE	338.5
GREAT WEST CASUALTY CO	NE	1,829.1
ICI MUTUAL INS CO RRG	VT	330.9
JEWELERS MUTUAL INS CO	WI	329.0
NATIONAL MORTGAGE INS CORP	WI	264.6
OLD REPUBLIC GENERAL INS CORP	IL	1,829.0
OLD REPUBLIC INS CO	PA	2,580.9
PROTECTIVE INS CO	IN	776.3
RETAILFIRST INS CO	FL	282.1
TRAVELERS CASUALTY & SURETY CO	CT	16,487.0
Rating:	**B+**	
ACA FINANCIAL GUARANTY CORP	MD	374.0
ALTERRA REINS USA INC	CT	1,467.0
AMICA MUTUAL INS CO	RI	5,054.3
BUILDERS MUTUAL INS CO	NC	625.9
CENTRAL STATES INDEMNITY CO OF OMAHA	NE	427.1
CENTURION CASUALTY CO	IA	140.4
EXECUTIVE RISK INDEMNITY INC	DE	3,025.1
FEDERAL INS CO	IN	32,714.5
FIRST COLONIAL INS CO	FL	355.0
GEICO GENERAL INS CO	MD	215.7
GEICO INDEMNITY CO	MD	6,922.7
GOVERNMENT EMPLOYEES INS CO	MD	22,729.4
HARTFORD UNDERWRITERS INS CO	CT	1,566.0
MERCURY CASUALTY CO	CA	1,993.8
MITSUI SUMITOMO INS CO OF AMER	NY	883.6

INSURANCE COMPANY NAME	DOM. STATE	TOTAL ASSETS ($MIL)
NATIONAL CASUALTY CO	WI	273.8
NATIONWIDE MUTUAL FIRE INS CO	OH	5,632.7
OLD REPUBLIC SURETY CO	WI	110.0
PACIFIC INDEMNITY CO	WI	6,857.3
SENTRY CASUALTY CO	WI	264.9
SENTRY SELECT INS CO	WI	676.5
STATE FARM MUTUAL AUTOMOBILE INS CO	IL	137,646.1
TOA-RE INS CO OF AMERICA	DE	1,812.3
USAA GENERAL INDEMNITY CO	TX	2,785.3
WESTFIELD NATIONAL INS CO	OH	593.0

Georgia

INSURANCE COMPANY NAME	DOM. STATE	TOTAL ASSETS ($MIL)
Rating: A+		
BERKSHIRE HATHAWAY ASR CORP	NY	2,246.2
DAIRYLAND INS CO	WI	1,212.4
MUNICIPAL ASR CORP	NY	1,528.4
OWNERS INS CO	OH	3,686.6
QUEEN CITY ASR INC	VT	2,149.3
STATE VOLUNTEER MUTUAL INS CO	TN	1,206.0
UNITED SERVICES AUTOMOBILE ASN	TX	30,759.0
USAA CASUALTY INS CO	TX	8,886.5
Rating: A		
AUTO-OWNERS INS CO	MI	11,867.2
CHURCH MUTUAL INS CO	WI	1,452.0
CINCINNATI INS CO	OH	10,791.2
FRANKENMUTH MUTUAL INS CO	MI	1,096.8
PROPERTY-OWNERS INS CO	IN	217.0
SENTRY INS A MUTUAL CO	WI	6,922.0
TOKIO MARINE AMERICA INS CO	NY	1,387.9
Rating: A-		
ALLSTATE INS CO	IL	44,425.2
BITCO GENERAL INS CORP	IL	796.8
BITCO NATIONAL INS CO	IL	468.3
BROTHERHOOD MUTUAL INS CO	IN	443.2
CINCINNATI INDEMNITY CO	OH	115.5
COUNTRY MUTUAL INS CO	IL	4,306.5
ESSENT GUARANTY INC	PA	767.9
FEDERATED MUTUAL INS CO	MN	4,726.6
GEICO CHOICE INS CO	NE	388.0
GEICO SECURE INSURANCE CO	NE	338.5
GREAT WEST CASUALTY CO	NE	1,829.1
HOME-OWNERS INS CO	MI	2,165.7
ICI MUTUAL INS CO RRG	VT	330.9
JEWELERS MUTUAL INS CO	WI	329.0
NATIONAL MORTGAGE INS CORP	WI	264.6
OLD REPUBLIC GENERAL INS CORP	IL	1,829.0
OLD REPUBLIC INS CO	PA	2,580.9
PROTECTIVE INS CO	IN	776.3
TRAVELERS CASUALTY & SURETY CO	CT	16,487.0
Rating: B+		
ACA FINANCIAL GUARANTY CORP	MD	374.0
ALFA INS CORP	AL	99.4
ALFA MUTUAL GENERAL INS CO	AL	100.9
ALL AMERICA INS CO	OH	256.6
ALTERRA REINS USA INC	CT	1,467.0
AMICA MUTUAL INS CO	RI	5,054.3
BUILDERS MUTUAL INS CO	NC	625.9
CENTRAL STATES INDEMNITY CO OF OMAHA	NE	427.1
COUNTRY CASUALTY INS CO	IL	78.1
EXECUTIVE RISK INDEMNITY INC	DE	3,025.1
FEDERAL INS CO	IN	32,714.5
FIRST COLONIAL INS CO	FL	355.0
GEICO GENERAL INS CO	MD	215.7
GEICO INDEMNITY CO	MD	6,922.7
GOVERNMENT EMPLOYEES INS CO	MD	22,729.4
GRANGE MUTUAL CAS CO	OH	2,088.9

INSURANCE COMPANY NAME	DOM. STATE	TOTAL ASSETS ($MIL)
HARTFORD UNDERWRITERS INS CO	CT	1,566.0
HOLYOKE MUTUAL INS CO IN SALEM	MA	224.3
MERCURY CASUALTY CO	CA	1,993.8
MITSUI SUMITOMO INS CO OF AMER	NY	883.6
NATIONAL CASUALTY CO	WI	273.8
NATIONWIDE MUTUAL FIRE INS CO	OH	5,632.7
OLD REPUBLIC SURETY CO	WI	110.0
PACIFIC INDEMNITY CO	WI	6,857.3
SENTRY CASUALTY CO	WI	264.9
SENTRY SELECT INS CO	WI	676.5
STATE FARM MUTUAL AUTOMOBILE INS CO	IL	137,646.1
TOA-RE INS CO OF AMERICA	DE	1,812.3
TRUSTGARD INS CO	OH	102.3
USAA GENERAL INDEMNITY CO	TX	2,785.3
WESTFIELD NATIONAL INS CO	OH	593.0

Hawaii

INSURANCE COMPANY NAME	DOM. STATE	TOTAL ASSETS ($MIL)
Rating:	**A+**	
BERKSHIRE HATHAWAY ASR CORP	NY	2,246.2
INTERINS EXCH OF THE AUTOMOBILE CLUB	CA	8,447.5
MUNICIPAL ASR CORP	NY	1,528.4
QUEEN CITY ASR INC	VT	2,149.3
UNITED SERVICES AUTOMOBILE ASN	TX	30,759.0
USAA CASUALTY INS CO	TX	8,886.5
Rating:	**A**	
CHURCH MUTUAL INS CO	WI	1,452.0
CINCINNATI INS CO	OH	10,791.2
SENTRY INS A MUTUAL CO	WI	6,922.0
TOKIO MARINE AMERICA INS CO	NY	1,387.0
Rating:	**A-**	
ALLSTATE INS CO	IL	44,425.2
BROTHERHOOD MUTUAL INS CO	IN	443.2
CINCINNATI INDEMNITY CO	OH	115.5
ESSENT GUARANTY INC	PA	767.9
GEICO CHOICE INS CO	NE	388.0
GEICO SECURE INSURANCE CO	NE	338.5
JEWELERS MUTUAL INS CO	WI	329.0
NATIONAL MORTGAGE INS CORP	WI	264.6
OLD REPUBLIC GENERAL INS CORP	IL	1,829.0
OLD REPUBLIC INS CO	PA	2,580.9
PROTECTIVE INS CO	IN	776.3
TRAVELERS CASUALTY & SURETY CO	CT	16,487.0
Rating:	**B+**	
ACA FINANCIAL GUARANTY CORP	MD	374.0
ALTERRA REINS USA INC	CT	1,467.0
CENTRAL STATES INDEMNITY CO OF OMAHA	NE	427.1
CENTURION CASUALTY CO	IA	140.4
EXECUTIVE RISK INDEMNITY INC	DE	3,025.1
FEDERAL INS CO	IN	32,714.5
FIRST COLONIAL INS CO	FL	355.0
GEICO GENERAL INS CO	MD	215.7
GEICO INDEMNITY CO	MD	6,922.7
GOVERNMENT EMPLOYEES INS CO	MD	22,729.4
HARTFORD UNDERWRITERS INS CO	CT	1,566.0
MITSUI SUMITOMO INS CO OF AMER	NY	883.6
NATIONAL CASUALTY CO	WI	273.8
NATIONWIDE MUTUAL FIRE INS CO	OH	5,632.7
PACIFIC INDEMNITY CO	WI	6,857.3
SENTRY CASUALTY CO	WI	264.9
SENTRY SELECT INS CO	WI	676.5
STATE FARM MUTUAL AUTOMOBILE INS CO	IL	137,646.1
TOA-RE INS CO OF AMERICA	DE	1,812.3
USAA GENERAL INDEMNITY CO	TX	2,785.3

Idaho

INSURANCE COMPANY NAME	DOM. STATE	TOTAL ASSETS ($MIL)
Rating: A+		
BERKSHIRE HATHAWAY ASR CORP	NY	2,246.2
DAIRYLAND INS CO	WI	1,212.4
MUNICIPAL ASR CORP	NY	1,528.4
OWNERS INS CO	OH	3,686.6
QUEEN CITY ASR INC	VT	2,149.3
UNITED SERVICES AUTOMOBILE ASN	TX	30,759.0
USAA CASUALTY INS CO	TX	8,886.5
Rating: A		
AUTO-OWNERS INS CO	MI	11,867.2
CHURCH MUTUAL INS CO	WI	1,452.0
CINCINNATI INS CO	OH	10,791.2
FRANKENMUTH MUTUAL INS CO	MI	1,096.8
SENTRY INS A MUTUAL CO	WI	6,922.0
TOKIO MARINE AMERICA INS CO	NY	1,387.9
Rating: A-		
ALLSTATE INS CO	IL	44,425.2
BITCO GENERAL INS CORP	IL	796.8
BITCO NATIONAL INS CO	IL	468.3
BROTHERHOOD MUTUAL INS CO	IN	443.2
CINCINNATI INDEMNITY CO	OH	115.5
COPIC INS CO	CO	548.6
COUNTRY MUTUAL INS CO	IL	4,306.5
ESSENT GUARANTY INC	PA	767.9
FARM BUREAU PROP & CAS INS CO	IA	2,012.0
FEDERATED MUTUAL INS CO	MN	4,726.6
GEICO CHOICE INS CO	NE	388.0
GEICO SECURE INSURANCE CO	NE	338.5
GREAT WEST CASUALTY CO	NE	1,829.1
JEWELERS MUTUAL INS CO	WI	329.0
MMIC INS INC	MN	701.8
NATIONAL MORTGAGE INS CORP	WI	264.6
OLD REPUBLIC GENERAL INS CORP	IL	1,829.0
OLD REPUBLIC INS CO	PA	2,580.9
PROTECTIVE INS CO	IN	776.3
TRAVELERS CASUALTY & SURETY CO	CT	16,487.0
Rating: B+		
ACA FINANCIAL GUARANTY CORP	MD	374.0
ALTERRA REINS USA INC	CT	1,467.0
AMERICAN FAMILY MUT INS CO	WI	14,543.2
AMERICAN STANDARD INS CO OF WI	WI	415.8
AMICA MUTUAL INS CO	RI	5,054.3
CENTRAL STATES INDEMNITY CO OF OMAHA	NE	427.1
CENTURION CASUALTY CO	IA	140.4
COUNTRY CASUALTY INS CO	IL	78.1
EXECUTIVE RISK INDEMNITY INC	DE	3,025.1
FARM BUREAU MUTUAL INS CO OF ID	ID	431.4
FEDERAL INS CO	IN	32,714.5
FIRST COLONIAL INS CO	FL	355.0
GEICO GENERAL INS CO	MD	215.7
GEICO INDEMNITY CO	MD	6,922.7
GOVERNMENT EMPLOYEES INS CO	MD	22,729.4
HARTFORD UNDERWRITERS INS CO	CT	1,566.0
HOLYOKE MUTUAL INS CO IN SALEM	MA	224.3

INSURANCE COMPANY NAME	DOM. STATE	TOTAL ASSETS ($MIL)
MITSUI SUMITOMO INS CO OF AMER	NY	883.6
NATIONAL CASUALTY CO	WI	273.8
NATIONWIDE MUTUAL FIRE INS CO	OH	5,632.7
OLD REPUBLIC SURETY CO	WI	110.0
PACIFIC INDEMNITY CO	WI	6,857.3
SENTRY CASUALTY CO	WI	264.9
SENTRY SELECT INS CO	WI	676.5
STATE FARM MUTUAL AUTOMOBILE INS CO	IL	137,646.1
TOA-RE INS CO OF AMERICA	DE	1,812.3
USAA GENERAL INDEMNITY CO	TX	2,785.3
WESTERN AGRICULTURAL INS CO	IA	178.2
WESTERN COMMUNITY INS CO	ID	36.2
WESTFIELD NATIONAL INS CO	OH	593.0

Illinois

INSURANCE COMPANY NAME	DOM. STATE	TOTAL ASSETS ($MIL)
Rating:	**A+**	
BERKSHIRE HATHAWAY ASR CORP	NY	2,246.2
DAIRYLAND INS CO	WI	1,212.4
MUNICIPAL ASR CORP	NY	1,528.4
OGLESBY REINSURANCE CO	IL	3,196.5
OWNERS INS CO	OH	3,686.6
QUEEN CITY ASR INC	VT	2,149.3
UNITED SERVICES AUTOMOBILE ASN	TX	30,759.0
USAA CASUALTY INS CO	TX	8,886.5
Rating:	**A**	
AUTO-OWNERS INS CO	MI	11,867.2
CHURCH MUTUAL INS CO	WI	1,452.0
CINCINNATI INS CO	OH	10,791.2
FRANKENMUTH MUTUAL INS CO	MI	1,096.8
PROPERTY-OWNERS INS CO	IN	217.0
SENTRY INS A MUTUAL CO	WI	6,922.0
TOKIO MARINE AMERICA INS CO	NY	1,387.9
Rating:	**A-**	
ALLSTATE INS CO	IL	44,425.2
BITCO GENERAL INS CORP	IL	796.8
BITCO NATIONAL INS CO	IL	468.3
BROTHERHOOD MUTUAL INS CO	IN	443.2
CINCINNATI INDEMNITY CO	OH	115.5
COUNTRY MUTUAL INS CO	IL	4,306.5
ESSENT GUARANTY INC	PA	767.9
FEDERATED MUTUAL INS CO	MN	4,726.6
GEICO CHOICE INS CO	NE	388.0
GEICO SECURE INSURANCE CO	NE	338.5
GREAT WEST CASUALTY CO	NE	1,829.1
HASTINGS MUTUAL INS CO	MI	777.9
HOME-OWNERS INS CO	MI	2,165.7
ICI MUTUAL INS CO RRG	VT	330.9
JEWELERS MUTUAL INS CO	WI	329.0
KENTUCKY FARM BUREAU MUTUAL INS CO	KY	2,214.4
MMIC INS INC	MN	701.8
MOTORISTS MUTUAL INS CO	OH	1,354.2
NATIONAL MORTGAGE INS CORP	WI	264.6
OLD REPUBLIC GENERAL INS CORP	IL	1,829.0
OLD REPUBLIC INS CO	PA	2,580.9
PROTECTIVE INS CO	IN	776.3
TRAVELERS CASUALTY & SURETY CO	CT	16,487.0
WEST BEND MUTUAL INS CO	WI	2,162.6
Rating:	**B+**	
ACA FINANCIAL GUARANTY CORP	MD	374.0
ALL AMERICA INS CO	OH	256.6
ALTERRA REINS USA INC	CT	1,467.0
AMERICAN FAMILY MUT INS CO	WI	14,543.2
AMERICAN STANDARD INS CO OF WI	WI	415.8
AMICA MUTUAL INS CO	RI	5,054.3
CENTRAL STATES INDEMNITY CO OF OMAHA	NE	427.1
CENTURION CASUALTY CO	IA	140.4
COUNTRY CASUALTY INS CO	IL	78.1
EXECUTIVE RISK INDEMNITY INC	DE	3,025.1
FARMERS AUTOMOBILE INS ASN	IL	1,172.9

INSURANCE COMPANY NAME	DOM. STATE	TOTAL ASSETS ($MIL)
FEDERAL INS CO	IN	32,714.5
FIRST COLONIAL INS CO	FL	355.0
GEICO GENERAL INS CO	MD	215.7
GEICO INDEMNITY CO	MD	6,922.7
GNY CUSTOM INS CO	AZ	55.8
GOVERNMENT EMPLOYEES INS CO	MD	22,729.4
GRANGE MUTUAL CAS CO	OH	2,088.9
HARTFORD UNDERWRITERS INS CO	CT	1,566.0
HOLYOKE MUTUAL INS CO IN SALEM	MA	224.3
MAINE EMPLOYERS MUTUAL INS CO	ME	813.8
MERCURY CASUALTY CO	CA	1,993.8
MITSUI SUMITOMO INS CO OF AMER	NY	883.6
NATIONAL CASUALTY CO	WI	273.8
NATIONWIDE MUTUAL FIRE INS CO	OH	5,632.7
OLD REPUBLIC SURETY CO	WI	110.0
PACIFIC INDEMNITY CO	WI	6,857.3
PEKIN INS CO	IL	286.1
SENTRY CASUALTY CO	WI	264.9
SENTRY SELECT INS CO	WI	676.5
STATE FARM MUTUAL AUTOMOBILE INS CO	IL	137,646.1
TOA-RE INS CO OF AMERICA	DE	1,812.3
TRUSTGARD INS CO	OH	102.3
USAA GENERAL INDEMNITY CO	TX	2,785.3
WESTERN AGRICULTURAL INS CO	IA	178.2
WESTFIELD NATIONAL INS CO	OH	593.0

Indiana

INSURANCE COMPANY NAME	DOM. STATE	TOTAL ASSETS ($MIL)
Rating: A+		
BERKSHIRE HATHAWAY ASR CORP	NY	2,246.2
DAIRYLAND INS CO	WI	1,212.4
MUNICIPAL ASR CORP	NY	1,528.4
OWNERS INS CO	OH	3,686.6
QUEEN CITY ASR INC	VT	2,149.3
STATE VOLUNTEER MUTUAL INS CO	TN	1,206.0
UNITED SERVICES AUTOMOBILE ASN	TX	30,759.0
USAA CASUALTY INS CO	TX	8,886.5
Rating: A		
AUTO-OWNERS INS CO	MI	11,867.2
CHURCH MUTUAL INS CO	WI	1,452.0
CINCINNATI INS CO	OH	10,791.2
FRANKENMUTH MUTUAL INS CO	MI	1,096.8
PIONEER STATE MUTUAL INS CO	MI	464.9
PROPERTY-OWNERS INS CO	IN	217.0
SENTRY INS A MUTUAL CO	WI	6,922.0
TOKIO MARINE AMERICA INS CO	NY	1,387.9
Rating: A-		
ALLSTATE INS CO	IL	44,425.2
BITCO GENERAL INS CORP	IL	796.8
BITCO NATIONAL INS CO	IL	468.3
BROTHERHOOD MUTUAL INS CO	IN	443.2
CINCINNATI INDEMNITY CO	OH	115.5
COUNTRY MUTUAL INS CO	IL	4,306.5
CSAA INS EXCHANGE	CA	6,956.8
ESSENT GUARANTY INC	PA	767.9
FEDERATED MUTUAL INS CO	MN	4,726.6
GEICO CHOICE INS CO	NE	388.0
GEICO SECURE INSURANCE CO	NE	338.5
GREAT WEST CASUALTY CO	NE	1,829.1
HASTINGS MUTUAL INS CO	MI	777.9
HOME-OWNERS INS CO	MI	2,165.7
JEWELERS MUTUAL INS CO	WI	329.0
MMIC INS INC	MN	701.8
MOTORISTS MUTUAL INS CO	OH	1,354.2
NATIONAL MORTGAGE INS CORP	WI	264.6
OLD REPUBLIC GENERAL INS CORP	IL	1,829.0
OLD REPUBLIC INS CO	PA	2,580.9
PROTECTIVE INS CO	IN	776.3
TRAVELERS CASUALTY & SURETY CO	CT	16,487.0
WEST BEND MUTUAL INS CO	WI	2,162.6
Rating: B+		
ACA FINANCIAL GUARANTY CORP	MD	374.0
ALL AMERICA INS CO	OH	256.6
ALTERRA REINS USA INC	CT	1,467.0
AMERICAN FAMILY MUT INS CO	WI	14,543.2
AMERICAN STANDARD INS CO OF WI	WI	415.8
AMICA MUTUAL INS CO	RI	5,054.3
CENTRAL STATES INDEMNITY CO OF OMAHA	NE	427.1
CENTURION CASUALTY CO	IA	140.4
COUNTRY CASUALTY INS CO	IL	78.1
EXECUTIVE RISK INDEMNITY INC	DE	3,025.1
FARMERS AUTOMOBILE INS ASN	IL	1,172.9

INSURANCE COMPANY NAME	DOM. STATE	TOTAL ASSETS ($MIL)
FEDERAL INS CO	IN	32,714.5
FIRST COLONIAL INS CO	FL	355.0
GEICO GENERAL INS CO	MD	215.7
GEICO INDEMNITY CO	MD	6,922.7
GNY CUSTOM INS CO	AZ	55.8
GOVERNMENT EMPLOYEES INS CO	MD	22,729.4
GRANGE MUTUAL CAS CO	OH	2,088.9
HARTFORD UNDERWRITERS INS CO	CT	1,566.0
INDIANA FARMERS MUTUAL INS CO	IN	351.6
MITSUI SUMITOMO INS CO OF AMER	NY	883.6
NATIONAL CASUALTY CO	WI	273.8
NATIONWIDE MUTUAL FIRE INS CO	OH	5,632.7
OLD REPUBLIC SURETY CO	WI	110.0
PACIFIC INDEMNITY CO	WI	6,857.3
PEKIN INS CO	IL	286.1
SENTRY CASUALTY CO	WI	264.9
SENTRY SELECT INS CO	WI	676.5
STATE FARM MUTUAL AUTOMOBILE INS CO	IL	137,646.1
TOA-RE INS CO OF AMERICA	DE	1,812.3
TRUSTGARD INS CO	OH	102.3
USAA GENERAL INDEMNITY CO	TX	2,785.3
WESTERN AGRICULTURAL INS CO	IA	178.2
WESTFIELD NATIONAL INS CO	OH	593.0

Iowa

INSURANCE COMPANY NAME	DOM. STATE	TOTAL ASSETS ($MIL)
Rating: A+		
BERKSHIRE HATHAWAY ASR CORP	NY	2,246.2
DAIRYLAND INS CO	WI	1,212.4
MUNICIPAL ASR CORP	NY	1,528.4
OWNERS INS CO	OH	3,686.6
QUEEN CITY ASR INC	VT	2,149.3
UNITED SERVICES AUTOMOBILE ASN	TX	30,759.0
USAA CASUALTY INS CO	TX	8,886.5
Rating: A		
AUTO-OWNERS INS CO	MI	11,867.2
CHURCH MUTUAL INS CO	WI	1,452.0
CINCINNATI INS CO	OH	10,791.2
FRANKENMUTH MUTUAL INS CO	MI	1,096.8
PROPERTY-OWNERS INS CO	IN	217.0
SENTRY INS A MUTUAL CO	WI	6,922.0
TOKIO MARINE AMERICA INS CO	NY	1,387.9
Rating: A-		
ALLSTATE INS CO	IL	44,425.2
BITCO GENERAL INS CORP	IL	796.8
BITCO NATIONAL INS CO	IL	468.3
BROTHERHOOD MUTUAL INS CO	IN	443.2
CINCINNATI INDEMNITY CO	OH	115.5
COPIC INS CO	CO	548.6
COUNTRY MUTUAL INS CO	IL	4,306.5
ESSENT GUARANTY INC	PA	767.9
FARM BUREAU PROP & CAS INS CO	IA	2,012.0
FEDERATED MUTUAL INS CO	MN	4,726.6
GEICO CHOICE INS CO	NE	388.0
GEICO SECURE INSURANCE CO	NE	338.5
GREAT WEST CASUALTY CO	NE	1,829.1
HASTINGS MUTUAL INS CO	MI	777.9
HOME-OWNERS INS CO	MI	2,165.7
ICI MUTUAL INS CO RRG	VT	330.9
JEWELERS MUTUAL INS CO	WI	329.0
KENTUCKY FARM BUREAU MUTUAL INS CO	KY	2,214.4
MMIC INS INC	MN	701.8
MOTORISTS MUTUAL INS CO	OH	1,354.2
NATIONAL MORTGAGE INS CORP	WI	264.6
OLD REPUBLIC GENERAL INS CORP	IL	1,829.0
OLD REPUBLIC INS CO	PA	2,580.9
PROTECTIVE INS CO	IN	776.3
TRAVELERS CASUALTY & SURETY CO	CT	16,487.0
WEST BEND MUTUAL INS CO	WI	2,162.6
Rating: B+		
ACA FINANCIAL GUARANTY CORP	MD	374.0
ALL AMERICA INS CO	OH	256.6
ALTERRA REINS USA INC	CT	1,467.0
AMERICAN FAMILY MUT INS CO	WI	14,543.2
AMERICAN STANDARD INS CO OF WI	WI	415.8
AMICA MUTUAL INS CO	RI	5,054.3
CENTRAL STATES INDEMNITY CO OF OMAHA	NE	427.1
CENTURION CASUALTY CO	IA	140.4
COUNTRY CASUALTY INS CO	IL	78.1
EXECUTIVE RISK INDEMNITY INC	DE	3,025.1

INSURANCE COMPANY NAME	DOM. STATE	TOTAL ASSETS ($MIL)
FARMERS AUTOMOBILE INS ASN	IL	1,172.9
FEDERAL INS CO	IN	32,714.5
FIRST COLONIAL INS CO	FL	355.0
GEICO GENERAL INS CO	MD	215.7
GEICO INDEMNITY CO	MD	6,922.7
GOVERNMENT EMPLOYEES INS CO	MD	22,729.4
GRANGE MUTUAL CAS CO	OH	2,088.9
HARTFORD UNDERWRITERS INS CO	CT	1,566.0
MITSUI SUMITOMO INS CO OF AMER	NY	883.6
NATIONAL CASUALTY CO	WI	273.8
NATIONWIDE MUTUAL FIRE INS CO	OH	5,632.7
OLD REPUBLIC SURETY CO	WI	110.0
PACIFIC INDEMNITY CO	WI	6,857.3
PEKIN INS CO	IL	286.1
SENTRY CASUALTY CO	WI	264.9
SENTRY SELECT INS CO	WI	676.5
STATE FARM MUTUAL AUTOMOBILE INS CO	IL	137,646.1
TOA-RE INS CO OF AMERICA	DE	1,812.3
TRUSTGARD INS CO	OH	102.3
USAA GENERAL INDEMNITY CO	TX	2,785.3
WESTERN AGRICULTURAL INS CO	IA	178.2
WESTFIELD NATIONAL INS CO	OH	593.0

Kansas

INSURANCE COMPANY NAME	DOM. STATE	TOTAL ASSETS ($MIL)
Rating: A+		
BERKSHIRE HATHAWAY ASR CORP	NY	2,246.2
DAIRYLAND INS CO	WI	1,212.4
MUNICIPAL ASR CORP	NY	1,528.4
OWNERS INS CO	OH	3,686.6
QUEEN CITY ASR INC	VT	2,149.3
UNITED SERVICES AUTOMOBILE ASN	TX	30,759.0
USAA CASUALTY INS CO	TX	8,886.5
Rating: A		
AUTO-OWNERS INS CO	MI	11,867.2
CHURCH MUTUAL INS CO	WI	1,452.0
CINCINNATI INS CO	OH	10,791.2
FRANKENMUTH MUTUAL INS CO	MI	1,096.8
SENTRY INS A MUTUAL CO	WI	6,922.0
TOKIO MARINE AMERICA INS CO	NY	1,387.9
Rating: A-		
ALLSTATE INS CO	IL	44,425.2
BITCO GENERAL INS CORP	IL	796.8
BITCO NATIONAL INS CO	IL	468.3
BROTHERHOOD MUTUAL INS CO	IN	443.2
CINCINNATI INDEMNITY CO	OH	115.5
COPIC INS CO	CO	548.6
COUNTRY MUTUAL INS CO	IL	4,306.5
ESSENT GUARANTY INC	PA	767.9
FARM BUREAU PROP & CAS INS CO	IA	2,012.0
FEDERATED MUTUAL INS CO	MN	4,726.6
GEICO CHOICE INS CO	NE	388.0
GEICO SECURE INSURANCE CO	NE	338.5
GREAT WEST CASUALTY CO	NE	1,829.1
ICI MUTUAL INS CO RRG	VT	330.9
JEWELERS MUTUAL INS CO	WI	329.0
MMIC INS INC	MN	701.8
NATIONAL MORTGAGE INS CORP	WI	264.6
OLD REPUBLIC GENERAL INS CORP	IL	1,829.0
OLD REPUBLIC INS CO	PA	2,580.9
PROTECTIVE INS CO	IN	776.3
TRAVELERS CASUALTY & SURETY CO	CT	16,487.0
WEST BEND MUTUAL INS CO	WI	2,162.6
Rating: B+		
ACA FINANCIAL GUARANTY CORP	MD	374.0
ALTERRA REINS USA INC	CT	1,467.0
AMERICAN FAMILY MUT INS CO	WI	14,543.2
AMERICAN STANDARD INS CO OF WI	WI	415.8
AMICA MUTUAL INS CO	RI	5,054.3
CENTRAL STATES INDEMNITY CO OF OMAHA	NE	427.1
CENTURION CASUALTY CO	IA	140.4
COUNTRY CASUALTY INS CO	IL	78.1
EXECUTIVE RISK INDEMNITY INC	DE	3,025.1
FEDERAL INS CO	IN	32,714.5
FIRST COLONIAL INS CO	FL	355.0
GEICO GENERAL INS CO	MD	215.7
GEICO INDEMNITY CO	MD	6,922.7
GOVERNMENT EMPLOYEES INS CO	MD	22,729.4
GRANGE MUTUAL CAS CO	OH	2,088.9

INSURANCE COMPANY NAME	DOM. STATE	TOTAL ASSETS ($MIL)
HARTFORD UNDERWRITERS INS CO	CT	1,566.0
MITSUI SUMITOMO INS CO OF AMER	NY	883.6
NATIONAL CASUALTY CO	WI	273.8
NATIONWIDE MUTUAL FIRE INS CO	OH	5,632.7
OLD REPUBLIC SURETY CO	WI	110.0
PACIFIC INDEMNITY CO	WI	6,857.3
SENTRY CASUALTY CO	WI	264.9
SENTRY SELECT INS CO	WI	676.5
STATE FARM MUTUAL AUTOMOBILE INS CO	IL	137,646.1
TOA-RE INS CO OF AMERICA	DE	1,812.3
TRUSTGARD INS CO	OH	102.3
USAA GENERAL INDEMNITY CO	TX	2,785.3
WESTERN AGRICULTURAL INS CO	IA	178.2
WESTFIELD NATIONAL INS CO	OH	593.0

Kentucky

INSURANCE COMPANY NAME	DOM. STATE	TOTAL ASSETS ($MIL)
Rating:	**A+**	
BERKSHIRE HATHAWAY ASR CORP	NY	2,246.2
DAIRYLAND INS CO	WI	1,212.4
MUNICIPAL ASR CORP	NY	1,528.4
OWNERS INS CO	OH	3,686.6
QUEEN CITY ASR INC	VT	2,149.3
STATE VOLUNTEER MUTUAL INS CO	TN	1,206.0
UNITED SERVICES AUTOMOBILE ASN	TX	30,759.0
USAA CASUALTY INS CO	TX	8,886.5
Rating:	**A**	
AUTO-OWNERS INS CO	MI	11,867.2
CHURCH MUTUAL INS CO	WI	1,452.0
CINCINNATI INS CO	OH	10,791.2
FRANKENMUTH MUTUAL INS CO	MI	1,096.8
PROPERTY-OWNERS INS CO	IN	217.0
SENTRY INS A MUTUAL CO	WI	6,922.0
TOKIO MARINE AMERICA INS CO	NY	1,387.9
Rating:	**A-**	
ALLSTATE INS CO	IL	44,425.2
BITCO GENERAL INS CORP	IL	796.8
BITCO NATIONAL INS CO	IL	468.3
BROTHERHOOD MUTUAL INS CO	IN	443.2
CINCINNATI INDEMNITY CO	OH	115.5
COUNTRY MUTUAL INS CO	IL	4,306.5
ESSENT GUARANTY INC	PA	767.9
FEDERATED MUTUAL INS CO	MN	4,726.6
GEICO CHOICE INS CO	NE	388.0
GEICO SECURE INSURANCE CO	NE	338.5
GREAT WEST CASUALTY CO	NE	1,829.1
HASTINGS MUTUAL INS CO	MI	777.9
HOME-OWNERS INS CO	MI	2,165.7
JEWELERS MUTUAL INS CO	WI	329.0
KENTUCKY FARM BUREAU MUTUAL INS CO	KY	2,214.4
MMIC INS INC	MN	701.8
MOTORISTS MUTUAL INS CO	OH	1,354.2
NATIONAL MORTGAGE INS CORP	WI	264.6
OLD REPUBLIC GENERAL INS CORP	IL	1,829.0
OLD REPUBLIC INS CO	PA	2,580.9
PROTECTIVE INS CO	IN	776.3
TRAVELERS CASUALTY & SURETY CO	CT	16,487.0
WEST BEND MUTUAL INS CO	WI	2,162.6
Rating:	**B+**	
ACA FINANCIAL GUARANTY CORP	MD	374.0
ALL AMERICA INS CO	OH	256.6
ALTERRA REINS USA INC	CT	1,467.0
AMICA MUTUAL INS CO	RI	5,054.3
CENTRAL STATES INDEMNITY CO OF OMAHA	NE	427.1
CENTURION CASUALTY CO	IA	140.4
COUNTRY CASUALTY INS CO	IL	78.1
EXECUTIVE RISK INDEMNITY INC	DE	3,025.1
FEDERAL INS CO	IN	32,714.5
FIRST COLONIAL INS CO	FL	355.0
GEICO GENERAL INS CO	MD	215.7
GEICO INDEMNITY CO	MD	6,922.7

INSURANCE COMPANY NAME	DOM. STATE	TOTAL ASSETS ($MIL)
GOVERNMENT EMPLOYEES INS CO	MD	22,729.4
GRANGE MUTUAL CAS CO	OH	2,088.9
HARTFORD UNDERWRITERS INS CO	CT	1,566.0
MITSUI SUMITOMO INS CO OF AMER	NY	883.6
NATIONAL CASUALTY CO	WI	273.8
NATIONWIDE MUTUAL FIRE INS CO	OH	5,632.7
PACIFIC INDEMNITY CO	WI	6,857.3
SENTRY CASUALTY CO	WI	264.9
SENTRY SELECT INS CO	WI	676.5
STATE FARM MUTUAL AUTOMOBILE INS CO	IL	137,646.1
TOA-RE INS CO OF AMERICA	DE	1,812.3
TRUSTGARD INS CO	OH	102.3
USAA GENERAL INDEMNITY CO	TX	2,785.3
WESTFIELD NATIONAL INS CO	OH	593.0

Louisiana

INSURANCE COMPANY NAME	DOM. STATE	TOTAL ASSETS ($MIL)
Rating: A+		
BERKSHIRE HATHAWAY ASR CORP	NY	2,246.2
MUNICIPAL ASR CORP	NY	1,528.4
QUEEN CITY ASR INC	VT	2,149.3
UNITED SERVICES AUTOMOBILE ASN	TX	30,759.0
USAA CASUALTY INS CO	TX	8,886.5
Rating: A		
CHURCH MUTUAL INS CO	WI	1,452.0
CINCINNATI INS CO	OH	10,791.2
FRANKENMUTH MUTUAL INS CO	MI	1,096.8
SENTRY INS A MUTUAL CO	WI	6,922.0
TOKIO MARINE AMERICA INS CO	NY	1,387.9
Rating: A-		
ALLSTATE INS CO	IL	44,425.2
BITCO GENERAL INS CORP	IL	796.8
BITCO NATIONAL INS CO	IL	468.3
BROTHERHOOD MUTUAL INS CO	IN	443.2
CINCINNATI INDEMNITY CO	OH	115.5
ESSENT GUARANTY INC	PA	767.9
FEDERATED MUTUAL INS CO	MN	4,726.6
GEICO CHOICE INS CO	NE	388.0
GEICO SECURE INSURANCE CO	NE	338.5
GREAT WEST CASUALTY CO	NE	1,829.1
JEWELERS MUTUAL INS CO	WI	329.0
LOUISIANA WORKERS COMPENSATION CORP	LA	1,576.2
NATIONAL MORTGAGE INS CORP	WI	264.6
OLD REPUBLIC GENERAL INS CORP	IL	1,829.0
OLD REPUBLIC INS CO	PA	2,580.9
PROTECTIVE INS CO	IN	776.3
TRAVELERS CASUALTY & SURETY CO	CT	16,487.0
Rating: B+		
ACA FINANCIAL GUARANTY CORP	MD	374.0
ALTERRA REINS USA INC	CT	1,467.0
AMICA MUTUAL INS CO	RI	5,054.3
CENTRAL STATES INDEMNITY CO OF OMAHA	NE	427.1
CENTURION CASUALTY CO	IA	140.4
EXECUTIVE RISK INDEMNITY INC	DE	3,025.1
FEDERAL INS CO	IN	32,714.5
FIRST COLONIAL INS CO	FL	355.0
GEICO GENERAL INS CO	MD	215.7
GEICO INDEMNITY CO	MD	6,922.7
GOVERNMENT EMPLOYEES INS CO	MD	22,729.4
HARTFORD UNDERWRITERS INS CO	CT	1,566.0
MITSUI SUMITOMO INS CO OF AMER	NY	883.6
NATIONAL CASUALTY CO	WI	273.8
NATIONWIDE MUTUAL FIRE INS CO	OH	5,632.7
PACIFIC INDEMNITY CO	WI	6,857.3
SENTRY CASUALTY CO	WI	264.9
SENTRY SELECT INS CO	WI	676.5
STATE FARM MUTUAL AUTOMOBILE INS CO	IL	137,646.1
TOA-RE INS CO OF AMERICA	DE	1,812.3
USAA GENERAL INDEMNITY CO	TX	2,785.3

Maine

INSURANCE COMPANY NAME	DOM. STATE	TOTAL ASSETS ($MIL)
STATE FARM MUTUAL AUTOMOBILE INS CO	IL	137,646.1
TOA-RE INS CO OF AMERICA	DE	1,812.3
USAA GENERAL INDEMNITY CO	TX	2,785.3

Rating: A+

INSURANCE COMPANY NAME	DOM. STATE	TOTAL ASSETS ($MIL)
BERKSHIRE HATHAWAY ASR CORP	NY	2,246.2
DAIRYLAND INS CO	WI	1,212.4
INTERINS EXCH OF THE AUTOMOBILE CLUB	CA	8,447.5
MUNICIPAL ASR CORP	NY	1,528.4
QUEEN CITY ASR INC	VT	2,149.3
UNITED SERVICES AUTOMOBILE ASN	TX	30,759.0
USAA CASUALTY INS CO	TX	8,886.5

Rating: A

INSURANCE COMPANY NAME	DOM. STATE	TOTAL ASSETS ($MIL)
CHURCH MUTUAL INS CO	WI	1,452.0
CINCINNATI INS CO	OH	10,791.2
FRANKENMUTH MUTUAL INS CO	MI	1,096.8
SENTRY INS A MUTUAL CO	WI	6,922.0
TOKIO MARINE AMERICA INS CO	NY	1,387.9

Rating: A-

INSURANCE COMPANY NAME	DOM. STATE	TOTAL ASSETS ($MIL)
ALLSTATE INS CO	IL	44,425.2
BITCO GENERAL INS CORP	IL	796.8
BROTHERHOOD MUTUAL INS CO	IN	443.2
CINCINNATI INDEMNITY CO	OH	115.5
COUNTRY MUTUAL INS CO	IL	4,306.5
ESSENT GUARANTY INC	PA	767.9
FEDERATED MUTUAL INS CO	MN	4,726.6
GEICO CHOICE INS CO	NE	388.0
GEICO SECURE INSURANCE CO	NE	338.5
GREAT WEST CASUALTY CO	NE	1,829.1
JEWELERS MUTUAL INS CO	WI	329.0
NATIONAL MORTGAGE INS CORP	WI	264.6
OLD REPUBLIC GENERAL INS CORP	IL	1,829.0
OLD REPUBLIC INS CO	PA	2,580.9
PROTECTIVE INS CO	IN	776.3
TRAVELERS CASUALTY & SURETY CO	CT	16,487.0

Rating: B+

INSURANCE COMPANY NAME	DOM. STATE	TOTAL ASSETS ($MIL)
ACA FINANCIAL GUARANTY CORP	MD	374.0
ALTERRA REINS USA INC	CT	1,467.0
AMICA MUTUAL INS CO	RI	5,054.3
CENTRAL STATES INDEMNITY CO OF OMAHA	NE	427.1
CENTURION CASUALTY CO	IA	140.4
COUNTRY CASUALTY INS CO	IL	78.1
EXECUTIVE RISK INDEMNITY INC	DE	3,025.1
FARM FAMILY CASUALTY INS CO	NY	1,067.1
FEDERAL INS CO	IN	32,714.5
FIRST COLONIAL INS CO	FL	355.0
GEICO GENERAL INS CO	MD	215.7
GEICO INDEMNITY CO	MD	6,922.7
GOVERNMENT EMPLOYEES INS CO	MD	22,729.4
HARTFORD UNDERWRITERS INS CO	CT	1,566.0
HOLYOKE MUTUAL INS CO IN SALEM	MA	224.3
MAINE EMPLOYERS MUTUAL INS CO	ME	813.8
MITSUI SUMITOMO INS CO OF AMER	NY	883.6
NATIONAL CASUALTY CO	WI	273.8
NATIONWIDE MUTUAL FIRE INS CO	OH	5,632.7
PACIFIC INDEMNITY CO	WI	6,857.3
SENTRY CASUALTY CO	WI	264.9
SENTRY SELECT INS CO	WI	676.5

Maryland

INSURANCE COMPANY NAME	DOM. STATE	TOTAL ASSETS ($MIL)
Rating: A+		
BERKSHIRE HATHAWAY ASR CORP	NY	2,246.2
DAIRYLAND INS CO	WI	1,212.4
MUNICIPAL ASR CORP	NY	1,528.4
QUEEN CITY ASR INC	VT	2,149.3
UNITED SERVICES AUTOMOBILE ASN	TX	30,759.0
USAA CASUALTY INS CO	TX	8,886.5
Rating: A		
CHURCH MUTUAL INS CO	WI	1,452.0
CINCINNATI INS CO	OH	10,791.2
FRANKENMUTH MUTUAL INS CO	MI	1,096.8
SENTRY INS A MUTUAL CO	WI	6,922.0
TOKIO MARINE AMERICA INS CO	NY	1,387.9
Rating: A-		
ALLSTATE INS CO	IL	44,425.2
BITCO GENERAL INS CORP	IL	796.8
BITCO NATIONAL INS CO	IL	468.3
BROTHERHOOD MUTUAL INS CO	IN	443.2
CINCINNATI INDEMNITY CO	OH	115.5
ESSENT GUARANTY INC	PA	767.9
FEDERATED MUTUAL INS CO	MN	4,726.6
GEICO CHOICE INS CO	NE	388.0
GEICO SECURE INSURANCE CO	NE	338.5
GREAT WEST CASUALTY CO	NE	1,829.1
ICI MUTUAL INS CO RRG	VT	330.9
JEWELERS MUTUAL INS CO	WI	329.0
NATIONAL MORTGAGE INS CORP	WI	264.6
OLD REPUBLIC GENERAL INS CORP	IL	1,829.0
OLD REPUBLIC INS CO	PA	2,580.9
PROTECTIVE INS CO	IN	776.3
TRAVELERS CASUALTY & SURETY CO	CT	16,487.0
Rating: B+		
ACA FINANCIAL GUARANTY CORP	MD	374.0
ALTERRA REINS USA INC	CT	1,467.0
AMICA MUTUAL INS CO	RI	5,054.3
BUILDERS MUTUAL INS CO	NC	625.9
CENTRAL STATES INDEMNITY CO OF OMAHA	NE	427.1
CENTURION CASUALTY CO	IA	140.4
COUNTRY CASUALTY INS CO	IL	78.1
EXECUTIVE RISK INDEMNITY INC	DE	3,025.1
FARM FAMILY CASUALTY INS CO	NY	1,067.1
FEDERAL INS CO	IN	32,714.5
FIRST COLONIAL INS CO	FL	355.0
GEICO GENERAL INS CO	MD	215.7
GEICO INDEMNITY CO	MD	6,922.7
GNY CUSTOM INS CO	AZ	55.8
GOVERNMENT EMPLOYEES INS CO	MD	22,729.4
HARTFORD UNDERWRITERS INS CO	CT	1,566.0
MAINE EMPLOYERS MUTUAL INS CO	ME	813.8
MITSUI SUMITOMO INS CO OF AMER	NY	883.6
NATIONAL CASUALTY CO	WI	273.8
NATIONWIDE MUTUAL FIRE INS CO	OH	5,632.7
OLD REPUBLIC SURETY CO	WI	110.0
PACIFIC INDEMNITY CO	WI	6,857.3

INSURANCE COMPANY NAME	DOM. STATE	TOTAL ASSETS ($MIL)
SENTRY CASUALTY CO	WI	264.9
SENTRY SELECT INS CO	WI	676.5
STATE FARM MUTUAL AUTOMOBILE INS CO	IL	137,646.1
TOA-RE INS CO OF AMERICA	DE	1,812.3
USAA GENERAL INDEMNITY CO	TX	2,785.3
WESTFIELD NATIONAL INS CO	OH	593.0

Massachusetts

INSURANCE COMPANY NAME	DOM. STATE	TOTAL ASSETS ($MIL)	INSURANCE COMPANY NAME	DOM. STATE	TOTAL ASSETS ($MIL)
Rating: A+			NATIONWIDE MUTUAL FIRE INS CO	OH	5,632.7
BERKSHIRE HATHAWAY ASR CORP	NY	2,246.2	PACIFIC INDEMNITY CO	WI	6,857.3
DAIRYLAND INS CO	WI	1,212.4	SAFETY INS CO	MA	1,429.1
MUNICIPAL ASR CORP	NY	1,528.4	SENTRY CASUALTY CO	WI	264.9
QUEEN CITY ASR INC	VT	2,149.3	SENTRY SELECT INS CO	WI	676.5
UNITED SERVICES AUTOMOBILE ASN	TX	30,759.0	STATE FARM MUTUAL AUTOMOBILE INS CO	IL	137,646.1
USAA CASUALTY INS CO	TX	8,886.5	TOA-RE INS CO OF AMERICA	DE	1,812.3
Rating: A			USAA GENERAL INDEMNITY CO	TX	2,785.3
CHURCH MUTUAL INS CO	WI	1,452.0			
CINCINNATI INS CO	OH	10,791.2			
FRANKENMUTH MUTUAL INS CO	MI	1,096.8			
SENTRY INS A MUTUAL CO	WI	6,922.0			
TOKIO MARINE AMERICA INS CO	NY	1,387.9			
Rating: A-					
ALLSTATE INS CO	IL	44,425.2			
BITCO GENERAL INS CORP	IL	796.8			
BITCO NATIONAL INS CO	IL	468.3			
BROTHERHOOD MUTUAL INS CO	IN	443.2			
CINCINNATI INDEMNITY CO	OH	115.5			
COUNTRY MUTUAL INS CO	IL	4,306.5			
ESSENT GUARANTY INC	PA	767.9			
FEDERATED MUTUAL INS CO	MN	4,726.6			
GEICO CHOICE INS CO	NE	388.0			
GEICO SECURE INSURANCE CO	NE	338.5			
GREAT WEST CASUALTY CO	NE	1,829.1			
ICI MUTUAL INS CO RRG	VT	330.9			
JEWELERS MUTUAL INS CO	WI	329.0			
MOTORISTS MUTUAL INS CO	OH	1,354.2			
NATIONAL MORTGAGE INS CORP	WI	264.6			
OLD REPUBLIC GENERAL INS CORP	IL	1,829.0			
OLD REPUBLIC INS CO	PA	2,580.9			
PROTECTIVE INS CO	IN	776.3			
TRAVELERS CASUALTY & SURETY CO	CT	16,487.0			
Rating: B+					
ACA FINANCIAL GUARANTY CORP	MD	374.0			
ALL AMERICA INS CO	OH	256.6			
ALTERRA REINS USA INC	CT	1,467.0			
AMICA MUTUAL INS CO	RI	5,054.3			
CENTRAL STATES INDEMNITY CO OF OMAHA	NE	427.1			
CENTURION CASUALTY CO	IA	140.4			
COUNTRY CASUALTY INS CO	IL	78.1			
EXECUTIVE RISK INDEMNITY INC	DE	3,025.1			
FARM FAMILY CASUALTY INS CO	NY	1,067.1			
FEDERAL INS CO	IN	32,714.5			
FIRST COLONIAL INS CO	FL	355.0			
GEICO GENERAL INS CO	MD	215.7			
GEICO INDEMNITY CO	MD	6,922.7			
GNY CUSTOM INS CO	AZ	55.8			
GOVERNMENT EMPLOYEES INS CO	MD	22,729.4			
HARTFORD UNDERWRITERS INS CO	CT	1,566.0			
HOLYOKE MUTUAL INS CO IN SALEM	MA	224.3			
MAINE EMPLOYERS MUTUAL INS CO	ME	813.8			
MITSUI SUMITOMO INS CO OF AMER	NY	883.6			
NATIONAL CASUALTY CO	WI	273.8			

Michigan

INSURANCE COMPANY NAME	DOM. STATE	TOTAL ASSETS ($MIL)
Rating: A+		
BERKSHIRE HATHAWAY ASR CORP	NY	2,246.2
DAIRYLAND INS CO	WI	1,212.4
INTERINS EXCH OF THE AUTOMOBILE CLUB	CA	8,447.5
MUNICIPAL ASR CORP	NY	1,528.4
OWNERS INS CO	OH	3,686.6
QUEEN CITY ASR INC	VT	2,149.3
UNITED SERVICES AUTOMOBILE ASN	TX	30,759.0
USAA CASUALTY INS CO	TX	8,886.5
Rating: A		
AUTO-OWNERS INS CO	MI	11,867.2
CHURCH MUTUAL INS CO	WI	1,452.0
CINCINNATI INS CO	OH	10,791.2
FRANKENMUTH MUTUAL INS CO	MI	1,096.8
PIONEER STATE MUTUAL INS CO	MI	464.9
PROPERTY-OWNERS INS CO	IN	217.0
SENTRY INS A MUTUAL CO	WI	6,922.0
SOUTHERN-OWNERS INS CO	MI	618.1
TOKIO MARINE AMERICA INS CO	NY	1,387.9
Rating: A-		
ALLSTATE INS CO	IL	44,425.2
BITCO GENERAL INS CORP	IL	796.8
BITCO NATIONAL INS CO	IL	468.3
BROTHERHOOD MUTUAL INS CO	IN	443.2
CINCINNATI INDEMNITY CO	OH	115.5
COUNTRY MUTUAL INS CO	IL	4,306.5
ESSENT GUARANTY INC	PA	767.9
FEDERATED MUTUAL INS CO	MN	4,726.6
GEICO CHOICE INS CO	NE	388.0
GEICO SECURE INSURANCE CO	NE	338.5
GREAT WEST CASUALTY CO	NE	1,829.1
HASTINGS MUTUAL INS CO	MI	777.9
HOME-OWNERS INS CO	MI	2,165.7
ICI MUTUAL INS CO RRG	VT	330.9
JEWELERS MUTUAL INS CO	WI	329.0
KENTUCKY FARM BUREAU MUTUAL INS CO	KY	2,214.4
MMIC INS INC	MN	701.8
MOTORISTS MUTUAL INS CO	OH	1,354.2
NATIONAL MORTGAGE INS CORP	WI	264.6
OLD REPUBLIC GENERAL INS CORP	IL	1,829.0
OLD REPUBLIC INS CO	PA	2,580.9
PROTECTIVE INS CO	IN	776.3
TRAVELERS CASUALTY & SURETY CO	CT	16,487.0
WEST BEND MUTUAL INS CO	WI	2,162.6
Rating: B+		
ACA FINANCIAL GUARANTY CORP	MD	374.0
ALL AMERICA INS CO	OH	256.6
ALTERRA REINS USA INC	CT	1,467.0
AMICA MUTUAL INS CO	RI	5,054.3
CENTRAL STATES INDEMNITY CO OF OMAHA	NE	427.1
COUNTRY CASUALTY INS CO	IL	78.1
EXECUTIVE RISK INDEMNITY INC	DE	3,025.1
FARMERS AUTOMOBILE INS ASN	IL	1,172.9
FEDERAL INS CO	IN	32,714.5

INSURANCE COMPANY NAME	DOM. STATE	TOTAL ASSETS ($MIL)
FIRST COLONIAL INS CO	FL	355.0
GEICO GENERAL INS CO	MD	215.7
GEICO INDEMNITY CO	MD	6,922.7
GNY CUSTOM INS CO	AZ	55.8
GOVERNMENT EMPLOYEES INS CO	MD	22,729.4
HARTFORD UNDERWRITERS INS CO	CT	1,566.0
MERCURY CASUALTY CO	CA	1,993.8
MITSUI SUMITOMO INS CO OF AMER	NY	883.6
NATIONAL CASUALTY CO	WI	273.8
NATIONWIDE MUTUAL FIRE INS CO	OH	5,632.7
PACIFIC INDEMNITY CO	WI	6,857.3
PEKIN INS CO	IL	286.1
SENTRY CASUALTY CO	WI	264.9
SENTRY SELECT INS CO	WI	676.5
STATE FARM MUTUAL AUTOMOBILE INS CO	IL	137,646.1
TOA-RE INS CO OF AMERICA	DE	1,812.3
USAA GENERAL INDEMNITY CO	TX	2,785.3
WESTERN AGRICULTURAL INS CO	IA	178.2
WESTFIELD NATIONAL INS CO	OH	593.0

Minnesota

INSURANCE COMPANY NAME	DOM. STATE	TOTAL ASSETS ($MIL)
Rating:	**A+**	
BERKSHIRE HATHAWAY ASR CORP	NY	2,246.2
DAIRYLAND INS CO	WI	1,212.4
MUNICIPAL ASR CORP	NY	1,528.4
OWNERS INS CO	OH	3,686.6
QUEEN CITY ASR INC	VT	2,149.3
UNITED SERVICES AUTOMOBILE ASN	TX	30,759.0
USAA CASUALTY INS CO	TX	8,886.5
Rating:	**A**	
AUTO-OWNERS INS CO	MI	11,867.2
CHURCH MUTUAL INS CO	WI	1,452.0
CINCINNATI INS CO	OH	10,791.2
FRANKENMUTH MUTUAL INS CO	MI	1,096.8
SENTRY INS A MUTUAL CO	WI	6,922.0
TOKIO MARINE AMERICA INS CO	NY	1,387.9
Rating:	**A-**	
ALLSTATE INS CO	IL	44,425.2
BITCO GENERAL INS CORP	IL	796.8
BITCO NATIONAL INS CO	IL	468.3
BROTHERHOOD MUTUAL INS CO	IN	443.2
CINCINNATI INDEMNITY CO	OH	115.5
COUNTRY MUTUAL INS CO	IL	4,306.5
ESSENT GUARANTY INC	PA	767.9
FARM BUREAU PROP & CAS INS CO	IA	2,012.0
FEDERATED MUTUAL INS CO	MN	4,726.6
GEICO CHOICE INS CO	NE	388.0
GEICO SECURE INSURANCE CO	NE	338.5
GREAT WEST CASUALTY CO	NE	1,829.1
ICI MUTUAL INS CO RRG	VT	330.9
JEWELERS MUTUAL INS CO	WI	329.0
MMIC INS INC	MN	701.8
NATIONAL MORTGAGE INS CORP	WI	264.6
OLD REPUBLIC GENERAL INS CORP	IL	1,829.0
OLD REPUBLIC INS CO	PA	2,580.9
PROTECTIVE INS CO	IN	776.3
TRAVELERS CASUALTY & SURETY CO	CT	16,487.0
WEST BEND MUTUAL INS CO	WI	2,162.6
Rating:	**B+**	
ACA FINANCIAL GUARANTY CORP	MD	374.0
ALTERRA REINS USA INC	CT	1,467.0
AMERICAN FAMILY MUT INS CO	WI	14,543.2
AMERICAN STANDARD INS CO OF WI	WI	415.8
AMICA MUTUAL INS CO	RI	5,054.3
CENTRAL STATES INDEMNITY CO OF OMAHA	NE	427.1
CENTURION CASUALTY CO	IA	140.4
COUNTRY CASUALTY INS CO	IL	78.1
EXECUTIVE RISK INDEMNITY INC	DE	3,025.1
FEDERAL INS CO	IN	32,714.5
FIRST COLONIAL INS CO	FL	355.0
GEICO GENERAL INS CO	MD	215.7
GEICO INDEMNITY CO	MD	6,922.7
GOVERNMENT EMPLOYEES INS CO	MD	22,729.4
GRANGE MUTUAL CAS CO	OH	2,088.9
HARTFORD UNDERWRITERS INS CO	CT	1,566.0

INSURANCE COMPANY NAME	DOM. STATE	TOTAL ASSETS ($MIL)
HOLYOKE MUTUAL INS CO IN SALEM	MA	224.3
MITSUI SUMITOMO INS CO OF AMER	NY	883.6
NATIONAL CASUALTY CO	WI	273.8
NATIONWIDE MUTUAL FIRE INS CO	OH	5,632.7
OLD REPUBLIC SURETY CO	WI	110.0
PACIFIC INDEMNITY CO	WI	6,857.3
SENTRY CASUALTY CO	WI	264.9
SENTRY SELECT INS CO	WI	676.5
STATE FARM MUTUAL AUTOMOBILE INS CO	IL	137,646.1
TOA-RE INS CO OF AMERICA	DE	1,812.3
TRUSTGARD INS CO	OH	102.3
USAA GENERAL INDEMNITY CO	TX	2,785.3
WESTERN AGRICULTURAL INS CO	IA	178.2
WESTFIELD NATIONAL INS CO	OH	593.0

Mississippi

INSURANCE COMPANY NAME	DOM. STATE	TOTAL ASSETS ($MIL)
Rating: A+		
BERKSHIRE HATHAWAY ASR CORP	NY	2,246.2
DAIRYLAND INS CO	WI	1,212.4
MUNICIPAL ASR CORP	NY	1,528.4
OWNERS INS CO	OH	3,686.6
QUEEN CITY ASR INC	VT	2,149.3
STATE VOLUNTEER MUTUAL INS CO	TN	1,206.0
UNITED SERVICES AUTOMOBILE ASN	TX	30,759.0
USAA CASUALTY INS CO	TX	8,886.5
Rating: A		
AUTO-OWNERS INS CO	MI	11,867.2
CHURCH MUTUAL INS CO	WI	1,452.0
CINCINNATI INS CO	OH	10,791.2
FRANKENMUTH MUTUAL INS CO	MI	1,096.8
SENTRY INS A MUTUAL CO	WI	6,922.0
TOKIO MARINE AMERICA INS CO	NY	1,387.9
Rating: A-		
ALLSTATE INS CO	IL	44,425.2
BITCO GENERAL INS CORP	IL	796.8
BITCO NATIONAL INS CO	IL	468.3
BROTHERHOOD MUTUAL INS CO	IN	443.2
CINCINNATI INDEMNITY CO	OH	115.5
ESSENT GUARANTY INC	PA	767.9
FEDERATED MUTUAL INS CO	MN	4,726.6
GEICO CHOICE INS CO	NE	388.0
GEICO SECURE INSURANCE CO	NE	338.5
GREAT WEST CASUALTY CO	NE	1,829.1
JEWELERS MUTUAL INS CO	WI	329.0
NATIONAL MORTGAGE INS CORP	WI	264.6
OLD REPUBLIC GENERAL INS CORP	IL	1,829.0
OLD REPUBLIC INS CO	PA	2,580.9
PROTECTIVE INS CO	IN	776.3
TRAVELERS CASUALTY & SURETY CO	CT	16,487.0
Rating: B+		
ACA FINANCIAL GUARANTY CORP	MD	374.0
ALFA INS CORP	AL	99.4
ALFA MUTUAL GENERAL INS CO	AL	100.9
ALTERRA REINS USA INC	CT	1,467.0
AMICA MUTUAL INS CO	RI	5,054.3
BUILDERS MUTUAL INS CO	NC	625.9
CENTRAL STATES INDEMNITY CO OF OMAHA	NE	427.1
CENTURION CASUALTY CO	IA	140.4
EXECUTIVE RISK INDEMNITY INC	DE	3,025.1
FEDERAL INS CO	IN	32,714.5
FIRST COLONIAL INS CO	FL	355.0
GEICO GENERAL INS CO	MD	215.7
GEICO INDEMNITY CO	MD	6,922.7
GOVERNMENT EMPLOYEES INS CO	MD	22,729.4
HARTFORD UNDERWRITERS INS CO	CT	1,566.0
MITSUI SUMITOMO INS CO OF AMER	NY	883.6
NATIONAL CASUALTY CO	WI	273.8
NATIONWIDE MUTUAL FIRE INS CO	OH	5,632.7
OLD REPUBLIC SURETY CO	WI	110.0
PACIFIC INDEMNITY CO	WI	6,857.3

INSURANCE COMPANY NAME	DOM. STATE	TOTAL ASSETS ($MIL)
SENTRY CASUALTY CO	WI	264.9
SENTRY SELECT INS CO	WI	676.5
STATE FARM MUTUAL AUTOMOBILE INS CO	IL	137,646.1
TOA-RE INS CO OF AMERICA	DE	1,812.3
USAA GENERAL INDEMNITY CO	TX	2,785.3
WESTFIELD NATIONAL INS CO	OH	593.0

Missouri

INSURANCE COMPANY NAME	DOM. STATE	TOTAL ASSETS ($MIL)
Rating:	**A+**	
BERKSHIRE HATHAWAY ASR CORP	NY	2,246.2
DAIRYLAND INS CO	WI	1,212.4
INTERINS EXCH OF THE AUTOMOBILE CLUB	CA	8,447.5
MUNICIPAL ASR CORP	NY	1,528.4
OWNERS INS CO	OH	3,686.6
QUEEN CITY ASR INC	VT	2,149.3
STATE VOLUNTEER MUTUAL INS CO	TN	1,206.0
UNITED SERVICES AUTOMOBILE ASN	TX	30,759.0
USAA CASUALTY INS CO	TX	8,886.5
Rating:	**A**	
AUTO-OWNERS INS CO	MI	11,867.2
CHURCH MUTUAL INS CO	WI	1,452.0
CINCINNATI INS CO	OH	10,791.2
FRANKENMUTH MUTUAL INS CO	MI	1,096.8
PROPERTY-OWNERS INS CO	IN	217.0
SENTRY INS A MUTUAL CO	WI	6,922.0
TOKIO MARINE AMERICA INS CO	NY	1,387.9
Rating:	**A-**	
ALLSTATE INS CO	IL	44,425.2
BITCO GENERAL INS CORP	IL	796.8
BITCO NATIONAL INS CO	IL	468.3
BROTHERHOOD MUTUAL INS CO	IN	443.2
CINCINNATI INDEMNITY CO	OH	115.5
COUNTRY MUTUAL INS CO	IL	4,306.5
ESSENT GUARANTY INC	PA	767.9
FARM BUREAU PROP & CAS INS CO	IA	2,012.0
FEDERATED MUTUAL INS CO	MN	4,726.6
GEICO CHOICE INS CO	NE	388.0
GEICO SECURE INSURANCE CO	NE	338.5
GREAT WEST CASUALTY CO	NE	1,829.1
HOME-OWNERS INS CO	MI	2,165.7
ICI MUTUAL INS CO RRG	VT	330.9
JEWELERS MUTUAL INS CO	WI	329.0
MMIC INS INC	MN	701.8
MOTORISTS MUTUAL INS CO	OH	1,354.2
NATIONAL MORTGAGE INS CORP	WI	264.6
OLD REPUBLIC GENERAL INS CORP	IL	1,829.0
OLD REPUBLIC INS CO	PA	2,580.9
PROTECTIVE INS CO	IN	776.3
TRAVELERS CASUALTY & SURETY CO	CT	16,487.0
WEST BEND MUTUAL INS CO	WI	2,162.6
Rating:	**B+**	
ACA FINANCIAL GUARANTY CORP	MD	374.0
ALTERRA REINS USA INC	CT	1,467.0
AMERICAN FAMILY MUT INS CO	WI	14,543.2
AMERICAN STANDARD INS CO OF WI	WI	415.8
AMICA MUTUAL INS CO	RI	5,054.3
CENTRAL STATES INDEMNITY CO OF OMAHA	NE	427.1
CENTURION CASUALTY CO	IA	140.4
COUNTRY CASUALTY INS CO	IL	78.1
EXECUTIVE RISK INDEMNITY INC	DE	3,025.1
FARM FAMILY CASUALTY INS CO	NY	1,067.1
FEDERAL INS CO	IN	32,714.5

INSURANCE COMPANY NAME	DOM. STATE	TOTAL ASSETS ($MIL)
FIRST COLONIAL INS CO	FL	355.0
GEICO GENERAL INS CO	MD	215.7
GEICO INDEMNITY CO	MD	6,922.7
GOVERNMENT EMPLOYEES INS CO	MD	22,729.4
GRANGE MUTUAL CAS CO	OH	2,088.9
HARTFORD UNDERWRITERS INS CO	CT	1,566.0
HOLYOKE MUTUAL INS CO IN SALEM	MA	224.3
MITSUI SUMITOMO INS CO OF AMER	NY	883.6
NATIONAL CASUALTY CO	WI	273.8
NATIONWIDE MUTUAL FIRE INS CO	OH	5,632.7
OLD REPUBLIC SURETY CO	WI	110.0
PACIFIC INDEMNITY CO	WI	6,857.3
SENTRY CASUALTY CO	WI	264.9
SENTRY SELECT INS CO	WI	676.5
STATE FARM MUTUAL AUTOMOBILE INS CO	IL	137,646.1
TOA-RE INS CO OF AMERICA	DE	1,812.3
TRUSTGARD INS CO	OH	102.3
USAA GENERAL INDEMNITY CO	TX	2,785.3
WESTERN AGRICULTURAL INS CO	IA	178.2
WESTFIELD NATIONAL INS CO	OH	593.0

Montana

INSURANCE COMPANY NAME	DOM. STATE	TOTAL ASSETS ($MIL)
Rating: A+		
BERKSHIRE HATHAWAY ASR CORP	NY	2,246.2
DAIRYLAND INS CO	WI	1,212.4
MUNICIPAL ASR CORP	NY	1,528.4
QUEEN CITY ASR INC	VT	2,149.3
UNITED SERVICES AUTOMOBILE ASN	TX	30,759.0
USAA CASUALTY INS CO	TX	8,886.5
Rating: A		
CHURCH MUTUAL INS CO	WI	1,452.0
CINCINNATI INS CO	OH	10,791.2
FRANKENMUTH MUTUAL INS CO	MI	1,096.8
SENTRY INS A MUTUAL CO	WI	6,922.0
TOKIO MARINE AMERICA INS CO	NY	1,387.9
Rating: A-		
ALLSTATE INS CO	IL	44,425.2
BITCO GENERAL INS CORP	IL	796.8
BITCO NATIONAL INS CO	IL	468.3
BROTHERHOOD MUTUAL INS CO	IN	443.2
CINCINNATI INDEMNITY CO	OH	115.5
COPIC INS CO	CO	548.6
COUNTRY MUTUAL INS CO	IL	4,306.5
ESSENT GUARANTY INC	PA	767.9
FEDERATED MUTUAL INS CO	MN	4,726.6
GEICO CHOICE INS CO	NE	388.0
GEICO SECURE INSURANCE CO	NE	338.5
GREAT WEST CASUALTY CO	NE	1,829.1
JEWELERS MUTUAL INS CO	WI	329.0
MMIC INS INC	MN	701.8
NATIONAL MORTGAGE INS CORP	WI	264.6
OLD REPUBLIC GENERAL INS CORP	IL	1,829.0
OLD REPUBLIC INS CO	PA	2,580.9
PROTECTIVE INS CO	IN	776.3
TRAVELERS CASUALTY & SURETY CO	CT	16,487.0
Rating: B+		
ACA FINANCIAL GUARANTY CORP	MD	374.0
ALTERRA REINS USA INC	CT	1,467.0
AMERICAN FAMILY MUT INS CO	WI	14,543.2
AMERICAN STANDARD INS CO OF WI	WI	415.8
AMICA MUTUAL INS CO	RI	5,054.3
CENTRAL STATES INDEMNITY CO OF OMAHA	NE	427.1
CENTURION CASUALTY CO	IA	140.4
COUNTRY CASUALTY INS CO	IL	78.1
EXECUTIVE RISK INDEMNITY INC	DE	3,025.1
FEDERAL INS CO	IN	32,714.5
FIRST COLONIAL INS CO	FL	355.0
GEICO GENERAL INS CO	MD	215.7
GEICO INDEMNITY CO	MD	6,922.7
GOVERNMENT EMPLOYEES INS CO	MD	22,729.4
HARTFORD UNDERWRITERS INS CO	CT	1,566.0
HOLYOKE MUTUAL INS CO IN SALEM	MA	224.3
MITSUI SUMITOMO INS CO OF AMER	NY	883.6
NATIONAL CASUALTY CO	WI	273.8
NATIONWIDE MUTUAL FIRE INS CO	OH	5,632.7
OLD REPUBLIC SURETY CO	WI	110.0

INSURANCE COMPANY NAME	DOM. STATE	TOTAL ASSETS ($MIL)
PACIFIC INDEMNITY CO	WI	6,857.3
SENTRY CASUALTY CO	WI	264.9
SENTRY SELECT INS CO	WI	676.5
STATE FARM MUTUAL AUTOMOBILE INS CO	IL	137,646.1
TOA-RE INS CO OF AMERICA	DE	1,812.3
USAA GENERAL INDEMNITY CO	TX	2,785.3
WESTERN AGRICULTURAL INS CO	IA	178.2
WESTFIELD NATIONAL INS CO	OH	593.0

Nebraska

INSURANCE COMPANY NAME	DOM. STATE	TOTAL ASSETS ($MIL)
Rating:　A+		
BERKSHIRE HATHAWAY ASR CORP	NY	2,246.2
DAIRYLAND INS CO	WI	1,212.4
MUNICIPAL ASR CORP	NY	1,528.4
OWNERS INS CO	OH	3,686.6
QUEEN CITY ASR INC	VT	2,149.3
UNITED SERVICES AUTOMOBILE ASN	TX	30,759.0
USAA CASUALTY INS CO	TX	8,886.5
Rating:　A		
AUTO-OWNERS INS CO	MI	11,867.2
CHURCH MUTUAL INS CO	WI	1,452.0
CINCINNATI INS CO	OH	10,791.2
FRANKENMUTH MUTUAL INS CO	MI	1,096.8
PROPERTY-OWNERS INS CO	IN	217.0
SENTRY INS A MUTUAL CO	WI	6,922.0
TOKIO MARINE AMERICA INS CO	NY	1,387.9
Rating:　A-		
ALLSTATE INS CO	IL	44,425.2
BITCO GENERAL INS CORP	IL	796.8
BITCO NATIONAL INS CO	IL	468.3
BROTHERHOOD MUTUAL INS CO	IN	443.2
CINCINNATI INDEMNITY CO	OH	115.5
COPIC INS CO	CO	548.6
COUNTRY MUTUAL INS CO	IL	4,306.5
ESSENT GUARANTY INC	PA	767.9
FARM BUREAU PROP & CAS INS CO	IA	2,012.0
FEDERATED MUTUAL INS CO	MN	4,726.6
GEICO CHOICE INS CO	NE	388.0
GEICO SECURE INSURANCE CO	NE	338.5
GREAT WEST CASUALTY CO	NE	1,829.1
HOME-OWNERS INS CO	MI	2,165.7
ICI MUTUAL INS CO RRG	VT	330.9
JEWELERS MUTUAL INS CO	WI	329.0
MMIC INS INC	MN	701.8
NATIONAL MORTGAGE INS CORP	WI	264.6
OLD REPUBLIC GENERAL INS CORP	IL	1,829.0
OLD REPUBLIC INS CO	PA	2,580.9
PROTECTIVE INS CO	IN	776.3
TRAVELERS CASUALTY & SURETY CO	CT	16,487.0
WEST BEND MUTUAL INS CO	WI	2,162.6
Rating:　B+		
ACA FINANCIAL GUARANTY CORP	MD	374.0
ALTERRA REINS USA INC	CT	1,467.0
AMERICAN FAMILY MUT INS CO	WI	14,543.2
AMERICAN STANDARD INS CO OF WI	WI	415.8
AMICA MUTUAL INS CO	RI	5,054.3
CENTRAL STATES INDEMNITY CO OF OMAHA	NE	427.1
CENTURION CASUALTY CO	IA	140.4
COUNTRY CASUALTY INS CO	IL	78.1
EXECUTIVE RISK INDEMNITY INC	DE	3,025.1
FEDERAL INS CO	IN	32,714.5
FIRST COLONIAL INS CO	FL	355.0
GEICO GENERAL INS CO	MD	215.7
GEICO INDEMNITY CO	MD	6,922.7

INSURANCE COMPANY NAME	DOM. STATE	TOTAL ASSETS ($MIL)
GOVERNMENT EMPLOYEES INS CO	MD	22,729.4
HARTFORD UNDERWRITERS INS CO	CT	1,566.0
HOLYOKE MUTUAL INS CO IN SALEM	MA	224.3
MITSUI SUMITOMO INS CO OF AMER	NY	883.6
NATIONAL CASUALTY CO	WI	273.8
NATIONWIDE MUTUAL FIRE INS CO	OH	5,632.7
OLD REPUBLIC SURETY CO	WI	110.0
PACIFIC INDEMNITY CO	WI	6,857.3
SENTRY CASUALTY CO	WI	264.9
SENTRY SELECT INS CO	WI	676.5
STATE FARM MUTUAL AUTOMOBILE INS CO	IL	137,646.1
TOA-RE INS CO OF AMERICA	DE	1,812.3
TRUSTGARD INS CO	OH	102.3
USAA GENERAL INDEMNITY CO	TX	2,785.3
WESTERN AGRICULTURAL INS CO	IA	178.2
WESTFIELD NATIONAL INS CO	OH	593.0

Nevada

INSURANCE COMPANY NAME	DOM. STATE	TOTAL ASSETS ($MIL)
Rating:	**A+**	
BERKSHIRE HATHAWAY ASR CORP	NY	2,246.2
DAIRYLAND INS CO	WI	1,212.4
MUNICIPAL ASR CORP	NY	1,528.4
OWNERS INS CO	OH	3,686.6
QUEEN CITY ASR INC	VT	2,149.3
UNITED SERVICES AUTOMOBILE ASN	TX	30,759.0
USAA CASUALTY INS CO	TX	8,886.5
Rating:	**A**	
AUTO-OWNERS INS CO	MI	11,867.2
CHURCH MUTUAL INS CO	WI	1,452.0
CINCINNATI INS CO	OH	10,791.2
FRANKENMUTH MUTUAL INS CO	MI	1,096.8
MUTUAL INS CO OF AZ	AZ	1,011.0
PROPERTY-OWNERS INS CO	IN	217.0
SENTRY INS A MUTUAL CO	WI	6,922.0
TOKIO MARINE AMERICA INS CO	NY	1,387.9
Rating:	**A-**	
ALLSTATE INS CO	IL	44,425.2
BITCO GENERAL INS CORP	IL	796.8
BITCO NATIONAL INS CO	IL	468.3
BROTHERHOOD MUTUAL INS CO	IN	443.2
CINCINNATI INDEMNITY CO	OH	115.5
COUNTRY MUTUAL INS CO	IL	4,306.5
CSAA INS EXCHANGE	CA	6,956.8
ESSENT GUARANTY INC	PA	767.9
FEDERATED MUTUAL INS CO	MN	4,726.6
GEICO CHOICE INS CO	NE	388.0
GEICO SECURE INSURANCE CO	NE	338.5
GREAT WEST CASUALTY CO	NE	1,829.1
HOME-OWNERS INS CO	MI	2,165.7
JEWELERS MUTUAL INS CO	WI	329.0
NATIONAL MORTGAGE INS CORP	WI	264.6
OLD REPUBLIC GENERAL INS CORP	IL	1,829.0
OLD REPUBLIC INS CO	PA	2,580.9
PROTECTIVE INS CO	IN	776.3
TRAVELERS CASUALTY & SURETY CO	CT	16,487.0
Rating:	**B+**	
ACA FINANCIAL GUARANTY CORP	MD	374.0
ALL AMERICA INS CO	OH	256.6
ALTERRA REINS USA INC	CT	1,467.0
AMERICAN FAMILY MUT INS CO	WI	14,543.2
AMERICAN STANDARD INS CO OF WI	WI	415.8
AMICA MUTUAL INS CO	RI	5,054.3
CENTRAL STATES INDEMNITY CO OF OMAHA	NE	427.1
CENTURION CASUALTY CO	IA	140.4
COUNTRY CASUALTY INS CO	IL	78.1
EXECUTIVE RISK INDEMNITY INC	DE	3,025.1
FEDERAL INS CO	IN	32,714.5
FIRST COLONIAL INS CO	FL	355.0
GEICO GENERAL INS CO	MD	215.7
GEICO INDEMNITY CO	MD	6,922.7
GOVERNMENT EMPLOYEES INS CO	MD	22,729.4
HARTFORD UNDERWRITERS INS CO	CT	1,566.0

INSURANCE COMPANY NAME	DOM. STATE	TOTAL ASSETS ($MIL)
HOLYOKE MUTUAL INS CO IN SALEM	MA	224.3
MERCURY CASUALTY CO	CA	1,993.8
MITSUI SUMITOMO INS CO OF AMER	NY	883.6
NATIONAL CASUALTY CO	WI	273.8
NATIONWIDE MUTUAL FIRE INS CO	OH	5,632.7
OLD REPUBLIC SURETY CO	WI	110.0
PACIFIC INDEMNITY CO	WI	6,857.3
SENTRY CASUALTY CO	WI	264.9
SENTRY SELECT INS CO	WI	676.5
STATE FARM MUTUAL AUTOMOBILE INS CO	IL	137,646.1
TOA-RE INS CO OF AMERICA	DE	1,812.3
USAA GENERAL INDEMNITY CO	TX	2,785.3
WESTERN AGRICULTURAL INS CO	IA	178.2
WESTFIELD NATIONAL INS CO	OH	593.0

New Hampshire

INSURANCE COMPANY NAME	DOM. STATE	TOTAL ASSETS ($MIL)
Rating: A+		
BERKSHIRE HATHAWAY ASR CORP	NY	2,246.2
DAIRYLAND INS CO	WI	1,212.4
INTERINS EXCH OF THE AUTOMOBILE CLUB	CA	8,447.5
MUNICIPAL ASR CORP	NY	1,528.4
QUEEN CITY ASR INC	VT	2,149.3
UNITED SERVICES AUTOMOBILE ASN	TX	30,759.0
USAA CASUALTY INS CO	TX	8,886.5
Rating: A		
CHURCH MUTUAL INS CO	WI	1,452.0
CINCINNATI INS CO	OH	10,791.2
FRANKENMUTH MUTUAL INS CO	MI	1,096.8
SENTRY INS A MUTUAL CO	WI	6,922.0
TOKIO MARINE AMERICA INS CO	NY	1,387.9
Rating: A-		
ALLSTATE INS CO	IL	44,425.2
BROTHERHOOD MUTUAL INS CO	IN	443.2
CINCINNATI INDEMNITY CO	OH	115.5
COUNTRY MUTUAL INS CO	IL	4,306.5
ESSENT GUARANTY INC	PA	767.9
FEDERATED MUTUAL INS CO	MN	4,726.6
GEICO CHOICE INS CO	NE	388.0
GEICO SECURE INSURANCE CO	NE	338.5
GREAT WEST CASUALTY CO	NE	1,829.1
JEWELERS MUTUAL INS CO	WI	329.0
MOTORISTS MUTUAL INS CO	OH	1,354.2
NATIONAL MORTGAGE INS CORP	WI	264.6
OLD REPUBLIC GENERAL INS CORP	IL	1,829.0
OLD REPUBLIC INS CO	PA	2,580.9
PROTECTIVE INS CO	IN	776.3
TRAVELERS CASUALTY & SURETY CO	CT	16,487.0
Rating: B+		
ACA FINANCIAL GUARANTY CORP	MD	374.0
ALTERRA REINS USA INC	CT	1,467.0
AMICA MUTUAL INS CO	RI	5,054.3
CENTRAL STATES INDEMNITY CO OF OMAHA	NE	427.1
EXECUTIVE RISK INDEMNITY INC	DE	3,025.1
FARM FAMILY CASUALTY INS CO	NY	1,067.1
FEDERAL INS CO	IN	32,714.5
FIRST COLONIAL INS CO	FL	355.0
GEICO GENERAL INS CO	MD	215.7
GEICO INDEMNITY CO	MD	6,922.7
GOVERNMENT EMPLOYEES INS CO	MD	22,729.4
HARTFORD UNDERWRITERS INS CO	CT	1,566.0
HOLYOKE MUTUAL INS CO IN SALEM	MA	224.3
MAINE EMPLOYERS MUTUAL INS CO	ME	813.8
MITSUI SUMITOMO INS CO OF AMER	NY	883.6
NATIONAL CASUALTY CO	WI	273.8
NATIONWIDE MUTUAL FIRE INS CO	OH	5,632.7
PACIFIC INDEMNITY CO	WI	6,857.3
SAFETY INS CO	MA	1,429.1
SENTRY CASUALTY CO	WI	264.9
SENTRY SELECT INS CO	WI	676.5
STATE FARM MUTUAL AUTOMOBILE INS CO	IL	137,646.1

INSURANCE COMPANY NAME	DOM. STATE	TOTAL ASSETS ($MIL)
TOA-RE INS CO OF AMERICA	DE	1,812.3
USAA GENERAL INDEMNITY CO	TX	2,785.3

New Jersey

INSURANCE COMPANY NAME	DOM. STATE	TOTAL ASSETS ($MIL)
Rating: A+		
BERKSHIRE HATHAWAY ASR CORP	NY	2,246.2
MUNICIPAL ASR CORP	NY	1,528.4
QUEEN CITY ASR INC	VT	2,149.3
UNITED SERVICES AUTOMOBILE ASN	TX	30,759.0
USAA CASUALTY INS CO	TX	8,886.5
Rating: A		
CHURCH MUTUAL INS CO	WI	1,452.0
CINCINNATI INS CO	OH	10,791.2
FRANKENMUTH MUTUAL INS CO	MI	1,096.8
SENTRY INS A MUTUAL CO	WI	6,922.0
TOKIO MARINE AMERICA INS CO	NY	1,387.9
Rating: A-		
BITCO GENERAL INS CORP	IL	796.8
BITCO NATIONAL INS CO	IL	468.3
BROTHERHOOD MUTUAL INS CO	IN	443.2
CINCINNATI INDEMNITY CO	OH	115.5
ESSENT GUARANTY INC	PA	767.9
FEDERATED MUTUAL INS CO	MN	4,726.6
GEICO CHOICE INS CO	NE	388.0
GEICO SECURE INSURANCE CO	NE	338.5
GREAT WEST CASUALTY CO	NE	1,829.1
ICI MUTUAL INS CO RRG	VT	330.9
JEWELERS MUTUAL INS CO	WI	329.0
NATIONAL MORTGAGE INS CORP	WI	264.6
OLD REPUBLIC GENERAL INS CORP	IL	1,829.0
OLD REPUBLIC INS CO	PA	2,580.9
PROTECTIVE INS CO	IN	776.3
TRAVELERS CASUALTY & SURETY CO	CT	16,487.0
Rating: B+		
ACA FINANCIAL GUARANTY CORP	MD	374.0
ALL AMERICA INS CO	OH	256.6
ALTERRA REINS USA INC	CT	1,467.0
AMICA MUTUAL INS CO	RI	5,054.3
CENTRAL STATES INDEMNITY CO OF OMAHA	NE	427.1
CENTURION CASUALTY CO	IA	140.4
EXECUTIVE RISK INDEMNITY INC	DE	3,025.1
FARM FAMILY CASUALTY INS CO	NY	1,067.1
FEDERAL INS CO	IN	32,714.5
FIRST COLONIAL INS CO	FL	355.0
GEICO GENERAL INS CO	MD	215.7
GEICO INDEMNITY CO	MD	6,922.7
GNY CUSTOM INS CO	AZ	55.8
GOVERNMENT EMPLOYEES INS CO	MD	22,729.4
HARTFORD UNDERWRITERS INS CO	CT	1,566.0
HOLYOKE MUTUAL INS CO IN SALEM	MA	224.3
MAINE EMPLOYERS MUTUAL INS CO	ME	813.8
MERCURY CASUALTY CO	CA	1,993.8
MITSUI SUMITOMO INS CO OF AMER	NY	883.6
NATIONAL CASUALTY CO	WI	273.8
NATIONWIDE MUTUAL FIRE INS CO	OH	5,632.7
PACIFIC INDEMNITY CO	WI	6,857.3
SENTRY CASUALTY CO	WI	264.9
SENTRY SELECT INS CO	WI	676.5

INSURANCE COMPANY NAME	DOM. STATE	TOTAL ASSETS ($MIL)
STATE FARM MUTUAL AUTOMOBILE INS CO	IL	137,646.1
TOA-RE INS CO OF AMERICA	DE	1,812.3
USAA GENERAL INDEMNITY CO	TX	2,785.3

New Mexico

INSURANCE COMPANY NAME	DOM. STATE	TOTAL ASSETS ($MIL)
Rating:	**A+**	
BERKSHIRE HATHAWAY ASR CORP	NY	2,246.2
DAIRYLAND INS CO	WI	1,212.4
INTERINS EXCH OF THE AUTOMOBILE CLUB	CA	8,447.5
OWNERS INS CO	OH	3,686.6
QUEEN CITY ASR INC	VT	2,149.3
UNITED SERVICES AUTOMOBILE ASN	TX	30,759.0
USAA CASUALTY INS CO	TX	8,886.5
Rating:	**A**	
AUTO-OWNERS INS CO	MI	11,867.2
CHURCH MUTUAL INS CO	WI	1,452.0
CINCINNATI INS CO	OH	10,791.2
FRANKENMUTH MUTUAL INS CO	MI	1,096.8
MUTUAL INS CO OF AZ	AZ	1,011.0
SENTRY INS A MUTUAL CO	WI	6,922.0
TOKIO MARINE AMERICA INS CO	NY	1,387.9
Rating:	**A-**	
ALLSTATE INS CO	IL	44,425.2
BITCO GENERAL INS CORP	IL	796.8
BITCO NATIONAL INS CO	IL	468.3
BROTHERHOOD MUTUAL INS CO	IN	443.2
CINCINNATI INDEMNITY CO	OH	115.5
COUNTRY MUTUAL INS CO	IL	4,306.5
ESSENT GUARANTY INC	PA	767.9
FARM BUREAU PROP & CAS INS CO	IA	2,012.0
FEDERATED MUTUAL INS CO	MN	4,726.6
GEICO CHOICE INS CO	NE	388.0
GEICO SECURE INSURANCE CO	NE	338.5
GREAT WEST CASUALTY CO	NE	1,829.1
JEWELERS MUTUAL INS CO	WI	329.0
NATIONAL MORTGAGE INS CORP	WI	264.6
OLD REPUBLIC GENERAL INS CORP	IL	1,829.0
OLD REPUBLIC INS CO	PA	2,580.9
PROTECTIVE INS CO	IN	776.3
TRAVELERS CASUALTY & SURETY CO	CT	16,487.0
Rating:	**B+**	
ACA FINANCIAL GUARANTY CORP	MD	374.0
ALTERRA REINS USA INC	CT	1,467.0
AMERICAN FAMILY MUT INS CO	WI	14,543.2
AMERICAN STANDARD INS CO OF WI	WI	415.8
AMICA MUTUAL INS CO	RI	5,054.3
CENTRAL STATES INDEMNITY CO OF OMAHA	NE	427.1
CENTURION CASUALTY CO	IA	140.4
COUNTRY CASUALTY INS CO	IL	78.1
EXECUTIVE RISK INDEMNITY INC	DE	3,025.1
FEDERAL INS CO	IN	32,714.5
FIRST COLONIAL INS CO	FL	355.0
GEICO GENERAL INS CO	MD	215.7
GEICO INDEMNITY CO	MD	6,922.7
GOVERNMENT EMPLOYEES INS CO	MD	22,729.4
HARTFORD UNDERWRITERS INS CO	CT	1,566.0
HOLYOKE MUTUAL INS CO IN SALEM	MA	224.3
MITSUI SUMITOMO INS CO OF AMER	NY	883.6
NATIONAL CASUALTY CO	WI	273.8

INSURANCE COMPANY NAME	DOM. STATE	TOTAL ASSETS ($MIL)
NATIONWIDE MUTUAL FIRE INS CO	OH	5,632.7
OLD REPUBLIC SURETY CO	WI	110.0
PACIFIC INDEMNITY CO	WI	6,857.3
SENTRY CASUALTY CO	WI	264.9
SENTRY SELECT INS CO	WI	676.5
STATE FARM MUTUAL AUTOMOBILE INS CO	IL	137,646.1
TOA-RE INS CO OF AMERICA	DE	1,812.3
USAA GENERAL INDEMNITY CO	TX	2,785.3
WESTERN AGRICULTURAL INS CO	IA	178.2
WESTFIELD NATIONAL INS CO	OH	593.0

New York

INSURANCE COMPANY NAME	DOM. STATE	TOTAL ASSETS ($MIL)
Rating: A+		
BERKSHIRE HATHAWAY ASR CORP	NY	2,246.2
DAIRYLAND INS CO	WI	1,212.4
MUNICIPAL ASR CORP	NY	1,528.4
QUEEN CITY ASR INC	VT	2,149.3
UNITED SERVICES AUTOMOBILE ASN	TX	30,759.0
USAA CASUALTY INS CO	TX	8,886.5
Rating: A		
CHURCH MUTUAL INS CO	WI	1,452.0
CINCINNATI INS CO	OH	10,791.2
FRANKENMUTH MUTUAL INS CO	MI	1,096.8
SENTRY INS A MUTUAL CO	WI	6,922.0
TOKIO MARINE AMERICA INS CO	NY	1,387.9
Rating: A-		
ALLSTATE INS CO	IL	44,425.2
BITCO GENERAL INS CORP	IL	796.8
BITCO NATIONAL INS CO	IL	468.3
BROTHERHOOD MUTUAL INS CO	IN	443.2
CINCINNATI INDEMNITY CO	OH	115.5
COUNTRY MUTUAL INS CO	IL	4,306.5
CSAA INS EXCHANGE	CA	6,956.8
ESSENT GUARANTY INC	PA	767.9
FEDERATED MUTUAL INS CO	MN	4,726.6
GEICO CHOICE INS CO	NE	388.0
GEICO SECURE INSURANCE CO	NE	338.5
GREAT WEST CASUALTY CO	NE	1,829.1
ICI MUTUAL INS CO RRG	VT	330.9
JEWELERS MUTUAL INS CO	WI	329.0
MOTORISTS MUTUAL INS CO	OH	1,354.2
NATIONAL MORTGAGE INS CORP	WI	264.6
OLD REPUBLIC GENERAL INS CORP	IL	1,829.0
OLD REPUBLIC INS CO	PA	2,580.9
OTSEGO MUTUAL FIRE INS CO	NY	110.3
PROTECTIVE INS CO	IN	776.3
TRAVELERS CASUALTY & SURETY CO	CT	16,487.0
Rating: B+		
ACA FINANCIAL GUARANTY CORP	MD	374.0
ALL AMERICA INS CO	OH	256.6
ALTERRA REINS USA INC	CT	1,467.0
AMICA MUTUAL INS CO	RI	5,054.3
CENTRAL STATES INDEMNITY CO OF OMAHA	NE	427.1
EXECUTIVE RISK INDEMNITY INC	DE	3,025.1
FARM FAMILY CASUALTY INS CO	NY	1,067.1
FEDERAL INS CO	IN	32,714.5
FIRST COLONIAL INS CO	FL	355.0
GEICO GENERAL INS CO	MD	215.7
GEICO INDEMNITY CO	MD	6,922.7
GNY CUSTOM INS CO	AZ	55.8
GOVERNMENT EMPLOYEES INS CO	MD	22,729.4
HARTFORD UNDERWRITERS INS CO	CT	1,566.0
HOLYOKE MUTUAL INS CO IN SALEM	MA	224.3
MAINE EMPLOYERS MUTUAL INS CO	ME	813.8
MERCURY CASUALTY CO	CA	1,993.8
MITSUI SUMITOMO INS CO OF AMER	NY	883.6

INSURANCE COMPANY NAME	DOM. STATE	TOTAL ASSETS ($MIL)
NATIONAL CASUALTY CO	WI	273.8
NATIONWIDE MUTUAL FIRE INS CO	OH	5,632.7
PACIFIC INDEMNITY CO	WI	6,857.3
SENTRY CASUALTY CO	WI	264.9
SENTRY SELECT INS CO	WI	676.5
STATE FARM MUTUAL AUTOMOBILE INS CO	IL	137,646.1
TOA-RE INS CO OF AMERICA	DE	1,812.3
USAA GENERAL INDEMNITY CO	TX	2,785.3

North Carolina

INSURANCE COMPANY NAME	DOM. STATE	TOTAL ASSETS ($MIL)
Rating: A+		
BERKSHIRE HATHAWAY ASR CORP	NY	2,246.2
DAIRYLAND INS CO	WI	1,212.4
MUNICIPAL ASR CORP	NY	1,528.4
OWNERS INS CO	OH	3,686.6
QUEEN CITY ASR INC	VT	2,149.3
STATE VOLUNTEER MUTUAL INS CO	TN	1,206.0
UNITED SERVICES AUTOMOBILE ASN	TX	30,759.0
USAA CASUALTY INS CO	TX	8,886.5
Rating: A		
AUTO-OWNERS INS CO	MI	11,867.2
CHURCH MUTUAL INS CO	WI	1,452.0
CINCINNATI INS CO	OH	10,791.2
FRANKENMUTH MUTUAL INS CO	MI	1,096.8
SENTRY INS A MUTUAL CO	WI	6,922.0
TOKIO MARINE AMERICA INS CO	NY	1,387.9
Rating: A-		
ALLSTATE INS CO	IL	44,425.2
BITCO GENERAL INS CORP	IL	796.8
BITCO NATIONAL INS CO	IL	468.3
BROTHERHOOD MUTUAL INS CO	IN	443.2
CINCINNATI INDEMNITY CO	OH	115.5
COUNTRY MUTUAL INS CO	IL	4,306.5
ESSENT GUARANTY INC	PA	767.9
FEDERATED MUTUAL INS CO	MN	4,726.6
GEICO CHOICE INS CO	NE	388.0
GEICO SECURE INSURANCE CO	NE	338.5
GREAT WEST CASUALTY CO	NE	1,829.1
JEWELERS MUTUAL INS CO	WI	329.0
KENTUCKY FARM BUREAU MUTUAL INS CO	KY	2,214.4
MOTORISTS MUTUAL INS CO	OH	1,354.2
NATIONAL MORTGAGE INS CORP	WI	264.6
OLD REPUBLIC GENERAL INS CORP	IL	1,829.0
OLD REPUBLIC INS CO	PA	2,580.9
PROTECTIVE INS CO	IN	776.3
TRAVELERS CASUALTY & SURETY CO	CT	16,487.0
Rating: B+		
ACA FINANCIAL GUARANTY CORP	MD	374.0
ALL AMERICA INS CO	OH	256.6
ALTERRA REINS USA INC	CT	1,467.0
AMERICAN FAMILY MUT INS CO	WI	14,543.2
AMERICAN STANDARD INS CO OF WI	WI	415.8
AMICA MUTUAL INS CO	RI	5,054.3
BUILDERS MUTUAL INS CO	NC	625.9
CENTRAL STATES INDEMNITY CO OF OMAHA	NE	427.1
CENTURION CASUALTY CO	IA	140.4
EXECUTIVE RISK INDEMNITY INC	DE	3,025.1
FEDERAL INS CO	IN	32,714.5
FIRST COLONIAL INS CO	FL	355.0
GEICO GENERAL INS CO	MD	215.7
GEICO INDEMNITY CO	MD	6,922.7
GNY CUSTOM INS CO	AZ	55.8
GOVERNMENT EMPLOYEES INS CO	MD	22,729.4
HARTFORD UNDERWRITERS INS CO	CT	1,566.0

INSURANCE COMPANY NAME	DOM. STATE	TOTAL ASSETS ($MIL)
HOLYOKE MUTUAL INS CO IN SALEM	MA	224.3
MITSUI SUMITOMO INS CO OF AMER	NY	883.6
NATIONAL CASUALTY CO	WI	273.8
NATIONWIDE MUTUAL FIRE INS CO	OH	5,632.7
OLD REPUBLIC SURETY CO	WI	110.0
PACIFIC INDEMNITY CO	WI	6,857.3
SENTRY CASUALTY CO	WI	264.9
SENTRY SELECT INS CO	WI	676.5
STATE FARM MUTUAL AUTOMOBILE INS CO	IL	137,646.1
TOA-RE INS CO OF AMERICA	DE	1,812.3
USAA GENERAL INDEMNITY CO	TX	2,785.3
WESTFIELD NATIONAL INS CO	OH	593.0

North Dakota

INSURANCE COMPANY NAME	DOM. STATE	TOTAL ASSETS ($MIL)
Rating: **A+**		
BERKSHIRE HATHAWAY ASR CORP	NY	2,246.2
DAIRYLAND INS CO	WI	1,212.4
MUNICIPAL ASR CORP	NY	1,528.4
OWNERS INS CO	OH	3,686.6
QUEEN CITY ASR INC	VT	2,149.3
UNITED SERVICES AUTOMOBILE ASN	TX	30,759.0
USAA CASUALTY INS CO	TX	8,886.5
Rating: **A**		
AUTO-OWNERS INS CO	MI	11,867.2
CHURCH MUTUAL INS CO	WI	1,452.0
CINCINNATI INS CO	OH	10,791.2
FRANKENMUTH MUTUAL INS CO	MI	1,096.8
PROPERTY-OWNERS INS CO	IN	217.0
SENTRY INS A MUTUAL CO	WI	6,922.0
TOKIO MARINE AMERICA INS CO	NY	1,387.9
Rating: **A-**		
ALLSTATE INS CO	IL	44,425.2
BITCO GENERAL INS CORP	IL	796.8
BITCO NATIONAL INS CO	IL	468.3
BROTHERHOOD MUTUAL INS CO	IN	443.2
CINCINNATI INDEMNITY CO	OH	115.5
COUNTRY MUTUAL INS CO	IL	4,306.5
ESSENT GUARANTY INC	PA	767.9
FEDERATED MUTUAL INS CO	MN	4,726.6
GEICO CHOICE INS CO	NE	388.0
GEICO SECURE INSURANCE CO	NE	338.5
GREAT WEST CASUALTY CO	NE	1,829.1
HOME-OWNERS INS CO	MI	2,165.7
ICI MUTUAL INS CO RRG	VT	330.9
JEWELERS MUTUAL INS CO	WI	329.0
MMIC INS INC	MN	701.8
NATIONAL MORTGAGE INS CORP	WI	264.6
OLD REPUBLIC GENERAL INS CORP	IL	1,829.0
OLD REPUBLIC INS CO	PA	2,580.9
PROTECTIVE INS CO	IN	776.3
TRAVELERS CASUALTY & SURETY CO	CT	16,487.0
Rating: **B+**		
ACA FINANCIAL GUARANTY CORP	MD	374.0
ALTERRA REINS USA INC	CT	1,467.0
AMERICAN FAMILY MUT INS CO	WI	14,543.2
AMERICAN STANDARD INS CO OF WI	WI	415.8
AMICA MUTUAL INS CO	RI	5,054.3
CENTRAL STATES INDEMNITY CO OF OMAHA	NE	427.1
CENTURION CASUALTY CO	IA	140.4
COUNTRY CASUALTY INS CO	IL	78.1
EXECUTIVE RISK INDEMNITY INC	DE	3,025.1
FEDERAL INS CO	IN	32,714.5
FIRST COLONIAL INS CO	FL	355.0
GEICO GENERAL INS CO	MD	215.7
GEICO INDEMNITY CO	MD	6,922.7
GOVERNMENT EMPLOYEES INS CO	MD	22,729.4
HARTFORD UNDERWRITERS INS CO	CT	1,566.0
HOLYOKE MUTUAL INS CO IN SALEM	MA	224.3

INSURANCE COMPANY NAME	DOM. STATE	TOTAL ASSETS ($MIL)
MAINE EMPLOYERS MUTUAL INS CO	ME	813.8
MITSUI SUMITOMO INS CO OF AMER	NY	883.6
NATIONAL CASUALTY CO	WI	273.8
NATIONWIDE MUTUAL FIRE INS CO	OH	5,632.7
OLD REPUBLIC SURETY CO	WI	110.0
PACIFIC INDEMNITY CO	WI	6,857.3
SENTRY CASUALTY CO	WI	264.9
SENTRY SELECT INS CO	WI	676.5
STATE FARM MUTUAL AUTOMOBILE INS CO	IL	137,646.1
TOA-RE INS CO OF AMERICA	DE	1,812.3
TRUSTGARD INS CO	OH	102.3
USAA GENERAL INDEMNITY CO	TX	2,785.3
WESTERN AGRICULTURAL INS CO	IA	178.2
WESTFIELD NATIONAL INS CO	OH	593.0

Ohio

INSURANCE COMPANY NAME	DOM. STATE	TOTAL ASSETS ($MIL)
Rating: A+		
BERKSHIRE HATHAWAY ASR CORP	NY	2,246.2
DAIRYLAND INS CO	WI	1,212.4
INTERINS EXCH OF THE AUTOMOBILE CLUB	CA	8,447.5
MUNICIPAL ASR CORP	NY	1,528.4
OWNERS INS CO	OH	3,686.6
QUEEN CITY ASR INC	VT	2,149.3
UNITED SERVICES AUTOMOBILE ASN	TX	30,759.0
USAA CASUALTY INS CO	TX	8,886.5
Rating: A		
AUTO-OWNERS INS CO	MI	11,867.2
CHURCH MUTUAL INS CO	WI	1,452.0
CINCINNATI INS CO	OH	10,791.2
FRANKENMUTH MUTUAL INS CO	MI	1,096.8
SENTRY INS A MUTUAL CO	WI	6,922.0
TOKIO MARINE AMERICA INS CO	NY	1,387.9
Rating: A-		
ALLSTATE INS CO	IL	44,425.2
BITCO GENERAL INS CORP	IL	796.8
BITCO NATIONAL INS CO	IL	468.3
BROTHERHOOD MUTUAL INS CO	IN	443.2
CINCINNATI INDEMNITY CO	OH	115.5
ESSENT GUARANTY INC	PA	767.9
FEDERATED MUTUAL INS CO	MN	4,726.6
GEICO CHOICE INS CO	NE	388.0
GEICO SECURE INSURANCE CO	NE	338.5
GREAT WEST CASUALTY CO	NE	1,829.1
HASTINGS MUTUAL INS CO	MI	777.9
HOME-OWNERS INS CO	MI	2,165.7
ICI MUTUAL INS CO RRG	VT	330.9
JEWELERS MUTUAL INS CO	WI	329.0
MMIC INS INC	MN	701.8
MOTORISTS MUTUAL INS CO	OH	1,354.2
NATIONAL MORTGAGE INS CORP	WI	264.6
OLD REPUBLIC GENERAL INS CORP	IL	1,829.0
OLD REPUBLIC INS CO	PA	2,580.9
PROTECTIVE INS CO	IN	776.3
TRAVELERS CASUALTY & SURETY CO	CT	16,487.0
WEST BEND MUTUAL INS CO	WI	2,162.6
Rating: B+		
ACA FINANCIAL GUARANTY CORP	MD	374.0
ALL AMERICA INS CO	OH	256.6
ALTERRA REINS USA INC	CT	1,467.0
AMERICAN FAMILY MUT INS CO	WI	14,543.2
AMERICAN STANDARD INS CO OF WI	WI	415.8
AMICA MUTUAL INS CO	RI	5,054.3
CENTRAL STATES INDEMNITY CO OF OMAHA	NE	427.1
CENTURION CASUALTY CO	IA	140.4
COUNTRY CASUALTY INS CO	IL	78.1
EXECUTIVE RISK INDEMNITY INC	DE	3,025.1
FARMERS AUTOMOBILE INS ASN	IL	1,172.9
FEDERAL INS CO	IN	32,714.5
FIRST COLONIAL INS CO	FL	355.0
GEICO GENERAL INS CO	MD	215.7

INSURANCE COMPANY NAME	DOM. STATE	TOTAL ASSETS ($MIL)
GEICO INDEMNITY CO	MD	6,922.7
GNY CUSTOM INS CO	AZ	55.8
GOVERNMENT EMPLOYEES INS CO	MD	22,729.4
GRANGE MUTUAL CAS CO	OH	2,088.9
HARTFORD UNDERWRITERS INS CO	CT	1,566.0
MAINE EMPLOYERS MUTUAL INS CO	ME	813.8
MITSUI SUMITOMO INS CO OF AMER	NY	883.6
NATIONAL CASUALTY CO	WI	273.8
NATIONWIDE MUTUAL FIRE INS CO	OH	5,632.7
OLD REPUBLIC SURETY CO	WI	110.0
PACIFIC INDEMNITY CO	WI	6,857.3
PEKIN INS CO	IL	286.1
SENTRY CASUALTY CO	WI	284.9
SENTRY SELECT INS CO	WI	676.5
STATE FARM MUTUAL AUTOMOBILE INS CO	IL	137,646.1
TOA-RE INS CO OF AMERICA	DE	1,812.3
TRUSTGARD INS CO	OH	102.3
TUSCARORA WAYNE INS CO	PA	91.3
USAA GENERAL INDEMNITY CO	TX	2,785.3
WESTERN AGRICULTURAL INS CO	IA	178.2
WESTFIELD NATIONAL INS CO	OH	593.0

Oklahoma

INSURANCE COMPANY NAME	DOM. STATE	TOTAL ASSETS ($MIL)
Rating: A+		
BERKSHIRE HATHAWAY ASR CORP	NY	2,246.2
MUNICIPAL ASR CORP	NY	1,528.4
QUEEN CITY ASR INC	VT	2,149.3
UNITED SERVICES AUTOMOBILE ASN	TX	30,759.0
USAA CASUALTY INS CO	TX	8,886.5
Rating: A		
CHURCH MUTUAL INS CO	WI	1,452.0
CINCINNATI INS CO	OH	10,791.2
FRANKENMUTH MUTUAL INS CO	MI	1,096.8
SENTRY INS A MUTUAL CO	WI	6,922.0
TOKIO MARINE AMERICA INS CO	NY	1,387.9
Rating: A-		
ALLSTATE INS CO	IL	44,425.2
BITCO GENERAL INS CORP	IL	796.8
BITCO NATIONAL INS CO	IL	468.3
BROTHERHOOD MUTUAL INS CO	IN	443.2
CINCINNATI INDEMNITY CO	OH	115.5
COUNTRY MUTUAL INS CO	IL	4,306.5
ESSENT GUARANTY INC	PA	767.9
FEDERATED MUTUAL INS CO	MN	4,726.6
GEICO CHOICE INS CO	NE	388.0
GEICO SECURE INSURANCE CO	NE	338.5
GREAT WEST CASUALTY CO	NE	1,829.1
JEWELERS MUTUAL INS CO	WI	329.0
MMIC INS INC	MN	701.8
NATIONAL MORTGAGE INS CORP	WI	264.6
OLD REPUBLIC GENERAL INS CORP	IL	1,829.0
OLD REPUBLIC INS CO	PA	2,580.9
PROTECTIVE INS CO	IN	776.3
TRAVELERS CASUALTY & SURETY CO	CT	16,487.0
Rating: B+		
ACA FINANCIAL GUARANTY CORP	MD	374.0
ALL AMERICA INS CO	OH	256.6
ALTERRA REINS USA INC	CT	1,467.0
AMICA MUTUAL INS CO	RI	5,054.3
CENTRAL STATES INDEMNITY CO OF OMAHA	NE	427.1
CENTURION CASUALTY CO	IA	140.4
COUNTRY CASUALTY INS CO	IL	78.1
EXECUTIVE RISK INDEMNITY INC	DE	3,025.1
FEDERAL INS CO	IN	32,714.5
FIRST COLONIAL INS CO	FL	355.0
GEICO GENERAL INS CO	MD	215.7
GEICO INDEMNITY CO	MD	6,922.7
GOVERNMENT EMPLOYEES INS CO	MD	22,729.4
HARTFORD UNDERWRITERS INS CO	CT	1,566.0
MERCURY CASUALTY CO	CA	1,993.8
MITSUI SUMITOMO INS CO OF AMER	NY	883.6
NATIONAL CASUALTY CO	WI	273.8
NATIONWIDE MUTUAL FIRE INS CO	OH	5,632.7
OLD REPUBLIC SURETY CO	WI	110.0
PACIFIC INDEMNITY CO	WI	6,857.3
SENTRY CASUALTY CO	WI	264.9
SENTRY SELECT INS CO	WI	676.5

INSURANCE COMPANY NAME	DOM. STATE	TOTAL ASSETS ($MIL)
STATE FARM MUTUAL AUTOMOBILE INS CO	IL	137,646.1
TOA-RE INS CO OF AMERICA	DE	1,812.3
USAA GENERAL INDEMNITY CO	TX	2,785.3
WESTERN AGRICULTURAL INS CO	IA	178.2
WESTFIELD NATIONAL INS CO	OH	593.0

Oregon

INSURANCE COMPANY NAME	DOM. STATE	TOTAL ASSETS ($MIL)
Rating:　　A+		
BERKSHIRE HATHAWAY ASR CORP	NY	2,246.2
DAIRYLAND INS CO	WI	1,212.4
MUNICIPAL ASR CORP	NY	1,528.4
OWNERS INS CO	OH	3,686.6
QUEEN CITY ASR INC	VT	2,149.3
UNITED SERVICES AUTOMOBILE ASN	TX	30,759.0
USAA CASUALTY INS CO	TX	8,886.5
Rating:　　A		
AUTO-OWNERS INS CO	MI	11,867.2
CHURCH MUTUAL INS CO	WI	1,452.0
OINOINNATI INS CO	OH	10,791.2
FRANKENMUTH MUTUAL INS CO	MI	1,096.8
SAIF CORP	OR	4,802.9
SENTRY INS A MUTUAL CO	WI	6,922.0
TOKIO MARINE AMERICA INS CO	NY	1,387.9
Rating:　　A-		
ALLSTATE INS CO	IL	44,425.2
BITCO GENERAL INS CORP	IL	796.8
BITCO NATIONAL INS CO	IL	468.3
BROTHERHOOD MUTUAL INS CO	IN	443.2
CINCINNATI INDEMNITY CO	OH	115.5
COUNTRY MUTUAL INS CO	IL	4,306.5
ESSENT GUARANTY INC	PA	767.9
FEDERATED MUTUAL INS CO	MN	4,726.6
GEICO CHOICE INS CO	NE	388.0
GEICO SECURE INSURANCE CO	NE	338.5
GREAT WEST CASUALTY CO	NE	1,829.1
JEWELERS MUTUAL INS CO	WI	329.0
MMIC INS INC	MN	701.8
NATIONAL MORTGAGE INS CORP	WI	264.6
OLD REPUBLIC GENERAL INS CORP	IL	1,829.0
OLD REPUBLIC INS CO	PA	2,580.9
PROTECTIVE INS CO	IN	776.3
TRAVELERS CASUALTY & SURETY CO	CT	16,487.0
Rating:　　B+		
ACA FINANCIAL GUARANTY CORP	MD	374.0
ALTERRA REINS USA INC	CT	1,467.0
AMERICAN FAMILY MUT INS CO	WI	14,543.2
AMERICAN STANDARD INS CO OF WI	WI	415.8
AMICA MUTUAL INS CO	RI	5,054.3
CENTRAL STATES INDEMNITY CO OF OMAHA	NE	427.1
CENTURION CASUALTY CO	IA	140.4
COUNTRY CASUALTY INS CO	IL	78.1
EXECUTIVE RISK INDEMNITY INC	DE	3,025.1
FEDERAL INS CO	IN	32,714.5
FIRST COLONIAL INS CO	FL	355.0
GEICO GENERAL INS CO	MD	215.7
GEICO INDEMNITY CO	MD	6,922.7
GOVERNMENT EMPLOYEES INS CO	MD	22,729.4
HARTFORD UNDERWRITERS INS CO	CT	1,566.0
HOLYOKE MUTUAL INS CO IN SALEM	MA	224.3
MITSUI SUMITOMO INS CO OF AMER	NY	883.6
NATIONAL CASUALTY CO	WI	273.8

INSURANCE COMPANY NAME	DOM. STATE	TOTAL ASSETS ($MIL)
NATIONWIDE MUTUAL FIRE INS CO	OH	5,632.7
OLD REPUBLIC SURETY CO	WI	110.0
PACIFIC INDEMNITY CO	WI	6,857.3
SENTRY CASUALTY CO	WI	264.9
SENTRY SELECT INS CO	WI	676.5
STATE FARM MUTUAL AUTOMOBILE INS CO	IL	137,646.1
TOA-RE INS CO OF AMERICA	DE	1,812.3
TRUSTGARD INS CO	OH	102.3
USAA GENERAL INDEMNITY CO	TX	2,785.3
WESTERN COMMUNITY INS CO	ID	36.2

Pennsylvania

INSURANCE COMPANY NAME	DOM. STATE	TOTAL ASSETS ($MIL)
Rating:	**A+**	
BERKSHIRE HATHAWAY ASR CORP	NY	2,246.2
DAIRYLAND INS CO	WI	1,212.4
INTERINS EXCH OF THE AUTOMOBILE CLUB	CA	8,447.5
MUNICIPAL ASR CORP	NY	1,528.4
OWNERS INS CO	OH	3,686.6
QUEEN CITY ASR INC	VT	2,149.3
UNITED SERVICES AUTOMOBILE ASN	TX	30,759.0
USAA CASUALTY INS CO	TX	8,886.5
Rating:	**A**	
AUTO-OWNERS INS CO	MI	11,867.2
CHURCH MUTUAL INS CO	WI	1,452.0
CINCINNATI INS CO	OH	10,791.2
FRANKENMUTH MUTUAL INS CO	MI	1,096.8
SENTRY INS A MUTUAL CO	WI	6,922.0
TOKIO MARINE AMERICA INS CO	NY	1,387.9
Rating:	**A-**	
ALLSTATE INS CO	IL	44,425.2
BITCO GENERAL INS CORP	IL	796.8
BITCO NATIONAL INS CO	IL	468.3
BROTHERHOOD MUTUAL INS CO	IN	443.2
CINCINNATI INDEMNITY CO	OH	115.5
COUNTRY MUTUAL INS CO	IL	4,306.5
ESSENT GUARANTY INC	PA	767.9
FEDERATED MUTUAL INS CO	MN	4,726.6
GEICO CHOICE INS CO	NE	388.0
GEICO SECURE INSURANCE CO	NE	338.5
GREAT WEST CASUALTY CO	NE	1,829.1
HASTINGS MUTUAL INS CO	MI	777.9
HOME-OWNERS INS CO	MI	2,165.7
ICI MUTUAL INS CO RRG	VT	330.9
JEWELERS MUTUAL INS CO	WI	329.0
MOTORISTS MUTUAL INS CO	OH	1,354.2
NATIONAL MORTGAGE INS CORP	WI	264.6
OLD REPUBLIC GENERAL INS CORP	IL	1,829.0
OLD REPUBLIC INS CO	PA	2,580.9
PROTECTIVE INS CO	IN	776.3
TRAVELERS CASUALTY & SURETY CO	CT	16,487.0
Rating:	**B+**	
ACA FINANCIAL GUARANTY CORP	MD	374.0
ALTERRA REINS USA INC	CT	1,467.0
AMICA MUTUAL INS CO	RI	5,054.3
CENTRAL STATES INDEMNITY CO OF OMAHA	NE	427.1
COUNTRY CASUALTY INS CO	IL	78.1
EXECUTIVE RISK INDEMNITY INC	DE	3,025.1
FEDERAL INS CO	IN	32,714.5
FIRST COLONIAL INS CO	FL	355.0
GEICO GENERAL INS CO	MD	215.7
GEICO INDEMNITY CO	MD	6,922.7
GNY CUSTOM INS CO	AZ	55.8
GOVERNMENT EMPLOYEES INS CO	MD	22,729.4
GRANGE MUTUAL CAS CO	OH	2,088.9
HARTFORD UNDERWRITERS INS CO	CT	1,566.0
MAINE EMPLOYERS MUTUAL INS CO	ME	813.8

INSURANCE COMPANY NAME	DOM. STATE	TOTAL ASSETS ($MIL)
MERCURY CASUALTY CO	CA	1,993.8
MITSUI SUMITOMO INS CO OF AMER	NY	883.6
NATIONAL CASUALTY CO	WI	273.8
NATIONWIDE MUTUAL FIRE INS CO	OH	5,632.7
OLD REPUBLIC SURETY CO	WI	110.0
PACIFIC INDEMNITY CO	WI	6,857.3
SENTRY CASUALTY CO	WI	264.9
SENTRY SELECT INS CO	WI	676.5
STATE FARM MUTUAL AUTOMOBILE INS CO	IL	137,646.1
TOA-RE INS CO OF AMERICA	DE	1,812.3
TRUSTGARD INS CO	OH	102.3
TUSCARORA WAYNE INS CO	PA	91.3
USAA GENERAL INDEMNITY CO	TX	2,785.3
WESTFIELD NATIONAL INS CO	OH	593.0

Rhode Island

INSURANCE COMPANY NAME	DOM. STATE	TOTAL ASSETS ($MIL)

Rating: A+

INSURANCE COMPANY NAME	DOM. STATE	TOTAL ASSETS ($MIL)
BERKSHIRE HATHAWAY ASR CORP	NY	2,246.2
DAIRYLAND INS CO	WI	1,212.4
MUNICIPAL ASR CORP	NY	1,528.4
QUEEN CITY ASR INC	VT	2,149.3
UNITED SERVICES AUTOMOBILE ASN	TX	30,759.0
USAA CASUALTY INS CO	TX	8,886.5

Rating: A

INSURANCE COMPANY NAME	DOM. STATE	TOTAL ASSETS ($MIL)
CHURCH MUTUAL INS CO	WI	1,452.0
CINCINNATI INS CO	OH	10,791.2
FRANKENMUTH MUTUAL INS CO	MI	1,096.8
SENTRY INS A MUTUAL CO	WI	6,922.0
TOKIO MARINE AMERICA INS CO	NY	1,387.9

Rating: A-

INSURANCE COMPANY NAME	DOM. STATE	TOTAL ASSETS ($MIL)
ALLSTATE INS CO	IL	44,425.2
BITCO GENERAL INS CORP	IL	796.8
BROTHERHOOD MUTUAL INS CO	IN	443.2
CINCINNATI INDEMNITY CO	OH	115.5
COUNTRY MUTUAL INS CO	IL	4,306.5
ESSENT GUARANTY INC	PA	767.9
FEDERATED MUTUAL INS CO	MN	4,726.6
GEICO CHOICE INS CO	NE	388.0
GEICO SECURE INSURANCE CO	NE	338.5
GREAT WEST CASUALTY CO	NE	1,829.1
JEWELERS MUTUAL INS CO	WI	329.0
MOTORISTS MUTUAL INS CO	OH	1,354.2
NATIONAL MORTGAGE INS CORP	WI	264.6
OLD REPUBLIC GENERAL INS CORP	IL	1,829.0
OLD REPUBLIC INS CO	PA	2,580.9
PROTECTIVE INS CO	IN	776.3
TRAVELERS CASUALTY & SURETY CO	CT	16,487.0

Rating: B+

INSURANCE COMPANY NAME	DOM. STATE	TOTAL ASSETS ($MIL)
ACA FINANCIAL GUARANTY CORP	MD	374.0
ALTERRA REINS USA INC	CT	1,467.0
AMICA MUTUAL INS CO	RI	5,054.3
CENTRAL STATES INDEMNITY CO OF OMAHA	NE	427.1
CENTURION CASUALTY CO	IA	140.4
COUNTRY CASUALTY INS CO	IL	78.1
EXECUTIVE RISK INDEMNITY INC	DE	3,025.1
FARM FAMILY CASUALTY INS CO	NY	1,067.1
FEDERAL INS CO	IN	32,714.5
FIRST COLONIAL INS CO	FL	355.0
GEICO GENERAL INS CO	MD	215.7
GEICO INDEMNITY CO	MD	6,922.7
GOVERNMENT EMPLOYEES INS CO	MD	22,729.4
HARTFORD UNDERWRITERS INS CO	CT	1,566.0
HOLYOKE MUTUAL INS CO IN SALEM	MA	224.3
MITSUI SUMITOMO INS CO OF AMER	NY	883.6
NATIONAL CASUALTY CO	WI	273.8
NATIONWIDE MUTUAL FIRE INS CO	OH	5,632.7
PACIFIC INDEMNITY CO	WI	6,857.3
SENTRY CASUALTY CO	WI	264.9
SENTRY SELECT INS CO	WI	676.5
STATE FARM MUTUAL AUTOMOBILE INS CO	IL	137,646.1

INSURANCE COMPANY NAME	DOM. STATE	TOTAL ASSETS ($MIL)
TOA-RE INS CO OF AMERICA	DE	1,812.3
USAA GENERAL INDEMNITY CO	TX	2,785.3

South Carolina

INSURANCE COMPANY NAME	DOM. STATE	TOTAL ASSETS ($MIL)
Rating: A+		
BERKSHIRE HATHAWAY ASR CORP	NY	2,246.2
DAIRYLAND INS CO	WI	1,212.4
MUNICIPAL ASR CORP	NY	1,528.4
OWNERS INS CO	OH	3,686.6
QUEEN CITY ASR INC	VT	2,149.3
UNITED SERVICES AUTOMOBILE ASN	TX	30,759.0
USAA CASUALTY INS CO	TX	8,886.5
Rating: A		
AUTO-OWNERS INS CO	MI	11,867.2
CHURCH MUTUAL INS CO	WI	1,452.0
CINCINNATI INS CO	OH	10,791.2
FRANKENMUTH MUTUAL INS CO	MI	1,096.8
PROPERTY-OWNERS INS CO	IN	217.0
SENTRY INS A MUTUAL CO	WI	6,922.0
TOKIO MARINE AMERICA INS CO	NY	1,387.9
Rating: A-		
ALLSTATE INS CO	IL	44,425.2
BITCO GENERAL INS CORP	IL	796.8
BITCO NATIONAL INS CO	IL	468.3
BROTHERHOOD MUTUAL INS CO	IN	443.2
CINCINNATI INDEMNITY CO	OH	115.5
ESSENT GUARANTY INC	PA	767.9
FEDERATED MUTUAL INS CO	MN	4,726.6
GEICO CHOICE INS CO	NE	388.0
GEICO SECURE INSURANCE CO	NE	338.5
GREAT WEST CASUALTY CO	NE	1,829.1
HOME-OWNERS INS CO	MI	2,165.7
ICI MUTUAL INS CO RRG	VT	330.9
JEWELERS MUTUAL INS CO	WI	329.0
NATIONAL MORTGAGE INS CORP	WI	264.6
OLD REPUBLIC GENERAL INS CORP	IL	1,829.0
OLD REPUBLIC INS CO	PA	2,580.9
PROTECTIVE INS CO	IN	776.3
TRAVELERS CASUALTY & SURETY CO	CT	16,487.0
Rating: B+		
ACA FINANCIAL GUARANTY CORP	MD	374.0
ALL AMERICA INS CO	OH	256.6
ALTERRA REINS USA INC	CT	1,467.0
AMERICAN FAMILY MUT INS CO	WI	14,543.2
AMERICAN STANDARD INS CO OF WI	WI	415.8
AMICA MUTUAL INS CO	RI	5,054.3
BUILDERS MUTUAL INS CO	NC	625.9
CENTRAL STATES INDEMNITY CO OF OMAHA	NE	427.1
CENTURION CASUALTY CO	IA	140.4
EXECUTIVE RISK INDEMNITY INC	DE	3,025.1
FEDERAL INS CO	IN	32,714.5
FIRST COLONIAL INS CO	FL	355.0
GEICO GENERAL INS CO	MD	215.7
GEICO INDEMNITY CO	MD	6,922.7
GOVERNMENT EMPLOYEES INS CO	MD	22,729.4
GRANGE MUTUAL CAS CO	OH	2,088.9
HARTFORD UNDERWRITERS INS CO	CT	1,566.0
HOLYOKE MUTUAL INS CO IN SALEM	MA	224.3

INSURANCE COMPANY NAME	DOM. STATE	TOTAL ASSETS ($MIL)
MITSUI SUMITOMO INS CO OF AMER	NY	883.6
NATIONAL CASUALTY CO	WI	273.8
NATIONWIDE MUTUAL FIRE INS CO	OH	5,632.7
OLD REPUBLIC SURETY CO	WI	110.0
PACIFIC INDEMNITY CO	WI	6,857.3
SENTRY CASUALTY CO	WI	264.9
SENTRY SELECT INS CO	WI	676.5
STATE FARM MUTUAL AUTOMOBILE INS CO	IL	137,646.1
TOA-RE INS CO OF AMERICA	DE	1,812.3
TRUSTGARD INS CO	OH	102.3
USAA GENERAL INDEMNITY CO	TX	2,785.3
WESTERN AGRICULTURAL INS CO	IA	178.2
WESTFIELD NATIONAL INS CO	OH	593.0

South Dakota

INSURANCE COMPANY NAME	DOM. STATE	TOTAL ASSETS ($MIL)
Rating: A+		
BERKSHIRE HATHAWAY ASR CORP	NY	2,246.2
DAIRYLAND INS CO	WI	1,212.4
MUNICIPAL ASR CORP	NY	1,528.4
OWNERS INS CO	OH	3,686.6
QUEEN CITY ASR INC	VT	2,149.3
UNITED SERVICES AUTOMOBILE ASN	TX	30,759.0
USAA CASUALTY INS CO	TX	8,886.5
Rating: A		
AUTO-OWNERS INS CO	MI	11,867.2
CHURCH MUTUAL INS CO	WI	1,452.0
CINCINNATI INS CO	OH	10,791.2
FRANKENMUTH MUTUAL INS CO	MI	1,096.8
PROPERTY-OWNERS INS CO	IN	217.0
SENTRY INS A MUTUAL CO	WI	6,922.0
TOKIO MARINE AMERICA INS CO	NY	1,387.9
Rating: A-		
ALLSTATE INS CO	IL	44,425.2
BITCO GENERAL INS CORP	IL	796.8
BITCO NATIONAL INS CO	IL	468.3
BROTHERHOOD MUTUAL INS CO	IN	443.2
CINCINNATI INDEMNITY CO	OH	115.5
COUNTRY MUTUAL INS CO	IL	4,306.5
ESSENT GUARANTY INC	PA	767.9
FARM BUREAU PROP & CAS INS CO	IA	2,012.0
FEDERATED MUTUAL INS CO	MN	4,726.6
GEICO CHOICE INS CO	NE	388.0
GEICO SECURE INSURANCE CO	NE	338.5
GREAT WEST CASUALTY CO	NE	1,829.1
HOME-OWNERS INS CO	MI	2,165.7
JEWELERS MUTUAL INS CO	WI	329.0
MMIC INS INC	MN	701.8
MOTORISTS MUTUAL INS CO	OH	1,354.2
NATIONAL MORTGAGE INS CORP	WI	264.6
OLD REPUBLIC GENERAL INS CORP	IL	1,829.0
OLD REPUBLIC INS CO	PA	2,580.9
PROTECTIVE INS CO	IN	776.3
TRAVELERS CASUALTY & SURETY CO	CT	16,487.0
Rating: B+		
ACA FINANCIAL GUARANTY CORP	MD	374.0
ALTERRA REINS USA INC	CT	1,467.0
AMERICAN FAMILY MUT INS CO	WI	14,543.2
AMERICAN STANDARD INS CO OF WI	WI	415.8
AMICA MUTUAL INS CO	RI	5,054.3
CENTRAL STATES INDEMNITY CO OF OMAHA	NE	427.1
CENTURION CASUALTY CO	IA	140.4
COUNTRY CASUALTY INS CO	IL	78.1
EXECUTIVE RISK INDEMNITY INC	DE	3,025.1
FEDERAL INS CO	IN	32,714.5
FIRST COLONIAL INS CO	FL	355.0
GEICO GENERAL INS CO	MD	215.7
GEICO INDEMNITY CO	MD	6,922.7
GOVERNMENT EMPLOYEES INS CO	MD	22,729.4
HARTFORD UNDERWRITERS INS CO	CT	1,566.0

INSURANCE COMPANY NAME	DOM. STATE	TOTAL ASSETS ($MIL)
HOLYOKE MUTUAL INS CO IN SALEM	MA	224.3
MITSUI SUMITOMO INS CO OF AMER	NY	883.6
NATIONAL CASUALTY CO	WI	273.8
NATIONWIDE MUTUAL FIRE INS CO	OH	5,632.7
OLD REPUBLIC SURETY CO	WI	110.0
PACIFIC INDEMNITY CO	WI	6,857.3
SENTRY CASUALTY CO	WI	264.9
SENTRY SELECT INS CO	WI	676.5
STATE FARM MUTUAL AUTOMOBILE INS CO	IL	137,646.1
TOA-RE INS CO OF AMERICA	DE	1,812.3
TRUSTGARD INS CO	OH	102.3
USAA GENERAL INDEMNITY CO	TX	2,785.3
WESTERN AGRICULTURAL INS CO	IA	170.2
WESTFIELD NATIONAL INS CO	OH	593.0

Tennessee

INSURANCE COMPANY NAME	DOM. STATE	TOTAL ASSETS ($MIL)
Rating: A+		
BERKSHIRE HATHAWAY ASR CORP	NY	2,246.2
DAIRYLAND INS CO	WI	1,212.4
MUNICIPAL ASR CORP	NY	1,528.4
OWNERS INS CO	OH	3,686.6
QUEEN CITY ASR INC	VT	2,149.3
STATE VOLUNTEER MUTUAL INS CO	TN	1,206.0
UNITED SERVICES AUTOMOBILE ASN	TX	30,759.0
USAA CASUALTY INS CO	TX	8,886.5
Rating: A		
AUTO-OWNERS INS CO	MI	11,867.2
CHURCH MUTUAL INS CO	WI	1,452.0
CINCINNATI INS CO	OH	10,791.2
FRANKENMUTH MUTUAL INS CO	MI	1,096.8
SENTRY INS A MUTUAL CO	WI	6,922.0
TOKIO MARINE AMERICA INS CO	NY	1,387.9
Rating: A-		
ALLSTATE INS CO	IL	44,425.2
BITCO GENERAL INS CORP	IL	796.8
BITCO NATIONAL INS CO	IL	468.3
BROTHERHOOD MUTUAL INS CO	IN	443.2
CINCINNATI INDEMNITY CO	OH	115.5
COUNTRY MUTUAL INS CO	IL	4,306.5
ESSENT GUARANTY INC	PA	767.9
FEDERATED MUTUAL INS CO	MN	4,726.6
GEICO CHOICE INS CO	NE	388.0
GEICO SECURE INSURANCE CO	NE	338.5
GREAT WEST CASUALTY CO	NE	1,829.1
HASTINGS MUTUAL INS CO	MI	777.9
ICI MUTUAL INS CO RRG	VT	330.9
JEWELERS MUTUAL INS CO	WI	329.0
MMIC INS INC	MN	701.8
NATIONAL MORTGAGE INS CORP	WI	264.6
OLD REPUBLIC GENERAL INS CORP	IL	1,829.0
OLD REPUBLIC INS CO	PA	2,580.9
PROTECTIVE INS CO	IN	776.3
TRAVELERS CASUALTY & SURETY CO	CT	16,487.0
Rating: B+		
ACA FINANCIAL GUARANTY CORP	MD	374.0
ALL AMERICA INS CO	OH	256.6
ALTERRA REINS USA INC	CT	1,467.0
AMICA MUTUAL INS CO	RI	5,054.3
BUILDERS MUTUAL INS CO	NC	625.9
CENTRAL STATES INDEMNITY CO OF OMAHA	NE	427.1
CENTURION CASUALTY CO	IA	140.4
COUNTRY CASUALTY INS CO	IL	78.1
EXECUTIVE RISK INDEMNITY INC	DE	3,025.1
FEDERAL INS CO	IN	32,714.5
FIRST COLONIAL INS CO	FL	355.0
GEICO GENERAL INS CO	MD	215.7
GEICO INDEMNITY CO	MD	6,922.7
GOVERNMENT EMPLOYEES INS CO	MD	22,729.4
GRANGE MUTUAL CAS CO	OH	2,088.9
HARTFORD UNDERWRITERS INS CO	CT	1,566.0

INSURANCE COMPANY NAME	DOM. STATE	TOTAL ASSETS ($MIL)
MITSUI SUMITOMO INS CO OF AMER	NY	883.6
NATIONAL CASUALTY CO	WI	273.8
NATIONWIDE MUTUAL FIRE INS CO	OH	5,632.7
OLD REPUBLIC SURETY CO	WI	110.0
PACIFIC INDEMNITY CO	WI	6,857.3
SENTRY CASUALTY CO	WI	264.9
SENTRY SELECT INS CO	WI	676.5
STATE FARM MUTUAL AUTOMOBILE INS CO	IL	137,646.1
TENNESSEE FARMERS ASR CO	TN	1,133.1
TENNESSEE FARMERS MUTUAL INS CO	TN	2,369.1
TOA-RE INS CO OF AMERICA	DE	1,812.3
TRUSTGARD INS CO	OH	102.3
USAA GENERAL INDEMNITY CO	TX	2,785.3
WESTERN AGRICULTURAL INS CO	IA	178.2
WESTFIELD NATIONAL INS CO	OH	593.0

Texas

INSURANCE COMPANY NAME	DOM. STATE	TOTAL ASSETS ($MIL)
Rating: A+		
BERKSHIRE HATHAWAY ASR CORP	NY	2,246.2
DAIRYLAND INS CO	WI	1,212.4
INTERINS EXCH OF THE AUTOMOBILE CLUB	CA	8,447.5
MUNICIPAL ASR CORP	NY	1,528.4
QUEEN CITY ASR INC	VT	2,149.3
UNITED SERVICES AUTOMOBILE ASN	TX	30,759.0
USAA CASUALTY INS CO	TX	8,886.5
Rating: A		
CHURCH MUTUAL INS CO	WI	1,452.0
CINCINNATI INS CO	OH	10,791.2
FRANKENMUTH MUTUAL INS CO	MI	1,096.8
SENTRY INS A MUTUAL CO	WI	6,922.0
TEXAS FARM BUREAU CASUALTY INS CO	TX	1,123.7
TOKIO MARINE AMERICA INS CO	NY	1,387.9
Rating: A-		
ALLSTATE INS CO	IL	44,425.2
AMICA LLOYDS OF TEXAS	TX	77.6
BITCO GENERAL INS CORP	IL	796.8
BITCO NATIONAL INS CO	IL	468.3
BROTHERHOOD MUTUAL INS CO	IN	443.2
CINCINNATI INDEMNITY CO	OH	115.5
COUNTRY MUTUAL INS CO	IL	4,306.5
ESSENT GUARANTY INC	PA	767.9
FEDERATED MUTUAL INS CO	MN	4,726.6
GEICO CHOICE INS CO	NE	388.0
GEICO SECURE INSURANCE CO	NE	338.5
GREAT WEST CASUALTY CO	NE	1,829.1
ICI MUTUAL INS CO RRG	VT	330.9
JEWELERS MUTUAL INS CO	WI	329.0
NATIONAL MORTGAGE INS CORP	WI	264.6
OLD REPUBLIC GENERAL INS CORP	IL	1,829.0
OLD REPUBLIC INS CO	PA	2,580.9
PROTECTIVE INS CO	IN	776.3
TRAVELERS CASUALTY & SURETY CO	CT	16,487.0
Rating: B+		
ACA FINANCIAL GUARANTY CORP	MD	374.0
ALL AMERICA INS CO	OH	256.6
ALTERRA REINS USA INC	CT	1,467.0
AMICA MUTUAL INS CO	RI	5,054.3
AUTO CLUB INDEMNITY CO	TX	21.8
CENTRAL STATES INDEMNITY CO OF OMAHA	NE	427.1
CENTURION CASUALTY CO	IA	140.4
COUNTRY CASUALTY INS CO	IL	78.1
EXECUTIVE RISK INDEMNITY INC	DE	3,025.1
FEDERAL INS CO	IN	32,714.5
FIRST COLONIAL INS CO	FL	355.0
GEICO GENERAL INS CO	MD	215.7
GEICO INDEMNITY CO	MD	6,922.7
GOVERNMENT EMPLOYEES INS CO	MD	22,729.4
HARTFORD UNDERWRITERS INS CO	CT	1,566.0
HOLYOKE MUTUAL INS CO IN SALEM	MA	224.3
MERCURY CASUALTY CO	CA	1,993.8
MITSUI SUMITOMO INS CO OF AMER	NY	883.6

INSURANCE COMPANY NAME	DOM. STATE	TOTAL ASSETS ($MIL)
NATIONAL CASUALTY CO	WI	273.8
NATIONWIDE MUTUAL FIRE INS CO	OH	5,632.7
OLD REPUBLIC SURETY CO	WI	110.0
PACIFIC INDEMNITY CO	WI	6,857.3
SENTRY CASUALTY CO	WI	264.9
SENTRY SELECT INS CO	WI	676.5
STATE FARM MUTUAL AUTOMOBILE INS CO	IL	137,646.1
TEXAS MUTUAL INS CO	TX	5,660.4
TOA-RE INS CO OF AMERICA	DE	1,812.3
TRUSTGARD INS CO	OH	102.3
USAA GENERAL INDEMNITY CO	TX	2,785.3
USAA TEXAS LLOYDS CO	TX	575.9
WESTERN AGRICULTURAL INS CO	IA	178.2
WESTFIELD NATIONAL INS CO	OH	593.0

Utah

INSURANCE COMPANY NAME	DOM. STATE	TOTAL ASSETS ($MIL)
Rating: A+		
BERKSHIRE HATHAWAY ASR CORP	NY	2,246.2
DAIRYLAND INS CO	WI	1,212.4
MUNICIPAL ASR CORP	NY	1,528.4
OWNERS INS CO	OH	3,686.6
QUEEN CITY ASR INC	VT	2,149.3
UNITED SERVICES AUTOMOBILE ASN	TX	30,759.0
USAA CASUALTY INS CO	TX	8,886.5
Rating: A		
AUTO-OWNERS INS CO	MI	11,867.2
CHURCH MUTUAL INS CO	WI	1,452.0
CINCINNATI INS CO	OH	10,791.2
FRANKENMUTH MUTUAL INS CO	MI	1,096.8
MUTUAL INS CO OF AZ	AZ	1,011.0
PROPERTY-OWNERS INS CO	IN	217.0
SENTRY INS A MUTUAL CO	WI	6,922.0
TOKIO MARINE AMERICA INS CO	NY	1,387.9
Rating: A-		
ALLSTATE INS CO	IL	44,425.2
BITCO GENERAL INS CORP	IL	796.8
BITCO NATIONAL INS CO	IL	468.3
BROTHERHOOD MUTUAL INS CO	IN	443.2
CINCINNATI INDEMNITY CO	OH	115.5
COPIC INS CO	CO	548.6
COUNTRY MUTUAL INS CO	IL	4,306.5
CSAA INS EXCHANGE	CA	6,956.8
ESSENT GUARANTY INC	PA	767.9
FARM BUREAU PROP & CAS INS CO	IA	2,012.0
FEDERATED MUTUAL INS CO	MN	4,726.6
GEICO CHOICE INS CO	NE	388.0
GEICO SECURE INSURANCE CO	NE	338.5
GREAT WEST CASUALTY CO	NE	1,829.1
HOME-OWNERS INS CO	MI	2,165.7
JEWELERS MUTUAL INS CO	WI	329.0
MMIC INS INC	MN	701.8
NATIONAL MORTGAGE INS CORP	WI	264.6
OLD REPUBLIC GENERAL INS CORP	IL	1,829.0
OLD REPUBLIC INS CO	PA	2,580.9
PROTECTIVE INS CO	IN	776.3
TRAVELERS CASUALTY & SURETY CO	CT	16,487.0
Rating: B+		
ACA FINANCIAL GUARANTY CORP	MD	374.0
ALTERRA REINS USA INC	CT	1,467.0
AMERICAN FAMILY MUT INS CO	WI	14,543.2
AMERICAN STANDARD INS CO OF WI	WI	415.8
AMICA MUTUAL INS CO	RI	5,054.3
CENTRAL STATES INDEMNITY CO OF OMAHA	NE	427.1
CENTURION CASUALTY CO	IA	140.4
EXECUTIVE RISK INDEMNITY INC	DE	3,025.1
FEDERAL INS CO	IN	32,714.5
FIRST COLONIAL INS CO	FL	355.0
GEICO GENERAL INS CO	MD	215.7
GEICO INDEMNITY CO	MD	6,922.7
GOVERNMENT EMPLOYEES INS CO	MD	22,729.4

INSURANCE COMPANY NAME	DOM. STATE	TOTAL ASSETS ($MIL)
HARTFORD UNDERWRITERS INS CO	CT	1,566.0
HOLYOKE MUTUAL INS CO IN SALEM	MA	224.3
MITSUI SUMITOMO INS CO OF AMER	NY	883.6
NATIONAL CASUALTY CO	WI	273.8
NATIONWIDE MUTUAL FIRE INS CO	OH	5,632.7
OLD REPUBLIC SURETY CO	WI	110.0
PACIFIC INDEMNITY CO	WI	6,857.3
SENTRY CASUALTY CO	WI	264.9
SENTRY SELECT INS CO	WI	676.5
STATE FARM MUTUAL AUTOMOBILE INS CO	IL	137,646.1
TOA-RE INS CO OF AMERICA	DE	1,812.3
USAA GENERAL INDEMNITY CO	TX	2,785.3
WESTERN AGRICULTURAL INS CO	IA	178.2
WESTFIELD NATIONAL INS CO	OH	593.0

Vermont

INSURANCE COMPANY NAME	DOM. STATE	TOTAL ASSETS ($MIL)
Rating: A+		
BERKSHIRE HATHAWAY ASR CORP	NY	2,246.2
DAIRYLAND INS CO	WI	1,212.4
INTERINS EXCH OF THE AUTOMOBILE CLUB	CA	8,447.5
MUNICIPAL ASR CORP	NY	1,528.4
QUEEN CITY ASR INC	VT	2,149.3
UNITED SERVICES AUTOMOBILE ASN	TX	30,759.0
USAA CASUALTY INS CO	TX	8,886.5
Rating: A		
CHURCH MUTUAL INS CO	WI	1,452.0
CINCINNATI INS CO	OH	10,791.2
FRANKENMUTH MUTUAL INS CO	MI	1,096.8
SENTRY INS A MUTUAL CO	WI	6,922.0
TOKIO MARINE AMERICA INS CO	NY	1,387.9
Rating: A-		
ALLSTATE INS CO	IL	44,425.2
BITCO GENERAL INS CORP	IL	796.8
BROTHERHOOD MUTUAL INS CO	IN	443.2
CINCINNATI INDEMNITY CO	OH	115.5
COUNTRY MUTUAL INS CO	IL	4,306.5
ESSENT GUARANTY INC	PA	767.9
FEDERATED MUTUAL INS CO	MN	4,726.6
GEICO CHOICE INS CO	NE	388.0
GEICO SECURE INSURANCE CO	NE	338.5
GREAT WEST CASUALTY CO	NE	1,829.1
ICI MUTUAL INS CO RRG	VT	330.9
JEWELERS MUTUAL INS CO	WI	329.0
KENTUCKY FARM BUREAU MUTUAL INS CO	KY	2,214.4
MOTORISTS MUTUAL INS CO	OH	1,354.2
NATIONAL MORTGAGE INS CORP	WI	264.6
OLD REPUBLIC GENERAL INS CORP	IL	1,829.0
OLD REPUBLIC INS CO	PA	2,580.9
PROTECTIVE INS CO	IN	776.3
TRAVELERS CASUALTY & SURETY CO	CT	16,487.0
Rating: B+		
ACA FINANCIAL GUARANTY CORP	MD	374.0
ALTERRA REINS USA INC	CT	1,467.0
AMICA MUTUAL INS CO	RI	5,054.3
CENTRAL STATES INDEMNITY CO OF OMAHA	NE	427.1
EXECUTIVE RISK INDEMNITY INC	DE	3,025.1
FARM FAMILY CASUALTY INS CO	NY	1,067.1
FEDERAL INS CO	IN	32,714.5
FIRST COLONIAL INS CO	FL	355.0
GEICO GENERAL INS CO	MD	215.7
GEICO INDEMNITY CO	MD	6,922.7
GNY CUSTOM INS CO	AZ	55.8
GOVERNMENT EMPLOYEES INS CO	MD	22,729.4
HARTFORD UNDERWRITERS INS CO	CT	1,566.0
HOLYOKE MUTUAL INS CO IN SALEM	MA	224.3
MAINE EMPLOYERS MUTUAL INS CO	ME	813.8
MITSUI SUMITOMO INS CO OF AMER	NY	883.6
NATIONAL CASUALTY CO	WI	273.8
NATIONWIDE MUTUAL FIRE INS CO	OH	5,632.7
PACIFIC INDEMNITY CO	WI	6,857.3

INSURANCE COMPANY NAME	DOM. STATE	TOTAL ASSETS ($MIL)
SENTRY CASUALTY CO	WI	264.9
SENTRY SELECT INS CO	WI	676.5
STATE FARM MUTUAL AUTOMOBILE INS CO	IL	137,646.1
TOA-RE INS CO OF AMERICA	DE	1,812.3
USAA GENERAL INDEMNITY CO	TX	2,785.3

Virginia

INSURANCE COMPANY NAME	DOM. STATE	TOTAL ASSETS ($MIL)
Rating: A+		
BERKSHIRE HATHAWAY ASR CORP	NY	2,246.2
DAIRYLAND INS CO	WI	1,212.4
INTERINS EXCH OF THE AUTOMOBILE CLUB	CA	8,447.5
MUNICIPAL ASR CORP	NY	1,528.4
OWNERS INS CO	OH	3,686.6
QUEEN CITY ASR INC	VT	2,149.3
STATE VOLUNTEER MUTUAL INS CO	TN	1,206.0
UNITED SERVICES AUTOMOBILE ASN	TX	30,759.0
USAA CASUALTY INS CO	TX	8,886.5
Rating: A		
AUTO-OWNERS INS CO	MI	11,867.2
CHURCH MUTUAL INS CO	WI	1,452.0
CINCINNATI INS CO	OH	10,791.2
FRANKENMUTH MUTUAL INS CO	MI	1,096.8
PROPERTY-OWNERS INS CO	IN	217.0
SENTRY INS A MUTUAL CO	WI	6,922.0
TOKIO MARINE AMERICA INS CO	NY	1,387.9
Rating: A-		
ALLSTATE INS CO	IL	44,425.2
BITCO GENERAL INS CORP	IL	796.8
BITCO NATIONAL INS CO	IL	468.3
BROTHERHOOD MUTUAL INS CO	IN	443.2
CINCINNATI INDEMNITY CO	OH	115.5
COUNTRY MUTUAL INS CO	IL	4,306.5
ESSENT GUARANTY INC	PA	767.9
FEDERATED MUTUAL INS CO	MN	4,726.6
GEICO CHOICE INS CO	NE	388.0
GEICO SECURE INSURANCE CO	NE	338.5
GREAT WEST CASUALTY CO	NE	1,829.1
HOME-OWNERS INS CO	MI	2,165.7
ICI MUTUAL INS CO RRG	VT	330.9
JEWELERS MUTUAL INS CO	WI	329.0
KENTUCKY FARM BUREAU MUTUAL INS CO	KY	2,214.4
MOTORISTS MUTUAL INS CO	OH	1,354.2
NATIONAL MORTGAGE INS CORP	WI	264.6
OLD REPUBLIC GENERAL INS CORP	IL	1,829.0
OLD REPUBLIC INS CO	PA	2,580.9
PROTECTIVE INS CO	IN	776.3
TRAVELERS CASUALTY & SURETY CO	CT	16,487.0
Rating: B+		
ACA FINANCIAL GUARANTY CORP	MD	374.0
ALL AMERICA INS CO	OH	256.6
ALTERRA REINS USA INC	CT	1,467.0
AMICA MUTUAL INS CO	RI	5,054.3
BUILDERS MUTUAL INS CO	NC	625.9
CENTRAL STATES INDEMNITY CO OF OMAHA	NE	427.1
CENTURION CASUALTY CO	IA	140.4
EXECUTIVE RISK INDEMNITY INC	DE	3,025.1
FARM FAMILY CASUALTY INS CO	NY	1,067.1
FEDERAL INS CO	IN	32,714.5
FIRST COLONIAL INS CO	FL	355.0
GEICO GENERAL INS CO	MD	215.7
GEICO INDEMNITY CO	MD	6,922.7

INSURANCE COMPANY NAME	DOM. STATE	TOTAL ASSETS ($MIL)
GNY CUSTOM INS CO	AZ	55.8
GOVERNMENT EMPLOYEES INS CO	MD	22,729.4
GRANGE MUTUAL CAS CO	OH	2,088.9
HARTFORD UNDERWRITERS INS CO	CT	1,566.0
MAINE EMPLOYERS MUTUAL INS CO	ME	813.8
MERCURY CASUALTY CO	CA	1,993.8
MITSUI SUMITOMO INS CO OF AMER	NY	883.6
NATIONAL CASUALTY CO	WI	273.8
NATIONWIDE MUTUAL FIRE INS CO	OH	5,632.7
OLD REPUBLIC SURETY CO	WI	110.0
PACIFIC INDEMNITY CO	WI	6,857.3
SENTRY CASUALTY CO	WI	264.9
SENTRY SELECT INS CO	WI	676.5
STATE FARM MUTUAL AUTOMOBILE INS CO	IL	137,646.1
TOA-RE INS CO OF AMERICA	DE	1,812.3
TRUSTGARD INS CO	OH	102.3
USAA GENERAL INDEMNITY CO	TX	2,785.3
WESTERN AGRICULTURAL INS CO	IA	178.2
WESTFIELD NATIONAL INS CO	OH	593.0

Washington

INSURANCE COMPANY NAME	DOM. STATE	TOTAL ASSETS ($MIL)
Rating: **A+**		
BERKSHIRE HATHAWAY ASR CORP	NY	2,246.2
DAIRYLAND INS CO	WI	1,212.4
MUNICIPAL ASR CORP	NY	1,528.4
OWNERS INS CO	OH	3,686.6
QUEEN CITY ASR INC	VT	2,149.3
UNITED SERVICES AUTOMOBILE ASN	TX	30,759.0
USAA CASUALTY INS CO	TX	8,886.5
Rating: **A**		
AUTO-OWNERS INS CO	MI	11,867.2
CHURCH MUTUAL INS CO	WI	1,452.0
CINCINNATI INS CO	OH	10,701.2
FRANKENMUTH MUTUAL INS CO	MI	1,096.8
SENTRY INS A MUTUAL CO	WI	6,922.0
TOKIO MARINE AMERICA INS CO	NY	1,387.9
Rating: **A-**		
ALLSTATE INS CO	IL	44,425.2
BITCO GENERAL INS CORP	IL	796.8
BITCO NATIONAL INS CO	IL	468.3
BROTHERHOOD MUTUAL INS CO	IN	443.2
CINCINNATI INDEMNITY CO	OH	115.5
COUNTRY MUTUAL INS CO	IL	4,306.5
ESSENT GUARANTY INC	PA	767.9
FEDERATED MUTUAL INS CO	MN	4,726.6
GEICO CHOICE INS CO	NE	388.0
GEICO SECURE INSURANCE CO	NE	338.5
GREAT WEST CASUALTY CO	NE	1,829.1
ICI MUTUAL INS CO RRG	VT	330.9
JEWELERS MUTUAL INS CO	WI	329.0
NATIONAL MORTGAGE INS CORP	WI	264.6
OLD REPUBLIC GENERAL INS CORP	IL	1,829.0
OLD REPUBLIC INS CO	PA	2,580.9
PROTECTIVE INS CO	IN	776.3
TRAVELERS CASUALTY & SURETY CO	CT	16,487.0
Rating: **B+**		
ACA FINANCIAL GUARANTY CORP	MD	374.0
ALTERRA REINS USA INC	CT	1,467.0
AMERICAN FAMILY MUT INS CO	WI	14,543.2
AMERICAN STANDARD INS CO OF WI	WI	415.8
AMICA MUTUAL INS CO	RI	5,054.3
CENTRAL STATES INDEMNITY CO OF OMAHA	NE	427.1
CENTURION CASUALTY CO	IA	140.4
COUNTRY CASUALTY INS CO	IL	78.1
EXECUTIVE RISK INDEMNITY INC	DE	3,025.1
FEDERAL INS CO	IN	32,714.5
FIRST COLONIAL INS CO	FL	355.0
GEICO GENERAL INS CO	MD	215.7
GEICO INDEMNITY CO	MD	6,922.7
GOVERNMENT EMPLOYEES INS CO	MD	22,729.4
HARTFORD UNDERWRITERS INS CO	CT	1,566.0
HOLYOKE MUTUAL INS CO IN SALEM	MA	224.3
MAINE EMPLOYERS MUTUAL INS CO	ME	813.8
MERCURY CASUALTY CO	CA	1,993.8
MITSUI SUMITOMO INS CO OF AMER	NY	883.6

INSURANCE COMPANY NAME	DOM. STATE	TOTAL ASSETS ($MIL)
NATIONAL CASUALTY CO	WI	273.8
NATIONWIDE MUTUAL FIRE INS CO	OH	5,632.7
OLD REPUBLIC SURETY CO	WI	110.0
PACIFIC INDEMNITY CO	WI	6,857.3
SENTRY CASUALTY CO	WI	264.9
SENTRY SELECT INS CO	WI	676.5
STATE FARM MUTUAL AUTOMOBILE INS CO	IL	137,646.1
TOA-RE INS CO OF AMERICA	DE	1,812.3
TRUSTGARD INS CO	OH	102.3
USAA GENERAL INDEMNITY CO	TX	2,785.3
WESTERN COMMUNITY INS CO	ID	36.2
WESTFIELD NATIONAL INS CO	OH	593.0

West Virginia

INSURANCE COMPANY NAME	DOM. STATE	TOTAL ASSETS ($MIL)
Rating: A+		
BERKSHIRE HATHAWAY ASR CORP	NY	2,246.2
DAIRYLAND INS CO	WI	1,212.4
MUNICIPAL ASR CORP	NY	1,528.4
QUEEN CITY ASR INC	VT	2,149.3
UNITED SERVICES AUTOMOBILE ASN	TX	30,759.0
USAA CASUALTY INS CO	TX	8,886.5
Rating: A		
CHURCH MUTUAL INS CO	WI	1,452.0
CINCINNATI INS CO	OH	10,791.2
FRANKENMUTH MUTUAL INS CO	MI	1,096.8
SENTRY INS A MUTUAL CO	WI	6,922.0
TOKIO MARINE AMERICA INS CO	NY	1,387.9
Rating: A-		
ALLSTATE INS CO	IL	44,425.2
BITCO GENERAL INS CORP	IL	796.8
BITCO NATIONAL INS CO	IL	468.3
BROTHERHOOD MUTUAL INS CO	IN	443.2
CINCINNATI INDEMNITY CO	OH	115.5
COUNTRY MUTUAL INS CO	IL	4,306.5
ESSENT GUARANTY INC	PA	767.9
FEDERATED MUTUAL INS CO	MN	4,726.6
GEICO CHOICE INS CO	NE	388.0
GEICO SECURE INSURANCE CO	NE	338.5
GREAT WEST CASUALTY CO	NE	1,829.1
JEWELERS MUTUAL INS CO	WI	329.0
KENTUCKY FARM BUREAU MUTUAL INS CO	KY	2,214.4
MOTORISTS MUTUAL INS CO	OH	1,354.2
NATIONAL MORTGAGE INS CORP	WI	264.6
OLD REPUBLIC GENERAL INS CORP	IL	1,829.0
OLD REPUBLIC INS CO	PA	2,580.9
PROTECTIVE INS CO	IN	776.3
TRAVELERS CASUALTY & SURETY CO	CT	16,487.0
Rating: B+		
ACA FINANCIAL GUARANTY CORP	MD	374.0
ALTERRA REINS USA INC	CT	1,467.0
AMICA MUTUAL INS CO	RI	5,054.3
CENTRAL STATES INDEMNITY CO OF OMAHA	NE	427.1
CENTURION CASUALTY CO	IA	140.4
EXECUTIVE RISK INDEMNITY INC	DE	3,025.1
FARM FAMILY CASUALTY INS CO	NY	1,067.1
FEDERAL INS CO	IN	32,714.5
FIRST COLONIAL INS CO	FL	355.0
GEICO GENERAL INS CO	MD	215.7
GEICO INDEMNITY CO	MD	6,922.7
GOVERNMENT EMPLOYEES INS CO	MD	22,729.4
HARTFORD UNDERWRITERS INS CO	CT	1,566.0
MITSUI SUMITOMO INS CO OF AMER	NY	883.6
NATIONAL CASUALTY CO	WI	273.8
NATIONWIDE MUTUAL FIRE INS CO	OH	5,632.7
OLD REPUBLIC SURETY CO	WI	110.0
PACIFIC INDEMNITY CO	WI	6,857.3
SENTRY CASUALTY CO	WI	264.9
SENTRY SELECT INS CO	WI	676.5

INSURANCE COMPANY NAME	DOM. STATE	TOTAL ASSETS ($MIL)
STATE FARM MUTUAL AUTOMOBILE INS CO	IL	137,646.1
TOA-RE INS CO OF AMERICA	DE	1,812.3
USAA GENERAL INDEMNITY CO	TX	2,785.3
WESTFIELD NATIONAL INS CO	OH	593.0

Wisconsin

INSURANCE COMPANY NAME	DOM. STATE	TOTAL ASSETS ($MIL)
Rating: A+		
BERKSHIRE HATHAWAY ASR CORP	NY	2,246.2
DAIRYLAND INS CO	WI	1,212.4
MUNICIPAL ASR CORP	NY	1,528.4
OWNERS INS CO	OH	3,686.6
QUEEN CITY ASR INC	VT	2,149.3
UNITED SERVICES AUTOMOBILE ASN	TX	30,759.0
USAA CASUALTY INS CO	TX	8,886.5
Rating: A		
AUTO-OWNERS INS CO	MI	11,867.2
CHURCH MUTUAL INS CO	WI	1,452.0
CINCINNATI INS CO	OH	10,791.2
FRANKENMUTH MUTUAL INS CO	MI	1,096.8
PROPERTY-OWNERS INS CO	IN	217.0
SENTRY INS A MUTUAL CO	WI	6,922.0
TOKIO MARINE AMERICA INS CO	NY	1,387.9
Rating: A-		
ALLSTATE INS CO	IL	44,425.2
BITCO GENERAL INS CORP	IL	796.8
BITCO NATIONAL INS CO	IL	468.3
BROTHERHOOD MUTUAL INS CO	IN	443.2
CINCINNATI INDEMNITY CO	OH	115.5
COUNTRY MUTUAL INS CO	IL	4,306.5
ESSENT GUARANTY INC	PA	767.9
FARM BUREAU PROP & CAS INS CO	IA	2,012.0
FEDERATED MUTUAL INS CO	MN	4,726.6
GEICO CHOICE INS CO	NE	388.0
GEICO SECURE INSURANCE CO	NE	338.5
GREAT WEST CASUALTY CO	NE	1,829.1
HASTINGS MUTUAL INS CO	MI	777.9
HOME-OWNERS INS CO	MI	2,165.7
ICI MUTUAL INS CO RRG	VT	330.9
JEWELERS MUTUAL INS CO	WI	329.0
KENTUCKY FARM BUREAU MUTUAL INS CO	KY	2,214.4
MMIC INS INC	MN	701.8
MOTORISTS MUTUAL INS CO	OH	1,354.2
NATIONAL MORTGAGE INS CORP	WI	264.6
OLD REPUBLIC GENERAL INS CORP	IL	1,829.0
OLD REPUBLIC INS CO	PA	2,580.9
PROTECTIVE INS CO	IN	776.3
TRAVELERS CASUALTY & SURETY CO	CT	16,487.0
WEST BEND MUTUAL INS CO	WI	2,162.6
Rating: B+		
ACA FINANCIAL GUARANTY CORP	MD	374.0
ALL AMERICA INS CO	OH	256.6
ALTERRA REINS USA INC	CT	1,467.0
AMERICAN FAMILY MUT INS CO	WI	14,543.2
AMERICAN STANDARD INS CO OF WI	WI	415.8
AMICA MUTUAL INS CO	RI	5,054.3
BUILDERS MUTUAL INS CO	NC	625.9
CENTRAL STATES INDEMNITY CO OF OMAHA	NE	427.1
CENTURION CASUALTY CO	IA	140.4
COUNTRY CASUALTY INS CO	IL	78.1
EXECUTIVE RISK INDEMNITY INC	DE	3,025.1

INSURANCE COMPANY NAME	DOM. STATE	TOTAL ASSETS ($MIL)
FARMERS AUTOMOBILE INS ASN	IL	1,172.9
FEDERAL INS CO	IN	32,714.5
FIRST COLONIAL INS CO	FL	355.0
GEICO GENERAL INS CO	MD	215.7
GEICO INDEMNITY CO	MD	6,922.7
GOVERNMENT EMPLOYEES INS CO	MD	22,729.4
GRANGE MUTUAL CAS CO	OH	2,088.9
HARTFORD UNDERWRITERS INS CO	CT	1,566.0
MITSUI SUMITOMO INS CO OF AMER	NY	883.6
NATIONAL CASUALTY CO	WI	273.8
NATIONWIDE MUTUAL FIRE INS CO	OH	5,632.7
OLD REPUBLIC SURETY CO	WI	110.0
PACIFIC INDEMNITY CO	WI	6,057.3
PEKIN INS CO	IL	286.1
SENTRY CASUALTY CO	WI	264.9
SENTRY SELECT INS CO	WI	676.5
STATE FARM MUTUAL AUTOMOBILE INS CO	IL	137,646.1
TOA-RE INS CO OF AMERICA	DE	1,812.3
TRUSTGARD INS CO	OH	102.3
USAA GENERAL INDEMNITY CO	TX	2,785.3
WESTERN AGRICULTURAL INS CO	IA	178.2
WESTFIELD NATIONAL INS CO	OH	593.0

Wyoming

INSURANCE COMPANY NAME	DOM. STATE	TOTAL ASSETS ($MIL)
Rating: A+		
BERKSHIRE HATHAWAY ASR CORP	NY	2,246.2
DAIRYLAND INS CO	WI	1,212.4
MUNICIPAL ASR CORP	NY	1,528.4
QUEEN CITY ASR INC	VT	2,149.3
UNITED SERVICES AUTOMOBILE ASN	TX	30,759.0
USAA CASUALTY INS CO	TX	8,886.5
Rating: A		
CHURCH MUTUAL INS CO	WI	1,452.0
CINCINNATI INS CO	OH	10,791.2
FRANKENMUTH MUTUAL INS CO	MI	1,096.8
SENTRY INS A MUTUAL CO	WI	6,922.0
TOKIO MARINE AMERICA INS CO	NY	1,387.9
Rating: A-		
ALLSTATE INS CO	IL	44,425.2
BITCO GENERAL INS CORP	IL	796.8
BITCO NATIONAL INS CO	IL	468.3
BROTHERHOOD MUTUAL INS CO	IN	443.2
CINCINNATI INDEMNITY CO	OH	115.5
COPIC INS CO	CO	548.6
COUNTRY MUTUAL INS CO	IL	4,306.5
CSAA INS EXCHANGE	CA	6,956.8
ESSENT GUARANTY INC	PA	767.9
FEDERATED MUTUAL INS CO	MN	4,726.6
GEICO CHOICE INS CO	NE	388.0
GEICO SECURE INSURANCE CO	NE	338.5
GREAT WEST CASUALTY CO	NE	1,829.1
JEWELERS MUTUAL INS CO	WI	329.0
MMIC INS INC	MN	701.8
NATIONAL MORTGAGE INS CORP	WI	264.6
OLD REPUBLIC GENERAL INS CORP	IL	1,829.0
OLD REPUBLIC INS CO	PA	2,580.9
PROTECTIVE INS CO	IN	776.3
TRAVELERS CASUALTY & SURETY CO	CT	16,487.0
Rating: B+		
ACA FINANCIAL GUARANTY CORP	MD	374.0
ALTERRA REINS USA INC	CT	1,467.0
AMERICAN FAMILY MUT INS CO	WI	14,543.2
AMERICAN STANDARD INS CO OF WI	WI	415.8
AMICA MUTUAL INS CO	RI	5,054.3
CENTRAL STATES INDEMNITY CO OF OMAHA	NE	427.1
CENTURION CASUALTY CO	IA	140.4
COUNTRY CASUALTY INS CO	IL	78.1
EXECUTIVE RISK INDEMNITY INC	DE	3,025.1
FEDERAL INS CO	IN	32,714.5
FIRST COLONIAL INS CO	FL	355.0
GEICO GENERAL INS CO	MD	215.7
GEICO INDEMNITY CO	MD	6,922.7
GOVERNMENT EMPLOYEES INS CO	MD	22,729.4
HARTFORD UNDERWRITERS INS CO	CT	1,566.0
HOLYOKE MUTUAL INS CO IN SALEM	MA	224.3
MITSUI SUMITOMO INS CO OF AMER	NY	883.6
NATIONAL CASUALTY CO	WI	273.8
NATIONWIDE MUTUAL FIRE INS CO	OH	5,632.7

INSURANCE COMPANY NAME	DOM. STATE	TOTAL ASSETS ($MIL)
OLD REPUBLIC SURETY CO	WI	110.0
PACIFIC INDEMNITY CO	WI	6,857.3
SENTRY CASUALTY CO	WI	264.9
SENTRY SELECT INS CO	WI	676.5
STATE FARM MUTUAL AUTOMOBILE INS CO	IL	137,646.1
TOA-RE INS CO OF AMERICA	DE	1,812.3
USAA GENERAL INDEMNITY CO	TX	2,785.3
WESTERN AGRICULTURAL INS CO	IA	178.2

Section VI

All Companies
Listed by Rating

A list of all rated and unrated

U.S. Property and Casualty Insurers.

Companies are ranked by Weiss Financial Strength Rating
and then listed alphabetically within each rating category.

Section VI Contents

This section sorts all companies by their Financial Strength Rating and then lists them alphabetically within each rating category. The purpose of this section is to provide in one place all of those companies receiving a given rating. Companies with the same rating should be viewed as having the same relative financial strength regardless of their order in this table.

1. **Insurance Company Name**

   The legally registered name, which can sometimes differ from the name that the company uses for advertising. An insurer's name can be very similar to that of another, so verify the company's exact name and state of domicile to make sure you are looking at the correct company.

2. **Domicile State**

   The state which has primary regulatory responsibility for the company. It may differ from the location of the company's corporate headquarters. You do not have to be living in the domicile state to purchase insurance from this firm, provided it is licensed to do business in your state.

3. **Total Assets**

   All assets admitted by state insurance regulators in millions of dollars. This includes investments and current business assets such as receivables from agents and reinsurers.

INSURANCE COMPANY NAME	DOM. STATE	TOTAL ASSETS ($MIL)
Rating: A+		
BERKSHIRE HATHAWAY ASR CORP	NY	2,246.2
CITIZENS PROPERTY INS CORP	FL	14,582.0
COPPERPOINT MUTUAL INS CO	AZ	3,581.2
DAIRYLAND INS CO	WI	1,212.4
INTERINS EXCH OF THE AUTOMOBILE CLUB	CA	8,447.5
MUNICIPAL ASR CORP	NY	1,528.4
OGLESBY REINSURANCE CO	IL	3,196.5
OWNERS INS CO	OH	3,686.6
QUEEN CITY ASR INC	VT	2,149.3
STATE VOLUNTEER MUTUAL INS CO	TN	1,206.0
UNITED SERVICES AUTOMOBILE ASN	TX	30,759.0
USAA CASUALTY INS CO	TX	8,886.5
Rating: A		
AUTO-OWNERS INS CO	MI	11,867.2
CHURCH MUTUAL INS CO	WI	1,452.0
CINCINNATI INS CO	OH	10,791.2
FRANKENMUTH MUTUAL INS CO	MI	1,096.8
MUTUAL INS CO OF AZ	AZ	1,011.0
PIONEER STATE MUTUAL INS CO	MI	464.9
PROPERTY-OWNERS INS CO	IN	217.0
SAIF CORP	OR	4,802.9
SENTRY INS A MUTUAL CO	WI	6,922.0
SOUTHERN-OWNERS INS CO	MI	618.1
TEXAS FARM BUREAU CASUALTY INS CO	TX	1,123.7
TOKIO MARINE AMERICA INS CO	NY	1,387.9
Rating: A-		
ALLSTATE INS CO	IL	44,425.2
AMICA LLOYDS OF TEXAS	TX	77.6
BITCO GENERAL INS CORP	IL	796.8
BITCO NATIONAL INS CO	IL	468.3
BROTHERHOOD MUTUAL INS CO	IN	443.2
CINCINNATI INDEMNITY CO	OH	115.5
COPIC INS CO	CO	548.6
COUNTRY MUTUAL INS CO	IL	4,306.5
CSAA INS EXCHANGE	CA	6,956.8
ESSENT GUARANTY INC	PA	767.9
FARM BUREAU PROP & CAS INS CO	IA	2,012.0
FEDERATED MUTUAL INS CO	MN	4,726.6
GEICO CHOICE INS CO	NE	388.0
GEICO SECURE INSURANCE CO	NE	338.5
GREAT WEST CASUALTY CO	NE	1,829.1
HASTINGS MUTUAL INS CO	MI	777.9
HOME-OWNERS INS CO	MI	2,165.7
ICI MUTUAL INS CO RRG	VT	330.9
JEWELERS MUTUAL INS CO	WI	329.0
KENTUCKY FARM BUREAU MUTUAL INS CO	KY	2,214.4
LOUISIANA WORKERS COMPENSATION CORP	LA	1,576.2
MERCURY INS CO	CA	1,591.4
MMIC INS INC	MN	701.8
MOTORISTS MUTUAL INS CO	OH	1,354.2
NATIONAL MORTGAGE INS CORP	WI	264.6
OLD REPUBLIC GENERAL INS CORP	IL	1,829.0
OLD REPUBLIC INS CO	PA	2,580.9
OTSEGO MUTUAL FIRE INS CO	NY	110.3

INSURANCE COMPANY NAME	DOM. STATE	TOTAL ASSETS ($MIL)
PROTECTIVE INS CO	IN	776.3
RETAILFIRST INS CO	FL	282.1
TRAVELERS CASUALTY & SURETY CO	CT	16,487.0
WEST BEND MUTUAL INS CO	WI	2,162.6
Rating: B+		
ACA FINANCIAL GUARANTY CORP	MD	374.0
ALFA INS CORP	AL	99.4
ALFA MUTUAL GENERAL INS CO	AL	100.9
ALL AMERICA INS CO	OH	256.6
ALTERRA REINS USA INC	CT	1,467.0
AMERICAN FAMILY MUT INS CO	WI	14,543.2
AMERICAN STANDARD INS CO OF WI	WI	415.8
AMICA MUTUAL INS CO	RI	5,054.3
AUTO CLUB INDEMNITY CO	TX	21.8
BUILDERS MUTUAL INS CO	NC	625.9
CENTRAL STATES INDEMNITY CO OF OMAHA	NE	427.1
CENTURION CASUALTY CO	IA	140.4
COUNTRY CASUALTY INS CO	IL	78.1
EXECUTIVE RISK INDEMNITY INC	DE	3,025.1
FARM BUREAU MUTUAL INS CO OF ID	ID	431.4
FARM FAMILY CASUALTY INS CO	NY	1,067.1
FARMERS AUTOMOBILE INS ASN	IL	1,172.9
FEDERAL INS CO	IN	32,714.5
FIRST COLONIAL INS CO	FL	355.0
GEICO GENERAL INS CO	MD	215.7
GEICO INDEMNITY CO	MD	6,922.7
GNY CUSTOM INS CO	AZ	55.8
GOVERNMENT EMPLOYEES INS CO	MD	22,729.4
GRANGE MUTUAL CAS CO	OH	2,088.9
HARTFORD UNDERWRITERS INS CO	CT	1,566.0
HOLYOKE MUTUAL INS CO IN SALEM	MA	224.3
INDIANA FARMERS MUTUAL INS CO	IN	351.6
MAINE EMPLOYERS MUTUAL INS CO	ME	813.8
MERCURY CASUALTY CO	CA	1,993.8
MITSUI SUMITOMO INS CO OF AMER	NY	883.6
NATIONAL CASUALTY CO	WI	273.8
NATIONWIDE MUTUAL FIRE INS CO	OH	5,632.7
OLD REPUBLIC SURETY CO	WI	110.0
PACIFIC INDEMNITY CO	WI	6,857.3
PEKIN INS CO	IL	286.1
SAFETY INS CO	MA	1,429.1
SENTRY CASUALTY CO	WI	264.9
SENTRY SELECT INS CO	WI	676.5
STATE FARM MUTUAL AUTOMOBILE INS CO	IL	137,646.1
TENNESSEE FARMERS ASR CO	TN	1,133.1
TENNESSEE FARMERS MUTUAL INS CO	TN	2,369.1
TEXAS MUTUAL INS CO	TX	5,660.4
TOA-RE INS CO OF AMERICA	DE	1,812.3
TRUSTGARD INS CO	OH	102.3
TUSCARORA WAYNE INS CO	PA	91.3
USAA GENERAL INDEMNITY CO	TX	2,785.3
USAA TEXAS LLOYDS CO	TX	575.9
WESTERN AGRICULTURAL INS CO	IA	178.2
WESTERN COMMUNITY INS CO	ID	36.2
WESTFIELD NATIONAL INS CO	OH	593.0

INSURANCE COMPANY NAME	DOM. STATE	TOTAL ASSETS ($MIL)
Rating: B		
21ST CENTURY ADVANTAGE INS CO	MN	28.5
21ST CENTURY ASR CO	DE	69.0
21ST CENTURY CASUALTY CO	CA	12.4
21ST CENTURY CENTENNIAL INS CO	PA	568.4
21ST CENTURY INDEMNITY INS CO	PA	64.9
21ST CENTURY INS CO	CA	889.9
21ST CENTURY NATIONAL INS CO INC	NY	24.2
21ST CENTURY NORTH AMERICA INS	NY	566.3
21ST CENTURY PACIFIC INS	CO	44.3
21ST CENTURY PINNACLE INS CO	NJ	42.2
21ST CENTURY PREFERRED INS CO	PA	41.3
21ST CENTURY SECURITY INS CO	PA	195.7
ACUITY A MUTUAL INS CO	WI	3,017.8
AIG ASR CO	PA	32.2
AIG INS CO - PUERTO RICO	PR	180.4
ALASKA NATIONAL INS CO	AK	853.2
ALFA MUTUAL FIRE INS CO	AL	687.7
ALFA MUTUAL INS CO	AL	1,293.2
ALLIED PROPERTY & CASUALTY INS CO	IA	362.1
ALLSTATE COUNTY MUTUAL INS CO	TX	14.6
ALLSTATE INDEMNITY CO	IL	154.3
ALLSTATE NJ INS CO	IL	2,569.7
ALLSTATE PROPERTY & CASUALTY INS CO	IL	218.3
ALLSTATE TEXAS LLOYDS	TX	17.1
ALLSTATE VEHICLE & PROPERTY INS CO	IL	25.4
ALPHA PROPERTY & CASUALTY INS CO	WI	34.3
ALTERRA AMERICA INS CO	DE	225.8
AMERICAN BANKERS INS CO OF FL	FL	2,020.9
AMERICAN CAPITAL ASR CORP	FL	200.2
AMERICAN CONTRACTORS INDEMNITY CO	CA	322.0
AMERICAN EQUITY SPECIALTY INS CO	CT	79.6
AMERICAN FAMILY INS CO	OH	27.8
AMERICAN MERCURY INS CO	OK	354.4
AMERICAN MERCURY LLOYDS INS CO	TX	5.7
AMERICAN MODERN PROPERTY & CASUALTY	OH	20.8
AMERICAN MODERN SURPLUS LINES INS CO	OH	84.4
AMERICAN NATIONAL LLOYDS INS CO	TX	77.4
AMERICAN NATIONAL PROPERTY & CAS CO	MO	1,216.0
AMERICAN NATL COUNTY MUT INS CO	TX	19.9
AMERICAN PACIFIC INS COMPANY	HI	11.6
AMERICAN SECURITY INS CO	DE	2,104.9
AMERICAN SOUTHERN HOME INS CO	FL	143.9
AMERICAN STANDARD INS CO OF OH	OH	8.8
AMERIPRISE INS CO	WI	48.0
AMEX ASSURANCE CO	IL	299.7
ANPAC LOUISIANA INS CO	LA	120.4
ANSUR AMERICA INS CO	MI	100.6
ANTILLES INS CO	PR	108.6
ARCH MORTGAGE ASR CO	WI	13.0
ARCH SPECIALTY INS CO	MO	577.2
AUTO CLUB INS ASSN	MI	3,680.4
AUTOMOBILE INS CO OF HARTFORD CT	CT	1,038.3
AVEMCO INS CO	MD	114.0

INSURANCE COMPANY NAME	DOM. STATE	TOTAL ASSETS ($MIL)
BCS INS CO	OH	291.2
BRETHREN MUTUAL INS CO	MD	240.0
CALIFORNIA AUTOMOBILE INS CO	CA	420.0
CALIFORNIA GENERAL UNDERWRITERS INS	CA	20.5
CANAL INDEMNITY CO	SC	44.4
CANAL INS CO	SC	858.0
CASTLE KEY INDEMNITY CO	IL	7.0
CENTENNIAL CASUALTY CO	AL	110.9
CENTRAL MUTUAL INS CO	OH	1,330.2
CENTURY INS CO GUAM LTD	GU	21.0
CENTURY-NATIONAL INS CO	CA	615.6
CHARTER INDEMNITY CO	TX	12.5
CHARTER OAK FIRE INS CO	CT	959.3
CHUBB INDEMNITY INS CO	NY	354.3
CHUBB INS CO OF NEW JERSEY	NJ	0.0
CHUBB LLOYDS INS CO OF TX	TX	38.8
CHUBB NATIONAL INS CO	IN	304.8
CINCINNATI CASUALTY CO	OH	362.0
CINCINNATI SPECIALTY UNDERWRITER	DE	531.6
CITATION INS CO	MA	250.8
CITIZENS INS CO OF AMERICA	MI	1,480.7
COLONIAL COUNTY MUTUAL INS CO	TX	120.6
COMPANION COMMERCIAL INS CO	SC	21.7
COMPANION SPECIALTY INS CO	DC	62.2
COUNTRY PREFERRED INS CO	IL	199.7
COURTESY INS CO	FL	718.2
COVINGTON SPECIALTY INS CO	NH	99.8
CRESTBROOK INS CO	OH	99.8
CUMIS INS SOCIETY INC	IA	2,309.5
CUMIS SPECIALTY INS CO INC	IA	147.6
DAIRYLAND COUNTY MUTUAL INS CO OF TX	TX	13.8
DENTISTS INS CO	CA	332.8
EAGLESTONE REINS CO	PA	5,539.9
ECONOMY PREFERRED INS CO	IL	32.8
ECONOMY PREMIER ASR CO	IL	85.1
EMPLOYERS COMPENSATION INS CO	CA	1,812.7
ENCOMPASS INDEMNITY CO	IL	27.7
ENDURANCE REINS CORP OF AMERICA	DE	1,568.6
ERIE INS CO OF NY	NY	90.1
ERIE INS EXCHANGE	PA	13,233.4
ERIE INS PROPERTY & CASUALTY CO	PA	96.1
EULER HERMES AMERICAN CREDIT IND CO	MD	428.5
FAIR AMERICAN INS & REINS CO	NY	257.2
FARM BU TOWN & COUNTRY INS CO OF MO	MO	330.8
FARM BUREAU GENERAL INS CO OF MI	MI	536.3
FARM BUREAU INS OF NC INC	NC	9.4
FARMERS & MECH MUTUAL INS CO	PA	5.2
FARMERS INS CO OF OR	OR	1,602.5
FARMERS INS HAWAII INC	HI	92.0
FARMERS MUTUAL INS CO OF NE	NE	506.0
FARMINGTON CASUALTY CO	CT	1,040.3
FARMLAND MUTUAL INS CO	IA	504.2
FEDERATED SERVICE INS CO	MN	422.2
FIRST FLORIDIAN AUTO & HOME INS CO	FL	282.9
FLORIDA FARM BUREAU GENERAL INS CO	FL	9.5
FOREMOST INS CO	MI	2,120.7

INSURANCE COMPANY NAME	DOM. STATE	TOTAL ASSETS ($MIL)	INSURANCE COMPANY NAME	DOM. STATE	TOTAL ASSETS ($MIL)
Rating: B (Continued)			METROPOLITAN LLOYDS INS CO TEXAS	TX	91.5
FORTUITY INS CO	MI	38.0	METROPOLITAN PROPERTY & CAS INS CO	RI	5,740.1
FRANKLIN MUTUAL INS CO	NJ	0.0	MHA INS CO	MI	539.0
FREEDOM SPECIALTY INS CO	OH	26.0	MIAMI MUTUAL INS CO	OH	52.1
GARRISON PROPERTY & CASUALTY INS CO	TX	1,435.4	MICO INS CO	OH	13.2
GENERAL STAR NATIONAL INS CO	DE	241.7	MID AMERICAN FIRE & CAS CO	NH	8.2
GEORGIA FARM BUREAU CASUALTY INS CO	GA	3.6	MIDDLESEX INS CO	WI	679.5
GERMANIA SELECT INS CO	TX	188.2	MIDDLESEX MUTUAL ASR CO	CT	250.8
GOVERNMENTAL INTERINSURANCE EXCHANGE	IL	68.9	MIDWEST BUILDERS CASUALTY MUTUAL CO	KS	77.7
GREAT NORTHERN INS CO	IN	1,661.0	MILWAUKEE CASUALTY INS CO	WI	48.0
GREEN MOUNTAIN INS CO INC	VT	11.2	MINNESOTA LAWYERS MUTUAL INS CO	MN	157.8
GUIDEONE PROPERTY & CASUALTY INS CO	IA	684.5	MISSISSIPPI FARM BUREAU CAS INS CO	MS	371.1
GUIDEONE SPECIALTY MUTUAL INS CO	IA	590.7	MODERN SERVICE INS CO	IL	28.3
HANOVER INS CO	NH	6,424.6	MOTORISTS COMMERCIAL MUTUAL INS CO	OH	342.1
HARTFORD ACCIDENT & INDEMNITY CO	CT	11,637.2	MUTUAL OF ENUMCLAW INS CO	WA	663.7
HARTFORD CASUALTY INS CO	IN	2,314.7	NATIONAL LIABILITY & FIRE INS CO	CT	2,144.3
HARTFORD FIRE INS CO	CT	25,686.8	NATIONAL PUBLIC FINANCE GUAR CORP	NY	5,398.3
HARTFORD INS CO OF IL	IL	3,895.9	NATIONWIDE AFFINITY INS CO OF AMER	OH	376.1
HARTFORD INS CO OF THE MIDWEST	IN	567.5	NATIONWIDE LLOYDS	TX	44.2
HARTFORD INS CO OF THE SOUTHEAST	CT	182.4	NATIONWIDE MUTUAL INS CO	OH	33,915.9
HARTFORD LLOYDS INS CO	TX	68.5	NAVIGATORS INS CO	NY	2,434.4
HARTFORD SM BOIL INSPECTION & INS	CT	1,348.6	NCMIC INS CO	IA	645.6
HARTFORD SM BOIL INSPECTION IC OF CT	CT	93.5	NEW JERSEY RE-INS CO	NJ	559.6
HIGH POINT PROPERTY & CASUALTY INS	NJ	0.0	NEW YORK SCHOOLS INS RECIPROCAL	NY	288.9
HOMELAND INS CO OF DE	DE	52.9	NORTHLAND CASUALTY CO	CT	109.2
HORACE MANN INS CO	IL	444.4	NORTHLAND INS CO	CT	1,210.2
HORACE MANN PROP & CAS INS CO	IL	282.7	OKLAHOMA ATTORNEYS MUTUAL INS CO	OK	54.8
HOUSTON SPECIALTY INS CO	TX	438.6	OLD REPUBLIC LLOYDS OF TX	TX	1.9
HSB SPECIALTY INS CO	CT	50.5	OLD REPUBLIC UNION INS CO	IL	56.1
HUDSON EXCESS INS CO	DE	58.8	OMNI INS CO	IL	208.6
IDS PROPERTY CASUALTY INS CO	WI	1,438.0	OPHTHALMIC MUTUAL INS CO RRG	VT	267.0
IMT INS CO	IA	300.9	PACIFIC INS CO LTD	CT	645.3
INFINITY INS CO	IN	2,031.5	PACIFIC PROPERTY & CASUALTY CO	CA	75.1
IOWA AMERICAN INS CO	IA	22.5	PATRIOT GENERAL INS CO	WI	27.4
IOWA MUTUAL INS CO	IA	101.6	PEAK PROP & CAS INS CORP	WI	51.2
KINSALE INS CO	AR	290.2	PENNSYLVANIA LUMBERMENS MUTUAL INS	PA	462.2
LIBERTY LLOYDS OF TX INS CO	TX	7.0	PHARMACISTS MUTUAL INS CO	IA	253.6
LIBERTY MUTUAL INS CO	MA	42,150.7	PHILADELPHIA INDEMNITY INS CO	PA	7,236.4
LIBERTY MUTUAL PERSONAL INS CO	MA	6.8	PHOENIX INS CO	CT	4,191.2
LION INS CO	FL	220.6	PREFERRED MUTUAL INS CO	NY	500.3
LOUISIANA FARM BUREAU CAS INS CO	LA	10.4	PREMIER INS CO OF MASSACHUSETTS	MA	361.7
LOUISIANA FARM BUREAU MUTUAL INS CO	LA	197.9	PROPERTY & CASUALTY I CO OF HARTFORD	IN	236.5
LUBA CASUALTY INS CO	LA	217.0	PROTECTIVE SPECIALTY INS CO	IN	76.3
MEDICAL INS EXCHANGE OF CALIFORNIA	CA	401.5	QBE REINSURANCE CORP	PA	1,269.9
MEDICAL PROTECTIVE CO	IN	2,672.6	QUINCY MUTUAL FIRE INS CO	MA	1,481.9
MENDAKOTA INS CO	MN	14.7	RED SHIELD INS CO	WA	41.8
MERCURY INDEMNITY CO OF GEORGIA	GA	13.4	RIVERPORT INS CO	MN	107.6
MERCURY INS CO OF GA	GA	19.8	RLI INS CO	IL	1,782.0
MERCURY INS CO OF IL	IL	32.6	RURAL COMMUNITY INS CO	MN	7,691.1
MERCURY NATIONAL INS CO	IL	16.3	SAFECO INS CO OF ILLINOIS	IL	185.7
MERRIMACK MUTUAL FIRE INS CO	MA	1,305.5	SAFECO INS CO OF OREGON	OR	13.7
METROPOLITAN CASUALTY INS CO	RI	198.2	SAFECO LLOYDS INS CO	TX	12.8
METROPOLITAN DIRECT PROP & CAS INS	RI	115.9	SCOTTSDALE INDEMNITY CO	OH	77.3
METROPOLITAN GENERAL INS CO	RI	40.7	SCOTTSDALE SURPLUS LINES INS CO	AZ	48.6
METROPOLITAN GROUP PROP & CAS INS CO	RI	616.7	SECURIAN CASUALTY CO	MN	192.1
			SELECTIVE CASUALTY INS CO	NJ	0.0

INSURANCE COMPANY NAME	DOM. STATE	TOTAL ASSETS ($MIL)
Rating: B (Continued)		
SELECTIVE INS CO OF NEW YORK	NY	377.5
SELECTIVE INS CO OF SC	IN	567.1
SELECTIVE INS CO OF THE SOUTHEAST	IN	438.2
SELECTIVE WAY INS CO	NJ	1,170.3
SENTINEL INS CO LTD	CT	220.3
SENTRY LLOYDS OF TX	TX	6.8
SERVICE INS CO	FL	48.3
SHELTER MUTUAL INS CO	MO	2,923.1
SOMPO JAPAN INS CO OF AMERICA	NY	1,244.3
SOUTHWEST MARINE & GEN INS CO	AZ	117.6
ST PAUL FIRE & MARINE INS CO	CT	18,981.1
STANDARD FIRE INS CO	CT	3,617.4
STATE AUTO INS CO OF WISCONSIN	WI	17.9
STATE FARM GENERAL INS CO	IL	6,749.8
SUNAPEE MUTUAL FIRE INS CO	NH	3.9
TEACHERS INS CO	IL	339.9
TEXAS PACIFIC INDEMNITY CO	TX	7.6
TRANS PACIFIC INS CO	NY	81.5
TRANSATLANTIC REINSURANCE CO	NY	14,695.1
TRANSGUARD INS CO OF AMERICA INC	IL	256.9
TRAVCO INS CO	CT	222.6
TRAVELERS CASUALTY CO OF CONNECTICUT	CT	330.8
TRAVELERS CASUALTY INS CO OF AMERICA	CT	1,972.9
TRAVELERS COMMERCIAL CASUALTY CO	CT	336.2
TRAVELERS COMMERCIAL INS CO	CT	352.9
TRAVELERS EXCESS & SURPLUS LINES CO	CT	219.6
TRAVELERS HOME & MARINE INS CO	CT	410.9
TRAVELERS INDEMNITY CO	CT	20,782.1
TRAVELERS INDEMNITY CO OF AMERICA	CT	639.2
TRAVELERS INDEMNITY CO OF CT	CT	1,161.8
TRAVELERS LLOYDS OF TEXAS INS CO	TX	25.1
TRAVELERS PERSONAL INS CO	CT	202.9
TRAVELERS PERSONAL SECURITY INS CO	CT	212.0
TRAVELERS PROPERTY CAS OF AMERICA	CT	946.6
TRAVELERS PROPERTY CASUALTY INS CO	CT	239.5
TRI-STATE CONSUMER INS CO	NY	120.9
TRINITY UNIVERSAL INS CO	TX	2,323.6
TRUMBULL INS CO	CT	223.1
TWIN CITY FIRE INS CO	IN	650.2
UFB CASUALTY INS CO	IN	8.5
UMIA INS INC	OR	279.3
UNION NATIONAL FIRE INS CO	LA	9.5
UNITED CASUALTY INS CO OF AMERICA	IL	11.4
UNITED FARM FAMILY INS CO	NY	29.2
UNITED FIRE & CAS CO	IA	1,620.3
UNITED STATES FIDELITY & GUARANTY CO	CT	4,798.7
UNITED SURETY & INDEMNITY CO	PR	101.7
UNITRIN DIRECT INS CO	IL	14.8
UNITRIN DIRECT PROPERTY & CAS CO	IL	17.6
UNITRIN SAFEGUARD INS CO	WI	26.9
USAA COUNTY MUTUAL INS CO	TX	5.7
UTICA LLOYDS OF TX	TX	10.0
VALLEY PROPERTY & CASUALTY INS CO	OR	12.1
VANLINER INS CO	MO	336.2

INSURANCE COMPANY NAME	DOM. STATE	TOTAL ASSETS ($MIL)
VERMONT ACCIDENT INS CO INC	VT	7.9
VICTORIA AUTOMOBILE INS CO	OH	26.9
VIGILANT INS CO	NY	489.2
VININGS INS CO	DE	71.2
WESTERN HERITAGE INS CO	AZ	144.1
WESTON INS CO	FL	48.3
WILSON MUTUAL INS CO	WI	98.6
Rating: B-		
21ST CENTURY PREMIER INS CO	PA	271.0
ACCIDENT FUND GENERAL INS CO	MI	247.0
ACE AMERICAN INS CO	PA	12,524.0
ACE INS CO	PR	137.8
AEGIS SECURITY INS CO	PA	106.3
AFFILIATES INS RECIPROCAL A RRG	VT	9.2
AGRICULTURAL WORKERS MUT AUTO INS CO	TX	78.1
AIX SPECIALTY INS CO	DE	52.4
ALAMANCE FARMERS MUTUAL INS CO	NC	7.7
ALFA GENERAL INS CORP	AL	98.0
ALLIED WORLD NATL ASR CO	NH	300.4
ALLSTATE NORTHBROOK INDEMNITY CO	IL	39.5
AMERICA FIRST INS CO	NH	13.9
AMERICAN EUROPEAN INS CO	NH	148.5
AMERICAN INTERSTATE INS CO	NE	1,214.8
AMERICAN MINING INS CO	IA	33.6
AMERICAN NATIONAL GENERAL INS CO	MO	103.3
AMERICAN STATES INS CO OF TX	TX	11.9
AMERICAN STATES LLOYDS INS CO	TX	3.5
AMERISURE INS CO	MI	745.1
AMERISURE MUTUAL INS CO	MI	2,027.5
AMTRUST INS CO OF KANSAS INC	KS	52.9
ARAG INS CO	IA	79.6
ARCH MORTGAGE GUARANTY CO	WI	9.0
ARISE BOILER INSPECT & INS CO RRG	KY	3.2
ARROW MUTUAL LIABILITY INS CO	MA	47.3
ASI HOME INS CORP	FL	16.7
ATHENS FINANCIAL INS CO	OK	2.1
ATLANTIC CASUALTY INS CO	NC	236.7
ATLANTIC CHARTER INS CO	MA	181.3
ATLANTIC STATES INS CO	PA	636.4
AUTO CLUB GROUP INS CO	MI	350.7
BARNSTABLE COUNTY MUTUAL INS CO	MA	102.0
BAY STATE INS CO	MA	429.0
BEAR RIVER MUTUAL INS CO	UT	233.8
BENCHMARK INS CO	KS	173.5
BENEFIT SECURITY INS CO	IL	8.1
BLACK DIAMOND INS CO	NV	0.0
BONDEX INS CO	NJ	5.2
BRIDGEFIELD EMPLOYERS INS CO	FL	156.7
CALIFORNIA CAPITAL INS CO	CA	590.0
CALIFORNIA INS CO	CA	614.3
CAMBRIDGE MUTUAL FIRE INS CO	MA	794.4
CANOPIUS US INS INC	DE	139.5
CAROLINA MUTUAL INS INC	NC	78.3
CASTLE KEY INS CO	IL	354.2
CATERPILLAR INS CO	MO	683.8

INSURANCE COMPANY NAME	DOM. STATE	TOTAL ASSETS ($MIL)

Rating: B- (Continued)

INSURANCE COMPANY NAME	DOM. STATE	TOTAL ASSETS ($MIL)
CHUBB CUSTOM INS CO	NJ	363.5
CMIC RRG	DC	3.8
CO-OPERATIVE INS COMPANIES	VT	122.2
COLUMBIA INS CO	NE	19,280.1
COMMERCE INS CO	MA	2,349.1
CONCORD GENERAL MUTUAL INS CO	NH	439.9
CONTRACTORS BONDING & INS CO	WA	198.5
COPPERPOINT GENERAL INS CO	AZ	16.1
COPPERPOINT WESTERN INS CO	AZ	8.3
CRUSADER INS CO	CA	120.0
CUMBERLAND INS CO INC	NJ	104.0
CUMBERLAND MUTUAL FIRE INS CO	NJ	258.5
DARWIN NATIONAL ASR CO	DE	777.1
DEALERS ASR CO	OH	88.0
DEPOSITORS INS CO	IA	278.0
DEVELOPERS SURETY & INDEMNITY CO	IA	137.5
DOCTORS CO AN INTERINSURANCE EXCH	CA	3,490.5
DONEGAL MUTUAL INS CO	PA	389.9
DONGBU INS CO LTD US GUAM BRANCH	GU	51.4
ECOLE INS CO	AZ	9.5
ECONOMY FIRE & CAS CO	IL	472.1
ELEMENTS PROPERTY INS CO	FL	38.8
EMC PROPERTY & CASUALTY CO	IA	160.0
EMCASCO INS CO	IA	443.0
EMPIRE BONDING & INS CO	NY	2.6
EMPLOYERS INS OF WAUSAU	WI	5,248.3
EMPLOYERS MUTUAL CAS CO	IA	2,711.2
ENCOMPASS HOME & AUTO INS CO	IL	13.8
ENCOMPASS INDEPENDENT INS CO	IL	7.7
ERIE INS CO	PA	837.4
ESSENT GUARANTY OF PA INC	PA	68.5
EXECUTIVE RISK SPECIALTY INS CO	CT	276.8
FARM BUREAU MUTUAL INS CO OF MI	MI	650.9
FARM CREDIT SYS ASSOC CAPTIVE INS CO	CO	103.1
FARMERS & MECHANICS MUTUAL IC OF WV	WV	58.4
FARMERS INS CO OF WA	WA	520.7
FARMERS INS OF COLUMBUS INC	OH	256.4
FARMERS MUTUAL HAIL INS CO OF IA	IA	844.6
FARMERS REINS CO	CA	1,445.7
FARMERS SPECIALTY INS CO	MI	16.4
FINANCIAL INDEMNITY CO	IL	82.7
FINANCIAL PACIFIC INS CO	CA	213.5
FIREMANS FUND INDEMNITY CORP	NJ	0.0
FIREMANS FUND INS CO OF HI INC	HI	11.3
FIRST GUARD INS CO	AZ	20.6
FIRST NATIONAL INS CO OF AMERICA	NH	55.7
FLAGSHIP CITY INS CO	PA	46.1
FLORIDA FARM BU CASUALTY INS CO	FL	530.4
FREDERICK MUTUAL INS CO	MD	54.7
GENERAL REINSURANCE CORP	DE	16,162.6
GENERAL STAR INDEMNITY CO	DE	827.5
GENWORTH MORTGAGE REINS CORP	NC	13.1
GERMAN AMERICAN FARM MUTUAL	TX	4.1
GERMANTOWN MUTUAL INS CO	WI	91.6
GOODVILLE MUTUAL CAS CO	PA	215.3
GOTHAM INS CO	NY	203.2
GOVT TECHNOLOGY INS CO RRG INC	NV	1.0
GRANITE STATE INS CO	PA	32.9
GREAT AMERICAN INS CO	OH	5,734.6
GREAT MIDWEST INS CO	TX	156.1
GREATER NEW YORK MUTUAL INS CO	NY	887.9
GRINNELL MUTUAL REINSURANCE CO	IA	910.5
GUIDEONE AMERICA INS CO	IA	11.6
GUIDEONE LLOYDS INS CO	TX	3.5
GUIDEONE MUTUAL INS CO	IA	2,459.2
HARCO NATIONAL INS CO	IL	344.2
HARFORD MUTUAL INS CO	MD	363.1
HISCOX INS CO INC	IL	141.6
HM CASUALTY INS CO	PA	29.5
HOSPITALITY MUTUAL INS CO	MA	52.7
HOUSTON CASUALTY CO	TX	3,216.5
HYUNDAI MARINE & FIRE INS CO LTD	CA	81.2
ILLINOIS NATIONAL INS CO	IL	39.3
INFINITY ASSURANCE INS CO	OH	7.2
INFINITY CASUALTY INS CO	OH	7.7
INFINITY SELECT INS CO	IN	6.7
INTEGRITY MUTUAL INS CO	WI	87.5
IRONSHORE INDEMNITY INC	MN	322.6
ISLAND INS CO LTD	HI	328.2
ISMIE MUTUAL INS CO	IL	1,679.1
KANSAS MEDICAL MUTUAL INS CO	KS	158.2
KEMPER INDEPENDENCE INS CO	IL	98.5
KESWICK GUARANTY INC	VI	4.6
LACKAWANNA CASUALTY CO	PA	213.5
LAFAYETTE INS CO	LA	174.8
LAWYERS MUTUAL LIAB INS CO OF NC	NC	94.0
LE MARS INS CO	IA	64.2
LIGHTNING ROD MUTUAL INS CO	OH	250.8
LITITZ MUTUAL INS CO	PA	223.7
LM GENERAL INS CO	IL	10.5
LYNDON PROPERTY INS CO	MO	371.1
LYNDON SOUTHERN INS CO	DE	87.6
MADISON MUTUAL INS CO	IL	64.6
MAG MUTUAL INS CO	GA	1,640.8
MAIDEN RE NORTH AMERICA INC	MO	1,233.1
MDOW INS CO	TX	8.8
MEDICAL MUTUAL INS CO OF MAINE	ME	263.7
MEDICAL MUTUAL INS CO OF NC	NC	481.0
MEDICAL MUTUAL LIAB INS SOC OF MD	MD	790.0
MEDICAL PROFESSIONAL MUTUAL INS CO	MA	3,054.0
MEDMAL DIRECT INS CO	FL	26.3
MEMBERSELECT INS CO	MI	498.8
MERASTAR INS CO	IL	25.8
MERCHANTS MUTUAL INS CO	NY	471.0
MICHIGAN MILLERS MUTUAL INS CO	MI	186.7
MID-CENTURY INS CO OF TEXAS	TX	37.8
MOUNTAIN LAKE RRG INC	VT	2.3
MOUNTAIN STATES MUTUAL CAS CO	NM	161.2
MSA INS CO	SC	18.0
MUTUAL BENEFIT INS CO	PA	194.1

Rating: B- (Continued)

INSURANCE COMPANY NAME	DOM. STATE	TOTAL ASSETS ($MIL)
NATIONAL INDEMNITY CO	NE	171,496.5
NATIONAL INDEMNITY CO OF MID-AMERICA	IA	230.4
NATIONAL LLOYDS INS CO	TX	217.2
NATIONWIDE AGRIBUSINESS INS CO	IA	456.3
NATIONWIDE ASR CO	WI	146.2
NATIONWIDE GENERAL INS CO	OH	225.4
NATIONWIDE INDEMNITY CO	OH	3,181.4
NATIONWIDE INS CO OF AMERICA	WI	499.8
NATIONWIDE PROPERTY & CAS INS CO	OH	612.6
NEW HAMPSHIRE EMPLOYERS INS CO	NH	3.8
NEW HOME WARRANTY INS CO RRG	DC	15.5
NEW JERSEY MANUFACTURERS INS CO	NJ	6,565.0
NEW LONDON COUNTY MUTUAL INS CO	CT	112.9
NEW MEXICO EMPLOYERS ASR CO	NM	7.5
NEW YORK CENTRAL MUTUAL FIRE INS CO	NY	1,014.9
NEW YORK MARINE & GENERAL INS CO	NY	1,046.5
NGM INS CO	FL	2,281.1
NLC MUTUAL INS CO	VT	310.1
NODAK MUTUAL INS CO	ND	236.5
NORCAL MUTUAL INS CO	CA	1,359.9
NORTH CAROLINA FARM BU MUTUAL INS CO	NC	1,735.1
NORTH LIGHT SPECIALTY INS CO	IL	48.1
NORTH STAR MUTUAL INS CO	MN	548.9
OASIS RECIPROCAL RRG	VT	12.0
OHIO BAR LIABILITY INS CO	OH	36.5
OHIO FARMERS INS CO	OH	2,470.1
OHIO MUTUAL INS ASSOC	OH	236.9
OLD AMERICAN INDEMNITY CO	KY	9.3
OLD DOMINION INS CO	FL	33.0
OLD UNITED CAS CO	KS	648.3
OMNI INDEMNITY CO	IL	70.5
OMS NATIONAL INS CO RRG	IL	374.2
OREGON MUTUAL INS CO	OR	247.3
PACIFIC EMPLOYERS INS CO	PA	3,430.5
PALMETTO SURETY CORP	SC	10.2
PEERLESS INS CO	NH	12,749.4
PEMCO MUTUAL INS CO	WA	660.8
PENN NATIONAL SECURITY INS CO	PA	879.0
PENNSYLVANIA NTL MUTUAL CAS INS CO	PA	1,171.8
PHILADELPHIA CBSP FOR INS OF HOUSES	PA	320.6
PHILADELPHIA CONTRIBUTIONSHIP INS CO	PA	203.8
PHYSICIANS INS A MUTUAL CO	WA	470.6
PIH INS CO A RECIP RRG	HI	13.2
PLATINUM UNDERWRITERS REINS CO	MD	1,652.7
PLYMOUTH ROCK ASR CORP	MA	485.6
PMSLIC INS CO	PA	467.5
PREFERRED PHYSICIANS MEDICAL RRG	MO	202.8
PRIVILEGE UNDERWRITERS RECIP EXCH	FL	208.2
PROASSURANCE CASUALTY CO	MI	1,291.9
PROASSURANCE INDEMNTIY CO INC	AL	1,737.4
PROCENTURY INS CO	MI	207.5
PROFESSIONALS ADVOCATE INS CO	MD	126.1
PROGRESSIVE MOUNTAIN INS CO	OH	228.7
PROGRESSIVE PREMIER INS CO OF IL	OH	203.4

INSURANCE COMPANY NAME	DOM. STATE	TOTAL ASSETS ($MIL)
PROVIDENCE MUTUAL FIRE INS CO	RI	194.6
PURE INS CO	FL	200.0
RAM MUTUAL INS CO	MN	88.6
RED CLAY RRG INC	SC	6.9
REPUBLIC VANGUARD INS CO	AZ	27.9
RLI INDEMNITY CO	IL	44.1
SAFECO INS CO OF AMERICA	NH	4,416.2
SAFECO INS CO OF INDIANA	IN	14.7
SAFECO NATIONAL INS CO	NH	17.9
SAFEWAY INS CO	IL	440.9
SAGAMORE INS CO	IN	155.7
SAMSUNG FIRE & MARINE INS CO LTD US	NY	206.2
SCOTTSDALE INS CO	OH	2,197.2
SEAWORTHY INS CO	MD	106.6
SECURA INS A MUTUAL CO	WI	933.2
SECURITY NATIONAL INS CO	DE	642.6
SELECTIVE AUTO INS CO OF NJ	NJ	329.7
SELECTIVE FIRE & CASUALTY INS CO	NJ	0.0
SELECTIVE INS CO OF AMERICA	NJ	2,040.8
SERVICE LLOYDS INS CO	TX	305.9
SHELTER GENERAL INS CO	MO	156.9
SIGMA RRG INC	DC	14.3
SOCIETY INS	WI	360.9
SOUTHERN FARM BUREAU CAS INS CO	MS	2,041.1
SOUTHERN TRUST INS CO	GA	43.5
ST PAUL MERCURY INS CO	CT	358.8
ST PAUL PROTECTIVE INS CO	CT	524.7
STANDARD GUARANTY INS CO	DE	443.0
STARR INDEMNITY & LIABILITY CO	TX	3,725.1
STARR SURPLUS LINES INS CO	IL	277.0
STATE FARM CTY MUTUAL INS CO OF TX	TX	196.8
STATE FARM FIRE & CAS CO	IL	33,186.6
STATE FARM INDEMNITY CO	IL	2,133.6
STATE FARM LLOYDS	TX	3,305.8
STILLWATER INS CO	CA	303.2
STRATFORD INS CO	NH	180.0
SUNLAND RRG INC	DE	5.8
SUTTER INS CO	CA	45.5
SWISS REINSURANCE AMERICA CORP	NY	12,939.3
TEXAS FARMERS INS CO	TX	282.6
TITAN INDEMNITY CO	TX	265.0
TNUS INS CO	NY	83.0
TOKIO MARINE PACIFIC INS LTD	GU	96.5
TOPA INS CO	CA	175.1
TRANSAMERICA CASUALTY INS CO	OH	341.8
TRAVELERS LLOYDS INS CO	TX	30.3
UNION INS CO OF PROVIDENCE	IA	114.5
UNION MUTUAL FIRE INS CO	VT	186.0
UNITED FARM FAMILY MUTUAL INS CO	IN	967.8
UNITED GUARANTY CREDIT INS CO	NC	23.7
UNITED OHIO INS CO	OH	280.2
UNITED SPECIALTY INS CO	DE	117.3
UNITRIN COUNTY MUTUAL INS CO	TX	31.4
UNIVERSAL INS CO	PR	823.2
US SPECIALTY INS CO	TX	2,023.8
UTICA MUTUAL INS CO	NY	2,254.6

INSURANCE COMPANY NAME	DOM. STATE	TOTAL ASSETS ($MIL)	INSURANCE COMPANY NAME	DOM. STATE	TOTAL ASSETS ($MIL)
Rating: B- (Continued)			BRITISH AMERICAN INS CO	TX	54.6
VERLAN FIRE INS CO	NH	25.3	BROADLINE RRG INC	VT	109.1
VICTORIA FIRE & CASUALTY CO	OH	176.6	CALIFORNIA CAS COMPENSATION INS CO	CA	72.7
VICTORIA SELECT INS CO	OH	38.3	CALIFORNIA CAS GEN INS CO OF OREGON	OR	103.8
VIRGINIA SENIOR CARE RRG	DC	0.0	CALIFORNIA CASUALTY INDEMNITY EXCH	CA	575.1
WEST BRANCH MUTUAL INS CO	PA	1.1	CALIFORNIA CASUALTY INS CO	OR	113.8
WESTERN MUTUAL FIRE INS CO	MN	6.4	CAPITOL SPECIALTY INS CORP	WI	106.6
WESTERN NATIONAL MUTUAL INS CO	MN	750.9	CARIBBEAN AMERICAN PROPERTY INS CO	PR	47.2
WESTERN RESERVE MUTUAL CAS CO	OH	180.7	CATLIN INS CO	TX	283.9
WESTFIELD INS CO	OH	2,510.3	CATLIN SPECIALTY INS CO	DE	628.7
WINTHROP PHYSICIANS RECIP RRG	VT	3.0	CENTURY SURETY CO	OH	630.7
WORKERS COMPENSATION FUND OF UTAH	UT	1,701.1	CITIZENS INS CO OF ILLINOIS	IL	4.6
Rating: C+			CIVIC PROPERTY & CASUALTY CO INC	CA	272.2
360 INS CO	CO	26.6	COLONIAL AMERICAN CAS & SURETY CO	MD	24.6
ACCIDENT FUND INS CO OF AMERICA	MI	2,514.9	COLORADO CASUALTY INS CO	NH	24.0
ACCIDENT FUND NATIONAL INS CO	MI	226.6	COLUMBIA MUTUAL INS CO	MO	369.7
ADDISON INS CO	IA	100.8	COLUMBIA NATIONAL INS CO	NE	90.9
AFFILIATES INS CO	IN	63.6	COMPANION PROPERTY & CASUALTY INS CO	SC	1,119.6
AG SECURITY INS CO	OK	58.0	CONNECTICUT MEDICAL INS CO	CT	476.3
AIG PROPERTY CASUALTY CO	PA	4,865.6	CONTINENTAL CASUALTY CO	IL	43,193.4
AIOI NISSAY DOWA INS CO OF AMERICA	NY	103.7	CONTINENTAL DIVIDE INS CO	CO	12.6
ALFA SPECIALTY INS CORP	VA	53.9	COOP OF AMER PHYS INS CO RRG	HI	0.0
ALFA VISION INS CORP	VA	97.0	COOPERATIVA D SEGUROS MULTIPLES D PR	PR	498.9
ALLEGANY CO-OP INS CO	NY	47.5	COPPERPOINT AMERICAN INS CO	AZ	7.5
ALLIANCE INDEMNITY CO	KS	9.5	COPPERPOINT CASUALTY INS CO	AZ	7.4
ALLIED EASTERN INDEMNITY CO	PA	68.4	COREPOINT INS CO	MI	207.1
ALLMERICA FINANCIAL ALLIANCE INS CO	NH	19.3	CROSSFIT RRG INC	MT	4.2
ALLMERICA FINANCIAL BENEFIT INS CO	MI	33.0	CSAA AFFINITY INS CO	PA	210.5
AMCO INS CO	IA	971.4	CSE SAFEGUARD INS CO	CA	100.7
AMERICAN AGRI BUSINESS INS CO	TX	1,387.1	DAKOTA TRUCK UNDERWRITERS	SD	108.1
AMERICAN AGRICULTURAL INS CO	IN	1,168.6	DIRECT GENERAL INS CO	IN	399.1
AMERICAN COMMERCE INS CO	OH	324.7	DIRECT NATIONAL INS CO	AR	17.1
AMERICAN FAMILY HOME INS CO	FL	551.7	DISCOVER PROPERTY & CASUALTY INS CO	CT	140.8
AMERICAN MODERN HOME INS CO	OH	1,235.6	DISCOVER SPECIALTY INS CO	CT	110.9
AMERICAN RELIABLE INS CO	AZ	275.3	DRIVE NEW JERSEY INS CO	NJ	0.0
AMERICAN ROAD INS CO	MI	589.2	DRYDEN MUTUAL INS CO	NY	174.1
AMERICAN SELECT INS CO	OH	226.9	EAGLE WEST INS CO	CA	120.1
AMERICAN SOUTHERN INS CO	KS	108.2	ELECTRIC INS CO	MA	1,533.4
AMERICAN STATES PREFERRED INS CO	IN	23.8	EMC REINSURANCE CO	IA	420.9
AMERICAN STRATEGIC INS CO	FL	812.0	EMPIRE INDEMNITY INS CO	OK	56.8
AMERICAN SUMMIT INS CO	TX	46.0	ENCOMPASS PROPERTY & CASUALTY CO	IL	11.3
AMERISURE PARTNERS INS CO	MI	73.8	EVEREST REINSURANCE CO	DE	10,434.6
AMGUARD INS CO	PA	404.3	EXACT PROPERTY & CASUALTY CO INC	CA	271.2
ARBELLA MUTUAL INS CO	MA	1,266.0	FARM BUREAU MUTUAL INS CO OF AR	AR	351.2
ARBELLA PROTECTION INS CO	MA	315.9	FARMERS INS CO INC	KS	284.2
ARCH MORTGAGE INS CO	WI	404.6	FARMERS INS CO OF AZ	AZ	40.1
ASI ASR CORP	FL	148.4	FARMERS INS CO OF FLEMINGTON	NJ	0.0
ASSURANCE COMPANY OF AMERICA	NY	26.9	FARMERS INS CO OF ID	ID	188.6
AXIS INS CO	IL	1,462.3	FARMERS NEW CENTURY INS CO	IL	185.3
AXIS REINS CO	NY	2,884.6	FARMERS TEXAS COUNTY MUTUAL INS CO	TX	139.3
BEAZLEY INS CO INC	CT	259.1	FARMERS UNION MUTUAL INS CO	MT	50.3
BERKLEY REGIONAL INS CO	DE	700.0	FCCI ADVANTAGE INS CO	FL	6.9
BERKSHIRE HATHAWAY HOMESTATE INS	NE	1,860.9	FCCI INS CO	FL	1,712.2
BERKSHIRE HATHAWAY SPECIALTY INS CO	NE	3,448.0	FEDERATED RURAL ELECTRIC INS EXCH	KS	483.0
BLOOMINGTON COMPENSATION INS CO	MN	17.0	FIDELITY & GUARANTY INS CO	IA	20.5
			FIDELITY & GUARANTY INS UDWRS INC	WI	167.8

INSURANCE COMPANY NAME	DOM. STATE	TOTAL ASSETS ($MIL)
Rating:	**C+**	**(Continued)**
FIDELITY MOHAWK INS CO	NJ	0.0
FIRE INS EXCHANGE	CA	2,270.3
FIRST LIBERTY INS CORP	IL	22.6
FIRST PROFESSIONALS INS CO INC	FL	397.2
FIRSTCOMP INS CO	NE	301.6
FIRSTLINE NATIONAL INS CO	MD	76.7
FMI INS CO	NJ	0.0
FOREMOST COUNTY MUTUAL INS CO	TX	90.2
FOREMOST LLOYDS OF TEXAS	TX	62.5
FOREMOST SIGNATURE INS CO	MI	103.7
FORTRESS INS CO	IL	137.4
FRANDISCO PROPERTY & CAS INS CO	GA	91.0
GEICO ADVANTAGE CO	NE	713.8
GERMANIA INS CO	TX	74.1
GERMANTOWN INS CO	PA	86.2
GRANGE INS ASN	WA	269.9
GRANITE MUTUAL INS CO	VT	4.3
GRAPHIC ARTS MUTUAL INS CO	NY	139.7
GRAY INS CO	LA	290.6
GREAT AMERICAN ASR CO	OH	19.1
GUARANTEE CO OF NORTH AMERICA USA	MI	191.5
GUIDEONE ELITE INS CO	IA	28.7
HANOVER LLOYDS INS CO	TX	5.8
HAWAIIAN INS & GUARANTY CO LTD	HI	24.6
HAWKEYE-SECURITY INS CO	WI	14.5
HCC SPECIALTY INS CO	OK	20.7
HEALTH PROVIDERS INS RECIPROCAL RRG	HI	75.1
HIGH POINT PREFERRED INS CO	NJ	0.0
HIGH POINT SAFETY & INS CO	NJ	0.0
HINGHAM MUTUAL FIRE INS CO	MA	63.4
HOOSIER MOTOR MUTUAL INS CO	IN	12.5
HOUSING AUTHORITY PROP A MUTUAL CO	VT	165.8
IL STATE BAR ASSOC MUTUAL INS CO	IL	71.6
ILLINOIS EMCASCO INS CO	IA	326.2
ILLINOIS FARMERS INS CO	IL	240.7
INDEPENDENT MUTUAL FIRE INS CO	IL	42.1
INFINITY SAFEGUARD INS CO	OH	5.6
INS CO OF GREATER NY	NY	110.7
INS CO OF ILLINOIS	IL	21.3
INTEGRAND ASR CO	PR	152.6
KENTUCKY EMPLOYERS MUTUAL INS	KY	881.2
LAMMICO	LA	395.1
LANCER INS CO	IL	576.6
LEXINGTON INS CO	DE	26,043.5
LIBERTY MUTUAL FIRE INS CO	WI	5,274.8
MADISON MUTUAL INS CO	NY	12.8
MAIDEN SPECIALTY INS CO	NC	83.3
MAPFRE INS CO OF NEW YORK	NY	139.9
MASSACHUSETTS BAY INS CO	NH	62.3
MEDICAL LIABILITY ALLIANCE	MO	71.0
MEDICAL SECURITY INS CO	NC	29.7
MERCHANTS BONDING CO (MUTUAL)	IA	140.9
MERCHANTS PREFERRED INS CO	NY	65.2
MICHIGAN INS CO	MI	113.9

INSURANCE COMPANY NAME	DOM. STATE	TOTAL ASSETS ($MIL)
MIDSTATE MUTUAL INS CO	NY	40.4
MIDWEST EMPLOYERS CAS CO	DE	129.4
MILLERS CAPITAL INS CO	PA	133.4
MISSOURI HOSPITAL PLAN	MO	194.6
MMG INS CO	ME	229.3
MONTEREY INS CO	CA	82.3
MOUNT VERNON FIRE INS CO	PA	562.4
MUNICH REINSURANCE AMERICA INC	DE	16,639.8
NAMIC INS CO INC	IN	54.4
NATIONAL AMERICAN INS CO	OK	175.1
NATIONAL INDEMNITY CO OF THE SOUTH	FL	305.0
NATIONAL INTERSTATE INS CO	OH	1,100.3
NATIONAL SECURITY FIRE & CAS CO	AL	72.8
NATIONWIDE INS CO OF FLORIDA	OH	338.6
NAVIGATORS SPECIALTY INS CO	NY	162.7
NEIGHBORHOOD SPIRIT PROP & CAS CO	CA	275.0
NEW ENGLAND GUARANTY INS CO INC	VT	40.5
NEW ENGLAND MUTUAL INS CO	MA	69.5
NEW JERSEY INDEMNITY INS CO	NJ	0.0
NEW MEXICO MUTUAL CASUALTY CO	NM	328.2
NEW MEXICO PREMIER INS CO	NM	2.2
NORFOLK & DEDHAM MUTUAL FIRE INS CO	MA	357.0
NORTH PACIFIC INS CO	OR	17.7
NORTHFIELD INS CO	IA	396.0
OLD GUARD INS CO	OH	405.7
PACIFIC SPECIALTY INS CO	CA	311.0
PEERLESS INDEMNITY INS CO	IL	192.5
PERSONAL EXPRESS INS CO	CA	21.8
PERSONAL SERVICE INS CO	PA	36.1
PHENIX MUTUAL FIRE INS CO	NH	62.3
PODIATRY INS CO OF AMERICA	IL	335.7
PREFERRED PROFESSIONAL INS CO	NE	300.7
PROGRESSIVE CASUALTY INS CO	OH	6,444.3
PROGRESSIVE GARDEN STATE INS CO	NJ	0.0
PROGRESSIVE NORTHERN INS CO	WI	1,437.1
PROGRESSIVE NORTHWESTERN INS CO	OH	1,391.0
PROGRESSIVE SOUTHEASTERN INS CO	IN	157.5
PROGRESSIVE UNIVERSAL INS CO	WI	308.4
RAINIER INS CO	AZ	25.8
REPUBLIC FIRE & CASUALTY INS CO	OK	8.3
REPUBLIC INDEMNITY CO OF AMERICA	CA	2,206.9
REPUBLIC UNDERWRITERS INS CO	TX	655.4
REPUBLIC-FRANKLIN INS CO	OH	102.4
ROCKFORD MUTUAL INS CO	IL	75.0
ROCKINGHAM INS CO	VA	111.0
RSUI INDEMNITY CO	NH	3,367.6
RURAL MUTUAL INS CO	WI	383.3
SAFEWAY INS CO OF LA	LA	126.0
SECURA SUPREME INS CO	WI	115.0
SENTRUITY CASUALTY CO	TX	130.5
SEQUOIA INS CO	CA	250.9
SFM MUTUAL INS CO	MN	499.5
SHEBOYGAN FALLS INS CO	WI	28.1
SILVER OAK CASUALTY INC	NE	223.8
SIRIUS AMERICA INS CO	NY	1,553.2
SOUTHERN FIDELITY INS CO INC	FL	195.2

INSURANCE COMPANY NAME	DOM. STATE	TOTAL ASSETS ($MIL)	INSURANCE COMPANY NAME	DOM. STATE	TOTAL ASSETS ($MIL)
Rating: C+ (Continued)			ALLEGHENY CASUALTY CO	PA	39.5
SOUTHERN FIDELITY P&C INC	FL	102.7	ALLIANCE INS CO INC	KS	22.3
SOUTHERN INS CO OF VIRGINIA	VA	133.1	ALLIED WORLD ASR CO (US) INC	DE	339.1
ST PAUL GUARDIAN INS CO	CT	78.3	ALLIED WORLD INS CO	NH	1,834.2
STATE AUTOMOBILE MUTUAL INS CO	OH	2,298.3	ALLIED WORLD SURPLUS LINES INS	AR	238.9
STATE NATIONAL INS CO INC	TX	285.5	ALLSTATE FIRE & CASUALTY INS CO	IL	150.7
SURETY BONDING CO OF AMERICA	SD	8.2	ALPS PROPERTY & CASUALTY INS CO	MT	98.8
TERRA INS CO RRG	VT	30.5	ALTERRA EXCESS & SURPLUS INS CO	DE	381.9
TITAN INS CO	MI	140.6	AMALGAMATED CASUALTY INS CO	DC	45.8
TRAVELERS CASUALTY & SURETY CO OF AM	CT	4,495.6	AMERICAN ACCESS CASUALTY CO	IL	228.3
TRAVELERS CASUALTY CO	CT	209.6	AMERICAN ALTERNATIVE INS CORP	DE	550.0
TRAVELERS CONSTITUTION STATE INS CO	CT	210.2	AMERICAN AUTOMOBILE INS CO	MO	181.7
TRITON INS CO	TX	550.4	AMERICAN CASUALTY CO OF READING	PA	145.1
TRUCK INS EXCHANGE	CA	2,001.7	AMERICAN ECONOMY INS CO	IN	65.5
TUDOR INS CO	NH	375.4	AMERICAN EMPIRE INS CO	OH	41.2
UMIALIK INS CO	AK	49.3	AMERICAN EMPIRE SURPLUS LINES INS CO	DE	299.6
UNITED FINANCIAL CASUALTY CO	OH	2,330.1	AMERICAN FARMERS & RANCHERS MUTUAL	OK	123.5
UNITED FIRE & INDEMNITY CO	TX	46.2	AMERICAN FREEDOM INS CO	IL	40.0
UNITED GUARANTY MORTGAGE INDEM CO	NC	286.3	AMERICAN GUARANTEE & LIABILITY INS	NY	251.0
UNITED STATES SURETY CO	MD	55.7	AMERICAN HALLMARK INS CO OF TX	TX	329.5
UNITED WISCONSIN INS CO	WI	358.8	AMERICAN HOME ASR CO	NY	26,660.0
UNIVERSAL UNDERWRITERS OF TX	IL	14.1	AMERICAN INTER FIDELITY EXCHANGE RRG	IN	51.3
US UNDERWRITERS INS CO	ND	175.6	AMERICAN INTERSTATE INS CO OF TEXAS	TX	58.6
UTICA NATIONAL INS CO OF TX	TX	32.9	AMERICAN MODERN INS CO OF FLORIDA	FL	31.0
UTICA SPECIALTY RISK INS CO	TX	36.0	AMERICAN MODERN LLOYDS INS CO	TX	7.0
VERMONT MUTUAL INS CO	VT	733.7	AMERICAN MODERN SELECT INS CO	OH	287.7
VIRGINIA SURETY CO INC	IL	1,059.2	AMERICAN PLATINUM PROP & CAS INS CO	FL	20.3
VOYAGER INDEMNITY INS CO	GA	96.0	AMERICAN SAFETY INS CO	GA	20.5
WADENA INS CO	IA	11.0	AMERICAN SENTINEL INS CO	PA	34.6
WAWANESA GENERAL INS CO	CA	585.4	AMERICAN STATES INS CO	IN	135.0
WESCO INS CO	DE	951.6	AMERICAN SURETY CO	IN	14.4
WESTERN PACIFIC MUT INS CO RISK RET	CO	142.6	AMERICAN WEST INS CO	ND	16.3
WESTPORT INS CORP	MO	5,352.8	AMERICAN WESTERN HOME INS CO	OK	202.5
WISCONSIN MUTUAL INS CO	WI	131.0	AMERICAN ZURICH INS CO	IL	236.8
ZALE INDEMNITY CO	TX	43.4	AMERIHEALTH CASUALTY INS CO	DE	268.8
ZURICH AMERICAN INS CO	NY	30,669.5	ANCHOR GENERAL INS CO	CA	93.6
			APOLLO CASUALTY CO	IL	17.5
Rating: C			APPALACHIAN INS CO	RI	281.6
1ST AUTO & CASUALTY INS CO	WI	29.8	ARBELLA INDEMNITY INS CO	MA	46.0
1ST CHOICE AUTO INS CO	PA	17.2	ARCH INDEMNITY INS CO	MO	41.1
ACADIA INS CO	NH	153.8	ARCH INS CO	MO	3,201.1
ACE FIRE UNDERWRITERS INS CO	PA	100.8	ARECA INS EXCHANGE	AK	28.9
ACE INS CO OF THE MIDWEST	IN	74.3	ARGONAUT INS CO	IL	1,294.7
ACE PROPERTY & CASUALTY INS CO	PA	7,350.7	ARI MUTUAL INS CO	PA	90.2
ACSTAR INS CO	IL	63.7	ARMED FORCES INS EXCHANGE	KS	134.4
ADMIRAL INDEMNITY CO	DE	51.3	ARTISAN & TRUCKERS CASUALTY CO	WI	287.9
ADRIATIC INS CO	ND	70.8	ASI LLOYDS	TX	197.1
ADVANTAGE WORKERS COMP INS CO	IN	104.1	ASI PREFERRED INS CORP	FL	57.9
AETNA INS CO OF CT	CT	15.7	ASOC DE SUSCRIPCION CONJUNTA DEL SEG	PR	256.5
AFFILIATED FM INS CO	RI	2,524.3	ASPEN AMERICAN INS CO	TX	481.1
AFFINITY MUTUAL INS CO	OH	15.4	ASPEN SPECIALTY INS CO	ND	291.9
AGENCY INS CO OF MARYLAND INC	MD	96.6	ASSOCIATED EMPLOYERS INS CO	MA	5.3
AIG SPECIALTY INS CO	IL	307.1	ASSOCIATED INDEMNITY CORP	CA	99.6
AIU INS CO	NY	243.7	ASSOCIATED INDUSTRIES OF MA MUT INS	MA	528.3
ALASKA TIMBER INS EXCHANGE	AK	19.2	ASSOCIATION CASUALTY INS CO	TX	46.7
ALFA ALLIANCE INS CORP	VA	27.6	ASSOCIATION INS CO	DE	112.4

INSURANCE COMPANY NAME	DOM. STATE	TOTAL ASSETS ($MIL)
Rating: C (Continued)		
ASURE WORLDWIDE INS CO	MI	37.0
ATAIN SPECIALTY INS CO	MI	292.1
ATLANTIC SPECIALTY INS CO	NY	2,431.5
ATRADIUS TRADE CREDIT INS CO	MD	91.4
ATX PREMIER INS CO	TX	9.7
AUTO CLUB FAMILY INS CO	MO	107.7
AUTO CLUB INS CO OF FL	FL	310.0
AUTO CLUB PROPERTY & CASUALTY INS CO	MI	80.4
AUTO CLUB SOUTH INS CO	FL	115.9
AUTOMOBILE CLUB INTERINSURANCE EXCH	MO	400.5
AVATAR PROPERTY & CASUALTY INS CO	FL	27.6
AXA ART INS CORP	NY	42.8
BADGER MUTUAL INS CO	WI	162.7
BANKERS INDEPENDENT INS CO	PA	24.8
BANKERS INS CO	FL	157.8
BANKERS STANDARD FIRE & MARINE CO	PA	195.1
BANKERS STANDARD INS CO	PA	415.4
BAR PLAN SURETY & FIDELITY CO	MO	4.9
BARNSTABLE COUNTY INS CO	MA	22.4
BEACON MUTUAL INS CO	RI	387.1
BELL UNITED INS CO	NV	34.9
BERKLEY INS CO	DE	16,852.4
BERKLEY NATIONAL INS CO	IA	84.9
BERKLEY REGIONAL SPECIALTY INS CO	DE	65.9
BLUE RIDGE INDEMNITY CO	WI	27.6
BREMEN FARMERS MUTUAL INS CO	KS	34.9
BRIDGEFIELD CASUALTY INS CO	FL	82.8
BRIERFIELD INS CO	MS	12.4
BROOKWOOD INS CO	IA	8.1
BUCKEYE STATE MUTUAL INS CO	OH	65.5
BUILDERS INS (A MUTUAL CAPTIVE CO)	GA	471.9
BUNKER HILL INS CO	MA	52.2
CALIFORNIA CASUALTY & FIRE INS CO	CA	62.2
CALIFORNIA HEALTHCARE INS CO INC RRG	HI	120.8
CALLICOON CO-OPERATIVE INS CO	NY	27.7
CAMERON MUTUAL INS CO	MO	78.2
CAMICO MUTUAL INS CO	CA	90.8
CAMPMED CAS & INDEM CO INC OF MD	NH	20.0
CAPITOL CASUALTY CO	NE	26.0
CAPITOL COUNTY MUTUAL FIRE INS CO	TX	14.2
CAPITOL INDEMNITY CORP	WI	450.7
CAROLINA CASUALTY INS CO	IA	186.0
CATLIN INDEMNITY CO	DE	143.2
CELINA MUTUAL INS CO	OH	67.0
CENTER MUTUAL INS CO	ND	46.8
CHICAGO INS CO	IL	108.3
CHUNG KUO INS CO LTD GUAM BRANCH	GU	35.7
CIM INS CORP	MI	18.6
CITIZENS INS CO OF OH	OH	15.0
CITIZENS INS CO OF THE MIDWEST	IN	45.3
CIVIL SERVICE EMPLOYEES INS CO	CA	231.6
CLARENDON NATIONAL INS CO	IL	607.4
CLERMONT INS CO	IA	23.4
CLUB INS CO	OH	13.8
COFACE NORTH AMERICA INS CO	MA	163.7
COLISEUM REINS CO	DE	323.3
COLONY INS CO	VA	1,367.1
COLORADO FARM BUREAU MUTUAL INS CO	CO	79.3
COLUMBIA CASUALTY CO	IL	240.2
COMMERCE & INDUSTRY INS CO	NY	4,847.9
COMMERCE WEST INS CO	CA	162.9
COMMERCIAL ALLIANCE INS CO	TX	60.2
COMMUNITY INS CORP	WI	10.5
COMPTRUST AGC MUT CAPTIVE INS CO	GA	30.1
CONSOLIDATED INS CO	IN	14.3
CONSUMERS INS USA INC	TN	50.5
CONTINENTAL HERITAGE INS CO	FL	7.4
CONTINENTAL INDEMNITY CO	IA	153.7
CONTINENTAL INS CO	PA	2,067.4
CONTINENTAL INS CO OF NJ	NJ	0.0
CONTINENTAL WESTERN INS CO	IA	181.6
CONTROLLED RISK INS CO OF VT RRG	VT	61.9
CONVENTUS INTER INS EXCHANGE	NJ	0.0
COPPERPOINT NATIONAL INS CO	AZ	7.4
CORNERSTONE NATIONAL INS CO	MO	38.4
COUNTRYWAY INS CO	NY	26.0
COVENANT INS CO	CT	82.2
CSAA FIRE & CASUALTY INS CO	IN	77.1
CSAA GENERAL INS CO	IN	254.1
CSAA MID-ATLANTIC INS CO OF NJ	NJ	48.5
CYPRESS INS CO	CA	1,184.6
DAILY UNDERWRITERS OF AMERICA	PA	36.6
DAKOTA FIRE INS CO	ND	210.0
DANBURY INS CO	MA	12.0
DE SMET FARM MUTUAL INS CO OF SD	SD	26.8
DENTISTS BENEFITS INS CO	OR	18.4
DIRECT AUTO INS CO	IL	29.6
DIRECT GENERAL INS CO OF MS	MS	33.8
DIRECT INS CO	TN	79.3
DOCTORS DIRECT INS INC	IL	14.0
DORCHESTER INS CO LTD	VI	20.0
DORCHESTER MUTUAL INS CO	MA	73.1
DTRIC INS CO LTD	HI	103.3
EASTERN ADVANTAGE ASR CO	PA	40.9
EASTERN MUTUAL INS CO	NY	22.1
ELEPHANT INS CO	VA	106.4
EMPIRE FIRE & MARINE INS CO	NE	94.2
EMPLOYERS ASSURANCE CO	FL	598.0
EMPLOYERS FIRE INS CO	PA	19.5
EMPLOYERS INS CO OF NEVADA INC	NV	2,299.8
EMPLOYERS PREFERRED INS CO	FL	717.9
ENCOMPASS INS CO	IL	11.1
ENCOMPASS INS CO OF AMERICA	IL	22.5
ENCOMPASS INS CO OF NJ	IL	31.7
ENCOMPASS PROP & CAS INS CO OF NJ	IL	14.2
ENDEAVOUR INS CO	MA	5.7
ENUMCLAW PROP & CAS INS CO	WA	8.3
EQUITY INS CO	TX	77.2
ERIE & NIAGARA INS ASSOC	NY	174.6
ESSENTIA INS CO	MO	60.3

INSURANCE COMPANY NAME	DOM. STATE	TOTAL ASSETS ($MIL)	INSURANCE COMPANY NAME	DOM. STATE	TOTAL ASSETS ($MIL)
Rating: C (Continued)			GENERAL INS CO OF AMERICA	NH	105.0
ESSEX INS CO	DE	1,353.3	GENESIS INS CO	CT	197.4
ESURANCE INS CO	WI	206.6	GENWORTH RESIDENTIAL MTG INS CORP NC	NC	220.6
EVANSTON INS CO	IL	2,395.2	GEORGIA CASUALTY & SURETY CO	GA	42.0
EVER-GREENE MUTUAL INS CO	PA	5.2	GEORGIA FARM BUREAU MUTUAL INS CO	GA	638.1
EVEREST INDEMNITY INS CO	DE	130.5	GEOVERA SPECIALTY INS CO	DE	108.4
EVEREST NATIONAL INS CO	DE	992.6	GERMANIA FIRE & CASUALTY CO	TX	30.2
EVEREST SECURITY INS CO	GA	32.7	GOLDEN EAGLE INS CORP	NH	64.5
EVERETT CASH MUTUAL INS CO	PA	104.8	GRANGE INDEMNITY INS CO	OH	94.0
EVERGREEN NATIONAL INDEMNITY CO	OH	46.6	GRANGE INS CO OF MI	OH	66.3
EXCELSIOR INS CO	NH	37.3	GRANGE PROPERTY & CASUALTY INS CO	OH	58.8
EXCESS SHARE INS CORP	OH	50.6	GRAY CASUALTY & SURETY CO	LA	16.7
EXPLORER INS CO	CA	248.1	GREAT AMERICAN ALLIANCE INS CO	OH	29.0
FACTORY MUTUAL INS CO	RI	15,135.4	GREAT AMERICAN E & S INS CO	DE	45.8
FAIRMONT FARMERS MUTUAL INS CO	MN	25.5	GREAT AMERICAN FIDELITY INS CO	DE	45.8
FALLS LAKE GENERAL INS CO	OH	6.0	GREAT AMERICAN INS CO OF NEW YORK	NY	47.0
FALLS LAKE NATIONAL INS CO	OH	252.5	GREAT AMERICAN LLOYDS INS CO	TX	1.4
FARM BUREAU CNTY MUTUAL INS CO OF TX	TX	19.7	GREAT AMERICAN PROTECTION INS CO	OH	25.9
FARMERS & MERCHANTS MUTUAL FIRE I C	MI	26.6	GREAT AMERICAN SECURITY INS CO	OH	17.9
FARMERS ALLIANCE MUTUAL INS CO	KS	281.3	GREAT AMERICAN SPIRIT INS CO	OH	19.9
FARMERS FIRE INS CO	PA	25.4	GREAT DIVIDE INS CO	ND	199.0
FARMERS INS EXCHANGE	CA	15,807.4	GREAT PLAINS CASUALTY INC	IA	16.0
FARMERS MUTUAL F I C OF OKARCHE OK	OK	17.1	GREENWICH INS CO	DE	1,036.8
FARMERS MUTUAL F I C OF SALEM CTY	NJ	131.0	GRINNELL SELECT INS CO	IA	40.5
FARMERS MUTUAL INS CO	WV	13.7	GUARDIAN INS CO INC	VI	35.2
FARMERS MUTUAL OF TENNESSEE	TN	21.5	GUIDEONE NATIONAL INS CO	IA	49.9
FARMERS UNION MUTUAL INS CO	ND	97.6	GULF GUARANTY INS CO	MS	4.7
FD INS CO	FL	81.5	GULFSTREAM PROP & CAS INS CO	FL	112.4
FHM INS CO	FL	97.5	HALLMARK COUNTY MUTUAL INS CO	TX	5.2
FIDELITY & DEPOSIT CO OF MARYLAND	MD	228.2	HALLMARK NATIONAL INS CO	OH	89.8
FINGER LAKES FIRE & CASUALTY CO	NY	35.5	HALLMARK SPECIALTY INS CO	OK	235.2
FIRE DISTRICTS OF NY MUT INS CO INC	NY	69.3	HAMILTON MUTUAL INS CO	IA	78.8
FIREMANS FUND INS CO	CA	9,903.6	HANOVER AMERICAN INS CO	NH	29.1
FIREMANS FUND INS CO OF OH	OH	50.2	HARLEYSVILLE INS CO	PA	113.8
FIREMENS INS CO OF WASHINGTON DC	DE	101.1	HARLEYSVILLE INS CO OF NEW YORK	PA	76.3
FIRST AMERICAN PROP & CAS INS CO	CA	97.6	HAULERS INS CO INC	TN	70.7
FIRST AMERICAN SPECIALTY INS CO	CA	103.6	HDI-GERLING AMERICA INS CO	IL	305.0
FIRST DAKOTA INDEMNITY CO	SD	42.3	HERITAGE INDEMNITY CO	CA	150.5
FIRST FIRE & CASUALTY INS OF HI INC	HI	8.9	HERITAGE PROPERTY & CASUALTY INS CO	FL	347.1
FIRST INDEMNITY INS OF HI INC	HI	7.3	HIGHMARK CASUALTY INS CO	PA	428.0
FIRST INS CO OF HI LTD	HI	652.6	HILLSTAR INS CO	IN	5.4
FIRST SECURITY INS OF HI INC	HI	5.4	HOCHHEIM PRAIRIE CASUALTY INS CO	TX	80.3
FIRST SPECIALTY INS CORP	MO	224.4	HOME STATE COUNTY MUTUAL INS CO	TX	299.9
FITCHBURG MUTUAL INS CO	MA	98.2	HOMELAND INS CO OF NEW YORK	NY	112.8
FLORIDA FAMILY INS CO	FL	108.3	HOMESITE INDEMNITY CO	KS	53.1
FLORIDA LAWYERS MUTUAL INS CO	FL	73.2	HOMESITE INS CO	CT	129.8
FLORISTS INS CO	IL	7.6	HOMESITE INS CO OF CA	CA	45.0
FLORISTS MUTUAL INS CO	IL	152.5	HOMESITE INS CO OF FL	IL	11.0
FOREMOST PROPERTY & CASUALTY INS CO	MI	76.6	HOMESITE INS CO OF GEORGIA	GA	14.3
FOUNDERS INS CO	NJ	0.0	HOMESITE INS CO OF IL	IL	12.9
FRANKLIN HOMEOWNERS ASR CO	DE	91.9	HOMESITE INS CO OF NY	NY	24.8
FRANKLIN INS CO	PA	25.6	HOMESITE INS CO OF THE MIDWEST	ND	340.0
GEMINI INS CO	DE	117.3	HORACE MANN LLOYDS	TX	4.6
GENERAL AUTOMOBILE INS CO	OH	49.3	HOUSING AUTHORITY RISK RET GROUP INC	VT	315.1
GENERAL CASUALTY CO OF WI	WI	893.2	HOUSING ENTERPRISE INS CO	VT	62.5
			ILLINOIS CASUALTY CO	IL	89.9

INSURANCE COMPANY NAME	DOM. STATE	TOTAL ASSETS ($MIL)
Rating: C **(Continued)**		
ILLINOIS UNION INS CO	IL	356.7
IMPERIAL FIRE & CASUALTY INS CO	LA	109.8
INDEMNITY CO OF CA	CA	23.9
INDEMNITY INS CO OF NORTH AMERICA	PA	410.3
INDEMNITY NATIONAL INS CO	MS	18.4
INDEPENDENCE AMERICAN INS CO	DE	101.3
INDEPENDENCE CASUALTY & SURETY CO	TX	44.6
INFINITY AUTO INS CO	OH	9.9
INFINITY COUNTY MUTUAL INS CO	TX	32.8
INFINITY INDEMNITY INS CO	IN	7.2
INFINITY PREFERRED INS CO	OH	5.3
INFINITY SECURITY INS CO	IN	6.1
INFINITY STANDARD INS CO	IN	7.0
INLAND INS CO	NE	258.7
INS CO OF NORTH AMERICA	PA	818.3
INS CO OF THE WEST	CA	1,565.5
INSURANCE CO OF THE SOUTH	GA	21.4
INTEGON CASUALTY INS CO	NC	48.2
INTEGON PREFERRED INS CO	NC	55.3
INTERNATIONAL FIDELITY INS CO	NJ	213.5
INTERSTATE FIRE & CAS CO	IL	184.0
IRONSHORE SPECIALTY INS CO	AZ	935.9
JAMES RIVER CASUALTY CO	VA	29.4
JAMES RIVER INS CO	OH	505.0
JEFFERSON INS CO	NY	71.9
KEY RISK INS CO	NC	50.6
KEYSTONE NATIONAL INS CO	PA	13.1
KINGSTONE INS CO	NY	82.7
KNIGHTBROOK INS CO	DE	221.9
LACKAWANNA AMERICAN INS CO	PA	77.7
LACKAWANNA NATIONAL INS CO	PA	29.6
LAKEVIEW INS CO	FL	34.9
LANCER INDEMNITY CO	NY	21.2
LANDMARK AMERICAN INS CO	OK	381.9
LAWYERS MUTUAL INS CO	CA	307.0
LAWYERS MUTUAL INS CO OF KENTUCKY	KY	22.8
LEAGUE OF WI MUNICIPALITIES MUT INS	WI	57.8
LIBERTY INS UNDERWRITERS INC	IL	163.3
LIBERTY MUTUAL MID ATLANTIC INS CO	MA	19.6
LIBERTY NORTHWEST INS CORP	OR	74.5
LIBERTY PERSONAL INS CO	NH	16.9
LIBERTY SURPLUS INS CORP	NH	136.5
LIVINGSTON MUTUAL INS CO	PA	3.1
LM INS CORP	IL	118.4
LUMBERMENS UNDERWRITING ALLIANCE	MO	316.6
LUTHERAN MUTUAL FIRE INS CO	IL	10.3
MAIN STREET AMERICA ASR CO	FL	37.6
MANUFACTURING TECHNOLOGY MUT INS CO	MI	44.6
MAPFRE INSURANCE CO	NJ	63.9
MAPFRE PAN AMERICAN INS CO	PR	14.7
MAPFRE PREFERRED RISK INS CO	PR	78.0
MAPLE VALLEY MUTUAL INS CO	WI	12.2
MARKEL AMERICAN INS CO	VA	329.8
MARKEL INS CO	IL	1,345.1

INSURANCE COMPANY NAME	DOM. STATE	TOTAL ASSETS ($MIL)
MARYLAND CASUALTY CO	MD	166.8
MARYSVILLE MUTUAL INS CO	KS	37.9
MASSACHUSETTS EMPLOYERS INS CO	MA	4.4
MASSACHUSETTS HOMELAND INS CO	MA	9.9
MAXUM INDEMNITY CO	DE	285.3
MCMILLAN WARNER MUTUAL INS CO	WI	14.5
MDADVANTAGE INS CO OF NJ	NJ	0.0
MEDICUS INS CO	TX	82.4
MEDMARC CASUALTY INS CO	VT	274.3
MEEMIC INS CO	MI	251.2
MEMIC CASUALTY CO	VT	27.0
MEMIC INDEMNITY CO	NH	300.2
MERCED PROPERTY & CASUALTY CO	CA	21.1
MERCER INS CO	PA	230.5
MERCER INS CO OF NJ INC	NJ	74.3
MERCHANTS NATIONAL INS CO	NH	109.5
MERCURY COUNTY MUTUAL INS CO	TX	9.5
MERIDIAN SECURITY INS CO	IN	117.1
MERITPLAN INS CO	CA	81.2
MGA INS CO INC	TX	240.6
MIC PROPERTY & CASUALTY INS CORP	MI	92.5
MICHIGAN PROFESSIONAL INS EXCHANGE	MI	102.2
MID-CENTURY INS CO	CA	3,719.4
MID-CONTINENT CAS CO	OH	485.0
MID-CONTINENT EXCESS & SURPLUS INS	DE	17.0
MID-CONTINENT INS CO	OH	33.3
MID-HUDSON CO-OPERTIVE INS CO	NY	19.9
MIDWEST FAMILY MUTUAL INS CO	IA	174.7
MIDWESTERN INDEMNITY CO	NH	30.0
MILBANK INS CO	IA	534.3
MILLVILLE MUTUAL INS CO	PA	71.4
MITSUI SUMITOMO INS USA INC	NY	122.6
MO EMPLOYERS MUTUAL INS CO	MO	552.5
MODERN USA INS CO	FL	37.9
MONROE GUARANTY INS CO	IN	47.8
MONTGOMERY MUTUAL INS CO	MA	51.0
MOTORS INS CORP	MI	2,494.5
MOUNTAIN LAUREL ASR CO	OH	127.9
MOUNTAIN STATES INDEMNITY CO	NM	55.4
MOUNTAIN WEST FARM BU MUTUAL INS CO	WY	365.6
MT HAWLEY INS CO	IL	818.9
MT WASHINGTON ASR CORP	NH	5.5
MUNICIPAL MUTUAL INS CO	WV	33.0
MUTUAL RRG INC	HI	90.3
MUTUALAID EXCHANGE	KS	25.3
NATIONAL BUILDING MATERIAL ASR CO	IN	6.5
NATIONAL CONTINENTAL INS CO	NY	176.3
NATIONAL FIRE & CASUALTY CO	IL	7.5
NATIONAL FIRE & MARINE INS CO	NE	8,030.5
NATIONAL FIRE INS CO OF HARTFORD	IL	120.0
NATIONAL GENERAL ASR CO	MO	41.3
NATIONAL GENERAL INS CO	MO	60.8
NATIONAL INS CO OF WISCONSIN INC	WI	43.6
NATIONAL MERIT INS CO	IL	6.6
NATIONAL MUTUAL INS CO	OH	70.1
NATIONAL SERVICE CONTRACT INS CO RRG	DC	12.6

INSURANCE COMPANY NAME	DOM. STATE	TOTAL ASSETS ($MIL)	INSURANCE COMPANY NAME	DOM. STATE	TOTAL ASSETS ($MIL)
Rating: C (Continued)			PILGRIM INS CO	MA	59.6
NATIONAL SPECIALTY INS CO	TX	68.7	PLANS LIABILITY INS CO	OH	81.2
NATIONAL SURETY CORP	IL	157.1	PLATEAU CASUALTY INS CO	TN	37.7
NATIONAL UNION FIRE INS CO OF PITTSB	PA	26,204.5	PLATTE RIVER INS CO	NE	126.4
NAU COUNTRY INS CO	MN	1,195.0	PLAZA INS CO	IA	55.4
NETHERLANDS INS CO	NH	95.5	PRE-PAID LEGAL CAS INC	OK	16.5
NEVADA CAPITAL INS CO	NV	105.3	PREFERRED EMPLOYERS INS CO	CA	89.8
NEVADA GENERAL INS CO	NV	22.0	PRINCETON EXCESS & SURPLUS LINES INS	DE	179.9
NEW CENTURY INS CO	TX	8.4	PRINCETON INS CO	NJ	658.9
NEW JERSEY CASUALTY INS CO	NJ	0.0	PRIORITY ONE INS CO	TX	20.8
NEW JERSEY SKYLANDS INS CO	NJ	0.0	PROASSURANCE SPECIALTY INS CO INC	AL	40.2
NEW SOUTH INS CO	NC	74.8	PRODUCERS LLOYDS INS CO	TX	7.0
NEW YORK MUNICIPAL INS RECIPROCAL	NY	140.9	PROFESSIONAL SECURITY INS CO	AZ	22.5
NEWPORT INS CO	AZ	47.8	PROGRESSIVE ADVANCED INS CO	OH	345.6
NOETIC SPECIALTY INS CO	VT	119.4	PROGRESSIVE AMERICAN INS CO	OH	409.1
NORGUARD INS CO	PA	479.7	PROGRESSIVE BAYSIDE INS CO	OH	112.7
NORTH AMERICAN CAPACITY INS CO	NH	113.7	PROGRESSIVE CHOICE INS CO	OH	13.4
NORTH AMERICAN ELITE INS CO	NH	110.5	PROGRESSIVE CLASSIC INS CO	WI	349.6
NORTH AMERICAN SPECIALTY INS CO	NH	544.5	PROGRESSIVE EXPRESS INS CO	OH	188.3
NORTHERN INS CO OF NY	NY	38.7	PROGRESSIVE FREEDOM INS CO	NJ	0.0
NORTHERN MUTUAL INS CO	MI	30.6	PROGRESSIVE GULF INS CO	OH	276.4
NORTHERN SECURITY INS CO INC	VT	8.2	PROGRESSIVE HAWAII INS CORP	OH	168.8
NORTHWEST DENTISTS INS CO	WA	21.1	PROGRESSIVE MARATHON INS CO	MI	413.3
NOVA CASUALTY CO	NY	98.7	PROGRESSIVE MAX INS CO	OH	385.1
OAK RIVER INS CO	NE	563.0	PROGRESSIVE MICHIGAN INS CO	MI	476.2
OBI NATIONAL INS CO	PA	13.1	PROGRESSIVE PALOVERDE INS CO	IN	118.6
OCEAN HARBOR CASUALTY INS CO	FL	213.1	PROGRESSIVE PREFERRED INS CO	OH	729.8
OCEANUS INS CO A RRG	SC	71.5	PROGRESSIVE SECURITY INS CO	LA	255.5
ODYSSEY REINSURANCE CO	CT	7,784.8	PROGRESSIVE SELECT INS CO	OH	504.6
OHIO CASUALTY INS CO	NH	5,392.1	PROGRESSIVE SPECIALTY INS CO	OH	1,037.0
OHIO INDEMNITY CO	OH	149.0	PROGRESSIVE WEST INS CO	OH	139.0
OKLAHOMA FARM BUREAU MUTUAL INS CO	OK	298.4	PROSELECT INS CO	MA	87.6
OKLAHOMA SPECIALTY INS CO	OK	43.6	QBE INS CORP	PA	2,576.0
OKLAHOMA SURETY CO	OH	28.9	RADIAN ASSET ASR CO	NY	1,343.9
ONEBEACON AMERICA INS CO	PA	96.1	REAL LEGACY ASR CO INC	PR	143.7
ONEBEACON INS CO	PA	1,074.1	REDWOOD FIRE & CAS INS CO	NE	1,181.0
OREGON AUTOMOBILE INS CO	OR	8.7	REPUBLIC INDEMNITY OF CA	CA	41.8
PACIFIC STAR INS CO	WI	9.6	REPUBLIC LLOYDS	TX	12.4
PALISADES SAFETY & INS ASSOC	NJ	0.0	RESPONSE WORLDWIDE DIRECT AUTO INS	IL	6.7
PALMETTO CASUALTY INS CO	SC	6.8	RESPONSE WORLDWIDE INS CO	IL	10.7
PARTNERRE AMERICA INS CO	DE	301.8	ROCKHILL INS CO	AZ	129.8
PARTNERRE INS CO OF NEW YORK	NY	135.6	ROCKINGHAM CASUALTY CO	VA	32.9
PATRIOT INS CO	ME	101.6	ROCKY MOUNTAIN FIRE & CAS CO	WA	22.6
PATRONS MUTUAL INS CO OF CT	CT	51.9	RVI AMERICA INS CO	CT	96.7
PATRONS-OXFORD INS CO	ME	18.7	SAFE AUTO INS CO	OH	385.4
PENINSULA INDEMNITY CO	MD	10.9	SAFETY FIRST INS CO	IL	18.3
PENINSULA INS CO	MD	82.9	SAFETY INDEMNITY INS CO	MA	115.7
PENN CHARTER MUTUAL INS CO	PA	12.5	SAFETY NATIONAL CASUALTY CORP	MO	4,823.4
PENN MILLERS INS CO	PA	153.5	SAFETY PROPERTY & CASUALTY INS CO	MA	43.3
PENNSYLVANIA INS CO	IA	28.6	SAFEWAY COUNTY MUTUAL INS CO	TX	12.4
PENNSYLVANIA MANUFACTURERS ASN INS	PA	810.9	SAFEWAY INS CO OF AL	IL	62.3
PENNSYLVANIA MANUFACTURERS IND CO	PA	192.6	SAFEWAY INS CO OF GEORGIA	GA	64.3
PERMANENT GEN ASR CORP OF OHIO	OH	162.0	SAFEWAY PROPERTY INS CO	IL	52.3
PERMANENT GENERAL ASR CORP	OH	249.0	SAVERS PROPERTY & CASUALTY INS CO	MO	268.3
PHYSICIANS PROFESSIONAL LIABILTY RRG	VT	40.2	SECURITY FIRST INS CO	FL	160.6
			SECURITY MUTUAL INS CO	NY	96.5

INSURANCE COMPANY NAME	DOM. STATE	TOTAL ASSETS ($MIL)
Rating: C (Continued)		
SELECT RISK INS CO	PA	37.6
SENECA SPECIALTY INS CO	AZ	48.5
SEQUOIA INDEMNITY CO	NV	21.2
SEVEN SEAS INS CO INC	FL	22.6
SHELTER REINSURANCE CO	MO	400.6
SLAVONIC MUTUAL FIRE INS ASN	TX	28.4
SOMPO JAPAN FIRE & MAR INS CO AMER	NY	76.1
SONNENBERG MUTUAL INS ASSOC	OH	22.7
SOUTH CAROLINA FARM BU MUTUAL INS CO	SC	112.1
SOUTHERN COUNTY MUTUAL INS CO	TX	41.3
SOUTHERN FIRE & CASUALTY CO	WI	19.1
SOUTHERN INS CO	TX	48.2
SOUTHERN MUTUAL CHURCH INS CO	SC	48.4
SOUTHERN MUTUAL INS CO	GA	15.9
SOUTHERN PILOT INS CO	WI	38.8
SOUTHERN STATES INS EXCHANGE	VA	45.3
SOUTHERN UNDERWRITERS INS CO	OK	5.4
SOUTHERN VANGUARD INS CO	TX	20.0
SPARTA AMERICAN INS CO	CA	44.8
SPARTA SPECIALTY INS CO	CT	103.2
SPARTAN PROPERTY INS CO	SC	51.9
ST PAUL SURPLUS LINES INS CO	DE	643.9
STANDARD CASUALTY CO	TX	31.3
STANDARD MUTUAL INS CO	IL	61.8
STAR INS CO	MI	1,010.1
STARNET INS CO	DE	216.7
STATE FARM FLORIDA INS CO	FL	1,895.7
STATE MUTUAL INS CO	ME	2.3
STATE NATIONAL FIRE INS CO	LA	2.0
STEADFAST INS CO	DE	553.3
STERLING INS CO	NY	148.3
STILLWATER P&C INS CO	NY	120.0
STONEWOOD INS CO	NC	79.9
STRATHMORE INS CO	NY	50.5
SU INS CO	WI	25.8
SUBLIMITY INS CO	OR	34.1
SURETEC INS CO	TX	171.4
T H E INS CO	LA	201.2
TDC SPECIALTY INS CO	DC	59.8
TEACHERS AUTO INS CO	NJ	0.0
TECHNOLOGY INS CO INC	NH	1,376.4
TEXAS FARM BUREAU UNDERWRITERS	TX	54.5
TEXAS HERITAGE INS CO	TX	24.6
TEXAS INS CO	TX	5.4
THAMES INS CO INC	CT	28.1
TOKIO MARINE SPECIALTY INS CO	DE	455.3
TORUS NATIONAL INS CO	DE	169.0
TOYOTA MOTOR INS CO	IA	450.5
TRADEWIND INS CO LTD	HI	15.5
TRANS CITY CASUALTY INS CO	AZ	17.3
TRANSPORTATION INS CO	IL	81.8
TRI STATE INS CO OF MINNESOTA	MN	35.5
TRIANGLE INS CO INC	OK	71.4
TRIPLE S PROPIEDAD INC	PR	283.7

INSURANCE COMPANY NAME	DOM. STATE	TOTAL ASSETS ($MIL)
TRIUMPHE CASUALTY CO	OH	35.6
UNDERWRITER FOR THE PROFESSIONS INS	OR	270.0
UNIGARD INS CO	WI	440.4
UNION INS CO	IA	117.5
UNION STANDARD LLOYDS	TX	2.2
UNITED EDUCATORS INS A RECIP RRG	VT	814.2
UNITED FIRE LLOYDS	TX	26.3
UNITED GUAR RESIDENTIAL INS CO OF NC	NC	454.6
UNITED GUARANTY INS CO	NC	148.3
UNITED GUARANTY MORTGAGE INS CO	NC	146.9
UNITED GUARANTY MTG INS CO OF NC	NC	149.3
UNITED NATIONAL INS CO	PA	373.6
UNITED NATIONAL SPECIALTY INS CO	WI	39.4
UNITED PROPERTY & CASUALTY INS CO	FL	344.7
UNITED STATES FIRE INS CO	DE	3,360.2
UNITED STATES LIABILITY INS CO	PA	845.9
UNIVERSAL SURETY CO	NE	181.9
UNIVERSAL SURETY OF AMERICA	SD	15.8
UNIVERSAL UNDERWRITERS INS CO	IL	390.3
USPLATE GLASS INS CO	IL	25.4
UTICA FIRST INS CO	NY	250.5
UTICA NATIONAL ASR CO	NY	62.8
VA FARM BUREAU TOWN & COUNTRY INS CO	VA	67.8
VALIANT INS CO	DE	34.2
VALLEY FORGE INS CO	PA	73.1
VERSANT CASUALTY INS CO	MS	28.2
VETERINARY PET INS CO	CA	273.1
VIKING INS CO OF WI	WI	397.9
VIRGINIA FARM BUREAU FIRE & CAS INS	VA	50.9
VIRGINIA FARM BUREAU MUTUAL INS CO	VA	359.7
WASHINGTON INTERNATIONAL INS CO	NH	110.5
WAUSAU BUSINESS INS CO	WI	38.7
WAUSAU GENERAL INS CO	WI	13.0
WAUSAU UNDERWRITERS INS CO	WI	95.9
WAYNE MUTUAL INS CO	OH	55.4
WESTCHESTER FIRE INS CO	PA	2,000.5
WESTCHESTER SURPLUS LINES INS CO	GA	365.8
WESTERN NATIONAL ASR CO	MN	56.3
WESTERN PROTECTORS INS CO	OR	11.4
WESTERN SELECT INS CO	CA	16.2
WESTERN SURETY CO	SD	2,003.0
WESTERN WORLD INS CO	NH	1,070.2
WESTGUARD INS CO	PA	38.8
WI LAWYERS MUTUAL INS CO	WI	31.4
WINDSOR MOUNT JOY MUTUAL INS CO	PA	64.2
WISCONSIN COUNTY MUTUAL INS CORP	WI	79.7
WOLVERINE MUTUAL INS CO	MI	51.4
WORTH CASUALTY CO	TX	11.2
XL INS AMERICA INC	DE	707.9
XL REINS AMERICA INC	NY	5,529.0
XL SPECIALTY INS CO	DE	410.3
YORK INS CO OF MAINE	ME	47.0
YOSEMITE INS CO	IN	265.7
YOUNG AMERICA INS CO	TX	44.6
ZNAT INS CO	CA	69.1
ZURICH AMERICAN INS CO OF IL	IL	47.0

INSURANCE COMPANY NAME	DOM. STATE	TOTAL ASSETS ($MIL)	INSURANCE COMPANY NAME	DOM. STATE	TOTAL ASSETS ($MIL)
Rating: C-			CAROLINA FARMERS MUTUAL INS CO	NC	8.8
			CASCO INDEMNITY CO	ME	26.7
			CASTLEPOINT NATIONAL INS CO	CA	415.2
AAA TEXAS COUNTY MUTUAL INS CO	TX	75.4	CENSTAT CASUALTY CO	NE	18.4
ACCEPTANCE INDEMNITY INS CO	NE	238.5	CHAUTAUQUA PATRONS INS CO	NY	20.2
ACCESS INS CO	TX	139.7	CHEROKEE INS CO	MI	430.1
ACCREDITED SURETY & CAS CO INC	FL	24.1	CLEARFIELD CTY GRNGE MUT FIRE INS CO	PA	3.8
ADM INS CO	AZ	438.6	COASTAL AMERICAN INS CO	MS	7.0
ADMIRAL INS CO	DE	682.0	COLONIAL SURETY CO	PA	49.0
AGENT ALLIANCE INS CO	AL	18.1	COMMUNITY BLOOD CENTERS EXCHANGE RRG	IN	23.7
AGRI GENERAL INS CO	IA	254.6	COMMUNITY HOSPITAL ALTERNATIVE RRG	VT	246.8
AGRI INS EXCHANGE RISK RETENTION GRP	IN	16.3	CONSTITUTION INS CO	NY	18.0
ALABAMA MUNICIPAL INS CORP	AL	94.5	COPPERPOINT INDEMNITY INS CO	AZ	11.3
ALAMANCE INS CO	IL	486.7	COPPERPOINT PREMIER INS CO	AZ	20.4
ALLIANZ GLOBAL RISKS US INS CO	IL	3,442.4	CPA MUTUAL INS CO OF AMERICA RRG	VT	23.7
ALLIANZ UNDERWRITERS INS CO	IL	96.3	CRYSTAL RUN RECIPROCAL RRG	VT	16.9
ALLSTATE NJ PROPERTY & CASUALTY INS	IL	49.7	CSAA MID-ATLANTIC INS CO	PA	36.7
AMERICA FIRST LLOYD'S INS CO	TX	6.9	CYPRESS PROPERTY & CASUALTY INS CO	FL	105.3
AMERICAN COASTAL INS CO	FL	357.4	CYPRESS TEXAS LLOYDS	TX	46.2
AMERICAN COLONIAL INS CO	FL	32.0	DANIELSON NATIONAL INS CO	CA	9.7
AMERICAN COUNTRY INS CO	IL	75.6	DE SMET INS CO OF SD	SD	13.5
AMERICAN FEDERATED INS CO	MS	36.7	DEALERS CHOICE MUTUAL INS INC	NC	26.3
AMERICAN FIRE & CASUALTY CO	NH	41.8	DEERFIELD INS CO	IL	114.2
AMERICAN INDEPENDENT INS CO	PA	58.0	DELTA FIRE & CAS INS CO	GA	6.6
AMERICAN INS CO	OH	330.2	DIAMOND STATE INS CO	IN	124.5
AMERICAN MUTUAL SHARE INS CORP	OH	221.7	DIRECT GENERAL INS CO OF LA	LA	33.2
AMERICAN RESOURCES INS CO INC	AL	21.9	DISTRIBUTORS INS CO	TN	0.0
AMERICAN SAFETY CASUALTY INS CO	OK	180.9	DTRIC INS UNDERWRITERS LTD	HI	19.2
AMERICAN TRADITIONS INS CO	FL	45.3	EASTERN ATLANTIC INS CO	PA	65.1
AMERITRUST INS CORP	MI	136.9	EASTERN DENTISTS INS CO RRG	VT	51.9
AMICA PROPERTY & CASUALTY INS CO	RI	30.0	ENCOMPASS FLORIDIAN INDEMNITY CO	IL	4.7
ANTHRACITE MUTUAL FIRE INS CO	PA	3.7	ENCOMPASS FLORIDIAN INS CO	IL	4.7
ARCH REINSURANCE CO	DE	1,724.7	ENCOMPASS INS CO OF MA	MA	6.9
ARCHITECTS & ENGINEERS INS CO RRG	DE	19.2	ENDURANCE AMERICAN INS CO	DE	1,896.0
ARGONAUT-SOUTHWEST INS CO	IL	17.6	ENDURANCE AMERICAN SPECIALTY INS CO	DE	485.9
ARK ROYAL INS CO	FL	91.4	FARMERS MUTUAL F I C OF MCCANDLESS	PA	8.9
ASSOCIATED INTERNATIONAL INS CO	IL	274.9	FARMERS MUTUAL FIRE INS CO OF MARBLE	PA	27.1
ASSOCIATED LOGGERS EXCHANGE	ID	30.4	FCCI COMMERCIAL INS CO	FL	14.0
ATAIN INS CO	TX	65.4	FFVA MUTUAL INS CO	FL	303.4
ATTORNEYS INS MUTUAL OF SOUTH RRG	DC	13.2	FIDELITY FIRE & CASUALTY CO	FL	79.8
ATTORNEYS LIAB ASR SOCIETY INC RRG	VT	1,997.4	FINANCIAL CASUALTY & SURETY INC	TX	20.8
AUTOONE INS CO	NY	47.5	FIRST ACCEPTANCE INS CO OF GEORGIA	GA	67.3
AXA INS CO	NY	224.9	FIRST FINANCIAL INS CO	IL	536.8
AXIS SURPLUS INS CO	IL	460.6	FIRST MEDICAL INS CO RRG	VT	103.3
BALBOA INS CO	CA	242.0	FIRST NONPROFIT INS CO	DE	142.2
BAR PLAN MUTUAL INS CO	MO	50.0	FORESTRY MUTUAL INS CO	NC	51.8
BEDFORD GRANGE MUTUAL INS CO	PA	7.6	FRIENDS COVE MUTUAL INS CO	PA	5.0
BERKLEY ASR CO	IA	57.1	GEM STATE INS CO	ID	10.1
BRIAR CREEK MUTUAL INS CO	PA	12.3	GENERAL CASUALTY CO OF IL	WI	89.3
BRICKSTREET MUTUAL INS CO	WV	1,873.7	GENERAL SECURITY NATIONAL INS CO	NY	264.3
BRISTOL WEST INS CO	OH	125.7	GENWORTH MORTGAGE INS CORP	NC	2,609.6
BROOME CO OPERATIVE INS CO	NY	18.9	GENWORTH MTG INS CORP OF NC	NC	332.9
BUILDERS PREMIER INS CO	NC	11.4	GRAIN DEALERS MUTUAL INS CO	IN	8.6
BURLINGTON INS CO	NC	388.6	GRANITE RE INC	OK	39.6
CAMERON NATIONAL INS CO	MO	11.6	GREAT NORTHWEST INS CO	MN	21.4
CARING COMMUNITIES RECIP RRG	DC	104.0	GUILFORD INS CO	IL	392.7

INSURANCE COMPANY NAME	DOM. STATE	TOTAL ASSETS ($MIL)
Rating: C- (Continued)		
HARLEYSVILLE INS CO OF NJ	NJ	93.8
HARLEYSVILLE LAKE STATES INS CO	MI	66.1
HARLEYSVILLE PREFERRED INS CO	PA	139.2
HARLEYSVILLE WORCESTER INS CO	PA	160.8
HAWAII EMPLOYERS MUTUAL INS CO	HI	337.7
HEALTH CARE INDEMNITY INC	CO	537.4
HEALTHCARE PROVIDERS INS EXCH	PA	85.3
HOME & FARM INS CO	IN	6.1
HOOSIER INS CO	IN	91.4
HOUSING & REDEVELOPMENT INS EXCH	PA	40.2
HUDSON INS CO	DE	1,014.1
ILLINOIS INS CO	IA	33.7
IMPERIUM INS CO	TX	377.1
INDIAN HARBOR INS CO	DE	207.2
INDIANA INS CO	IN	69.8
INDIANA OLD NATIONAL INS CO	VT	2,068.3
INLAND MUTUAL INS CO	WV	6.5
INTEGON GENERAL INS CORP	NC	28.3
INTEGON INDEMNITY CORP	NC	53.5
ISLAND PREMIER INS CO LTD	HI	9.8
JOHN DEERE INS CO	IA	639.0
KANSAS MUTUAL INS CO	KS	0.0
LANDCAR CASUALTY CO	UT	36.2
LEBANON VALLEY INS CO	PA	23.7
LEXON INS CO	TX	144.1
LIBERTY AMERICAN SELECT INS CO	FL	8.5
LIBERTY COUNTY MUTUAL INS CO	TX	8.2
LIGHTHOUSE PROPERTY INS CORP	LA	54.3
MAIDSTONE INS CO	NY	14.5
MAISON INS CO	LA	27.4
MANUFACTURERS ALLIANCE INS CO	PA	179.8
MAPFRE INS CO OF FLORIDA	FL	79.3
MENNONITE MUTUAL INS CO	OH	21.8
MENTAL HEALTH RISK RETENTION GROUP	VT	28.1
MERCURY INS CO OF FL	FL	46.8
MESA UNDERWRITERS SPECIALTY INS CO	NJ	286.4
MFS MUTUAL INS CO	IA	3.5
MIC GENERAL INS CORP	MI	37.3
MICHIGAN COMMERCIAL INS MUTUAL	MI	90.7
MIDWEST INS CO	IL	78.6
MILLVILLE INS CO OF NEW YORK	NY	2.8
MULTINATIONAL INS CO	PR	30.2
MUTUAL OF WAUSAU INS CORP	WI	21.2
NATIONAL FARMERS UNION PROP & CAS CO	WI	192.9
NATIONAL FIRE & INDEMNITY EXCHANGE	MO	11.0
NATIONAL GENERAL INS ONLINE INC	MO	30.9
NATIONAL MORTGAGE RE INC ONE	WI	11.3
NATIONAL TRUST INS CO	IN	35.1
NATIONS INS CO	CA	26.5
NAUTILUS INS CO	AZ	256.7
NEW JERSEY SKYLANDS INS ASSN	NJ	0.0
NEW MEXICO ASR CO	NM	5.4
NEW MEXICO FOUNDATION INS CO	NM	23.0
NEW MEXICO SOUTHWEST CASUALTY CO	NM	18.4

INSURANCE COMPANY NAME	DOM. STATE	TOTAL ASSETS ($MIL)
NORTH COUNTRY INS CO	NY	24.1
NORTH POINTE INS CO	PA	105.3
NORTH RIVER INS CO	NJ	946.2
NUTMEG INS CO	CT	403.3
OCCIDENTAL FIRE & CAS CO OF NC	NC	444.7
OCEAN MARINE INDEMNITY INS CO	LA	12.6
OHA INS SOLUTIONS	OH	43.5
OHIO SECURITY INS CO	NH	16.7
OLD RELIABLE CAS CO	MO	6.0
ONTARIO INS CO	NY	16.0
OSWEGO COUNTY MUTUAL INS CO	NY	22.0
PACIFIC COMPENSATION INS CO	CA	243.4
PACIFIC INDEMNITY INS CO	GU	30.0
PANHANDLE FARMERS MUT INS CO OF WV	WV	4.4
PARAMOUNT INS CO	NY	53.7
PARTNER REINSURANCE CO OF THE US	NY	4,984.4
PENN PATRIOT INS CO	VA	38.2
PENN-AMERICA INS CO	PA	190.6
PENN-STAR INS CO	PA	94.9
PETROLEUM CAS CO	TX	33.2
PINNACLEPOINT INS CO	WV	54.5
PIONEER SPECIALTY INS CO	MN	56.9
PRAETORIAN INS CO	PA	1,261.3
PREMIER GROUP INS CO INC	TN	54.2
PREPARED INS CO	FL	54.5
PRIME P&C INS INC	IL	18.6
PRIMEONE INS CO	MI	16.7
PROFESSIONAL CASUALTY ASSN	PA	52.8
PROGRESSIVE COUNTY MUTUAL INS CO	TX	434.1
PROGRESSIVE DIRECT INS CO	OH	5,269.8
RADIAN INS INC	PA	321.9
RANCHERS & FARMERS INS CO	TX	6.2
REGENT INS CO	WI	144.0
RESIDENCE MUTUAL INS CO	CA	111.8
RESPONSIVE AUTO INS CO	FL	24.5
RESTORATION RRG INC	VT	63.4
ROAD CONTRACTORS MUTUAL INS CO	TN	8.0
ROCHDALE INS CO OF NEW YORK NY	NY	262.4
ROCKWOOD CASUALTY INS CO	PA	251.2
RUTGERS CASUALTY INS CO	NJ	25.2
SAFE HARBOR INS CO	FL	61.9
SAUQUOIT VALLEY INS CO	NY	4.8
SCRUBS MUTUAL ASR CO RRG	NV	13.1
SOUTHERN PIONEER PROP & CAS INS CO	AR	29.4
SPARTA INS CO	CT	418.8
SPECIALTY RISK OF AMERICA	IL	9.9
STATE AUTO INS CO OF OHIO	OH	32.7
STATE AUTO PROPERTY & CASUALTY INS	IA	2,108.4
STATE FARM GUARANTY INS CO	IL	32.4
STEADPOINT INS CO	TN	21.0
SUMMITPOINT INS CO	WV	47.8
SURETEC INDEMNITY CO	CA	20.5
TANK OWNER MEMBERS INS CO	TX	27.3
TORUS SPECIALTY INS CO	DE	174.9
TPA CAPTIVE INSURANCE CO INC	GA	0.0
TRI CENTURY INS CO	PA	61.2

INSURANCE COMPANY NAME	DOM. STATE	TOTAL ASSETS ($MIL)
Rating: C- (Continued)		
UNIGARD INDEMNITY CO	WI	57.9
UNIQUE INS CO	IL	69.5
UNITED FRONTIER MUTUAL INS CO	NY	14.5
UNIVERSAL CASUALTY CO	IL	30.8
UNIVERSAL FIRE & CASUALTY INS CO	IN	14.0
UNIVERSAL INS CO OF NORTH AMERICA	FL	126.0
UNIVERSAL NORTH AMERICA INS CO	TX	190.2
UPLAND MUTUAL INS INC	KS	23.3
UTICA NATIONAL INS CO OF OHIO	OH	14.5
WAYNE COOPERATIVE INS CO	NY	27.3
WEA PROPERTY & CASUALTY INS CO	WI	16.7
WELLINGTON INS CO	TX	37.1
WEST AMERICAN INSURANCE CO	IN	77.2
WEST VIRGINIA FARMERS MUT INS ASSOC	WV	6.8
WESTERN HOME INS CO	MN	57.3
WESTERN MUTUAL INS CO	CA	73.4
WESTMINSTER AMERICAN INS CO	MD	19.0
WHITE PINE INS CO	MI	46.6
WILLIAMSBURG NATIONAL INS CO	MI	144.9
WILSHIRE INS CO	NC	217.3
WISCONSIN MUNICIPAL MUTUAL INS CO	WI	55.6
WISCONSIN REINSURANCE CORP	WI	82.8
WRIGHT NATIONAL FLOOD INS CO	TX	18.4
YEL CO INS	FL	15.7
ZENITH INS CO	CA	1,866.5
Rating: D+		
ACIG INS CO	IL	412.6
ADIRONDACK INS EXCH	NY	196.9
AGCS MARINE INS CO	IL	368.1
AIOI NISSAY DOWA INS CO LTD	GU	24.3
ALLIED PROFESSIONALS INS CO RRG	AZ	39.3
AMERICAN BUS & MERCANTILE INS MUT	DE	58.7
AMERICAN MILLENNIUM INS CO	NJ	17.2
AMERICAN RISK INS CO INC	TX	21.1
AMERICAN UNDERWRITERS INS CO	AR	7.5
AMERICAS INS CO	LA	21.1
APOLLO MUTUAL FIRE INS CO	PA	0.0
ASSOCIATED MUTUAL INS CO	NY	26.9
ASSURED GUARANTY CORP	MD	2,485.9
ASSURED GUARANTY MUNICIPAL CORP	NY	5,751.6
AVIATION ALLIANCE INS RRG INC	MT	3.1
BANKERS SPECIALTY INS CO	LA	58.2
BEARING MIDWEST CASUALTY CO	KS	5.8
BLOOMFIELD MUTUAL INS CO	MN	9.6
BRISTOL WEST CASUALTY INS CO	OH	19.6
BUILD AMERICA MUTUAL ASR CO	NY	492.2
BUNKER HILL INS CASUALTY CO	MA	14.0
BUSINESSFIRST INS CO	FL	37.9
CAPITOL INS CO	PA	20.7
CASTLEPOINT FLORIDA INS	FL	40.2
CENTER VALLEY MUTUAL FIRE INS CO	PA	0.0
CENTRE COUNTY MUTUAL FIRE INS CO	PA	5.3
CENTURY CASUALTY CO	GA	6.5
CENTURY MUTUAL INS CO	NC	8.5

INSURANCE COMPANY NAME	DOM. STATE	TOTAL ASSETS ($MIL)
CITIES & VILLAGES MUTUAL INS CO	WI	52.8
COAST NATIONAL INS CO	CA	613.8
COASTAL SELECT INS CO	CA	110.1
COLLEGE RRG INC	VT	22.3
COLONIAL MORTGAGE INS CO	TX	2.9
COLONY SPECIALTY INS CO	OH	71.0
COMPWEST INS CO	CA	230.8
CONSOLIDATED INS ASN	TX	4.7
CONSOLIDATED LLOYDS	TX	1.7
CONTINUING CARE RRG INC	SC	5.3
CRUM & FORSTER INDEMNITY CO	DE	46.6
CRUM & FORSTER INS CO	NJ	0.0
CRUM & FORSTER SPECIALTY INS CO	AZ	61.9
DORINCO REINSURANCE CO	MI	1,586.7
EASTGUARD INS CO	PA	93.6
ECHELON PROP & CAS INS CO	IL	11.5
ELLINGTON MUTUAL INS CO	WI	5.5
ENDURANCE RISK SOLUTIONS ASR CO	DE	337.9
EVERGREEN USA RRG INC	VT	14.7
FALCON INS CO	IL	12.9
FAMILY SECURITY INS CO	HI	20.9
FINANCIAL AMERICAN PROP & CAS INS CO	TX	13.2
FINIAL REINS CO	CT	1,240.9
FIRST ACCEPTANCE INS CO INC	TX	215.4
FIRST ACCEPTANCE INS CO OF TN INC	TN	24.5
FIRST COMMUNITY INS CO	FL	132.6
FIRST PROTECTIVE INS CO	FL	88.8
FIRST SURETY CORP	WV	10.2
FOUNDERS INS CO	IL	166.7
GENEVA INS CO	IN	3.9
GLOBAL REINS CORP OF AMERICA	NY	415.1
GOLDEN BEAR INS CO	CA	114.6
GRANGE MUTUAL FIRE INS CO	PA	4.0
GREAT CENTRAL FIRE INS CO	LA	0.0
HANOVER FIRE & CASUALTY INS CO	PA	4.3
HARBOR INS CO	OK	13.9
HARTLAND MUT INS CO	ND	11.9
HEALTHCARE UNDERWRITERS GROUP OF KY	KY	23.1
HEALTHCARE UNDERWRITERS GRP MUT OH	OH	27.5
HEREFORD INS CO	NY	150.1
HOSPITALITY INS CO	MA	8.3
HUDSON SPECIALTY INS CO	NY	371.6
INSUREMAX INS CO	IN	11.7
INTEGON NATIONAL INS CO	NC	1,720.3
JUNIATA MUTUAL INS CO	PA	7.9
KEY INS CO	KS	25.3
LEATHERSTOCKING COOP INS CO	NY	24.0
MAPFRE PRAICO INS CO	PR	386.8
MAXUM CASUALTY INS CO	DE	56.0
MEDICAL LIABILITY MUTUAL INS CO	NY	6,271.6
MEDPRO RRG	DC	27.2
MENDOTA INS CO	MN	123.1
MERCHANTS NATIONAL BONDING INC	IA	20.4
MGIC CREDIT ASR CORP	WI	44.4
MGIC INDEMNITY CORP	WI	496.0
MGIC MORTGAGE REINSURANCE CORP	WI	13.4

INSURANCE COMPANY NAME	DOM. STATE	TOTAL ASSETS ($MIL)
US AGENCIES CASUALTY INS CO INC	LA	35.3
WARRANTY UNDERWRITERS INS CO	TX	39.3
WESTERN GENERAL INS CO	CA	53.1
WRIGHT SPECIALTY INS CO	NY	24.9
X L INS CO OF NY	NY	205.2
XL SELECT INS CO	DE	136.1

Rating: D

INSURANCE COMPANY NAME	DOM. STATE	TOTAL ASSETS ($MIL)
ACADEMIC MEDICAL PROFESSIONALS RRG	VT	3.1
ACCC INS CO	TX	315.2
ACCEPTANCE CASUALTY INS CO	NE	69.1
ACCESS HOME INS CO	LA	29.6
ADVANCED PHYSICIANS INS RRG INC	AZ	1.9
AFFIRMATIVE INS CO	IL	197.5
AGENTS MUTUAL INS CO	AR	3.6
AGIC INC	FL	6.9
ALLEGHENY SURETY CO	PA	4.6
ALLIANCE MUTUAL INS CO	NC	2.1
ALLIANCE OF NONPROFITS FOR INS RRG	VT	73.2
ALLIANCE UNITED INS CO	CA	252.4
AMERICAN ASSOC OF ORTHODONTIST RRG	AZ	41.9
AMERICAN COMPENSATION INS CO	MN	71.5
AMERICAN CONTRACTORS INS CO RISK RET	TX	21.1
AMERICAN EXCESS INS EXCHANGE RRG	VT	388.5
AMERICAN FOREST CASUALTY CO RRG	SC	9.8
AMERICAN INTEGRITY INS CO OF FL	FL	195.3
AMERICAN PET INS CO INC	NY	37.0
AMERICAN SAFETY INDEMNITY CO	OK	282.8
AMERICAN SAFETY RRG INC	VT	11.7
AMERICAN SERVICE INS CO INC	IL	118.3
AMERICAN STEAMSHIP O M PROT & IND AS	NY	313.1
AMFED CAS INS CO	MS	4.4
AMFED NATIONAL INS CO	MS	69.6
APPLIED MEDICO LEGAL SOLUTIONS RRG	AZ	116.1
ARGONAUT GREAT CENTRAL INS CO	IL	52.6
ARGONAUT-MIDWEST INS CO	IL	29.6
ARIZONA AUTOMOBILE INS CO	AZ	20.1
ARIZONA HOME INS CO	AZ	23.6
ARKANSAS MUTUAL INS CO	AR	7.2
ASI SELECT INS CORP	DE	6.3
ASSOCIATED INDUSTRIES INS CO INC	FL	202.8
ASSURANCEAMERICA INS CO	SC	51.3
ATLANTIC BONDING CO	MD	11.8
ATTPRO RRG RECIPROCAL RRG	DC	1.7
BAR VERMONT RRG INC	VT	25.1
BATTLE CREEK MUTUAL INS CO	NE	5.9
BEDFORD PHYSICIANS RRG INC	VT	39.3
BOND SAFEGUARD INS CO	SD	70.9
BONDED BUILDERS INS CO RRG	NV	3.5
BOSTON INDEMNITY CO INC	SD	6.8
BRISTOL WEST PREFERRED INS CO	MI	22.0
BROADWAY INS & SURETY CO	NJ	0.0
BUSINESS ALLIANCE INS CO	CA	23.8
CAPACITY INS CO	FL	19.5
CAPITOL PREFERRED INS CO	FL	42.5
CAPSON PHYSICIANS INS CO	TX	20.1

Rating: D+ (Continued)

INSURANCE COMPANY NAME	DOM. STATE	TOTAL ASSETS ($MIL)
MGIC REINSURANCE CORP	WI	167.6
MGIC RESIDENTIAL REINSURANCE CORP	WI	12.7
MIDDLE STATES INS CO INC	OK	5.7
MIDROX INS CO	NY	7.3
MIDSOUTH MUTUAL INS CO	TN	14.0
MIDWESTERN EQUITY TITLE INS CO	IN	3.3
MORTGAGE GUARANTY INS CORP	WI	4,175.5
MUTUAL FIRE INS CO OF S BEND TOWNSHP	PA	0.0
NATIONAL HERITAGE INS CO	IL	3.9
NATIONAL INDEPENDENT TRUCKERS IC RRG	SC	11.5
NAZARETH MUTUAL INS CO	PA	12.3
NEW HAMPSHIRE INS CO	PA	272.1
NEW JERSEY PHYS UNITED RECIP EXCH	NJ	40.7
NORMANDY HARBOR INS CO INC	FL	29.6
NORTHSTONE INS CO	PA	52.1
OLYMPUS INS CO	FL	58.6
PACIFIC PIONEER INSURANCE CO	CA	26.2
PACO ASR CO INC	IL	74.4
PALISADES INS CO	NJ	0.0
PATRONS MUTUAL FIRE INS CO OF IN PA	PA	0.0
PEACHTREE CASUALTY INS CO	FL	29.1
PENINSULAR SURETY CO	FL	2.3
PHYSICIANS CASUALTY RRG INC	NV	6.9
PRIME INS CO	IL	68.9
PUBLIC SERVICE INS CO	IL	515.2
PUERTO RICO MED DEFENSE MUT INS CO	PR	13.5
PYMATUNING MUTUAL FIRE INS CO	PA	0.0
QUANTA INDEMNITY CO	CO	59.1
RADIAN MORTGAGE INS INC	PA	142.9
RANCHERS & FARMERS MUTUAL INS CO	TX	12.9
RED ROCK RISK RETENTION GROUP INC	AZ	6.7
RELIABLE LLOYDS INS CO	TX	15.4
RETAILERS CASUALTY INS CO	LA	73.5
ROCHE SURETY & CASUALTY INC	FL	22.1
SEABRIGHT INS CO	IL	497.1
SEAVIEW INS CO	CA	20.4
SECURITY NATIONAL INS CO	FL	120.5
SENECA INS CO INC	DE	192.9
SIMED	PR	165.7
SOUTHERN GUARANTY INS CO	WI	126.5
SOUTHERN OAK INS CO	FL	118.0
SPRINGFIELD INS CO INC	CA	94.2
STAR CASUALTY INS CO	FL	18.1
STONETRUST COMMERCIAL INS CO	LA	115.9
TEXAS LAWYERS INS EXCHANGE	TX	88.2
TITLE REINSURANCE CO	VT	0.0
TOWER HILL SELECT INS CO	FL	83.2
TRADERS INS CO	MO	44.5
UNITED EQUITABLE INS CO	IL	21.4
UNITED GUARANTY RESIDENTIAL INS CO	NC	3,230.8
UNITED HERITAGE PROP & CAS CO	ID	38.9
UNITED INS CO	UT	27.3
UNITRIN AUTO & HOME INS CO	NY	97.1
UNITRIN PREFERRED INS CO	NY	26.8

INSURANCE COMPANY NAME	DOM. STATE	TOTAL ASSETS ($MIL)	INSURANCE COMPANY NAME	DOM. STATE	TOTAL ASSETS ($MIL)
Rating: D (Continued)			FIRST MUTUAL INS CO	NC	5.5
CARE RRG INC	DC	20.3	FLORIDA PENINSULA INS CO	FL	338.2
CARECONCEPTS INS INC A RRG	MT	3.0	FORT WAYNE MEDICAL ASR CO RRG	AZ	4.6
CASUALTY UNDERWRITERS INS CO	UT	4.4	FRANK WINSTON CRUM INS CO	FL	47.8
CATTLEMANS INS CO A RRG	MT	1.6	FREDERICKSBURG PROFESSIONAL RISK EXC	VT	19.5
CBIA COMP SERVICES INC	CT	23.5	FREEDOM ADVANTAGE INS CO	PA	11.3
CENTAURI SPECIALTY INS CO	FL	58.7	FREMONT INS CO	MI	137.3
CENTRAL CO-OPERATIVE INS CO	NY	14.5	GENERAL SECURITY IND CO OF AZ	AZ	181.6
CENTRAL PA PHYSICIANS RRG INC	SC	60.0	GENERALI - US BRANCH	NY	78.0
CHARITABLE SERVICE PROVIDERS RRG	AZ	3.5	GEORGIA DEALERS INS CO	GA	9.9
CHATTAHOCHEE RRG CAPTIVE INS CO	GA	0.0	GEORGIA MUNICIPAL CAPTIVE INS CO	GA	7.6
CHEROKEE GUARANTEE CO INC A RRG	AZ	13.6	GEORGIA TRANSPORTATION CAPTIVE INS	GA	2.5
CHERRY VALLEY COOPERATIVE INS CO	NY	1.7	GEOVERA INS CO	CA	92.8
CIMARRON INS EXCH RRG	VT	0.0	GERMANIA FARM MUTUAL INS ASN	TX	397.6
CITIZENS UNITED RECIP EXCH	NJ	90.4	GOAUTO INS CO	LA	25.9
CLEARWATER INS CO	DE	1,197.0	GOLDEN INS CO RRG	NV	8.5
CLEARWATER SELECT INS CO	CT	1,167.6	GOVERNMENT ENTITIES MUTUAL INC	DC	74.0
COLLEGE LIAB INS CO LTD RRG	HI	15.5	GREAT FALLS INS CO	ME	6.8
COLONIAL LLOYDS	TX	9.1	GREAT LAKES CASUALTY INS CO	MI	16.6
COLUMBIA FEDERAL INS CO	DC	3.5	GREAT LAKES MUTUAL INS CO	MI	9.4
COLUMBIA LLOYDS INS CO	TX	38.4	GROWERS AUTOMOBILE INS ASN	IN	5.9
COMMUNITIES OF FAITH RRG INC	SC	13.6	GUTHRIE RRG	SC	54.2
COMP OPTIONS INS CO INC	FL	117.0	HALLMARK INS CO	AZ	238.5
COMPANION INC	VI	0.0	HANNAHSTOWN MUTUAL INS CO	PA	3.5
CONEMAUGH VALLEY MUTUAL INS CO	PA	7.5	HAY CREEK MUTUAL INS CO	MN	4.4
CONIFER INS CO	MI	62.5	HEALTH CARE INS RECIPROCAL	MN	23.2
CONSUMER SPECIALTIES INS CO RRG	VT	5.1	HEALTHCARE PROFESSIONAL INS CO INC	NY	294.6
CONSUMERS COUNTY MUTUAL INS CO	TX	111.4	HEALTHCARE PROVIDERS INS CO RRG	SC	75.6
CONTINENTAL MUTUAL INS CO	PA	1.4	HEALTHCARE UNDERWRITERS GRP OF FL	FL	43.1
COVERYS RRG INC	DC	6.8	HEARTLAND HEALTHCARE RECIPROCAL RRG	VT	14.8
CROWN CAPTIVE INS CO	GA	1.3	HOMEOWNERS CHOICE PROP & CAS INS CO	FL	387.2
DELAWARE GRANGE MUTUAL FIRE INS CO	DE	1.5	HOMESITE LLOYDS OF TEXAS	TX	15.1
DELPHI CASUALTY CO	IL	7.1	HOSPITALS INS CO INC	NY	0.0
DELTA LLOYDS INS CO OF HOUSTON	TX	10.7	ID COUNTIES RISK MGMT PROGRAM UNDW	ID	58.3
DISCOVERY INS CO	NC	25.3	IFA INS CO	NJ	63.0
DIST-CO INS CO INC RRG	HI	2.2	INDIANA HEALTHCARE RECIPROCAL RRG	VT	30.6
DONGBU INS CO LTD	HI	194.9	INDIANA LUMBERMENS MUTUAL INS CO	IN	66.3
DUBOIS MEDICAL RRG	DC	11.4	INNOVATIVE PHYSICIAN SOLUTIONS RRG	AZ	5.2
EASTERN ALLIANCE INS CO	PA	246.5	INS CO OF THE STATE OF PA	PA	315.2
EMERGENCY CAP MGMT LLC A RRG	DE	4.2	INSURORS INDEMNITY CO	TX	22.5
EMERGENCY MEDICINE PROFESSIONAL ASR	NV	23.9	INSURORS INDEMNITY LLOYDS	TX	4.1
EMERGENCY PHYSICIANS INS CO RRG	NV	35.0	INTEGRA INS INC	MN	2.0
ESURANCE INS CO OF NEW JERSEY	WI	14.8	IQS INS RRG INC	VT	1.6
FARM BUREAU NEW HORIZONS INS CO MO	MO	39.7	IRONSHORE RRG INC	DE	2.3
FARMERS & MECH MU I ASN OF CECIL CTY	MD	1.1	LANCET IND RRG INC	NV	20.1
FARMERS & MECHANICS FIRE & CAS INS	WV	10.5	LAUNDRY OWNERS MUTUAL LIAB INS ASN	PA	15.1
FARMINGTON MUTUAL INS CO	WI	6.8	LENDERS PROTECTION ASR CO RRG	NE	2.4
FDM PREFERRED INS CO	NY	7.0	LIBERTY INS CORP	IL	225.6
FEDERATED NATIONAL INS CO	FL	331.9	LIGHTHOUSE CASUALTY CO	IL	9.0
FINANCIAL GUARANTY INS CO	NY	2,539.9	LOYA CASUALTY INS CO	CA	101.5
FIRE DISTRICTS INS CO	NY	10.7	LOYA INS CO	TX	261.8
FIRST CHICAGO INS CO	IL	43.9	MADISON INS CO	SC	73.5
FIRST FOUNDERS ASR CO	NJ	0.0	MARATHON FINANCIAL INS INC RRG	DE	7.4
FIRST JERSEY CASUALTY INS CO INC	NJ	0.0	MBIA INS CORP	NY	933.4
FIRST MERCURY INS CO	IL	146.1	MED MAL RRG INC	TN	5.1
			MEDICAL ALLIANCE INS CO	IL	9.0

INSURANCE COMPANY NAME	DOM. STATE	TOTAL ASSETS ($MIL)
Rating:	**D**	**(Continued)**
MEDICAL PROVIDERS MUTUAL INS CO RRG	DC	7.3
MIC REINS CORP	WI	4.3
MIC REINS CORP OF WISCONSIN	WI	7.0
MIDWEST INS GROUP INC RRG	VT	6.6
MILLBROOK NMF RRG INC	SC	3.2
MISSOURI VALLEY MUTUAL INS CO	SD	5.6
MONTOUR MUTUAL INS CO	PA	1.0
MOUND PRAIRIE MUTUAL INS CO	MN	5.6
MOUNT CARROLL MUTUAL INS CO	IL	6.0
MOUNTAIN VALLEY INDEMNITY CO	NH	31.2
MOWER COUNTY FARMERS MUT INS CO	MN	4.4
MT MORRIS MUTUAL INS CO	WI	28.1
MUTUAL INS CO OF LEHIGH CTY	PA	3.1
MUTUAL SAVINGS FIRE INS CO	AL	6.8
NASW RISK RETENTION GROUP INC	DC	2.7
NATIONAL AMERICAN INS CO OF CA	CA	40.3
NATIONAL ASSISTED LIVING RRG INC	DC	8.7
NATIONAL DIRECT INS CO	NV	4.7
NATIONAL GUARDIAN RRG INC	HI	18.3
NATIONAL INTERSTATE INS CO OF HAWAII	OH	46.1
NATIONAL MEDICAL PROFESSIONAL RRG	SC	6.2
NATIONAL UNITY INS CO	TX	67.4
NCMIC RRG INC	VT	6.0
NHRMA MUTUAL INS CO	IL	39.4
NIPPONKOA INS CO LTD (GUAM)	GU	0.0
NORTH EAST INS CO	ME	72.7
NORTH SHORE LIJ PHYSICIANS INS RRG	VT	15.6
OLD GLORY INS CO	TX	21.9
OMEGA INS CO	FL	39.1
ONTARIO REINS CO LTD	GA	27.8
ONYX INS CO INC A RRG	TN	16.5
OOIDA RISK RETENTION GROUP INC	VT	84.5
OTSEGO COUNTY PATRONS CO-OP F R ASN	NY	1.8
PALISADES PROPERTY & CASUALTY INS	NJ	0.0
PARATRANSIT INS CO A MUTUAL RRG	TN	24.1
PARTNERS MUTUAL INS CO	WI	42.9
PENN RESERVE INS CO LTD	PA	1.8
PEOPLES TRUST INS CO	FL	242.8
PETROLEUM MARKETERS MGMT INS CO	IA	31.5
PHYSICIANS INS CO	FL	13.0
PHYSICIANS INS PROGRAM RECIP EXCH	PA	26.4
PHYSICIANS PROACTIVE PROTECTION INC	SC	62.9
PIA PROFESSIONAL LIABILITY INS RRG	MT	2.1
PIEDMONT MUTUAL INS CO	NC	3.7
PINNACLE CONSORTIUM OF HIGHER ED RRG	VT	8.4
PLICO INC	OK	152.1
POINT GUARD INS CO	PR	23.5
PONCE DE LEON LTC RRG INC	FL	11.1
POSITIVE PHYSICIANS INS EXCHANGE	PA	48.9
PRESERVER INS CO	NJ	146.4
PRIMERO INS CO	NV	12.4
PROFESSIONAL INS EXCHANGE MUTUAL	UT	8.0
PROFESSIONAL QUALITY LIABILITY INS	VT	2.2
PROFESSIONAL SOLUTIONS INS CO	IA	21.1

INSURANCE COMPANY NAME	DOM. STATE	TOTAL ASSETS ($MIL)
PROFESSIONALS RRG INC	MT	3.4
QBE OPTIMA INS CO	PR	65.7
QBE SPECIALTY INS CO	ND	957.4
QUALITY CASUALTY INS CO INC	AL	1.1
R&Q REINS CO	PA	156.1
RADIAN GUARANTY INC	PA	3,530.5
REAMSTOWN MUTUAL INS CO	PA	8.0
RELIAMAX INS CO	SD	9.8
RELIAMAX SURETY CO	SD	55.5
REPUBLIC CREDIT INDEMNITY CO	IL	60.6
REPUBLIC MORTGAGE INS CO OF FLORIDA	FL	27.6
RESPONSE INS CO	IL	26.8
RIDER INS CO	NJ	40.4
RPX RRG INC	HI	5.5
RUTGERS ENHANCED INS CO	NJ	0.0
SAFECARD SERVICE INS CO	ND	0.0
SAINT LUKES HEALTH SYSTEM RRG	SC	23.9
SAMARITAN RRG INC	SC	29.7
SAWGRASS MUTUAL INS CO	FL	27.4
SCHOOL BOARDS INS CO OF PA INC	PA	196.2
SCOR REINSURANCE CO	NY	2,254.6
SECURITY AMERICA RRG INC	VT	5.5
SECURITY PLAN FIRE INS CO	LA	6.8
SELECT MARKETS INS CO	IL	15.5
SELECT MD RRG INC	MT	2.2
SELECTIVE INS CO OF NEW ENGLAND	NJ	167.4
SOMERSET CASUALTY INS CO	PA	32.8
SOUTHERN GENERAL INS CO	GA	46.0
SOUTHWEST GENERAL INS CO	NM	3.0
SPARTAN INS CO	TX	5.8
SPIRIT COMMERCIAL AUTO RRG INC	NV	48.5
ST JOHNS INS CO INC	FL	123.8
STICO MUTUAL INS CO A RRG	VT	24.0
STONEGATE INS CO	IL	12.2
SUN SURETY INS CO	SD	17.5
SUNDERLAND MARINE INS CO LTD	AK	10.2
TERRAFIRMA RRG LLC	VT	5.6
TEXAS FARM BUREAU MUTUAL INS CO	TX	682.4
TEXAS HOSPITAL INS EXCHANGE	TX	33.3
TIFT AREA CAPTIVE INS CO	GA	0.0
TIG INS CO	CA	2,315.8
TITAN INS CO INC RRG	SC	47.6
TITLE INDUSTRY ASR CO RRG	VT	6.2
TOWER HILL PREFERRED INS CO	FL	110.7
TOWER HILL PRIME INS CO	FL	144.0
TOWER HILL SIGNATURE INS CO	FL	134.7
TRANSIT GENERAL INS CO	IL	21.2
TRANSIT MUTUAL INS CORP OF WI	WI	14.0
TRINITY RISK SOLUTIONS RECIP INS RRG	DC	8.4
TWIN LIGHTS INS CO	NJ	0.0
U S LLOYDS INS CO	TX	23.6
UNDERWRITERS AT LLOYDS	KY	213.7
UNDERWRITERS AT LLOYDS LONDON	IL	369.8
UNITED AUTOMOBILE INS CO	FL	347.1
UNITED BUSINESS INS CO	GA	6.3
UNITED CASUALTY & SURETY CO INC	MA	9.5

INSURANCE COMPANY NAME	DOM. STATE	TOTAL ASSETS ($MIL)	INSURANCE COMPANY NAME	DOM. STATE	TOTAL ASSETS ($MIL)
Rating: D (Continued)			HEALTH CARE INDUSTRY LIAB RECIP INS	DC	44.6
UNITED GROUP CAPTIVE INS CO	GA	1.8	HEALTHCARE UNDERWRITING CO RRG	VT	131.2
UNITED HOME INS CO	AR	28.2	HOMEOWNERS OF AMERICA INS CO	TX	29.0
UPMC WORK ALLIANCE INC	PA	2.3	INTEGRITY PROP & CAS INS CO	WI	20.3
URGENT CARE ASR CO RRG INC	NV	4.8	INTERBORO MUTUAL INDEMNITY INS CO	NY	90.5
US LEGAL SERVICES INC	TN	2.0	INTERMODAL INS CO RRG	DC	0.0
UV INS RRG INC	HI	1.1	IU HEALTH RRG INC	SC	9.3
VICTORIA SPECIALTY INSURANCE CO	OH	22.3	JOLIET AREA RRG CAPTIVE INS CO	GA	0.0
VICTORY INS CO INC	MT	14.3	KENTUCKY HOSPITAL INS CO RRG	KY	20.5
WACO FIRE & CAS INS CO	GA	26.8	LAKE STREET RRG INC	VT	2.9
WARNER INS CO	IL	11.7	LEXINGTON NATIONAL INS CORP	MD	53.4
WASHINGTON CASUALTY CO	WA	27.2	LITTLE BLACK MUTUAL INS CO	WI	4.6
WEST VIRGINIA INS CO	WV	47.8	LONE STAR NATIONAL INS CO	IN	6.0
WEST VIRGINIA NATIONAL AUTO INS CO	WV	11.1	MACHINERY INS INC AN ASSESSABLE MUT	FL	2.8
WILMINGTON INS CO	DE	4.7	MD RRG INC	MT	17.7
Rating: D-			MEDSTAR LIABILITY LTD INS CO INC RRG	DC	3.7
AMERICAN ALLIANCE CASUALTY CO	IL	12.7	MERCURY INDEMNITY CO OF AMERICA	FL	54.8
AMERICAN HEARTLAND INS CO	IL	17.3	MOUNTAIN STATES HEALTHCARE RECIP RRG	MT	116.0
AMERICAN TRUCKING & TRANSP INS RRG	MT	19.8	MOUNTAINEER FREEDOM RRG INC	WV	34.2
AMERIGUARD RRG INC	VT	11.2	NATIONAL CATHOLIC RRG	VT	69.9
ARCH MORTGAGE REINS CO	WI	26.8	NEVADA MUTUAL INS CO INC	NV	27.5
ATTORNEYS INS MUTUAL RRG	HI	16.5	NEW MEXICO PROPERTY & CASUALTY CO	NM	2.4
BUTTE MUTUAL INS CO	NM	1.1	NORTHWESTERN NATL INS CO SEG ACCNT	WI	31.8
CALIFORNIA MUTUAL INS CO	CA	14.3	NUCLEAR ELECTRIC INS LTD	DE	0.0
CAREGIVERS UNITED LIAB INS CO RRG	SC	40.6	ORANGE COUNTY MEDICAL RECIP INS RRG	AZ	7.4
CASSATT RISK RETENTION GROUP INC	VT	12.4	ORTHOFORUM INS CO RRG	SC	15.5
CASUALTY CORP OF AMERICA	OK	7.2	PARAMOUNT INS CO	MD	6.9
CATASTROPHE REINS CO	TX	1,979.8	PEACE CHURCH RRG INC	VT	22.5
CEM INS CO	IL	31.5	PELICAN INS RRG	VT	18.6
CENTURION MEDICAL LIAB PROTECT RRG	AZ	19.6	PHYSICIANS IND RRG INC	NV	7.8
CIRCLE STAR INS CO RRG	VT	4.9	PHYSICIANS REIMBURSEMENT FUND RRG	VT	29.5
COASTAL INS RRG INC	AL	43.4	PHYSICIANS SPECIALTY LTD RRG	SC	14.2
COMCARE PRO INS RECIPROCAL RRG	VT	5.3	PINE TREE INS RECIPROCAL RRG	VT	11.3
COMMONWEALTH CASUALTY CO	AZ	7.2	PREFERRED AUTO INS CO INC	TN	7.5
COMMUNITY MUTUAL INS CO	NY	2.6	REPWEST INS CO	AZ	298.7
COUNTRYWIDE INS CO	NY	228.2	RETAILERS INS CO	MI	19.7
CRUDEN BAY RRG INC	VT	11.7	SAFE INS CO	WV	9.7
DIAMOND INS CO	IL	46.0	SENTINEL ASR RRG INC	HI	16.5
DOCTORS & SURGEONS NATL RRG INC	KY	11.0	SERVICE INS CO INC	NJ	12.1
EMERGENCY MEDICINE RRG INC	SC	8.5	SFM SELECT INS CO	MN	4.8
EQUITABLE LIABILITY INS CO	DC	3.5	SPIRIT MOUNTAIN INS CO RRG INC	DC	6.7
ESURANCE PROP & CAS INS CO	CA	91.4	STATES SELF-INSURERS RISK RET GROUP	VT	27.0
FAIRWAY PHYSICIANS INS CO RRG	DC	25.3	SYNERGY COMP INS CO	PA	26.1
FIRST BENEFITS INS MUTUAL INC	NC	35.4	SYNERGY INS CO	NC	53.1
FIRST INDEMNITY OF AMERICA INS CO	NJ	7.9	SYSTEMS PROTECTION ASR RRG INC	MT	0.0
FULMONT MUTUAL INS CO	NY	5.4	TEXAS MEDICAL INS CO	TX	37.1
GALEN INS CO	MO	16.1	TOWER INS CO OF NEW YORK	NY	426.2
GATEWAY INS CO	MO	43.5	US INS CO OF AMERICA	IL	5.9
GEICO CASUALTY CO	MD	2,376.6	UTAH BUSINESS INS CO INC	UT	17.1
GENESEE PATRONS COOP INS	NY	8.8	VASA SPRING GARDEN MUTUAL INS CO	MN	4.0
GLOBAL HAWK INS CO RRG	VT	34.5	WEST VIRGINIA MUTUAL INS CO	WV	179.0
GLOBAL LIBERTY INS CO OF NY	NY	54.9	WESTERN CATHOLIC INS CO RRG	VT	7.1
GREENVILLE CASUALTY INS CO INC	SC	14.6	WHITECAP SURETY CO	MN	1.3
GUARDIAN RRG INC	MT	5.8	WINDHAVEN INS CO	FL	107.5
HEALTH CARE CASUALTY RRG INC	DC	16.4	WORK FIRST CASUALTY CO	DE	41.1
			WORKMENS AUTO INS CO	CA	30.5

INSURANCE COMPANY NAME	DOM. STATE	TOTAL ASSETS ($MIL)
Rating: D- (Continued)		
YELLOWSTONE INS EXCH RRG	VT	20.5
ZEPHYR INS CO INC	HI	84.2
Rating: E+		
A CENTRAL INS CO	NY	98.2
ACCIDENT INS CO INC	SC	143.9
AMERICAN TRANSIT INS CO	NY	145.2
ASCENDANT COMMERCIAL INS INC	FL	40.0
AVERA PROPERTY INS INC	SD	0.0
BALDWIN MUTUAL INS CO	AL	11.3
CARE WEST INS CO	CA	117.7
CLAIM PROFESSIONALS LIAB INS CO RRG	VT	3.6
OROWN CAPTIVE INS CO INC	DC	5.5
DELAWARE PROFESSIONAL INS CO	DE	7.3
DISTRICTS MUTUAL INS	WI	23.8
ETHIO AMERICAN INS CO	GA	7.9
FAITH AFFILIATED RRG INC	VT	9.6
FARMERS MUTUAL F I C OF BRANCH CTY	MI	1.5
FIRST NET INS CO	GU	17.9
FRANKLIN CASUALTY INS CO RRG	VT	42.6
GOOD SHEPHERD RECIPROCAL RRG	SC	6.8
GRANADA INS CO	FL	33.9
GUARANTEE INS CO	FL	424.4
INDEPENDENCE CASUALTY INS CO	MA	4.4
ISLAND HOME INS CO	GU	26.4
JM WOODWORTH RRG INC	NV	14.6
KENSINGTON INS CO	NY	14.9
KENTUCKY NATIONAL INS CO	KY	27.9
LINCOLN GENERAL INS CO	PA	83.4
MAKE TRANSPORTATION INS INC RRG	DE	4.4
MAYA ASR CO	NY	14.3
MEMBERS INS CO	NC	21.1
MOUNTAIN LAUREL RRG INC	VT	26.6
MPM INS CO OF KANSAS	KS	21.2
NEW YORK HEALTHCARE INS CO INC RRG	DC	23.4
NORTH CAROLINA GRANGE MUTUAL INS CO	NC	25.2
OKLAHOMA PROPERTY & CAS INS CO	OK	3.6
OLD AMERICAN CTY MUTUAL FIRE INS CO	TX	66.6
ORISKA INS CO	NY	71.7
PACE RRG INC	VT	13.2
PCH MUTUAL INS CO INC RRG	DC	9.7
PENNSYLVANIA PHYSICIANS RECIP INS	PA	13.9
PHYSICIANS INS MUTUAL	MO	4.9
PREFERRED CONTRACTORS INS CO RRG LLC	MT	92.0
PREMIER PHYSICIANS INS CO INC A RRG	NV	11.8
PROFESSIONAL EXCHANGE ASR CO (A RRG)	HI	4.2
RADIAN GUARANTY REINS INC	PA	373.6
RVOS FARM MUTUAL INS CO	TX	73.3
SOUTHWEST PHYSICIANS RRG INC	SC	79.9
SPRING VALLEY MUTUAL INS CO	MN	3.9
STAR & SHIELD INS EXCHANGE	FL	21.8
STONINGTON INS CO	TX	195.0
TOWER BONDING & SURETY CO	PR	4.0
TOWER NATIONAL INS CO	MA	33.3
UNITRIN ADVANTAGE INS CO	NY	3.5

INSURANCE COMPANY NAME	DOM. STATE	TOTAL ASSETS ($MIL)
UNIVERSAL PROPERTY & CASUALTY INS	FL	657.6
USA INS CO	MS	14.9
VFH CAPTIVE INS CO	GA	6.3
VIRGINIA PHYSICIANS RRG INC	MT	1.7
WASHINGTON COUNTY CO-OPERATIVE INS	NY	7.3
WELLSPAN RRG	VT	25.2
Rating: E		
AEGIS HEALTHCARE RRG INC	DC	3.3
AGRINATIONAL INS CO	VT	1,114.9
ALLEGIANT INS CO INC A RRG	HI	20.2
ALLIANCE NATIONAL INS CO	NY	47.5
ALLIED SERVICES RRG	SC	7.4
AMBAC ASSURANCE CORP	WI	5,940.7
AMERICAN LIBERTY INS CO	UT	10.5
APPLIED UNDERWRITERS CAPTIVE RISK	IA	611.7
ARCOA RRG INC	NV	11.4
AUSTIN MUTUAL INS CO	MN	45.3
BUILDING INDUSTRY INS ASSN INC	VA	20.0
CALIFORNIA MEDICAL GROUP INS CO RRG	AZ	13.4
CIFG ASR NORTH AMERICA INC	NY	785.1
COLUMBIA NATIONAL RRG INC	VT	1.7
COMMUNITY HEALTH ALLIANCE RECIP RRG	VT	95.5
CONTRACTORS INS CO OF NORTH AMER RRG	HI	43.3
CTLIC RRG INC	DC	0.0
FARMERS MUTUAL INS CO OF ELLINWOOD	KS	3.1
FARMERS UNION MUTUAL INS CO	AR	3.6
GABLES RRG INC	VT	8.0
GEISINGER INS CORP RRG	VT	21.7
GERMAN MUTUAL INS CO	OH	34.0
GHS INS CO	OK	19.7
GREEN HILLS INS CO RRG	VT	11.8
HALIFAX MUTUAL INS CO	NC	6.4
HEALTH CARE MUT CAPTIVE INS CO	GA	11.8
HEARTLAND MUTUAL INS CO	MN	4.9
HOCHHEIM PRAIRIE FARM MUT INS ASN	TX	153.8
INS PLACEMENT FACILITY OF PA	PA	0.0
KENTUCKIANA MEDICAL RRG & INS CO INC	KY	51.4
KEYSTONE MUTUAL INS CO	MO	2.1
LEADING INS GROUP INS CO LTD US BR	NY	225.0
MGIC REINSURANCE CORP OF WI	WI	363.6
MIDWEST PROVIDER INS CO RRG INC	AZ	4.2
MILLERS CLASSIFIED INS CO	IL	2.7
MISSOURI DOCTORS MUTUAL INS CO	MO	7.0
MISSOURI PROFESSIONALS MUTUAL INS CO	MO	17.7
NARRAGANSETT BAY INS CO	RI	135.9
NATIONAL AUTOMOTIVE INS	LA	23.7
NATIONAL BUILDERS & CONTRACTORS INS	NV	3.5
NATIONAL CONTRACTORS INS CO INC RRG	MT	5.3
NEVADA DOCS MEDICAL RRG INC	NV	2.1
NEWPORT BONDING & SURETY CO	PR	5.8
NORTHWEST GF MUTUAL INS CO	SD	15.1
NOVANT HEALTH RRG INC	SC	11.7
PACIFIC SPECIALTY PROPERTY & CAS CO	TX	4.6
PARK INS CO	NY	27.1
PHOEBE RECIPROCAL RRG	SC	5.5

INSURANCE COMPANY NAME	DOM. STATE	TOTAL ASSETS ($MIL)
Rating: E (Continued)		
PHYSICIANS INS EXCHANGE RESOURCE RRG	VT	4.9
PHYSICIANS PROFESSIONAL IND ASSN	MO	10.9
PINELANDS INS CO RRG INC	DC	3.4
PUBLIC UTILITY MUTUAL INS CO RRG	VT	6.1
PXRE REINSURANCE CO	CT	26.2
REGIS INS CO	PA	2.8
REPUBLIC MORTGAGE INS CO OF NC	NC	233.0
ST CHARLES INS CO RRG	SC	13.7
ST LUKES HEALTH NETWORK INS CO RRG	VT	57.0
STERLING CAS INS CO	CA	15.6
SUNZ INS CO	FL	66.2
SYNCORA CAPITAL ASR INC	NY	523.7
UNITED CENTRAL PA RRG	VT	17.5
UNIVERSAL INS CO	NC	25.2
UPPER HUDSON NATIONAL INS CO	NY	3.3
VISION INS CO	TX	20.8
WORKERS COMPENSATION EXCHANGE	ID	8.4
Rating: E-		
ACADEMIC HLTH PROFESSIONALS INS ASSO	NY	288.7
AF&L INS CO	PA	157.9
AGGREGATE SECURITY INS GROUP A RRG	NV	4.0
CASTLEPOINT INS CO	NY	194.0
DRIVERS INS CO	NY	4.3
EVEREADY INS CO	NY	0.0
EXCALIBUR REINS CORP	PA	18.6
FIDUCIARY INS CO OF AMERICA	NY	100.2
HERMITAGE INS CO	NY	142.4
PHYSICIANS RECIPROCAL INSURERS	NY	1,447.3
SENIOR AMERICAN INS CO	PA	17.7
SYNCORA GUARANTEE INC	NY	1,210.4
TEXAS FAIR PLAN ASSN	TX	103.1
Rating: F		
ACCEPTANCE INS CO	NE	29.1
ARGUS FIRE & CASUALTY INS CO	FL	5.1
CAGC INS CO	NC	0.0
COMMERCIAL MUT INS CO	GA	0.0
COMMONWEALTH INS CO	PA	0.0
FIRST KEYSTONE RRG INC	SC	13.6
FLORIDA SELECT INS CO	FL	0.0
FREESTONE INS CO	DE	0.0
GEORGIA MUTUAL INS CO	GA	0.0
GULF BUILDERS RRG INC	SC	0.0
HIGHLANDS INS CO	TX	0.0
HOME VALUE INS CO	OH	0.0
ICM INS CO	NY	0.0
INDEMNITY INS CORP RRG	DE	0.0
INTERSTATE BANKERS CASUALTY CO	IL	0.0
LEMIC INS CO	LA	0.0
LIBERTY FIRST RRG INS CO	UT	0.0
LION INS CO	NY	0.0
LUMBER MUTUAL INS CO	MA	0.0
MANHATTAN RE-INS CO	DE	0.0
MILLERS FIRST INS CO	IL	7.8

INSURANCE COMPANY NAME	DOM. STATE	TOTAL ASSETS ($MIL)
NATIONAL INS CO	PR	0.0
NORTHWESTERN NTL INS CO MILWAUKEE	WI	32.1
PAFCO GENERAL INS CO	IN	0.0
PHOENIX FUND INC	NC	0.0
PMI INS CO	AZ	95.4
PMI MORTGAGE INS CO	AZ	1,370.8
PROFESSIONAL LIAB INS CO OF AMERICA	NY	0.0
RED ROCK INS CO	OK	57.1
REPUBLIC MORTGAGE INS CO	NC	845.6
SAN ANTONIO INDEMNITY CO	TX	0.0
SHELBY INS CO	TX	0.0
SUNSHINE STATE INS CO	FL	22.9
TRIAD GUARANTY ASR CORP	IL	0.0
TRIAD GUARANTY INS CORP	IL	0.0
UNION AMERICAN INS CO	FL	0.0
UNION MUTUAL INS CO	OK	0.0
VESTA INS CORP	TX	0.0
Rating: U		
1ST ATLANTIC SURETY CO	NC	3.2
2-10 HOME BUYERS WARRANTY OF VA	VA	0.0
21ST CENTURY AUTO INS CO OF NJ	NJ	25.6
21ST CENTURY INS CO OF THE SW	TX	5.4
21ST CENTURY SUPERIOR INS CO	CA	30.4
A-ONE COMM INS RRG GROUP INC	TN	3.0
AFFIRMATIVE INS CO OF MI	MI	9.2
AIMCO MUTUAL INS CO	NC	9.1
ALEA NORTH AMERICA INS CO	NY	146.2
ALICOT INS CO	TX	0.0
ALINSCO INS CO	TX	20.2
ALLIED INS CO OF AMERICA	OH	13.9
ALLSTATE NORTH AMERICAN INS CO	IL	11.0
AMBAC ASR CORP SEGREGATED ACCT	WI	13.6
AMC RE INC	AR	0.0
AMERICAN BUILDERS INS CO RRG INC	MT	1.0
AMERICAN CENTENNIAL INS CO	DE	40.6
AMERICAN EQUITY INS CO	AZ	103.8
AMERICAN FARMERS & RANCHERS INS CO	OK	8.7
AMERICAN FEED INDUSTRY INS CO RRG	IA	1.5
AMERICAN HEALTHCARE INDEMNITY CO	DE	105.1
AMERICAN INTERNATIONAL OVERSEAS LTD		0.0
AMERICAN MEDICAL ASR CO	IL	3.5
AMERICAN MEDICAL INS EXCHANGE	IN	0.5
AMERICAN PHYSICIANS ASR CORP	MI	455.1
AMERICAN PROPERTY INS CO	NJ	28.3
AMERICAN SHIELD INS CO	MO	5.0
AMERICAN SPECIAL RISK INS CO	DE	0.9
AMTRUST LLOYDS INS CO OF TEXAS	TX	2.2
APPLIANCE MANUFACTURERS ASR CO RRG	IA	0.0
AQUAGARDIAN INS CO INC	AZ	0.0
ARCH EXCESS & SURPLUS INS CO	MO	61.5
ARGONAUT LIMITED RISK INS CO	IL	11.4
ARI CASUALTY CO	NJ	7.8
ARROWOOD INDEMNITY CO	DE	1,499.6
ARROWOOD SURPLUS LINES INS CO	DE	174.6
ARTISAN CONTRACTORS INS CO RRG LLC	MT	0.0

INSURANCE COMPANY NAME	DOM. STATE	TOTAL ASSETS ($MIL)	INSURANCE COMPANY NAME	DOM. STATE	TOTAL ASSETS ($MIL)
Rating: U (Continued)			EXCELA RECIPROCAL RRG	VT	4.3
ASHLAND MUTUAL FIRE INS CO OF PA	PA	0.5	EXECUTIVE INS CO	NY	2.3
ASHMERE INS CO	IL	36.5	EXPLORER AMERICAN INS CO	CA	2.6
ASPEN SPECIALTY RRG INC	DC	1.0	FACILITY INS CORP	TX	115.8
ASSET PROTECTION PROGRAM RRG INC	SC	1.5	FAIR AMERICAN SELECT INS CO	DE	49.0
ASSN OF CERTIFIED MTG ORIG RRG	NV	1.2	FAIRMONT INS CO	CA	26.6
ATLANTA INTERNATIONAL INS CO	NY	44.1	FAIRMONT PREMIER INS CO	CA	133.0
ATRIUM INS CORP	NY	1.8	FAIRMONT SPECIALTY INS CO	CA	151.2
AUTO CLUB CASUALTY CO	TX	2.8	FB INS CO	KY	1.3
AVIVA INS CO OF CANADA (US BR)	NY	16.3	FIRST AMERICAN HOME BUYERS PRO CORP	CA	0.0
AXIS SPECIALTY INS CO	CT	80.4	FIRST CHOICE CASUALTY INS CO	NV	5.5
AZTEC INS CO	FL	0.0	FIRST MORTGAGE INS CO	NC	8.2
BALTIMORE EQUITABLE SOCIETY	MD	157.6	FIRST STATE INS CO	OT	370.9
BAY INS RRG INC	SC	0.6	FIRST WASHINGTON INS CO INC	DC	2.0
BEACONHARBOR MUTUAL RRG	ME	1.0	FMH INS CO OF IOWA	IA	6.7
BLUESHORE INS CO	CO	5.5	FOUNDERS INS CO OF MICHIGAN	MI	6.1
BOLD LEGAL DEFENSE INS INC	FL	0.0	FRONTLINE INS UNLIMITED CO	IL	25.3
BRACKEN HILL SPECIALTY INS CO INC	IL	45.6	GEICO COUNTY MUTUAL INS CO	TX	31.9
BROWARD FACTORY SERVICE INC	NV	0.0	GENERAL FIDELITY INS CO	SC	406.5
BTTS INS RRG GROUP INC	SC	0.6	GENWORTH FINANCIAL ASR CORP	NC	14.3
BUCKS COUNTY CONTRIBUTIONSHIP	PA	6.5	GLOBAL HAWK PROPERTY CAS INS CO	DE	5.0
CAMBRIA COUNTY MUTUAL INS CO	PA	0.0	GLOBAL INS CO	GA	3.5
CASTLE HILL INS CO	RI	0.0	GOLDSTREET INS CO	NY	5.9
CATAWBA INS CO	SC	7.1	GRACO RRG INC	SC	1.0
CENTRE INS CO	DE	89.8	GREAT AMERICAN CASUALTY INS CO	OH	12.7
CENTURY INDEMNITY CO	PA	890.2	GREAT AMERICAN CONTEMPORARY INS CO	OH	10.3
CGB INS CO	IN	187.2	GREEN TREE PERPETUAL ASR CO	PA	0.2
CHURCH INS CO	NY	25.4	GREENPATH INS CO	CA	11.7
CINCINNATI EQUITABLE INS CO	OH	4.1	GUILDERLAND REINSURANCE CO	NY	3.3
CLAREMONT LIABILITY INS CO	CA	15.0	GULF UNDERWRITERS INS CO	CT	55.9
CLARENDON AMERICA INS CO	IL	250.8	HAMDEN ASR RRG INC	VT	94.5
CLINIC MUTUAL INS CO RRG	HI	4.8	HANOVER NATIONAL INS CO	NH	12.0
CLOISTER MUTUAL CASUALTY INS CO	PA	4.7	HANOVER NJ INS CO	NH	30.6
COLONY NATIONAL INS CO	VA	87.6	HERITAGE CASUALTY INS CO	KS	61.2
COMMERCIAL CASUALTY INS CO	CA	117.6	HERITAGE WARRANTY INS RRG INC	SC	0.6
COMMERCIAL GUARANTY INS CO	DE	34.8	HOME CONSTRUCTION INS CO RRG	NV	6.1
COMMONWEALTH INS CO OF AMERICA	WA	22.1	HOMEOWNERS CHOICE ASR CO INC	AL	2.0
COMMONWEALTH MUTUAL INS CO	MD	0.5	HOMESHIELD FIRE & CASUALTY INS CO	OK	1.1
COMPANION CAPTIVE INS CO	SC	0.0	HOMESTEAD INS CO	PA	6.5
COMPASS INS CO	NY	11.9	HOMESURE OF VIRGINIA INC	VA	0.0
COMPSOURCE OKLAHOMA	OK	0.0	HORIZON MIDWEST CASUALTY CO	KS	2.5
COMPUTER INS CO	RI	24.0	HOSPITALITY MUT CAPT INS CO	GA	0.0
CONSTELLATION REINSURANCE CO	NY	15.3	HOUSING SPECIALTY INS CO	VT	15.8
CONTINENTAL AMERICAN INS CO	IN	0.0	HOUSTON GENERAL INS EXCH	TX	2.4
CONTINENTAL RISK UNDERWRITERS RRG IN	NV	0.8	HOW INS CO A RRG	VA	122.6
COPIC A RRG	DC	0.9	HUTTERIAN BRETHREN MUTUAL INS CORP	IL	2.2
CORNERSTONE MUTUAL INS CO	GA	0.0	IDAHO STATE INS FUND	ID	0.0
COVENTRY INSURANCE CO	RI	1.9	INDEPENDENT TRUCKERS INS CO	IA	0.0
CUMIS MORTGAGE REINS CO	WI	9.9	INS CO OF THE AMERICAS	FL	11.0
DR INS CO	KY	0.0	INTERMED INS CO	MO	27.2
EDISON INS CO	FL	20.6	INTREPID INS CO	MI	33.2
ELITE TRANSPORTATION RRG INC	AZ	10.4	ISMIE INDEMNITY CO	IL	16.8
ELIZABETHTOWN INS CO	DE	3.8	KNIGHT SPECIALTY INS CO	DE	23.6
EMPIRE INS CO	NY	27.4	LAMMICO RRG INC	DC	6.1
EVERSPAN FINANCIAL GUARANTEE CORP	WI	219.8	LEGAL MUTUAL LIAB INS SOCIETY OF MD	MD	0.5
			LEON HIX INS CO	SC	3.4

INSURANCE COMPANY NAME	DOM. STATE	TOTAL ASSETS ($MIL)	INSURANCE COMPANY NAME	DOM. STATE	TOTAL ASSETS ($MIL)
Rating: U (Continued)			PHYSICIANS RRG LLC	MT	0.0
LIBERTY AMERICAN INS CO	FL	8.5	PINNACOL ASR CO	CO	2,094.0
LITTLE RIVER INS CO	DE	3.2	PLICO RRG INC	OK	1.6
LM PROPERTY & CASUALTY INS CO	IN	63.0	POLICYHOLDERS MUTUAL INS CO	WI	0.3
LOCUST MUTUAL FIRE INS CO	PA	0.0	POTOMAC INS CO	PA	11.4
LONE STAR ALLIANCE INC A RRG	DC	1.3	PREFERRED MANAGED RISK LTD	DC	0.0
LR INS INC	DE	8.7	PREFERRED PROFESSIONAL RRG	DC	0.6
LVHN RRG	SC	60.3	PREMIER INS EXCHANGE RRG	VT	0.0
MADA INS EXCHANGE	MN	0.5	PREVISOR INS CO	CO	5.3
MAIN STREET AMER PROTECTION INS CO	FL	14.9	PROAIR RRG INC	NV	0.5
MANAGED CARE MUT CAPTIVE INS CO	GA	0.0	PROBUILDERS SPECIALTY INS CO RRG	DC	36.8
MERCHANTS PROPERTY INS CO OF IN	IN	72.7	PRODUCERS AGRICULTURE INS CO	TX	432.2
MGIC ASSURANCE CORP	WI	10.5	PROFESSIONALS DIRECT INS CO	MI	22.2
MICA RRG INC	DC	1.0	PROGRESSIVE COMMERCIAL CASUALTY CO	OH	9.4
MICHIGAN AUTO INS PLACEMENT FACILITY	MI	0.0	PROSELECT NATIONAL INS CO INC	AZ	15.3
MICHIGAN BASIC PROPERTY INS ASN	MI	0.0	PROTECTION MUT INS CO	PA	0.7
MIDSTATES REINSURANCE CORP	IL	85.8	PROVIDENCE PLANTATIONS INS CO	RI	1.2
MIDVALE INDEMNITY CO	IL	13.2	PROVIDENCE WASHINGTON INS CO	RI	125.6
MISSISSIPPI FARM BU MUTUAL INS CO	MS	0.0	QUALITAS INS CO	CA	15.9
MISSOURI PHYSICIANS ASSOCIATES	MO	1.8	RADIAN MORTGAGE ASR INC	PA	17.6
MMIC RRG INC	DC	0.7	RAMPART INS CO	NY	35.4
MOSAIC INS CO	DE	21.7	REPUBLIC RRG	SC	0.0
MOTOR CLUB INS CO	RI	47.8	RESPONSE INDEMNITY CO OF CA	CA	6.3
MOUNT BEACON INS CO	FL	25.0	RISK MGMT INDEMNITY INC	DE	0.0
MOUNT VERNON SPECIALTY INS CO	PA	19.7	RURAL TRUST INS CO	TX	11.8
MOUNTAINPOINT INS CO	AZ	11.8	SAFECO SURPLUS LINES INS CO	NH	42.1
MT MCKINLEY INS CO	DE	24.4	SAFEPOINT INS CO	FL	59.8
NATIONAL HOME INS CO RRG	CO	35.5	SALEM COUNTY MUTUAL FIRE INS CO	NJ	0.0
NATIONAL INS ASN	IN	13.1	SAN DIEGO INS CO	CA	66.2
NEW ENGLAND INS CO	CT	37.6	SAN FRANCISCO REINSURANCE CO	CA	97.2
NEW ENGLAND REINSURANCE CORP	CT	38.3	SANILAC MUTUAL INS CO	MI	0.8
NEW JERSEY CAR RRG	DC	0.0	SAUCON MUTUAL INS CO	PA	0.0
NEW MEXICO SAFETY CASUALTY CO	NM	2.8	SEATON INS CO	RI	56.3
NEW MEXICO SECURITY INS CO	NM	2.1	SEAWAY MUTUAL INS CO	PA	0.0
NEW YORK TRANSPORTATION INS CORP	NY	0.0	SELECT INS CO	TX	73.3
NORTH STAR GENERAL INS CO	MN	4.3	SHAMOKIN TOWNSHIP MUTUAL FIRE INS CO	PA	0.0
OAKWOOD INS CO	TN	50.7	SLAVONIC INS CO OF TX	TX	4.1
OBSTETRICIANS & GYNECOLOGISTS RRG	MT	0.8	SOUTH CAROLINA FARM BUREAU INS	SC	3.1
OHIC INS CO	OH	102.4	SOUTHEAST EMPLOYERS MUT CAP INS CO	GA	0.0
OHIO FAIR PLAN UNDERWRITING ASN	OH	0.0	SOUTHERN FARM BUREAU PROPERTY	MS	54.6
OKLAHOMA TRANSIT INS CO	OK	0.0	SOUTHLAND LLOYDS INS CO	TX	0.0
OLD ELIZABETH MUTUAL FIRE INS CO	PA	0.0	SPECIALTY SURPLUS INS CO	IL	22.2
OLD REPUBLIC SECURITY ASR CO	AZ	6.5	ST CLAIR INS CO	NY	1.2
OMAHA INDEMNITY CO	WI	14.6	ST PAUL FIRE & CAS INS CO	WI	16.7
OMEGA ONE INS CO	AL	10.1	STATE COMPENSATION INS FUND	CA	19,387.8
ONECIS INS CO	IL	24.3	STATE INS FUND	NY	0.0
ORDINARY MUTUAL A RRG CORP	VT	8.7	STATE INS FUND DISABILITY BENEFITS	NY	0.0
PALADIN REINSURANCE CORP	NY	1.5	STATE WORKERS INS FUND	PA	0.0
PALLADIUM RRG INC	VT	21.8	STEWARD RRG	DC	0.0
PALOMAR SPECIALTY INS CO	OR	80.3	STONE VALLEY MUTUAL FIRE INS CO	PA	0.0
PASSPORT INS CO	ND	0.0	SUBURBAN HEALTH ORG RRG LLC	SC	0.9
PAWTUCKET INS CO	RI	4.2	SUECIA INS CO	NY	46.9
PENNSYLVANIA PROFESSIONAL LIAB JUA	PA	279.4	SUPERIOR GUARANTY INS CO	FL	0.0
PHILADELPHIA REINSURANCE CORP	PA	214.3	SUPERIOR INS CO	FL	0.0
PHP RRG LTD	AZ	27.0	TEXAS BUILDERS INS CO	TX	12.7
			TEXAS GENERAL INDEMNITY CO	CO	26.1

INSURANCE COMPANY NAME	DOM. STATE	TOTAL ASSETS ($MIL)	INSURANCE COMPANY NAME	DOM. STATE	TOTAL ASSETS ($MIL)
Rating: U (Continued)					
TEXAS MEDICAL LIAB INS UNDWRG ASN	TX	293.1			
TEXAS WINDSTORM INS ASN	TX	0.0			
THIRD COAST INS CO	IL	17.8			
THOMSON SECURITY INS CO	DE	0.0			
TM SPECIALTY INS CO	AZ	38.3			
TOKIO MILLENNIUM RE AG (US BRANCH)	NY	56.5			
TRANSPORT INS CO	OH	36.7			
TRAVEL AIR INS CO KANSAS	KS	5.4			
TRENWICK AMERICA REINSURANCE CORP	CT	77.0			
TRUSTSTAR INS CO	MD	1.0			
TRYGG-HANSA INS CO LTD US BR	NY	2.4			
UNIONE ITALIANA REINS CO OF AMERICA	NY	60.8			
UNITED AMERICAS INS CO	NY	7.4			
UNITED GUARANTY COML INS CO OF NC	NC	54.2			
UNITED HOME INS CO A RRG	VT	2.3			
UNITED INTERNATIONAL INS CO	NY	4.7			
UNIVERSAL INS EXCHANGE	TX	0.0			
UPMC HEALTH BENEFITS	PA	79.7			
US COASTAL INS CO	NY	8.9			
USA UNDERWRITERS	MI	6.2			
USAGENCIES DIRECT INS CO	NY	5.3			
VALIANT SPECIALTY INS CO	DE	5.3			
VANTAGE CASUALTY INS CO	IN	86.0			
VANTAPRO SPECIALTY INS CO	AR	23.6			
VEHICULAR SERVICE INS CO RRG	OK	2.6			
VICTORIA NATIONAL INS CO	OH	3.5			
WALLROSE MUTUAL INS CO	PA	0.9			
WESCAP INS CO	CO	4.2			
WESTERN BONDING CO	UT	0.0			
WESTERN INS RRG INC	AZ	0.0			
WESTERN PROFESSIONAL INS CO	WA	13.8			
WISCONSIN HEALTH CARE LIAB INS PLAN	WI	0.0			
WOODLANDS INS CO	TX	10.0			
WOODRIDGE INS CO	IL	8.4			
YORK INS CO	RI	17.0			

Section VII

Rating Upgrades
and Downgrades

A list of all

U.S. Property and Casualty Insurers

receiving a rating upgrade or downgrade
during the current quarter.

Section VII Contents

This section identifies those companies receiving a rating change since the previous edition of this publication, whether it is a rating upgrade, rating downgrade, newly rated company or the withdrawal of a rating. A rating may be withdrawn due to a merger, dissolution, or liquidation. A rating upgrade or downgrade may entail a change from one letter grade to another, or it may mean the addition or deletion of a plus or minus sign within the same letter grade previously assigned to the company. Ratings are normally updated once each quarter of the year. In some instances, however, a company's rating may be downgraded outside of the normal updates due to overriding circumstances.

Unlike other rating agencies, Weiss ratings are reviewed each and every quarter to ensure that the company's current rating reflects the most recent information available. This allows us to react more promptly and with greater flexibility to changing conditions as they occur. In addition, we are not inhibited to upgrade or downgrade a company as soon as its financial condition warrants the change. You should therefore consider the magnitude of the rating change along with the meaning of the new rating when evaluating the significance of a rating upgrade or downgrade.

1. Insurance Company Name	The legally-registered name, which can sometimes differ from the name that the company uses for advertising. An insurer's name can be very similar to that of another, so verify the company's exact name and state of domicile to make sure you are looking at the correct company.	
2. Domicile State	The state which has primary regulatory responsibility for the company. It may differ from the location of the company's corporate headquarters. You do not have to be living in the domicile state to purchase insurance from this firm, provided it is licensed to do business in your state.	
3. Total Assets	All assets admitted by state insurance regulators in millions of dollars. This includes investments and current business assets such as receivables from agents and reinsurers.	
4. New Financial Strength Rating	The rating assigned to the company as of the date of this Guide's publication. Our rating is measured on a scale from A to F and considers a wide range of factors. Highly-rated companies are, in our opinion, less likely to experience financial difficulties than lower-rated firms. See *About Weiss Financial Strength Ratings* for more information.	
5. Previous Financial Strength Rating	The rating assigned to the company prior to its most recent change.	
6. Date of Change	The date that the rating upgrade or downgrade officially occurred. Normally, all rating changes are put into effect on a single day each quarter of the year. In some instances, however, a rating may have been changed outside of this normal update.	

Withdrawn Ratings

INSURANCE COMPANY NAME	DOM. STATE	TOTAL ASSETS ($MIL)	NEW RATING	PREVIOUS RATING	DATE OF CHANGE
ADVOCATE MD INS OF THE SW INC	TX	56.4	U	D+	07/09/14
AMERICAN FELLOWSHIP MUT INS CO	MI	0.0	U	F	10/30/13
COMMONWEALTH MUTUAL INS CO	MA	5.6	U	U	07/09/14
COMMONWEALTH REINS CO	MA	43.1	U	C-	07/09/14
FARMERS UNION COOPERATIVE INS CO	IA	7.6	U	U	07/09/14
GENERAL EASTERN SKI INS RRG INC	VT	1.0	U	U	07/09/14
GENWORTH RESIDENTIAL MTG ASR CORP	NC	107.5	U	C	07/09/14
GRAMERCY INS CO	TX	0.0	U	F	01/28/13
KODIAK INS CO	NJ	21.8	U	U	05/19/14
OCEAN RRG INC	DC	0.0	U	F	10/30/13
PRIDE NATIONAL INS CO	OK	0.0	U	F	10/30/13
STATE CAPITOL INS RRG INC	NV	0.5	U	U	07/09/14

Rating Upgrades

GOODVILLE MUTUAL CAS CO was upgraded to B- from C+ in January 2015 based on an increase in the profitability index from a 5.60(good) to 8.30(excellent), stability index from a 4.70(fair) to 5.10(good), and capitalization index from a 9.30(excellent) to 9.40(excellent).

PROFESSIONAL EXCHANGE ASR CO (A RRG) was upgraded to E+ from E in January 2015 based on an increase in the stability index from a 0.00(weak) to 0.40(weak) and capitalization index from a 0.20(weak) to 0.40(weak). Other factors: The company's net asset base increased during the period by 24.4%, from $3.3 million to $4.2 million. Capital and surplus increased during the period by 88.6%, from $0.6 million to $1.2 million.

AF&L INS CO was downgraded to E- from E in January 2015 based on a decrease in the profitability index from a 1.90(weak) to 1.50(weak).

AMERICAN BUS & MERCANTILE INS MUT was downgraded to D+ from B in January 2015 based on a decrease in the stability index from a 4.40(fair) to 2.40(weak), capitalization index from a 1.90(weak) to 1.50(weak), and profitability index from a 3.40(fair) to 3.10(fair).

ARKANSAS MUTUAL INS CO was downgraded to D from C- in January 2015 based on a decrease in the profitability index from a 2.40(weak) to 1.70(weak) and capitalization index from a 2.40(weak) to 1.80(weak). Other factors: Capital and surplus decreased during the period by 11.8%, from $2.3 million to $2.1 million.

CASTLEPOINT INS CO was downgraded to E- from D+ in January 2015 based on a decrease in the profitability index from a 2.80(weak) to 0.90(weak) and stability index from a 1.00(weak) to 0.00(weak). Other factors: The company's net asset base decreased during the period by 44.7%, from $280.8 million to $194.0 million.

COMPANION PROPERTY & CASUALTY INS CO was downgraded to C+ from B in January 2015 based on a decrease in the capitalization index from a 6.90(excellent) to 5.30(good), stability index from a 5.40(good) to 4.50(fair), and profitability index from a 3.30(fair) to 2.70(weak).

DOCTORS & SURGEONS NATL RRG INC was downgraded to D- from D in January 2015 based on a decrease in the profitability index from a 2.80(weak) to 1.10(weak), stability index from a 1.70(weak) to 1.00(weak), and capitalization index from a 1.20(weak) to 0.70(weak). Other factors: Capital and surplus decreased during the period by 48.1%, from $1.8 million to $1.2 million.

FIDUCIARY INS CO OF AMERICA was downgraded to E- from E in January 2015 based on a decrease in the profitability index from a 0.60(weak) to 0.40(weak). Other factors: The company's net asset base decreased during the period by 7.6%, from $107.8 million to $100.2 million.

FIRST KEYSTONE RRG INC was downgraded to F having been placed into liquidation by the state insurance regulator in October 2014.

HARLEYSVILLE LAKE STATES INS CO was downgraded to C- from C in January 2015 based on a decrease in the profitability index from a 2.70(weak) to 1.90(weak) and stability index from a 3.80(fair) to 3.10(fair). Other factors: The company's net asset base decreased during the period by 71.2%, from $113.1 million to $66.1 million.

HARLEYSVILLE PREFERRED INS CO was downgraded to C- from C in January 2015 based on a decrease in the profitability index from a 2.50(weak) to 1.90(weak) and stability index from a 3.70(fair) to 3.10(fair). Other factors: The company's net asset base decreased during the period by 111.6%, from $294.7 million to $139.2 million.

HARLEYSVILLE WORCESTER INS CO was downgraded to C- from C in January 2015 based on a decrease in the stability index from a 3.80(fair) to 3.10(fair) and profitability index from a 2.50(weak) to 1.90(weak). Other factors: The company's net asset base decreased during the period by 114.1%, from $344.2 million to $160.8 million.

HERITAGE INDEMNITY CO was downgraded to C from B- in January 2015 based on a decrease in the profitability index from a 8.30(excellent) to 2.90(fair) and stability index from a 5.10(good) to 4.20(fair). Other factors: The company's net asset base decreased during the period by 38.7%, from $208.7 million to $150.5 million. Capital and surplus decreased during the period by 116.3%, from $108.6 million to $50.2 million.

LIBERTY AMERICAN SELECT INS CO was downgraded to C- from C in January 2015 based on a decrease in the profitability index from a 3.40(fair) to 1.90(weak) and stability index from a 3.60(fair) to 3.10(fair).

NATIONAL LIABILITY & FIRE INS CO was downgraded to B from B+ in January 2015 based on a decrease in the profitability index from a 6.70(good) to 5.40(good) and capitalization index from a 9.20(excellent) to 9.00(excellent).

NEW HAMPSHIRE INS CO was downgraded to D+ from C in January 2015 based on a decrease in the capitalization index from a 6.60(good) to 3.90(fair) and stability index from a 4.20(fair) to 2.40(weak). Other factors: The company's net asset base decreased during the period by 105.9%, from $560.1 million to $272.1 million. Capital and surplus decreased during the period by 68.1%, from $233.4 million to $138.9 million.

PRIMEONE INS CO was downgraded to C- from C in January 2015 based on a decrease in the profitability index from a 2.40(weak) to 1.80(weak) and capitalization index from a 4.60(fair) to 4.50(fair). Other factors: The company's net asset base decreased during the period by 14.5%, from $19.1 million to $16.7 million. Capital and surplus decreased during the period by 9.8%, from $9.9 million to $9.0 million.

Rating Downgrades (Continued)

RIDER INS CO was downgraded to D from D+ in January 2015 based on a decrease in the capitalization index from a 4.10(fair) to 3.20(fair), stability index from a 2.60(weak) to 2.10(weak), and profitability index from a 1.30(weak) to 0.90(weak). Other factors: The company's net asset base decreased during the period by 6.2%, from $49.3 million to $46.4 million. Capital and surplus decreased during the period by 27.0%, from $10.6 million to $8.3 million.

SAMSUNG FIRE & MARINE INS CO LTD US was downgraded to B- from B in January 2015 based on a decrease in the capitalization index from a 5.70(good) to 5.00(good) and stability index from a 4.00(fair) to 3.50(fair). Other factors: Capital and surplus decreased during the period by 12.9%, from $58.0 million to $51.4 million.

SOUTHERN VANGUARD INS CO was downgraded to C from B- in January 2015 based on a decrease in the stability index from a 4.30(fair) to 2.90(fair). Other factors: The company's net asset base decreased during the period by 6.6%, from $21.3 million to $20.0 million.

WRIGHT SPECIALTY INS CO was downgraded to D+ from C in January 2015 based on a decrease in the capitalization index from a 9.00(excellent) to 7.80(excellent), stability index from a 3.50(fair) to 2.70(weak), and profitability index from a 2.10(weak) to 1.50(weak). Other factors: Capital and surplus decreased during the period by 9.6%, from $14.8 million to $13.5 million.

Appendix

State Guaranty Associations

The states have established insurance guaranty associations to help pay claims to policyholders of failed insurance companies. However, there are several cautions which you must be aware of with respect to this coverage:

1. Most of the guaranty associations do not set aside funds in advance. Rather, states assess contributions from other insurance companies after an insolvency occurs.

2. There can be an unacceptably long delay before claims are paid.

3. Each state has different levels and types of coverage, often governed by legislation unique to that state that can sometimes conflict with coverage of other states. Generally speaking, most property and casualty lines of business written by licensed insurers are covered by guaranty associations subject to the conditions and limitations set forth in the various acts. The Guaranty Funds do not cover non-admitted carriers (except in the state of New Jersey). Most state guaranty funds will not cover title, surety, credit, mortgage guarantee or ocean marine insurance.

The table on the following page is designed to help you sort out these issues. However, it is not intended to handle all of them. If your carrier has failed and you need a complete answer, we recommend you contact your State Insurance Official.

Following is a brief explanation of each of the columns in the table.

1.	**Maximum Per Claim**	The maximum amount payable by the State Guaranty Fund on a single covered claim, with the exception of workers' compensation claims, which are paid in full in most states.
2.	**Workers' Comp. Paid in Full**	"Yes" indicates that there is no cap on the amount paid for workers' compensation claims.
3.	**Net Worth Provision**	A net worth provision gives the association the right to seek reimbursement from an insured if the insured's net worth exceeds $50 million, essentially excluding certain large organizations from coverage by the guaranty association. Roughly half of the states have a net worth provision. If a state has a provision, marked "yes", there are other conditions applicable; contact your local department of insurance for further information.
4.	**Guaranty Fund Trigger**	The action that triggers the guaranty fund process.

COVERAGE OF STATE GUARANTY FUNDS

STATE	MAXIMUM PER CLAIM	WORKERS' COMP. PAID IN FULL	NET WORTH PROVISION	GUARANTY FUND TRIGGER		
				FINAL ORDER OF LIQUIDATION WITH FINDING OF INSOLVENCY	FINDING OF INSOLVENCY ONLY	OTHER
Alabama	$150,000	Yes	Yes	X		(21)
Alaska	$500,000	Yes	None	X		
Arizona	$300,000	(8)	None	X		(21)
Arkansas	$300,000	(9)	Yes		X	
California	$500,000	Yes	None	X		
Colorado	$300,000	Yes	Yes	X		(21)
Connecticut	$400,000	Yes	Yes		X	
Delaware	$300,000	Yes	Yes	X		(21)
Dist. of Colombia	$300,000	Yes	Yes	X		(21)
Florida	$300,000 (1)	(10)	None	X		(16)
Georgia	$300,000	Yes	Yes	X		(21)
Hawaii	$300,000	Yes	Yes	X		
Idaho	$300,000	Yes	None	X		
Illinois	$500,000	Yes	Yes	X		
Indiana	$100,000	(9)	Yes	X		(16)
Iowa	$500,000	Yes	yes (13)	X		
Kansas	$300,000	Yes	None	X		
Kentucky	$300,000	Yes	Yes	X		
Louisiana	$500,000 (2)	Yes	Yes	X		(15)
Maine	$300,000	Yes	Yes	X		
Maryland	$300,000	Yes	Yes	X		
Massachusetts	$300,000	Yes	Yes		X	
Michigan	(3)	Yes	Yes	X		(19)
Minnesota	$300,000	yes	Yes	X		
Mississippi	$300,000	yes	Yes	X		(21)
Missouri	$300,000	yes	Yes	X		(21)
Montana	$300,000	yes	Yes	X		
Nebraska	$300,000	yes	None	X		
Nevada	$300,000	yes	Yes	X		(17)
New Hampshire	$300,000	yes	yes (24)	X		(25)
New Jersey	$300,000 (4)	(10)	Yes			(23)
New Mexico	$100,000	yes	None	X		(21)
New York	$1,000,000 (5)	(10)	None			(20)
North Carolina	$300,000	yes	Yes	X		(21)
North Dakota	$300,000	(12)	Yes	X		
Ohio	$300,000	(12)	Yes			(14)
Oklahoma	$150,000	yes	Yes	X		
Oregon	$300,000	yes	Yes	X		
Pennsylvania	$300,000	(10)	Yes	X		
Puerto Rico	$300,000	yes	None	X		(21)
Rhode Island	$500,000	yes	Yes	X		
South Carolina	$300,000	yes	Yes		X	(22)
South Dakota	$300,000	yes	Yes	X		
Tennessee	$100,000	yes	Yes	X		
Texas	$300,000	yes	Yes		X	(18)
Utah	$300,000	yes	Yes			(23)
Vermont	$500,000	yes	None	X		
Virgin Island	$50,000	(9)	None		X	
Virginia	$300,000	yes	yes			(23)
Washington	$300,000	(12)	None			(14)
West Virginia	$300,000	Yes	None			(14)
Wisconsin	$300,000 (6)	(11)	yes			(14)
Wyoming	$150,000 (7)	yes	None	X		

N O T E S

1. Limit of $100,000 per residential unit for policies covering condominium associations or homeowners' associations.Policies providing coverage for homeowner's insurance shall provide for an additional 200,000 for the portion of covered claim which relates only to the damage to the structure and contents.

2. Maximum claim per occurrence is $300,000.

3. $5,000,000 – Subject to Consumer Price Index.

4. Maximum per auto claim is $75,000. This applies only to No Fault Personal Injury Protection Claims. The difference between the Maximum Per Claim and the $75,000 is covered by the Unsatisfied Claim & Judgement Fund.

5. Maximum of $5,000,000 for all claims arising out of any one policy, for policies issued to residents insuring property or risks located outside the state.

6. $300,000 is the limit on a single risk, loss or life.

7. $150,000 limit per claimant for each covered claim.

8. Workers' compensation claims of insolvent insurers paid by Arizona's state fund.

9. Workers' compensation payments limited to the maximum claim amount.

10. Workers' compensation claims covered by a separate workers' compensation security fund that is not intermingled with any other state funds and is administered by the state insurance commissioner.

11. Workers Compensation payments subject only to deductible.

12. Only a state fund is permitted to write workers' compensation insurance. In Washington, WC not covered except Longshore Harbor Workers'

13. Iowa does not cover claims of a person whose net worth is greater than that allowed by guaranty fund law of his or her state of residence.

14. Triggered by finding of insolvency and liquidation order.

15. The State Guaranty Association is also obligated to pay claims of an insurer that is in rehabilitation upon joint motion of association and receiver.

16. Liquidation order not final until there is no further right of appeal.

17. Also triggered if the insolvent insurer is involved in a court proceeding to determine its status of solvency, rehabilitation or liquidation, and the court has prohibited the insurer from paying claims for more than thirty days.

18. Triggered if (1) insurer is placed in receivership based on finding of insolvency, or (2) conservatorship after being deemed by commissioner to be insolvent and an impared insurer.

19. Final Order of Liquidation.

20. Insolvency of Insurer.

21. Order not stayed or subject to supersedeas.

22. Fails to meet obligation to policyholders and state.

23. Order of liquidation with finding of insolvency.

24. A new act (NH Act of 2004) was enacted for insolvencies occurring after 8-6-2004 and gives the association the right to recover from the following persons the amount of any covered claim paid, whether for defense, indemnity, or otherwise, on behalf of such person, any insured whose net worth exceeds $25 million, provided the insured's net worth shall be deemed to include the net worth of the insured and all of its affiliates on a consolidated basis. The prior act does not

cover a claim of an insured or third party liability claimant whose net worth exceeds $25 million.

25. A new act (NH Act of 2004) was enacted for insolvencies occurring after 8-6-2004 and defines an insolvent insurer as a licensed insurer against whom a final order of liquidation has been entered with a finding of insolvency by a court of competent jurisdiction in the insurer's state of domicile. The prior act requires a finding of insolvency only.

Information provided in the Coverage of State Guaranty Funds chart was obtained from the National Conference of Insurance Guaranty Funds (NCIGF).

State Insurance Commissioners'
Departmental Contact Information

State	Official's Title	Website Address	Phone Number
Alabama	Commissioner	www.aldoi.org	(334) 269-3550
Alaska	Director	http://commerce.alaska.gov/dnn/ins/Home.aspx	(800) 467-8725
Arizona	Director	http://www.azinsurance.gov/	(800) 325-2548
Arkansas	Commissioner	www.insurance.arkansas.gov	(800) 282-9134
California	Commissioner	www.insurance.ca.gov	(800) 927-4357
Colorado	Commissioner	www.dora.state.co.us/insurance/	(800) 886-7675
Connecticut	Commissioner	www.ct.gov/cid/	(800) 203-3447
Delaware	Commissioner	http://delawareinsurance.gov/	(800) 282-8611
Dist. of Columbia	Commissioner	http://disb.dc.gov/	(202) 727-8000
Florida	Commissioner	www.floir.com/	(850) 413-3140
Georgia	Commissioner	www.oci.ga.gov/	(800) 656-2298
Hawaii	Commissioner	http://hawaii.gov/dcca/ins/	(808) 586-2790
Idaho	Director	www.doi.idaho.gov	(800) 721-3272
Illinois	Director	www.insurance.illinois.gov/	(877) 527-9431
Indiana	Commissioner	www.in.gov/idoi/	(317) 232-2385
Iowa	Commissioner	www.iid.state.ia.us	(877) 955-1212
Kansas	Commissioner	www.ksinsurance.org	(800) 432-2484
Kentucky	Commissioner	http://insurance.ky.gov/	(800) 595-6053
Louisiana	Commissioner	www.ldi.la.gov/	(800) 259-5300
Maine	Superintendent	www.maine.gov/pfr/insurance/	(800) 300-5000
Maryland	Commissioner	www.mdinsurance.state.md.us	(800) 492-6116
Massachusetts	Commissioner	www.mass.gov/ocabr/government/oca-agencies/doi-lp/	(877) 563-4467
Michigan	Director	www.michigan.gov/cis/	(877) 999-6442
Minnesota	Commissioner	http://mn.gov/commerce/insurance/	(651) 539-1500
Mississippi	Commissioner	www.mid.state.ms.us/	(601) 359-3569
Missouri	Director	www.insurance.mo.gov	(800) 726-7390
Montana	Commissioner	www.csi.mt.gov/	(800) 332-6148
Nebraska	Director	www.doi.nebraska.gov/	(402) 471-2201
Nevada	Commissioner	www.doi.nv.gov/	(888) 872-3234
New Hampshire	Commissioner	www.nh.gov/insurance/	(800) 852-3416
New Jersey	Commissioner	www.state.nj.us/dobi/	(800) 446-7467
New Mexico	Superintendent	www.osi.state.nm.us/	(855) 427-5674
New York	Superintendent	www.dfs.ny.gov/	(800) 342-3736
North Carolina	Commissioner	www.ncdoi.com	(800) 546-5664
North Dakota	Commissioner	www.nd.gov/ndins/	(800) 247-0560
Ohio	Lieutenant Governor	www.insurance.ohio.gov/	(800) 686-1526
Oklahoma	Commissioner	www.ok.gov/oid/	(800) 522-0071
Oregon	Insurance Commissioner	www.oregon.gov/dcbs/insurance/Pages/index.aspx	(888) 877-4894
Pennsylvania	Commissioner	www.insurance.pa.gov/	(877) 881-6388
Puerto Rico	Commissioner	www.ocs.gobierno.pr	(787) 304-8686
Rhode Island	Superintendent	www.dbr.state.ri.us/divisions/insurance/	(401) 462-9500
South Carolina	Director	www.doi.sc.gov	(803) 737-6160
South Dakota	Director	http://dlr.sd.gov/insurance/default.aspx	(605) 773-3563
Tennessee	Commissioner	www.tn.gov/insurance/	(800) 342-4029
Texas	Commissioner	www.tdi.texas.gov/	(800) 252-3439
Utah	Commissioner	www.insurance.utah.gov	(800) 439-3805
Vermont	Commissioner	www.dfr.vermont.gov/	(802) 828-3301
Virgin Islands	Lieutenant Governor	www.ltg.gov.vi	(340) 774-7166
Virginia	Commissioner	www.scc.virginia.gov/boi/	(804) 371-9741
Washington	Commissioner	www.insurance.wa.gov	(800) 562-6900
West Virginia	Commissioner	www.wvinsurance.gov	(888) 879-9842
Wisconsin	Commissioner	oci.wi.gov	(800) 236-8517
Wyoming	Commissioner	http://doi.wyo.gov/	(800) 438-5768

Risk-Adjusted Capital for Property and Casualty Insurers in Weiss Rating Model

Among the most important indicators used in the analysis of an individual company are our two risk-adjusted capital ratios, which are useful tools in determining exposure to investment, liquidity and insurance risk in relation to the capital the company has to cover those risks.

The first risk-adjusted capital ratio evaluates the company's ability to withstand a moderate loss scenario. The second ratio evaluates the company's ability to withstand a severe loss scenario.

In order to calculate these Risk-Adjusted Capital Ratios, we follow these steps:

1. Capital Resources

First, we find out how much capital a company actually has by adding the company's resources which could be used to cover unexpected losses. These resources are primarily composed of stock issued by the company (capital) and accumulated funds from prior year profits (retained earnings or surplus). Additional credit can also be given for conservative reserving practices and other "hidden capital" where applicable.

Conservative policy reserves can be an important source of capital and can contribute significantly to the financial strength of a company. Companies that set aside more than is necessary in their reserves year after year are less likely to be over run with claims and forced to dip into capital to pay them. Conversely, a company that understates its reserves year after year will be forced to routinely withdraw from capital to pay claims. Accordingly, we give companies credit for consistent over- reserving and penalize companies for consistent under-reserving.

2. Target Capital

Next, we determine how much capital the company should have to cover moderate losses based upon the company's level of risk in both its insurance business and its investment portfolio. We examine each of the company's risk areas and determine how much capital is needed for each area, based on how risky it is and how much exposure it has in that area. Then we combine these amounts to arrive at a total risk figure.

Credit is given for the company's diversification, since it is unlikely that "the worst" will happen in all areas at once.

3. Risk-Adjusted Capital Ratio #1

We compare the results of Step 1 with those of Step 2. Specifically, we divide the "capital resources" by the "target capital" and express it in terms of a ratio. This ratio is called RACR #1.

If a company has a Risk-Adjusted Capital Ratio of 1.0 or more, it means the company has all of the capital we believe it requires to withstand potential losses which could be inflicted by a moderate economic decline. If the company has a ratio of less than 1.0, it does not currently have all of the capital resources we think it needs. During times of financial distress, companies often have access to additional capital through contributions from a parent or holding company, current profits or reductions in dividends. Therefore, we make an allowance for firms with Risk-Adjusted Capital Ratios of somewhat less than 1.0.

4. Risk-Adjusted Capital Ratio #2 We repeat Steps 2 and 3 but now assume a severe loss scenario. This ratio is called RACR #2.

5. Risk-Adjusted Capital Index We convert RACR #1 and #2 into an index. It is measured on a scale of zero to ten, with ten being the best and seven or better considered strong. A company whose capital resources exactly equal its target capital will have a Risk-Adjusted Capital Ratio of 1.0 and a Risk-Adjusted Capital Index of 7.0.

How We Determine Target Capital

The basic procedure for determining target capital is to identify the risk areas where the company is exposed to loss such as: (1) the risk of receiving more claims than expected; (2) the risk of not being able to collect from reinsurers or others who owe the company money; (3) the risk of losses on investments and (4) the risk of having inadequate reserves. Then we ask questions, such as:

- What is the breakdown of the company's investment portfolio? What types of policies does the company offer? Who owes the company money and how likely are they to pay? What losses has the company experienced on its underwriting (when claims and expenses exceeded premiums)? How accurate have reserve estimates been? What exposure does the company have to catastrophic property losses, such as Hurricane Andrew or the Los Angeles earthquake? What exposure does the company have to catastrophic liability losses such as asbestos pollution?

- For each category, what are the potential losses which could be incurred in both a moderate loss and a severe loss scenario?

- In order to cover those potential losses, how much in capital resources does the company need? It stands to reason that more capital is needed as a cushion for losses on high-risk investments, such as junk bonds, than on low-risk investments, such as AAA-rated utility bonds.

Amounts from each separate risk area are added together and adjustments are made to take into account the low likelihood that all risk areas would suffer severe losses at the same time. Finally, target capital is adjusted for the company's spread of risk in the diversification of its investment portfolio, the size and number of the policies it writes and the diversification of its business.

Table 1 on the next page shows target capital percentages used by the National Association of Insurance Commissioners (NAIC) in relation to Weiss Ratings Risk-Adjusted Capital Ratios #1 and #2 (RACR #1 and RACR #2).

The percentages shown in the table answer the question: How much should the firm hold in capital resources for every $100 it has committed to each category? Several of the items in Table 1 are expressed as ranges. The actual percentages used in the calculation of target capital for an individual company are determined by the levels of risk in the operations, investments or policy obligations of that specific company.

Table 1. Target Capital Percentages

Invested Asset Risk	Weiss Ratings		NAIC
Bonds	RACR#1	RACR#2	
	(%)	(%)	(%)
Government guaranteed bonds	0	0	0
Class 1	.5-.75	1-1.5	0.3
Class 2	2	5	1
Class 3	5	15	2
Class 4	10	30	4.5
Class 5	20	60	10
Class 6	20	60	30
Preferred Stock	7	9.1	2.3-30
Common Stock			
Unaffiliated	25	33	15
Affiliated	25-100	33-100	N/A
Mortgages	5	15	5
Real Estate	10	33	10
Short-term investment	0.5	1	0.3
Collateral loans	2	5	5
Other invested assets	5	10	20
Credit Risk			
Agents' Balances	0.5	1	
Premium Notes	2	5	
Receivable Investment Income	2	3	5
Misc. Non-invested Assets	5	10	5
Reinsurance Recov. Current	1	1.5	10
30 to 90 Days Overdue	2	3	10
90 to 180 Days Overdue	5	7.5	10
More Than 180 Days Overdue	10	15	10
Rein Recov on Unpaid Losses	5	7.5	10
Rein Recov on IBNR	10	15	10
Rein Recov on UEP	5	7.5	10
Off Balance Sheet RBC			
Noncontrolled assets	1	2	1
Guarantee for affiliates	2	5	1
Contingent Liabilities	2	5	1
Reserve Risk*			
Homeowner Reserves	19-152	22-176	19-154
Private Auto Reserves	10-80	14-108	13-107
Commercial Auto Reserves	11-88	14-108	14-108
Worker's Comp Reserves	8-60	21-168	6-48
Commercial Multiple Peril Res.	19-152	22-176	19-153
Medical Malpractice Res.	26-208	39-312	26-201
Special Liability Res.	13-100	15-120	13-102
Other Liability Res.	24-192	26-208	24-190
International Reserves	16-128	19-152	16-127
Product Liability Reserves	24-192	39-312	24-192
Health Lines Reserves	15-116	23-180	20-157
Other Lines Reserves	20-156	25-196	20-157
Premium Risk*			
Homeowners NPW	29-260	43-260	43-260
Auto Liability NPW	34-304	35-319	52-304
Worker's Comp NPW	34-303	40-363	50-303
Commercial Multiperil NPW	30-272	39-347	45-272
Medical Malpractice NPW	53-478	79-478	80-478
Special Liabilities NPW	29-266	32-281	44-266
Other Liabilities NPW	38-342	49-441	57-342
International NPW	41-373	43-388	62-373
Product Liabilities NPW	41-365	52-464	61-365
Other Lines NPW	24-220	26-234	27-220

* All numbers are shown for illustrative purposes. Figures actually used in the formula vary annually based on industry experience.

Investment Class   Description

Investment Class		Description
Government guaranteed bonds		Guaranteed bonds issued by U.S. and other governments which receive the top rating of state insurance commissioners
Bonds	Class 1	Investment grade bonds rated AAA, AA or A by Moody's or Standard & Poor's or deemed AAA - A equivalent by state insurance regulators
	Class 2	Investment grade bonds with some speculative elements rated BBB or equivalent
	Class 3	Noninvestment grade bonds, rated BB or equivalent
	Class 4	Noninvestment grade bonds, rated B or equivalent
	Class 5	Noninvestment grade bonds, rated CCC, C, C- or equivalent
	Class 6	Noninvestment grade bonds, in or near default
Preferred Stock		
Common Stock		Unaffiliated common stock Affiliated common stock
Mortgages		
Real Estate		Company occupied and other investment properties
Short-term Investments		All investments whose maturities at the time of acquisition were one year or less
Collateral Loans		Loans made to a company or individual where the underlying security is in the form of bonds, stocks or other marketable securities
Other Invested Assets		Any invested assets that do not fit under the main categories above

Credit Risk

	Description
Agents' Balances	Amounts which have been booked as written and billed to agents
Premium Notes	Loans to policyholders for payments of premiums
Receivable Interest Income	Interest income due but not yet received
Misc. Noninvested Income	Misc. income that is not related to invested assets
Reinsurance Recov. Current	Current receivables from reinsurers for their portion of the recorded losses
30 to 90 Days Overdue	Receivables from reinsurers 30 - 90 days overdue
90 to 180 Days Overdue	Receivables from reinsurers 90 - 180 days overdue
More Than 180 Days Overdue	Receivables from reinsurers more than 180 days overdue
Rein. Recov. on Unpaid Losses	Receivables from reinsurers for unpaid losses
Rein. Recov. on IBNR	Receivables from reinsurers for incurred but not reported losses
Rein. Recov. on UEP	Receivables from reinsurers for unearned premium

Off Balance Sheet Risk

	Description
Noncontrolled Assets	Assets not subject to complete insurer control
Guarantee for Affiliates	Guarantees on behalf of affiliates
Contingent Liabilities	Liabilities that are likely to happen but are not certain

Table 2. Bond Default Rates - potential losses as a percent of bond portfolio

	(1)	(2)	(3)	(4)	(5)	(6)	(7)	(8)
Bond Rating	Moody's 15 Yr Rate (%)	Moody's 12 Yr Rate (%)	Worst Year (%)	3 Cum. Recession Years (%)	Weiss Ratings 15 Year Rate (%)	Assumed Loss Rate (%)	Losses as % of Holdings (%)	RACR #2 Rate (%)
Aaa	2.80	1.60	0.10	0.30	1.89	50	0.95	1.00
Aa	2.00	1.60	0.20	0.60	2.19	50	1.09	1.00
A	3.30	2.50	0.40	1.20	3.67	55	2.02	1.00
Baa	7.20	5.50	1.10	3.26	8.58	60	5.15	5.00
Ba	20.10	17.90	8.40	23.08	36.47	65	23.71	15.00
B	33.70	32.50	21.60	50.80	62.24	70	43.57	30.00

Comments on Target Capital Percentages

The factors in the RACR calculations can be grouped into five categories: (1) Investment Risks; (2) Credit Risks; (3) Off Balance Sheet Risks; (4) Reserve Risks and (5) Premium Risks. Each of these has numerous subcomponents. The five categories are discussed below along with specific comments on some of the most important subcomponents.

Investment Risks:

Bonds Target capital percentages for bonds are derived from a model that factors in historical cumulative bond default rates from the last twenty years and the additional loss potential during a prolonged economic decline. The continuance of post-World War II prosperity is by no means certain. Realistic analysis of potential losses must factor in the possibility of a severe economic recession.

Table 2 shows how this was done for each bond rating classification. A 15-year cumulative default rate is used (column 1). These are historical default rates for 1970-1990 for each bond class, taken from Moody's Studies of Loss Potential of Life Insurance Assets.

To factor in the additional loss potential of a severe three-year-long economic decline, we reduced the base to Moody's 12-year rate (column 2), determined the worst single year experience (column 3), spread that experience over three years (column 4) and added the historical 12-year rate to the 3-year projection to derive Weiss Ratings 15-year default rate (column 5). Note: Due to the shrinking base of nondefaulted bonds in each year, column 4 may be somewhat less than three times column 3; and column 5 may be somewhat less than the sum of column 2 and column 4.

The next step was to determine the losses that could be expected from these defaults. This would be equivalent to the capital a company should have to cover those losses. Loss rates were assigned for each bond class (column 6), based on the fact that higher rated issues generally carry less debt and the fact that the debt is also better secured, leading to higher recovery rates upon default.

Column 7 shows losses as a percent of holdings for each bond class. Column 8 shows the target capital percentages that are used in RACR #2 (Table 1, RACR #2 column, Bonds -classes 1 to 6).

Regulations limiting junk bond holdings of insurers to a set percent of assets are a tacit acknowledgement that the maximum reserve requirements used by State Insurance Commissioners (Table 1, NAIC column, Bonds — classes 4, 5 and 6) are inadequate. If the figure adequately represented full loss potential, there would be no need to limit holdings through legislation since an adequate loss reserve would provide sufficient capital to absorb potential losses.

Affiliate Common Stock

These stocks are often only "paper" assets, difficult to sell, and not truly available to pay insurance claims. The appropriate value of the stock may also be difficult to determine unless the stock is publicly traded.

The target capital rate on affiliate common stock for RACR #2 can vary between 33% and 100% (Table 1, RACR #2 column, Common stock — Affiliated), depending on the financial strength of the affiliate and the prospects for obtaining capital from the affiliate should the need arise.

Credit Risk

This category refers to the financial risk faced if the company cannot collect funds it is owed. These include funds owed to the company by its agents and funds owed to the company by its reinsurers.

Off Balance Sheet Risk

A miscellaneous category of risk that is developed from data not found on the company's balance sheet. It includes risks associated with rapid premium growth, unsettled lawsuits against the company, guarantees to affiliates and investment risks such as interest rate swaps.

Reserve Risk

The risk that reserve estimates are too low to pay all outstanding claims. Target capital percentages used for each line of business are based on the historical experience of both the company and industry, for that line.

Rather than basing our figures solely on the company's average experience over the last nine years, as is done in the NAIC formula, we factor in the company's worst results over the same period. We believe that this gives a more realistic appraisal of the company's loss potential. Of two companies with identical averages, one may have greater ups and downs than the other. Under the NAIC formula, the companies would have the same target capital, while our formula would require more target capital from the company with the more volatile history.

Target capital requirements have been reduced for each line of business in order to reflect the time value of money. As claims are generally paid months or years after premiums are received, insurers invest those premium funds, accumulating investment income until the claims must be paid. The discount given varies from 9% for private auto liability, a "short-tail" line where claims are paid shortly after receipt of premiums, to 21% for medical malpractice, a "long-tail" line where claims are generally paid many years after receipt of premiums.

Premium Risk

The risk that premium levels are not sufficient to pay claims and related expenses. Individual target capital percentages are used for each line of business based on the riskiness of the line and the company's own experience with reserve risk. Target capital requirements are reduced to account for the time value of money, using a technique similar to that used for reserve risk.

Risky Lines of Business and Catastrophic Losses

These include fire, earthquake, multiple peril (including storm damage) and similar personal and commercial property coverages. Even excluding Hurricane Andrew, the insured losses from natural disasters since 1989 have been far greater than in previous decades. Yet, too many insurance companies are basing their risk calculations on the assumption that losses will return to more normal levels. They are not ready for the possibility that the pattern of increasing disasters might be a real, continuing trend.

Also considered high risk lines are medical malpractice, general liability, product liability and other similar liability coverages. Court awards for damages often run into the millions. These settlement amounts can be very difficult to predict. This uncertainty hinders an insurer's ability to accurately assess how much to charge policyholders and how much to set aside to pay claims. Of special concern are large, unexpected liabilities related to environmental damages such as asbestos. Similar risk may lie hidden in coverage for medical equipment and procedures, industrial wastes, carcinogens and other substances found in products previously viewed as benign.

RECENT INDUSTRY FAILURES

2014

Institution	Headquarters	Industry	Date of Failure	At Date of Failure	
				Total Assets ($Mil)	Financial Strength Rating
Union Mutual Ins Co	Oklahoma	P&C	01/24/14	5.1	E+ (Very Weak)
Commonwealth Ins Co	Pennsylvania	P&C	03/20/14	1.1	E (Very Weak)
LEMIC Ins Co	Louisiana	P&C	03/31/14	51.6	D (Weak)
Interstate Bankers Casualty Co	Illinois	P&C	04/16/14	16.2	D+ (Weak)
Freestone Ins Co	Delaware	P&C	04/28/14	421.2	D- (Weak)
Alameda Alliance For Health	California	Health	05/05/14	176.3	D (Weak)
National Guaranty Ins Co	Nevada	P&C	05/06/14	10.4	N/A
Physicians Ben. Resources RRG	Nevada	P&C	05/09/14	.6	U (Unrated)
Sunshine State Ins Co	Florida	P&C	06/03/14	22.9	E+ (Very Weak)
Physicians United Plan Inc	Florida	Health	06/09/14	110.7	E (Very Weak)
Professional Aviation Ins Co	Nevada	P&C	07/03/14	N/A	N/A
Red Rock Ins Co	Oklahoma	P&C	08/01/14	28.5	E+ (Very Weak)
UHAB Mutual Ins Co	New York	P&C	09/26/14	N/A	N/A
First Keystone RRG Inc	South Carolina	P&C	10/21/14	13.6	E+ (Very Weak)
SeeChange Health Ins Co	California	Health	11/19/14	23.4	D (Weak)
Florida Healthcare Plus, Inc	Florida	Health	12/10/14	11.1	U (Unrated)
CoOportunity Health, Inc	Iowa	Health	12/23/14	195.7	U (Unrated)

2013

Institution	Headquarters	Industry	Date of Failure	Total Assets ($Mil)	Financial Strength Rating
				At Date of Failure	
Partnership Health Plan Inc	Wisconsin	Health	01/18/13	27.1	D (Weak)
Driver's Insurance Co	Oklahoma	P&C	02/21/13	33.1	D+ (Weak)
Lewis & Clark LTC RRG	Nevada	P&C	02/28/13	16.4	E (Very Weak)
Pride National Ins Co	Oklahoma	P&C	03/08/13	17.1	E+ (Very Weak)
Santa Fe Auto	Texas	P&C	03/08/13	22.9	E (Very Weak)
Ullico Casualty Co	Delaware	P&C	03/11/13	327.7	D (Weak)
Builders Ins Co Inc	Nevada	P&C	03/15/13	15.0	U (Unrated)
Nevada Contractors Ins Co Inc	Nevada	P&C	03/15/13	49.0	U (Unrated)
Universal Health Care Ins Co Inc	Florida	Health	03/22/13	106.1	C (Fair)
Universal Health Care Inc	Florida	Health	03/25/13	109.0	D (Weak)
Universal HMO of Texas	Texas	Health	04/18/13	15.3	C- (Fair)
Universal Health Care of NV Inc	Nevada	Health	06/03/13	1.9	D+ (Weak)
Liberty First RRG Ins Co	Utah	P&C	08/06/13	2.5	E (Very Weak)
United Contrs Ins Co Inc, RRG	Delaware	P&C	08/22/13	17.0	E (Very Weak)
Georgia Mutual Ins Co	Georgia	P&C	09/10/13	3.3	D (Weak)
Ocean Risk Retention Group	D.C.	P&C	09/06/13	7.9	E (Very Weak)
Gertrude Geddes Willis Life Ins Co	Louisiana	L&H	10/24/13	4.9	U (Unrated)
San Antonio Indemnity Co	Texas	P&C	10/31/13	2.8	E+ (Very Weak)
Higginbotham Burial Ins Co	Arkansas	L&H	11/04/13	1.3	U (Unrated)
Indemnity Ins Corp RRG	Delaware	P&C	11/07/13	83.2	D- (Weak)
Concert Health Plan Ins Co	Illinois	L&H	12/10/13	1.8	D- (Weak)
ICM Insurance Co	New York	P&C	12/23/13	5.0	E+ (Very Weak)

2012

Institution	Headquarters	Industry	Date of Failure	At Date of Failure Total Assets ($Mil)	Financial Strength Rating
Autoglass Ins Co	New York	P&C	01/09/12	29.7	E+ (Very Weak)
Hlth Facilities of CA Mut I C RRG	Nevada	P&C	01/10/12	1.9	U (Unrated)
Republic Mortgage Ins Co	North Carolina	P&C	01/19/12	1.41	E (Very Weak)
CAGC Ins Co	North Carolina	P&C	01/26/12	11.8	U (Unrated)
First Sealord Surety Inc	Pennsylvania	P&C	02/08/12	15.2	U (Unrated)
Scaffold Industry Ins Co RRG Inc	D.C.	P&C	05/01/12	5.1	E+ (Very Weak)
Financial Guaranty Ins Co	New York	P&C	06/11/12	2054.0	E- (Very Weak)
Global Health Plan & Ins Co	Puerto Rico	Health	06/13/12	1.1	U (Unrated)
Garden State Indemnity Co, Inc	New Jersey	P&C	06/22/12	2.93	E- (Very Weak)
AvaHealth Inc	Florida	HMO	06/27/12	3.3	E (Very Weak)
American Manufacturers Mutual	Illinois	P&C	07/02/12	10.3	E+ (Very Weak)
Lumbermens Mutual Casualty Co	Illinois	P&C	07/02/12	789.4	E (Very Weak)
Millers First Ins Co	Illinois	P&C	07/24/12	23.0	E (Very Weak)
American Motorists Ins Co	Illinois	P&C	08/16/12	19.7	D (Weak)
Home Value Ins Co	Ohio	P&C	08/31/12	3.5	U (Unrated)
Northern Plains Ins Co	South Dakota	P&C	09/18/12	1.4	D (Weak)
Jamestown Ins Co RRG	South Carolina	P&C	09/24/12	5.9	E+ (Very Weak)
Interstate Auto Ins Co	Maryland	P&C	10/11/12	4.6	D (Weak)
Regional Health Ins Co, RRG	D.C.	P&C	10/18/12	0.6	U (Unrated)
DC Chartered Health Plan Inc	D.C.	HMO	10/19/12	65.4	E- (Very Weak)
American Fellowship Mut Ins Co	Michigan	P&C	10/29/20	50.0	D (Weak)
Gramercy Ins Co	Texas	P&C	12/04/12	41.8	D (Weak)
Triad Guaranty Ins Corp	Illinois	P&C	12/11/12	766.7	E (Very Weak)
Triad Guaranty ASR Corp	Illinois	P&C	12/11/12	16.1	B (Good)

2011

Institution	Headquarters	Industry	Date of Failure	Total Assets ($Mil)	Financial Strength Rating
Comm. Ins. Alliance Reciprocal	Florida	P&C	01/26/11	N/A	N/A
Aequicap Ins Co	Florida	P&C	02/28/11	29.7	E+ (Very Weak)
US Rail Ins Co a RRG	Vermont	P&C	03/04/11	3.2	E (Very Weak)
Seminole Casualty Ins Co	Florida	P&C	03/15/11	35.6	D (Weak)
Qualicare Self-Insurance Trust	Georgia	HMO	04/21/11	N/A	N/A
Majestic Insurance Co	California	P&C	04/21/11	313.1	D+ (Weak)
Reinsurance Co of America Inc	Illinois	P&C	04/27/11	7.1	D (Weak)
National Insurance Co	Puerto Rico	P&C	05/24/11	79.4	D+ (Weak)
Argus Fire & Casualty Ins Co	Florida	P&C	05/27/11	33.8	D (Weak)
Security Pacific Ins Co	Delaware	P&C	06/15/11	N/A	N/A
Great Republic Life Ins Co	Washington	L&H	07/07/11	16.9	E+ (Very Weak)
National Group Ins Co	Florida	P&C	08/01/11	9.53	E- (Very Weak)
Federal Motors Carriers RRG Inc	Delaware	P&C	08/18/11	11.9	E (Very Weak)
PMI Insurance Co	Arizona	P&C	08/19/11	436.9	D (Weak)
PMI Mortgage Ins Co	Arizona	P&C	08/19/11	2841.2	D (Weak)
Western Insurance Co	Utah	P&C	08/25/11	21.66	U (Unrated)
Homewise Preferred Ins Co	Florida	P&C	09/02/11	11.1	E (Very Weak)
American Sterling Ins Co	California	P&C	09/26/11	15.4	D (Weak)
Quality Health Plans Inc	Florida	HMO	10/17/11	45.0	E+ (Very Weak)
HomeWise Ins Co	Florida	P&C	11/18/11	84.7	D (Weak)
Minnesota Surety & Trust Co	Minnesota	P&C	12/02/11	1.5	E(Very Weak)
Southern Eagle Ins Co	Florida	P&C	12/06/11	18.6	D (Weak)

2010

Institution	Headquarters	Industry	Date of Failure	At Date of Failure	
				Total Assets ($Mil)	Financial Strength Rating
First American Life Ins Co	Texas	L&H	02/18/10	9.4	E- (Very Weak)
Colonial Cooperative Ins Co	New York	P&C	02/25/10	7.0	E (Very Weak)
Northern Capital Ins Co	Florida	P&C	02/25/10	78.2	E+ (Very Weak)
Gibraltar National Ins Co	Arkansas	P&C	03/11/10	4.9	E+ (Very Weak)
Imperial Casualty & Ind Co	Oklahoma	P&C	03/18/10	39.6	C- (Fair)
National States Ins Co	Missouri	L&H	04/01/10	70.5	E (Very Weak)
American Comm. Mutual Ins Co	Michigan	L&H	04/08/10	128.7	B (Good)
Financial Advisors ASR Select RRG	Nevada	P&C	04/26/10	0.9	E (Very Weak)
Prof. Liability Ins Co of America	New York	P&C	04/28/10	39.5	D- (Weak)
Pegasus Insurance Co. Inc.	Oklahoma	P&C	06/18/10	9.9	C- (Fair)
Gulf Builders RRG, Inc	South Carolina	P&C	08/02/10	N/A	U (Unrated)
Carrier Solutions RRG	Delaware	P&C	08/09/10	N/A	N/A
Georgia Restaurant Mut Cap Ins Co	Georgia	P&C	08/26/10	1.2	U (Unrated)
Atlantic Mutual Ins Co	New York	P&C	09/16/10	205.4	E- (Very Weak)
Centennial Ins Co	New York	P&C	09/16/10	74.9	E- (Very Weak)
Georgia Timber Harvesters' Mut Cap	Georgia	P&C	09/21/10	N/A	N/A
Peoples Assd Family Life Ins Co	Mississippi	L&H	09/23/10	N/A	N/A
Southern Casualty Ins Co	Georgia	P&C	09/29/10	6.3	D (Weak)
Guardian Health Care Inc	South Carolina	HMO	10/12/10	11.0	U (Unrated)
Long Island Insurance Co	New York	P&C	10/19/10	6.7	E- (Very Weak)
Constitutional Casualty Co	Illinois	P&C	11/04/10	15.6	E+ (Very Weak)

2009

Institution	Headquarters	Industry	Date of Failure	At Date of Failure	
				Total Assets ($Mil)	Financial Strength Rating
Scottish RE US Inc	Delaware	L&H	01/05/09	2950.6	D (Weak)
American Network Ins Co	Pennsylvania	L&H	01/06/09	125.8	D+ (Weak)
Penn Treaty Network Am.Ins Co	Pennsylvania	L&H	01/06/09	1037.6	C- (Fair)
Shenandoah Life Ins Co	Virginia	L&H	02/12/09	1735.0	B (Good)
NSA Rrg Inc.	Vermont	P&C	03/09/09	23.4	D(Weak)
Cosmopolitan Life Ins Co	Arkansas	L&H	03/19/09	2.6	E+ (Very Weak)
Wonder State Life Ins Co	Arkansas	L&H	03/23/09	N/A	U (Unrated)
The Transportation Liability Ins Co	South Carolina	P&C	03/16/09	0.8	E- (Very Weak)
Coral Ins Co	Florida	P&C	04/09/09	15.4	E+ (Very Weak)
Consumer First Ins Co	New Jersey	P&C	04/22/09	10.7	D- (Weak)
Universal Life Ins. Co.	Alabama	L&H	04/24/09	13.1	E (Very Weak)
Continental Life Ins Co of SC	South Carolina	L&H	04/27/09	2.2	E (Very Weak)
Eastern Casualty Ins Co	Massachusetts	P&C	04/27/09	28.2	U (Unrated)
Escude Life Ins Co	Louisiana	L&H	04/27/09	3.0	E- (Very Weak)
Texas Memorial Life Ins Co	Texas	L&H	06/10/09	3.80	E- (Very Weak)
Insurance Corp of New York	New York	P&C	06/29/09	87.3	E (Very Weak)
Old American County Mu Fire Ins Co	Texas	P&C	07/02/09	82.8	E+ (Very Weak)
First Commercial Ins Co	Florida	P&C	07/10/09	87.1	E+ (Very Weak)
First Comm Trans & Prop Ins Co	Florida	P&C	07/10/09	19.6	E+ (Very Weak)
Newburyport Mutual Fire Ins Co	Massachusetts	P&C	07/26/09	N/A	U (Unrated)
Medcore HP	California	HMO	07/30/09	5.5	D (Weak)
Preferred Health	Puerto Rico	HMO	07/30/09	16.2	D- (Weak)
Physicians Assurance Corp	Ohio	HMO	08/18/09	3.4	D+ (Weak)
Golden State Mutual Life Ins Co	California	L&H	09/30/09	90.0	D (Weak)
American Keystone Ins Co	Florida	P&C	10/09/09	24.1	C- (Fair)
Southeastern US Ins Co	Georgia	P&C	10/28/09	42.5	E (Very Weak)
Imerica Life & Health Ins Co	Arkansas	HMO	11/18/09	8.4	D (Weak)
Park Avenue Prop & Cas Ins Co	Oklahoma	P&C	11/18/09	92.0	C- (Fair)
SDM HealthCare	Puerto Rico	HMO	12/07/09	N/A	U (Unrated)
Magnolia Ins	Florida	P&C	12/14/09	N/A	N/A
ProSalud HMO Care	Puerto Rico	HMO	12/21/09	N/A	U (Unrated)
Astraea RRGroup, Inc	Arizona	P&C	12/30/09	3.5	E+ (Very Weak)

Glossary

This glossary contains the most important terms used in this publication.

Admitted Assets   The total of all investments and business interests which are acceptable under statutory accounting rules.

Asset/Liability Matching   Management of cash flows so that investments pay interest or mature at just the right time to meet the need for cash to pay claims and expenses.

Average Recession   A recession involving a decline in real GDP which is approximately equivalent to the average of the postwar recessions of 1957-58, 1960, 1970, 1974-75, 1980 and 1981-82. It is assumed, however, that in today's market, the financial losses suffered from a recession of that magnitude would be greater than those experienced in previous decades. (See also "Severe Recession.")

Capital   Strictly speaking, capital refers to funds raised through the sale of common and preferred stock. Mutual companies have capital in the form of retained earnings. In a more general sense, the term capital is commonly used to refer to a company's equity or net worth, that is, the difference between assets and liabilities (i.e., capital and surplus as shown on the balance sheet).

Capital Resources   The sum of various resources which serve as a capital cushion to losses, including capital and surplus.

Cash and Demand Deposits   Includes cash on hand and on deposit. A negative figure indicates that the company has more checks outstanding than current funds to cover those checks. This is not an unusual situation for an insurance company.

Common and Preferred Stocks   See "Stocks".

Direct Premiums Written   Premiums derived from policies issued directly by the company. This figure excludes the impact of reinsurance.

Financial Strength Rating   Weiss Financial Strength Ratings grade insurers on a scale from A (Excellent) to F (Failed). Ratings for property and casualty insurers are based on five major factors: liquidity, reserve adequacy, capitalization, profitability, and stability of operations.

Five-Year Profitability Index   See "Profitability Index".

Government Securities

Securities issued and/or guaranteed by U.S. and foreign governments which are rated as highest quality (class 1) by state insurance commissioners. Included in this category are bonds issued by governmental agencies and guaranteed with the full faith and credit of the government. Regardless of the issuing entity, they are viewed as being relatively safer than the other investment categories.

Interest Rate Risk

The risk that, due to changes in interest rates, investment income will not meet the needs of policy commitments. This risk can be reduced by effective asset/liability matching.

Invested Assets

The total size of the firm's investment portfolio.

Investments in Affiliates

Includes bonds, preferred stocks and common stocks, as well as other vehicles which many insurance companies use to invest in—and establish a corporate link with—affiliated companies.

Line of Business

Types of insurance coverage such as fire, inland marine, group accident and health, auto physical damage and auto liability. Statutory accounting uses over 30 different lines of business. A particular insurer may write coverage in any or all of these lines.

Liquidity Index

An index, expressed on a scale of zero to ten, with seven or higher considered excellent, that measures a company's ability to raise the necessary cash to settle claims. It is possible for a company to have the resources to pay claims on paper, but be unable to raise the cash. This can occur when a company is owed a great deal of money by its agents or reinsurers, or when it cannot sell its investments at the anticipated price.

Our liquidity tests examine how the company might fare under various cash flow scenarios.

Long/Short-Tail Lines

Time periods over which claims are paid out. For example, auto physical damage is considered a short-tail line, since claims are generally paid within one year of an accident. On the other hand, medical malpractice is considered a long-tail line as claims are typically paid five years or more after the occurrence of the incident giving rise to the claim.

For the insurer, the risks associated with long-tail lines are greater than with short-tail lines because the period of uncertainty in which unexpected claims can arise is longer.

Moderate Loss Scenario

Possible future events that would result in loss levels comparable to those experienced in recent history. (Compare with "Severe Loss Scenario.")

Net Premiums Written

The dollar volume of premiums retained by the company. This figure is equal to direct premiums written, plus reinsurance assumed, less reinsurance ceded to other companies.

Noninvestment Grade Bonds	Low-rated issues, commonly known as "junk bonds," which carry a high risk as defined by the state insurance commissioners. These include bond classes 3 - 6.
Other Investments	Items not included in any of the other categories, such as premium notes, collateral loans, short-term investments and other miscellaneous items.
Premium Risk	The risk that, for a particular group of policies, premiums will not be sufficient to meet the level of claims and related expenses.
Profitability Index	An index, expressed on a scale of zero to ten, with seven or higher considered excellent, that measures the soundness of the company's operations and the contribution of profits to the company's fiscal strength. The Profitability Index is a composite of five factors: (1) gain or loss on underwriting (core insurance business); (2) gain or loss on overall operations; (3) consistency of operating results; (4) impact of operating results on surplus and (5) expenses in relation to industry averages for the types of policies that the company offers.
Real Estate	Direct real estate investments, including property (a) occupied by the company; (b) acquired through foreclosure of a mortgage and (c) purchased as an investment.
Reinsurance Assumed	Insurance risk acquired by taking on partial or full responsibility for claims on policies written by other companies. (See "Reinsurance Ceded.")
Reinsurance Ceded	Insurance risk sold to another company. When there is a claim on a reinsured policy, the original company generally pays the claim and then is reimbursed by its reinsurer.
Reserve Adequacy Index	An index, expressed on a scale of zero to ten with seven or higher considered excellent, that measures the adequacy of the company's reserves over the last five years. Companies that have a history of inadequate reserves will receive a low score. Reserves are company estimates of unsettled claims in each year, including both claims that have been received but not yet settled, as well as claims that the company expects to receive. A company that underestimates its claims inflates profits and capital. Additionally, chronically deficient reserves call into question the company's ability to manage its policy risk effectively.
Risk-Adjusted Capital	The capital resources that would be needed to deal with unexpected claims or other adverse developments (same as "Target Capital").
Risk-Adjusted Capital Ratio #1	The capital resources which a company currently has, expressed as a ratio, to the resources that would be needed to deal with a moderate loss scenario. (See "Moderate Loss Scenario.")

**Risk-Adjusted
Capital Ratio #2**
The capital resources which a company currently has, expressed as a ratio, to the resources that would be needed to deal with a severe loss scenario. (See "Severe Loss Scenario.")

Severe Loss Scenario
Possible future events that could result in loss levels that are somewhat higher than recent experience. These levels are developed from examination of current trends. (Compare with "Moderate Loss Scenario.")

Severe Recession
A prolonged economic slowdown in which the single worst year of the postwar period is extended for a period of three years. (See also "Average Recession.")

Short-Tail Lines
See "Long/Short-Tail Lines".

Stability Index
An index, measured on a scale of zero to ten, integrating a wide variety of factors that reflect the company's stability and diversification of risk.

State of Domicile
Although most insurance companies are licensed to do business in many states, they have only one state of domicile. This is the state which has primary regulatory responsibility for the company. Use the state of domicile to make absolutely sure that you have the correct company. Bear in mind, however, that this need not be the state where the company's main offices are located.

State Guaranty Funds
Funds that are designed to raise cash from existing insurance carriers to cover policy claims of bankrupt insurance companies.

Stocks
Common and preferred equities, including stocks in affiliates.

Surplus
Accumulated funds from prior years' profits (retained earnings) plus additional amounts paid-in by a parent or other corporation. The term "surplus" is also sometimes used broadly to include capital such as common stock.

Target Capital
See "Risk-Adjusted Capital."

Total Assets
Total admitted assets, including investments and other business assets. (See "Admitted Assets.")